# Peterson's Vocational and Technical Schools West

## 9th Edition

**About Peterson's**

To succeed on your lifelong educational journey, you will need accurate, dependable, and practical tools and resources. That is why Peterson's is everywhere education happens. Because whenever and however you need education content delivered, you can rely on Peterson's to provide the information, know-how, and guidance to help you reach your goals. Tools to match the right students with the right school. It's here. Personalized resources and expert guidance. It's here. Comprehensive and dependable education content—delivered whenever and however you need it. It's all here.

For more information, contact Peterson's, 2000 Lenox Drive, Lawrenceville, NJ 08648; 800-338-3282; or find us on the World Wide Web at www.petersons.com/about.



Stephen Clemente, President; Bernadette Webster, Director of Publishing; Mark D. Snider, Editor; John Wells, Research Project Manager; Tim Nelson, Programmer; Ray Golaszewski, Manufacturing Manager; Linda M. Williams, Composition Manager



ISBN-13: 978-0-7689-2810-5
ISBN-10: 0-7689-2810-9

Printed in the United States of America

10 9 8 7 6 5 4 3 2 1 11 10 09

Ninth Edition

By producing this book on recycled paper (40% post-consumer waste) 80 trees were saved.

# Contents

# A Note from the Peterson's Editors

If you're thinking of attending a vocational-technical school, you have probably decided to enter a specific trade, occupation, or profession and found that it requires you to have certain entry-level skills or training. With so many schools to choose from, you may be wondering how you will find the right one. Or maybe you're undecided on a career and are looking for guidance as to which career or occupation is right for you. And if you're a working adult thinking of going back to school, there is even more to consider. *Peterson's Vocational and Technical Schools East* has the information you need to make the right decisions.

The **Choosing a Vo-Tech Program** section contains insightful articles on preparing for a career—how careers, income, and education relate; which are the fastest-growing occupations; and much more. There is valuable advice about apprenticeships and financial aid and tips on how to manage being an adult student. In this section you also will find descriptions of various career areas and lists of occupations within each one. Included are six of the most popular areas, as well as new and emerging occupations you may not have considered. Finally, the "How to Use This Guide" article provides explanations of each element in the school profiles, the criteria used to select the programs in the book, and our data collection procedures.

The **Profiles of Vo-Tech Schools** section contains detailed profiles of more than 2,300 vocational-technical schools and programs located east of the Mississippi River. Each profile contains comprehensive information about the school, including a list of the vo-tech programs offered and the name and phone number of the person to contact.

The **Appendixes** contain two listings. The first lists the State Offices of Apprenticeship Contacts. The second listing contains the accrediting organizations that are recognized by the Council for Higher Education Accreditation (CHEA) of the U.S. Department of Education.

The **Indexes** make it easy to locate a school by program and state or alphabetically.

Peterson's publishes a full line of resources to help gather all the information you need to make informed career and education decisions. Peterson's publications can be found at your local bookstore or library; you can access us online at **www.petersons.com.**

We welcome any comments or suggestions you may have about this publication and invite you to complete our online survey at **www.petersons.com/booksurvey.** Your feedback will help us make your educational dreams possible.

The editors at Peterson's wish you the best of luck in your search for the perfect vo-tech school for you!

# Choosing a Vo-Tech Program

# The Expanding Role of America's Career Colleges

**Nicholas Glakas**

***Former President, Career College Association***

*Editor's Note: Career colleges are privately owned and operated schools and colleges that provide postsecondary (after high school) technical and vocational training. Most of the institutions represented in this publication are career colleges, but publicly supported two-year and four-year colleges and private nonprofit institutions also are represented. Mr. Glakas's comments about the advantages of a vocational or technical education apply whether you are considering a career college or another kind of vocational and technical career training institution.*

Most of us have been told all of our lives, "If you don't go to college, you'll never get a good job." Many of us have been conditioned to equate a traditional four-year college degree with a guarantee of professional success. This is not necessarily the case.

Most employers look upon a person with a college degree as a person with persistence and stamina. With a degree as a credential, the newly graduated enter the workforce with a reasonably proven ability to learn but often without a marketable skill. To overcome that pitfall, many college graduates attend career colleges to expand their experience and learn skills that will get them a job. In fact, on many career college campuses, more than 40 percent of the students already have their baccalaureate degrees.

Recent statistics indicate that nearly 65 percent of the workforce in this country is made up of skilled laborers. Only 20 percent of that same workforce are considered professionals. These figures show that the majority of this nation's new jobs in the next decade will require strong technical skills—the exact type of skills taught in this country's career colleges.

If you lack the time and financial resources to spend four years in a traditional college or university, a career college is an excellent alternative. Whether this choice is made directly after high school or after spending a few years in the workforce, successful completion of the program is not likely to be affected.

In good economic times or bad, you will always have a distinct advantage if you have a skill and can be immediately productive while continuing to learn and improve. If you are technologically savvy, work collaboratively, and find creative solutions to difficult problems, you will always be in demand. Less than half of the students who start at a traditional college ever obtain their degree. One half or two thirds of a degree is of little value; all the time and financial resources invested help to produce no dividend because they do not develop marketable skills.

Like most of us, you will spend more of your waking hours in the workplace than anywhere else. If you don't like what you are doing—the financial, emotional, and spiritual rewards will not be there—it is likely that you will be unhappy and not do well. As you begin to decide on how to prepare for your future, consider the following guidelines:

- Identify what interests you, and consider careers that relate to these interests
- Seek the counsel of individuals working in the jobs in which you are interested
- Try to combine school and real-world work experience during your training
- Understand that skills are transferable, and your initial job choice may prepare you for other opportunities

Career colleges offer scores of opportunities to learn the technical skills required by many of today's top jobs. This is especially true in the areas of computer and information technology, health care, and hospitality (culinary arts, travel and tourism, and hotel and motel management). Career colleges range in size from those with a handful of students to universities with enrollments in the thousands. They are located in every state in the nation and share one common objective—to prepare students for a successful career in the world of work through a focused, intensive curriculum. America's career colleges are privately owned and operated for-profit companies. Instead of using tax support to operate, career colleges pay taxes. Because career colleges are businesses, they must be responsive to the needs of the workforce and of their communities, or they will cease to exist.

When choosing an institution of higher education, consider the following:

- What percentage of the students who begin programs actually graduate?
- Of those who graduate, how many get jobs in their chosen career, and how long does it take to be hired?
- Is there full-service placement assistance available at the school?

Today's jobs demand skills that are ever changing. In the future, this demand will be even greater. The education system necessary to provide you with the skills you need exists. It is made up of this country's career and technical colleges.

# How Career, Income, and Education Relate

The relationship between education and work—the more you invest in your education, the more you will earn—has been repeated so often that it has almost lost its meaning. Here are the most recent figures from the U.S. Census Bureau:

| Level of Education Attained | Average Annual Income |
|---|---|
| Bachelor's Degree | $58,613 |
| Associate Degree | 39,506 |
| High School Graduate | 31,283 |
| Not a High School Graduate | 21,056 |

Source: U.S. Census Bureau, *Current Population Survey, 2009 Annual Social and Economic Supplement.*

Reliable data on the incomes of vocational-technical school graduates are not available, but there are other data that might provide some clues as to what these might be. A study of two-year college graduates showed that associate degree earners who took vocational programs had higher incomes than graduates from nonvocational programs. This difference in incomes expanded from 16 percent greater within five years after graduation to 37 percent greater within nine years after graduation. Approximately 59 percent of two-year college graduates in 1992 earned degrees in vocational programs.

## Fastest-Growing Occupations Require Vocational Training

The table on the next page shows the latest projections from the Bureau of Labor Statistics of the fastest-growing occupations in the ten years from 2006 to 2016. Programs for many of these occupations are offered by schools that are represented in this book.

## College Is Not For Everybody

Forty years ago, most young people went directly to work after high school. Today, most young people first go to school for more training. The above figures on income and education demonstrate why this is a good idea. They also demonstrate that earning a bachelor's degree is a better option than going to vocational-technical school, but we know that college is not for everybody.

Life events often can interfere with plans to attend college. Responsibilities to a family may materialize that make it impossible to delay earning an income for four years. One may have to work and go to school. In this situation, as demonstrated below, career training that is measured in months instead of years can be the best choice.

Also, let's be real. College demands certain conventions, behaviors, and attitudes that do not fit every kind of person. Some people need a lot of physical activity to feel satisfied, while others just are not academically attuned. Whether the reasons are rooted in personality or upbringing, for these individuals, the intellectual path of college life is dry, cold, and unsatisfying; day after day of sitting, reading, memorizing, and analyzing is pure agony. Years of strict time management and postponed rewards are more than they can stand. On the other hand, the clear structure and demands of a worker in a real career might be an appealing and satisfying alternative to the vague, indefinite life of a student who lacks career direction.

Certainly, the college world has made great attempts to be more inclusive. It is no longer a world of kids under the age of 23, but at their heart, from their standardized tests through to their campus social life, most colleges are defined by the standards and norms of the majority culture, which remains largely younger than age 23. Adults who have lived in the "real world," although aware of the rewards that are promised by spending a few years in college, may not want to go through the years of self-denial, isolation, and cultural displacement that a college experience seems to entail.

## FASTEST-GROWING OCCUPATIONS, 2006–2016

**The 10 fastest-growing occupations, 2006–2016**
**[Numbers in thousands of jobs]**

| Occupation | Employment | | Change | |
|---|---|---|---|---|
| | 2006 | 2016 | Number | Percent |
| Network systems and data communications analyst | 262 | 402 | 140 | 53.4 |
| Personal and home care aides | 767 | 1,156 | 389 | 50.6 |
| Home health aides | 787 | 1,171 | 384 | 48.7 |
| Computer software engineers, applications | 507 | 733 | 226 | 44.6 |
| Veterinary technologists and technicians | 71 | 100 | 29 | 41.0 |
| Personal financial advisors | 176 | 248 | 72 | 41.0 |
| Makeup artists, theatrical and performance | 2 | 3 | 1 | 39.8 |
| Medical assistants | 417 | 565 | 148 | 35.4 |
| Veterinarians | 62 | 84 | 22 | 35.0 |
| Substance abuse and behavioral disorder counselors | 83 | 112 | 29 | 34.3 |

*Source: U.S. Department of Labor Statistics, Occupational Employment Projections 2006 to 2016.*

## Vocational-Technical Students Achieve Their Goals

A truly positive aspect of vocational-technical education is that most students who enter it are likely to complete their educational goals. Fifty-five percent of all students working toward an educational certificate (the category defining vo-tech students) complete their educational program. By contrast, only 24 percent of all students working toward an associate degree complete their degree work, while 54 percent of all students working toward a bachelor's degree complete their degree work. As the following chart demonstrates, these differences become even more dramatic when factors such as delaying one's education for more than a year after high school, studying part-time, or working while studying are considered.

For most students, vocational-technical education programs offer a truer chance of achievement than other alternative paths of education. The range of possible careers provides the satisfaction of a fulfilling work life with exceptional compensation. Vocational-technical education can be a lifesaver for the men and women who choose to refrain from or postpone going to a two- or four-year college.

## POSTSECONDARY STUDENTS WHO ATTAINED THEIR INITIAL DEGREE OBJECTIVE

| | Vocational-Technical (Certificate) Programs | Associate Degree Programs | Bachelor's Degree Programs |
|---|---|---|---|
| Enrollment More Than a Year After High School | 54% | 14% | 50% |
| Part-Time Student | 41% | 18% | 13% |
| Also Worked 1–20 Hours per Week | 75% | 42% | 51% |
| Also Worked More Than 20 Hours per Week | 47% | 28% | 40% |

Source: U.S. Department of Education, National Center for Education Statistics.

# Student Financial Aid: Paying for Your College Education

**Heidi B. Granger**
***Director of Financial Aid***
***College of the Desert, Palm Desert, CA***

The decision to attend a vocational-technical college is an extremely important one. The specialized education and training will provide you with the necessary tools and knowledge to be successful in the career of your choice. You will have the opportunity to grow in many areas. You will learn the skills needed to prosper, and your abilities will be developed to their greatest potential.

Education is an investment in your future. Before you choose your career, it is necessary to consider how much time, money, and commitment you have to prepare yourself for a career. Remember, your career goals should be reasonable and realistic in terms of your ability, interests, and values. All students are encouraged to think about the amount of educational debt that might be necessary to achieve one's educational goals and objectives. In addition, students should also look at the effect that student loan indebtedness can have on one's future lifestyle. Choosing the right career and paying for college takes planning, forethought, dedication, and commitment.

This article is designed to assist you with your college plans and to familiarize you with the various kinds of financial aid programs available to help you meet the costs of attending a vocational institution. Understanding the policies and procedures necessary to obtain financial assistance is essential. Although the process may seem confusing and complicated, the purpose of financial aid is to assist students with their educational expenses so that financial barriers do not prevent them from achieving their educational goals.

## What Is Financial Aid?

Financial aid is the assistance available to help students pay for the costs of attending a vocational-technical institution. Financial aid is provided by federal, state, institutional, or private sources and may consist of grants, loans, work study, or scholarships. Qualified students may be offered combinations of the various types of aid or aid from a single source. Each year, billions of dollars are given or lent to students, and about half of all college students receive some sort of financial aid.

Most financial aid is awarded based on an individual's financial need, college costs, and the availability of funds. This aid is provided to students because neither they nor their families have all of the resources needed to pay for a college education. This kind of aid is referred to as need-based aid.

Merit-based aid is awarded to students who may or may not have financial need. Students are given assistance because they have a special skill or ability, display a particular talent, have a certain grade point average, or are enrolled in a specific program.

## Types and Sources of Financial Aid

There are several types of financial aid offered to help pay for educational expenses: grants, loans, student employment (work), and scholarships. Grants and scholarships are "gifts" and do not have to be repaid. Loans are borrowed money that must be paid back over a period of time, usually after the student leaves school. Student employment is normally part-time work arranged for a student during the school year.

### WHAT ARE THE ELIGIBILITY REQUIREMENTS?

**In general, to be considered eligible for federal financial aid, you must:**

- ❑ **Be a United States citizen or eligible noncitizen**
- ❑ **Be enrolled or accepted for enrollment in an accredited institution**
- ❑ **Be making satisfactory academic progress in your course of study**
- ❑ **Not be in default on any loan or owe a refund or repayment on any previous financial aid received at any institution attended**
- ❑ **Be registered with the Selective Service, if you are required to do so**

Wages received by the student are used for specific college expenses.

The primary source of aid for students attending a vocational institution of higher education is from the federal government. The federal government offers both grant and loan financial aid programs. Another source of aid is state assistance. Many states across the country provide some aid for students attending colleges in their own home states. Most state aid programs are grants, although there are a few states that offer special loan and work-study programs. Other sources of aid that award money to students come from private foundations such as corporations, civic associations, unions, fraternal organizations, and religious groups. Most of these awards are not based solely on need, although the amount of the award may vary depending on your financial need. In addition, many companies offer tuition reimbursement to their employees and/or their employees' dependents. The personnel department at either your or your parent's place of employment can tell you whether or not the company offers this benefit and who may be eligible. Lastly, there are some colleges that offer awards from their own funds or from money received from various organizations. This type of aid is often referred to as "institutional aid." Although most vocational institutions have little or no institutional aid available, the student should still be sure to ask the college about this type of assistance.

## Grants

**Federal Pell Grant**—Funded by the federal government, this need-based grant is available for undergraduate students who have financial need. Award amounts vary according to an eligibility index. The maximum award amount based on congressional appropriations for the 2009–10 award year is $5350.

> **Note:** The actual amount of a student's Federal Pell Grant depends upon several factors in addition to eligibility. These include the calculated expected family contribution (EFC), your cost of attendance, your enrollment status (full-time, half-time, etc.), the length of your period of enrollment, the college's definition of the academic year for your program of study, and the structure and length of your program of study.

**Federal Supplemental Educational Opportunity Grant (FSEOG)**—Funded by the federal government, this need-based grant is available for undergraduate students who have exceptional financial need. Although the maximum award per year can be $4000, few vocational schools have an abundance of FSEOG funds, and therefore the average award is usually around $760 as of 2008.

## Loans

**Federal Perkins Loan**—The Federal Perkins Loan is awarded on the basis of demonstrated financial need. The interest rate is 5 percent, and the first payment is due nine months after you leave school or drop below half-time status. The maximum award is $4000 for undergraduate students but, like the FSEOG funds, most vocational schools have limited Perkins funding and will award what they can to the neediest students.

**Subsidized Federal Stafford Student Loans**—Subsidized Federal Stafford Student Loans are for students who demonstrate financial need. FFEL Stafford Loans are made to students through lending institutions such as banks and credit unions. Direct Stafford Loans are made to students by the Department of Education. Not every college participates in the Direct Loan Program. The interest rate for undergraduate Direct and Stafford Loans first disbursed between July 1, 2009, and June 30, 2010, is 5.6 percent. This rate became fixed on July 1, 2006 (for loans with a first disbursement on or after that date). The fixed interest rate will drop on new loans each year until it reaches

3.4 percent for loans first disbursed between July 1, 2011, and June 30, 2012. After that the interest rate reverts to 6.8 percent. All lenders offer the same rate for the Stafford Loan, although some give discounts for on-time and electronic payments. Stafford Loans have loan fees of 1.5 percent, which are deducted from the disbursement check. These fees consist of a 0.5 percent origination fee and a 1 percent default fee, which was previously called a "guarantee fee." The origination fee will be phased out entirely on July 1, 2010. Loan repayment begins six months after you leave school or drop below half-time status. The government pays the interest while you are in school and during the six-month grace period. Both FFEL and Direct Stafford Loans have a basic ten-year repayment period. The borrower may select from a variety of repayment plans, some of which will lengthen the repayment period, and thus increase the amount of interest paid.

**Unsubsidized Federal Stafford Loans**—Unsubsidized Federal Stafford Loans are for students who do not demonstrate financial need. Students may borrow within the same loan limits and at the same interest rates as the subsidized Stafford Loan program. The interest rate is 6.8 percent, which became fixed on July 1, 2006. A 1.5 percent fee is deducted and interest payments begin immediately. Students may defer payments while enrolled at least part-time at school, but most lenders allow students to defer payments while in school, but interest continues to accrue and is added to the principle balance. Regular payments begin six months after the student either leaves school or drops below half-time status.

Borrowers of additional unsubsidized loan amounts must meet the federal definition of independent or have exceptional circumstances as documented by the financial aid office.

**Note:** The loan amounts for which you are eligible may be prorated if your program's length is less than thirty weeks.

**Federal PLUS Loans**—The Federal PLUS Loan program enables parents of dependent students to obtain loans to pay for their child's educational costs. The interest rate for the FFELP PLUS loan is now fixed at 8.5 percent; the interest rate for a Direct PLUS Loan is fixed at 7.9 percent. Parents may borrow up to the cost of attendance minus any other financial aid received by the student.

***FINANCIAL AID ELIGIBILITY FORMULA:***

**Cost of Attendance**
**– Expected Family Contribution (student and parents)**
**= Financial Need (Financial Aid Eligibility)**

**Primary responsibility for financing a college education must be assumed by the student and often by the student's parents. Students and their families are expected to make a maximum effort to pay for college expenses. Financial assistance should be viewed as supplementary to the efforts of the family. Financial aid is available to assist students with educational costs, and students should be aware that financial aid usually does not cover 100 percent of educational expenses.**

## Work

**Federal Work-Study Program**—The Federal Work-Study Program provides jobs for students with financial aid eligibility. It gives students a chance to earn money to help pay for educational expenses while providing valuable work experience. All eligible students are also afforded the opportunity to perform community service work. Many vocational schools offer the Federal Work-Study Program, but the number of jobs available tend to be limited.

## Understanding the Cost of Attendance

Every college establishes an estimate of what it will cost each student to attend the school. There are usually several types of budgets: one for students living on campus (if a school has dormitories), one for students living off campus, and one for students living with their parents. The expenses included in the cost of attendance are tuition and fees, books and supplies, room and board (includes food, rent, and utilities), personal expenses, and transportation. The total educational expenses or budgets are referred to as the student's cost of attendance.

## Determining Financial Aid Eligibility and Financial Need

Eligibility for financial aid is determined by subtracting the amount you and your parents can contribute from the cost of attendance (the "budget" as explained in the previous section). An assessment of your family's ability to contribute toward educational expenses is made based on the information you provide when applying for financial aid. Income, assets, family size, and number of family members in college are some of the factors considered in this calculation. This assessment, referred to as need analysis, determines your financial need, which is defined as the difference between the total cost of attendance and what you are expected to pay. The need analysis uses a formula mandated by legislation. It determines the ability, not the willingness, of the student and parents to finance the cost of attendance. Everyone who applies is treated equally under this analysis. The end result of the need analysis is your expected family contribution and represents the amount your family should be able to contribute toward the cost of attendance. The cost of attendance will vary at each college, but the amount your family is expected to contribute should stay the same. Financial need will vary between colleges because of each school's different costs of attendance.

## Determining the Student's Status: Independent or Dependent?

Remember that both students and parents are expected to help pay for college costs. This means that you, the student, will be expected to contribute to your educational expenses.

If you are considered dependent by federal definition, then your parents' income and assets, as well as yours, will be counted toward the family contribution. If you are considered independent of your parents, only your income (and that of your spouse, if you are married) will count in the need analysis formula.

To be considered independent for financial aid, you must meet one of the following criteria:

- Be at least 24 years old.
- Be a veteran of the U.S. armed forces.
- Be married.
- Be an orphan or ward of the court.
- Have legal dependents other than a spouse.
- Be a graduate professional student.

If you can document extraordinary circumstances that might indicate independent status, you will need to show this information to the financial aid administrator at the college you will be attending. Only the financial aid administrator has the authority to make exceptions to the requirements listed above.

## Applying for Financial Aid

To apply for financial aid, it is essential that you properly complete the necessary forms so that your individual financial need can be evaluated. It is important to read all application materials and instructions very carefully. The application process can be a bit long and confusing, so remember to take one step at a time. If you run into any problems or have specific questions, contact the financial aid office at the college you will be attending. The financial aid office will be happy to provide you with guidance and assistance.

Most vocational schools use just one financial aid application called the Free Application for Federal Student Aid (FAFSA). This form is a four-page application available at your college's financial aid office, local high school guidance offices, and state education department offices. Students can apply for federal student aid via the Internet by using FAFSA on the Web. FAFSA on the Web can be accessed at www.fafsa.ed.gov. The process is self-paced and interactive, with step-by-step guidance. Depending on the availability of information about your income and financial situation, the process can take as little as 20 minutes to complete. The FAFSA that students will use to apply for aid for each school year becomes available in the December prior to the year in which aid is needed. However, do *not* fill out the form until after January 1 of the year you will require aid.

> **Note:** You want to complete the FAFSA as soon as possible after January 1, 2010. Although you may apply for aid at any time during the year, many state agencies have early cut-off dates for state aid funding.

To complete this application, you will need to gather specific family information and financial records, such as tax forms, if they are available. If they are not, use estimates. You can make corrections later. Be sure to answer all questions. Omitted information may delay the processing of your application. Be sure that you and your parents (if needed) have signed the form and that you keep a copy of the form for your records. The FAFSA processing center will calculate your expected family contribution and will distribute the information back to the college.

About two to four weeks after you submit your completed FAFSA, you will receive a Student Aid Report (SAR) that shows the information you reported and your calculated EFC. If you need to make any corrections, you may do so at this time. The college may also have this same information in an ISIR (Institutional Student Information Record) or electronic Student Aid Report (ESAR).

If you are chosen for verification by the school, you may be asked to submit documentation that will verify the information you reported on the FAFSA. Once the financial aid office is satisfied that all of the information is correct, the college can then determine your financial need and provide you with a financial aid offer for funding your education. If you are eligible to receive aid, most schools will either mail you an award letter or will ask you to come into the financial aid office to discuss your financial aid eligibility.

> **Note:** Financial aid is not renewed automatically; you must apply each year. Often, if you are in a program that lasts longer than one year, a renewal application will automatically be mailed to you by the federal processor.

## Student Loans and Debt Management

More than ever before, loans have become an important part of financial assistance. The majority of students find that they must borrow money to finance their education. If you accept a loan, you are incurring a financial obligation. You will have to repay the loan in full, along with any interest and additional fees (collection, legal, etc.). Since you will be making loan payments to satisfy the loan obligation, carefully consider the burden your loan amount will impose on you after you leave school. Defaulting on a student loan can jeopardize your entire future by harming your credit history. Borrow intelligently.

## Your Rights and Responsibilities as a Financial Aid Recipient

**As a student consumer, you have a right to:**

- be informed of the correct procedures for applying for aid, cost of attendance, types of aid available, how financial need is determined, criteria for awarding aid, how satisfactory academic progress is determined, and what you need to do to continue receiving aid.
- be informed of the type and amount of assistance you will receive, how much of your need has been met, and how and when you will be paid.
- appeal any decision of the financial aid office if you feel you have been treated unfairly with regard to your application.
- view the contents in your financial aid file, in accordance with the Family Educational Rights and Privacy Act.
- know the conditions of any loan you accept.

**It is your responsibility to:**

- complete all application materials truthfully and accurately and comply with deadline dates.
- review all materials sent to you and read and understand all documents. Be sure to keep copies of all forms you sign.
- know and comply with the rules governing the aid you receive.
- provide additional documentation and/or new information requested by the financial aid office.
- maintain satisfactory academic progress.
- keep your local and permanent addresses current with all pertinent school offices.
- use financial aid only for expenses related to the college.

Remember that your dreams can come true when you act to turn them into realities. Financial aid is the means by which you can achieve your dream of obtaining an education and pursuing your career. Use it wisely and you will succeed.

# Apprenticeships: Valuable Training for Higher-Paying Jobs

**Kenneth Edwards**

***Former Director of Technical Services, International Brotherhood of Electrical Workers***

To remain competitive, America needs highly skilled workers. One of the best possible ways to obtain the skills that will lead to a career in a high-paying occupation is through a formal apprenticeship program.

Apprenticeship provides structured on-the-job training under the supervision of a qualified craftsperson, technician, or professional. This training is supplemented by related classroom instruction conducted either by the sponsor or by an educational institution.

The advantages of apprenticeships are numerous. First and foremost, an apprenticeship leads to a lasting lifetime skill. As a highly trained worker, you can take your skill anywhere. The more creative, exciting, and challenging jobs are put in the hands of the fully skilled worker, the all-around person who knows his or her trade inside and out.

Skilled workers advance much more quickly than those who are semiskilled or whose skills are not broad enough to equip them to assume additional responsibilities. Those who complete an apprenticeship have also acquired the skills and judgment necessary to go into business for themselves, if they choose.

## About Apprenticeships

Although there are more than 20,000 occupations listed in the *Dictionary of Occupational Titles,* the Employment and Training Administration's Office of Apprenticeship and state apprenticeship registration agencies consider only 1,000 of these "apprenticeable." To be apprenticeable, an occupation must be commonly practiced in industry and must lend itself to sequential learning experiences accompanied by a program of related instruction.

Currently, approximately 468,000 apprentices are being trained by 28,000 programs registered with either the Office of Apprenticeship or with state apprenticeship registration agencies.

## How Apprenticeships Are Regulated

Registration of an apprenticeship program with the Office of Apprenticeship or with a state apprenticeship registration agency is purely voluntary. Having such status is significant, however, a "registered apprenticeship" must meet certain minimum standards of training established by federal regulations. Registration thus serves as an official stamp of approval.

This does not mean, however, that nonregistered apprenticeships are not quality programs. Quite a number of major corporations have outstanding apprenticeship programs that have never been registered. If you want to inquire about the validity of a certain apprenticeship, you should contact a state apprenticeship registration agency or a regional office of the Office of Apprenticeship; addresses of state offices are listed in an appendix in this book.

National guideline standards are in place for many recognized occupations. These standards are established in each field by a nationally recognized association of employers or by a recognized labor organization and an employer association. For example, the International Brotherhood of Electrical Workers and the National Electrical Contractors Association have established national guideline standards for training apprentices in the electrical construction industry. National guideline standards ensure uniformity of training across the country, so an apprentice can seek employment anywhere in the United States and have his or her training accepted without questions.

In general, apprenticeship is legally recognized only if it is recorded in a written contract or agreement called an "indenture," in which the employer promises to teach the worker the processes of his or her trade in return for services rendered to the employer. Standards of a registered apprenticeship program are defined in Title 29, Code of Federal Regulations (CFR) Parts 29 and 30. A total of twenty-two standards identified in Title 29 CFR Part 29 must be incorporated into an apprenticeship program before it can be registered with the Office of Apprenticeship or a state-recognized registration agency. Standards include such provisions as the term/length of apprenticeship, a progressive wage scale, the ratio of apprentices to journey worker, credit for prior experience, safety on the job, and related classroom instruction.

## What to Do If You're Interested in an Apprenticeship

A person seeking an apprenticeship fills out what amounts to an application for employment. These applications may be available year-round or at certain times during the year. Because an apprentice must be trained in an area where work actually exists and where a certain pay scale is guaranteed upon completion of the program, waits for application acceptance may be quite lengthy in areas of low employment. Such a standard works to the advantage of the potential apprentice; certainly no one would want to encourage you to spend one to six years of your life learning an occupation where no work exists or where the wage is the same as, or a little above, that of the common laborer.

Federal regulations prohibit anyone younger than age 16 from being considered as an apprentice. Some programs require that the individual receive a high school degree or complete certain course work. Other requirements could include passing certain validated aptitude tests or proof of physical ability to perform the essential functions of the occupation.

Program sponsors register different procedures with the registration agency. An example of a selection procedure is an interview process. The apprentice is rated during the oral interview process based on responses directly related to determining the ability to perform in the apprenticeable occupation. Apprentices are then placed based on rank.

## For More Information

If you're considering an apprenticeship, the best sources of assistance and information are vocational or career counselors, local one-stop career centers, field offices of state apprenticeship agencies, and regional offices of the Office of Apprenticeship.

# Placement Rate Data

## Philip Roush

*Former Commissioner for the Indiana Commission on Proprietary Education*

When you undertake the complex task of selecting the "right" vocational-technical school, you must collect as much information as possible about each school you are considering. One major piece of information you should obtain is the placement rate data, which is available from most, if not all, vocational-technical schools. This information indicates how effective the school's academic programs are in meeting the needs of today's employers. Because you want the skills you acquire at the school you choose to lead to a great job, this data will be very important as you decide which school to attend.

The school's placement rates may be obtained in several ways. Most schools will provide this data as an integral part of their prospective student-orientation program. If not, ask for it. Be cautious about considering a school that does not make its placement rates readily available.

All fifty states, the District of Columbia, and Puerto Rico have laws requiring state authorization, approval, or registration to offer educational programs to the general public. Ask the school's administration which state agency provides the required legal authority to operate its educational program; you may be able to obtain placement information from that state agency. If you are considering an occupation that requires a state license, such as a cosmetologist, barber, or medical assistant, you should also inquire about the percent of graduates who have passed or failed required licensing examinations.

Keep in mind that, while placement rate data reflects the success rate of the school's graduates, this is not the only criterion you should use in your school-selection process. Placement services are an integral part of most schools' education programs. You should remember, however, that no school can guarantee you a job upon graduation. A high placement rate simply indicates that a large number of the school's graduates are employed—as determined by a calculation method selected by the school. Currently, since there is not a nationally prescribed method of computing placement rates, placement rate data may include three categories of graduates: graduates placed in the specific vocation for which they were trained, graduates placed in a vocation related to their training, or graduates employed prior to their enrollment. It is very important to identify the method the school used to calculate its placement rates.

As you contact schools during your search, it is also important that you obtain the names and addresses of any graduates employed in your vocational interest and the names of their employers. Although placement rate data will provide you with a statistical basis from which to begin, alumni and employer comments about the school and opinions about the quality of its vocational programs will also be integral to your decision-making process.

# Returning to School: Advice for Adult Students

**Sandra Cook, Ph.D.**

***Executive Director of Enrollment Services, San Diego State University***

Many adults think for a long time about returning to school without taking any action. One purpose of this article is to help the "thinkers" finally make some decisions by examining what is keeping them from action. Another purpose is to describe not only some of the difficulties and obstacles that adult students may face when returning to school, but also to explore tactics for coping with them.

If you have been thinking about going back to school and feel as though you are the only person your age contemplating this, you should know that approximately 8 million adult students are currently enrolled in higher education institutions. This number represents 46 percent of total higher education enrollments. The majority of adult students are enrolled at two-year colleges.

There are many reasons why adult students choose to return to school. Studies have shown that the three most important criteria that adult students consider when choosing a school are location, cost, and availability of the major or program desired. Most two-year colleges are public institutions that serve a geographic district, making them readily accessible to the community. Costs at most two-year colleges are far less than at other types of higher education institutions. If you are interested in a vocational or technical program, two-year colleges excel in providing this type of training.

## Uncertainty, Choice, and Support

There are three different "stages" in the process of adults returning to school. The first stage is uncertainty. Do I really want to go back to school? What will my friends or family think? Can I compete with those 18-year-old whiz kids? Am I too old? The second stage is choice. Once you make the decision to return, you must choose where you will attend. There are many criteria to use in making this decision. The third stage is support. You have just added another role to your already-too-busy life. There are, however, strategies that will help you accomplish your goals—perhaps not without struggle, but with grace and humor nonetheless. Let's look at each of these stages.

## Uncertainty

Why are you thinking about returning to school? Is it to:

- fulfill a dream that had to be delayed?
- become more educationally well-rounded?

These reasons focus on *personal growth.*

If you are returning to school to:

- meet people and make friends;
- attain and enjoy higher social status and prestige among friends, relatives, and associates;
- understand/study a cultural heritage; or
- have a medium in which to exchange ideas,

you are interested in *social and cultural opportunities.*

If you are like most adult students, you want to:

- qualify for a new occupation;
- enter or reenter the job market;
- increase earnings potential; or
- qualify for a more challenging position in the same field of work,

you are seeking *career growth.*

Understanding the reasons why you want to go back to school is an important step in setting your educational goals and will help you to establish some criteria for selecting a college. However, don't delay your decision because you have not been able to clearly define your motives. Many times, these aren't clear until you have already begun the process, and they may change as you move through your college experience.

Assuming you agree that additional education will benefit you, what is it that prevents you from returning to school? You may have a litany of excuses running through your mind:

- I don't have time.
- I can't afford it.
- I'm too old to learn.
- My friends will think I'm crazy.
- The teachers will be younger than I.
- My family can't survive without me to take care of them every minute.
- I'll be *x* years old when I finish.
- I'm afraid.
- I don't know what to expect.

And that is just what these are—excuses. You can make school, like anything else in your life, a priority or not. If you really want to return, you can. The more you understand your motivation for returning to school and the more you understand what excuses are keeping you from taking action, the easier your task will be.

**If you think you don't have time:** The best way to decide how attending class and studying can fit into your schedule is to keep track of what you do with your time each day for several weeks. Completing a standard time-management grid (each day is plotted out by the half hour) is helpful for visualizing how your time is spent. For each 3-credit-hour class you take, you will need to find 3 hours for class, plus 6 to 9 hours for reading-studying-library time. This study time should be spaced evenly throughout the week, not loaded up on one day. It is not possible to learn or retain the material that way. When you examine your grid, see where there are activities that could be replaced with school and study time. You may decide to give up your bowling league or some time in front of the TV. Try not to give up sleeping, and don't cut out every moment of free time. Here are some suggestions that have come from adults who have returned to school:

- Enroll in a time-management workshop. It helps you rethink how you use your time.
- Don't think you have to take more than one course at a time. You may eventually want to work up to taking more, but consider starting with one. (It is more than you are taking now!)
- If you have a family, start assigning to them those household chores that you usually do—and don't redo what they do.
- Use your lunch hour or commuting time for reading.

**If you think you cannot afford it:** As mentioned earlier, two-year colleges are extremely affordable. If you cannot afford the tuition, look into the various financial aid options. Most federal and state funds are available to full- and part-time students. Loans are also available. While many people prefer not to accumulate a debt for school, these same people will think nothing of taking out a loan to buy a car. After five or six years, which is the better investment? Adult students who work should look into whether their company has a tuition-reimbursement policy. There are also private scholarships, available through foundations, service organizations, and clubs, that are focused on adult learners. Your public library and a college financial aid adviser are two excellent sources for reference materials regarding financial aid.

**If you think you are too old to learn:** This is pure myth. A number of studies have shown that adult learners perform as well as or better than traditional-age students.

**If you are afraid your friends will think you're crazy:** Who cares? Maybe they will, maybe they won't. They may admire your courage and even be just a little jealous of your ambition (although they'll never tell you that). Follow your dreams, not theirs.

**If you are concerned because the teachers or students will be younger than you:** Don't be. The age differences that may be apparent in other settings evaporate in the classroom. If anything, an adult in the classroom strikes fear into the hearts of some 18-year-olds. Adult students have been known to be more prepared, ask better questions, be truly motivated, and be there to learn!

**If you think your family members will have a difficult time surviving while you are in school:** If you have done everything for them up to now, they might struggle. Consider this an opportunity to help them become independent and self-sufficient. Your family members can only make you feel guilty if you let them. You are not abandoning them; you are becoming an educational role model. When you are happy and working toward your goals, everyone benefits. Admittedly, it sometimes takes time for family members to realize this. For single parents, there are schools that offer support groups, child care, and cooperative babysitting.

**If you're appalled at the thought of being X years old when you graduate in Y years:** How old will you be in Y years if you *don't* go back to school?

**If you are afraid or don't know what to expect:** These are natural feelings when one encounters any new situation. Adult students find that their fears usually dissipate once they begin classes. Fear of trying is usually the biggest roadblock to the reentry process.

No doubt you have dreamed up a few more reasons for not deciding to return to school. Keep in mind that what you are doing is making up excuses, and you are using these excuses to release you from the obligation to make a decision about your life. The thought of returning to college can be scary. Anytime you venture into unknown territory, you take a risk, but taking risks is a necessary component of personal and professional growth. It is your life, and you alone are responsible for making the decisions that determine its course. Education is an investment in your future.

## Choice

Once you have decided to go back to school, your next task is to decide where to go. If your educational goals are well defined (e.g., you want to pursue a degree to change careers), then your task is a bit easier.

Most students who attend a public two-year college choose the community college in the district in which they live. This is generally the closest and least expensive option if the school offers the programs you want. If you are planning to begin your education at a two-year college and then transfer to a four-year school, there are distinct advantages to choosing your four-year school early. Many community and four-year colleges have "articulation" agreements that designate what credits from the two-year school will transfer to the four-year college, and how they can be transferred. Some four-year institutions accept an associate degree as equivalent to the freshman and sophomore years, regardless of the courses you have taken. Some four-year schools accept two-year college work only on a course-by-course basis. If you can identify which school you will transfer to, you can know in advance exactly how your two-year credits will apply and prevent an unexpected loss of credit or time.

Each institution of higher education is distinctive. Your goal in choosing a school is to come up with the best student-institution fit—matching your needs with the offerings and characteristics of the school. The first step is to determine what criteria are most important to you in attaining your educational goals. Location, cost, and program availability are the three main factors that influence an adult student's college choice. In considering location, don't forget that some colleges have conveniently located branch campuses. In considering cost, remember to explore your financial aid options before ruling out an institution because of its tuition. Program availability should include not only the area in which you are interested, but also whether or not classes in that area are available when you can take them.

Here are some additional considerations beyond location, cost, and programs:

- Does the school have a commitment to adult students and offer appropriate services, such as child care, tutoring, and advising?
- Are classes offered at times when you can take them?
- Is the faculty sensitive to the needs of adult learners?

Once you determine which criteria are vital in your choice of an institution, you can begin to narrow your choices. There are myriad ways for you to locate the information you desire. Many urban newspapers publish a "School Guide" several times a year in which colleges and universities advertise to an adult student market. In addition, schools themselves publish catalogs, class schedules, and promotional materials that contain much of the information you need, and they are yours for the asking. Many colleges sponsor information sessions and open houses that allow you to visit the campus and ask questions. An appointment with an adviser is a good way to assess the fit between you and the institution. Be sure to bring your questions with you to your interview.

## Support

Once you have made the decision to return to school and have chosen the institution that best meets your needs, take some additional steps to ensure your success during your crucial first semester. Take advantage of institutional support and build some social support systems of your own. Here are some ways to do that:

- Plan to participate in orientation programs. These serve the threefold purpose of providing you with a great deal of important information, familiarizing you with the school and its facilities, and giving you the opportunity to meet and begin networking with other students.
- Build new support networks by joining an adult student organization, making a point of meeting other adult students through workshops, or actively seeking out a "study buddy" in each class—that invaluable friend who shares and understands your experience.
- Incorporate your new status as student into your family life. Doing your homework with your

children at a designated homework time is a valuable family activity and reinforces the importance of education.

- Make sure you take a reasonable course load in your first semester. It is far better to have some extra time on your hands and to succeed magnificently than to spend the entire semester on the brink of a breakdown. Also, whenever possible, try to focus your first courses not only on requirements, but also on areas of personal interest.
- Seek out faculty members, advisers, and student affairs personnel who are there to help you during difficult times—let them assist you as often as necessary.

After completing your first semester, you will probably look back in wonder why you feared returning to school. Certainly, it's not without its occasional exasperations. But keeping things in perspective and maintaining your sense of humor will make the difference between merely coping and succeeding brilliantly.

# Careers in Business

When it comes to work environments, people's tastes generally fall into three categories. There are those who enjoy structure, working at a desk, and dressing in suits; those who appreciate some routine but want a certain amount of freedom in their schedule and appearance; and those who prefer to work in a workshop or outdoors. If you fall into the first category, you may find a career in business well-suited to your personality.

The good news is that you don't need Ivy League connections or an M.B.A. to land a good job in the business arena. In fact, many vocational school programs will teach you the ins and outs of the white-collar world and prepare you to be, for example, an administrative assistant, accounting technician, real-estate agent, or paralegal.

Now that most offices are computerized, administrative assistants—who used to be called secretaries—have much larger roles than ever before. They perform a wide range of administrative and clerical jobs that keep an organization running smoothly, including scheduling appointments, organizing and maintaining files, filling out forms, and operating office equipment such as personal computers, fax machines, scanners, and photocopiers.

Accounting technicians, who are perhaps more "behind the scenes" but very important for a business's success, keep track of a company's finances using computers, calculators, and ledger books. Accounting technicians may also prepare financial reports and handle bank deposits. With computerization, accounting work is faster and more efficient. Those who are well trained on the latest equipment stand a good chance of finding great jobs.

Another important business occupation is that of the paralegal, who assists lawyers in legal research. Paralegals help prepare cases by searching for information in law books, public records, computer databases, and various documents. They may also work on wills, inheritances, and income tax returns. Some paralegals write drafts of important documents, including contracts, mortgages, and separation agreements.

Many businesspeople dream of being their own boss one day, and in the field of real estate, they have a good chance of achieving that goal. Real estate agents that have a thorough knowledge of the housing market in their community, including information about neighborhoods, zoning, and tax laws, work with buyers and sellers of homes.

With the variety of business professions available to vocational school graduates, you're sure to find a career that suits you.

## Business Professions

Accounting

Accounting technical services

Administrative and secretarial services

Administrative assistant/secretarial science

Advertising

Agricultural and food products processing operations and management

Agricultural business/agribusiness operations

Agricultural business and management

Agricultural business and production

Apparel and accessories marketing operations

Auctioneering

Aviation and airway science

Aviation management

Banking and financial support services

Broadcast journalism

Business administration and management

Business and personal services marketing operations

Business communications
Business management and administrative services
Business marketing and marketing management
Business services marketing operations
Business systems networking and telecommunications
Buying operations
Child-care services management
Communications
Computer and information sciences
Court reporting
Distribution operations
Enterprise management and operation
Entrepreneurship
Executive assistant/secretarial services
Farm and ranch management
Fashion merchandising
Finance
Financial management and services
Financial services marketing operations
Fire services administration
Floristry marketing operations
Food and beverage/restaurant operations management
Food products retailing and wholesaling operations
Food sales operations
Franchise operation
General office/clerical and typing services
Home and office products marketing operations
Home products marketing operations
Hospitality/administration management
Hospitality and recreation marketing operations
Hospitality services management
Hotel/motel and restaurant management
Hotel/motel services marketing operations
Human resources management
Information processing/data entry services
Institutional food service and administration
Insurance and risk management
Insurance marketing operations
Journalism
Journalism and mass communication
Labor/personnel relations and studies
Legal administrative assistant/secretarial services
Library assistance
Logistics and materials management
Marketing management and research
Marketing operations/marketing and distribution
Medical administrative assistant/secretarial services
Natural resource management and protective services
Nonprofit and public management
Office management and supervision
Operations management and supervision
Paralegal/legal assistance
Parks, recreation, and leisure facilities management
Personal services marketing operations
Purchasing, procurement, and contracts management
Radio and television broadcasting
Real estate
Reception
Recreation products/services marketing operations
Retailing and wholesaling operations and skills
Retailing operations
Sales operations
Security and loss prevention services
Taxation
Tourism and travel services marketing operations
Tourism promotion operations
Travel services marketing operations
Travel-tourism management
Vehicle and petroleum products marketing operations
Vehicle parts and accessories marketing operations
Wildlife and wildlands management

# Careers in Health Care

Do you enjoy watching TV shows and movies about hospitals and doctors? Do you feel a thrill when you see an ambulance race down the street with its lights flashing? Do you like helping family members or friends when they are sick or injured? If so, you can find a fulfilling career in the rapidly growing health-care industry—without the time and expense involved in attending medical school.

Many vocational school programs, ranging from licensed practical nurse training to emergency medical technical preparation, are currently available to guide those interested in health care.

Licensed practical nurses (LPNs) care for sick, injured, recovering, and disabled people under the guidance of physicians and registered nurses. Most LPNs work at the patient's bedside, checking blood pressure, pulse, and respiration. They may also give injections and change bandages. Their responsibilities may include bathing, dressing, and feeding patients and helping to keep them comfortable.

The responsibilities of medical assistants are closely tied to the routine of a doctor's office. While duties vary from office to office, medical assistants generally perform a combination of clerical and clinical duties. Clerical duties might include answering telephones, keeping patient files, filling out insurance forms, and scheduling appointments, while clinical tasks could involve collecting and preparing laboratory specimens, instructing patients about medication, taking EKGs, and removing stitches.

Dental assistants, like medical assistants, perform a variety of clinical, office, and laboratory duties. They work beside the dentist at the patient's chair, preparing trays with dental tools, assisting the dentist, and instructing patients in brushing and flossing. They may also make impressions of teeth and take and develop X-rays. Dental assistants often schedule appointments, keep records, receive payments from patients, and order supplies.

Emergency medical technicians (EMTs) work with sick and injured people before they reach a doctor's office or hospital. Their job is to treat the problem immediately—whether it's a wound, a heart attack, or poisoning—and then transport the patient to the proper place as quickly as possible. EMTs generally work in teams of 2 to assess and treat the illness or injury. They are also trained to perform a variety of emergency procedures, including restoring breathing, controlling bleeding, and assisting in childbirth.

As the population increases and the average lifespan lengthens, jobs in health care will be interesting and plentiful for those with the right preparation. Employment opportunities in these professions are expected to increase much more quickly through the year 2016 than the average compared to other professions.

## Health-Care Professions

Acupuncture and Oriental medicine
Alcohol/drug abuse counseling
Athletic training and sports medicine
Blood bank technical services
Cardiovascular technology
Child care and guidance work and management
Child-care service/assistance
Community health liaison
Cytotechnology
Dental assistance
Dental hygiene
Dental laboratory technical services
Dental services
Dietetics/human nutritional services

Diagnostic medical sonography
Elder-care provider/companion services
Electrocardiograph technology
Electroencephalograph technology
Emergency medical technical services
Environmental health
Health aide services
Health and medical administrative services
Health and medical assistance
Health and medical diagnostic and treatment services
Health and medical laboratory technologies
Health and physical education/fitness
Health physics/radiologic health
Health professions and related sciences
Health unit coordination/ward clerk
Health unit management/ward supervision
Hematology technology
Home health aide services
Hypnotherapy
Medical assistance
Medical dietician
Medical laboratory assistance
Medical laboratory technical services
Medical office management
Medical radiologic technology
Medical records administration
Medical records technical services
Medical transcription
Mental health services
Naturopathic medicine
Nuclear medical technology
Nurse assistance/aide
Nursing
Nursing (RN training)
Occupational health and industrial hygiene
Occupational therapy assistance
Ophthalmic medical assistance
Ophthalmic medical technical services
Ophthalmic/optometric laboratory technology
Ophthalmic/optometric services
Optical technical services/assistance
Opticianry/dispense opticianry
Orthotics/prosthetics
Parks, recreation, leisure, and fitness studies
Pharmacy technical services/assistance
Physical therapy
Physical therapy assistance
Physician assistance
Practical nursing (LPN training)
Psychiatric/mental health services technical services
Recreational therapy
Rehabilitation/therapeutic services
Respiratory therapy technology
Surgical/operating room technical services
Vocational rehabilitation counseling

# Careers in Technology

It's hard to go a single day without noticing the huge role technology plays in our daily lives. Even something as familiar as the mail demonstrates the impact of technology: Bills are computed on lightning-fast machines, letters are written with word-processing programs, mailing lists are kept on huge electronic databases, and barcode readers help scan and sort mail. If you're interested in how computers streamline any of these or a million other processes, you can excel in a technology-related career.

People interested in learning how electronic systems work might consider jobs as data-processing technicians—people who install, maintain, and repair computers. They also keep records of repairs and order parts. Data-processing technicians often work for computer manufacturers, but they also find employment with businesses that maintain large computer systems, such as banks, insurance firms, and public utility companies.

Electronics engineering technicians need to be familiar with technical machines other than computers, because they help design, build, install, maintain, and repair electronic equipment such as radios, televisions, control devices, and sonar, radar, and navigational equipment, as well as computers. Electronics engineering technicians often rely on high-tech measuring and diagnostic devices to get the job done. Employment opportunities in this field are expected to rise more quickly than the average for many other professions through the year 2016.

People who are more interested in the "brains" of the machine than in the "muscle" may want to consider a career in computer programming. Computer programmers write step-by-step instructions that direct computers to process information in a series of logical steps. Programmers work in all types of businesses, from hospitals to schools, since just about every line of work relies on computer power these days.

Whether you're interested in the miniature silicon chips inside computers or the larger parts that make technical equipment function correctly, a vocational school program could help prepare you for a career in one of the most exciting, fastest-growing fields.

## Technology Professions

Aeronautical and aerospace engineering technology

Air traffic control

Architectural engineering technology

Automotive engineering technology

Aviation science

Aviation systems and avionics maintenance technology

Biological technology

Biomedical engineering-related technology

Business computer facilities operation

Business computer programming

Business information and data processing services

Chemical technology

Civil engineering

Civil engineering/civil technology

Communications technology

Computer and information sciences

Computer engineering technology

Computer maintenance technology

Computer typography and composition equipment operation

Construction/building technology

Data processing technology

Desktop publishing equipment operation

Educational/instructional media technology

Electrical and electronic engineering-related technologies

Electrical, electronic, and communications engineering technology

Electromechanical instrumentation and maintenance technologies

Electromechanical technology

Energy management and systems technology

Engineering-related technologies

Environmental and pollution control technologies

Forensic technical services

Forest harvesting and production technology

Forest products technology

Heating, air conditioning, and refrigeration technology

Hydraulic technology

Industrial production technologies

Industrial/manufacturing technology

Laser and optical technology

Management information systems and business data processing

Mechanical engineering/mechanical technology

Mechanical engineering-related technologies

Metallurgical technology

Mining technology

Nuclear and industrial radiologic technologies

Nuclear/nuclear power technology

Occupational safety and health technology

Petroleum technology

Photographic technology

Physical science technologies

Plastics technology

Quality control and safety technology

Quality control technology

Radio and television broadcasting technology

Robotics technology

Science technologies

Solar technology

Surveying

Water quality and wastewater treatment technology

# Careers in the Trade

For some people, a day's work doesn't count for much if it doesn't involve getting their hands dirty or breaking a sweat. To these achievers, work means a lot more than wearing a suit and shuffling papers at a desk. If you're a get-down-to-the-nitty-gritty kind of person, you might consider a career in auto mechanics, electrical work, carpentry, or law enforcement. Many vocational school programs are available to give you the information and training you need to break into these and other related fields.

Auto mechanics, also called automotive service technicians, repair and service automobiles and light trucks. Mechanics must have in-depth knowledge about how vehicles work to be able to identify what caused a car or truck to break down and to perform routine tasks that keep automobiles running smoothly.

Those who are fascinated by wires and connections might consider a career as an electrician. Although the main responsibility of an electrician is to install and maintain electrical systems, specific systems can range from climate control to communications. Some electricians specialize in preventive maintenance; they routinely inspect equipment, searching for problems before systems break down.

Within the building trade, the most plentiful positions are for carpenters—people who cut, shape, and assemble wood to construct buildings or create other products such as cabinets and doors. Carpenters work on construction sites, inside buildings, in factories, and in woodworking shops. The majority of those employed as carpenters work for contractors who build, remodel, or repair buildings and other structures.

If you're interested in challenging, physical work outside of a traditional office environment, you might find that a trade career will satisfy these needs.

## Trade Professions

Agricultural animal husbandry and production management
Agricultural mechanization
Agricultural power machinery operation
Agricultural production work and management
Agricultural supplies and related services
Agricultural supplies retailing and wholesaling
Agriculture/agricultural sciences
Air transportation services
Animal training
Aquaculture operations and production management
Architectural drafting
Auto/automotive body repair
Auto/automotive mechanical/technical services
Building/property maintenance and management
Business machine repair
Cabinet making and millworking
Carpentry
Civil/structural drafting
Clothing, apparel, and textile work and management
Commercial garment and apparel services
Commercial photography
Communication systems installation and repair
Computer installation and repair
Conservation and renewable natural resources
Construction and building finishing and management
Construction/building inspecting
Construction equipment operating
Construction trades
Crop production operations and management
Custodial, housekeeping, and home services and management

Custodial services/caretaking
Custom tailoring
Diesel engine mechanical and repair services
Dietitian assistance
Diving (professional)
Drafting
Dry cleaning and laundering (commercial)
Electrical and electronics equipment installation and repair
Electrical and power transmission installation
Electrical/electronics drafting
Electrician
Equestrian/equine studies, horse management, and training
Fire protection
Fire protection and safety technology
Fire science/firefighting
Fishing technology/commercial fishing
Food catering
Forest production and processing
Forestry
Furniture design and craft
Graphic and printing equipment operation
Greenhouse operations and management
Gunsmithing
Heating, air conditioning, and refrigeration mechanical and repair services
Heavy equipment maintenance and repair
Home furnishings and equipment installation and consultation
Horseshoeing
Horticulture services operations and management
Industrial design
Industrial electronics installation and repair
Industrial equipment maintenance and repair
Industrial machinery maintenance and repair
Instrument calibration and repair
Landscaping operations and management
Leather working and upholstering
Line work
Lithography and platemaking
Locksmithing and safe repair
Logging/timber harvesting
Machine shop assistance
Machinist/machine technology
Major appliance installation and repair
Marine maintenance and ship repair
Masonry and tile setting
Mechanical and repair services
Mechanical drafting
Mechanical typesetting and composing
Mechanical and repair services
Motorcycle mechanical and repair services
Musical instrument repair
Nursery operations and management
Ornamental horticulture operations and management
Painting and wall covering
Plumbing and pipe fitting
Precision metal working
Precision production trades
Printing press operation
Sheet metal working
Shoe, boot, and leather repair
Small engine mechanical and repair services
Stationary energy sources installation and operation
Tool- and die-making/technology
Transportation and materials moving
Truck, bus, and other commercial vehicle operation
Vehicle and equipment operation
Vehicle and mobile equipment mechanical and repair services
Watch, clock, and jewelry repair
Water transportation services
Welding
Window treatment making and installation
Woodworking

# Careers in Visual and Performing Arts

If you feel the need to express yourself on canvas or on a stage, or you enjoy making your own clothes or jewelry, taking photographs, singing, dancing, or doodling, chances are that a career in visual and performing arts is for you.

There are numerous careers where you can use your creativity and self-expression as a service to others. For example, some visual artists use computer techniques to create art to meet clients' needs, whether for packaging and promotional displays, company logos and stationery, or newspaper or magazine ads.

In addition to the programs listed here, you may want to consult *Peterson's College Guide for Performing Arts Majors* or *Peterson's College Guide for Visual Arts Majors.*

## Visual and Performing Arts Professions

Acting and directing

Ceramic arts and ceramics

Crafts, folk art, and artisanry

Design and applied arts

Design and visual communications

Dramatic/theater arts and stagecraft

Drawing

Fashion and fabric consultation

Fashion design and illustration

Fashion modeling

Film/video and photographic arts

Film-video making/cinematography and production

Fine arts and art studies

Fine/studio arts

Graphic design, commercial art, and illustration

Interior design

Intermedia

Metal and jewelry arts

Music

Music—piano and organ performance

Music—voice and choral/opera performance

Painting

Photography

Printmaking

Technical theater/theater design and stagecraft

# Careers in Personal Services

It's hard for some people to believe they can earn a living doing something they enjoy, particularly when it involves helping or serving others in a calm environment. Are you one of those people who cuts your friends' hair for free? Would you enjoy using your artistic talent to enhance the looks of other people through cosmetics? If so, many vocational school programs can help you turn these interests into a steady paycheck.

Barbers and hairstylists shampoo and cut hair, shave and cut beards and mustaches, give facial massages and hair and scalp treatments, and recommend and sell grooming products. Cosmetologists—who may also be called beauty operators, hairdressers, and beauticians—perform many similar duties: They care for their clients' skin and nails by giving massages and facials, shaping eyebrows, and offering makeup advice.

If you have the talent and the patience necessary to figure out what others need and want, consider checking out vocational programs for personal service careers, which are fun—and profitable.

---

**Personal Services Professions**

Barbering/hairstyling

Cosmetic services

Cosmetology

Electrolysis technician services

Executive housekeeping

Funeral services and mortuary science

Homemaker's aide services

Make-up artistry

Massage services

# Careers in Other Fields

A number of career areas do not fall neatly into any of the six major categories already covered. These careers include criminal justice and law enforcement, teacher education, language instruction, culinary arts, fashion modeling, and bartending.

Police officers are charged with protecting the lives and property of citizens, and their days are filled with work aimed at preventing crime. Officers may work in investigation, at police departments, in traffic control, or for crime prevention. The majority of police officers, detectives, and special agents are employed by local city governments.

Bartenders prepare alcoholic drinks for restaurant, bar, and cocktail lounge patrons and need to know exact recipes for a multitude of drinks. Busy workers in this profession take drink orders, mix and serve the drinks, and collect money; they may also wash and dry glasses behind the bar and be responsible for keeping the bar area clean and well-stocked.

If you are interested in an unconventional work schedule and enjoy interacting with people, consider enrolling in programs in these areas.

### Other Professions

Adult and continuing teacher education
Agriculture/agricultural sciences
Animal sciences
Baking/pastry chef training
Bartending/mixology
Card dealing
Corrections/correctional administration
Criminal justice and corrections
Criminal justice/law enforcement administration
Culinary arts/chef training
Custodial, housekeeping, and home services work and management
Education
Elementary teacher education
Flight attending
Foreign language interpretation and translation
Gaming and sports officiating services
Home economics
Kitchen personnel/cook and assistant training
Law enforcement/police science
Marine science/merchant marine official
Meatcutting
Pet grooming
Pre-elementary/early childhood/kindergarten teacher education
Protective services
Public administration and services
Sign language interpretation
Social work
Special education
Teacher assistance
Veterinarian assistant/animal health technician services
Vocational home economics
Waiter/waitress and dining room management

# New and Emerging Careers

As the job market continues to expand and redefine itself, several new employment opportunities have become available. Emerging occupations can be characterized as new occupations created by changes in technology, society, markets, or regulations. Emerging occupations may also describe existing occupations that have been substantially modified by the same changes and are increasing in employment opportunities. The following are a few of the new and emerging occupations identified by the U.S. Department of Labor, Bureau of Labor Statistics.

Now with the emerging employment trend of "going green," many new and exciting careers have emerged in regards to the environment and environmental protection. Environmental engineers, environmental compliance managers, regulatory compliance managers, and environmental scientists and technicians work together to ensure compliance with environmental regulations and company policy. Environmental compliance managers direct the work of scientists, technicians and hazardous materials removal workers and field technicians. The work may involve the disposal of hazardous materials, monitoring emissions of pollutants, or protecting the safety of employees on the job. Environmental engineers and scientists may also work on environmental impact statements or environmental assessments. Some may work as contractors advising clients on how to ensure compliance with environmental law and regulations. These environmental professionals were mostly reported in industries that must adhere to environmental regulations, such as the paper and allied products; fabricated metal products; industrial machinery and equipment; electric, gas, and sanitary services; construction; wholesale trade; business services; health services; and engineering and management services industries.

Consumer credit counselors provide advice on personal finance, such as budgeting, money management, mortgages, and financial planning, especially to those with money management or credit problems. They may help negotiate with creditors to arrange a debt repayment plan to help clients avoid personal bankruptcy. They may conduct public education workshops and seminars on personal finance subjects. They are employed in the nonprofit social services industry.

Convention managers, meeting planners, conference planners, and convention coordinators convention planning personnel serve as liaisons between their own organization and various outside vendors that provide goods and services for a convention. Convention managers coordinate activities of convention center/hotel/banquet personnel to make arrangements for group meetings and conventions. Convention managers were most prominent in the membership organizations industry. They were also reported in the following industries: business services; educational services; printing and publishing; social services; health services; transportation services; wholesale trade; depository institutions; insurance carriers; and hotels, rooming houses, camps, and other lodging industries.

Continued technological advances in computer hardware, software, printers, and related equipment now allow firms to do more document production in-house and on demand. Doing the work this way is faster than sending it to an outside vendor. Desktop publishing specialists and desktop publishing operators use advanced computer graphics and word processing computer systems to produce documents such as reports, proposals, benefit books, advertisements, brochures, and flyers. Firms in the finance, insurance and real estate, and wholesale trade industries, among others, reported desktop publishing occupations.

Nonprofit organizations are the primary employers of volunteer coordinators. Volunteer coordinators and volunteer directors work to recruit, train, schedule, and organize volunteers in the educational services, local government, health services, residential care, membership organizations, and social services industries.

Web masters, web site technicians, and web site coordinators write the computer code necessary to publish or update text and images on Web sites. They also design and maintain Web sites. As more organizations project a presence on the Internet, more Web workers are being reported. Establishments in the printing and publishing, wholesale trade, retail trade, business services, and membership organizations industries have reported employment of Internet publishing personnel.

More specialized fields will continue to emerge, making the job market even more attractive to students of vocational and technical schools.

# How to Use This Guide

## Profiles of Vo-Tech Schools

**Institution Name:** The heading for each institution gives the name of the school or institution, the street address, the Web address (if available), the chief officer to contact for admissions information, and the admissions phone number.

**General Information:** This section lists key facts and figures about the institution, including institution type, when it was founded, the type of accreditation it has, the total enrollment of students in its vo-tech programs as of the official fall reporting date, and the application fee.

**Program(s) Offered:** Programs that a school offers are listed, followed by their individual program enrollment or their length and cost. The Integrated Postsecondary Education Data System (IPEPS) collects and collates data in two different ways depending on whether a school is a degree-granting institute or if it grants certificates. Therefore, the type of data presented may differ from program to program.

**Student Services:** This section details support services, ranging from career counseling to child day care, that are offered to program participants.

## Appendixes

The Appendixes contain two listings. The first lists the State Offices of Apprenticeship Contacts. The second listing contains the accrediting organizations that are recognized by the Council for Higher Education Accreditation (CHEA) of the U.S. Department of Education. Recognition by CHEA affirms that the standards and processes of the accrediting organization are consistent with the academic quality, improvement, and accountability expectations that CHEA has established. The organizations are listed alphabetically by their region or by their field of specialization and include contact information, should you wish to check on a particular program's accreditation.

## Indexes

The Career Training Programs index allows you to search by a given career area to see which schools offer training programs in your field of interest. Career areas are listed alphabetically. Within each career area, institution names are broken down by state to facilitate your search. The location of each school appears after the school name.

If you can't find the career area you're looking for, refer to the "Careers in..." articles. Career areas found in the index are listed at the end of each of the articles. Be sure to look at all the lists to make sure you're not forgetting any career opportunities you hadn't thought of previously.

The Alphabetical Listing of Vo-Tech Schools index of institutions can help you find a particular school by name.

## Data Collection Procedures

Information for schools was obtained from IPEDS (The Integrated Postsecondary Education Data System) 2007–08 data file. All usable information received in time for publication has been included. The omission of a particular item from a profile means either that it is not applicable to that particular school or not available or usable. Because of the system of checks performed on the data collected by Peterson's, we believe that the information presented in this guide is accurate. Nonetheless, errors and omissions are possible in a data collection endeavor of this scope. Also, facts and figures are subject to change. Therefore, students should check at the time of application with the specific institution to verify all pertinent information.

## Criteria for Inclusion in This Book

*Peterson's Vocational and Technical Schools East* profiles more than 2,300 U.S. institutions of higher education that offer postsecondary awards, certificates, or diplomas requiring less than two years of study. Institutions that are included meet the qualifications of having been in operation for at least two years and must be accredited by a national, regional, state, or specialized accrediting body.

The programs included are defined as instructional and designed to prepare individuals with entry-level skills and training required for employment in a specific trade, occupation, or profession.

This definition of vocational and technical schools includes private colleges (also called career colleges), public colleges, and regional technical training centers. For information on schools offering associate degree programs in the career areas listed in this book, refer to *Peterson's Two-Year Colleges.*

# Profiles of Vo-Tech Schools

# ALASKA

## Alaska Pacific University

4101 University Drive, Anchorage, AK 99508-4672
http://www.alaskapacific.edu/

**CONTACT** Douglas M. North, President
**Telephone:** 907-561-1266

**GENERAL INFORMATION** Private Institution. Founded 1959. **Accreditation:** Regional (NCCU/NCCU). **Total program enrollment:** 467. **Application fee:** $25.

**PROGRAM(S) OFFERED**
• **Entrepreneurship/Entrepreneurial Studies** • **Finance, General**

**STUDENT SERVICES** Academic or career counseling, employment services for current students, remedial services.

## Alaska Vocational Technical Center

PO Box 889, Seward, AK 99664
http://avtec.labor.state.ak.us/

**CONTACT** Fred Esposito, Director
**Telephone:** 907-224-3322

**GENERAL INFORMATION** Public Institution. Founded 1970. **Total program enrollment:** 324. **Application fee:** $25.

**PROGRAM(S) OFFERED**
• **Administrative Assistant and Secretarial Science, General** *1281 hrs./$2835* • **Automobile/Automotive Mechanics Technology/Technician** *6 students enrolled* • **Building/Property Maintenance and Management** *6 students enrolled* • **Design and Visual Communications, General** *7 students enrolled* • **Diesel Mechanics Technology/Technician** *1281 hrs./$2835* • **Heating, Air Conditioning, Ventilation and Refrigeration Maintenance Technology/Technician (HAC, HACR, HVAC, HVACR)** *4 students enrolled* • **Industrial Electronics Technology/Technician** *1379 hrs./$2835* • **Information Science/Studies** *15 students enrolled* • **Licensed Practical/Vocational Nurse Training (LPN, LVN, Cert, Dipl, AAS)** *23 students enrolled* • **Marine Science/Merchant Marine Officer** *15 students enrolled* • **Nurse/Nursing Assistant/Aide and Patient Care Assistant** *230 hrs./$1736* • **Restaurant, Culinary, and Catering Management/Manager** *1470 hrs./$2835* • **Welding Technology/Welder** *630 hrs./$2310*

**STUDENT SERVICES** Academic or career counseling, daycare for children of students, employment services for current students, placement services for program completers, remedial services.

## Career Academy

1415 East Tudor Road, Anchorage, AK 99507
http://www.careeracademy.edu/

**CONTACT** Jennifer Deitz, President
**Telephone:** 907-563-7575

**GENERAL INFORMATION** Private Institution. **Total program enrollment:** 339. **Application fee:** $50.

**PROGRAM(S) OFFERED**
• **Aviation/Airway Management and Operations** *306 hrs./$5905* • **Business Administration and Management, General** *914 hrs./$9705* • **Massage Therapy/Therapeutic Massage** *915 hrs./$10,005* • **Medical Insurance Coding Specialist/Coder** *362 hrs./$7705* • **Medical/Clinical Assistant** *946 hrs./$10,005* • **Phlebotomy/Phlebotomist** *521 hrs./$7705* • **Tourism and Travel Services Management**

**STUDENT SERVICES** Employment services for current students, placement services for program completers.

## Charter College

2221 East Northern Lights Boulevard, Suite 120, Anchorage, AK 99508-4140
http://www.chartercollege.edu/

**CONTACT** Terrance Harris, President
**Telephone:** 907-277-1000

**GENERAL INFORMATION** Private Institution. Founded 1985. **Accreditation:** State accredited or approved. **Total program enrollment:** 210.

**PROGRAM(S) OFFERED**
• **Accounting** *5 students enrolled* • **Business/Office Automation/Technology/Data Entry** *5 students enrolled* • **CAD/CADD Drafting and/or Design Technology/Technician** *2 students enrolled* • **Computer and Information Systems Security** • **General Office Occupations and Clerical Services** • **Medical Insurance Coding Specialist/Coder** *14 students enrolled* • **Medical/Clinical Assistant** *6 students enrolled*

**STUDENT SERVICES** Academic or career counseling, employment services for current students, placement services for program completers.

## Ilisagvik College

UIC/Narl, Barrow, AK 99723
http://www.ilisagvik.cc/

**CONTACT** Beverly Patkotak Grinage, President
**Telephone:** 907-852-3333

**GENERAL INFORMATION** Public Institution. Founded 1995. **Accreditation:** Regional (NCCU/NCCU). **Total program enrollment:** 30.

**PROGRAM(S) OFFERED**
• **Accounting Technology/Technician and Bookkeeping** *6 students enrolled* • **American Indian/Native American Languages, Literatures, and Linguistics** *1 student enrolled* • **Business Administration and Management, General** • **Carpentry/Carpenter** *2 students enrolled* • **Construction Trades, General** • **Construction Trades, Other** *15 students enrolled* • **Crafts/Craft Design, Folk Art and Artisanry** • **Electrician** *3 students enrolled* • **Health Services/Allied Health/Health Sciences, General** *2 students enrolled* • **Information Technology** *6 students enrolled* • **Medical Insurance Coding Specialist/Coder** • **Non-Profit/Public/Organizational Management** • **Office Management and Supervision** *2 students enrolled* • **Pipefitting/Pipefitter and Sprinkler Fitter** *6 students enrolled* • **Plumbing Technology/Plumber** • **Truck and Bus Driver/Commercial Vehicle Operation** *1 student enrolled*

**STUDENT SERVICES** Academic or career counseling, employment services for current students, remedial services.

## University of Alaska Anchorage

3211 Providence Drive, Anchorage, AK 99508-8060
http://www.uaa.alaska.edu/

**CONTACT** Fran Ulmer, Chancellor
**Telephone:** 907-786-1800

**GENERAL INFORMATION** Public Institution. Founded 1954. **Accreditation:** Regional (NCCU/NCCU); art and design (NASAD); dental assisting (ADA); dental hygiene (ADA); dietetics: postbaccalaureate internship (ADtA/CAADE); engineering-related programs (ABET/RAC); journalism and mass communications (ACEJMC); medical assisting (AAMAE); medical laboratory technology (NAACLS); medical technology (NAACLS); music (NASM). **Total program enrollment:** 7374. **Application fee:** $40.

**PROGRAM(S) OFFERED**
• **Accounting Technology/Technician and Bookkeeping** *3 students enrolled* • **Administrative Assistant and Secretarial Science, General** • **Airframe Mechanics and Aircraft Maintenance Technology/Technician** *6 students enrolled* • **Architectural Drafting and Architectural CAD/CADD** *4 students enrolled* • **Architectural Engineering Technology/Technician** • **Automobile/Automotive Mechanics Technology/Technician** • **Business/Corporate Communications** • **CAD/CADD Drafting and/or Design Technology/Technician** *3 students enrolled* • **Child Care Provider/Assistant** *4 students enrolled* • **Civil Drafting and Civil Engineering CAD/CADD** • **Computer Systems Networking and Telecommunica-**

*University of Alaska Anchorage (continued)*

**tions** *2 students enrolled* • **Dental Assisting/Assistant** *9 students enrolled* • **Diesel Mechanics Technology/Technician** • **Drafting and Design Technology/Technician, General** *2 students enrolled* • **Drafting/Design Engineering Technologies/Technicians, Other** *4 students enrolled* • **Early Childhood Education and Teaching** • **Electrical/Electronics Drafting and Electrical/Electronics CAD/CADD** *4 students enrolled* • **Electrical/Electronics Maintenance and Repair Technology, Other** • **Entrepreneurship/Entrepreneurial Studies** *4 students enrolled* • **General Office Occupations and Clerical Services** *5 students enrolled* • **Geotechnical Engineering** *3 students enrolled* • **Heating, Air Conditioning, Ventilation and Refrigeration Maintenance Technology/Technician (HAC, HACR, HVAC, HVACR)** *3 students enrolled* • **Heavy Equipment Maintenance Technology/Technician** • **Legal Administrative Assistant/Secretary** • **Legal Assistant/Paralegal** *10 students enrolled* • **Licensed Practical/Vocational Nurse Training (LPN, LVN, Cert, Dipl, AAS)** *23 students enrolled* • **Logistics and Materials Management** *3 students enrolled* • **Management Information Systems, General** *4 students enrolled* • **Massage Therapy/Therapeutic Massage** • **Mechanical Engineering** • **Mechanical Engineering/Mechanical Technology/Technician** • **Medical Office Assistant/Specialist** *2 students enrolled* • **Nursing—Registered Nurse Training (RN, ASN, BSN, MSN)** • **Office Management and Supervision** • **Petroleum Technology/Technician** • **Pharmacy Technician/Assistant** *1 student enrolled* • **Philosophy** • **Phlebotomy/Phlebotomist** *6 students enrolled* • **Radiologic Technology/Science—Radiographer** *11 students enrolled* • **System, Networking, and LAN/WAN Management/Manager** *8 students enrolled* • **Web Page, Digital/Multimedia and Information Resources Design** *4 students enrolled* • **Welding Technology/Welder** *1 student enrolled*

**STUDENT SERVICES** Academic or career counseling, daycare for children of students, employment services for current students, placement services for program completers, remedial services.

## University of Alaska Fairbanks

PO Box 757500, Fairbanks, AK 99775-7520
http://www.uaf.edu/

**CONTACT** Brian Rogers, Interim Chancellor
**Telephone:** 907-474-7211

**GENERAL INFORMATION** Public Institution. Founded 1917. **Accreditation:** Regional (NCCU/NCCU); computer science (ABET/CSAC); forestry (SAF); journalism and mass communications (ACEJMC); medical assisting (AAMAE); music (NASM). **Total program enrollment:** 4022. **Application fee:** $40.

**PROGRAM(S) OFFERED**
• **Accounting Technology/Technician and Bookkeeping** *13 students enrolled* • **Administrative Assistant and Secretarial Science, General** *1 student enrolled* • **Aircraft Powerplant Technology/Technician** • **Airframe Mechanics and Aircraft Maintenance Technology/Technician** *7 students enrolled* • **American Indian/Native American Languages, Literatures, and Linguistics** *7 students enrolled* • **Automobile/Automotive Mechanics Technology/Technician** *13 students enrolled* • **Business Administration and Management, General** *14 students enrolled* • **Carpentry/Carpenter** *23 students enrolled* • **Child Care Provider/Assistant** • **Clinical/Medical Laboratory Assistant** • **Community Organization and Advocacy** *2 students enrolled* • **Computer Installation and Repair Technology/Technician** • **Culinary Arts/Chef Training** *1 student enrolled* • **Dental Assisting/Assistant** *1 student enrolled* • **Diesel Mechanics Technology/Technician** *6 students enrolled* • **Drafting and Design Technology/Technician, General** *18 students enrolled* • **Early Childhood Education and Teaching** *7 students enrolled* • **Fire Science/Firefighting** • **Foreign Languages, Literatures, and Linguistics, Other** *1 student enrolled* • **Health and Medical Administrative Services, Other** *4 students enrolled* • **Industrial Safety Technology/Technician** *11 students enrolled* • **Instrumentation Technology/Technician** *12 students enrolled* • **Kindergarten/Preschool Education and Teaching** • **Medical Administrative/Executive Assistant and Medical Secretary** *2 students enrolled* • **Medical/Clinical Assistant** *4 students enrolled* • **Mental and Social Health Services and Allied Professions, Other** *19 students enrolled* • **Teacher Assistant/Aide** • **Vehicle Maintenance and Repair Technologies, Other**

**STUDENT SERVICES** Academic or career counseling, employment services for current students, placement services for program completers, remedial services.

## University of Alaska, Prince William Sound Community College

PO Box 97, Valdez, AK 99686-0097
http://www.pwscc.edu/

**CONTACT** Douglas A. Desorcie, President
**Telephone:** 907-834-1600

**GENERAL INFORMATION** Public Institution. Founded 1978. **Accreditation:** Regional (NCCU/NCCU). **Total program enrollment:** 70. **Application fee:** $25.

**PROGRAM(S) OFFERED**
• **Administrative Assistant and Secretarial Science, General** • **Broadcast Journalism** • **Industrial Production Technologies/Technicians, Other** • **Management Information Systems, General** *1 student enrolled* • **Special Education and Teaching, General** *2 students enrolled*

**STUDENT SERVICES** Academic or career counseling, employment services for current students, placement services for program completers, remedial services.

## University of Alaska Southeast

11120 Glacier Highway, Juneau, AK 99801
http://www.uas.alaska.edu/

**CONTACT** John Pugh, Chancellor
**Telephone:** 877-465-4827

**GENERAL INFORMATION** Public Institution. Founded 1972. **Accreditation:** Regional (NCCU/NCCU). **Total program enrollment:** 769. **Application fee:** $40.

**PROGRAM(S) OFFERED**
• **Accounting Technology/Technician and Bookkeeping** *4 students enrolled* • **Accounting** *1 student enrolled* • **Art/Art Studies, General** *22 students enrolled* • **Automobile/Automotive Mechanics Technology/Technician** • **Building/Home/Construction Inspection/Inspector** *1 student enrolled* • **Carpentry/Carpenter** • **Criminal Justice/Police Science** • **Diesel Mechanics Technology/Technician** *1 student enrolled* • **Drafting and Design Technology/Technician, General** *1 student enrolled* • **Early Childhood Education and Teaching** *5 students enrolled* • **Educational/Instructional Media Design** *5 students enrolled* • **Electrical and Power Transmission Installation/Installer, General** • **Elementary Education and Teaching** *5 students enrolled* • **Entrepreneurship/Entrepreneurial Studies** *1 student enrolled* • **Environmental Control Technologies/Technicians, Other** • **General Office Occupations and Clerical Services** • **Health Aide** *8 students enrolled* • **Health Information/Medical Records Administration/Administrator** *2 students enrolled* • **Management Information Systems, General** • **Marine Maintenance/Fitter and Ship Repair Technology/Technician** • **Mathematics Teacher Education** *1 student enrolled* • **Medical Office Assistant/Specialist** • **Nursing—Registered Nurse Training (RN, ASN, BSN, MSN)** *2 students enrolled* • **Parks, Recreation, Leisure and Fitness Studies, Other** *11 students enrolled* • **Reading Teacher Education** *6 students enrolled* • **Tourism Promotion Operations** • **Welding Technology/Welder**

**STUDENT SERVICES** Academic or career counseling, employment services for current students, placement services for program completers, remedial services.

## University of Alaska System

202 Butrovich Building, Fairbanks, AK 99775

**CONTACT** Mark Hamilton, President
**Telephone:** 907-450-8000

**GENERAL INFORMATION** Public Institution.

# AMERICAN SAMOA

## American Samoa Community College

PO Box 2609, Pago Pago, AS 96799-2609
http://www.amsamoa.edu/

**CONTACT** Seth P. Galea'i, President
**Telephone:** 684-699-9155 Ext. 412

**GENERAL INFORMATION** Public Institution. Founded 1969. **Accreditation:** Regional (WASC/ACCJC). **Total program enrollment:** 719.

**PROGRAM(S) OFFERED**
• **Accounting** • **Architectural Drafting and Architectural CAD/CADD** • **Area, Ethnic, Cultural, and Gender Studies, Other** • **Autobody/Collision and Repair Technology/Technician** • **Automobile/Automotive Mechanics Technology/ Technician** • **Civil Engineering, General** *1 student enrolled* • **Construction Trades, General** • **Counselor Education/School Counseling and Guidance Services** *1 student enrolled* • **Criminal Justice/Safety Studies** • **Electrical and Electronic Engineering Technologies/Technicians, Other** • **Elementary Education and Teaching** • **General Office Occupations and Clerical Services** • **Nursing, Other** • **Welding Technology/Welder**

**STUDENT SERVICES** Academic or career counseling, employment services for current students, placement services for program completers, remedial services.

# ARIZONA

## American Institute of Technology

440 South 54th Avenue, Phoenix, AZ 85043
http://www.ait-schools.com/

**CONTACT** Charles R. Wirth, President
**Telephone:** 602-233-2222

**GENERAL INFORMATION** Private Institution. Founded 1981. **Total program enrollment:** 483. **Application fee:** $100.

**PROGRAM(S) OFFERED**
• **Truck and Bus Driver/Commercial Vehicle Operation** *360 hrs./$6220*

**STUDENT SERVICES** Employment services for current students, placement services for program completers.

## Apollo College–Phoenix

8503 North 27th Avenue, Phoenix, AZ 85051
http://www.apollocollege.edu/

**CONTACT** Jeffrey Gearhart, Executive Director
**Telephone:** 602-324-5505

**GENERAL INFORMATION** Private Institution. Founded 1976. **Accreditation:** State accredited or approved. **Total program enrollment:** 4533. **Application fee:** $95.

**PROGRAM(S) OFFERED**
• **Athletic Training/Trainer** *26 students enrolled* • **Dental Assisting/Assistant** *30 hrs./$12,360* • **Health Information/Medical Records Administration/ Administrator** *30 hrs./$12,360* • **Massage Therapy/Therapeutic Massage** *233 students enrolled* • **Medical Office Management/Administration** *33 students enrolled* • **Medical/Clinical Assistant** *30 hrs./$12,745* • **Nursing—Registered Nurse Training (RN, ASN, BSN, MSN)** *71 hrs./$43,165* • **Pharmacy Technician/Assistant** *30 hrs./$12,360* • **Physical Therapist Assistant** *30 hrs./ $12,360* • **Veterinary/Animal Health Technology/Technician and Veterinary Assistant** *103 students enrolled*

**STUDENT SERVICES** Academic or career counseling, employment services for current students, placement services for program completers.

## Arizona Academy of Beauty

5631 East Speedway Boulevard, Tucson, AZ 85712

**CONTACT** Stewart White, Owner
**Telephone:** 520-885-4120

**GENERAL INFORMATION** Private Institution. Founded 1965. **Total program enrollment:** 55. **Application fee:** $100.

**PROGRAM(S) OFFERED**
• **Cosmetology and Related Personal Grooming Arts, Other** • **Cosmetology, Barber/Styling, and Nail Instructor** *650 hrs./$4450* • **Cosmetology/ Cosmetologist, General** *1600 hrs./$14,060* • **Nail Technician/Specialist and Manicurist** *600 hrs./$3855*

**STUDENT SERVICES** Academic or career counseling, employment services for current students, placement services for program completers.

## Arizona Academy of Beauty–North

4046 North Oracle Road, Tucson, AZ 85705

**CONTACT** Stewart White, President/Owner
**Telephone:** 520-888-0170

**GENERAL INFORMATION** Private Institution. Founded 1961. **Total program enrollment:** 64. **Application fee:** $100.

**PROGRAM(S) OFFERED**
• **Cosmetology and Related Personal Grooming Arts, Other** • **Cosmetology, Barber/Styling, and Nail Instructor** *650 hrs./$4450* • **Cosmetology/ Cosmetologist, General** *1600 hrs./$14,160* • **Nail Technician/Specialist and Manicurist** *600 hrs./$3855*

**STUDENT SERVICES** Academic or career counseling, employment services for current students, placement services for program completers.

## Arizona Automotive Institute

6829 North 46th Avenue, Glendale, AZ 85301-3597
http://www.aai.edu/

**CONTACT** Dennis Del Valle, Executive Director
**Telephone:** 800-528-0717

**GENERAL INFORMATION** Private Institution. **Accreditation:** State accredited or approved. **Total program enrollment:** 341. **Application fee:** $100.

**PROGRAM(S) OFFERED**
• **Automobile/Automotive Mechanics Technology/Technician** *174 students enrolled* • **Diesel Mechanics Technology/Technician** *32 students enrolled* • **Heating, Air Conditioning and Refrigeration Technology/Technician (ACH/ACR/ ACHR/HRAC/HVAC/AC Technology)** *23 students enrolled*

**STUDENT SERVICES** Academic or career counseling, employment services for current students, placement services for program completers, remedial services.

## Arizona College of Allied Health

4425 West Olive Avenue, Suite 300, Glendale, AZ 85302-3843
http://www.arizonacollege.edu/

**CONTACT** C. Larkin Hicks, President
**Telephone:** 602-222-9300

**GENERAL INFORMATION** Private Institution. Founded 1992. **Accreditation:** State accredited or approved. **Total program enrollment:** 205. **Application fee:** $25.

**PROGRAM(S) OFFERED**
• **Dental Assisting/Assistant** *25 students enrolled* • **Health Information/Medical Records Administration/Administrator** *8 students enrolled* • **Massage Therapy/Therapeutic Massage** *2 students enrolled* • **Medical Administrative/Executive Assistant and Medical Secretary** *10 students enrolled* • **Medical/Clinical Assistant** *28 students enrolled* • **Pharmacy Technician/Assistant** *20 students enrolled* • **Phlebotomy/Phlebotomist** *51 students enrolled*

**STUDENT SERVICES** Academic or career counseling, employment services for current students, placement services for program completers.

## Arizona Culinary Institute

10585 North 114th Street, Suite 401, Scottsdale, AZ 85259
http://www.azculinary.com/

**CONTACT** Robert Wilson, President
**Telephone:** 480-603-1066

**GENERAL INFORMATION** Private Institution. **Total program enrollment:** 153. **Application fee:** $25.

**PROGRAM(S) OFFERED**
• **Culinary Arts/Chef Training** *135 students enrolled*

**STUDENT SERVICES** Employment services for current students, placement services for program completers.

## Arizona Western College

PO Box 929, Yuma, AZ 85366-0929
http://www.azwestern.edu/

**CONTACT** Don Schoening, President
**Telephone:** 928-317-6000

**GENERAL INFORMATION** Public Institution. Founded 1962. **Accreditation:** Regional (NCA). **Total program enrollment:** 2270.

**PROGRAM(S) OFFERED**
• **American Sign Language (ASL)** *9 students enrolled* • **Automobile/Automotive Mechanics Technology/Technician** *2 students enrolled* • **CAD/CADD Drafting and/or Design Technology/Technician** *2 students enrolled* • **Carpentry/Carpenter** *13 students enrolled* • **Child Care Provider/Assistant** • **Child Development** *1 student enrolled* • **Computer Systems Networking and Telecommunications** *1 student enrolled* • **Computer and Information Sciences, General** • **Construction Trades, Other** *77 students enrolled* • **Data Entry/Microcomputer Applications, General** • **Dietetics and Clinical Nutrition Services, Other** *1 student enrolled* • **Early Childhood Education and Teaching** *48 students enrolled* • **Electrician** *28 students enrolled* • **Emergency Medical Technology/Technician (EMT Paramedic)** *33 students enrolled* • **Family and Consumer Sciences/Human Sciences, General** • **Fire Science/Firefighting** • **Heating, Air Conditioning, Ventilation and Refrigeration Maintenance Technology/Technician (HAC, HACR, HVAC, HVACR)** *1 student enrolled* • **Licensed Practical/Vocational Nurse Training (LPN, LVN, Cert, Dipl, AAS)** • **Massage Therapy/Therapeutic Massage** *5 students enrolled* • **Nurse/Nursing Assistant/Aide and Patient Care Assistant** *6 students enrolled* • **Office Management and Supervision** *2 students enrolled* • **Plumbing and Related Water Supply Services, Other** *1 student enrolled* • **Restaurant, Culinary, and Catering Management/Manager** *3 students enrolled* • **Water Quality and Wastewater Treatment Management and Recycling Technology/Technician** *19 students enrolled* • **Welding Technology/Welder** *1 student enrolled*

**STUDENT SERVICES** Academic or career counseling, daycare for children of students, employment services for current students, placement services for program completers, remedial services.

## The Art Center Design College

2525 North Country Club Road, Tucson, AZ 85716-2505
http://www.theartcenter.edu/

**CONTACT** Sharmon R. Woods, President
**Telephone:** 520-325-0123

**GENERAL INFORMATION** Private Institution. Founded 1983. **Accreditation:** Interior design: professional (CIDA); state accredited or approved. **Total program enrollment:** 253. **Application fee:** $25.

**PROGRAM(S) OFFERED**
• **Interior Design**

**STUDENT SERVICES** Academic or career counseling, employment services for current students, placement services for program completers, remedial services.

## The Art Institute of Phoenix

2233 West Dunlap Avenue, Phoenix, AZ 85021-2859
http://www.artinstitutes.edu/phoenix/

**CONTACT** Kevin LaMountain, President
**Telephone:** 602-331-7500

**GENERAL INFORMATION** Private Institution. Founded 1995. **Accreditation:** State accredited or approved. **Total program enrollment:** 850. **Application fee:** $50.

**PROGRAM(S) OFFERED**
• **Baking and Pastry Arts/Baker/Pastry Chef** *18 students enrolled* • **Culinary Arts/Chef Training** *12 students enrolled*

**STUDENT SERVICES** Academic or career counseling, employment services for current students, placement services for program completers, remedial services.

## The Art Institute of Tucson

5099 E. Grant Road, Suite 100, Tucson, AZ 85712
http://www.artinstitutes.edu/tucson/

**CONTACT** Karen Habblitz, President
**Telephone:** 520-318-2719

**GENERAL INFORMATION** Private Institution. Founded 2007. **Total program enrollment:** 74. **Application fee:** $50.

**STUDENT SERVICES** Academic or career counseling, employment services for current students, remedial services.

## Artistic Beauty Colleges–Chandler

2390 North Alma School Road, Suite 101, Chandler, AZ 85224
http://artisticbeautycolleges.com/

**CONTACT** Michael Bouman, President/COO
**Telephone:** 570-429-4321 Ext. 2414

**GENERAL INFORMATION** Private Institution. Founded 1985. **Total program enrollment:** 81. **Application fee:** $100.

**PROGRAM(S) OFFERED**
• **Aesthetician/Esthetician and Skin Care Specialist** *600 hrs./$5600* • **Cosmetology, Barber/Styling, and Nail Instructor** • **Cosmetology/Cosmetologist, General** *1600 hrs./$15,554* • **Nail Technician/Specialist and Manicurist** *37 students enrolled*

**STUDENT SERVICES** Academic or career counseling, employment services for current students, placement services for program completers.

## Artistic Beauty Colleges–Flagstaff

1790 Route 66, Flagstaff, AZ 86004
http://artisticbeautycolleges.com/

**CONTACT** Michael Bouman, President/COO
**Telephone:** 570-429-4321 Ext. 2414

**GENERAL INFORMATION** Private Institution. Founded 1963. **Total program enrollment:** 42. **Application fee:** $100.

**PROGRAM(S) OFFERED**
• **Aesthetician/Esthetician and Skin Care Specialist** • **Cosmetology, Barber/Styling, and Nail Instructor** • **Cosmetology/Cosmetologist, General** *1600 hrs./$15,554* • **Nail Technician/Specialist and Manicurist**

**STUDENT SERVICES** Academic or career counseling, employment services for current students, placement services for program completers.

## Artistic Beauty Colleges–Phoenix

10820 North 43rd Avenue, Suite 12, Glendale, AZ 85304
http://artisticbeautycolleges.com/

**CONTACT** Michael Bouman, President/COO
**Telephone:** 570-429-4321 Ext. 2414

**GENERAL INFORMATION** Private Institution. **Total program enrollment:** 105. **Application fee:** $100.

**PROGRAM(S) OFFERED**
• **Cosmetology, Barber/Styling, and Nail Instructor** • **Cosmetology/Cosmetologist, General** *1600 hrs./$15,554* • **Nail Technician/Specialist and Manicurist** *600 hrs./$3600*

**STUDENT SERVICES** Academic or career counseling, employment services for current students, placement services for program completers.

## Artistic Beauty Colleges–Phoenix North Central

402 E. Greenway Parkway, #21, 28, & 6, Phoenix, AZ 85022
http://artisticbeautycolleges.com/

**CONTACT** Michael Bouman, President/COO
**Telephone:** 570-429-4321 Ext. 2414

**GENERAL INFORMATION** Private Institution. **Total program enrollment:** 132. **Application fee:** $100.

**PROGRAM(S) OFFERED**
• **Aesthetician/Esthetician and Skin Care Specialist** *3 students enrolled*
• **Cosmetology, Barber/Styling, and Nail Instructor** • **Cosmetology/Cosmetologist, General** *1600 hrs./$15,554* • **Nail Technician/Specialist and Manicurist**

**STUDENT SERVICES** Academic or career counseling, employment services for current students, placement services for program completers.

## Artistic Beauty Colleges–Prescott

410 West Goodwin, Prescott, AZ 86301
http://artisticbeautycolleges.com/

**CONTACT** Michael Bouman, President/COO
**Telephone:** 570-429-4321 Ext. 2414

**GENERAL INFORMATION** Private Institution. Founded 1986. **Total program enrollment:** 77. **Application fee:** $100.

**PROGRAM(S) OFFERED**
• **Aesthetician/Esthetician and Skin Care Specialist** *22 students enrolled*
• **Cosmetology, Barber/Styling, and Nail Instructor** • **Cosmetology/Cosmetologist, General** *1600 hrs./$15,554* • **Nail Technician/Specialist and Manicurist** *600 hrs./$3600*

**STUDENT SERVICES** Academic or career counseling, employment services for current students, placement services for program completers.

## Artistic Beauty Colleges–Scottsdale

7730 E. McDowell, #106, Scottsdale, AZ 85257
http://artisticbeautycolleges.com/

**CONTACT** Michael Bouman, President/COO
**Telephone:** 570-429-4321 Ext. 2414

**GENERAL INFORMATION** Private Institution. **Total program enrollment:** 61. **Application fee:** $100.

**PROGRAM(S) OFFERED**
• **Aesthetician/Esthetician and Skin Care Specialist** *1 student enrolled*
• **Cosmetology, Barber/Styling, and Nail Instructor** • **Cosmetology/Cosmetologist, General** *1600 hrs./$15,554* • **Nail Technician/Specialist and Manicurist**

**STUDENT SERVICES** Academic or career counseling, employment services for current students, placement services for program completers.

## Artistic Beauty Colleges–Tucson

3210 East Speedway Boulevard, Tucson, AZ 85716
http://artisticbeautycolleges.com/

**CONTACT** Michael Bouman, President/COO
**Telephone:** 570-429-4321 Ext. 2414

**GENERAL INFORMATION** Private Institution. Founded 1972. **Total program enrollment:** 157. **Application fee:** $100.

**PROGRAM(S) OFFERED**
• **Aesthetician/Esthetician and Skin Care Specialist** *600 hrs./$5600*
• **Cosmetology, Barber/Styling, and Nail Instructor** • **Cosmetology/Cosmetologist, General** *1600 hrs./$15,554* • **Nail Technician/Specialist and Manicurist** *20 students enrolled*

**STUDENT SERVICES** Academic or career counseling, employment services for current students, placement services for program completers.

## Artistic Beauty Colleges–Tucson North

4343 N. Oracle Road, # I, Tucson, AZ 85705
http://artisticbeautycolleges.com/

**CONTACT** Michael Bouman, President/COO
**Telephone:** 570-429-4321 Ext. 2414

**GENERAL INFORMATION** Private Institution. **Total program enrollment:** 44. **Application fee:** $100.

**PROGRAM(S) OFFERED**
• **Aesthetician/Esthetician and Skin Care Specialist** *600 hrs./$5600*
• **Cosmetology, Barber/Styling, and Nail Instructor** • **Cosmetology/Cosmetologist, General** *1600 hrs./$15,554* • **Nail Technician/Specialist and Manicurist** *1 student enrolled*

**STUDENT SERVICES** Academic or career counseling, employment services for current students, placement services for program completers.

## Artistic Beauty School

4533 West Glendale Avenue, Glendale, AZ 85301-2808

**CONTACT** Michael Bouman, President/COO
**Telephone:** 570-429-4321 Ext. 2414

**GENERAL INFORMATION** Private Institution. **Total program enrollment:** 114. **Application fee:** $100.

**PROGRAM(S) OFFERED**
• **Aesthetician/Esthetician and Skin Care Specialist** *38 students enrolled*
• **Cosmetology, Barber/Styling, and Nail Instructor** • **Cosmetology/Cosmetologist, General** *1600 hrs./$15,554* • **Nail Technician/Specialist and Manicurist**

**STUDENT SERVICES** Academic or career counseling, employment services for current students, placement services for program completers.

## Axia College

3157 East Elwood Street, Phoenix, AZ 85034
http://www.axiacollege.com/

**CONTACT** William Pepicello, PhD, President
**Telephone:** 800-366-9699

**GENERAL INFORMATION** Private Institution. **Total program enrollment:** 301323.

**PROGRAM(S) OFFERED**
• **Business Administration and Management, General** *124 students enrolled* • **Customer Service Support/Call Center/Teleservice Operation** *18 students enrolled* • **Human Resources Management/Personnel Administration, General** *194 students enrolled* • **Web Page, Digital/Multimedia and Information Resources Design** *1 student enrolled*

**STUDENT SERVICES** Academic or career counseling, remedial services.

## Brookline College

925 South Gilbert Road, Suite 201, Mesa, AZ 85204-4448
http://brooklinecollege.edu/

**CONTACT** Ken Guerrero, Director
**Telephone:** 480-545-8755 Ext. 201

**GENERAL INFORMATION** Private Institution. Founded 1982. **Accreditation:** State accredited or approved. **Total program enrollment:** 213. **Application fee:** $50.

**PROGRAM(S) OFFERED**
• **Business Administration and Management, General** *61 hrs./$22,375* • **Criminal Justice/Law Enforcement Administration** *64 hrs./$24,600* • **Legal Administrative Assistant/Secretary** *28 hrs./$12,160* • **Medical Administrative/Executive Assistant and Medical Secretary** *12 students enrolled* • **Medical/Clinical Assistant** *28 hrs./$11,760* • **Security and Loss Prevention Services** *28 hrs./$12,160*

**STUDENT SERVICES** Academic or career counseling, employment services for current students, placement services for program completers, remedial services.

## Brookline College

4240 West Bethany Home Road, Phoenix, AZ 85019-1600
http://brooklinecollege.edu/

**CONTACT** Oleg Bortman, Campus Director
**Telephone:** 602-242-6265

**GENERAL INFORMATION** Private Institution. Founded 1979. **Accreditation:** State accredited or approved. **Total program enrollment:** 914. **Application fee:** $50.

**PROGRAM(S) OFFERED**
• **Business Administration and Management, General** *25 hrs./$10,900* • **Criminal Justice/Law Enforcement Administration** *64 hrs./$24,600* • **Legal Administrative Assistant/Secretary** • **Medical Administrative/Executive Assistant and Medical Secretary** *33 students enrolled* • **Medical/Clinical Assistant** *28 hrs./$11,760* • **Nurse/Nursing Assistant/Aide and Patient Care Assistant** *28 students enrolled* • **Nursing—Registered Nurse Training (RN, ASN, BSN, MSN)** *67 hrs./$34,280* • **Security and Loss Prevention Services** *8 students enrolled*

**STUDENT SERVICES** Academic or career counseling, employment services for current students, placement services for program completers, remedial services.

## Brookline College

5441 East 22nd Street, Suite 125, Tucson, AZ 85711-5444
http://brooklinecollege.edu/

**CONTACT** Leigh Anne Pechota, Director
**Telephone:** 520-748-9799

**GENERAL INFORMATION** Private Institution. Founded 1979. **Accreditation:** State accredited or approved. **Total program enrollment:** 394. **Application fee:** $50.

**PROGRAM(S) OFFERED**
• **Accounting Technology/Technician and Bookkeeping** *1 student enrolled* • **Business Administration and Management, General** *61 hrs./$23,375* • **Criminal Justice/Law Enforcement Administration** *64 hrs./$24,600* • **Legal Administrative Assistant/Secretary** • **Legal Assistant/Paralegal** *69 hrs./$26,425* • **Medical Administrative/Executive Assistant and Medical Secretary** *30 students enrolled* • **Medical/Clinical Assistant** *28 hrs./$11,760* • **Security and Loss Prevention Services** *28 hrs./$12,260*

**STUDENT SERVICES** Academic or career counseling, daycare for children of students, employment services for current students, placement services for program completers, remedial services.

## Brown Mackie College–Tucson

4585 East Speedway, No 204, Tucson, AZ 85712
http://www.brownmackie.edu/tucson/

**CONTACT** Holly Helscher, PhD, President
**Telephone:** 520-319-3300

**GENERAL INFORMATION** Private Institution. Founded 1972. **Accreditation:** State accredited or approved. **Total program enrollment:** 386.

**PROGRAM(S) OFFERED**
• **Accounting** *5 students enrolled* • **Computer and Information Sciences, General** *1 student enrolled* • **Emergency Medical Technology/Technician (EMT Paramedic)** • **General Office Occupations and Clerical Services** *5 students enrolled* • **Health Information/Medical Records Technology/Technician** *2 students enrolled*

**STUDENT SERVICES** Academic or career counseling, employment services for current students, placement services for program completers, remedial services.

## The Bryman School of Arizona

2250 West Peoria Avenue, Phoenix, AZ 85029
http://www.brymanschool.edu/

**CONTACT** Melissa Gray, Executive Assistant
**Telephone:** 602-274-4300

**GENERAL INFORMATION** Private Institution. Founded 1964. **Accreditation:** Medical assisting (AAMAE); state accredited or approved. **Total program enrollment:** 744. **Application fee:** $50.

**PROGRAM(S) OFFERED**
• **Dental Assisting/Assistant** *746 hrs./$11,740* • **Massage Therapy/Therapeutic Massage** *7 students enrolled* • **Medical Insurance Specialist/Medical Biller** *720 hrs./$11,316* • **Medical Radiologic Technology/Science—Radiation Therapist** *964 hrs./$12,724* • **Medical/Clinical Assistant** *746 hrs./$11,550* • **Pharmacy Technician/Assistant** *720 hrs./$11,537* • **Surgical Technology/Technologist** *1160 hrs./$22,681*

**STUDENT SERVICES** Placement services for program completers.

## Carsten Institute of Hair and Beauty

3345 South Rural Road, Tempe, AZ 85282
http://carsteninstitute.com/

**CONTACT** Carsten Wilms, CEO/Owner
**Telephone:** 480-491-0449

**GENERAL INFORMATION** Private Institution. Founded 1989. **Total program enrollment:** 103.

**PROGRAM(S) OFFERED**

- **Aesthetician/Esthetician and Skin Care Specialist** *600 hrs./$7600*
- **Cosmetology, Barber/Styling, and Nail Instructor** *500 hrs./$5100*
- **Cosmetology/Cosmetologist, General** *1600 hrs./$14,000*

**STUDENT SERVICES** Academic or career counseling, placement services for program completers.

## Central Arizona College

8470 North Overfield Road, Coolidge, AZ 85228-9779
http://www.centralaz.edu/

**CONTACT** Dennis Jenkins, President
**Telephone:** 520-494-5444

**GENERAL INFORMATION** Public Institution. Founded 1961. **Accreditation:** Regional (NCA). **Total program enrollment:** 1400.

**PROGRAM(S) OFFERED**

- **Accounting Technology/Technician and Bookkeeping** *5 students enrolled*
- **Agricultural Business and Management, General** *1 student enrolled*
- **Automobile/Automotive Mechanics Technology/Technician** *61 students enrolled* • **Building/Property Maintenance and Management** *28 students enrolled*
- **Business Administration and Management, General** *5 students enrolled*
- **Business/Commerce, General** *11 students enrolled* • **Carpentry/Carpenter** *41 students enrolled* • **Child Development** *51 students enrolled* • **Computer Programming/Programmer, General** *9 students enrolled* • **Computer Software and Media Applications, Other** *21 students enrolled* • **Computer and Information Sciences, General** *1 student enrolled* • **Construction Trades, Other** *48 students enrolled* • **Construction/Heavy Equipment/Earthmoving Equipment Operation** *14 students enrolled* • **Criminal Justice/Police Science** *113 students enrolled* • **Diesel Mechanics Technology/Technician** *8 students enrolled* • **Family and Consumer Sciences/Human Sciences, Other** *3 students enrolled* • **Fire Protection and Safety Technology/Technician** *2 students enrolled* • **Food Preparation/Professional Cooking/Kitchen Assistant** *2 students enrolled*
- **Foods, Nutrition, and Wellness Studies, General** *118 students enrolled*
- **Foodservice Systems Administration/Management** *3 students enrolled*
- **Ground Transportation, Other** *2 students enrolled* • **Hotel/Motel Administration/Management** *3 students enrolled* • **Human Development, Family Studies, and Related Services, Other** *371 students enrolled* • **Industrial Electronics Technology/Technician** *1 student enrolled* • **Mason/Masonry** *7 students enrolled* • **Massage Therapy/Therapeutic Massage** *5 students enrolled*
- **Medical Administrative/Executive Assistant and Medical Secretary** *6 students enrolled* • **Medical Transcription/Transcriptionist** *3 students enrolled*
- **Nursing, Other** *1 student enrolled* • **Pharmacy Technician/Assistant**
- **Pipefitting/Pipefitter and Sprinkler Fitter** *101 students enrolled* • **Upholstery/Upholsterer** *14 students enrolled* • **Welding Technology/Welder** *44 students enrolled*

**STUDENT SERVICES** Academic or career counseling, daycare for children of students, employment services for current students, remedial services.

## Chandler-Gilbert Community College

2626 East Pecos Road, Chandler, AZ 85225-2479
http://www.cgc.maricopa.edu/

**CONTACT** Maria Hesse, President
**Telephone:** 480-732-7000

**GENERAL INFORMATION** Public Institution. Founded 1985. **Accreditation:** Regional (NCA). **Total program enrollment:** 3314.

**PROGRAM(S) OFFERED**

- **Aircraft Powerplant Technology/Technician** *47 students enrolled* • **Airframe Mechanics and Aircraft Maintenance Technology/Technician** *31 students enrolled* • **Airline/Commercial/Professional Pilot and Flight Crew** • **Art/Art Studies, General** *167 students enrolled* • **Business/Commerce, General** *34 students enrolled* • **Commercial Photography** *1 student enrolled* • **Commercial and Advertising Art** *1 student enrolled* • **Computer Installation and Repair Technology/Technician** *7 students enrolled* • **Computer Programming, Specific Applications** • **Computer Programming, Vendor/Product Certification**
- **Computer Programming/Programmer, General** *1 student enrolled* • **Computer Systems Analysis/Analyst** • **Computer Systems Networking and Telecommunications** *18 students enrolled* • **Computer and Information Sciences and Support Services, Other** • **Computer and Information Systems Security**
- **Computer/Information Technology Services Administration and Management, Other** *8 students enrolled* • **Criminal Justice/Police Science**
- **Criminal Justice/Safety Studies** *6 students enrolled* • **Criminology** • **Data Entry/Microcomputer Applications, General** *5 students enrolled* • **Data Modeling/Warehousing and Database Administration** *3 students enrolled*
- **Licensed Practical/Vocational Nurse Training (LPN, LVN, Cert, Dipl, AAS)** *38 students enrolled* • **Lineworker** *9 students enrolled* • **Management Information Systems, General** • **Marketing/Marketing Management, General** • **Massage Therapy/Therapeutic Massage** *8 students enrolled* • **Mental and Social Health Services and Allied Professions, Other** • **Security and Protective Services, Other** *2 students enrolled* • **System Administration/Administrator** • **Teacher Assistant/Aide**

**STUDENT SERVICES** Academic or career counseling, employment services for current students, placement services for program completers, remedial services.

## Charles of Italy Beauty College

1987 McCulloch Boulevard, Lake Havasu City, AZ 86403
http://www.charlesofitaly.edu/

**CONTACT** Charles Bartolomeo, Owner
**Telephone:** 928-453-6666

**GENERAL INFORMATION** Private Institution. Founded 1980. **Total program enrollment:** 28. **Application fee:** $100.

**PROGRAM(S) OFFERED**

- **Cosmetology, Barber/Styling, and Nail Instructor** *650 hrs./$3900*
- **Cosmetology/Cosmetologist, General** *1600 hrs./$10,900* • **Massage Therapy/Therapeutic Massage** *700 hrs./$6700* • **Nail Technician/Specialist and Manicurist**

**STUDENT SERVICES** Academic or career counseling, placement services for program completers.

## Cochise College

4190 West Highway 80, Douglas, AZ 85607-9724
http://www.cochise.edu/

**CONTACT** Karen A. Nicodemus, President
**Telephone:** 520-515-0500

**GENERAL INFORMATION** Public Institution. Founded 1962. **Accreditation:** Regional (NCA). **Total program enrollment:** 1122.

**PROGRAM(S) OFFERED**

- **Airframe Mechanics and Aircraft Maintenance Technology/Technician**
- **Airline/Commercial/Professional Pilot and Flight Crew** *1 student enrolled*
- **Animation, Interactive Technology, Video Graphics and Special Effects**
- **Automobile/Automotive Mechanics Technology/Technician** *3 students enrolled*
- **Avionics Maintenance Technology/Technician** *1 student enrolled* • **Baking and Pastry Arts/Baker/Pastry Chef** *1 student enrolled* • **Building/Property Maintenance and Management** *7 students enrolled* • **Business Administration and Management, General** • **Business/Commerce, General** *1 student enrolled*
- **CAD/CADD Drafting and/or Design Technology/Technician** *2 students enrolled*
- **Carpentry/Carpenter** *2 students enrolled* • **Communications Systems Installation and Repair Technology** *5 students enrolled* • **Community Health Services/Liaison/Counseling** *2 students enrolled* • **Computer Installation and Repair Technology/Technician** *9 students enrolled* • **Computer Programming/Programmer, General** • **Computer Systems Networking and Telecommunications** • **Computer Technology/Computer Systems Technology** • **Computer and Information Sciences, General** *48 students enrolled* • **Computer and Information Systems Security** *5 students enrolled* • **Customer Service Support/Call Center/Teleservice Operation** • **Data Entry/Microcomputer Applications, General** *8 students enrolled* • **Early Childhood Education and Teaching** *2 students enrolled* • **Electrical and Power Transmission Installers, Other**
- **Electrical, Electronic and Communications Engineering Technology/Technician** *47 students enrolled* • **Electrical/Electronics Equipment Installation and Repair, General** • **Electrician** *4 students enrolled* • **Emergency Medical**

*Cochise College (continued)*

**Technology/Technician (EMT Paramedic)** • **Equestrian/Equine Studies** *2 students enrolled* • **Fire Protection and Safety Technology/Technician** *15 students enrolled* • **Fire Science/Firefighting** *2 students enrolled* • **Fire Services Administration** *3 students enrolled* • **Food Preparation/Professional Cooking/Kitchen Assistant** *4 students enrolled* • **General Office Occupations and Clerical Services** *1 student enrolled* • **Hazardous Materials Management and Waste Technology/Technician** • **Heating, Air Conditioning, Ventilation and Refrigeration Maintenance Technology/Technician (HAC, HACR, HVAC, HVACR)** *15 students enrolled* • **Hospitality Administration/Management, General** • **Housing and Human Environments, Other** *310 students enrolled* • **Information Technology** *21 students enrolled* • **International Business/Trade/Commerce** *1 student enrolled* • **Language Interpretation and Translation** *2 students enrolled* • **Licensed Practical/Vocational Nurse Training (LPN, LVN, Cert, Dipl, AAS)** *50 students enrolled* • **Manufacturing Technology/Technician** • **Mason/Masonry** • **Medical Transcription/Transcriptionist** • **Medical/Clinical Assistant** *1 student enrolled* • **Office Management and Supervision** • **Receptionist** *1 student enrolled* • **Sales, Distribution and Marketing Operations, General** *1 student enrolled* • **Social Work** *1 student enrolled* • **Spanish Language and Literature** • **System Administration/Administrator** *10 students enrolled* • **System, Networking, and LAN/WAN Management/Manager** *15 students enrolled* • **Teacher Assistant/Aide** *27 students enrolled* • **Web/Multimedia Management and Webmaster** *2 students enrolled* • **Welding Technology/Welder** *7 students enrolled*

**STUDENT SERVICES** Academic or career counseling, employment services for current students, placement services for program completers, remedial services.

## Coconino Community College

2800 South Lonetree Road, Flagstaff, AZ 86001
http://www.coconino.edu/

**CONTACT** Dr. Leah L. Bornstein, President
**Telephone:** 928-527-1222

**GENERAL INFORMATION** Public Institution. Founded 1991. **Accreditation:** Regional (NCA). **Total program enrollment:** 840.

**PROGRAM(S) OFFERED**

• **Accounting Technology/Technician and Bookkeeping** *1 student enrolled* • **Accounting** • **Architectural Drafting and Architectural CAD/CADD** • **Business Administration and Management, General** *1 student enrolled* • **CAD/CADD Drafting and/or Design Technology/Technician** *3 students enrolled* • **Carpentry/Carpenter** • **Computer Software Technology/Technician** *1 student enrolled* • **Computer Software and Media Applications, Other** • **Computer Technology/Computer Systems Technology** • **Construction Trades, Other** *1 student enrolled* • **Corrections and Criminal Justice, Other** *1 student enrolled* • **Early Childhood Education and Teaching** *4 students enrolled* • **Fire Science/Firefighting** *1 student enrolled* • **Forensic Science and Technology** *2 students enrolled* • **General Office Occupations and Clerical Services** • **Medical Insurance Specialist/Medical Biller** *2 students enrolled* • **Medical Transcription/Transcriptionist** • **Nurse/Nursing Assistant/Aide and Patient Care Assistant** *1 student enrolled* • **Phlebotomy/Phlebotomist** *1 student enrolled* • **Prepress/Desktop Publishing and Digital Imaging Design** *1 student enrolled* • **Sheet Metal Technology/Sheetworking** • **System Administration/Administrator**

**STUDENT SERVICES** Academic or career counseling, daycare for children of students, employment services for current students, placement services for program completers, remedial services.

## Conservatory of Recording Arts and Sciences

2300 East Broadway Road, Tempe, AZ 85282-1707
http://www.audiorecordingschool.com/

**CONTACT** Kirt R. Hamm, Administrator
**Telephone:** 480-858-9400

**GENERAL INFORMATION** Private Institution. **Total program enrollment:** 303.

**PROGRAM(S) OFFERED**

• **Music, Other** *23 hrs./$9620*

**STUDENT SERVICES** Employment services for current students, placement services for program completers.

## Cortiva Institute—School of Massage Therapy

609 N. Scottsdale Road, Scottsdale, AZ 85257
http://cortiva.com/

**CONTACT** Mark Elliott, Campus President
**Telephone:** 480-945-9461

**GENERAL INFORMATION** Private Institution. **Total program enrollment:** 88. **Application fee:** $100.

**PROGRAM(S) OFFERED**

• **Health and Physical Education/Fitness, Other** *$1500* • **Massage Therapy/Therapeutic Massage** *56 hrs./$9400*

**STUDENT SERVICES** Academic or career counseling, employment services for current students, placement services for program completers.

## Desert Institute of the Healing Arts

639 North 6th Avenue, Tucson, AZ 85705
http://www.diha.org/

**CONTACT** Joann Rockwell MacMaster, President
**Telephone:** 520-623-2160

**GENERAL INFORMATION** Private Institution. Founded 1982. **Total program enrollment:** 69. **Application fee:** $100.

**PROGRAM(S) OFFERED**

• **Massage Therapy/Therapeutic Massage** *56 hrs./$11,550*

**STUDENT SERVICES** Academic or career counseling, placement services for program completers.

## Earl's Academy of Beauty

2111 South Alma School Road, Suite 21, Mesa, AZ 85210
http://www.earlsacademy.com/

**CONTACT** April Montes, President-Owner
**Telephone:** 480-897-1722

**GENERAL INFORMATION** Private Institution. Founded 1967. **Total program enrollment:** 149. **Application fee:** $100.

**PROGRAM(S) OFFERED**

• **Cosmetology, Barber/Styling, and Nail Instructor** *650 hrs./$4875* • **Cosmetology/Cosmetologist, General** *1600 hrs./$14,595* • **Nail Technician/Specialist and Manicurist** *600 hrs./$3240*

**STUDENT SERVICES** Academic or career counseling, placement services for program completers.

## Eastern Arizona College

PO Box 769, Thatcher, AZ 85552-0769
http://www.eac.edu/

**CONTACT** Mark Bryce, President
**Telephone:** 928-428-8322

**GENERAL INFORMATION** Public Institution. Founded 1888. **Accreditation:** Regional (NCA). **Total program enrollment:** 1787.

**PROGRAM(S) OFFERED**

• **Accounting Technology/Technician and Bookkeeping** *5 students enrolled* • **Administrative Assistant and Secretarial Science, General** *6 students enrolled* • **Allied Health and Medical Assisting Services, Other** *2 students enrolled* • **Applied Horticulture/Horticultural Operations, General** • **Architectural Drafting and Architectural CAD/CADD** • **Automobile/Automotive Mechanics Technology/Technician** *3 students enrolled* • **Building/Construction Finishing, Management, and Inspection, Other** *47 students enrolled* • **Building/Property Maintenance and Management** • **Business Administration and Management, General** *5 students enrolled* • **Business/Commerce, General** *21 students enrolled* • **CAD/CADD Drafting and/or Design Technology/Technician** 6 *students enrolled* • **Carpentry/Carpenter** *24 students enrolled* • **Child Care and Support Services Management** • **Child Development** • **Clinical/Medical Laboratory Assistant** • **Communications Technology/Technician** • **Computer Programming/Programmer, General** • **Computer Software and Media Applications, Other** • **Computer and Information Sciences, General** • **Criminal Justice/Police Science** *1 student enrolled* • **Data Processing and Data Processing Technology/Technician** • **Diesel Mechanics Technology/Technician** *25 students enrolled* • **Drafting and Design Technology/Technician, General** • **Early Childhood Education and Teaching** *8 students enrolled* • **Entrepreneurship/Entrepreneurial Studies** *1 student enrolled* • **Fire Science/Firefighting** • **General Office Occupations and Clerical Services** • **Health Aide** • **Heating, Air Conditioning, Ventilation and Refrigeration Maintenance Technology/Technician (HAC, HACR, HVAC, HVACR)** *35 students enrolled* • **Horticultural Science** *34 students enrolled* • **Industrial Electronics Technology/Technician** *38 students enrolled* • **Industrial Mechanics and Maintenance Technology** *24 students enrolled* • **Information Science/Studies** *1 student enrolled* • **Licensed Practical/Vocational Nurse Training (LPN, LVN, Cert, Dipl, AAS)** • **Machine Shop Technology/Assistant** • **Machine Tool Technology/Machinist** • **Mason/Masonry** *17 students enrolled* • **Medical Transcription/Transcriptionist** *2 students enrolled* • **Medical/Clinical Assistant** *6 students enrolled* • **Nurse/Nursing Assistant/Aide and Patient Care Assistant** *19 students enrolled* • **Operations Management and Supervision** • **Pharmacy Technician/Assistant** *9 students enrolled* • **Retailing and Retail Operations** • **Sheet Metal Technology/Sheetworking** *1 student enrolled* • **Small Business Administration/Management** • **Web Page, Digital/Multimedia and Information Resources Design** • **Web/Multimedia Management and Webmaster**

**STUDENT SERVICES** Academic or career counseling, employment services for current students, placement services for program completers, remedial services.

## East Valley Institute of Technology

1601 W. Main Street, Mesa, AZ 85201
http://www.evit.com/

**CONTACT** Dr. Sally E. Downey, Superintendent
**Telephone:** 480-461-4000

**GENERAL INFORMATION** Public Institution. **Total program enrollment:** 37. **Application fee:** $100.

**PROGRAM(S) OFFERED**
• **Administrative Assistant and Secretarial Science, General** • **Aesthetician/Esthetician and Skin Care Specialist** *1 student enrolled* • **Animation, Interactive Technology, Video Graphics and Special Effects** *3 students enrolled* • **Autobody/Collision and Repair Technology/Technician** *900 hrs./$4000* • **Automobile/Automotive Mechanics Technology/Technician** *1 student enrolled* • **Building/Property Maintenance and Management** *1 student enrolled* • **Child Care and Support Services Management** *2 students enrolled* • **Commercial Photography** • **Commercial and Advertising Art** *2 students enrolled* • **Communications Technologies/Technicians and Support Services, Other** • **Computer Installation and Repair Technology/Technician** • **Construction Trades, Other** *1 student enrolled* • **Cosmetology/Cosmetologist, General** *1600 hrs./$11,521* • **Criminal Justice/Police Science** *1 student enrolled* • **Culinary Arts/Chef Training** *3 students enrolled* • **Drafting and Design Technology/Technician, General** *2 students enrolled* • **Educational/Instructional Media Design** • **Electrical, Electronic and Communications Engineering Technology/Technician** • **Fire Protection, Other** • **Heating, Air Conditioning, Ventilation and Refrigeration Maintenance Technology/Technician (HAC, HACR, HVAC, HVACR)** • **Interior Design** • **Licensed Practical/Vocational Nurse Training (LPN, LVN, Cert, Dipl, AAS)** *18 students enrolled* • **Machine Tool Technology/Machinist** *1 student enrolled* • **Management Information Systems, General** *1 student enrolled* • **Massage Therapy/Therapeutic Massage** *720 hrs./$5600* • **Nurse/Nursing Assistant/Aide and Patient Care Assistant** *163 hrs./$1000* • **Nursing, Other** *650 hrs./$7526* • **Radio and Television Broadcasting Technology/Technician** *2 students enrolled* • **Welding Technology/Welder** *900 hrs./$4000*

**STUDENT SERVICES** Academic or career counseling, employment services for current students, placement services for program completers.

## Estrella Mountain Community College

3000 North Dysart Road, Avondale, AZ 85392
http://www.emc.maricopa.edu/

**CONTACT** Dr. Ernie Laura, President
**Telephone:** 623-935-8000

**GENERAL INFORMATION** Public Institution. Founded 1992. **Accreditation:** Regional (NCA). **Total program enrollment:** 1631.

**PROGRAM(S) OFFERED**
• **Art/Art Studies, General** *180 students enrolled* • **Business Administration, Management and Operations, Other** *35 students enrolled* • **Business, Management, Marketing, and Related Support Services, Other** • **Business/Commerce, General** *4 students enrolled* • **Business/Office Automation/Technology/Data Entry** *2 students enrolled* • **Computer Installation and Repair Technology/Technician** • **Computer Programming, Vendor/Product Certification** • **Computer Systems Analysis/Analyst** • **Computer Systems Networking and Telecommunications** *30 students enrolled* • **Computer and Information Sciences and Support Services, Other** • **Computer/Information Technology Services Administration and Management, Other** *3 students enrolled* • **Criminal Justice/Safety Studies** *7 students enrolled* • **Culinary Arts/Chef Training** *5 students enrolled* • **Hotel/Motel Administration/Management** *1 student enrolled* • **Licensed Practical/Vocational Nurse Training (LPN, LVN, Cert, Dipl, AAS)** *15 students enrolled* • **Management Information Systems, General** • **Organizational Behavior Studies** • **Personal and Culinary Services, Other** • **Speech-Language Pathology/Pathologist** • **System Administration/Administrator** • **System, Networking, and LAN/WAN Management/Manager**

**STUDENT SERVICES** Academic or career counseling, employment services for current students, placement services for program completers, remedial services.

## Everest College

5416 E. Baseline Road, Suite 200, Mesa, AZ 85206
http://www.everest.edu/

**CONTACT** Mary Ritter, President
**Telephone:** 480-830-5151

**GENERAL INFORMATION** Private Institution. **Total program enrollment:** 116.

**PROGRAM(S) OFFERED**
• **Allied Health and Medical Assisting Services, Other** *62 students enrolled* • **Medical Office Assistant/Specialist** *80 students enrolled*

**STUDENT SERVICES** Academic or career counseling, employment services for current students, placement services for program completers, remedial services.

## Everest College

10400 North 25th Avenue, Suite 190, Phoenix, AZ 85021
http://www.everest.edu/

**CONTACT** Todd McDonald, President
**Telephone:** 602-942-4141

**GENERAL INFORMATION** Private Institution. Founded 1982. **Accreditation:** Regional (NCA); state accredited or approved. **Total program enrollment:** 2152.

**PROGRAM(S) OFFERED**
• **Allied Health and Medical Assisting Services, Other** *70 students enrolled* • **Health Information/Medical Records Technology/Technician** *54 students enrolled*

**STUDENT SERVICES** Academic or career counseling, employment services for current students, placement services for program completers, remedial services.

## GateWay Community College

108 North 40th Street, Phoenix, AZ 85034-1795
http://www.gwc.maricopa.edu/

**CONTACT** Eugene Giovannini, EdD, President
**Telephone:** 602-392-5000

**GENERAL INFORMATION** Public Institution. Founded 1968. **Accreditation:** Regional (NCA); physical therapy assisting (APTA); radiologic technology: radiography (JRCERT). **Total program enrollment:** 989.

**PROGRAM(S) OFFERED**
• **Accounting Technology/Technician and Bookkeeping** *7 students enrolled* • **Administrative Assistant and Secretarial Science, General** • **Allied Health Diagnostic, Intervention, and Treatment Professions, Other** *26 students enrolled* • **Art/Art Studies, General** *33 students enrolled* • **Automobile/Automotive Mechanics Technology/Technician** *140 students enrolled* • **Building/Construction Finishing, Management, and Inspection, Other** *4 students enrolled* • **Business Administration, Management and Operations, Other** *1 student enrolled* • **Business/Commerce, General** *1 student enrolled* • **Business/Office Automation/Technology/Data Entry** *2 students enrolled* • **Carpentry/Carpenter** • **Computer Systems Analysis/Analyst** • **Computer Systems Networking and Telecommunications** *17 students enrolled* • **Computer Teacher Education** • **Computer and Information Sciences and Support Services, Other** • **Computer and Information Sciences, General** • **Computer/Information Technology Services Administration and Management, Other** *3 students enrolled* • **Construction Trades, Other** *1 student enrolled* • **Court Reporting/Court Reporter** • **Electrician** *24 students enrolled* • **Electroneurodiagnostic/Electroencephalographic Technology/Technologist** *10 students enrolled* • **Emergency Medical Technology/Technician (EMT Paramedic)** • **Health Unit Coordinator/Ward Clerk** *44 students enrolled* • **Health and Medical Administrative Services, Other** *57 students enrolled* • **Heating, Air Conditioning and Refrigeration Technology/Technician (ACH/ACR/ACHR/HRAC/HVAC/AC Technology)** • **Heating, Air Conditioning, Ventilation and Refrigeration Maintenance Technology/Technician (HAC, HACR, HVAC, HVACR)** *10 students enrolled* • **Industrial Technology/Technician** • **Licensed Practical/Vocational Nurse Training (LPN, LVN, Cert, Dipl, AAS)** *82 students enrolled* • **Lineworker** *1 student enrolled* • **Logistics and Materials Management** • **Management Information Systems, General** • **Manufacturing Technology/Technician** *19 students enrolled* • **Marketing/Marketing Management, General** *1 student enrolled* • **Mason/Masonry** • **Medical Administrative/Executive Assistant and Medical Secretary** • **Medical Radiologic Technology/Science—Radiation Therapist** *11 students enrolled* • **Medical Transcription/Transcriptionist** *3 students enrolled* • **Nuclear Medical Technology/Technologist** • **Nurse/Nursing Assistant/Aide and Patient Care Assistant** *144 students enrolled* • **Nursing—Registered Nurse Training (RN, ASN, BSN, MSN)** • **Occupational Safety and Health Technology/Technician** *3 students enrolled* • **Office Management and Supervision** • **Operations Management and Supervision** • **Organizational Behavior Studies** • **Painting/Painter and Wall Coverer** • **Perioperative/Operating Room and Surgical Nurse/Nursing** *7 students enrolled* • **Personal and Culinary Services, Other** • **Pharmacy Technician/Assistant** • **Pipefitting/Pipefitter and Sprinkler Fitter** *1 student enrolled* • **Plumbing Technology/Plumber** • **Radiologic Technology/Science—Radiographer** *2 students enrolled* • **Respiratory Care Therapy/Therapist** • **Sheet Metal Technology/Sheetworking** *21 students enrolled* • **Surgical Technology/Technologist** *10 students enrolled* • **Water Quality and Wastewater Treatment Management and Recycling Technology/Technician** *2 students enrolled*

**STUDENT SERVICES** Academic or career counseling, daycare for children of students, remedial services.

## Glendale Community College

6000 West Olive Avenue, Glendale, AZ 85302-3090
http://www.gc.maricopa.edu/

**CONTACT** Velvie Green, PhD, President
**Telephone:** 623-845-3000

**GENERAL INFORMATION** Public Institution. Founded 1965. **Accreditation:** Regional (NCA). **Total program enrollment:** 5830.

**PROGRAM(S) OFFERED**
• **Administrative Assistant and Secretarial Science, General** • **Applied Horticulture/Horticultural Operations, General** • **Architectural Drafting and Architectural CAD/CADD** *8 students enrolled* • **Art/Art Studies, General** *419 students enrolled* • **Automobile/Automotive Mechanics Technology/Technician** *136 students enrolled* • **Business Administration and Management, General** • **Business/Commerce, General** *17 students enrolled* • **Business/Office Automation/Technology/Data Entry** *1 student enrolled* • **Child Care and Support Services Management** • **Commercial and Advertising Art** • **Computer Engineering Technology/Technician** • **Computer Programming, Specific Applications** • **Computer Systems Analysis/Analyst** *1 student enrolled* • **Computer Systems Networking and Telecommunications** • **Computer and Information Sciences and Support Services, Other** • **Computer and Information Sciences, General** • **Computer/Information Technology Services Administration and Management, Other** • **Criminal Justice/Police Science** *28 students enrolled* • **Data Modeling/Warehousing and Database Administration** • **Drafting/Design Engineering Technologies/Technicians, Other** • **Early Childhood Education and Teaching** *32 students enrolled* • **Emergency Medical Technology/Technician (EMT Paramedic)** • **Entrepreneurship/Entrepreneurial Studies** *2 students enrolled* • **Fire Science/Firefighting** *90 students enrolled* • **Foods, Nutrition, and Wellness Studies, General** *6 students enrolled* • **Health Teacher Education** • **Human Development, Family Studies, and Related Services, Other** *1 student enrolled* • **Interior Design** • **Kinesiology and Exercise Science** *50 students enrolled* • **Landscaping and Groundskeeping** • **Licensed Practical/Vocational Nurse Training (LPN, LVN, Cert, Dipl, AAS)** • **Management Information Systems, General** • **Mental and Social Health Services and Allied Professions, Other** *7 students enrolled* • **Music, General** *2 students enrolled* • **Nurse/Nursing Assistant/Aide and Patient Care Assistant** *1 student enrolled* • **Office Management and Supervision** • **Plant Nursery Operations and Management** • **Receptionist** • **System Administration/Administrator** • **System, Networking, and LAN/WAN Management/Manager** • **Truck and Bus Driver/Commercial Vehicle Operation** *12 students enrolled*

**STUDENT SERVICES** Academic or career counseling, daycare for children of students, employment services for current students, remedial services.

## Grand Canyon University

3300 West Camelback Road, PO Box 11097, Phoenix, AZ 85017-1097
http://www.gcu.edu/

**CONTACT** Brian Mueller, Chief Executive Officer
**Telephone:** 800-800-9776

**GENERAL INFORMATION** Private Institution. Founded 1949. **Accreditation:** Regional (NCA). **Total program enrollment:** 3890. **Application fee:** $100.

**STUDENT SERVICES** Academic or career counseling, employment services for current students, placement services for program completers, remedial services.

## Hair Academy of Safford

1550 West Thatcher Boulevard, Safford, AZ 85546

**CONTACT** Joey Scott, Owner
**Telephone:** 928-428-0331

**GENERAL INFORMATION** Private Institution. **Total program enrollment:** 55. **Application fee:** $100.

**PROGRAM(S) OFFERED**
• **Cosmetology, Barber/Styling, and Nail Instructor** *650 hrs./$4550* • **Cosmetology/Cosmetologist, General** *1500 hrs./$9810* • **Nail Technician/Specialist and Manicurist** *600 hrs./$4300*

**STUDENT SERVICES** Academic or career counseling, placement services for program completers.

## HDS Truck Driving Institute

6251 S. Wilmot Road, Tucson, AZ 85706
http://www.hdsdrivers.com/

**CONTACT** Robert Knapp, School Administrator
**Telephone:** 520-721-5825 Ext. 219

**GENERAL INFORMATION** Private Institution. **Total program enrollment:** 143. **Application fee:** $100.

**PROGRAM(S) OFFERED**
• **Truck and Bus Driver/Commercial Vehicle Operation** *80 hrs./$1705*

**STUDENT SERVICES** Academic or career counseling, employment services for current students, placement services for program completers.

## High-Tech Institute

1515 East Indian School Road, Phoenix, AZ 85014-4901
http://www.high-techinstitute.com/

**CONTACT** Fred Pressel, Campus President
**Telephone:** 602-279-9700

**GENERAL INFORMATION** Private Institution. Founded 1982. **Accreditation:** State accredited or approved. **Total program enrollment:** 2280. **Application fee:** $50.

**PROGRAM(S) OFFERED**
• **Computer and Information Systems Security** *900 hrs./$17,325* • **Criminal Justice/Police Science** *1236 hrs./$26,789* • **Industrial Electronics Technology/Technician** *900 hrs./$16,900* • **Mechanical Drafting and Mechanical Drafting CAD/CADD** *900 hrs./$17,653* • **Medical Insurance Specialist/Medical Biller** *1210 hrs./$23,950* • **Medical/Clinical Assistant** *746 hrs./$11,361*

**STUDENT SERVICES** Placement services for program completers.

## International Academy of Hair Design

4415 South Rural Road, Suite 2, Tempe, AZ 85282
http://www.intlacademy.biz/

**CONTACT** Gerald Johnson, Chief Executive Officer
**Telephone:** 480-820-9422

**GENERAL INFORMATION** Private Institution. Founded 1977. **Total program enrollment:** 190. **Application fee:** $100.

**PROGRAM(S) OFFERED**
• **Aesthetician/Esthetician and Skin Care Specialist** *600 hrs./$12,500* • **Cosmetology and Related Personal Grooming Arts, Other** • **Cosmetology, Barber/Styling, and Nail Instructor** *650 hrs./$4000* • **Cosmetology/Cosmetologist, General** *1600 hrs./$16,095* • **Teacher Education and Professional Development, Specific Subject Areas, Other** *2 students enrolled*

**STUDENT SERVICES** Academic or career counseling, employment services for current students, placement services for program completers.

## Kaplan College–Phoenix Campus

13610 North Black Canyon Highway, Suite 104, Phoenix, AZ 85029
http://www.kc-phoenix.com

**CONTACT** Debra Thibodeaux, Executive Director
**Telephone:** 602-548-1955

**GENERAL INFORMATION** Private Institution. Founded 1972. **Accreditation:** State accredited or approved. **Total program enrollment:** 560.

**PROGRAM(S) OFFERED**
• **Allied Health and Medical Assisting Services, Other** *2 students enrolled* • **Computer and Information Sciences and Support Services, Other** *54 hrs./$11,347* • **Medical/Clinical Assistant** *47 hrs./$10,724* • **Pharmacy Technician/Assistant** *53 hrs./$13,116* • **Respiratory Care Therapy/Therapist** *128 hrs./$36,115* • **Veterinary/Animal Health Technology/Technician and Veterinary Assistant** *132 hrs./$33,491*

**STUDENT SERVICES** Academic or career counseling, employment services for current students, placement services for program completers.

## Lamson College

1126 North Scottsdale Road, Suite 17, Tempe, AZ 85281
http://www.lamsoncollege.com/

**CONTACT** Donna Green, School President
**Telephone:** 480-898-7000

**GENERAL INFORMATION** Private Institution. Founded 1889. **Accreditation:** State accredited or approved. **Total program enrollment:** 643. **Application fee:** $30.

**PROGRAM(S) OFFERED**
• **Administrative Assistant and Secretarial Science, General** • **Business Administration and Management, General** *1080 hrs./$20,745* • **Legal Assistant/Paralegal** *940 hrs./$20,745* • **Medical Insurance Specialist/Medical Biller** *49 hrs./$12,202* • **Medical/Clinical Assistant** *49 hrs./$12,475* • **Surgical Technology/Technologist** *77 hrs./$22,353*

**STUDENT SERVICES** Academic or career counseling, employment services for current students, placement services for program completers.

## Maricopa Beauty College

515 West Western Avenue, Avondale, AZ 85323
http://www.maricopabeautycollege.com/

**CONTACT** Glen E. Mehlhorn, Sole Member
**Telephone:** 623-932-4414

**GENERAL INFORMATION** Private Institution. **Total program enrollment:** 68.

**PROGRAM(S) OFFERED**
• **Aesthetician/Esthetician and Skin Care Specialist** *600 hrs./$5900* • **Cosmetology, Barber/Styling, and Nail Instructor** *650 hrs./$4900* • **Cosmetology/Cosmetologist, General** *1600 hrs./$11,700* • **Hair Styling/Stylist and Hair Design** *1600 hrs./$10,900* • **Nail Technician/Specialist and Manicurist** *600 hrs./$3700*

**STUDENT SERVICES** Academic or career counseling, employment services for current students, placement services for program completers.

## Maricopa County Community Colleges System

2411 West 14th Street, Tempe, AZ 85281-6941
http://www.maricopa.edu/

**CONTACT** Rufus Glasper, Chancellor
**Telephone:** 480-731-8000

**GENERAL INFORMATION** Public Institution.

## Maricopa Skill Center

1245 East Buckeye Road, Phoenix, AZ 85034-4101
http://www.gwc.maricopa.edu/msc/index.html/

**CONTACT** John Underwood, Executive Director
**Telephone:** 602-238-4300

**GENERAL INFORMATION** Private Institution. Founded 1962. **Total program enrollment:** 565.

**PROGRAM(S) OFFERED**
• **Accounting Technology/Technician and Bookkeeping** *1376 hrs./$6330* • **Administrative Assistant and Secretarial Science, General** *4 students enrolled* • **Autobody/Collision and Repair Technology/Technician** *1448 hrs./$6661* • **CAD/CADD Drafting and/or Design Technology/Technician** *7 students enrolled* • **Computer Hardware Technology/Technician** *6 students enrolled* • **Construction Trades, Other** *4 students enrolled* • **Cosmetology/Cosmetologist, General** *1661 hrs./$7641* • **Electrical/Electronics Maintenance and Repair Technology, Other** *6 students enrolled* • **Electrician** *8 students enrolled* • **Graphic Communications, Other** *2 students enrolled* • **Institutional Food Workers** *3 students enrolled* • **Legal Administrative Assistant/Secretary** *1641 hrs./$7549* • **Machine Tool Technology/Machinist** *23 students enrolled* • **Manufacturing**

*Maricopa Skill Center (continued)*

**Technology/Technician** *2 students enrolled* • **Meat Cutting/Meat Cutter** *7 students enrolled* • **Medical/Clinical Assistant** *50 students enrolled* • **Nursing, Other** *84 students enrolled* • **Orthoptics/Orthoptist** *1 student enrolled* • **Plumbing Technology/Plumber** *1 student enrolled* • **Welding Technology/Welder** *1326 hrs./$6100*

**STUDENT SERVICES** Academic or career counseling, employment services for current students, placement services for program completers, remedial services.

## Mesa Community College

1833 West Southern Avenue, Mesa, AZ 85202-4866
http://www.mc.maricopa.edu/

**CONTACT** Dr. Shouan Pan, President
**Telephone:** 602-461-7000

**GENERAL INFORMATION** Public Institution. Founded 1965. **Accreditation:** Regional (NCA); funeral service (ABFSE). **Total program enrollment:** 7348.

**PROGRAM(S) OFFERED**
• **Accounting Technology/Technician and Bookkeeping** • **Administrative Assistant and Secretarial Science, General** *3 students enrolled* • **Animal/Livestock Husbandry and Production** • **Apparel and Textile Manufacture** • **Applied Horticulture/Horticultural Operations, General** • **Architectural Drafting and Architectural CAD/CADD** *7 students enrolled* • **Art/Art Studies, General** *598 students enrolled* • **Automobile/Automotive Mechanics Technology/Technician** *39 students enrolled* • **Business Administration and Management, General** *4 students enrolled* • **Business Administration, Management and Operations, Other** *14 students enrolled* • **Business/Commerce, General** *4 students enrolled* • **Child Care and Support Services Management** *1 student enrolled* • **Commercial Photography** *2 students enrolled* • **Commercial and Advertising Art** *3 students enrolled* • **Communication, Journalism and Related Programs, Other** • **Community Health and Preventive Medicine** • **Computer Programming, Other** *3 students enrolled* • **Computer Programming, Specific Applications** • **Computer Systems Networking and Telecommunications** • **Computer and Information Sciences, General** • **Criminal Justice/Police Science** *4 students enrolled* • **Criminal Justice/Safety Studies** *5 students enrolled* • **Design and Visual Communications, General** • **Diesel Mechanics Technology/Technician** • **Drafting and Design Technology/Technician, General** *10 students enrolled* • **Drafting/Design Engineering Technologies/Technicians, Other** • **Education, Other** • **Electrical, Electronic and Communications Engineering Technology/Technician** • **Electromechanical Technology/Electromechanical Engineering Technology** • **Emergency Medical Technology/Technician (EMT Paramedic)** *1 student enrolled* • **Fire Science/Firefighting** *1 student enrolled* • **Foods, Nutrition, and Wellness Studies, General** • **Forensic Science and Technology** *10 students enrolled* • **Geography** • **Interior Design** *12 students enrolled* • **International Business/Trade/Commerce** *1 student enrolled* • **Kinesiology and Exercise Science** *5 students enrolled* • **Landscaping and Groundskeeping** • **Library Assistant/Technician** *4 students enrolled* • **Licensed Practical/Vocational Nurse Training (LPN, LVN, Cert, Dipl, AAS)** • **Machine Tool Technology/Machinist** • **Management Information Systems, General** • **Marketing, Other** • **Marketing/Marketing Management, General** *1 student enrolled* • **Mechanical Drafting and Mechanical Drafting CAD/CADD** • **Music Management and Merchandising** *1 student enrolled* • **Music, General** *4 students enrolled* • **Music, Other** • **Nurse/Nursing Assistant/Aide and Patient Care Assistant** *45 students enrolled* • **Organizational Behavior Studies** • **Personal and Culinary Services, Other** • **Public Health, Other** • **Real Estate** *2 students enrolled* • **Selling Skills and Sales Operations** • **Sociology** *6 students enrolled* • **Teacher Assistant/Aide** • **Tool and Die Technology/Technician** • **Web Page, Digital/Multimedia and Information Resources Design** • **Welding Technology/Welder** *1 student enrolled*

**STUDENT SERVICES** Academic or career counseling, daycare for children of students, employment services for current students, remedial services.

## Mohave Community College

1971 Jagerson Avenue, Kingman, AZ 86401
http://www.mohave.edu/

**CONTACT** Michael Kearns, Chancellor
**Telephone:** 928-757-4331

**GENERAL INFORMATION** Public Institution. Founded 1971. **Accreditation:** Regional (NCA). **Total program enrollment:** 1532.

**PROGRAM(S) OFFERED**
• **Accounting Technology/Technician and Bookkeeping** • **Accounting** *14 students enrolled* • **Administrative Assistant and Secretarial Science, General** *6 students enrolled* • **Architectural Drafting and Architectural CAD/CADD** *1 student enrolled* • **Art/Art Studies, General** • **Blood Bank Technology Specialist** *3 students enrolled* • **Business Administration and Management, General** *10 students enrolled* • **Business/Commerce, General** • **Business/Office Automation/Technology/Data Entry** *9 students enrolled* • **Child Care Provider/Assistant** • **Child Care and Support Services Management** • **Computer Installation and Repair Technology/Technician** *11 students enrolled* • **Computer Programming/Programmer, General** *2 students enrolled* • **Computer Systems Analysis/Analyst** *5 students enrolled* • **Computer and Information Sciences and Support Services, Other** *7 students enrolled* • **Criminalistics and Criminal Science** *2 students enrolled* • **Culinary Arts/Chef Training** *13 students enrolled* • **Dental Assisting/Assistant** *11 students enrolled* • **Drafting and Design Technology/Technician, General** *3 students enrolled* • **Drama and Dramatics/Theatre Arts, General** *1 student enrolled* • **E-Commerce/Electronic Commerce** • **Education, General** • **Electrical and Power Transmission Installation/Installer, General** *1 student enrolled* • **Emergency Medical Technology/Technician (EMT Paramedic)** • **Fire Science/Firefighting** • **General Office Occupations and Clerical Services** • **Heating, Air Conditioning, Ventilation and Refrigeration Maintenance Technology/Technician (HAC, HACR, HVAC, HVACR)** *33 students enrolled* • **Legal Administrative Assistant/Secretary** • **Marketing/Marketing Management, General** • **Medical Administrative/Executive Assistant and Medical Secretary** *8 students enrolled* • **Medical Insurance Specialist/Medical Biller** *6 students enrolled* • **Medical Transcription/Transcriptionist** • **Medical/Clinical Assistant** *3 students enrolled* • **Metal and Jewelry Arts** *6 students enrolled* • **Nursing—Registered Nurse Training (RN, ASN, BSN, MSN)** *40 students enrolled* • **Photography** • **Retailing and Retail Operations** *7 students enrolled* • **Social Work** • **Social Work, Other** • **Sociology** *1 student enrolled* • **Surgical Technology/Technologist** *9 students enrolled* • **Truck and Bus Driver/Commercial Vehicle Operation** *96 students enrolled* • **Web Page, Digital/Multimedia and Information Resources Design** *10 students enrolled* • **Welding Technology/Welder** *3 students enrolled*

**STUDENT SERVICES** Academic or career counseling, employment services for current students, remedial services.

## Motorcycle Mechanics Institute–Division of Universal Technical Institute

2844 West Deer Valley Road, Phoenix, AZ 85027
http://www.uticorp.com/

**CONTACT** Bryan Fishkind, Campus President
**Telephone:** 623-869-9644

**GENERAL INFORMATION** Private Institution. **Total program enrollment:** 1758.

**PROGRAM(S) OFFERED**
• **Motorcycle Maintenance and Repair Technology/Technician** *48 hrs./$17,500*

**STUDENT SERVICES** Academic or career counseling, employment services for current students, placement services for program completers.

## Northern Arizona University

South San Francisco Street, Flagstaff, AZ 86011
http://www.nau.edu/

**CONTACT** John D. Haeger, President
**Telephone:** 928-523-9011

**GENERAL INFORMATION** Public Institution. Founded 1899. **Accreditation:** Regional (NCA); computer science (ABET/CSAC); counseling (ACA); dental hygiene (ADA); forestry (SAF); music (NASM); recreation and parks (NRPA); speech-language pathology (ASHA). **Total program enrollment:** 15764. **Application fee:** $25.

**PROGRAM(S) OFFERED**
• **Accounting** *41 students enrolled* • **American/United States Studies/Civilization** • **Business Administration and Management, General** *1 student enrolled* • **Business/Managerial Economics** *8 students enrolled* • **Ceramic Arts and Ceramics** *2 students enrolled* • **Communication Studies/Speech Communication and Rhetoric** • **Customer Service Management** *6 students enrolled* • **Elementary Education and Teaching** *1 student enrolled* • **Engineering, General** *1 student enrolled* • **Entrepreneurship/Entrepreneurial Studies** *14*

*students enrolled* • **Finance and Financial Management Services, Other** *14 students enrolled* • **Hospitality Administration/Management, General** *2 students enrolled* • **Human Resources Management/Personnel Administration, General** *18 students enrolled* • **International Business/Trade/Commerce** *2 students enrolled* • **International Marketing** • **Investments and Securities** *25 students enrolled* • **Management Information Systems, General** *12 students enrolled* • **Marketing/Marketing Management, General** • **Metal and Jewelry Arts** • **Painting** • **Parks, Recreation and Leisure Studies** *8 students enrolled* • **Printmaking** • **Public Relations/Image Management** *18 students enrolled* • **Radio and Television** *4 students enrolled* • **Speech-Language Pathology/Pathologist** *35 students enrolled* • **Tourism and Travel Services Management** *3 students enrolled*

**STUDENT SERVICES** Academic or career counseling, employment services for current students, placement services for program completers.

## Northland Pioneer College

PO Box 610, Holbrook, AZ 86025-0610
http://www.npc.edu/

**CONTACT** Jeanne Swarthout, President
**Telephone:** 928-524-7600

**GENERAL INFORMATION** Public Institution. Founded 1974. **Accreditation:** Regional (NCA). **Total program enrollment:** 1083.

**PROGRAM(S) OFFERED**

• **Accounting Technology/Technician and Bookkeeping** • **Administrative Assistant and Secretarial Science, General** • **Agriculture, General** • **Animal Sciences, General** • **Archeology** • **Architectural Drafting and Architectural CAD/CADD** • **Building/Home/Construction Inspection/Inspector** • **Building/Property Maintenance and Management** *4 students enrolled* • **Business Administration and Management, General** • **Business/Office Automation/Technology/Data Entry** • **CAD/CADD Drafting and/or Design Technology/Technician** • **Cabinetmaking and Millwork/Millwright** • **Carpentry/Carpenter** *32 students enrolled* • **Child Care Provider/Assistant** • **Child Care and Support Services Management** *4 students enrolled* • **Child Development** • **Commercial Photography** • **Commercial and Advertising Art** • **Community Health Services/Liaison/Counseling** • **Computer Graphics** • **Computer Installation and Repair Technology/Technician** • **Computer Systems Networking and Telecommunications** • **Construction Trades, General** *5 students enrolled* • **Corrections** • **Cosmetology, Barber/Styling, and Nail Instructor** • **Cosmetology/Cosmetologist, General** • **Court Reporting/Court Reporter** • **Criminal Justice/Police Science** • **Data Modeling/Warehousing and Database Administration** • **Drafting and Design Technology/Technician, General** • **Early Childhood Education and Teaching** • **Education/Teaching of Individuals in Early Childhood Special Education Programs** • **Electrical, Electronic and Communications Engineering Technology/Technician** • **Electrical/Electronics Equipment Installation and Repair, General** • **Electrician** • **Emergency Medical Technology/Technician (EMT Paramedic)** • **Entrepreneurial and Small Business Operations, Other** • **Fire Science/Firefighting** • **Health Information/Medical Records Administration/Administrator** *1 student enrolled* • **Horticultural Science** • **Hospitality and Recreation Marketing Operations** • **Housing and Human Environments, Other** • **Industrial Electronics Technology/Technician** • **Industrial Mechanics and Maintenance Technology** • **Industrial Technology/Technician** • **Information Science/Studies** • **Instrumentation Technology/Technician** • **Kindergarten/Preschool Education and Teaching** *10 students enrolled* • **Legal Administrative Assistant/Secretary** • **Legal Professions and Studies, Other** • **Library Assistant/Technician** • **Licensed Practical/Vocational Nurse Training (LPN, LVN, Cert, Dipl, AAS)** *5 students enrolled* • **Machine Tool Technology/Machinist** • **Massage Therapy/Therapeutic Massage** • **Medical Office Assistant/Specialist** • **Medical Reception/Receptionist** • **Medical Transcription/Transcriptionist** • **Nail Technician/Specialist and Manicurist** • **Parks, Recreation and Leisure Facilities Management** • **Photography** • **Public Administration** • **Range Science and Management** • **Restaurant, Culinary, and Catering Management/Manager** • **Small Business Administration/Management** • **Specialized Merchandising, Sales, and Marketing Operations, Other** • **Substance Abuse/Addiction Counseling** • **Teacher Assistant/Aide** • **Teaching Assistants/Aides, Other** • **Turf and Turfgrass Management** • **Upholstery/Upholsterer** *13 students enrolled* • **Water Quality and Wastewater Treatment Management and Recycling Technology/Technician** • **Welding Technology/Welder** • **Word Processing**

**STUDENT SERVICES** Academic or career counseling, employment services for current students, placement services for program completers, remedial services.

## Ottawa University–Phoenix

10020 North 25th Avenue, Phoenix, AZ 85021
http://www.ottawa.edu/

**CONTACT** Dr. Allan Hoffman, Campus Executive Officer
**Telephone:** 602-371-1188

**GENERAL INFORMATION** Private Institution (Affiliated with American Baptist Churches in the U.S.A.). **Total program enrollment:** 277. **Application fee:** $50.

**STUDENT SERVICES** Academic or career counseling.

## Paradise Valley Community College

18401 North 32nd Street, Phoenix, AZ 85032-1200
http://www.pvc.maricopa.edu/

**CONTACT** Dr. Mary Kathryn Kickels, President
**Telephone:** 602-787-6500

**GENERAL INFORMATION** Public Institution. Founded 1985. **Accreditation:** Regional (NCA). **Total program enrollment:** 2534.

**PROGRAM(S) OFFERED**

• **Accounting Technology/Technician and Bookkeeping** *2 students enrolled* • **Administrative Assistant and Secretarial Science, General** • **Art/Art Studies, General** *155 students enrolled* • **Business Administration and Management, General** • **Business Administration, Management and Operations, Other** *1 student enrolled* • **Business/Commerce, General** *1 student enrolled* • **Business/Office Automation/Technology/Data Entry** • **Commercial and Advertising Art** • **Computer Installation and Repair Technology/Technician** *1 student enrolled* • **Computer Programming, Specific Applications** *1 student enrolled* • **Computer Systems Analysis/Analyst** • **Computer Systems Networking and Telecommunications** • **Computer and Information Sciences and Support Services, Other** • **Computer and Information Sciences, General** *2 students enrolled* • **Computer/Information Technology Services Administration and Management, Other** *1 student enrolled* • **Early Childhood Education and Teaching** *2 students enrolled* • **Emergency Medical Technology/Technician (EMT Paramedic)** *189 students enrolled* • **Environmental Control Technologies/Technicians, Other** • **Fine Arts and Art Studies, Other** • **Fire Science/Firefighting** *40 students enrolled* • **Health Professions and Related Clinical Sciences, Other** • **International Business/Trade/Commerce** • **Journalism** *2 students enrolled* • **Kindergarten/Preschool Education and Teaching** • **Kinesiology and Exercise Science** *1 student enrolled* • **Licensed Practical/Vocational Nurse Training (LPN, LVN, Cert, Dipl, AAS)** *28 students enrolled* • **Music, General** • **Nurse/Nursing Assistant/Aide and Patient Care Assistant** *47 students enrolled* • **Organizational Behavior Studies** • **Personal and Culinary Services, Other** • **System Administration/Administrator**

**STUDENT SERVICES** Academic or career counseling, daycare for children of students, employment services for current students, placement services for program completers, remedial services.

## Phoenix College

1202 West Thomas Road, Phoenix, AZ 85013-4234
http://www.pc.maricopa.edu/

**CONTACT** Dr. Anna Solley, President
**Telephone:** 602-264-2492

**GENERAL INFORMATION** Public Institution. Founded 1920. **Accreditation:** Regional (NCA); dental assisting (ADA); dental hygiene (ADA); health information technology (AHIMA). **Total program enrollment:** 2428.

**PROGRAM(S) OFFERED**

• **Accounting Technology/Technician and Bookkeeping** • **Administrative Assistant and Secretarial Science, General** *1 student enrolled* • **Adult Development and Aging** • **Allied Health Diagnostic, Intervention, and Treatment Professions, Other** • **Allied Health and Medical Assisting Services, Other** *60 students enrolled* • **American Indian/Native American Studies** • **American Sign Language (ASL)** • **Apparel and Textile Manufacture** • **Apparel and Textiles, General** • **Architectural Drafting and Architectural CAD/CADD** *11 students enrolled* • **Art/Art Studies, General** *245 students enrolled* • **Baking and Pastry Arts/Baker/Pastry Chef** *1 student enrolled* • **Banking and Financial Support Services** • **Building/Home/Construction Inspection/Inspector** • **Business**

*Phoenix College (continued)*

**Administration and Management, General • Business/Commerce, General** 8 *students enrolled* • **Business/Office Automation/Technology/Data Entry** 2 *students enrolled* • **Cartography** 11 *students enrolled* • **Child Care and Support Services Management • Child Development** 3 *students enrolled* • **Civil Engineering Technology/Technician • Clinical/Medical Laboratory Assistant** 30 *students enrolled* • **Clinical/Medical Laboratory Science and Allied Professions, Other • Clinical/Medical Laboratory Technician** 6 *students enrolled* • **Commercial Photography • Commercial and Advertising Art** 1 *student enrolled* • **Computer Programming, Specific Applications • Computer Systems Analysis/Analyst • Computer Systems Networking and Telecommunications • Computer and Information Sciences and Support Services, Other • Computer and Information Sciences, General • Computer/Information Technology Services Administration and Management, Other** 1 *student enrolled* • **Construction Management** 5 *students enrolled* • **Court Reporting/Court Reporter • Criminal Justice/Police Science • Criminal Justice/Safety Studies** 20 *students enrolled* • **Culinary Arts/Chef Training** 3 *students enrolled* • **Dental Assisting/Assistant** 17 *students enrolled* • **Design and Visual Communications, General** 1 *student enrolled* • **Early Childhood Education and Teaching** 2 *students enrolled* • **Educational Administration and Supervision, Other • Emergency Medical Technology/Technician (EMT Paramedic)** 192 *students enrolled* • **Family and Community Services** 1 *student enrolled* • **Fashion Merchandising • Fashion/Apparel Design** 1 *student enrolled* • **Fire Protection and Safety Technology/Technician • Fire Science/Firefighting** 40 *students enrolled* • **Food Preparation/Professional Cooking/Kitchen Assistant** 1 *student enrolled* • **Foodservice Systems Administration/Management** 1 *student enrolled* • **Forensic Science and Technology** 75 *students enrolled* • **General Office Occupations and Clerical Services • Health Information/Medical Records Technology/Technician** 1 *student enrolled* • **Health and Medical Administrative Services, Other** 18 *students enrolled* • **Health and Physical Education/Fitness, Other • Histologic Technician • Histologic Technology/Histotechnologist** 11 *students enrolled* • **Hospitality and Recreation Marketing Operations • Hotel/Motel Administration/Management • Human Services, General • Institutional Food Workers • Insurance • Interior Design • Kindergarten/Preschool Education and Teaching** 1 *student enrolled* • **Landscaping and Groundskeeping • Legal Administrative Assistant/Secretary • Legal Assistant/Paralegal • Legal Professions and Studies, Other • Licensed Practical/Vocational Nurse Training (LPN, LVN, Cert, Dipl, AAS) • Management Information Systems, General • Marketing/Marketing Management, General** 2 *students enrolled* • **Massage Therapy/Therapeutic Massage** 20 *students enrolled* • **Medical Administrative/Executive Assistant and Medical Secretary • Medical Transcription/Transcriptionist** 1 *student enrolled* • **Medical/Clinical Assistant** 57 *students enrolled* • **Music Performance, General • Music, General** 1 *student enrolled* • **Music, Other • Nurse/Nursing Assistant/Aide and Patient Care Assistant • Phlebotomy/Phlebotomist** 99 *students enrolled* • **Real Estate** 2 *students enrolled* • **Rehabilitation and Therapeutic Professions, Other • Sign Language Interpretation and Translation** 3 *students enrolled* • **Survey Technology/Surveying • System Administration/Administrator • Tourism and Travel Services Marketing Operations • Welding Technology/Welder** 2 *students enrolled*

**STUDENT SERVICES** Academic or career counseling, daycare for children of students, employment services for current students, placement services for program completers, remedial services.

## Pima Community College

4905 East Broadway, Tucson, AZ 85709-1010
http://www.pima.edu/

**CONTACT** Roy Flores, Chancellor
**Telephone:** 520-206-4500

**GENERAL INFORMATION** Public Institution. Founded 1966. **Accreditation:** Regional (NCA); dental assisting (ADA); dental hygiene (ADA); dental laboratory technology (ADA); radiologic technology: radiography (JRCERT). **Total program enrollment:** 9893.

**PROGRAM(S) OFFERED**

• **Accounting** 9 *students enrolled* • **Administrative Assistant and Secretarial Science, General** 5 *students enrolled* • **Aircraft Powerplant Technology/Technician** 25 *students enrolled* • **Allied Health and Medical Assisting Services, Other** 14 *students enrolled* • **Archeology** 26 *students enrolled* • **Architectural Drafting and Architectural CAD/CADD** 12 *students enrolled* • **Automobile/Automotive Mechanics Technology/Technician** 13 *students enrolled* • **Avionics Maintenance Technology/Technician • Baking and Pastry Arts/Baker/Pastry Chef** 5 *students enrolled* • **Bilingual and Multilingual Education • Biology Technician/Biotechnology Laboratory Technician** 1 *student enrolled* • **Building/Property Maintenance and Management** 15 *students enrolled* • **Business Administration and Management, General** 9 *students enrolled* • **Business Administration, Management and Operations, Other** 7 *students enrolled* • **Business Operations Support and Secretarial Services, Other** 13 *students enrolled* • **Business, Management, Marketing, and Related Support Services, Other** 12 *students enrolled* • **Cabinetmaking and Millwork/Millwright • Child Development** 28 *students enrolled* • **Clinical/Medical Laboratory Science and Allied Professions, Other • Clinical/Medical Social Work** 14 *students enrolled* • **Community Health Services/Liaison/Counseling** 26 *students enrolled* • **Computer Software and Media Applications, Other** 12 *students enrolled* • **Computer Systems Analysis/Analyst** 2 *students enrolled* • **Computer Systems Networking and Telecommunications** 13 *students enrolled* • **Computer and Information Sciences, General** 9 *students enrolled* • **Corrections and Criminal Justice, Other** 2 *students enrolled* • **Criminal Justice/Police Science • Culinary Arts and Related Services, Other** 1 *student enrolled* • **Customer Service Management • Data Processing and Data Processing Technology/Technician • Dental Assisting/Assistant** 26 *students enrolled* • **Dental Laboratory Technology/Technician** 2 *students enrolled* • **Design and Visual Communications, General** 1 *student enrolled* • **Drafting and Design Technology/Technician, General • Early Childhood Education and Teaching** 4 *students enrolled* • **Education, General** 66 *students enrolled* • **Education, Other • Electrical/Electronics Drafting and Electrical/Electronics CAD/CADD • Emergency Medical Technology/Technician (EMT Paramedic)** 3 *students enrolled* • **Environmental Engineering Technology/Environmental Technology** 2 *students enrolled* • **Fashion Merchandising • Fire Science/Firefighting** 6 *students enrolled* • **Foreign Languages, Literatures, and Linguistics, Other • Forensic Science and Technology** 8 *students enrolled* • **Graphic Communications, General** 2 *students enrolled* • **Health and Medical Administrative Services, Other** 14 *students enrolled* • **Health and Physical Education/Fitness, Other** 9 *students enrolled* • **Heating, Air Conditioning, Ventilation and Refrigeration Maintenance Technology/Technician (HAC, HACR, HVAC, HVACR)** 10 *students enrolled* • **Histologic Technician** 1 *student enrolled* • **Home Health Aide/Home Attendant • Hospitality Administration/Management, General** 1 *student enrolled* • **Human Resources Management/Personnel Administration, General** 12 *students enrolled* • **Industrial Electronics Technology/Technician** 1 *student enrolled* • **Industrial Production Technologies/Technicians, Other** 3 *students enrolled* • **International Business/Trade/Commerce** 1 *student enrolled* • **Language Interpretation and Translation** 8 *students enrolled* • **Laser and Optical Technology/Technician** 3 *students enrolled* • **Legal Assistant/Paralegal** 12 *students enrolled* • **Machine Shop Technology/Assistant** 9 *students enrolled* • **Massage Therapy/Therapeutic Massage** 5 *students enrolled* • **Medical/Health Management and Clinical Assistant/Specialist • Nursing—Registered Nurse Training (RN, ASN, BSN, MSN)** 9 *students enrolled* • **Nursing, Other** 63 *students enrolled* • **Pharmacy Technician/Assistant** 5 *students enrolled* • **Physical Education Teaching and Coaching** 4 *students enrolled* • **Radio and Television** 2 *students enrolled* • **Radiologic Technology/Science—Radiographer** 3 *students enrolled* • **Restaurant, Culinary, and Catering Management/Manager** 11 *students enrolled* • **Retailing and Retail Operations** 3 *students enrolled* • **Security and Protective Services, Other** 7 *students enrolled* • **Special Education and Teaching, General • Teacher Education and Professional Development, Specific Levels and Methods, Other • Technical and Business Writing • Truck and Bus Driver/Commercial Vehicle Operation** 49 *students enrolled* • **Vehicle Maintenance and Repair Technologies, Other • Web Page, Digital/Multimedia and Information Resources Design** 2 *students enrolled*

**STUDENT SERVICES** Academic or career counseling, daycare for children of students, placement services for program completers, remedial services.

## Pima Medical Institute

957 South Dobson Road, Mesa, AZ 85202
http://www.pmi.edu/

**CONTACT** Kristen Torres, Director
**Telephone:** 480-644-0267

**GENERAL INFORMATION** Private Institution. Founded 1985. **Accreditation:** Radiologic technology: radiography (JRCERT); respiratory therapy technology (CoARC); state accredited or approved. **Total program enrollment:** 860.

**PROGRAM(S) OFFERED**

• **Dental Assisting/Assistant** 720 *hrs.*/$9580 • **Massage Therapy/Therapeutic Massage** 17 *students enrolled* • **Medical Administrative/Executive Assistant and Medical Secretary** 560 *hrs.*/$6430 • **Medical/Clinical Assistant** 800 *hrs.*/$9995 • **Pharmacy Technician/Assistant** 800 *hrs.*/$9380 • **Phlebotomy/Phlebotomist** 300 *hrs.*/$2900 • **Physical Therapist Assistant** 18 *students enrolled* • **Veterinary/Animal Health Technology/Technician and Veterinary Assistant** 720 *hrs.*/$9380

**STUDENT SERVICES** Academic or career counseling, employment services for current students, placement services for program completers, remedial services.

## Pima Medical Institute

3350 East Grant Road, Tucson, AZ 85716-2800
http://www.pmi.edu/

**CONTACT** Dale Berg, Campus Director
**Telephone:** 520-326-1600

**GENERAL INFORMATION** Private Institution. Founded 1972. **Accreditation:** Radiologic technology: radiography (JRCERT); respiratory therapy technology (CoARC); state accredited or approved. **Total program enrollment:** 1062.

**PROGRAM(S) OFFERED**
• **Dental Assisting/Assistant** *720 hrs./$9530* • **Health Unit Coordinator/Ward Clerk** *4 students enrolled* • **Medical Administrative/Executive Assistant and Medical Secretary** *560 hrs./$6430* • **Medical/Clinical Assistant** *800 hrs./$9995* • **Pharmacy Technician/Assistant** *800 hrs./$9380* • **Phlebotomy/Phlebotomist** *300 hrs./$2900* • **Physical Therapist Assistant** *38 students enrolled* • **Veterinary/Animal Health Technology/Technician and Veterinary Assistant** *720 hrs./$9380*

**STUDENT SERVICES** Academic or career counseling, employment services for current students, placement services for program completers, remedial services.

## The Refrigeration School

4210 East Washington Street, Phoenix, AZ 85034-1816
http://www.refrigerationschool.com/

**CONTACT** Elizabeth Loney-Cline, President Director
**Telephone:** 602-275-7133

**GENERAL INFORMATION** Private Institution. Founded 1965. **Accreditation:** State accredited or approved. **Total program enrollment:** 442.

**PROGRAM(S) OFFERED**
• **Electrician** *13 students enrolled* • **Electromechanical Technology/Electromechanical Engineering Technology** *42 hrs./$13,710* • **Energy Management and Systems Technology/Technician** *72 hrs./$21,630* • **Heating, Air Conditioning and Refrigeration Technology/Technician (ACH/ACR/ACHR/HRAC/HVAC/AC Technology)** *34 hrs./$11,220*

**STUDENT SERVICES** Academic or career counseling, employment services for current students, placement services for program completers.

## Regency Beauty Institute

1457 W. Southern Avenue, Suite 113, Mesa, AZ 85203

**CONTACT** J. Hayes Batson
**Telephone:** 480-273-8087

**GENERAL INFORMATION** Private Institution. **Total program enrollment:** 40. **Application fee:** $100.

**PROGRAM(S) OFFERED**
• **Cosmetology/Cosmetologist, General** *1600 hrs./$17,011*

**STUDENT SERVICES** Academic or career counseling, placement services for program completers.

## Regency Beauty Institute

10217 N. Metro Parkway West, Phoenix, AZ 85710

**GENERAL INFORMATION** Private Institution. **Total program enrollment:** 70. **Application fee:** $100.

**PROGRAM(S) OFFERED**
• **Cosmetology/Cosmetologist, General** *1600 hrs./$16,011*

**STUDENT SERVICES** Academic or career counseling, placement services for program completers.

## Regency Beauty Institute

7910 W. Thomas Road, Phoenix, AZ 85033

**CONTACT** J. Hayes Batson, CEO
**Telephone:** 623-215-0807

**GENERAL INFORMATION** Private Institution. **Total program enrollment:** 19. **Application fee:** $100.

**PROGRAM(S) OFFERED**
• **Cosmetology/Cosmetologist, General** *1600 hrs./$17,011*

## Regency Beauty Institute

7225 E. Broadway Boulevard, Suite 170, Tucson, AZ 85710

**GENERAL INFORMATION** Private Institution. **Total program enrollment:** 81. **Application fee:** $100.

**PROGRAM(S) OFFERED**
• **Cosmetology/Cosmetologist, General** *1600 hrs./$16,011*

**STUDENT SERVICES** Academic or career counseling, placement services for program completers.

## Rio Salado College

2323 West 14th Street, Tempe, AZ 85281-6950
http://www.rio.maricopa.edu/

**CONTACT** Linda Thor, President
**Telephone:** 480-517-8000

**GENERAL INFORMATION** Public Institution. Founded 1978. **Accreditation:** Regional (NCA); dental hygiene (ADA). **Total program enrollment:** 1888.

**PROGRAM(S) OFFERED**
• **Administrative Assistant and Secretarial Science, General** • **Airline Flight Attendant** *66 students enrolled* • **Art/Art Studies, General** *51 students enrolled* • **Aviation/Airway Management and Operations** *311 students enrolled* • **Banking and Financial Support Services** *76 students enrolled* • **Business Administration and Management, General** • **Business Administration, Management and Operations, Other** *137 students enrolled* • **Business/Commerce, General** • **Business/Office Automation/Technology/Data Entry** *49 students enrolled* • **Carpentry/Carpenter** *12 students enrolled* • **Computer Installation and Repair Technology/Technician** *6 students enrolled* • **Computer Programming/Programmer, General** • **Computer Systems Analysis/Analyst** • **Computer Systems Networking and Telecommunications** *12 students enrolled* • **Computer and Information Sciences and Support Services, Other** *2 students enrolled* • **Cooking and Related Culinary Arts, General** *4 students enrolled* • **Corrections** *705 students enrolled* • **Criminal Justice/Police Science** *100 students enrolled* • **Customer Service Management** *290 students enrolled* • **Customer Service Support/Call Center/Teleservice Operation** *456 students enrolled* • **Data Processing and Data Processing Technology/Technician** *202 students enrolled* • **Dental Assisting/Assistant** *15 students enrolled* • **Dental Hygiene/Hygienist** • **Electrical, Electronic and Communications Engineering Technology/Technician** • **Fire Science/Firefighting** *31 students enrolled* • **Graphic Communications, General** *19 students enrolled* • **Industrial Production Technologies/Technicians, Other** • **Licensed Practical/Vocational Nurse Training (LPN, LVN, Cert, Dipl, AAS)** *29 students enrolled* • **Management Information Systems, General** • **Nurse/Nursing Assistant/Aide and Patient Care Assistant** *1 student enrolled* • **Operations Management and Supervision** • **Organizational Behavior Studies** • **Personal and Culinary Services, Other** *47 students enrolled* • **Public Administration and Social Service Professions, Other** • **Public Administration** *23 students enrolled* • **Sheet Metal Technology/Sheetworking** • **Substance Abuse/Addiction Counseling** *47 students enrolled* • **Water Quality and Wastewater Treatment Management and Recycling Technology/Technician** • **Web Page, Digital/Multimedia and Information Resources Design** *5 students enrolled* • **Welding Technology/Welder** *6 students enrolled*

**STUDENT SERVICES** Academic or career counseling, remedial services.

## Roberto–Venn School of Luthiery

4011 S. 16th Street, Phoenix, AZ 85040
http://www.roberto-venn.com/

**CONTACT** William Eaton, Director
**Telephone:** 602-243-1179

**GENERAL INFORMATION** Private Institution. **Total program enrollment:** 35. **Application fee:** $50.

**PROGRAM(S) OFFERED**
• **Musical Instrument Fabrication and Repair** *880 hrs./$11,450*

**STUDENT SERVICES** Academic or career counseling, placement services for program completers.

## Scottsdale Community College

9000 East Chaparral Road, Scottsdale, AZ 85256-2626
http://www.sc.maricopa.edu/

**CONTACT** Dr. Jan L. Gehler, President
**Telephone:** 480-423-6000

**GENERAL INFORMATION** Public Institution. Founded 1969. **Accreditation:** Regional (NCA). **Total program enrollment:** 3248.

**PROGRAM(S) OFFERED**
• **Accounting Technology/Technician and Bookkeeping** *14 students enrolled* • **Acting** *1 student enrolled* • **Administrative Assistant and Secretarial Science, General** *2 students enrolled* • **Animal/Livestock Husbandry and Production** • **Architectural Drafting and Architectural CAD/CADD** *8 students enrolled* • **Art/Art Studies, General** *318 students enrolled* • **Broadcast Journalism** *6 students enrolled* • **Building/Home/Construction Inspection/Inspector** • **Business Administration and Management, General** • **Business/Commerce, General** • **Child Care Provider/Assistant** • **Child Development** *1 student enrolled* • **Cinematography and Film/Video Production** *39 students enrolled* • **Computer Programming/Programmer, General** *1 student enrolled* • **Computer Systems Networking and Telecommunications** • **Computer and Information Sciences and Support Services, Other** • **Computer/Information Technology Services Administration and Management, Other** • **Corrections and Criminal Justice, Other** • **Criminal Justice/Police Science** *10 students enrolled* • **Criminal Justice/Safety Studies** *1 student enrolled* • **Culinary Arts/Chef Training** *31 students enrolled* • **Dance, General** • **Drafting/Design Engineering Technologies/Technicians, Other** • **Emergency Medical Technology/Technician (EMT Paramedic)** *56 students enrolled* • **Equestrian/Equine Studies** *5 students enrolled* • **Film/Cinema Studies** *3 students enrolled* • **Fire Science/Firefighting** *1 student enrolled* • **Forensic Science and Technology** *9 students enrolled* • **General Office Occupations and Clerical Services** *1 student enrolled* • **Graphic Design** *2 students enrolled* • **Hospitality Administration/Management, General** • **Hotel/Motel Administration/Management** *1 student enrolled* • **Institutional Food Workers** • **Interior Design** *23 students enrolled* • **International Business/Trade/Commerce** • **Journalism** *1 student enrolled* • **Kinesiology and Exercise Science** *4 students enrolled* • **Licensed Practical/Vocational Nurse Training (LPN, LVN, Cert, Dipl, AAS)** • **Lineworker** • **Management Information Systems, General** • **Marketing, Other** • **Marketing/Marketing Management, General** *3 students enrolled* • **Music, General** *1 student enrolled* • **Nurse/Nursing Assistant/Aide and Patient Care Assistant** *11 students enrolled* • **Parks, Recreation and Leisure Studies** *1 student enrolled* • **Playwriting and Screenwriting** *25 students enrolled* • **Radio and Television Broadcasting Technology/Technician** • **Resort Management** *1 student enrolled* • **Small Business Administration/Management** *2 students enrolled* • **Speech-Language Pathology/Pathologist** • **Web Page, Digital/Multimedia and Information Resources Design** • **Yoga Teacher Training/Yoga Therapy** *4 students enrolled*

**STUDENT SERVICES** Academic or career counseling, remedial services.

## Scottsdale Culinary Institute

8100 East Camelback Road, Suite 1001, Scottsdale, AZ 85251-3940
http://www.scichefs.com/

**CONTACT** Jacob Elsen, President
**Telephone:** 480-425-3000

**GENERAL INFORMATION** Private Institution. Founded 1986. **Accreditation:** State accredited or approved. **Total program enrollment:** 1204. **Application fee:** $50.

**PROGRAM(S) OFFERED**
• **Baking and Pastry Arts/Baker/Pastry Chef** *60 hrs./$38,700* • **Culinary Arts and Related Services, Other** *36 hrs./$19,450* • **Culinary Arts/Chef Training** *60 hrs./$40,500* • **Hospitality Administration/Management, General** *120 hrs./$54,400*

**STUDENT SERVICES** Academic or career counseling, employment services for current students, placement services for program completers.

## South Mountain Community College

7050 South Twenty-fourth Street, Phoenix, AZ 85040
http://www.smc.maricopa.edu/

**CONTACT** Ken Atwater, President
**Telephone:** 602-243-8135

**GENERAL INFORMATION** Public Institution. Founded 1979. **Accreditation:** Regional (NCA). **Total program enrollment:** 949.

**PROGRAM(S) OFFERED**
• **Administrative Assistant and Secretarial Science, General** • **Art/Art Studies, General** *122 students enrolled* • **Business Administration and Management, General** • **Business/Commerce, General** • **Business/Office Automation/Technology/Data Entry** • **Child Care Provider/Assistant** • **Child Development** • **Computer Systems Analysis/Analyst** • **Computer Systems Networking and Telecommunications** *27 students enrolled* • **Computer and Information Sciences and Support Services, Other** • **Computer and Information Systems Security** • **Early Childhood Education and Teaching** • **Education, Other** • **Entrepreneurship/Entrepreneurial Studies** *1 student enrolled* • **Information Technology** *1 student enrolled* • **Management Information Systems, General** • **Marketing/Marketing Management, General** *1 student enrolled* • **Radio and Television Broadcasting Technology/Technician** • **Web Page, Digital/Multimedia and Information Resources Design**

**STUDENT SERVICES** Academic or career counseling, daycare for children of students, employment services for current students, placement services for program completers, remedial services.

## Southwestern College

2625 East Cactus Road, Phoenix, AZ 85032-7042
http://www.swcaz.edu/

**CONTACT** Brent Garrison, President
**Telephone:** 602-489-5300

**GENERAL INFORMATION** Private Institution. Founded 1960. **Accreditation:** Regional (NCA). **Total program enrollment:** 352. **Application fee:** $30.

**PROGRAM(S) OFFERED**
• **Bible/Biblical Studies** *2 students enrolled*

**STUDENT SERVICES** Academic or career counseling, placement services for program completers, remedial services.

## Southwest Institute of Healing Arts

1100 East Apache Boulevard, Tempe, AZ 85281
http://www.swiha.org/

**CONTACT** K. C. Miller, CEO
**Telephone:** 480-994-9244

**GENERAL INFORMATION** Private Institution. Founded 1992. **Accreditation:** State accredited or approved. **Total program enrollment:** 445. **Application fee:** $75.

**PROGRAM(S) OFFERED**
• **Aesthetician/Esthetician and Skin Care Specialist** *74 students enrolled* • **Alternative and Complementary Medicine and Medical Systems, Other** *60 hrs./$14,675* • **Asian Bodywork Therapy** *1 student enrolled* • **Herbalism/Herbalist** *5 students enrolled* • **Hypnotherapy/Hypnotherapist** *22 students*

*enrolled* • **Massage Therapy/Therapeutic Massage** *750 hrs./$9075* • **Movement and Mind-Body Therapies and Education, Other** *600 hrs./$7875* • **Nutrition Sciences** • **Yoga Teacher Training/Yoga Therapy** *200 hrs./$2475*

**STUDENT SERVICES** Academic or career counseling, placement services for program completers.

## Southwest Skill Center

3000 N. Dysart Road, Avondale, AZ 85323

**CONTACT** President
**Telephone:** 623-535-2700

**GENERAL INFORMATION** Public Institution. **Total program enrollment:** 204.

**PROGRAM(S) OFFERED**
• **Emergency Medical Technology/Technician (EMT Paramedic)** *20 students enrolled* • **Licensed Practical/Vocational Nurse Training (LPN, LVN, Cert, Dipl, AAS)** *1008 hrs./$7210* • **Medical Insurance Coding Specialist/Coder** *665 hrs./$3207* • **Medical/Clinical Assistant** *851 hrs./$4411* • **Nurse/Nursing Assistant/Aide and Patient Care Assistant** *144 hrs./$1006* • **Parts, Warehousing, and Inventory Management Operations** *160 hrs./$1466* • **Phlebotomy/Phlebotomist** *410 hrs./$2265*

**STUDENT SERVICES** Academic or career counseling, remedial services.

## Tohono O'odham Community College

PO Box 3129, Sells, AZ 85634
http://www.tocc.cc.az.us/

**CONTACT** Olivia Vanegas-Funcheon, President
**Telephone:** 520-383-8401

**GENERAL INFORMATION** Private Institution. Founded 1998. **Accreditation:** Regional (NCA). **Total program enrollment:** 14. **Application fee:** $25.

**PROGRAM(S) OFFERED**
• **Administrative Assistant and Secretarial Science, General** • **Carpentry/Carpenter** • **Child Care Provider/Assistant** *3 students enrolled* • **Construction Trades, General** • **Electrical/Electronics Maintenance and Repair Technology, Other** *5 students enrolled* • **General Office Occupations and Clerical Services** • **Plumbing Technology/Plumber** • **Welding Technology/Welder**

**STUDENT SERVICES** Academic or career counseling, employment services for current students, placement services for program completers, remedial services.

## Toni & Guy Hairdressing Academy

7201 East Camelback Road, Suite 100, Scottsdale, AZ 85251
http://attheacademy.com/

**CONTACT** Michael A. Smith, Chief Executive Officer
**Telephone:** 480-994-4222

**GENERAL INFORMATION** Private Institution. Founded 1995. **Total program enrollment:** 288. **Application fee:** $100.

**PROGRAM(S) OFFERED**
• **Cosmetology/Cosmetologist, General** *1600 hrs./$16,360* • **Trade and Industrial Teacher Education** *650 hrs./$3010*

**STUDENT SERVICES** Academic or career counseling, employment services for current students, placement services for program completers.

## Tucson College

7310 East 22nd Street, Tucson, AZ 85710
http://www.tucsoncollege.edu/

**CONTACT** Alan Sussna, President, Chief Executive Officer
**Telephone:** 520-296-3261

**GENERAL INFORMATION** Private Institution. **Total program enrollment:** 355. **Application fee:** $75.

**PROGRAM(S) OFFERED**
• **Computer and Information Sciences and Support Services, Other** *720 hrs./$10,733* • **Criminal Justice/Law Enforcement Administration** *8 students enrolled* • **Electrician** *720 hrs./$9825* • **Medical Office Management/Administration** *720 hrs./$10,733* • **Medical/Clinical Assistant** *800 hrs./$13,422* • **Nurse/Nursing Assistant/Aide and Patient Care Assistant** *640 hrs./$10,733* • **Nursing, Other** *29 students enrolled* • **Pharmacy Technician/Assistant** *720 hrs./$10,733*

**STUDENT SERVICES** Academic or career counseling, employment services for current students, placement services for program completers.

## Tucson College of Beauty

3955 N. Flowing Wells Road, Tucson, AZ 85705
http://tucsoncollegeofbeauty.com/

**CONTACT** Rochelle Carr, Director
**Telephone:** 520-887-8262

**GENERAL INFORMATION** Private Institution. **Total program enrollment:** 77. **Application fee:** $50.

**PROGRAM(S) OFFERED**
• **Aesthetician/Esthetician and Skin Care Specialist** *600 hrs./$7285*
• **Cosmetology/Cosmetologist, General** *1600 hrs./$14,085*

**STUDENT SERVICES** Academic or career counseling, employment services for current students, placement services for program completers.

## Turning Point Beauty College

1226 E. Florence Boulevard, Casa Grande, AZ 85222

**CONTACT** Jan Haner
**Telephone:** 520-836-1476

**GENERAL INFORMATION** Private Institution. **Total program enrollment:** 62. **Application fee:** $50.

**PROGRAM(S) OFFERED**
• **Cosmetology, Barber/Styling, and Nail Instructor** *650 hrs./$6500*
• **Cosmetology/Cosmetologist, General** *1600 hrs./$14,600*

**STUDENT SERVICES** Academic or career counseling, employment services for current students, placement services for program completers.

## University of Phoenix–Phoenix Campus

4635 East Elwood Street, Phoenix, AZ 85040-1958
http://www.phoenix.edu/

**CONTACT** William Pepicello, PhD, President
**Telephone:** 800-776-4867

**GENERAL INFORMATION** Private Institution. Founded 1976. **Accreditation:** Regional (NCA); counseling (ACA). **Total program enrollment:** 5868.

**PROGRAM(S) OFFERED**
• **Business Administration and Management, General** *17 students enrolled*
• **Human Resources Management/Personnel Administration, General** *51 students enrolled*

**STUDENT SERVICES** Academic or career counseling, remedial services.

## University of Phoenix–Southern Arizona Campus

300 South Craycroft Road, Tucson, AZ 85711
http://www.phoenix.edu/

**CONTACT** William Pepicello, PhD, President
**Telephone:** 800-659-8988

**GENERAL INFORMATION** Private Institution. Founded 1979. **Accreditation:** Regional (NCA); counseling (ACA). **Total program enrollment:** 2325.

**STUDENT SERVICES** Academic or career counseling, remedial services.

## Yavapai College

1100 East Sheldon Street, Prescott, AZ 86301-3297
http://www2.yc.edu/

**CONTACT** Dr. James Horton, President
**Telephone:** 928-445-7300

**GENERAL INFORMATION** Public Institution. Founded 1966. **Accreditation:** Regional (NCA). **Total program enrollment:** 1600.

**PROGRAM(S) OFFERED**
• **Accounting** *3 students enrolled* • **Administrative Assistant and Secretarial Science, General** • **Agricultural Production Operations, General** *2 students enrolled* • **Architecture and Related Services, Other** *1 student enrolled* • **Automobile/Automotive Mechanics Technology/Technician** *1 student enrolled* • **Business Family and Consumer Sciences/Human Sciences** • **Business, Management, Marketing, and Related Support Services, Other** *3 students enrolled* • **Business/Commerce, General** *7 students enrolled* • **Cinematography and Film/Video Production** *25 students enrolled* • **Commercial and Advertising Art** • **Computer Installation and Repair Technology/Technician** *1 student enrolled* • **Computer Programming, Vendor/Product Certification** *2 students enrolled* • **Computer Systems Networking and Telecommunications** *9 students enrolled* • **Computer and Information Sciences, General** • **Construction Trades, Other** *3 students enrolled* • **Criminal Justice/Police Science** *44 students enrolled* • **Design and Applied Arts, Other** • **Early Childhood Education and Teaching** *2 students enrolled* • **Emergency Medical Technology/Technician (EMT Paramedic)** • **Fire Science/Firefighting** • **Gunsmithing/Gunsmith** *5 students enrolled* • **Legal Assistant/Paralegal** *7 students enrolled* • **Mechanic and Repair Technologies/Technicians, Other** *24 students enrolled* • **Medical Administrative/Executive Assistant and Medical Secretary** • **Medical Insurance Coding Specialist/Coder** *3 students enrolled* • **Medical Transcription/Transcriptionist** *2 students enrolled* • **Welding Technology/Welder** *3 students enrolled*

**STUDENT SERVICES** Academic or career counseling, daycare for children of students, employment services for current students, placement services for program completers, remedial services.

# ARKANSAS

## Arkadelphia Beauty College

2708 West Pine, Arkadelphia, AR 71923

**CONTACT** Charles Kirkpatrick, Owner
**Telephone:** 870-246-6726

**GENERAL INFORMATION** Private Institution. **Total program enrollment:** 52. **Application fee:** $50.

**PROGRAM(S) OFFERED**
• **Barbering/Barber** *1500 hrs./$7900* • **Cosmetology, Barber/Styling, and Nail Instructor** *600 hrs./$5000* • **Cosmetology/Cosmetologist, General** *1500 hrs./$8725* • **Nail Technician/Specialist and Manicurist** *600 hrs./$4416*

## Arkansas Beauty School

1007 Oak, Conway, AR 72032

**CONTACT** Tamara Harrison, Owner
**Telephone:** 501-329-8303

**GENERAL INFORMATION** Private Institution. **Total program enrollment:** 45.

**PROGRAM(S) OFFERED**
• **Cosmetology and Related Personal Grooming Arts, Other** *5 students enrolled* • **Cosmetology, Barber/Styling, and Nail Instructor** *600 hrs./$2750* • **Cosmetology/Cosmetologist, General** *1500 hrs./$8550* • **Nail Technician/Specialist and Manicurist** *600 hrs./$2750* • **Trade and Industrial Teacher Education** *2 students enrolled*

**STUDENT SERVICES** Academic or career counseling.

## Arkansas Beauty School

5108 Baseline Road, Little Rock, AR 72209

**CONTACT** Patricia Ray, Owner
**Telephone:** 501-562-5673

**GENERAL INFORMATION** Private Institution. Founded 1959. **Total program enrollment:** 30.

**PROGRAM(S) OFFERED**
• **Cosmetology, Barber/Styling, and Nail Instructor** *600 hrs./$3500* • **Cosmetology/Cosmetologist, General** *1500 hrs./$8450* • **Nail Technician/Specialist and Manicurist** *600 hrs./$3500*

**STUDENT SERVICES** Academic or career counseling, placement services for program completers.

## Arkansas Beauty School

109 North Commerce Street, Russellville, AR 72801
http://arkansasbeautycollege@cox-internet.net/

**CONTACT** Barbara Ward, Owner & Instructor
**Telephone:** 479-968-3075

**GENERAL INFORMATION** Private Institution. **Total program enrollment:** 44.

**PROGRAM(S) OFFERED**
• **Cosmetology, Barber/Styling, and Nail Instructor** *600 hrs./$3825* • **Cosmetology/Cosmetologist, General** *1500 hrs./$9945* • **Nail Technician/Specialist and Manicurist** *600 hrs./$3825*

## Arkansas College of Barbering and Hair Design

200 Washington Avenue, North Little Rock, AR 72114-5615

**CONTACT** Larry Little, President
**Telephone:** 501-376-9696

**GENERAL INFORMATION** Private Institution. Founded 1975. **Total program enrollment:** 90.

**PROGRAM(S) OFFERED**
• **Barbering/Barber** *1500 hrs./$10,410* • **Cosmetology, Barber/Styling, and Nail Instructor** *600 hrs./$3900*

**STUDENT SERVICES** Placement services for program completers.

## Arkansas Northeastern College

PO Box 1109, Blytheville, AR 72316-1109
http://www.anc.edu/

**CONTACT** Robert Myers, President
**Telephone:** 870-762-1020 Ext. 1114

**GENERAL INFORMATION** Public Institution. Founded 1975. **Accreditation:** Regional (NCA). **Total program enrollment:** 753.

**PROGRAM(S) OFFERED**

• **Accounting** *2 students enrolled* • **Applied Horticulture/Horticultural Operations, General** *1 student enrolled* • **Automobile/Automotive Mechanics Technology/Technician** *2 students enrolled* • **Business/Commerce, General** *2 students enrolled* • **Child Development** *3 students enrolled* • **Dental Assisting/Assistant** *11 students enrolled* • **Emergency Medical Technology/Technician (EMT Paramedic)** *22 students enrolled* • **Heating, Air Conditioning, Ventilation and Refrigeration Maintenance Technology/Technician (HAC, HACR, HVAC, HVACR)** *5 students enrolled* • **Industrial Electronics Technology/Technician** *17 students enrolled* • **Industrial Mechanics and Maintenance Technology** *1 student enrolled* • **Licensed Practical/Vocational Nurse Training (LPN, LVN, Cert, Dipl, AAS)** *32 students enrolled* • **Medical Transcription/Transcriptionist** *3 students enrolled* • **Nurse/Nursing Assistant/Aide and Patient Care Assistant** *57 students enrolled* • **Retailing and Retail Operations** *2 students enrolled* • **Truck and Bus Driver/Commercial Vehicle Operation** *22 students enrolled* • **Welding Technology/Welder** *9 students enrolled*

**STUDENT SERVICES** Academic or career counseling, daycare for children of students, employment services for current students, placement services for program completers, remedial services.

## Arkansas State University

PO Box 600, State University, AR 72467
http://www.astate.edu/

**CONTACT** Dr. Robert Potts, Chancellor
**Telephone:** 870-972-2100

**GENERAL INFORMATION** Public Institution. Founded 1909. **Accreditation:** Regional (NCA); art and design (NASAD); athletic training (JRCAT); counseling (ACA); journalism and mass communications (ACEJMC); medical laboratory technology (NAACLS); medical technology (NAACLS); music (NASM); physical therapy assisting (APTA); radiologic technology: radiation therapy technology (JRCERT); radiologic technology: radiography (JRCERT); speech-language pathology (ASHA). **Total program enrollment:** 8171. **Application fee:** $15.

**PROGRAM(S) OFFERED**

• **Administrative Assistant and Secretarial Science, General** *8 students enrolled* • **Autobody/Collision and Repair Technology/Technician** *3 students enrolled* • **Automobile/Automotive Mechanics Technology/Technician** *3 students enrolled* • **Cosmetology/Cosmetologist, General** *5 students enrolled* • **Electrical, Electronic and Communications Engineering Technology/Technician** *6 students enrolled* • **Emergency Medical Technology/Technician (EMT Paramedic)** *1 student enrolled* • **Heating, Air Conditioning, Ventilation and Refrigeration Maintenance Technology/Technician (HAC, HACR, HVAC, HVACR)** *7 students enrolled* • **Licensed Practical/Vocational Nurse Training (LPN, LVN, Cert, Dipl, AAS)** *19 students enrolled* • **Phlebotomy/Phlebotomist** *6 students enrolled*

**STUDENT SERVICES** Academic or career counseling, daycare for children of students, employment services for current students, placement services for program completers, remedial services.

## Arkansas State University–Beebe

PO Box 1000, Beebe, AR 72012-1000
http://www.asub.edu/

**CONTACT** Eugene McKay, Chancellor
**Telephone:** 501-882-3600

**GENERAL INFORMATION** Public Institution. Founded 1927. **Accreditation:** Regional (NCA); engineering technology (ABET/TAC); medical laboratory technology (NAACLS). **Total program enrollment:** 2349.

**PROGRAM(S) OFFERED**

• **Accounting Technology/Technician and Bookkeeping** *1 student enrolled* • **Autobody/Collision and Repair Technology/Technician** *13 students enrolled* • **Automobile/Automotive Mechanics Technology/Technician** *10 students enrolled* • **Child Care Provider/Assistant** *18 students enrolled* • **Computer Technology/Computer Systems Technology** *69 students enrolled* • **Corrections** *2 students enrolled* • **Criminal Justice/Law Enforcement Administration** *17 students enrolled* • **Criminal Justice/Police Science** *4 students enrolled* • **Diesel Mechanics Technology/Technician** *11 students enrolled* • **Drafting and Design Technology/Technician, General** *26 students enrolled* • **Early Childhood Education and Teaching** *6 students enrolled* • **Emergency Medical Technology/Technician (EMT Paramedic)** *20 students enrolled* • **General Office Occupations and Clerical Services** *20 students enrolled* • **Health Information/Medical Records Technology/Technician** *37 students enrolled* • **Heating, Air Conditioning, Ventilation and Refrigeration Maintenance Technology/Technician (HAC, HACR, HVAC, HVACR)** *18 students enrolled* • **Industrial Electronics Technology/Technician** *16 students enrolled* • **Licensed Practical/Vocational Nurse Training (LPN, LVN, Cert, Dipl, AAS)** *34 students enrolled* • **Machine Tool Technology/Machinist** *11 students enrolled* • **Nurse/Nursing Assistant/Aide and Patient Care Assistant** *47 students enrolled* • **Petroleum Technology/Technician** *7 students enrolled* • **Pharmacy Technician/Assistant** *7 students enrolled* • **Upholstery/Upholsterer** *4 students enrolled* • **Welding Technology/Welder** *23 students enrolled*

**STUDENT SERVICES** Academic or career counseling, employment services for current students, placement services for program completers, remedial services.

## Arkansas State University–Mountain Home

1600 South College Street, Mountain Home, AR 72653
http://www.asumh.edu/

**CONTACT** William E. Coulter, Chancellor
**Telephone:** 870-508-6100

**GENERAL INFORMATION** Public Institution. Founded 2000. **Accreditation:** Regional (NCA); funeral service (ABFSE). **Total program enrollment:** 794.

**PROGRAM(S) OFFERED**

• **Banking and Financial Support Services** • **Business, Management, Marketing, and Related Support Services, Other** • **Computer Installation and Repair Technology/Technician** *16 students enrolled* • **Computer Systems Networking and Telecommunications** *4 students enrolled* • **Criminal Justice/Law Enforcement Administration** • **Drafting and Design Technology/Technician, General** • **Electrical, Electronic and Communications Engineering Technology/Technician** • **Emergency Medical Technology/Technician (EMT Paramedic)** *12 students enrolled* • **Forensic Science and Technology** • **Graphic Design** • **Health Services/Allied Health/Health Sciences, General** *7 students enrolled* • **Health Unit Coordinator/Ward Clerk** *7 students enrolled* • **Industrial Mechanics and Maintenance Technology** • **Information Science/Studies** • **Licensed Practical/Vocational Nurse Training (LPN, LVN, Cert, Dipl, AAS)** *17 students enrolled* • **Management Information Systems, General** *1 student enrolled* • **Medical Insurance Coding Specialist/Coder** *17 students enrolled* • **Medical Office Management/Administration** • **Medication Aide** *6 students enrolled* • **Nurse/Nursing Assistant/Aide and Patient Care Assistant** *148 students enrolled* • **Office Management and Supervision** • **Phlebotomy/Phlebotomist** *22 students enrolled* • **Welding Technology/Welder**

**STUDENT SERVICES** Academic or career counseling, remedial services.

## Arkansas State University–Newport

7648 Victory Boulevard, Newport, AR 72112
http://www.asun.edu/

**CONTACT** Larry Williams, Chancellor
**Telephone:** 870-512-7800

**GENERAL INFORMATION** Public Institution. Founded 1989. **Accreditation:** Regional (NCA). **Total program enrollment:** 634.

**PROGRAM(S) OFFERED**

• **Diesel Mechanics Technology/Technician** *6 students enrolled* • **General Office Occupations and Clerical Services** *1 student enrolled* • **Licensed Practical/Vocational Nurse Training (LPN, LVN, Cert, Dipl, AAS)** *60 students enrolled*

*Arkansas State University–Newport (continued)*

• **Lineworker** *13 students enrolled* • **Nurse/Nursing Assistant/Aide and Patient Care Assistant** *20 students enrolled* • **Truck and Bus Driver/Commercial Vehicle Operation** *798 students enrolled*

**STUDENT SERVICES** Academic or career counseling, remedial services.

## Arkansas State University System Office

2626 U Street, Jonesboro, AR 72401
http://www.astate.edu

**CONTACT** Dr. Leslie Wyatt, President Arkansas State University System
**Telephone:** 870-933-7900

**GENERAL INFORMATION** Public Institution.

## Arkansas Tech University

Russellville, AR 72801
http://www.atu.edu/

**CONTACT** Robert C. Brown, President
**Telephone:** 479-968-0389

**GENERAL INFORMATION** Public Institution. Founded 1909. **Accreditation:** Regional (NCA); health information administration (AHIMA); medical assisting (AAMAE); music (NASM); recreation and parks (NRPA). **Total program enrollment:** 5827.

**PROGRAM(S) OFFERED**
• **Administrative Assistant and Secretarial Science, General** *19 students enrolled* • **Autobody/Collision and Repair Technology/Technician** *16 students enrolled* • **Automobile/Automotive Mechanics Technology/Technician** *11 students enrolled* • **Cosmetology/Cosmetologist, General** *13 students enrolled* • **Criminal Justice/Law Enforcement Administration** • **Electrical and Electronic Engineering Technologies/Technicians, Other** *7 students enrolled* • **Electrical, Electronic and Communications Engineering Technology/Technician** • **Emergency Medical Technology/Technician (EMT Paramedic)** *38 students enrolled* • **Heating, Air Conditioning, Ventilation and Refrigeration Maintenance Technology/Technician (HAC, HACR, HVAC, HVACR)** *6 students enrolled* • **Licensed Practical/Vocational Nurse Training (LPN, LVN, Cert, Dipl, AAS)** *50 students enrolled* • **Management Information Systems, General** *2 students enrolled* • **Medical Administrative/Executive Assistant and Medical Secretary** *7 students enrolled* • **Medical Transcription/Transcriptionist** *1 student enrolled* • **Nurse/Nursing Assistant/Aide and Patient Care Assistant** *1 student enrolled* • **Welding Technology/Welder** *7 students enrolled*

**STUDENT SERVICES** Academic or career counseling, employment services for current students, placement services for program completers, remedial services.

## Arthur's Beauty College

2600 John Harden Drive, Jacksonville, AR 72076
http://arthursbeautycollege.com/

**CONTACT** Chris Strawn, Owner
**Telephone:** 501-982-8987

**GENERAL INFORMATION** Private Institution. Founded 1952. **Total program enrollment:** 80. **Application fee:** $100.

**PROGRAM(S) OFFERED**
• **Aesthetician/Esthetician and Skin Care Specialist** *600 hrs./$5000*
• **Cosmetology, Barber/Styling, and Nail Instructor** *600 hrs./$2310*
• **Cosmetology/Cosmetologist, General** *1500 hrs./$10,225* • **Nail Technician/Specialist and Manicurist** *600 hrs./$4000*

**STUDENT SERVICES** Placement services for program completers.

## Arthur's Beauty College–Fort Smith

2000 North B Street, Ft. Smith, AR 72901-3342
http://www.arthursbeautycollege.com/

**CONTACT** Chris Strawn, Owner
**Telephone:** 479-783-6245

**GENERAL INFORMATION** Private Institution. **Total program enrollment:** 56. **Application fee:** $100.

**PROGRAM(S) OFFERED**
• **Aesthetician/Esthetician and Skin Care Specialist** *600 hrs./$5000*
• **Cosmetology, Barber/Styling, and Nail Instructor** *600 hrs./$2310*
• **Cosmetology/Cosmetologist, General** *1500 hrs./$10,225* • **Nail Technician/Specialist and Manicurist** *600 hrs./$4000*

**STUDENT SERVICES** Placement services for program completers.

## Arthur's Beauty School–Conway

2320 Washington Avenue, Conway, AR 72032
http://www.arthursbeautycollege.com/

**CONTACT** Chris Strawn, Owner
**Telephone:** 501-329-7770

**GENERAL INFORMATION** Private Institution. **Total program enrollment:** 68. **Application fee:** $100.

**PROGRAM(S) OFFERED**
• **Aesthetician/Esthetician and Skin Care Specialist** *600 hrs./$5000*
• **Cosmetology, Barber/Styling, and Nail Instructor** *600 hrs./$2310*
• **Cosmetology/Cosmetologist, General** *1500 hrs./$10,225* • **Nail Technician/Specialist and Manicurist** *600 hrs./$4000*

**STUDENT SERVICES** Placement services for program completers.

## Arthur's Beauty School–Pine Bluff

2710 Commerce Circle, Pine Bluff, AR 70601
http://www.arthursbeautycollege.com/

**CONTACT** Chris Strawn, Owner
**Telephone:** 870-534-0498

**GENERAL INFORMATION** Private Institution. **Total program enrollment:** 39. **Application fee:** $100.

**PROGRAM(S) OFFERED**
• **Aesthetician/Esthetician and Skin Care Specialist** *600 hrs./$5000*
• **Cosmetology, Barber/Styling, and Nail Instructor** *600 hrs./$2310*
• **Cosmetology/Cosmetologist, General** *1500 hrs./$10,225* • **Nail Technician/Specialist and Manicurist** *600 hrs./$4000*

**STUDENT SERVICES** Placement services for program completers.

## Askins Vo-Tech

7716 Highway 271, S, Fort Smith, AR 72908

**CONTACT** Troy Askins, Administrator
**Telephone:** 479-646-4803

**GENERAL INFORMATION** Private Institution. Founded 1991. **Application fee:** $100.

**PROGRAM(S) OFFERED**
• **Heating, Air Conditioning and Refrigeration Technology/Technician (ACH/ACR/ACHR/HRAC/HVAC/AC Technology)** *600 hrs.*

**STUDENT SERVICES** Academic or career counseling, placement services for program completers.

## Baptist Schools of Nursing and Allied Health

11900 Colonel Glenn Road, Suite 100, Little Rock, AR 72210-2820
http://www.baptist-health.org/

**CONTACT** Judy Pile, Director
**Telephone:** 501-202-6200

**GENERAL INFORMATION** Private Institution (Affiliated with Baptist Church). Founded 1921. **Total program enrollment:** 663.

**PROGRAM(S) OFFERED**
• **Clinical/Medical Laboratory Technician** *8 students enrolled* • **Histologic Technology/Histotechnologist** *4 students enrolled* • **Licensed Practical/Vocational Nurse Training (LPN, LVN, Cert, Dipl, AAS)** *109 students enrolled* • **Nuclear Medical Technology/Technologist** *5 students enrolled* • **Surgical Technology/Technologist** *15 students enrolled*

**STUDENT SERVICES** Academic or career counseling, employment services for current students.

## Bee Jay's Academy

1907 Hinson Loop, Little Rock, AR 72212
http://bjacademy.net/

**CONTACT** Terry Yarbrough, Chief Operations Officer
**Telephone:** 501-224-2442

**GENERAL INFORMATION** Private Institution. Founded 1973. **Total program enrollment:** 48. **Application fee:** $50.

**PROGRAM(S) OFFERED**
• **Aesthetician/Esthetician and Skin Care Specialist** *600 hrs./$6150*
• **Cosmetology, Barber/Styling, and Nail Instructor** *600 hrs./$6150*
• **Cosmetology/Cosmetologist, General** *1500 hrs./$10,600* • **Electrolysis/Electrology and Electrolysis Technician** *350 hrs./$6150* • **Nail Technician/Specialist and Manicurist** *600 hrs./$4150*

**STUDENT SERVICES** Academic or career counseling, placement services for program completers.

## Black River Technical College

1410 Highway 304 East, Pocahontas, AR 72455
http://www.blackrivertech.edu/

**CONTACT** Richard Gaines, President
**Telephone:** 870-248-4000

**GENERAL INFORMATION** Public Institution. Founded 1972. **Accreditation:** Regional (NCA); respiratory therapy technology (CoARC). **Total program enrollment:** 1182.

**PROGRAM(S) OFFERED**
• **Accounting Technology/Technician and Bookkeeping** *5 students enrolled* • **Administrative Assistant and Secretarial Science, General** *3 students enrolled* • **Aircraft Powerplant Technology/Technician** *6 students enrolled* • **Airframe Mechanics and Aircraft Maintenance Technology/Technician** *13 students enrolled* • **Autobody/Collision and Repair Technology/Technician** *13 students enrolled* • **Automobile/Automotive Mechanics Technology/Technician** *17 students enrolled* • **Clinical/Medical Laboratory Assistant** *2 students enrolled* • **Dietitian Assistant** *5 students enrolled* • **Emergency Medical Technology/Technician (EMT Paramedic)** *2 students enrolled* • **Industrial Electronics Technology/Technician** *16 students enrolled* • **Licensed Practical/Vocational Nurse Training (LPN, LVN, Cert, Dipl, AAS)** *24 students enrolled* • **Machine Tool Technology/Machinist** *9 students enrolled* • **Management Information Systems and Services, Other** *1 student enrolled* • **Medical Insurance Coding Specialist/Coder** *3 students enrolled* • **Medical Transcription/Transcriptionist** *5 students enrolled* • **Nurse/Nursing Assistant/Aide and Patient Care Assistant** *69 students enrolled* • **Phlebotomy/Phlebotomist** *19 students enrolled* • **Welding Technology/Welder** *19 students enrolled*

**STUDENT SERVICES** Academic or career counseling, employment services for current students, placement services for program completers, remedial services.

## Blytheville Academy of Cosmetology

224 West Main Street, Blytheville, AR 72315

**CONTACT** Lucille Coleman, Owner
**Telephone:** 870-763-4012

**GENERAL INFORMATION** Private Institution. Founded 1965. **Total program enrollment:** 29. **Application fee:** $50.

**PROGRAM(S) OFFERED**
• **Cosmetology and Related Personal Grooming Arts, Other** *600 hrs./$2300*
• **Cosmetology, Barber/Styling, and Nail Instructor** *600 hrs./$2275*
• **Cosmetology/Cosmetologist, General** *1500 hrs./$6260*

**STUDENT SERVICES** Academic or career counseling.

## Bryan College

3704 W. Walnut Street, Rogers, AR 72756

**CONTACT** Brian Stewart, President/CEO
**Telephone:** 479-899-6644

**GENERAL INFORMATION** Private Institution. **Total program enrollment:** 160. **Application fee:** $30.

**PROGRAM(S) OFFERED**
• **Business Administration and Management, General** • **Computer Systems Networking and Telecommunications** • **Health and Physical Education/Fitness, Other** • **Medical Office Assistant/Specialist** *1 student enrolled*

**STUDENT SERVICES** Academic or career counseling, employment services for current students, placement services for program completers.

## Career Academy of Hair Design

109 West Emma Street, Springdale, AR 72764
http://beautyschool.edu/

**CONTACT** Jim Butenschoen, Administrator
**Telephone:** 479-756-6060

**GENERAL INFORMATION** Private Institution. Founded 1978. **Total program enrollment:** 165.

**PROGRAM(S) OFFERED**
• **Aesthetician/Esthetician and Skin Care Specialist** *600 hrs./$5235*
• **Cosmetology, Barber/Styling, and Nail Instructor** *600 hrs./$2800*
• **Cosmetology/Cosmetologist, General** *1500 hrs./$9625* • **Nail Technician/Specialist and Manicurist** *600 hrs./$2800*

**STUDENT SERVICES** Academic or career counseling, placement services for program completers.

## Cossatot Community College of the University of Arkansas

PO Box 960, De Queen, AR 71832
http://www.cccua.edu/

**CONTACT** Frank Adams, Chancellor
**Telephone:** 870-584-4471

**GENERAL INFORMATION** Public Institution. Founded 1991. **Accreditation:** Regional (NCA). **Total program enrollment:** 507.

**PROGRAM(S) OFFERED**
• **Administrative Assistant and Secretarial Science, General** *1 student enrolled*
• **Autobody/Collision and Repair Technology/Technician** *3 students enrolled*
• **Automobile/Automotive Mechanics Technology/Technician** *3 students enrolled*
• **Carpentry/Carpenter** *4 students enrolled* • **Child Development** *19 students enrolled* • **Computer Programming, Vendor/Product Certification** *7 students enrolled* • **Licensed Practical/Vocational Nurse Training (LPN, LVN, Cert, Dipl,**

*Cossatot Community College of the University of Arkansas (continued)*

**AAS)** *25 students enrolled* • **Medical Transcription/Transcriptionist** *7 students enrolled* • **Teaching English as a Second or Foreign Language/ESL Language Instructor** *17 students enrolled* • **Welding Technology/Welder** *7 students enrolled*

**STUDENT SERVICES** Academic or career counseling, daycare for children of students, employment services for current students, placement services for program completers, remedial services.

## Crossett School of Cosmetology

121 Pine Street, Crossett, AR 71635

**CONTACT** Lori Freeman, Owner
**Telephone:** 870-304-2545

**GENERAL INFORMATION** Private Institution. **Total program enrollment:** 28.

**PROGRAM(S) OFFERED**
• **Cosmetology, Barber/Styling, and Nail Instructor** *600 hrs./$4600* • **Cosmetology/Cosmetologist, General** *1500 hrs./$9000*

**STUDENT SERVICES** Academic or career counseling.

## Crowley's Ridge Technical Institute

PO Box 925, Forrest City, AR 72336-0925
http://www.crti.tec.ar.us/

**CONTACT** Burl Lieblong, President
**Telephone:** 870-633-5411

**GENERAL INFORMATION** Public Institution. Founded 2001. **Total program enrollment:** 232.

**PROGRAM(S) OFFERED**
• **Accounting** *5 students enrolled* • **Administrative Assistant and Secretarial Science, General** *4 students enrolled* • **Appliance Installation and Repair Technology/Technician** *2 students enrolled* • **Autobody/Collision and Repair Technology/Technician** *6 students enrolled* • **Automobile/Automotive Mechanics Technology/Technician** *4 students enrolled* • **Carpentry/Carpenter** *5 students enrolled* • **Child Care Provider/Assistant** *4 students enrolled* • **Computer Installation and Repair Technology/Technician** *11 students enrolled* • **Cosmetology/Cosmetologist, General** *14 students enrolled* • **Drafting and Design Technology/Technician, General** *5 students enrolled* • **Emergency Medical Technology/Technician (EMT Paramedic)** *12 students enrolled* • **Heating, Air Conditioning, Ventilation and Refrigeration Maintenance Technology/Technician (HAC, HACR, HVAC, HVACR)** *3 students enrolled* • **Industrial Mechanics and Maintenance Technology** *8 students enrolled* • **Licensed Practical/Vocational Nurse Training (LPN, LVN, Cert, Dipl, AAS)** *16 students enrolled* • **Machine Tool Technology/Machinist** *3 students enrolled* • **Nurse/Nursing Assistant/Aide and Patient Care Assistant** *17 students enrolled* • **Truck and Bus Driver/Commercial Vehicle Operation** *24 students enrolled* • **Welding Technology/Welder** *11 students enrolled*

**STUDENT SERVICES** Academic or career counseling, daycare for children of students, employment services for current students, remedial services.

## De Luxe Beauty School

1609 West 26th Street, Pine Bluff, AR 71601

**CONTACT** Dorothy Jackson, Director
**Telephone:** 870-534-7609

**GENERAL INFORMATION** Private Institution. **Total program enrollment:** 10. **Application fee:** $100.

**PROGRAM(S) OFFERED**
• **Cosmetology/Cosmetologist, General** *1500 hrs./$6830*

**STUDENT SERVICES** Academic or career counseling, placement services for program completers.

## East Arkansas Community College

1700 Newcastle Road, Forrest City, AR 72335-2204
http://www.eacc.edu/

**CONTACT** Coy Grace, President
**Telephone:** 870-633-4480

**GENERAL INFORMATION** Public Institution. Founded 1974. **Accreditation:** Regional (NCA). **Total program enrollment:** 763.

**PROGRAM(S) OFFERED**
• **Administrative Assistant and Secretarial Science, General** *2 students enrolled* • **CAD/CADD Drafting and/or Design Technology/Technician** *11 students enrolled* • **Criminal Justice/Law Enforcement Administration** *4 students enrolled* • **Criminal Justice/Police Science** *8 students enrolled* • **Electrical, Electronic and Communications Engineering Technology/Technician** *49 students enrolled* • **Emergency Medical Technology/Technician (EMT Paramedic)** *6 students enrolled* • **Engineering Technology, General** *1 student enrolled* • **General Office Occupations and Clerical Services** *6 students enrolled* • **Health Services/Allied Health/Health Sciences, General** *3 students enrolled* • **Hospitality Administration/Management, General** *2 students enrolled* • **Hotel/Motel Administration/Management** *2 students enrolled* • **Management Information Systems, General** *1 student enrolled* • **Manufacturing Technology/Technician** *1 student enrolled* • **Medication Aide** *1 student enrolled* • **Web Page, Digital/Multimedia and Information Resources Design** *1 student enrolled*

**STUDENT SERVICES** Academic or career counseling, employment services for current students, placement services for program completers, remedial services.

## Eastern College of Health Vocations

6423 Forbing Road, Little Rock, AR 72209
http://www.echv.com/

**CONTACT** Joseph P. Dalto, III, Owner
**Telephone:** 501-568-0211

**GENERAL INFORMATION** Private Institution. Founded 1983. **Total program enrollment:** 265. **Application fee:** $100.

**PROGRAM(S) OFFERED**
• **Dental Assisting/Assistant** *592 hrs./$6900* • **Medical/Clinical Assistant** *736 hrs./$9160*

**STUDENT SERVICES** Academic or career counseling, placement services for program completers.

## Fayetteville Beauty College

1200 North College Avenue, Fayetteville, AR 72703
http://www.fayettevillebeautycollege.edu/

**CONTACT** Tammy Sisemore, Manager
**Telephone:** 479-521-3571

**GENERAL INFORMATION** Private Institution. Founded 1965. **Total program enrollment:** 44. **Application fee:** $100.

**PROGRAM(S) OFFERED**
• **Cosmetology and Related Personal Grooming Arts, Other** *4 students enrolled* • **Cosmetology, Barber/Styling, and Nail Instructor** *600 hrs./$3360* • **Cosmetology/Cosmetologist, General** *1500 hrs./$9005* • **Nail Technician/Specialist and Manicurist** *600 hrs./$3360*

**STUDENT SERVICES** Academic or career counseling, employment services for current students, placement services for program completers.

## Hot Springs Beauty College

100 Cones Road, Hot Springs, AR 71901

**CONTACT** Wentz Akard, Chief Executive Officer
**Telephone:** 501-624-4258

**GENERAL INFORMATION** Private Institution. **Total program enrollment:** 31.

**PROGRAM(S) OFFERED**

• **Cosmetology and Related Personal Grooming Arts, Other** *600 hrs./$4500* • **Cosmetology/Cosmetologist, General** *1500 hrs./$10,345* • **Nail Technician/ Specialist and Manicurist** *600 hrs./$3700* • **Technical Teacher Education** *600 hrs./$3000*

## Lees School of Cosmetology

2700 West Perishing Boulevard, North Little Rock, AR 72114
http://lsctraining.com/

**CONTACT** Linda Lee, Director
**Telephone:** 501-758-2800

**GENERAL INFORMATION** Private Institution. **Total program enrollment:** 37.

**PROGRAM(S) OFFERED**

• **Cosmetology, Barber/Styling, and Nail Instructor** *$2800* • **Cosmetology/ Cosmetologist, General** *1500 hrs./$11,750*

**STUDENT SERVICES** Academic or career counseling, employment services for current students, placement services for program completers.

## Lynndale Fundamentals of Beauty School

1729 Champagnolle Road, El Dorado, AR 71730

**CONTACT** Jacquita Hayden, Owner
**Telephone:** 870-863-3919

**GENERAL INFORMATION** Public Institution. **Total program enrollment:** 15. **Application fee:** $100.

**PROGRAM(S) OFFERED**

• **Cosmetology, Barber/Styling, and Nail Instructor** *600 hrs./$4360* • **Cosmetology/Cosmetologist, General** *1500 hrs./$9345* • **Nail Technician/ Specialist and Manicurist** *600 hrs./$4360*

**STUDENT SERVICES** Academic or career counseling.

## Margaret's Hair Academy

200 North Moose, Morrilton, AR 72110

**CONTACT** Margaret Thomas, Director
**Telephone:** 870-367-5533

**GENERAL INFORMATION** Private Institution. **Total program enrollment:** 79. **Application fee:** $100.

**PROGRAM(S) OFFERED**

• **Cosmetology/Cosmetologist, General** *1500 hrs./$9500* • **Nail Technician/ Specialist and Manicurist** *600 hrs./$2200* • **Technical Teacher Education** *600 hrs./$4150* • **Trade and Industrial Teacher Education** *2 students enrolled*

**STUDENT SERVICES** Academic or career counseling.

## Marsha Kay Beauty College

408 Highway 201 North, Mountain Home, AR 72653

**CONTACT** Marsha Kay Snedecor, Director
**Telephone:** 870-425-7575

**GENERAL INFORMATION** Private Institution. **Total program enrollment:** 15.

**PROGRAM(S) OFFERED**

• **Cosmetology/Cosmetologist, General** *1500 hrs./$8125*

**STUDENT SERVICES** Academic or career counseling, placement services for program completers.

## Mellie's Beauty College

311 South 16th Street, Fort Smith, AR 72901

**CONTACT** Patricia Anderson, Owner
**Telephone:** 479-782-5059

**GENERAL INFORMATION** Private Institution. **Total program enrollment:** 86. **Application fee:** $50.

**PROGRAM(S) OFFERED**

• **Aesthetician/Esthetician and Skin Care Specialist** *600 hrs./$7700* • **Cosmetology, Barber/Styling, and Nail Instructor** *600 hrs./$4500* • **Cosmetology/Cosmetologist, General** *1500 hrs./$10,590* • **Nail Technician/ Specialist and Manicurist** *600 hrs./$5100*

**STUDENT SERVICES** Academic or career counseling, employment services for current students, placement services for program completers.

## Mid-South Community College

2000 West Broadway, West Memphis, AR 72301
http://www.midsouthcc.edu/

**CONTACT** Dr. Glen F. Fenter, President
**Telephone:** 870-733-6722

**GENERAL INFORMATION** Public Institution. Founded 1993. **Accreditation:** Regional (NCA). **Total program enrollment:** 462.

**PROGRAM(S) OFFERED**

• **Child Care Provider/Assistant** *5 students enrolled* • **Child Development** *1 student enrolled* • **Computer Installation and Repair Technology/Technician** *2 students enrolled* • **Computer Systems Networking and Telecommunications** *6 students enrolled* • **Emergency Medical Technology/Technician (EMT Paramedic)** *1 student enrolled* • **General Office Occupations and Clerical Services** *12 students enrolled* • **Manufacturing Technology/Technician** *1 student enrolled* • **Nurse/Nursing Assistant/Aide and Patient Care Assistant** *5 students enrolled* • **Radio and Television Broadcasting Technology/Technician** *1 student enrolled* • **Web/Multimedia Management and Webmaster** *1 student enrolled*

**STUDENT SERVICES** Academic or career counseling, employment services for current students, remedial services.

## National Park Community College

101 College Drive, Hot Springs, AR 71913
http://www.npcc.edu/

**CONTACT** Sally Carder, President
**Telephone:** 501-760-4222

**GENERAL INFORMATION** Public Institution. Founded 1973. **Accreditation:** Regional (NCA); health information technology (AHIMA); medical laboratory technology (NAACLS); radiologic technology: radiography (JRCERT). **Total program enrollment:** 1529.

**PROGRAM(S) OFFERED**

• **Accounting Technology/Technician and Bookkeeping** *1 student enrolled* • **Automobile/Automotive Mechanics Technology/Technician** *14 students enrolled* • **Carpentry/Carpenter** *11 students enrolled* • **Child Care Provider/ Assistant** *1 student enrolled* • **Computer and Information Sciences, General** *2 students enrolled* • **Emergency Medical Technology/Technician (EMT Paramedic)** *7 students enrolled* • **Health Information/Medical Records Technology/Technician** *1 student enrolled* • **Health Services/Allied Health/ Health Sciences, General** *49 students enrolled* • **Heating, Air Conditioning, Ventilation and Refrigeration Maintenance Technology/Technician (HAC, HACR, HVAC, HVACR)** *11 students enrolled* • **Hospitality Administration/ Management, General** *3 students enrolled* • **Licensed Practical/Vocational Nurse Training (LPN, LVN, Cert, Dipl, AAS)** *32 students enrolled* • **Marine Maintenance/Fitter and Ship Repair Technology/Technician** *11 students enrolled* • **Medical Administrative/Executive Assistant and Medical Secretary** *2 students enrolled* • **Medical Transcription/Transcriptionist** *1 student enrolled* • **Phlebotomy/Phlebotomist** *3 students enrolled* • **Welding Technology/Welder** *12 students enrolled*

**STUDENT SERVICES** Academic or career counseling, employment services for current students, placement services for program completers, remedial services.

## New Tyler Barber College

1221 East 7th Street, North Little Rock, AR 72114

**CONTACT** Ricky Bryant, President
**Telephone:** 501-375-0377

**GENERAL INFORMATION** Private Institution. **Total program enrollment:** 70.

**PROGRAM(S) OFFERED**
• **Barbering/Barber** *1500 hrs./$10,825* • **Cosmetology, Barber/Styling, and Nail Instructor** *600 hrs./$4350*

**STUDENT SERVICES** Academic or career counseling, employment services for current students, placement services for program completers.

## North Arkansas College

1515 Pioneer Drive, Harrison, AR 72601
http://www.northark.edu/

**CONTACT** Jeff Olson, President
**Telephone:** 870-743-3000

**GENERAL INFORMATION** Public Institution. Founded 1974. **Accreditation:** Regional (NCA); medical laboratory technology (NAACLS); radiologic technology: radiography (JRCERT); surgical technology (ARCST). **Total program enrollment:** 1301.

**PROGRAM(S) OFFERED**
• **Accounting** *4 students enrolled* • **Administrative Assistant and Secretarial Science, General** *6 students enrolled* • **Autobody/Collision and Repair Technology/Technician** *1 student enrolled* • **Automobile/Automotive Mechanics Technology/Technician** *1 student enrolled* • **CAD/CADD Drafting and/or Design Technology/Technician** *1 student enrolled* • **Computer Systems Networking and Telecommunications** *1 student enrolled* • **Computer and Information Sciences, General** *2 students enrolled* • **Construction Trades, General** *2 students enrolled* • **Construction/Heavy Equipment/Earthmoving Equipment Operation** *14 students enrolled* • **Criminal Justice/Law Enforcement Administration** *1 student enrolled* • **Drafting and Design Technology/Technician, General** *5 students enrolled* • **Electrical, Electronic and Communications Engineering Technology/Technician** *1 student enrolled* • **Health Information/Medical Records Technology/Technician** *9 students enrolled* • **Health Services/Allied Health/Health Sciences, General** *34 students enrolled* • **Heating, Air Conditioning, Ventilation and Refrigeration Maintenance Technology/Technician (HAC, HACR, HVAC, HVACR)** *1 student enrolled* • **Licensed Practical/Vocational Nurse Training (LPN, LVN, Cert, Dipl, AAS)** *26 students enrolled* • **Phlebotomy/Phlebotomist** *4 students enrolled* • **Surgical Technology/Technologist** *3 students enrolled* • **Truck and Bus Driver/Commercial Vehicle Operation** *38 students enrolled* • **Welding Technology/Welder** *1 student enrolled*

**STUDENT SERVICES** Academic or career counseling, employment services for current students, placement services for program completers, remedial services.

## NorthWest Arkansas Community College

One College Drive, Bentonville, AR 72712
http://www.nwacc.edu/

**CONTACT** Dr. Becky Paneitz, President
**Telephone:** 479-636-9222

**GENERAL INFORMATION** Public Institution. Founded 1989. **Accreditation:** Regional (NCA); emergency medical services (JRCEMTP); respiratory therapy technology (CoARC). **Total program enrollment:** 2466. **Application fee:** $10.

**PROGRAM(S) OFFERED**
• **Aircraft Powerplant Technology/Technician** *3 students enrolled* • **Airframe Mechanics and Aircraft Maintenance Technology/Technician** *1 student enrolled* • **Child Development** *1 student enrolled* • **Corrections and Criminal Justice, Other** *2 students enrolled* • **Criminal Justice/Police Science** *1 student enrolled* • **Culinary Arts/Chef Training** *2 students enrolled* • **Drafting and Design Technology/Technician, General** *6 students enrolled* • **Early Childhood Education and Teaching** *10 students enrolled* • **Emergency Medical Technology/Technician (EMT Paramedic)** *60 students enrolled* • **Environmental Engineering Technology/Environmental Technology** *4 students enrolled* • **Forensic Science and Technology** *3 students enrolled* • **Hospitality Administration/Management, General** *1 student enrolled* • **Security and Protective Services, Other** *2 students enrolled*

**STUDENT SERVICES** Academic or career counseling, employment services for current students, placement services for program completers, remedial services.

## Northwest Technical Institute

PO Box A, Springdale, AR 72765-2000
http://www.nti.tec.ar.us/

**CONTACT** George V. Burch, President
**Telephone:** 479-751-8824 Ext. 0

**GENERAL INFORMATION** Public Institution. Founded 1975. **Total program enrollment:** 218.

**PROGRAM(S) OFFERED**
• **Accounting** *2 students enrolled* • **Administrative Assistant and Secretarial Science, General** *11 students enrolled* • **Architectural Drafting and Architectural CAD/CADD** *7 students enrolled* • **Automobile/Automotive Mechanics Technology/Technician** *9 students enrolled* • **Computer Programming/Programmer, General** *2 students enrolled* • **Computer and Information Sciences, General** *13 students enrolled* • **Construction/Heavy Equipment/Earthmoving Equipment Operation** *3 students enrolled* • **Diesel Mechanics Technology/Technician** *4 students enrolled* • **Electrical, Electronic and Communications Engineering Technology/Technician** *3 students enrolled* • **Electrical/Electronics Equipment Installation and Repair, General** *1 student enrolled* • **Electromechanical Technology/Electromechanical Engineering Technology** • **Heating, Air Conditioning and Refrigeration Technology/Technician (ACH/ACR/ACHR/HRAC/HVAC/AC Technology)** *10 students enrolled* • **Heating, Air Conditioning, Ventilation and Refrigeration Maintenance Technology/Technician (HAC, HACR, HVAC, HVACR)** *12 students enrolled* • **Industrial Mechanics and Maintenance Technology** *8 students enrolled* • **Licensed Practical/Vocational Nurse Training (LPN, LVN, Cert, Dipl, AAS)** *39 students enrolled* • **Machine Shop Technology/Assistant** *7 students enrolled* • **Management Information Systems, General** • **Medical Office Computer Specialist/Assistant** *9 students enrolled* • **Surgical Technology/Technologist** *2 students enrolled* • **Truck and Bus Driver/Commercial Vehicle Operation** *48 students enrolled* • **Web Page, Digital/Multimedia and Information Resources Design** *1 student enrolled* • **Welding Technology/Welder** *32 students enrolled*

**STUDENT SERVICES** Academic or career counseling, employment services for current students, placement services for program completers, remedial services.

## Ouachita Technical College

One College Circle, Malvern, AR 72104
http://www.otcweb.edu/

**CONTACT** Barry Ballard, President
**Telephone:** 501-337-5000 Ext. 1100

**GENERAL INFORMATION** Public Institution. Founded 1972. **Accreditation:** Regional (NCA). **Total program enrollment:** 564.

**PROGRAM(S) OFFERED**
• **Accounting** *4 students enrolled* • **Automobile/Automotive Mechanics Technology/Technician** *11 students enrolled* • **Business, Management, Marketing, and Related Support Services, Other** *7 students enrolled* • **Child Care Provider/Assistant** *8 students enrolled* • **Computer Systems Networking and Telecommunications** *1 student enrolled* • **Computer Technology/Computer Systems Technology** *2 students enrolled* • **Computer and Information Systems Security** *1 student enrolled* • **Cosmetology/Cosmetologist, General** *11 students enrolled* • **Criminal Justice/Law Enforcement Administration** *8 students enrolled* • **Electrical/Electronics Equipment Installation and Repair, General** *1 student enrolled* • **Electrician** *18 students enrolled* • **General Office Occupations and Clerical Services** *1 student enrolled* • **Health Information/Medical Records Technology/Technician** *2 students enrolled* • **Industrial Mechanics and Maintenance Technology** *4 students enrolled* • **Licensed Practical/Vocational Nurse Training (LPN, LVN, Cert, Dipl, AAS)** *54 students enrolled* • **Medical Office Management/Administration** *8 students enrolled* • **Medical Transcription/Transcriptionist** *4 students enrolled* • **Medication Aide** *5 students enrolled* • **Nurse/Nursing Assistant/Aide and Patient Care Assistant** *74 students enrolled*

• **Small Engine Mechanics and Repair Technology/Technician** *8 students enrolled* • **Truck and Bus Driver/Commercial Vehicle Operation** *5 students enrolled* • **Welding Technology/Welder** *7 students enrolled*

**STUDENT SERVICES** Academic or career counseling, employment services for current students, placement services for program completers, remedial services.

## Ozarka College

PO Box 10, Melbourne, AR 72556
http://www.ozarka.edu/

**CONTACT** Dr. Dusty R. Johnston, President
**Telephone:** 870-368-7371

**GENERAL INFORMATION** Public Institution. Founded 1973. **Accreditation:** Regional (NCA). **Total program enrollment:** 753.

**PROGRAM(S) OFFERED**
• **Accounting Technology/Technician and Bookkeeping** *6 students enrolled* • **Automobile/Automotive Mechanics Technology/Technician** *2 students enrolled* • **Business, Management, Marketing, and Related Support Services, Other** *4 students enrolled* • **Business/Office Automation/Technology/Data Entry** *12 students enrolled* • **Child Development** *9 students enrolled* • **Culinary Arts/Chef Training** *1 student enrolled* • **Health Services/Allied Health/Health Sciences, General** *1 student enrolled* • **Information Resources Management/CIO Training** *2 students enrolled* • **Licensed Practical/Vocational Nurse Training (LPN, LVN, Cert, Dipl, AAS)** *38 students enrolled*

**STUDENT SERVICES** Academic or career counseling, daycare for children of students, remedial services.

## Phillips Community College of the University of Arkansas

PO Box 785, Helena, AR 72342-0785
http://www.pccua.edu/

**CONTACT** Dr. Steven Murray, Chancellor
**Telephone:** 870-338-6474

**GENERAL INFORMATION** Public Institution. Founded 1965. **Accreditation:** Regional (NCA); medical laboratory technology (NAACLS). **Total program enrollment:** 832.

**PROGRAM(S) OFFERED**
• **Child Care Provider/Assistant** *27 students enrolled* • **Computer Systems Networking and Telecommunications** *12 students enrolled* • **Computer and Information Sciences and Support Services, Other** *2 students enrolled* • **Cosmetology/Cosmetologist, General** *13 students enrolled* • **Early Childhood Education and Teaching** *19 students enrolled* • **Emergency Medical Technology/Technician (EMT Paramedic)** *5 students enrolled* • **Graphic and Printing Equipment Operator, General Production** *4 students enrolled* • **Health Information/Medical Records Technology/Technician** *11 students enrolled* • **Health Services/Allied Health/Health Sciences, General** *4 students enrolled* • **Industrial Technology/Technician** *1 student enrolled* • **Licensed Practical/Vocational Nurse Training (LPN, LVN, Cert, Dipl, AAS)** *3 students enrolled* • **Make-Up Artist/Specialist** *1 student enrolled* • **Management Information Systems, General** *2 students enrolled* • **Nurse/Nursing Assistant/Aide and Patient Care Assistant** *17 students enrolled* • **Phlebotomy/Phlebotomist** *5 students enrolled* • **Social Work** *2 students enrolled* • **System, Networking, and LAN/WAN Management/Manager** *2 students enrolled* • **Welding Technology/Welder** *9 students enrolled*

**STUDENT SERVICES** Academic or career counseling, employment services for current students, placement services for program completers, remedial services.

## Professional Cosmetology Education Center

115 East Washington Street, Camden, AR 71701-4009

**CONTACT** Robert F. Kelley, Registrar
**Telephone:** 870-864-9292

**GENERAL INFORMATION** Private Institution. **Total program enrollment:** 39. **Application fee:** $100.

**PROGRAM(S) OFFERED**
• **Cosmetology and Related Personal Grooming Arts, Other** *50 hrs./$8025*
• **Cosmetology/Cosmetologist, General** *30 hrs./$3060*

**STUDENT SERVICES** Employment services for current students, placement services for program completers.

## Pulaski Technical College

3000 West Scenic Drive, North Little Rock, AR 72118
http://www.pulaskitech.edu/

**CONTACT** Dr. Dan F. Bakke, President
**Telephone:** 501-812-2200

**GENERAL INFORMATION** Public Institution. Founded 1945. **Accreditation:** Regional (NCA); dental assisting (ADA); respiratory therapy technology (CoARC). **Total program enrollment:** 3995.

**PROGRAM(S) OFFERED**
• **Accounting Technology/Technician and Bookkeeping** *16 students enrolled* • **Accounting** *11 students enrolled* • **Aircraft Powerplant Technology/Technician** *33 students enrolled* • **Airframe Mechanics and Aircraft Maintenance Technology/Technician** *35 students enrolled* • **Autobody/Collision and Repair Technology/Technician** *21 students enrolled* • **Automobile/Automotive Mechanics Technology/Technician** *11 students enrolled* • **Baking and Pastry Arts/Baker/Pastry Chef** *3 students enrolled* • **Child Development** *31 students enrolled* • **Cosmetology/Cosmetologist, General** *16 students enrolled* • **Culinary Arts/Chef Training** *2 students enrolled* • **Dental Assisting/Assistant** *26 students enrolled* • **Diesel Mechanics Technology/Technician** *16 students enrolled* • **Drafting and Design Technology/Technician, General** *7 students enrolled* • **Electrical/Electronics Equipment Installation and Repair, General** *1 student enrolled* • **General Office Occupations and Clerical Services** *10 students enrolled* • **Heating, Air Conditioning, Ventilation and Refrigeration Maintenance Technology/Technician (HAC, HACR, HVAC, HVACR)** *1 student enrolled* • **Legal Administrative Assistant/Secretary** *3 students enrolled* • **Licensed Practical/Vocational Nurse Training (LPN, LVN, Cert, Dipl, AAS)** *30 students enrolled* • **Machine Tool Technology/Machinist** *8 students enrolled* • **Management Information Systems, General** *59 students enrolled* • **Medical Transcription/Transcriptionist** *29 students enrolled* • **Medium/Heavy Vehicle and Truck Technology/Technician** • **Nail Technician/Specialist and Manicurist** *15 students enrolled* • **Small Engine Mechanics and Repair Technology/Technician** *9 students enrolled* • **Welding Technology/Welder** *12 students enrolled*

**STUDENT SERVICES** Academic or career counseling, daycare for children of students, employment services for current students, placement services for program completers, remedial services.

## Remington College–Little Rock Campus

19 Remington Drive, Little Rock, AR 72204
http://www.remingtoncollege.edu/

**CONTACT** Edna Higgins, Campus President
**Telephone:** 501-312-0007

**GENERAL INFORMATION** Private Institution. **Accreditation:** State accredited or approved. **Total program enrollment:** 496. **Application fee:** $50.

**PROGRAM(S) OFFERED**
• **Electrical, Electronic and Communications Engineering Technology/Technician** • **Medical Insurance Coding Specialist/Coder** *106 students enrolled* • **Medical/Clinical Assistant** *142 students enrolled* • **Pharmacy Technician/Assistant** *32 students enrolled*

**STUDENT SERVICES** Academic or career counseling, employment services for current students, placement services for program completers.

## Rich Mountain Community College

1100 College Drive, Mena, AR 71953
http://www.rmcc.edu/

**CONTACT** Dr. Wayne Hatcher, President
**Telephone:** 479-394-7622

**GENERAL INFORMATION** Public Institution. Founded 1983. **Accreditation:** Regional (NCA). **Total program enrollment:** 377.

**PROGRAM(S) OFFERED**
• **Administrative Assistant and Secretarial Science, General** *1 student enrolled* • **Child Development** *1 student enrolled* • **Licensed Practical/Vocational Nurse Training (LPN, LVN, Cert, Dipl, AAS)** *26 students enrolled* • **Web/Multimedia Management and Webmaster** *1 student enrolled*

**STUDENT SERVICES** Academic or career counseling, daycare for children of students, employment services for current students, placement services for program completers, remedial services.

## Searcy Beauty College

1004 South Main Street, Searcy, AR 72143

**CONTACT** Colita Moye, Owner Secretary Director
**Telephone:** 501-268-6300

**GENERAL INFORMATION** Private Institution. Founded 1983. **Total program enrollment:** 59.

**PROGRAM(S) OFFERED**
• **Cosmetology, Barber/Styling, and Nail Instructor** *600 hrs./$3750* • **Cosmetology/Cosmetologist, General** *1500 hrs./$8865* • **Nail Technician/ Specialist and Manicurist** *600 hrs./$3750*

**STUDENT SERVICES** Academic or career counseling, placement services for program completers.

## South Arkansas Community College

PO Box 7010, El Dorado, AR 71731-7010
http://www.southark.edu/

**CONTACT** Dr. Alan Rasco, President
**Telephone:** 870-862-8131

**GENERAL INFORMATION** Public Institution. Founded 1975. **Accreditation:** Regional (NCA); medical laboratory technology (NAACLS); physical therapy assisting (APTA); radiologic technology: radiography (JRCERT). **Total program enrollment:** 735.

**PROGRAM(S) OFFERED**
• **Accounting Technology/Technician and Bookkeeping** *1 student enrolled* • **Administrative Assistant and Secretarial Science, General** *1 student enrolled* • **Automobile/Automotive Mechanics Technology/Technician** *15 students enrolled* • **Business, Management, Marketing, and Related Support Services, Other** *4 students enrolled* • **Early Childhood Education and Teaching** *11 students enrolled* • **Electrical/Electronics Equipment Installation and Repair, General** • **Emergency Medical Technology/Technician (EMT Paramedic)** *1 student enrolled* • **Industrial Electronics Technology/Technician** • **Licensed Practical/ Vocational Nurse Training (LPN, LVN, Cert, Dipl, AAS)** *58 students enrolled* • **Medical Insurance Coding Specialist/Coder** *20 students enrolled* • **Medical Transcription/Transcriptionist** *6 students enrolled* • **Nurse/Nursing Assistant/ Aide and Patient Care Assistant** *22 students enrolled* • **Truck and Bus Driver/ Commercial Vehicle Operation** *16 students enrolled* • **Welding Technology/ Welder** *12 students enrolled*

**STUDENT SERVICES** Academic or career counseling, employment services for current students, placement services for program completers, remedial services.

## Southeast Arkansas College

1900 Hazel Street, Pine Bluff, AR 71603
http://www.seark.edu/

**CONTACT** Phil E. Shirley, President
**Telephone:** 870-543-5900

**GENERAL INFORMATION** Public Institution. Founded 1991. **Accreditation:** Regional (NCA); radiologic technology: radiography (JRCERT); surgical technology (ARCST). **Total program enrollment:** 994.

**PROGRAM(S) OFFERED**
• **Accounting Technology/Technician and Bookkeeping** *4 students enrolled* • **Administrative Assistant and Secretarial Science, General** *7 students enrolled* • **Business Administration and Management, General** *8 students enrolled* • **Business/Office Automation/Technology/Data Entry** *4 students enrolled* • **Child Care Provider/Assistant** *8 students enrolled* • **Computer Systems Networking and Telecommunications** *7 students enrolled* • **Computer Technology/Computer Systems Technology** *6 students enrolled* • **Drafting and Design Technology/Technician, General** *3 students enrolled* • **Emergency Medical Technology/Technician (EMT Paramedic)** *9 students enrolled* • **Forensic Science and Technology** *1 student enrolled* • **Heating, Air Conditioning, Ventilation and Refrigeration Maintenance Technology/Technician (HAC, HACR, HVAC, HVACR)** *8 students enrolled* • **Industrial Electronics Technology/ Technician** • **Industrial Mechanics and Maintenance Technology** *2 students enrolled* • **Information Science/Studies** *1 student enrolled* • **Licensed Practical/ Vocational Nurse Training (LPN, LVN, Cert, Dipl, AAS)** *46 students enrolled* • **Management Information Systems and Services, Other** *1 student enrolled* • **Medication Aide** *5 students enrolled* • **Nurse/Nursing Assistant/Aide and Patient Care Assistant** *82 students enrolled* • **Phlebotomy/Phlebotomist** *19 students enrolled* • **Quality Control Technology/Technician** *1 student enrolled* • **Surgical Technology/Technologist** *13 students enrolled* • **Welding Technology/ Welder** *4 students enrolled*

**STUDENT SERVICES** Academic or career counseling, employment services for current students, placement services for program completers, remedial services.

## Southern Arkansas University–Magnolia

100 East University, Magnolia, AR 71753
http://www.saumag.edu/

**CONTACT** David Rankin, President
**Telephone:** 870-235-4000

**GENERAL INFORMATION** Public Institution. Founded 1909. **Accreditation:** Regional (NCA); music (NASM). **Total program enrollment:** 2351.

**STUDENT SERVICES** Academic or career counseling, employment services for current students, placement services for program completers, remedial services.

## Southern Arkansas University Tech

100 Carr Road, PO Box 3499, Camden, AR 71701
http://www.sautech.edu/

**CONTACT** Corbet Lamkin, Chancellor
**Telephone:** 870-574-4500

**GENERAL INFORMATION** Public Institution. Founded 1967. **Accreditation:** Regional (NCA). **Total program enrollment:** 589.

**PROGRAM(S) OFFERED**
• **Aircraft Powerplant Technology/Technician** *10 students enrolled* • **Airframe Mechanics and Aircraft Maintenance Technology/Technician** *14 students enrolled* • **Automobile/Automotive Mechanics Technology/Technician** • **Building/Construction Finishing, Management, and Inspection, Other** • **Business/Office Automation/Technology/Data Entry** *5 students enrolled* • **Child Care Provider/Assistant** *7 students enrolled* • **Commercial and Advertising Art** *3 students enrolled* • **Computer Installation and Repair Technology/Technician** • **Computer Science** *9 students enrolled* • **Computer Systems Networking and Telecommunications** *4 students enrolled* • **Computer and Information Sciences and Support Services, Other** *3 students enrolled* • **Cosmetology/Cosmetologist, General** • **Criminal Justice/Law Enforcement Administration** • **Criminal Justice/Police Science** *254 students enrolled* • **Drafting/Design Engineering Technologies/Technicians, Other** • **Educational/Instructional Media Design** *1*

*student enrolled* • **Electrical, Electronic and Communications Engineering Technology/Technician** *1 student enrolled* • **Fire Science/Firefighting** *88 students enrolled* • **Hazardous Materials Management and Waste Technology/Technician** *6 students enrolled* • **Health Services/Allied Health/Health Sciences, General** • **Industrial Electronics Technology/Technician** • **Industrial Mechanics and Maintenance Technology** *4 students enrolled* • **Licensed Practical/Vocational Nurse Training (LPN, LVN, Cert, Dipl, AAS)** *25 students enrolled* • **Logistics and Materials Management** • **Manufacturing Technology/Technician** *1 student enrolled* • **Nurse/Nursing Assistant/Aide and Patient Care Assistant** *87 students enrolled* • **Purchasing, Procurement/Acquisitions and Contracts Management** • **Radio and Television Broadcasting Technology/Technician** • **System, Networking, and LAN/WAN Management/Manager** • **Water Quality and Wastewater Treatment Management and Recycling Technology/Technician** • **Welding Technology/Welder**

**STUDENT SERVICES** Academic or career counseling, employment services for current students, placement services for program completers, remedial services.

## University of Arkansas at Fort Smith

PO Box 3649, Fort Smith, AR 72913-3649
http://www.uafortsmith.edu/

**CONTACT** Paul Beran, Chancellor
**Telephone:** 479-788-7000

**GENERAL INFORMATION** Public Institution. Founded 1928. **Accreditation:** Regional (NCA); dental hygiene (ADA); radiologic technology: radiography (JRCERT); surgical technology (ARCST). **Total program enrollment:** 4447.

**PROGRAM(S) OFFERED**

• **Automobile/Automotive Mechanics Technology/Technician** *11 students enrolled* • **Business Administration and Management, General** *19 students enrolled* • **CAD/CADD Drafting and/or Design Technology/Technician** *16 students enrolled* • **Computer Installation and Repair Technology/Technician** *29 students enrolled* • **Computer Programming, Specific Applications** *1 student enrolled* • **Criminal Justice/Law Enforcement Administration** *1 student enrolled* • **Data Entry/Microcomputer Applications, General** *3 students enrolled* • **Executive Assistant/Executive Secretary** *18 students enrolled* • **Industrial Electronics Technology/Technician** *9 students enrolled* • **Industrial Mechanics and Maintenance Technology** *1 student enrolled* • **Licensed Practical/Vocational Nurse Training (LPN, LVN, Cert, Dipl, AAS)** *22 students enrolled* • **Welding Technology/Welder** *113 students enrolled*

**STUDENT SERVICES** Academic or career counseling, employment services for current students, placement services for program completers, remedial services.

## University of Arkansas at Little Rock

2801 South University Avenue, Little Rock, AR 72204-1099
http://www.ualr.edu/

**CONTACT** Joel E. Anderson, Chancellor
**Telephone:** 501-569-3000

**GENERAL INFORMATION** Public Institution. Founded 1927. **Accreditation:** Regional (NCA); art and design (NASAD); audiology (ASHA); computer science (ABET/CSAC); engineering technology (ABET/TAC); music (NASM); speech-language pathology (ASHA); theater (NAST). **Total program enrollment:** 6280.

**STUDENT SERVICES** Academic or career counseling, employment services for current students, placement services for program completers, remedial services.

## University of Arkansas at Monticello

Monticello, AR 71656
http://www.uamont.edu/

**CONTACT** Dr. Jack Lassiter, Chancellor
**Telephone:** 870-367-6811

**GENERAL INFORMATION** Public Institution. Founded 1909. **Accreditation:** Regional (NCA); forestry (SAF); music (NASM). **Total program enrollment:** 2307.

**PROGRAM(S) OFFERED**

• **Administrative Assistant and Secretarial Science, General** *17 students enrolled* • **Automobile/Automotive Mechanics Technology/Technician** *1 student enrolled* • **Child Care and Support Services Management** *9 students enrolled* • **Child Development** *22 students enrolled* • **Computer Technology/Computer Systems Technology** *12 students enrolled* • **Electromechanical Technology/Electromechanical Engineering Technology** *2 students enrolled* • **Electromechanical and Instrumentation and Maintenance Technologies/Technicians, Other** *20 students enrolled* • **Emergency Medical Technology/Technician (EMT Paramedic)** *23 students enrolled* • **Hospitality Administration/Management, General** *4 students enrolled* • **Industrial Mechanics and Maintenance Technology** *6 students enrolled* • **Licensed Practical/Vocational Nurse Training (LPN, LVN, Cert, Dipl, AAS)** *25 students enrolled* • **Nurse/Nursing Assistant/Aide and Patient Care Assistant** *32 students enrolled* • **Welding Technology/Welder** *11 students enrolled*

**STUDENT SERVICES** Academic or career counseling, employment services for current students, placement services for program completers, remedial services.

## University of Arkansas at Pine Bluff

1200 North University Drive, Pine Bluff, AR 71601-2799
http://www.uapb.edu/

**CONTACT** Lawrence A. Davis, Jr., Chancellor
**Telephone:** 870-575-8000

**GENERAL INFORMATION** Public Institution. Founded 1873. **Accreditation:** Regional (NCA); art and design (NASAD); home economics (AAFCS); music (NASM). **Total program enrollment:** 3054.

**STUDENT SERVICES** Academic or career counseling, daycare for children of students, employment services for current students, placement services for program completers, remedial services.

## University of Arkansas Community College at Batesville

PO Box 3350, Batesville, AR 72503
http://www.uaccb.edu/

**CONTACT** Deborah Frazier, Chancellor
**Telephone:** 870-612-2000

**GENERAL INFORMATION** Public Institution. **Accreditation:** Regional (NCA). **Total program enrollment:** 950.

**PROGRAM(S) OFFERED**

• **Accounting** *4 students enrolled* • **Administrative Assistant and Secretarial Science, General** *9 students enrolled* • **Business/Commerce, General** *15 students enrolled* • **Early Childhood Education and Teaching** *49 students enrolled* • **Electrical/Electronics Equipment Installation and Repair, General** *1 student enrolled* • **Emergency Medical Technology/Technician (EMT Paramedic)** *14 students enrolled* • **Finance, General** *1 student enrolled* • **Licensed Practical/Vocational Nurse Training (LPN, LVN, Cert, Dipl, AAS)** *40 students enrolled* • **Nurse/Nursing Assistant/Aide and Patient Care Assistant** *97 students enrolled*

**STUDENT SERVICES** Academic or career counseling, employment services for current students, remedial services.

## University of Arkansas Community College at Hope

PO Box 140, Hope, AR 71802-0140
http://www.uacch.edu/

**CONTACT** Chris Thomason, JD, Chancellor
**Telephone:** 870-777-5722

**GENERAL INFORMATION** Public Institution. Founded 1966. **Accreditation:** Regional (NCA); funeral service (ABFSE); respiratory therapy technology (CoARC). **Total program enrollment:** 698.

**PROGRAM(S) OFFERED**

• **Accounting Technology/Technician and Bookkeeping** *3 students enrolled* • **Child Care Provider/Assistant** *21 students enrolled* • **Computer and Information Sciences, General** *2 students enrolled* • **Diesel Mechanics Technology/**

*University of Arkansas Community College at Hope (continued)*

**Technician** *5 students enrolled* • **Emergency Care Attendant (EMT Ambulance)** *15 students enrolled* • **Emergency Medical Technology/Technician (EMT Paramedic)** *2 students enrolled* • **General Office Occupations and Clerical Services** *1 student enrolled* • **Heating, Air Conditioning, Ventilation and Refrigeration Maintenance Technology/Technician (HAC, HACR, HVAC, HVACR)** *2 students enrolled* • **Heavy/Industrial Equipment Maintenance Technologies, Other** *3 students enrolled* • **Industrial Electronics Technology/ Technician** *6 students enrolled* • **Industrial Mechanics and Maintenance Technology** *2 students enrolled* • **Licensed Practical/Vocational Nurse Training (LPN, LVN, Cert, Dipl, AAS)** *26 students enrolled* • **Medical Office Management/Administration** *3 students enrolled* • **Welding Technology/Welder** *4 students enrolled*

**STUDENT SERVICES** Academic or career counseling, employment services for current students, placement services for program completers, remedial services.

## University of Arkansas Community College at Morrilton

1537 University Boulevard, Morrilton, AR 72110
http://www.uaccm.edu/

**CONTACT** Nathan Crook, Chancellor
**Telephone:** 501-977-2000

**GENERAL INFORMATION** Public Institution. Founded 1961. **Accreditation:** Regional (NCA). **Total program enrollment:** 1299.

**PROGRAM(S) OFFERED**
• **Autobody/Collision and Repair Technology/Technician** *5 students enrolled* • **Automobile/Automotive Mechanics Technology/Technician** *3 students enrolled* • **Business/Commerce, General** *3 students enrolled* • **Child Development** *4 students enrolled* • **Computer Technology/Computer Systems Technology** *9 students enrolled* • **Criminal Justice/Law Enforcement Administration** • **Dietitian Assistant** • **Drafting and Design Technology/Technician, General** *4 students enrolled* • **Emergency Medical Technology/Technician (EMT Paramedic)** *7 students enrolled* • **Forensic Science and Technology** • **Heating, Air Conditioning, Ventilation and Refrigeration Maintenance Technology/ Technician (HAC, HACR, HVAC, HVACR)** *5 students enrolled* • **Licensed Practical/Vocational Nurse Training (LPN, LVN, Cert, Dipl, AAS)** *43 students enrolled* • **Nurse/Nursing Assistant/Aide and Patient Care Assistant** *2 students enrolled* • **Petroleum Technology/Technician** *36 students enrolled* • **Survey Technology/Surveying** *16 students enrolled* • **System, Networking, and LAN/ WAN Management/Manager** *4 students enrolled* • **Welding Technology/Welder** *13 students enrolled*

**STUDENT SERVICES** Academic or career counseling, daycare for children of students, employment services for current students, placement services for program completers, remedial services.

## University of Arkansas for Medical Sciences

4301 West Markham, Little Rock, AR 72205-7199
http://www.uams.edu/

**CONTACT** I. Dodd Wilson, MD, Chancellor
**Telephone:** 501-296-1275

**GENERAL INFORMATION** Public Institution. Founded 1879. **Accreditation:** Regional (NCA); cytotechnology (ASC); dental hygiene (ADA); dietetics: postbaccalaureate internship (ADtA/CAADE); emergency medical services (JRCEMTP); medical technology (NAACLS); nuclear medicine technology (JRCNMT); radiologic technology: radiography (JRCERT); respiratory therapy technology (CoARC); surgical technology (ARCST). **Total program enrollment:** 1976. **Application fee:** $30.

**PROGRAM(S) OFFERED**
• **Emergency Medical Technology/Technician (EMT Paramedic)** *14 students enrolled* • **Surgical Technology/Technologist** *5 students enrolled*

**STUDENT SERVICES** Academic or career counseling, employment services for current students, remedial services.

## University of Central Arkansas

201 Donaghey Avenue, Conway, AR 72035-0001
http://www.uca.edu/

**CONTACT** Tom Courtway, Interim President
**Telephone:** 501-450-5000

**GENERAL INFORMATION** Public Institution. Founded 1907. **Accreditation:** Regional (NCA); art and design (NASAD); dietetics: postbaccalaureate internship (ADtA/CAADE); home economics (AAFCS); music (NASM); speech-language pathology (ASHA); theater (NAST). **Total program enrollment:** 9893.

**PROGRAM(S) OFFERED**
• **Substance Abuse/Addiction Counseling**

**STUDENT SERVICES** Academic or career counseling, employment services for current students, placement services for program completers, remedial services.

## Velvatex College of Beauty Culture

1520 Martin Luther King Drive, Little Rock, AR 72202

**CONTACT** Barbara Douglas, Owner
**Telephone:** 501-372-9678

**GENERAL INFORMATION** Private Institution. Founded 1929. **Total program enrollment:** 17. **Application fee:** $100.

**PROGRAM(S) OFFERED**
• **Cosmetology, Barber/Styling, and Nail Instructor** • **Cosmetology/ Cosmetologist, General** *1500 hrs./$5895* • **Nail Technician/Specialist and Manicurist** • **Teacher Education and Professional Development, Specific Subject Areas, Other**

**STUDENT SERVICES** Academic or career counseling, placement services for program completers.

## White River School of Massage

2503 Hiram Davis Place, Fayetteville, AR 72703
http://www.wrsm.com/

**CONTACT** Lynnlee Hutchinson, Director
**Telephone:** 479-521-2250

**GENERAL INFORMATION** Private Institution. **Total program enrollment:** 83.

**PROGRAM(S) OFFERED**
• **Massage Therapy/Therapeutic Massage** *102 students enrolled*

**STUDENT SERVICES** Academic or career counseling, placement services for program completers.

# CALIFORNIA

## Academy of Barbering Arts

19557 Parthenia Street, Northridge, CA 91324

**CONTACT** Mohammad Mihandoust, President
**Telephone:** 818-775-9951

**GENERAL INFORMATION** Private Institution. **Total program enrollment:** 98. **Application fee:** $75.

**PROGRAM(S) OFFERED**
• **Barbering/Barber** *1500 hrs./$10,900* • **Cosmetology and Related Personal Grooming Arts, Other** *400 hrs./$3075* • **Cosmetology/Cosmetologist, General** *1600 hrs./$10,075*

**STUDENT SERVICES** Academic or career counseling, employment services for current students, placement services for program completers.

## Academy of Hair Design

14010 Poway Road, Suite J, Poway, CA 92064
http://www.sandiegobeautyacademy.com/

**CONTACT** Lynelle Lynch, President
**Telephone:** 858-748-1490 Ext. 0

**GENERAL INFORMATION** Private Institution. **Total program enrollment:** 311. **Application fee:** $75.

**PROGRAM(S) OFFERED**
• **Aesthetician/Esthetician and Skin Care Specialist** *750 hrs./$10,550* • **Cosmetology and Related Personal Grooming Arts, Other** *1000 hrs./$10,125* • **Cosmetology/Cosmetologist, General** *1750 hrs./$16,550* • **Facial Treatment Specialist/Facialist** *800 hrs./$10,250* • **Health Services/Allied Health/Health Sciences, General** *1 student enrolled* • **Make-Up Artist/Specialist** *15 students enrolled* • **Massage Therapy/Therapeutic Massage** *700 hrs./$5925* • **Nail Technician/Specialist and Manicurist** *6 students enrolled*

**STUDENT SERVICES** Employment services for current students, placement services for program completers.

## Academy of Professional Careers

45-691 Monroe Avenue, Indio, CA 92201

**CONTACT** Gary Yasuda, President
**Telephone:** 760-347-5000

**GENERAL INFORMATION** Private Institution. **Total program enrollment:** 227. **Application fee:** $100.

**PROGRAM(S) OFFERED**
• **Massage Therapy/Therapeutic Massage** *720 hrs./$10,042* • **Medical Administrative/Executive Assistant and Medical Secretary** *720 hrs./$10,113* • **Medical/Clinical Assistant** *720 hrs./$11,034* • **Pharmacy Technician/Assistant** *720 hrs./$10,817*

**STUDENT SERVICES** Academic or career counseling, employment services for current students, placement services for program completers.

## Academy of Radio Broadcasting

16052 Beach Boulevard, # 263N, Huntington Beach, CA 92647
http://www.arbradio.com/

**CONTACT** Tom Gillenwater, Financial Aid Director
**Telephone:** 714-842-0100

**GENERAL INFORMATION** Private Institution. **Total program enrollment:** 106. **Application fee:** $100.

**PROGRAM(S) OFFERED**
• **Radio and Television Broadcasting Technology/Technician** *36 hrs./$11,800* • **Radio and Television** *36 hrs./$11,800*

**STUDENT SERVICES** Academic or career counseling, placement services for program completers, remedial services.

## Adelante Career Institute

14547 Titus, Van Nuys, CA 91402
http://adelantecareerinstitute.com/

**CONTACT** Merrill Lyons, President
**Telephone:** 818-908-9912

**GENERAL INFORMATION** Private Institution. **Total program enrollment:** 166.

**PROGRAM(S) OFFERED**
• **Accounting Technology/Technician and Bookkeeping** *9 students enrolled* • **General Office Occupations and Clerical Services** *2 students enrolled* • **Health and Medical Administrative Services, Other** *32 students enrolled* • **Pharmacy Technician/Assistant** *5 students enrolled* • **Physical Therapist Assistant** *12 students enrolled*

**STUDENT SERVICES** Employment services for current students, placement services for program completers.

## Adrians Beauty College of Turlock

2253 Geer Road, Turlock, CA 95380

**CONTACT** Sherri A. Cytanovich, Director
**Telephone:** 209-632-2233

**GENERAL INFORMATION** Private Institution. **Total program enrollment:** 161.

**PROGRAM(S) OFFERED**
• **Aesthetician/Esthetician and Skin Care Specialist** *600 hrs./$8395* • **Cosmetology and Related Personal Grooming Arts, Other** *400 hrs./$3645* • **Cosmetology, Barber/Styling, and Nail Instructor** *600 hrs./$9000* • **Cosmetology/Cosmetologist, General** *1600 hrs./$14,598*

**STUDENT SERVICES** Placement services for program completers.

## Advance Beauty College

10121 Westminster Avenue, Garden Grove, CA 92643
http://www.advancebeautycollege.com/

**CONTACT** Tam Nguyen, President
**Telephone:** 714-530-2131

**GENERAL INFORMATION** Private Institution. **Total program enrollment:** 441. **Application fee:** $75.

**PROGRAM(S) OFFERED**
• **Aesthetician/Esthetician and Skin Care Specialist** *600 hrs./$2325* • **Cosmetology, Barber/Styling, and Nail Instructor** *600 hrs./$1875* • **Cosmetology/Cosmetologist, General** *1600 hrs./$7748* • **Massage Therapy/Therapeutic Massage** *1000 hrs./$6075* • **Nail Technician/Specialist and Manicurist** *400 hrs./$425*

**STUDENT SERVICES** Academic or career counseling, placement services for program completers.

## Advanced College

13180 Paramount Boulevard, South Gate, CA 90280
http://www.advancedcollege.edu/

**CONTACT** Dr. Mehdi Karimpour, CEO/Director
**Telephone:** 562-408-6969

**GENERAL INFORMATION** Private Institution. **Total program enrollment:** 118. **Application fee:** $75.

**PROGRAM(S) OFFERED**
• **Accounting** *720 hrs./$10,700* • **Administrative Assistant and Secretarial Science, General** • **Computer Installation and Repair Technology/Technician** • **Computer Systems Networking and Telecommunications** *1 student enrolled* • **Licensed Practical/Vocational Nurse Training (LPN, LVN, Cert, Dipl, AAS)**

*Advanced College (continued)*

*1536 hrs./$25,835* • **Massage Therapy/Therapeutic Massage** *740 hrs./$10,700* • **Medical Insurance Specialist/Medical Biller** *720 hrs./$10,700* • **Medical/Clinical Assistant** *720 hrs./$10,700* • **Physical Therapy/Therapist** *720 hrs./$10,700*

**STUDENT SERVICES** Placement services for program completers.

## Advanced Training Associates

1900 Joe Crosson Drive, El Cajon, CA 92020
http://www.advancedtraining.edu/

**CONTACT** Joann Ferrera, President/Director
**Telephone:** 619-596-2766

**GENERAL INFORMATION** Private Institution. **Total program enrollment:** 22. **Application fee:** $75.

**PROGRAM(S) OFFERED**
• **Accounting and Business/Management** *600 hrs./$6070* • **Computer Systems Networking and Telecommunications** *340 hrs./$5070* • **Computer and Information Sciences, General** *720 hrs./$9570* • **Massage Therapy/Therapeutic Massage** • **Medical Administrative/Executive Assistant and Medical Secretary** *760 hrs./$9570* • **Medical/Clinical Assistant** *760 hrs./$9570* • **Teaching English as a Second or Foreign Language/ESL Language Instructor** *760 hrs./$4500*

**STUDENT SERVICES** Academic or career counseling, placement services for program completers, remedial services.

## Alameda Beauty College

2318 Central Avenue, Alameda, CA 94501

**CONTACT** Tracy Stoddard Becker, President
**Telephone:** 510-523-1050

**GENERAL INFORMATION** Private Institution. Founded 1960. **Total program enrollment:** 137.

**PROGRAM(S) OFFERED**
• **Aesthetician/Esthetician and Skin Care Specialist** • **Cosmetology/Cosmetologist, General** *1600 hrs./$12,800* • **Nail Technician/Specialist and Manicurist**

**STUDENT SERVICES** Academic or career counseling, employment services for current students, remedial services.

## Alhambra Beauty College

200 West Main Street, Alhambra, CA 91801

**GENERAL INFORMATION** Private Institution. **Total program enrollment:** 110.

**PROGRAM(S) OFFERED**
• **Aesthetician/Esthetician and Skin Care Specialist** *600 hrs./$2850* • **Cosmetology, Barber/Styling, and Nail Instructor** *600 hrs./$1525* • **Cosmetology/Cosmetologist, General** *1600 hrs./$8675* • **Nail Technician/Specialist and Manicurist** *400 hrs./$1200*

**STUDENT SERVICES** Academic or career counseling, placement services for program completers.

## Allan Hancock College

800 South College Drive, Santa Maria, CA 93454-6399
http://www.hancockcollege.edu/

**CONTACT** Dr. Jose Ortiz, Superintendent/President
**Telephone:** 805-922-6966

**GENERAL INFORMATION** Public Institution. Founded 1920. **Accreditation:** Regional (WASC/ACCJC). **Total program enrollment:** 3340.

**PROGRAM(S) OFFERED**
• **Accounting** *31 students enrolled* • **Administrative Assistant and Secretarial Science, General** *44 students enrolled* • **Apparel and Textiles, General** *2 students enrolled* • **Architectural Drafting and Architectural CAD/CADD** *5 students enrolled* • **Autobody/Collision and Repair Technology/Technician** *2 students enrolled* • **Business/Commerce, General** *122 students enrolled* • **Child Development** *21 students enrolled* • **Computer Systems Networking and Telecommunications** *1 student enrolled* • **Computer and Information Sciences, General** *4 students enrolled* • **Cooking and Related Culinary Arts, General** *1 student enrolled* • **Cosmetology/Cosmetologist, General** *79 students enrolled* • **Criminal Justice/Police Science** *61 students enrolled* • **Dental Assisting/Assistant** *18 students enrolled* • **Drafting and Design Technology/Technician, General** *5 students enrolled* • **Education/Teaching of Individuals in Early Childhood Special Education Programs** *1 student enrolled* • **Electrical/Electronics Equipment Installation and Repair, General** *2 students enrolled* • **Emergency Medical Technology/Technician (EMT Paramedic)** • **Fire Science/Firefighting** *60 students enrolled* • **Hazardous Materials Management and Waste Technology/Technician** *1 student enrolled* • **Health Unit Coordinator/Ward Clerk** • **Home Health Aide/Home Attendant** • **Human Services, General** *4 students enrolled* • **Information Technology** *1 student enrolled* • **Legal Administrative Assistant/Secretary** *1 student enrolled* • **Licensed Practical/Vocational Nurse Training (LPN, LVN, Cert, Dipl, AAS)** *36 students enrolled* • **Medical/Clinical Assistant** *20 students enrolled* • **Music Management and Merchandising** *2 students enrolled* • **Nurse/Nursing Assistant/Aide and Patient Care Assistant** *115 students enrolled* • **Nursing—Registered Nurse Training (RN, ASN, BSN, MSN)** *35 students enrolled* • **Restaurant, Culinary, and Catering Management/Manager** *1 student enrolled* • **Substance Abuse/Addiction Counseling** *7 students enrolled*

**STUDENT SERVICES** Academic or career counseling, daycare for children of students, employment services for current students, placement services for program completers, remedial services.

## American Academy of Dramatic Arts/Hollywood

1336 North La Brea Avenue, Hollywood, CA 90028
http://www.aada.org/

**CONTACT** Roger Croucher, President
**Telephone:** 323-464-2777 Ext. 109

**GENERAL INFORMATION** Private Institution. Founded 1974. **Accreditation:** Regional (WASC/ACCJC); theater (NAST). **Total program enrollment:** 162. **Application fee:** $50.

**STUDENT SERVICES** Academic or career counseling.

## American Auto Institute

17522 Studebaker Road, Cerritos, CA 90703
http://americanautoinstitute.com/

**CONTACT** Dr. Nagui B. Elyas, Owner
**Telephone:** 562-403-2660

**GENERAL INFORMATION** Private Institution. **Total program enrollment:** 42.

**PROGRAM(S) OFFERED**
• **Automobile/Automotive Mechanics Technology/Technician** *51 students enrolled* • **Vehicle Emissions Inspection and Maintenance Technology/Technician** *11 students enrolled* • **Vehicle Maintenance and Repair Technologies, Other** *1 student enrolled*

**STUDENT SERVICES** Employment services for current students, placement services for program completers.

## American Beauty College

16512 Bellflower Boulevard, Bellflower, CA 90706

**CONTACT** Tanya Rhiner, Chief Financial Officer
**Telephone:** 562-866-0728

**GENERAL INFORMATION** Private Institution. **Total program enrollment:** 37. **Application fee:** $75.

**PROGRAM(S) OFFERED**
• **Cosmetology/Cosmetologist, General** *1600 hrs./$8395*

**STUDENT SERVICES** Placement services for program completers.

## American Career College

1200 North Magnolia Avenue, Anaheim, CA 92801-2607
http://www.americancareer.com/

**CONTACT** David A. Pyle, President/CEO
**Telephone:** 714-952-9066

**GENERAL INFORMATION** Private Institution. **Total program enrollment:** 1512.

**PROGRAM(S) OFFERED**
• **Dental Assisting/Assistant** *89 students enrolled* • **Health and Medical Administrative Services, Other** *720 hrs./$12,575* • **Massage Therapy/Therapeutic Massage** *720 hrs./$12,575* • **Medical/Clinical Assistant** *720 hrs./$12,575* • **Nursing, Other** *1560 hrs./$30,075* • **Opticianry/Ophthalmic Dispensing Optician** *720 hrs./$12,150* • **Pharmacy Technician/Assistant** *720 hrs./$12,575* • **Surgical Technology/Technologist** *107 students enrolled*

**STUDENT SERVICES** Academic or career counseling, employment services for current students, placement services for program completers, remedial services.

## American Career College

4021 Rosewood Avenue, First Floor, Los Angeles, CA 90004-2932
http://www.americancareer.com/

**CONTACT** David Pyle, President/CEO
**Telephone:** 323-668-7555

**GENERAL INFORMATION** Private Institution. Founded 1978. **Total program enrollment:** 1732.

**PROGRAM(S) OFFERED**
• **Dental Assisting/Assistant** *726 hrs./$12,975* • **Health Information/Medical Records Technology/Technician** *720 hrs./$12,575* • **Health and Medical Administrative Services, Other** *175 students enrolled* • **Massage Therapy/Therapeutic Massage** *89 students enrolled* • **Medical/Clinical Assistant** *720 hrs./$12,575* • **Nursing, Other** *1560 hrs./$30,000* • **Opticianry/Ophthalmic Dispensing Optician** *129 students enrolled* • **Pharmacy Technician/Assistant** *720 hrs./$12,575* • **Surgical Technology/Technologist** *1540 hrs./$28,075*

**STUDENT SERVICES** Academic or career counseling, employment services for current students, placement services for program completers, remedial services.

## American Career College

3299 Horseless Carriage Road, #C, Norco, CA 92860
http://www.americancareer.com/

**CONTACT** David A. Pyle, President/CEO
**Telephone:** 951-739-0788

**GENERAL INFORMATION** Private Institution. **Total program enrollment:** 735.

**PROGRAM(S) OFFERED**
• **Diagnostic Medical Sonography/Sonographer and Ultrasound Technician** *1856 hrs./$30,075* • **Health Information/Medical Records Technology/Technician** *103 students enrolled* • **Health and Medical Administrative Services, Other** *720 hrs./$12,575* • **Massage Therapy/Therapeutic Massage** *720 hrs./$12,575* • **Medical/Clinical Assistant** *720 hrs./$12,575* • **Opticianry/Ophthalmic Dispensing Optician** *720 hrs./$12,150* • **Pharmacy Technician/Assistant** *720 hrs./$12,575*

**STUDENT SERVICES** Academic or career counseling, employment services for current students, placement services for program completers, remedial services.

## American College of Health Professions

1200 Arizona Street, Suite A-1, Redlands, CA 92374
http://achp.edu/

**CONTACT** Michele Brooks, President/CEO
**Telephone:** 951-637-6900

**GENERAL INFORMATION** Private Institution. **Total program enrollment:** 12. **Application fee:** $75.

**PROGRAM(S) OFFERED**
• **Surgical Technology/Technologist** *80 hrs./$25,120*

**STUDENT SERVICES** Academic or career counseling, placement services for program completers.

## American Conservatory Theater

30 Grant Avenue, San Francisco, CA 94108-5800
http://www.act-sfbay.org/

**CONTACT** Heather Kitchen, Executive Director
**Telephone:** 415-439-2350

**GENERAL INFORMATION** Private Institution. Founded 1969. **Accreditation:** Regional (WASC/ACSCU). **Total program enrollment:** 44. **Application fee:** $65.

**PROGRAM(S) OFFERED**
• **Acting** *89 students enrolled*

**STUDENT SERVICES** Academic or career counseling, employment services for current students, placement services for program completers.

## American Institute of Health Sciences

3711 Long Beach Boulevard, Suite 200, Long Beach, CA 90807
http://aihs.edu/

**CONTACT** Kim Dang, President
**Telephone:** 562-988-2278 Ext. 112

**GENERAL INFORMATION** Private Institution. **Total program enrollment:** 22. **Application fee:** $25.

**PROGRAM(S) OFFERED**
• **Allied Health and Medical Assisting Services, Other** *50 hrs./$11,950* • **Medical/Clinical Assistant** *74 hrs./$20,000* • **Medical/Health Management and Clinical Assistant/Specialist** *84 hrs./$25,000* • **Nursing—Registered Nurse Training (RN, ASN, BSN, MSN)** *130 hrs./$84,000* • **Pharmacy Technician/Assistant** *54 hrs./$12,175*

**STUDENT SERVICES** Academic or career counseling, placement services for program completers, remedial services.

## American Institute of Massage Therapy

1570 E. Warner Avenue, Suite 200, Santa Ana, CA 92705-5465
http://www.aimtinc.com/

**CONTACT** Thanh H. Nguyen, Chief Operating Officer
**Telephone:** 714-432-7879

**GENERAL INFORMATION** Private Institution. **Total program enrollment:** 39. **Application fee:** $25.

**PROGRAM(S) OFFERED**
• **Massage Therapy/Therapeutic Massage** *624 hrs./$6575*

**STUDENT SERVICES** Academic or career counseling, employment services for current students, placement services for program completers.

## American Pacific College

14435 Sherman Way, Suite 208, Van Nuys, CA 91405
http://www.apc.edu

**CONTACT** Augusto V. Guerra, President
**Telephone:** 818-781-0001

**GENERAL INFORMATION** Private Institution. **Total program enrollment:** 85. **Application fee:** $75.

**PROGRAM(S) OFFERED**
• **Accounting Technology/Technician and Bookkeeping** *560 hrs./$5600* • **Accounting** *1 student enrolled* • **Automobile/Automotive Mechanics Technology/Technician** *560 hrs./$5600* • **Computer Installation and Repair Technology/Technician** *600 hrs./$6000* • **Computer Software and Media Applications, Other** • **Computer and Information Sciences and Support Services, Other** *1015 hrs./$10,150* • **Data Entry/Microcomputer Applications, Other** *560 hrs./$5600* • **Electrical/Electronics Maintenance and Repair Technology, Other** *11 students enrolled* • **General Office Occupations and Clerical Services** *3 students enrolled* • **Prepress/Desktop Publishing and Digital Imaging Design** • **Vehicle Maintenance and Repair Technologies, Other** *6 students enrolled*

**STUDENT SERVICES** Academic or career counseling, employment services for current students, placement services for program completers.

## American River College

4700 College Oak Drive, Sacramento, CA 95841-4286
http://www.arc.losrios.edu/

**CONTACT** David Viar, President
**Telephone:** 916-484-8011

**GENERAL INFORMATION** Public Institution. Founded 1955. **Accreditation:** Regional (WASC/ACCJC); funeral service (ABFSE). **Total program enrollment:** 8712.

**PROGRAM(S) OFFERED**
• **Accounting** *16 students enrolled* • **Adult Development and Aging** *2 students enrolled* • **American Sign Language (ASL)** *2 students enrolled* • **Animation, Interactive Technology, Video Graphics and Special Effects** *3 students enrolled* • **Apparel and Textile Marketing Management** *2 students enrolled* • **Autobody/Collision and Repair Technology/Technician** *1 student enrolled* • **Automobile/Automotive Mechanics Technology/Technician** *24 students enrolled* • **Biology Technician/Biotechnology Laboratory Technician** *3 students enrolled* • **Business Administration and Management, General** *3 students enrolled* • **Business/Commerce, General** *5 students enrolled* • **Carpentry/Carpenter** *41 students enrolled* • **Child Development** *31 students enrolled* • **Computer Graphics** *3 students enrolled* • **Computer Programming/Programmer, General** *1 student enrolled* • **Computer Systems Networking and Telecommunications** *1 student enrolled* • **Data Entry/Microcomputer Applications, General** *2 students enrolled* • **Data Modeling/Warehousing and Database Administration** *4 students enrolled* • **Diesel Mechanics Technology/Technician** *2 students enrolled* • **Drafting and Design Technology/Technician, General** *9 students enrolled* • **Drawing** *1 student enrolled* • **Drywall Installation/Drywaller** *103 students enrolled* • **Electrical/Electronics Equipment Installation and Repair, General** *1 student enrolled* • **Electrician** *45 students enrolled* • **Fashion/Apparel Design** *2 students enrolled* • **Fire Science/Firefighting** *9 students enrolled* • **Geography, Other** *18 students enrolled* • **Human Services, General** *16 students enrolled* • **Interior Design** *12 students enrolled* • **International Relations and Affairs** *2 students enrolled* • **Landscaping and Groundskeeping** *4 students enrolled* • **Legal Assistant/Paralegal** *8 students enrolled* • **Music Management and Merchandising** *3 students enrolled* • **Natural Resources/Conservation, General** *4 students enrolled* • **Plant Nursery Operations and Management** *1 student enrolled* • **Real Estate** *9 students enrolled* • **Restaurant, Culinary, and Catering Management/Manager** *6 students enrolled* • **Retailing and Retail Operations** *1 student enrolled* • **Sheet Metal Technology/Sheetworking** *46 students enrolled* • **Sign Language Interpretation and Translation** *11 students enrolled* • **Substance Abuse/Addiction Counseling** *13 students enrolled* • **System Administration/Administrator** *5 students enrolled* • **Technical and Business Writing** *3 students enrolled* • **Web Page, Digital/Multimedia and Information Resources Design** *1 student enrolled* • **Web/Multimedia Management and Webmaster** *1 student enrolled*

**STUDENT SERVICES** Academic or career counseling, daycare for children of students, employment services for current students, placement services for program completers, remedial services.

## Antelope Valley College

3041 West Avenue K, Lancaster, CA 93536-5426
http://www.avc.edu/

**CONTACT** Ms. Deborah Wallace, Vice President, Business Services
**Telephone:** 661-722-6300

**GENERAL INFORMATION** Public Institution. Founded 1929. **Accreditation:** Regional (WASC/ACCJC). **Total program enrollment:** 4802.

**PROGRAM(S) OFFERED**
• **Accounting** *2 students enrolled* • **Administrative Assistant and Secretarial Science, General** *5 students enrolled* • **Aircraft Powerplant Technology/Technician** *20 students enrolled* • **Airframe Mechanics and Aircraft Maintenance Technology/Technician** *14 students enrolled* • **American Sign Language (ASL)** *3 students enrolled* • **Animation, Interactive Technology, Video Graphics and Special Effects** *5 students enrolled* • **Apparel and Textiles, General** *11 students enrolled* • **Autobody/Collision and Repair Technology/Technician** *11 students enrolled* • **Automobile/Automotive Mechanics Technology/Technician** *5 students enrolled* • **Business/Commerce, General** *2 students enrolled* • **Child Development** *19 students enrolled* • **Computer Graphics** *5 students enrolled* • **Computer Systems Networking and Telecommunications** *3 students enrolled* • **Electrical/Electronics Equipment Installation and Repair, General** *2 students enrolled* • **Electrician** *10 students enrolled* • **Emergency Medical Technology/Technician (EMT Paramedic)** • **Fire Science/Firefighting** *28 students enrolled* • **Geography, Other** *4 students enrolled* • **Heating, Air Conditioning and Refrigeration Technology/Technician (ACH/ACR/ACHR/HRAC/HVAC/AC Technology)** *29 students enrolled* • **Home Health Aide/Home Attendant** • **Industrial Production Technologies/Technicians, Other** *13 students enrolled* • **Information Technology** *1 student enrolled* • **Interior Design** *8 students enrolled* • **Licensed Practical/Vocational Nurse Training (LPN, LVN, Cert, Dipl, AAS)** *2 students enrolled* • **Medical/Clinical Assistant** *1 student enrolled* • **Music Management and Merchandising** *2 students enrolled* • **Nurse/Nursing Assistant/Aide and Patient Care Assistant** • **Photography** *1 student enrolled* • **Prepress/Desktop Publishing and Digital Imaging Design** *1 student enrolled* • **Real Estate** *2 students enrolled* • **Sales, Distribution and Marketing Operations, General** *1 student enrolled* • **Teacher Assistant/Aide** *10 students enrolled* • **Welding Technology/Welder** *4 students enrolled*

**STUDENT SERVICES** Academic or career counseling, daycare for children of students, employment services for current students, placement services for program completers, remedial services.

## Antelope Valley Medical College

44201 10th Street West, Lancaster, CA 93534

**CONTACT** Araceli Jimenez, Financial Aid Director
**Telephone:** 661-726-1911 Ext. 106

**GENERAL INFORMATION** Private Institution. **Total program enrollment:** 663. **Application fee:** $75.

**PROGRAM(S) OFFERED**
• **Corrections and Criminal Justice, Other** *1140 hrs./$25,105* • **Culinary Arts/Chef Training** *750 hrs./$12,075* • **Emergency Medical Technology/Technician (EMT Paramedic)** *135 hrs./$950* • **Health and Medical Administrative Services, Other** *129 students enrolled* • **Licensed Practical/Vocational Nurse Training (LPN, LVN, Cert, Dipl, AAS)** *1530 hrs./$21,000* • **Massage Therapy/Therapeutic Massage** *38 students enrolled* • **Medical Insurance Specialist/Medical Biller** *810 hrs./$11,850* • **Medical/Clinical Assistant** *720 hrs./$11,525* • **Nurse/Nursing Assistant/Aide and Patient Care Assistant** *61 students enrolled* • **Pharmacy Technician/Assistant** *56 students enrolled*

**STUDENT SERVICES** Academic or career counseling, employment services for current students, placement services for program completers.

## Antioch University Los Angeles

400 Corporate Pointe, Culver City, CA 90230
http://www.antiochla.edu/

**CONTACT** Neal King, President
**Telephone:** 310-578-1080

**GENERAL INFORMATION** Private Institution. Founded 1972. **Accreditation:** Regional (NCA). **Total program enrollment:** 468. **Application fee:** $60.

**STUDENT SERVICES** Academic or career counseling, remedial services.

## The Art Institute of California–Los Angeles

2900 31st Street, Santa Monica, CA 90405-3035
http://www.artinstitutes.edu/losangeles/

**CONTACT** Laura Soloff, President
**Telephone:** 310-752-4700

**GENERAL INFORMATION** Private Institution. **Accreditation:** State accredited or approved. **Total program enrollment:** 1473. **Application fee:** $50.

**PROGRAM(S) OFFERED**
• **Baking and Pastry Arts/Baker/Pastry Chef** *4 students enrolled* • **Cooking and Related Culinary Arts, General** *4 students enrolled*

**STUDENT SERVICES** Academic or career counseling, employment services for current students, placement services for program completers, remedial services.

## The Art Institute of California–Orange County

3601 West Sunflower Avenue, Santa Ana, CA 92704-9888
http://www.artinstitutes.edu/orangecounty/

**CONTACT** Daniel A. Levinson, President
**Telephone:** 714-830-0200

**GENERAL INFORMATION** Private Institution. Founded 2000. **Accreditation:** State accredited or approved. **Total program enrollment:** 1303. **Application fee:** $50.

**PROGRAM(S) OFFERED**
• **Baking and Pastry Arts/Baker/Pastry Chef** *15 students enrolled* • **Cooking and Related Culinary Arts, General** *7 students enrolled*

**STUDENT SERVICES** Academic or career counseling, employment services for current students, placement services for program completers, remedial services.

## Asian-American International Beauty College

7871 Westminster Boulevard, Westminster, CA 92683
http://www.aabeautycollege.com/

**CONTACT** Minh Trieu, Asst. Gen. Manager
**Telephone:** 714-891-0508

**GENERAL INFORMATION** Private Institution. Founded 1986. **Total program enrollment:** 113. **Application fee:** $75.

**PROGRAM(S) OFFERED**
• **Aesthetician/Esthetician and Skin Care Specialist** *600 hrs./$2250*
• **Cosmetology, Barber/Styling, and Nail Instructor** *600 hrs./$2250*
• **Cosmetology/Cosmetologist, General** *1600 hrs./$7200* • **Nail Technician/Specialist and Manicurist** *400 hrs./$1300*

**STUDENT SERVICES** Academic or career counseling, placement services for program completers.

## Associated Technical College

1670 Wilshire Boulevard, Los Angeles, CA 90017-1690

**CONTACT** Samuel Romano, President
**Telephone:** 213-413-6808

**GENERAL INFORMATION** Private Institution. Founded 1967. **Total program enrollment:** 305. **Application fee:** $75.

**PROGRAM(S) OFFERED**
• **Cardiovascular Technology/Technologist** *30 hrs./$9500* • **Telecommunications Technology/Technician** *30 hrs./$9500*

**STUDENT SERVICES** Academic or career counseling, employment services for current students, placement services for program completers.

## Associated Technical College

1445 6th Avenue, San Diego, CA 92101
http://www.associatedtechcollege.com/

**CONTACT** Ali Pourhosseini, Director
**Telephone:** 619-234-2181 Ext. 309

**GENERAL INFORMATION** Private Institution. **Total program enrollment:** 86. **Application fee:** $100.

**PROGRAM(S) OFFERED**
• **Communications Technology/Technician** *24 hrs./$10,230* • **Computer and Information Sciences and Support Services, Other** *24 hrs./$10,100*

**STUDENT SERVICES** Academic or career counseling, employment services for current students, placement services for program completers.

## Athena Education Corporation

1720 E. Garry Avenue, Suite 101, Santa Ana, CA 92705
http://www.career-college.net

**CONTACT** Ramona Adams, CEO
**Telephone:** 949-222-1033

**GENERAL INFORMATION** Private Institution. **Total program enrollment:** 17.

**PROGRAM(S) OFFERED**
• **General Office Occupations and Clerical Services** *36 hrs./$6950* • **Legal Support Services, Other** *36 hrs./$6950* • **Medical Administrative/Executive Assistant and Medical Secretary** *36 hrs./$7200*

**STUDENT SERVICES** Academic or career counseling, placement services for program completers.

## ATI College

12440 Firestone Boulevard, Suite 2001, Norwalk, CA 90650
http://www.ati.edu/

**CONTACT** Lisa Jee, Executive Director
**Telephone:** 562-864-0506 Ext. 10

**GENERAL INFORMATION** Private Institution. **Total program enrollment:** 106. **Application fee:** $75.

**PROGRAM(S) OFFERED**
• **Aesthetician/Esthetician and Skin Care Specialist** *26 hrs./$5200*
• **Cardiovascular Technology/Technologist** *84 hrs./$27,025* • **Computer Programming/Programmer, General** • **Computer Systems Networking and Telecommunications** *36 hrs./$12,015* • **Cosmetology/Cosmetologist, General** *66 hrs./$9425* • **Diagnostic Medical Sonography/Sonographer and Ultrasound Technician** *84 hrs./$26,425* • **Medical Office Assistant/Specialist** *30 hrs./$5495* • **Systems Engineering**

**STUDENT SERVICES** Placement services for program completers.

## ATI College–SantaAna

1125 East 17th Street, Suite N251, Santa Ana, CA 92701
http://www.ati.edu

**CONTACT** Myung Jong Kim, CEO/President
**Telephone:** 714-730-7080

**GENERAL INFORMATION** Private Institution. **Total program enrollment:** 47. **Application fee:** $75.

**PROGRAM(S) OFFERED**
• **Diagnostic Medical Sonography/Sonographer and Ultrasound Technician** *84 hrs./$26,425*

**STUDENT SERVICES** Placement services for program completers.

## Avalon Beauty College

504 N. Milpas Street, Santa Barbara, CA 93103

**CONTACT** Jenn Johnson, Director
**Telephone:** 801-302-8801 Ext. 1021

**GENERAL INFORMATION** Private Institution. **Total program enrollment:** 104. **Application fee:** $75.

**PROGRAM(S) OFFERED**
• **Cosmetology/Cosmetologist, General** *1600 hrs./$17,925*

**STUDENT SERVICES** Academic or career counseling, employment services for current students, placement services for program completers, remedial services.

## Avance Beauty College

750 Beyer Way, San Diego, CA 92154

**CONTACT** James Duckham, Chief Administrator
**Telephone:** 619-575-1511

**GENERAL INFORMATION** Private Institution. **Total program enrollment:** 69. **Application fee:** $75.

**PROGRAM(S) OFFERED**
• **Cosmetology/Cosmetologist, General** *1600 hrs./$12,400*

**STUDENT SERVICES** Placement services for program completers.

## Bakersfield College

1801 Panorama Drive, Bakersfield, CA 93305-1299
http://www.bakersfieldcollege.edu/

**CONTACT** Dr. Greg A. Chamberlain, President
**Telephone:** 661-395-4011

**GENERAL INFORMATION** Public Institution. Founded 1913. **Accreditation:** Regional (WASC/ACCJC); radiologic technology: radiography (JRCERT). **Total program enrollment:** 6496.

**PROGRAM(S) OFFERED**
• **Accounting** *13 students enrolled* • **Administrative Assistant and Secretarial Science, General** *10 students enrolled* • **Animal/Livestock Husbandry and Production** *1 student enrolled* • **Architectural Technology/Technician** *55 students enrolled* • **Automobile/Automotive Mechanics Technology/Technician** *54 students enrolled* • **Business, Management, Marketing, and Related Support Services, Other** *2 students enrolled* • **Business/Commerce, General** *22 students enrolled* • **Cabinetmaking and Millwork/Millwright** *13 students enrolled* • **Carpentry/Carpenter** *1 student enrolled* • **Child Development** *1 student enrolled* • **Computer Science** *2 students enrolled* • **Construction Trades, General** *1 student enrolled* • **Cooking and Related Culinary Arts, General** *3 students enrolled* • **Criminal Justice/Police Science** *3 students enrolled* • **Drafting and Design Technology/Technician, General** *38 students enrolled* • **Electrical/Electronics Equipment Installation and Repair, General** *6 students enrolled* • **Electrician** *6 students enrolled* • **Emergency Medical Technology/Technician (EMT Paramedic)** • **Fire Science/Firefighting** *22 students enrolled* • **Forestry, General** *1 student enrolled* • **Graphic Design** *5 students enrolled* • **Health/Medical Preparatory Programs, Other** *4 students enrolled* • **Human Services, General** *4 students enrolled* • **Licensed Practical/Vocational Nurse Training (LPN, LVN, Cert, Dipl, AAS)** *27 students enrolled* • **Machine Tool Technology/Machinist** *28 students enrolled* • **Manufacturing Technology/Technician** *15 students enrolled* • **Mass Communication/Media Studies** *128 students enrolled* • **Nurse/Nursing Assistant/Aide and Patient Care Assistant** *47 students enrolled* • **Plumbing Technology/Plumber** *9 students enrolled* • **Real Estate** *2 students enrolled* • **Sheet Metal Technology/Sheetworking** *1 student enrolled* • **Welding Technology/Welder** *25 students enrolled*

**STUDENT SERVICES** Academic or career counseling, daycare for children of students, employment services for current students, placement services for program completers, remedial services.

## Barstow College

2700 Barstow Road, Barstow, CA 92311-6699
http://www.barstow.edu/

**CONTACT** Clifford Brock, President
**Telephone:** 760-252-2411

**GENERAL INFORMATION** Public Institution. Founded 1959. **Accreditation:** Regional (WASC/ACCJC). **Total program enrollment:** 889.

**PROGRAM(S) OFFERED**
• **Accounting** *2 students enrolled* • **Administrative Assistant and Secretarial Science, General** *6 students enrolled* • **Child Development** *9 students enrolled* • **Cosmetology/Cosmetologist, General** *2 students enrolled* • **Criminal Justice/Police Science** *2 students enrolled* • **Electrical/Electronics Equipment Installation and Repair, General** *1 student enrolled* • **Medical/Clinical Assistant** *2 students enrolled* • **Welding Technology/Welder** *1 student enrolled*

**STUDENT SERVICES** Academic or career counseling, employment services for current students, remedial services.

## Bay Vista College of Beauty

1520 Plaza Boulevard, National City, CA 91950
http://www.sandiegobeautyacademy.com/

**CONTACT** Lynelle Lynch, President
**Telephone:** 619-474-6607 Ext. 0

**GENERAL INFORMATION** Private Institution. **Total program enrollment:** 197. **Application fee:** $75.

**PROGRAM(S) OFFERED**
• **Cosmetology/Cosmetologist, General** *1750 hrs./$15,050* • **Make-Up Artist/Specialist** *150 hrs./$3125* • **Nail Technician/Specialist and Manicurist** *600 hrs./$7225*

**STUDENT SERVICES** Employment services for current students, placement services for program completers.

## Berkeley City College

2050 Center Street, Berkeley, CA 94704-5102
http://www.berkeleycitycollege.edu/

**CONTACT** Dr. Betty Inclan, President
**Telephone:** 510-981-2800

**GENERAL INFORMATION** Public Institution. Founded 1974. **Accreditation:** Regional (WASC/ACCJC). **Total program enrollment:** 1220.

**PROGRAM(S) OFFERED**
• **Administrative Assistant and Secretarial Science, General** *1 student enrolled* • **Adult Development and Aging** *1 student enrolled* • **American Sign Language (ASL)** *9 students enrolled* • **Business Administration and Management, General** *1 student enrolled* • **Business/Commerce, General** *1 student enrolled* • **Digital Communication and Media/Multimedia** *9 students enrolled* • **Human Services, General** *4 students enrolled* • **International Business/Trade/Commerce** *2 students enrolled* • **Spanish Language and Literature** *2 students enrolled* • **Tourism and Travel Services Marketing Operations** *14 students enrolled* • **Web Page, Digital/Multimedia and Information Resources Design** *2 students enrolled*

**STUDENT SERVICES** Academic or career counseling, remedial services.

## Bethany University

800 Bethany Drive, Scotts Valley, CA 95066-2820
http://www.bethany.edu/

**CONTACT** Lew Shelton, President
**Telephone:** 831-438-3800

**GENERAL INFORMATION** Private Institution. Founded 1919. **Accreditation:** Regional (WASC/ACSCU). **Total program enrollment:** 419. **Application fee:** $35.

**PROGRAM(S) OFFERED**

• **Substance Abuse/Addiction Counseling** *8 students enrolled*

**STUDENT SERVICES** Academic or career counseling, daycare for children of students, employment services for current students, placement services for program completers, remedial services.

## Bethesda Christian University

730 North Euclid Street, Anaheim, CA 92801
http://www.bcu.edu/

**CONTACT** Dr. John Stetz, President
**Telephone:** 714-517-1945

**GENERAL INFORMATION** Private Institution (Affiliated with Full Gospel World Mission). Founded 1978. **Accreditation:** State accredited or approved. **Total program enrollment:** 277. **Application fee:** $35.

**PROGRAM(S) OFFERED**

• **Early Childhood Education and Teaching** *11 students enrolled*

**STUDENT SERVICES** Academic or career counseling.

## Bridges Academy of Beauty

423 East Main Street, Barstow, CA 92311

**CONTACT** Vicki Bridges, Owner
**Telephone:** 760-256-0515

**GENERAL INFORMATION** Private Institution. **Total program enrollment:** 10. **Application fee:** $75.

**PROGRAM(S) OFFERED**

• **Aesthetician/Esthetician and Skin Care Specialist** *600 hrs./$4183* • **Cosmetology/Cosmetologist, General** *1600 hrs./$9645* • **Nail Technician/Specialist and Manicurist** *400 hrs./$1875*

**STUDENT SERVICES** Placement services for program completers.

## Brownson Technical School

1110 Technology Circle, Suite D, Anaheim, CA 92805
http://brownsontechnicalschool.com/

**CONTACT** Donald P. Brown, Administrator
**Telephone:** 714-774-9443

**GENERAL INFORMATION** Private Institution. Founded 1984. **Total program enrollment:** 48.

**PROGRAM(S) OFFERED**

• **CAD/CADD Drafting and/or Design Technology/Technician** • **Heating, Air Conditioning and Refrigeration Technology/Technician (ACH/ACR/ACHR/HRAC/HVAC/AC Technology)** *600 hrs./$7250* • **Heating, Air Conditioning, Ventilation and Refrigeration Maintenance Technology/Technician (HAC, HACR, HVAC, HVACR)** *780 hrs./$9535*

**STUDENT SERVICES** Academic or career counseling, placement services for program completers.

## Butte College

3536 Butte Campus Drive, Oroville, CA 95965-8399
http://www.butte.edu/

**CONTACT** Dr. Diana J. Van Der Ploeg, President
**Telephone:** 530-895-2511

**GENERAL INFORMATION** Public Institution. Founded 1966. **Accreditation:** Regional (WASC/ACCJC). **Total program enrollment:** 5150.

**PROGRAM(S) OFFERED**

• **Accounting Technology/Technician and Bookkeeping** *16 students enrolled* • **Administrative Assistant and Secretarial Science, General** *45 students enrolled* • **Agribusiness/Agricultural Business Operations** • **Agricultural Mechanics and Equipment/Machine Technology** *6 students enrolled* • **Agriculture, General** *4 students enrolled* • **Animation, Interactive Technology, Video Graphics and Special Effects** • **Apparel and Textile Marketing Management** • **Applied Horticulture/Horticultural Operations, General** • **Automobile/Automotive Mechanics Technology/Technician** • **Building/Home/Construction Inspection/Inspector** *50 students enrolled* • **Business Administration and Management, General** *1 student enrolled* • **Ceramic Arts and Ceramics** *2 students enrolled* • **Child Care Provider/Assistant** *49 students enrolled* • **Child Care and Support Services Management** *37 students enrolled* • **Classics and Languages, Literatures and Linguistics, General** • **Computer Systems Networking and Telecommunications** • **Computer and Information Sciences, General** • **Construction/Heavy Equipment/Earthmoving Equipment Operation** *96 students enrolled* • **Corrections and Criminal Justice, Other** • **Cosmetology/Cosmetologist, General** *20 students enrolled* • **Criminal Justice/Police Science** *70 students enrolled* • **Data Entry/Microcomputer Applications, General** *6 students enrolled* • **Drafting and Design Technology/Technician, General** *2 students enrolled* • **E-Commerce/Electronic Commerce** • **Emergency Medical Technology/Technician (EMT Paramedic)** *15 students enrolled* • **Engineering Technology, General** • **Family and Consumer Sciences/Human Sciences, General** • **Fire Science/Firefighting** *658 students enrolled* • **Floriculture/Floristry Operations and Management** *1 student enrolled* • **Hazardous Materials Management and Waste Technology/Technician** *112 students enrolled* • **Home Health Aide/Home Attendant** • **Information Technology** *50 students enrolled* • **Interior Design** • **Landscaping and Groundskeeping** • **Legal Administrative Assistant/Secretary** *10 students enrolled* • **Licensed Practical/Vocational Nurse Training (LPN, LVN, Cert, Dipl, AAS)** • **Medical Administrative/Executive Assistant and Medical Secretary** *9 students enrolled* • **Natural Resources/Conservation, General** • **Nurse/Nursing Assistant/Aide and Patient Care Assistant** • **Nursing—Registered Nurse Training (RN, ASN, BSN, MSN)** • **Parks, Recreation and Leisure Facilities Management** • **Photography** • **Radio and Television** • **Real Estate** *1 student enrolled* • **Retailing and Retail Operations** • **Sales, Distribution and Marketing Operations, General** *1 student enrolled* • **Small Business Administration/Management** • **Substance Abuse/Addiction Counseling** *12 students enrolled* • **System Administration/Administrator** • **Taxation** • **Tourism and Travel Services Marketing Operations** *8 students enrolled* • **Welding Technology/Welder**

**STUDENT SERVICES** Academic or career counseling, daycare for children of students, employment services for current students, remedial services.

## Cabrillo College

6500 Soquel Drive, Aptos, CA 95003-3194
http://www.cabrillo.edu/

**CONTACT** Brian King, Superintendent/President
**Telephone:** 831-479-6100

**GENERAL INFORMATION** Public Institution. Founded 1959. **Accreditation:** Regional (WASC/ACCJC); dental hygiene (ADA); medical assisting (AAMAE); radiologic technology: radiography (JRCERT). **Total program enrollment:** 4069.

**PROGRAM(S) OFFERED**

• **Accounting** *21 students enrolled* • **Administrative Assistant and Secretarial Science, General** *15 students enrolled* • **Animation, Interactive Technology, Video Graphics and Special Effects** • **Applied Horticulture/Horticultural Operations, General** *5 students enrolled* • **Archeology** *3 students enrolled* • **Architectural Drafting and Architectural CAD/CADD** • **Building/Construction Site Management/Manager** *5 students enrolled* • **Building/Home/Construction Inspection/Inspector** *10 students enrolled* • **Business/Commerce, General** • **Child Development** *31 students enrolled* • **Civil Drafting and Civil Engineering CAD/CADD** *2 students enrolled* • **Clinical/Medical Laboratory Technician** *5 students enrolled* • **Computer Graphics** • **Computer Programming/Programmer, General** *4 students enrolled* • **Computer Systems Networking and Telecommunications** *9 students enrolled* • **Cooking and Related Culinary Arts, General** *4 students enrolled* • **Corrections and Criminal Justice, Other** • **Data Modeling/Warehousing and Database Administration** • **Digital Communication and Media/Multimedia** *8 students enrolled* • **Drafting and Design Technology/Technician, General** *1 student enrolled* • **E-Commerce/Electronic Commerce** • **Electrocardiograph Technology/Technician** • **Emergency Medical Technology/Technician (EMT Paramedic)** • **Engineering Technology, General** • **Fire Science/Firefighting** • **Human Services, General** *5 students enrolled* • **Journalism** • **Landscaping and Groundskeeping** • **Manufacturing Technology/Technician** • **Medical Administrative/Executive Assistant and Medical Secretary** *5 students enrolled* • **Medical/Clinical Assistant** *20 students enrolled* • **Phlebotomy/Phlebotomist** • **Plant Nursery Operations and Man-**

*Cabrillo College (continued)*

**agement • Radiologic Technology/Science—Radiographer • Real Estate • System Administration/Administrator** *1 student enrolled* **• Web Page, Digital/ Multimedia and Information Resources Design** *5 students enrolled* **• Welding Technology/Welder** *5 students enrolled*

**STUDENT SERVICES** Academic or career counseling, daycare for children of students, employment services for current students, placement services for program completers, remedial services.

## California Beauty College

1115 15th Street, Modesto, CA 95354

**CONTACT** Donna McElroy, Director
**Telephone:** 209-524-5184 Ext. 216

**GENERAL INFORMATION** Private Institution. Founded 1961. **Total program enrollment:** 53. **Application fee:** $25.

**PROGRAM(S) OFFERED**
**• Cosmetology/Cosmetologist, General** *1600 hrs./$13,435* **• Nail Technician/ Specialist and Manicurist** *400 hrs./$4100*

**STUDENT SERVICES** Academic or career counseling, placement services for program completers.

## California Career College

7108 De Soto Avenue, Suite 207, Canoga Park, CA 91303

**GENERAL INFORMATION** Private Institution. **Application fee:** $50.

**PROGRAM(S) OFFERED**
**• Licensed Practical/Vocational Nurse Training (LPN, LVN, Cert, Dipl, AAS)** *1600 hrs.*

## California Career Schools

1100 Technology Circle, Anaheim, CA 92805-6550
http://californiacareerschool.edu/

**CONTACT** Chuck Emanuele, President
**Telephone:** 714-635-6585

**GENERAL INFORMATION** Private Institution. Founded 1970. **Total program enrollment:** 334.

**PROGRAM(S) OFFERED**
**• Automobile/Automotive Mechanics Technology/Technician** *600 hrs./$6255* **• Machine Tool Technology/Machinist** *6 students enrolled* **• Precision Production Trades, General** *720 hrs./$7185* **• Security and Loss Prevention Services** *500 hrs./$4313* **• Truck and Bus Driver/Commercial Vehicle Operation** *80 hrs./ $2520* **• Vehicle Emissions Inspection and Maintenance Technology/ Technician** *21 students enrolled*

**STUDENT SERVICES** Academic or career counseling, placement services for program completers.

## California College of Vocational Careers

2822 F Street, Suite L, Bakersfield, CA 93301
http://www.californiacollegevc.com/

**CONTACT** Rudy Fernandez
**Telephone:** 661-323-6791

**GENERAL INFORMATION** Private Institution. **Total program enrollment:** 71. **Application fee:** $200.

**PROGRAM(S) OFFERED**
**• Allied Health and Medical Assisting Services, Other** *41 students enrolled* **• Dental Assisting/Assistant** *752 hrs./$11,856* **• Medical/Clinical Assistant** *720 hrs./$12,330*

**STUDENT SERVICES** Academic or career counseling, employment services for current students, placement services for program completers, remedial services.

## California Community Colleges System

1102 Q Street, Fourth Floor, Sacramento, CA 95814-3607

**CONTACT** Mark Drummond, Chancellor
**Telephone:** 213-891-2000

**GENERAL INFORMATION** Public Institution.

## California Cosmetology College

955 Monroe Street, Santa Clara, CA 95050
http://www.cacosmetologycollege.com/

**CONTACT** Dr. Nagui Elyas, President
**Telephone:** 408-247-2200

**GENERAL INFORMATION** Private Institution. Founded 1968. **Total program enrollment:** 103.

**PROGRAM(S) OFFERED**
**• Aesthetician/Esthetician and Skin Care Specialist** *600 hrs./$8475* **• Cosmetology/Cosmetologist, General** *1600 hrs./$10,945*

**STUDENT SERVICES** Academic or career counseling, placement services for program completers.

## California Culinary Academy

625 Polk Street, San Francisco, CA 94102-3368
http://www.baychef.com/

**CONTACT** Jennifer White, President
**Telephone:** 415-771-3500

**GENERAL INFORMATION** Private Institution. Founded 1977. **Accreditation:** State accredited or approved. **Total program enrollment:** 821. **Application fee:** $65.

**PROGRAM(S) OFFERED**
**• Baking and Pastry Arts/Baker/Pastry Chef** *42 hrs./$23,500* **• Culinary Arts/ Chef Training** *61 hrs./$46,886* **• Hospitality Administration/Management, General** *65 hrs./$32,000*

**STUDENT SERVICES** Academic or career counseling, employment services for current students, placement services for program completers.

## California Hair Design Academy

5315 El Cajon Boulevard, San Diego, CA 92115

**CONTACT** Len Steinbarth, President
**Telephone:** 619-461-8600

**GENERAL INFORMATION** Private Institution. **Total program enrollment:** 189. **Application fee:** $75.

**PROGRAM(S) OFFERED**
**• Aesthetician/Esthetician and Skin Care Specialist** *600 hrs./$6195* **• Cosmetology, Barber/Styling, and Nail Instructor • Cosmetology/ Cosmetologist, General** *1600 hrs./$11,995* **• Nail Technician/Specialist and Manicurist** *400 hrs./$3375* **• Trade and Industrial Teacher Education** *600 hrs./ $5995*

**STUDENT SERVICES** Academic or career counseling, placement services for program completers, remedial services.

## California Healing Arts College

12217 Santa Monica Boulevard, Suite 206, West Los Angeles, CA 90025
http://www.chac.edu/

**CONTACT** Dr. Paul Schwinghamer, President/Director
**Telephone:** 310-826-7622

**GENERAL INFORMATION** Private Institution. **Total program enrollment:** 129. **Application fee:** $50.

**PROGRAM(S) OFFERED**
• **Massage Therapy/Therapeutic Massage** *33 hrs./$15,430*

**STUDENT SERVICES** Academic or career counseling, employment services for current students, placement services for program completers.

## California Lutheran University

60 West Olsen Road, Thousand Oaks, CA 91360-2787
http://www.callutheran.edu/

**CONTACT** Dr. Christopher Kimball, President
**Telephone:** 805-492-2411

**GENERAL INFORMATION** Private Institution. Founded 1959. **Accreditation:** Regional (WASC/ACSCU). **Total program enrollment:** 2844. **Application fee:** $45.

**STUDENT SERVICES** Academic or career counseling, employment services for current students, placement services for program completers.

## California School of Culinary Arts

521 East Green Street, Pasadena, CA 91101
http://www.csca.edu/

**CONTACT** Anthony Bondi, President
**Telephone:** 626-229-1300

**GENERAL INFORMATION** Private Institution. Founded 1994. **Total program enrollment:** 1682. **Application fee:** $75.

**PROGRAM(S) OFFERED**
• **Baking and Pastry Arts/Baker/Pastry Chef** *39 hrs./$25,920* • **Cooking and Related Culinary Arts, General** *40 hrs./$21,950* • **Culinary Arts/Chef Training** *90 hrs./$48,432* • **Hospitality Administration/Management, General** *90 hrs./$32,940* • **Restaurant/Food Services Management** *39 students enrolled*

**STUDENT SERVICES** Academic or career counseling, employment services for current students, placement services for program completers, remedial services.

## Cambridge Career College

990-A Klamath Lane, Yuba City, CA 95993
http://cambridge.edu/

**CONTACT** Tonya Flores, Director
**Telephone:** 530-674-9199

**GENERAL INFORMATION** Private Institution. **Total program enrollment:** 150. **Application fee:** $100.

**PROGRAM(S) OFFERED**
• **Accounting** *99 hrs./$22,670* • **Administrative Assistant and Secretarial Science, General** *48 hrs./$13,975* • **Business/Office Automation/Technology/Data Entry** *14 students enrolled* • **Medical Office Assistant/Specialist** *480 hrs./$8435*

**STUDENT SERVICES** Academic or career counseling, employment services for current students, placement services for program completers.

## Cañada College

4200 Farm Hill Boulevard, Redwood City, CA 94061-1099
http://www.canadacollege.net/

**CONTACT** Tom Mohr, President
**Telephone:** 650-306-3100

**GENERAL INFORMATION** Public Institution. Founded 1968. **Accreditation:** Regional (WASC/ACCJC); radiologic technology: radiography (JRCERT). **Total program enrollment:** 1156.

**PROGRAM(S) OFFERED**
• **Accounting** *7 students enrolled* • **Administrative Assistant and Secretarial Science, General** *5 students enrolled* • **Child Development** *93 students enrolled* • **Digital Communication and Media/Multimedia** *1 student enrolled* • **Fashion/Apparel Design** *2 students enrolled* • **Health Information/Medical Records Technology/Technician** *8 students enrolled* • **Human Services, General** *24 students enrolled* • **Interior Design** *1 student enrolled* • **Legal Assistant/Paralegal** *17 students enrolled* • **Medical/Clinical Assistant** *7 students enrolled* • **Real Estate** *1 student enrolled* • **Small Business Administration/Management** *1 student enrolled*

**STUDENT SERVICES** Academic or career counseling, employment services for current students, remedial services.

## Career Academy of Beauty

663 North Euclid Avenue, Anaheim, CA 92801
http://beautycareers.com/

**CONTACT** Dayna Pattison, Director
**Telephone:** 714-776-8400

**GENERAL INFORMATION** Private Institution. **Total program enrollment:** 18.

**PROGRAM(S) OFFERED**
• **Aesthetician/Esthetician and Skin Care Specialist** *600 hrs./$7170*
• **Cosmetology and Related Personal Grooming Arts, Other** *400 hrs./$2200*
• **Cosmetology, Barber/Styling, and Nail Instructor** *600 hrs./$2200*
• **Cosmetology/Cosmetologist, General** *160 hrs./$15,486*

**STUDENT SERVICES** Academic or career counseling, employment services for current students, placement services for program completers, remedial services.

## Career Academy of Beauty

12375 Seal Beach Boulevard, Seal Beach, CA 90740
http://beautycareers.com/

**CONTACT** Dayna Pattison, Financial Aid Director
**Telephone:** 714-897-3010 Ext. 106

**GENERAL INFORMATION** Private Institution. Founded 1968. **Total program enrollment:** 54.

**PROGRAM(S) OFFERED**
• **Aesthetician/Esthetician and Skin Care Specialist** *600 hrs./$7170*
• **Cosmetology and Related Personal Grooming Arts, Other** *400 hrs./$2200*
• **Cosmetology, Barber/Styling, and Nail Instructor** *600 hrs./$2200*
• **Cosmetology/Cosmetologist, General** *160 hrs./$15,486* • **Nail Technician/Specialist and Manicurist** *37 students enrolled*

**STUDENT SERVICES** Academic or career counseling, employment services for current students, placement services for program completers, remedial services.

## Career Care Institute

43770 Fifteenth Street W., Suite 205, Lancaster, CA 93534
http://www.careercareinstitute.com/

**CONTACT** Edmund Carrasco, Owner/Director
**Telephone:** 661-942-6204

**GENERAL INFORMATION** Private Institution. **Total program enrollment:** 255. **Application fee:** $80.

**PROGRAM(S) OFFERED**
• **Allied Health and Medical Assisting Services, Other** *720 hrs./$9450* • **Clinical/Medical Laboratory Technician** *768 hrs./$14,388* • **Dental Assisting/Assistant** *720 hrs./$8023* • **Licensed Practical/Vocational Nurse Training (LPN, LVN, Cert, Dipl, AAS)** *1564 hrs./$25,111* • **Massage Therapy/Therapeutic Massage** *720 hrs./$11,160* • **Medical Insurance Coding Specialist/Coder** *720 hrs./$9490* • **Medical Insurance Specialist/Medical Biller** *10 students enrolled* • **Medical/Clinical Assistant** *26 students enrolled*

**STUDENT SERVICES** Placement services for program completers, remedial services.

## Career College Consultants

5015 Eagle Rock Boulevard, Suite 302, Los Angeles, CA 90041
http://www.sticcc.com

**CONTACT** David Montoya, President
**Telephone:** 323-254-2203

**GENERAL INFORMATION** Private Institution. **Total program enrollment:** 50. **Application fee:** $75.

**PROGRAM(S) OFFERED**
• **Medical Insurance Coding Specialist/Coder** • **Office Management and Supervision**

**STUDENT SERVICES** Academic or career counseling, placement services for program completers.

## Career College of America

5612 E. Imperial Highway, South Gate, CA 90280
http://careercolleges.org/

**CONTACT** Avi Paladino, Director of Operations
**Telephone:** 562-861-8702

**GENERAL INFORMATION** Private Institution. **Total program enrollment:** 417. **Application fee:** $100.

**PROGRAM(S) OFFERED**
• **Administrative Assistant and Secretarial Science, General** *3 students enrolled* • **Diagnostic Medical Sonography/Sonographer and Ultrasound Technician** *56 hrs./$34,928* • **Licensed Practical/Vocational Nurse Training (LPN, LVN, Cert, Dipl, AAS)** *52 hrs./$33,250* • **Medical Insurance Specialist/Medical Biller** *24 hrs./$12,980* • **Medical/Clinical Assistant** *24 hrs./$12,630* • **Pharmacy Technician/Assistant** *25 hrs./$13,080* • **Surgical Technology/Technologist** *54 hrs./$27,115*

**STUDENT SERVICES** Academic or career counseling, employment services for current students, placement services for program completers.

## Career College of San Diego

3350 Market Street, Suite C, San Diego, CA 92102

**GENERAL INFORMATION** Private Institution. **Total program enrollment:** 26.

**PROGRAM(S) OFFERED**
• **Clinical/Medical Laboratory Assistant** *9 students enrolled* • **Data Entry/Microcomputer Applications, General** *32 hrs./$7165* • **Medical/Clinical Assistant** *32 hrs./$7800*

**STUDENT SERVICES** Academic or career counseling, placement services for program completers.

## Career Networks Institute

3420 Bristol Street, Suite 209, Costa Mesa, CA 92626
http://www.cnicollege.edu/

**CONTACT** James Buffington, President
**Telephone:** 714-437-9697

**GENERAL INFORMATION** Private Institution. **Total program enrollment:** 606.

**PROGRAM(S) OFFERED**
• **Athletic Training/Trainer** *24 hrs./$12,383* • **Health Information/Medical Records Administration/Administrator** *24 hrs./$9100* • **Health Professions and Related Clinical Sciences, Other** *24 hrs./$11,664* • **Licensed Practical/Vocational Nurse Training (LPN, LVN, Cert, Dipl, AAS)** *52 hrs./$31,768* • **Massage Therapy/Therapeutic Massage** *24 hrs./$11,558* • **Medical Administrative/Executive Assistant and Medical Secretary** *1 student enrolled* • **Medical/Clinical Assistant** *24 hrs./$9175* • **Surgical Technology/Technologist** *25 students enrolled*

**STUDENT SERVICES** Placement services for program completers.

## Casa Loma College–Van Nuys

6850 Van Nuys Boulevard, Suite 318, Van Nuys, CA 91405
http://www.casalomacollege.edu/

**CONTACT** V. Gregory Malone, Chief Executive Officer
**Telephone:** 818-785-2726

**GENERAL INFORMATION** Private Institution. **Total program enrollment:** 598. **Application fee:** $100.

**PROGRAM(S) OFFERED**
• **Allied Health and Medical Assisting Services, Other** *66 hrs./$7598* • **Diagnostic Medical Sonography/Sonographer and Ultrasound Technician** *125 hrs./$29,175* • **Fire Protection and Safety Technology/Technician** *66 hrs./$13,900* • **Licensed Practical/Vocational Nurse Training (LPN, LVN, Cert, Dipl, AAS)** *1531 hrs./$25,870* • **Medical Insurance Specialist/Medical Biller** *69 hrs./$7598* • **Medical/Clinical Assistant** *33 students enrolled* • **Radiologic Technology/Science—Radiographer** *68 hrs./$26,338*

**STUDENT SERVICES** Academic or career counseling, employment services for current students, placement services for program completers, remedial services.

## Center for Employment Training–Coachella

49-111 Highway 111, Suite 5, Coachella, CA 92236

**CONTACT** Mirna Flores, Director
**Telephone:** 408-287-7924

**GENERAL INFORMATION** Private Institution. **Total program enrollment:** 64.

**PROGRAM(S) OFFERED**
• **Administrative Assistant and Secretarial Science, General** *900 hrs./$8864* • **Building/Property Maintenance and Management** *900 hrs./$8864* • **Heating, Air Conditioning, Ventilation and Refrigeration Maintenance Technology/Technician (HAC, HACR, HVAC, HVACR)** *810 hrs./$8270*

**STUDENT SERVICES** Academic or career counseling, employment services for current students, placement services for program completers, remedial services.

## Center for Employment Training–El Centro

294 South 3rd Street, El Centro, CA 92243

**CONTACT** Judy Siquieros, Director
**Telephone:** 408-287-7924

**GENERAL INFORMATION** Private Institution. **Total program enrollment:** 320.

**PROGRAM(S) OFFERED**
• **Accounting and Related Services, Other** *42 students enrolled* • **Accounting** *900 hrs./$8864* • **Building/Property Maintenance and Management** *900 hrs./$8864* • **Retailing and Retail Operations** *630 hrs./$7083* • **Truck and Bus Driver/Commercial Vehicle Operation** *630 hrs./$8361* • **Welding Technology/Welder** *900 hrs./$8864*

**STUDENT SERVICES** Academic or career counseling, employment services for current students, placement services for program completers, remedial services.

## Center for Employment Training–Gilroy

7800 Arroyo Circle, Gilroy, CA 95020

**CONTACT** Vernice Estrada, Director
**Telephone:** 408-287-7924

**GENERAL INFORMATION** Private Institution. **Total program enrollment:** 162.

**PROGRAM(S) OFFERED**
• **Accounting** *900 hrs./$8864* • **Building/Property Maintenance and Management** *900 hrs./$8864* • **Construction Trades, Other** *720 hrs./$7676* • **Health/Health Care Administration/Management** *720 hrs./$7676* • **Medical Administrative/Executive Assistant and Medical Secretary** *27 students enrolled* • **Truck and Bus Driver/Commercial Vehicle Operation** *630 hrs./$8361*

**STUDENT SERVICES** Academic or career counseling, employment services for current students, placement services for program completers, remedial services.

## Center for Employment Training–Oxnard

730 South A Street, Oxnard, CA 93030

**CONTACT** Johnny Rodriguez, Director
**Telephone:** 408-287-7924

**GENERAL INFORMATION** Private Institution. Founded 1967. **Total program enrollment:** 131.

**PROGRAM(S) OFFERED**
• **Building/Property Maintenance and Management** *900 hrs./$8864* • **Business/Office Automation/Technology/Data Entry** *900 hrs./$8864* • **Machine Shop Technology/Assistant** *900 hrs./$8864* • **Machine Tool Technology/Machinist** *500 hrs./$6226* • **Medical/Clinical Assistant** *900 hrs./$8864* • **Truck and Bus Driver/Commercial Vehicle Operation** *630 hrs./$8361*

**STUDENT SERVICES** Academic or career counseling, employment services for current students, placement services for program completers, remedial services.

## Center for Employment Training–Riverside

9960 Indiana Avenue, Suite # 9, Riverside, CA 92503

**CONTACT** Pat Pendergraph, Director
**Telephone:** 408-287-7924

**GENERAL INFORMATION** Private Institution. **Total program enrollment:** 138.

**PROGRAM(S) OFFERED**
• **Building/Property Maintenance and Management** *900 hrs./$8864* • **Heating, Air Conditioning, Ventilation and Refrigeration Maintenance Technology/Technician (HAC, HACR, HVAC, HVACR)** *810 hrs./$8270* • **Machine Shop Technology/Assistant** *900 hrs./$8864* • **Machine Tool Technology/Machinist** *500 hrs./$6226* • **Precision Metal Working, Other** • **Welding Technology/Welder** *900 hrs./$8864*

**STUDENT SERVICES** Academic or career counseling, employment services for current students, placement services for program completers, remedial services.

## Center for Employment Training–Salinas

421 Monterey Street, Salinas, CA 93901

**CONTACT** Diana Carillo, Director
**Telephone:** 408-287-7924

**GENERAL INFORMATION** Private Institution. **Total program enrollment:** 189.

**PROGRAM(S) OFFERED**
• **Building/Property Maintenance and Management** *900 hrs./$8864* • **Business/Office Automation/Technology/Data Entry** *900 hrs./$8864* • **Computer and Information Sciences and Support Services, Other** *420 hrs./$5700* • **Construction Trades, Other** *720 hrs./$7676* • **Data Processing and Data Processing Technology/Technician** • **Health and Medical Administrative Services, Other** *720 hrs./$7676* • **Medical Administrative/Executive Assistant and Medical Secretary** *33 students enrolled* • **Transportation and Materials Moving, Other** *720 hrs./$7676*

**STUDENT SERVICES** Academic or career counseling, employment services for current students, placement services for program completers, remedial services.

## Center for Employment Training–San Diego

3295 Market Street, San Diego, CA 92102

**CONTACT** Dora Mendivil, Director
**Telephone:** 408-287-7924

**GENERAL INFORMATION** Private Institution. **Total program enrollment:** 153.

**PROGRAM(S) OFFERED**
• **Building/Property Maintenance and Management** *900 hrs./$8864* • **Medical/Clinical Assistant** *900 hrs./$8864* • **Welding Technology/Welder** *900 hrs./$8864*

**STUDENT SERVICES** Academic or career counseling, employment services for current students, placement services for program completers, remedial services.

## Center for Employment Training–Santa Maria

509 West Morrison, Santa Maria, CA 93454

**CONTACT** Gabriel Morales, Director
**Telephone:** 408-287-7924

**GENERAL INFORMATION** Private Institution. **Total program enrollment:** 114.

**PROGRAM(S) OFFERED**
• **Building/Property Maintenance and Management** *900 hrs./$8864* • **Business/Office Automation/Technology/Data Entry** *900 hrs./$8864* • **Computer and Information Sciences and Support Services, Other** *420 hrs./$5700* • **Electrical and Power Transmission Installers, Other** • **Medical/Clinical Assistant** *900 hrs./$8864* • **Truck and Bus Driver/Commercial Vehicle Operation** *630 hrs./$8361*

**STUDENT SERVICES** Academic or career counseling, employment services for current students, placement services for program completers, remedial services.

## Center for Employment Training–Sobrato

701 Vine Street, San Jose, CA 95110

**CONTACT** Elsa Garcia De Leon, Director
**Telephone:** 408-287-7924

**GENERAL INFORMATION** Private Institution. **Total program enrollment:** 419.

*Center for Employment Training–Sobrato (continued)*

**PROGRAM(S) OFFERED**

• **Accounting and Related Services, Other** *12 students enrolled* • **Accounting** *1 student enrolled* • **Building/Property Maintenance and Management** *900 hrs./$8864* • **Business/Office Automation/Technology/Data Entry** • **Child Care Provider/Assistant** *900 hrs./$8864* • **Culinary Arts and Related Services, Other** *810 hrs./$9810* • **Electrical and Power Transmission Installers, Other** *13 students enrolled* • **Graphic Communications, Other** *7 students enrolled* • **Mechanic and Repair Technologies/Technicians, Other** *810 hrs./$8270* • **Medical Administrative/Executive Assistant and Medical Secretary** *720 hrs./$7676* • **Medical/Clinical Assistant** *900 hrs./$8864* • **Transportation and Materials Moving, Other**

**STUDENT SERVICES** Academic or career counseling, daycare for children of students, employment services for current students, placement services for program completers, remedial services.

## Center for Employment Training–Temecula

42066 Avenida Alvarado, Unit A, Temecula, CA 92390

**CONTACT** Alicia Ramirez, Director
**Telephone:** 408-287-7924

**GENERAL INFORMATION** Private Institution. **Total program enrollment:** 32.

**PROGRAM(S) OFFERED**

• **Accounting and Related Services, Other** *605 hrs./$6919* • **Accounting** *900 hrs./$8864* • **Business, Management, Marketing, and Related Support Services, Other** • **Business/Office Automation/Technology/Data Entry** *900 hrs./$8864* • **Computer and Information Sciences and Support Services, Other** *420 hrs./$5700* • **Ground Transportation, Other** *330 hrs./$5106* • **Transportation and Materials Moving, Other** *720 hrs./$7676*

**STUDENT SERVICES** Academic or career counseling, employment services for current students, placement services for program completers, remedial services.

## Center for Employment Training–Watsonville

10 Blanca Lane, Watsonville, CA 95076

**CONTACT** Alia Ayyad, Director
**Telephone:** 408-287-7924

**GENERAL INFORMATION** Private Institution. **Total program enrollment:** 157.

**PROGRAM(S) OFFERED**

• **Building/Property Maintenance and Management** *900 hrs./$8864* • **Construction Trades, Other** *720 hrs./$7676* • **Health/Health Care Administration/Management** *720 hrs./$7676* • **Medical Office Assistant/Specialist** *22 students enrolled* • **Welding Technology/Welder** *900 hrs./$8864*

**STUDENT SERVICES** Academic or career counseling, employment services for current students, placement services for program completers, remedial services.

## Central California School

3195 McMillan, Suite F, San Luis Obispo, CA 93401
http://ccsce.org/

**CONTACT** Gene Appleby, Administrator
**Telephone:** 805-543-9123

**GENERAL INFORMATION** Private Institution. Founded 1989. **Total program enrollment:** 200.

**PROGRAM(S) OFFERED**

• **Dental Assisting/Assistant** *8 students enrolled* • **Medical Radiologic Technology/Science—Radiation Therapist** *51 students enrolled* • **Medical/Clinical Assistant** *4 students enrolled*

**STUDENT SERVICES** Academic or career counseling, placement services for program completers.

## Central Coast College of Business Data Processing

480 South Main Street, Salinas, CA 93901
http://www.centralcoastcollege.edu/

**CONTACT** Robert H. Schaefer, President
**Telephone:** 831-424-6767

**GENERAL INFORMATION** Private Institution. Founded 1983. **Total program enrollment:** 191. **Application fee:** $75.

**PROGRAM(S) OFFERED**

• **Accounting Technology/Technician and Bookkeeping** *28 hrs./$9360* • **Administrative Assistant and Secretarial Science, General** *42 hrs./$11,375* • **Medical Insurance Specialist/Medical Biller** *36 hrs./$10,920* • **Medical Office Assistant/Specialist** *33 hrs./$9360* • **Medical/Clinical Assistant** *37 hrs./$11,940* • **Pharmacy Technician/Assistant** *30 hrs./$10,920*

**STUDENT SERVICES** Academic or career counseling, employment services for current students, placement services for program completers, remedial services.

## Cerritos College

11110 Alondra Boulevard, Norwalk, CA 90650-6298
http://www.cerritos.edu/

**CONTACT** William Farmer, Acting President
**Telephone:** 562-860-2451

**GENERAL INFORMATION** Public Institution. Founded 1956. **Accreditation:** Regional (WASC/ACCJC); dental assisting (ADA); dental hygiene (ADA); physical therapy assisting (APTA). **Total program enrollment:** 6931.

**PROGRAM(S) OFFERED**

• **Accounting** *3 students enrolled* • **Administrative Assistant and Secretarial Science, General** *1 student enrolled* • **Architectural Technology/Technician** *6 students enrolled* • **Audiology/Audiologist and Speech-Language Pathology/Pathologist** *3 students enrolled* • **Autobody/Collision and Repair Technology/Technician** *7 students enrolled* • **Automobile/Automotive Mechanics Technology/Technician** *39 students enrolled* • **Business Administration and Management, General** *10 students enrolled* • **Cabinetmaking and Millwork/Millwright** *4 students enrolled* • **Child Development** *8 students enrolled* • **Computer Systems Analysis/Analyst** *1 student enrolled* • **Computer Systems Networking and Telecommunications** *3 students enrolled* • **Cooking and Related Culinary Arts, General** *7 students enrolled* • **Cosmetology/Cosmetologist, General** *29 students enrolled* • **Dental Assisting/Assistant** *8 students enrolled* • **Drafting and Design Technology/Technician, General** *6 students enrolled* • **Education/Teaching of Individuals in Early Childhood Special Education Programs** *2 students enrolled* • **Electrical/Electronics Equipment Installation and Repair, General** *3 students enrolled* • **Emergency Medical Technology/Technician (EMT Paramedic)** • **Human Services, General** *3 students enrolled* • **Industrial Electronics Technology/Technician** *1 student enrolled* • **Legal Administrative Assistant/Secretary** *1 student enrolled* • **Legal Assistant/Paralegal** *24 students enrolled* • **Machine Tool Technology/Machinist** *11 students enrolled* • **Medical/Clinical Assistant** *12 students enrolled* • **Pharmacy Technician/Assistant** *11 students enrolled* • **Plastics Engineering Technology/Technician** *2 students enrolled* • **Real Estate** *9 students enrolled* • **Retailing and Retail Operations** *1 student enrolled* • **Selling Skills and Sales Operations** *1 student enrolled* • **Sport and Fitness Administration/Management** *2 students enrolled* • **Welding Technology/Welder** *7 students enrolled*

**STUDENT SERVICES** Academic or career counseling, daycare for children of students, employment services for current students, placement services for program completers, remedial services.

## Cerro Coso Community College

3000 College Heights Boulevard, Ridgecrest, CA 93555-9571
http://www.cerrocoso.edu/

**CONTACT** Dr. Mary Retterer, President
**Telephone:** 760-384-6100

**GENERAL INFORMATION** Public Institution. Founded 1973. **Accreditation:** Regional (WASC/ACCJC). **Total program enrollment:** 1310.

**PROGRAM(S) OFFERED**

• **Animation, Interactive Technology, Video Graphics and Special Effects** *2 students enrolled* • **Business Administration and Management, General** *4 students enrolled* • **Child Development** *2 students enrolled* • **Criminal Justice/Police Science** *8 students enrolled* • **Emergency Medical Technology/Technician (EMT Paramedic)** • **Legal Assistant/Paralegal** *2 students enrolled* • **Licensed Practical/Vocational Nurse Training (LPN, LVN, Cert, Dipl, AAS)** *1 student enrolled* • **Medical/Clinical Assistant** • **Nurse/Nursing Assistant/Aide and Patient Care Assistant** • **Web Page, Digital/Multimedia and Information Resources Design** *1 student enrolled*

**STUDENT SERVICES** Academic or career counseling, daycare for children of students, employment services for current students, placement services for program completers, remedial services.

## CET–Sacramento

6853 65th Street, Sacramento, CA 95828

**CONTACT** Thomas Anderson, Center Director
**Telephone:** 408-287-7924

**GENERAL INFORMATION** Private Institution. **Total program enrollment:** 179.

**PROGRAM(S) OFFERED**

• **Accounting and Related Services, Other** • **Accounting** • **Automobile/Automotive Mechanics Technology/Technician** *810 hrs./$8270* • **Business/Office Automation/Technology/Data Entry** *900 hrs./$8864* • **Computer and Information Sciences and Support Services, Other** *420 hrs./$5700* • **Heating, Air Conditioning, Ventilation and Refrigeration Maintenance Technology/Technician (HAC, HACR, HVAC, HVACR)** *810 hrs./$8270* • **Medical/Clinical Assistant** *900 hrs./$8864* • **Precision Systems Maintenance and Repair Technologies, Other** • **Truck and Bus Driver/Commercial Vehicle Operation** *630 hrs./$8361*

**STUDENT SERVICES** Academic or career counseling, employment services for current students, placement services for program completers, remedial services.

## Chabot College

25555 Hesperian Boulevard, Hayward, CA 94545-5001
http://www.chabotcollege.edu/

**CONTACT** Dr. Celia Barberena, President
**Telephone:** 510-723-6600

**GENERAL INFORMATION** Public Institution. Founded 1961. **Accreditation:** Regional (WASC/ACCJC); dental hygiene (ADA); health information technology (AHIMA); medical assisting (AAMAE). **Total program enrollment:** 3427.

**PROGRAM(S) OFFERED**

• **Accounting** *11 students enrolled* • **Administrative Assistant and Secretarial Science, General** *19 students enrolled* • **Automobile/Automotive Mechanics Technology/Technician** *3 students enrolled* • **Child Development** *72 students enrolled* • **Commercial Photography** *2 students enrolled* • **Commercial and Advertising Art** *3 students enrolled* • **Computer Installation and Repair Technology/Technician** *2 students enrolled* • **Computer and Information Sciences, General** *1 student enrolled* • **Data Entry/Microcomputer Applications, General** *1 student enrolled* • **Electrical/Electronics Equipment Installation and Repair, General** *1 student enrolled* • **Fire Science/Firefighting** *3 students enrolled* • **Graphic Design** *2 students enrolled* • **Human Services, General** *4 students enrolled* • **Interior Design** *2 students enrolled* • **Machine Tool Technology/Machinist** *5 students enrolled* • **Medical Insurance Coding Specialist/Coder** *1 student enrolled* • **Medical/Clinical Assistant** *1 student enrolled* • **Office Management and Supervision** *15 students enrolled* • **Public Administration and Social Service Professions, Other** *3 students enrolled* • **Real Estate** *4 students enrolled* • **Retailing and Retail Operations** *8 students enrolled* • **Sales, Distribution and Marketing Operations, General** *2 students enrolled* • **Small Business Administration/Management** *1 student enrolled* • **Sport and Fitness Administration/Management** *4 students enrolled* • **Tourism and Travel Services Marketing Operations** *1 student enrolled* • **Welding Technology/Welder** *2 students enrolled*

**STUDENT SERVICES** Academic or career counseling, daycare for children of students, employment services for current students, placement services for program completers, remedial services.

## Chaffey College

5885 Haven Avenue, Rancho Cucamonga, CA 91737-3002
http://www.chaffey.edu/

**CONTACT** Henry D. Shannon, PhD, Superintendent/President
**Telephone:** 909-987-1737

**GENERAL INFORMATION** Public Institution. Founded 1883. **Accreditation:** Regional (WASC/ACCJC); dental assisting (ADA); radiologic technology: radiography (JRCERT). **Total program enrollment:** 6642.

**PROGRAM(S) OFFERED**

• **Accounting** *6 students enrolled* • **Administrative Assistant and Secretarial Science, General** *39 students enrolled* • **Adult Development and Aging** *4 students enrolled* • **Aircraft Powerplant Technology/Technician** *9 students enrolled* • **Airframe Mechanics and Aircraft Maintenance Technology/Technician** *4 students enrolled* • **Apparel and Textile Manufacture** *1 student enrolled* • **Apparel and Textile Marketing Management** *1 student enrolled* • **Autobody/Collision and Repair Technology/Technician** *4 students enrolled* • **Automobile/Automotive Mechanics Technology/Technician** *28 students enrolled* • **Business Administration and Management, General** *13 students enrolled* • **Business Family and Consumer Sciences/Human Sciences** *1 student enrolled* • **Child Development** *2 students enrolled* • **Commercial Photography** *2 students enrolled* • **Communications Systems Installation and Repair Technology** *8 students enrolled* • **Computer Graphics** *1 student enrolled* • **Computer Programming/Programmer, General** *1 student enrolled* • **Computer Systems Networking and Telecommunications** *23 students enrolled* • **Cooking and Related Culinary Arts, General** *3 students enrolled* • **Corrections** *15 students enrolled* • **Criminal Justice/Police Science** *3 students enrolled* • **Data Entry/Microcomputer Applications, General** *2 students enrolled* • **Dental Assisting/Assistant** *3 students enrolled* • **Digital Communication and Media/Multimedia** *1 student enrolled* • **Electrical and Power Transmission Installation/Installer, General** *6 students enrolled* • **Electromechanical Technology/Electromechanical Engineering Technology** *4 students enrolled* • **Fire Science/Firefighting** *2 students enrolled* • **Foods, Nutrition, and Wellness Studies, General** *2 students enrolled* • **Foodservice Systems Administration/Management** *24 students enrolled* • **Health Teacher Education** *1 student enrolled* • **Hotel/Motel Administration/Management** *1 student enrolled* • **Information Technology** *11 students enrolled* • **Interior Design** *7 students enrolled* • **Mechanical Engineering/Mechanical Technology/Technician** *3 students enrolled* • **Medical Administrative/Executive Assistant and Medical Secretary** *9 students enrolled* • **Music Management and Merchandising** *1 student enrolled* • **Nurse/Nursing Assistant/Aide and Patient Care Assistant** *71 students enrolled* • **Office Management and Supervision** *1 student enrolled* • **Pharmacy Technician/Assistant** *16 students enrolled* • **Prepress/Desktop Publishing and Digital Imaging Design** *1 student enrolled* • **Radio and Television** *5 students enrolled* • **Real Estate** *11 students enrolled* • **Restaurant, Culinary, and Catering Management/Manager** *6 students enrolled* • **Retailing and Retail Operations** *1 student enrolled* • **Sales, Distribution and Marketing Operations, General** *5 students enrolled* • **Small Business Administration/Management** *2 students enrolled* • **Sport and Fitness Administration/Management** *1 student enrolled* • **System Administration/Administrator** *9 students enrolled* • **Taxation** *8 students enrolled* • **Teacher Assistant/Aide** *15 students enrolled* • **Web/Multimedia Management and Webmaster** *7 students enrolled*

**STUDENT SERVICES** Academic or career counseling, daycare for children of students, employment services for current students, placement services for program completers, remedial services.

## Charles R. Drew University of Medicine and Science

1731 East 120th Street, Los Angeles, CA 90059
http://www.cdrewu.edu/

**CONTACT** Susan Kelly, PhD, President and Chief Executive Officer
**Telephone:** 323-563-4800

**GENERAL INFORMATION** Private Institution. Founded 1966. **Accreditation:** Regional (WASC/ACSCU); health information technology (AHIMA); medical assisting (AAMAE); radiologic technology: radiography (JRCERT). **Total program enrollment:** 178. **Application fee:** $35.

**PROGRAM(S) OFFERED**

• **Diagnostic Medical Sonography/Sonographer and Ultrasound Technician** *9 students enrolled* • **Health Professions and Related Clinical Sciences, Other** *20*

*Charles R. Drew University of Medicine and Science (continued)*

*students enrolled* • **Nuclear Medical Technology/Technologist** *22 students enrolled* • **Physician Assistant** • **Substance Abuse/Addiction Counseling** *1 student enrolled*

**STUDENT SERVICES** Academic or career counseling, employment services for current students, placement services for program completers, remedial services.

## Citrus College

1000 West Foothill Boulevard, Glendora, CA 91741-1899
http://www.citruscollege.edu/

**CONTACT** Dr. Geraldine M. Perri, Superintendent/President
**Telephone:** 626-963-0323

**GENERAL INFORMATION** Public Institution. Founded 1915. **Accreditation:** Regional (WASC/ACCJC); dental assisting (ADA). **Total program enrollment:** 5116.

**PROGRAM(S) OFFERED**

• **Accounting** *6 students enrolled* • **Automobile/Automotive Mechanics Technology/Technician** *1 student enrolled* • **Child Development** *18 students enrolled* • **Computer Graphics** *1 student enrolled* • **Construction Trades, Other** *3 students enrolled* • **Cosmetology/Cosmetologist, General** *47 students enrolled* • **Criminal Justice/Police Science** *19 students enrolled* • **Dance, Other** *1 student enrolled* • **Dental Assisting/Assistant** *22 students enrolled* • **Diesel Mechanics Technology/Technician** *31 students enrolled* • **Electrical/Electronics Equipment Installation and Repair, General** *3 students enrolled* • **Forestry, General** *7 students enrolled* • **Health Professions and Related Clinical Sciences, Other** • **Health Services/Allied Health/Health Sciences, General** • **Health Unit Coordinator/Ward Clerk** • **Heating, Air Conditioning and Refrigeration Technology/Technician (ACH/ACR/ACHR/HRAC/HVAC/AC Technology)** *5 students enrolled* • **Home Health Aide/Home Attendant** • **Library Science/Librarianship** *4 students enrolled* • **Licensed Practical/Vocational Nurse Training (LPN, LVN, Cert, Dipl, AAS)** *52 students enrolled* • **Medical/Clinical Assistant** • **Music Management and Merchandising** *51 students enrolled* • **Nurse/Nursing Assistant/Aide and Patient Care Assistant** • **Office Management and Supervision** *1 student enrolled* • **Photography** *1 student enrolled* • **Sales, Distribution and Marketing Operations, General** *1 student enrolled* • **Water Quality and Wastewater Treatment Management and Recycling Technology/Technician** *5 students enrolled*

**STUDENT SERVICES** Academic or career counseling, daycare for children of students, employment services for current students, placement services for program completers, remedial services.

## City College of San Francisco

50 Phelan Avenue, San Francisco, CA 94112-1821
http://www.ccsf.edu/

**CONTACT** Don Q. Griffin, Chancellor
**Telephone:** 415-239-3000

**GENERAL INFORMATION** Public Institution. Founded 1935. **Accreditation:** Regional (WASC/ACCJC); dental assisting (ADA); health information technology (AHIMA); medical assisting (AAMAE); radiologic technology: radiation therapy technology (JRCERT); radiologic technology: radiography (JRCERT). **Total program enrollment:** 8914.

**PROGRAM(S) OFFERED**

• **Accounting** *12 students enrolled* • **Administrative Assistant and Secretarial Science, General** *3 students enrolled* • **Aircraft Powerplant Technology/Technician** *5 students enrolled* • **Airframe Mechanics and Aircraft Maintenance Technology/Technician** *9 students enrolled* • **Animation, Interactive Technology, Video Graphics and Special Effects** *3 students enrolled* • **Apparel and Textile Marketing Management** *1 student enrolled* • **Automobile/Automotive Mechanics Technology/Technician** *68 students enrolled* • **Banking and Financial Support Services** *2 students enrolled* • **Biology Technician/Biotechnology Laboratory Technician** *32 students enrolled* • **Business, Management, Marketing, and Related Support Services, Other** *4 students enrolled* • **Cardiovascular Technology/Technologist** *40 students enrolled* • **Child Development** *80 students enrolled* • **Chinese Language and Literature** *6 students enrolled* • **Computer Programming/Programmer, General** *4 students enrolled* • **Computer Systems Networking and Telecommunications** *4 students enrolled* • **Computer and Information Sciences and Support Services, Other** *13 students enrolled* • **Computer and Information Sciences, General** *2 students enrolled* • **Criminal Justice/Police Science** *9 students enrolled* • **Dance, General** *5 students enrolled* • **Digital Communication and Media/Multimedia** *6 students enrolled* • **Drafting and Design Technology/Technician, General** *11 students enrolled* • **Electrical/Electronics Equipment Installation and Repair, General** *7 students enrolled* • **Fashion/Apparel Design** *9 students enrolled* • **Film/Cinema Studies** *4 students enrolled* • **Fire Science/Firefighting** *3 students enrolled* • **Floriculture/Floristry Operations and Management** *1 student enrolled* • **Forensic Science and Technology** *7 students enrolled* • **French Language and Literature** *1 student enrolled* • **Geography, Other** *11 students enrolled* • **German Language and Literature** *1 student enrolled* • **Graphic Design** *7 students enrolled* • **Health Information/Medical Records Technology/Technician** *22 students enrolled* • **Health Professions and Related Clinical Sciences, Other** *86 students enrolled* • **International Business/Trade/Commerce** *7 students enrolled* • **Italian Language and Literature** *2 students enrolled* • **Japanese Language and Literature** *5 students enrolled* • **Journalism** *1 student enrolled* • **Landscaping and Groundskeeping** *4 students enrolled* • **Legal Assistant/Paralegal** *27 students enrolled* • **Library Assistant/Technician** *8 students enrolled* • **Licensed Practical/Vocational Nurse Training (LPN, LVN, Cert, Dipl, AAS)** *9 students enrolled* • **Mass Communication/Media Studies** *1 student enrolled* • **Medical Insurance Coding Specialist/Coder** *16 students enrolled* • **Medical/Clinical Assistant** *24 students enrolled* • **Office Management and Supervision** *12 students enrolled* • **Pharmacy Technician/Assistant** *23 students enrolled* • **Plumbing Technology/Plumber** *5 students enrolled* • **Radio and Television** *4 students enrolled* • **Real Estate** *5 students enrolled* • **Sales, Distribution and Marketing Operations, General** *3 students enrolled* • **Sociology** *3 students enrolled* • **Spanish Language and Literature** *5 students enrolled* • **Substance Abuse/Addiction Counseling** *14 students enrolled* • **System Administration/Administrator** *2 students enrolled* • **Tourism and Travel Services Marketing Operations** *13 students enrolled*

**STUDENT SERVICES** Academic or career counseling, daycare for children of students, employment services for current students, placement services for program completers, remedial services.

## Clarita Career College

27125 Sierra Highway, Suite 329, Canyon Country, CA 91351
http://claritacareercollege.com/

**CONTACT** Raelene Vanek, President
**Telephone:** 661-252-1864

**GENERAL INFORMATION** Private Institution. **Total program enrollment:** 519. **Application fee:** $75.

**PROGRAM(S) OFFERED**

• **Dental Assisting/Assistant** *29 hrs./$13,687* • **Legal Assistant/Paralegal** *43 hrs./$16,174* • **Licensed Practical/Vocational Nurse Training (LPN, LVN, Cert, Dipl, AAS)** *72 hrs./$33,705* • **Massage Therapy/Therapeutic Massage** *33 hrs./$14,178* • **Medical Insurance Coding Specialist/Coder** *31 hrs./$13,674* • **Medical/Clinical Assistant** *84 students enrolled* • **Pharmacy Technician/Assistant** *39 hrs./$17,137*

**STUDENT SERVICES** Academic or career counseling, placement services for program completers.

## Clovis Adult Education

1452 David East Cook Way, Clovis, CA 93611

**CONTACT** John Ballinger, Director
**Telephone:** 559-327-2800

**GENERAL INFORMATION** Private Institution. **Total program enrollment:** 615.

**PROGRAM(S) OFFERED**

• **Business/Commerce, General** *725 hrs./$712* • **Licensed Practical/Vocational Nurse Training (LPN, LVN, Cert, Dipl, AAS)** *1443 hrs./$6440* • **Medical Insurance Specialist/Medical Biller** *930 hrs./$937* • **Medical/Clinical Assistant** *820 hrs./$734*

**STUDENT SERVICES** Academic or career counseling, remedial services.

## Coachella Valley Beauty College

47-120 Dune Palms Road, Suite D, La Quinta, CA 92253

**CONTACT** Denise Harker, Financial Aid Officer
**Telephone:** 760-772-5950

**GENERAL INFORMATION** Private Institution. **Total program enrollment:** 117.

**PROGRAM(S) OFFERED**
• **Aesthetician/Esthetician and Skin Care Specialist** *600 hrs./$3600* • **Cosmetology/Cosmetologist, General** *1600 hrs./$6225* • **Nail Technician/ Specialist and Manicurist** *400 hrs./$2400* • **Personal and Culinary Services, Other** *600 hrs./$3000*

**STUDENT SERVICES** Academic or career counseling, employment services for current students, placement services for program completers.

## Coast Career Institute

1354 S. Hill Street, Los Angeles, CA 90015-3040

**CONTACT** Brigitte Illingworth, Director
**Telephone:** 213-747-8676

**GENERAL INFORMATION** Private Institution. **Total program enrollment:** 12.

**PROGRAM(S) OFFERED**
• **Baking and Pastry Arts/Baker/Pastry Chef** *24 hrs./$3599* • **Crafts/Craft Design, Folk Art and Artisanry** *24 hrs./$3400* • **Opticianry/Ophthalmic Dispensing Optician** *30 hrs./$4575* • **Security and Protective Services, Other** *52 hrs./$606*

**STUDENT SERVICES** Academic or career counseling, placement services for program completers.

## Coast Community College District

1370 Adams Avenue, Costa Mesa, CA 92626

**CONTACT** Kenneth D. Yglesias, EdD, Chancellor
**Telephone:** 714-438-4600

**GENERAL INFORMATION** Public Institution.

## Coastline Beauty College

10840 Warner Avenue, Suite 207, Fountain Valley, CA 92708
http://www.coastlinebeautycollege.com

**CONTACT** Tom Do, President
**Telephone:** 714-963-4000

**GENERAL INFORMATION** Private Institution. **Total program enrollment:** 90. **Application fee:** $75.

**PROGRAM(S) OFFERED**
• **Aesthetician/Esthetician and Skin Care Specialist** *600 hrs./$3075* • **Cosmetology/Cosmetologist, General** *1600 hrs./$7775* • **Massage Therapy/ Therapeutic Massage** *300 hrs./$1875* • **Nail Technician/Specialist and Manicurist** *400 hrs./$875*

**STUDENT SERVICES** Academic or career counseling, placement services for program completers, remedial services.

## Coastline Community College

11460 Warner Avenue, Fountain Valley, CA 92708-2597
http://coastline.cccd.edu/

**CONTACT** Ding-Jo Currie, President
**Telephone:** 714-546-7600

**GENERAL INFORMATION** Public Institution. Founded 1976. **Accreditation:** Regional (WASC/ACCJC). **Total program enrollment:** 911.

**PROGRAM(S) OFFERED**
• **Accounting** *1 student enrolled* • **Administrative Assistant and Secretarial Science, General** *3 students enrolled* • **Adult Development and Aging** *3 students enrolled* • **Building/Home/Construction Inspection/Inspector** *17 students enrolled* • **Business Administration and Management, General** *1 student enrolled* • **Chemical Technology/Technician** *5 students enrolled* • **Computer Systems Networking and Telecommunications** *2 students enrolled* • **Legal Assistant/ Paralegal** *37 students enrolled* • **Real Estate** *1 student enrolled*

**STUDENT SERVICES** Academic or career counseling, employment services for current students, placement services for program completers, remedial services.

## COBA Academy

102 North Glassell Street, Orange, CA 92666
http://www.coba.edu/

**CONTACT** Mrs. A. E. Williams, Owner
**Telephone:** 714-633-5950

**GENERAL INFORMATION** Private Institution. **Total program enrollment:** 101. **Application fee:** $75.

**PROGRAM(S) OFFERED**
• **Cosmetology/Cosmetologist, General** *1600 hrs./$14,825*

**STUDENT SERVICES** Academic or career counseling, placement services for program completers.

## Coleman University

8888 Balboa Avenue, San Diego, CA 92123
http://www.coleman.edu/

**CONTACT** Pritpal Panesar, President
**Telephone:** 858-499-0202

**GENERAL INFORMATION** Private Institution. Founded 1963. **Accreditation:** State accredited or approved. **Total program enrollment:** 425. **Application fee:** $100.

**PROGRAM(S) OFFERED**
• **Computer Graphics** *34 students enrolled* • **Computer Systems Networking and Telecommunications** *35 students enrolled* • **Computer and Information Sciences, General** *22 students enrolled*

**STUDENT SERVICES** Academic or career counseling, placement services for program completers.

## Colleen O'Haras Beauty Academy

109 West 4th Street, Santa Ana, CA 92701
http://californiabeautyschool.com/

**CONTACT** Jim Buffington, President
**Telephone:** 714-568-5399

**GENERAL INFORMATION** Private Institution. **Total program enrollment:** 213.

**PROGRAM(S) OFFERED**
• **Cosmetology/Cosmetologist, General** *1600 hrs./$18,400*

**STUDENT SERVICES** Placement services for program completers.

## College of Alameda

555 Ralph Appezzato Memorial Parkway, Alameda, CA 94501-2109
http://www.peralta.cc.ca.us/

**CONTACT** Dr. George Herring, President
**Telephone:** 510-748-2334

**GENERAL INFORMATION** Public Institution. Founded 1970. **Accreditation:** Regional (WASC/ACCJC); dental assisting (ADA). **Total program enrollment:** 1139.

**PROGRAM(S) OFFERED**
• **Accounting** *11 students enrolled* • **Administrative Assistant and Secretarial Science, General** *1 student enrolled* • **Airframe Mechanics and Aircraft Maintenance Technology/Technician** *1 student enrolled* • **American Sign Language (ASL)** *1 student enrolled* • **Apparel and Textiles, General** *11 students enrolled* • **Automobile/Automotive Mechanics Technology/Technician** *19 students enrolled* • **Business Administration and Management, General** *3 students enrolled* • **Computer Systems Networking and Telecommunications** *2 students enrolled* • **Dental Assisting/Assistant** *7 students enrolled* • **Diesel Mechanics Technology/Technician** *4 students enrolled* • **Information Technology** *3 students enrolled* • **Public Administration and Social Service Professions, Other** *1 student enrolled* • **Small Business Administration/Management** *1 student enrolled*

**STUDENT SERVICES** Academic or career counseling, daycare for children of students, employment services for current students, placement services for program completers, remedial services.

## College of Information Technology

2701 E. Chapman Avenue, Suite 101, Fullerton, CA 92831
http://collegeofit.com/

**CONTACT** Mohammad Qamaruddin, Owner/President
**Telephone:** 714-879-5100

**GENERAL INFORMATION** Private Institution. **Total program enrollment:** 361. **Application fee:** $75.

**PROGRAM(S) OFFERED**
• **Computer Programming/Programmer, General** *36 hrs./$9900* • **Medical/Clinical Assistant** *37 hrs./$9900* • **Nursing, Other** *79 hrs./$25,830*

**STUDENT SERVICES** Placement services for program completers.

## College of Marin

835 College Avenue, Kentfield, CA 94904
http://www.marin.edu/

**CONTACT** Frances L. White, Superintendent/President
**Telephone:** 415-457-8811

**GENERAL INFORMATION** Public Institution. Founded 1926. **Accreditation:** Regional (WASC/ACCJC); dental assisting (ADA). **Total program enrollment:** 1039.

**PROGRAM(S) OFFERED**
• **Accounting** *1 student enrolled* • **Automobile/Automotive Mechanics Technology/Technician** *4 students enrolled* • **Business Administration and Management, General** *3 students enrolled* • **Child Development** *2 students enrolled* • **Court Reporting/Court Reporter** *1 student enrolled* • **Criminal Justice/Police Science** *1 student enrolled* • **Dental Assisting/Assistant** *18 students enrolled* • **Emergency Medical Technology/Technician (EMT Paramedic)** • **Health Services/Allied Health/Health Sciences, General** *19 students enrolled* • **Landscaping and Groundskeeping** *2 students enrolled* • **Medical/Clinical Assistant** *5 students enrolled* • **Phlebotomy/Phlebotomist** • **Prepress/Desktop Publishing and Digital Imaging Design** *1 student enrolled*

**STUDENT SERVICES** Academic or career counseling, daycare for children of students, employment services for current students, placement services for program completers, remedial services.

## College of San Mateo

1700 West Hillsdale Boulevard, San Mateo, CA 94402-3784
http://www.collegeofsanmateo.edu/

**CONTACT** Michael Claire, President
**Telephone:** 650-574-6161

**GENERAL INFORMATION** Public Institution. Founded 1922. **Accreditation:** Regional (WASC/ACCJC); dental assisting (ADA). **Total program enrollment:** 2693.

**PROGRAM(S) OFFERED**
• **Accounting** *68 students enrolled* • **Administrative Assistant and Secretarial Science, General** *3 students enrolled* • **Building/Home/Construction Inspection/Inspector** *1 student enrolled* • **Chinese Language and Literature** *5 students enrolled* • **Computer Programming/Programmer, General** *3 students enrolled* • **Computer Systems Networking and Telecommunications** *1 student enrolled* • **Cosmetology/Cosmetologist, General** *42 students enrolled* • **Criminal Justice/Police Science** *53 students enrolled* • **Dental Assisting/Assistant** *14 students enrolled* • **Digital Communication and Media/Multimedia** *1 student enrolled* • **Drafting and Design Technology/Technician, General** *1 student enrolled* • **Electrical/Electronics Equipment Installation and Repair, General** *1 student enrolled* • **Fire Science/Firefighting** *5 students enrolled* • **Floriculture/Floristry Operations and Management** *3 students enrolled* • **Foreign Languages, Literatures, and Linguistics, Other** *4 students enrolled* • **French Language and Literature** *2 students enrolled* • **German Language and Literature** *2 students enrolled* • **Graphic Design** *4 students enrolled* • **Heating, Air Conditioning and Refrigeration Technology/Technician (ACH/ACR/ACHR/HRAC/HVAC/AC Technology)** *8 students enrolled* • **Human Services, General** *28 students enrolled* • **Japanese Language and Literature** *10 students enrolled* • **Landscaping and Groundskeeping** *6 students enrolled* • **Nursing—Registered Nurse Training (RN, ASN, BSN, MSN)** *40 students enrolled* • **Plumbing Technology/Plumber** *14 students enrolled* • **Radio and Television** *3 students enrolled* • **Real Estate** *2 students enrolled* • **Retailing and Retail Operations** *4 students enrolled* • **Substance Abuse/Addiction Counseling** *10 students enrolled*

**STUDENT SERVICES** Academic or career counseling, daycare for children of students, employment services for current students, placement services for program completers, remedial services.

## College of the Canyons

26455 Rockwell Canyon Road, Santa Clarita, CA 91355-1803
http://www.canyons.edu/

**CONTACT** Dianne G. Van Hook, Chancellor-President
**Telephone:** 661-259-7800

**GENERAL INFORMATION** Public Institution. Founded 1969. **Accreditation:** Regional (WASC/ACCJC). **Total program enrollment:** 6023.

**PROGRAM(S) OFFERED**
• **Administrative Assistant and Secretarial Science, General** *1 student enrolled* • **Criminal Justice/Police Science** *1 student enrolled* • **Fire Science/Firefighting** *1 student enrolled* • **Home Health Aide/Home Attendant** • **Interior Design** *2 students enrolled* • **Nurse/Nursing Assistant/Aide and Patient Care Assistant** • **Photography** *1 student enrolled*

**STUDENT SERVICES** Academic or career counseling, daycare for children of students, employment services for current students, placement services for program completers, remedial services.

## College of the Desert

43-500 Monterey Avenue, Palm Desert, CA 92260-9305
http://desert.cc.ca.us/

**CONTACT** Jerry R. Patton, President
**Telephone:** 760-346-8041

**GENERAL INFORMATION** Public Institution. Founded 1959. **Accreditation:** Regional (WASC/ACCJC). **Total program enrollment:** 3410.

**PROGRAM(S) OFFERED**
• **Accounting** *8 students enrolled* • **Applied Horticulture/Horticultural Operations, General** *3 students enrolled* • **Automobile/Automotive Mechanics Technology/Technician** • **Building/Construction Site Management/Manager** *3 students enrolled* • **Building/Home/Construction Inspection/Inspector** *5 students*

enrolled • **Child Development** *10 students enrolled* • **Computer Graphics** *3 students enrolled* • **Cooking and Related Culinary Arts, General** *2 students enrolled* • **Criminal Justice/Police Science** *8 students enrolled* • **Fire Science/Firefighting** *2 students enrolled* • **Heating, Air Conditioning and Refrigeration Technology/Technician (ACH/ACR/ACHR/HRAC/HVAC/AC Technology)** *6 students enrolled* • **Home Health Aide/Home Attendant** • **Human Services, General** *1 student enrolled* • **Information Technology** *5 students enrolled* • **Licensed Practical/Vocational Nurse Training (LPN, LVN, Cert, Dipl, AAS)** *24 students enrolled* • **Music, General** *2 students enrolled* • **Natural Resources/Conservation, General** *1 student enrolled* • **Office Management and Supervision** *5 students enrolled* • **Substance Abuse/Addiction Counseling** *15 students enrolled* • **Turf and Turfgrass Management** *8 students enrolled*

**STUDENT SERVICES** Academic or career counseling, daycare for children of students, employment services for current students, placement services for program completers, remedial services.

## College of the Redwoods

7351 Tompkins Hill Road, Eureka, CA 95501-9300
http://www.redwoods.edu/

**CONTACT** Dr. Jeff Marsee, President/Superintendent
**Telephone:** 707-476-4100

**GENERAL INFORMATION** Public Institution. Founded 1964. **Accreditation:** Regional (WASC/ACCJC); dental assisting (ADA). **Total program enrollment:** 2526.

**PROGRAM(S) OFFERED**
• **Accounting** • **Agriculture, General** *1 student enrolled* • **Business/Commerce, General** *1 student enrolled* • **Cabinetmaking and Millwork/Millwright** *17 students enrolled* • **Child Development** *21 students enrolled* • **Construction Trades, General** *7 students enrolled* • **Criminal Justice/Police Science** *60 students enrolled* • **Dental Assisting/Assistant** *10 students enrolled* • **Electrical/Electronics Equipment Installation and Repair, General** *1 student enrolled* • **Electrician** *3 students enrolled* • **Heavy Equipment Maintenance Technology/Technician** *6 students enrolled* • **Legal Assistant/Paralegal** *2 students enrolled* • **Licensed Practical/Vocational Nurse Training (LPN, LVN, Cert, Dipl, AAS)** *15 students enrolled* • **Manufacturing Technology/Technician** *2 students enrolled* • **Mechanical Drafting and Mechanical Drafting CAD/CADD** *1 student enrolled* • **Medical/Clinical Assistant** *10 students enrolled* • **Plant Nursery Operations and Management** • **Real Estate** *1 student enrolled* • **Restaurant, Culinary, and Catering Management/Manager** • **Science Technologies/Technicians, Other** *1 student enrolled* • **Substance Abuse/Addiction Counseling** *4 students enrolled*

**STUDENT SERVICES** Academic or career counseling, daycare for children of students, employment services for current students, placement services for program completers, remedial services.

## College of the Sequoias

915 South Mooney Boulevard, Visalia, CA 93277-2234
http://www.cos.edu/

**CONTACT** William Scroggins, PhD, Superintendent/President
**Telephone:** 559-730-3700

**GENERAL INFORMATION** Public Institution. Founded 1925. **Accreditation:** Regional (WASC/ACCJC). **Total program enrollment:** 5147.

**PROGRAM(S) OFFERED**
• **Accounting** *3 students enrolled* • **Agribusiness/Agricultural Business Operations** *2 students enrolled* • **Agricultural Mechanics and Equipment/Machine Technology** *1 student enrolled* • **Agricultural Production Operations, Other** *1 student enrolled* • **Animal/Livestock Husbandry and Production** *1 student enrolled* • **Apparel and Textile Marketing Management** *1 student enrolled* • **Automobile/Automotive Mechanics Technology/Technician** *1 student enrolled* • **Building/Home/Construction Inspection/Inspector** *5 students enrolled* • **Child Development** *82 students enrolled* • **Computer and Information Sciences, General** *1 student enrolled* • **Cosmetology/Cosmetologist, General** *3 students enrolled* • **Criminal Justice/Police Science** *63 students enrolled* • **Crop Production** *1 student enrolled* • **Data Entry/Microcomputer Applications, General** *1 student enrolled* • **Emergency Medical Technology/Technician (EMT Paramedic)** *100 students enrolled* • **Equestrian/Equine Studies** *1 student enrolled* • **Fashion/Apparel Design** *3 students enrolled* • **Fire Science/Firefighting** *1 student enrolled* • **Floriculture/Floristry Operations and Management** *1 student enrolled* • **Human Services, General** *8 students enrolled* • **Landscaping and Groundskeeping** *1 student enrolled* • **Legal Administrative Assistant/Secretary** *59 students enrolled* • **Mechanical Engineering/Mechanical Technology/Technician** *2 students enrolled* • **Nurse/Nursing Assistant/Aide and Patient Care Assistant** *36 students enrolled* • **Nursing—Registered Nurse Training (RN, ASN, BSN, MSN)** *24 students enrolled* • **Phlebotomy/Phlebotomist** • **Spanish Language and Literature** *5 students enrolled* • **Veterinary/Animal Health Technology/Technician and Veterinary Assistant** *2 students enrolled* • **Welding Technology/Welder** *2 students enrolled*

**STUDENT SERVICES** Academic or career counseling, daycare for children of students, employment services for current students, placement services for program completers, remedial services.

## College of the Siskiyous

800 College Avenue, Weed, CA 96094-2899
http://www.siskiyous.edu/

**CONTACT** Randall Lawrence, EdD, Superintendent President
**Telephone:** 530-938-5555

**GENERAL INFORMATION** Public Institution. Founded 1957. **Accreditation:** Regional (WASC/ACCJC). **Total program enrollment:** 920.

**PROGRAM(S) OFFERED**
• **Accounting** *1 student enrolled* • **Administrative Assistant and Secretarial Science, General** *2 students enrolled* • **Child Development** *2 students enrolled* • **Computer Graphics** *1 student enrolled* • **Computer and Information Sciences and Support Services, Other** *2 students enrolled* • **Customer Service Support/Call Center/Teleservice Operation** *2 students enrolled* • **Drama and Dramatics/Theatre Arts, General** *1 student enrolled* • **Emergency Medical Technology/Technician (EMT Paramedic)** *17 students enrolled* • **Fire Science/Firefighting** *76 students enrolled* • **Graphic Design** *2 students enrolled* • **Nurse/Nursing Assistant/Aide and Patient Care Assistant** *23 students enrolled* • **Welding Technology/Welder** *1 student enrolled*

**STUDENT SERVICES** Academic or career counseling, daycare for children of students, employment services for current students, remedial services.

## Columbia College

11600 Columbia College Drive, Sonora, CA 95370
http://www.gocolumbia.org/

**CONTACT** Joan Smith, President
**Telephone:** 209-588-5100

**GENERAL INFORMATION** Public Institution. Founded 1968. **Accreditation:** Regional (WASC/ACCJC); emergency medical services (JRCEMTP). **Total program enrollment:** 865.

**PROGRAM(S) OFFERED**
• **Automobile/Automotive Mechanics Technology/Technician** *15 students enrolled* • **Business/Commerce, General** *3 students enrolled* • **Child Development** *10 students enrolled* • **Computer and Information Sciences, General** *1 student enrolled* • **Emergency Medical Technology/Technician (EMT Paramedic)** • **Fire Science/Firefighting** *9 students enrolled* • **Forestry, General** *2 students enrolled* • **Geography, Other** *1 student enrolled* • **Natural Resources/Conservation, General** *4 students enrolled* • **Restaurant, Culinary, and Catering Management/Manager** *3 students enrolled* • **Tourism and Travel Services Marketing Operations** *2 students enrolled* • **Web Page, Digital/Multimedia and Information Resources Design** *1 student enrolled*

**STUDENT SERVICES** Academic or career counseling, daycare for children of students, employment services for current students, remedial services.

## Community Based Education Development

5724 W. Third Street, # 314, Los Angeles, CA 90036
http://www.cbd.edu/

**CONTACT** Alan Heshel, President
**Telephone:** 323-937-7772

**GENERAL INFORMATION** Private Institution. **Total program enrollment:** 338.

*Community Based Education Development (continued)*

**PROGRAM(S) OFFERED**

• **Computer and Information Sciences and Support Services, Other** *32 students enrolled* • **Education, Other** *720 hrs./$4050* • **Licensed Practical/Vocational Nurse Training (LPN, LVN, Cert, Dipl, AAS)** *120 hrs./$27,320* • **Medical/Clinical Assistant** • **Surgical Technology/Technologist** *1500 hrs./$20,350*

**STUDENT SERVICES** Academic or career counseling, placement services for program completers.

## Computer Tutor Business and Technical Institute

4306 Sisk Road, Modesto, CA 95356
http://www.com/putertutor.com/

**CONTACT** George Rawe, Director
**Telephone:** 209-545-5200

**GENERAL INFORMATION** Private Institution. **Total program enrollment:** 146. **Application fee:** $75.

**PROGRAM(S) OFFERED**

• **Accounting Technology/Technician and Bookkeeping** *24 hrs./$4875* • **Administrative Assistant and Secretarial Science, General** *36 hrs./$7275* • **Computer Systems Networking and Telecommunications** *36 hrs./$7275* • **General Office Occupations and Clerical Services** *20 hrs./$4075* • **Medical Administrative/Executive Assistant and Medical Secretary** *36 hrs./$7575*

**STUDENT SERVICES** Academic or career counseling, placement services for program completers, remedial services.

## Concorde Career College

12951 Euclid Street, Suite 101, Garden Grove, CA 92840
http://www.concorde.edu/

**CONTACT** Cindy Gordon, Campus President
**Telephone:** 714-703-1900

**GENERAL INFORMATION** Private Institution. **Total program enrollment:** 587.

**PROGRAM(S) OFFERED**

• **Dental Assisting/Assistant** *800 hrs./$11,755* • **Health and Medical Administrative Services, Other** *720 hrs./$11,755* • **Licensed Practical/Vocational Nurse Training (LPN, LVN, Cert, Dipl, AAS)** *1600 hrs./$31,548* • **Medical/Clinical Assistant** *720 hrs./$12,175* • **Nursing, Other** *168 students enrolled* • **Respiratory Care Therapy/Therapist** *450 hrs./$8920* • **Respiratory Therapy Technician/Assistant** *1865 hrs./$34,881*

**STUDENT SERVICES** Academic or career counseling, employment services for current students, placement services for program completers, remedial services.

## Concorde Career Institute

12412 Victory Boulevard, North Hollywood, CA 91606
http://www.concordecareercolleges.com/

**CONTACT** Madeline Volker, Campus President
**Telephone:** 818-766-8151

**GENERAL INFORMATION** Private Institution. Founded 1955. **Accreditation:** Respiratory therapy technology (CoARC); state accredited or approved. **Total program enrollment:** 579.

**PROGRAM(S) OFFERED**

• **Dental Assisting/Assistant** *800 hrs./$11,997* • **Health Information/Medical Records Administration/Administrator** *720 hrs./$11,885* • **Health and Medical Administrative Services, Other** *44 students enrolled* • **Licensed Practical/Vocational Nurse Training (LPN, LVN, Cert, Dipl, AAS)** *1600 hrs./$26,381* • **Massage Therapy/Therapeutic Massage** *23 students enrolled* • **Medical/Clinical Assistant** *720 hrs./$13,090* • **Respiratory Care Therapy/Therapist** *1650 hrs./$27,316* • **Respiratory Therapy Technician/Assistant** *9 students enrolled* • **Surgical Technology/Technologist** *1440 hrs./$21,730*

**STUDENT SERVICES** Academic or career counseling, employment services for current students, placement services for program completers, remedial services.

## Concorde Career Institute

570 West 4th Street, San Bernardino, CA 92401
http://www.concorde.edu/

**CONTACT** Ron Johnson, Campus President
**Telephone:** 909-884-8891

**GENERAL INFORMATION** Private Institution. Founded 1967. **Total program enrollment:** 796.

**PROGRAM(S) OFFERED**

• **Dental Assisting/Assistant** *720 hrs./$12,779* • **Licensed Practical/Vocational Nurse Training (LPN, LVN, Cert, Dipl, AAS)** *1600 hrs./$26,482* • **Massage Therapy/Therapeutic Massage** *63 students enrolled* • **Medical Office Management/Administration** *720 hrs./$12,063* • **Medical/Clinical Assistant** *720 hrs./$13,437* • **Respiratory Care Therapy/Therapist** *450 hrs./$8500* • **Surgical Technology/Technologist** *1440 hrs./$22,050*

**STUDENT SERVICES** Academic or career counseling, employment services for current students, placement services for program completers, remedial services.

## Concorde Career Institute

123 Camino De Lane Reina, Suite E125, San Diego, CA 92108
http://www.concorde.edu/sandiego/

**CONTACT** Shawn Traudt, Campus President
**Telephone:** 800-852-8434

**GENERAL INFORMATION** Private Institution. **Total program enrollment:** 649.

**PROGRAM(S) OFFERED**

• **Dental Assisting/Assistant** *800 hrs./$13,015* • **Health Information/Medical Records Administration/Administrator** *720 hrs./$12,543* • **Health and Medical Administrative Services, Other** *92 students enrolled* • **Licensed Practical/Vocational Nurse Training (LPN, LVN, Cert, Dipl, AAS)** *1600 hrs./$27,453* • **Massage Therapy/Therapeutic Massage** *720 hrs./$13,231* • **Medical/Clinical Assistant** *720 hrs./$13,559* • **Nursing, Other** *75 students enrolled* • **Surgical Technology/Technologist** *1440 hrs./$13,231*

**STUDENT SERVICES** Academic or career counseling, employment services for current students, placement services for program completers, remedial services.

## Contra Costa College

2600 Mission Bell Drive, San Pablo, CA 94806-3195
http://www.contracosta.edu/

**CONTACT** McKinley Williams, President
**Telephone:** 510-235-7800

**GENERAL INFORMATION** Public Institution. Founded 1948. **Accreditation:** Regional (WASC/ACCJC); dental assisting (ADA). **Total program enrollment:** 2146.

**PROGRAM(S) OFFERED**

• **Accounting** *8 students enrolled* • **Administrative Assistant and Secretarial Science, General** *2 students enrolled* • **Autobody/Collision and Repair Technology/Technician** *7 students enrolled* • **Automobile/Automotive Mechanics Technology/Technician** *7 students enrolled* • **Biology Technician/Biotechnology Laboratory Technician** *1 student enrolled* • **Biology/Biological Sciences, General** *1 student enrolled* • **Business Administration and Management, General** *26 students enrolled* • **Child Development** *32 students enrolled* • **Computer Programming/Programmer, General** *1 student enrolled* • **Computer Systems Networking and Telecommunications** • **Cooking and Related**

**Culinary Arts, General** *16 students enrolled* • **Corrections** *2 students enrolled* • **Criminal Justice/Police Science** *8 students enrolled* • **Data Entry/Microcomputer Applications, General** *1 student enrolled* • **Dental Assisting/Assistant** *2 students enrolled* • **Electrical/Electronics Equipment Installation and Repair, General** • **Health Services/Allied Health/Health Sciences, General** *21 students enrolled* • **Health and Physical Education, General** • **Human Services, General** *19 students enrolled* • **Journalism** *1 student enrolled* • **Medical/Clinical Assistant** *13 students enrolled* • **Nurse/Nursing Assistant/Aide and Patient Care Assistant** *21 students enrolled* • **Real Estate** *4 students enrolled* • **Security and Loss Prevention Services**

**STUDENT SERVICES** Academic or career counseling, daycare for children of students, employment services for current students, placement services for program completers, remedial services.

## Contra Costa Community College District

500 Court Street, Martinez, CA 94553

**CONTACT** Dr. Helen Benjamin, Chancellor
**Telephone:** 925-229-1000

**GENERAL INFORMATION** Public Institution.

## Copper Mountain College

6162 Rotary Way, Joshua Tree, CA 92252
http://www.cmccd.edu/

**CONTACT** Dr. Roger Wagner, Superintendent/President
**Telephone:** 760-366-3791

**GENERAL INFORMATION** Public Institution. Founded 1966. **Total program enrollment:** 712.

**STUDENT SERVICES** Academic or career counseling, employment services for current students, remedial services.

## Cosumnes River College

8401 Center Parkway, Sacramento, CA 95823-5799
http://www.crc.losrios.edu/

**CONTACT** Francisco C. Rodriguez, President
**Telephone:** 916-688-7344

**GENERAL INFORMATION** Public Institution. Founded 1970. **Accreditation:** Regional (WASC/ACCJC); health information technology (AHIMA); medical assisting (AAMAE). **Total program enrollment:** 4295.

**PROGRAM(S) OFFERED**

• **Accounting** *19 students enrolled* • **Administrative Assistant and Secretarial Science, General** *6 students enrolled* • **Agribusiness/Agricultural Business Operations** *1 student enrolled* • **Agriculture, General** *1 student enrolled* • **Architectural Drafting and Architectural CAD/CADD** *2 students enrolled* • **Architectural Technology/Technician** *2 students enrolled* • **Automobile/Automotive Mechanics Technology/Technician** *199 students enrolled* • **Building/Construction Site Management/Manager** *2 students enrolled* • **Building/Home/Construction Inspection/Inspector** *4 students enrolled* • **Child Development** *29 students enrolled* • **Commercial Photography** *14 students enrolled* • **Computer Programming/Programmer, General** *6 students enrolled* • **Computer Systems Networking and Telecommunications** *5 students enrolled* • **Data Entry/Microcomputer Applications, General** *2 students enrolled* • **Data Modeling/Warehousing and Database Administration** *4 students enrolled* • **Dietetic Technician (DTR)** *2 students enrolled* • **Emergency Medical Technology/Technician (EMT Paramedic)** *1 student enrolled* • **Fire Science/Firefighting** *5 students enrolled* • **Geography, Other** *5 students enrolled* • **Human Services, General** *3 students enrolled* • **Information Technology** *1 student enrolled* • **Landscaping and Groundskeeping** *5 students enrolled* • **Medical Insurance Coding Specialist/Coder** *1 student enrolled* • **Medical/Clinical Assistant** *9 students enrolled* • **Photography** *5 students enrolled* • **Plant Nursery Operations and Management** *3 students enrolled* • **Radio and Television** *2 students enrolled* • **Real Estate** *6 students enrolled* • **Restaurant, Culinary, and Catering Management/Manager** *1 student enrolled* • **Small Engine Mechanics and Repair Technology/Technician** *6 students enrolled* • **System Administration/Administrator** *5 students enrolled* • **Veterinary/Animal Health Technology/Technician and Veterinary Assistant** *2 students enrolled* • **Web Page, Digital/Multimedia and Information Resources Design** *1 student enrolled*

**STUDENT SERVICES** Academic or career counseling, daycare for children of students, employment services for current students, placement services for program completers, remedial services.

## Crafton Hills College

11711 Sand Canyon Road, Yucaipa, CA 92399-1799
http://www.craftonhills.edu/

**CONTACT** Gloria Macías Harrison, President
**Telephone:** 909-794-2161

**GENERAL INFORMATION** Public Institution. Founded 1972. **Accreditation:** Regional (WASC/ACCJC); emergency medical services (JRCEMTP); respiratory therapy technology (CoARC). **Total program enrollment:** 2260.

**PROGRAM(S) OFFERED**

• **Accounting** *1 student enrolled* • **Child Development** *3 students enrolled* • **Computer and Information Sciences and Support Services, Other** *1 student enrolled* • **Computer and Information Sciences, General** *1 student enrolled* • **Emergency Medical Technology/Technician (EMT Paramedic)** *131 students enrolled* • **Fire Science/Firefighting** *64 students enrolled* • **Information Technology** *14 students enrolled* • **Nursing—Registered Nurse Training (RN, ASN, BSN, MSN)** • **Retailing and Retail Operations** *3 students enrolled* • **Sales, Distribution and Marketing Operations, General** *1 student enrolled*

**STUDENT SERVICES** Academic or career counseling, daycare for children of students, employment services for current students, remedial services.

## CSI Career College

611-K Orange Drive, Vacaville, CA 95687
http://www.traincsi.com/

**CONTACT** Joanie French-Reed, Owner/Director
**Telephone:** 707-455-0557

**GENERAL INFORMATION** Private Institution. **Total program enrollment:** 254.

**PROGRAM(S) OFFERED**

• **Accounting Technology/Technician and Bookkeeping** *3 students enrolled* • **Allied Health and Medical Assisting Services, Other** *39 hrs./$11,445* • **Clinical/Medical Laboratory Assistant** • **Computer Graphics** • **Electrocardiograph Technology/Technician** • **Executive Assistant/Executive Secretary** *38 hrs./$10,305* • **General Office Occupations and Clerical Services** *2 students enrolled* • **Licensed Practical/Vocational Nurse Training (LPN, LVN, Cert, Dipl, AAS)** *75 hrs./$38,985* • **Medical Office Assistant/Specialist** *39 hrs./$11,130* • **Medical/Clinical Assistant** *37 hrs./$11,445* • **Pharmacy Technician/Assistant** *32 hrs./$11,445* • **Phlebotomy/Phlebotomist** *1 student enrolled*

**STUDENT SERVICES** Academic or career counseling, placement services for program completers.

## Cuesta College

PO Box 8106, San Luis Obispo, CA 93403-8106
http://www.cuesta.edu/

**CONTACT** Dr. Dave Pelham, President Superintendent
**Telephone:** 805-546-3100

**GENERAL INFORMATION** Public Institution. Founded 1964. **Accreditation:** Regional (WASC/ACCJC). **Total program enrollment:** 4804.

**PROGRAM(S) OFFERED**

• **Administrative Assistant and Secretarial Science, General** *1 student enrolled* • **Agricultural Production Operations, Other** • **Apparel and Textile Marketing Management** *1 student enrolled* • **Autobody/Collision and Repair Technology/Technician** *2 students enrolled* • **Automobile/Automotive Mechanics Technology/Technician** *5 students enrolled* • **Business Administration and Management, General** *21 students enrolled* • **Child Development** *9 students enrolled*

*Cuesta College (continued)*

• **Construction Trades, General** *2 students enrolled* • **Cooking and Related Culinary Arts, General** *1 student enrolled* • **Crop Production** *2 students enrolled* • **Drafting and Design Technology/Technician, General** *3 students enrolled* • **Electrical/Electronics Equipment Installation and Repair, General** *1 student enrolled* • **Electrician** • **Electrocardiograph Technology/Technician** • **Emergency Medical Technology/Technician (EMT Paramedic)** *257 students enrolled* • **Fashion/Apparel Design** *1 student enrolled* • **Health Professions and Related Clinical Sciences, Other** • **Health Unit Coordinator/Ward Clerk** • **Legal Assistant/Paralegal** *2 students enrolled* • **Library Assistant/Technician** *10 students enrolled* • **Licensed Practical/Vocational Nurse Training (LPN, LVN, Cert, Dipl, AAS)** *29 students enrolled* • **Mason/Masonry** • **Medical Insurance Coding Specialist/Coder** • **Medical/Clinical Assistant** *90 students enrolled* • **Nurse/Nursing Assistant/Aide and Patient Care Assistant** *51 students enrolled* • **Nursing—Registered Nurse Training (RN, ASN, BSN, MSN)** *1 student enrolled* • **Phlebotomy/Phlebotomist** • **Plumbing Technology/Plumber** • **Sales, Distribution and Marketing Operations, General** • **Water Quality and Wastewater Treatment Management and Recycling Technology/Technician** • **Welding Technology/Welder** *15 students enrolled*

**STUDENT SERVICES** Academic or career counseling, daycare for children of students, employment services for current students, placement services for program completers, remedial services.

## Cuyamaca College

900 Rancho San Diego Parkway, El Cajon, CA 92019-4304
http://www.cuyamaca.net/

**CONTACT** Gerri Perri, President
**Telephone:** 619-660-4000

**GENERAL INFORMATION** Public Institution. Founded 1978. **Accreditation:** Regional (WASC/ACCJC). **Total program enrollment:** 1636.

**PROGRAM(S) OFFERED**

• **Accounting** *5 students enrolled* • **Administrative Assistant and Secretarial Science, General** *19 students enrolled* • **Architectural Drafting and Architectural CAD/CADD** *9 students enrolled* • **Automobile/Automotive Mechanics Technology/Technician** *1 student enrolled* • **Business Administration and Management, General** *53 students enrolled* • **Child Development** *14 students enrolled* • **Computer Systems Networking and Telecommunications** *5 students enrolled* • **Graphic Design** *10 students enrolled* • **Hazardous Materials Management and Waste Technology/Technician** *23 students enrolled* • **Industrial Safety Technology/Technician** *5 students enrolled* • **Landscaping and Groundskeeping** *5 students enrolled* • **Mathematics, General** *3 students enrolled* • **Plant Nursery Operations and Management** *2 students enrolled* • **Real Estate** *12 students enrolled* • **Small Business Administration/Management** *1 student enrolled* • **Survey Technology/Surveying** *1 student enrolled* • **Turf and Turfgrass Management** *3 students enrolled* • **Web Page, Digital/Multimedia and Information Resources Design** *2 students enrolled*

**STUDENT SERVICES** Academic or career counseling, daycare for children of students, employment services for current students, placement services for program completers, remedial services.

## Cynthia's Beauty Academy

4130 East Gage Avenue, Bell, CA 90201

**CONTACT** Juana Roman, President
**Telephone:** 323-560-2207

**GENERAL INFORMATION** Private Institution. **Total program enrollment:** 106.

**PROGRAM(S) OFFERED**

• **Cosmetology/Cosmetologist, General** *1600 hrs./$17,650*

**STUDENT SERVICES** Academic or career counseling, employment services for current students, placement services for program completers.

## Cypress College

9200 Valley View, Cypress, CA 90630-5897
http://www.cypress.cc.ca.us/

**CONTACT** Michael Kasler, President
**Telephone:** 714-484-7000

**GENERAL INFORMATION** Public Institution. Founded 1966. **Accreditation:** Regional (WASC/ACCJC); dental assisting (ADA); dental hygiene (ADA); funeral service (ABFSE); health information technology (AHIMA); radiologic technology: radiography (JRCERT). **Total program enrollment:** 5208.

**PROGRAM(S) OFFERED**

• **Accounting** *5 students enrolled* • **Administrative Assistant and Secretarial Science, General** *1 student enrolled* • **Airline Flight Attendant** *21 students enrolled* • **Airline/Commercial/Professional Pilot and Flight Crew** *1 student enrolled* • **Autobody/Collision and Repair Technology/Technician** *8 students enrolled* • **Automobile/Automotive Mechanics Technology/Technician** *86 students enrolled* • **Aviation/Airway Management and Operations** *2 students enrolled* • **Business Administration and Management, General** *16 students enrolled* • **Commercial Photography** *2 students enrolled* • **Computer Graphics** *10 students enrolled* • **Computer Programming/Programmer, General** *2 students enrolled* • **Computer and Information Sciences, General** *15 students enrolled* • **Cooking and Related Culinary Arts, General** *7 students enrolled* • **Criminal Justice/Police Science** *1 student enrolled* • **Dental Assisting/Assistant** *11 students enrolled* • **Dental Hygiene/Hygienist** *12 students enrolled* • **Diagnostic Medical Sonography/Sonographer and Ultrasound Technician** *11 students enrolled* • **Graphic Design** *5 students enrolled* • **Health Information/Medical Records Technology/Technician** *4 students enrolled* • **Heating, Air Conditioning and Refrigeration Technology/Technician (ACH/ACR/ACHR/HRAC/HVAC/AC Technology)** *1 student enrolled* • **Hospital and Health Care Facilities Administration/Management** *1 student enrolled* • **Hospitality Administration/Management, General** *15 students enrolled* • **Human Services, General** *12 students enrolled* • **Legal Administrative Assistant/Secretary** *1 student enrolled* • **Medical Insurance Coding Specialist/Coder** *10 students enrolled* • **Music Management and Merchandising** *2 students enrolled* • **Music, General** *1 student enrolled* • **Photography** *12 students enrolled* • **Prepress/Desktop Publishing and Digital Imaging Design** *2 students enrolled* • **Psychiatric/Mental Health Services Technician** *49 students enrolled* • **Radiologic Technology/Science—Radiographer** *31 students enrolled* • **Resort Management** *2 students enrolled* • **Restaurant, Culinary, and Catering Management/Manager** *1 student enrolled* • **Sales, Distribution and Marketing Operations, General** *16 students enrolled* • **Selling Skills and Sales Operations** *1 student enrolled* • **Small Business Administration/Management** *2 students enrolled* • **Substance Abuse/Addiction Counseling** *21 students enrolled* • **Tourism and Travel Services Marketing Operations** *5 students enrolled*

**STUDENT SERVICES** Academic or career counseling, employment services for current students, remedial services.

## De Anza College

21250 Stevens Creek Boulevard, Cupertino, CA 95014-5793
http://www.deanza.fhda.edu/

**CONTACT** Brian Murphy, President
**Telephone:** 408-864-5678

**GENERAL INFORMATION** Public Institution. Founded 1967. **Accreditation:** Regional (WASC/ACCJC); medical assisting (AAMAE); physical therapy assisting (APTA). **Total program enrollment:** 10424.

**PROGRAM(S) OFFERED**

• **Accounting** *11 students enrolled* • **Administrative Assistant and Secretarial Science, General** *12 students enrolled* • **Animation, Interactive Technology, Video Graphics and Special Effects** *2 students enrolled* • **Automobile/Automotive Mechanics Technology/Technician** *5 students enrolled* • **Business Administration and Management, General** *40 students enrolled* • **Business, Management, Marketing, and Related Support Services, Other** *1 student enrolled* • **Ceramic Arts and Ceramics** *4 students enrolled* • **Child Development** *49 students enrolled* • **Commercial Photography** *2 students enrolled* • **Computer Programming/Programmer, General** *2 students enrolled* • **Computer Systems Networking and Telecommunications** *18 students enrolled* • **Data Entry/Microcomputer Applications, General** *3 students enrolled* • **Drafting and Design Technology/Technician, General** *23 students enrolled* • **Drawing** *1 student enrolled* • **Education/Teaching of Individuals in Early Childhood Special Education Programs** *1 student enrolled* • **Energy Management and Systems Technology/Technician** *1 student enrolled* • **Environmental Science** *1 student enrolled* • **Graphic Design** *3 students enrolled* • **Hazardous Materials Man-**

agement and Waste Technology/Technician *4 students enrolled* • **Health and Physical Education, General** *1 student enrolled* • **Legal Assistant/Paralegal** *39 students enrolled* • **Library Science/Librarianship** *1 student enrolled* • **Machine Tool Technology/Machinist** *47 students enrolled* • **Manufacturing Technology/ Technician** *2 students enrolled* • **Massage Therapy/Therapeutic Massage** *5 students enrolled* • **Mechanical Drafting and Mechanical Drafting CAD/CADD** *2 students enrolled* • **Medical/Clinical Assistant** *73 students enrolled* • **Radio and Television** *2 students enrolled* • **Real Estate** *4 students enrolled* • **Sales, Distribution and Marketing Operations, General** *8 students enrolled* • **Sculpture** *1 student enrolled* • **Security and Loss Prevention Services** *1 student enrolled* • **Taxation** *8 students enrolled* • **Technical and Business Writing** *8 students enrolled*

**STUDENT SERVICES** Academic or career counseling, daycare for children of students, employment services for current students, placement services for program completers, remedial services.

## Dell'Arte School of Physical Theatre

PO Box 816, Blue Lake, CA 95525
http://www.dellarte.com/

**CONTACT** Bobbi Ricca, Administrative Director
**Telephone:** 707-668-5663

**GENERAL INFORMATION** Private Institution. Founded 1971. **Total program enrollment:** 44. **Application fee:** $35.

**PROGRAM(S) OFFERED**
• **Drama and Dramatics/Theatre Arts, General** *20 students enrolled*

**STUDENT SERVICES** Employment services for current students, placement services for program completers.

## Design's School of Cosmetology

715 24th Street, Suite E, Paso Robles, CA 93446
http://designsschool.com/

**CONTACT** Sharon Skinner, Administrator
**Telephone:** 805-237-8575

**GENERAL INFORMATION** Private Institution. **Total program enrollment:** 46. **Application fee:** $50.

**PROGRAM(S) OFFERED**
• **Aesthetician/Esthetician and Skin Care Specialist** *6 hrs./$5950* • **Cosmetology/Cosmetologist, General** *12 hrs./$9650* • **Nail Technician/ Specialist and Manicurist** *3 hrs./$1500*

**STUDENT SERVICES** Academic or career counseling, placement services for program completers.

## Diablo Valley College

321 Golf Club Road, Pleasant Hill, CA 94523-1544
http://www.dvc.edu/

**CONTACT** Judy Walters, President
**Telephone:** 925-685-1230

**GENERAL INFORMATION** Public Institution. Founded 1949. **Accreditation:** Regional (WASC/ACCJC); dental assisting (ADA); dental hygiene (ADA). **Total program enrollment:** 7145.

**PROGRAM(S) OFFERED**
• **Accounting** *30 students enrolled* • **Administrative Assistant and Secretarial Science, General** *8 students enrolled* • **Animation, Interactive Technology, Video Graphics and Special Effects** *2 students enrolled* • **Applied Horticulture/ Horticultural Operations, General** *2 students enrolled* • **Building/Construction Site Management/Manager** *2 students enrolled* • **Building/Home/Construction Inspection/Inspector** *5 students enrolled* • **Business Administration and Management, General** *1 student enrolled* • **Business/Commerce, General** *12 students enrolled* • **Child Development** *69 students enrolled* • **Chinese Language and Literature** *7 students enrolled* • **Civil Drafting and Civil Engineering CAD/ CADD** *1 student enrolled* • **Computer Programming/Programmer, General** *1 student enrolled* • **Computer Systems Networking and Telecommunications** *1 student enrolled* • **Cooking and Related Culinary Arts, General** *37 students enrolled* • **Corrections and Criminal Justice, Other** *2 students enrolled* • **Corrections** *3 students enrolled* • **Criminal Justice/Police Science** *23 students enrolled* • **Dental Assisting/Assistant** *13 students enrolled* • **Dental Laboratory Technology/Technician** *16 students enrolled* • **Digital Communication and Media/Multimedia** *12 students enrolled* • **Drafting and Design Technology/ Technician, General** *2 students enrolled* • **Electrical/Electronics Equipment Installation and Repair, General** *4 students enrolled* • **Family Systems** *1 student enrolled* • **Forensic Science and Technology** *4 students enrolled* • **French Language and Literature** *1 student enrolled* • **Geography, Other** *2 students enrolled* • **German Language and Literature** *1 student enrolled* • **Human Services, General** *1 student enrolled* • **Italian Language and Literature** *6 students enrolled* • **Japanese Language and Literature** *6 students enrolled* • **Landscaping and Groundskeeping** *5 students enrolled* • **Library Assistant/ Technician** *17 students enrolled* • **Mechanical Drafting and Mechanical Drafting CAD/CADD** *1 student enrolled* • **Music Management and Merchandising** *25 students enrolled* • **Radio and Television** *2 students enrolled* • **Real Estate** *1 student enrolled* • **Restaurant, Culinary, and Catering Management/Manager** *19 students enrolled* • **Retailing and Retail Operations** *2 students enrolled* • **Small Business Administration/Management** *4 students enrolled* • **Spanish Language and Literature** *7 students enrolled* • **Special Education and Teaching, General** *5 students enrolled* • **Sport and Fitness Administration/Management** *9 students enrolled* • **Substance Abuse/Addiction Counseling** *20 students enrolled* • **System Administration/Administrator** *7 students enrolled*

**STUDENT SERVICES** Academic or career counseling, daycare for children of students, employment services for current students, placement services for program completers, remedial services.

## East Los Angeles College

1301 Avenida Cesar Chavez, Monterey Park, CA 91754-6099
http://www.elac.edu/

**CONTACT** Ernest H. Moreno, President
**Telephone:** 323-265-8650

**GENERAL INFORMATION** Public Institution. Founded 1945. **Accreditation:** Regional (WASC/ACCJC); health information technology (AHIMA). **Total program enrollment:** 6640.

**PROGRAM(S) OFFERED**
• **Accounting** *136 students enrolled* • **Administrative Assistant and Secretarial Science, General** *20 students enrolled* • **Architectural Technology/Technician** *20 students enrolled* • **Architecture and Related Services, Other** • **Automobile/ Automotive Mechanics Technology/Technician** *4 students enrolled* • **Biology Technician/Biotechnology Laboratory Technician** *2 students enrolled* • **Business Administration and Management, General** *1 student enrolled* • **Child Development** *96 students enrolled* • **Commercial Photography** *23 students enrolled* • **Computer Programming/Programmer, General** *1 student enrolled* • **Computer and Information Sciences, General** *1 student enrolled* • **Criminal Justice/Police Science** *1254 students enrolled* • **Drafting and Design Technology/Technician, General** *8 students enrolled* • **Electrical/Electronics Equipment Installation and Repair, General** *28 students enrolled* • **Emergency Medical Technology/ Technician (EMT Paramedic)** *12 students enrolled* • **Fire Science/Firefighting** *2 students enrolled* • **Health Information/Medical Records Technology/Technician** *1 student enrolled* • **Heating, Air Conditioning and Refrigeration Technology/ Technician (ACH/ACR/ACHR/HRAC/HVAC/AC Technology)** *15 students enrolled* • **Human Services, General** *34 students enrolled* • **Journalism** *2 students enrolled* • **Legal Administrative Assistant/Secretary** *2 students enrolled* • **Medical Insurance Coding Specialist/Coder** *48 students enrolled* • **Medical/Clinical Assistant** *3 students enrolled* • **Nursing—Registered Nurse Training (RN, ASN, BSN, MSN)** *14 students enrolled* • **Real Estate** *48 students enrolled* • **Respiratory Care Therapy/Therapist** *15 students enrolled* • **Science Technologies/ Technicians, Other** *1 student enrolled* • **Substance Abuse/Addiction Counseling** *1 student enrolled*

**STUDENT SERVICES** Academic or career counseling, daycare for children of students, employment services for current students, placement services for program completers, remedial services.

## East San Gabriel Valley Regional Occupational Program & Technical Center

1501 West Del Norte Avenue, West Covina, CA 91790
http://www.esgvrop.org/

**CONTACT** Laurel Adler, Superintendent
**Telephone:** 626-472-5195

**GENERAL INFORMATION** Private Institution. **Total program enrollment:** 541.

**PROGRAM(S) OFFERED**
• **Communication, Journalism and Related Programs, Other** *51 students enrolled* • **Computer Science** *21 students enrolled* • **Cosmetology/Cosmetologist, General** *10 students enrolled* • **Criminal Justice/Police Science** *11 students enrolled* • **Environmental/Environmental Health Engineering** *11 students enrolled* • **Marketing/Marketing Management, General** *9 students enrolled* • **Medical/Clinical Assistant** *36 students enrolled*

**STUDENT SERVICES** Academic or career counseling, employment services for current students, placement services for program completers, remedial services.

## El Camino College

16007 Crenshaw Boulevard, Torrance, CA 90506-0001
http://www.elcamino.edu/

**CONTACT** Thomas M. Fallo, Superintendent/President
**Telephone:** 310-532-3670

**GENERAL INFORMATION** Public Institution. Founded 1947. **Accreditation:** Regional (WASC/ACCJC); radiologic technology: radiography (JRCERT). **Total program enrollment:** 8468.

**PROGRAM(S) OFFERED**
• **Accounting** *8 students enrolled* • **Administrative Assistant and Secretarial Science, General** *2 students enrolled* • **Applied Horticulture/Horticultural Operations, General** *3 students enrolled* • **Automobile/Automotive Mechanics Technology/Technician** *5 students enrolled* • **Business Administration and Management, General** *13 students enrolled* • **Child Development** *10 students enrolled* • **Computer Installation and Repair Technology/Technician** *8 students enrolled* • **Computer Programming/Programmer, General** *1 student enrolled* • **Construction Trades, General** *4 students enrolled* • **Cosmetology/Cosmetologist, General** *6 students enrolled* • **Criminal Justice/Police Science** *14 students enrolled* • **Drafting and Design Technology/Technician, General** *4 students enrolled* • **Electrical/Electronics Equipment Installation and Repair, General** *3 students enrolled* • **Emergency Medical Technology/Technician (EMT Paramedic)** *62 students enrolled* • **Fashion/Apparel Design** *1 student enrolled* • **Fire Science/Firefighting** *30 students enrolled* • **Graphic Design** *3 students enrolled* • **Heating, Air Conditioning and Refrigeration Technology/Technician (ACH/ACR/ACHR/HRAC/HVAC/AC Technology)** *24 students enrolled* • **Information Technology** *2 students enrolled* • **Legal Assistant/Paralegal** *2 students enrolled* • **Machine Tool Technology/Machinist** *2 students enrolled* • **Radio and Television** *3 students enrolled* • **Real Estate** *2 students enrolled* • **Respiratory Care Therapy/Therapist** *4 students enrolled* • **Sales, Distribution and Marketing Operations, General** *13 students enrolled* • **Sign Language Interpretation and Translation** *19 students enrolled* • **Special Education and Teaching, General** *1 student enrolled* • **Technical Theatre/Theatre Design and Technology** *1 student enrolled* • **Welding Technology/Welder** *5 students enrolled*

**STUDENT SERVICES** Academic or career counseling, daycare for children of students, employment services for current students, placement services for program completers, remedial services.

## El Camino College Compton Center

1111 East Artesia Boulevard, Compton, CA 90221-5393
http://www.compton.edu/

**CONTACT** Dr. Lawrence M. Cox, CEO/Provost
**Telephone:** 310-900-1600

**GENERAL INFORMATION** Public Institution. Founded 1927. **Accreditation:** Regional (WASC/ACCJC). **Total program enrollment:** 1414.

**PROGRAM(S) OFFERED**
• **Automobile/Automotive Mechanics Technology/Technician** *3 students enrolled* • **Child Development** *18 students enrolled* • **Criminal Justice/Police Science** *4 students enrolled* • **Real Estate** *1 student enrolled* • **Welding Technology/Welder** *2 students enrolled*

**STUDENT SERVICES** Academic or career counseling, daycare for children of students, employment services for current students, placement services for program completers, remedial services.

## Elegance Academy of Makeup

4929 Wilshire Boulevard, Suite 520, Los Angeles, CA 90010-1734
http://www.ei.edu/

**CONTACT** Mary Hagen, Director
**Telephone:** 323-871-8318

**GENERAL INFORMATION** Private Institution. Founded 1966. **Total program enrollment:** 113. **Application fee:** $75.

**PROGRAM(S) OFFERED**
• **Make-Up Artist/Specialist** *500 hrs./$11,125*

**STUDENT SERVICES** Academic or career counseling, placement services for program completers.

## Elite Progressive School of Cosmetology

5522 Garfield Avenue, Sacramento, CA 95841

**CONTACT** Steve Mucciaro, Executive Director, Financial Aid
**Telephone:** 916-338-1885

**GENERAL INFORMATION** Private Institution. **Total program enrollment:** 301. **Application fee:** $75.

**PROGRAM(S) OFFERED**
• **Cosmetology, Barber/Styling, and Nail Instructor** *600 hrs./$3900*
• **Cosmetology/Cosmetologist, General** *1600 hrs./$13,319*

**STUDENT SERVICES** Academic or career counseling, employment services for current students, remedial services.

## Empire College

3035 Cleveland Avenue, Santa Rosa, CA 95403
http://www.empcol.com/

**CONTACT** Roy O. Hurd, President
**Telephone:** 707-546-4000

**GENERAL INFORMATION** Private Institution. Founded 1961. **Accreditation:** State accredited or approved. **Total program enrollment:** 823. **Application fee:** $75.

**PROGRAM(S) OFFERED**
• **Accounting Technology/Technician and Bookkeeping** *15 students enrolled* • **Accounting** *1750 hrs./$20,825* • **Administrative Assistant and Secretarial Science, General** *2 students enrolled* • **Computer Installation and Repair Technology/Technician** *750 hrs./$8925* • **Executive Assistant/Executive Secretary** *2 students enrolled* • **General Office Occupations and Clerical Services** • **Hospitality Administration/Management, General** *4 students enrolled* • **Information Technology** *1500 hrs./$17,850* • **Legal Administrative Assistant/Secretary** *2 students enrolled* • **Legal Assistant/Paralegal** *1750 hrs./$20,825* • **Medical Administrative/Executive Assistant and Medical Secretary** *12 students enrolled* • **Medical Insurance Coding Specialist/Coder** *13 students enrolled* • **Medical Office Assistant/Specialist** *1750 hrs./$20,825* • **Medical Transcription/Transcriptionist** *1 student enrolled* • **Medical/Clinical Assistant** *1250 hrs./$17,875* • **Receptionist** *9 students enrolled* • **Tourism and Travel Services Management** *19 students enrolled*

**STUDENT SERVICES** Academic or career counseling, employment services for current students, placement services for program completers.

## English Center for International Women

66 Franklin Street, Suite 300, Jack London Square, Oakland, CA 94607
http://www.eciw.org/

**CONTACT** Marcy Jackson, Executive Director
**Telephone:** 510-836-6700

**GENERAL INFORMATION** Private Institution. **Total program enrollment:** 89. **Application fee:** $50.

**PROGRAM(S) OFFERED**
• **General Office Occupations and Clerical Services** *78 students enrolled*

**STUDENT SERVICES** Academic or career counseling, employment services for current students, placement services for program completers, remedial services.

## Estes Institute of Cosmetology Arts and Science

324 East Main Street, Visalia, CA 93291

**CONTACT** Susan Estes Hedstrom, Fiscal Operations Director
**Telephone:** 559-733-3617

**GENERAL INFORMATION** Private Institution. **Total program enrollment:** 120. **Application fee:** $25.

**PROGRAM(S) OFFERED**
• **Cosmetology/Cosmetologist, General** *1600 hrs./$8220* • **Nail Technician/Specialist and Manicurist** *400 hrs./$1475*

## Everest College

2215 W. Mission Road, Alhambra, CA 91803
http://www.everest.edu/

**CONTACT** Linnea Ray, School President
**Telephone:** 626-979-4940

**GENERAL INFORMATION** Private Institution. **Total program enrollment:** 333.

**PROGRAM(S) OFFERED**
• **Business Administration and Management, General** *720 hrs./$12,964* • **Business/Commerce, General** *21 students enrolled* • **Dental Assisting/Assistant** *720 hrs./$14,193* • **Health and Medical Administrative Services, Other** *70 students enrolled* • **Licensed Practical/Vocational Nurse Training (LPN, LVN, Cert, Dipl, AAS)** *21 students enrolled* • **Massage Therapy/Therapeutic Massage** *720 hrs./$14,586* • **Medical Insurance Coding Specialist/Coder** *720 hrs./$13,409* • **Medical Office Management/Administration** *35 students enrolled* • **Medical/Clinical Assistant** *720 hrs./$14,514* • **Pharmacy Technician/Assistant** *720 hrs./$13,469*

**STUDENT SERVICES** Academic or career counseling, placement services for program completers.

## Everest College

511 North Brookhurst Street, #300, Anaheim, CA 92801
http://www.everest.edu/

**CONTACT** Staci K. Mall, School President
**Telephone:** 714-953-6500

**GENERAL INFORMATION** Private Institution. **Total program enrollment:** 430.

**PROGRAM(S) OFFERED**
• **Dental Assisting/Assistant** *720 hrs./$14,606* • **Massage Therapy/Therapeutic Massage** *720 hrs./$14,314* • **Medical Insurance Coding Specialist/Coder** *720 hrs./$12,786* • **Medical Insurance Specialist/Medical Biller** *51 students enrolled* • **Medical Office Assistant/Specialist** *2 students enrolled* • **Medical/Clinical Assistant** *720 hrs./$15,402* • **Nursing, Other** *1536 hrs./$27,877* • **Pharmacy Technician/Assistant** *44 students enrolled*

**STUDENT SERVICES** Academic or career counseling, placement services for program completers, remedial services.

## Everest College

12801 Crossroads Parkway South, City of Industry, CA 91746
http://www.everest.edu/

**CONTACT** Michelle Lisoskie, School President
**Telephone:** 562-908-2500

**GENERAL INFORMATION** Private Institution. Founded 1969. **Total program enrollment:** 314.

**PROGRAM(S) OFFERED**
• **Business Administration and Management, General** *648 hrs./$12,964* • **Dental Assisting/Assistant** *720 hrs./$14,193* • **Massage Therapy/Therapeutic Massage** *720 hrs./$14,586* • **Medical Insurance Specialist/Medical Biller** *720 hrs./$13,409* • **Medical/Clinical Assistant** *720 hrs./$14,691* • **Pharmacy Technician/Assistant** *720 hrs./$13,464*

**STUDENT SERVICES** Academic or career counseling, employment services for current students, placement services for program completers, remedial services.

## Everest College

1045 West Redondo Beach Boulevard, Suite 275, Gardena, CA 90247
http://www.everest.edu/

**CONTACT** Revina Miller, College President
**Telephone:** 310-527-7105

**GENERAL INFORMATION** Private Institution. **Total program enrollment:** 398.

**PROGRAM(S) OFFERED**
• **Dental Assisting/Assistant** *720 hrs./$14,193* • **Massage Therapy/Therapeutic Massage** *720 hrs./$14,376* • **Medical Insurance Coding Specialist/Coder** *720 hrs./$13,409* • **Medical Insurance Specialist/Medical Biller** *136 students enrolled* • **Medical Office Management/Administration** *37 students enrolled* • **Medical/Clinical Assistant** *720 hrs./$15,282*

**STUDENT SERVICES** Academic or career counseling, employment services for current students, placement services for program completers, remedial services.

## Everest College

3000 South Robertson Boulevard, Suite 300, Los Angeles, CA 90034
http://www.everest.edu/

**CONTACT** Tom Azimzadeh, President
**Telephone:** 310-840-5777

**GENERAL INFORMATION** Private Institution. Founded 1987. **Accreditation:** State accredited or approved. **Total program enrollment:** 211.

**PROGRAM(S) OFFERED**
• **Criminal Justice/Law Enforcement Administration** *96 hrs./$26,928* • **Dental Assisting/Assistant** *47 hrs./$12,903* • **Massage Therapy/Therapeutic Massage** *54 hrs./$13,260* • **Medical Insurance Specialist/Medical Biller** *47 hrs./$12,190* • **Medical/Clinical Assistant** *54 hrs./$13,808* • **Pharmacy Technician/Assistant** *720 hrs./$12,240*

**STUDENT SERVICES** Academic or career counseling, employment services for current students, placement services for program completers, remedial services.

## Everest College

3460 Wilshire Boulevard, #500, Los Angeles, CA 90010
http://www.everest.edu/

**CONTACT** Bob Bosic, Regional Vice President of Operations
**Telephone:** 213-388-9950

**GENERAL INFORMATION** Private Institution. Founded 1960. **Total program enrollment:** 362.

**PROGRAM(S) OFFERED**
• **Dental Assisting/Assistant** *720 hrs./$14,193* • **Health Information/Medical Records Administration/Administrator** *720 hrs./$14,193* • **Massage Therapy/Therapeutic Massage** *720 hrs./$14,586* • **Medical Insurance Specialist/Medical Biller** *720 hrs./$13,446* • **Medical/Clinical Assistant** *720 hrs./$15,300* • **Pharmacy Technician/Assistant** *50 students enrolled*

**STUDENT SERVICES** Academic or career counseling, employment services for current students, placement services for program completers, remedial services.

## Everest College

1460 South Milliken Avenue, Ontario, CA 91761
http://www.everest.edu/

**CONTACT** Scott Wardall, President
**Telephone:** 909-984-5027

**GENERAL INFORMATION** Private Institution. Founded 1991. **Accreditation:** State accredited or approved. **Total program enrollment:** 1140.

**PROGRAM(S) OFFERED**
• **Business Administration and Management, General** *648 hrs./$11,554* • **Dental Assisting/Assistant** *720 hrs./$14,960* • **Massage Therapy/Therapeutic Massage** *720 hrs./$14,575* • **Medical Insurance Coding Specialist/Coder** *560 hrs./$9250* • **Medical Insurance Specialist/Medical Biller** *152 students enrolled* • **Medical Office Management/Administration** • **Medical/Clinical Assistant** *720 hrs./$16,064* • **Pharmacy Technician/Assistant** *720 hrs./$12,000*

**STUDENT SERVICES** Academic or career counseling, employment services for current students, placement services for program completers, remedial services.

## Everest College

18040 Sherman Way, #400, Reseda, CA 91335
http://www.everest.edu/

**CONTACT** Lani Townsend, President
**Telephone:** 818-774-0550

**GENERAL INFORMATION** Private Institution. **Total program enrollment:** 294.

**PROGRAM(S) OFFERED**
• **Dental Assisting/Assistant** *720 hrs./$14,190* • **Massage Therapy/Therapeutic Massage** *750 hrs./$14,588* • **Medical Insurance Coding Specialist/Coder** *21 students enrolled* • **Medical Office Management/Administration** *720 hrs./$14,190* • **Medical/Clinical Assistant** *720 hrs./$15,297* • **Pharmacy Technician/Assistant** *720 hrs./$13,675* • **Surgical Technology/Technologist** *1220 hrs./$28,700*

**STUDENT SERVICES** Academic or career counseling, employment services for current students, placement services for program completers, remedial services.

## Everest College

217 E. Club Center Drive, Suite A, San Bernardino, CA 92408
http://www.everest.edu/

**CONTACT** Fred Faridian, President
**Telephone:** 909-777-3300

**GENERAL INFORMATION** Private Institution. **Total program enrollment:** 790.

**PROGRAM(S) OFFERED**
• **Corrections and Criminal Justice, Other** *96 hrs./$29,040* • **Dental Assisting/Assistant** *720 hrs./$13,775* • **Electrician** *720 hrs./$16,275* • **Massage Therapy/Therapeutic Massage** *720 hrs./$14,300* • **Medical Administrative/Executive Assistant and Medical Secretary** *720 hrs./$14,190* • **Medical Office Management/Administration** *79 students enrolled* • **Medical/Clinical Assistant** *720 hrs./$15,347*

**STUDENT SERVICES** Employment services for current students, placement services for program completers, remedial services.

## Everest College

814 Mission Street, #500, San Francisco, CA 94103
http://www.everest.edu/

**CONTACT** Stephanie Hunt, Director of Student Finance
**Telephone:** 415-777-2500 Ext. 275

**GENERAL INFORMATION** Private Institution. **Total program enrollment:** 652.

**PROGRAM(S) OFFERED**
• **Dental Assisting/Assistant** *720 hrs./$14,280* • **Massage Therapy/Therapeutic Massage** *720 hrs./$14,465* • **Medical Administrative/Executive Assistant and Medical Secretary** *43 students enrolled* • **Medical/Clinical Assistant** *720 hrs./$15,667* • **Pharmacy Technician/Assistant** *720 hrs./$14,190*

**STUDENT SERVICES** Academic or career counseling, employment services for current students, placement services for program completers, remedial services.

## Everest College

1245 South Winchester Boulevard, Suite 102, San Jose, CA 95128
http://www.everest.edu/

**CONTACT** Bill Grady, School President
**Telephone:** 510-582-9500

**GENERAL INFORMATION** Private Institution. **Total program enrollment:** 180.

**PROGRAM(S) OFFERED**
• **Massage Therapy/Therapeutic Massage** *720 hrs./$14,465* • **Medical Insurance Specialist/Medical Biller** *720 hrs./$14,190* • **Medical Office Assistant/Specialist** *720 hrs./$14,750* • **Medical/Clinical Assistant** *720 hrs./$14,465* • **Surgical Technology/Technologist** *1221 hrs./$27,134*

**STUDENT SERVICES** Placement services for program completers, remedial services.

## Everest College

1231 Cabrillo Avenue, Suite 201, Torrance, CA 90501
http://www.everest.edu/

**CONTACT** Duemand Edwards, College President
**Telephone:** 310-320-3200

**GENERAL INFORMATION** Private Institution. **Total program enrollment:** 104.

**PROGRAM(S) OFFERED**
• **Massage Therapy/Therapeutic Massage** *54 hrs./$14,480* • **Pharmacy Technician/Assistant** *49 hrs./$14,150*

**STUDENT SERVICES** Academic or career counseling, employment services for current students, placement services for program completers, remedial services.

## Everest Institute

2161 Technology Place, Long Beach, CA 90810
http://www.everest.edu/

**CONTACT** Lawrence Peyser, College President
**Telephone:** 562-624-9530 Ext. 200

**GENERAL INFORMATION** Private Institution. Founded 1969. **Accreditation:** State accredited or approved. **Total program enrollment:** 1933.

**PROGRAM(S) OFFERED**
• **Allied Health and Medical Assisting Services, Other** *720 hrs./$13,145* • **Automobile/Automotive Mechanics Technology/Technician** *1000 hrs./$23,417* • **Electrician** *720 hrs./$18,400* • **Heating, Air Conditioning and Refrigeration Technology/Technician (ACH/ACR/ACHR/HRAC/HVAC/AC Technology)** *600 hrs./$14,532* • **Heating, Air Conditioning, Ventilation and Refrigeration Maintenance Technology/Technician (HAC, HACR, HVAC, HVACR)** *104 students enrolled* • **Massage Therapy/Therapeutic Massage** *720 hrs./$15,424* • **Medical/Clinical Assistant** *36 students enrolled* • **Plumbing Technology/Plumber** *720 hrs./$16,106*

**STUDENT SERVICES** Academic or career counseling, employment services for current students, placement services for program completers, remedial services.

## Evergreen Valley College

3095 Yerba Buena Road, San Jose, CA 95135-1598
http://www.evc.edu/

**CONTACT** David Wain Coon, EdD, President
**Telephone:** 408-274-7900

**GENERAL INFORMATION** Public Institution. Founded 1975. **Accreditation:** Regional (WASC/ACCJC). **Total program enrollment:** 3105.

**PROGRAM(S) OFFERED**
• **Accounting** *3 students enrolled* • **Administrative Assistant and Secretarial Science, General** *17 students enrolled* • **Automobile/Automotive Mechanics Technology/Technician** *22 students enrolled* • **Computer Programming/Programmer, General** *1 student enrolled* • **Computer and Information Sciences, General** *5 students enrolled* • **Drafting and Design Technology/Technician, General** *11 students enrolled* • **Engineering Technology, General** *4 students enrolled* • **Legal Assistant/Paralegal** *26 students enrolled* • **Medical/Clinical Assistant** *1 student enrolled*

**STUDENT SERVICES** Academic or career counseling, daycare for children of students, employment services for current students, placement services for program completers, remedial services.

## Fashion Careers College

1923 Morena Boulevard, San Diego, CA 92110
http://www.fashioncareerscollege.com/

**CONTACT** Judith Thacker, President
**Telephone:** 619-275-4700 Ext. 301

**GENERAL INFORMATION** Private Institution. Founded 1979. **Accreditation:** State accredited or approved. **Total program enrollment:** 78. **Application fee:** $25.

**PROGRAM(S) OFFERED**
• **Fashion Merchandising** *22 students enrolled* • **Fashion/Apparel Design** *7 students enrolled*

**STUDENT SERVICES** Academic or career counseling, employment services for current students, placement services for program completers.

## Feather River College

570 Golden Eagle Avenue, Quincy, CA 95971-9124
http://www.frc.edu/

**CONTACT** Ron Taylor, Superintendent/President
**Telephone:** 530-283-0202

**GENERAL INFORMATION** Public Institution. Founded 1968. **Accreditation:** Regional (WASC/ACCJC). **Total program enrollment:** 520.

**PROGRAM(S) OFFERED**
• **Accounting** *6 students enrolled* • **Administrative Assistant and Secretarial Science, General** *2 students enrolled* • **Banking and Financial Support Services** *1 student enrolled* • **Business Administration and Management, General** *7 students enrolled* • **Business/Commerce, General** *3 students enrolled* • **Child Development** *1 student enrolled* • **Economics, General** *3 students enrolled* • **Equestrian/Equine Studies** *29 students enrolled* • **Licensed Practical/Vocational Nurse Training (LPN, LVN, Cert, Dipl, AAS)** *22 students enrolled*

**STUDENT SERVICES** Academic or career counseling, daycare for children of students, employment services for current students, remedial services.

## Federico College of Hairstyling

2100 Arden Way, Suite 265, Sacramento, CA 95825
http://federico.edu/

**CONTACT** Gary Federico, President
**Telephone:** 916-929-4242

**GENERAL INFORMATION** Private Institution. **Total program enrollment:** 151. **Application fee:** $100.

**PROGRAM(S) OFFERED**
• **Cosmetology/Cosmetologist, General** *1600 hrs./$16,885*

**STUDENT SERVICES** Academic or career counseling, placement services for program completers.

## Folsom Lake College

10 College Parkway, Folsom, CA 95630
http://www.flc.losrios.edu/

**CONTACT** Thelma Scott-Skillman, President
**Telephone:** 916-608-6572

**GENERAL INFORMATION** Public Institution. Founded 2004. **Total program enrollment:** 2553.

**PROGRAM(S) OFFERED**
• **Accounting** *20 students enrolled* • **Administrative Assistant and Secretarial Science, General** *2 students enrolled* • **Child Development** *76 students enrolled* • **Computer Graphics** *2 students enrolled* • **Computer Programming/Programmer, General** *7 students enrolled* • **Data Entry/Microcomputer Applications, General** *2 students enrolled* • **Data Modeling/Warehousing and Database Administration** *10 students enrolled* • **Real Estate** *4 students enrolled* • **Small Business Administration/Management** *1 student enrolled* • **Web/Multimedia Management and Webmaster** *3 students enrolled*

**STUDENT SERVICES** Academic or career counseling, employment services for current students, placement services for program completers, remedial services.

## Foothill College

12345 El Monte Road, Los Altos Hills, CA 94022-4599
http://www.foothill.edu/

**CONTACT** Judy C. Miner, President
**Telephone:** 650-949-7777

**GENERAL INFORMATION** Public Institution. Founded 1958. **Accreditation:** Regional (WASC/ACCJC); dental assisting (ADA); dental hygiene (ADA); radiologic technology: radiography (JRCERT). **Total program enrollment:** 4481.

*Foothill College (continued)*

**PROGRAM(S) OFFERED**

• **Accounting** *7 students enrolled* • **Administrative Assistant and Secretarial Science, General** *1 student enrolled* • **Anthropology** *2 students enrolled* • **Applied Horticulture/Horticultural Operations, General** *9 students enrolled* • **Art/Art Studies, General** *1 student enrolled* • **Biology Technician/Biotechnology Laboratory Technician** *3 students enrolled* • **Business Administration and Management, General** • **Child Development** *4 students enrolled* • **Chinese Language and Literature** *7 students enrolled* • **Computer Programming/Programmer, General** *1 student enrolled* • **Computer Systems Networking and Telecommunications** *4 students enrolled* • **Data Modeling/Warehousing and Database Administration** *3 students enrolled* • **Dental Assisting/Assistant** *20 students enrolled* • **Diagnostic Medical Sonography/Sonographer and Ultrasound Technician** • **Digital Communication and Media/Multimedia** *1 student enrolled* • **Drama and Dramatics/Theatre Arts, General** *8 students enrolled* • **E-Commerce/Electronic Commerce** *2 students enrolled* • **Electrician** *12 students enrolled* • **Film/Cinema Studies** *2 students enrolled* • **French Language and Literature** *4 students enrolled* • **Geography** *3 students enrolled* • **Geography, Other** *2 students enrolled* • **Graphic Design** *2 students enrolled* • **Health and Physical Education, General** *1 student enrolled* • **International Business/Trade/Commerce** *1 student enrolled* • **Korean Language and Literature** *1 student enrolled* • **Music Management and Merchandising** *1 student enrolled* • **Phlebotomy/Phlebotomist** • **Physician Assistant** *42 students enrolled* • **Plumbing Technology/Plumber** *11 students enrolled* • **Radiologic Technology/Science—Radiographer** • **Real Estate** *2 students enrolled* • **Respiratory Care Therapy/Therapist** • **Sheet Metal Technology/Sheetworking** *44 students enrolled* • **Sociology** *3 students enrolled* • **Spanish Language and Literature** *3 students enrolled* • **Special Education and Teaching, General** *13 students enrolled* • **Tourism and Travel Services Marketing Operations** *66 students enrolled* • **Web/Multimedia Management and Webmaster** *1 student enrolled*

**STUDENT SERVICES** Academic or career counseling, employment services for current students, placement services for program completers, remedial services.

## Foothill-DeAnza Community College District

12345 El Monte Road, Los Altos Hills, CA 94022-4599

**CONTACT** Martha Kanter, Chancellor
**Telephone:** 650-949-6106

**GENERAL INFORMATION** Public Institution.

## Four-D Success Academy

1020 East Washington Street, Colton, CA 92324
http://www.4dddd.com/

**CONTACT** Linda L. Smith, President/CEO
**Telephone:** 909-783-9331

**GENERAL INFORMATION** Private Institution. **Total program enrollment:** 142.

**PROGRAM(S) OFFERED**

• **Dental Assisting/Assistant** *32 hrs./$14,000* • **Health/Medical Claims Examiner** • **Licensed Practical/Vocational Nurse Training (LPN, LVN, Cert, Dipl, AAS)** *62 hrs./$30,000* • **Massage Therapy/Therapeutic Massage** *39 hrs./$14,000* • **Medical Insurance Coding Specialist/Coder** *60 students enrolled* • **Medical Office Assistant/Specialist** *34 hrs./$14,000* • **Medical/Clinical Assistant** *97 students enrolled* • **Nurse/Nursing Assistant/Aide and Patient Care Assistant** • **Pharmacy Technician/Assistant** *33 hrs./$14,000*

**STUDENT SERVICES** Academic or career counseling, daycare for children of students, employment services for current students, placement services for program completers, remedial services.

## Fredrick and Charles Beauty College

831 F Street, Eureka, CA 95501

**CONTACT** Jeanie Scott, Owner
**Telephone:** 707-443-2733

**GENERAL INFORMATION** Private Institution. Founded 1955. **Total program enrollment:** 89.

**PROGRAM(S) OFFERED**

• **Aesthetician/Esthetician and Skin Care Specialist** *600 hrs./$4000* • **Cosmetology/Cosmetologist, General** *1600 hrs./$9660* • **Education, Other** *600 hrs./$4000* • **Nail Technician/Specialist and Manicurist** *400 hrs./$2700*

**STUDENT SERVICES** Academic or career counseling, placement services for program completers.

## Fremont College

18000 Studebaker Road, 9th Floor, Cerritos, CA 90703
http://www.fremont.edu/

**CONTACT** Sabrina Kay, Chairman & CEO
**Telephone:** 562-809-5100

**GENERAL INFORMATION** Private Institution. **Total program enrollment:** 171. **Application fee:** $75.

**PROGRAM(S) OFFERED**

• **Business Administration and Management, General** *90 hrs./$22,800* • **Legal Assistant/Paralegal** *105 hrs./$26,636* • **Massage Therapy/Therapeutic Massage** *60 hrs./$14,400* • **Therapeutic Recreation/Recreational Therapy** *90 hrs./$21,600*

**STUDENT SERVICES** Academic or career counseling, employment services for current students, placement services for program completers.

## Fresno City College

1101 East University Avenue, Fresno, CA 93741-0002
http://www.fresnocitycollege.edu/

**CONTACT** Dr. Guy Lease, Interim President
**Telephone:** 559-442-4600

**GENERAL INFORMATION** Public Institution. Founded 1910. **Accreditation:** Regional (WASC/ACCJC); dental hygiene (ADA); health information technology (AHIMA); radiologic technology: radiography (JRCERT). **Total program enrollment:** 8648.

**PROGRAM(S) OFFERED**

• **Accounting** *18 students enrolled* • **Administrative Assistant and Secretarial Science, General** *26 students enrolled* • **Advertising** *2 students enrolled* • **Applied Horticulture/Horticultural Operations, General** *5 students enrolled* • **Archeology** *2 students enrolled* • **Autobody/Collision and Repair Technology/Technician** *25 students enrolled* • **Automobile/Automotive Mechanics Technology/Technician** *1 student enrolled* • **Building/Home/Construction Inspection/Inspector** *6 students enrolled* • **Business Administration and Management, General** *28 students enrolled* • **Business, Management, Marketing, and Related Support Services, Other** *2 students enrolled* • **Child Development** *36 students enrolled* • **Commercial Photography** *14 students enrolled* • **Communications Systems Installation and Repair Technology** *17 students enrolled* • **Computer Installation and Repair Technology/Technician** *1 student enrolled* • **Computer Systems Networking and Telecommunications** *2 students enrolled* • **Construction Trades, General** *1 student enrolled* • **Cooking and Related Culinary Arts, General** *4 students enrolled* • **Corrections and Criminal Justice, Other** *36 students enrolled* • **Corrections** *28 students enrolled* • **Criminal Justice/Police Science** *186 students enrolled* • **Data Entry/Microcomputer Applications, General** *7 students enrolled* • **Drafting and Design Technology/Technician, General** *1 student enrolled* • **Education/Teaching of Individuals in Early Childhood Special Education Programs** *5 students enrolled* • **Electrical/Electronics Equipment Installation and Repair, General** *5 students enrolled* • **Emergency Medical Technology/Technician (EMT Paramedic)** *92 students enrolled* • **Family Systems** *2 students enrolled* • **Fire Science/Firefighting** *68 students enrolled* • **Foods, Nutrition, and Wellness Studies, General** *1 student enrolled* • **Foodservice Systems Administration/Management** *9 students enrolled* • **Graphic Communications, General** *1 student enrolled* • **Heating, Air Conditioning and Refrigeration Technology/Technician (ACH/ACR/ACHR/HRAC/HVAC/AC Technology)** *12 students enrolled* • **Human Services, General** *1 student enrolled* • **Industrial Electronics Technology/Technician** *2 students enrolled* • **Legal Assistant/Paralegal** *10 students enrolled* • **Library Assistant/Technician** *7 students enrolled* • **Machine Tool Technology/Machinist** *22 students enrolled* • **Mechanical Engineering/Mechanical Technology/Technician** *1 student enrolled* • **Medical Administrative/Executive Assistant and Medical Secretary** *18 students enrolled* • **Office Management and Supervision** *2 students enrolled* • **Personal and Culinary Services, Other** *34 students enrolled* • **Photography** *6 students enrolled* • **Real Estate** *2 students enrolled* • **Retailing and Retail Operations** *2 students enrolled* • **Selling Skills and Sales Operations** *2 students* enrolled • **Special Education and Teaching, General** *8 students enrolled* • **Substance Abuse/Addiction Counseling** *63 students enrolled* • **Surgical Technology/Technologist** *8 students enrolled* • **Teacher Assistant/Aide** *10 students enrolled* • **Visual and Performing Arts, Other** *1 student enrolled* • **Web/Multimedia Management and Webmaster** *3 students enrolled* • **Welding Technology/Welder** *5 students enrolled*

**STUDENT SERVICES** Academic or career counseling, daycare for children of students, employment services for current students, placement services for program completers, remedial services.

## Fullerton College

321 East Chapman Avenue, Fullerton, CA 92832-2095
http://www.fullcoll.edu/

**CONTACT** Kathleen O'Connell Hodge, EdD, President
**Telephone:** 714-992-7000

**GENERAL INFORMATION** Public Institution. Founded 1913. **Accreditation:** Regional (WASC/ACCJC). **Total program enrollment:** 8802.

**PROGRAM(S) OFFERED**

• **Accounting** *4 students enrolled* • **Advertising** *2 students enrolled* • **Animation, Interactive Technology, Video Graphics and Special Effects** *1 student enrolled* • **Apparel and Textile Marketing Management** *1 student enrolled* • **Architectural Technology/Technician** *1 student enrolled* • **Automobile/Automotive Mechanics Technology/Technician** *9 students enrolled* • **Building/Construction Site Management/Manager** *1 student enrolled* • **Cabinetmaking and Millwork/Millwright** *1 student enrolled* • **Child Development** *5 students enrolled* • **Computer Graphics** *4 students enrolled* • **Computer and Information Sciences and Support Services, Other** *1 student enrolled* • **Construction Trades, General** *2 students enrolled* • **Cosmetology/Cosmetologist, General** *19 students enrolled* • **Criminal Justice/Police Science** *53 students enrolled* • **Data Entry/Microcomputer Applications, General** *1 student enrolled* • **Drafting and Design Technology/Technician, General** *2 students enrolled* • **E-Commerce/Electronic Commerce** *1 student enrolled* • **Fashion/Apparel Design** *1 student enrolled* • **Graphic Communications, General** *10 students enrolled* • **Interior Design** *4 students enrolled* • **International Business/Trade/Commerce** *3 students enrolled* • **Journalism** *1 student enrolled* • **Legal Assistant/Paralegal** *19 students enrolled* • **Machine Tool Technology/Machinist** *6 students enrolled* • **Massage Therapy/Therapeutic Massage** *12 students enrolled* • **Music Management and Merchandising** *4 students enrolled* • **Public Relations/Image Management** *1 student enrolled* • **Radio and Television** *6 students enrolled* • **Real Estate** *1 student enrolled* • **Sales, Distribution and Marketing Operations, General** *1 student enrolled* • **Small Business Administration/Management** *2 students enrolled* • **Sport and Fitness Administration/Management** *3 students enrolled* • **Welding Technology/Welder** *7 students enrolled*

**STUDENT SERVICES** Academic or career counseling, daycare for children of students, employment services for current students, placement services for program completers, remedial services.

## Galen College of Medical and Dental Assistants

1325 North Wishon Avenue, Fresno, CA 93728-2381

**CONTACT** Stella Mesple, President
**Telephone:** 559-264-9700

**GENERAL INFORMATION** Private Institution. Founded 1969. **Total program enrollment:** 130. **Application fee:** $75.

**PROGRAM(S) OFFERED**

• **Dental Assisting/Assistant** *720 hrs./$12,500* • **Medical/Clinical Assistant** *720 hrs./$10,800*

**STUDENT SERVICES** Placement services for program completers.

## Gavilan College

5055 Santa Teresa Boulevard, Gilroy, CA 95020-9599
http://www.gavilan.edu/

**CONTACT** Steve Kinsella, President/Superintendent
**Telephone:** 408-848-4800

**GENERAL INFORMATION** Public Institution. Founded 1919. **Accreditation:** Regional (WASC/ACCJC). **Total program enrollment:** 1049.

**PROGRAM(S) OFFERED**

• **Accounting** *5 students enrolled* • **Administrative Assistant and Secretarial Science, General** *4 students enrolled* • **Airframe Mechanics and Aircraft Maintenance Technology/Technician** *5 students enrolled* • **Business/Commerce, General** *2 students enrolled* • **Child Development** *14 students enrolled* • **Computer Programming/Programmer, General** *2 students enrolled* • **Cosmetology/Cosmetologist, General** *33 students enrolled* • **Criminal Justice/Police Science** *8 students enrolled* • **Data Entry/Microcomputer Applications, General** *3 students enrolled* • **Drafting and Design Technology/Technician, General** *1 student enrolled* • **Licensed Practical/Vocational Nurse Training (LPN, LVN, Cert, Dipl, AAS)** *23 students enrolled* • **Nursing—Registered Nurse Training (RN, ASN, BSN, MSN)** *17 students enrolled*

**STUDENT SERVICES** Academic or career counseling, daycare for children of students, employment services for current students, remedial services.

## Gemological Institute of America

5345 Armada Drive, Carlsbad, CA 92008
http://www.gia.edu/

**CONTACT** Donna Baker, President
**Telephone:** 760-603-4000

**GENERAL INFORMATION** Private Institution. **Total program enrollment:** 204. **Application fee:** $75.

**PROGRAM(S) OFFERED**

• **Business Administration, Management and Operations, Other** *37 students enrolled* • **Metal and Jewelry Arts** *210 hrs./$5100* • **Selling Skills and Sales Operations** *3497 students enrolled*

**STUDENT SERVICES** Employment services for current students.

## Glendale Career College

1015 Grandview Avenue, Glendale, CA 91201
http://www.success.edu/

**CONTACT** Serjik Kesachekian, Campus Director
**Telephone:** 818-956-4915 Ext. 220

**GENERAL INFORMATION** Private Institution. **Total program enrollment:** 213.

**PROGRAM(S) OFFERED**

• **Allied Health and Medical Assisting Services, Other** *720 hrs./$12,315* • **Computer and Information Sciences, General** *720 hrs./$11,595* • **Instrumentation Technology/Technician** *15 students enrolled* • **Massage Therapy/Therapeutic Massage** *720 hrs./$12,315* • **Medical Office Management/Administration** *720 hrs./$12,315* • **Medical/Clinical Assistant** *35 students enrolled* • **Nursing, Other** *1560 hrs./$26,595* • **Surgical Technology/Technologist** *1440 hrs./$23,115*

**STUDENT SERVICES** Placement services for program completers, remedial services.

## Glendale Community College

1500 North Verdugo Road, Glendale, CA 91208-2894
http://www.glendale.edu/

**CONTACT** Audre Levy, Superintendent President
**Telephone:** 818-240-1000

**GENERAL INFORMATION** Public Institution. Founded 1927. **Accreditation:** Regional (WASC/ACCJC). **Total program enrollment:** 5589.

**PROGRAM(S) OFFERED**

• **Accounting** *25 students enrolled* • **Administrative Assistant and Secretarial Science, General** *70 students enrolled* • **Aircraft Powerplant Technology/Technician** *1 student enrolled* • **Airline Flight Attendant** *11 students enrolled* • **Airline/Commercial/Professional Pilot and Flight Crew** *3 students enrolled* • **Architectural Technology/Technician** *12 students enrolled* • **Art/Art Studies, General** *2 students enrolled* • **Aviation/Airway Management and Operations** *1 student enrolled* • **Banking and Financial Support Services** *2 students enrolled* • **Business Administration and Management, General** *4 students enrolled* • **Business/Commerce, General** *1 student enrolled* • **Ceramic Arts and Ceramics** *3 students enrolled* • **Child Development** *15 students enrolled* • **Commercial and Advertising Art** *4 students enrolled* • **Computer Graphics** *5 students enrolled* • **Cooking and Related Culinary Arts, General** *11 students enrolled* • **Criminal**

*Glendale Community College (continued)*

**Justice/Police Science** *2 students enrolled* • **Dance, General** *1 student enrolled* • **Drafting and Design Technology/Technician, General** *2 students enrolled* • **Fire Science/Firefighting** *5 students enrolled* • **Foodservice Systems Administration/Management** *4 students enrolled* • **Hospitality Administration/Management, General** *10 students enrolled* • **Insurance** *1 student enrolled* • **International Business/Trade/Commerce** *1 student enrolled* • **Machine Tool Technology/Machinist** *4 students enrolled* • **Manufacturing Technology/Technician** *1 student enrolled* • **Mass Communication/Media Studies** *15 students enrolled* • **Medical Administrative/Executive Assistant and Medical Secretary** *9 students enrolled* • **Medical/Clinical Assistant** *5 students enrolled* • **Music, General** *1 student enrolled* • **Nursing—Registered Nurse Training (RN, ASN, BSN, MSN)** *36 students enrolled* • **Photography** *1 student enrolled* • **Public Relations/Image Management** *3 students enrolled* • **Radio and Television** *1 student enrolled* • **Real Estate** *11 students enrolled* • **Small Business Administration/Management** *1 student enrolled* • **Sport and Fitness Administration/Management** *2 students enrolled* • **Substance Abuse/Addiction Counseling** *15 students enrolled* • **Welding Technology/Welder** *2 students enrolled*

**STUDENT SERVICES** Academic or career counseling, daycare for children of students, employment services for current students, placement services for program completers, remedial services.

## Gnomon School of Visual Effects

1015 N. Cahuenga Boulevard, Suite 54301, Hollywood, CA 90038
gnomonschool.com

**CONTACT** Darrin Krumweide, Chief Administrator Officer/Director of Education
**Telephone:** 323-466-6663 Ext. 11

**GENERAL INFORMATION** Private Institution. **Total program enrollment:** 76. **Application fee:** $25.

**PROGRAM(S) OFFERED**
• **Computer Graphics** *32 students enrolled*

**STUDENT SERVICES** Academic or career counseling, employment services for current students, placement services for program completers.

## Golden Gate University

536 Mission Street, San Francisco, CA 94105-2968
http://www.ggu.edu/

**CONTACT** Dan Angel, President
**Telephone:** 415-442-7800

**GENERAL INFORMATION** Private Institution. Founded 1901. **Accreditation:** Regional (WASC/ACSCU). **Total program enrollment:** 1212. **Application fee:** $55.

**PROGRAM(S) OFFERED**
• **Accounting** *7 students enrolled* • **Business Administration and Management, General** *2 students enrolled* • **Computer and Information Sciences and Support Services, Other** *5 students enrolled* • **Human Resources Management/Personnel Administration, General** *3 students enrolled* • **Marketing/Marketing Management, General** *3 students enrolled*

**STUDENT SERVICES** Academic or career counseling, employment services for current students, placement services for program completers, remedial services.

## Golden State College

3356 South Fairway, Visalia, CA 93277
http://www.goldenstatecollege.com/

**CONTACT** Gary Yasuda, President
**Telephone:** 559-733-4040

**GENERAL INFORMATION** Private Institution. **Total program enrollment:** 356. **Application fee:** $100.

**PROGRAM(S) OFFERED**
• **Accounting and Related Services, Other** *720 hrs./$10,750* • **Business/Office Automation/Technology/Data Entry** *720 hrs./$10,750* • **Massage Therapy/Therapeutic Massage** *720 hrs./$11,049* • **Medical Administrative/Executive Assistant and Medical Secretary** *720 hrs./$10,750* • **Medical/Clinical Assistant** *720 hrs./$10,341*

**STUDENT SERVICES** Academic or career counseling, employment services for current students, placement services for program completers.

## Golden West College

PO Box 2748, 15744 Golden West Street, Huntington Beach, CA 92647-2748
http://www.gwc.cccd.edu/

**CONTACT** Wes Bryan, President
**Telephone:** 714-892-7711

**GENERAL INFORMATION** Public Institution. Founded 1966. **Accreditation:** Regional (WASC/ACCJC). **Total program enrollment:** 3958.

**PROGRAM(S) OFFERED**
• **Accounting** *18 students enrolled* • **Administrative Assistant and Secretarial Science, General** *4 students enrolled* • **Architectural Technology/Technician** *8 students enrolled* • **Autobody/Collision and Repair Technology/Technician** *13 students enrolled* • **Automobile/Automotive Mechanics Technology/Technician** *1 student enrolled* • **Business Administration and Management, General** *11 students enrolled* • **Cosmetology/Cosmetologist, General** *43 students enrolled* • **Criminal Justice/Police Science** *101 students enrolled* • **Diesel Mechanics Technology/Technician** *15 students enrolled* • **Drafting and Design Technology/Technician, General** *8 students enrolled* • **Floriculture/Floristry Operations and Management** *10 students enrolled* • **Graphic Design** *11 students enrolled* • **Legal Administrative Assistant/Secretary** *1 student enrolled* • **Music Management and Merchandising** *4 students enrolled* • **Nursing—Registered Nurse Training (RN, ASN, BSN, MSN)** *5 students enrolled* • **Office Management and Supervision** *1 student enrolled* • **Sign Language Interpretation and Translation** *19 students enrolled*

**STUDENT SERVICES** Academic or career counseling, daycare for children of students, employment services for current students, placement services for program completers, remedial services.

## Grossmont College

8800 Grossmont College Drive, El Cajon, CA 92020-1799
http://www.grossmont.edu/

**CONTACT** Sunita V. Cooke, President
**Telephone:** 619-644-7000

**GENERAL INFORMATION** Public Institution. Founded 1961. **Accreditation:** Regional (WASC/ACCJC); cardiovascular technology (JRCECT). **Total program enrollment:** 4375.

**PROGRAM(S) OFFERED**
• **Administrative Assistant and Secretarial Science, General** *109 students enrolled* • **Arabic Language and Literature** *5 students enrolled* • **Business Administration and Management, General** *4 students enrolled* • **Business/Commerce, General** *6 students enrolled* • **Cardiovascular Technology/Technologist** *28 students enrolled* • **Child Development** *6 students enrolled* • **Computer Programming/Programmer, General** *4 students enrolled* • **Computer Systems Networking and Telecommunications** *2 students enrolled* • **Cooking and Related Culinary Arts, General** *115 students enrolled* • **Corrections** *1 student enrolled* • **Criminal Justice/Police Science** *11 students enrolled* • **Dance, General** *5 students enrolled* • **Data Entry/Microcomputer Applications, General** *1 student enrolled* • **Digital Communication and Media/Multimedia** *1 student enrolled* • **Drama and Dramatics/Theatre Arts, General** *2 students enrolled* • **Forensic Science and Technology** *64 students enrolled* • **French Language and Literature** *4 students enrolled* • **German Language and Literature** *17 students enrolled* • **Health and Physical Education, General** *3 students enrolled* • **Hospitality Administration/Management, General** *7 students enrolled* • **International Business/Trade/Commerce** *11 students enrolled* • **Japanese Language and Literature** *5 students enrolled* • **Medical Administrative/Executive Assistant and Medical Secretary** *3 students enrolled* • **Music, General** *2 students enrolled* • **Orthotist/Prosthetist** *5 students enrolled* • **Public Administration and Social Service Professions, Other** *4 students enrolled* • **Radio and Television** *8 students enrolled* • **Restaurant, Culinary, and Catering Management/Manager** *2 students enrolled* • **Retailing and Retail Operations** *1 student enrolled* • **Russian**

**Language and Literature** *1 student enrolled* • **Sales, Distribution and Marketing Operations, General** *4 students enrolled* • **Spanish Language and Literature** *11 students enrolled* • **Web/Multimedia Management and Webmaster** *2 students enrolled*

**STUDENT SERVICES** Academic or career counseling, daycare for children of students, employment services for current students, placement services for program completers, remedial services.

## Grossmont-Cuyamaca Community College District

8800 Grossmont College Drive, El Cajon, CA 92020-1799

**CONTACT** Omero Suarez, Chancellor
**Telephone:** 619-644-7010

**GENERAL INFORMATION** Public Institution.

## Hacienda La Puente Unified School District–Adult Education

PO Box 60002, City of Industry, CA 91716-0002
http://www.hlpusd.k12.ca.us/

**CONTACT** Cynthia Parulan-Colfer, Assistant Superintendent-Adult Education
**Telephone:** 626-933-3914

**GENERAL INFORMATION** Public Institution. Founded 1956. **Total program enrollment:** 899.

**PROGRAM(S) OFFERED**
• **Accounting Technology/Technician and Bookkeeping** *1600 hrs./$600* • **Accounting** *79 students enrolled* • **Adult Health Nurse/Nursing** *1530 hrs./$1200* • **Aesthetician/Esthetician and Skin Care Specialist** *1440 hrs./$600* • **Allied Health and Medical Assisting Services, Other** *500 hrs./$550* • **Cosmetology, Barber/Styling, and Nail Instructor** *160 hrs./$1208* • **Dental Assisting/Assistant** *94 students enrolled* • **Electrical and Electronic Engineering Technologies/Technicians, Other** *1440 hrs./$550* • **Licensed Practical/Vocational Nurse Training (LPN, LVN, Cert, Dipl, AAS)** *64 students enrolled* • **Medical/Clinical Assistant** *87 students enrolled* • **Psychiatric/Mental Health Nurse/Nursing** *69 students enrolled*

**STUDENT SERVICES** Academic or career counseling, employment services for current students, placement services for program completers, remedial services.

## Hair California Beauty Academy

1110 N. Tustin Street, Orange, CA 92867

**GENERAL INFORMATION** Private Institution. **Total program enrollment:** 111.

**PROGRAM(S) OFFERED**
• **Aesthetician/Esthetician and Skin Care Specialist** *600 hrs./$6100* • **Barbering/Barber** *1500 hrs./$16,100* • **Cosmetology, Barber/Styling, and Nail Instructor** *600 hrs./$6100* • **Cosmetology/Cosmetologist, General** *1600 hrs./$17,300* • **Massage Therapy/Therapeutic Massage** *600 hrs./$6100* • **Nail Technician/Specialist and Manicurist** *400 hrs./$4100*

## Hair Masters University

208 West Highland Avenue, San Bernardino, CA 92405
http://www.gotobeautyschool.com/

**CONTACT** Robert P. Gross, President
**Telephone:** 909-982-4200

**GENERAL INFORMATION** Private Institution. **Total program enrollment:** 50. **Application fee:** $100.

**PROGRAM(S) OFFERED**
• **Cosmetology/Cosmetologist, General** *1600 hrs./$15,424* • **Nail Technician/Specialist and Manicurist**

**STUDENT SERVICES** Academic or career counseling, placement services for program completers.

## Hartnell College

156 Homestead Avenue, Salinas, CA 93901-1697
http://www.hartnell.edu/

**CONTACT** Phoebe K. Helm, Superintendent President
**Telephone:** 831-755-6700

**GENERAL INFORMATION** Public Institution. Founded 1920. **Accreditation:** Regional (WASC/ACCJC); medical laboratory technology (NAACLS). **Total program enrollment:** 2848.

**PROGRAM(S) OFFERED**
• **Accounting** *2 students enrolled* • **Administrative Assistant and Secretarial Science, General** *3 students enrolled* • **Architectural Drafting and Architectural CAD/CADD** *1 student enrolled* • **Automobile/Automotive Mechanics Technology/Technician** *1 student enrolled* • **Building/Construction Site Management/Manager** *1 student enrolled* • **Carpentry/Carpenter** *2 students enrolled* • **Child Development** *29 students enrolled* • **Construction Trades, General** *1 student enrolled* • **Criminal Justice/Police Science** *24 students enrolled* • **Digital Communication and Media/Multimedia** *4 students enrolled* • **Electrical/Electronics Equipment Installation and Repair, General** *2 students enrolled* • **Licensed Practical/Vocational Nurse Training (LPN, LVN, Cert, Dipl, AAS)** *20 students enrolled* • **Mechanical Drafting and Mechanical Drafting CAD/CADD** *2 students enrolled* • **Real Estate** *1 student enrolled* • **Substance Abuse/Addiction Counseling** *1 student enrolled* • **Welding Technology/Welder** *1 student enrolled*

**STUDENT SERVICES** Academic or career counseling, daycare for children of students, employment services for current students, remedial services.

## Heald College–Concord

2150 John Glenn Drive, Concord, CA 94520-5618
http://www.heald.edu/

**CONTACT** Shirley Llafet, Campus President
**Telephone:** 925-288-5800

**GENERAL INFORMATION** Private Institution. Founded 1863. **Accreditation:** Regional (WASC/ACCJC). **Total program enrollment:** 882.

**PROGRAM(S) OFFERED**
• **Accounting and Business/Management** *2 students enrolled* • **Accounting and Related Services, Other** • **Accounting** • **Business Administration, Management and Operations, Other** • **Business Operations Support and Secretarial Services, Other** *8 students enrolled* • **Computer Engineering Technology/Technician** • **Computer and Information Sciences and Support Services, Other** *5 students enrolled* • **Criminal Justice/Law Enforcement Administration** • **General Office Occupations and Clerical Services** • **Management Information Systems, General** • **Medical Administrative/Executive Assistant and Medical Secretary** • **Medical Insurance Coding Specialist/Coder** *6 students enrolled* • **Medical Office Assistant/Specialist** *6 students enrolled* • **Medical/Clinical Assistant** *6 students enrolled* • **Phlebotomy/Phlebotomist** • **System Administration/Administrator** *2 students enrolled*

**STUDENT SERVICES** Academic or career counseling, employment services for current students, placement services for program completers, remedial services.

## Heald College–Fresno

255 West Bullard Avenue, Fresno, CA 93704-1706
http://www.heald.edu/

**CONTACT** Carolyn Kovalski, President
**Telephone:** 209-438-4222

**GENERAL INFORMATION** Private Institution. Founded 1863. **Accreditation:** Regional (WASC/ACCJC). **Total program enrollment:** 898.

*Heald College–Fresno (continued)*

**PROGRAM(S) OFFERED**

• **Accounting and Business/Management** *2 students enrolled* • **Business Administration, Management and Operations, Other** *1 student enrolled* • **Business Operations Support and Secretarial Services, Other** *3 students enrolled* • **Hospitality Administration/Management, General** *6 students enrolled* • **Medical Insurance Coding Specialist/Coder** *22 students enrolled* • **Medical Office Assistant/Specialist** *1 student enrolled* • **Medical/Clinical Assistant** *3 students enrolled*

**STUDENT SERVICES** Academic or career counseling, employment services for current students, placement services for program completers, remedial services.

## Heald College–Hayward

25500 Industrial Boulevard, Hayward, CA 94545
http://www.heald.edu/

**CONTACT** Nick Davis, Campus President
**Telephone:** 510-783-2100

**GENERAL INFORMATION** Private Institution. Founded 1863. **Accreditation:** Regional (WASC/ACCJC). **Total program enrollment:** 947.

**PROGRAM(S) OFFERED**

• **Accounting and Business/Management** *2 students enrolled* • **Business Administration, Management and Operations, Other** *8 students enrolled* • **Business Operations Support and Secretarial Services, Other** *1 student enrolled* • **Computer and Information Sciences and Support Services, Other** • **Medical Insurance Coding Specialist/Coder** *21 students enrolled* • **Medical Office Assistant/Specialist** *6 students enrolled* • **System Administration/Administrator** *3 students enrolled*

**STUDENT SERVICES** Academic or career counseling, employment services for current students, placement services for program completers, remedial services.

## Heald College–Rancho Cordova

2910 Prospect Park Drive, Rancho Cordova, CA 95670-6005
http://www.heald.edu/

**CONTACT** Guy R. Adams, Executive Director of Campus Operations
**Telephone:** 916-638-1616 Ext. 2325

**GENERAL INFORMATION** Private Institution. Founded 1863. **Accreditation:** Regional (WASC/ACCJC). **Total program enrollment:** 645.

**PROGRAM(S) OFFERED**

• **Accounting and Business/Management** *1 student enrolled* • **Business Administration, Management and Operations, Other** *5 students enrolled* • **Medical Insurance Coding Specialist/Coder** *17 students enrolled*

**STUDENT SERVICES** Academic or career counseling, employment services for current students, placement services for program completers, remedial services.

## Heald College–Roseville

Seven Sierra Gate Plaza, Roseville, CA 95678
http://www.heald.edu/

**CONTACT** Guy R. Adams, Campus President
**Telephone:** 916-789-8600

**GENERAL INFORMATION** Private Institution. Founded 1863. **Accreditation:** Regional (WASC/ACCJC). **Total program enrollment:** 490.

**PROGRAM(S) OFFERED**

• **Accounting and Business/Management** *1 student enrolled* • **Accounting and Related Services, Other** • **Business Administration, Management and Operations, Other** • **Computer and Information Sciences and Support Services, Other** *11 students enrolled* • **General Office Occupations and Clerical Services** • **Medical Insurance Coding Specialist/Coder** *23 students enrolled* • **Medical Office Assistant/Specialist** *1 student enrolled*

**STUDENT SERVICES** Academic or career counseling, employment services for current students, placement services for program completers, remedial services.

## Heald College–Salinas

1450 North Main Street, Salinas, CA 93906
http://www.heald.edu/

**CONTACT** Maria Embry, Campus President
**Telephone:** 831-443-1700

**GENERAL INFORMATION** Private Institution. Founded 1863. **Accreditation:** Regional (WASC/ACCJC). **Total program enrollment:** 574.

**PROGRAM(S) OFFERED**

• **Business Administration, Management and Operations, Other** *2 students enrolled* • **Business Operations Support and Secretarial Services, Other** *3 students enrolled* • **Medical Insurance Coding Specialist/Coder** *3 students enrolled* • **Medical Office Assistant/Specialist** *5 students enrolled*

**STUDENT SERVICES** Academic or career counseling, employment services for current students, placement services for program completers, remedial services.

## Heald College–San Francisco

350 Mission Street, San Francisco, CA 94105-2206
http://www.heald.edu/

**CONTACT** Daniel Waterman, Director of Campus Operations
**Telephone:** 415-808-3000

**GENERAL INFORMATION** Private Institution. Founded 1863. **Accreditation:** Regional (WASC/ACCJC). **Total program enrollment:** 571.

**PROGRAM(S) OFFERED**

• **Accounting and Business/Management** *3 students enrolled* • **Medical Insurance Coding Specialist/Coder** *3 students enrolled*

**STUDENT SERVICES** Academic or career counseling, employment services for current students, placement services for program completers, remedial services.

## Heald College–San Jose

341 Great Mall Parkway, Milpitas, CA 95035
http://www.heald.edu/

**CONTACT** John Luotto, Campus President
**Telephone:** 408-934-4900

**GENERAL INFORMATION** Private Institution. Founded 1863. **Accreditation:** Regional (WASC/ACCJC). **Total program enrollment:** 809.

**PROGRAM(S) OFFERED**

• **Accounting and Business/Management** *1 student enrolled* • **Business Operations Support and Secretarial Services, Other** *1 student enrolled* • **Medical Insurance Coding Specialist/Coder** *7 students enrolled* • **Medical Office Assistant/Specialist** *2 students enrolled* • **Medical/Clinical Assistant** *1 student enrolled*

**STUDENT SERVICES** Academic or career counseling, employment services for current students, placement services for program completers, remedial services.

## Heald College–Stockton

1605 East March Lane, Stockton, CA 95210
http://www.heald.edu/

**CONTACT** Bob Nodolf, Campus President
**Telephone:** 209-473-5200

**GENERAL INFORMATION** Private Institution. Founded 1863. **Accreditation:** Regional (WASC/ACCJC). **Total program enrollment:** 840.

**PROGRAM(S) OFFERED**
• **Accounting and Business/Management** *2 students enrolled* • **Business Administration, Management and Operations, Other** *1 student enrolled* • **Business Operations Support and Secretarial Services, Other** *1 student enrolled* • **Computer and Information Sciences and Support Services, Other** *4 students enrolled* • **Dental Assisting/Assistant** • **Medical Insurance Coding Specialist/Coder** *20 students enrolled* • **Medical Office Assistant/Specialist** *1 student enrolled* • **Medical/Clinical Assistant** *2 students enrolled* • **System Administration/Administrator**

**STUDENT SERVICES** Academic or career counseling, employment services for current students, placement services for program completers, remedial services.

## Healthy Hair Academy

2648 W. Imperial Highway, Inglewood, CA 90303

**CONTACT** Lory Hillyard, CEO
**Telephone:** 323-757-9597

**GENERAL INFORMATION** Private Institution. **Total program enrollment:** 35. **Application fee:** $75.

**PROGRAM(S) OFFERED**
• **Barbering/Barber** *1500 hrs./$7650* • **Cosmetology/Cosmetologist, General** *1600 hrs./$9430*

**STUDENT SERVICES** Academic or career counseling, placement services for program completers.

## High-Tech Institute

9738 Lincoln Village Drive, Suite 100, Sacramento, CA 95827
http://www.high-techinstitute.com/

**CONTACT** Gordon Kent, Campus President
**Telephone:** 916-929-9700

**GENERAL INFORMATION** Private Institution. Founded 1992. **Accreditation:** State accredited or approved. **Total program enrollment:** 752. **Application fee:** $50.

**PROGRAM(S) OFFERED**
• **Dental Assisting/Assistant** *720 hrs./$12,040* • **Massage Therapy/Therapeutic Massage** *820 hrs./$11,583* • **Medical Insurance Specialist/Medical Biller** *720 hrs./$11,316* • **Medical/Clinical Assistant** *746 hrs./$11,361* • **Pharmacy Technician/Assistant** *720 hrs./$11,937* • **Surgical Technology/Technologist** *1160 hrs./$23,850*

**STUDENT SERVICES** Placement services for program completers.

## Hilltop Beauty School

6317 Mission Street, Daly City, CA 94014

**CONTACT** Tina M. Perry, Owner
**Telephone:** 650-992-4949

**GENERAL INFORMATION** Private Institution. **Total program enrollment:** 36. **Application fee:** $75.

**PROGRAM(S) OFFERED**
• **Cosmetology, Barber/Styling, and Nail Instructor** *600 hrs./$2075*
• **Cosmetology/Cosmetologist, General** *1600 hrs./$10,250*

**STUDENT SERVICES** Academic or career counseling, employment services for current students, placement services for program completers.

## Hope International University

2500 East Nutwood Avenue, Fullerton, CA 92831-3138
http://www.hiu.edu/

**CONTACT** John L. Derry, President
**Telephone:** 714-879-3901

**GENERAL INFORMATION** Private Institution (Affiliated with Christian Churches and Churches of Christ). Founded 1928. **Accreditation:** Regional (WASC/ACSCU). **Total program enrollment:** 608. **Application fee:** $40.

**PROGRAM(S) OFFERED**
• **Theological and Ministerial Studies, Other** *1 student enrolled*

**STUDENT SERVICES** Academic or career counseling, employment services for current students, placement services for program completers, remedial services.

## Humphreys College

6650 Inglewood Avenue, Stockton, CA 95207-3896
http://www.humphreys.edu/

**CONTACT** Robert Humphreys, President
**Telephone:** 209-478-0800

**GENERAL INFORMATION** Private Institution. Founded 1896. **Accreditation:** Regional (WASC/ACSCU). **Total program enrollment:** 448. **Application fee:** $35.

**PROGRAM(S) OFFERED**
• **Accounting** • **Executive Assistant/Executive Secretary** • **Legal Administrative Assistant/Secretary** • **Legal Assistant/Paralegal** *17 students enrolled* • **Medical Administrative/Executive Assistant and Medical Secretary** • **Medical Transcription/Transcriptionist**

**STUDENT SERVICES** Academic or career counseling, daycare for children of students, employment services for current students, placement services for program completers, remedial services.

## Hypnosis Motivation Institute

18607 Ventura Boulevard, Suite 310, Tarzana, CA 91356
http://www.hypnosis.edu/

**CONTACT** George Kappas, Director
**Telephone:** 818-758-2720

**GENERAL INFORMATION** Private Institution. **Total program enrollment:** 105. **Application fee:** $100.

**PROGRAM(S) OFFERED**
• **Hypnotherapy/Hypnotherapist** *720 hrs./$13,577*

**STUDENT SERVICES** Academic or career counseling.

## ICDC College

6363 Wilshire Boulevard, Los Angeles, CA 90048
http://www.learncareer.com/

**CONTACT** Anna Berger, President/CEO
**Telephone:** 323-468-0404

**GENERAL INFORMATION** Private Institution. **Total program enrollment:** 1727.

*ICDC College (continued)*

**PROGRAM(S) OFFERED**

• **Accounting and Related Services, Other** *720 hrs./$13,400* • **Administrative Assistant and Secretarial Science, General** *66 students enrolled* • **Commercial and Advertising Art** *73 students enrolled* • **Computer Systems Networking and Telecommunications** *7 students enrolled* • **Computer Technology/Computer Systems Technology** *2 students enrolled* • **Dental Laboratory Technology/ Technician** *26 students enrolled* • **Legal Assistant/Paralegal** *720 hrs./$13,400* • **Massage Therapy/Therapeutic Massage** *720 hrs./$13,400* • **Medical Administrative/Executive Assistant and Medical Secretary** *34 students enrolled* • **Medical/Clinical Assistant** *720 hrs./$13,400* • **Physical Therapist Assistant** *720 hrs./$13,400* • **Substance Abuse/Addiction Counseling** *810 hrs./$13,400*

**STUDENT SERVICES** Academic or career counseling, placement services for program completers.

## Imperial Valley College

380 East Aten Road, PO Box 158, Imperial, CA 92251-0158
http://www.imperial.cc.ca.us/

**CONTACT** Ed Gould, President
**Telephone:** 760-352-8320

**GENERAL INFORMATION** Public Institution. Founded 1922. **Accreditation:** Regional (WASC/ACCJC). **Total program enrollment:** 2234. **Application fee:** $20.

**PROGRAM(S) OFFERED**

• **Automobile/Automotive Mechanics Technology/Technician** *20 students enrolled* • **Business Administration and Management, General** *7 students enrolled* • **Child Development** *30 students enrolled* • **Computer and Information Sciences, General** *2 students enrolled* • **Corrections** *1 student enrolled* • **Court Reporting/Court Reporter** *4 students enrolled* • **Criminal Justice/Police Science** *3 students enrolled* • **Electrical and Power Transmission Installation/Installer, General** *4 students enrolled* • **Electrical, Electronic and Communications Engineering Technology/Technician** *10 students enrolled* • **Fire Science/ Firefighting** *1 student enrolled* • **Home Health Aide/Home Attendant** • **Legal Administrative Assistant/Secretary** *1 student enrolled* • **Library Assistant/ Technician** *2 students enrolled* • **Medical/Clinical Assistant** *28 students enrolled* • **Pharmacy Technician/Assistant** *4 students enrolled* • **Special Education and Teaching, General** *1 student enrolled* • **Substance Abuse/Addiction Counseling** *5 students enrolled* • **Water Quality and Wastewater Treatment Management and Recycling Technology/Technician** *7 students enrolled*

**STUDENT SERVICES** Academic or career counseling, daycare for children of students, employment services for current students, placement services for program completers, remedial services.

## InfoTech Career College

16900 Lakewood Boulevard, Suite 209, Bellflower, CA 90706
http://www.infotechinst.com/

**CONTACT** Amita Garg
**Telephone:** 562-804-1239

**GENERAL INFORMATION** Private Institution. **Total program enrollment:** 173. **Application fee:** $75.

**PROGRAM(S) OFFERED**

• **Accounting Technology/Technician and Bookkeeping** *5 students enrolled* • **Computer Technology/Computer Systems Technology** *1 student enrolled* • **Crafts/Craft Design, Folk Art and Artisanry** *2 students enrolled* • **General Office Occupations and Clerical Services** *5 students enrolled* • **Graphic Design** *4 students enrolled* • **Licensed Practical/Vocational Nurse Training (LPN, LVN, Cert, Dipl, AAS)** *16 students enrolled* • **Massage Therapy/Therapeutic Massage** *1 student enrolled* • **Medical/Clinical Assistant** *13 students enrolled* • **Nurse/ Nursing Assistant/Aide and Patient Care Assistant** *3 students enrolled* • **Opticianry/Ophthalmic Dispensing Optician** *3 students enrolled*

**STUDENT SERVICES** Academic or career counseling, placement services for program completers.

## Institute for Business and Technology

2550 Scott Boulevard, Santa Clara, CA 95050-2551
http://www.ibttech.com/

**CONTACT** Keith Cravens, Regional Operations Director
**Telephone:** 408-727-1060 Ext. 260

**GENERAL INFORMATION** Private Institution. **Total program enrollment:** 718. **Application fee:** $30.

**PROGRAM(S) OFFERED**

• **Clinical/Medical Laboratory Assistant** *720 hrs./$12,617* • **Electrician** *720 hrs./$14,608* • **Heating, Air Conditioning and Refrigeration Technology/ Technician (ACH/ACR/ACHR/HRAC/HVAC/AC Technology)** *1080 hrs./$17,075* • **Heating, Air Conditioning, Ventilation and Refrigeration Maintenance Technology/Technician (HAC, HACR, HVAC, HVACR)** *66 students enrolled* • **Massage Therapy/Therapeutic Massage** *760 hrs./$12,021* • **Medical Insurance Specialist/Medical Biller** *720 hrs./$12,519* • **Medical/Clinical Assistant** *720 hrs./$12,426* • **Phlebotomy/Phlebotomist** *116 students enrolled*

**STUDENT SERVICES** Academic or career counseling, employment services for current students, placement services for program completers, remedial services.

## Institute of Technology

731 W. Shaw, Clovis, CA 93612
http://www.it-colleges.edu/

**CONTACT** James Haga, President/CEO
**Telephone:** 559-297-4500

**GENERAL INFORMATION** Private Institution. **Total program enrollment:** 1768. **Application fee:** $75.

**PROGRAM(S) OFFERED**

• **Accounting Technology/Technician and Bookkeeping** *37 students enrolled* • **Administrative Assistant and Secretarial Science, General** *23 students enrolled* • **Allied Health and Medical Assisting Services, Other** *860 hrs./ $14,016* • **Baking and Pastry Arts/Baker/Pastry Chef** *38 students enrolled* • **Computer Systems Networking and Telecommunications** *800 hrs./$14,016* • **Culinary Arts/Chef Training** *780 hrs./$17,085* • **Early Childhood Education and Teaching** *2 students enrolled* • **Heating, Air Conditioning, Ventilation and Refrigeration Maintenance Technology/Technician (HAC, HACR, HVAC, HVACR)** *800 hrs./$14,723* • **Human Resources Management/Personnel Administration, General** *31 students enrolled* • **Medical Insurance Coding Specialist/Coder** *49 students enrolled* • **Medical Office Assistant/Specialist** *73 students enrolled* • **Medical/Clinical Assistant** *214 students enrolled* • **Pharmacy Technician/Assistant** *860 hrs./$14,016* • **System, Networking, and LAN/WAN Management/Manager** *57 students enrolled* • **Web Page, Digital/Multimedia and Information Resources Design** *54 students enrolled*

**STUDENT SERVICES** Academic or career counseling, employment services for current students, placement services for program completers.

## Intercoast Colleges

401 S. Glenoaks Boulevard, #211, Burbank, CA 91502
http://intercoastcolleges.com/

**CONTACT** Sheila Swanson, Vice President, Student Financial Services
**Telephone:** 818-500-8400

**GENERAL INFORMATION** Private Institution. **Total program enrollment:** 25. **Application fee:** $75.

**PROGRAM(S) OFFERED**

• **Accounting Technology/Technician and Bookkeeping** *24 hrs./$13,750* • **Accounting** *1 student enrolled* • **Legal Assistant/Paralegal** *30 hrs./$14,520* • **Massage Therapy/Therapeutic Massage** *26 hrs./$14,465* • **Medical/Clinical Assistant** *30 hrs./$15,750* • **Pharmacy Technician/Assistant** • **Substance Abuse/ Addiction Counseling** *21 hrs./$8635*

**STUDENT SERVICES** Academic or career counseling, employment services for current students, placement services for program completers.

## Intercoast Colleges

One Civic Plaza, Suite 110, Carson, CA 90745
http://www.intercoastcolleges.com

**CONTACT** Sheila Swanson, Vice President, Student Financial Services
**Telephone:** 310-847-8400

**GENERAL INFORMATION** Private Institution. **Total program enrollment:** 172. **Application fee:** $75.

**PROGRAM(S) OFFERED**
• **Accounting Technology/Technician and Bookkeeping** *24 hrs./$13,750* • **Legal Assistant/Paralegal** *30 hrs./$14,520* • **Massage Therapy/Therapeutic Massage** *26 hrs./$14,465* • **Medical Administrative/Executive Assistant and Medical Secretary** *26 students enrolled* • **Medical/Clinical Assistant** *30 hrs./$15,750* • **Pharmacy Technician/Assistant** *27 hrs./$14,685* • **Substance Abuse/Addiction Counseling** *30 hrs./$16,300*

**STUDENT SERVICES** Academic or career counseling, employment services for current students, placement services for program completers.

## Intercoast Colleges

1115 Spruce Street, Suite A, Riverside, CA 92507
http://www.intercoastcolleges.com/

**CONTACT** Sheila Swanson, Vice President, Student Financial Services
**Telephone:** 951-779-0700

**GENERAL INFORMATION** Private Institution. **Total program enrollment:** 183. **Application fee:** $75.

**PROGRAM(S) OFFERED**
• **Accounting** *4 students enrolled* • **Administrative Assistant and Secretarial Science, General** *24 hrs./$13,750* • **Legal Assistant/Paralegal** *30 hrs./$14,520* • **Massage Therapy/Therapeutic Massage** *26 hrs./$14,465* • **Medical/Clinical Assistant** *30 hrs./$15,750* • **Pharmacy Technician/Assistant** *27 hrs./$14,685* • **Substance Abuse/Addiction Counseling** *30 hrs./$16,300*

**STUDENT SERVICES** Academic or career counseling, employment services for current students, placement services for program completers.

## Intercoast Colleges

1631 North Bristol Street, Suite 200, Santa Ana, CA 92706
http://www.intercoastcolleges.com/

**CONTACT** Sheila Swanson, Vice President, Student Financial Services
**Telephone:** 714-712-7900

**GENERAL INFORMATION** Private Institution. **Total program enrollment:** 134. **Application fee:** $75.

**PROGRAM(S) OFFERED**
• **Accounting Technology/Technician and Bookkeeping** *24 hrs./$13,750* • **Accounting** *1 student enrolled* • **Medical/Clinical Assistant** *30 hrs./$14,320* • **Substance Abuse/Addiction Counseling** *30 hrs./$16,300*

**STUDENT SERVICES** Academic or career counseling, employment services for current students, placement services for program completers.

## Intercoast Colleges

1400 W. West Covina Parkway, 2nd Floor, West Covina, CA 91790
http://intercoastcolleges.com/

**CONTACT** Sheila Swanson, Vice President, Student Financial Services
**Telephone:** 626-337-6800

**GENERAL INFORMATION** Private Institution. **Total program enrollment:** 89. **Application fee:** $75.

**PROGRAM(S) OFFERED**
• **Accounting** *2 students enrolled* • **Legal Assistant/Paralegal** *30 hrs./$14,520* • **Massage Therapy/Therapeutic Massage** *26 hrs./$14,465* • **Medical/Clinical Assistant** *15 students enrolled* • **Pharmacy Technician/Assistant** *27 hrs./$14,685* • **Substance Abuse/Addiction Counseling** *30 hrs./$16,300*

**STUDENT SERVICES** Academic or career counseling, employment services for current students, placement services for program completers.

## Interior Designers Institute

1061 Camelback Road, Newport Beach, CA 92660
http://www.idi.edu/

**CONTACT** Judy Deaton, Executive Director
**Telephone:** 949-675-4451

**GENERAL INFORMATION** Private Institution. Founded 1984. **Accreditation:** Interior design: professional (CIDA); state accredited or approved. **Total program enrollment:** 107. **Application fee:** $95.

**PROGRAM(S) OFFERED**
• **Interior Design** *299 students enrolled*

**STUDENT SERVICES** Academic or career counseling, placement services for program completers.

## International School of Beauty

72261 Hwy 111, Suite 121-B, Palm Desert, CA 92260
http://internationalschoolofbeauty.com/

**CONTACT** Kimberly Beardsley, Associate Director/Financial Aid Officer
**Telephone:** 760-674-1624 Ext. 45

**GENERAL INFORMATION** Private Institution. **Total program enrollment:** 149. **Application fee:** $75.

**PROGRAM(S) OFFERED**
• **Aesthetician/Esthetician and Skin Care Specialist** *600 hrs./$6738* • **Cosmetology/Cosmetologist, General** *1600 hrs./$9925* • **Nail Technician/Specialist and Manicurist** *400 hrs./$2000*

**STUDENT SERVICES** Placement services for program completers.

## International School of Cosmetology

13613 Hawthorne Boulevard, Hawthorne, CA 90250
http://isoc.edu/

**CONTACT** David Evans, Director
**Telephone:** 310-451-0101

**GENERAL INFORMATION** Private Institution. **Total program enrollment:** 27.

**PROGRAM(S) OFFERED**
• **Aesthetician/Esthetician and Skin Care Specialist** • **Cosmetology, Barber/Styling, and Nail Instructor** • **Cosmetology/Cosmetologist, General** *1600 hrs./$18,040* • **Nail Technician/Specialist and Manicurist**

**STUDENT SERVICES** Placement services for program completers.

## Irvine Valley College

5500 Irvine Center Drive, Irvine, CA 92618
http://www.ivc.edu/

**CONTACT** Glenn R. Roquemore, PhD, President
**Telephone:** 949-451-5100

**GENERAL INFORMATION** Public Institution. Founded 1979. **Accreditation:** Regional (WASC/ACCJC). **Total program enrollment:** 2317.

*Irvine Valley College (continued)*

**PROGRAM(S) OFFERED**

• **Accounting** *17 students enrolled* • **Administrative Assistant and Secretarial Science, General** *2 students enrolled* • **Business Administration and Management, General** *2 students enrolled* • **Child Development** *5 students enrolled* • **Computer Programming/Programmer, General** *1 student enrolled* • **Computer Systems Analysis/Analyst** *1 student enrolled* • **Criminal Justice/Police Science** *4 students enrolled* • **Data Entry/Microcomputer Applications, General** *2 students enrolled* • **Electrical/Electronics Equipment Installation and Repair, General** *5 students enrolled* • **Graphic Design** *6 students enrolled* • **Manufacturing Technology/Technician** *2 students enrolled* • **Real Estate** *2 students enrolled* • **Sport and Fitness Administration/Management** *10 students enrolled* • **Web Page, Digital/Multimedia and Information Resources Design** *1 student enrolled*

**STUDENT SERVICES** Academic or career counseling, daycare for children of students, employment services for current students, placement services for program completers, remedial services.

## James Albert School of Cosmetology

2289 W. Ball Road, Anaheim, CA 92804

**CONTACT** James A. Nasser, President
**Telephone:** 714-774-8736

**GENERAL INFORMATION** Private Institution. **Total program enrollment:** 42.

**PROGRAM(S) OFFERED**

• **Aesthetician/Esthetician and Skin Care Specialist** *600 hrs./$6575* • **Cosmetology, Barber/Styling, and Nail Instructor** • **Cosmetology/Cosmetologist, General** *1600 hrs./$13,437* • **Nail Technician/Specialist and Manicurist** *400 hrs./$2075*

**STUDENT SERVICES** Academic or career counseling, placement services for program completers.

## James Albert School of Cosmetology

281 E. 17th Street, Costa Mesa, CA 92627-3831

**CONTACT** James Albert, President
**Telephone:** 949-642-0606

**GENERAL INFORMATION** Private Institution. **Total program enrollment:** 61.

**PROGRAM(S) OFFERED**

• **Aesthetician/Esthetician and Skin Care Specialist** *600 hrs./$8075* • **Cosmetology, Barber/Styling, and Nail Instructor** • **Cosmetology/Cosmetologist, General** *1600 hrs./$15,175* • **Nail Technician/Specialist and Manicurist** *400 hrs./$2075*

**STUDENT SERVICES** Academic or career counseling, placement services for program completers.

## James Albert School of Cosmetology

9170 Foothill Boulevard, Ranch Cucamonga, CA 91730
http://www.jamesalbertschools.biz/

**CONTACT** James A. Nasser, President
**Telephone:** 909-989-9933

**GENERAL INFORMATION** Private Institution. **Total program enrollment:** 48.

**PROGRAM(S) OFFERED**

• **Aesthetician/Esthetician and Skin Care Specialist** *600 hrs./$7575* • **Cosmetology/Cosmetologist, General** *160 hrs./$17,525* • **Nail Technician/Specialist and Manicurist** *400 hrs./$2075*

**STUDENT SERVICES** Academic or career counseling, placement services for program completers.

## Je Boutique College of Beauty

1073 East Main Street, El Cajon, CA 92021
http://www.sandiegobeautyacademy.com/

**CONTACT** Lynelle Lynch, President
**Telephone:** 619-442-3407

**GENERAL INFORMATION** Private Institution. Founded 1968. **Total program enrollment:** 148. **Application fee:** $75.

**PROGRAM(S) OFFERED**

• **Aesthetician/Esthetician and Skin Care Specialist** *600 hrs./$7425* • **Cosmetology/Cosmetologist, General** *1750 hrs./$15,050* • **Facial Treatment Specialist/Facialist** *46 students enrolled* • **Make-Up Artist/Specialist** *150 hrs./$3125* • **Nail Technician/Specialist and Manicurist** *600 hrs./$7225*

**STUDENT SERVICES** Employment services for current students, placement services for program completers.

## John F. Kennedy University

100 Ellinwood Way, Pleasant Hill, CA 94523-4817
http://www.jfku.edu/

**CONTACT** Steven Stargardter, President
**Telephone:** 925-969-3300

**GENERAL INFORMATION** Private Institution. Founded 1964. **Accreditation:** Regional (WASC/ACSCU). **Total program enrollment:** 586. **Application fee:** $60.

**PROGRAM(S) OFFERED**

• **Business Administration and Management, General** • **Business, Management, Marketing, and Related Support Services, Other** • **Legal Assistant/Paralegal** *13 students enrolled*

**STUDENT SERVICES** Academic or career counseling.

## John Wesley International Barber and Beauty College

717 Pine Avenue, Long Beach, CA 90813

**CONTACT** Aruni S. Blount, Director Administrator
**Telephone:** 562-435-7060

**GENERAL INFORMATION** Private Institution. **Total program enrollment:** 59.

**PROGRAM(S) OFFERED**

• **Barbering/Barber** *1500 hrs./$11,325* • **Cosmetology/Cosmetologist, General** *1600 hrs./$12,675*

**STUDENT SERVICES** Academic or career counseling, employment services for current students, placement services for program completers.

## Kaplan College

6180 Laurel Canyon Boulevard, Suite 101, North Hollywood, CA 91606
http://getinfo.kaplancollege.com/KaplanCollegePortal/

**CONTACT** Mark Newman, Campus President
**Telephone:** 818-763-2563 Ext. 221

**GENERAL INFORMATION** Private Institution. Founded 1982. **Accreditation:** State accredited or approved. **Total program enrollment:** 1182. **Application fee:** $20.

**PROGRAM(S) OFFERED**

• **Diagnostic Medical Sonography/Sonographer and Ultrasound Technician** *152 hrs./$38,898* • **Licensed Practical/Vocational Nurse Training (LPN, LVN, Cert, Dipl, AAS)** *89 hrs./$25,200* • **Medical/Clinical Assistant** *45 hrs./$10,616* • **Nurse/Nursing Assistant/Aide and Patient Care Assistant** *16 students enrolled* • **Radiologic Technology/Science—Radiographer** *123 hrs./$38,081*

**STUDENT SERVICES** Academic or career counseling, employment services for current students, placement services for program completers, remedial services.

## Kaplan College–Bakersfield

1914 Wible Road, Bakersfield, CA 93304
http://getinfo.kaplancollege.com/KaplanCollegePortal/

**CONTACT** Becky Anderson, Executive Director
**Telephone:** 661-836-6300

**GENERAL INFORMATION** Private Institution. **Total program enrollment:** 711. **Application fee:** $20.

**PROGRAM(S) OFFERED**
• **Computer and Information Sciences and Support Services, Other** *54 hrs./$12,176* • **Criminal Justice/Law Enforcement Administration** *95 hrs./$24,364* • **Dental Assisting/Assistant** *46 hrs./$13,220* • **Medical Office Computer Specialist/Assistant** *50 hrs./$13,220* • **Medical/Clinical Assistant** *720 hrs./$14,896*

**STUDENT SERVICES** Employment services for current students, placement services for program completers, remedial services.

## Kaplan College–Fresno Campus

44 Shaw Avenue, Rodeo Plaza Shopping Center, Clovis, CA 93612
http://www.kc-fresno.com

**CONTACT** Chris VanEs, Executive Director
**Telephone:** 559-325-5100

**GENERAL INFORMATION** Private Institution. **Total program enrollment:** 631. **Application fee:** $20.

**PROGRAM(S) OFFERED**
• **Criminal Justice/Safety Studies** *60 hrs./$24,535* • **Dental Assisting/Assistant** *29 hrs./$13,848* • **Medical Office Assistant/Specialist** *30 hrs./$12,660* • **Medical/Clinical Assistant** *720 hrs./$13,617* • **Rehabilitation and Therapeutic Professions, Other** *20 students enrolled*

**STUDENT SERVICES** Academic or career counseling, employment services for current students, placement services for program completers, remedial services.

## Kaplan College–Modesto Campus

5172 Kiernan Court, Salida, CA 95368
http://www.kc-modesto.com

**CONTACT** Kevin Puls, Executive Director
**Telephone:** 209-543-7000

**GENERAL INFORMATION** Private Institution. **Total program enrollment:** 1147.

**PROGRAM(S) OFFERED**
• **Criminal Justice/Safety Studies** *60 hrs./$25,146* • **Dental Assisting/Assistant** *29 hrs./$12,740* • **Health and Medical Administrative Services, Other** *30 hrs./$12,670* • **Medical/Clinical Assistant** *720 hrs./$13,555* • **Rehabilitation and Therapeutic Professions, Other** *32 hrs./$12,550* • **Respiratory Care Therapy/Therapist** *77 hrs./$33,551*

**STUDENT SERVICES** Academic or career counseling, employment services for current students, placement services for program completers, remedial services.

## Kaplan College–Palm Springs

2475 East Tahquitz Canyon Way, Palm Springs, CA 92262-7011
http://getinfo.kaplancollege.com/KaplanCollegePortal/

**CONTACT** Kevin Quirk, Executive Director
**Telephone:** 760-778-3540

**GENERAL INFORMATION** Private Institution. **Total program enrollment:** 552.

**PROGRAM(S) OFFERED**
• **Allied Health and Medical Assisting Services, Other** *720 hrs./$13,463* • **Dental Assisting/Assistant** *46 hrs./$15,395* • **Legal Assistant/Paralegal** *108 hrs./$33,248* • **Massage Therapy/Therapeutic Massage** *54 hrs./$13,942* • **Medical Insurance Specialist/Medical Biller** *50 hrs./$13,305* • **Pharmacy Technician/Assistant** *48 hrs./$13,420*

**STUDENT SERVICES** Academic or career counseling, employment services for current students, placement services for program completers, remedial services.

## Kaplan College–Panorama City Campus

14355 Roscoe Boulevard, Panorama City, CA 91402
http://www.kc-panoramacity.com

**CONTACT** Jeff Conlon, President
**Telephone:** 818-672-3000

**GENERAL INFORMATION** Private Institution. Founded 1996. **Accreditation:** State accredited or approved. **Total program enrollment:** 285.

**PROGRAM(S) OFFERED**
• **Business/Commerce, General** • **Computer and Information Sciences, General** • **Legal Assistant/Paralegal** *102 hrs./$30,205* • **Legal Professions and Studies, Other** *51 hrs./$14,750* • **Medical Insurance Specialist/Medical Biller** *47 hrs./$14,000* • **Medical Office Assistant/Specialist** *720 hrs./$14,000* • **Medical/Clinical Assistant** *133 students enrolled*

**STUDENT SERVICES** Academic or career counseling, employment services for current students, placement services for program completers.

## Kaplan College–Sacramento Campus

4330 Watt Avenue, Suite 400, Sacramento, CA 95821
http://www.kc-sacramento.com

**CONTACT** Sue Powell, Executive Director
**Telephone:** 916-649-8168

**GENERAL INFORMATION** Private Institution. **Accreditation:** State accredited or approved. **Total program enrollment:** 624.

**PROGRAM(S) OFFERED**
• **Computer and Information Sciences and Support Services, Other** *54 hrs./$13,095* • **Corrections and Criminal Justice, Other** *95 hrs./$25,295* • **Dental Assisting/Assistant** *46 hrs./$12,625* • **Medical Office Assistant/Specialist** *50 hrs./$12,225* • **Medical/Clinical Assistant** *720 hrs./$13,714*

**STUDENT SERVICES** Academic or career counseling, employment services for current students, placement services for program completers.

## Kaplan College–San Diego Campus

9055 Balboa Avenue, San Diego, CA 92123
http://www.kc-sandiego.com

**CONTACT** Mike Seifert, President
**Telephone:** 858-279-4500

**GENERAL INFORMATION** Private Institution. Founded 1976. **Accreditation:** State accredited or approved. **Total program enrollment:** 1307.

**PROGRAM(S) OFFERED**
• **Computer and Information Sciences and Support Services, Other** *48 hrs./$15,475* • **Corrections and Criminal Justice, Other** *98 hrs./$25,515* • **Licensed Practical/Vocational Nurse Training (LPN, LVN, Cert, Dipl, AAS)** *91 hrs./$25,691* • **Massage Therapy/Therapeutic Massage** *16 students enrolled* • **Medical Insurance Specialist/Medical Biller** *29 students enrolled* • **Medical/Clinical Assistant** *48 hrs./$12,299* • **Nurse/Nursing Assistant/Aide and Patient Care Assistant** *48 hrs./$13,163* • **Nursing—Registered Nurse Training (RN, ASN, BSN, MSN)** *70 hrs./$50,334*

**STUDENT SERVICES** Academic or career counseling, employment services for current students, placement services for program completers, remedial services.

## Kaplan College–Stockton Campus

722 West March Lane, Stockton, CA 95207
http://www.kc-stockton.com

**CONTACT** Bill Jones, Executive Director
**Telephone:** 209-462-8777

**GENERAL INFORMATION** Private Institution. **Total program enrollment:** 555.

**PROGRAM(S) OFFERED**
• **Criminal Justice/Law Enforcement Administration** *60 hrs./$25,426* • **Dental Assisting/Assistant** *800 hrs./$13,273* • **Health and Medical Administrative Services, Other** *720 hrs./$12,787* • **Licensed Practical/Vocational Nurse Training (LPN, LVN, Cert, Dipl, AAS)** *93 hrs./$24,145* • **Medical/Clinical Assistant** *720 hrs./$13,534*

**STUDENT SERVICES** Academic or career counseling, employment services for current students, placement services for program completers.

## Kaplan College–Vista Campus

2022 University Drive, Vista, CA 92083
http://www.kc-vista.com

**CONTACT** Jann Underwood-Mitchell, Executive Director
**Telephone:** 760-630-1555

**GENERAL INFORMATION** Private Institution. **Total program enrollment:** 1074.

**PROGRAM(S) OFFERED**
• **Allied Health and Medical Assisting Services, Other** *71 hrs./$18,020* • **Clinical/Medical Laboratory Technician** *1320 hrs./$24,703* • **Computer and Information Sciences and Support Services, Other** • **Licensed Practical/ Vocational Nurse Training (LPN, LVN, Cert, Dipl, AAS)** *86 hrs./$28,953* • **Massage Therapy/Therapeutic Massage** *29 students enrolled* • **Medical Insurance Coding Specialist/Coder** *50 hrs./$13,070* • **Medical/Clinical Assistant** *48 hrs./$13,070* • **Nursing, Other** *29 students enrolled* • **Pharmacy Technician/ Assistant** *45 students enrolled*

**STUDENT SERVICES** Academic or career counseling, employment services for current students, placement services for program completers, remedial services.

## Kensington College

2428 North Grand Avenue, Suite D, Santa Ana, CA 92705
http://www.kensingtoncollege.net/

**CONTACT** Larry D. Madoski, President
**Telephone:** 714-542-8086

**GENERAL INFORMATION** Private Institution. Founded 1991. **Total program enrollment:** 33.

**PROGRAM(S) OFFERED**
• **Legal Administrative Assistant/Secretary** *480 hrs./$7095* • **Legal Assistant/ Paralegal** *480 hrs./$6795* • **Legal Professions and Studies, Other**

**STUDENT SERVICES** Placement services for program completers.

## The King's College and Seminary

14800 Sherman Way, Van Nuys, CA 91405-8040
http://www.kingscollege.edu/

**CONTACT** Paul Chappell, PhD, Executive Vice President
**Telephone:** 818-779-8040

**GENERAL INFORMATION** Private Institution (Affiliated with International Church of the Foursquare Gospel). **Accreditation:** State accredited or approved. **Total program enrollment:** 118. **Application fee:** $45.

**PROGRAM(S) OFFERED**
• **Bible/Biblical Studies** *15 students enrolled*

**STUDENT SERVICES** Academic or career counseling, employment services for current students, placement services for program completers, remedial services.

## Kitchen Academy–Sacramento

2450 Del Paso Road, Sacramento, CA 95834
http://www.kitchenacademy.com/

**CONTACT** Kris DiGiacomo, Campus President
**Telephone:** 916-830-6220 Ext. 6230

**GENERAL INFORMATION** Private Institution. **Total program enrollment:** 339.

**PROGRAM(S) OFFERED**
• **Baking and Pastry Arts/Baker/Pastry Chef** • **Culinary Arts/Chef Training** *235 students enrolled*

**STUDENT SERVICES** Academic or career counseling, employment services for current students, placement services for program completers, remedial services.

## LA College International

3200 Wilshire Boulevard, # 400, Los Angeles, CA 90010-1308
http://www.lac.edu/

**CONTACT** Harish Amar, Executive Director
**Telephone:** 213-381-3333

**GENERAL INFORMATION** Private Institution. Founded 1981. **Accreditation:** State accredited or approved. **Total program enrollment:** 63. **Application fee:** $35.

**PROGRAM(S) OFFERED**
• **Business Administration and Management, General** *68 hrs./$21,938* • **Computer Science** *65 hrs./$24,188* • **Graphic Design** *65 hrs./$24,188* • **Health/Health Care Administration/Management** *60 hrs./$22,380* • **Massage Therapy/Therapeutic Massage** *36 hrs./$9943* • **Medical Office Assistant/ Specialist** *32 hrs./$9943* • **Medical Office Management/Administration** *11 students enrolled*

**STUDENT SERVICES** Academic or career counseling, employment services for current students, placement services for program completers, remedial services.

## Ladera Career Paths Training Centers

6820 La Tijera Boulevard, Suite 217, Los Angeles, CA 90045
http://laderacareerpathsinc.com/

**CONTACT** Anna E. Little, Director
**Telephone:** 310-568-0244 Ext. 135

**GENERAL INFORMATION** Private Institution. **Total program enrollment:** 20. **Application fee:** $100.

**PROGRAM(S) OFFERED**
• **Health/Medical Claims Examiner** *909 hrs./$9758* • **Medical Insurance Coding Specialist/Coder** *766 hrs./$7319* • **Medical Insurance Specialist/Medical Biller** *784 hrs./$6902* • **Medical Transcription/Transcriptionist** *530 hrs./$4642*

**STUDENT SERVICES** Academic or career counseling, placement services for program completers.

## Lake College

2655 Bechelli Lanr, Redding, CA 96002
http://www.lakecollege.edu/

**CONTACT** Jennifer Cannon, President
**Telephone:** 530-224-7227

**GENERAL INFORMATION** Private Institution. **Total program enrollment:** 46.

**PROGRAM(S) OFFERED**
• **Accounting Technology/Technician and Bookkeeping** *638 hrs./$10,280* • **Business Administration, Management and Operations, Other** *1080 hrs./$20,479* • **Computer and Information Sciences, General** *6 students enrolled* • **Health/Health Care Administration/Management** *13 students enrolled* • **Licensed Practical/Vocational Nurse Training (LPN, LVN, Cert, Dipl, AAS)** *17 students enrolled* • **Medical Office Assistant/Specialist** *725 hrs./$11,261* • **Medical/Clinical Assistant** *722 hrs./$12,518* • **Medical/Health Management and Clinical Assistant/Specialist** *1092 hrs./$17,006* • **Occupational and Environmental Health Nursing** *1575 hrs./$23,075* • **Phlebotomy/Phlebotomist**

**STUDENT SERVICES** Academic or career counseling, employment services for current students, placement services for program completers.

## Lake Tahoe Community College

One College Drive, South Lake Tahoe, CA 96150-4524
http://www.ltcc.edu/

**CONTACT** Paul Killpatrick, Superintendent President
**Telephone:** 530-541-4660

**GENERAL INFORMATION** Public Institution. Founded 1975. **Accreditation:** Regional (WASC/ACCJC). **Total program enrollment:** 685.

**PROGRAM(S) OFFERED**
• **Accounting** *2 students enrolled* • **Child Development** *1 student enrolled* • **Commercial Photography** *1 student enrolled* • **Criminal Justice/Police Science** *1 student enrolled* • **Fire Science/Firefighting** *1 student enrolled* • **Home Health Aide/Home Attendant** • **Spanish Language and Literature** *3 students enrolled* • **Substance Abuse/Addiction Counseling** *1 student enrolled*

**STUDENT SERVICES** Academic or career counseling, daycare for children of students, employment services for current students, placement services for program completers, remedial services.

## Lancaster Beauty School

44646 10th Street, West, Lancaster, CA 93534

**CONTACT** Gail Miner, Owner/Director
**Telephone:** 661-948-1672

**GENERAL INFORMATION** Private Institution. Founded 1960. **Total program enrollment:** 206.

**PROGRAM(S) OFFERED**
• **Aesthetician/Esthetician and Skin Care Specialist** *600 hrs./$5500* • **Barbering/Barber** *8 students enrolled* • **Cosmetology and Related Personal Grooming Arts, Other** • **Cosmetology/Cosmetologist, General** *400 hrs./$2200* • **Nail Technician/Specialist and Manicurist** *20 students enrolled* • **Trade and Industrial Teacher Education**

**STUDENT SERVICES** Academic or career counseling, placement services for program completers.

## Laney College

900 Fallon Street, Oakland, CA 94607-4893
http://www.peralta.cc.ca.us/

**CONTACT** Dr. Frank Chong, President
**Telephone:** 510-834-5740

**GENERAL INFORMATION** Public Institution. Founded 1953. **Accreditation:** Regional (WASC/ACCJC). **Total program enrollment:** 2649.

**PROGRAM(S) OFFERED**
• **Accounting** *19 students enrolled* • **Biology Technician/Biotechnology Laboratory Technician** *6 students enrolled* • **Building/Construction Site Management/Manager** *3 students enrolled* • **Building/Home/Construction Inspection/Inspector** *3 students enrolled* • **Business Administration and Management, General** *36 students enrolled* • **Carpentry/Carpenter** *8 students enrolled* • **Commercial Photography** *3 students enrolled* • **Computer Programming/Programmer, General** *1 student enrolled* • **Cooking and Related Culinary Arts, General** *28 students enrolled* • **Cosmetology/Cosmetologist, General** *35 students enrolled* • **Graphic Communications, General** *2 students enrolled* • **Heating, Air Conditioning and Refrigeration Technology/Technician (ACH/ACR/ACHR/HRAC/HVAC/AC Technology)** *8 students enrolled* • **Hospitality Administration/Management, General** *11 students enrolled* • **Information Technology** *3 students enrolled* • **Labor and Industrial Relations** *5 students enrolled* • **Machine Tool Technology/Machinist** *2 students enrolled* • **Office Management and Supervision** *55 students enrolled* • **Radio and Television** *5 students enrolled* • **System Administration/Administrator** *1 student enrolled* • **Welding Technology/Welder** *1 student enrolled*

**STUDENT SERVICES** Academic or career counseling, daycare for children of students, employment services for current students, placement services for program completers, remedial services.

## La Sierra University

4500 Riverwalk Parkway, Riverside, CA 92515
http://www.lasierra.edu/

**CONTACT** Randal Wisbey, President
**Telephone:** 951-785-2000

**GENERAL INFORMATION** Private Institution. Founded 1922. **Accreditation:** Regional (WASC/ACSCU); music (NASM). **Total program enrollment:** 1516. **Application fee:** $30.

**PROGRAM(S) OFFERED**
• **Music Performance, General**

**STUDENT SERVICES** Academic or career counseling, employment services for current students, placement services for program completers, remedial services.

## Las Positas College

3033 Collier Canyon Road, Livermore, CA 94551-7650
http://www.laspositascollege.edu/

**CONTACT** Dr. DeRionne Pollard, President
**Telephone:** 925-424-1000

**GENERAL INFORMATION** Public Institution. Founded 1988. **Accreditation:** Regional (WASC/ACCJC). **Total program enrollment:** 2557.

**PROGRAM(S) OFFERED**
• **Accounting** *4 students enrolled* • **Administrative Assistant and Secretarial Science, General** *1 student enrolled* • **Applied Horticulture/Horticultural Operations, General** *1 student enrolled* • **Automobile/Automotive Mechanics Technology/Technician** *4 students enrolled* • **Child Development** *44 students enrolled* • **Commercial Photography** *4 students enrolled* • **Computer Systems Networking and Telecommunications** *6 students enrolled* • **Data Entry/Microcomputer Applications, General** *3 students enrolled* • **Digital Communication and Media/Multimedia** *8 students enrolled* • **Engineering Technologies/Technicians, Other** *3 students enrolled* • **Fire Science/Firefighting** *2 students enrolled* • **Industrial Safety Technology/Technician** *5 students enrolled* • **Interior Design** *9 students enrolled* • **Journalism** *1 student enrolled* • **Laser and Optical Technology/Technician** *1 student enrolled* • **Music, General** *2 students enrolled* • **Small Business Administration/Management** *1 student enrolled* • **Welding Technology/Welder** *2 students enrolled*

**STUDENT SERVICES** Academic or career counseling, employment services for current students, placement services for program completers, remedial services.

## Lassen Community College District

Highway 139, PO Box 3000, Susanville, CA 96130
http://www.lassencollege.edu/

**CONTACT** Douglas Houston, District Superintendent President
**Telephone:** 530-257-6181

**GENERAL INFORMATION** Public Institution. Founded 1925. **Accreditation:** Regional (WASC/ACCJC). **Total program enrollment:** 532.

**PROGRAM(S) OFFERED**
• **Agriculture, General** *3 students enrolled* • **Animal/Livestock Husbandry and Production** *1 student enrolled* • **Automobile/Automotive Mechanics Technology/Technician** *1 student enrolled* • **Child Development** *4 students enrolled* • **Corrections** *8 students enrolled* • **Criminal Justice/Police Science** *8 students enrolled* • **Engineering Technologies/Technicians, Other** *13 students enrolled* • **Human Services, General** *7 students enrolled* • **Journalism** *1 student enrolled* • **Licensed Practical/Vocational Nurse Training (LPN, LVN, Cert, Dipl, AAS)** *25 students enrolled* • **Substance Abuse/Addiction Counseling** *6 students enrolled*

**STUDENT SERVICES** Academic or career counseling, daycare for children of students, remedial services.

## Liberty Training Institute

2706 Wilshire Boulevard, Los Angeles, CA 90057

**CONTACT** Julio Betbeder, Associate Director, CEO
**Telephone:** 213-383-9545

**GENERAL INFORMATION** Private Institution. **Total program enrollment:** 282.

**PROGRAM(S) OFFERED**
• **Accounting** *480 hrs./$8350* • **Automobile/Automotive Mechanics Technology/Technician** *480 hrs./$8350* • **Data Entry/Microcomputer Applications, General** *4 students enrolled* • **Electrical and Electronic Engineering Technologies/Technicians, Other** *480 hrs./$8350* • **Metal and Jewelry Arts** *480 hrs./$8500* • **Precision Systems Maintenance and Repair Technologies, Other** *480 hrs./$8350* • **Watchmaking and Jewelrymaking** *480 hrs./$8350*

**STUDENT SERVICES** Academic or career counseling, employment services for current students, placement services for program completers.

## Lincoln University

401 15th Street, Oakland, CA 94612
http://www.lincolnuca.edu/

**CONTACT** Peggy Au, Director of Admissions
**Telephone:** 510-628-8010

**GENERAL INFORMATION** Private Institution. Founded 1919. **Accreditation:** State accredited or approved. **Total program enrollment:** 395. **Application fee:** $75.

**PROGRAM(S) OFFERED**
• **Medical Staff Services Technology/Technician** *1 student enrolled* • **Medical/Clinical Assistant** *1 student enrolled*

**STUDENT SERVICES** Academic or career counseling, placement services for program completers.

## Lola Beauty College

11883 Valley View Street, Garden Grove, CA 92641

**CONTACT** Aruni Blount, President
**Telephone:** 714-894-3344

**GENERAL INFORMATION** Private Institution. Founded 1990. **Total program enrollment:** 7.

**PROGRAM(S) OFFERED**
• **Aesthetician/Esthetician and Skin Care Specialist** *600 hrs./$5075* • **Barbering/Barber** *1500 hrs./$11,325* • **Cosmetology/Cosmetologist, General** *160 hrs./$12,675* • **Make-Up Artist/Specialist**

**STUDENT SERVICES** Placement services for program completers.

## Loma Linda University

Loma Linda, CA 92350
http://www.llu.edu/

**CONTACT** Richard H. Hart, MD, DrPH, Chancellor and President
**Telephone:** 909-558-1000

**GENERAL INFORMATION** Private Institution. Founded 1905. **Accreditation:** Regional (WASC/ACSCU); cytotechnology (ASC); dental hygiene (ADA); health information administration (AHIMA); medical technology (NAACLS); physical therapy assisting (APTA); radiologic technology: radiography (JRCERT); speech-language pathology (ASHA); surgical technology (ARCST). **Total program enrollment:** 3168. **Application fee:** $60.

**PROGRAM(S) OFFERED**
• **Allied Health Diagnostic, Intervention, and Treatment Professions, Other** *8 students enrolled* • **Chinese Studies** *1 student enrolled* • **Cytotechnology/Cytotechnologist** *2 students enrolled* • **Diagnostic Medical Sonography/Sonographer and Ultrasound Technician** • **Dietetic Technician (DTR)** • **Dietetics/Dietitians** *6 students enrolled* • **Health Information/Medical Records Administration/Administrator** *1 student enrolled* • **Medical Insurance Coding Specialist/Coder** *15 students enrolled* • **Medical Radiologic Technology/Science—Radiation Therapist** *2 students enrolled* • **Nuclear Medical Technology/Technologist** *17 students enrolled* • **Spanish and Iberian Studies** *1 student enrolled*

**STUDENT SERVICES** Academic or career counseling, daycare for children of students, employment services for current students, placement services for program completers.

## Long Beach City College

4901 East Carson Street, Long Beach, CA 90808-1780
http://www.lbcc.edu/

**CONTACT** Eloy Oakley, Superintendent-President
**Telephone:** 562-938-4111

**GENERAL INFORMATION** Public Institution. Founded 1927. **Accreditation:** Regional (WASC/ACCJC); radiologic technology: radiography (JRCERT). **Total program enrollment:** 7856.

**PROGRAM(S) OFFERED**
• **Accounting** *24 students enrolled* • **Administrative Assistant and Secretarial Science, General** *35 students enrolled* • **Airframe Mechanics and Aircraft Maintenance Technology/Technician** *4 students enrolled* • **Airline/Commercial/Professional Pilot and Flight Crew** *1 student enrolled* • **Alternative Fuel Vehicle Technology/Technician** *1 student enrolled* • **Apparel and Textile Manufacture** *1 student enrolled* • **Apparel and Textile Marketing Management** *1 student enrolled* • **Applied Horticulture/Horticultural Operations, General** *4 students enrolled* • **Architectural Drafting and Architectural CAD/CADD** *6 students enrolled* • **Architectural Technology/Technician** *3 students enrolled* • **Autobody/Collision and Repair Technology/Technician** *1 student enrolled* • **Automobile/Automotive Mechanics Technology/Technician** *56 students enrolled* • **Broadcast Journalism** *1 student enrolled* • **Business Administration and Management, General** *2 students enrolled* • **Business/Commerce, General** *3 students enrolled* • **Cabinetmaking and Millwork/Millwright** *1 student enrolled* • **Carpentry/Carpenter** *2 students enrolled* • **Child Development** *121 students enrolled* • **Commercial Photography** *4 students enrolled* • **Communications Systems Installation and Repair Technology** *18 students enrolled* • **Computer Programming/Programmer, General** *1 student enrolled* • **Computer Systems Networking and Telecommunications** *6 students enrolled* • **Computer and Information Sciences, General** *1 student enrolled* • **Cooking and Related Culinary Arts, General** *298 students enrolled* • **Criminal Justice/Police Science** *21 students enrolled* • **Diesel Mechanics Technology/Technician** *3 students enrolled* • **Dietetic Technician (DTR)** *4 students enrolled* • **Digital Communication and Media/Multimedia** *2 students enrolled* • **Education/Teaching of Individuals in Early Childhood Special Education Programs** *2 students enrolled* • **Electrical/Electronics Equipment Installation and Repair, General** *39*

*students enrolled* • **Emergency Medical Technology/Technician (EMT Paramedic)** • **Family Systems** *6 students enrolled* • **Fashion/Apparel Design** *2 students enrolled* • **Fire Science/Firefighting** *15 students enrolled* • **Floriculture/Floristry Operations and Management** *1 student enrolled* • **Foodservice Systems Administration/Management** *21 students enrolled* • **Forensic Science and Technology** *9 students enrolled* • **Heating, Air Conditioning and Refrigeration Technology/Technician (ACH/ACR/ACHR/HRAC/HVAC/AC Technology)** *17 students enrolled* • **Home Health Aide/Home Attendant** • **Hotel/Motel Administration/Management** *3 students enrolled* • **Human Services, General** *22 students enrolled* • **Interior Design** *3 students enrolled* • **International Business/Trade/Commerce** *1 student enrolled* • **Journalism** *1 student enrolled* • **Legal Administrative Assistant/Secretary** *1 student enrolled* • **Licensed Practical/Vocational Nurse Training (LPN, LVN, Cert, Dipl, AAS)** *81 students enrolled* • **Mechanical Drafting and Mechanical Drafting CAD/CADD** *7 students enrolled* • **Mechanical Engineering/Mechanical Technology/Technician** *3 students enrolled* • **Medical Administrative/Executive Assistant and Medical Secretary** *1 student enrolled* • **Medical/Clinical Assistant** *40 students enrolled* • **Music Management and Merchandising** *15 students enrolled* • **Nurse/Nursing Assistant/Aide and Patient Care Assistant** *2 students enrolled* • **Phlebotomy/Phlebotomist** *1 student enrolled* • **Prepress/Desktop Publishing and Digital Imaging Design** *1 student enrolled* • **Radio and Television** *1 student enrolled* • **Radiologic Technology/Science—Radiographer** • **Real Estate** *3 students enrolled* • **Sales, Distribution and Marketing Operations, General** *2 students enrolled* • **Special Education and Teaching, General** *1 student enrolled* • **Substance Abuse/Addiction Counseling** *23 students enrolled* • **System Administration/Administrator** *2 students enrolled* • **Welding Technology/Welder** *3 students enrolled*

**STUDENT SERVICES** Academic or career counseling, daycare for children of students, employment services for current students, placement services for program completers, remedial services.

## Los Angeles City College

855 North Vermont Avenue, Los Angeles, CA 90029-3590
http://www.lacitycollege.edu/

**CONTACT** Jamillah Moore, President
**Telephone:** 323-953-4000

**GENERAL INFORMATION** Public Institution. Founded 1929. **Accreditation:** Regional (WASC/ACCJC); dental laboratory technology (ADA); radiologic technology: radiography (JRCERT). **Total program enrollment:** 5233.

**PROGRAM(S) OFFERED**

• **Child Development** *122 students enrolled* • **Cinematography and Film/Video Production** *28 students enrolled* • **Commercial Photography** *4 students enrolled* • **Computer Programming/Programmer, General** *1 student enrolled* • **Computer Systems Networking and Telecommunications** • **Criminal Justice/Police Science** *7 students enrolled* • **Data Entry/Microcomputer Applications, General** *2 students enrolled* • **Data Modeling/Warehousing and Database Administration** • **Digital Communication and Media/Multimedia** • **E-Commerce/Electronic Commerce** • **Education/Teaching of Individuals in Early Childhood Special Education Programs** • **Electrical/Electronics Equipment Installation and Repair, General** *1 student enrolled* • **Foodservice Systems Administration/Management** *14 students enrolled* • **Forensic Science and Technology** • **Human Services, General** *11 students enrolled* • **Legal Assistant/Paralegal** *10 students enrolled* • **Music Management and Merchandising** • **Radio and Television** *24 students enrolled* • **Retailing and Retail Operations** • **Security and Loss Prevention Services** • **Substance Abuse/Addiction Counseling** *15 students enrolled* • **System Administration/Administrator** *4 students enrolled* • **Web Page, Digital/Multimedia and Information Resources Design** • **Web/Multimedia Management and Webmaster**

**STUDENT SERVICES** Academic or career counseling, daycare for children of students, employment services for current students, placement services for program completers, remedial services.

## Los Angeles County College of Nursing and Allied Health

1237 North Mission Road, Los Angeles, CA 90033
http://www.ladhs.org/lacusc/lacnah/

**CONTACT** Nancy Miller, Provost
**Telephone:** 323-226-4911

**GENERAL INFORMATION** Public Institution. Founded 1895. **Accreditation:** Regional (WASC/ACCJC). **Application fee:** $5.

**PROGRAM(S) OFFERED**

• **Nursing—Registered Nurse Training (RN, ASN, BSN, MSN)** *11 students enrolled*

**STUDENT SERVICES** Academic or career counseling, employment services for current students, placement services for program completers.

## Los Angeles Film School

6363 Sunset Boulevard, Hollywood, CA 90028
http://www.lafilm.com/

**CONTACT** Diana Derycz-Kessler, CEO
**Telephone:** 877-952-3456

**GENERAL INFORMATION** Private Institution. **Total program enrollment:** 346. **Application fee:** $75.

**PROGRAM(S) OFFERED**

• **Film/Video and Photographic Arts, Other** *1100 hrs./$38,210*

**STUDENT SERVICES** Academic or career counseling, employment services for current students, placement services for program completers.

## Los Angeles Harbor College

1111 Figueroa Place, Wilmington, CA 90744-2397
http://www.lahc.edu/

**CONTACT** Linda Spink, President
**Telephone:** 310-233-4000

**GENERAL INFORMATION** Public Institution. Founded 1949. **Accreditation:** Regional (WASC/ACCJC). **Total program enrollment:** 2872.

**PROGRAM(S) OFFERED**

• **Administrative Assistant and Secretarial Science, General** *2 students enrolled* • **Architectural Technology/Technician** *2 students enrolled* • **Computer and Information Sciences, General** *1 student enrolled* • **Mechanical Engineering/Mechanical Technology/Technician** *35 students enrolled* • **Nurse/Nursing Assistant/Aide and Patient Care Assistant** • **Real Estate** *1 student enrolled*

**STUDENT SERVICES** Academic or career counseling, daycare for children of students, employment services for current students, placement services for program completers, remedial services.

## Los Angeles Mission College

13356 Eldridge Avenue, Sylmar, CA 91342-3245
http://www.lamission.edu/

**CONTACT** Judith Valles, President
**Telephone:** 818-364-7600

**GENERAL INFORMATION** Public Institution. Founded 1974. **Accreditation:** Regional (WASC/ACCJC). **Total program enrollment:** 2657.

**PROGRAM(S) OFFERED**

• **Administrative Assistant and Secretarial Science, General** *2 students enrolled* • **Adult Development and Aging** *2 students enrolled* • **Child Development** *114 students enrolled* • **Computer Programming/Programmer, General** *2 students enrolled* • **Computer and Information Sciences, General** *2 students enrolled* • **Cooking and Related Culinary Arts, General** *8 students enrolled* • **Criminal Justice/Police Science** *1 student enrolled* • **Data Entry/Microcomputer Applications, General** *3 students enrolled* • **Drafting and Design Technology/**

*Los Angeles Mission College (continued)*

**Technician, General** *1 student enrolled* • **Engineering Technology, General** *1 student enrolled* • **Graphic Design** • **Hospitality Administration/Management, General** *12 students enrolled* • **Hotel/Motel Administration/Management** • **Interior Design** *3 students enrolled* • **Legal Administrative Assistant/Secretary** • **Legal Assistant/Paralegal** *48 students enrolled* • **Retailing and Retail Operations** • **Teacher Assistant/Aide** *1 student enrolled* • **Tourism and Travel Services Marketing Operations** • **Visual and Performing Arts, Other** *12 students enrolled*

**STUDENT SERVICES** Academic or career counseling, daycare for children of students, employment services for current students, placement services for program completers, remedial services.

## Los Angeles Music Academy

370 S. Fair Oaks Avenue, Pasadena, CA 91105
http://www.lamusicacademy.edu/

**CONTACT** C. Thomas Aylesbury, Director
**Telephone:** 626-568-8850

**GENERAL INFORMATION** Private Institution. **Total program enrollment:** 73. **Application fee:** $100.

**PROGRAM(S) OFFERED**
• **Music Performance, General** *71 students enrolled*

**STUDENT SERVICES** Academic or career counseling, remedial services.

## Los Angeles ORT Technical Institute

6435 Wilshire Boulevard, Los Angeles, CA 90048
http://www.laort.edu/

**CONTACT** Joseph Neman, Director
**Telephone:** 323-966-5444

**GENERAL INFORMATION** Private Institution (Affiliated with Jewish faith). Founded 1985. **Total program enrollment:** 177. **Application fee:** $100.

**PROGRAM(S) OFFERED**
• **Accounting Technology/Technician and Bookkeeping** *720 hrs./$9950* • **Accounting and Business/Management** *1200 hrs./$15,550* • **Clinical/Medical Laboratory Assistant** *720 hrs./$9950* • **Commercial and Advertising Art** *721 hrs./$9950* • **Drafting and Design Technology/Technician, General** *720 hrs./$9950* • **Executive Assistant/Executive Secretary** *14 students enrolled* • **Medical Administrative/Executive Assistant and Medical Secretary** • **Pharmacy Technician/Assistant** *720 hrs./$9950*

**STUDENT SERVICES** Academic or career counseling, employment services for current students, placement services for program completers.

## Los Angeles ORT Technical Institute–Sherman Oaks Branch

15130 Ventura Boulevard, Suite 250, Sherman Oaks, CA 91403
http://www.laort.edu/

**CONTACT** Joseph Neman, Director
**Telephone:** 818-382-6000

**GENERAL INFORMATION** Private Institution (Affiliated with Jewish faith). **Total program enrollment:** 49. **Application fee:** $100.

**PROGRAM(S) OFFERED**
• **Accounting Technology/Technician and Bookkeeping** *720 hrs./$9950* • **Accounting and Business/Management** *1200 hrs./$15,550* • **Clinical/Medical Laboratory Assistant** *720 hrs./$9950* • **Commercial and Advertising Art** *721 hrs./$9950* • **Drafting and Design Technology/Technician, General** *720 hrs./$9950* • **Executive Assistant/Executive Secretary** *8 students enrolled* • **Medical Administrative/Executive Assistant and Medical Secretary** *8 students enrolled* • **Pharmacy Technician/Assistant** *720 hrs./$9950*

**STUDENT SERVICES** Academic or career counseling, employment services for current students, placement services for program completers.

## Los Angeles Pierce College

6201 Winnetka Avenue, Woodland Hills, CA 91371-0001
http://www.lapc.cc.ca.us/

**CONTACT** Mr. Robert Garber, President
**Telephone:** 818-347-6401

**GENERAL INFORMATION** Public Institution. Founded 1947. **Accreditation:** Regional (WASC/ACCJC). **Total program enrollment:** 6275.

**PROGRAM(S) OFFERED**
• **Accounting** *30 students enrolled* • **Administrative Assistant and Secretarial Science, General** *5 students enrolled* • **Anthropology** *6 students enrolled* • **Applied Horticulture/Horticultural Operations, General** *11 students enrolled* • **Architectural Technology/Technician** *1 student enrolled* • **Automobile/Automotive Mechanics Technology/Technician** *48 students enrolled* • **Banking and Financial Support Services** *1 student enrolled* • **Biology Technician/Biotechnology Laboratory Technician** *1 student enrolled* • **Biology/Biological Sciences, General** *2 students enrolled* • **Business Administration and Management, General** *11 students enrolled* • **Business/Commerce, General** *6 students enrolled* • **Child Development** *166 students enrolled* • **Communications Systems Installation and Repair Technology** *12 students enrolled* • **Computer Programming/Programmer, General** *4 students enrolled* • **Computer and Information Sciences and Support Services, Other** *5 students enrolled* • **Computer and Information Sciences, General** *8 students enrolled* • **Dance, General** *1 student enrolled* • **Drafting and Design Technology/Technician, General** *1 student enrolled* • **Electrical/Electronics Equipment Installation and Repair, General** *17 students enrolled* • **Equestrian/Equine Studies** *1 student enrolled* • **Film/Cinema Studies** • **Geography, Other** • **Graphic Design** *2 students enrolled* • **International Business/Trade/Commerce** *10 students enrolled* • **Landscaping and Groundskeeping** *3 students enrolled* • **Machine Tool Technology/Machinist** *1 student enrolled* • **Manufacturing Technology/Technician** *5 students enrolled* • **Mass Communication/Media Studies** *2 students enrolled* • **Mathematics, General** *7 students enrolled* • **Music Management and Merchandising** *2 students enrolled* • **Retailing and Retail Operations** *1 student enrolled* • **Sales, Distribution and Marketing Operations, General** *3 students enrolled* • **Small Business Administration/Management** • **Substance Abuse/Addiction Counseling** *7 students enrolled* • **System Administration/Administrator** • **Taxation** • **Technical and Business Writing** *1 student enrolled* • **Web Page, Digital/Multimedia and Information Resources Design** • **Web/Multimedia Management and Webmaster** • **Welding Technology/Welder** • **Women's Studies**

**STUDENT SERVICES** Academic or career counseling, daycare for children of students, employment services for current students, placement services for program completers, remedial services.

## Los Angeles Recording Workshop

5278 Lankershim Boulevard, North Hollywood, CA 91601
http://www.larecordingschool.com/

**CONTACT** Darren Millar, Chief Operations Officer
**Telephone:** 323-464-5200

**GENERAL INFORMATION** Private Institution. Founded 1985. **Total program enrollment:** 261. **Application fee:** $75.

**PROGRAM(S) OFFERED**
• **Communications Technologies/Technicians and Support Services, Other** *361 students enrolled* • **Educational/Instructional Media Design** *904 hrs./$22,845*

**STUDENT SERVICES** Academic or career counseling, placement services for program completers.

## Los Angeles Southwest College

1600 West Imperial Highway, Los Angeles, CA 90047-4810
http://www.lasc.edu/

**CONTACT** Dr. Jack E. Daniels, III, President
**Telephone:** 323-241-5225

**GENERAL INFORMATION** Public Institution. Founded 1967. **Accreditation:** Regional (WASC/ACCJC). **Total program enrollment:** 1599.

**PROGRAM(S) OFFERED**

• **Accounting** *1 student enrolled* • **Administrative Assistant and Secretarial Science, General** *1 student enrolled* • **Audiology/Audiologist and Speech-Language Pathology/Pathologist** • **Banking and Financial Support Services** *1 student enrolled* • **Business Administration and Management, General** *1 student enrolled* • **Child Development** *6 students enrolled* • **Communications Systems Installation and Repair Technology** • **Computer Installation and Repair Technology/Technician** • **Criminal Justice/Police Science** *19 students enrolled* • **Education, General** *1 student enrolled* • **Education/Teaching of Individuals in Early Childhood Special Education Programs** • **Electrical/Electronics Equipment Installation and Repair, General** *8 students enrolled* • **Health and Physical Education, General** *1 student enrolled* • **Human Services, General** *13 students enrolled* • **Legal Administrative Assistant/Secretary** • **Manufacturing Technology/Technician** • **Office Management and Supervision** *2 students enrolled* • **Quality Control Technology/Technician** • **Real Estate** *9 students enrolled* • **Small Business Administration/Management** • **Spanish Language and Literature** *1 student enrolled* • **Sport and Fitness Administration/Management** • **Substance Abuse/Addiction Counseling** *6 students enrolled* • **Taxation** • **Teacher Assistant/Aide**

**STUDENT SERVICES** Academic or career counseling, daycare for children of students, employment services for current students, placement services for program completers, remedial services.

## Los Angeles Trade-Technical College

400 West Washington Boulevard, Los Angeles, CA 90015-4108
http://www.lattc.edu/

**CONTACT** Roland Chapdelaine, President
**Telephone:** 213-763-7000

**GENERAL INFORMATION** Public Institution. Founded 1925. **Accreditation:** Regional (WASC/ACCJC). **Total program enrollment:** 3779.

**PROGRAM(S) OFFERED**

• **Accounting** *19 students enrolled* • **Administrative Assistant and Secretarial Science, General** *12 students enrolled* • **Apparel and Textile Manufacture** *2 students enrolled* • **Apparel and Textile Marketing Management** *2 students enrolled* • **Apparel and Textiles, General** *10 students enrolled* • **Architectural Technology/Technician** *1 student enrolled* • **Art/Art Studies, General** *1 student enrolled* • **Autobody/Collision and Repair Technology/Technician** *7 students enrolled* • **Automobile/Automotive Mechanics Technology/Technician** *130 students enrolled* • **Banking and Financial Support Services** *8 students enrolled* • **Business Administration and Management, General** *5 students enrolled* • **Cabinetmaking and Millwork/Millwright** *2 students enrolled* • **Carpentry/Carpenter** *4 students enrolled* • **Chemical Technology/Technician** *9 students enrolled* • **Child Development** *10 students enrolled* • **Commercial and Advertising Art** *9 students enrolled* • **Communications Systems Installation and Repair Technology** *6 students enrolled* • **Computer Installation and Repair Technology/Technician** *5 students enrolled* • **Construction Trades, General** *11 students enrolled* • **Construction Trades, Other** *4 students enrolled* • **Cooking and Related Culinary Arts, General** *98 students enrolled* • **Cosmetology/Cosmetologist, General** *48 students enrolled* • **Diesel Mechanics Technology/Technician** *10 students enrolled* • **Electrical/Electronics Equipment Installation and Repair, General** *29 students enrolled* • **Electrician** *65 students enrolled* • **Electromechanical Technology/Electromechanical Engineering Technology** *7 students enrolled* • **Engineering Technologies/Technicians, Other** *5 students enrolled* • **Fashion/Apparel Design** *43 students enrolled* • **Geography** *3 students enrolled* • **Geography, Other** *1 student enrolled* • **Heating, Air Conditioning and Refrigeration Technology/Technician (ACH/ACR/ACHR/HRAC/HVAC/AC Technology)** *33 students enrolled* • **Information Technology** *6 students enrolled* • **Labor and Industrial Relations** *14 students enrolled* • **Licensed Practical/Vocational Nurse Training (LPN, LVN, Cert, Dipl, AAS)** *8 students enrolled* • **Machine Tool Technology/Machinist** *5 students enrolled* • **Medical Administrative/Executive Assistant and Medical Secretary** *3 students enrolled* • **Office Management and Supervision** *1 student enrolled* • **Plumbing Technology/Plumber** *1 student enrolled* • **Public Administration and Social Service Professions, Other** *1 student enrolled* • **Public Administration** *1 student enrolled* • **Real Estate** *1 student enrolled* • **Sales, Distribution and Marketing Operations, General** *1 student enrolled* • **Small Engine Mechanics and Repair Technology/Technician** *6 students enrolled* • **System Administration/Administrator** *6 students enrolled* • **Water Quality and Wastewater Treatment Management and Recycling Technology/Technician** *5 students enrolled* • **Web/Multimedia Management and Webmaster** *1 student enrolled* • **Welding Technology/Welder** *18 students enrolled*

**STUDENT SERVICES** Academic or career counseling, daycare for children of students, employment services for current students, placement services for program completers, remedial services.

## Los Angeles Valley College

5800 Fulton Avenue, Van Nuys, CA 91401-4096
http://www.lavc.cc.ca.us/

**CONTACT** Dr. Tyree Wieder, President
**Telephone:** 818-947-2600

**GENERAL INFORMATION** Public Institution. Founded 1949. **Accreditation:** Regional (WASC/ACCJC). **Total program enrollment:** 4592.

**PROGRAM(S) OFFERED**

• **Accounting** *13 students enrolled* • **Administrative Assistant and Secretarial Science, General** *5 students enrolled* • **Anthropology** *2 students enrolled* • **Architectural Technology/Technician** *3 students enrolled* • **Banking and Financial Support Services** *1 student enrolled* • **Business Administration and Management, General** *4 students enrolled* • **Child Development** *339 students enrolled* • **Cinematography and Film/Video Production** *1 student enrolled* • **Computer Programming/Programmer, General** *4 students enrolled* • **Criminal Justice/Police Science** *5 students enrolled* • **Drafting and Design Technology/Technician, General** *1 student enrolled* • **Electrical/Electronics Equipment Installation and Repair, General** *10 students enrolled* • **Fire Science/Firefighting** *1 student enrolled* • **Graphic Design** *8 students enrolled* • **Industrial Electronics Technology/Technician** *1 student enrolled* • **Machine Tool Technology/Machinist** *2 students enrolled* • **Manufacturing Technology/Technician** *2 students enrolled* • **Mass Communication/Media Studies** *2 students enrolled* • **Mechanical Drafting and Mechanical Drafting CAD/CADD** *2 students enrolled* • **Music Management and Merchandising** *3 students enrolled* • **Real Estate** *4 students enrolled* • **Sales, Distribution and Marketing Operations, General** *1 student enrolled* • **System Administration/Administrator** *4 students enrolled*

**STUDENT SERVICES** Academic or career counseling, daycare for children of students, employment services for current students, placement services for program completers, remedial services.

## Los Medanos College

2700 East Leland Road, Pittsburg, CA 94565-5197
http://www.losmedanos.net/

**CONTACT** Peter Garcia, President
**Telephone:** 925-439-2181

**GENERAL INFORMATION** Public Institution. Founded 1974. **Accreditation:** Regional (WASC/ACCJC). **Total program enrollment:** 2743.

**PROGRAM(S) OFFERED**

• **Accounting** *1 student enrolled* • **Administrative Assistant and Secretarial Science, General** *1 student enrolled* • **Appliance Installation and Repair Technology/Technician** *1 student enrolled* • **Automobile/Automotive Mechanics Technology/Technician** *19 students enrolled* • **Business Administration and Management, General** *2 students enrolled* • **Business/Commerce, General** *2 students enrolled* • **Child Development** *163 students enrolled* • **Computer and Information Sciences, General** *1 student enrolled* • **Criminal Justice/Police Science** *89 students enrolled* • **Emergency Medical Technology/Technician (EMT Paramedic)** • **Fire Science/Firefighting** *31 students enrolled* • **Information Technology** *1 student enrolled* • **Licensed Practical/Vocational Nurse Training (LPN, LVN, Cert, Dipl, AAS)** *25 students enrolled* • **Mechanical Engineering/Mechanical Technology/Technician** *5 students enrolled* • **Music Management and Merchandising** *3 students enrolled* • **Office Management and Supervision** *8 students enrolled* • **Small Business Administration/Management** *1 student enrolled* • **Tourism and Travel Services Marketing Operations** *17 students enrolled*

**STUDENT SERVICES** Academic or career counseling, daycare for children of students, employment services for current students, placement services for program completers, remedial services.

## Los Rios Community College District

1919 Spanos Court, Sacramento, CA 95825-3981

**CONTACT** Brice W. Harris, Chancellor
**Telephone:** 916-568-3041

**GENERAL INFORMATION** Public Institution.

## Lyle's Bakersfield College of Beauty

2935 F Street, Bakersfield, CA 93301

**CONTACT** Odulia Dee Upton, President
**Telephone:** 661-327-9784

**GENERAL INFORMATION** Private Institution. **Total program enrollment:** 169.

**PROGRAM(S) OFFERED**
- **Aesthetician/Esthetician and Skin Care Specialist** *600 hrs./$10,475*
- **Cosmetology and Related Personal Grooming Arts, Other** *400 hrs./$3075*
- **Cosmetology/Cosmetologist, General** *1600 hrs./$11,975* • **Nail Technician/Specialist and Manicurist** *400 hrs./$4875*

**STUDENT SERVICES** Academic or career counseling, placement services for program completers.

## Lyle's College of Beauty

6735 North First Avenue, Suite 112, Fresno, CA 93710

**CONTACT** Odulia Dee Upton, President
**Telephone:** 559-431-6060

**GENERAL INFORMATION** Private Institution. Founded 1972. **Total program enrollment:** 39.

**PROGRAM(S) OFFERED**
- **Aesthetician/Esthetician and Skin Care Specialist** *600 hrs./$9575*
- **Cosmetology and Related Personal Grooming Arts, Other** *400 hrs./$3075*
- **Cosmetology/Cosmetologist, General** *1600 hrs./$11,977* • **Nail Technician/Specialist and Manicurist** *400 hrs./$4275*

**STUDENT SERVICES** Academic or career counseling, placement services for program completers.

## Lytle's Redwood Empire Beauty College, Inc.

186 Wikiup Drive, Santa Rosa, CA 95403
http://www.lytles-rebc.com/

**CONTACT** Amanda Keith, Financial Aid Officer/Director of Student Affairs
**Telephone:** 707-545-8490

**GENERAL INFORMATION** Private Institution. Founded 1936. **Total program enrollment:** 101. **Application fee:** $75.

**PROGRAM(S) OFFERED**
- **Aesthetician/Esthetician and Skin Care Specialist** *600 hrs./$8394*
- **Cosmetology/Cosmetologist, General** *1600 hrs./$18,901* • **Facial Treatment Specialist/Facialist** *26 students enrolled*

**STUDENT SERVICES** Academic or career counseling, employment services for current students.

## Madera Beauty College

200 West Olive Avenue, Madera, CA 93637

**CONTACT** Wendell N. Berke, President
**Telephone:** 559-673-9201

**GENERAL INFORMATION** Private Institution. **Total program enrollment:** 28. **Application fee:** $100.

**PROGRAM(S) OFFERED**
- **Cosmetology and Related Personal Grooming Arts, Other** • **Cosmetology, Barber/Styling, and Nail Instructor** *600 hrs./$3200* • **Cosmetology/Cosmetologist, General** *1600 hrs./$8808* • **Nail Technician/Specialist and Manicurist** *400 hrs./$2400*

**STUDENT SERVICES** Academic or career counseling, employment services for current students, placement services for program completers.

## Make-up Designory

129 S. San Fernando Boulevard, Burbank, CA 91502
http://www.mud.edu

**CONTACT** Karl Zundel, School Director
**Telephone:** 818-729-9420

**GENERAL INFORMATION** Private Institution. **Total program enrollment:** 244. **Application fee:** $100.

**PROGRAM(S) OFFERED**
- **Make-Up Artist/Specialist** *400 hrs./$7450*

**STUDENT SERVICES** Academic or career counseling, employment services for current students, placement services for program completers.

## Manchester Beauty College

3756 North Blackstone Avenue, Fresno, CA 93726

**CONTACT** Wendell N. Berke, President
**Telephone:** 559-224-4242

**GENERAL INFORMATION** Private Institution. **Total program enrollment:** 10. **Application fee:** $100.

**PROGRAM(S) OFFERED**
- **Aesthetician/Esthetician and Skin Care Specialist** *600 hrs./$5500*
- **Cosmetology, Barber/Styling, and Nail Instructor** *600 hrs./$3200*
- **Cosmetology/Cosmetologist, General** *1600 hrs./$8910* • **Make-Up Artist/Specialist** *15 students enrolled* • **Nail Technician/Specialist and Manicurist** *400 hrs./$2400*

**STUDENT SERVICES** Academic or career counseling, employment services for current students, placement services for program completers.

## Marian Health Career Centers

3325 Wilshire Boulevard, Suite 1213, Los Angeles, CA 90010
http://www.mariancollege-california.com/

**CONTACT** Jo Anne R. Mutia, President
**Telephone:** 213-388-3566

**GENERAL INFORMATION** Private Institution. **Total program enrollment:** 169.

**PROGRAM(S) OFFERED**
- **Licensed Practical/Vocational Nurse Training (LPN, LVN, Cert, Dipl, AAS)** *1534 hrs./$20,500*

**STUDENT SERVICES** Academic or career counseling, placement services for program completers, remedial services.

## Marinello School of Beauty

19022 Brookhurst Street, Huntington Beach, CA 92646
http://www.marinello.com/

**CONTACT** Dr. Nagui Elyas, President
**Telephone:** 714-962-8831

**GENERAL INFORMATION** Private Institution. **Total program enrollment:** 51.

**PROGRAM(S) OFFERED**
- **Aesthetician/Esthetician and Skin Care Specialist** *600 hrs./$8400*
- **Cosmetology/Cosmetologist, General** *1600 hrs./$17,650*

**STUDENT SERVICES** Academic or career counseling, placement services for program completers.

## Marinello School of Beauty

240 South Market Street, Inglewood, CA 90301
http://www.marinello.com/

**CONTACT** Dr. Nagui Elyas, President
**Telephone:** 310-674-8100

**GENERAL INFORMATION** Private Institution. **Total program enrollment:** 79.

**PROGRAM(S) OFFERED**
- **Cosmetology/Cosmetologist, General** *1600 hrs./$17,650*

**STUDENT SERVICES** Academic or career counseling, placement services for program completers.

## Marinello School of Beauty

6111 Wilshire Boulevard, Los Angeles, CA 90048
http://www.marinello.com/

**CONTACT** Dr. Nagui Elyas, President
**Telephone:** 323-938-2005

**GENERAL INFORMATION** Private Institution. **Total program enrollment:** 67.

**PROGRAM(S) OFFERED**
- **Aesthetician/Esthetician and Skin Care Specialist** *600 hrs./$9475*
- **Cosmetology and Related Personal Grooming Arts, Other** *41 students enrolled* • **Cosmetology/Cosmetologist, General** *1600 hrs./$17,650*

**STUDENT SERVICES** Academic or career counseling, placement services for program completers.

## Marinello School of Beauty

716 South Broadway, Los Angeles, CA 90014
http://www.marinello.com/

**CONTACT** Dr. Nagui Elyas, President
**Telephone:** 323-980-9253

**GENERAL INFORMATION** Private Institution. **Total program enrollment:** 158.

**PROGRAM(S) OFFERED**
- **Aesthetician/Esthetician and Skin Care Specialist** *600 hrs./$8475*
- **Cosmetology/Cosmetologist, General** *1600 hrs./$17,650*

**STUDENT SERVICES** Academic or career counseling, placement services for program completers.

## Marinello School of Beauty

6219 Laurel Cyn Boulevard, North Hollywood, CA 91606
http://www.marinello.com/

**CONTACT** Dr. Nagui Elyas, President
**Telephone:** 818-980-1300

**GENERAL INFORMATION** Private Institution. **Total program enrollment:** 100.

**PROGRAM(S) OFFERED**
- **Cosmetology/Cosmetologist, General** *1600 hrs./$17,650* • **Nail Technician/Specialist and Manicurist**

**STUDENT SERVICES** Academic or career counseling, placement services for program completers.

## Marinello School of Beauty

940 North Mountain Avenue, Ontario, CA 91764
http://www.marinello.com/

**CONTACT** Dr. Nagui Elyas, President
**Telephone:** 909-984-5884

**GENERAL INFORMATION** Private Institution. **Total program enrollment:** 114.

**PROGRAM(S) OFFERED**
- **Cosmetology/Cosmetologist, General** *1600 hrs./$17,650* • **Nail Technician/Specialist and Manicurist** *400 hrs./$3475*

**STUDENT SERVICES** Academic or career counseling, placement services for program completers.

## Marinello School of Beauty

18442 Sherman Way, Reseda, CA 91335
http://www.marinello.com/

**CONTACT** Dr. Nagui Elyas, President
**Telephone:** 818-881-2521

**GENERAL INFORMATION** Private Institution. **Total program enrollment:** 81.

**PROGRAM(S) OFFERED**
- **Cosmetology/Cosmetologist, General** *1600 hrs./$17,650*

**STUDENT SERVICES** Academic or career counseling, placement services for program completers.

## Marinello School of Beauty

721e West 2nd Street, San Bernardino, CA 92410
http://www.marinello.com/

**CONTACT** Dr. Nagui Elyas, President
**Telephone:** 909-884-8747

**GENERAL INFORMATION** Private Institution. **Total program enrollment:** 270.

**PROGRAM(S) OFFERED**
- **Aesthetician/Esthetician and Skin Care Specialist** *600 hrs./$8475*
- **Cosmetology/Cosmetologist, General** *1600 hrs./$17,650*

**STUDENT SERVICES** Academic or career counseling, placement services for program completers.

## Marinello School of Beauty

1226 University Avenue, San Diego, CA 92103
http://www.marinello.com/

**CONTACT** Dr. Nagui Elyas, President
**Telephone:** 858-547-9260

**GENERAL INFORMATION** Private Institution. Founded 1905. **Total program enrollment:** 247.

*Marinello School of Beauty (continued)*

**PROGRAM(S) OFFERED**
• **Aesthetician/Esthetician and Skin Care Specialist** *600 hrs./$8475*
• **Cosmetology/Cosmetologist, General** *1600 hrs./$17,650* • **Nail Technician/Specialist and Manicurist** *4 students enrolled*

**STUDENT SERVICES** Academic or career counseling, placement services for program completers.

## Marinello School of Beauty

118 Plaza Drive, West Covina, CA 91790
http://www.marinello.com/

**CONTACT** Dr. Nagui Elyas, President
**Telephone:** 626-962-1021

**GENERAL INFORMATION** Private Institution. **Total program enrollment:** 111.

**PROGRAM(S) OFFERED**
• **Cosmetology/Cosmetologist, General** *1600 hrs./$17,650*

**STUDENT SERVICES** Academic or career counseling, placement services for program completers.

## Marinello School of Beauty

6538 Greenleaf Avenue, Whittier, CA 90601
http://www.marinello.com/

**CONTACT** Dr. Nagui Elyas, President
**Telephone:** 562-698-0068

**GENERAL INFORMATION** Private Institution. **Total program enrollment:** 226.

**PROGRAM(S) OFFERED**
• **Cosmetology/Cosmetologist, General** *1600 hrs./$17,650* • **Massage Therapy/Therapeutic Massage** *36 hrs./$10,155*

**STUDENT SERVICES** Academic or career counseling, placement services for program completers.

## Marinello Schools of Beauty

23635 El Toro Road, Suite K, Lake Forest, CA 92553
http://www.marinello.com/

**CONTACT** Dr. Nagui Elyas, President
**Telephone:** 949-586-4900

**GENERAL INFORMATION** Private Institution. Founded 1987. **Total program enrollment:** 75.

**PROGRAM(S) OFFERED**
• **Cosmetology/Cosmetologist, General** *1600 hrs./$17,650*

**STUDENT SERVICES** Academic or career counseling, placement services for program completers.

## Marinello Schools of Beauty

17337 East Valley Boulevard, La Puente, CA 91744
http://www.marinello.com/

**CONTACT** Dr. Nagui Elyas, President
**Telephone:** 626-965-2532

**GENERAL INFORMATION** Private Institution. Founded 1973. **Total program enrollment:** 94.

**PROGRAM(S) OFFERED**
• **Aesthetician/Esthetician and Skin Care Specialist** *600 hrs./$8475*
• **Cosmetology/Cosmetologist, General** *1600 hrs./$17,650* • **Nail Technician/Specialist and Manicurist** *400 hrs./$3475*

**STUDENT SERVICES** Academic or career counseling, placement services for program completers.

## Marinello Schools of Beauty

505 Long Beach Boulevard, Long Beach, CA 90802
http://www.marinello.com/

**CONTACT** Dr. Nagui Elyas, President
**Telephone:** 818-954-8894

**GENERAL INFORMATION** Private Institution. Founded 1972. **Total program enrollment:** 170.

**PROGRAM(S) OFFERED**
• **Aesthetician/Esthetician and Skin Care Specialist** *600 hrs./$8475*
• **Cosmetology/Cosmetologist, General** *1600 hrs./$17,650*

**STUDENT SERVICES** Academic or career counseling, placement services for program completers.

## Marinello Schools of Beauty

24741 Alessandro Boulevard, Moreno Valley, CA 92553
http://www.marinello.com/

**CONTACT** Dr. Nagui Elyas, President
**Telephone:** 909-247-2047

**GENERAL INFORMATION** Private Institution. Founded 1989. **Total program enrollment:** 173.

**PROGRAM(S) OFFERED**
• **Cosmetology/Cosmetologist, General** *1600 hrs./$17,650*

**STUDENT SERVICES** Academic or career counseling, placement services for program completers.

## Marinello Schools of Beauty

8527 Alondra Boulevard, Suite 129, Paramount, CA 90723
http://www.marinello.com/

**CONTACT** Dr. Nagui Elyas, President
**Telephone:** 562-531-1800

**GENERAL INFORMATION** Private Institution. **Total program enrollment:** 185.

**PROGRAM(S) OFFERED**
• **Cosmetology/Cosmetologist, General** *1600 hrs./$17,650*

**STUDENT SERVICES** Academic or career counseling, placement services for program completers.

## Martinez Adult School

600 F Street, Martinez, CA 94553-3298
http://www.martinez-ed.org/

**CONTACT** Kathy Farwell, Director
**Telephone:** 925-228-3276 Ext. 263

**GENERAL INFORMATION** Public Institution. Founded 1919. **Total program enrollment:** 274.

**PROGRAM(S) OFFERED**
• **Accounting Technology/Technician and Bookkeeping** *900 hrs./$1200*
• **Administrative Assistant and Secretarial Science, General** *900 hrs./$900*
• **CAD/CADD Drafting and/or Design Technology/Technician** *50 students enrolled* • **Criminal Justice/Police Science** *20 students enrolled* • **Data Entry/**

**Microcomputer Applications, General** *900 hrs./$1200* • **Executive Assistant/Executive Secretary** *15 students enrolled* • **General Office Occupations and Clerical Services** *6 students enrolled* • **Medical Insurance Coding Specialist/Coder** *900 hrs./$1870* • **Medical Office Management/Administration** *51 students enrolled* • **Nurse/Nursing Assistant/Aide and Patient Care Assistant** *225 hrs./$665* • **Opticianry/Ophthalmic Dispensing Optician** *700 hrs./$4200* • **Pharmacy Technician/Assistant** *10 students enrolled*

**STUDENT SERVICES** Academic or career counseling, placement services for program completers, remedial services.

## The Master's College and Seminary

21726 Placerita Canyon Road, Santa Clarita, CA 91321-1200
http://www.masters.edu/

**CONTACT** John MacArthur, President
**Telephone:** 661-259-3540

**GENERAL INFORMATION** Private Institution. Founded 1927. **Accreditation:** Regional (WASC/ACSCU); home economics (AAFCS). **Total program enrollment:** 1017. **Application fee:** $40.

**PROGRAM(S) OFFERED**
• **Bible/Biblical Studies** *10 students enrolled*

**STUDENT SERVICES** Academic or career counseling, employment services for current students, placement services for program completers, remedial services.

## Maxine Waters Employment Preparation Center

10925 South Central Avenue, Los Angeles, CA 90059

**CONTACT** Dr. Janet Clark, Principal
**Telephone:** 323-564-1431 Ext. 300

**GENERAL INFORMATION** Public Institution. **Total program enrollment:** 536.

**PROGRAM(S) OFFERED**
• **Automobile/Automotive Mechanics Technology/Technician** • **Banking and Financial Support Services** *20 students enrolled* • **Child Development** *31 students enrolled* • **Computer Installation and Repair Technology/Technician** *1200 hrs./$148* • **Construction Trades, General** *1200 hrs./$128* • **Electrical/Electronics Maintenance and Repair Technology, Other** • **Landscaping and Groundskeeping** *1200 hrs./$88* • **Licensed Practical/Vocational Nurse Training (LPN, LVN, Cert, Dipl, AAS)** *1530 hrs./$2513* • **Medical Office Management/Administration** *600 hrs./$138* • **Welding Technology/Welder** *1200 hrs./$1318*

**STUDENT SERVICES** Academic or career counseling, daycare for children of students, employment services for current students, placement services for program completers, remedial services.

## MCed Career College

2002 North Gateway Boulevard, Fresno, CA 93727
http://www.mced.edu/

**CONTACT** Rick Trevino, CEO
**Telephone:** 559-456-0623

**GENERAL INFORMATION** Private Institution. **Total program enrollment:** 1486. **Application fee:** $75.

**PROGRAM(S) OFFERED**
• **Accounting Technology/Technician and Bookkeeping** *5 students enrolled* • **Business Administration and Management, General** *6 students enrolled* • **Cardiovascular Technology/Technologist** *44 hrs./$10,150* • **Computer Systems Networking and Telecommunications** *6 students enrolled* • **Dental Assisting/Assistant** *44 hrs./$10,150* • **Legal Assistant/Paralegal** *44 hrs./$10,150* • **Medical Administrative/Executive Assistant and Medical Secretary** *32 students enrolled* • **Medical Insurance Coding Specialist/Coder** *71 hrs./$13,920* • **Medical/Clinical Assistant** *44 hrs./$10,150* • **Pharmacy Technician/Assistant** *44 hrs./$10,150*

**STUDENT SERVICES** Academic or career counseling, employment services for current students, placement services for program completers, remedial services.

## Mendocino College

1000 Hensley Creek Road, Ukiah, CA 95482-0300
http://www.mendocino.edu/

**CONTACT** Kathryn G. Lehner, Superintendent/President
**Telephone:** 707-468-3000

**GENERAL INFORMATION** Public Institution. Founded 1973. **Accreditation:** Regional (WASC/ACCJC). **Total program enrollment:** 1141.

**PROGRAM(S) OFFERED**
• **Accounting** *2 students enrolled* • **Apparel and Textiles, General** *2 students enrolled* • **Automobile/Automotive Mechanics Technology/Technician** *9 students enrolled* • **Business Administration and Management, General** *6 students enrolled* • **Ceramic Arts and Ceramics** *1 student enrolled* • **Child Development** *4 students enrolled* • **Computer Systems Networking and Telecommunications** *2 students enrolled* • **Computer and Information Sciences, General** *1 student enrolled* • **Criminal Justice/Police Science** *5 students enrolled* • **Data Entry/Microcomputer Applications, General** *3 students enrolled* • **Human Services, General** *5 students enrolled* • **Landscaping and Groundskeeping** *2 students enrolled* • **Medical Administrative/Executive Assistant and Medical Secretary** *1 student enrolled* • **Medical Insurance Coding Specialist/Coder** *1 student enrolled* • **Plant Nursery Operations and Management** *1 student enrolled* • **Restaurant, Culinary, and Catering Management/Manager** *5 students enrolled* • **Substance Abuse/Addiction Counseling** *3 students enrolled* • **Web Page, Digital/Multimedia and Information Resources Design** *2 students enrolled*

**STUDENT SERVICES** Academic or career counseling, daycare for children of students, employment services for current students, remedial services.

## Merced College

3600 M Street, Merced, CA 95348-2898
http://www.mccd.edu/

**CONTACT** Benjamin T. Duran, Superintendent President
**Telephone:** 209-384-6000

**GENERAL INFORMATION** Public Institution. Founded 1962. **Accreditation:** Regional (WASC/ACCJC); radiologic technology: radiography (JRCERT). **Total program enrollment:** 4886.

**PROGRAM(S) OFFERED**
• **Accounting** *5 students enrolled* • **Administrative Assistant and Secretarial Science, General** *1 student enrolled* • **Agricultural Mechanics and Equipment/Machine Technology** *51 students enrolled* • **Applied Horticulture/Horticultural Operations, General** *1 student enrolled* • **Architectural Drafting and Architectural CAD/CADD** *5 students enrolled* • **Autobody/Collision and Repair Technology/Technician** *1 student enrolled* • **Biology Technician/Biotechnology Laboratory Technician** *1 student enrolled* • **Computer Installation and Repair Technology/Technician** *2 students enrolled* • **Cooking and Related Culinary Arts, General** *1 student enrolled* • **Criminal Justice/Police Science** *1 student enrolled* • **Drawing** *1 student enrolled* • **Electrical/Electronics Equipment Installation and Repair, General** *1 student enrolled* • **Emergency Medical Technology/Technician (EMT Paramedic)** • **Fire Science/Firefighting** *2 students enrolled* • **Hazardous Materials Management and Waste Technology/Technician** *1 student enrolled* • **Heating, Air Conditioning and Refrigeration Technology/Technician (ACH/ACR/ACHR/HRAC/HVAC/AC Technology)** *2 students enrolled* • **Human Services, General** *3 students enrolled* • **Industrial Electronics Technology/Technician** *1 student enrolled* • **Instrumentation Technology/Technician** *1 student enrolled* • **Licensed Practical/Vocational Nurse Training (LPN, LVN, Cert, Dipl, AAS)** *37 students enrolled* • **Mechanical Drafting and Mechanical Drafting CAD/CADD** *3 students enrolled* • **Mechanical Engineering/Mechanical Technology/Technician** *1 student enrolled* • **Nurse/Nursing Assistant/Aide and Patient Care Assistant** • **Radiologic Technology/Science—Radiographer** *15 students enrolled* • **Substance Abuse/Addiction Counseling** *6 students enrolled* • **Welding Technology/Welder** *1 student enrolled*

**STUDENT SERVICES** Academic or career counseling, daycare for children of students, employment services for current students, placement services for program completers, remedial services.

## Meridian Institute

4201 Wilshire Boulevard, Suite 515, Los Angeles, CA 90010

**GENERAL INFORMATION** Private Institution. **Total program enrollment:** 44. **Application fee:** $75.

**PROGRAM(S) OFFERED**
• **Massage Therapy/Therapeutic Massage** *20 hrs./$3192* • **Medical Office Management/Administration** *28 hrs./$4802* • **Phlebotomy/Phlebotomist** *11 hrs./$1831* • **Physical Therapist Assistant** *26 hrs./$4822*

**STUDENT SERVICES** Academic or career counseling, employment services for current students, placement services for program completers, remedial services.

## Merritt College

12500 Campus Drive, Oakland, CA 94619-3196
http://www.merritt.edu/

**CONTACT** Dr. Robert Adams, President
**Telephone:** 510-531-4911

**GENERAL INFORMATION** Public Institution. Founded 1953. **Accreditation:** Regional (WASC/ACCJC); radiologic technology: radiography (JRCERT). **Total program enrollment:** 1263.

**PROGRAM(S) OFFERED**
• **Administrative Assistant and Secretarial Science, General** *1 student enrolled* • **Applied Horticulture/Horticultural Operations, General** *1 student enrolled* • **Child Development** *129 students enrolled* • **Computer and Information Sciences, General** *1 student enrolled* • **Corrections** *3 students enrolled* • **Criminal Justice/Police Science** *5 students enrolled* • **Dietetic Technician (DTR)** *9 students enrolled* • **Emergency Medical Technology/Technician (EMT Paramedic)** • **Foodservice Systems Administration/Management** *1 student enrolled* • **Hazardous Materials Management and Waste Technology/Technician** *1 student enrolled* • **Human Services, General** *34 students enrolled* • **Landscaping and Groundskeeping** *17 students enrolled* • **Legal Assistant/Paralegal** *20 students enrolled* • **Licensed Practical/Vocational Nurse Training (LPN, LVN, Cert, Dipl, AAS)** *16 students enrolled* • **Nurse/Nursing Assistant/Aide and Patient Care Assistant** *1 student enrolled* • **Plant Nursery Operations and Management** *1 student enrolled* • **Real Estate** *25 students enrolled* • **Substance Abuse/Addiction Counseling** *23 students enrolled*

**STUDENT SERVICES** Academic or career counseling, daycare for children of students, employment services for current students, placement services for program completers, remedial services.

## Milan Institute of Cosmetology

731 W. Shaw Avenue, Clovis, CA 93612
http://www.milaninstitute.edu/

**CONTACT** Gary Yasuda, President
**Telephone:** 559-323-2800

**GENERAL INFORMATION** Private Institution. **Total program enrollment:** 427. **Application fee:** $100.

**PROGRAM(S) OFFERED**
• **Aesthetician/Esthetician and Skin Care Specialist** *600 hrs./$6999* • **Cosmetology/Cosmetologist, General** *1600 hrs./$16,193* • **Massage Therapy/Therapeutic Massage** *720 hrs./$9820* • **Medical/Clinical Assistant** *720 hrs./$10,338*

**STUDENT SERVICES** Academic or career counseling, employment services for current students, placement services for program completers.

## Milan Institute of Cosmetology

934 Missouri Street, Fairfield, CA 94533
http://www.milaninstitute.edu

**CONTACT** Gary Yasuda, President
**Telephone:** 707-425-2288

**GENERAL INFORMATION** Private Institution. **Total program enrollment:** 129. **Application fee:** $100.

**PROGRAM(S) OFFERED**
• **Aesthetician/Esthetician and Skin Care Specialist** *600 hrs./$6999* • **Cosmetology/Cosmetologist, General** *1600 hrs./$16,180* • **Massage Therapy/Therapeutic Massage** *720 hrs./$9819*

**STUDENT SERVICES** Academic or career counseling, employment services for current students, placement services for program completers.

## Milan Institute of Cosmetology

3238 South Fairway Street, Visalia, CA 93277
http://www.milaninstitute.edu

**CONTACT** Gary Yasuda, President
**Telephone:** 559-730-5350

**GENERAL INFORMATION** Private Institution. **Total program enrollment:** 139. **Application fee:** $75.

**PROGRAM(S) OFFERED**
• **Cosmetology/Cosmetologist, General** *1600 hrs./$16,189*

**STUDENT SERVICES** Academic or career counseling, employment services for current students, placement services for program completers.

## MiraCosta College

One Barnard Drive, Oceanside, CA 92056-3899
http://www.miracosta.edu/

**CONTACT** Dr. Susan Cota, Interim Superintendent/President
**Telephone:** 760-757-2121

**GENERAL INFORMATION** Public Institution. Founded 1934. **Accreditation:** Regional (WASC/ACCJC). **Total program enrollment:** 4769.

**PROGRAM(S) OFFERED**
• **Accounting** *11 students enrolled* • **Administrative Assistant and Secretarial Science, General** *32 students enrolled* • **Agribusiness/Agricultural Business Operations** *1 student enrolled* • **Agriculture, Agriculture Operations and Related Sciences, Other** *2 students enrolled* • **Architectural Technology/Technician** *8 students enrolled* • **Automobile/Automotive Mechanics Technology/Technician** *49 students enrolled* • **Biology Technician/Biotechnology Laboratory Technician** *3 students enrolled* • **Child Development** *71 students enrolled* • **Computer Systems Networking and Telecommunications** *7 students enrolled* • **Computer and Information Sciences and Support Services, Other** *2 students enrolled* • **Cosmetology/Cosmetologist, General** *53 students enrolled* • **Criminal Justice/Police Science** *7 students enrolled* • **Dance, General** *1 student enrolled* • **Data Entry/Microcomputer Applications, General** *3 students enrolled* • **Digital Communication and Media/Multimedia** *7 students enrolled* • **Drafting and Design Technology/Technician, General** *10 students enrolled* • **E-Commerce/Electronic Commerce** *3 students enrolled* • **Education/Teaching of Individuals in Early Childhood Special Education Programs** *2 students enrolled* • **Floriculture/Floristry Operations and Management** *2 students enrolled* • **Health Services/Allied Health/Health Sciences, General** *7 students enrolled* • **Health and Physical Education, General** *1 student enrolled* • **Home Health Aide/Home Attendant** *1 student enrolled* • **Hospitality Administration/Management, General** *6 students enrolled* • **Landscaping and Groundskeeping** *7 students enrolled* • **Licensed Practical/Vocational Nurse Training (LPN, LVN, Cert, Dipl, AAS)** *20 students enrolled* • **Music Management and Merchandising** *13 students enrolled* • **Music, General** *3 students enrolled* • **Nurse/Nursing Assistant/Aide and Patient Care Assistant** *14 students enrolled* • **Nursing—Registered Nurse Training (RN, ASN, BSN, MSN)** *28 students enrolled* • **Office Management and Supervision** *1 student enrolled* • **Phlebotomy/Phlebotomist** • **Physical Therapist Assistant** • **Plant Nursery Operations and Management** *3 students enrolled* • **Real Estate** *28 students enrolled* • **Restaurant, Culinary, and Catering Management/Manager** *2 students enrolled* • **Retailing and Retail Operations** *1 student enrolled* • **Sales, Distribution and Marketing Operations, General** *3 students enrolled* • **Small Business Administration/Management** *9*

*students enrolled* • **Spanish Language and Literature** *1 student enrolled* • **Surgical Technology/Technologist** *6 students enrolled* • **Taxation** *10 students enrolled* • **Technical Theatre/Theatre Design and Technology** *1 student enrolled* • **Tourism and Travel Services Marketing Operations** *3 students enrolled* • **Web Page, Digital/Multimedia and Information Resources Design** *1 student enrolled*

**STUDENT SERVICES** Academic or career counseling, daycare for children of students, employment services for current students, placement services for program completers, remedial services.

## Mission College

3000 Mission College Boulevard, Santa Clara, CA 95054-1897
http://www.missioncollege.org/

**CONTACT** Harriett Robles, President
**Telephone:** 408-988-2200

**GENERAL INFORMATION** Public Institution. Founded 1977. **Accreditation:** Regional (WASC/ACCJC). **Total program enrollment:** 2419.

**PROGRAM(S) OFFERED**

• **Accounting** *20 students enrolled* • **Administrative Assistant and Secretarial Science, General** *6 students enrolled* • **Business/Commerce, General** *3 students enrolled* • **Child Development** *3 students enrolled* • **Community Health and Preventive Medicine** *3 students enrolled* • **Computer Graphics** *2 students enrolled* • **Computer Programming/Programmer, General** *1 student enrolled* • **Data Modeling/Warehousing and Database Administration** *4 students enrolled* • **Education/Teaching of Individuals in Early Childhood Special Education Programs** *1 student enrolled* • **Electrical/Electronics Drafting and Electrical/Electronics CAD/CADD** *1 student enrolled* • **Floriculture/Floristry Operations and Management** *7 students enrolled* • **Foodservice Systems Administration/Management** *1 student enrolled* • **Graphic Design** *2 students enrolled* • **Licensed Practical/Vocational Nurse Training (LPN, LVN, Cert, Dipl, AAS)** *50 students enrolled* • **Mechanical Drafting and Mechanical Drafting CAD/CADD** *1 student enrolled* • **Music, General** *1 student enrolled* • **Nurse/Nursing Assistant/Aide and Patient Care Assistant** *56 students enrolled* • **Office Management and Supervision** *8 students enrolled* • **Psychiatric/Mental Health Services Technician** *14 students enrolled* • **Real Estate** *5 students enrolled* • **Restaurant, Culinary, and Catering Management/Manager** *2 students enrolled* • **Sales, Distribution and Marketing Operations, General** *1 student enrolled* • **Sociology** *2 students enrolled* • **Sport and Fitness Administration/Management** *8 students enrolled* • **System Administration/Administrator** *5 students enrolled* • **Teacher Assistant/Aide** *1 student enrolled* • **Web Page, Digital/Multimedia and Information Resources Design** *2 students enrolled*

**STUDENT SERVICES** Academic or career counseling, daycare for children of students, employment services for current students, placement services for program completers, remedial services.

## Miss Marty's School of Beauty

1087 Mission Street, San Francisco, CA 94103
http://www.missmartys.com/page5.html/

**CONTACT** Dorothy Bell, Director
**Telephone:** 415-227-4240

**GENERAL INFORMATION** Private Institution. Founded 1957. **Total program enrollment:** 52. **Application fee:** $75.

**PROGRAM(S) OFFERED**

• **Aesthetician/Esthetician and Skin Care Specialist** *600 hrs./$8675* • **Cosmetology, Barber/Styling, and Nail Instructor** • **Cosmetology/Cosmetologist, General** *1600 hrs./$18,325* • **Massage Therapy/Therapeutic Massage** • **Nail Technician/Specialist and Manicurist**

**STUDENT SERVICES** Academic or career counseling, placement services for program completers.

## Modern Beauty Academy

699 South C Street, Oxnard, CA 93030

**CONTACT** Duane Davis, President
**Telephone:** 805-483-4994

**GENERAL INFORMATION** Private Institution. **Total program enrollment:** 59. **Application fee:** $75.

**PROGRAM(S) OFFERED**

• **Cosmetology/Cosmetologist, General** *1600 hrs./$11,032*

**STUDENT SERVICES** Academic or career counseling, placement services for program completers.

## Modern Technology School

1232 East Katella Avenue, Anaheim, CA 92805-6623

**CONTACT** Susan L. Shannon, Campus Director
**Telephone:** 714-418-9100

**GENERAL INFORMATION** Private Institution. Founded 1982. **Total program enrollment:** 196. **Application fee:** $75.

**PROGRAM(S) OFFERED**

• **Cardiovascular Technology/Technologist** *632 hrs./$8237* • **Diagnostic Medical Sonography/Sonographer and Ultrasound Technician** *2172 hrs./$30,488* • **Medical Office Management/Administration** *1 student enrolled* • **Medical Radiologic Technology/Science—Radiation Therapist** *1159 hrs./$14,414* • **Medical/Clinical Assistant** *480 hrs./$4850*

**STUDENT SERVICES** Academic or career counseling, placement services for program completers.

## Modesto Junior College

435 College Avenue, Modesto, CA 95350-5800
http://www.mjc.edu/

**CONTACT** Richard Rose, President
**Telephone:** 209-575-6550

**GENERAL INFORMATION** Public Institution. Founded 1921. **Accreditation:** Regional (WASC/ACCJC); dental assisting (ADA); medical assisting (AAMAE). **Total program enrollment:** 6874.

**PROGRAM(S) OFFERED**

• **Administrative Assistant and Secretarial Science, General** *4 students enrolled* • **Agricultural Mechanics and Equipment/Machine Technology** *1 student enrolled* • **Agricultural Production Operations, Other** *1 student enrolled* • **Animal/Livestock Husbandry and Production** *3 students enrolled* • **Architectural Technology/Technician** *11 students enrolled* • **Autobody/Collision and Repair Technology/Technician** *3 students enrolled* • **Automobile/Automotive Mechanics Technology/Technician** *7 students enrolled* • **Building/Home/Construction Inspection/Inspector** *2 students enrolled* • **Child Development** *5 students enrolled* • **Computer Installation and Repair Technology/Technician** *1 student enrolled* • **Computer and Information Sciences, General** *8 students enrolled* • **Construction Trades, General** *3 students enrolled* • **Cooking and Related Culinary Arts, General** *5 students enrolled* • **Criminal Justice/Police Science** *1 student enrolled* • **Dental Assisting/Assistant** *18 students enrolled* • **Education/Teaching of Individuals in Early Childhood Special Education Programs** *10 students enrolled* • **Emergency Medical Technology/Technician (EMT Paramedic)** • **Ethnic, Cultural Minority, and Gender Studies, Other** *1 student enrolled* • **Fire Science/Firefighting** *8 students enrolled* • **Forestry, General** *1 student enrolled* • **Graphic Design** *3 students enrolled* • **Human Services, General** *6 students enrolled* • **Industrial Electronics Technology/Technician** *8 students enrolled* • **Interior Design** *6 students enrolled* • **Licensed Practical/Vocational Nurse Training (LPN, LVN, Cert, Dipl, AAS)** *29 students enrolled* • **Machine Tool Technology/Machinist** *5 students enrolled* • **Mechanical Engineering/Mechanical Technology/Technician** *2 students enrolled* • **Medical/Clinical Assistant** *24 students enrolled* • **Nurse/Nursing Assistant/Aide and Patient Care Assistant** • **Office Management and Supervision** *1 student enrolled* • **Parks, Recreation and Leisure Facilities Management** *1 student enrolled* • **Radio and Television** *5 students enrolled* • **Sheet Metal Technology/Sheetworking** *1 student enrolled* • **Technical Theatre/Theatre Design and Technology** *1 student enrolled* • **Welding Technology/Welder** *10 students enrolled*

**STUDENT SERVICES** Academic or career counseling, daycare for children of students, employment services for current students, remedial services.

## Mojave Barber College

15505 7th Street, Victorville, CA 92395
http://mojavebarbercollege.com/

**CONTACT** Nancy J. Reyes, Financial Aid Officer
**Telephone:** 760-955-2934

**GENERAL INFORMATION** Private Institution. **Total program enrollment:** 9. **Application fee:** $65.

**PROGRAM(S) OFFERED**

• **Barbering/Barber** *1500 hrs./$10,573*

## Moler Barber College

3500 Broadway Street, Oakland, CA 94611-5729

**CONTACT** Elsia Curry, Owner/Director
**Telephone:** 510-652-4177

**GENERAL INFORMATION** Private Institution. Founded 1979. **Total program enrollment:** 29.

**PROGRAM(S) OFFERED**
• **Barbering/Barber** *1500 hrs./$6925*

**STUDENT SERVICES** Academic or career counseling, remedial services.

## Montebello Beauty College

2201 West Whitier Boulevard, Montebello, CA 90640

**CONTACT** Florence G. Hernandez, Owner
**Telephone:** 323-727-7851

**GENERAL INFORMATION** Private Institution. Founded 1987. **Total program enrollment:** 67.

**PROGRAM(S) OFFERED**
• **Cosmetology and Related Personal Grooming Arts, Other** *62 students enrolled* • **Cosmetology/Cosmetologist, General** *160 hrs./$11,475*

**STUDENT SERVICES** Academic or career counseling, placement services for program completers.

## Monterey Peninsula College

980 Fremont Street, Monterey, CA 93940-4799
http://www.mpc.edu/

**CONTACT** Douglas Garrison, President Superintendent
**Telephone:** 831-646-4000

**GENERAL INFORMATION** Public Institution. Founded 1947. **Accreditation:** Regional (WASC/ACCJC); dental assisting (ADA). **Total program enrollment:** 2175.

**PROGRAM(S) OFFERED**
• **Administrative Assistant and Secretarial Science, General** *2 students enrolled* • **Apparel and Textile Manufacture** *1 student enrolled* • **Applied Horticulture/Horticultural Operations, General** *4 students enrolled* • **Automobile/Automotive Mechanics Technology/Technician** *1 student enrolled* • **Child Development** *2 students enrolled* • **Computer and Information Sciences, General** *2 students enrolled* • **Criminal Justice/Police Science** *24 students enrolled* • **Data Entry/Microcomputer Applications, General** *1 student enrolled* • **Dental Assisting/Assistant** *5 students enrolled* • **Emergency Medical Technology/Technician (EMT Paramedic)** • **Fashion/Apparel Design** *1 student enrolled* • **Fire Science/Firefighting** *2 students enrolled* • **Graphic Design** *2 students enrolled* • **Hospitality Administration/Management, General** *3 students enrolled* • **Human Services, General** *1 student enrolled* • **Interior Design** *2 students enrolled* • **International Business/Trade/Commerce** *1 student enrolled* • **Massage Therapy/Therapeutic Massage** *2 students enrolled* • **Metal and Jewelry Arts** *1 student enrolled* • **Technical Theatre/Theatre Design and Technology** *1 student enrolled*

**STUDENT SERVICES** Academic or career counseling, daycare for children of students, employment services for current students, placement services for program completers, remedial services.

## Moorpark College

7075 Campus Road, Moorpark, CA 93021-1695
http://www.moorpark.cc.ca.us/

**CONTACT** Pam Eddinger, President
**Telephone:** 805-378-1400

**GENERAL INFORMATION** Public Institution. Founded 1967. **Accreditation:** Regional (WASC/ACCJC); radiologic technology: radiography (JRCERT). **Total program enrollment:** 6378.

**PROGRAM(S) OFFERED**
• **Accounting** *2 students enrolled* • **Business Administration and Management, General** *1 student enrolled* • **Child Development** *1 student enrolled* • **Computer Science** *1 student enrolled* • **Computer Systems Networking and Telecommunications** *5 students enrolled* • **Emergency Medical Technology/Technician (EMT Paramedic)** • **Information Technology** *3 students enrolled* • **Interior Design** *22 students enrolled*

**STUDENT SERVICES** Academic or career counseling, daycare for children of students, employment services for current students, placement services for program completers, remedial services.

## Mt. Diablo Adult Education

1266 San Carlos, Concord, CA 94518
http://www.mdusd.k12.ca.us/adulted/

**CONTACT** Joanne Durkee, Director
**Telephone:** 925-685-7340 Ext. 2744

**GENERAL INFORMATION** Private Institution. **Total program enrollment:** 176.

**PROGRAM(S) OFFERED**
• **Accounting Technology/Technician and Bookkeeping** *82 students enrolled* • **Allied Health and Medical Assisting Services, Other** *21 students enrolled* • **Computer and Information Sciences and Support Services, Other** *616 hrs./$755* • **Dental Assisting/Assistant** *922 hrs./$3350* • **Emergency Medical Technology/Technician (EMT Paramedic)** *25 students enrolled* • **General Office Occupations and Clerical Services** *77 students enrolled* • **Hospitality Administration/Management, Other** *142 students enrolled* • **Medical/Clinical Assistant** *700 hrs./$1719* • **Nurse/Nursing Assistant/Aide and Patient Care Assistant** *320 hrs./$709* • **Pharmacy Technician/Assistant** *700 hrs./$2731* • **Surgical Technology/Technologist** *1100 hrs./$6070* • **Veterinary/Animal Health Technology/Technician and Veterinary Assistant** *5 students enrolled*

**STUDENT SERVICES** Remedial services.

## Mt. San Antonio College

1100 North Grand Avenue, Walnut, CA 91789-1399
http://www.mtsac.edu/

**CONTACT** John Nixon, Interim President/CEO
**Telephone:** 909-594-5611

**GENERAL INFORMATION** Public Institution. Founded 1946. **Accreditation:** Regional (WASC/ACCJC); histologic technology (NAACLS); radiologic technology: radiography (JRCERT). **Total program enrollment:** 9827.

**PROGRAM(S) OFFERED**
• **Accounting** *27 students enrolled* • **Administrative Assistant and Secretarial Science, General** *7 students enrolled* • **Aircraft Powerplant Technology/Technician** *2 students enrolled* • **Airframe Mechanics and Aircraft Maintenance Technology/Technician** *4 students enrolled* • **Animation, Interactive Technology, Video Graphics and Special Effects** *6 students enrolled* • **Apparel and Textile Marketing Management** *2 students enrolled* • **Architectural Technology/Technician** *3 students enrolled* • **Building/Home/Construction Inspection/Inspector** *2 students enrolled* • **Business Administration and Management, General** *44 students enrolled* • **Child Development** *62 students enrolled* • **Commercial Photography** *1 student enrolled* • **Communications Systems Installation and Repair Technology** *12 students enrolled* • **Computer Graphics** *1 student enrolled* • **Computer Installation and Repair Technology/Technician** *1 student enrolled* • **Computer Programming/Programmer, General** *15 students enrolled* • **Computer Systems Networking and Telecommunications** *1 student enrolled* • **Computer and Information Sciences and Support Services, Other** *5 students enrolled* • **Computer and Information Sciences, General** *3 students enrolled* • **Cooking and Related Culinary Arts, General** *2 students enrolled* • **Criminal Justice/Police Science** *6 students enrolled* • **Design and Visual Communications, General** *2 students enrolled* • **Electrical/Electronics Equipment Installation and Repair, General** *14 students enrolled* • **Emergency Medical Technology/Technician (EMT Paramedic)** *1 student enrolled* • **Equestrian/Equine Studies** *2 students enrolled* • **Fashion/Apparel Design** *3 students enrolled* • **Fire Science/Firefighting** *38 students enrolled* • **Foods, Nutrition, and Wellness Studies, General** *3 students enrolled* • **Health and Physical Education, General** *6 students enrolled* • **Heating, Air Conditioning and Refrigeration Technology/Technician (ACH/ACR/ACHR/HRAC/HVAC/AC Technology)** *24 students enrolled* • **Hospitality Administration/Management, General** *14*

students enrolled • **Industrial Electronics Technology/Technician** *1 student enrolled* • **Interior Design** *7 students enrolled* • **International Business/Trade/Commerce** *20 students enrolled* • **Landscaping and Groundskeeping** *4 students enrolled* • **Manufacturing Technology/Technician** *3 students enrolled* • **Parks, Recreation and Leisure Facilities Management** *1 student enrolled* • **Plant Nursery Operations and Management** *2 students enrolled* • **Psychiatric/Mental Health Services Technician** *6 students enrolled* • **Real Estate** *6 students enrolled* • **Restaurant, Culinary, and Catering Management/Manager** *10 students enrolled* • **Retailing and Retail Operations** *1 student enrolled* • **Sales, Distribution and Marketing Operations, General** *3 students enrolled* • **Sign Language Interpretation and Translation** *5 students enrolled* • **Small Business Administration/Management** *1 student enrolled* • **Substance Abuse/Addiction Counseling** *17 students enrolled* • **Teacher Assistant/Aide** *1 student enrolled* • **Turf and Turfgrass Management** *4 students enrolled* • **Water Quality and Wastewater Treatment Management and Recycling Technology/Technician** *6 students enrolled* • **Web Page, Digital/Multimedia and Information Resources Design** *2 students enrolled* • **Welding Technology/Welder** *16 students enrolled*

**STUDENT SERVICES** Academic or career counseling, daycare for children of students, employment services for current students, placement services for program completers, remedial services.

## Mt. San Jacinto College

1499 North State Street, San Jacinto, CA 92583-2399
http://www.msjc.edu/

**CONTACT** Mr. Roger Schultz, Superintendent/President
**Telephone:** 951-487-3002

**GENERAL INFORMATION** Public Institution. Founded 1963. **Accreditation:** Regional (WASC/ACCJC). **Total program enrollment:** 5522.

**PROGRAM(S) OFFERED**
• **Accounting** *2 students enrolled* • **Administrative Assistant and Secretarial Science, General** *5 students enrolled* • **Automobile/Automotive Mechanics Technology/Technician** *1 student enrolled* • **Business Administration and Management, General** *3 students enrolled* • **Child Development** *11 students enrolled* • **Computer Programming/Programmer, General** *4 students enrolled* • **Computer Systems Networking and Telecommunications** *2 students enrolled* • **Computer and Information Sciences, General** *2 students enrolled* • **Criminal Justice/Police Science** *4 students enrolled* • **Data Entry/Microcomputer Applications, General** *1 student enrolled* • **Design and Visual Communications, General** *1 student enrolled* • **Diagnostic Medical Sonography/Sonographer and Ultrasound Technician** *4 students enrolled* • **Digital Communication and Media/Multimedia** *3 students enrolled* • **Drafting and Design Technology/Technician, General** *3 students enrolled* • **Geography, Other** *9 students enrolled* • **Human Services, General** *5 students enrolled* • **Information Technology** *3 students enrolled* • **Legal Assistant/Paralegal** *2 students enrolled* • **Licensed Practical/Vocational Nurse Training (LPN, LVN, Cert, Dipl, AAS)** *33 students enrolled* • **Medical/Clinical Assistant** *2 students enrolled* • **Music Management and Merchandising** *13 students enrolled* • **Photography** *4 students enrolled* • **Real Estate** *4 students enrolled* • **Small Business Administration/Management** *1 student enrolled* • **Substance Abuse/Addiction Counseling** *7 students enrolled* • **System Administration/Administrator** *3 students enrolled* • **Taxation** *1 student enrolled* • **Technical Theatre/Theatre Design and Technology** *1 student enrolled* • **Turf and Turfgrass Management** *1 student enrolled* • **Water Quality and Wastewater Treatment Management and Recycling Technology/Technician** *3 students enrolled* • **Web Page, Digital/Multimedia and Information Resources Design** *1 student enrolled* • **Web/Multimedia Management and Webmaster** *1 student enrolled*

**STUDENT SERVICES** Academic or career counseling, daycare for children of students, employment services for current students, remedial services.

## MTI Business College

6006 North El Dorado Street, Stockton, CA 95207-4349
http://www.mtistockton.com/

**CONTACT** Steven J. Brenner, Director/President
**Telephone:** 209-957-3030

**GENERAL INFORMATION** Private Institution. Founded 1968. **Total program enrollment:** 251.

**PROGRAM(S) OFFERED**
• **Administrative Assistant and Secretarial Science, General** *71 hrs./$6468* • **Business/Office Automation/Technology/Data Entry** *71 hrs./$7295* • **Computer and Information Sciences and Support Services, Other** *84 hrs./$10,043* • **General Office Occupations and Clerical Services** *66 hrs./$7220* • **Legal Administrative Assistant/Secretary** *77 hrs./$6770* • **Medical Administrative/Executive Assistant and Medical Secretary** *74 hrs./$6870* • **Medical Office Management/Administration** *12 students enrolled* • **Medical/Clinical Assistant** *52 students enrolled*

**STUDENT SERVICES** Academic or career counseling, employment services for current students, placement services for program completers, remedial services.

## MTI College

2011 West Chapman Avenue, Suite 100, Orange, CA 92868-2632

**CONTACT** Jean Gonzalez, President
**Telephone:** 714-867-5009

**GENERAL INFORMATION** Private Institution. **Total program enrollment:** 194. **Application fee:** $99.

**PROGRAM(S) OFFERED**
• **Court Reporting/Court Reporter** *4452 hrs./$14,166* • **Legal Administrative Assistant/Secretary** *760 hrs./$9524* • **Legal Assistant/Paralegal** *1344 hrs./$18,999* • **Medical Transcription/Transcriptionist** *2070 hrs./$8400* • **Medical/Clinical Assistant** *720 hrs./$9559*

**STUDENT SERVICES** Academic or career counseling, placement services for program completers.

## MTI College of Business & Technology

5221 Madison Avenue, Sacramento, CA 95841
http://www.mticollege.com/

**CONTACT** John Zimmerman, President
**Telephone:** 916-339-1500

**GENERAL INFORMATION** Private Institution. Founded 1965. **Accreditation:** Regional (WASC/ACCJC). **Total program enrollment:** 616. **Application fee:** $50.

**PROGRAM(S) OFFERED**
• **Accounting** *53 hrs./$12,150* • **Business Administration and Management, General** *99 hrs./$22,200* • **Computer Systems Analysis/Analyst** *37 students enrolled* • **Computer and Information Sciences, General** *57 students enrolled* • **Computer and Information Systems Security** *111 hrs./$24,400* • **Cosmetology/Cosmetologist, General** *78 hrs./$17,200* • **Health Professions and Related Clinical Sciences, Other** *52 hrs./$11,850* • **Legal Administrative Assistant/Secretary** *46 students enrolled* • **Legal Assistant/Paralegal** *112 hrs./$29,327* • **Medical Administrative/Executive Assistant and Medical Secretary** *23 students enrolled* • **Medical Insurance Specialist/Medical Biller** • **Medical/Clinical Assistant** *74 students enrolled* • **Phlebotomy/Phlebotomist** *23 students enrolled*

**STUDENT SERVICES** Academic or career counseling, placement services for program completers.

## Mueller College of Holistic Studies

4607 Park Boulevard, San Diego, CA 92116
http://www.mueller.edu/

**CONTACT** David Taylor, Registrar
**Telephone:** 619-291-9811

**GENERAL INFORMATION** Private Institution. Founded 1976. **Total program enrollment:** 30. **Application fee:** $100.

**PROGRAM(S) OFFERED**
• **Massage Therapy/Therapeutic Massage** *83 students enrolled*

**STUDENT SERVICES** Academic or career counseling, employment services for current students, placement services for program completers, remedial services.

## Musicians Institute

1655 North McCadden Place, Hollywood, CA 90028
http://www.mi.edu/

**CONTACT** Hisatake Shibuya, President
**Telephone:** 323-462-1384

**GENERAL INFORMATION** Private Institution. Founded 1976. **Accreditation:** Music (NASM). **Total program enrollment:** 1124. **Application fee:** $100.

**PROGRAM(S) OFFERED**
• **Music Performance, General** *52 students enrolled* • **Music, Other** *344 students enrolled*

**STUDENT SERVICES** Academic or career counseling, employment services for current students, placement services for program completers, remedial services.

## My Le's Beauty College

5972 Stockton Boulevard, Sacramento, CA 95824

**CONTACT** John Thai Tran, CEO/Owner
**Telephone:** 916-422-0223

**GENERAL INFORMATION** Private Institution. **Total program enrollment:** 74. **Application fee:** $75.

**PROGRAM(S) OFFERED**
• **Aesthetician/Esthetician and Skin Care Specialist** *600 hrs./$2175*
• **Cosmetology, Barber/Styling, and Nail Instructor** *600 hrs./$2175*
• **Cosmetology/Cosmetologist, General** *1600 hrs./$7550* • **Nail Technician/Specialist and Manicurist** *400 hrs./$975*

**STUDENT SERVICES** Placement services for program completers.

## Napa Valley College

2277 Napa-Vallejo Highway, Napa, CA 94558-6236
http://www.napavalley.edu/

**CONTACT** Dr. Christopher McCarthy, Superintendent President
**Telephone:** 707-253-3000

**GENERAL INFORMATION** Public Institution. Founded 1942. **Accreditation:** Regional (WASC/ACCJC). **Total program enrollment:** 2166.

**PROGRAM(S) OFFERED**
• **Accounting** *3 students enrolled* • **Administrative Assistant and Secretarial Science, General** *1 student enrolled* • **Agricultural Production Operations, Other** *3 students enrolled* • **Commercial Photography** *1 student enrolled* • **Criminal Justice/Police Science** *111 students enrolled* • **Drafting and Design Technology/Technician, General** *4 students enrolled* • **Emergency Medical Technology/Technician (EMT Paramedic)** • **Human Development and Family Studies, General** *3 students enrolled* • **Human Services, General** *7 students enrolled* • **Information Technology** *5 students enrolled* • **Legal Assistant/Paralegal** *7 students enrolled* • **Machine Tool Technology/Machinist** *1 student enrolled* • **Psychiatric/Mental Health Services Technician** *49 students enrolled* • **Welding Technology/Welder** *2 students enrolled*

**STUDENT SERVICES** Academic or career counseling, daycare for children of students, employment services for current students, placement services for program completers, remedial services.

## National Career Education

6060 Sunrise Vista Drive, #3000, Citrus Heights, CA 95610
http://www.ncecollege.com/

**CONTACT** Donald Fraser, Director
**Telephone:** 916-969-4900 Ext. 115

**GENERAL INFORMATION** Private Institution. **Total program enrollment:** 421. **Application fee:** $75.

**PROGRAM(S) OFFERED**
• **Allied Health and Medical Assisting Services, Other** *720 hrs./$11,857* • **Medical Insurance Specialist/Medical Biller** *41 students enrolled* • **Medical/Clinical Assistant** *67 students enrolled* • **Optometric Technician/Assistant** *720 hrs./$12,902* • **Pharmacy Technician/Assistant** *720 hrs./$12,487* • **Phlebotomy/Phlebotomist** *720 hrs./$13,545*

**STUDENT SERVICES** Employment services for current students, placement services for program completers.

## The National Hispanic University

14271 Story Road, San Jose, CA 95127-3823
http://www.nhu.edu/

**CONTACT** Dr. David P. Lopez, President
**Telephone:** 408-254-6900

**GENERAL INFORMATION** Private Institution. Founded 1981. **Accreditation:** Regional (WASC/ACSCU); state accredited or approved. **Total program enrollment:** 312. **Application fee:** $50.

**STUDENT SERVICES** Academic or career counseling, remedial services.

## National Holistic Institute

5900 Hollis Street, Suite J, Emeryville, CA 94608-2008
http://www.nhimassage.com/

**CONTACT** Mason Myers, President
**Telephone:** 510-547-6442

**GENERAL INFORMATION** Private Institution. Founded 1977. **Total program enrollment:** 196. **Application fee:** $50.

**PROGRAM(S) OFFERED**
• **Health Professions and Related Clinical Sciences, Other** *36 hrs./$13,736*
• **Massage Therapy/Therapeutic Massage** *524 students enrolled*

**STUDENT SERVICES** Academic or career counseling, employment services for current students, placement services for program completers.

## National Polytechnic College

2465 W. Whittier Boulevard, Suite 201, Montebello, CA 90640
http://www.npcollege.edu/

**CONTACT** David Maddahi, Director
**Telephone:** 323-728-9636

**GENERAL INFORMATION** Private Institution. **Total program enrollment:** 74.

**PROGRAM(S) OFFERED**
• **Computer Science** *1 student enrolled* • **Dental Assisting/Assistant** *9 students enrolled* • **Massage Therapy/Therapeutic Massage** *21 students enrolled* • **Medical/Clinical Assistant** *31 students enrolled*

**STUDENT SERVICES** Employment services for current students, placement services for program completers.

## National Polytechnic College of Engineering and Oceaneering

272 South Fries Avenue, Wilmington, CA 90744-6399
http://www.coo.edu/

**CONTACT** Kevin Casey, President
**Telephone:** 310-816-5700 Ext. 5721

**GENERAL INFORMATION** Private Institution. **Accreditation:** Regional (WASC/ACCJC). **Total program enrollment:** 310. **Application fee:** $60.

**PROGRAM(S) OFFERED**
• **Diver, Professional and Instructor** *63 hrs./$18,290* • **Physiology, Pathology, and Related Sciences, Other** *99 hrs./$25,975*

**STUDENT SERVICES** Academic or career counseling, employment services for current students, placement services for program completers.

## Newberry School of Beauty

6633 Fallbrook Avenue, West Hills, CA 91307

**CONTACT** Deanne Jacobson, President
**Telephone:** 818-366-3211

**GENERAL INFORMATION** Private Institution. Founded 1949. **Total program enrollment:** 101. **Application fee:** $75.

**PROGRAM(S) OFFERED**
• **Aesthetician/Esthetician and Skin Care Specialist** *600 hrs./$7275*
• **Cosmetology, Barber/Styling, and Nail Instructor** *600 hrs./$2835*
• **Cosmetology/Cosmetologist, General** *1600 hrs./$11,933* • **Nail Technician/Specialist and Manicurist** *400 hrs./$1275*

**STUDENT SERVICES** Academic or career counseling, placement services for program completers.

## Newbridge College–Long Beach

3799 E. Burnett Street, Long Beach, CA 90815
http://www.newbridgecollege.edu

**CONTACT** C. Duncan Thomas, CEO
**Telephone:** 562-498-4500

**GENERAL INFORMATION** Private Institution. **Total program enrollment:** 429.

**PROGRAM(S) OFFERED**
• **Allied Health and Medical Assisting Services, Other** *41 students enrolled*
• **Clinical/Medical Laboratory Assistant** *42 hrs./$11,975* • **Clinical/Medical Laboratory Technician** *46 students enrolled* • **Diagnostic Medical Sonography/Sonographer and Ultrasound Technician** *115 hrs./$31,975* • **Medical Insurance Specialist/Medical Biller** *42 hrs./$11,975* • **Medical Office Assistant/Specialist** *42 hrs./$11,975* • **Surgical Technology/Technologist** *103 hrs./$23,925*

**STUDENT SERVICES** Employment services for current students, placement services for program completers.

## Newbridge College–Santa Ana

1840 East 17th Street, Suite 140, Santa Ana, CA 92705
http://www.newbridgecollege.edu/

**CONTACT** Dr. C. Duncan Thomas, President/CEO
**Telephone:** 714-550-8000

**GENERAL INFORMATION** Private Institution. **Total program enrollment:** 415.

**PROGRAM(S) OFFERED**
• **Clinical/Medical Laboratory Assistant** *42 hrs./$11,975* • **Diagnostic Medical Sonography/Sonographer and Ultrasound Technician** *115 hrs./$31,975* • **Medical Insurance Specialist/Medical Biller** *42 hrs./$11,975* • **Medical Office Assistant/Specialist** *42 hrs./$11,975* • **Medical/Clinical Assistant** *110 students enrolled* • **Surgical Technology/Technologist** *103 hrs./$23,925*

**STUDENT SERVICES** Employment services for current students, placement services for program completers.

## North Adrians Beauty College

124 Floyd Avenue, Modesto, CA 95350
http://www.alle.com/adrians

**CONTACT** Rebecca Abinales, Vice President
**Telephone:** 209-526-2040

**GENERAL INFORMATION** Private Institution. Founded 1961. **Total program enrollment:** 251.

**PROGRAM(S) OFFERED**
• **Aesthetician/Esthetician and Skin Care Specialist** *600 hrs./$8395*
• **Cosmetology, Barber/Styling, and Nail Instructor** • **Cosmetology/Cosmetologist, General** *1600 hrs./$14,598* • **Nail Technician/Specialist and Manicurist** *400 hrs./$3645* • **Teacher Education and Professional Development, Specific Subject Areas, Other** *600 hrs./$9145*

## North Orange County Community College District

1000 North Lemon Street, Fullerton, CA 92832-1351

**CONTACT** Jerome Hunter, Chancellor
**Telephone:** 714-808-4500

**GENERAL INFORMATION** Public Institution.

## North-West College

124 South Glendale Avenue, Glendale, CA 91205
http://www.north-westcollege.com/

**CONTACT** Marsha Fuerst, CEO/Executive Director
**Telephone:** 818-242-0205

**GENERAL INFORMATION** Private Institution. Founded 1966. **Total program enrollment:** 148. **Application fee:** $100.

**PROGRAM(S) OFFERED**
• **Dental Assisting/Assistant** *736 hrs./$9004* • **Licensed Practical/Vocational Nurse Training (LPN, LVN, Cert, Dipl, AAS)** *1701 hrs./$26,950* • **Medical Administrative/Executive Assistant and Medical Secretary** *760 hrs./$8935*
• **Medical Insurance Specialist/Medical Biller** *736 hrs./$8324* • **Medical Reception/Receptionist** • **Medical/Clinical Assistant** *736 hrs./$8648*
• **Pharmacy Technician/Assistant** *768 hrs./$9750*

**STUDENT SERVICES** Academic or career counseling, placement services for program completers, remedial services.

## North-West College

530 East Union Street, Pasadena, CA 91101
http://www.north-westcollege.com/

**CONTACT** Marsha Fuerst, CEO/Executive Director
**Telephone:** 626-796-5815

**GENERAL INFORMATION** Private Institution. Founded 1966. **Total program enrollment:** 80. **Application fee:** $100.

**PROGRAM(S) OFFERED**
• **Accounting and Related Services, Other** • **Allied Health and Medical Assisting Services, Other** *22 students enrolled* • **Dental Assisting/Assistant** *8 students enrolled* • **Legal Assistant/Paralegal** *874 hrs./$1236* • **Licensed Practical/Vocational Nurse Training (LPN, LVN, Cert, Dipl, AAS)** *1701 hrs./$26,450*
• **Massage Therapy/Therapeutic Massage** *720 hrs./$9275* • **Medical Administrative/Executive Assistant and Medical Secretary** *3 students enrolled*
• **Medical Insurance Specialist/Medical Biller** *736 hrs./$8324* • **Medical/Clinical Assistant** *736 hrs./$9150* • **Pharmacy Technician/Assistant** *768 hrs./$9258*

**STUDENT SERVICES** Academic or career counseling, placement services for program completers, remedial services.

## North-West College

134 West Holt Avenue, Pomona, CA 91768
http://www.north-westcollege.com/

**CONTACT** Marsha Fuerst, CEO/Executive Director
**Telephone:** 909-623-1552

**GENERAL INFORMATION** Private Institution. Founded 1966. **Total program enrollment:** 153. **Application fee:** $100.

**PROGRAM(S) OFFERED**
• **Dental Assisting/Assistant** *736 hrs./$9004* • **Licensed Practical/Vocational Nurse Training (LPN, LVN, Cert, Dipl, AAS)** *1701 hrs./$26,450* • **Medical Administrative/Executive Assistant and Medical Secretary** *760 hrs./$9550* • **Medical Insurance Specialist/Medical Biller** *736 hrs./$8324* • **Medical Reception/Receptionist** • **Medical/Clinical Assistant** *736 hrs./$9150* • **Pharmacy Technician/Assistant** *768 hrs./$9258*

**STUDENT SERVICES** Academic or career counseling, placement services for program completers, remedial services.

## North-West College

10020 Indiana Street, Riverside, CA 92503
http://www.north-westcollege.com/

**CONTACT** Marsha Fuerst, Executive Director/CEO
**Telephone:** 951-351-7750

**GENERAL INFORMATION** Private Institution. **Total program enrollment:** 137. **Application fee:** $100.

**PROGRAM(S) OFFERED**
• **Allied Health and Medical Assisting Services, Other** *736 hrs./$8648* • **Licensed Practical/Vocational Nurse Training (LPN, LVN, Cert, Dipl, AAS)** *1701 hrs./$27,750*

**STUDENT SERVICES** Academic or career counseling, placement services for program completers, remedial services.

## North-West College

2121 West Garvey Avenue, West Covina, CA 91790
http://www.north-westcollege.com/

**CONTACT** Marsha Fuerst, CEO/Executive Director
**Telephone:** 626-960-5046

**GENERAL INFORMATION** Private Institution. Founded 1966. **Total program enrollment:** 309. **Application fee:** $100.

**PROGRAM(S) OFFERED**
• **Allied Health and Medical Assisting Services, Other** *736 hrs./$8648* • **Dental Assisting/Assistant** *736 hrs./$8648* • **Licensed Practical/Vocational Nurse Training (LPN, LVN, Cert, Dipl, AAS)** *170 hrs./$27,750* • **Massage Therapy/Therapeutic Massage** *720 hrs./$9250* • **Medical Administrative/Executive Assistant and Medical Secretary** • **Medical Insurance Specialist/Medical Biller** *736 hrs./$8324* • **Medical Reception/Receptionist** • **Medical/Clinical Assistant** *37 students enrolled* • **Ophthalmic Laboratory Technology/Technician** *5 students enrolled* • **Pharmacy Technician/Assistant** *768 hrs./$9258*

**STUDENT SERVICES** Academic or career counseling, placement services for program completers, remedial services.

## Notre Dame de Namur University

1500 Ralston Avenue, Belmont, CA 94002-1908
http://www.ndnu.edu/

**CONTACT** Judith Maxwell Greig, PhD, Acting President
**Telephone:** 650-508-3500

**GENERAL INFORMATION** Private Institution. Founded 1851. **Accreditation:** Regional (WASC/ACSCU); music (NASM). **Total program enrollment:** 676. **Application fee:** $50.

**STUDENT SERVICES** Academic or career counseling, employment services for current students, placement services for program completers, remedial services.

## NTMA Training Centers of Southern California

13230 E. Firestone Boulevard, Unit A, Santa Fe Springs, CA 90650
http://www.trainingcenters.org/

**CONTACT** Michael Kerwin, President
**Telephone:** 562-404-4295 Ext. 0

**GENERAL INFORMATION** Private Institution. **Total program enrollment:** 341.

**PROGRAM(S) OFFERED**
• **Machine Tool Technology/Machinist** *725 hrs./$11,495*

**STUDENT SERVICES** Academic or career counseling, placement services for program completers, remedial services.

## Oceanside College of Beauty

1575 South Coast Highway, Oceanside, CA 92054
http://ocb.edu/

**CONTACT** Raymond R. Stainback, President
**Telephone:** 760-757-6161 Ext. 14

**GENERAL INFORMATION** Private Institution. **Total program enrollment:** 92.

**PROGRAM(S) OFFERED**
• **Cosmetology, Barber/Styling, and Nail Instructor** *600 hrs./$3875* • **Cosmetology/Cosmetologist, General** *1600 hrs./$9795* • **Nail Technician/Specialist and Manicurist** *400 hrs./$3475*

**STUDENT SERVICES** Academic or career counseling, placement services for program completers.

## Ohlone College

43600 Mission Boulevard, Fremont, CA 94539-5884
http://www.ohlone.edu/

**CONTACT** Gari Browning, President/Superintendent
**Telephone:** 510-659-6000

**GENERAL INFORMATION** Public Institution. Founded 1967. **Accreditation:** Regional (WASC/ACCJC); physical therapy assisting (APTA). **Total program enrollment:** 3279. **Application fee:** $5.

**PROGRAM(S) OFFERED**
• **Accounting** *7 students enrolled* • **Animation, Interactive Technology, Video Graphics and Special Effects** *1 student enrolled* • **Anthropology** *2 students enrolled* • **Astronomy** *2 students enrolled* • **Biology Technician/Biotechnology Laboratory Technician** *5 students enrolled* • **Biology/Biological Sciences, General** *2 students enrolled* • **Chemistry, General** *42 students enrolled* • **Child Development** *2 students enrolled* • **Computer Graphics** *1 student enrolled* • **Computer Programming/Programmer, General** *4 students enrolled* • **Computer Systems Networking and Telecommunications** *2 students enrolled* • **Criminal Justice/Police Science** *2 students enrolled* • **Digital Communication and Media/Multimedia** *2 students enrolled* • **Drawing** *1 student enrolled* • **Education, Other** *1 student enrolled* • **Geology/Earth Science, General** *2 students enrolled* • **Mathematics, General** *21 students enrolled* • **Music Management and Merchandising** *3 students enrolled* • **Music, General** *4 students enrolled* • **Office Management and Supervision** *4 students enrolled* • **Real Estate** *4 students enrolled* • **Sign Language Interpretation and Translation** *1 student enrolled* • **Sociology** *1 student enrolled* • **Special Education and Teaching, General** *2 students enrolled* • **Visual and Performing Arts, General** *1 student enrolled* • **Web Page, Digital/Multimedia and Information Resources Design** *2 students enrolled*

**STUDENT SERVICES** Academic or career counseling, daycare for children of students, employment services for current students, placement services for program completers, remedial services.

## Orange Coast College

2701 Fairview Road, PO Box 5005, Costa Mesa, CA 92628-5005
http://www.orangecoastcollege.com/

**CONTACT** Bob Dees, President
**Telephone:** 714-432-5072

**GENERAL INFORMATION** Public Institution. Founded 1947. **Accreditation:** Regional (WASC/ACCJC); cardiovascular technology (JRCECT); dental assisting (ADA); diagnostic medical sonography (JRCEDMS); electroneurodiagnostic technology (JRCEND); radiologic technology: radiography (JRCERT). **Total program enrollment:** 9776.

**PROGRAM(S) OFFERED**

• **Accounting** *4 students enrolled* • **Administrative Assistant and Secretarial Science, General** *3 students enrolled* • **Aircraft Powerplant Technology/Technician** *1 student enrolled* • **Airframe Mechanics and Aircraft Maintenance Technology/Technician** *2 students enrolled* • **Airline Flight Attendant** *11 students enrolled* • **Airline/Commercial/Professional Pilot and Flight Crew** *2 students enrolled* • **Apparel and Textile Manufacture** *2 students enrolled* • **Apparel and Textile Marketing Management** *2 students enrolled* • **Applied Horticulture/Horticultural Operations, General** *2 students enrolled* • **Architectural Technology/Technician** *13 students enrolled* • **Audiology/Audiologist and Speech-Language Pathology/Pathologist** *1 student enrolled* • **Business Administration and Management, General** *4 students enrolled* • **Cardiovascular Technology/Technologist** *2 students enrolled* • **Child Development** *18 students enrolled* • **Cinematography and Film/Video Production** *5 students enrolled* • **Commercial Photography** *12 students enrolled* • **Commercial and Advertising Art** *1 student enrolled* • **Computer Graphics** *4 students enrolled* • **Computer Programming/Programmer, General** *1 student enrolled* • **Computer Science** *1 student enrolled* • **Computer and Information Sciences, General** *1 student enrolled* • **Construction Trades, General** *1 student enrolled* • **Cooking and Related Culinary Arts, General** *27 students enrolled* • **Dance, General** *1 student enrolled* • **Dental Assisting/Assistant** *21 students enrolled* • **Drafting and Design Technology/Technician, General** *3 students enrolled* • **Education/Teaching of Individuals in Early Childhood Special Education Programs** *1 student enrolled* • **Electrical/Electronics Equipment Installation and Repair, General** *3 students enrolled* • **Electrocardiograph Technology/Technician** *18 students enrolled* • **Electroneurodiagnostic/Electroencephalographic Technology/Technologist** *1 student enrolled* • **Fashion/Apparel Design** *9 students enrolled* • **Film/Cinema Studies** *4 students enrolled* • **Foods, Nutrition, and Wellness Studies, General** *1 student enrolled* • **Foodservice Systems Administration/Management** *10 students enrolled* • **Heating, Air Conditioning and Refrigeration Technology/Technician (ACH/ACR/ACHR/HRAC/HVAC/AC Technology)** *5 students enrolled* • **Interior Design** *7 students enrolled* • **International Business/Trade/Commerce** *7 students enrolled* • **Machine Tool Technology/Machinist** *8 students enrolled* • **Mechanical Drafting and Mechanical Drafting CAD/CADD** *2 students enrolled* • **Medical/Clinical Assistant** *3 students enrolled* • **Music Management and Merchandising** *2 students enrolled* • **Real Estate** *1 student enrolled* • **Restaurant, Culinary, and Catering Management/Manager** *2 students enrolled* • **Sales, Distribution and Marketing Operations, General** *1 student enrolled* • **Sport and Fitness Administration/Management** *9 students enrolled*

**STUDENT SERVICES** Academic or career counseling, daycare for children of students, employment services for current students, placement services for program completers, remedial services.

## Oxnard College

4000 South Rose Avenue, Oxnard, CA 93033-6699
http://www.oxnardcollege.edu/

**CONTACT** Richard Duran, President
**Telephone:** 805-986-5800

**GENERAL INFORMATION** Public Institution. Founded 1975. **Accreditation:** Regional (WASC/ACCJC); dental hygiene (ADA). **Total program enrollment:** 2195.

**PROGRAM(S) OFFERED**

• **Accounting** *7 students enrolled* • **Administrative Assistant and Secretarial Science, General** *6 students enrolled* • **Autobody/Collision and Repair Technology/Technician** *9 students enrolled* • **Automobile/Automotive Mechanics Technology/Technician** *1 student enrolled* • **Business Administration and Management, General** *7 students enrolled* • **Child Development** *70 students enrolled* • **Computer Systems Networking and Telecommunications** *2 students enrolled* • **Cooking and Related Culinary Arts, General** *1 student enrolled* • **Dental Assisting/Assistant** *19 students enrolled* • **Dental Hygiene/Hygienist** *1 student enrolled* • **Fire Science/Firefighting** *1 student enrolled* • **Heating, Air Conditioning and Refrigeration Technology/Technician (ACH/ACR/ACHR/HRAC/HVAC/AC Technology)** *21 students enrolled* • **Legal Assistant/Paralegal** *13 students enrolled* • **Radio and Television** *1 student enrolled* • **Restaurant, Culinary, and Catering Management/Manager** *1 student enrolled* • **Science Technologies/Technicians, Other** *7 students enrolled* • **Substance Abuse/Addiction Counseling** *23 students enrolled*

**STUDENT SERVICES** Academic or career counseling, daycare for children of students, employment services for current students, placement services for program completers, remedial services.

## Pacific Coast Trade School

1690 Universe Circle, Oxnard, CA 93033

**CONTACT** Leticia Cazares, Director
**Telephone:** 805-487-9260

**GENERAL INFORMATION** Private Institution. **Total program enrollment:** 226. **Application fee:** $75.

**PROGRAM(S) OFFERED**

• **Business/Office Automation/Technology/Data Entry** *24 hrs./$6975* • **Child Care Provider/Assistant** *22 hrs./$5775* • **Electrical/Electronics Equipment Installation and Repair, General** *9 students enrolled* • **Electrical/Electronics Maintenance and Repair Technology, Other** *30 hrs./$7550* • **Medical/Clinical Assistant** *30 hrs./$9170* • **Welding Technology/Welder** *30 hrs./$9250*

**STUDENT SERVICES** Academic or career counseling, daycare for children of students, employment services for current students, placement services for program completers.

## Pacific College

3160 Red Hill Avenue, Costa Mesa, CA 92626
http://pacific-college.com/

**CONTACT** William L. Nelson, Director
**Telephone:** 714-662-4402

**GENERAL INFORMATION** Private Institution. **Total program enrollment:** 229. **Application fee:** $75.

**PROGRAM(S) OFFERED**

• **Cardiovascular Technology/Technologist** *1140 hrs./$13,950* • **Licensed Practical/Vocational Nurse Training (LPN, LVN, Cert, Dipl, AAS)** *1542 hrs./$26,900* • **Massage Therapy/Therapeutic Massage** *720 hrs./$9950* • **Physical Therapist Assistant** *1040 hrs./$12,950*

**STUDENT SERVICES** Academic or career counseling, employment services for current students, placement services for program completers.

## Pacific College of Oriental Medicine

7445 Mission Valley Road, Suite 105, San Diego, CA 92108
http://www.pacificcollege.edu/

**CONTACT** Jack Miller, President
**Telephone:** 619-574-6909 Ext. 104

**GENERAL INFORMATION** Private Institution. Founded 1986. **Accreditation:** Acupuncture and Oriental Medicine (ACAOM). **Total program enrollment:** 373. **Application fee:** $50.

**PROGRAM(S) OFFERED**

• **Massage Therapy/Therapeutic Massage** *29 students enrolled*

**STUDENT SERVICES** Academic or career counseling, remedial services.

## Pacific States University

1516 South Western Avenue, Los Angeles, CA 90006
http://www.psuca.edu/

**CONTACT** Jae Duk Kim, President
**Telephone:** 323-731-2383 Ext. 11

**GENERAL INFORMATION** Private Institution. Founded 1928. **Accreditation:** State accredited or approved. **Total program enrollment:** 216. **Application fee:** $100.

**STUDENT SERVICES** Academic or career counseling, employment services for current students, placement services for program completers, remedial services.

## Palace Beauty College

1517 S. Western Avenue, Los Angeles, CA 90006

**CONTACT** Norma Cerano, Financial Aid Officer
**Telephone:** 323-731-2075

**GENERAL INFORMATION** Private Institution. **Total program enrollment:** 82.

**PROGRAM(S) OFFERED**
• **Aesthetician/Esthetician and Skin Care Specialist** *600 hrs./$5475*
• **Cosmetology and Related Personal Grooming Arts, Other** *1600 hrs./$12,075*
• **Cosmetology, Barber/Styling, and Nail Instructor** *600 hrs./$3075*
• **Cosmetology/Cosmetologist, General** *22 students enrolled* • **Nail Technician/Specialist and Manicurist** *400 hrs./$2075*

**STUDENT SERVICES** Employment services for current students, placement services for program completers.

## Palladium Technical Academy

10507 Valley Boulevard, Suite 806, El Monte, CA 91731

**CONTACT** Dani Duncan, Associate Director
**Telephone:** 626-444-0880

**GENERAL INFORMATION** Private Institution. **Total program enrollment:** 52. **Application fee:** $75.

**PROGRAM(S) OFFERED**
• **Computer Graphics** *38 hrs./$8200* • **Computer and Information Sciences, General** *38 hrs./$8200* • **Licensed Practical/Vocational Nurse Training (LPN, LVN, Cert, Dipl, AAS)** *78 hrs./$21,804* • **Medical Insurance Specialist/Medical Biller** *36 hrs./$8015* • **Medical Office Assistant/Specialist** *24 hrs./$5000* • **Medical/Clinical Assistant** *36 hrs./$8500*

**STUDENT SERVICES** Academic or career counseling, placement services for program completers.

## Palomar College

1140 West Mission Road, San Marcos, CA 92069-1487
http://www.palomar.edu/

**CONTACT** Robert Deegan, Superintendent/President
**Telephone:** 760-744-1150

**GENERAL INFORMATION** Public Institution. Founded 1946. **Accreditation:** Regional (WASC/ACCJC); dental assisting (ADA). **Total program enrollment:** 8681.

**PROGRAM(S) OFFERED**
• **Accounting** *27 students enrolled* • **Administrative Assistant and Secretarial Science, General** *2 students enrolled* • **Advertising** *2 students enrolled* • **Airline/Commercial/Professional Pilot and Flight Crew** *3 students enrolled* • **Animation, Interactive Technology, Video Graphics and Special Effects** *6 students enrolled* • **Apparel and Textile Marketing Management** *8 students enrolled* • **Archeology** *7 students enrolled* • **Architectural Drafting and Architectural CAD/CADD** *3 students enrolled* • **Autobody/Collision and Repair Technology/Technician** *2 students enrolled* • **Automobile/Automotive Mechanics Technology/Technician** *5 students enrolled* • **Aviation/Airway Management and Operations** *3 students enrolled* • **Biology/Biological Sciences, General** *1 student enrolled* • **Building/Home/Construction Inspection/Inspector** *9 students enrolled* • **Business Administration and Management, General** *15 students enrolled* • **Cabinetmaking and Millwork/Millwright** *4 students enrolled* • **Carpentry/Carpenter** *52 students enrolled* • **Child Development** *19 students enrolled* • **Commercial Photography** *4 students enrolled* • **Computer Graphics** *4 students enrolled* • **Computer Installation and Repair Technology/Technician** *4 students enrolled* • **Computer Programming/Programmer, General** *10 students enrolled* • **Computer Systems Networking and Telecommunications** *4 students enrolled* • **Cooking and Related Culinary Arts, General** *1 student enrolled* • **Criminal Justice/Police Science** *17 students enrolled* • **Data Entry/Microcomputer Applications, General** *7 students enrolled* • **Data Modeling/Warehousing and Database Administration** *4 students enrolled* • **Dental Assisting/Assistant** *23 students enrolled* • **Diesel Mechanics Technology/Technician** *2 students enrolled* • **Digital Communication and Media/Multimedia** *4 students enrolled* • **Drafting and Design Technology/Technician, General** *5 students enrolled* • **Economics, General** *2 students enrolled* • **Electrical/Electronics Equipment Installation and Repair, General** *3 students enrolled* • **Electrician** *85 students enrolled* • **Emergency Medical Technology/Technician (EMT Paramedic)** *10 students enrolled* • **Ethnic, Cultural Minority, and Gender Studies, Other** *6 students enrolled* • **Fashion/Apparel Design** *3 students enrolled* • **Film/Cinema Studies** *2 students enrolled* • **Fire Science/Firefighting** *29 students enrolled* • **French Language and Literature** *13 students enrolled* • **Geography, Other** *2 students enrolled* • **Graphic Communications, General** *3 students enrolled* • **Hazardous Materials Management and Waste Technology/Technician** *1 student enrolled* • **Heating, Air Conditioning and Refrigeration Technology/Technician (ACH/ACR/ACHR/HRAC/HVAC/AC Technology)** *2 students enrolled* • **Industrial Electronics Technology/Technician** *5 students enrolled* • **Interior Design** *6 students enrolled* • **International Business/Trade/Commerce** *4 students enrolled* • **Legal Administrative Assistant/Secretary** *1 student enrolled* • **Legal Assistant/Paralegal** *2 students enrolled* • **Library Assistant/Technician** *22 students enrolled* • **Mason/Masonry** *31 students enrolled* • **Medical/Clinical Assistant** *11 students enrolled* • **Music, General** *1 student enrolled* • **Parks, Recreation and Leisure Facilities Management** *2 students enrolled* • **Parks, Recreation and Leisure Studies** *2 students enrolled* • **Prepress/Desktop Publishing and Digital Imaging Design** *2 students enrolled* • **Public Administration** *1 student enrolled* • **Radio and Television** *5 students enrolled* • **Real Estate** *8 students enrolled* • **Retailing and Retail Operations** *1 student enrolled* • **Selling Skills and Sales Operations** *1 student enrolled* • **Sheet Metal Technology/Sheetworking** *16 students enrolled* • **Sign Language Interpretation and Translation** *6 students enrolled* • **Substance Abuse/Addiction Counseling** *11 students enrolled* • **Survey Technology/Surveying** *1 student enrolled* • **System Administration/Administrator** *20 students enrolled* • **Technical Theatre/Theatre Design and Technology** *1 student enrolled* • **Water Quality and Wastewater Treatment Management and Recycling Technology/Technician** *20 students enrolled* • **Web Page, Digital/Multimedia and Information Resources Design** *2 students enrolled* • **Web/Multimedia Management and Webmaster** *6 students enrolled* • **Welding Technology/Welder** *11 students enrolled*

**STUDENT SERVICES** Academic or career counseling, daycare for children of students, employment services for current students, remedial services.

## Palomar Institute of Cosmetology

355 Via Vera Cruz, Suite 3, San Marcos, CA 92069
http://www.pic.edu/

**CONTACT** Raymond Stainback, President
**Telephone:** 760-744-7900 Ext. 14

**GENERAL INFORMATION** Private Institution. **Total program enrollment:** 151.

**PROGRAM(S) OFFERED**
• **Aesthetician/Esthetician and Skin Care Specialist** *600 hrs./$5795*
• **Cosmetology, Barber/Styling, and Nail Instructor** *600 hrs./$4295*
• **Cosmetology/Cosmetologist, General** *1600 hrs./$14,995* • **Nail Technician/Specialist and Manicurist** *400 hrs./$3495*

**STUDENT SERVICES** Academic or career counseling, placement services for program completers.

## Palo Verde College

One College Drive, Blythe, CA 92225-9561
http://www.paloverde.edu/

**CONTACT** James Hottois, Superintendent/President
**Telephone:** 760-921-5500

**GENERAL INFORMATION** Public Institution. Founded 1947. **Accreditation:** Regional (WASC/ACCJC). **Total program enrollment:** 658.

**PROGRAM(S) OFFERED**
• **Administrative Assistant and Secretarial Science, General** *2 students enrolled* • **Animation, Interactive Technology, Video Graphics and Special Effects** *1 student enrolled* • **Automobile/Automotive Mechanics Technology/Technician** *9 students enrolled* • **Business Administration and Management, General** *34 students enrolled* • **Child Development** *10 students enrolled* • **Emergency Medical Technology/Technician (EMT Paramedic)** • **Fire Science/Firefighting** *1 student enrolled* • **Home Health Aide/Home Attendant** *11 students enrolled* • **Information Technology** *1 student enrolled* • **Licensed Practical/Vocational Nurse Training (LPN, LVN, Cert, Dipl, AAS)** *12 students enrolled* • **Nurse/Nursing Assistant/Aide and Patient Care Assistant** *34 students enrolled* • **Phlebotomy/Phlebotomist** • **Substance Abuse/Addiction Counseling** *55 students enrolled* • **Welding Technology/Welder** *4 students enrolled*

**STUDENT SERVICES** Academic or career counseling, remedial services.

## Paris Beauty College

1950e Market Street, Concord, CA 94520
http://parisbeautycollege.com/

**CONTACT** Rhonda Baines, Owner
**Telephone:** 925-685-7600

**GENERAL INFORMATION** Private Institution. **Total program enrollment:** 50.

**PROGRAM(S) OFFERED**
• **Aesthetician/Esthetician and Skin Care Specialist** *600 hrs./$4875* • **Cosmetology/Cosmetologist, General** *1600 hrs./$11,370* • **Nail Technician/Specialist and Manicurist** *400 hrs./$3475*

**STUDENT SERVICES** Academic or career counseling.

## Pasadena City College

1570 East Colorado Boulevard, Pasadena, CA 91106-2041
http://www.pasadena.edu/

**CONTACT** Paulette Perfumo, President
**Telephone:** 626-585-7123

**GENERAL INFORMATION** Public Institution. Founded 1924. **Accreditation:** Regional (WASC/ACCJC); dental assisting (ADA); dental hygiene (ADA); dental laboratory technology (ADA); radiologic technology: radiography (JRCERT). **Total program enrollment:** 9187.

**PROGRAM(S) OFFERED**
• **Administrative Assistant and Secretarial Science, General** *35 students enrolled* • **Apparel and Textiles, General** *16 students enrolled* • **Audiology/Audiologist and Speech-Language Pathology/Pathologist** *10 students enrolled* • **Automobile/Automotive Mechanics Technology/Technician** *54 students enrolled* • **Banking and Financial Support Services** *3 students enrolled* • **Biology Technician/Biotechnology Laboratory Technician** *2 students enrolled* • **Building/Home/Construction Inspection/Inspector** *12 students enrolled* • **Child Development** *42 students enrolled* • **Commercial Photography** *10 students enrolled* • **Computer Programming/Programmer, General** *3 students enrolled* • **Cooking and Related Culinary Arts, General** *1 student enrolled* • **Cosmetology/Cosmetologist, General** *9 students enrolled* • **Dental Assisting/Assistant** *14 students enrolled* • **Dental Hygiene/Hygienist** *14 students enrolled* • **Dental Laboratory Technology/Technician** *14 students enrolled* • **Digital Communication and Media/Multimedia** *7 students enrolled* • **Electrical/Electronics Equipment Installation and Repair, General** *12 students enrolled* • **Emergency Medical Technology/Technician (EMT Paramedic)** • **Fire Science/Firefighting** *2 students enrolled* • **Graphic Communications, General** *3 students enrolled* • **Graphic Design** *5 students enrolled* • **Hospitality Administration/Management, General** *5 students enrolled* • **Information Technology** *1 student enrolled* • **International Business/Trade/Commerce** *6 students enrolled* • **Journalism** *3 students enrolled* • **Legal Assistant/Paralegal** *52 students enrolled* • **Library Assistant/Technician** *19 students enrolled* • **Licensed Practical/Vocational Nurse Training (LPN, LVN, Cert, Dipl, AAS)** *22 students enrolled* • **Nurse/Nursing Assistant/Aide and Patient Care Assistant** • **Nursing—Registered Nurse Training (RN, ASN, BSN, MSN)** *97 students enrolled* • **Office Management and Supervision** *10 students enrolled* • **Radio and Television** *1 student enrolled* • **Small Business Administration/Management** *4 students enrolled* • **System Administration/Administrator** *2 students enrolled* • **Technical Theatre/Theatre Design and Technology** *1 student enrolled* • **Welding Technology/Welder** *1 student enrolled*

**STUDENT SERVICES** Academic or career counseling, daycare for children of students, employment services for current students, placement services for program completers, remedial services.

## Patten University

2433 Coolidge Avenue, Oakland, CA 94601-2699
http://www.patten.edu/

**CONTACT** Gary Moncher, President
**Telephone:** 510-261-8500 Ext. 0

**GENERAL INFORMATION** Private Institution. Founded 1944. **Accreditation:** Regional (WASC/ACSCU). **Total program enrollment:** 504. **Application fee:** $30.

**PROGRAM(S) OFFERED**
• **Bible/Biblical Studies** *9 students enrolled* • **Child Development** *17 students enrolled*

**STUDENT SERVICES** Academic or career counseling, remedial services.

## Paul Mitchell the School—Costa Mesa

1534 Adams Avenue, Costa Mesa, CA 92626
http://www.paulmitchelltheschool.com/

**CONTACT** Nate Meador, Director
**Telephone:** 801-302-8801 Ext. 1001

**GENERAL INFORMATION** Private Institution. **Total program enrollment:** 223. **Application fee:** $75.

**PROGRAM(S) OFFERED**
• **Aesthetician/Esthetician and Skin Care Specialist** *600 hrs./$10,075* • **Cosmetology/Cosmetologist, General** *1600 hrs./$19,625*

**STUDENT SERVICES** Academic or career counseling, employment services for current students, placement services for program completers, remedial services.

## Paul Mitchell the School—San Diego

410 A Street, San Diego, CA 92101

**CONTACT** Joyce Douglas, Director
**Telephone:** 801-302-8801 Ext. 1021

**GENERAL INFORMATION** Private Institution. **Total program enrollment:** 218. **Application fee:** $75.

**PROGRAM(S) OFFERED**
• **Cosmetology/Cosmetologist, General** *1800 hrs./$20,925*

**STUDENT SERVICES** Academic or career counseling, employment services for current students, placement services for program completers, remedial services.

## PCI College

17215 Studebaker Road #310, Cerritos, CA 90703
http://www.pci-ed.com/

**CONTACT** Ray Khan, Financial Aid Director
**Telephone:** 562-916-5055

**GENERAL INFORMATION** Private Institution. **Total program enrollment:** 180. **Application fee:** $75.

**PROGRAM(S) OFFERED**
• **Computer Systems Networking and Telecommunications** *6 students enrolled* • **Computer Technology/Computer Systems Technology** *24 hrs./$7495* • **Dental Assisting/Assistant** *10 students enrolled* • **Diagnostic Medical Sonography/Sonographer and Ultrasound Technician** *94 hrs./$25,600* • **Medical Insurance Coding Specialist/Coder** *36 hrs./$5650* • **Medical Insurance Specialist/Medical Biller** *36 hrs./$9850* • **Medical/Clinical Assistant** *24 hrs./$5650*

**STUDENT SERVICES** Placement services for program completers.

## Peralta Community College District

333 East Eighth Street, Oakland, CA 94606
http://www.peralta.cc.ca.us/

**CONTACT** Elihu Harris, Chancellor
**Telephone:** 510-466-7300

**GENERAL INFORMATION** Public Institution.

## Pima Medical Institute

780 Bay Boulevard, Suite 101, Chula Vista, CA 91910
http://www.pmi.edu/

**CONTACT** Jim Volpe, Campus Director
**Telephone:** 619-425-3200

**GENERAL INFORMATION** Private Institution. Founded 1998. **Accreditation:** State accredited or approved. **Total program enrollment:** 853.

**PROGRAM(S) OFFERED**
• **Dental Assisting/Assistant** *720 hrs./$10,110* • **Medical Administrative/Executive Assistant and Medical Secretary** *560 hrs./$6880* • **Medical/Clinical Assistant** *800 hrs./$10,195* • **Pharmacy Technician/Assistant** *800 hrs./$9805* • **Respiratory Therapy Technician/Assistant** *88 hrs./$28,780* • **Veterinary/Animal Health Technology/Technician and Veterinary Assistant** *720 hrs./$9480*

**STUDENT SERVICES** Academic or career counseling, employment services for current students, placement services for program completers, remedial services.

## Platt College

3700 Inland Empire Boulevard, Suite 400, Ontario, CA 91764
http://www.plattcollege.edu/

**CONTACT** Daryl Goldberg, Campus Director
**Telephone:** 909-941-9410

**GENERAL INFORMATION** Private Institution. **Accreditation:** State accredited or approved. **Total program enrollment:** 385. **Application fee:** $75.

**PROGRAM(S) OFFERED**
• **Design and Visual Communications, General** *4 students enrolled* • **Legal Assistant/Paralegal**

**STUDENT SERVICES** Academic or career counseling, employment services for current students, placement services for program completers, remedial services.

## Platt College Los Angeles

1000 South Fremont A9W, Alhambra, CA 91803
http://www.plattcollege.edu/

**CONTACT** Sam Alahmad, Campus Director
**Telephone:** 626-300-5444

**GENERAL INFORMATION** Private Institution. Founded 1987. **Accreditation:** State accredited or approved. **Total program enrollment:** 223. **Application fee:** $75.

**PROGRAM(S) OFFERED**
• **Design and Visual Communications, General** *10 students enrolled*

**STUDENT SERVICES** Academic or career counseling, employment services for current students, placement services for program completers, remedial services.

## Platt College San Diego

6250 El Cajon Boulevard, San Diego, CA 92115-3919
http://www.platt.edu/

**CONTACT** Robert D. Leiker, Chairman
**Telephone:** 619-265-0107

**GENERAL INFORMATION** Private Institution. Founded 1879. **Accreditation:** State accredited or approved. **Total program enrollment:** 289.

**PROGRAM(S) OFFERED**
• **Animation, Interactive Technology, Video Graphics and Special Effects** *4 students enrolled* • **Computer Software and Media Applications, Other** • **Photographic and Film/Video Technology/Technician and Assistant** *5 students enrolled* • **Prepress/Desktop Publishing and Digital Imaging Design** *12 students enrolled* • **Web Page, Digital/Multimedia and Information Resources Design** *12 students enrolled*

**STUDENT SERVICES** Academic or career counseling, employment services for current students, placement services for program completers.

## Pomona Unified School District Adult and Career Education

1515 West Mission Boulevard, Pomona, CA 91766
http://www.pusd.org/

**CONTACT** Barbara Thompson, Principal
**Telephone:** 909-469-2333

**GENERAL INFORMATION** Public Institution. Founded 1936. **Total program enrollment:** 1340.

**PROGRAM(S) OFFERED**
• **Automobile/Automotive Mechanics Technology/Technician** *1750 hrs./$70* • **Barbering/Barber** *1500 hrs./$70* • **Cosmetology and Related Personal Grooming Arts, Other** *144 students enrolled* • **Cosmetology/Cosmetologist, General** *1600 hrs./$987* • **Executive Assistant/Executive Secretary** *900 hrs./$70* • **Mechanics and Repairers, General** *17 students enrolled* • **Medical Office Assistant/Specialist** *21 students enrolled* • **Welding Technology/Welder** *900 hrs./$70* • **Word Processing** *900 hrs./$40*

**STUDENT SERVICES** Academic or career counseling, remedial services.

## Porterville College

100 East College Avenue, Porterville, CA 93257-6058
http://www.pc.cc.ca.us/

**CONTACT** Dr. Rosa Carlson, President
**Telephone:** 559-791-2200

**GENERAL INFORMATION** Public Institution. Founded 1927. **Accreditation:** Regional (WASC/ACCJC). **Total program enrollment:** 1731.

**PROGRAM(S) OFFERED**

• **Accounting** *1 student enrolled* • **Adult Development and Aging** *1 student enrolled* • **Child Development** *5 students enrolled* • **Criminal Justice/Police Science** *5 students enrolled* • **Licensed Practical/Vocational Nurse Training (LPN, LVN, Cert, Dipl, AAS)** *26 students enrolled* • **Psychiatric/Mental Health Services Technician** *57 students enrolled* • **Substance Abuse/Addiction Counseling** *5 students enrolled* • **Teacher Assistant/Aide** *1 student enrolled*

**STUDENT SERVICES** Academic or career counseling, daycare for children of students, employment services for current students, placement services for program completers, remedial services.

## Premiere Career College

12901 Ramona Boulevard, Irwindale, CA 91706-3746
http://www.premierecollege.edu/

**CONTACT** Fe Ludovico-Aragon, Executive Director
**Telephone:** 626-814-2080

**GENERAL INFORMATION** Private Institution. **Total program enrollment:** 388. **Application fee:** $75.

**PROGRAM(S) OFFERED**

• **Accounting and Related Services, Other** *5 students enrolled* • **Accounting** *27 hrs./$5200* • **Administrative Assistant and Secretarial Science, General** *27 hrs./$5200* • **Clinical/Medical Laboratory Assistant** *83 students enrolled* • **General Office Occupations and Clerical Services** *16 students enrolled* • **Hospital and Health Care Facilities Administration/Management** *36 hrs./$7930* • **Licensed Practical/Vocational Nurse Training (LPN, LVN, Cert, Dipl, AAS)** *77 hrs./$23,524* • **Medical Administrative/Executive Assistant and Medical Secretary** *4 students enrolled* • **Medical Office Assistant/Specialist** *32 hrs./$6470* • **Medical/Clinical Assistant** *4 students enrolled* • **Surgical Technology/Technologist** *65 hrs./$18,925*

**STUDENT SERVICES** Academic or career counseling, employment services for current students, placement services for program completers, remedial services.

## Professional Institute of Beauty

10801 East Valley Mall, El Monte, CA 91731
http://www.pibschool.com/

**CONTACT** Willie Quinonez, Owner
**Telephone:** 626-443-9401

**GENERAL INFORMATION** Private Institution. Founded 1962. **Total program enrollment:** 99. **Application fee:** $75.

**PROGRAM(S) OFFERED**

• **Cosmetology, Barber/Styling, and Nail Instructor** *600 hrs./$3225* • **Cosmetology/Cosmetologist, General** *1600 hrs./$8900*

**STUDENT SERVICES** Placement services for program completers.

## Proteus

1830 N. Dinuba Boulevard, Visalia, CA 93291-3014
proteusinc.org

**CONTACT** Michael E. McCann, Chief Executive Officer
**Telephone:** 559-733-5423

**GENERAL INFORMATION** Private Institution. **Total program enrollment:** 40. **Application fee:** $100.

**PROGRAM(S) OFFERED**

• **Business/Office Automation/Technology/Data Entry** *630 hrs./$5934* • **Parts, Warehousing, and Inventory Management Operations** *300 hrs./$3130* • **Retailing and Retail Operations** *615 hrs./$4643* • **Truck and Bus Driver/Commercial Vehicle Operation** *240 hrs./$3252*

**STUDENT SERVICES** Academic or career counseling, employment services for current students, placement services for program completers.

## Rancho Santiago Community College District Office

2323 N. Broadway, Santa Ana, CA 92706-1640
http://www.rsccd.org

**CONTACT** Edward Hernandez, Jr., Chancellor
**Telephone:** 714-480-7450

**GENERAL INFORMATION** Public Institution.

## Reedley College

995 North Reed Avenue, Reedley, CA 93654-2099
http://www.reedleycollege.com/

**CONTACT** Dr. Barbara Hioco, President
**Telephone:** 559-638-3641

**GENERAL INFORMATION** Public Institution. Founded 1926. **Accreditation:** Regional (WASC/ACCJC). **Total program enrollment:** 5661.

**PROGRAM(S) OFFERED**

• **Accounting** *2 students enrolled* • **Administrative Assistant and Secretarial Science, General** *17 students enrolled* • **Agribusiness/Agricultural Business Operations** *5 students enrolled* • **Agricultural Mechanics and Equipment/Machine Technology** *11 students enrolled* • **Airframe Mechanics and Aircraft Maintenance Technology/Technician** *2 students enrolled* • **Animal/Livestock Husbandry and Production** *1 student enrolled* • **Automobile/Automotive Mechanics Technology/Technician** *28 students enrolled* • **Business Administration and Management, General** *1 student enrolled* • **Child Development** *36 students enrolled* • **Criminal Justice/Police Science** *1 student enrolled* • **Dental Assisting/Assistant** *19 students enrolled* • **Forestry, General** *16 students enrolled* • **Information Technology** *2 students enrolled* • **Machine Tool Technology/Machinist** *7 students enrolled* • **Welding Technology/Welder** *2 students enrolled*

**STUDENT SERVICES** Academic or career counseling, daycare for children of students, employment services for current students, placement services for program completers, remedial services.

## Rio Hondo College

3600 Workman Mill Road, Whittier, CA 90601-1699
http://www.rh.cc.ca.us/

**CONTACT** Dr. Ted Martinez, Jr., Superintendent/President
**Telephone:** 562-692-0921

**GENERAL INFORMATION** Public Institution. Founded 1960. **Accreditation:** Regional (WASC/ACCJC). **Total program enrollment:** 4999.

**PROGRAM(S) OFFERED**

• **Accounting** *1 student enrolled* • **Animation, Interactive Technology, Video Graphics and Special Effects** *1 student enrolled* • **Architectural Technology/Technician** *12 students enrolled* • **Autobody/Collision and Repair Technology/Technician** *4 students enrolled* • **Automobile/Automotive Mechanics Technology/Technician** *2 students enrolled* • **Child Development** *133 students enrolled* • **Criminal Justice/Police Science** *225 students enrolled* • **Drafting and Design Technology/Technician, General** *12 students enrolled* • **Emergency Medical Technology/Technician (EMT Paramedic)** *72 students enrolled* • **Fire Science/Firefighting** *157 students enrolled* • **Geography** *6 students enrolled* • **Hazardous Materials Management and Waste Technology/Technician** *1 student enrolled* • **Human Services, General** *3 students enrolled* • **Information Technology** *1 student enrolled* • **Journalism** *2 students enrolled* • **Licensed Practical/Vocational Nurse Training (LPN, LVN, Cert, Dipl, AAS)** *3 students enrolled* • **Office Management and Supervision** *6 students enrolled* • **Small Business Administration/Management** *1 student enrolled* • **Sport and Fitness Administration/Management** *4 students enrolled* • **Substance Abuse/Addiction Counseling** *9 students enrolled*

**STUDENT SERVICES** Academic or career counseling, daycare for children of students, employment services for current students, placement services for program completers, remedial services.

## Riverside Community College District

4800 Magnolia Avenue, Riverside, CA 92506-1299
http://www.rcc.edu/

**CONTACT** Dr. Irving Hendrick, Interim Chancellor
**Telephone:** 951-222-8000 Ext. 8979

**GENERAL INFORMATION** Public Institution. Founded 1916. **Accreditation:** Regional (WASC/ACCJC); dental hygiene (ADA). **Total program enrollment:** 10270.

**PROGRAM(S) OFFERED**

• **Accounting** *15 students enrolled* • **Administrative Assistant and Secretarial Science, General** *2 students enrolled* • **Architectural Technology/Technician** *36 students enrolled* • **Automobile/Automotive Mechanics Technology/Technician** *10 students enrolled* • **Building/Home/Construction Inspection/Inspector** *12 students enrolled* • **Business Administration and Management, General** *12 students enrolled* • **Business, Management, Marketing, and Related Support Services, Other** *2 students enrolled* • **Business/Commerce, General** *12 students enrolled* • **Child Development** *596 students enrolled* • **Commercial Photography** *6 students enrolled* • **Computer Programming/Programmer, General** *14 students enrolled* • **Computer and Information Sciences and Support Services, Other** *18 students enrolled* • **Computer and Information Sciences, General** *25 students enrolled* • **Cooking and Related Culinary Arts, General** *5 students enrolled* • **Corrections** *29 students enrolled* • **Cosmetology/Cosmetologist, General** *29 students enrolled* • **Criminal Justice/Police Science** *246 students enrolled* • **Data Entry/Microcomputer Applications, General** *7 students enrolled* • **Dental Assisting/Assistant** *5 students enrolled* • **Dental Laboratory Technology/Technician** *7 students enrolled* • **Drafting and Design Technology/Technician, General** *6 students enrolled* • **Education/Teaching of Individuals in Early Childhood Special Education Programs** *3 students enrolled* • **Emergency Medical Technology/Technician (EMT Paramedic)** *24 students enrolled* • **Engineering Technology, General** *1 student enrolled* • **Fire Science/Firefighting** *69 students enrolled* • **Forensic Science and Technology** *26 students enrolled* • **Graphic Communications, General** *5 students enrolled* • **Graphic Design** *25 students enrolled* • **Heating, Air Conditioning and Refrigeration Technology/Technician (ACH/ACR/ACHR/HRAC/HVAC/AC Technology)** *16 students enrolled* • **Human Services, General** *18 students enrolled* • **International Business/Trade/Commerce** *3 students enrolled* • **Language Interpretation and Translation** *9 students enrolled* • **Licensed Practical/Vocational Nurse Training (LPN, LVN, Cert, Dipl, AAS)** *56 students enrolled* • **Logistics and Materials Management** *6 students enrolled* • **Medical/Clinical Assistant** *148 students enrolled* • **Music, General** *7 students enrolled* • **Nursing—Registered Nurse Training (RN, ASN, BSN, MSN)** *89 students enrolled* • **Public Administration and Social Service Professions, Other** *47 students enrolled* • **Radio and Television** *4 students enrolled* • **Real Estate** *6 students enrolled* • **Sales, Distribution and Marketing Operations, General** *7 students enrolled* • **Security and Loss Prevention Services** • **Sign Language Interpretation and Translation** *5 students enrolled* • **Sport and Fitness Administration/Management** *4 students enrolled* • **Teacher Assistant/Aide** *3 students enrolled*

**STUDENT SERVICES** Academic or career counseling, daycare for children of students, employment services for current students, placement services for program completers, remedial services.

## Rosemead Beauty School

8531 East Valley Boulevard, Rosemead, CA 91770

**CONTACT** Eva Wu Su, CEO/Owner
**Telephone:** 626-286-2146

**GENERAL INFORMATION** Private Institution. Founded 1957. **Total program enrollment:** 140. **Application fee:** $75.

**PROGRAM(S) OFFERED**

• **Aesthetician/Esthetician and Skin Care Specialist** *600 hrs./$27,500* • **Cosmetology/Cosmetologist, General** *1600 hrs./$7921* • **Nail Technician/Specialist and Manicurist** *400 hrs./$570*

**STUDENT SERVICES** Academic or career counseling, placement services for program completers.

## Royale College of Beauty

27485 Commerce Center Drive, Temecula, CA 92590

**CONTACT** Barbara Kruis, Owner
**Telephone:** 951-676-0833

**GENERAL INFORMATION** Private Institution. **Total program enrollment:** 80.

**PROGRAM(S) OFFERED**

• **Aesthetician/Esthetician and Skin Care Specialist** *600 hrs./$6070* • **Cosmetology and Related Personal Grooming Arts, Other** • **Cosmetology/Cosmetologist, General** *160 hrs./$11,970* • **Make-Up Artist/Specialist** *19 students enrolled* • **Nail Technician/Specialist and Manicurist** *400 hrs./$3675*

**STUDENT SERVICES** Academic or career counseling, placement services for program completers.

## Sacramento City College

3835 Freeport Boulevard, Sacramento, CA 95822-1386
http://www.scc.losrios.edu/

**CONTACT** Kathryn E. Jeffrey, President
**Telephone:** 916-558-2111

**GENERAL INFORMATION** Public Institution. Founded 1916. **Accreditation:** Regional (WASC/ACCJC); dental assisting (ADA); dental hygiene (ADA); physical therapy assisting (APTA). **Total program enrollment:** 7054.

**PROGRAM(S) OFFERED**

• **Accounting** *1 student enrolled* • **Administrative Assistant and Secretarial Science, General** *1 student enrolled* • **Adult Development and Aging** *1 student enrolled* • **Aircraft Powerplant Technology/Technician** *1 student enrolled* • **Airframe Mechanics and Aircraft Maintenance Technology/Technician** *2 students enrolled* • **Apparel and Textile Manufacture** *1 student enrolled* • **Business Administration and Management, General** *5 students enrolled* • **Business/Commerce, General** *6 students enrolled* • **Child Development** *17 students enrolled* • **Commercial Photography** *11 students enrolled* • **Communications Systems Installation and Repair Technology** *4 students enrolled* • **Computer Science** *1 student enrolled* • **Computer Systems Networking and Telecommunications** *6 students enrolled* • **Computer and Information Sciences, General** *3 students enrolled* • **Corrections** *3 students enrolled* • **Cosmetology/Cosmetologist, General** *38 students enrolled* • **Data Entry/Microcomputer Applications, General** *1 student enrolled* • **Dental Assisting/Assistant** *4 students enrolled* • **Digital Communication and Media/Multimedia** *9 students enrolled* • **Drafting and Design Technology/Technician, General** *8 students enrolled* • **Electrical/Electronics Equipment Installation and Repair, General** *5 students enrolled* • **Environmental Studies** *7 students enrolled* • **Graphic Communications, General** *31 students enrolled* • **Ground Transportation, Other** *11 students enrolled* • **Human Services, General** *7 students enrolled* • **Information Technology** *10 students enrolled* • **Interior Design** *1 student enrolled* • **Library Assistant/Technician** *9 students enrolled* • **Licensed Practical/Vocational Nurse Training (LPN, LVN, Cert, Dipl, AAS)** *2 students enrolled* • **Mechanical Engineering/Mechanical Technology/Technician** *19 students enrolled* • **Music Management and Merchandising** *1 student enrolled* • **Office Management and Supervision** *8 students enrolled* • **Real Estate** *2 students enrolled* • **Sales, Distribution and Marketing Operations, General** *2 students enrolled* • **Security and Loss Prevention Services** *1 student enrolled* • **Small Business Administration/Management** *1 student enrolled* • **Small Engine Mechanics and Repair Technology/Technician** *10 students enrolled* • **Survey Technology/Surveying** *5 students enrolled* • **System Administration/Administrator** *7 students enrolled*

**STUDENT SERVICES** Academic or career counseling, daycare for children of students, employment services for current students, placement services for program completers, remedial services.

## Sacramento City Unified School District–Skills and Business Education Center

5451 Lemon Hill Avenue, Sacramento, CA 95824
http://www.scusd.edu/

**CONTACT** Nancy Compton, Principal
**Telephone:** 916-433-2600 Ext. 1011

**GENERAL INFORMATION** Private Institution. **Total program enrollment:** 1928.

**PROGRAM(S) OFFERED**

• **Accounting Technology/Technician and Bookkeeping** *62 students enrolled* • **Allied Health and Medical Assisting Services, Other** *402 students enrolled*

• **Anatomy** *145 students enrolled* • **Autobody/Collision and Repair Technology/Technician** *214 students enrolled* • **Barbering/Barber** *28 students enrolled* • **Business/Office Automation/Technology/Data Entry** *69 students enrolled* • **Clinical/Medical Laboratory Assistant** *93 students enrolled* • **Construction Trades, General** *259 students enrolled* • **Cooking and Related Culinary Arts, General** *200 students enrolled* • **Court Reporting/Court Reporter** *4050 hrs./$1800* • **Customer Service Support/Call Center/Teleservice Operation** *447 students enrolled* • **Data Entry/Microcomputer Applications, General** *1069 students enrolled* • **Diesel Mechanics Technology/Technician** *147 students enrolled* • **Electrical/Electronics Maintenance and Repair Technology, Other** *1170 hrs./$980* • **Emergency Care Attendant (EMT Ambulance)** *160 students enrolled* • **General Office Occupations and Clerical Services** *157 students enrolled* • **Ground Transportation, Other** *67 students enrolled* • **Health Information/Medical Records Technology/Technician** • **Health and Medical Administrative Services, Other** *474 students enrolled* • **Heating, Air Conditioning, Ventilation and Refrigeration Maintenance Technology/Technician (HAC, HACR, HVAC, HVACR)** *1260 hrs./$1125* • **Human Nutrition** *62 students enrolled* • **Interior Design** *153 students enrolled* • **Legal Administrative Assistant/Secretary** *15 students enrolled* • **Licensed Practical/Vocational Nurse Training (LPN, LVN, Cert, Dipl, AAS)** *1532 hrs./$15,000* • **Medical Insurance Coding Specialist/Coder** *39 students enrolled* • **Medical Insurance Specialist/Medical Biller** *38 students enrolled* • **Medical Office Assistant/Specialist** *74 students enrolled* • **Medical/Clinical Assistant** *1440 hrs./$2048* • **Nurse/Nursing Assistant/Aide and Patient Care Assistant** *158 students enrolled* • **Optometric Technician/Assistant** *16 students enrolled* • **Pharmacy Technician/Assistant** *115 students enrolled* • **Pharmacy, Pharmaceutical Sciences, and Administration, Other** *1500 hrs./$1437* • **Pre-Nursing Studies** *24 students enrolled* • **Real Estate** *49 students enrolled* • **Truck and Bus Driver/Commercial Vehicle Operation** *581 students enrolled*

**STUDENT SERVICES** Academic or career counseling, employment services for current students, placement services for program completers, remedial services.

## Saddleback College

28000 Marguerite Parkway, Mission Viejo, CA 92692-3635
http://www.saddleback.cc.ca.us/

**CONTACT** Tod Burnett, EdD, President
**Telephone:** 949-582-4500

**GENERAL INFORMATION** Public Institution. Founded 1967. **Accreditation:** Regional (WASC/ACCJC). **Total program enrollment:** 4573.

**PROGRAM(S) OFFERED**
• **Accounting** *17 students enrolled* • **Administrative Assistant and Secretarial Science, General** *3 students enrolled* • **Apparel and Textile Marketing Management** *7 students enrolled* • **Apparel and Textiles, General** *3 students enrolled* • **Applied Horticulture/Horticultural Operations, General** *7 students enrolled* • **Architectural Technology/Technician** *5 students enrolled* • **Automobile/Automotive Mechanics Technology/Technician** *4 students enrolled* • **Building/Home/Construction Inspection/Inspector** *3 students enrolled* • **Child Development** *11 students enrolled* • **Computer Graphics** *1 student enrolled* • **Computer Installation and Repair Technology/Technician** *2 students enrolled* • **Computer Programming/Programmer, General** *1 student enrolled* • **Computer Systems Networking and Telecommunications** *3 students enrolled* • **Cooking and Related Culinary Arts, General** *4 students enrolled* • **Cosmetology/Cosmetologist, General** *29 students enrolled* • **Data Entry/Microcomputer Applications, General** *1 student enrolled* • **Drafting and Design Technology/Technician, General** *3 students enrolled* • **E-Commerce/Electronic Commerce** *1 student enrolled* • **Electrical/Electronics Equipment Installation and Repair, General** *6 students enrolled* • **Emergency Medical Technology/Technician (EMT Paramedic)** *41 students enrolled* • **Fashion/Apparel Design** *6 students enrolled* • **Foods, Nutrition, and Wellness Studies, General** *3 students enrolled* • **Graphic Communications, General** *2 students enrolled* • **Graphic Design** *4 students enrolled* • **Human Services, General** *1 student enrolled* • **Interior Design** *22 students enrolled* • **International Business/Trade/Commerce** *1 student enrolled* • **Landscaping and Groundskeeping** *6 students enrolled* • **Marine Transportation, Other** *2 students enrolled* • **Medical/Clinical Assistant** *13 students enrolled* • **Office Management and Supervision** *1 student enrolled* • **Real Estate** *2 students enrolled* • **Sales, Distribution and Marketing Operations, General** *2 students enrolled* • **Science Technologies/Technicians, Other** *5 students enrolled* • **Sign Language Interpretation and Translation** *9 students enrolled* • **Small Business Administration/Management** *2 students enrolled* • **Substance Abuse/Addiction Counseling** *17 students enrolled* • **Taxation** *5 students enrolled* • **Teacher Assistant/Aide** *1 student enrolled* • **Tourism and Travel Services Marketing Operations** *1 student enrolled* • **Web Page, Digital/Multimedia and Information Resources Design** *9 students enrolled* • **Web/Multimedia Management and Webmaster** *1 student enrolled*

**STUDENT SERVICES** Academic or career counseling, daycare for children of students, employment services for current students, placement services for program completers, remedial services.

## Saddleback Community College District

28000 Marguerite Parkway, Mission Viejo, CA 92692

**CONTACT** Dr. Raghu P. Mather, Chancellor
**Telephone:** 949-582-4999

**GENERAL INFORMATION** Public Institution.

## Sage College

12125 Day Street, Building L, Moreno Valley, CA 92557-6720
http://www.sagecollege.edu/

**CONTACT** Lauren Somma, CEO
**Telephone:** 951-781-2727

**GENERAL INFORMATION** Private Institution. Founded 1973. **Accreditation:** State accredited or approved. **Total program enrollment:** 270. **Application fee:** $100.

**PROGRAM(S) OFFERED**
• **Legal Administrative Assistant/Secretary** *16 students enrolled*

**STUDENT SERVICES** Academic or career counseling, employment services for current students, placement services for program completers.

## Saint Francis Career College

3680 E. Imperial Highway, Lynwood, CA 90262

**CONTACT** Gerald T. Kozai, President
**Telephone:** 310-900-8050

**GENERAL INFORMATION** Private Institution. **Total program enrollment:** 133.

**PROGRAM(S) OFFERED**
• **Licensed Practical/Vocational Nurse Training (LPN, LVN, Cert, Dipl, AAS)** *1551 hrs./$31,575* • **Nurse/Nursing Assistant/Aide and Patient Care Assistant** *150 hrs./$2659*

**STUDENT SERVICES** Academic or career counseling, employment services for current students, placement services for program completers, remedial services.

## Salon Success Academy

16803 Arrow Boulevard, Fontana, CA 92335
http://www.gotobeautyschool.com/

**CONTACT** Robert P. Gross, President
**Telephone:** 909-982-4200

**GENERAL INFORMATION** Private Institution. **Total program enrollment:** 50. **Application fee:** $100.

**PROGRAM(S) OFFERED**
• **Aesthetician/Esthetician and Skin Care Specialist** • **Cosmetology/Cosmetologist, General** *1600 hrs./$15,424*

**STUDENT SERVICES** Academic or career counseling, placement services for program completers.

## Salon Success Academy—Upland Campus

1385 E. Foothill Boulevard, Upland, CA 91786

**CONTACT** Robert P. Gross, President
**Telephone:** 909-982-4200

**GENERAL INFORMATION** Private Institution. **Total program enrollment:** 117. **Application fee:** $100.

**PROGRAM(S) OFFERED**
• **Aesthetician/Esthetician and Skin Care Specialist** *600 hrs./$6700*
• **Cosmetology/Cosmetologist, General** *1600 hrs./$15,424*

**STUDENT SERVICES** Academic or career counseling, placement services for program completers.

## San Bernardino Community College District

441 West Eighth Street, San Bernardino, CA 92401-1007

**CONTACT** Donald Averill, Chancellor
**Telephone:** 909-382-4000

**GENERAL INFORMATION** Public Institution.

## San Bernardino Valley College

701 South Mount Vernon Avenue, San Bernardino, CA 92410-2748
http://www.valleycollege.edu/

**CONTACT** Debra Daniels, President
**Telephone:** 909-384-4400

**GENERAL INFORMATION** Public Institution. Founded 1926. **Accreditation:** Regional (WASC/ACCJC). **Total program enrollment:** 4006.

**PROGRAM(S) OFFERED**
• **Accounting** *3 students enrolled* • **Administrative Assistant and Secretarial Science, General** *4 students enrolled* • **Aircraft Powerplant Technology/Technician** *9 students enrolled* • **Airframe Mechanics and Aircraft Maintenance Technology/Technician** *13 students enrolled* • **Automobile/Automotive Mechanics Technology/Technician** *7 students enrolled* • **Building/Home/Construction Inspection/Inspector** *6 students enrolled* • **Business Administration and Management, General** *4 students enrolled* • **Child Development** *39 students enrolled* • **Cinematography and Film/Video Production** *1 student enrolled* • **Communications Systems Installation and Repair Technology** *3 students enrolled* • **Computer Installation and Repair Technology/Technician** *4 students enrolled* • **Criminal Justice/Police Science** *16 students enrolled* • **Diesel Mechanics Technology/Technician** *1 student enrolled* • **Digital Communication and Media/Multimedia** *5 students enrolled* • **Electrical and Power Transmission Installation/Installer, General** *18 students enrolled* • **Electrical/Electronics Equipment Installation and Repair, General** *15 students enrolled* • **Graphic Design** *3 students enrolled* • **Heating, Air Conditioning and Refrigeration Technology/Technician (ACH/ACR/ACHR/HRAC/HVAC/AC Technology)** *17 students enrolled* • **Human Services, General** *5 students enrolled* • **Library Assistant/Technician** *8 students enrolled* • **Logistics and Materials Management** *40 students enrolled* • **Machine Tool Technology/Machinist** *2 students enrolled* • **Manufacturing Technology/Technician** *3 students enrolled* • **Pharmacy Technician/Assistant** *13 students enrolled* • **Psychiatric/Mental Health Services Technician** *41 students enrolled* • **Radio and Television** *1 student enrolled* • **Real Estate** *4 students enrolled* • **Retailing and Retail Operations** *5 students enrolled* • **Substance Abuse/Addiction Counseling** *37 students enrolled* • **Water Quality and Wastewater Treatment Management and Recycling Technology/Technician** *3 students enrolled* • **Welding Technology/Welder** *8 students enrolled*

**STUDENT SERVICES** Academic or career counseling, daycare for children of students, employment services for current students, placement services for program completers, remedial services.

## San Diego City College

1313 Park Boulevard, San Diego, CA 92101-4787
http://www.sdcity.edu/

**CONTACT** Terrence Burgess, President
**Telephone:** 619-388-3400

**GENERAL INFORMATION** Public Institution. Founded 1914. **Accreditation:** Regional (WASC/ACCJC). **Total program enrollment:** 3510.

**PROGRAM(S) OFFERED**
• **Accounting** • **Administrative Assistant and Secretarial Science, General** *5 students enrolled* • **Adult Development and Aging** *2 students enrolled* • **Archeology** • **Banking and Financial Support Services** • **Biology Technician/Biotechnology Laboratory Technician** • **Broadcast Journalism** • **Business Administration and Management, General** • **Business/Commerce, General** • **Child Development** *78 students enrolled* • **Cinematography and Film/Video Production** • **Commercial Photography** *2 students enrolled* • **Communications Systems Installation and Repair Technology** *1 student enrolled* • **Computer Installation and Repair Technology/Technician** *1 student enrolled* • **Computer Programming/Programmer, General** • **Computer Systems Networking and Telecommunications** • **Cosmetology/Cosmetologist, General** *19 students enrolled* • **Dance, General** • **Data Entry/Microcomputer Applications, General** • **Digital Communication and Media/Multimedia** • **Drafting and Design Technology/Technician, General** • **E-Commerce/Electronic Commerce** • **Electrical and Power Transmission Installation/Installer, General** *30 students enrolled* • **Electrical/Electronics Equipment Installation and Repair, General** *4 students enrolled* • **Electrician** *55 students enrolled* • **Engineering Technologies/Technicians, Other** *1 student enrolled* • **Graphic Design** *4 students enrolled* • **Ground Transportation, Other** • **Heating, Air Conditioning and Refrigeration Technology/Technician (ACH/ACR/ACHR/HRAC/HVAC/AC Technology)** *12 students enrolled* • **Human Services, General** • **Illustration** • **Labor and Industrial Relations** *3 students enrolled* • **Legal Administrative Assistant/Secretary** *1 student enrolled* • **Legal Assistant/Paralegal** • **Licensed Practical/Vocational Nurse Training (LPN, LVN, Cert, Dipl, AAS)** • **Machine Tool Technology/Machinist** *4 students enrolled* • **Manufacturing Technology/Technician** • **Music Management and Merchandising** • **Plumbing Technology/Plumber** *46 students enrolled* • **Public Administration and Social Service Professions, Other** • **Radio and Television** • **Real Estate** • **Retailing and Retail Operations** *1 student enrolled* • **Sheet Metal Technology/Sheetworking** *1 student enrolled* • **Small Business Administration/Management** • **Sport and Fitness Administration/Management** *8 students enrolled* • **Substance Abuse/Addiction Counseling** *47 students enrolled* • **System Administration/Administrator** • **Taxation** • **Technical Theatre/Theatre Design and Technology**

**STUDENT SERVICES** Academic or career counseling, daycare for children of students, employment services for current students, placement services for program completers, remedial services.

## San Diego Community College District

3375 Camino del Rio South, San Diego, CA 92108
http://www.sdccd.edu/

**CONTACT** Constance M. Carroll, Chancellor
**Telephone:** 619-388-6500

**GENERAL INFORMATION** Public Institution.

## San Diego Mesa College

7250 Mesa College Drive, San Diego, CA 92111-4998
http://www.sandiegomesacollege.net/

**CONTACT** Rita Cepeda, President
**Telephone:** 619-388-2604

**GENERAL INFORMATION** Public Institution. Founded 1964. **Accreditation:** Regional (WASC/ACCJC); dental assisting (ADA); health information technology (AHIMA); medical assisting (AAMAE); physical therapy assisting (APTA). **Total program enrollment:** 5634.

**PROGRAM(S) OFFERED**
• **Accounting** *13 students enrolled* • **Administrative Assistant and Secretarial Science, General** *6 students enrolled* • **Animation, Interactive Technology, Video Graphics and Special Effects** • **Apparel and Textile Marketing Management** *7 students enrolled* • **Apparel and Textiles, General** • **Architectural Technology/Technician** *6 students enrolled* • **Art/Art Studies, General** • **Biology Technician/Biotechnology Laboratory Technician** • **Building/Construction Site Management/Manager** *4 students enrolled* • **Building/Home/Construction Inspection/Inspector** *7 students enrolled* • **Business Administration and Management, General** *60 students enrolled* • **Chemical Technology/Technician** *1 student enrolled* • **Chemistry, General** *2 students enrolled* • **Child Development** *1 student enrolled* • **Computer Programming/Programmer, General** • **Computer Systems Networking and Telecommunications** • **Cooking and Related Culinary Arts, General** *3 students enrolled* • **Dance, General** • **Dental Assisting/Assistant** *15 students enrolled* • **Digital Communication and Media/Multimedia** • **Drafting and Design Technology/Technician, General** • **Drawing** • **Engineering, General** *1 student enrolled* • **Family and Consumer Sciences/Human Sciences, General** • **Fashion/Apparel Design** *1 student enrolled* • **Foods, Nutrition, and Wellness Studies, General** *4 students enrolled* • **Foodservice Systems Administration/Management** • **Geography, Other** *1 student enrolled*

• **Hotel/Motel Administration/Management** *1 student enrolled* • **Information Technology** *11 students enrolled* • **International Relations and Affairs** • **Landscaping and Groundskeeping** • **Legal Administrative Assistant/Secretary** • **Medical Administrative/Executive Assistant and Medical Secretary** • **Medical/Clinical Assistant** *17 students enrolled* • **Music Management and Merchandising** • **Music, General** • **Physical Sciences** • **Radiologic Technology/Science—Radiographer** *10 students enrolled* • **Real Estate** *17 students enrolled* • **Sales, Distribution and Marketing Operations, General** *2 students enrolled* • **Sign Language Interpretation and Translation** *3 students enrolled* • **Sport and Fitness Administration/Management** *7 students enrolled* • **Tourism and Travel Services Marketing Operations** • **Web Page, Digital/Multimedia and Information Resources Design**

**STUDENT SERVICES** Academic or career counseling, daycare for children of students, employment services for current students, placement services for program completers, remedial services.

## San Diego Miramar College

10440 Black Mountain Road, San Diego, CA 92126-2999
http://www.sdmiramar.edu/

**CONTACT** Patricia Hsieh, President
**Telephone:** 619-388-7800

**GENERAL INFORMATION** Public Institution. Founded 1969. **Accreditation:** Regional (WASC/ACCJC). **Total program enrollment:** 1972.

**PROGRAM(S) OFFERED**
• **Administrative Assistant and Secretarial Science, General** *4 students enrolled* • **Aircraft Powerplant Technology/Technician** *8 students enrolled* • **Airframe Mechanics and Aircraft Maintenance Technology/Technician** *12 students enrolled* • **Airline/Commercial/Professional Pilot and Flight Crew** *1 student enrolled* • **Automobile/Automotive Mechanics Technology/Technician** *32 students enrolled* • **Aviation/Airway Management and Operations** *2 students enrolled* • **Banking and Financial Support Services** *6 students enrolled* • **Business Administration and Management, General** *33 students enrolled* • **Child Development** *3 students enrolled* • **Corrections** *1 student enrolled* • **Criminal Justice/Police Science** *11 students enrolled* • **Diesel Mechanics Technology/Technician** *12 students enrolled* • **Fire Science/Firefighting** *68 students enrolled* • **Forensic Science and Technology** *10 students enrolled* • **Heavy Equipment Maintenance Technology/Technician** *9 students enrolled* • **Information Technology** *5 students enrolled* • **Legal Assistant/Paralegal** *5 students enrolled* • **Sport and Fitness Administration/Management** *9 students enrolled*

**STUDENT SERVICES** Academic or career counseling, daycare for children of students, employment services for current students, placement services for program completers, remedial services.

## San Joaquin Delta College

5151 Pacific Avenue, Stockton, CA 95207-6370
http://www.deltacollege.edu/

**CONTACT** Raul Rodriguez, PhD, Superintendent/President
**Telephone:** 209-954-5151

**GENERAL INFORMATION** Public Institution. Founded 1935. **Accreditation:** Regional (WASC/ACCJC). **Total program enrollment:** 7715.

**PROGRAM(S) OFFERED**
• **Accounting** *2 students enrolled* • **Administrative Assistant and Secretarial Science, General** *3 students enrolled* • **Adult Development and Aging** *5 students enrolled* • **American Sign Language (ASL)** *15 students enrolled* • **Architectural Technology/Technician** *19 students enrolled* • **Autobody/Collision and Repair Technology/Technician** *2 students enrolled* • **Automobile/Automotive Mechanics Technology/Technician** *26 students enrolled* • **Carpentry/Carpenter** *5 students enrolled* • **Child Development** *1 student enrolled* • **Computer Programming/Programmer, General** *4 students enrolled* • **Computer Systems Networking and Telecommunications** *3 students enrolled* • **Computer and Information Sciences, General** *1 student enrolled* • **Cooking and Related Culinary Arts, General** *11 students enrolled* • **Corrections** *11 students enrolled* • **Data Entry/Microcomputer Applications, General** *1 student enrolled* • **Diesel Mechanics Technology/Technician** *4 students enrolled* • **Drafting and Design Technology/Technician, General** *16 students enrolled* • **Electrical/Electronics Drafting and Electrical/Electronics CAD/CADD** *3 students enrolled* • **Electrical/Electronics Equipment Installation and Repair, General** *9 students enrolled* • **Engineering, General** *2 students enrolled* • **Family and Consumer Sciences/Human Sciences, General** *1 student enrolled* • **Fashion/Apparel Design** *4 students enrolled* • **Fire Science/Firefighting** *1 student enrolled* • **Graphic Design** *6 students enrolled* • **Heating, Air Conditioning and Refrigeration Technology/Technician (ACH/ACR/ACHR/HRAC/HVAC/AC Technology)** *20 students enrolled* • **Heavy Equipment Maintenance Technology/Technician** *2 students enrolled* • **Human Services, General** *13 students enrolled* • **Information Technology** *1 student enrolled* • **Interior Design** *2 students enrolled* • **International Business/Trade/Commerce** *1 student enrolled* • **Landscaping and Groundskeeping** *1 student enrolled* • **Licensed Practical/Vocational Nurse Training (LPN, LVN, Cert, Dipl, AAS)** *15 students enrolled* • **Logistics and Materials Management** *3 students enrolled* • **Machine Tool Technology/Machinist** *3 students enrolled* • **Manufacturing Technology/Technician** *1 student enrolled* • **Mechanical Drafting and Mechanical Drafting CAD/CADD** *2 students enrolled* • **Nurse/Nursing Assistant/Aide and Patient Care Assistant** • **Office Management and Supervision** *1 student enrolled* • **Parks, Recreation and Leisure Studies** *1 student enrolled* • **Psychiatric/Mental Health Services Technician** *7 students enrolled* • **Radio and Television** *4 students enrolled* • **Real Estate** *6 students enrolled* • **Retailing and Retail Operations** *1 student enrolled* • **Sales, Distribution and Marketing Operations, General** *7 students enrolled* • **Science Technologies/Technicians, Other** *8 students enrolled* • **Sport and Fitness Administration/Management** *4 students enrolled* • **Substance Abuse/Addiction Counseling** *4 students enrolled* • **Taxation** *18 students enrolled* • **Welding Technology/Welder** *2 students enrolled*

**STUDENT SERVICES** Academic or career counseling, daycare for children of students, employment services for current students, remedial services.

## San Joaquin Valley College

201 New Stine Road, Bakersfield, CA 93309
http://www.sjvc.edu/

**CONTACT** Mark A. Perry, President
**Telephone:** 661-834-0126

**GENERAL INFORMATION** Private Institution. Founded 1977. **Total program enrollment:** 541.

**PROGRAM(S) OFFERED**
• **Building/Property Maintenance and Management** *2 students enrolled*

**STUDENT SERVICES** Academic or career counseling, employment services for current students, placement services for program completers, remedial services.

## San Joaquin Valley College

295 East Sierra Avenue, Fresno, CA 93710-3616
http://www.sjvc.edu/

**CONTACT** Mark A. Perry, President
**Telephone:** 559-448-8282

**GENERAL INFORMATION** Private Institution. **Total program enrollment:** 786.

**PROGRAM(S) OFFERED**
• **Medical/Clinical Assistant** • **Veterinary/Animal Health Technology/Technician and Veterinary Assistant**

**STUDENT SERVICES** Academic or career counseling, employment services for current students, placement services for program completers, remedial services.

## San Joaquin Valley College

11050 Olson Drive, Suite 100, Rancho Cordova, CA 95670
http://www.sjvc.edu/

**CONTACT** Mark Perry, President
**Telephone:** 916-638-7582

**GENERAL INFORMATION** Private Institution. **Total program enrollment:** 287.

*San Joaquin Valley College (continued)*

**PROGRAM(S) OFFERED**
• **Business Administration and Management, General** *9 students enrolled* • **Medical Office Management/Administration** *39 students enrolled* • **Medical/Clinical Assistant** *13 students enrolled*

**STUDENT SERVICES** Academic or career counseling, employment services for current students, placement services for program completers, remedial services.

## San Joaquin Valley College

10641 Church Street, Rancho Cucamonga, CA 91730
http://www.sjvc.edu/

**CONTACT** Mark Perry, President
**Telephone:** 909-948-7582

**GENERAL INFORMATION** Private Institution. **Total program enrollment:** 588.

**PROGRAM(S) OFFERED**
• **Business Administration and Management, General** • **Medical Office Management/Administration** • **Medical/Clinical Assistant** *2 students enrolled* • **Pharmacy Technician/Assistant**

**STUDENT SERVICES** Academic or career counseling, employment services for current students, placement services for program completers, remedial services.

## San Joaquin Valley College

5380 Pirrone Road, Salida, CA 95368
http://www.sjvc.edu/

**CONTACT** Mark Perry, President
**Telephone:** 209-543-8800

**GENERAL INFORMATION** Private Institution. **Total program enrollment:** 310.

**PROGRAM(S) OFFERED**
• **Business Administration and Management, General** *21 students enrolled* • **Medical Office Management/Administration** *78 students enrolled* • **Medical/Clinical Assistant** *105 students enrolled*

**STUDENT SERVICES** Academic or career counseling, employment services for current students, placement services for program completers, remedial services.

## San Joaquin Valley College

8400 West Mineral King Avenue, Visalia, CA 93291
http://www.sjvc.edu/

**CONTACT** Mark A. Perry, President
**Telephone:** 559-651-2500

**GENERAL INFORMATION** Private Institution. Founded 1977. **Accreditation:** Regional (WASC/ACCJC); dental hygiene (ADA); surgical technology (ARCST). **Total program enrollment:** 887.

**PROGRAM(S) OFFERED**
• **Business Administration and Management, General** *11 students enrolled* • **Industrial Technology/Technician** *46 students enrolled* • **Medical Office Management/Administration** *29 students enrolled* • **Medical/Clinical Assistant** *83 students enrolled*

**STUDENT SERVICES** Academic or career counseling, employment services for current students, placement services for program completers, remedial services.

## San Joaquin Valley College–Online

3808 W. Caldwell Avenue, Suite A, Visalia, CA 93277
http://www.sjvconline.edu/

**CONTACT** Mark Perry, President
**Telephone:** 559-734-7582

**GENERAL INFORMATION** Private Institution. **Total program enrollment:** 303.

**PROGRAM(S) OFFERED**
• **Business Administration and Management, General** *20 students enrolled* • **Human Resources Management/Personnel Administration, General** *10 students enrolled* • **Medical Office Management/Administration** *76 students enrolled* • **Medical/Clinical Assistant** *60 students enrolled*

**STUDENT SERVICES** Academic or career counseling, employment services for current students, placement services for program completers, remedial services.

## San Jose City College

2100 Moorpark Avenue, San Jose, CA 95128-2799
http://www.sjcc.edu/

**CONTACT** Dr. Michael Burke, President
**Telephone:** 408-298-2181

**GENERAL INFORMATION** Public Institution. Founded 1921. **Accreditation:** Regional (WASC/ACCJC); dental assisting (ADA). **Total program enrollment:** 3062.

**PROGRAM(S) OFFERED**
• **Accounting** *6 students enrolled* • **Administrative Assistant and Secretarial Science, General** *3 students enrolled* • **Business Administration and Management, General** *1 student enrolled* • **Child Development** *41 students enrolled* • **Communication, Journalism and Related Programs, Other** *1 student enrolled* • **Computer Programming/Programmer, General** *1 student enrolled* • **Computer Systems Networking and Telecommunications** *3 students enrolled* • **Computer and Information Sciences and Support Services, Other** *1 student enrolled* • **Construction Trades, General** *17 students enrolled* • **Cosmetology/Cosmetologist, General** *68 students enrolled* • **Dental Assisting/Assistant** *38 students enrolled* • **Digital Communication and Media/Multimedia** *2 students enrolled* • **Electrical/Electronics Equipment Installation and Repair, General** *3 students enrolled* • **Health Professions and Related Clinical Sciences, Other** • **Heating, Air Conditioning and Refrigeration Technology/Technician (ACH/ACR/ACHR/HRAC/HVAC/AC Technology)** *17 students enrolled* • **Industrial Electronics Technology/Technician** *2 students enrolled* • **Laser and Optical Technology/Technician** *3 students enrolled* • **Machine Tool Technology/Machinist** *14 students enrolled* • **Mechanical Engineering/Mechanical Technology/Technician** *1 student enrolled* • **Real Estate** *4 students enrolled* • **Substance Abuse/Addiction Counseling** *8 students enrolled* • **Web Page, Digital/Multimedia and Information Resources Design** *2 students enrolled*

**STUDENT SERVICES** Academic or career counseling, daycare for children of students, employment services for current students, placement services for program completers, remedial services.

## San Jose-Evergreen Community College District

4750 San Felipe Road, San Jose, CA 95135-1599

**CONTACT** Rosa G. Perez, Chancellor
**Telephone:** 408-270-6700

**GENERAL INFORMATION** Public Institution.

## San Mateo County Community College District

3401 CSM Drive, San Mateo, CA 94402-3699

**CONTACT** Ron Galatolo, Chancellor/Superintendent
**Telephone:** 650-574-6550

**GENERAL INFORMATION** Public Institution.

## Santa Ana College

1530 West 17th Street, Santa Ana, CA 92706-3398
http://www.sac.edu/

**CONTACT** Erlinda Martinez, President
**Telephone:** 714-564-6000

**GENERAL INFORMATION** Public Institution. Founded 1915. **Accreditation:** Regional (WASC/ACCJC). **Total program enrollment:** 4587.

**PROGRAM(S) OFFERED**
• **Accounting** *12 students enrolled* • **Administrative Assistant and Secretarial Science, General** *8 students enrolled* • **Advertising** *2 students enrolled* • **American Sign Language (ASL)** *5 students enrolled* • **Animation, Interactive Technology, Video Graphics and Special Effects** *3 students enrolled* • **Apparel and Textile Marketing Management** *2 students enrolled* • **Architectural Drafting and Architectural CAD/CADD** *2 students enrolled* • **Audiology/Audiologist and Speech-Language Pathology/Pathologist** *1 student enrolled* • **Automobile/Automotive Mechanics Technology/Technician** *78 students enrolled* • **Broadcast Journalism** *2 students enrolled* • **Business Administration and Management, General** *16 students enrolled* • **Child Development** *16 students enrolled* • **Commercial and Advertising Art** *1 student enrolled* • **Communications Systems Installation and Repair Technology** *1 student enrolled* • **Computer Graphics** *5 students enrolled* • **Computer Programming/Programmer, General** *2 students enrolled* • **Corrections** *5 students enrolled* • **Data Modeling/Warehousing and Database Administration** *2 students enrolled* • **Drafting and Design Technology/Technician, General** *5 students enrolled* • **Fashion/Apparel Design** *2 students enrolled* • **Fire Science/Firefighting** *36 students enrolled* • **Health and Physical Education, General** *1 student enrolled* • **Heavy Equipment Maintenance Technology/Technician** *1 student enrolled* • **Information Technology** *3 students enrolled* • **International Business/Trade/Commerce** *11 students enrolled* • **Legal Administrative Assistant/Secretary** *1 student enrolled* • **Legal Assistant/Paralegal** *13 students enrolled* • **Library Assistant/Technician** *7 students enrolled* • **Machine Tool Technology/Machinist** *16 students enrolled* • **Manufacturing Technology/Technician** *1 student enrolled* • **Medical/Clinical Assistant** *30 students enrolled* • **Metal and Jewelry Arts** *1 student enrolled* • **Music Management and Merchandising** *2 students enrolled* • **Office Management and Supervision** *7 students enrolled* • **Pharmacy Technician/Assistant** *27 students enrolled* • **Photography** *3 students enrolled* • **Prepress/Desktop Publishing and Digital Imaging Design** *3 students enrolled* • **Radio and Television** *3 students enrolled* • **Sales, Distribution and Marketing Operations, General** *4 students enrolled* • **Small Business Administration/Management** *1 student enrolled* • **Technical Theatre/Theatre Design and Technology** *1 student enrolled* • **Web Page, Digital/Multimedia and Information Resources Design** *2 students enrolled* • **Welding Technology/Welder** *1 student enrolled*

**STUDENT SERVICES** Academic or career counseling, daycare for children of students, employment services for current students, remedial services.

## Santa Barbara Business College

211 South Real Road, Bakersfield, CA 93309
http://www.sbbcollege.edu/

**CONTACT** Corey Doxey, Campus Director
**Telephone:** 661-835-1100

**GENERAL INFORMATION** Private Institution. **Total program enrollment:** 708. **Application fee:** $25.

**PROGRAM(S) OFFERED**
• **Athletic Training/Trainer** *5 students enrolled* • **Business Operations Support and Secretarial Services, Other** • **Business/Commerce, General** *102 hrs./$25,090* • **Criminal Justice/Safety Studies** *95 hrs./$26,097* • **Legal Administrative Assistant/Secretary** • **Legal Assistant/Paralegal** *102 hrs./$25,090* • **Licensed Practical/Vocational Nurse Training (LPN, LVN, Cert, Dipl, AAS)** *97 hrs./$27,745* • **Massage Therapy/Therapeutic Massage** • **Medical Office Assistant/Specialist** *8 students enrolled* • **Medical/Clinical Assistant** *101 hrs./$24,820* • **Pharmacy Technician/Assistant** *92 hrs./$22,640* • **System Administration/Administrator** *6 students enrolled*

**STUDENT SERVICES** Academic or career counseling, employment services for current students, placement services for program completers.

## Santa Barbara Business College

303 Plaza Drive, Santa Maria, CA 93454
http://www.sbbcollege.edu/

**CONTACT** Matthew Johnston, President
**Telephone:** 805-922-8256

**GENERAL INFORMATION** Private Institution. **Total program enrollment:** 216. **Application fee:** $25.

**PROGRAM(S) OFFERED**
• **Athletic Training/Trainer** • **Business Operations Support and Secretarial Services, Other** *7 students enrolled* • **Business/Commerce, General** *102 hrs./$25,090* • **Criminal Justice/Safety Studies** *95 hrs./$23,375* • **Legal Administrative Assistant/Secretary** • **Legal Assistant/Paralegal** • **Licensed Practical/Vocational Nurse Training (LPN, LVN, Cert, Dipl, AAS)** *97 hrs./$27,745* • **Massage Therapy/Therapeutic Massage** *53 hrs./$9905* • **Medical Office Assistant/Specialist** *8 students enrolled* • **Medical/Clinical Assistant** *101 hrs./$27,535* • **Pharmacy Technician/Assistant** *92 hrs./$22,640*

**STUDENT SERVICES** Academic or career counseling, employment services for current students, placement services for program completers.

## Santa Barbara Business College

4839 Market Street, Ventura, CA 93003
http://www.sbbcollege.com/

**CONTACT** Joe Liddicote, Campus Director
**Telephone:** 805-339-2999

**GENERAL INFORMATION** Private Institution. **Total program enrollment:** 373. **Application fee:** $25.

**PROGRAM(S) OFFERED**
• **Business Operations Support and Secretarial Services, Other** *4 students enrolled* • **Business/Commerce, General** *102 hrs./$25,090* • **Criminal Justice/Safety Studies** *95 hrs./$23,375* • **Health and Physical Education/Fitness, Other** *51 hrs./$9535* • **Legal Administrative Assistant/Secretary** *2 students enrolled* • **Legal Assistant/Paralegal** *102 hrs./$25,090* • **Massage Therapy/Therapeutic Massage** *53 hrs./$9905* • **Medical Office Assistant/Specialist** *1 student enrolled* • **Medical/Clinical Assistant** *101 hrs./$27,535* • **Pharmacy Technician/Assistant** *6 students enrolled*

**STUDENT SERVICES** Academic or career counseling, employment services for current students, placement services for program completers.

## Santa Barbara City College

721 Cliff Drive, Santa Barbara, CA 93109-2394
http://www.sbcc.edu/

**CONTACT** Andreea Serban, Superintendent President
**Telephone:** 805-965-0581

**GENERAL INFORMATION** Public Institution. Founded 1908. **Accreditation:** Regional (WASC/ACCJC); health information technology (AHIMA); radiologic technology: radiography (JRCERT). **Total program enrollment:** 6778.

**PROGRAM(S) OFFERED**
• **Accounting** *1 student enrolled* • **Administrative Assistant and Secretarial Science, General** *4 students enrolled* • **Animation, Interactive Technology, Video Graphics and Special Effects** *2 students enrolled* • **Applied Horticulture/Horticultural Operations, General** *5 students enrolled* • **Automobile/Automotive Mechanics Technology/Technician** *10 students enrolled* • **Banking and Financial Support Services** *2 students enrolled* • **Broadcast Journalism** *1 student enrolled* • **Business Administration and Management, General** *5 students enrolled* • **Child Development** *25 students enrolled* • **Computer Science** *3 students enrolled* • **Computer Systems Networking and Telecommunications** *4 students enrolled* • **Cooking and Related Culinary Arts, General** *23 students enrolled* • **Cosmetology/Cosmetologist, General** *36 students enrolled* • **Criminal Justice/Police Science** *5 students enrolled* • **Crop Production** • **Diagnostic Medical Sonography/Sonographer and Ultrasound Technician** *13 students enrolled* • **Digital Communication and Media/Multimedia** *2 students enrolled* • **Diver, Professional and Instructor** *28 students enrolled* • **Drafting and Design Technology/Technician, General** *7 students enrolled* • **Emergency Medical Technology/Technician (EMT Paramedic)** • **Health Information/Medical**

*Santa Barbara City College (continued)*

**Records Technology/Technician** *13 students enrolled* • **Home Health Aide/Home Attendant** • **Hospitality Administration/Management, General** *1 student enrolled* • **Interior Design** *6 students enrolled* • **International Business/Trade/Commerce** *8 students enrolled* • **Journalism** *1 student enrolled* • **Licensed Practical/Vocational Nurse Training (LPN, LVN, Cert, Dipl, AAS)** *36 students enrolled* • **Medical Insurance Coding Specialist/Coder** *47 students enrolled* • **Music Management and Merchandising** *2 students enrolled* • **Nurse/Nursing Assistant/Aide and Patient Care Assistant** *97 students enrolled* • **Real Estate** *1 student enrolled* • **Sales, Distribution and Marketing Operations, General** *28 students enrolled* • **Small Business Administration/Management** *1 student enrolled* • **Substance Abuse/Addiction Counseling** *13 students enrolled*

**STUDENT SERVICES** Academic or career counseling, daycare for children of students, employment services for current students, placement services for program completers, remedial services.

## Santa Monica College

1900 Pico Boulevard, Santa Monica, CA 90405-1628
http://www.smc.edu/

**CONTACT** Chui L. Tsang, Superintendent/President
**Telephone:** 310-434-4000

**GENERAL INFORMATION** Public Institution. Founded 1929. **Accreditation:** Regional (WASC/ACCJC). **Total program enrollment:** 11139.

**PROGRAM(S) OFFERED**

• **Accounting** *21 students enrolled* • **Apparel and Textile Marketing Management** *3 students enrolled* • **Business Administration and Management, General** *5 students enrolled* • **Child Development** *67 students enrolled* • **Commercial Photography** *9 students enrolled* • **Computer Programming/Programmer, General** *4 students enrolled* • **Cosmetology/Cosmetologist, General** *7 students enrolled* • **Data Entry/Microcomputer Applications, General** *3 students enrolled* • **Data Modeling/Warehousing and Database Administration** *1 student enrolled* • **Fashion/Apparel Design** *1 student enrolled* • **Graphic Design** *45 students enrolled* • **Interior Design** *39 students enrolled* • **International Business/Trade/Commerce** *3 students enrolled* • **Office Management and Supervision** *3 students enrolled* • **Sales, Distribution and Marketing Operations, General** *5 students enrolled*

**STUDENT SERVICES** Academic or career counseling, daycare for children of students, employment services for current students, placement services for program completers, remedial services.

## Santa Rosa Junior College

1501 Mendocino Avenue, Santa Rosa, CA 95401-4395
http://www.santarosa.edu/

**CONTACT** Robert F. Agrella, EdD, Superintendent/President
**Telephone:** 707-527-4011

**GENERAL INFORMATION** Public Institution. Founded 1918. **Accreditation:** Regional (WASC/ACCJC); dental assisting (ADA); dental hygiene (ADA); radiologic technology: radiography (JRCERT). **Total program enrollment:** 6007.

**PROGRAM(S) OFFERED**

• **Accounting** *27 students enrolled* • **Administrative Assistant and Secretarial Science, General** *4 students enrolled* • **Agricultural Production Operations, Other** *6 students enrolled* • **Agriculture, Agriculture Operations and Related Sciences, Other** *1 student enrolled* • **Airline/Commercial/Professional Pilot and Flight Crew** *1 student enrolled* • **Architectural Technology/Technician** *3 students enrolled* • **Art/Art Studies, General** *2 students enrolled* • **Automobile/Automotive Mechanics Technology/Technician** *74 students enrolled* • **Building/Construction Site Management/Manager** *2 students enrolled* • **Business Administration and Management, General** *20 students enrolled* • **Business, Management, Marketing, and Related Support Services, Other** *63 students enrolled* • **Child Development** *87 students enrolled* • **Communication, Journalism and Related Programs, Other** *2 students enrolled* • **Community Health and Preventive Medicine** *3 students enrolled* • **Computer Graphics** *1 student enrolled* • **Computer and Information Sciences and Support Services, Other** *31 students enrolled* • **Computer and Information Sciences, General** *17 students enrolled* • **Cooking and Related Culinary Arts, General** *55 students enrolled* • **Corrections and Criminal Justice, Other** *12 students enrolled* • **Corrections** *76 students enrolled* • **Criminal Justice/Police Science** *13 students enrolled* • **Dance, General** *2 students enrolled* • **Data Entry/Microcomputer Applications, General** *34 students enrolled* • **Dental Assisting/Assistant** *20 students enrolled* • **Diesel Mechanics Technology/Technician** *2 students enrolled* • **Drama and Dramatics/Theatre Arts, General** *3 students enrolled* • **Drawing** *5 students enrolled* • **E-Commerce/Electronic Commerce** *1 student enrolled* • **Electrical/Electronics Equipment Installation and Repair, General** *8 students enrolled* • **Emergency Medical Technology/Technician (EMT Paramedic)** *399 students enrolled* • **Fire Science/Firefighting** *286 students enrolled* • **Floriculture/Floristry Operations and Management** *1 student enrolled* • **Foodservice Systems Administration/Management** *6 students enrolled* • **Graphic Design** *3 students enrolled* • **Hospitality Administration/Management, General** *3 students enrolled* • **Human Services, General** *2 students enrolled* • **Interior Design** *1 student enrolled* • **International Business/Trade/Commerce** *2 students enrolled* • **Landscaping and Groundskeeping** *1 student enrolled* • **Legal Administrative Assistant/Secretary** *4 students enrolled* • **Machine Tool Technology/Machinist** *18 students enrolled* • **Medical/Clinical Assistant** *3 students enrolled* • **Natural Resources/Conservation, General** *1 student enrolled* • **Nurse/Nursing Assistant/Aide and Patient Care Assistant** *1 student enrolled* • **Office Management and Supervision** *8 students enrolled* • **Pharmacy Technician/Assistant** *19 students enrolled* • **Phlebotomy/Phlebotomist** • **Photography** *4 students enrolled* • **Plant Nursery Operations and Management** *1 student enrolled* • **Psychiatric/Mental Health Services Technician** *22 students enrolled* • **Real Estate** *8 students enrolled* • **Restaurant, Culinary, and Catering Management/Manager** *39 students enrolled* • **Selling Skills and Sales Operations** *5 students enrolled* • **Small Business Administration/Management** *2 students enrolled* • **Substance Abuse/Addiction Counseling** *12 students enrolled* • **Survey Technology/Surveying** *9 students enrolled* • **System Administration/Administrator** *3 students enrolled* • **Veterinary/Animal Health Technology/Technician and Veterinary Assistant** *3 students enrolled* • **Web/Multimedia Management and Webmaster** *2 students enrolled* • **Welding Technology/Welder** *2 students enrolled*

**STUDENT SERVICES** Academic or career counseling, daycare for children of students, employment services for current students, placement services for program completers, remedial services.

## Santiago Canyon College

8045 East Chapman Avenue, Orange, CA 92869
http://www.sccollege.edu/

**CONTACT** Juan Vazquez, President
**Telephone:** 714-628-4900

**GENERAL INFORMATION** Public Institution. Founded 2000. **Accreditation:** Regional (WASC/ACCJC). **Total program enrollment:** 2645.

**PROGRAM(S) OFFERED**

• **Advertising** *3 students enrolled* • **American Sign Language (ASL)** *1 student enrolled* • **Business Administration and Management, General** *1 student enrolled* • **Business, Management, Marketing, and Related Support Services, Other** *20 students enrolled* • **Child Development** *1 student enrolled* • **Construction Trades, Other** *2 students enrolled* • **Cosmetology/Cosmetologist, General** *42 students enrolled* • **Engineering Technologies/Technicians, Other** *10 students enrolled* • **Mechanical Engineering/Mechanical Technology/Technician** *1 student enrolled* • **Radio and Television** *1 student enrolled* • **Real Estate** *4 students enrolled* • **Survey Technology/Surveying** *34 students enrolled* • **Tourism and Travel Services Marketing Operations** *2 students enrolled* • **Water Quality and Wastewater Treatment Management and Recycling Technology/Technician** *55 students enrolled*

**STUDENT SERVICES** Academic or career counseling, daycare for children of students, employment services for current students, remedial services.

## Shasta Bible College

2951 Goodwater Avenue, Redding, CA 96002
http://www.shasta.edu/

**CONTACT** David R. Nicholas, President
**Telephone:** 530-221-4275

**GENERAL INFORMATION** Private Institution. Founded 1971. **Accreditation:** State accredited or approved. **Total program enrollment:** 42. **Application fee:** $50.

**PROGRAM(S) OFFERED**

• **Bible/Biblical Studies** *4 students enrolled* • **Early Childhood Education and Teaching**

**STUDENT SERVICES** Academic or career counseling, employment services for current students.

## Shasta College

PO Box 496006, 11555 Old Oregon Trail, Redding, CA 96049-6006
http://www.shastacollege.edu/

**CONTACT** Gary Lewis, Superintendent/President
**Telephone:** 530-242-7500

**GENERAL INFORMATION** Public Institution. Founded 1948. **Accreditation:** Regional (WASC/ACCJC); dental hygiene (ADA). **Total program enrollment:** 3916.

**PROGRAM(S) OFFERED**
• **Accounting** *1 student enrolled* • **Administrative Assistant and Secretarial Science, General** *8 students enrolled* • **Agricultural Mechanics and Equipment/Machine Technology** *11 students enrolled* • **Child Development** *1 student enrolled* • **Computer Systems Networking and Telecommunications** *3 students enrolled* • **Construction Trades, General** *3 students enrolled* • **Cooking and Related Culinary Arts, General** *7 students enrolled* • **Diesel Mechanics Technology/Technician** *3 students enrolled* • **Equestrian/Equine Studies** *1 student enrolled* • **Medical Administrative/Executive Assistant and Medical Secretary** *8 students enrolled*

**STUDENT SERVICES** Academic or career counseling, daycare for children of students, employment services for current students, placement services for program completers, remedial services.

## Sierra College

5000 Rocklin Road, Rocklin, CA 95677-3397
http://www.sierracollege.edu/

**CONTACT** Leo Chavez, Superintendent/President
**Telephone:** 916-624-3333

**GENERAL INFORMATION** Public Institution. Founded 1936. **Accreditation:** Regional (WASC/ACCJC). **Total program enrollment:** 7246.

**PROGRAM(S) OFFERED**
• **Accounting** *21 students enrolled* • **Administrative Assistant and Secretarial Science, General** *1 student enrolled* • **Apparel and Textile Manufacture** *1 student enrolled* • **Applied Horticulture/Horticultural Operations, General** *3 students enrolled* • **Architectural Drafting and Architectural CAD/CADD** *1 student enrolled* • **Automobile/Automotive Mechanics Technology/Technician** *3 students enrolled* • **Business Administration and Management, General** *4 students enrolled* • **Business/Commerce, General** *2 students enrolled* • **Cabinetmaking and Millwork/Millwright** *6 students enrolled* • **Carpentry/Carpenter** *5 students enrolled* • **Child Development** *4 students enrolled* • **Commercial Photography** *1 student enrolled* • **Computer Programming/Programmer, General** *3 students enrolled* • **Computer Systems Networking and Telecommunications** *3 students enrolled* • **Computer and Information Sciences and Support Services, Other** *4 students enrolled* • **Construction Trades, General** *4 students enrolled* • **Data Entry/Microcomputer Applications, General** *5 students enrolled* • **Digital Communication and Media/Multimedia** *2 students enrolled* • **Electrical/Electronics Equipment Installation and Repair, General** *1 student enrolled* • **Emergency Medical Technology/Technician (EMT Paramedic)** • **Fire Science/Firefighting** *12 students enrolled* • **Graphic Design** *2 students enrolled* • **Industrial Electronics Technology/Technician** *8 students enrolled* • **Library Assistant/Technician** *4 students enrolled* • **Licensed Practical/Vocational Nurse Training (LPN, LVN, Cert, Dipl, AAS)** *9 students enrolled* • **Mechanical Drafting and Mechanical Drafting CAD/CADD** *1 student enrolled* • **Nurse/Nursing Assistant/Aide and Patient Care Assistant** • **Real Estate** *1 student enrolled* • **Small Business Administration/Management** *7 students enrolled* • **Sport and Fitness Administration/Management** *5 students enrolled* • **System Administration/Administrator** *8 students enrolled* • **Welding Technology/Welder** *9 students enrolled*

**STUDENT SERVICES** Academic or career counseling, daycare for children of students, employment services for current students, placement services for program completers, remedial services.

## Sierra College of Beauty

1340 West 18th Street, Merced, CA 95340

**CONTACT** Burna Burnthorne, Owner
**Telephone:** 209-723-2989

**GENERAL INFORMATION** Private Institution. Founded 1969. **Total program enrollment:** 97. **Application fee:** $100.

**PROGRAM(S) OFFERED**
• **Cosmetology and Related Personal Grooming Arts, Other** *21 students enrolled* • **Cosmetology/Cosmetologist, General** *1600 hrs./$8300* • **Nail Technician/Specialist and Manicurist** *400 hrs./$1900*

**STUDENT SERVICES** Academic or career counseling.

## Silicon Valley University

2160 Lundy Avenue, Suite 110, San Jose, CA 95131
http://www.svuca.edu/

**CONTACT** Seiko Cheng, Administrative Officer
**Telephone:** 408-435-8989 Ext. 102

**GENERAL INFORMATION** Private Institution. **Accreditation:** State accredited or approved. **Total program enrollment:** 584. **Application fee:** $50.

**PROGRAM(S) OFFERED**
• **Computer Engineering, General** *1 student enrolled* • **Teaching English as a Second or Foreign Language/ESL Language Instructor** *10 students enrolled*

**STUDENT SERVICES** Academic or career counseling, employment services for current students, placement services for program completers.

## Simpson University

2211 College View Drive, Redding, CA 96003-8606
http://www.simpsonuniversity.edu/

**CONTACT** Larry J. McKinney, President
**Telephone:** 530-224-5600

**GENERAL INFORMATION** Private Institution (Affiliated with The Christian and Missionary Alliance). Founded 1921. **Accreditation:** Regional (WASC/ACSCU). **Total program enrollment:** 985. **Application fee:** $25.

**STUDENT SERVICES** Academic or career counseling, employment services for current students, remedial services.

## Skyline College

3300 College Drive, San Bruno, CA 94066-1698
http://skylinecollege.net/

**CONTACT** Victoria Morrow, President
**Telephone:** 650-738-4100

**GENERAL INFORMATION** Public Institution. Founded 1969. **Accreditation:** Regional (WASC/ACCJC); surgical technology (ARCST). **Total program enrollment:** 2574.

**PROGRAM(S) OFFERED**
• **Accounting** *23 students enrolled* • **Administrative Assistant and Secretarial Science, General** *11 students enrolled* • **Automobile/Automotive Mechanics Technology/Technician** *245 students enrolled* • **Biology Technician/Biotechnology Laboratory Technician** *33 students enrolled* • **Business Administration and Management, General** *6 students enrolled* • **Child Development** *28 students enrolled* • **Computer Systems Networking and Telecommunications** *9 students enrolled* • **Cosmetology/Cosmetologist, General** *5 students enrolled* • **Criminal Justice/Police Science** *8 students enrolled* • **Electrical/Electronics Equipment Installation and Repair, General** *9 students enrolled* • **Electromechanical Technology/Electromechanical Engineering Technology** *8 students enrolled* • **Emergency Medical Technology/Technician (EMT Paramedic)** *54 students enrolled* • **Health and Medical Administrative**

*Skyline College (continued)*

**Services, Other** *16 students enrolled* • **International Business/Trade/Commerce** *3 students enrolled* • **Legal Assistant/Paralegal** *9 students enrolled* • **Medical Administrative/Executive Assistant and Medical Secretary** *4 students enrolled* • **Surgical Technology/Technologist** *11 students enrolled* • **Web Page, Digital/Multimedia and Information Resources Design** *2 students enrolled*

**STUDENT SERVICES** Academic or career counseling, daycare for children of students, employment services for current students, placement services for program completers, remedial services.

## Solano Community College

4000 Suisun Valley Road, Suisun City, CA 94534-3197
http://www.solano.edu/

**CONTACT** Gerald F. Fisher, Superintendent- President
**Telephone:** 707-864-7000

**GENERAL INFORMATION** Public Institution. Founded 1945. **Accreditation:** Regional (WASC/ACCJC). **Total program enrollment:** 2630.

**PROGRAM(S) OFFERED**
• **Accounting** *7 students enrolled* • **Banking and Financial Support Services** *1 student enrolled* • **Biology Technician/Biotechnology Laboratory Technician** *12 students enrolled* • **Business Administration and Management, General** *8 students enrolled* • **Business/Commerce, General** *5 students enrolled* • **Child Development** *20 students enrolled* • **Computer Installation and Repair Technology/Technician** *1 student enrolled* • **Computer Programming/Programmer, General** *4 students enrolled* • **Corrections** *24 students enrolled* • **Cosmetology/Cosmetologist, General** *31 students enrolled* • **Criminal Justice/Police Science** *31 students enrolled* • **Data Entry/Microcomputer Applications, General** *7 students enrolled* • **Drafting and Design Technology/Technician, General** *1 student enrolled* • **Electrical/Electronics Equipment Installation and Repair, General** *1 student enrolled* • **Emergency Medical Technology/Technician (EMT Paramedic)** • **Fire Science/Firefighting** *11 students enrolled* • **Floriculture/Floristry Operations and Management** • **Hazardous Materials Management and Waste Technology/Technician** • **Human Services, General** *22 students enrolled* • **Insurance** *1 student enrolled* • **Interior Design** *8 students enrolled* • **Landscaping and Groundskeeping** • **Medical Administrative/Executive Assistant and Medical Secretary** *6 students enrolled* • **Office Management and Supervision** *1 student enrolled* • **Real Estate** *2 students enrolled* • **Small Business Administration/Management** *2 students enrolled* • **Welding Technology/Welder** *1 student enrolled*

**STUDENT SERVICES** Academic or career counseling, daycare for children of students, employment services for current students, placement services for program completers, remedial services.

## Sound Master Recording Engineer School-Audio/Video

10747 Magnolia Boulevard, North Hollywood, CA 91601
http://www.soundmasterrecording.com/

**CONTACT** Saleh Younis, Chief Operating Officer
**Telephone:** 626-284-0050

**GENERAL INFORMATION** Private Institution. Founded 1972. **Total program enrollment:** 68. **Application fee:** $75.

**PROGRAM(S) OFFERED**
• **Radio and Television Broadcasting Technology/Technician** *720 hrs./$17,885*

**STUDENT SERVICES** Academic or career counseling, placement services for program completers, remedial services.

## South Baylo University

1126 North Brookhurst Street, Anaheim, CA 92801-1701
http://www.southbaylo.edu/

**CONTACT** Jason Shin, President/CEO
**Telephone:** 714-533-1495

**GENERAL INFORMATION** Private Institution. Founded 1977. **Accreditation:** Acupuncture and Oriental Medicine (ACAOM). **Total program enrollment:** 531. **Application fee:** $100.

**STUDENT SERVICES** Academic or career counseling, employment services for current students, remedial services.

## Southern California Institute of Technology

1900 West Crescent Avenue, Building B, Anaheim, CA 92801
http://www.scitcollege.com/

**CONTACT** Parviz Shams, President
**Telephone:** 714-300-0300

**GENERAL INFORMATION** Private Institution. Founded 1987. **Accreditation:** State accredited or approved. **Total program enrollment:** 604. **Application fee:** $100.

**PROGRAM(S) OFFERED**
• **Accounting** *33 students enrolled* • **Administrative Assistant and Secretarial Science, General** *29 students enrolled* • **Computer Science** • **Electrical, Electronics and Communications Engineering** *10 students enrolled* • **Electrician** *140 students enrolled*

**STUDENT SERVICES** Academic or career counseling, employment services for current students, placement services for program completers.

## Southwestern College

900 Otay Lakes Road, Chula Vista, CA 91910-7299
http://www.swc.edu/

**CONTACT** Raj K. Chopra, Superintendent/President
**Telephone:** 619-482-6550

**GENERAL INFORMATION** Public Institution. Founded 1961. **Accreditation:** Regional (WASC/ACCJC); dental hygiene (ADA); surgical technology (ARCST). **Total program enrollment:** 4860.

**PROGRAM(S) OFFERED**
• **Accounting** *22 students enrolled* • **Administrative Assistant and Secretarial Science, General** *40 students enrolled* • **Architectural Technology/Technician** *2 students enrolled* • **Automobile/Automotive Mechanics Technology/Technician** *5 students enrolled* • **Banking and Financial Support Services** *5 students enrolled* • **Biology Technician/Biotechnology Laboratory Technician** *1 student enrolled* • **Building/Construction Site Management/Manager** *2 students enrolled* • **Building/Home/Construction Inspection/Inspector** *10 students enrolled* • **Business Administration and Management, General** *5 students enrolled* • **Chemical Technology/Technician** *3 students enrolled* • **Child Development** *99 students enrolled* • **Communications Systems Installation and Repair Technology** *1 student enrolled* • **Computer Installation and Repair Technology/Technician** *2 students enrolled* • **Computer Programming/Programmer, General** *2 students enrolled* • **Computer and Information Sciences, General** *1 student enrolled* • **Corrections** *22 students enrolled* • **Criminal Justice/Police Science** *31 students enrolled* • **Data Entry/Microcomputer Applications, General** *1 student enrolled* • **Drafting and Design Technology/Technician, General** *15 students enrolled* • **Electrical/Electronics Equipment Installation and Repair, General** *3 students enrolled* • **Emergency Medical Technology/Technician (EMT Paramedic)** *5 students enrolled* • **Fire Science/Firefighting** *12 students enrolled* • **Geography, Other** *2 students enrolled* • **Graphic Design** *4 students enrolled* • **Hazardous Materials Management and Waste Technology/Technician** *2 students enrolled* • **Industrial Safety Technology/Technician** *4 students enrolled* • **International Business/Trade/Commerce** *1 student enrolled* • **Landscaping and Groundskeeping** *3 students enrolled* • **Language Interpretation and Translation** *6 students enrolled* • **Legal Administrative Assistant/Secretary** *10 students enrolled* • **Legal Assistant/Paralegal** *19 students enrolled* • **Licensed Practical/Vocational Nurse Training (LPN, LVN, Cert, Dipl, AAS)** *19 students enrolled* • **Medical Administrative/Executive Assistant and Medical Secretary** *9 students enrolled* • **Medical Insurance Coding Specialist/Coder** *5 students enrolled* • **Music Management and Merchandising** *2 students enrolled* • **Nurse/Nursing Assistant/Aide and Patient Care Assistant** *2 students enrolled* • **Office Management and Supervision** *10 students enrolled* • **Ornamental Horticulture** *3 students enrolled* • **Public Administration and Social Service Professions, Other** *10 students enrolled* • **Radio and Television** *12 students enrolled* • **Real Estate** *7 students enrolled* • **Sales, Distribution and Marketing Operations, General** *3 students enrolled* • **Small Business Administration/Management** *6 students enrolled* • **Spanish Language and Literature** *3 students enrolled* • **Sport and Fitness Administration/Management** *13 students enrolled* • **Surgical Technology/Technologist** *2 students enrolled* • **System Administration/Administrator** *2 students enrolled* • **Tourism and Travel Services Marketing Operations** *6 students enrolled* • **Transportation and Materials Moving, Other** *10 students enrolled* • **Web Page, Digital/Multimedia and Information Resources Design** *15 students enrolled* • **Web/Multimedia Management and Webmaster** *3 students enrolled*

**STUDENT SERVICES** Academic or career counseling, daycare for children of students, employment services for current students, remedial services.

## Stanbridge College

2041 Business Center Drive, Irvine, CA 92612
http://www.stanbridge.edu/

**CONTACT** Yasith Weerasuriya, Director of Training
**Telephone:** 949-794-9090

**GENERAL INFORMATION** Private Institution. **Total program enrollment:** 151.

**PROGRAM(S) OFFERED**
• **Accounting Technology/Technician and Bookkeeping** *480 hrs./$13,235* • **Accounting** *90 hrs./$27,105* • **Computer and Information Systems Security** *90 hrs./$25,320* • **Information Technology** *17 students enrolled* • **Licensed Practical/Vocational Nurse Training (LPN, LVN, Cert, Dipl, AAS)** *1664 hrs./$27,995* • **System, Networking, and LAN/WAN Management/Manager** *432 hrs./$10,300*

**STUDENT SERVICES** Placement services for program completers.

## State Center Community College District

1525 East Weldon Avenue, Fresno, CA 93704

**CONTACT** Dr. Thomas A. Crow, Chancellor
**Telephone:** 559-226-0720

**GENERAL INFORMATION** Public Institution.

## Summit Career College

1250 East Cooley Drive, Colton, CA 92324
http://www.summitcollege.edu/

**CONTACT** Jay Murvine, Chief Executive Officer
**Telephone:** 909-422-8950

**GENERAL INFORMATION** Private Institution. Founded 1991. **Total program enrollment:** 1696. **Application fee:** $75.

**PROGRAM(S) OFFERED**
• **Administrative Assistant and Secretarial Science, General** *92 students enrolled* • **Dental Assisting/Assistant** *41 hrs./$11,637* • **Legal Assistant/Paralegal** *47 hrs./$10,980* • **Licensed Practical/Vocational Nurse Training (LPN, LVN, Cert, Dipl, AAS)** *1586 hrs./$24,944* • **Massage Therapy/Therapeutic Massage** *45 hrs./$10,948* • **Medical Administrative/Executive Assistant and Medical Secretary** • **Medical Insurance Specialist/Medical Biller** *41 hrs./$11,242* • **Medical/Clinical Assistant** *41 hrs./$11,293*

**STUDENT SERVICES** Employment services for current students, placement services for program completers, remedial services.

## Taft College

29 Emmons Park Drive, Taft, CA 93268-2317
http://www.taftcollege.edu/

**CONTACT** William Duncan, Superintendent-President
**Telephone:** 661-763-7700

**GENERAL INFORMATION** Public Institution. Founded 1922. **Accreditation:** Regional (WASC/ACCJC); dental hygiene (ADA). **Total program enrollment:** 987.

**PROGRAM(S) OFFERED**
• **Accounting** *2 students enrolled* • **Administrative Assistant and Secretarial Science, General** *1 student enrolled* • **Automobile/Automotive Mechanics Technology/Technician** *4 students enrolled* • **Child Development** *22 students enrolled* • **Criminal Justice/Police Science** *1 student enrolled* • **Emergency Medical Technology/Technician (EMT Paramedic)** • **Petroleum Technology/Technician** *2 students enrolled*

**STUDENT SERVICES** Academic or career counseling, daycare for children of students, employment services for current students, placement services for program completers, remedial services.

## TechSkills–Sacramento

1510 Arden Way, Suite 102, Sacramento, CA 95815
http://www.techskills-sac.com/

**GENERAL INFORMATION** Private Institution. **Total program enrollment:** 2. **Application fee:** $100.

**PROGRAM(S) OFFERED**
• **Computer Installation and Repair Technology/Technician** *721 hrs./$8075*
• **Computer Systems Networking and Telecommunications** *750 hrs./$6595*
• **Computer/Information Technology Services Administration and Management, Other** *840 hrs./$11,850* • **Medical Insurance Coding Specialist/Coder** *750 hrs./$8095* • **Medical Transcription/Transcriptionist** *660 hrs./$8095*
• **Pharmacy Technician/Assistant** *750 hrs./$8095*

**STUDENT SERVICES** Placement services for program completers.

## Thanh Le College School of Cosmetology

12875 Chapman Avenue, Garden Grove, CA 92840

**CONTACT** Joanna Chiapparine, Director
**Telephone:** 714-748-7019

**GENERAL INFORMATION** Private Institution. **Total program enrollment:** 25. **Application fee:** $75.

**PROGRAM(S) OFFERED**
• **Aesthetician/Esthetician and Skin Care Specialist** *600 hrs./$3000*
• **Cosmetology and Related Personal Grooming Arts, Other** • **Cosmetology/Cosmetologist, General** *1600 hrs./$10,025* • **Make-Up Artist/Specialist** *8 students enrolled* • **Nail Technician/Specialist and Manicurist** *400 hrs./$700*

**STUDENT SERVICES** Academic or career counseling, employment services for current students, placement services for program completers, remedial services.

## Thuy Princess Beauty College

252 Second Street, Pomona, CA 91766
http://pomonabeautycollege.com/

**CONTACT** Thuy Bich Luu, Owner
**Telephone:** 909-620-6893

**GENERAL INFORMATION** Private Institution. **Total program enrollment:** 50. **Application fee:** $75.

**PROGRAM(S) OFFERED**
• **Aesthetician/Esthetician and Skin Care Specialist** *600 hrs./$3675*
• **Cosmetology, Barber/Styling, and Nail Instructor** *600 hrs./$4275*
• **Cosmetology/Cosmetologist, General** *1600 hrs./$9275* • **Massage Therapy/Therapeutic Massage** *600 hrs./$3675* • **Nail Technician/Specialist and Manicurist** *400 hrs./$975*

**STUDENT SERVICES** Academic or career counseling, employment services for current students, placement services for program completers.

## Trinity Life Bible College

5225 Hillsdale Boulevard, Sacramento, CA 95842
http://www.tlbc.edu/

**CONTACT** Ronald W. Harden, President
**Telephone:** 916-348-4689

**GENERAL INFORMATION** Private Institution. Founded 1974. **Accreditation:** State accredited or approved. **Total program enrollment:** 57. **Application fee:** $50.

**PROGRAM(S) OFFERED**
• **Pastoral Studies/Counseling** *3 students enrolled* • **Pre-Theology/Pre-Ministerial Studies** • **Religious Education** • **Theology and Religious Vocations, Other** *3 students enrolled*

**STUDENT SERVICES** Academic or career counseling.

## Tulare Beauty College

1400 W. Inyo Street, Tulare, CA 93274

**CONTACT** Wendell N. Berke, President
**Telephone:** 559-229-7480

**GENERAL INFORMATION** Private Institution. **Total program enrollment:** 20. **Application fee:** $100.

**PROGRAM(S) OFFERED**
• **Cosmetology/Cosmetologist, General** *1600 hrs./$8812* • **Nail Technician/Specialist and Manicurist** *400 hrs./$2400*

**STUDENT SERVICES** Academic or career counseling, employment services for current students, placement services for program completers.

## United Beauty College

9324 E. Garvey Avenue, South El Monte, CA 91733

**CONTACT** Scott Yang, CEO
**Telephone:** 626-443-0900

**GENERAL INFORMATION** Private Institution. **Total program enrollment:** 67.

**PROGRAM(S) OFFERED**
• **Aesthetician/Esthetician and Skin Care Specialist** *600 hrs./$3075* • **Cosmetology/Cosmetologist, General** *1600 hrs./$8625* • **Massage Therapy/Therapeutic Massage** *600 hrs./$3273* • **Nail Technician/Specialist and Manicurist** *400 hrs./$575*

**STUDENT SERVICES** Academic or career counseling, placement services for program completers.

## United Education Institute

3727 West Sixth Street, Suite 317, Los Angeles, CA 90020

**CONTACT** Fardad Fateri, Chief Executive Officer
**Telephone:** 323-277-8000

**GENERAL INFORMATION** Private Institution. **Total program enrollment:** 2191. **Application fee:** $75.

**PROGRAM(S) OFFERED**
• **Administrative Assistant and Secretarial Science, General** *132 students enrolled* • **Business/Office Automation/Technology/Data Entry** *24 hrs./$13,640* • **Computer Technology/Computer Systems Technology** *24 hrs./$13,640* • **Computer and Information Sciences, General** *186 students enrolled* • **Dental Assisting/Assistant** *24 hrs./$13,640* • **Massage Therapy/Therapeutic Massage** *24 hrs./$13,640* • **Medical Insurance Coding Specialist/Coder** *222 students enrolled* • **Medical Insurance Specialist/Medical Biller** *24 hrs./$13,640* • **Medical/Clinical Assistant** *24 hrs./$13,640* • **Pharmacy Technician/Assistant** *250 students enrolled*

**STUDENT SERVICES** Academic or career counseling, employment services for current students, placement services for program completers.

## Universal College of Beauty

718 West Compton Boulevard, Compton, CA 90220

**CONTACT** Loretta C. Williams, Chief Administrative Officer
**Telephone:** 323-299-1737

**GENERAL INFORMATION** Private Institution. **Total program enrollment:** 62. **Application fee:** $85.

**PROGRAM(S) OFFERED**
• **Cosmetology/Cosmetologist, General** *1600 hrs./$12,870* • **Personal and Culinary Services, Other** *400 hrs./$1276* • **Teacher Education and Professional Development, Specific Levels and Methods, Other** *600 hrs./$3900* • **Teacher Education and Professional Development, Specific Subject Areas, Other** *1 student enrolled*

**STUDENT SERVICES** Academic or career counseling, employment services for current students, placement services for program completers.

## Universal College of Beauty

3419 West 43rd Place, Los Angeles, CA 90008

**CONTACT** John C. Willliams, President
**Telephone:** 323-298-0045

**GENERAL INFORMATION** Private Institution. Founded 1964. **Total program enrollment:** 38. **Application fee:** $80.

**PROGRAM(S) OFFERED**
• **Cosmetology, Barber/Styling, and Nail Instructor** *30 hrs./$3900* • **Cosmetology/Cosmetologist, General** *75 hrs./$12,870* • **Nail Technician/Specialist and Manicurist** *21 hrs./$1276*

**STUDENT SERVICES** Placement services for program completers.

## Universal College of Beauty

8619 South Vermont Avenue, Los Angeles, CA 90044

**CONTACT** John C. Williams, President
**Telephone:** 323-750-5750

**GENERAL INFORMATION** Private Institution. **Total program enrollment:** 25. **Application fee:** $80.

**PROGRAM(S) OFFERED**
• **Cosmetology, Barber/Styling, and Nail Instructor** *30 hrs./$3900* • **Cosmetology/Cosmetologist, General** *75 hrs./$12,870* • **Nail Technician/Specialist and Manicurist** *21 hrs./$1276*

**STUDENT SERVICES** Placement services for program completers.

## Universal Technical Institute of Northern California

4100 Duchhorn Drive, Sacramento, CA 95834
http://www.uticorp.com/

**CONTACT** Ms. Kim Pablo, Campus President
**Telephone:** 916-263-9100

**GENERAL INFORMATION** Private Institution. **Total program enrollment:** 1567.

**PROGRAM(S) OFFERED**
• **Autobody/Collision and Repair Technology/Technician** *125 students enrolled* • **Automobile/Automotive Mechanics Technology/Technician** *85 hrs./$32,725* • **Diesel Mechanics Technology/Technician** *2 students enrolled*

**STUDENT SERVICES** Academic or career counseling, employment services for current students, placement services for program completers.

## Universal Technical Institute of Southern California

11530 6th Street, Suite 110, Rancho Cucamonga, CA 91730
http://www.uticorp.com/

**CONTACT** Michael Fontaine, Campus President
**Telephone:** 909-484-1929

**GENERAL INFORMATION** Private Institution. **Total program enrollment:** 1502.

**PROGRAM(S) OFFERED**
• **Automobile/Automotive Mechanics Technology/Technician** *73 hrs./$28,525*

**STUDENT SERVICES** Academic or career counseling, employment services for current students, placement services for program completers.

## University of California System

1111 Franklin Street, Oakland, CA 94607-5200

**CONTACT** Mark Yudof, President
**Telephone:** 510-987-0700

**GENERAL INFORMATION** Public Institution.

## University of Phoenix–Bay Area Campus

Stoneridge Business Center, Pleasanton, CA 94588-3677
http://www.phoenix.edu/

**CONTACT** William Pepicello, PhD, President
**Telephone:** 877-478-8336

**GENERAL INFORMATION** Private Institution. **Accreditation:** Regional (NCA). **Total program enrollment:** 2344.

**PROGRAM(S) OFFERED**
- **Human Resources Management/Personnel Administration, General** 6 *students enrolled*

**STUDENT SERVICES** Academic or career counseling, remedial services.

## University of Phoenix–Central Valley Campus

45 River Park Place West, Suite 101, Fresno, CA 93720-1562
http://phoenix.edu/

**CONTACT** William Pepicello, PhD, President
**Telephone:** 888-722-0055

**GENERAL INFORMATION** Private Institution. Founded 2004. **Total program enrollment:** 2328.

**STUDENT SERVICES** Academic or career counseling, remedial services.

## University of Phoenix–Sacramento Valley Campus

2890 Gateway Oaks Drive, Suite 200, Sacramento, CA 95833-3632
http://www.phoenix.edu/

**CONTACT** William Pepicello, PhD, President
**Telephone:** 800-266-2107

**GENERAL INFORMATION** Private Institution. Founded 1993. **Accreditation:** Regional (NCA). **Total program enrollment:** 3933.

**PROGRAM(S) OFFERED**
- **Business Administration and Management, General** *1 student enrolled*
- **Human Resources Management/Personnel Administration, General** 7 *students enrolled*

**STUDENT SERVICES** Academic or career counseling, remedial services.

## University of Phoenix–San Diego Campus

3870 Murphy Canyon Road, Suite 210, San Diego, CA 92123
http://www.phoenix.edu/

**CONTACT** William Pepicello, PhD, President
**Telephone:** 800-473-4346

**GENERAL INFORMATION** Private Institution. Founded 1988. **Accreditation:** Regional (NCA). **Total program enrollment:** 3367.

**PROGRAM(S) OFFERED**
- **Business Administration and Management, General** *13 students enrolled*
- **Human Resources Management/Personnel Administration, General** 15 *students enrolled*

**STUDENT SERVICES** Academic or career counseling, remedial services.

## University of Phoenix–Southern California Campus

3150 Bristol Street, Suite 340, Costa Mesa, CA 92626
http://www.phoenix.edu/

**CONTACT** William Pepicello, PhD, President
**Telephone:** 800-888-1968

**GENERAL INFORMATION** Private Institution. Founded 1980. **Accreditation:** Regional (NCA). **Total program enrollment:** 12339.

**PROGRAM(S) OFFERED**
- **Business Administration and Management, General** *4 students enrolled*
- **Human Resources Management/Personnel Administration, General** 14 *students enrolled*

**STUDENT SERVICES** Academic or career counseling, remedial services.

## University of the West

1409 North Walnut Grove Avenue, Rosemead, CA 91770
http://www.uwest.edu/

**CONTACT** Dr. Allen Huang, President
**Telephone:** 626-571-8811 Ext. 119

**GENERAL INFORMATION** Private Institution. Founded 1991. **Accreditation:** Regional (WASC/ACSCU). **Total program enrollment:** 113. **Application fee:** $75.

**PROGRAM(S) OFFERED**
- **Business Administration and Management, General** *1 student enrolled*

**STUDENT SERVICES** Remedial services.

## Vallecitos CET

597 C Street, Hayward, CA 94541

**CONTACT** John Olachea, Executive Director
**Telephone:** 510-537-8400 Ext. 224

**GENERAL INFORMATION** Private Institution. **Total program enrollment:** 39. **Application fee:** $20.

**PROGRAM(S) OFFERED**
- **Building/Property Maintenance and Management** *900 hrs./$7500* • **Computer Software and Media Applications, Other** *930 hrs./$6000* • **Construction Trades, General** *600 hrs./$4350* • **Medical/Clinical Assistant** *900 hrs./$8500* • **Word Processing** *480 hrs./$3000*

**STUDENT SERVICES** Academic or career counseling, employment services for current students, placement services for program completers, remedial services.

## Valley Career College

878 Jackman Street, El Cajon, CA 92020-3057
http://valleycareercollege.com/

**CONTACT** Thomas Mueller, President
**Telephone:** 619-593-5111

**GENERAL INFORMATION** Private Institution. **Total program enrollment:** 373. **Application fee:** $75.

**PROGRAM(S) OFFERED**
- **Business Operations Support and Secretarial Services, Other** *720 hrs./$11,974* • **Computer Technology/Computer Systems Technology** *720 hrs./$12,400* • **Dental Assisting/Assistant** *760 hrs./$12,618* • **Medical Administrative/Executive Assistant and Medical Secretary** *720 hrs./$11,952* • **Medical/Clinical Assistant** *720 hrs./$12,551* • **Pharmacy Technician/Assistant** *720 hrs./$11,954*

**STUDENT SERVICES** Academic or career counseling, employment services for current students, placement services for program completers.

## Valley College of Medical Careers

8399 Topanga Canyon Boulevard, Suite 200, West Hills, CA 91304

**CONTACT** Tim O'Neil, Campus Director
**Telephone:** 818-883-9002

**GENERAL INFORMATION** Private Institution. **Total program enrollment:** 102.

**PROGRAM(S) OFFERED**
• **Medical Insurance Specialist/Medical Biller** *19 students enrolled* • **Medical Office Management/Administration** *720 hrs./$8100* • **Medical/Clinical Assistant** *720 hrs./$8200* • **Nursing, Other** *1560 hrs./$22,150* • **Pharmacy Technician/Assistant** *720 hrs./$8500*

**STUDENT SERVICES** Academic or career counseling, employment services for current students, placement services for program completers.

## Vanguard University of Southern California

55 Fair Drive, Costa Mesa, CA 92626-9601
http://www.vanguard.edu/

**CONTACT** Murray W. Dempster, President
**Telephone:** 714-556-3610

**GENERAL INFORMATION** Private Institution (Affiliated with Assemblies of God). Founded 1920. **Accreditation:** Regional (WASC/ACSCU); athletic training (JRCAT). **Total program enrollment:** 1581. **Application fee:** $45.

**STUDENT SERVICES** Academic or career counseling, employment services for current students, placement services for program completers, remedial services.

## Ventura Adult and Continuing Education

5200 Valentine Road, Ventura, CA 93003
http://tdctraining.com/

**CONTACT** Teresa Johnson, Director/Principal
**Telephone:** 805-289-7925

**GENERAL INFORMATION** Public Institution. Founded 1987. **Total program enrollment:** 120.

**PROGRAM(S) OFFERED**
• **Accounting and Related Services, Other** *4 students enrolled* • **Accounting** *10 students enrolled* • **Administrative Assistant and Secretarial Science, General** *5 students enrolled* • **Business Administration and Management, General** *1190 hrs./$6500* • **Business Administration, Management and Operations, Other** *1 student enrolled* • **Business Operations Support and Secretarial Services, Other** • **Commercial and Advertising Art** *9 students enrolled* • **Computer Installation and Repair Technology/Technician** *1120 hrs./$6250* • **Data Processing and Data Processing Technology/Technician** *1 student enrolled* • **Digital Communication and Media/Multimedia** *1330 hrs./$7584* • **Drafting/Design Engineering Technologies/Technicians, Other** • **Electrical/Electronics Drafting and Electrical/Electronics CAD/CADD** *15 students enrolled* • **Electrical/Electronics Equipment Installation and Repair, General** • **General Office Occupations and Clerical Services** *11 students enrolled* • **Health Information/Medical Records Administration/Administrator** • **Health Information/Medical Records Technology/Technician** *7 students enrolled* • **Human Resources Management and Services, Other** *3 students enrolled* • **Legal Administrative Assistant/Secretary** • **Medical Transcription/Transcriptionist** • **Medical/Clinical Assistant** *1120 hrs./$6000* • **Pharmacy Technician/Assistant** *1 student enrolled* • **Physical Therapist Assistant** *3 students enrolled* • **Prepress/Desktop Publishing and Digital Imaging Design** *1050 hrs./$5700* • **Radio and Television** *6 students enrolled* • **Receptionist** • **System Administration/Administrator** *1330 hrs./$7775*

**STUDENT SERVICES** Academic or career counseling, employment services for current students, placement services for program completers, remedial services.

## Ventura College

4667 Telegraph Road, Ventura, CA 93003-3899
http://www.venturacollege.edu/

**CONTACT** Robin Calote, President
**Telephone:** 805-654-6400

**GENERAL INFORMATION** Public Institution. Founded 1925. **Accreditation:** Regional (WASC/ACCJC). **Total program enrollment:** 4696.

**PROGRAM(S) OFFERED**
• **Accounting** *1 student enrolled* • **Architectural Technology/Technician** *2 students enrolled* • **Art/Art Studies, General** *1 student enrolled* • **Automobile/Automotive Mechanics Technology/Technician** *9 students enrolled* • **Biology Technician/Biotechnology Laboratory Technician** *1 student enrolled* • **Building/Construction Site Management/Manager** *2 students enrolled* • **Business Administration and Management, General** *3 students enrolled* • **Child Development** *15 students enrolled* • **Criminal Justice/Police Science** *1 student enrolled* • **Emergency Medical Technology/Technician (EMT Paramedic)** *16 students enrolled* • **Medical Administrative/Executive Assistant and Medical Secretary** *2 students enrolled* • **Office Management and Supervision** *1 student enrolled* • **Water Quality and Wastewater Treatment Management and Recycling Technology/Technician** *2 students enrolled* • **Welding Technology/Welder** *1 student enrolled*

**STUDENT SERVICES** Academic or career counseling, daycare for children of students, employment services for current students, placement services for program completers, remedial services.

## Ventura County Community College System Office

333 Skyway Drive, Camarillo, CA 93010-8552
http://www.vcccd.net

**CONTACT** James Meznek, Chancellor
**Telephone:** 805-652-5500

**GENERAL INFORMATION** Public Institution.

## Victor Valley Beauty College

16515 Mojave Drive, Victorville, CA 92392
http://www.victorvalleybeautycollege.com/

**CONTACT** Irma Silva, School Administrator
**Telephone:** 760-245-2522

**GENERAL INFORMATION** Private Institution. **Total program enrollment:** 154. **Application fee:** $75.

**PROGRAM(S) OFFERED**
• **Cosmetology/Cosmetologist, General** *1600 hrs./$12,955* • **Nail Technician/Specialist and Manicurist** *400 hrs./$2275*

**STUDENT SERVICES** Academic or career counseling, placement services for program completers.

## Victor Valley College

18422 Bear Valley Road, Victorville, CA 92392-5849
http://www.vvc.edu/

**CONTACT** Dr. Robert M. Silverman, Superintendent President
**Telephone:** 760-245-4271 Ext. 2225

**GENERAL INFORMATION** Public Institution. Founded 1961. **Accreditation:** Regional (WASC/ACCJC). **Total program enrollment:** 2970.

**PROGRAM(S) OFFERED**
• **Accounting** *16 students enrolled* • **Administrative Assistant and Secretarial Science, General** *110 students enrolled* • **Applied Horticulture/Horticultural Operations, General** *20 students enrolled* • **Automobile/Automotive Mechanics Technology/Technician** *23 students enrolled* • **Biology Technician/Biotechnology Laboratory Technician** *1 student enrolled* • **Building/Construction Site Management/Manager** *2 students enrolled* • **Business Administration and Man-**

agement, General *7 students enrolled* • **Child Development** *25 students enrolled* • **Computer Installation and Repair Technology/Technician** *2 students enrolled* • **Construction Trades, General** *8 students enrolled* • **Criminal Justice/Police Science** *204 students enrolled* • **Drafting and Design Technology/Technician, General** *27 students enrolled* • **Electrical/Electronics Equipment Installation and Repair, General** *10 students enrolled* • **Legal Assistant/Paralegal** *6 students enrolled* • **Medical/Clinical Assistant** *5 students enrolled* • **Nursing, Other** *2 students enrolled* • **Real Estate** *8 students enrolled* • **Restaurant, Culinary, and Catering Management/Manager** *4 students enrolled* • **Web/Multimedia Management and Webmaster** *3 students enrolled* • **Welding Technology/Welder** *5 students enrolled*

**STUDENT SERVICES** Academic or career counseling, daycare for children of students, employment services for current students, placement services for program completers, remedial services.

## Video Symphony EnterTraining

266 E. Magnolia Boulevard, Burbank, CA 91502
http://www.videosymphony.com

**CONTACT** R. Andrew Webb, Chief Operations Officer
**Telephone:** 818-557-7200

**GENERAL INFORMATION** Private Institution. **Total program enrollment:** 46.

**PROGRAM(S) OFFERED**
• **Animation, Interactive Technology, Video Graphics and Special Effects** *720 hrs./$19,398* • **Cinematography and Film/Video Production** *720 hrs./$22,261* • **Film/Video and Photographic Arts, Other** *720 hrs./$17,902*

**STUDENT SERVICES** Academic or career counseling, employment services for current students, placement services for program completers.

## Virginia Sewing Machines and School Center

1033 S. Broadway Street, Los Angeles, CA 90015-4001

**CONTACT** Sara Cristi, Director
**Telephone:** 213-747-8292

**GENERAL INFORMATION** Private Institution. **Total program enrollment:** 70. **Application fee:** $75.

**PROGRAM(S) OFFERED**
• **Administrative Assistant and Secretarial Science, General** *24 hrs./$6699* • **Apparel and Textile Manufacture** *24 hrs./$6699* • **Apparel and Textiles, Other** *11 students enrolled* • **Appliance Installation and Repair Technology/Technician** *24 hrs./$6410* • **Fashion/Apparel Design** *24 hrs./$6949* • **Medical/Clinical Assistant** *30 hrs./$8797*

**STUDENT SERVICES** Placement services for program completers.

## Walter J. M.D. Institute, an Educational Center

1930 Wilshire Boulevard, Suite 700, Los Angeles, CA 90057

**CONTACT** Prassana Silva, President/COO
**Telephone:** 213-388-1369

**GENERAL INFORMATION** Private Institution. **Total program enrollment:** 117. **Application fee:** $75.

**PROGRAM(S) OFFERED**
• **Licensed Practical/Vocational Nurse Training (LPN, LVN, Cert, Dipl, AAS)** *79 hrs./$25,835* • **Massage Therapy/Therapeutic Massage** *36 hrs./$10,595* • **Medical/Clinical Assistant** *36 hrs./$10,695* • **Office Management and Supervision** *36 hrs./$9685*

**STUDENT SERVICES** Placement services for program completers.

## West Coast Ultrasound Institute

291 S. La Cienega Boulevard, Suite 500, Beverly Hills, CA 90211
http://wcui.edu/

**CONTACT** Myra Chason, Campus Director
**Telephone:** 310-289-5123

**GENERAL INFORMATION** Private Institution. **Total program enrollment:** 508. **Application fee:** $75.

**PROGRAM(S) OFFERED**
• **Cardiovascular Technology/Technologist** *73 students enrolled* • **Diagnostic Medical Sonography/Sonographer and Ultrasound Technician** *126 students enrolled*

**STUDENT SERVICES** Academic or career counseling, employment services for current students, placement services for program completers.

## Westech College

500 West Mission Boulevard, Pomona, CA 91766-1532
http://www.westech.edu/

**CONTACT** Barry Maleki, Executive Director
**Telephone:** 909-980-4474

**GENERAL INFORMATION** Private Institution. Founded 1988. **Total program enrollment:** 300. **Application fee:** $75.

**PROGRAM(S) OFFERED**
• **Allied Health and Medical Assisting Services, Other** *900 hrs./$12,470* • **CAD/CADD Drafting and/or Design Technology/Technician** *900 hrs./$12,445* • **Drafting and Design Technology/Technician, General** *52 students enrolled* • **Health and Medical Administrative Services, Other** *204 students enrolled* • **Medical Insurance Specialist/Medical Biller** *600 hrs./$7250* • **Office Management and Supervision** *800 hrs./$9815*

**STUDENT SERVICES** Placement services for program completers.

## Western Beauty Institute

13714 Foothill Boulevard, Sylmar, CA 91342
http://wbi.edu/

**CONTACT** Christina Diaz, President Owner
**Telephone:** 818-894-9550

**GENERAL INFORMATION** Private Institution. **Total program enrollment:** 681. **Application fee:** $75.

**PROGRAM(S) OFFERED**
• **Aesthetician/Esthetician and Skin Care Specialist** *600 hrs./$6575* • **Barbering/Barber** *1500 hrs./$10,675* • **Cosmetology/Cosmetologist, General** *1600 hrs./$15,295*

**STUDENT SERVICES** Academic or career counseling, placement services for program completers.

## Western Career College

7301 Greenback Lane, Suite A, Citrus Heights, CA 95621
http://www.westerncollege.edu/california/citrus-heights-vocational-career-college-campus.php

**CONTACT** Jeff Akens, President
**Telephone:** 916-722-8200

**GENERAL INFORMATION** Private Institution. **Total program enrollment:** 739. **Application fee:** $100.

**PROGRAM(S) OFFERED**
• **Allied Health and Medical Assisting Services, Other** *36 hrs./$16,479* • **Criminal Justice/Safety Studies** *60 hrs./$24,066* • **Dental Assisting/Assistant** *36 hrs./$16,092* • **Diagnostic Medical Sonography/Sonographer and Ultrasound Technician** *21 students enrolled* • **Health Information/Medical Records Technology/Technician** *16 students enrolled* • **Massage Therapy/Therapeutic**

*Western Career College (continued)*

**Massage** *31 students enrolled* • **Pharmacy Technician/Assistant** *60 hrs./$24,066* • **Surgical Technology/Technologist** *59 hrs./$32,863* • **Veterinary/Animal Health Technology/Technician and Veterinary Assistant** *53 hrs./$29,253*

**STUDENT SERVICES** Academic or career counseling, employment services for current students, placement services for program completers.

## Western Career College

1400 65th Street, Suite 200, Emeryville, CA 94608
http://www.westerncollege.edu/

**CONTACT** Jeff Akens, President
**Telephone:** 510-601-0133

**GENERAL INFORMATION** Private Institution. Founded 2001. **Accreditation:** State accredited or approved. **Total program enrollment:** 423. **Application fee:** $100.

**PROGRAM(S) OFFERED**

• **Allied Health and Medical Assisting Services, Other** *36 hrs./$16,479* • **Architectural Drafting and Architectural CAD/CADD** *36 hrs./$16,092* • **Biology Technician/Biotechnology Laboratory Technician** • **Computer Graphics** *45 hrs./$20,115* • **Criminal Justice/Safety Studies** *60 hrs./$24,066* • **Drafting and Design Technology/Technician, General** *10 students enrolled* • **Graphic Design** *11 students enrolled* • **Health/Health Care Administration/Management** *18 students enrolled* • **Massage Therapy/Therapeutic Massage** • **Medical Office Assistant/Specialist** *43 students enrolled* • **Medical Office Management/Administration** *36 hrs./$16,092* • **Pharmacy Technician/Assistant** *60 hrs./$24,066*

**STUDENT SERVICES** Academic or career counseling, employment services for current students, placement services for program completers.

## Western Career College

380 Civic Drive, Suite 300, Pleasant Hill, CA 94523
http://www.westerncollege.edu/

**CONTACT** Jeff Akens, President
**Telephone:** 925-609-6650

**GENERAL INFORMATION** Private Institution. Founded 1997. **Accreditation:** Regional (WASC/ACCJC); medical assisting (AAMAE). **Total program enrollment:** 514. **Application fee:** $100.

**PROGRAM(S) OFFERED**

• **Allied Health and Medical Assisting Services, Other** • **Dental Assisting/Assistant** *36 hrs./$16,092* • **Graphic Design** • **Health Information/Medical Records Administration/Administrator** *16 students enrolled* • **Health/Health Care Administration/Management** *22 students enrolled* • **Massage Therapy/Therapeutic Massage** *34 hrs./$14,751* • **Medical/Clinical Assistant** *36 hrs./$16,479* • **Pharmacy Technician/Assistant** *60 hrs./$14,066* • **Respiratory Therapy Technician/Assistant** *96 hrs./$45,132* • **Veterinary/Animal Health Technology/Technician and Veterinary Assistant** *63 hrs./$29,253*

**STUDENT SERVICES** Academic or career counseling, employment services for current students, placement services for program completers.

## Western Career College

8909 Folsom Boulevard, Sacramento, CA 95826
http://www.westerncollege.edu/

**CONTACT** Jeff Akens, President
**Telephone:** 916-361-1660

**GENERAL INFORMATION** Private Institution. Founded 1967. **Accreditation:** Regional (WASC/ACCJC); medical assisting (AAMAE). **Total program enrollment:** 1548. **Application fee:** $100.

**PROGRAM(S) OFFERED**

• **Dental Assisting/Assistant** *36 hrs./$16,092* • **Dental Hygiene/Hygienist** *61 hrs./$51,972* • **Health Professions and Related Clinical Sciences, Other** *4 students enrolled* • **Health and Medical Administrative Services, Other** *25 students enrolled* • **Massage Therapy/Therapeutic Massage** *41 students enrolled* • **Medical/Clinical Assistant** *36 hrs./$16,479* • **Nursing, Other** *65 hrs./$41,470* • **Pharmacy Technician/Assistant** *60 hrs./$24,066* • **Veterinary/Animal Health Technology/Technician and Veterinary Assistant** *63 hrs./$29,253*

**STUDENT SERVICES** Academic or career counseling, employment services for current students, placement services for program completers.

## Western Career College

6201 San Ignacio Boulevard, San Jose, CA 95119
http://www.westerncollege.edu/

**CONTACT** Jeff Akens, President
**Telephone:** 408-360-0840

**GENERAL INFORMATION** Private Institution. Founded 1999. **Accreditation:** State accredited or approved. **Total program enrollment:** 782. **Application fee:** $100.

**PROGRAM(S) OFFERED**

• **Allied Health and Medical Assisting Services, Other** *36 hrs./$16,479* • **Architectural Drafting and Architectural CAD/CADD** *20 students enrolled* • **Computer Graphics** *12 students enrolled* • **Dental Assisting/Assistant** *36 hrs./$16,092* • **Dental Hygiene/Hygienist** *61 hrs./$51,972* • **Massage Therapy/Therapeutic Massage** *18 students enrolled* • **Medical Office Management/Administration** *24 students enrolled* • **Nursing, Other** *65 hrs./$41,470* • **Surgical Technology/Technologist** *59 hrs./$32,863* • **Veterinary/Animal Health Technology/Technician and Veterinary Assistant** *63 hrs./$29,253*

**STUDENT SERVICES** Academic or career counseling, employment services for current students, placement services for program completers, remedial services.

## Western Career College

15555 E. 14th Street, Suite 500, San Leandro, CA 94578
http://www.westerncollege.edu/

**CONTACT** Jeff Akens, President
**Telephone:** 510-276-3888

**GENERAL INFORMATION** Private Institution. Founded 1986. **Accreditation:** Regional (WASC/ACCJC); medical assisting (AAMAE). **Total program enrollment:** 838. **Application fee:** $100.

**PROGRAM(S) OFFERED**

• **Dental Assisting/Assistant** *36 hrs./$16,092* • **Massage Therapy/Therapeutic Massage** *21 students enrolled* • **Medical Administrative/Executive Assistant and Medical Secretary** *60 students enrolled* • **Medical Office Management/Administration** *36 hrs./$16,092* • **Medical/Clinical Assistant** *36 hrs./$16,449* • **Nursing, Other** *65 hrs./$41,470* • **Pharmacy Technician/Assistant** *60 hrs./$24,066* • **Veterinary/Animal Health Technology/Technician and Veterinary Assistant** *63 hrs./$29,253*

**STUDENT SERVICES** Academic or career counseling, employment services for current students, placement services for program completers.

## Western Career College

1313 West Robinhood Drive, Suite B, Stockton, CA 95207
http://www.westerncollege.edu/campus_locations/stockton_campus.html

**CONTACT** Jeff Akens, President
**Telephone:** 209-956-1240

**GENERAL INFORMATION** Private Institution. **Total program enrollment:** 472. **Application fee:** $100.

**PROGRAM(S) OFFERED**

• **Allied Health and Medical Assisting Services, Other** *36 hrs./$16,479* • **Criminal Justice/Safety Studies** *60 hrs./$24,066* • **Health Information/Medical Records Administration/Administrator** *24 students enrolled* • **Massage**

**Therapy/Therapeutic Massage** *33 hrs./$14,751* • **Medical Office Management/Administration** *36 hrs./$16,092* • **Pharmacy Technician/Assistant** *60 hrs./$24,066* • **Veterinary/Animal Health Technology/Technician and Veterinary Assistant** *63 hrs./$29,253*

**STUDENT SERVICES** Academic or career counseling, employment services for current students, placement services for program completers.

## Western Career College

2800 Mitchell Drive, Walnut Creek, CA 94598
http://www.westerncollege.edu/

**CONTACT** Jeff Akens, President
**Telephone:** 925-522-7777

**GENERAL INFORMATION** Private Institution. Founded 1997. **Accreditation:** State accredited or approved. **Total program enrollment:** 685. **Application fee:** $100.

**PROGRAM(S) OFFERED**
• **Allied Health and Medical Assisting Services, Other** *36 hrs./$16,479* • **Criminal Justice/Safety Studies** *60 hrs./$24,066* • **Dental Assisting/Assistant** *36 hrs./$16,092* • **Health/Health Care Administration/Management** *36 hrs./$16,092* • **Massage Therapy/Therapeutic Massage** *55 students enrolled* • **Medical Office Management/Administration** *41 students enrolled* • **Nursing, Other** *65 hrs./$41,470* • **Pharmacy Technician/Assistant** *60 hrs./$24,066*

**STUDENT SERVICES** Academic or career counseling, employment services for current students, placement services for program completers, remedial services.

## West Hills Community College

300 Cherry Lane, Coalinga, CA 93210-1399
http://www.westhillscollege.com/

**CONTACT** Willard Lewallen, President
**Telephone:** 559-934-2000

**GENERAL INFORMATION** Public Institution. Founded 1932. **Accreditation:** Regional (WASC/ACCJC). **Total program enrollment:** 950.

**PROGRAM(S) OFFERED**
• **Administrative Assistant and Secretarial Science, General** *8 students enrolled* • **Agriculture, General** *3 students enrolled* • **Business Administration and Management, General** *2 students enrolled* • **Child Development** *3 students enrolled* • **Data Entry/Microcomputer Applications, General** *7 students enrolled* • **Psychiatric/Mental Health Services Technician** *73 students enrolled* • **Teacher Assistant/Aide** *2 students enrolled*

**STUDENT SERVICES** Academic or career counseling, daycare for children of students, remedial services.

## West Hills Community College District

9900 Cody Street, Coalinga, CA 93210
http://www.westhillscollege.com/

**CONTACT** Frank Gornick, Chancellor
**Telephone:** 559-934-2100

**GENERAL INFORMATION** Public Institution.

## West Hills Community College–Lemoore

555 College Avenue, Lemoore, CA 93245
http://www.westhillscollege.com/

**CONTACT** Don Warkentin, President
**Telephone:** 559-925-3000

**GENERAL INFORMATION** Public Institution. **Total program enrollment:** 1157.

**PROGRAM(S) OFFERED**
• **Accounting** *3 students enrolled* • **Administrative Assistant and Secretarial Science, General** *6 students enrolled* • **Child Development** *25 students enrolled*

**STUDENT SERVICES** Academic or career counseling, daycare for children of students, remedial services.

## West Los Angeles College

9000 Overland Avenue, Culver City, CA 90230-3519
http://www.lacolleges.net/

**CONTACT** Mark W. Rocha, President
**Telephone:** 310-287-4200

**GENERAL INFORMATION** Public Institution. Founded 1969. **Accreditation:** Regional (WASC/ACCJC); dental hygiene (ADA). **Total program enrollment:** 2657.

**PROGRAM(S) OFFERED**
• **Accounting** *4 students enrolled* • **Aircraft Powerplant Technology/Technician** *32 students enrolled* • **Airframe Mechanics and Aircraft Maintenance Technology/Technician** *34 students enrolled* • **Business/Commerce, General** *2 students enrolled* • **Child Development** *8 students enrolled* • **Computer Science** *2 students enrolled* • **Corrections** • **Drama and Dramatics/Theatre Arts, General** *1 student enrolled* • **Film/Cinema Studies** *2 students enrolled* • **Graphic Design** *1 student enrolled* • **Information Technology** *1 student enrolled* • **Legal Assistant/Paralegal** *14 students enrolled* • **Real Estate** *4 students enrolled* • **Substance Abuse/Addiction Counseling** *2 students enrolled* • **System Administration/Administrator** *1 student enrolled* • **Tourism and Travel Services Marketing Operations** *34 students enrolled*

**STUDENT SERVICES** Academic or career counseling, daycare for children of students, employment services for current students, placement services for program completers, remedial services.

## West Valley College

14000 Fruitvale Avenue, Saratoga, CA 95070-5698
http://www.westvalley.edu/

**CONTACT** Philip Hartley, President
**Telephone:** 408-867-2200

**GENERAL INFORMATION** Public Institution. Founded 1963. **Accreditation:** Regional (WASC/ACCJC); interior design: professional (CIDA); medical assisting (AAMAE). **Total program enrollment:** 3489.

**PROGRAM(S) OFFERED**
• **Accounting** *6 students enrolled* • **Administrative Assistant and Secretarial Science, General** *7 students enrolled* • **Advertising** *2 students enrolled* • **Animation, Interactive Technology, Video Graphics and Special Effects** *1 student enrolled* • **Architectural Technology/Technician** *6 students enrolled* • **Business Administration and Management, General** *13 students enrolled* • **Business/Commerce, General** *15 students enrolled* • **Commercial Photography** *2 students enrolled* • **Computer Programming/Programmer, General** *1 student enrolled* • **Digital Communication and Media/Multimedia** *2 students enrolled* • **Drafting and Design Technology/Technician, General** *16 students enrolled* • **Fashion/Apparel Design** *8 students enrolled* • **French Language and Literature** *1 student enrolled* • **Geography, Other** *3 students enrolled* • **Health and Physical Education, General** *2 students enrolled* • **Massage Therapy/Therapeutic Massage** *5 students enrolled* • **Medical/Clinical Assistant** *13 students enrolled* • **Office Management and Supervision** *2 students enrolled* • **Photography** *2 students enrolled* • **Prepress/Desktop Publishing and Digital Imaging Design** *2 students enrolled* • **Retailing and Retail Operations** *2 students enrolled* • **Selling Skills and Sales Operations** *2 students enrolled* • **Spanish Language and Literature** *1 student enrolled*

**STUDENT SERVICES** Academic or career counseling, daycare for children of students, employment services for current students, placement services for program completers, remedial services.

## West Valley-Mission College District

14000 Fruitvale Avenue, Saratoga, CA 95070

**GENERAL INFORMATION** Public Institution.

## William Jessup University

333 Sunset Boulevard, Rocklin, CA 95765
http://www.jessup.edu/

**CONTACT** Bryce Jessup, President
**Telephone:** 916-577-2200

**GENERAL INFORMATION** Private Institution. Founded 1939. **Accreditation:** Regional (WASC/ACSCU); state accredited or approved. **Total program enrollment:** 360. **Application fee:** $35.

**PROGRAM(S) OFFERED**
• **Bible/Biblical Studies** • **Missions/Missionary Studies and Missiology** • **Music, General** • **Pastoral Counseling and Specialized Ministries, Other** • **Religious Education** *2 students enrolled* • **Theology and Religious Vocations, Other** • **Youth Ministry**

**STUDENT SERVICES** Academic or career counseling, employment services for current students, placement services for program completers, remedial services.

## World Mission University

500 Shatto Plaza, Suite 600, Los Angeles, CA 90020
http://www.wmu.edu/

**CONTACT** Dong Sun Lim, President
**Telephone:** 213-385-2322

**GENERAL INFORMATION** Private Institution. **Total program enrollment:** 187. **Application fee:** $50.

**PROGRAM(S) OFFERED**
• **Early Childhood Education and Teaching** *4 students enrolled*

**STUDENT SERVICES** Academic or career counseling.

## WyoTech

200 Whitney Place, Fremont, CA 94539-7663
http://www.wyotech.com/

**CONTACT** Joe Pappaly, President
**Telephone:** 800-248-8585

**GENERAL INFORMATION** Private Institution. Founded 1966. **Accreditation:** State accredited or approved. **Total program enrollment:** 490.

**PROGRAM(S) OFFERED**
• **Automobile/Automotive Mechanics Technology/Technician** *1560 hrs./$32,156* • **Heating, Air Conditioning, Ventilation and Refrigeration Maintenance Technology/Technician (HAC, HACR, HVAC, HVACR)** *600 hrs./$12,776* • **Motorcycle Maintenance and Repair Technology/Technician** *1500 hrs./ $25,245* • **Plumbing Technology/Plumber** *35 students enrolled*

**STUDENT SERVICES** Employment services for current students, placement services for program completers, remedial services.

## WyoTech

980 Riverside Parkway, West Sacramento, CA 95605-1507
http://www.wyotech.com/

**CONTACT** John Hurd, President
**Telephone:** 916-376-8888

**GENERAL INFORMATION** Private Institution. Founded 2003. **Accreditation:** State accredited or approved. **Total program enrollment:** 794.

**PROGRAM(S) OFFERED**
• **Autobody/Collision and Repair Technology/Technician** *1500 hrs./$25,700* • **Automobile/Automotive Mechanics Technology/Technician** *1500 hrs./$25,700* • **Precision Systems Maintenance and Repair Technologies, Other** *1500 hrs./ $25,700*

**STUDENT SERVICES** Employment services for current students, placement services for program completers.

## Yosemite Community College District

PO Box 4065, Modesto, CA 95352-4065
http://www.yosemite.cc.ca.us/

**CONTACT** Dr. Roe Darnell, Chancellor
**Telephone:** 209-575-6550

**GENERAL INFORMATION** Public Institution.

## Yuba College

2088 North Beale Road, Marysville, CA 95901-7699
http://www.yccd.edu/

**CONTACT** Virginia Harrington, Chancellor
**Telephone:** 530-741-6700

**GENERAL INFORMATION** Public Institution. Founded 1927. **Accreditation:** Regional (WASC/ACCJC); radiologic technology: radiography (JRCERT). **Total program enrollment:** 3196.

**PROGRAM(S) OFFERED**
• **Accounting** *12 students enrolled* • **Administrative Assistant and Secretarial Science, General** *28 students enrolled* • **Architectural Drafting and Architectural CAD/CADD** *1 student enrolled* • **Art/Art Studies, General** *1 student enrolled* • **Autobody/Collision and Repair Technology/Technician** *4 students enrolled* • **Automobile/Automotive Mechanics Technology/Technician** *24 students enrolled* • **Business Administration and Management, General** *2 students enrolled* • **Child Development** *88 students enrolled* • **Commercial Photography** *2 students enrolled* • **Cooking and Related Culinary Arts, General** *6 students enrolled* • **Cosmetology/Cosmetologist, General** *56 students enrolled* • **Emergency Medical Technology/Technician (EMT Paramedic)** • **Fire Science/Firefighting** *2 students enrolled* • **Legal Administrative Assistant/ Secretary** *3 students enrolled* • **Medical Administrative/Executive Assistant and Medical Secretary** *4 students enrolled* • **Office Management and Supervision** *4 students enrolled* • **Small Business Administration/Management** *1 student enrolled* • **Substance Abuse/Addiction Counseling** *22 students enrolled* • **Taxation** *7 students enrolled* • **Welding Technology/Welder** *4 students enrolled*

**STUDENT SERVICES** Academic or career counseling, daycare for children of students, employment services for current students, placement services for program completers, remedial services.

# COLORADO

## Academy of Beauty Culture

2992 North Avenue, Grand Junction, CO 81504
http://www.thesalonprofessionalacademy.net/

**CONTACT** Angela Lema, Owner/Director
**Telephone:** 970-245-1110

**GENERAL INFORMATION** Private Institution. Founded 1977. **Total program enrollment:** 73.

**PROGRAM(S) OFFERED**
• **Aesthetician/Esthetician and Skin Care Specialist** *20 hrs./$7990* • **Cosmetology/Cosmetologist, General** *60 hrs./$14,190* • **Nail Technician/ Specialist and Manicurist** *20 hrs./$3990*

**STUDENT SERVICES** Academic or career counseling, placement services for program completers.

## Academy of Natural Therapy

625 8th Avenue, Greeley, CO 80631
http://www.natural-therapy.com

**CONTACT** James Mongan, CEO/Director
**Telephone:** 970-352-1181

**GENERAL INFORMATION** Private Institution. **Total program enrollment:** 54. **Application fee:** $25.

**PROGRAM(S) OFFERED**
• **Massage Therapy/Therapeutic Massage** *1000 hrs./$9000*

**STUDENT SERVICES** Academic or career counseling, employment services for current students, placement services for program completers.

## Aims Community College

Box 69, 5401 West 20th Street, Greeley, CO 80632-0069
http://www.aims.edu/

**CONTACT** Dr. Marilynn Liddell, President
**Telephone:** 970-330-8008

**GENERAL INFORMATION** Public Institution. Founded 1967. **Accreditation:** Regional (NCA); radiologic technology: radiography (JRCERT). **Total program enrollment:** 1814.

**PROGRAM(S) OFFERED**
• **Accounting Technology/Technician and Bookkeeping** *14 students enrolled* • **Allied Health Diagnostic, Intervention, and Treatment Professions, Other** *5 students enrolled* • **Animation, Interactive Technology, Video Graphics and Special Effects** *2 students enrolled* • **Autobody/Collision and Repair Technology/Technician** *16 students enrolled* • **Automobile/Automotive Mechanics Technology/Technician** *40 students enrolled* • **Building/Construction Site Management/Manager** *1 student enrolled* • **Business/Office Automation/Technology/Data Entry** *13 students enrolled* • **Child Development** *18 students enrolled* • **Communications Technology/Technician** *2 students enrolled* • **Criminal Justice/Police Science** *20 students enrolled* • **Emergency Medical Technology/Technician (EMT Paramedic)** *104 students enrolled* • **Engineering Technology, General** *5 students enrolled* • **Fire Science/Firefighting** *74 students enrolled* • **Graphic Communications, General** *6 students enrolled* • **Licensed Practical/Vocational Nurse Training (LPN, LVN, Cert, Dipl, AAS)** *26 students enrolled* • **Management Information Systems, General** *11 students enrolled* • **Marketing/Marketing Management, General** *2 students enrolled* • **Medical Office Management/Administration** *2 students enrolled* • **Medical/Health Management and Clinical Assistant/Specialist** *3 students enrolled* • **Nuclear Medical Technology/Technologist** *3 students enrolled* • **Nurse/Nursing Assistant/Aide and Patient Care Assistant** *295 students enrolled* • **Phlebotomy/Phlebotomist** *57 students enrolled* • **Web Page, Digital/Multimedia and Information Resources Design** *1 student enrolled* • **Welding Technology/Welder** *18 students enrolled*

**STUDENT SERVICES** Academic or career counseling, daycare for children of students, employment services for current students, placement services for program completers, remedial services.

## Anthem College Aurora

350 Blackhawk Street, Aurora, CO 80011
http://www.anthem.edu/locations/anthem-college-aurora/

**CONTACT** Erin Henry, Campus President
**Telephone:** 720-859-7900

**GENERAL INFORMATION** Private Institution. **Accreditation:** State accredited or approved. **Total program enrollment:** 294. **Application fee:** $50.

**PROGRAM(S) OFFERED**
• **Massage Therapy/Therapeutic Massage** *820 hrs./$11,083* • **Medical Insurance Specialist/Medical Biller** *720 hrs./$11,316* • **Medical Radiologic Technology/Science—Radiation Therapist** *970 hrs./$13,424* • **Medical/Clinical Assistant** *746 hrs./$11,550* • **Surgical Technology/Technologist** *1340 hrs./$23,381*

**STUDENT SERVICES** Placement services for program completers.

## Arapahoe Community College

5900 South Santa Fe Drive, PO Box 9002, Littleton, CO 80160-9002
http://www.arapahoe.edu/

**CONTACT** Bert Glandon, President
**Telephone:** 303-797-4222

**GENERAL INFORMATION** Public Institution. Founded 1965. **Accreditation:** Regional (NCA); funeral service (ABFSE); health information technology (AHIMA); medical laboratory technology (NAACLS); physical therapy assisting (APTA). **Total program enrollment:** 2066.

**PROGRAM(S) OFFERED**
• **Allied Health and Medical Assisting Services, Other** *10 students enrolled* • **Architectural Engineering Technology/Technician** *51 students enrolled* • **Automobile/Automotive Mechanics Technology/Technician** *1 student enrolled* • **Banking and Financial Support Services** *3 students enrolled* • **Business Administration and Management, General** *9 students enrolled* • **Business Administration, Management and Operations, Other** *1 student enrolled* • **Carpentry/Carpenter** *3 students enrolled* • **Child Development** *10 students enrolled* • **Computer Engineering Technology/Technician** *55 students enrolled* • **Computer and Information Sciences, General** *1 student enrolled* • **Criminal Justice/Law Enforcement Administration** *2 students enrolled* • **Criminal Justice/Police Science** *64 students enrolled* • **Emergency Medical Technology/Technician (EMT Paramedic)** *100 students enrolled* • **Graphic Design** *1 student enrolled* • **Health Information/Medical Records Technology/Technician** *24 students enrolled* • **Health and Physical Education, General** *4 students enrolled* • **Human Resources Management/Personnel Administration, General** *1 student enrolled* • **Legal Assistant/Paralegal** *35 students enrolled* • **Medical Office Management/Administration** *5 students enrolled* • **Nurse/Nursing Assistant/Aide and Patient Care Assistant** *99 students enrolled* • **Nursing—Registered Nurse Training (RN, ASN, BSN, MSN)** *3 students enrolled* • **Office Management and Supervision** *9 students enrolled* • **Pharmacy Technician/Assistant** *6 students enrolled* • **Phlebotomy/Phlebotomist** *29 students enrolled* • **Real Estate** *12 students enrolled* • **Sales, Distribution and Marketing Operations, General** *3 students enrolled* • **System, Networking, and LAN/WAN Management/Manager** *5 students enrolled* • **Tourism and Travel Services Marketing Operations** *1 student enrolled*

**STUDENT SERVICES** Academic or career counseling, daycare for children of students, employment services for current students, placement services for program completers, remedial services.

## The Art Institute of Colorado

1200 Lincoln Street, Denver, CO 80203
http://www.artinstitutes.edu/denver/

**CONTACT** David C. Zorn, President
**Telephone:** 303-837-0825

**GENERAL INFORMATION** Private Institution. Founded 1952. **Accreditation:** State accredited or approved. **Total program enrollment:** 1407. **Application fee:** $50.

**PROGRAM(S) OFFERED**
• **Baking and Pastry Arts/Baker/Pastry Chef** *4 students enrolled* • **Commercial Photography** *1 student enrolled* • **Culinary Arts/Chef Training** *15 students enrolled* • **Graphic Design** *4 students enrolled* • **Web Page, Digital/Multimedia and Information Resources Design** *4 students enrolled*

**STUDENT SERVICES** Academic or career counseling, employment services for current students, placement services for program completers, remedial services.

## Artistic Beauty Colleges–Arvada

5801 West 44th, Denver, CO 80212
http://artisticbeautycolleges.com/

**CONTACT** Michael Bouman, President/COO
**Telephone:** 570-429-4321 Ext. 2414

**GENERAL INFORMATION** Private Institution. **Total program enrollment:** 52. **Application fee:** $100.

*Artistic Beauty Colleges–Arvada (continued)*

**PROGRAM(S) OFFERED**
• **Aesthetician/Esthetician and Skin Care Specialist** *3 students enrolled* • **Cosmetology/Cosmetologist, General** *60 hrs./$17,266* • **Nail Technician/Specialist and Manicurist** *2 students enrolled*

**STUDENT SERVICES** Academic or career counseling, employment services for current students, placement services for program completers.

## Artistic Beauty Colleges–Aurora

16800 E. Mississippi Avenue, Aurora, CO 80017
http://artisticbeautycolleges.com/

**CONTACT** Michael Bouman, President/COO
**Telephone:** 570-429-4321 Ext. 2414

**GENERAL INFORMATION** Private Institution. **Total program enrollment:** 66. **Application fee:** $100.

**PROGRAM(S) OFFERED**
• **Aesthetician/Esthetician and Skin Care Specialist** • **Cosmetology/Cosmetologist, General** *60 hrs./$17,266* • **Nail Technician/Specialist and Manicurist** *1 student enrolled*

**STUDENT SERVICES** Academic or career counseling, employment services for current students, placement services for program completers.

## Artistic Beauty Colleges–Lakewood

1225 Wadsworth Boulevard, Lakewood, CO 80215
http://artisticbeautycolleges.com/

**CONTACT** Michael Bouman, President/COO
**Telephone:** 570-429-4321 Ext. 2414

**GENERAL INFORMATION** Private Institution. **Total program enrollment:** 73. **Application fee:** $100.

**PROGRAM(S) OFFERED**
• **Aesthetician/Esthetician and Skin Care Specialist** • **Cosmetology/Cosmetologist, General** *60 hrs./$17,266* • **Nail Technician/Specialist and Manicurist**

**STUDENT SERVICES** Academic or career counseling, employment services for current students, placement services for program completers.

## Artistic Beauty Colleges–Littleton

8996 W. Bowles Avenue, # E & F, Littleton, CO 80123
http://artisticbeautycolleges.com/

**CONTACT** Michael Bouman, President/COO
**Telephone:** 570-429-4321 Ext. 2414

**GENERAL INFORMATION** Private Institution. **Total program enrollment:** 56. **Application fee:** $100.

**PROGRAM(S) OFFERED**
• **Aesthetician/Esthetician and Skin Care Specialist** *21 students enrolled* • **Cosmetology/Cosmetologist, General** *60 hrs./$17,266* • **Nail Technician/Specialist and Manicurist**

**STUDENT SERVICES** Academic or career counseling, employment services for current students, placement services for program completers.

## Artistic Beauty Colleges–Thornton

3811 East 120th, Thornton, CO 80229
http://artisticbeautycolleges.com/

**CONTACT** Michael Bouman, President/COO
**Telephone:** 570-429-4321 Ext. 2414

**GENERAL INFORMATION** Private Institution. **Total program enrollment:** 90. **Application fee:** $100.

**PROGRAM(S) OFFERED**
• **Aesthetician/Esthetician and Skin Care Specialist** • **Cosmetology/Cosmetologist, General** *60 hrs./$17,266* • **Nail Technician/Specialist and Manicurist**

**STUDENT SERVICES** Academic or career counseling, employment services for current students, placement services for program completers.

## Artistic Beauty Colleges–Westminster

3049-A West 74th Avenue, Westminster, CO 80030
http://artisticbeautycolleges.com/

**CONTACT** Michael Bouman, President/COO
**Telephone:** 570-429-4321 Ext. 2414

**GENERAL INFORMATION** Private Institution. Founded 1967. **Total program enrollment:** 23. **Application fee:** $100.

**PROGRAM(S) OFFERED**
• **Aesthetician/Esthetician and Skin Care Specialist** *2 students enrolled* • **Cosmetology/Cosmetologist, General** *60 hrs./$17,266* • **Nail Technician/Specialist and Manicurist**

**STUDENT SERVICES** Academic or career counseling, employment services for current students, placement services for program completers.

## Boulder College of Massage Therapy

6255 Longbow Drive, Boulder, CO 80301
http://www.bcmt.org/

**CONTACT** Jan Combs, President
**Telephone:** 303-530-2100 Ext. 100

**GENERAL INFORMATION** Private Institution. Founded 1975. **Accreditation:** State accredited or approved. **Total program enrollment:** 132. **Application fee:** $75.

**PROGRAM(S) OFFERED**
• **Massage Therapy/Therapeutic Massage** *118 students enrolled*

**STUDENT SERVICES** Academic or career counseling.

## Cheeks International Academy of Beauty Culture

4025 South Mason Street, Unit 5, Fort Collins, CO 80525
http://cheeksusa.com/

**CONTACT** Robert M. Stevenson, Financial Aid Administrator
**Telephone:** 970-226-1416

**GENERAL INFORMATION** Private Institution. Founded 1988. **Total program enrollment:** 21. **Application fee:** $100.

**PROGRAM(S) OFFERED**
• **Aesthetician/Esthetician and Skin Care Specialist** *22 hrs./$6900* • **Cosmetology/Cosmetologist, General** *60 hrs./$16,550* • **Hair Styling/Stylist and Hair Design** *40 hrs./$9700* • **Nail Technician/Specialist and Manicurist** *22 hrs./$5400*

**STUDENT SERVICES** Academic or career counseling, placement services for program completers.

## Cheeks International Academy of Beauty Culture

2547b 11th Avenue, Greeley, CO 80631

**CONTACT** Robert M. Stevenson, Financial Aid Administrator
**Telephone:** 970-352-4550

**GENERAL INFORMATION** Private Institution. **Total program enrollment:** 32. **Application fee:** $100.

**PROGRAM(S) OFFERED**
• **Cosmetology/Cosmetologist, General** *60 hrs./$16,550* • **Hair Styling/Stylist and Hair Design** *40 hrs./$9700* • **Nail Technician/Specialist and Manicurist**

**STUDENT SERVICES** Academic or career counseling, placement services for program completers.

## The Colorado Center for Medical Laboratory Science

1719 E. 19th Avenue, Denver, CO 80218
http://www.health1.org/

**CONTACT** Anne Warhover, President
**Telephone:** 303-839-6485

**GENERAL INFORMATION** Private Institution. **Total program enrollment:** 18. **Application fee:** $50.

**PROGRAM(S) OFFERED**
• **Clinical Laboratory Science/Medical Technology/Technologist** *2 students enrolled*

**STUDENT SERVICES** Academic or career counseling, employment services for current students, placement services for program completers.

## Colorado Christian University

8787 West Alameda, Lakewood, CO 80226
http://www.ccu.edu/

**CONTACT** William L. Armstrong, President
**Telephone:** 303-963-3000

**GENERAL INFORMATION** Private Institution. Founded 1914. **Accreditation:** Regional (NCA). **Total program enrollment:** 1566. **Application fee:** $50.

**PROGRAM(S) OFFERED**
• **Accounting** • **Bible/Biblical Studies** *7 students enrolled* • **Early Childhood Education and Teaching** *1 student enrolled* • **Education, Other** • **Elementary Education and Teaching** *13 students enrolled* • **Organizational Behavior Studies** *14 students enrolled* • **Religious/Sacred Music**

**STUDENT SERVICES** Academic or career counseling, employment services for current students, placement services for program completers, remedial services.

## Colorado Heights University

3001 South Federal Boulevard, Denver, CO 80236-2711
http://www.chu.edu/

**CONTACT** Mr. Tony Sanichara, Chief Executive Officer
**Telephone:** 303-937-4200

**GENERAL INFORMATION** Private Institution. Founded 1989. **Accreditation:** State accredited or approved. **Total program enrollment:** 373. **Application fee:** $50.

**STUDENT SERVICES** Academic or career counseling, employment services for current students, placement services for program completers.

## Colorado Mountain College

831 Grand Avenue, Glenwood Springs, CO 81601
http://www.coloradomtn.edu/

**CONTACT** Robert Spuhler, President
**Telephone:** 970-945-8691

**GENERAL INFORMATION** Public Institution. Founded 1965. **Accreditation:** Regional (NCA). **Total program enrollment:** 1218.

**PROGRAM(S) OFFERED**
• **Accounting Technology/Technician and Bookkeeping** *3 students enrolled* • **Business Administration and Management, General** *1 student enrolled* • **Business/Office Automation/Technology/Data Entry** • **Child Development** *7 students enrolled* • **Computer and Information Systems Security** *3 students enrolled* • **Computer/Information Technology Services Administration and Management, Other** *3 students enrolled* • **Criminal Justice/Police Science** *55 students enrolled* • **Culinary Arts/Chef Training** *2 students enrolled* • **Data Entry/Microcomputer Applications, General** *6 students enrolled* • **Electrician** *4 students enrolled* • **Emergency Medical Technology/Technician (EMT Paramedic)** *168 students enrolled* • **Graphic Design** *1 student enrolled* • **Historic Preservation and Conservation** *1 student enrolled* • **Mechanic and Repair Technologies/Technicians, Other** *4 students enrolled* • **Natural Resources/Conservation, General** *1 student enrolled* • **Nurse/Nursing Assistant/Aide and Patient Care Assistant** *27 students enrolled* • **Real Estate** *109 students enrolled* • **Resort Management** *1 student enrolled* • **Tourism and Travel Services Management** *6 students enrolled* • **Veterinary/Animal Health Technology/Technician and Veterinary Assistant** *6 students enrolled* • **Web Page, Digital/Multimedia and Information Resources Design** *1 student enrolled*

**STUDENT SERVICES** Academic or career counseling, employment services for current students, placement services for program completers, remedial services.

## Colorado Northwestern Community College

500 Kennedy Drive, Rangely, CO 81648-3598
http://www.cncc.edu/

**CONTACT** John Boyd, President
**Telephone:** 970-675-2261

**GENERAL INFORMATION** Public Institution. Founded 1962. **Accreditation:** Regional (NCA); dental hygiene (ADA). **Total program enrollment:** 495.

**PROGRAM(S) OFFERED**
• **Accounting** *4 students enrolled* • **Administrative Assistant and Secretarial Science, General** *2 students enrolled* • **Aesthetician/Esthetician and Skin Care Specialist** *3 students enrolled* • **Aircraft Powerplant Technology/Technician** *6 students enrolled* • **Airline/Commercial/Professional Pilot and Flight Crew** *2 students enrolled* • **Cosmetology/Cosmetologist, General** *3 students enrolled* • **Criminal Justice/Law Enforcement Administration** *5 students enrolled* • **Emergency Medical Technology/Technician (EMT Paramedic)** *17 students enrolled* • **Geography, Other** *1 student enrolled* • **Massage Therapy/Therapeutic Massage** *6 students enrolled*

**STUDENT SERVICES** Academic or career counseling, employment services for current students, placement services for program completers, remedial services.

## Colorado School of Healing Arts

7655 West Mississippi Avenue, Suite 100, Lakewood, CO 80226
http://www.csha.net/

**CONTACT** Victoria Steere, Director
**Telephone:** 303-986-2320

**GENERAL INFORMATION** Private Institution. Founded 1986. **Accreditation:** State accredited or approved. **Total program enrollment:** 120. **Application fee:** $50.

**PROGRAM(S) OFFERED**
• **Massage Therapy/Therapeutic Massage** *6 students enrolled*

**STUDENT SERVICES** Academic or career counseling, placement services for program completers.

## Community College of Aurora

16000 East Centre Tech Parkway, Aurora, CO 80011-9036
http://www.ccaurora.edu/

**CONTACT** Linda S. Bowman, President
**Telephone:** 303-360-4700

**GENERAL INFORMATION** Public Institution. Founded 1983. **Accreditation:** Regional (NCA). **Total program enrollment:** 1416.

**PROGRAM(S) OFFERED**
• **Biology Technician/Biotechnology Laboratory Technician** *1 student enrolled* • **Child Development** *14 students enrolled* • **Cinematography and Film/Video Production** *4 students enrolled* • **Criminal Justice/Law Enforcement Administration** *13 students enrolled* • **Fire Science/Firefighting** *34 students enrolled* • **Legal Assistant/Paralegal** *4 students enrolled* • **Management Information Systems, General** *15 students enrolled* • **Manufacturing Technology/Technician** *1 student enrolled* • **Office Management and Supervision** *30 students enrolled* • **Science, Technology and Society** *5 students enrolled*

**STUDENT SERVICES** Academic or career counseling, employment services for current students, placement services for program completers, remedial services.

## Community College of Denver

PO Box 173363, Denver, CO 80217-3363
http://www.ccd.edu/

**CONTACT** Karén Bleeker, President
**Telephone:** 303-556-2600

**GENERAL INFORMATION** Public Institution. Founded 1970. **Accreditation:** Regional (NCA); dental hygiene (ADA); radiologic technology: radiography (JRCERT); surgical technology (ARCST). **Total program enrollment:** 1923.

**PROGRAM(S) OFFERED**
• **Accounting Technology/Technician and Bookkeeping** *2 students enrolled* • **Administrative Assistant and Secretarial Science, General** *5 students enrolled* • **Child Development** *116 students enrolled* • **Computer and Information Sciences, General** *2 students enrolled* • **Drafting and Design Technology/Technician, General** *7 students enrolled* • **Graphic Design** *1 student enrolled* • **Legal Assistant/Paralegal** *7 students enrolled* • **Licensed Practical/Vocational Nurse Training (LPN, LVN, Cert, Dipl, AAS)** *165 students enrolled* • **Machine Shop Technology/Assistant** *1 student enrolled* • **Massage Therapy/Therapeutic Massage** *3 students enrolled* • **Medical/Clinical Assistant** *1 student enrolled* • **Mental Health Counseling/Counselor** *6 students enrolled* • **Nurse/Nursing Assistant/Aide and Patient Care Assistant** *26 students enrolled* • **Security and Loss Prevention Services** *2 students enrolled* • **Technical Theatre/Theatre Design and Technology** *1 student enrolled* • **Welding Technology/Welder** *4 students enrolled*

**STUDENT SERVICES** Academic or career counseling, daycare for children of students, employment services for current students, placement services for program completers, remedial services.

## Concorde Career Institute

770 Grant Street, Denver, CO 80203-3517
http://www.concorde.edu/

**CONTACT** Barbara Kearns, Campus President
**Telephone:** 303-861-1151

**GENERAL INFORMATION** Private Institution. Founded 1966. **Total program enrollment:** 751.

**PROGRAM(S) OFFERED**
• **Dental Assisting/Assistant** *720 hrs./$11,860* • **Health Information/Medical Records Administration/Administrator** *720 hrs./$11,335* • **Health and Medical Administrative Services, Other** *81 students enrolled* • **Licensed Practical/Vocational Nurse Training (LPN, LVN, Cert, Dipl, AAS)** *1563 hrs./$26,450* • **Medical/Clinical Assistant** *720 hrs./$13,768* • **Nursing—Registered Nurse Training (RN, ASN, BSN, MSN)** *1748 hrs./$39,239* • **Respiratory Care Therapy/Therapist** *2 students enrolled* • **Surgical Technology/Technologist** *1220 hrs./$24,592*

**STUDENT SERVICES** Academic or career counseling, employment services for current students, placement services for program completers, remedial services.

## Cuttin' Up Beauty Academy

8101 E. Colfax Avenue, Denver, CO 80220
http://cubacuttinup@aol.com/

**GENERAL INFORMATION** Private Institution. **Total program enrollment:** 19. **Application fee:** $50.

**PROGRAM(S) OFFERED**
• **Aesthetician/Esthetician and Skin Care Specialist** *21 hrs./$4100* • **Barbering/Barber** *50 hrs./$9750* • **Cosmetology/Cosmetologist, General** *60 hrs./$14,100* • **Hair Styling/Stylist and Hair Design** *40 hrs./$8600* • **Nail Technician/Specialist and Manicurist** *21 hrs./$4100*

## Delta-Montrose Area Vocational Technical Center

1765 US Highway 50, Delta, CO 81416
http://www.dmtc.edu/

**CONTACT** Caryn Gibson, Center Manager
**Telephone:** 970-874-7671

**GENERAL INFORMATION** Private Institution. **Total program enrollment:** 81.

**PROGRAM(S) OFFERED**
• **Administrative Assistant and Secretarial Science, General** *60 hrs./$4054* • **Agricultural Mechanization, Other** • **Applied Horticulture/Horticultural Operations, General** *58 hrs./$4077* • **Cosmetology/Cosmetologist, General** *60 hrs./$5492* • **Criminal Justice/Police Science** *32 hrs./$2584* • **Drafting and Design Technology/Technician, General** *60 hrs./$4193* • **Licensed Practical/Vocational Nurse Training (LPN, LVN, Cert, Dipl, AAS)** *46 hrs./$4819*

**STUDENT SERVICES** Academic or career counseling, remedial services.

## Denver Automotive and Diesel College

460 South Lipan Street, Denver, CO 80223-2025
http://www.dadc.com/

**CONTACT** Robert Lantzy, Executive Director
**Telephone:** 303-722-5724

**GENERAL INFORMATION** Private Institution. Founded 1963. **Accreditation:** State accredited or approved. **Total program enrollment:** 915.

**PROGRAM(S) OFFERED**
• **Automobile/Automotive Mechanics Technology/Technician** *58 hrs./$23,676* • **Diesel Mechanics Technology/Technician** *62 hrs./$23,676*

**STUDENT SERVICES** Academic or career counseling, employment services for current students, placement services for program completers, remedial services.

## Emily Griffith Opportunity School

1250 Welton Street, Denver, CO 80204
http://www.egos-school.com/

**CONTACT** Les Lindauer, Executive Director
**Telephone:** 720-423-4700

**GENERAL INFORMATION** Public Institution. **Total program enrollment:** 389.

**PROGRAM(S) OFFERED**

• **Accounting Technology/Technician and Bookkeeping** • **Administrative Assistant and Secretarial Science, General** *2 students enrolled* • **Aesthetician/Esthetician and Skin Care Specialist** *20 students enrolled* • **Aircraft Powerplant Technology/Technician** *18 students enrolled* • **Apparel and Textile Manufacture** *5 students enrolled* • **Autobody/Collision and Repair Technology/Technician** *2 students enrolled* • **Automobile/Automotive Mechanics Technology/Technician** *50 students enrolled* • **Barbering/Barber** *28 students enrolled* • **Cabinetmaking and Millwork/Millwright** • **Carpentry/Carpenter** *59 students enrolled* • **Child Care and Support Services Management** *10 students enrolled* • **Communications Systems Installation and Repair Technology** • **Computer Systems Networking and Telecommunications** *1 student enrolled* • **Concrete Finishing/Concrete Finisher** • **Construction Trades, General** *7 students enrolled* • **Construction Trades, Other** *7 students enrolled* • **Construction/Heavy Equipment/Earthmoving Equipment Operation** • **Cosmetology/Cosmetologist, General** *50 students enrolled* • **Culinary Arts/Chef Training** *17 students enrolled* • **Dental Assisting/Assistant** *17 students enrolled* • **Dental Services and Allied Professions, Other** • **Electrical and Power Transmission Installers, Other** • **Electrical/Electronics Maintenance and Repair Technology, Other** • **Electrician** *811 students enrolled* • **Floriculture/Floristry Operations and Management** *6 students enrolled* • **Glazier** *34 students enrolled* • **Hair Styling/Stylist and Hair Design** *15 students enrolled* • **Health and Physical Education/Fitness, Other** *1 student enrolled* • **Heating, Air Conditioning, Ventilation and Refrigeration Maintenance Technology/Technician (HAC, HACR, HVAC, HVACR)** *15 students enrolled* • **Home Health Aide/Home Attendant** *124 students enrolled* • **Housing and Human Environments, Other** *26 students enrolled* • **Ironworking/Ironworker** *25 students enrolled* • **Licensed Practical/Vocational Nurse Training (LPN, LVN, Cert, Dipl, AAS)** *41 students enrolled* • **Lineworker** *36 students enrolled* • **Mason/Masonry** • **Medical Office Assistant/Specialist** *3 students enrolled* • **Medical Transcription/Transcriptionist** *14 students enrolled* • **Medical/Clinical Assistant** *11 students enrolled* • **Nurse/Nursing Assistant/Aide and Patient Care Assistant** *215 students enrolled* • **Opticianry/Ophthalmic Dispensing Optician** *3 students enrolled* • **Painting/Painter and Wall Coverer** • **Pharmacy Technician/Assistant** *3 students enrolled* • **Pipefitting/Pipefitter and Sprinkler Fitter** *161 students enrolled* • **Plumbing Technology/Plumber** *164 students enrolled* • **Plumbing and Related Water Supply Services, Other** *54 students enrolled* • **Real Estate** *8 students enrolled* • **Restaurant, Culinary, and Catering Management/Manager** *13 students enrolled* • **Science Technologies/Technicians, Other** • **Sheet Metal Technology/Sheetworking** *161 students enrolled* • **Welding Technology/Welder** *4 students enrolled*

**STUDENT SERVICES** Academic or career counseling, employment services for current students, placement services for program completers, remedial services.

## Everest College

14280 East Jewell Avenue, Suite 100, Aurora, CO 80014
http://www.everest.edu/

**CONTACT** Patricia Schlotter, President
**Telephone:** 303-745-6244

**GENERAL INFORMATION** Private Institution. Founded 1989. **Accreditation:** State accredited or approved. **Total program enrollment:** 1078.

**PROGRAM(S) OFFERED**

• **Allied Health and Medical Assisting Services, Other** *96 students enrolled* • **Medical Administrative/Executive Assistant and Medical Secretary** *2 students enrolled* • **Medical Insurance Coding Specialist/Coder** *37 students enrolled* • **Pharmacy Technician/Assistant** *35 students enrolled*

**STUDENT SERVICES** Academic or career counseling, employment services for current students, placement services for program completers.

## Everest College

1815 Jet Wing Drive, Colorado Springs, CO 80916
http://www.everest.edu/

**CONTACT** James Hadley, PhD, President
**Telephone:** 719-638-6580

**GENERAL INFORMATION** Private Institution. Founded 1897. **Accreditation:** Medical assisting (AAMAE); state accredited or approved. **Total program enrollment:** 438.

**PROGRAM(S) OFFERED**

• **Accounting Technology/Technician and Bookkeeping** *1 student enrolled* • **Medical Insurance Specialist/Medical Biller** *50 students enrolled* • **Medical Office Assistant/Specialist** *34 students enrolled*

**STUDENT SERVICES** Academic or career counseling, employment services for current students, placement services for program completers.

## Everest College

9065 Grant Street, Denver, CO 80229-4339
http://www.everest.edu/

**CONTACT** Bruce Pileggi, President
**Telephone:** 303-457-2757

**GENERAL INFORMATION** Private Institution. Founded 1895. **Accreditation:** Medical assisting (AAMAE); state accredited or approved. **Total program enrollment:** 550.

**PROGRAM(S) OFFERED**

• **Business, Management, Marketing, and Related Support Services, Other** *6 students enrolled* • **Criminal Justice/Safety Studies** *4 students enrolled* • **Massage Therapy/Therapeutic Massage** • **Medical Administrative/Executive Assistant and Medical Secretary** *54 students enrolled* • **Medical Insurance Coding Specialist/Coder** *39 students enrolled*

**STUDENT SERVICES** Academic or career counseling, employment services for current students, placement services for program completers, remedial services.

## Front Range Community College

3645 West 112th Avenue, Westminster, CO 80031-2105
http://frcc.cc.co.us/

**CONTACT** Michael Kupcho, Chief Administrative Officer
**Telephone:** 303-466-8811

**GENERAL INFORMATION** Public Institution. Founded 1968. **Accreditation:** Regional (NCA); dental assisting (ADA). **Total program enrollment:** 5582.

**PROGRAM(S) OFFERED**

• **Accounting Technology/Technician and Bookkeeping** *16 students enrolled* • **Administrative Assistant and Secretarial Science, General** *4 students enrolled* • **Animation, Interactive Technology, Video Graphics and Special Effects** *9 students enrolled* • **Applied Horticulture/Horticultural Operations, General** *3 students enrolled* • **Architectural Engineering Technology/Technician** *10 students enrolled* • **Automobile/Automotive Mechanics Technology/Technician** *9 students enrolled* • **CAD/CADD Drafting and/or Design Technology/Technician** *19 students enrolled* • **Child Care and Support Services Management** *46 students enrolled* • **Dental Assisting/Assistant** *14 students enrolled* • **Electrical, Electronic and Communications Engineering Technology/Technician** *5 students enrolled* • **Emergency Medical Technology/Technician (EMT Paramedic)** *419 students enrolled* • **Heating, Air Conditioning and Refrigeration Technology/Technician (ACH/ACR/ACHR/HRAC/HVAC/AC Technology)** *1 student enrolled* • **Homeopathic Medicine/Homeopathy** *6 students enrolled* • **Hospitality Administration/Management, General** *2 students enrolled* • **Information Science/Studies** *12 students enrolled* • **Interior Design** *1 student enrolled* • **Legal Assistant/Paralegal** *6 students enrolled* • **Licensed Practical/Vocational Nurse Training (LPN, LVN, Cert, Dipl, AAS)** *5 students enrolled* • **Machine Shop Technology/Assistant** *3 students enrolled* • **Management Information Systems, General** *50 students enrolled* • **Medical Office Assistant/Specialist** *8 students enrolled* • **Nurse/Nursing Assistant/Aide and Patient Care Assistant** *502 students enrolled* • **Office Management and Supervision** *16 students enrolled* • **Pharmacy Technician/Assistant** *22 students enrolled* • **Phlebotomy/Phlebotomist** *13 students enrolled* • **Teacher Assistant/Aide** *5 students enrolled* • **Teaching English as a Second or Foreign Language/ESL Language Instructor** *5 students enrolled* • **Welding Technology/Welder** *32 students enrolled* • **Wildlife and Wildlands Science and Management** *12 students enrolled*

**STUDENT SERVICES** Academic or career counseling, daycare for children of students, employment services for current students, placement services for program completers, remedial services.

## Glenwood Beauty Academy

51241 Highway 6 and 24, Suite 1, Glenwood Springs, CO 81601

**CONTACT** Karen Fiolkoski, President
**Telephone:** 970-945-0485

**GENERAL INFORMATION** Private Institution. Founded 1982. **Total program enrollment:** 21.

**PROGRAM(S) OFFERED**
• **Aesthetician/Esthetician and Skin Care Specialist** *600 hrs./$7859* • **Barbering/Barber** • **Cosmetology/Cosmetologist, General** *60 hrs./$9904* • **Hair Styling/Stylist and Hair Design** *40 hrs./$7500* • **Nail Technician/Specialist and Manicurist** *600 hrs./$6785*

**STUDENT SERVICES** Academic or career counseling, placement services for program completers.

## Hair Dynamics Education Center

6464 South College, Ft. Collins, CO 80525

**CONTACT** Tina Matuska, Owner
**Telephone:** 970-223-9943

**GENERAL INFORMATION** Private Institution. **Total program enrollment:** 195. **Application fee:** $100.

**PROGRAM(S) OFFERED**
• **Aesthetician/Esthetician and Skin Care Specialist** *21 hrs./$6640* • **Cosmetology/Cosmetologist, General** *60 hrs./$17,320* • **Hair Styling/Stylist and Hair Design** *40 hrs./$9020* • **Nail Technician/Specialist and Manicurist** *21 hrs./$4560*

**STUDENT SERVICES** Placement services for program completers.

## Heritage College

12 Lakeside Lane, Denver, CO 80212-7413
http://www.heritage-education.com/

**CONTACT** Jennifer Sprague, School Director
**Telephone:** 303-477-7240

**GENERAL INFORMATION** Private Institution. Founded 1986. **Accreditation:** State accredited or approved. **Total program enrollment:** 695.

**PROGRAM(S) OFFERED**
• **Aesthetician/Esthetician and Skin Care Specialist** *95 hrs./$20,336* • **Allied Health and Medical Assisting Services, Other** *100 hrs./$22,850* • **Health and Physical Education, General** *96 hrs./$20,953* • **Health and Physical Education/Fitness, Other** *95 hrs./$19,005* • **Massage Therapy/Therapeutic Massage** • **Medical/Clinical Assistant** • **Pharmacy Technician/Assistant** *54 hrs./$12,053*

**STUDENT SERVICES** Academic or career counseling, employment services for current students, placement services for program completers.

## Institute of Business & Medical Careers

1609 Oakridge Drive, Suite 102, Fort Collins, CO 80525
http://www.ibmcedu.com/

**CONTACT** Richard B. Laub, CEO
**Telephone:** 970-223-2669

**GENERAL INFORMATION** Private Institution. Founded 1987. **Accreditation:** State accredited or approved. **Total program enrollment:** 393. **Application fee:** $75.

**PROGRAM(S) OFFERED**
• **Accounting Technology/Technician and Bookkeeping** • **Administrative Assistant and Secretarial Science, General** • **Computer/Information Technology Services Administration and Management, Other** • **Massage Therapy/Therapeutic Massage** *42 students enrolled* • **Medical Administrative/Executive Assistant and Medical Secretary** *2 students enrolled* • **Medical/Clinical Assistant** *19 students enrolled*

**STUDENT SERVICES** Academic or career counseling, employment services for current students, placement services for program completers.

## IntelliTec College

772 Horizon Drive, Grand Junction, CO 81506
http://www.intelliteccollege.edu/

**CONTACT** Ed Kraus, Executive Director
**Telephone:** 970-245-8101

**GENERAL INFORMATION** Private Institution. **Accreditation:** State accredited or approved. **Total program enrollment:** 744.

**PROGRAM(S) OFFERED**
• **Accounting and Business/Management** *96 hrs./$19,390* • **Architectural Drafting and Architectural CAD/CADD** *110 hrs./$23,158* • **Automobile/Automotive Mechanics Technology/Technician** *93 hrs./$18,738* • **Dental Assisting/Assistant** *19 students enrolled* • **Massage Therapy/Therapeutic Massage** *73 hrs./$14,800* • **Mechanical Drafting and Mechanical Drafting CAD/CADD** *110 hrs./$22,125* • **Medical Insurance Coding Specialist/Coder** *11 students enrolled* • **Medical/Clinical Assistant** *91 hrs./$18,315*

**STUDENT SERVICES** Academic or career counseling, employment services for current students, placement services for program completers, remedial services.

## IntelliTec Medical Institute

2345 North Academy Boulevard, Colorado Springs, CO 80909
http://www.intelliteccollege.edu/

**CONTACT** Mary A. Jefferson, Campus Director
**Telephone:** 719-596-7400

**GENERAL INFORMATION** Private Institution. Founded 1966. **Accreditation:** State accredited or approved. **Total program enrollment:** 301.

**PROGRAM(S) OFFERED**
• **Clinical/Medical Laboratory Technician** *126 hrs./$22,880* • **Dental Assisting/Assistant** *1020 hrs./$12,573* • **Massage Therapy/Therapeutic Massage** *92 hrs./$16,425* • **Medical Administrative/Executive Assistant and Medical Secretary** *92 hrs./$16,870* • **Medical/Clinical Assistant** *92 hrs./$19,378* • **Pharmacy Technician/Assistant** *2 students enrolled*

**STUDENT SERVICES** Academic or career counseling, employment services for current students, placement services for program completers.

## International Beauty Academy

1360 North Academy Boulevard, Colorado Springs, CO 80909
http://www.csbeautyschools.com/

**CONTACT** Thomas J. Twardowski, President
**Telephone:** 719-597-1413

**GENERAL INFORMATION** Private Institution. Founded 1971. **Total program enrollment:** 166.

**PROGRAM(S) OFFERED**
• **Aesthetician/Esthetician and Skin Care Specialist** *21 hrs./$5203* • **Barbering/Barber** *50 hrs./$11,600* • **Cosmetology/Cosmetologist, General** *60 hrs./$15,770* • **Hair Styling/Stylist and Hair Design** *40 hrs./$9300* • **Massage Therapy/Therapeutic Massage** *40 hrs./$9820* • **Nail Technician/Specialist and Manicurist** *20 hrs./$5200*

**STUDENT SERVICES** Academic or career counseling, placement services for program completers.

## Kaplan College–Denver Campus

500 East 84th Avenue, Suite W-200, Thornton, CO 80229
http://www.kc-denver.com

**CONTACT** Todd Smith, Executive Director
**Telephone:** 303-295-0550

**GENERAL INFORMATION** Private Institution. Founded 1977. **Accreditation:** State accredited or approved. **Total program enrollment:** 365.

PROGRAM(S) OFFERED

• **Allied Health and Medical Assisting Services, Other** *47 hrs./$14,581* • **Corrections and Criminal Justice, Other** *99 hrs./$33,838* • **Legal Assistant/Paralegal** *45 hrs./$13,858* • **Massage Therapy/Therapeutic Massage** *2 students enrolled* • **Medical Office Assistant/Specialist** *51 hrs./$14,431* • **Medical/Clinical Assistant** *77 students enrolled* • **Pharmacy Technician/Assistant** *53 hrs./$14,431*

**STUDENT SERVICES** Academic or career counseling, employment services for current students, placement services for program completers, remedial services.

## Lamar Community College

2401 South Main Street, Lamar, CO 81052-3999
http://www.lamarcc.edu/

**CONTACT** John Marrin, President
**Telephone:** 719-336-2248

**GENERAL INFORMATION** Public Institution. Founded 1937. **Accreditation:** Regional (NCA). **Total program enrollment:** 459.

**PROGRAM(S) OFFERED**

• **Cosmetology/Cosmetologist, General** *1 student enrolled* • **Licensed Practical/Vocational Nurse Training (LPN, LVN, Cert, Dipl, AAS)** *10 students enrolled* • **Small Business Administration/Management** *24 students enrolled*

**STUDENT SERVICES** Academic or career counseling, employment services for current students, placement services for program completers, remedial services.

## Massage Therapy Institute of Colorado

1441 York Street, Suite 301, Denver, CO 80206
http://www.mtic.edu/

**CONTACT** Elia Fisher, Chief Administrator
**Telephone:** 303-329-6345

**GENERAL INFORMATION** Private Institution. Founded 1986. **Application fee:** $25.

**PROGRAM(S) OFFERED**

• **Massage Therapy/Therapeutic Massage** *616 hrs.*

**STUDENT SERVICES** Employment services for current students.

## Mesa State College

1100 North Avenue, Grand Junction, CO 81501-3122
http://www.mesastate.edu/

**CONTACT** Timothy E. Foster, President
**Telephone:** 970-248-1020

**GENERAL INFORMATION** Public Institution. Founded 1925. **Accreditation:** Regional (NCA); radiologic technology: radiography (JRCERT). **Total program enrollment:** 4391. **Application fee:** $30.

**PROGRAM(S) OFFERED**

• **Automobile/Automotive Mechanics Technology/Technician** *2 students enrolled* • **Cartography** *10 students enrolled* • **Cooking and Related Culinary Arts, General** *3 students enrolled* • **Criminal Justice/Police Science** *46 students enrolled* • **Licensed Practical/Vocational Nurse Training (LPN, LVN, Cert, Dipl, AAS)** *27 students enrolled* • **Lineworker** *24 students enrolled* • **Machine Tool Technology/Machinist** *25 students enrolled* • **Office Management and Supervision** *10 students enrolled*

**STUDENT SERVICES** Academic or career counseling, daycare for children of students, employment services for current students, placement services for program completers, remedial services.

## Montessori Centre International Denver

9351 E. Arbor Drive, Greenwood Village, CO 80111

**CONTACT** Punum Bhatia, Director
**Telephone:** 303-523-7590

**GENERAL INFORMATION** Private Institution. **Total program enrollment:** 20. **Application fee:** $50.

**PROGRAM(S) OFFERED**

• **Early Childhood Education and Teaching** *720 hrs./$5600*

**STUDENT SERVICES** Academic or career counseling.

## Montessori Education Center of the Rockies

3300 Redstone Road, Boulder, CO 80305
http://www.mecr.edu/

**CONTACT** Dorothy Thompson, Director
**Telephone:** 303-494-3002

**GENERAL INFORMATION** Private Institution. **Total program enrollment:** 75. **Application fee:** $100.

**PROGRAM(S) OFFERED**

• **Montessori Teacher Education** *610 hrs./$5100*

**STUDENT SERVICES** Academic or career counseling, employment services for current students, placement services for program completers.

## Morgan Community College

920 Barlow Road, Fort Morgan, CO 80701-4399
http://www.morgancc.edu/

**CONTACT** Kerry Hart, President
**Telephone:** 970-542-3100

**GENERAL INFORMATION** Public Institution. Founded 1967. **Accreditation:** Regional (NCA); physical therapy assisting (APTA). **Total program enrollment:** 381.

**PROGRAM(S) OFFERED**

• **Agribusiness/Agricultural Business Operations** *8 students enrolled* • **Agricultural Business Technology** *26 students enrolled* • **Agricultural/Farm Supplies Retailing and Wholesaling** *18 students enrolled* • **Animation, Interactive Technology, Video Graphics and Special Effects** *1 student enrolled* • **Automobile/Automotive Mechanics Technology/Technician** *5 students enrolled* • **Business Administration and Management, General** *2 students enrolled* • **Child Development** *4 students enrolled* • **Construction Trades, Other** *12 students enrolled* • **Emergency Medical Technology/Technician (EMT Paramedic)** *66 students enrolled* • **Entrepreneurship/Entrepreneurial Studies** *1 student enrolled* • **Farm/Farm and Ranch Management** *9 students enrolled* • **Health Aide** *5 students enrolled* • **Licensed Practical/Vocational Nurse Training (LPN, LVN, Cert, Dipl, AAS)** *32 students enrolled* • **Massage Therapy/Therapeutic Massage** *3 students enrolled* • **Medical/Clinical Assistant** *2 students enrolled* • **Nurse/Nursing Assistant/Aide and Patient Care Assistant** *88 students enrolled* • **Phlebotomy/Phlebotomist** *5 students enrolled* • **Welding Technology/Welder** *3 students enrolled*

**STUDENT SERVICES** Academic or career counseling, placement services for program completers, remedial services.

## Naropa University

2130 Arapahoe Avenue, Boulder, CO 80302-6697
http://www.naropa.edu/

**CONTACT** Thomas B. Coburn, President
**Telephone:** 303-444-0202

**GENERAL INFORMATION** Private Institution. Founded 1974. **Accreditation:** Regional (NCA). **Total program enrollment:** 794. **Application fee:** $50.

*Naropa University (continued)*

**PROGRAM(S) OFFERED**

• **Music, General**

**STUDENT SERVICES** Academic or career counseling, employment services for current students, placement services for program completers.

## Nazarene Bible College

1111 Academy Park Loop, Colorado Springs, CO 80910-3704
http://www.nbc.edu/

**CONTACT** Harold B. Graves, President
**Telephone:** 719-884-5000

**GENERAL INFORMATION** Private Institution (Affiliated with Church of the Nazarene). Founded 1967. **Accreditation:** State accredited or approved. **Total program enrollment:** 178.

**PROGRAM(S) OFFERED**

• **Pastoral Counseling and Specialized Ministries, Other** • **Religious/Sacred Music**

**STUDENT SERVICES** Academic or career counseling, daycare for children of students, employment services for current students, placement services for program completers, remedial services.

## Northeastern Junior College

100 College Avenue, Sterling, CO 80751-2399
http://www.njc.edu/

**CONTACT** Lance Bolton, PhD, President
**Telephone:** 970-521-6600

**GENERAL INFORMATION** Public Institution. Founded 1941. **Accreditation:** Regional (NCA). **Total program enrollment:** 910.

**PROGRAM(S) OFFERED**

• **Agricultural Business Technology** *11 students enrolled* • **Agricultural/Farm Supplies Retailing and Wholesaling** *5 students enrolled* • **Applied Horticulture/Horticultural Operations, General** *1 student enrolled* • **Cosmetology/Cosmetologist, General** *17 students enrolled* • **Emergency Medical Technology/Technician (EMT Paramedic)** *18 students enrolled* • **Licensed Practical/Vocational Nurse Training (LPN, LVN, Cert, Dipl, AAS)** *4 students enrolled*

**STUDENT SERVICES** Academic or career counseling, remedial services.

## Ohio Center for Broadcasting–Colorado Campus

1310 Wadsworth Boulevard, Suite 100, Lakewood, CO 80214
http://www.beonair.com/

**CONTACT** Robert Mills, President
**Telephone:** 303-937-7070

**GENERAL INFORMATION** Private Institution. **Total program enrollment:** 160. **Application fee:** $125.

**PROGRAM(S) OFFERED**

• **Radio and Television Broadcasting Technology/Technician** *111 students enrolled* • **Radio and Television** *36 hrs./$14,889*

**STUDENT SERVICES** Academic or career counseling, employment services for current students, placement services for program completers, remedial services.

## Otero Junior College

1802 Colorado Avenue, La Junta, CO 81050-3415
http://www.ojc.edu/

**CONTACT** Jim Rizzuto, President
**Telephone:** 719-384-6831

**GENERAL INFORMATION** Public Institution. Founded 1941. **Accreditation:** Regional (NCA). **Total program enrollment:** 802.

**PROGRAM(S) OFFERED**

• **Agribusiness/Agricultural Business Operations** *6 students enrolled* • **Agricultural Business Technology** *8 students enrolled* • **Agricultural/Farm Supplies Retailing and Wholesaling** *43 students enrolled* • **Automobile/Automotive Mechanics Technology/Technician** *48 students enrolled* • **Business Administration and Management, General** *1 student enrolled* • **Business/Office Automation/Technology/Data Entry** *1 student enrolled* • **Child Development** *9 students enrolled* • **Computer and Information Sciences, General** *7 students enrolled* • **Cosmetology/Cosmetologist, General** *6 students enrolled* • **Criminal Justice/Police Science** *21 students enrolled* • **Emergency Medical Technology/Technician (EMT Paramedic)** *12 students enrolled* • **Farm/Farm and Ranch Management** *7 students enrolled* • **Licensed Practical/Vocational Nurse Training (LPN, LVN, Cert, Dipl, AAS)** *22 students enrolled* • **Massage Therapy/Therapeutic Massage** *2 students enrolled* • **Nurse/Nursing Assistant/Aide and Patient Care Assistant** *36 students enrolled* • **Small Business Administration/Management** *16 students enrolled*

**STUDENT SERVICES** Academic or career counseling, employment services for current students, remedial services.

## Pickens Technical College

500 Airport Boulevard, Aurora, CO 80011
http://www.pickenstech.org/

**CONTACT** Dean Stecklein, Executive Director
**Telephone:** 303-344-4910 Ext. 27734

**GENERAL INFORMATION** Public Institution. Founded 1970. **Total program enrollment:** 884.

**PROGRAM(S) OFFERED**

• **Administrative Assistant and Secretarial Science, General** *28 students enrolled* • **Aesthetician/Esthetician and Skin Care Specialist** *27 students enrolled* • **Applied Horticulture/Horticultural Operations, General** *35 students enrolled* • **Autobody/Collision and Repair Technology/Technician** *12 students enrolled* • **Automobile/Automotive Mechanics Technology/Technician** *48 students enrolled* • **Barbering/Barber** *12 students enrolled* • **Building/Property Maintenance and Management** *22 students enrolled* • **CAD/CADD Drafting and/or Design Technology/Technician** *68 students enrolled* • **Cabinetmaking and Millwork/Millwright** *6 students enrolled* • **Carpentry/Carpenter** *9 students enrolled* • **Commercial and Advertising Art** *28 students enrolled* • **Computer Installation and Repair Technology/Technician** *96 students enrolled* • **Cosmetology/Cosmetologist, General** *29 students enrolled* • **Dental Assisting/Assistant** *18 students enrolled* • **Diesel Mechanics Technology/Technician** *13 students enrolled* • **Electrician** *17 students enrolled* • **Hair Styling/Stylist and Hair Design** *15 students enrolled* • **Heating, Air Conditioning and Refrigeration Technology/Technician (ACH/ACR/ACHR/HRAC/HVAC/AC Technology)** *48 students enrolled* • **Licensed Practical/Vocational Nurse Training (LPN, LVN, Cert, Dipl, AAS)** *36 students enrolled* • **Machine Shop Technology/Assistant** *13 students enrolled* • **Nail Technician/Specialist and Manicurist** *15 students enrolled* • **Natural Resources Management/Development** *20 students enrolled* • **Photography** *39 students enrolled* • **Respiratory Care Therapy/Therapist** *11 students enrolled* • **Small Engine Mechanics and Repair Technology/Technician** *6 students enrolled* • **Welding Technology/Welder** *52 students enrolled*

**STUDENT SERVICES** Academic or career counseling, employment services for current students.

## Pikes Peak Community College

5675 South Academy Boulevard, Colorado Springs, CO 80906-5498
http://www.ppcc.edu/

**CONTACT** Dr. Tony Kinkel, President
**Telephone:** 719-502-2000

**GENERAL INFORMATION** Public Institution. Founded 1968. **Accreditation:** Regional (NCA); dental assisting (ADA). **Total program enrollment:** 4401.

**PROGRAM(S) OFFERED**

• **Accounting Technology/Technician and Bookkeeping** *1 student enrolled* • **Animation, Interactive Technology, Video Graphics and Special Effects** *15* students enrolled • **Architectural Engineering Technology/Technician** *14 students enrolled* • **Autobody/Collision and Repair Technology/Technician** *13 students enrolled* • **Automobile/Automotive Mechanics Technology/Technician** *16 students enrolled* • **Building/Construction Finishing, Management, and Inspection, Other** *13 students enrolled* • **CAD/CADD Drafting and/or Design Technology/Technician** *32 students enrolled* • **Child Development** *11 students enrolled* • **Computer Systems Networking and Telecommunications** *1 student enrolled* • **Computer/Information Technology Services Administration and Management, Other** *12 students enrolled* • **Cooking and Related Culinary Arts, General** *17 students enrolled* • **Criminal Justice/Law Enforcement Administration** *4 students enrolled* • **Criminal Justice/Police Science** *21 students enrolled* • **Dental Assisting/Assistant** *3 students enrolled* • **Emergency Medical Technology/Technician (EMT Paramedic)** *269 students enrolled* • **Fire Science/Firefighting** *19 students enrolled* • **International Business/Trade/Commerce** *3 students enrolled* • **Legal Assistant/Paralegal** *2 students enrolled* • **Medical Office Management/Administration** *27 students enrolled* • **Nursing—Registered Nurse Training (RN, ASN, BSN, MSN)** *118 students enrolled* • **Office Management and Supervision** *1 student enrolled* • **Pharmacy Technician/Assistant** *5 students enrolled* • **Phlebotomy/Phlebotomist** *26 students enrolled* • **Radio and Television Broadcasting Technology/Technician** *5 students enrolled* • **Security and Protective Services, Other** *1 student enrolled* • **Sign Language Interpretation and Translation** *12 students enrolled* • **Welding Technology/Welder** *2 students enrolled*

**STUDENT SERVICES** Academic or career counseling, daycare for children of students, employment services for current students, placement services for program completers, remedial services.

## Pima Medical Institute

370 Printer Parkway, Colorado Springs, CO 80910
http://www.pmi.edu/

**CONTACT** Sam Pedregon, Campus Director
**Telephone:** 719-482-7462

**GENERAL INFORMATION** Private Institution. Founded 2002. **Total program enrollment:** 536.

**PROGRAM(S) OFFERED**
• **Dental Assisting/Assistant** *720 hrs./$9530* • **Dental Services and Allied Professions, Other** *45 hrs./$1500* • **Medical Administrative/Executive Assistant and Medical Secretary** *560 hrs./$6430* • **Medical/Clinical Assistant** *800 hrs./$9995* • **Pharmacy Technician/Assistant** *800 hrs./$9380* • **Veterinary/Animal Health Technology/Technician and Veterinary Assistant** *720 hrs./$9380*

**STUDENT SERVICES** Academic or career counseling, employment services for current students, placement services for program completers, remedial services.

## Pima Medical Institute

1701 West 72nd Avenue, Suite 130, Denver, CO 80221
http://www.pmi.edu/

**CONTACT** Susan Anderson, Campus Director
**Telephone:** 303-426-1800

**GENERAL INFORMATION** Private Institution. Founded 1988. **Accreditation:** Radiologic technology: radiography (JRCERT); respiratory therapy technology (CoARC); state accredited or approved. **Total program enrollment:** 809.

**PROGRAM(S) OFFERED**
• **Dental Assisting/Assistant** *720 hrs./$9530* • **Dental Services and Allied Professions, Other** *31 students enrolled* • **Medical Administrative/Executive Assistant and Medical Secretary** *560 hrs./$6430* • **Medical/Clinical Assistant** *800 hrs./$9995* • **Pharmacy Technician/Assistant** *800 hrs./$9380* • **Phlebotomy/Phlebotomist** *300 hrs./$2900* • **Veterinary/Animal Health Technology/Technician and Veterinary Assistant** *720 hrs./$9380*

**STUDENT SERVICES** Academic or career counseling, employment services for current students, placement services for program completers, remedial services.

## Pueblo Community College

900 West Orman Avenue, Pueblo, CO 81004-1499
http://www.pueblocc.edu/

**CONTACT** Dr. John D. Garvin, President
**Telephone:** 719-549-3200

**GENERAL INFORMATION** Public Institution. Founded 1933. **Accreditation:** Regional (NCA); dental assisting (ADA); dental hygiene (ADA); emergency medical services (JRCEMTP); ophthalmic medical technology (JCAHPO); physical therapy assisting (APTA). **Total program enrollment:** 1976.

**PROGRAM(S) OFFERED**
• **Airline/Commercial/Professional Pilot and Flight Crew** *1 student enrolled* • **Animation, Interactive Technology, Video Graphics and Special Effects** *1 student enrolled* • **Autobody/Collision and Repair Technology/Technician** *5 students enrolled* • **Automobile/Automotive Mechanics Technology/Technician** *4 students enrolled* • **Business Administration and Management, General** *2 students enrolled* • **Business/Office Automation/Technology/Data Entry** *3 students enrolled* • **Child Development** *12 students enrolled* • **Computer and Information Sciences, General** *1 student enrolled* • **Computer/Information Technology Services Administration and Management, Other** *6 students enrolled* • **Criminal Justice/Law Enforcement Administration** *32 students enrolled* • **Dental Assisting/Assistant** *15 students enrolled* • **Dental Hygiene/Hygienist** *13 students enrolled* • **E-Commerce/Electronic Commerce** *8 students enrolled* • **Electrical, Electronic and Communications Engineering Technology/Technician** *1 student enrolled* • **Emergency Medical Technology/Technician (EMT Paramedic)** *58 students enrolled* • **Engineering Technology, General** *3 students enrolled* • **Fire Science/Firefighting** *4 students enrolled* • **Hospitality and Recreation Marketing Operations** *2 students enrolled* • **Library Assistant/Technician** *5 students enrolled* • **Licensed Practical/Vocational Nurse Training (LPN, LVN, Cert, Dipl, AAS)** *28 students enrolled* • **Machine Shop Technology/Assistant** *2 students enrolled* • **Massage Therapy/Therapeutic Massage** *6 students enrolled* • **Nurse/Nursing Assistant/Aide and Patient Care Assistant** *18 students enrolled* • **Pharmacy Technician/Assistant** *26 students enrolled* • **Phlebotomy/Phlebotomist** *35 students enrolled* • **Psychiatric/Mental Health Services Technician** *6 students enrolled* • **Welding Technology/Welder** *1 student enrolled*

**STUDENT SERVICES** Academic or career counseling, employment services for current students, remedial services.

## Red Rocks Community College

13300 West 6th Avenue, Lakewood, CO 80228-1255
http://www.rrcc.edu/

**CONTACT** Dr. Michele Haney, President
**Telephone:** 303-914-6600

**GENERAL INFORMATION** Public Institution. Founded 1969. **Accreditation:** Regional (NCA); medical assisting (AAMAE). **Total program enrollment:** 2471.

**PROGRAM(S) OFFERED**
• **Accounting Technology/Technician and Bookkeeping** *3 students enrolled* • **Automobile/Automotive Mechanics Technology/Technician** *53 students enrolled* • **Business Administration and Management, General** *1 student enrolled* • **Business/Office Automation/Technology/Data Entry** *1 student enrolled* • **Child Development** *26 students enrolled* • **Cinematography and Film/Video Production** *7 students enrolled* • **Clinical/Medical Laboratory Science and Allied Professions, Other** *21 students enrolled* • **Construction Trades, General** *45 students enrolled* • **Criminal Justice/Police Science** *49 students enrolled* • **Diagnostic Medical Sonography/Sonographer and Ultrasound Technician** *7 students enrolled* • **Drafting and Design Technology/Technician, General** *9 students enrolled* • **Emergency Medical Technology/Technician (EMT Paramedic)** *133 students enrolled* • **Fire Protection and Safety Technology/Technician** *43 students enrolled* • **Health Professions and Related Clinical Sciences, Other** *5 students enrolled* • **Management Information Systems, General** *2 students enrolled* • **Manufacturing Technology/Technician** *1 student enrolled* • **Medical Office Management/Administration** *11 students enrolled* • **Natural Resources Management/Development** *3 students enrolled* • **Nurse/Nursing Assistant/Aide and Patient Care Assistant** *96 students enrolled* • **Nursing, Other** *34 students enrolled* • **Physician Assistant** *27 students enrolled* • **Plumbing Technology/Plumber** *1 student enrolled* • **Real Estate** *18 students enrolled* • **Small Business Administration/Management** *19 students enrolled* • **Technical Theatre/Theatre Design and Technology** *2 students enrolled* • **Water Quality**

*Red Rocks Community College (continued)*

**and Wastewater Treatment Management and Recycling Technology/ Technician** *13 students enrolled* • **Welding Technology/Welder** *32 students enrolled*

**STUDENT SERVICES** Academic or career counseling, daycare for children of students, employment services for current students, placement services for program completers, remedial services.

## Redstone College–Denver

10851 West 120th Avenue, Broomfield, CO 80021-3465
http://www.redstone.edu/

**CONTACT** Mike Couling, Executive Director
**Telephone:** 800-888-3995

**GENERAL INFORMATION** Private Institution. Founded 1965. **Accreditation:** State accredited or approved. **Total program enrollment:** 567. **Application fee:** $25.

**PROGRAM(S) OFFERED**
• **Airframe Mechanics and Aircraft Maintenance Technology/Technician** *1269 hrs./$20,940* • **Avionics Maintenance Technology/Technician** *2100 hrs./ $32,311* • **Construction Trades, General** *99 hrs./$39,059* • **Heating, Air Conditioning, Ventilation and Refrigeration Maintenance Technology/ Technician (HAC, HACR, HVAC, HVACR)** *63 hrs./$20,190*

**STUDENT SERVICES** Academic or career counseling, employment services for current students, placement services for program completers.

## Regency Beauty Institute

2236 E. Harmony Road, Fort Collins, CO 80528

**CONTACT** J. Hayes Batson, CEO
**Telephone:** 970-530-3044

**GENERAL INFORMATION** Private Institution. **Total program enrollment:** 58. **Application fee:** $100.

**PROGRAM(S) OFFERED**
• **Cosmetology/Cosmetologist, General** *1799 hrs./$17,011*

## Regency Beauty Institute

98 Wadsworth Boulevard, Lakewood, CO 80226

**GENERAL INFORMATION** Private Institution. **Total program enrollment:** 48. **Application fee:** $100.

**PROGRAM(S) OFFERED**
• **Cosmetology/Cosmetologist, General** *1799 hrs./$16,011*

**STUDENT SERVICES** Academic or career counseling, placement services for program completers.

## Regency Beauty Institute

6755 West 88th Avenue, Westminster, CO 80031

**GENERAL INFORMATION** Private Institution. **Total program enrollment:** 71. **Application fee:** $100.

**PROGRAM(S) OFFERED**
• **Cosmetology/Cosmetologist, General** *1799 hrs./$16,011*

**STUDENT SERVICES** Academic or career counseling, placement services for program completers.

## Regis University

3333 Regis Boulevard, Denver, CO 80221-1099
http://www.regis.edu/

**CONTACT** Rev. Michael J. Sheeran, SJ, President
**Telephone:** 800-388-2366 Ext. 2111

**GENERAL INFORMATION** Private Institution. Founded 1877. **Accreditation:** Regional (NCA); health information administration (AHIMA). **Total program enrollment:** 5157. **Application fee:** $40.

**STUDENT SERVICES** Academic or career counseling, employment services for current students.

## Remington College–Colorado Springs Campus

6050 Erin Park Drive, #250, Colorado Springs, CO 80918
http://www.remingtoncollege.edu/

**CONTACT** Ms. Shirley McCray, Campus Vice-President
**Telephone:** 719-532-1234

**GENERAL INFORMATION** Private Institution. **Accreditation:** State accredited or approved. **Total program enrollment:** 188. **Application fee:** $50.

**PROGRAM(S) OFFERED**
• **Computer and Information Sciences and Support Services, Other** *4 students enrolled* • **Medical/Clinical Assistant** *53 students enrolled* • **Pharmacy Technician/Assistant** *17 students enrolled*

**STUDENT SERVICES** Academic or career counseling, employment services for current students, placement services for program completers, remedial services.

## San Juan Basin Area Vocational School

PO Box 970, Cortez, CO 81321
http://www.sjbtc.edu/

**CONTACT** Shannon L. South, President
**Telephone:** 970-565-8457

**GENERAL INFORMATION** Public Institution. Founded 1972. **Total program enrollment:** 182. **Application fee:** $25.

**PROGRAM(S) OFFERED**
• **Accounting** *2 students enrolled* • **Administrative Assistant and Secretarial Science, General** *28 students enrolled* • **Agricultural Business Technology** • **Agricultural/Farm Supplies Retailing and Wholesaling** • **Agriculture, Agriculture Operations and Related Sciences, Other** • **Automobile/Automotive Mechanics Technology/Technician** *8 students enrolled* • **Carpentry/Carpenter** *14 students enrolled* • **Computer Systems Networking and Telecommunications** *18 students enrolled* • **Diesel Mechanics Technology/Technician** *10 students enrolled* • **Electrical, Electronic and Communications Engineering Technology/ Technician** *33 students enrolled* • **Emergency Medical Technology/Technician (EMT Paramedic)** *608 students enrolled* • **Farm/Farm and Ranch Management** • **Fire Protection and Safety Technology/Technician** *224 students enrolled* • **Health Professions and Related Clinical Sciences, Other** *18 students enrolled* • **Industrial Mechanics and Maintenance Technology** • **Licensed Practical/ Vocational Nurse Training (LPN, LVN, Cert, Dipl, AAS)** *91 students enrolled* • **Medical Insurance Coding Specialist/Coder** *6 students enrolled* • **Pharmacy Technician/Assistant** *14 students enrolled* • **Radio and Television Broadcasting Technology/Technician** • **Small Business Administration/Management** *5 students enrolled* • **Welding Technology/Welder** *7 students enrolled*

**STUDENT SERVICES** Academic or career counseling, employment services for current students, placement services for program completers, remedial services.

## Toni & Guy Hairdressing Academy

322 Main Street, Colorado Springs, CO 80911
http://toniguyco.com/

**CONTACT** Sandra Chandler, President
**Telephone:** 719-390-9898

**GENERAL INFORMATION** Private Institution. **Total program enrollment:** 42. **Application fee:** $100.

**PROGRAM(S) OFFERED**
• **Cosmetology/Cosmetologist, General** *40 hrs./$9250* • **Hair Styling/Stylist and Hair Design** *6 students enrolled*

## Trinidad State Junior College

600 Prospect, Trinidad, CO 81082-2396
http://www.trinidadstate.edu/

**CONTACT** Ruth Ann Woods, President
**Telephone:** 719-846-5011

**GENERAL INFORMATION** Public Institution. Founded 1925. **Accreditation:** Regional (NCA); engineering-related programs (ABET/RAC). **Total program enrollment:** 783.

**PROGRAM(S) OFFERED**
• **Aesthetician/Esthetician and Skin Care Specialist** *3 students enrolled* • **Aquaculture** *1 student enrolled* • **Automobile/Automotive Mechanics Technology/Technician** *11 students enrolled* • **Barbering/Barber** *1 student enrolled* • **Business/Office Automation/Technology/Data Entry** *3 students enrolled* • **Child Care and Support Services Management** *2 students enrolled* • **Construction Trades, General** *1 student enrolled* • **Construction/Heavy Equipment/Earthmoving Equipment Operation** *20 students enrolled* • **Cosmetology/Cosmetologist, General** *7 students enrolled* • **Criminal Justice/Law Enforcement Administration** *17 students enrolled* • **Emergency Medical Technology/Technician (EMT Paramedic)** *39 students enrolled* • **Engineering Technology, General** *1 student enrolled* • **Farm/Farm and Ranch Management** *15 students enrolled* • **Gunsmithing/Gunsmith** *8 students enrolled* • **Hair Styling/Stylist and Hair Design** *3 students enrolled* • **Manufacturing Technology/Technician** *18 students enrolled* • **Massage Therapy/Therapeutic Massage** *20 students enrolled* • **Mechanic and Repair Technologies/Technicians, Other** *12 students enrolled* • **Nail Technician/Specialist and Manicurist** *4 students enrolled* • **Nurse/Nursing Assistant/Aide and Patient Care Assistant** *54 students enrolled* • **Nursing—Registered Nurse Training (RN, ASN, BSN, MSN)** *16 students enrolled* • **Occupational Safety and Health Technology/Technician** *5 students enrolled* • **Welding Technology/Welder** *31 students enrolled*

**STUDENT SERVICES** Academic or career counseling, employment services for current students, placement services for program completers, remedial services.

## University of Denver

2199 South University Park Boulevard, Denver, CO 80208
http://www.du.edu/

**CONTACT** Robert D. Coombe, Chancellor
**Telephone:** 303-871-2000

**GENERAL INFORMATION** Private Institution. Founded 1864. **Accreditation:** Regional (NCA); art and design (NASAD); music (NASM). **Total program enrollment:** 8164. **Application fee:** $50.

**STUDENT SERVICES** Academic or career counseling, employment services for current students, placement services for program completers.

## University of Phoenix–Denver Campus

10004 Park Meadows Drive, Lone Tree, CO 80124-5453
http://www.phoenix.edu/

**CONTACT** William Pepicello, PhD, President
**Telephone:** 800-441-2981

**GENERAL INFORMATION** Private Institution. **Accreditation:** Regional (NCA). **Total program enrollment:** 2373.

**PROGRAM(S) OFFERED**
• **Human Resources Management/Personnel Administration, General** *1 student enrolled*

**STUDENT SERVICES** Academic or career counseling, remedial services.

## University of Phoenix–Southern Colorado Campus

5725 Mark Dabling Boulevard, Suite 150, Colorado Springs, CO 80919-2335
http://www.phoenix.edu/

**CONTACT** William Pepicello, PhD, President
**Telephone:** 800-834-4646

**GENERAL INFORMATION** Private Institution. Founded 1999. **Accreditation:** Regional (NCA). **Total program enrollment:** 594.

**STUDENT SERVICES** Academic or career counseling, remedial services.

## Westwood College–Denver North

7350 North Broadway, Denver, CO 80221-3653
http://www.westwood.edu/

**CONTACT** Natalie Williams, President
**Telephone:** 303-426-7000

**GENERAL INFORMATION** Private Institution. Founded 1953. **Accreditation:** Medical assisting (AAMAE); state accredited or approved. **Total program enrollment:** 4226. **Application fee:** $25.

**STUDENT SERVICES** Academic or career counseling, employment services for current students, placement services for program completers, remedial services.

## Westwood College–Denver South

3150 South Sheridan Boulevard, Denver, CO 80227
http://www.westwood.edu/

**CONTACT** Daniel Snyder, Interim Executive Director
**Telephone:** 303-934-1122

**GENERAL INFORMATION** Private Institution. **Accreditation:** State accredited or approved. **Total program enrollment:** 391. **Application fee:** $25.

**PROGRAM(S) OFFERED**
• **Medical/Clinical Assistant** *5 students enrolled*

**STUDENT SERVICES** Academic or career counseling, employment services for current students, placement services for program completers, remedial services.

## Xenon International School of Hair Design III

2231 South Peoria Street, Aurora, CO 80014
http://www.xenonintl.com/

**CONTACT** Donna Loghry, Director
**Telephone:** 303-752-1560

**GENERAL INFORMATION** Private Institution. Founded 1988. **Total program enrollment:** 81.

**PROGRAM(S) OFFERED**
• **Aesthetician/Esthetician and Skin Care Specialist** *20 hrs./$5800* • **Cosmetology/Cosmetologist, General** *60 hrs./$15,875* • **Hair Styling/Stylist and Hair Design** *40 hrs./$12,000* • **Nail Technician/Specialist and Manicurist** *20 hrs./$4000*

**STUDENT SERVICES** Academic or career counseling, placement services for program completers.

# GUAM

## Guam Community College

PO Box 23069 Guam Main Facility, Barrigada, GU 96921-3069
http://www.guamcc.net/

**CONTACT** Mary A.Y. Okada, President
**Telephone:** 671-735-5500

**GENERAL INFORMATION** Public Institution. Founded 1977. **Accreditation:** Regional (WASC/ACCJC); medical assisting (AAMAE). **Total program enrollment:** 687.

**PROGRAM(S) OFFERED**
• **Accounting Technology/Technician and Bookkeeping** *2 students enrolled* • **Automobile/Automotive Mechanics Technology/Technician** *1 student enrolled* • **Business Administration and Management, General** *1 student enrolled* • **Carpentry/Carpenter** • **Child Care Provider/Assistant** • **Clinical/Medical Social Work** • **Computer Science** *2 students enrolled* • **Computer Systems Networking and Telecommunications** *1 student enrolled* • **Cosmetology/Cosmetologist, General** • **Criminal Justice/Police Science** *11 students enrolled* • **Early Childhood Education and Teaching** *1 student enrolled* • **Education, General** *1 student enrolled* • **Electrical and Power Transmission Installation/Installer, General** • **Electrical, Electronic and Communications Engineering Technology/Technician** • **Electrician** • **Family Resource Management Studies, General** • **Fire Science/Firefighting** • **General Office Occupations and Clerical Services** • **Heating, Air Conditioning, Ventilation and Refrigeration Maintenance Technology/Technician (HAC, HACR, HVAC, HVACR)** • **Hotel/Motel Administration/Management** • **Licensed Practical/Vocational Nurse Training (LPN, LVN, Cert, Dipl, AAS)** *12 students enrolled* • **Medical/Clinical Assistant** *5 students enrolled* • **Restaurant, Culinary, and Catering Management/Manager** • **Restaurant/Food Services Management** • **Sales, Distribution and Marketing Operations, General** • **Tourism and Travel Services Management**

**STUDENT SERVICES** Academic or career counseling, employment services for current students, placement services for program completers, remedial services.

# HAWAII

## Hawaii Community College

200 West Kawili Street, Hilo, HI 96720-4091
http://www.hawcc.hawaii.edu/

**CONTACT** Rockne Freitas, Chancellor
**Telephone:** 808-974-7611

**GENERAL INFORMATION** Public Institution. Founded 1954. **Accreditation:** Regional (WASC/ACCJC). **Total program enrollment:** 1331. **Application fee:** $25.

**PROGRAM(S) OFFERED**
• **Accounting** *1 student enrolled* • **Administrative Assistant and Secretarial Science, General** *1 student enrolled* • **Agricultural Production Operations, General** • **Autobody/Collision and Repair Technology/Technician** *4 students enrolled* • **Automobile/Automotive Mechanics Technology/Technician** *16 students enrolled* • **Carpentry/Carpenter** *1 student enrolled* • **Cooking and Related Culinary Arts, General** *10 students enrolled* • **Diesel Mechanics Technology/Technician** *5 students enrolled* • **Early Childhood Education and Teaching** *3 students enrolled* • **Electrical/Electronics Equipment Installation and Repair, General** *9 students enrolled* • **Forestry, Other** *3 students enrolled* • **Hospitality Administration/Management, General** • **Hotel/Motel Administration/Management** *1 student enrolled* • **Information Technology** • **Licensed Practical/Vocational Nurse Training (LPN, LVN, Cert, Dipl, AAS)** *17 students enrolled* • **Marketing/Marketing Management, General** *2 students enrolled* • **Welding Technology/Welder** *2 students enrolled*

**STUDENT SERVICES** Academic or career counseling, daycare for children of students, employment services for current students, placement services for program completers, remedial services.

## Hawaii Institute of Hair Design

71 South Hotel Street, Honolulu, HI 96813-3112
http://www.hihd.net/

**CONTACT** Margaret Williams, President
**Telephone:** 808-533-6596

**GENERAL INFORMATION** Private Institution. **Total program enrollment:** 60. **Application fee:** $25.

**PROGRAM(S) OFFERED**
• **Barbering/Barber** *1500 hrs./$9487*

**STUDENT SERVICES** Academic or career counseling, placement services for program completers.

## Hawai'i Pacific University

1164 Bishop Street, Honolulu, HI 96813
http://www.hpu.edu/

**CONTACT** Chatt G. Wright, President
**Telephone:** 808-544-0200

**GENERAL INFORMATION** Private Institution. Founded 1965. **Accreditation:** Regional (WASC/ACSCU). **Total program enrollment:** 4315. **Application fee:** $50.

**PROGRAM(S) OFFERED**
• **American Indian/Native American Studies** *1 student enrolled* • **Anthropology** • **Forensic Science and Technology** *14 students enrolled* • **Nursing, Other** *1 student enrolled* • **Social Sciences, Other** • **Teaching English as a Second or Foreign Language/ESL Language Instructor** *2 students enrolled* • **Tourism and Travel Services Management** *1 student enrolled*

**STUDENT SERVICES** Academic or career counseling, employment services for current students, placement services for program completers, remedial services.

## Hawaii Technology Institute

629 Pohukaina Street, Honolulu, HI 96813
http://www.hti.edu/

**CONTACT** Naomi Digitaki, President/CEO
**Telephone:** 808-527-2700

**GENERAL INFORMATION** Private Institution. **Total program enrollment:** 14.

**PROGRAM(S) OFFERED**
• **Allied Health and Medical Assisting Services, Other** *48 hrs./$5700* • **Data Processing and Data Processing Technology/Technician** *27 hrs./$5200* • **Medical/Clinical Assistant** *6 students enrolled*

**STUDENT SERVICES** Academic or career counseling, employment services for current students, placement services for program completers, remedial services.

## Heald College–Honolulu

1500 Kapiolani Boulevard, Honolulu, HI 96814-3797
http://www.heald.edu/

**CONTACT** Evelyn A. Schemmel, Regional Vice President, Campus Operations-Hawaii
**Telephone:** 808-955-1500

**GENERAL INFORMATION** Private Institution. Founded 1863. **Accreditation:** Regional (WASC/ACCJC); medical assisting (AAMAE). **Total program enrollment:** 812.

**PROGRAM(S) OFFERED**
• **Accounting and Business/Management** • **Business Administration, Management and Operations, Other** *1 student enrolled* • **Business Operations Support and Secretarial Services, Other** *3 students enrolled* • **Computer and Information Sciences and Support Services, Other** *10 students enrolled* • **Hospitality Administration/Management, General** *1 student enrolled* • **Medical Office Assistant/Specialist** *1 student enrolled* • **System Administration/Administrator** *1 student enrolled* • **Web Page, Digital/Multimedia and Information Resources Design** *6 students enrolled*

**STUDENT SERVICES** Academic or career counseling, employment services for current students, placement services for program completers, remedial services.

## Honolulu Community College

874 Dillingham Boulevard, Honolulu, HI 96817-4598
http://www.honolulu.hawaii.edu/

**CONTACT** Michael Rota, Interim Chancellor
**Telephone:** 808-845-9129

**GENERAL INFORMATION** Public Institution. Founded 1920. **Accreditation:** Regional (WASC/ACCJC). **Total program enrollment:** 1481. **Application fee:** $25.

**PROGRAM(S) OFFERED**
• **Aeronautical/Aerospace Engineering Technology/Technician** *6 students enrolled* • **Apparel and Textile Manufacture** *1 student enrolled* • **Architectural Drafting and Architectural CAD/CADD** *2 students enrolled* • **Autobody/Collision and Repair Technology/Technician** *3 students enrolled* • **Automobile/Automotive Mechanics Technology/Technician** • **Carpentry/Carpenter** *1 student enrolled* • **Cosmetology/Cosmetologist, General** *17 students enrolled* • **Diesel Mechanics Technology/Technician** • **Early Childhood Education and Teaching** • **Electrical/Electronics Equipment Installation and Repair, General** *1 student enrolled* • **Fire Science/Firefighting** *3 students enrolled* • **Heating, Air Conditioning, Ventilation and Refrigeration Maintenance Technology/Technician (HAC, HACR, HVAC, HVACR)** *4 students enrolled* • **Human Services, General** *1 student enrolled* • **Occupational Safety and Health Technology/Technician** *3 students enrolled* • **Sheet Metal Technology/Sheetworking** *13 students enrolled* • **Welding Technology/Welder** *5 students enrolled*

**STUDENT SERVICES** Academic or career counseling, daycare for children of students, employment services for current students, placement services for program completers, remedial services.

## Kapiolani Community College

4303 Diamond Head Road, Honolulu, HI 96816-4421
http://www.kcc.hawaii.edu/

**CONTACT** Leon Richards, Chancellor
**Telephone:** 808-734-9000

**GENERAL INFORMATION** Public Institution. Founded 1957. **Accreditation:** Regional (WASC/ACCJC); medical assisting (AAMAE); medical laboratory technology (NAACLS); physical therapy assisting (APTA); radiologic technology: radiography (JRCERT). **Total program enrollment:** 2921. **Application fee:** $25.

**PROGRAM(S) OFFERED**
• **Accounting** • **Cooking and Related Culinary Arts, General** *4 students enrolled* • **Information Technology** • **Kinesiology and Exercise Science** • **Licensed Practical/Vocational Nurse Training (LPN, LVN, Cert, Dipl, AAS)** *21 students enrolled* • **Marketing/Marketing Management, General** *1 student enrolled* • **Medical/Clinical Assistant** *5 students enrolled* • **Tourism and Travel Services Management** *4 students enrolled*

**STUDENT SERVICES** Academic or career counseling, daycare for children of students, employment services for current students, placement services for program completers, remedial services.

## Kauai Community College

3-1901 Kaumualii Highway, Lihue, HI 96766
http://kauai.hawaii.edu/

**CONTACT** Helen Cox, Chancellor
**Telephone:** 808-245-8311

**GENERAL INFORMATION** Public Institution. Founded 1965. **Accreditation:** Regional (WASC/ACCJC). **Total program enrollment:** 443. **Application fee:** $25.

**PROGRAM(S) OFFERED**
• **Accounting** • **Administrative Assistant and Secretarial Science, General** *2 students enrolled* • **Autobody/Collision and Repair Technology/Technician** *1 student enrolled* • **Automobile/Automotive Mechanics Technology/Technician** *1 student enrolled* • **Carpentry/Carpenter** • **Cooking and Related Culinary Arts, General** *2 students enrolled* • **Early Childhood Education and Teaching** • **Electrical, Electronic and Communications Engineering Technology/Technician** *3 students enrolled* • **Electrical/Electronics Equipment Installation and Repair, General** • **Hotel/Motel Administration/Management** • **Licensed Practical/Vocational Nurse Training (LPN, LVN, Cert, Dipl, AAS)** *25 students enrolled*

**STUDENT SERVICES** Academic or career counseling, daycare for children of students, employment services for current students, placement services for program completers, remedial services.

## Leeward Community College

96-045 Ala Ike, Pearl City, HI 96782-3393
http://www.lcc.hawaii.edu/

**CONTACT** Manuel Cabral, Chancellor
**Telephone:** 808-455-0011

**GENERAL INFORMATION** Public Institution. Founded 1968. **Accreditation:** Regional (WASC/ACCJC). **Total program enrollment:** 2882. **Application fee:** $25.

**PROGRAM(S) OFFERED**
• **Accounting** *4 students enrolled* • **Administrative Assistant and Secretarial Science, General** *8 students enrolled* • **Automobile/Automotive Mechanics Technology/Technician** *17 students enrolled* • **Cooking and Related Culinary Arts, General** *3 students enrolled* • **Radio and Television Broadcasting Technology/Technician** *1 student enrolled*

**STUDENT SERVICES** Academic or career counseling, daycare for children of students, employment services for current students, placement services for program completers, remedial services.

## Maui Community College

310 Kaahumanu Avenue, Kahului, HI 96732
http://mauicc.hawaii.edu/

**CONTACT** Clyde Sakamoto, Chancellor
**Telephone:** 808-984-3267

**GENERAL INFORMATION** Public Institution. Founded 1967. **Accreditation:** Regional (WASC/ACCJC); dental assisting (ADA). **Total program enrollment:** 1328. **Application fee:** $25.

**PROGRAM(S) OFFERED**
• **Accounting** *8 students enrolled* • **Administrative Assistant and Secretarial Science, General** *7 students enrolled* • **Agricultural Production Operations, General** *3 students enrolled* • **Apparel and Textile Manufacture** *1 student enrolled* • **Autobody/Collision and Repair Technology/Technician** • **Automobile/**

*Maui Community College (continued)*

**Automotive Mechanics Technology/Technician** *5 students enrolled* • **Building/Property Maintenance and Management** *2 students enrolled* • **Business/Commerce, General** *4 students enrolled* • **Carpentry/Carpenter** • **Computer Technology/Computer Systems Technology** *5 students enrolled* • **Cooking and Related Culinary Arts, General** *9 students enrolled* • **Criminal Justice/Police Science** • **Energy Management and Systems Technology/Technician** *2 students enrolled* • **Hospitality Administration/Management, General** *3 students enrolled* • **Hotel/Motel Administration/Management** *1 student enrolled* • **Human Services, General** *16 students enrolled* • **Licensed Practical/Vocational Nurse Training (LPN, LVN, Cert, Dipl, AAS)** *74 students enrolled*

**STUDENT SERVICES** Academic or career counseling, daycare for children of students, employment services for current students, placement services for program completers, remedial services.

## Med-Assist School of Hawaii

33 South King Street, #223, Honolulu, HI 96813
http://staging.mash.edu/

**CONTACT** Helene Takemoto, President
**Telephone:** 808-524-3363

**GENERAL INFORMATION** Private Institution. Founded 1974. **Total program enrollment:** 73. **Application fee:** $15.

**PROGRAM(S) OFFERED**

• **Medical/Clinical Assistant** *33 hrs./$12,397*

**STUDENT SERVICES** Academic or career counseling, placement services for program completers, remedial services.

## Remington College–Honolulu Campus

1111 Bishop Street, Suite 400, Honolulu, HI 96813
http://www.remingtoncollege.edu/

**CONTACT** Kenneth G. Heinemann, Campus President
**Telephone:** 808-942-1000

**GENERAL INFORMATION** Private Institution. **Accreditation:** State accredited or approved. **Total program enrollment:** 557. **Application fee:** $50.

**PROGRAM(S) OFFERED**

• **Massage Therapy/Therapeutic Massage** *61 students enrolled*

**STUDENT SERVICES** Academic or career counseling, employment services for current students, placement services for program completers.

## Travel Institute of the Pacific

1314 South King Street, Suite 1164, Honolulu, HI 96814-4401
http://www.tiphawaii.com/

**CONTACT** James E. Hughes, Chief Executive Officer
**Telephone:** 808-591-2708

**GENERAL INFORMATION** Private Institution. Founded 1974. **Total program enrollment:** 145. **Application fee:** $100.

**PROGRAM(S) OFFERED**

• **Culinary Arts and Related Services, Other** *900 hrs./$15,727* • **Culinary Arts/Chef Training** *900 hrs./$9093* • **Hotel/Motel Administration/Management** *42 hrs./$4160* • **Tourism and Travel Services Management** *900 hrs./$7684*

**STUDENT SERVICES** Academic or career counseling, employment services for current students, placement services for program completers.

## University of Hawaii System

2444 Dole Street, Honolulu, HI 96822-2330
http://www.hawaii.edu/

**CONTACT** David McClain, President
**Telephone:** 808-956-4153

**GENERAL INFORMATION** Public Institution.

## University of Phoenix–Hawaii Campus

827 Fort Street, Honolulu, HI 96813-4317
http://www.phoenix.edu/

**CONTACT** William Pepicello, PhD, President
**Telephone:** 800-483-5444

**GENERAL INFORMATION** Private Institution. **Accreditation:** Regional (NCA). **Total program enrollment:** 993.

**STUDENT SERVICES** Academic or career counseling, remedial services.

# IDAHO

## Academy of Professional Careers

8590 West Fairview Avenue, Boise, ID 83704
http://www.academyofhealthcareers.com/

**CONTACT** Gary Yasuda, President
**Telephone:** 208-672-9500

**GENERAL INFORMATION** Private Institution. **Total program enrollment:** 373. **Application fee:** $100.

**PROGRAM(S) OFFERED**

• **Aesthetician/Esthetician and Skin Care Specialist** *700 hrs./$8212* • **Dental Assisting/Assistant** *720 hrs./$10,684* • **Health/Health Care Administration/Management** *720 hrs./$10,801* • **Legal Administrative Assistant/Secretary** *12 students enrolled* • **Massage Therapy/Therapeutic Massage** *720 hrs./$10,019* • **Medical Administrative/Executive Assistant and Medical Secretary** *720 hrs./$10,901* • **Medical/Clinical Assistant** *720 hrs./$11,823* • **Pharmacy Technician/Assistant** *7 students enrolled*

**STUDENT SERVICES** Academic or career counseling, employment services for current students, placement services for program completers.

## Apollo College–Boise

1200 North Liberty Road, Boise, ID 83704
http://www.apollocollege.edu/

**CONTACT** Lois Hine, Executive Campus Director
**Telephone:** 208-377-8080

**GENERAL INFORMATION** Private Institution. Founded 1980. **Accreditation:** Dental assisting (ADA); dental hygiene (ADA); state accredited or approved. **Total program enrollment:** 833. **Application fee:** $100.

**PROGRAM(S) OFFERED**

• **Dental Assisting/Assistant** *38 hrs./$13,229* • **Dental Hygiene/Hygienist** *83 hrs./$49,785* • **Health Information/Medical Records Administration/Administrator** *18 students enrolled* • **Licensed Practical/Vocational Nurse Training (LPN, LVN, Cert, Dipl, AAS)** *45 hrs./$25,896* • **Massage Therapy/Therapeutic Massage** *36 hrs./$11,764* • **Medical Office Assistant/Specialist** *36 hrs./$12,060* • **Medical Office Management/Administration** • **Medical/Clinical Assistant** *62 students enrolled* • **Pharmacy Technician/Assistant** *38 hrs./$12,321*

**STUDENT SERVICES** Academic or career counseling, employment services for current students, placement services for program completers, remedial services.

## Boise Bible College

8695 West Marigold Street, Boise, ID 83714-1220
http://www.boisebible.edu/

**CONTACT** Terry Stine, President
**Telephone:** 208-376-7731

**GENERAL INFORMATION** Private Institution. Founded 1945. **Accreditation:** State accredited or approved. **Total program enrollment:** 150. **Application fee:** $25.

**PROGRAM(S) OFFERED**
• **Bible/Biblical Studies** *12 students enrolled*

**STUDENT SERVICES** Academic or career counseling, employment services for current students, placement services for program completers, remedial services.

## Boise State University

1910 University Drive, Boise, ID 83725-0399
http://www.boisestate.edu/

**CONTACT** Dr. Bob Kustra, President
**Telephone:** 208-426-1011

**GENERAL INFORMATION** Public Institution. Founded 1932. **Accreditation:** Regional (NCCU/NCCU); athletic training (JRCAT); computer science (ABET/CSAC); counseling (ACA); dental assisting (ADA); diagnostic medical sonography (JRCEDMS); health information technology (AHIMA); music (NASM); radiologic technology: radiography (JRCERT); respiratory therapy technology (CoARC); theater (NAST). **Total program enrollment:** 12160. **Application fee:** $40.

**PROGRAM(S) OFFERED**
• **Accounting Technology/Technician and Bookkeeping** *4 students enrolled* • **Administrative Assistant and Secretarial Science, General** • **Applied Horticulture/Horticultural Operations, General** *4 students enrolled* • **Autobody/Collision and Repair Technology/Technician** *6 students enrolled* • **Automobile/Automotive Mechanics Technology/Technician** *14 students enrolled* • **Child Care and Support Services Management** *1 student enrolled* • **Computer Systems Networking and Telecommunications** • **Computer Technology/Computer Systems Technology** • **Culinary Arts/Chef Training** *3 students enrolled* • **Dental Assisting/Assistant** *19 students enrolled* • **Diesel Mechanics Technology/Technician** *4 students enrolled* • **Drafting and Design Technology/Technician, General** *6 students enrolled* • **Electrical, Electronic and Communications Engineering Technology/Technician** *1 student enrolled* • **General Office Occupations and Clerical Services** *3 students enrolled* • **Heating, Air Conditioning, Ventilation and Refrigeration Maintenance Technology/Technician (HAC, HACR, HVAC, HVACR)** • **Industrial Mechanics and Maintenance Technology** *2 students enrolled* • **Industrial Technology/Technician** • **Licensed Practical/Vocational Nurse Training (LPN, LVN, Cert, Dipl, AAS)** *35 students enrolled* • **Lineworker** *2 students enrolled* • **Machine Tool Technology/Machinist** • **Manufacturing Technology/Technician** • **Retailing and Retail Operations** *3 students enrolled* • **Small Engine Mechanics and Repair Technology/Technician** *3 students enrolled* • **Surgical Technology/Technologist** *15 students enrolled* • **Truck and Bus Driver/Commercial Vehicle Operation** *17 students enrolled* • **Welding Technology/Welder** *6 students enrolled*

**STUDENT SERVICES** Academic or career counseling, daycare for children of students, employment services for current students, placement services for program completers, remedial services.

## Career Beauty College

57 College Avenue, Rexburg, ID 83440
http://careerbeautycollege.com/

**CONTACT** Grant D. Gardner, Owner-Administrator
**Telephone:** 208-356-0222

**GENERAL INFORMATION** Private Institution. Founded 1979. **Total program enrollment:** 74. **Application fee:** $50.

**PROGRAM(S) OFFERED**
• **Cosmetology, Barber/Styling, and Nail Instructor** *1000 hrs./$4200*
• **Cosmetology/Cosmetologist, General** *2000 hrs./$9000*

**STUDENT SERVICES** Academic or career counseling, placement services for program completers.

## College of Southern Idaho

PO Box 1238, Twin Falls, ID 83303-1238
http://www.csi.edu/

**CONTACT** Jerry Beck, President
**Telephone:** 208-733-9554

**GENERAL INFORMATION** Public Institution. Founded 1964. **Accreditation:** Regional (NCCU/NCCU); medical assisting (AAMAE). **Total program enrollment:** 2881.

**PROGRAM(S) OFFERED**
• **Administrative Assistant and Secretarial Science, General** *3 students enrolled* • **Agricultural Business and Management, General** • **Agricultural and Food Products Processing** *3 students enrolled* • **Applied Horticulture/Horticultural Operations, General** *5 students enrolled* • **Aquaculture** • **Autobody/Collision and Repair Technology/Technician** *3 students enrolled* • **Automobile/Automotive Mechanics Technology/Technician** • **Building/Construction Finishing, Management, and Inspection, Other** *1 student enrolled* • **CAD/CADD Drafting and/or Design Technology/Technician** • **Cabinetmaking and Millwork/Millwright** *3 students enrolled* • **Child Care and Support Services Management** *1 student enrolled* • **Computer Systems Networking and Telecommunications** *8 students enrolled* • **Criminal Justice/Police Science** *9 students enrolled* • **Dental Assisting/Assistant** *14 students enrolled* • **Diesel Mechanics Technology/Technician** *2 students enrolled* • **Electrical, Electronic and Communications Engineering Technology/Technician** • **Emergency Medical Technology/Technician (EMT Paramedic)** *8 students enrolled* • **Equestrian/Equine Studies** • **Farm/Farm and Ranch Management** • **Health Professions and Related Clinical Sciences, Other** • **Heating, Air Conditioning, Ventilation and Refrigeration Maintenance Technology/Technician (HAC, HACR, HVAC, HVACR)** *3 students enrolled* • **Institutional Food Workers** *4 students enrolled* • **Licensed Practical/Vocational Nurse Training (LPN, LVN, Cert, Dipl, AAS)** *53 students enrolled* • **Medical/Clinical Assistant** *5 students enrolled* • **Psychiatric/Mental Health Services Technician** *1 student enrolled* • **Surgical Technology/Technologist** *13 students enrolled* • **Teacher Assistant/Aide** *2 students enrolled* • **Teacher Education and Professional Development, Specific Subject Areas, Other** • **Water Quality and Wastewater Treatment Management and Recycling Technology/Technician** *2 students enrolled* • **Welding Technology/Welder** *15 students enrolled*

**STUDENT SERVICES** Academic or career counseling, daycare for children of students, employment services for current students, placement services for program completers, remedial services.

## Cosmetology School of Arts and Sciences

529 Overland Avenue, Burley, ID 83318

**CONTACT** Rhonda Clark, CEO
**Telephone:** 208-678-4454

**GENERAL INFORMATION** Private Institution. **Total program enrollment:** 39. **Application fee:** $120.

**PROGRAM(S) OFFERED**
• **Aesthetician/Esthetician and Skin Care Specialist** *600 hrs./$4620*
• **Cosmetology, Barber/Styling, and Nail Instructor** *1000 hrs./$5000*
• **Cosmetology/Cosmetologist, General** *2000 hrs./$9280* • **Nail Technician/Specialist and Manicurist** *400 hrs./$2500*

## Eastern Idaho Technical College

1600 South 25th East, Idaho Falls, ID 83404-5788
http://www.eitc.edu/

**CONTACT** Burton Waite, President
**Telephone:** 208-524-3000 Ext. 3371

**GENERAL INFORMATION** Public Institution. Founded 1970. **Accreditation:** Regional (NCCU/NCCU); medical assisting (AAMAE); surgical technology (ARCST). **Total program enrollment:** 296. **Application fee:** $10.

**PROGRAM(S) OFFERED**
• **Accounting** *1 student enrolled* • **Administrative Assistant and Secretarial Science, General** *5 students enrolled* • **Automobile/Automotive Mechanics**

*Eastern Idaho Technical College (continued)*

**Technology/Technician • Computer Systems Networking and Telecommunications • Dental Assisting/Assistant** *14 students enrolled* **• Diesel Mechanics Technology/Technician** *1 student enrolled* **• Electrical, Electronic and Communications Engineering Technology/Technician** *1 student enrolled* **• Legal Assistant/Paralegal • Medical/Clinical Assistant** *5 students enrolled* **• Nuclear and Industrial Radiologic Technologies/Technicians, Other** *15 students enrolled* **• Truck and Bus Driver/Commercial Vehicle Operation** *30 students enrolled* **• Welding Technology/Welder** *2 students enrolled*

**STUDENT SERVICES** Academic or career counseling, employment services for current students, placement services for program completers, remedial services.

## The Headmasters School of Hair Design

317 Coeur d'Alene, Coeur d'Alene, ID 83814
http://www.headmastersschool.com/

**CONTACT** Barbara Lyon, Director
**Telephone:** 208-664-0541 Ext. 5

**GENERAL INFORMATION** Private Institution. Founded 1982. **Total program enrollment:** 79.

**PROGRAM(S) OFFERED**
**• Cosmetology and Related Personal Grooming Arts, Other** *3 students enrolled* **• Cosmetology, Barber/Styling, and Nail Instructor** *1000 hrs./$3100* **• Cosmetology/Cosmetologist, General** *2000 hrs./$13,214*

**STUDENT SERVICES** Academic or career counseling, placement services for program completers.

## Headmasters School of Hair Design

602 Main Street, Lewiston, ID 83501
http://www.headmastersschoolhairdesign.com/

**CONTACT** Peggy Foster, President
**Telephone:** 208-743-1512

**GENERAL INFORMATION** Private Institution. Founded 1981. **Total program enrollment:** 41. **Application fee:** $100.

**PROGRAM(S) OFFERED**
**• Cosmetology, Barber/Styling, and Nail Instructor** *1000 hrs./$4250* **• Cosmetology/Cosmetologist, General** *2000 hrs./$11,297* **• Technical Teacher Education** *1 student enrolled*

**STUDENT SERVICES** Academic or career counseling, employment services for current students, placement services for program completers, remedial services.

## Headmasters School of Hair Design–Boise

5823 W. Franklin Road, Boise, ID 83709
http://www.headmastersschool.com/

**CONTACT** Barbara Lyon, Director
**Telephone:** 208-429-8070

**GENERAL INFORMATION** Private Institution. **Total program enrollment:** 132. **Application fee:** $100.

**PROGRAM(S) OFFERED**
**• Aesthetician/Esthetician and Skin Care Specialist** *600 hrs./$5050* **• Cosmetology, Barber/Styling, and Nail Instructor** *1000 hrs./$3000* **• Cosmetology/Cosmetologist, General** *2000 hrs./$14,114* **• Nail Technician/Specialist and Manicurist** *450 hrs./$3000*

**STUDENT SERVICES** Academic or career counseling, employment services for current students, placement services for program completers.

## Idaho State University

921 South 8th Avenue, Pocatello, ID 83209
http://www.isu.edu/

**CONTACT** Dr. Arthur C. Vailas, President
**Telephone:** 208-282-3620

**GENERAL INFORMATION** Public Institution. Founded 1901. **Accreditation:** Regional (NCCU/NCCU); audiology (ASHA); counseling (ACA); dental hygiene (ADA); dental laboratory technology (ADA); dietetics: postbaccalaureate internship (ADtA/CAADE); engineering-related programs (ABET/RAC); health information technology (AHIMA); medical assisting (AAMAE); medical technology (NAACLS); music (NASM); physical therapy assisting (APTA); public health: community health education (CEPH); speech-language pathology (ASHA). **Total program enrollment:** 8128. **Application fee:** $40.

**PROGRAM(S) OFFERED**
**• Administrative Assistant and Secretarial Science, General** *26 students enrolled* **• Aircraft Powerplant Technology/Technician** *1 student enrolled* **• Autobody/Collision and Repair Technology/Technician** *1 student enrolled* **• Automobile/Automotive Mechanics Technology/Technician** *15 students enrolled* **• Business Machine Repairer** *3 students enrolled* **• Carpentry/Carpenter • Child Care and Support Services Management** *17 students enrolled* **• Communications Systems Installation and Repair Technology • Computer Programming, Specific Applications • Cosmetology/Cosmetologist, General** *10 students enrolled* **• Culinary Arts/Chef Training • Drafting and Design Technology/Technician, General • Drafting/Design Engineering Technologies/Technicians, Other • Electrician** *5 students enrolled* **• Emergency Medical Technology/Technician (EMT Paramedic) • Graphic and Printing Equipment Operator, General Production** *1 student enrolled* **• Health Information/Medical Records Technology/Technician** *5 students enrolled* **• Licensed Practical/Vocational Nurse Training (LPN, LVN, Cert, Dipl, AAS) • Machine Tool Technology/Machinist • Massage Therapy/Therapeutic Massage** *6 students enrolled* **• Pharmacy Technician/Assistant • Welding Technology/Welder** *10 students enrolled*

**STUDENT SERVICES** Academic or career counseling, daycare for children of students, employment services for current students, placement services for program completers, remedial services.

## Lewis-Clark State College

500 Eighth Avenue, Lewiston, ID 83501-2698
http://www.lcsc.edu/

**CONTACT** Dene Kay Thomas, President
**Telephone:** 208-792-5272

**GENERAL INFORMATION** Public Institution. Founded 1893. **Accreditation:** Regional (NCCU/NCCU). **Total program enrollment:** 2354. **Application fee:** $35.

**PROGRAM(S) OFFERED**
**• Administrative Assistant and Secretarial Science, General** *3 students enrolled* **• Autobody/Collision and Repair Technology/Technician • Automobile/Automotive Mechanics Technology/Technician** *1 student enrolled* **• CAD/CADD Drafting and/or Design Technology/Technician • Diesel Mechanics Technology/Technician • Graphic and Printing Equipment Operator, General Production • Heating, Air Conditioning, Ventilation and Refrigeration Maintenance Technology/Technician (HAC, HACR, HVAC, HVACR) • Hospitality and Recreation Marketing Operations • Industrial Electronics Technology/Technician** *1 student enrolled* **• Legal Administrative Assistant/Secretary • Legal Assistant/Paralegal • Manufacturing Technology/Technician • Marketing/Marketing Management, General** *2 students enrolled* **• Medical Office Assistant/Specialist • Web Page, Digital/Multimedia and Information Resources Design • Welding Technology/Welder** *2 students enrolled*

**STUDENT SERVICES** Academic or career counseling, daycare for children of students, employment services for current students, placement services for program completers, remedial services.

## Mr. Juan's College of Hair Design

577 Lynwood Mall, Twin Falls, ID 83301

**CONTACT** E. Scholes, Jr., President
**Telephone:** 208-733-7777

**GENERAL INFORMATION** Private Institution. Founded 1965. **Total program enrollment:** 31. **Application fee:** $100.

**PROGRAM(S) OFFERED**
- **Cosmetology, Barber/Styling, and Nail Instructor** *500 hrs./$1250*
- **Cosmetology/Cosmetologist, General** *2000 hrs./$9955*

**STUDENT SERVICES** Academic or career counseling, placement services for program completers.

## Mr. Leon's School of Hair Design

205 10th Street, Lewiston, ID 83501

**CONTACT** Lisa Salisbury, Owner
**Telephone:** 208-882-2923

**GENERAL INFORMATION** Private Institution. **Total program enrollment:** 32. **Application fee:** $100.

**PROGRAM(S) OFFERED**
- **Cosmetology/Cosmetologist, General** *2000 hrs./$10,285*

**STUDENT SERVICES** Placement services for program completers.

## North Idaho College

1000 West Garden Avenue, Coeur d'Alene, ID 83814-2199
http://www.nic.edu/

**CONTACT** Priscilla Bell, President
**Telephone:** 208-769-3300

**GENERAL INFORMATION** Public Institution. Founded 1933. **Accreditation:** Regional (NCCU/NCCU). **Total program enrollment:** 2657. **Application fee:** $25.

**PROGRAM(S) OFFERED**
- **Accounting Technology/Technician and Bookkeeping** *1 student enrolled*
- **Autobody/Collision and Repair Technology/Technician** *11 students enrolled*
- **Automobile/Automotive Mechanics Technology/Technician** *6 students enrolled*
- **Carpentry/Carpenter** *8 students enrolled* • **Computer Programming, Specific Applications** *2 students enrolled* • **Criminal Justice/Law Enforcement Administration** *2 students enrolled* • **Culinary Arts/Chef Training** *12 students enrolled* • **Diesel Mechanics Technology/Technician** *8 students enrolled* • **Drafting and Design Technology/Technician, General** *3 students enrolled* • **Electrical, Electronic and Communications Engineering Technology/Technician**
- **General Office Occupations and Clerical Services** *3 students enrolled* • **Heating, Air Conditioning, Ventilation and Refrigeration Maintenance Technology/Technician (HAC, HACR, HVAC, HVACR)** *9 students enrolled* • **Industrial Mechanics and Maintenance Technology** *5 students enrolled* • **Landscaping and Groundskeeping** *1 student enrolled* • **Licensed Practical/Vocational Nurse Training (LPN, LVN, Cert, Dipl, AAS)** *25 students enrolled* • **Machine Tool Technology/Machinist** *4 students enrolled* • **Medical Administrative/Executive Assistant and Medical Secretary** *2 students enrolled* • **Medical Transcription/Transcriptionist** *1 student enrolled* • **Motorcycle Maintenance and Repair Technology/Technician** *2 students enrolled* • **Pharmacy Technician/Assistant** *11 students enrolled* • **Psychiatric/Mental Health Services Technician** *1 student enrolled* • **Welding Technology/Welder** *12 students enrolled*

**STUDENT SERVICES** Academic or career counseling, daycare for children of students, employment services for current students, placement services for program completers, remedial services.

## Razzle Dazzle College of Hair Design

214 Holly Street, Nampa, ID 83651
http://www.razzledazzlecollege.com/

**CONTACT** Christina Brown, President
**Telephone:** 208-465-7660

**GENERAL INFORMATION** Private Institution. Founded 1985. **Total program enrollment:** 83.

**PROGRAM(S) OFFERED**
- **Cosmetology and Related Personal Grooming Arts, Other** *600 hrs./$4470*
- **Cosmetology, Barber/Styling, and Nail Instructor** *500 hrs./$1499*
- **Cosmetology/Cosmetologist, General** *2000 hrs./$11,304* • **Facial Treatment Specialist/Facialist** *16 students enrolled* • **Nail Technician/Specialist and Manicurist** *400 hrs./$2410*

**STUDENT SERVICES** Academic or career counseling, employment services for current students, placement services for program completers.

## The School of Hairstyling

257 North Main Street, Pocatello, ID 83204
http://www.theschoolofhairstyling.com/

**CONTACT** Linda K. Mottishaw, President Treasurer
**Telephone:** 208-232-9170

**GENERAL INFORMATION** Private Institution. Founded 1976. **Total program enrollment:** 51. **Application fee:** $100.

**PROGRAM(S) OFFERED**
- **Cosmetology, Barber/Styling, and Nail Instructor** *1000 hrs./$3000*
- **Cosmetology/Cosmetologist, General** *2000 hrs./$8500* • **Nail Technician/Specialist and Manicurist** *400 hrs./$3000* • **Technical Teacher Education**

**STUDENT SERVICES** Academic or career counseling.

## University of Idaho

875 Perimeter Drive, PO Box 442282, Moscow, ID 83844-2282
http://www.uidaho.edu/

**CONTACT** Steven Daley-Laursen, President
**Telephone:** 208-885-6111

**GENERAL INFORMATION** Public Institution. Founded 1889. **Accreditation:** Regional (NCCU/NCCU); art and design (NASAD); computer science (ABET/CSAC); counseling (ACA); forestry (SAF); home economics (AAFCS); music (NASM); recreation and parks (NRPA). **Total program enrollment:** 9343. **Application fee:** $40.

**STUDENT SERVICES** Academic or career counseling, daycare for children of students, employment services for current students, placement services for program completers, remedial services.

# ILLINOIS

## Alvareitas College of Cosmetology

5400 West Main, Belleville, IL 62226

**CONTACT** Alvareita Giles, President
**Telephone:** 618-257-9193

**GENERAL INFORMATION** Private Institution. **Total program enrollment:** 19. **Application fee:** $50.

*Alvareitas College of Cosmetology (continued)*

**PROGRAM(S) OFFERED**

• **Cosmetology, Barber/Styling, and Nail Instructor** *1000 hrs./$3300* • **Hair Styling/Stylist and Hair Design** *1540 hrs./$11,500*

**STUDENT SERVICES** Academic or career counseling.

## Alvareita's College of Cosmetology

333 South Kansas Street, Edwardsville, IL 62025

**CONTACT** Alavreita Giles, President
**Telephone:** 618-656-2593

**GENERAL INFORMATION** Private Institution. Founded 1965. **Total program enrollment:** 29. **Application fee:** $50.

**PROGRAM(S) OFFERED**

• **Cosmetology, Barber/Styling, and Nail Instructor** *1000 hrs./$3300* • **Hair Styling/Stylist and Hair Design** *1540 hrs./$11,500*

**STUDENT SERVICES** Academic or career counseling.

## Alvareita's College of Cosmetology

5711 Godfrey Road, Godfrey, IL 62035

**CONTACT** Alvareita Giles, President
**Telephone:** 618-466-9723

**GENERAL INFORMATION** Private Institution. Founded 1984. **Total program enrollment:** 35. **Application fee:** $50.

**PROGRAM(S) OFFERED**

• **Cosmetology, Barber/Styling, and Nail Instructor** *1000 hrs./$4000* • **Hair Styling/Stylist and Hair Design** *1540 hrs./$11,450* • **Massage Therapy/Therapeutic Massage** *720 hrs./$5500*

**STUDENT SERVICES** Academic or career counseling.

## American Career College

7000 W. Cermak Road, Berwyn, IL 60402

**CONTACT** Patricia Caraballo, President
**Telephone:** 708-795-1500

**GENERAL INFORMATION** Private Institution. **Total program enrollment:** 35.

**PROGRAM(S) OFFERED**

• **Cosmetology, Barber/Styling, and Nail Instructor** *500 hrs./$2500* • **Cosmetology/Cosmetologist, General** *1500 hrs./$10,800* • **Nail Technician/Specialist and Manicurist** *350 hrs./$2400*

**STUDENT SERVICES** Academic or career counseling, placement services for program completers, remedial services.

## Beck Area Career Center–Red Bud

6137 Beck Road, Red Bud, IL 62278
http://www.schools.lth5.k12.il.us/beck/

**CONTACT** Dian Albert, Director
**Telephone:** 618-473-2222

**GENERAL INFORMATION** Public Institution. Founded 1972. **Total program enrollment:** 98.

**PROGRAM(S) OFFERED**

• **Licensed Practical/Vocational Nurse Training (LPN, LVN, Cert, Dipl, AAS)** *1463 hrs./$10,962* • **Nurse/Nursing Assistant/Aide and Patient Care Assistant** *138 hrs./$550*

**STUDENT SERVICES** Academic or career counseling, placement services for program completers, remedial services.

## Bell Mar Beauty College

5717 West Cermak, Cicero, IL 60804

**CONTACT** Vincent Guarna, President
**Telephone:** 708-863-6644

**GENERAL INFORMATION** Private Institution.

**PROGRAM(S) OFFERED**

• **Cosmetology, Barber/Styling, and Nail Instructor** *1500 hrs./$8801* • **Cosmetology/Cosmetologist, General** *250 hrs./$1000*

**STUDENT SERVICES** Academic or career counseling, placement services for program completers, remedial services.

## BIR Training Center

3601 West Devon, Suite 210, Chicago, IL 60659
http://www.birtraining.com/

**CONTACT** Irene Zakon, CEO
**Telephone:** 773-866-0111

**GENERAL INFORMATION** Private Institution. **Total program enrollment:** 693. **Application fee:** $80.

**PROGRAM(S) OFFERED**

• **Accounting and Related Services, Other** *22 hrs./$5480* • **English Language and Literature, General** *35 hrs./$5680* • **Finance and Financial Management Services, Other** • **Health Information/Medical Records Technology/Technician** *23 hrs./$6790* • **Mechanical Engineering Related Technologies/Technicians, Other** *23 hrs./$8280* • **Medical Office Assistant/Specialist** *31 hrs./$9035* • **Medical Office Computer Specialist/Assistant** *36 students enrolled*

**STUDENT SERVICES** Academic or career counseling, placement services for program completers, remedial services.

## Black Hawk College

6600 34th Avenue, Moline, IL 61265-5899
http://www.bhc.edu/

**CONTACT** Dr. R. Gene Gardner, Interim President
**Telephone:** 309-796-5000

**GENERAL INFORMATION** Public Institution. Founded 1946. **Accreditation:** Regional (NCA); physical therapy assisting (APTA). **Total program enrollment:** 2622.

**PROGRAM(S) OFFERED**

• **Accounting Technology/Technician and Bookkeeping** *3 students enrolled* • **Agricultural Mechanization, General** *3 students enrolled* • **Animal/Livestock Husbandry and Production** *17 students enrolled* • **Automobile/Automotive Mechanics Technology/Technician** *5 students enrolled* • **CAD/CADD Drafting and/or Design Technology/Technician** *2 students enrolled* • **Child Care Provider/Assistant** *5 students enrolled* • **Computer Systems Networking and Telecommunications** *3 students enrolled* • **Criminal Justice/Police Science** *1 student enrolled* • **Electromechanical Technology/Electromechanical Engineering Technology** *4 students enrolled* • **Emergency Medical Technology/Technician (EMT Paramedic)** *1 student enrolled* • **Legal Administrative Assistant/Secretary** *1 student enrolled* • **Licensed Practical/Vocational Nurse Training (LPN, LVN, Cert, Dipl, AAS)** *41 students enrolled* • **Machine Tool Technology/Machinist** *1 student enrolled* • **Manufacturing Technology/Technician** *8 students enrolled* • **Massage Therapy/Therapeutic Massage** *13 students enrolled* • **Medical Insurance Coding Specialist/Coder** *13 students enrolled* • **Medical Insurance Specialist/Medical Biller** *6 students enrolled* • **Medical Transcription/Transcriptionist** *9 students enrolled* • **Retailing and Retail Operations** *2 students enrolled* • **Welding Technology/Welder** *4 students enrolled*

**STUDENT SERVICES** Academic or career counseling, employment services for current students, placement services for program completers, remedial services.

## Brown Mackie College–Moline

1527 47th Avenue, Moline, IL 61265-7062
http://www.brownmackie.edu/Moline/

**CONTACT** Kareem Odukale, Campus President
**Telephone:** 309-762-2100

**GENERAL INFORMATION** Private Institution. **Total program enrollment:** 165.

**PROGRAM(S) OFFERED**
• **Accounting** *4 students enrolled* • **Business Administration and Management, General** *16 students enrolled* • **Computer Software Technology/Technician** *4 students enrolled* • **Legal Assistant/Paralegal** *11 students enrolled* • **Medical Office Management/Administration** *13 students enrolled* • **Medical/Clinical Assistant** *47 students enrolled*

**STUDENT SERVICES** Academic or career counseling, employment services for current students, placement services for program completers, remedial services.

## Cain's Barber College

365 East 51st Street, Chicago, IL 60615-3510
http://www.cainbarber1.org/

**CONTACT** Jessica Pearson-Cain, President/CEO
**Telephone:** 773-536-4441

**GENERAL INFORMATION** Private Institution. Founded 1985. **Total program enrollment:** 129. **Application fee:** $100.

**PROGRAM(S) OFFERED**
• **Barbering/Barber** *1500 hrs./$8985* • **Cosmetology, Barber/Styling, and Nail Instructor** *2 students enrolled*

**STUDENT SERVICES** Placement services for program completers.

## CALC Institute of Technology

235-A E. Center Drive, Alton, IL 62002
http://www.calc4it.com/

**CONTACT** Fred Albrecht, Director
**Telephone:** 618-474-0616

**GENERAL INFORMATION** Private Institution.

**PROGRAM(S) OFFERED**
• **Computer Systems Networking and Telecommunications** *550 hrs./$7800* • **Medical Office Assistant/Specialist** *580 hrs./$7872* • **Medical/Clinical Assistant** *900 hrs.* • **System, Networking, and LAN/WAN Management/Manager** *850 hrs./$12,000*

**STUDENT SERVICES** Placement services for program completers.

## Cameo Beauty Academy

9714 South Cicero Avenue, Oak Lawn, IL 60453
http://www.cameobeautyacademy.com/

**CONTACT** Herman A. Harrison, President
**Telephone:** 708-636-4660

**GENERAL INFORMATION** Private Institution. Founded 1960. **Total program enrollment:** 75.

**PROGRAM(S) OFFERED**
• **Cosmetology, Barber/Styling, and Nail Instructor** *5 students enrolled* • **Cosmetology/Cosmetologist, General** *1500 hrs./$17,300* • **Trade and Industrial Teacher Education** *1000 hrs./$10,700*

**STUDENT SERVICES** Academic or career counseling, placement services for program completers.

## Cannella School of Hair Design

12840 South Western Avenue, Blue Island, IL 60406
http://djosephcannella@aol.com/

**CONTACT** Joseph Cannella, President
**Telephone:** 708-388-4949

**GENERAL INFORMATION** Private Institution. **Total program enrollment:** 18.

**PROGRAM(S) OFFERED**
• **Cosmetology/Cosmetologist, General** *1500 hrs./$12,990* • **Teacher Education and Professional Development, Specific Subject Areas, Other** *1000 hrs./$5750*

**STUDENT SERVICES** Academic or career counseling, placement services for program completers.

## Cannella School of Hair Design

4217 West North Avenue, Chicago, IL 60639
http://djosephcannella@aol.com/

**CONTACT** Joseph Cannella, Owner
**Telephone:** 773-278-4477

**GENERAL INFORMATION** Private Institution. **Total program enrollment:** 8.

**PROGRAM(S) OFFERED**
• **Cosmetology/Cosmetologist, General** *1500 hrs./$10,900* • **Teacher Education and Professional Development, Specific Subject Areas, Other** *1000 hrs./$5750*

**STUDENT SERVICES** Academic or career counseling, placement services for program completers.

## Cannella School of Hair Design

4269 South Archer Avenue, Chicago, IL 60632
http://djosephcannella@aol.com/

**CONTACT** Joseph Cannella, President
**Telephone:** 773-890-0412

**GENERAL INFORMATION** Private Institution. **Total program enrollment:** 23.

**PROGRAM(S) OFFERED**
• **Cosmetology/Cosmetologist, General** *1500 hrs./$10,900* • **Teacher Education and Professional Development, Specific Subject Areas, Other** *1000 hrs./$5750*

**STUDENT SERVICES** Academic or career counseling, placement services for program completers.

## Cannella School of Hair Design

9012 South Commercial, Chicago, IL 60617
http://djosephcannella@aol.com/

**CONTACT** Joseph Cannella, Owner
**Telephone:** 773-221-4700

**GENERAL INFORMATION** Private Institution. **Total program enrollment:** 15.

**PROGRAM(S) OFFERED**
• **Cosmetology/Cosmetologist, General** *1500 hrs./$12,990* • **Teacher Education and Professional Development, Specific Subject Areas, Other** *1000 hrs./$5750*

**STUDENT SERVICES** Academic or career counseling, placement services for program completers.

## Cannella School of Hair Design

113-117 West Chicago Street, Elgin, IL 60120
http://djosephcannella@aol.com/

**CONTACT** Joseph Cannella, Owner
**Telephone:** 708-742-6611

**GENERAL INFORMATION** Private Institution. **Total program enrollment:** 7.

**PROGRAM(S) OFFERED**
• **Cosmetology/Cosmetologist, General** *1500 hrs./$12,990* • **Teacher Education and Professional Development, Specific Subject Areas, Other** *1000 hrs./$5750*

**STUDENT SERVICES** Academic or career counseling, placement services for program completers.

## Cannella School of Hair Design

191 North York Road, Elmhurst, IL 60126
http://djosephcannella@aol.com/

**CONTACT** Joseph Cannella, Owner
**Telephone:** 708-833-6118

**GENERAL INFORMATION** Private Institution. **Total program enrollment:** 13.

**PROGRAM(S) OFFERED**
• **Cosmetology/Cosmetologist, General** *1500 hrs./$10,900* • **Teacher Education and Professional Development, Specific Subject Areas, Other** *1000 hrs./$5750*

**STUDENT SERVICES** Academic or career counseling, placement services for program completers.

## Capital Area School of Practical Nursing

2201 Toronto Road, Springfield, IL 62707

**CONTACT** Karen Riddell, Office Manager/Administrative Assistant
**Telephone:** 217-585-2160

**GENERAL INFORMATION** Public Institution. Founded 1958. **Total program enrollment:** 65. **Application fee:** $70.

**PROGRAM(S) OFFERED**
• **Licensed Practical/Vocational Nurse Training (LPN, LVN, Cert, Dipl, AAS)** *1330 hrs./$7688*

**STUDENT SERVICES** Academic or career counseling.

## Capri Garfield Ridge School of Beauty Culture

6301 South Washtenaw, Chicago, IL 60629
http://www.capribeautyschool.com/

**CONTACT** Frederick Seil, President
**Telephone:** 773-778-0882 Ext. 225

**GENERAL INFORMATION** Private Institution. Founded 1966. **Total program enrollment:** 96. **Application fee:** $100.

**PROGRAM(S) OFFERED**
• **Cosmetology, Barber/Styling, and Nail Instructor** *1000 hrs./$8100*
• **Cosmetology/Cosmetologist, General** *1500 hrs./$15,700*

**STUDENT SERVICES** Academic or career counseling, placement services for program completers.

## Capri Oak Forest School of Beauty Culture

15815 South Robroy Drive, Oak Forest, IL 60452
http://www.capribeautycollege.com/

**CONTACT** Frederick C. Seil, President
**Telephone:** 708-687-3020

**GENERAL INFORMATION** Private Institution. Founded 1978. **Total program enrollment:** 110. **Application fee:** $100.

**PROGRAM(S) OFFERED**
• **Cosmetology, Barber/Styling, and Nail Instructor** *1000 hrs./$9714*
• **Cosmetology/Cosmetologist, General** *1500 hrs./$17,750*

**STUDENT SERVICES** Academic or career counseling, employment services for current students, placement services for program completers.

## Carl Sandburg College

2400 Tom L. Wilson Boulevard, Galesburg, IL 61401-9576
http://www.sandburg.edu/

**CONTACT** Thomas A. Schmidt, President
**Telephone:** 309-344-2518

**GENERAL INFORMATION** Public Institution. Founded 1967. **Accreditation:** Regional (NCA); dental hygiene (ADA); funeral service (ABFSE); radiologic technology: radiography (JRCERT). **Total program enrollment:** 1178.

**PROGRAM(S) OFFERED**
• **Accounting** *4 students enrolled* • **Administrative Assistant and Secretarial Science, General** *5 students enrolled* • **Automobile/Automotive Mechanics Technology/Technician** *2 students enrolled* • **Business Administration and Management, General** *1 student enrolled* • **Cosmetology, Barber/Styling, and Nail Instructor** *1 student enrolled* • **Cosmetology/Cosmetologist, General** *13 students enrolled* • **Criminal Justice/Police Science** *1 student enrolled* • **Diagnostic Medical Sonography/Sonographer and Ultrasound Technician** *7 students enrolled* • **Diesel Mechanics Technology/Technician** *1 student enrolled* • **Licensed Practical/Vocational Nurse Training (LPN, LVN, Cert, Dipl, AAS)** *66 students enrolled* • **Massage Therapy/Therapeutic Massage** *6 students enrolled* • **Medical Administrative/Executive Assistant and Medical Secretary** *11 students enrolled* • **Medical/Clinical Assistant** *10 students enrolled* • **Nuclear Medical Technology/Technologist** *3 students enrolled* • **Radiologic Technology/Science—Radiographer** *5 students enrolled* • **Social Work** *3 students enrolled* • **Welding Technology/Welder** *2 students enrolled*

**STUDENT SERVICES** Academic or career counseling, daycare for children of students, employment services for current students, placement services for program completers, remedial services.

## Center for Employment Training–Chicago

3301 West Arthington, Suite 101, Chicago, IL 60624

**CONTACT** Marie Pickett, Director
**Telephone:** 408-287-7924

**GENERAL INFORMATION** Private Institution. **Total program enrollment:** 400.

**PROGRAM(S) OFFERED**
• **Administrative Assistant and Secretarial Science, General** • **Building/Property Maintenance and Management** *630 hrs./$7083* • **Medical/Clinical Assistant** *900 hrs./$8864*

**STUDENT SERVICES** Academic or career counseling, employment services for current students, placement services for program completers, remedial services.

## Christian Life College

400 East Gregory Street, Mount Prospect, IL 60056
http://www.christianlifecollege.edu/

**CONTACT** Harry Schmidt, President
**Telephone:** 847-259-1840

**GENERAL INFORMATION** Private Institution. Founded 1950. **Accreditation:** State accredited or approved. **Total program enrollment:** 36. **Application fee:** $35.

**STUDENT SERVICES** Academic or career counseling, employment services for current students, placement services for program completers, remedial services.

## City Colleges of Chicago, Harold Washington College

30 East Lake Street, Chicago, IL 60601-2449
http://hwashington.ccc.edu/

**CONTACT** John R. Wozniak, President
**Telephone:** 312-553-5600

**GENERAL INFORMATION** Public Institution. Founded 1962. **Accreditation:** Regional (NCA). **Total program enrollment:** 4173.

**PROGRAM(S) OFFERED**
• **Accounting** *3 students enrolled* • **Animation, Interactive Technology, Video Graphics and Special Effects** *4 students enrolled* • **Architectural Drafting and Architectural CAD/CADD** *1 student enrolled* • **Business Administration and Management, General** *2 students enrolled* • **Child Care Provider/Assistant** *8 students enrolled* • **Criminal Justice/Safety Studies** *1 student enrolled* • **Foodservice Systems Administration/Management** *1027 students enrolled* • **Information Science/Studies** *2 students enrolled* • **Marketing/Marketing Management, General** *3 students enrolled* • **Music, General** *1 student enrolled* • **Nurse/Nursing Assistant/Aide and Patient Care Assistant** *61 students enrolled* • **Social Work** *3 students enrolled* • **Substance Abuse/Addiction Counseling** *13 students enrolled* • **Truck and Bus Driver/Commercial Vehicle Operation** *3183 students enrolled*

**STUDENT SERVICES** Academic or career counseling, employment services for current students, placement services for program completers, remedial services.

## City Colleges of Chicago, Harry S. Truman College

1145 West Wilson Avenue, Chicago, IL 60640-5616
http://www.trumancollege.cc/

**CONTACT** Lynn Walker, President
**Telephone:** 773-907-4700

**GENERAL INFORMATION** Public Institution. Founded 1956. **Accreditation:** Regional (NCA). **Total program enrollment:** 2569.

**PROGRAM(S) OFFERED**
• **Accounting** *3 students enrolled* • **Appliance Installation and Repair Technology/Technician** *4 students enrolled* • **Automobile/Automotive Mechanics Technology/Technician** *13 students enrolled* • **Business Administration and Management, General** *1 student enrolled* • **Child Care Provider/Assistant** *20 students enrolled* • **Computer Systems Networking and Telecommunications** *1 student enrolled* • **Cosmetology/Cosmetologist, General** *39 students enrolled* • **Information Science/Studies** *11 students enrolled* • **Mechanical Drafting and Mechanical Drafting CAD/CADD** *2 students enrolled* • **Pharmacy Technician/Assistant** *48 students enrolled* • **Phlebotomy/Phlebotomist** *11 students enrolled* • **Web Page, Digital/Multimedia and Information Resources Design** *2 students enrolled*

**STUDENT SERVICES** Academic or career counseling, daycare for children of students, employment services for current students, placement services for program completers, remedial services.

## City Colleges of Chicago, Kennedy-King College

6800 South Wentworth Avenue, Chicago, IL 60621-3733
http://kennedyking.ccc.edu/

**CONTACT** Clyde El-Amin, President
**Telephone:** 773-602-5000

**GENERAL INFORMATION** Public Institution. Founded 1935. **Accreditation:** Regional (NCA); dental hygiene (ADA). **Total program enrollment:** 3090.

**PROGRAM(S) OFFERED**
• **Animation, Interactive Technology, Video Graphics and Special Effects** *1 student enrolled* • **Autobody/Collision and Repair Technology/Technician** *4 students enrolled* • **Automobile/Automotive Mechanics Technology/Technician** *9 students enrolled* • **Baking and Pastry Arts/Baker/Pastry Chef** *24 students enrolled* • **Building/Home/Construction Inspection/Inspector** *4 students enrolled* • **Carpentry/Carpenter** *61 students enrolled* • **Child Care Provider/Assistant** *16 students enrolled* • **Criminal Justice/Safety Studies** *14 students enrolled* • **Culinary Arts/Chef Training** *35 students enrolled* • **Graphic Communications, General** *1 student enrolled* • **Heating, Air Conditioning, Ventilation and Refrigeration Maintenance Technology/Technician (HAC, HACR, HVAC, HVACR)** *1 student enrolled* • **Information Science/Studies** *2 students enrolled* • **Lineworker** *30 students enrolled* • **Mason/Masonry** *44 students enrolled* • **Medical Insurance Coding Specialist/Coder** *5 students enrolled* • **Mental Health Counseling/Counselor** *1 student enrolled* • **Nurse/Nursing Assistant/Aide and Patient Care Assistant** *8 students enrolled* • **Painting/Painter and Wall Coverer** *9 students enrolled* • **Phlebotomy/Phlebotomist** *11 students enrolled* • **Platemaker/Imager** *1 student enrolled* • **Substance Abuse/Addiction Counseling** *28 students enrolled* • **Web Page, Digital/Multimedia and Information Resources Design** *1 student enrolled* • **Welding Technology/Welder** *11 students enrolled*

**STUDENT SERVICES** Academic or career counseling, daycare for children of students, employment services for current students, placement services for program completers, remedial services.

## City Colleges of Chicago, Malcolm X College

1900 West Van Buren Street, Chicago, IL 60612-3145
http://malcolmx.ccc.edu/

**CONTACT** Ghingo Brooks, President
**Telephone:** 312-850-7000

**GENERAL INFORMATION** Public Institution. Founded 1911. **Accreditation:** Regional (NCA); funeral service (ABFSE); radiologic technology: radiography (JRCERT); surgical technology (ARCST). **Total program enrollment:** 2584.

**PROGRAM(S) OFFERED**
• **Child Care Provider/Assistant** *14 students enrolled* • **Emergency Care Attendant (EMT Ambulance)** *128 students enrolled* • **Nurse/Nursing Assistant/Aide and Patient Care Assistant** *126 students enrolled* • **Pharmacy Technician/Assistant** *14 students enrolled* • **Phlebotomy/Phlebotomist** *6 students enrolled* • **Renal/Dialysis Technologist/Technician** *8 students enrolled* • **Surgical Technology/Technologist** *9 students enrolled*

**STUDENT SERVICES** Academic or career counseling, daycare for children of students, employment services for current students, placement services for program completers, remedial services.

## City Colleges of Chicago, Olive-Harvey College

10001 South Woodlawn Avenue, Chicago, IL 60628-1645
http://oliveharvey.ccc.edu/

**CONTACT** Dr. Valerie Roberson, President
**Telephone:** 773-291-6100

**GENERAL INFORMATION** Public Institution. Founded 1970. **Accreditation:** Regional (NCA). **Total program enrollment:** 1758.

*City Colleges of Chicago, Olive-Harvey College (continued)*

**PROGRAM(S) OFFERED**

• **Accounting** *1 student enrolled* • **Child Care Provider/Assistant** *29 students enrolled* • **Criminal Justice/Safety Studies** *2 students enrolled* • **Emergency Medical Technology/Technician (EMT Paramedic)** *30 students enrolled* • **Ground Transportation, Other** *31 students enrolled* • **Information Science/Studies** *1 student enrolled* • **Marketing/Marketing Management, General** *1 student enrolled* • **Medical Insurance Coding Specialist/Coder** *8 students enrolled* • **Nurse/Nursing Assistant/Aide and Patient Care Assistant** *22 students enrolled* • **Pharmacy Technician/Assistant** *6 students enrolled* • **Phlebotomy/Phlebotomist** *6 students enrolled*

**STUDENT SERVICES** Academic or career counseling, daycare for children of students, employment services for current students, placement services for program completers, remedial services.

## City Colleges of Chicago, Richard J. Daley College

7500 South Pulaski Road, Chicago, IL 60652-1242
http://daley.ccc.edu/

**CONTACT** Dr. Sylvia Ramos, President
**Telephone:** 773-838-7500

**GENERAL INFORMATION** Public Institution. Founded 1960. **Accreditation:** Regional (NCA). **Total program enrollment:** 3507.

**PROGRAM(S) OFFERED**

• **Accounting** *7 students enrolled* • **Business Administration and Management, General** *5 students enrolled* • **Business/Office Automation/Technology/Data Entry** *1 student enrolled* • **Child Care Provider/Assistant** *23 students enrolled* • **Computer Installation and Repair Technology/Technician** *12 students enrolled* • **Computer Systems Networking and Telecommunications** *2 students enrolled* • **Criminal Justice/Police Science** *1 student enrolled* • **Criminal Justice/Safety Studies** *4 students enrolled* • **Emergency Medical Technology/Technician (EMT Paramedic)** *1 student enrolled* • **Industrial Mechanics and Maintenance Technology** *12 students enrolled* • **Information Science/Studies** *20 students enrolled* • **Machine Tool Technology/Machinist** *4 students enrolled* • **Marketing/Marketing Management, General** *44 students enrolled* • **Medical Insurance Coding Specialist/Coder** *29 students enrolled* • **Medical Staff Services Technology/Technician** *2 students enrolled* • **Nurse/Nursing Assistant/Aide and Patient Care Assistant** *95 students enrolled* • **Pharmacy Technician/Assistant** *26 students enrolled* • **Phlebotomy/Phlebotomist** *28 students enrolled* • **Real Estate** *1 student enrolled* • **Security and Loss Prevention Services** *2 students enrolled*

**STUDENT SERVICES** Academic or career counseling, daycare for children of students, employment services for current students, placement services for program completers, remedial services.

## City Colleges of Chicago System

226 West Jackson Boulevard, Chicago, IL 60606-6998
http://www.ccc.edu

**CONTACT** Dr. Wayne Watson, Chancellor
**Telephone:** 312-553-2500

**GENERAL INFORMATION** Public Institution.

## City Colleges of Chicago, Wilbur Wright College

4300 North Narragansett Avenue, Chicago, IL 60634-1591
http://wright.ccc.edu/

**CONTACT** Charles Guengerich, President
**Telephone:** 773-777-7900

**GENERAL INFORMATION** Public Institution. Founded 1934. **Accreditation:** Regional (NCA); radiologic technology: radiography (JRCERT). **Total program enrollment:** 3547.

**PROGRAM(S) OFFERED**

• **Accounting** *3 students enrolled* • **Architectural Drafting and Architectural CAD/CADD** *11 students enrolled* • **Business Administration and Management, General** *2 students enrolled* • **Business/Office Automation/Technology/Data Entry** *5 students enrolled* • **Computer Installation and Repair Technology/Technician** *2 students enrolled* • **Criminal Justice/Safety Studies** *2 students enrolled* • **Criminalistics and Criminal Science** *1 student enrolled* • **Dental Assisting/Assistant** *6 students enrolled* • **Emergency Medical Technology/Technician (EMT Paramedic)** *56 students enrolled* • **Energy Management and Systems Technology/Technician** *10 students enrolled* • **Environmental Engineering Technology/Environmental Technology** *2 students enrolled* • **Hospital and Health Care Facilities Administration/Management** *1 student enrolled* • **Industrial Mechanics and Maintenance Technology** *11 students enrolled* • **Information Science/Studies** *3 students enrolled* • **Library Assistant/Technician** *1 student enrolled* • **Licensed Practical/Vocational Nurse Training (LPN, LVN, Cert, Dipl, AAS)** *40 students enrolled* • **Marketing/Marketing Management, General** *4 students enrolled* • **Mechanical Drafting and Mechanical Drafting CAD/CADD** *6 students enrolled* • **Medical Insurance Coding Specialist/Coder** *8 students enrolled* • **Nurse/Nursing Assistant/Aide and Patient Care Assistant** *98 students enrolled* • **Pharmacy Technician/Assistant** *3 students enrolled* • **Phlebotomy/Phlebotomist** *49 students enrolled* • **Psychiatric/Mental Health Services Technician** *17 students enrolled* • **Substance Abuse/Addiction Counseling** *6 students enrolled*

**STUDENT SERVICES** Academic or career counseling, employment services for current students, placement services for program completers, remedial services.

## College of DuPage

425 Fawell Boulevard, Glen Ellyn, IL 60137-6599
http://www.cod.edu/

**CONTACT** Dr. Robert Breuder, President
**Telephone:** 630-942-2800

**GENERAL INFORMATION** Public Institution. Founded 1967. **Accreditation:** Regional (NCA); dental hygiene (ADA); health information technology (AHIMA); physical therapy assisting (APTA); radiologic technology: radiography (JRCERT); respiratory therapy technology (CoARC). **Total program enrollment:** 9882. **Application fee:** $10.

**PROGRAM(S) OFFERED**

• **Accounting Technology/Technician and Bookkeeping** *14 students enrolled* • **Administrative Assistant and Secretarial Science, General** *50 students enrolled* • **Applied Horticulture/Horticultural Operations, General** *5 students enrolled* • **Architectural Drafting and Architectural CAD/CADD** *2 students enrolled* • **Automobile/Automotive Mechanics Technology/Technician** *23 students enrolled* • **Baking and Pastry Arts/Baker/Pastry Chef** *2 students enrolled* • **Building/Property Maintenance and Management** *4 students enrolled* • **Business Administration and Management, General** *65 students enrolled* • **Child Care Provider/Assistant** *2 students enrolled* • **Child Care and Support Services Management** *7 students enrolled* • **Commercial Photography** *10 students enrolled* • **Commercial and Advertising Art** *47 students enrolled* • **Computer Installation and Repair Technology/Technician** *127 students enrolled* • **Computer Programming, Specific Applications** *12 students enrolled* • **Computer Technology/Computer Systems Technology** *2 students enrolled* • **Criminal Justice/Police Science** *12 students enrolled* • **Culinary Arts/Chef Training** *8 students enrolled* • **Data Entry/Microcomputer Applications, General** *1 student enrolled* • **Diagnostic Medical Sonography/Sonographer and Ultrasound Technician** *8 students enrolled* • **Electrocardiograph Technology/Technician** *1 student enrolled* • **Emergency Medical Technology/Technician (EMT Paramedic)** *212 students enrolled* • **Entrepreneurship/Entrepreneurial Studies** *2 students enrolled* • **Fashion Merchandising** *4 students enrolled* • **Fashion and Fabric Consultant** *12 students enrolled* • **Fire Protection and Safety Technology/Technician** *4 students enrolled* • **Heating, Air Conditioning, Ventilation and Refrigeration Maintenance Technology/Technician (HAC, HACR, HVAC, HVACR)** *20 students enrolled* • **Home Health Aide/Home Attendant** *27 students enrolled* • **Hospital and Health Care Facilities Administration/Management** *9 students enrolled* • **Hotel/Motel Administration/Management** *3 students enrolled* • **Illustration** *1 student enrolled* • **Interior Design** *40 students enrolled* • **Landscaping and Groundskeeping** *7 students enrolled* • **Library Assistant/Technician** *21 students enrolled* • **Massage Therapy/Therapeutic Massage** *9 students enrolled* • **Medical Insurance Coding Specialist/Coder** *12 students enrolled* • **Medical Radiologic Technology/Science—Radiation Therapist** *15 students enrolled* • **Medical Transcription/Transcriptionist** *76 students enrolled* • **Nuclear Medical Technology/Technologist** *17 students enrolled* • **Nurse/Nursing Assistant/Aide and Patient Care Assistant** *184 students enrolled* • **Ornamental Horticulture** *2 students enrolled* • **Pharmacy Technician/Assistant** *65 students enrolled* • **Photographic and Film/Video Technology/Technician and Assistant** *5 students enrolled* • **Plant Nursery Operations and Management** *3 students* enrolled • **Plastics Engineering Technology/Technician** *1 student enrolled* • **Platemaker/Imager** *1 student enrolled* • **Prepress/Desktop Publishing and Digital Imaging Design** *8 students enrolled* • **Restaurant, Culinary, and Catering Management/Manager** *3 students enrolled* • **Robotics Technology/Technician** *1 student enrolled* • **Sales, Distribution and Marketing Operations, General** *8 students enrolled* • **Selling Skills and Sales Operations** *14 students enrolled* • **Social Work** *5 students enrolled* • **Substance Abuse/Addiction Counseling** *2 students enrolled* • **Surgical Technology/Technologist** *23 students enrolled* • **Technical and Business Writing** *1 student enrolled* • **Tourism and Travel Services Marketing Operations** *32 students enrolled* • **Web Page, Digital/Multimedia and Information Resources Design** *4 students enrolled* • **Welding Technology/Welder** *1 student enrolled*

**STUDENT SERVICES** Academic or career counseling, daycare for children of students, employment services for current students, remedial services.

## College of Lake County

19351 West Washington Street, Grayslake, IL 60030-1198
http://www.clcillinois.edu/

**CONTACT** James Rock, Interim President
**Telephone:** 847-543-2000

**GENERAL INFORMATION** Public Institution. Founded 1967. **Accreditation:** Regional (NCA); dental hygiene (ADA); health information technology (AHIMA); radiologic technology: radiography (JRCERT). **Total program enrollment:** 5206.

**PROGRAM(S) OFFERED**

• **Accounting Technology/Technician and Bookkeeping** *2 students enrolled* • **Accounting** *5 students enrolled* • **Administrative Assistant and Secretarial Science, General** *49 students enrolled* • **Architectural Drafting and Architectural CAD/CADD** *1 student enrolled* • **Autobody/Collision and Repair Technology/Technician** *1 student enrolled* • **Automobile/Automotive Mechanics Technology/Technician** *6 students enrolled* • **Business/Office Automation/Technology/Data Entry** *39 students enrolled* • **CAD/CADD Drafting and/or Design Technology/Technician** *5 students enrolled* • **Child Care Provider/Assistant** *5 students enrolled* • **Computer Installation and Repair Technology/Technician** *14 students enrolled* • **Computer Programming, Specific Applications** *1 student enrolled* • **Computer Systems Networking and Telecommunications** *6 students enrolled* • **Computer and Information Systems Security** *4 students enrolled* • **Construction Engineering Technology/Technician** *1 student enrolled* • **Criminal Justice/Police Science** *3 students enrolled* • **Culinary Arts/Chef Training** *7 students enrolled* • **Diagnostic Medical Sonography/Sonographer and Ultrasound Technician** *12 students enrolled* • **Early Childhood Education and Teaching** *3 students enrolled* • **Electrical, Electronic and Communications Engineering Technology/Technician** *1 student enrolled* • **Emergency Medical Technology/Technician (EMT Paramedic)** *7 students enrolled* • **Food Service, Waiter/Waitress, and Dining Room Management/Manager** *3 students enrolled* • **Forestry Technology/Technician** *4 students enrolled* • **Heating, Air Conditioning, Ventilation and Refrigeration Maintenance Technology/Technician (HAC, HACR, HVAC, HVACR)** *193 students enrolled* • **Industrial Mechanics and Maintenance Technology** *2 students enrolled* • **Landscaping and Groundskeeping** *3 students enrolled* • **Legal Assistant/Paralegal** *53 students enrolled* • **Library Assistant/Technician** *2 students enrolled* • **Machine Tool Technology/Machinist** *2 students enrolled* • **Manufacturing Technology/Technician** *2 students enrolled* • **Medical Administrative/Executive Assistant and Medical Secretary** *1 student enrolled* • **Medical Insurance Coding Specialist/Coder** *11 students enrolled* • **Medical Insurance Specialist/Medical Biller** *27 students enrolled* • **Medical Transcription/Transcriptionist** *5 students enrolled* • **Medical/Clinical Assistant** *1 student enrolled* • **Nurse/Nursing Assistant/Aide and Patient Care Assistant** *152 students enrolled* • **Office Management and Supervision** *6 students enrolled* • **Phlebotomy/Phlebotomist** *71 students enrolled* • **Securities Services Administration/Management** *3 students enrolled* • **Selling Skills and Sales Operations** *5 students enrolled* • **Small Business Administration/Management** *7 students enrolled* • **Social Work** *2 students enrolled* • **Substance Abuse/Addiction Counseling** *1 student enrolled* • **Surgical Technology/Technologist** *8 students enrolled* • **System Administration/Administrator** *1 student enrolled* • **Teacher Assistant/Aide** *8 students enrolled* • **Teaching English as a Second or Foreign Language/ESL Language Instructor** *3 students enrolled* • **Technical and Business Writing** *4 students enrolled* • **Web Page, Digital/Multimedia and Information Resources Design** *4 students enrolled* • **Welding Technology/Welder** *4 students enrolled*

**STUDENT SERVICES** Academic or career counseling, daycare for children of students, employment services for current students, placement services for program completers, remedial services.

## The College of Office Technology

1520 West Division Street, Chicago, IL 60622
http://www.cotedu.com/

**CONTACT** Pedro Galva, President
**Telephone:** 773-278-0042

**GENERAL INFORMATION** Private Institution. **Accreditation:** State accredited or approved. **Total program enrollment:** 365. **Application fee:** $50.

**PROGRAM(S) OFFERED**

• **Computer Systems Networking and Telecommunications** • **Data Entry/Microcomputer Applications, General** *55 hrs./$10,533* • **Data Entry/Microcomputer Applications, Other** *75 students enrolled* • **Data Processing and Data Processing Technology/Technician** *36 hrs./$9763* • **Medical Office Assistant/Specialist** *45 hrs./$10,368* • **Medical/Clinical Assistant** *70 hrs./$10,995* • **Nurse/Nursing Assistant/Aide and Patient Care Assistant** *42 hrs./$10,368* • **Phlebotomy/Phlebotomist** *46 students enrolled*

**STUDENT SERVICES** Academic or career counseling, employment services for current students, placement services for program completers, remedial services.

## Columbia College Chicago

600 South Michigan Avenue, Chicago, IL 60605-1996
http://www.colum.edu/

**CONTACT** Warrick Carter, President
**Telephone:** 312-663-1600

**GENERAL INFORMATION** Private Institution. Founded 1890. **Accreditation:** Regional (NCA). **Total program enrollment:** 10933. **Application fee:** $35.

**PROGRAM(S) OFFERED**

• **Arts Management** *1 student enrolled* • **Cinematography and Film/Video Production** *5 students enrolled* • **Fashion/Apparel Design** *1 student enrolled* • **Graphic Design** *3 students enrolled* • **Industrial Design** *1 student enrolled* • **Journalism** *1 student enrolled* • **Marketing/Marketing Management, General** *1 student enrolled* • **Photography** • **Radio and Television** *3 students enrolled* • **Recording Arts Technology/Technician** *2 students enrolled* • **Web Page, Digital/Multimedia and Information Resources Design** *1 student enrolled*

**STUDENT SERVICES** Academic or career counseling, employment services for current students, placement services for program completers, remedial services.

## Computer Systems Institute

8930 Gross Point Road, Skokie, IL 60077

**CONTACT** Julia Lowder, Executive Vice President
**Telephone:** 847-967-5030

**GENERAL INFORMATION** Private Institution. **Total program enrollment:** 266. **Application fee:** $35.

**PROGRAM(S) OFFERED**

• **Business/Office Automation/Technology/Data Entry** *36 hrs./$10,950* • **Medical Insurance Specialist/Medical Biller** *36 hrs./$11,700* • **Medical Office Management/Administration** *12 students enrolled* • **System, Networking, and LAN/WAN Management/Manager** *36 hrs./$10,950*

**STUDENT SERVICES** Academic or career counseling, placement services for program completers.

## Concept College of Cosmetology

2500 Georgetown Road, Danville, IL 61832
http://conceptcollege.com/

**CONTACT** Janet Trosper, President
**Telephone:** 217-442-9329

**GENERAL INFORMATION** Private Institution. **Total program enrollment:** 48. **Application fee:** $25.

**PROGRAM(S) OFFERED**
• **Cosmetology, Barber/Styling, and Nail Instructor** *1000 hrs./$3800* • **Cosmetology/Cosmetologist, General** *1500 hrs./$11,200* • **Teacher Education and Professional Development, Specific Subject Areas, Other**

**STUDENT SERVICES** Academic or career counseling.

## Concept College of Cosmetology

129 North Race Street, Urbana, IL 61802
http://conceptcollege.com/

**CONTACT** Janet Trosper, President
**Telephone:** 217-344-7550

**GENERAL INFORMATION** Private Institution. **Total program enrollment:** 42. **Application fee:** $25.

**PROGRAM(S) OFFERED**
• **Cosmetology, Barber/Styling, and Nail Instructor** *1000 hrs./$3800* • **Cosmetology/Cosmetologist, General** *1500 hrs./$11,200* • **Teacher Education and Professional Development, Specific Subject Areas, Other** *1 student enrolled*

**STUDENT SERVICES** Academic or career counseling.

## The Cooking and Hospitality Institute of Chicago

361 West Chestnut, Chicago, IL 60610-3050
http://www.chicnet.org/

**CONTACT** Lloyd Kirsch, President
**Telephone:** 312-944-0882

**GENERAL INFORMATION** Private Institution. Founded 1983. **Accreditation:** Regional (NCA); state accredited or approved. **Total program enrollment:** 1004. **Application fee:** $100.

**PROGRAM(S) OFFERED**
• **Culinary Arts/Chef Training** *76 students enrolled*

**STUDENT SERVICES** Academic or career counseling, employment services for current students, placement services for program completers, remedial services.

## Cortiva Institute—Chicago School of Massage Therapy

17 N. State Street, Suite 500, Chicago, IL 60602
http://www.cortiva.com/locations/csmt/

**CONTACT** Paul Myer, President
**Telephone:** 312-753-7900

**GENERAL INFORMATION** Private Institution. **Application fee:** $100.

**PROGRAM(S) OFFERED**
• **Massage Therapy/Therapeutic Massage** *750 hrs./$13,315*

**STUDENT SERVICES** Academic or career counseling, placement services for program completers.

## Coyne American Institute Incorporated

1235 West Fullerton Avenue, Chicago, IL 60614
http://www.coyneamerican.edu/

**CONTACT** Russell T. Freeman, President
**Telephone:** 773-577-8100

**GENERAL INFORMATION** Private Institution. **Total program enrollment:** 785. **Application fee:** $25.

**PROGRAM(S) OFFERED**
• **Allied Health and Medical Assisting Services, Other** *101 hrs./$18,507* • **Communications Systems Installation and Repair Technology** *103 hrs./$19,077* • **Electrician** *58 hrs./$10,764* • **Heating, Air Conditioning, Ventilation and Refrigeration Maintenance Technology/Technician (HAC, HACR, HVAC, HVACR)** *99 hrs./$18,433* • **Medical Administrative/Executive Assistant and Medical Secretary** *17 students enrolled* • **Medical Insurance Specialist/Medical Biller** *21 students enrolled* • **Medical/Clinical Assistant** *22 students enrolled* • **Pharmacy Technician/Assistant**

**STUDENT SERVICES** Academic or career counseling, employment services for current students, placement services for program completers.

## CSI The Cosmetology and Spa Institute

4320 West Elm Street, Suite 9, McHenry, IL 60050
http://csicl.com/

**CONTACT** Inaet Halimi, President
**Telephone:** 815-455-5900 Ext. 12

**GENERAL INFORMATION** Private Institution. Founded 1998. **Total program enrollment:** 129. **Application fee:** $100.

**PROGRAM(S) OFFERED**
• **Cosmetology, Barber/Styling, and Nail Instructor** *1000 hrs./$10,000* • **Cosmetology/Cosmetologist, General** *1500 hrs./$17,500* • **Facial Treatment Specialist/Facialist** *21 students enrolled*

**STUDENT SERVICES** Academic or career counseling, employment services for current students.

## Danville Area Community College

2000 East Main Street, Danville, IL 61832-5199
http://www.dacc.cc.il.us/

**CONTACT** Alice Jacobs, President
**Telephone:** 217-443-3222

**GENERAL INFORMATION** Public Institution. Founded 1946. **Accreditation:** Regional (NCA). **Total program enrollment:** 1178.

**PROGRAM(S) OFFERED**
• **Accounting Technology/Technician and Bookkeeping** *1 student enrolled* • **Administrative Assistant and Secretarial Science, General** *1 student enrolled* • **Agricultural Mechanics and Equipment/Machine Technology** *13 students enrolled* • **Business Administration and Management, General** *5 students enrolled* • **Computer Programming/Programmer, General** *1 student enrolled* • **Construction Engineering Technology/Technician** *6 students enrolled* • **Culinary Arts/Chef Training** *6 students enrolled* • **E-Commerce/Electronic Commerce** *1 student enrolled* • **Heating, Air Conditioning, Ventilation and Refrigeration Maintenance Technology/Technician (HAC, HACR, HVAC, HVACR)** *7 students enrolled* • **Machine Tool Technology/Machinist** *3 students enrolled* • **Medical Administrative/Executive Assistant and Medical Secretary** *3 students enrolled* • **Nurse/Nursing Assistant/Aide and Patient Care Assistant** *135 students enrolled* • **Office Management and Supervision** *9 students enrolled* • **Selling Skills and Sales Operations** *2 students enrolled* • **Truck and Bus Driver/Commercial Vehicle Operation** *29 students enrolled* • **Welding Technology/Welder** *3 students enrolled*

**STUDENT SERVICES** Academic or career counseling, daycare for children of students, employment services for current students, placement services for program completers, remedial services.

## DePaul University

1 East Jackson Boulevard, Chicago, IL 60604-2287
http://www.depaul.edu/

**CONTACT** Dennis H. Holtschneider, President
**Telephone:** 312-362-8000

**GENERAL INFORMATION** Private Institution. Founded 1898. **Accreditation:** Regional (NCA); music (NASM). **Total program enrollment:** 17850. **Application fee:** $40.

**PROGRAM(S) OFFERED**
• **Cartography** • **Music Teacher Education** *9 students enrolled*

**STUDENT SERVICES** Academic or career counseling, employment services for current students, placement services for program completers, remedial services.

## Dominican University

7900 West Division Street, River Forest, IL 60305-1099
http://www.dom.edu/

**CONTACT** Dr. Donna M. Carroll, President
**Telephone:** 708-366-2490

**GENERAL INFORMATION** Private Institution. Founded 1901. **Accreditation:** Regional (NCA); library and information science (ALA). **Total program enrollment:** 2022. **Application fee:** $25.

**PROGRAM(S) OFFERED**
• **Computer Science** • **Dietetics/Dietitians** • **Information Science/Studies** • **Pastoral Studies/Counseling**

**STUDENT SERVICES** Academic or career counseling, daycare for children of students, employment services for current students, placement services for program completers, remedial services.

## East-West University

816 South Michigan Avenue, Chicago, IL 60605-2103
http://www.eastwest.edu/

**CONTACT** M. Wasi Khan, Chancellor
**Telephone:** 312-939-0111 Ext. 1800

**GENERAL INFORMATION** Private Institution. Founded 1978. **Accreditation:** Regional (NCA). **Total program enrollment:** 1141. **Application fee:** $40.

**PROGRAM(S) OFFERED**
• **Accounting** • **Business Administration and Management, General** *21 students enrolled* • **Computer and Information Sciences, General** *5 students enrolled* • **Digital Communication and Media/Multimedia** • **Electrical, Electronic and Communications Engineering Technology/Technician** *6 students enrolled* • **Medical Insurance Specialist/Medical Biller** *8 students enrolled* • **Nurse/Nursing Assistant/Aide and Patient Care Assistant** *30 students enrolled*

**STUDENT SERVICES** Academic or career counseling, employment services for current students, remedial services.

## Educators of Beauty

122 Wright Street, La Salle, IL 61301
http://www.educatorsofbeauty.com/

**CONTACT** Diane Chamberlain, Director
**Telephone:** 815-223-7326

**GENERAL INFORMATION** Private Institution. Founded 1969. **Total program enrollment:** 57. **Application fee:** $100.

**PROGRAM(S) OFFERED**
• **Cosmetology, Barber/Styling, and Nail Instructor** *625 hrs./$4475* • **Cosmetology/Cosmetologist, General** *1500 hrs./$14,775* • **Nail Technician/Specialist and Manicurist** *350 hrs./$3100*

**STUDENT SERVICES** Academic or career counseling, employment services for current students, placement services for program completers.

## Educators of Beauty

128 South Fifth Street, Rockford, IL 61104
http://www.educatorsofbeauty.com/

**CONTACT** Rhonda Renner Loos, Owner
**Telephone:** 815-969-7030

**GENERAL INFORMATION** Private Institution. **Total program enrollment:** 81. **Application fee:** $100.

**PROGRAM(S) OFFERED**
• **Cosmetology, Barber/Styling, and Nail Instructor** *625 hrs./$4475* • **Cosmetology/Cosmetologist, General** *1500 hrs./$14,675* • **Nail Technician/Specialist and Manicurist** *350 hrs./$3100*

**STUDENT SERVICES** Academic or career counseling, employment services for current students, placement services for program completers.

## Educators of Beauty

211 East Third Street, Sterling, IL 61081
http://www.educatorsofbeauty.com/

**CONTACT** Rhonda Renner Reese, Owner
**Telephone:** 815-625-0247

**GENERAL INFORMATION** Private Institution. Founded 1946. **Total program enrollment:** 69. **Application fee:** $100.

**PROGRAM(S) OFFERED**
• **Cosmetology, Barber/Styling, and Nail Instructor** *650 hrs./$4475* • **Cosmetology/Cosmetologist, General** *1500 hrs./$14,675* • **Nail Technician/Specialist and Manicurist** *350 hrs./$3100*

**STUDENT SERVICES** Academic or career counseling, employment services for current students, placement services for program completers.

## Elgin Community College

1700 Spartan Drive, Elgin, IL 60123-7193
http://www.elgin.edu/

**CONTACT** David Sam, President
**Telephone:** 847-697-1000

**GENERAL INFORMATION** Public Institution. Founded 1949. **Accreditation:** Regional (NCA); dental assisting (ADA); medical laboratory technology (NAACLS). **Total program enrollment:** 3624.

**PROGRAM(S) OFFERED**
• **Accounting and Business/Management** *1 student enrolled* • **Administrative Assistant and Secretarial Science, General** *4 students enrolled* • **Automobile/Automotive Mechanics Technology/Technician** *145 students enrolled* • **Baking and Pastry Arts/Baker/Pastry Chef** *18 students enrolled* • **Business/Office Automation/Technology/Data Entry** *4 students enrolled* • **CAD/CADD Drafting and/or Design Technology/Technician** *20 students enrolled* • **Child Care Provider/Assistant** *54 students enrolled* • **Clinical/Medical Laboratory Technician** *2 students enrolled* • **Computer Installation and Repair Technology/Technician** *1 student enrolled* • **Corrections and Criminal Justice, Other** *21 students enrolled* • **Culinary Arts/Chef Training** *19 students enrolled* • **Dental Assisting/Assistant** *33 students enrolled* • **Emergency Medical Technology/Technician (EMT Paramedic)** *70 students enrolled* • **Entrepreneurship/Entrepreneurial Studies** *1 student enrolled* • **Executive Assistant/Executive Secretary** *1 student enrolled* • **Fire Science/Firefighting** *35 students enrolled* • **Food Preparation/Professional Cooking/Kitchen Assistant** *58 students enrolled* • **General Office Occupations and Clerical Services** *5 students enrolled* • **Heating, Air Conditioning, Ventilation and Refrigeration Maintenance Technology/Technician (HAC, HACR, HVAC, HVACR)** *82 students enrolled* • **Hospitality**

*Elgin Community College (continued)*

**Administration/Management, General** *12 students enrolled* • **Hotel/Motel Administration/Management** *1 student enrolled* • **Industrial Mechanics and Maintenance Technology** *10 students enrolled* • **Kinesiology and Exercise Science** *7 students enrolled* • **Legal Assistant/Paralegal** *18 students enrolled* • **Licensed Practical/Vocational Nurse Training (LPN, LVN, Cert, Dipl, AAS)** *90 students enrolled* • **Machine Tool Technology/Machinist** *2 students enrolled* • **Manufacturing Technology/Technician** *2 students enrolled* • **Marketing/Marketing Management, General** *1 student enrolled* • **Nurse/Nursing Assistant/Aide and Patient Care Assistant** *79 students enrolled* • **Office Management and Supervision** *7 students enrolled* • **Phlebotomy/Phlebotomist** *17 students enrolled* • **Plastics Engineering Technology/Technician** *1 student enrolled* • **Prepress/Desktop Publishing and Digital Imaging Design** *3 students enrolled* • **Psychiatric/Mental Health Services Technician** *1 student enrolled* • **Restaurant, Culinary, and Catering Management/Manager** *3 students enrolled* • **Retailing and Retail Operations** *1 student enrolled* • **Small Business Administration/Management** *3 students enrolled* • **Social Work** *2 students enrolled* • **Substance Abuse/Addiction Counseling** *5 students enrolled* • **Surgical Technology/Technologist** *12 students enrolled* • **Tool and Die Technology/Technician** *2 students enrolled* • **Truck and Bus Driver/Commercial Vehicle Operation** *49 students enrolled* • **Web Page, Digital/Multimedia and Information Resources Design** *2 students enrolled* • **Welding Technology/Welder** *31 students enrolled* • **Word Processing** *2 students enrolled*

**STUDENT SERVICES** Academic or career counseling, daycare for children of students, employment services for current students, placement services for program completers, remedial services.

## Empire Beauty School–Arlington Heights

264 West Rand Road, Arlington Heights, IL 60004
http://www.empire.edu

**CONTACT** Michael Bouman, President
**Telephone:** 847-394-8359

**GENERAL INFORMATION** Private Institution. **Total program enrollment:** 141. **Application fee:** $100.

**PROGRAM(S) OFFERED**
• **Cosmetology, Barber/Styling, and Nail Instructor** *1000 hrs./$6900* • **Cosmetology/Cosmetologist, General** *1530 hrs./$18,845* • **Nail Technician/Specialist and Manicurist** *1 student enrolled*

**STUDENT SERVICES** Placement services for program completers.

## Empire Beauty School–Hanover Park

1166 West Lake Street, Hanover Park, IL 60133-5421
http://www.empire.edu/

**CONTACT** Michael Bouman, President
**Telephone:** 800-223-3271

**GENERAL INFORMATION** Private Institution. **Total program enrollment:** 68. **Application fee:** $100.

**PROGRAM(S) OFFERED**
• **Cosmetology/Cosmetologist, General** *1530 hrs./$18,845* • **Nail Technician/Specialist and Manicurist**

**STUDENT SERVICES** Placement services for program completers.

## Empire Beauty School–Lisle

2709 Maple Avenue, Lisle, IL 60532
http://www.empire.edu

**CONTACT** Michael Bouman, President
**Telephone:** 570-429-4321 Ext. 2414

**GENERAL INFORMATION** Private Institution. **Total program enrollment:** 52. **Application fee:** $100.

**PROGRAM(S) OFFERED**
• **Cosmetology, Barber/Styling, and Nail Instructor** *1530 hrs./$18,845* • **Cosmetology/Cosmetologist, General** *17 students enrolled* • **Nail Technician/Specialist and Manicurist**

**STUDENT SERVICES** Placement services for program completers.

## Environmental Technical Institute

1101 West Thorndale Avenue, Itasca, IL 60143-1334
http://eticampus.com/

**CONTACT** Camille M. Tortorello, Administration Director
**Telephone:** 630-285-9100

**GENERAL INFORMATION** Private Institution. Founded 1985. **Total program enrollment:** 98. **Application fee:** $75.

**PROGRAM(S) OFFERED**
• **Heating, Air Conditioning and Refrigeration Technology/Technician (ACH/ACR/ACHR/HRAC/HVAC/AC Technology)** *906 hrs./$12,517* • **Heating, Air Conditioning, Ventilation and Refrigeration Maintenance Technology/Technician (HAC, HACR, HVAC, HVACR)** *616 hrs./$9845*

**STUDENT SERVICES** Employment services for current students, placement services for program completers.

## Environmental Technical Institute–Blue Island Campus

13010 South Division Street, Blue Island, IL 60406-2606
http://eticampus.com/

**CONTACT** Camille M. Tortorello, Administration Director
**Telephone:** 630-285-9100

**GENERAL INFORMATION** Private Institution. Founded 1985. **Total program enrollment:** 125. **Application fee:** $75.

**PROGRAM(S) OFFERED**
• **Heating, Air Conditioning and Refrigeration Technology/Technician (ACH/ACR/ACHR/HRAC/HVAC/AC Technology)** *906 hrs./$12,517* • **Heating, Air Conditioning, Ventilation and Refrigeration Maintenance Technology/Technician (HAC, HACR, HVAC, HVACR)** *616 hrs./$9845*

**STUDENT SERVICES** Employment services for current students, placement services for program completers.

## European Massage Therapy School

8707 Skokie Boulevard, Suite 106, Skokie, IL 60077
http://www.school-for-massage.com/

**CONTACT** Arkady Khazin, Director
**Telephone:** 847-673-7595

**GENERAL INFORMATION** Private Institution. **Application fee:** $100.

**PROGRAM(S) OFFERED**
• **Massage Therapy/Therapeutic Massage** *110 students enrolled*

**STUDENT SERVICES** Academic or career counseling, employment services for current students, placement services for program completers.

## Everest College

6880 Frontgate Road, Suite 400, Burr Ridge, IL 60527
http://www.everest.edu/

**CONTACT** Mark Sullivan, President
**Telephone:** 630-920-1102

**GENERAL INFORMATION** Private Institution. **Total program enrollment:** 527.

**PROGRAM(S) OFFERED**
• **Dental Assisting/Assistant** *720 hrs./$13,414* • **Massage Therapy/Therapeutic Massage** *720 hrs./$13,414* • **Medical Administrative/Executive Assistant and Medical Secretary** *720 hrs./$13,362* • **Medical Insurance Coding Specialist/Coder** *720 hrs./$13,414* • **Medical Office Assistant/Specialist** *258 students enrolled* • **Medical/Clinical Assistant** *720 hrs./$14,507*

**STUDENT SERVICES** Academic or career counseling, employment services for current students, placement services for program completers.

## Everest College

247 South State Street, Suite 400, Chicago, IL 60604
http://www.everest.edu/

**CONTACT** Jeff Jarmes, President
**Telephone:** 312-913-1616

**GENERAL INFORMATION** Private Institution. **Total program enrollment:** 1745.

**PROGRAM(S) OFFERED**
• **Dental Assisting/Assistant** *720 hrs./$12,913* • **Massage Therapy/Therapeutic Massage** *750 hrs./$13,290* • **Medical Insurance Specialist/Medical Biller** *720 hrs./$12,735* • **Medical Office Assistant/Specialist** *165 students enrolled* • **Medical Office Management/Administration** *720 hrs./$13,290* • **Medical/Clinical Assistant** *720 hrs./$14,403* • **Pharmacy Technician/Assistant** *720 hrs./$12,913*

**STUDENT SERVICES** Academic or career counseling, placement services for program completers.

## Everest College

11560 South Kedzie Avenue, Merrionette Park, IL 60803
http://www.everest.edu/

**CONTACT** Deann Fitzgerald, President
**Telephone:** 708-239-0055

**GENERAL INFORMATION** Private Institution. **Total program enrollment:** 358.

**PROGRAM(S) OFFERED**
• **Allied Health and Medical Assisting Services, Other** *720 hrs./$14,403* • **Massage Therapy/Therapeutic Massage** *750 hrs./$13,274* • **Medical Insurance Coding Specialist/Coder** *720 hrs./$13,274* • **Medical Office Assistant/Specialist** *237 students enrolled* • **Pharmacy Technician/Assistant** *720 hrs./$12,913*

**STUDENT SERVICES** Employment services for current students, placement services for program completers.

## Everest College

150 South Lincolnway, Suite 100, North Aurora, IL 60542
http://www.everest.edu/

**CONTACT** Robert Van Elsen, Campus President
**Telephone:** 630-896-2140

**GENERAL INFORMATION** Private Institution. **Total program enrollment:** 80.

**PROGRAM(S) OFFERED**
• **Accounting and Related Services, Other** *720 hrs./$11,797* • **Massage Therapy/Therapeutic Massage** *76 students enrolled* • **Medical Administrative/Executive Assistant and Medical Secretary** *720 hrs./$13,211* • **Medical Insurance Coding Specialist/Coder** *720 hrs./$13,251* • **Medical/Clinical Assistant** *720 hrs./$14,295*

**STUDENT SERVICES** Academic or career counseling, employment services for current students, placement services for program completers, remedial services.

## Everest College

9811 Woods Drive, Suite 200, Skokie, IL 60077
http://www.everest.edu/

**CONTACT** Jeanette Prickett, School President
**Telephone:** 847-470-0277

**GENERAL INFORMATION** Private Institution. **Total program enrollment:** 896.

**PROGRAM(S) OFFERED**
• **Accounting and Related Services, Other** *720 hrs./$11,797* • **Health Information/Medical Records Administration/Administrator** *720 hrs./$13,251* • **Massage Therapy/Therapeutic Massage** *750 hrs./$13,236* • **Medical Administrative/Executive Assistant and Medical Secretary** *720 hrs./$13,104* • **Medical Insurance Specialist/Medical Biller** *36 students enrolled* • **Medical/Clinical Assistant** *720 hrs./$14,215* • **Pharmacy Technician/Assistant** *720 hrs./$12,913*

**STUDENT SERVICES** Academic or career counseling, employment services for current students, placement services for program completers.

## First Institute of Travel

790 McHenry Avenue, Crystal Lake, IL 60014
http://www.firstinstitute.com/

**CONTACT** Ron Beier, President
**Telephone:** 815-459-3500

**GENERAL INFORMATION** Private Institution. Founded 1982. **Total program enrollment:** 153. **Application fee:** $100.

**PROGRAM(S) OFFERED**
• **Allied Health and Medical Assisting Services, Other** *36 hrs./$13,050* • **Massage Therapy/Therapeutic Massage** *33 hrs./$11,815* • **Medical Office Assistant/Specialist** *24 hrs./$8620*

**STUDENT SERVICES** Employment services for current students, placement services for program completers.

## Fox College

6640 South Cicero, Bedford Park, IL 60638
http://www.foxcollege.edu/

**CONTACT** Carey Cranston, President
**Telephone:** 708-636-7700

**GENERAL INFORMATION** Private Institution. Founded 1932. **Accreditation:** State accredited or approved. **Total program enrollment:** 345. **Application fee:** $50.

**PROGRAM(S) OFFERED**
• **Accounting Technology/Technician and Bookkeeping** • **Administrative Assistant and Secretarial Science, General** *9 students enrolled* • **Allied Health and Medical Assisting Services, Other** *5 students enrolled*

**STUDENT SERVICES** Academic or career counseling, employment services for current students, placement services for program completers.

## Gem City College

PO Box 179, Quincy, IL 62301
http://www.gemcitycollege.com/

**CONTACT** Russell H. Hagenah, President
**Telephone:** 217-222-0391

**GENERAL INFORMATION** Private Institution. Founded 1870. **Accreditation:** State accredited or approved. **Total program enrollment:** 60. **Application fee:** $50.

*Gem City College (continued)*

**PROGRAM(S) OFFERED**
• **Business/Office Automation/Technology/Data Entry** • **Cosmetology/Cosmetologist, General** *50 hrs./$7200* • **Watchmaking and Jewelrymaking** *21 hrs./$7200*

**STUDENT SERVICES** Academic or career counseling, placement services for program completers.

## Hairmasters Institute of Cosmetology

506 South McClun Street, Bloomington, IL 61701

**CONTACT** Julie A. Fritzsche, Chief Executive Officer
**Telephone:** 309-828-1884

**GENERAL INFORMATION** Private Institution. **Total program enrollment:** 99. **Application fee:** $50.

**PROGRAM(S) OFFERED**
• **Cosmetology, Barber/Styling, and Nail Instructor** *500 hrs./$4000*
• **Cosmetology/Cosmetologist, General** *1500 hrs./$13,500*

**STUDENT SERVICES** Academic or career counseling, employment services for current students, placement services for program completers.

## Hair Professional Career College

1734 Sycamore Road, De Kalb, IL 60115
http://www.hairpros.edu/

**CONTACT** Wanda Zachary, President
**Telephone:** 815-756-3596

**GENERAL INFORMATION** Private Institution. Founded 1983. **Total program enrollment:** 39. **Application fee:** $100.

**PROGRAM(S) OFFERED**
• **Aesthetician/Esthetician and Skin Care Specialist** *750 hrs./$9800*
• **Cosmetology, Barber/Styling, and Nail Instructor** *1000 hrs./$8100*
• **Cosmetology/Cosmetologist, General** *1500 hrs./$17,400* • **Nail Technician/Specialist and Manicurist**

**STUDENT SERVICES** Academic or career counseling, placement services for program completers.

## Hair Professionals Academy of Cosmetology

440 Airport Road, Suite C, Elgin, IL 60123

**CONTACT** Carol Westphal, President
**Telephone:** 847-836-5900

**GENERAL INFORMATION** Private Institution. **Total program enrollment:** 110.

**PROGRAM(S) OFFERED**
• **Aesthetician/Esthetician and Skin Care Specialist** *750 hrs./$9800*
• **Cosmetology, Barber/Styling, and Nail Instructor** *500 hrs./$5100*
• **Cosmetology/Cosmetologist, General** *250 hrs./$2832* • **Nail Technician/Specialist and Manicurist**

**STUDENT SERVICES** Academic or career counseling, employment services for current students, placement services for program completers.

## Hair Professionals Academy of Cosmetology

1145 East Butterfield Road, Wheaton, IL 60187

**CONTACT** Carol Westphal, President
**Telephone:** 630-653-6630

**GENERAL INFORMATION** Private Institution. **Total program enrollment:** 25.

**PROGRAM(S) OFFERED**
• **Aesthetician/Esthetician and Skin Care Specialist** *750 hrs./$9800*
• **Cosmetology, Barber/Styling, and Nail Instructor** *1000 hrs./$10,000*
• **Cosmetology/Cosmetologist, General** *250 hrs./$2833*

**STUDENT SERVICES** Academic or career counseling, employment services for current students, placement services for program completers.

## Hair Professionals Career College

10321 S. Roberts Road, Palos Hills, IL 60485
http://www.hairpros.edu/

**CONTACT** Wanda S. Zachary, President
**Telephone:** 708-430-1755

**GENERAL INFORMATION** Private Institution. **Total program enrollment:** 73. **Application fee:** $100.

**PROGRAM(S) OFFERED**
• **Aesthetician/Esthetician and Skin Care Specialist** *750 hrs./$9800*
• **Cosmetology, Barber/Styling, and Nail Instructor** *1000 hrs./$8100*
• **Cosmetology/Cosmetologist, General** *1500 hrs./$17,400* • **Nail Technician/Specialist and Manicurist** *350 hrs./$2550* • **Teacher Education and Professional Development, Specific Subject Areas, Other** *2 students enrolled*

**STUDENT SERVICES** Academic or career counseling, placement services for program completers.

## Hair Professionals School of Cosmetology

5460 Route 34, Box 40, Oswego, IL 60543
http://www.hairpros.edu/

**CONTACT** Wanda Zachary, Secretary-Treasurer
**Telephone:** 630-554-2266

**GENERAL INFORMATION** Private Institution. Founded 1979. **Total program enrollment:** 36. **Application fee:** $100.

**PROGRAM(S) OFFERED**
• **Cosmetology, Barber/Styling, and Nail Instructor** *1000 hrs./$8100*
• **Cosmetology/Cosmetologist, General** *1500 hrs./$17,400* • **Teacher Education and Professional Development, Specific Subject Areas, Other** *4 students enrolled*

**STUDENT SERVICES** Academic or career counseling, placement services for program completers.

## Harper College

1200 West Algonquin Road, Palatine, IL 60067-7398
http://www.harpercollege.edu/

**CONTACT** Dr. John Pickelman, Interim President
**Telephone:** 847-925-6000

**GENERAL INFORMATION** Public Institution. Founded 1965. **Accreditation:** Regional (NCA); dental hygiene (ADA); medical assisting (AAMAE); music (NASM). **Total program enrollment:** 6753. **Application fee:** $25.

**PROGRAM(S) OFFERED**
• **Accounting Technology/Technician and Bookkeeping** *68 students enrolled* • **Accounting** *4 students enrolled* • **Applied Horticulture/Horticultural Operations, General** *13 students enrolled* • **Architectural Drafting and Architectural CAD/CADD** *23 students enrolled* • **Baking and Pastry Arts/Baker/Pastry Chef** *5 students enrolled* • **Banking and Financial Support Services** *5 students enrolled* • **Building/Home/Construction Inspection/Inspector** *3 students enrolled* • **Building/Property Maintenance and Management** *6 students enrolled* • **Business Administration and Management, General** *122 students enrolled* • **Child Care Provider/Assistant** *69 students enrolled* • **Computer Programming/Programmer, General** *5 students enrolled* • **Computer Systems Networking and Telecommunications** *10 students enrolled* • **Computer and Information Systems Security** *1 student enrolled* • **Criminal Justice/Police Science** *4 students enrolled* • **Culinary Arts/Chef Training** *6 students enrolled* • **Dietetic Technician (DTR)** *11 students enrolled* • **Electrical/Electronics Equipment Installation and Repair, General** *25 students enrolled* • **Emergency Care Attendant (EMT Ambulance)** *1*

*student enrolled* • **Emergency Medical Technology/Technician (EMT Paramedic)** *1 student enrolled* • **Fashion and Fabric Consultant** *21 students enrolled* • **Floriculture/Floristry Operations and Management** *4 students enrolled* • **Food Service, Waiter/Waitress, and Dining Room Management/Manager** *7 students enrolled* • **Forestry Technology/Technician** *7 students enrolled* • **General Office Occupations and Clerical Services** *2 students enrolled* • **Graphic and Printing Equipment Operator, General Production** *1 student enrolled* • **Heating, Air Conditioning, Ventilation and Refrigeration Maintenance Technology/Technician (HAC, HACR, HVAC, HVACR)** *65 students enrolled* • **Hotel/Motel Administration/Management** *4 students enrolled* • **Human Resources Management/Personnel Administration, General** *4 students enrolled* • **Industrial Electronics Technology/Technician** *26 students enrolled* • **Information Science/Studies** *22 students enrolled* • **International Business/Trade/Commerce** *1 student enrolled* • **Landscaping and Groundskeeping** *1 student enrolled* • **Legal Administrative Assistant/Secretary** *1 student enrolled* • **Legal Assistant/Paralegal** *70 students enrolled* • **Licensed Practical/Vocational Nurse Training (LPN, LVN, Cert, Dipl, AAS)** *25 students enrolled* • **Medical Administrative/Executive Assistant and Medical Secretary** *4 students enrolled* • **Medical Insurance Coding Specialist/Coder** *16 students enrolled* • **Medical Transcription/Transcriptionist** *4 students enrolled* • **Medical/Clinical Assistant** *23 students enrolled* • **Nurse/Nursing Assistant/Aide and Patient Care Assistant** *190 students enrolled* • **Parts, Warehousing, and Inventory Management Operations** *18 students enrolled* • **Phlebotomy/Phlebotomist** *20 students enrolled* • **Plant Nursery Operations and Management** *1 student enrolled* • **Purchasing, Procurement/Acquisitions and Contracts Management** *14 students enrolled* • **Retailing and Retail Operations** *5 students enrolled* • **Sales, Distribution and Marketing Operations, General** *8 students enrolled* • **Selling Skills and Sales Operations** *23 students enrolled* • **Sign Language Interpretation and Translation** *9 students enrolled* • **System, Networking, and LAN/WAN Management/Manager** *2 students enrolled* • **Turf and Turfgrass Management** *8 students enrolled* • **Web Page, Digital/Multimedia and Information Resources Design** *3 students enrolled* • **Welding Technology/Welder** *10 students enrolled*

**STUDENT SERVICES** Academic or career counseling, daycare for children of students, employment services for current students, remedial services.

## Harrington College of Design

200 West Madison Street, Chicago, IL 60606
http://www.interiordesign.edu/

**CONTACT** Erik Parks, President
**Telephone:** 312-939-4975

**GENERAL INFORMATION** Private Institution. Founded 1931. **Accreditation:** Art and design (NASAD); interior design: professional (CIDA). **Total program enrollment:** 540. **Application fee:** $60.

**PROGRAM(S) OFFERED**
• **Interior Design** *1 student enrolled*

**STUDENT SERVICES** Academic or career counseling, employment services for current students, placement services for program completers.

## Heartland Community College

1500 West Raab Road, Normal, IL 61761
http://www.heartland.edu/

**CONTACT** Jonathan Astroth, President
**Telephone:** 309-268-8000

**GENERAL INFORMATION** Public Institution. Founded 1990. **Accreditation:** Regional (NCA). **Total program enrollment:** 2273.

**PROGRAM(S) OFFERED**
• **Accounting** *4 students enrolled* • **Administrative Assistant and Secretarial Science, General** *1 student enrolled* • **Business/Office Automation/Technology/Data Entry** *4 students enrolled* • **CAD/CADD Drafting and/or Design Technology/Technician** *1 student enrolled* • **Child Care Provider/Assistant** *10 students enrolled* • **Computer Technology/Computer Systems Technology** *10 students enrolled* • **Corrections** *4 students enrolled* • **Drafting and Design Technology/Technician, General** *2 students enrolled* • **Electrical, Electronic and Communications Engineering Technology/Technician** *3 students enrolled* • **Heating, Air Conditioning, Ventilation and Refrigeration Maintenance Technology/Technician (HAC, HACR, HVAC, HVACR)** *1 student enrolled* • **Licensed Practical/Vocational Nurse Training (LPN, LVN, Cert, Dipl, AAS)** *22 students enrolled* • **Manufacturing Technology/Technician** *5 students enrolled* • **Nurse/Nursing Assistant/Aide and Patient Care Assistant** *107 students enrolled* • **System Administration/Administrator** *1 student enrolled* • **Welding Technology/Welder** *1 student enrolled*

**STUDENT SERVICES** Academic or career counseling, daycare for children of students, employment services for current students, placement services for program completers, remedial services.

## Hebrew Theological College

7135 North Carpenter Road, Skokie, IL 60077-3263
http://www.htc.edu/

**CONTACT** Rabbi Dr. Jerold Isenberg, Chancellor
**Telephone:** 847-982-2500

**GENERAL INFORMATION** Private Institution. Founded 1922. **Accreditation:** Regional (NCA). **Total program enrollment:** 530. **Application fee:** $75.

**PROGRAM(S) OFFERED**
• **Data Entry/Microcomputer Applications, General** • **Teacher Education and Professional Development, Specific Subject Areas, Other** *1 student enrolled*

**STUDENT SERVICES** Academic or career counseling, placement services for program completers.

## Highland Community College

2998 West Pearl City Road, Freeport, IL 61032-9341
http://www.highland.edu/

**CONTACT** Joe M. Kanosky, President
**Telephone:** 815-235-6121

**GENERAL INFORMATION** Public Institution. Founded 1962. **Accreditation:** Regional (NCA). **Total program enrollment:** 1111.

**PROGRAM(S) OFFERED**
• **Accounting Technology/Technician and Bookkeeping** *8 students enrolled* • **Accounting** *3 students enrolled* • **Autobody/Collision and Repair Technology/Technician** *1 student enrolled* • **Child Care Provider/Assistant** *2 students enrolled* • **Computer Installation and Repair Technology/Technician** *3 students enrolled* • **Cosmetology/Cosmetologist, General** *10 students enrolled* • **General Office Occupations and Clerical Services** *2 students enrolled* • **Graphic Design** *1 student enrolled* • **Industrial Mechanics and Maintenance Technology** *1 student enrolled* • **Industrial Technology/Technician** *1 student enrolled* • **Licensed Practical/Vocational Nurse Training (LPN, LVN, Cert, Dipl, AAS)** *16 students enrolled* • **Manufacturing Technology/Technician** *6 students enrolled* • **Medical Insurance Coding Specialist/Coder** *2 students enrolled* • **Medical Transcription/Transcriptionist** *2 students enrolled* • **Nail Technician/Specialist and Manicurist** *2 students enrolled* • **Welding Technology/Welder** *2 students enrolled*

**STUDENT SERVICES** Academic or career counseling, daycare for children of students, employment services for current students, placement services for program completers, remedial services.

## Illinois Center for Broadcasting

200 West 22nd Street, Suite 202, Lombard, IL 60148
http://www.beonair.com/

**CONTACT** Robert Mills, President
**Telephone:** 630-916-1700 Ext. 104

**GENERAL INFORMATION** Private Institution. **Total program enrollment:** 219. **Application fee:** $125.

**PROGRAM(S) OFFERED**
• **Radio and Television** *36 hrs./$14,889*

**STUDENT SERVICES** Academic or career counseling, employment services for current students, placement services for program completers, remedial services.

## Illinois Central College

One College Drive, East Peoria, IL 61635-0001
http://www.icc.edu/

**CONTACT** Dr. John S. Erwin, President
**Telephone:** 309-694-5422

**GENERAL INFORMATION** Public Institution. Founded 1967. **Accreditation:** Regional (NCA); dental hygiene (ADA); medical laboratory technology (NAACLS); music (NASM); physical therapy assisting (APTA); radiologic technology: radiography (JRCERT); respiratory therapy technology (CoARC). **Total program enrollment:** 4798.

**PROGRAM(S) OFFERED**
• **Accounting Technology/Technician and Bookkeeping** *6 students enrolled* • **Administrative Assistant and Secretarial Science, General** *3 students enrolled* • **Applied Horticulture/Horticultural Operations, General** *27 students enrolled* • **Architectural Drafting and Architectural CAD/CADD** *1 student enrolled* • **Automobile/Automotive Mechanics Technology/Technician** *8 students enrolled* • **Banking and Financial Support Services** *4 students enrolled* • **Business Administration and Management, General** *39 students enrolled* • **Business/Office Automation/Technology/Data Entry** *20 students enrolled* • **Child Care Provider/Assistant** *5 students enrolled* • **Computer Systems Networking and Telecommunications** *24 students enrolled* • **Construction Trades, General** *15 students enrolled* • **Culinary Arts/Chef Training** *1 student enrolled* • **Data Entry/Microcomputer Applications, General** *1 student enrolled* • **E-Commerce/Electronic Commerce** *4 students enrolled* • **Electrical, Electronic and Communications Engineering Technology/Technician** *4 students enrolled* • **Emergency Care Attendant (EMT Ambulance)** *7 students enrolled* • **Food Service, Waiter/Waitress, and Dining Room Management/Manager** *17 students enrolled* • **Forensic Science and Technology** *3 students enrolled* • **General Office Occupations and Clerical Services** *7 students enrolled* • **Geography, Other** *5 students enrolled* • **Heating, Air Conditioning, Ventilation and Refrigeration Maintenance Technology/Technician (HAC, HACR, HVAC, HVACR)** *31 students enrolled* • **Housing and Human Environments, Other** *14 students enrolled* • **Industrial Mechanics and Maintenance Technology** *1 student enrolled* • **Legal Assistant/Paralegal** *9 students enrolled* • **Licensed Practical/Vocational Nurse Training (LPN, LVN, Cert, Dipl, AAS)** *25 students enrolled* • **Logistics and Materials Management** *7 students enrolled* • **Massage Therapy/Therapeutic Massage** *22 students enrolled* • **Medical Insurance Coding Specialist/Coder** *9 students enrolled* • **Medical Office Assistant/Specialist** *17 students enrolled* • **Medical Transcription/Transcriptionist** *3 students enrolled* • **Nurse/Nursing Assistant/Aide and Patient Care Assistant** *139 students enrolled* • **Phlebotomy/Phlebotomist** *17 students enrolled* • **Prepress/Desktop Publishing and Digital Imaging Design** *1 student enrolled* • **Psychiatric/Mental Health Services Technician** *2 students enrolled* • **Security and Loss Prevention Services** *3 students enrolled* • **Sign Language Interpretation and Translation** *1 student enrolled* • **Small Business Administration/Management** *3 students enrolled* • **Substance Abuse/Addiction Counseling** *6 students enrolled* • **Surgical Technology/Technologist** *11 students enrolled* • **Tourism and Travel Services Management** *1 student enrolled* • **Web Page, Digital/Multimedia and Information Resources Design** *6 students enrolled* • **Welding Technology/Welder** *11 students enrolled*

**STUDENT SERVICES** Academic or career counseling, daycare for children of students, employment services for current students, placement services for program completers, remedial services.

## Illinois Eastern Community Colleges, Frontier Community College

Frontier Drive, Fairfield, IL 62837-2601
http://www.iecc.edu/fcc/

**CONTACT** Terry Bruce, Chief Executive Officer
**Telephone:** 618-393-2982

**GENERAL INFORMATION** Public Institution. Founded 1976. **Accreditation:** Regional (NCA). **Total program enrollment:** 303. **Application fee:** $10.

**PROGRAM(S) OFFERED**
• **Administrative Assistant and Secretarial Science, General** *1 student enrolled* • **Automobile/Automotive Mechanics Technology/Technician** *4 students enrolled* • **Electrical and Power Transmission Installation/Installer, General** *18 students enrolled* • **Emergency Care Attendant (EMT Ambulance)** *30 students enrolled* • **Fire Science/Firefighting** *1 student enrolled* • **Nurse/Nursing Assistant/Aide and Patient Care Assistant** *92 students enrolled* • **Psychiatric/Mental Health Services Technician** *6 students enrolled* • **Quality Control Technology/Technician** *13 students enrolled* • **Teacher Assistant/Aide** *1 student enrolled* • **Truck and Bus Driver/Commercial Vehicle Operation** *2 students enrolled*

**STUDENT SERVICES** Academic or career counseling, employment services for current students, placement services for program completers, remedial services.

## Illinois Eastern Community Colleges, Lincoln Trail College

11220 State Highway 1, Robinson, IL 62454
http://www.iecc.edu/ltc/

**CONTACT** Terry Bruce, Chief Executive Officer
**Telephone:** 618-393-2982

**GENERAL INFORMATION** Public Institution. Founded 1969. **Accreditation:** Regional (NCA). **Total program enrollment:** 504. **Application fee:** $10.

**PROGRAM(S) OFFERED**
• **Administrative Assistant and Secretarial Science, General** *1 student enrolled* • **Applied Horticulture/Horticultural Operations, General** *6 students enrolled* • **Business Administration and Management, General** *20 students enrolled* • **Business/Office Automation/Technology/Data Entry** *15 students enrolled* • **Communications Systems Installation and Repair Technology** *20 students enrolled* • **Computer Installation and Repair Technology/Technician** *2 students enrolled* • **Food Service, Waiter/Waitress, and Dining Room Management/Manager** *16 students enrolled* • **Housing and Human Environments, Other** *72 students enrolled* • **Medical Transcription/Transcriptionist** *1 student enrolled* • **Medical/Clinical Assistant** *12 students enrolled* • **Nurse/Nursing Assistant/Aide and Patient Care Assistant** *71 students enrolled* • **Pharmacy Technician/Assistant** *9 students enrolled* • **Restaurant, Culinary, and Catering Management/Manager** *1 student enrolled* • **System, Networking, and LAN/WAN Management/Manager** *1 student enrolled*

**STUDENT SERVICES** Academic or career counseling, employment services for current students, placement services for program completers, remedial services.

## Illinois Eastern Community Colleges, Olney Central College

305 North West Street, Olney, IL 62450
http://www.iecc.edu/occ/

**CONTACT** Terry Bruce, Chief Executive Officer
**Telephone:** 618-393-2982

**GENERAL INFORMATION** Public Institution. Founded 1962. **Accreditation:** Regional (NCA); radiologic technology: radiography (JRCERT). **Total program enrollment:** 745. **Application fee:** $10.

**PROGRAM(S) OFFERED**
• **Automobile/Automotive Mechanics Technology/Technician** *2 students enrolled* • **Cosmetology/Cosmetologist, General** *10 students enrolled* • **Emergency Care Attendant (EMT Ambulance)** *2 students enrolled* • **Heating, Air Conditioning, Ventilation and Refrigeration Maintenance Technology/Technician (HAC, HACR, HVAC, HVACR)** *10 students enrolled* • **Industrial Mechanics and Maintenance Technology** *4 students enrolled* • **Licensed Practical/Vocational Nurse Training (LPN, LVN, Cert, Dipl, AAS)** *111 students enrolled* • **Massage Therapy/Therapeutic Massage** *6 students enrolled* • **Medical Transcription/Transcriptionist** *14 students enrolled* • **Nurse/Nursing Assistant/Aide and Patient Care Assistant** *102 students enrolled* • **Phlebotomy/Phlebotomist** *23 students enrolled* • **Web Page, Digital/Multimedia and Information Resources Design** *1 student enrolled* • **Welding Technology/Welder** *15 students enrolled*

**STUDENT SERVICES** Academic or career counseling, daycare for children of students, employment services for current students, placement services for program completers, remedial services.

## Illinois Eastern Community Colleges, Wabash Valley College

2200 College Drive, Mount Carmel, IL 62863-2657
http://www.iecc.edu/wvc/

**CONTACT** Terry Bruce, Chief Executive Officer
**Telephone:** 618-393-2982

**GENERAL INFORMATION** Public Institution. Founded 1960. **Accreditation:** Regional (NCA). **Total program enrollment:** 665. **Application fee:** $10.

**PROGRAM(S) OFFERED**
• **Administrative Assistant and Secretarial Science, General** *1 student enrolled* • **Agricultural Business Technology** *3 students enrolled* • **Emergency Care Attendant (EMT Ambulance)** *1 student enrolled* • **Industrial Technology/Technician** *1 student enrolled* • **Machine Shop Technology/Assistant** *1 student enrolled* • **Mining Technology/Technician** *3 students enrolled* • **Nurse/Nursing Assistant/Aide and Patient Care Assistant** *54 students enrolled* • **Selling Skills and Sales Operations** *6 students enrolled* • **Truck and Bus Driver/Commercial Vehicle Operation** *9 students enrolled* • **Turf and Turfgrass Management** *4 students enrolled* • **Web Page, Digital/Multimedia and Information Resources Design** *1 student enrolled*

**STUDENT SERVICES** Academic or career counseling, daycare for children of students, employment services for current students, placement services for program completers, remedial services.

## Illinois Eastern Community College System

Olney, IL 62450-2298

**CONTACT** Terry Bruce, Chief Executive Officer
**Telephone:** 618-393-2982

**GENERAL INFORMATION** Public Institution.

## The Illinois Institute of Art–Chicago

350 North Orleans, Chicago, IL 60654
http://www.artinstitutes.edu/chicago

**CONTACT** John Jenkins, President
**Telephone:** 312-280-3500

**GENERAL INFORMATION** Private Institution. Founded 1916. **Accreditation:** Interior design: professional (CIDA); state accredited or approved. **Total program enrollment:** 1938. **Application fee:** $50.

**PROGRAM(S) OFFERED**
• **Baking and Pastry Arts/Baker/Pastry Chef** *20 students enrolled* • **Food Preparation/Professional Cooking/Kitchen Assistant** *7 students enrolled*

**STUDENT SERVICES** Academic or career counseling, employment services for current students, placement services for program completers, remedial services.

## The Illinois Institute of Art–Schaumburg

1000 Plaza Drive, Schaumburg, IL 60173
http://www.artinstitutes.edu/schaumburg

**CONTACT** David Ray, President
**Telephone:** 847-619-3450

**GENERAL INFORMATION** Private Institution. **Accreditation:** Interior design: professional (CIDA); state accredited or approved. **Total program enrollment:** 961. **Application fee:** $50.

**PROGRAM(S) OFFERED**
• **Graphic Design** *4 students enrolled* • **Interior Design** *3 students enrolled* • **Web Page, Digital/Multimedia and Information Resources Design** *5 students enrolled*

**STUDENT SERVICES** Academic or career counseling, employment services for current students, placement services for program completers, remedial services.

## Illinois School of Health Careers

220 South State Street, #600, Chicago, IL 60604
http://www.ishc.edu/

**CONTACT** Steve Strong, Executive Director
**Telephone:** 312-913-1230

**GENERAL INFORMATION** Private Institution. Founded 1990. **Total program enrollment:** 869. **Application fee:** $100.

**PROGRAM(S) OFFERED**
• **Allied Health and Medical Assisting Services, Other** *59 hrs./$14,400* • **Dental Assisting/Assistant** *59 hrs./$13,000* • **Medical/Clinical Assistant** *241 students enrolled*

**STUDENT SERVICES** Academic or career counseling, employment services for current students, placement services for program completers, remedial services.

## Illinois School of Health Careers–O'Hare Campus

8750 W. Bryn Mawr, Suite 300, Chicago, IL 60631
http://www.ishc.edu/

**CONTACT** Geralyn M. Randich, Executive Director
**Telephone:** 773-458-1111

**GENERAL INFORMATION** Private Institution. **Total program enrollment:** 276. **Application fee:** $100.

**PROGRAM(S) OFFERED**
• **Dental Assisting/Assistant** *880 hrs./$13,000* • **Medical/Clinical Assistant** *880 hrs./$14,400*

**STUDENT SERVICES** Academic or career counseling, employment services for current students, placement services for program completers, remedial services.

## Illinois Valley Community College

815 North Orlando Smith Avenue, Oglesby, IL 61348-9692
http://www.ivcc.edu/

**CONTACT** Dr. Jerry Corcoran, President
**Telephone:** 815-224-2720

**GENERAL INFORMATION** Public Institution. Founded 1924. **Accreditation:** Regional (NCA); dental assisting (ADA). **Total program enrollment:** 1775.

**PROGRAM(S) OFFERED**
• **Accounting Technology/Technician and Bookkeeping** *4 students enrolled* • **Applied Horticulture/Horticultural Operations, General** *20 students enrolled* • **Architectural Drafting and Architectural CAD/CADD** *5 students enrolled* • **Automobile/Automotive Mechanics Technology/Technician** *7 students enrolled* • **Business/Office Automation/Technology/Data Entry** *3 students enrolled* • **CAD/CADD Drafting and/or Design Technology/Technician** *6 students enrolled* • **Child Care Provider/Assistant** *1 student enrolled* • **Computer Systems Networking and Telecommunications** *6 students enrolled* • **Computer Technology/Computer Systems Technology** *32 students enrolled* • **Criminal Justice/Police Science** *3 students enrolled* • **Dental Assisting/Assistant** *7 students enrolled* • **Electrician** *6 students enrolled* • **Food Service, Waiter/Waitress, and Dining Room Management/Manager** *15 students enrolled* • **Forensic Science and Technology** *4 students enrolled* • **General Office Occupations and Clerical Services** *7 students enrolled* • **Graphic Design** *3 students enrolled* • **Heating, Air Conditioning, Ventilation and Refrigeration Maintenance Technology/Technician (HAC, HACR, HVAC, HVACR)** *11 students enrolled* • **Housing and Human Environments, Other** *25 students enrolled* • **Industrial Mechanics and Maintenance Technology** *2 students enrolled* • **Licensed Practical/Vocational Nurse Training (LPN, LVN, Cert, Dipl, AAS)** *38 students enrolled* • **Machine Tool Technology/Machinist** *1 student enrolled* • **Manufacturing Technology/Technician** *1 student enrolled* • **Massage Therapy/Therapeutic Massage** *2 students enrolled* • **Nurse/Nursing Assistant/Aide and Patient Care Assistant** *213 students enrolled* • **Parts, Warehousing, and Inventory Management Operations** *7 students enrolled* • **Phlebotomy/Phlebotomist** *10 students enrolled* • **Selling Skills and Sales Operations** *1 student enrolled* • **Social Work** *2 students enrolled*

*Illinois Valley Community College (continued)*

• **Substance Abuse/Addiction Counseling** *2 students enrolled* • **Truck and Bus Driver/Commercial Vehicle Operation** *45 students enrolled* • **Welding Technology/Welder** *69 students enrolled*

**STUDENT SERVICES** Academic or career counseling, daycare for children of students, employment services for current students, placement services for program completers, remedial services.

## John A. Logan College

700 Logan College Road, Carterville, IL 62918-9900
http://www.jalc.edu/

**CONTACT** Robert Mees, President
**Telephone:** 618-985-3741

**GENERAL INFORMATION** Public Institution. Founded 1967. **Accreditation:** Regional (NCA); dental assisting (ADA); dental hygiene (ADA); health information technology (AHIMA); medical laboratory technology (NAACLS). **Total program enrollment:** 2418.

**PROGRAM(S) OFFERED**

• **Accounting Technology/Technician and Bookkeeping** *3 students enrolled* • **Administrative Assistant and Secretarial Science, General** *16 students enrolled* • **Autobody/Collision and Repair Technology/Technician** *34 students enrolled* • **Automobile/Automotive Mechanics Technology/Technician** *1 student enrolled* • **Business/Commerce, General** *3 students enrolled* • **Business/Office Automation/Technology/Data Entry** *10 students enrolled* • **CAD/CADD Drafting and/or Design Technology/Technician** *2 students enrolled* • **Child Care Provider/Assistant** *1 student enrolled* • **Computer Engineering Technology/Technician** *8 students enrolled* • **Cosmetology/Cosmetologist, General** *35 students enrolled* • **Criminal Justice/Police Science** *22 students enrolled* • **Dental Assisting/Assistant** *16 students enrolled* • **Diagnostic Medical Sonography/Sonographer and Ultrasound Technician** *1 student enrolled* • **Electrical, Electronic and Communications Engineering Technology/Technician** *13 students enrolled* • **General Office Occupations and Clerical Services** *9 students enrolled* • **Heating, Air Conditioning, Ventilation and Refrigeration Maintenance Technology/Technician (HAC, HACR, HVAC, HVACR)** *2 students enrolled* • **Industrial Electronics Technology/Technician** *1 student enrolled* • **Information Science/Studies** *2 students enrolled* • **Legal Administrative Assistant/Secretary** *6 students enrolled* • **Licensed Practical/Vocational Nurse Training (LPN, LVN, Cert, Dipl, AAS)** *86 students enrolled* • **Machine Shop Technology/Assistant** *9 students enrolled* • **Massage Therapy/Therapeutic Massage** *10 students enrolled* • **Medical Administrative/Executive Assistant and Medical Secretary** *14 students enrolled* • **Medical Transcription/Transcriptionist** *8 students enrolled* • **Medical/Clinical Assistant** *9 students enrolled* • **Nurse/Nursing Assistant/Aide and Patient Care Assistant** *144 students enrolled* • **Retailing and Retail Operations** *1 student enrolled* • **Sign Language Interpretation and Translation** *7 students enrolled* • **Surgical Technology/Technologist** *3 students enrolled* • **Tool and Die Technology/Technician** *4 students enrolled* • **Welding Technology/Welder** *9 students enrolled*

**STUDENT SERVICES** Academic or career counseling, daycare for children of students, employment services for current students, placement services for program completers, remedial services.

## John Wood Community College

1301 South 48th Street, Quincy, IL 62305-8736
http://www.jwcc.edu/

**CONTACT** Thomas D. Klincar, DA, President
**Telephone:** 217-224-6500

**GENERAL INFORMATION** Public Institution. Founded 1974. **Accreditation:** Regional (NCA). **Total program enrollment:** 1216.

**PROGRAM(S) OFFERED**

• **Accounting** *1 student enrolled* • **Administrative Assistant and Secretarial Science, General** *5 students enrolled* • **Animal/Livestock Husbandry and Production** *4 students enrolled* • **Applied Horticulture/Horticultural Operations, General** *2 students enrolled* • **Business Administration and Management, General** *4 students enrolled* • **Culinary Arts/Chef Training** *3 students enrolled* • **Electrician** *3 students enrolled* • **Licensed Practical/Vocational Nurse Training (LPN, LVN, Cert, Dipl, AAS)** *18 students enrolled* • **Medical Office Management/Administration** *1 student enrolled* • **Nurse/Nursing Assistant/Aide and Patient Care Assistant** *90 students enrolled* • **Selling Skills and Sales Operations** *1 student enrolled* • **Surgical Technology/Technologist** *7 students enrolled* • **Truck and Bus Driver/Commercial Vehicle Operation** *57 students enrolled*

**STUDENT SERVICES** Academic or career counseling, employment services for current students, remedial services.

## Joliet Junior College

1215 Houbolt Road, Joliet, IL 60431-8938
http://www.jjc.edu/

**CONTACT** Dr. Eugenia Proulx, President
**Telephone:** 815-729-9020

**GENERAL INFORMATION** Public Institution. Founded 1901. **Accreditation:** Regional (NCA); music (NASM). **Total program enrollment:** 6054.

**PROGRAM(S) OFFERED**

• **Accounting** *2 students enrolled* • **Automobile/Automotive Mechanics Technology/Technician** *10 students enrolled* • **Child Care Provider/Assistant** *7 students enrolled* • **Computer Installation and Repair Technology/Technician** *3 students enrolled* • **Computer Systems Networking and Telecommunications** *1 student enrolled* • **Construction Trades, General** *13 students enrolled* • **Construction/Heavy Equipment/Earthmoving Equipment Operation** *2 students enrolled* • **Cosmetology/Cosmetologist, General** *1 student enrolled* • **Criminal Justice/Police Science** *3 students enrolled* • **Data Processing and Data Processing Technology/Technician** *4 students enrolled* • **Electrician** *5 students enrolled* • **Electrocardiograph Technology/Technician** *1 student enrolled* • **Entrepreneurship/Entrepreneurial Studies** *2 students enrolled* • **Finance, General** *3 students enrolled* • **Fire Science/Firefighting** *2 students enrolled* • **Fire Services Administration** *1 student enrolled* • **Floriculture/Floristry Operations and Management** *3 students enrolled* • **Food Preparation/Professional Cooking/Kitchen Assistant** *3 students enrolled* • **Heating, Air Conditioning, Ventilation and Refrigeration Maintenance Technology/Technician (HAC, HACR, HVAC, HVACR)** *3 students enrolled* • **Heavy Equipment Maintenance Technology/Technician** *2 students enrolled* • **Hospitality Administration/Management, General** *2 students enrolled* • **Human Resources Management/Personnel Administration, General** *5 students enrolled* • **Industrial Electronics Technology/Technician** *21 students enrolled* • **Instrumentation Technology/Technician** *4 students enrolled* • **Library Assistant/Technician** *3 students enrolled* • **Licensed Practical/Vocational Nurse Training (LPN, LVN, Cert, Dipl, AAS)** *143 students enrolled* • **Manufacturing Technology/Technician** *9 students enrolled* • **Mechanical Engineering/Mechanical Technology/Technician** *3 students enrolled* • **Medical Insurance Coding Specialist/Coder** *11 students enrolled* • **Medical Transcription/Transcriptionist** *4 students enrolled* • **Nurse/Nursing Assistant/Aide and Patient Care Assistant** *3 students enrolled* • **Operations Management and Supervision** *8 students enrolled* • **Phlebotomy/Phlebotomist** *5 students enrolled* • **Plant Nursery Operations and Management** *2 students enrolled* • **Prepress/Desktop Publishing and Digital Imaging Design** *1 student enrolled* • **Word Processing** *3 students enrolled*

**STUDENT SERVICES** Academic or career counseling, daycare for children of students, employment services for current students, placement services for program completers, remedial services.

## Kankakee Community College

PO Box 888, Kankakee, IL 60901-0888
http://www.kcc.cc.il.us/

**CONTACT** G. Weber, President
**Telephone:** 815-802-8500

**GENERAL INFORMATION** Public Institution. Founded 1966. **Accreditation:** Regional (NCA); medical laboratory technology (NAACLS). **Total program enrollment:** 1537.

**PROGRAM(S) OFFERED**

• **Accounting Technology/Technician and Bookkeeping** *3 students enrolled* • **Architectural Drafting and Architectural CAD/CADD** *2 students enrolled* • **Automobile/Automotive Mechanics Technology/Technician** *2 students enrolled* • **Business Administration and Management, General** *2 students enrolled* • **Business/Office Automation/Technology/Data Entry** *2 students enrolled* • **CAD/CADD Drafting and/or Design Technology/Technician** *3 students enrolled* • **Child Care Provider/Assistant** *2 students enrolled* • **Computer Installation and Repair Technology/Technician** *1 student enrolled* • **Construction Engineering Technology/Technician** *3 students enrolled* • **Criminal Justice/Police Science** 3 *students enrolled* • **Data Entry/Microcomputer Applications, General** *1 student enrolled* • **Drafting and Design Technology/Technician, General** *4 students enrolled* • **Emergency Care Attendant (EMT Ambulance)** *1 student enrolled* • **Heating, Air Conditioning, Ventilation and Refrigeration Maintenance Technology/Technician (HAC, HACR, HVAC, HVACR)** *7 students enrolled* • **Industrial Electronics Technology/Technician** *14 students enrolled* • **Industrial Mechanics and Maintenance Technology** *2 students enrolled* • **Legal Assistant/Paralegal** *4 students enrolled* • **Licensed Practical/Vocational Nurse Training (LPN, LVN, Cert, Dipl, AAS)** *45 students enrolled* • **Mechanical Drafting and Mechanical Drafting CAD/CADD** *1 student enrolled* • **Medical Insurance Coding Specialist/Coder** *19 students enrolled* • **Medical Office Assistant/Specialist** *5 students enrolled* • **Nurse/Nursing Assistant/Aide and Patient Care Assistant** *39 students enrolled* • **Teacher Assistant/Aide** *1 student enrolled* • **Welding Technology/Welder** *5 students enrolled*

**STUDENT SERVICES** Academic or career counseling, daycare for children of students, employment services for current students, placement services for program completers, remedial services.

## Kaskaskia College

27210 College Road, Centralia, IL 62801-7878
http://www.kaskaskia.edu/

**CONTACT** Dr. James Underwood, President
**Telephone:** 618-545-3000

**GENERAL INFORMATION** Public Institution. Founded 1966. **Accreditation:** Regional (NCA); dental assisting (ADA); physical therapy assisting (APTA); radiologic technology: radiography (JRCERT); respiratory therapy technology (CoARC). **Total program enrollment:** 1922.

**PROGRAM(S) OFFERED**

• **Accounting and Business/Management** *1 student enrolled* • **Accounting** *4 students enrolled* • **Administrative Assistant and Secretarial Science, General** *1 student enrolled* • **Architectural Drafting and Architectural CAD/CADD** *1 student enrolled* • **Autobody/Collision and Repair Technology/Technician** *3 students enrolled* • **Automobile/Automotive Mechanics Technology/Technician** *1 student enrolled* • **Business/Office Automation/Technology/Data Entry** *3 students enrolled* • **CAD/CADD Drafting and/or Design Technology/Technician** *12 students enrolled* • **Carpentry/Carpenter** *2 students enrolled* • **Computer Systems Networking and Telecommunications** *10 students enrolled* • **Construction Trades, General** *17 students enrolled* • **Cosmetology/Cosmetologist, General** *20 students enrolled* • **Criminal Justice/Law Enforcement Administration** *7 students enrolled* • **Culinary Arts/Chef Training** *5 students enrolled* • **Dental Assisting/Assistant** *20 students enrolled* • **Diagnostic Medical Sonography/Sonographer and Ultrasound Technician** *10 students enrolled* • **Electrical, Electronic and Communications Engineering Technology/Technician** *15 students enrolled* • **Electrical/Electronics Drafting and Electrical/Electronics CAD/CADD** *19 students enrolled* • **Entrepreneurship/Entrepreneurial Studies** *1 student enrolled* • **Food Preparation/Professional Cooking/Kitchen Assistant** *3 students enrolled* • **Food Service, Waiter/Waitress, and Dining Room Management/Manager** *8 students enrolled* • **General Office Occupations and Clerical Services** *3 students enrolled* • **Graphic and Printing Equipment Operator, General Production** *4 students enrolled* • **Heating, Air Conditioning, Ventilation and Refrigeration Maintenance Technology/Technician (HAC, HACR, HVAC, HVACR)** *18 students enrolled* • **Housing and Human Environments, Other** *3 students enrolled* • **Industrial Mechanics and Maintenance Technology** *3 students enrolled* • **Instrumentation Technology/Technician** *1 student enrolled* • **Legal Administrative Assistant/Secretary** *1 student enrolled* • **Licensed Practical/Vocational Nurse Training (LPN, LVN, Cert, Dipl, AAS)** *43 students enrolled* • **Massage Therapy/Therapeutic Massage** *7 students enrolled* • **Mechanical Drafting and Mechanical Drafting CAD/CADD** *12 students enrolled* • **Medical Administrative/Executive Assistant and Medical Secretary** *7 students enrolled* • **Medical Transcription/Transcriptionist** *5 students enrolled* • **Nurse/Nursing Assistant/Aide and Patient Care Assistant** *213 students enrolled* • **Office Management and Supervision** *3 students enrolled* • **Retailing and Retail Operations** *2 students enrolled* • **System Administration/Administrator** *4 students enrolled* • **Truck and Bus Driver/Commercial Vehicle Operation** *15 students enrolled* • **Welding Technology/Welder** *2 students enrolled*

**STUDENT SERVICES** Academic or career counseling, daycare for children of students, employment services for current students, placement services for program completers, remedial services.

## Kendall College

900 North Branch Street, Chicago, IL 60622
http://www.kendall.edu/

**CONTACT** Nivine Megahed, President
**Telephone:** 312-752-2000

**GENERAL INFORMATION** Private Institution. Founded 1934. **Accreditation:** Regional (NCA). **Total program enrollment:** 1222. **Application fee:** $50.

**PROGRAM(S) OFFERED**

• **Business/Commerce, General** • **Culinary Arts/Chef Training** *66 students enrolled*

**STUDENT SERVICES** Academic or career counseling, employment services for current students, placement services for program completers, remedial services.

## Kishwaukee College

21193 Malta Road, Malta, IL 60150-9699
http://www.kishwaukeecollege.edu/

**CONTACT** Tom Choice, President
**Telephone:** 815-825-2086

**GENERAL INFORMATION** Public Institution. Founded 1967. **Accreditation:** Regional (NCA); radiologic technology: radiography (JRCERT). **Total program enrollment:** 2031.

**PROGRAM(S) OFFERED**

• **Administrative Assistant and Secretarial Science, General** *6 students enrolled* • **Agricultural Power Machinery Operation** *28 students enrolled* • **Airline/Commercial/Professional Pilot and Flight Crew** *1 student enrolled* • **Autobody/Collision and Repair Technology/Technician** *5 students enrolled* • **Automobile/Automotive Mechanics Technology/Technician** *3 students enrolled* • **CAD/CADD Drafting and/or Design Technology/Technician** *1 student enrolled* • **Carpentry/Carpenter** *2 students enrolled* • **Computer Installation and Repair Technology/Technician** *3 students enrolled* • **Computer Systems Networking and Telecommunications** *1 student enrolled* • **Electrical, Electronic and Communications Engineering Technology/Technician** *2 students enrolled* • **Electrician** *3 students enrolled* • **Emergency Care Attendant (EMT Ambulance)** *39 students enrolled* • **Floriculture/Floristry Operations and Management** *1 student enrolled* • **General Office Occupations and Clerical Services** *2 students enrolled* • **Greenhouse Operations and Management** *1 student enrolled* • **Licensed Practical/Vocational Nurse Training (LPN, LVN, Cert, Dipl, AAS)** *13 students enrolled* • **Massage Therapy/Therapeutic Massage** *22 students enrolled* • **Mechanical Drafting and Mechanical Drafting CAD/CADD** *1 student enrolled* • **Medical Insurance Coding Specialist/Coder** *15 students enrolled* • **Medical Transcription/Transcriptionist** *3 students enrolled* • **Nurse/Nursing Assistant/Aide and Patient Care Assistant** *165 students enrolled* • **Welding Technology/Welder** *1 student enrolled*

**STUDENT SERVICES** Academic or career counseling, daycare for children of students, employment services for current students, placement services for program completers, remedial services.

## La' James College of Hairstyling

485 42nd Avenue, East Moline, IL 61244
http://www.lajames.net/

**CONTACT** Cynthia Becher, President
**Telephone:** 309-755-1313

**GENERAL INFORMATION** Private Institution. Founded 1986. **Total program enrollment:** 25. **Application fee:** $50.

**PROGRAM(S) OFFERED**

• **Aesthetician/Esthetician and Skin Care Specialist** *600 hrs./$8860* • **Cosmetology, Barber/Styling, and Nail Instructor** *1000 hrs./$7565* • **Cosmetology/Cosmetologist, General** *1500 hrs./$18,365* • **Massage Therapy/Therapeutic Massage** *625 hrs./$8860* • **Nail Technician/Specialist and Manicurist** *350 hrs./$3925*

**STUDENT SERVICES** Academic or career counseling, employment services for current students, placement services for program completers.

## Lake Land College

5001 Lake Land Boulevard, Mattoon, IL 61938-9366
http://www.lakelandcollege.edu/

**CONTACT** Scott Lensink, President
**Telephone:** 217-234-5253

**GENERAL INFORMATION** Public Institution. Founded 1966. **Accreditation:** Regional (NCA); dental hygiene (ADA); physical therapy assisting (APTA); practical nursing (NLN). **Total program enrollment:** 3009.

**PROGRAM(S) OFFERED**
• **Accounting** *4 students enrolled* • **Administrative Assistant and Secretarial Science, General** *27 students enrolled* • **Agricultural Business and Management, General** *1 student enrolled* • **Agricultural Power Machinery Operation** *1 student enrolled* • **Animal Training** *19 students enrolled* • **Applied Horticulture/Horticultural Operations, General** *48 students enrolled* • **Autobody/Collision and Repair Technology/Technician** *28 students enrolled* • **Automobile/Automotive Mechanics Technology/Technician** *106 students enrolled* • **Building/Property Maintenance and Management** *4 students enrolled* • **Business Administration and Management, General** *18 students enrolled* • **Business/Office Automation/Technology/Data Entry** *142 students enrolled* • **CAD/CADD Drafting and/or Design Technology/Technician** *8 students enrolled* • **Child Care Provider/Assistant** *1 student enrolled* • **Communications Systems Installation and Repair Technology** *3 students enrolled* • **Computer Technology/Computer Systems Technology** *1 student enrolled* • **Construction Trades, General** *97 students enrolled* • **Cosmetology, Barber/Styling, and Nail Instructor** *1 student enrolled* • **Cosmetology/Cosmetologist, General** *48 students enrolled* • **Crop Production** *2 students enrolled* • **Dog/Pet/Animal Grooming** *10 students enrolled* • **Entrepreneurship/Entrepreneurial Studies** *2 students enrolled* • **Food Service, Waiter/Waitress, and Dining Room Management/Manager** *47 students enrolled* • **General Office Occupations and Clerical Services** *6 students enrolled* • **Graphic and Printing Equipment Operator, General Production** *14 students enrolled* • **Heating, Air Conditioning, Ventilation and Refrigeration Maintenance Technology/Technician (HAC, HACR, HVAC, HVACR)** *31 students enrolled* • **Housing and Human Environments, Other** *126 students enrolled* • **Information Science/Studies** *4 students enrolled* • **Licensed Practical/Vocational Nurse Training (LPN, LVN, Cert, Dipl, AAS)** *28 students enrolled* • **Massage Therapy/Therapeutic Massage** *10 students enrolled* • **Medical Transcription/Transcriptionist** *7 students enrolled* • **Nail Technician/Specialist and Manicurist** *7 students enrolled* • **Parts, Warehousing, and Inventory Management Operations** *5 students enrolled* • **Prepress/Desktop Publishing and Digital Imaging Design** *1 student enrolled* • **Radio and Television** *4 students enrolled* • **Selling Skills and Sales Operations** *5 students enrolled*

**STUDENT SERVICES** Academic or career counseling, daycare for children of students, employment services for current students, placement services for program completers, remedial services.

## Lakeview College of Nursing

903 North Logan Avenue, Danville, IL 61832
http://www.lakeviewcol.edu/

**CONTACT** Dick Shockey, CEO
**Telephone:** 217-443-5238

**GENERAL INFORMATION** Private Institution. Founded 1987. **Accreditation:** Regional (NCA). **Total program enrollment:** 226. **Application fee:** $100.

**STUDENT SERVICES** Academic or career counseling, remedial services.

## Lewis and Clark Community College

5800 Godfrey Road, Godfrey, IL 62035-2466
http://www.lc.edu/

**CONTACT** Dale T. Chapman, President
**Telephone:** 618-468-3411

**GENERAL INFORMATION** Public Institution. Founded 1970. **Accreditation:** Regional (NCA); dental assisting (ADA); dental hygiene (ADA). **Total program enrollment:** 2813.

**PROGRAM(S) OFFERED**
• **Accounting Technology/Technician and Bookkeeping** *3 students enrolled* • **Accounting** *2 students enrolled* • **Administrative Assistant and Secretarial Science, General** *153 students enrolled* • **Automobile/Automotive Mechanics Technology/Technician** *9 students enrolled* • **Banking and Financial Support Services** *11 students enrolled* • **Business Administration and Management, General** *6 students enrolled* • **Business/Office Automation/Technology/Data Entry** *56 students enrolled* • **CAD/CADD Drafting and/or Design Technology/Technician** *5 students enrolled* • **Child Care Provider/Assistant** *1 student enrolled* • **Computer Installation and Repair Technology/Technician** *41 students enrolled* • **Computer Programming, Specific Applications** *6 students enrolled* • **Computer Systems Networking and Telecommunications** *26 students enrolled* • **Criminal Justice/Police Science** *19 students enrolled* • **Dental Assisting/Assistant** *25 students enrolled* • **Electrician** *43 students enrolled* • **Emergency Medical Technology/Technician (EMT Paramedic)** *8 students enrolled* • **Fire Science/Firefighting** *30 students enrolled* • **Fire Services Administration** *7 students enrolled* • **General Office Occupations and Clerical Services** *2 students enrolled* • **Graphic Design** *7 students enrolled* • **Human Resources Management/Personnel Administration, General** *13 students enrolled* • **Legal Administrative Assistant/Secretary** *2 students enrolled* • **Legal Assistant/Paralegal** *12 students enrolled* • **Library Assistant/Technician** *2 students enrolled* • **Machine Tool Technology/Machinist** *11 students enrolled* • **Massage Therapy/Therapeutic Massage** *9 students enrolled* • **Medical Insurance Specialist/Medical Biller** *11 students enrolled* • **Medical Transcription/Transcriptionist** *2 students enrolled* • **Nurse/Nursing Assistant/Aide and Patient Care Assistant** *162 students enrolled* • **Prepress/Desktop Publishing and Digital Imaging Design** *10 students enrolled* • **Radio and Television** *6 students enrolled* • **Selling Skills and Sales Operations** *15 students enrolled* • **System Administration/Administrator** *11 students enrolled* • **Web Page, Digital/Multimedia and Information Resources Design** *8 students enrolled* • **Welding Technology/Welder** *71 students enrolled*

**STUDENT SERVICES** Academic or career counseling, daycare for children of students, employment services for current students, placement services for program completers, remedial services.

## Lewis University

One University Parkway, Romeoville, IL 60446
http://www.lewisu.edu/

**CONTACT** Brother James Gaffney, FSC, President
**Telephone:** 815-838-0500

**GENERAL INFORMATION** Private Institution (Affiliated with Roman Catholic Church). Founded 1932. **Accreditation:** Regional (NCA). **Total program enrollment:** 3219. **Application fee:** $40.

**PROGRAM(S) OFFERED**
• **Airframe Mechanics and Aircraft Maintenance Technology/Technician**

**STUDENT SERVICES** Academic or career counseling, employment services for current students, placement services for program completers, remedial services.

## Lincoln Christian College

100 Campus View Drive, Lincoln, IL 62656-2167
http://www.lccs.edu/

**CONTACT** Keith Ray, President
**Telephone:** 217-732-3168

**GENERAL INFORMATION** Private Institution (Affiliated with Christian Churches and Churches of Christ). Founded 1944. **Accreditation:** Regional (NCA); state accredited or approved. **Total program enrollment:** 700. **Application fee:** $20.

**PROGRAM(S) OFFERED**
• **Bible/Biblical Studies** *3 students enrolled*

**STUDENT SERVICES** Academic or career counseling, employment services for current students, placement services for program completers, remedial services.

## Lincoln College

300 Keokuk Street, Lincoln, IL 62656-1699
http://www.lincolncollege.edu/

**CONTACT** John Hutchinson, President
**Telephone:** 217-732-3155 Ext. 242

**GENERAL INFORMATION** Private Institution. Founded 1865. **Accreditation:** Regional (NCA). **Total program enrollment:** 983. **Application fee:** $25.

**PROGRAM(S) OFFERED**
• **Cosmetology/Cosmetologist, General** *31 students enrolled* • **Medical Administrative/Executive Assistant and Medical Secretary** • **Office Management and Supervision** • **Tourism and Travel Services Marketing Operations**

**STUDENT SERVICES** Academic or career counseling, employment services for current students, remedial services.

## Lincoln Land Community College

5250 Shepherd Road, PO Box 19256, Springfield, IL 62794-9256
http://www.llcc.edu/

**CONTACT** Dr. Charlotte Warren, President
**Telephone:** 217-786-2200

**GENERAL INFORMATION** Public Institution. Founded 1967. **Accreditation:** Regional (NCA); radiologic technology: radiography (JRCERT). **Total program enrollment:** 2921.

**PROGRAM(S) OFFERED**
• **Architectural Drafting and Architectural CAD/CADD** *2 students enrolled* • **Autobody/Collision and Repair Technology/Technician** *21 students enrolled* • **Automobile/Automotive Mechanics Technology/Technician** *6 students enrolled* • **Baking and Pastry Arts/Baker/Pastry Chef** *5 students enrolled* • **Building/Property Maintenance and Management** *2 students enrolled* • **Business Administration and Management, General** *5 students enrolled* • **Business/Office Automation/Technology/Data Entry** *10 students enrolled* • **CAD/CADD Drafting and/or Design Technology/Technician** *3 students enrolled* • **Computer Engineering Technology/Technician** *4 students enrolled* • **Computer Programming/Programmer, General** *2 students enrolled* • **Computer Technology/Computer Systems Technology** *2 students enrolled* • **Criminal Justice/Police Science** *2 students enrolled* • **Dietitian Assistant** *1 student enrolled* • **Electrical, Electronic and Communications Engineering Technology/Technician** *3 students enrolled* • **Emergency Care Attendant (EMT Ambulance)** *59 students enrolled* • **Emergency Medical Technology/Technician (EMT Paramedic)** *23 students enrolled* • **Fire Protection and Safety Technology/Technician** *8 students enrolled* • **Fire Science/Firefighting** *72 students enrolled* • **Fire Services Administration** *15 students enrolled* • **General Office Occupations and Clerical Services** *7 students enrolled* • **Heating, Air Conditioning, Ventilation and Refrigeration Maintenance Technology/Technician (HAC, HACR, HVAC, HVACR)** *12 students enrolled* • **Hotel/Motel Administration/Management** *2 students enrolled* • **Industrial Electronics Technology/Technician** *10 students enrolled* • **Landscaping and Groundskeeping** *5 students enrolled* • **Legal Administrative Assistant/Secretary** *2 students enrolled* • **Licensed Practical/Vocational Nurse Training (LPN, LVN, Cert, Dipl, AAS)** *21 students enrolled* • **Medical Administrative/Executive Assistant and Medical Secretary** *3 students enrolled* • **Medical Insurance Coding Specialist/Coder** *2 students enrolled* • **Medical Transcription/Transcriptionist** *10 students enrolled* • **Nurse/Nursing Assistant/Aide and Patient Care Assistant** *323 students enrolled* • **Restaurant, Culinary, and Catering Management/Manager** *4 students enrolled* • **Security and Loss Prevention Services** *146 students enrolled* • **System Administration/Administrator** *3 students enrolled* • **Truck and Bus Driver/Commercial Vehicle Operation** *154 students enrolled* • **Web Page, Digital/Multimedia and Information Resources Design** *1 student enrolled* • **Welding Technology/Welder** *9 students enrolled* • **Word Processing** *4 students enrolled*

**STUDENT SERVICES** Academic or career counseling, daycare for children of students, employment services for current students, placement services for program completers, remedial services.

## Lincoln Technical Institute

7320 West Agatite Avenue, Norridge, IL 60656-9975
http://www.lincolnedu.com/

**CONTACT** Helen Carver, President
**Telephone:** 203-582-8200

**GENERAL INFORMATION** Private Institution. Founded 1946. **Total program enrollment:** 1292. **Application fee:** $150.

**PROGRAM(S) OFFERED**
• **Automobile/Automotive Mechanics Technology/Technician** *30 hrs./$10,767* • **Construction Trades, Other** *52 hrs./$18,304* • **Health Services/Allied Health/Health Sciences, General** *40 hrs./$14,210* • **Medical/Clinical Assistant** *270 students enrolled*

**STUDENT SERVICES** Academic or career counseling, employment services for current students, placement services for program completers, remedial services.

## Loyola University Chicago

1032 West Sheridan Road, Chicago, IL 60660
http://www.luc.edu/

**CONTACT** Michael J. Garanzini, SJ, President
**Telephone:** 312-915-6000

**GENERAL INFORMATION** Private Institution. Founded 1870. **Accreditation:** Regional (NCA); dietetics: postbaccalaureate internship (ADtA/CAADE); theater (NAST). **Total program enrollment:** 13561. **Application fee:** $25.

**STUDENT SERVICES** Academic or career counseling, employment services for current students, placement services for program completers, remedial services.

## MacCormac College

506 South Wabash Avenue, Chicago, IL 60605-1667
http://www.maccormac.edu/

**CONTACT** Dr. Leo Loughead, President
**Telephone:** 312-922-1884 Ext. 401

**GENERAL INFORMATION** Private Institution. Founded 1904. **Accreditation:** Regional (NCA). **Total program enrollment:** 99. **Application fee:** $20.

**PROGRAM(S) OFFERED**
• **Business Administration and Management, General** • **Business/Office Automation/Technology/Data Entry** • **Information Science/Studies** • **International Business/Trade/Commerce** • **Legal Administrative Assistant/Secretary** • **Legal Assistant/Paralegal** • **Legal Support Services, Other** • **Medical Transcription/Transcriptionist** • **Tourism and Travel Services Marketing Operations**

**STUDENT SERVICES** Academic or career counseling, employment services for current students, placement services for program completers.

## MacDaniel's Beauty School

5228 North Clark Street, Chicago, IL 60640

**CONTACT** Steven Papageorge, Director
**Telephone:** 773-561-2376

**GENERAL INFORMATION** Private Institution. Founded 1965. **Total program enrollment:** 37. **Application fee:** $100.

*MacDaniel's Beauty School (continued)*

**PROGRAM(S) OFFERED**

• **Cosmetology, Barber/Styling, and Nail Instructor** *1000 hrs./$7600* • **Cosmetology/Cosmetologist, General** *1500 hrs./$11,750* • **Nail Technician/Specialist and Manicurist** *350 hrs./$2750*

**STUDENT SERVICES** Academic or career counseling, employment services for current students, placement services for program completers.

## McHenry County College

8900 US Highway 14, Crystal Lake, IL 60012-2761
http://www.mchenry.edu/

**CONTACT** Walter Packard, President
**Telephone:** 815-455-3700

**GENERAL INFORMATION** Public Institution. Founded 1967. **Accreditation:** Regional (NCA). **Total program enrollment:** 2283. **Application fee:** $15.

**PROGRAM(S) OFFERED**

• **Accounting Technology/Technician and Bookkeeping** *1 student enrolled* • **Accounting** *1 student enrolled* • **Administrative Assistant and Secretarial Science, General** *5 students enrolled* • **Animation, Interactive Technology, Video Graphics and Special Effects** *4 students enrolled* • **Applied Horticulture/Horticultural Operations, General** *4 students enrolled* • **Automobile/Automotive Mechanics Technology/Technician** *10 students enrolled* • **Building/Home/Construction Inspection/Inspector** *11 students enrolled* • **Business Administration and Management, General** *53 students enrolled* • **Business/Office Automation/Technology/Data Entry** *5 students enrolled* • **CAD/CADD Drafting and/or Design Technology/Technician** *5 students enrolled* • **Child Care Provider/Assistant** *1 student enrolled* • **Computer Systems Networking and Telecommunications** *1 student enrolled* • **Computer Technology/Computer Systems Technology** *2 students enrolled* • **Emergency Care Attendant (EMT Ambulance)** *14 students enrolled* • **Fire Science/Firefighting** *56 students enrolled* • **Fire Services Administration** *1 student enrolled* • **Floriculture/Floristry Operations and Management** *4 students enrolled* • **Greenhouse Operations and Management** *2 students enrolled* • **Health and Physical Education, General** *14 students enrolled* • **International Business/Trade/Commerce** *1 student enrolled* • **Landscaping and Groundskeeping** *3 students enrolled* • **Mechanical Engineering/Mechanical Technology/Technician** *1 student enrolled* • **Medical Office Assistant/Specialist** *9 students enrolled* • **Nurse/Nursing Assistant/Aide and Patient Care Assistant** *175 students enrolled* • **Operations Management and Supervision** *2 students enrolled* • **Selling Skills and Sales Operations** *7 students enrolled*

**STUDENT SERVICES** Academic or career counseling, daycare for children of students, employment services for current students, placement services for program completers, remedial services.

## Midstate College

411 West Northmoor Road, Peoria, IL 61614
http://www.midstate.edu/

**CONTACT** R. Dale Bunch, President
**Telephone:** 309-692-4092

**GENERAL INFORMATION** Private Institution. Founded 1888. **Accreditation:** Regional (NCA); medical assisting (AAMAE). **Total program enrollment:** 292. **Application fee:** $25.

**PROGRAM(S) OFFERED**

• **Computer Software and Media Applications, Other** • **Computer Systems Networking and Telecommunications** • **General Office Occupations and Clerical Services** *7 students enrolled* • **Medical Insurance Coding Specialist/Coder** *16 students enrolled* • **Medical Transcription/Transcriptionist** *3 students enrolled* • **Web Page, Digital/Multimedia and Information Resources Design**

**STUDENT SERVICES** Academic or career counseling, employment services for current students, placement services for program completers.

## Midwest Institute of Massage Therapy

4715 W. Main Street, Belleville, IL 62223

**CONTACT** Vinomani Gaddam, President
**Telephone:** 618-239-6468 Ext. 0

**GENERAL INFORMATION** Private Institution. **Total program enrollment:** 30. **Application fee:** $100.

**PROGRAM(S) OFFERED**

• **Massage Therapy/Therapeutic Massage** *700 hrs./$5660*

**STUDENT SERVICES** Academic or career counseling, placement services for program completers.

## Midwest Technical Institute

405 N. Limit Street., Lincoln, IL 62656-0506
http://midwesttechnicalinstitute.edu/

**CONTACT** Kathy Steinberg, President
**Telephone:** 217-527-8324

**GENERAL INFORMATION** Private Institution. **Total program enrollment:** 635. **Application fee:** $100.

**PROGRAM(S) OFFERED**

• **Dental Assisting/Assistant** *32 hrs./$9600* • **Heating, Air Conditioning, Ventilation and Refrigeration Maintenance Technology/Technician (HAC, HACR, HVAC, HVACR)** *30 hrs./$9315* • **Massage Therapy/Therapeutic Massage** *39 hrs./$9550* • **Medical Insurance Coding Specialist/Coder** *38 hrs./$9260* • **Medical/Clinical Assistant** *34 hrs./$9550* • **Nurse/Nursing Assistant/Aide and Patient Care Assistant** *36 students enrolled* • **Pharmacy Technician/Assistant** *11 students enrolled* • **Welding Technology/Welder** *30 hrs./$10,400*

**STUDENT SERVICES** Academic or career counseling, employment services for current students, placement services for program completers.

## Moraine Valley Community College

9000 W. College Parkway, Palos Hills, IL 60465
http://www.morainevalley.edu/

**CONTACT** Dr. Vernon O. Crawley, President
**Telephone:** 708-974-4300

**GENERAL INFORMATION** Public Institution. Founded 1967. **Accreditation:** Regional (NCA); health information technology (AHIMA); radiologic technology: radiography (JRCERT). **Total program enrollment:** 7368.

**PROGRAM(S) OFFERED**

• **Accounting Technology/Technician and Bookkeeping** *9 students enrolled* • **Administrative Assistant and Secretarial Science, General** *12 students enrolled* • **Animation, Interactive Technology, Video Graphics and Special Effects** *4 students enrolled* • **Automobile/Automotive Mechanics Technology/Technician** *9 students enrolled* • **Business/Commerce, General** *18 students enrolled* • **Business/Office Automation/Technology/Data Entry** *15 students enrolled* • **CAD/CADD Drafting and/or Design Technology/Technician** *9 students enrolled* • **Computer Engineering Technology/Technician** *5 students enrolled* • **Computer Programming, Specific Applications** *4 students enrolled* • **Computer Systems Networking and Telecommunications** *7 students enrolled* • **Computer and Information Systems Security** *6 students enrolled* • **E-Commerce/Electronic Commerce** *3 students enrolled* • **Electrical, Electronic and Communications Engineering Technology/Technician** *2 students enrolled* • **Emergency Medical Technology/Technician (EMT Paramedic)** *1 student enrolled* • **Executive Assistant/Executive Secretary** *3 students enrolled* • **Heating, Air Conditioning, Ventilation and Refrigeration Maintenance Technology/Technician (HAC, HACR, HVAC, HVACR)** *5 students enrolled* • **Hospitality Administration/Management, General** *9 students enrolled* • **Human Resources Management/Personnel Administration, General** *1 student enrolled* • **Kinesiology and Exercise Science** *6 students enrolled* • **Legal Administrative Assistant/Secretary** *3 students enrolled* • **Massage Therapy/Therapeutic Massage** *25 students enrolled* • **Mechanical Drafting and Mechanical Drafting CAD/CADD** *3 students enrolled* • **Medical Insurance Coding Specialist/Coder** *59 students enrolled* • **Medical Transcription/Transcriptionist** *10 students enrolled* • **Medical/Clinical Assistant** *12 students enrolled* • **Phlebotomy/Phlebotomist** *92 students enrolled* • **Psychiatric/Mental Health Services Technician** *2 students enrolled* • **Respiratory Care Therapy/Therapist** *14 students enrolled* • **Restaurant, Culinary, and Catering Management/Manager** *3 students enrolled* • **Security** and Loss Prevention Services *1 student enrolled* • Substance Abuse/Addiction Counseling *2 students enrolled* • System Administration/Administrator *4 students enrolled* • System, Networking, and LAN/WAN Management/Manager *4 students enrolled* • Teacher Assistant/Aide *5 students enrolled* • Tourism and Travel Services Management *11 students enrolled* • Web Page, Digital/Multimedia and Information Resources Design *4 students enrolled* • Welding Technology/Welder *26 students enrolled*

**STUDENT SERVICES** Academic or career counseling, daycare for children of students, employment services for current students, placement services for program completers, remedial services.

## Morton College

3801 South Central Avenue, Cicero, IL 60804-4398
http://www.morton.edu/

**CONTACT** Leslie Navarro, President
**Telephone:** 708-656-8000

**GENERAL INFORMATION** Public Institution. Founded 1924. **Accreditation:** Regional (NCA); physical therapy assisting (APTA). **Total program enrollment:** 1332. **Application fee:** $10.

**PROGRAM(S) OFFERED**
• **Administrative Assistant and Secretarial Science, General** *5 students enrolled* • **Automobile/Automotive Mechanics Technology/Technician** *1 student enrolled* • **Business/Office Automation/Technology/Data Entry** *10 students enrolled* • **CAD/CADD Drafting and/or Design Technology/Technician** *2 students enrolled* • **Child Care Provider/Assistant** *37 students enrolled* • **Computer Installation and Repair Technology/Technician** *2 students enrolled* • **Computer Programming, Vendor/Product Certification** *24 students enrolled* • **Computer Programming/Programmer, General** *1 student enrolled* • **Computer Systems Networking and Telecommunications** *1 student enrolled* • **Computer Technology/Computer Systems Technology** *1 student enrolled* • **General Office Occupations and Clerical Services** *3 students enrolled* • **Health Information/Medical Records Technology/Technician** *8 students enrolled* • **Heating, Air Conditioning, Ventilation and Refrigeration Maintenance Technology/Technician (HAC, HACR, HVAC, HVACR)** *7 students enrolled* • **Licensed Practical/Vocational Nurse Training (LPN, LVN, Cert, Dipl, AAS)** *41 students enrolled* • **Massage Therapy/Therapeutic Massage** *13 students enrolled* • **Mechanical Drafting and Mechanical Drafting CAD/CADD** *1 student enrolled* • **Nurse/Nursing Assistant/Aide and Patient Care Assistant** *56 students enrolled*

**STUDENT SERVICES** Academic or career counseling, daycare for children of students, employment services for current students, placement services for program completers, remedial services.

## Mr. John's School of Cosmetology

1745 East Eldorado Street, Decatur, IL 62521
http://www.mrjohns.com/

**CONTACT** John W. Stubblefield, President
**Telephone:** 217-423-8173

**GENERAL INFORMATION** Private Institution. Founded 1967. **Total program enrollment:** 76. **Application fee:** $100.

**PROGRAM(S) OFFERED**
• **Aesthetician/Esthetician and Skin Care Specialist** *750 hrs./$6095* • **Cosmetology and Related Personal Grooming Arts, Other** • **Cosmetology, Barber/Styling, and Nail Instructor** *1000 hrs./$5870* • **Cosmetology/Cosmetologist, General** *1900 hrs./$11,595* • **Make-Up Artist/Specialist** *4 students enrolled* • **Nail Technician/Specialist and Manicurist** *400 hrs./$2770*

**STUDENT SERVICES** Academic or career counseling, employment services for current students, placement services for program completers.

## Mr. John's School of Cosmetology & Nails

1429 S. Main Street, Suite F, Jacksonville, IL 62650
http://mrjohns.com/

**CONTACT** John W. Stubblefield, President
**Telephone:** 217-243-1744

**GENERAL INFORMATION** Private Institution. **Total program enrollment:** 27. **Application fee:** $100.

**PROGRAM(S) OFFERED**
• **Cosmetology and Related Personal Grooming Arts, Other** *6 students enrolled* • **Cosmetology, Barber/Styling, and Nail Instructor** *1000 hrs./$5870* • **Cosmetology/Cosmetologist, General** *1700 hrs./$13,350* • **Nail Technician/Specialist and Manicurist** *400 hrs./$2745*

**STUDENT SERVICES** Academic or career counseling, employment services for current students, placement services for program completers.

## Ms. Robert's Academy of Beauty Culture–Villa Park

17 East Park Boulevard, Villa Park, IL 60181

**CONTACT** Phil Sparagna, President
**Telephone:** 630-941-3880

**GENERAL INFORMATION** Private Institution. **Total program enrollment:** 55. **Application fee:** $100.

**PROGRAM(S) OFFERED**
• **Aesthetician/Esthetician and Skin Care Specialist** *750 hrs./$8150* • **Cosmetology and Related Personal Grooming Arts, Other** *87 students enrolled* • **Cosmetology/Cosmetologist, General** *1500 hrs./$11,000*

**STUDENT SERVICES** Academic or career counseling, placement services for program completers.

## National-Louis University

122 South Michigan Avenue, Chicago, IL 60603
http://www.nl.edu/

**CONTACT** Richard Pappas, President
**Telephone:** 800-443-5522

**GENERAL INFORMATION** Private Institution. Founded 1886. **Accreditation:** Regional (NCA); radiologic technology: radiation therapy technology (JRCERT). **Total program enrollment:** 2287. **Application fee:** $40.

**STUDENT SERVICES** Academic or career counseling, employment services for current students, placement services for program completers, remedial services.

## National University of Health Sciences

200 East Roosevelt Road, Lombard, IL 60148-4583
http://www.nuhs.edu/

**CONTACT** James F. Winterstein, President
**Telephone:** 630-629-2000

**GENERAL INFORMATION** Private Institution. Founded 1906. **Accreditation:** Regional (NCA). **Total program enrollment:** 499. **Application fee:** $55.

**PROGRAM(S) OFFERED**
• **Chiropractic Assistant/Technician** *6 students enrolled* • **Massage Therapy/Therapeutic Massage** *69 students enrolled*

**STUDENT SERVICES** Academic or career counseling, employment services for current students, remedial services.

## Niles School of Cosmetology

8057 North Milwaukee Avenue, Niles, IL 60714
http://nilesschoolofcosmetology.com/

**CONTACT** Filippo Livolsi, President
**Telephone:** 847-965-8061

**GENERAL INFORMATION** Private Institution. Founded 1975. **Total program enrollment:** 30. **Application fee:** $100.

*Niles School of Cosmetology (continued)*

**PROGRAM(S) OFFERED**

• **Cosmetology, Barber/Styling, and Nail Instructor** *1000 hrs./$4175* • **Cosmetology/Cosmetologist, General** *1500 hrs./$9000* • **Education, Other** *53 students enrolled*

**STUDENT SERVICES** Placement services for program completers.

## Northwestern Business College–Southwestern Campus

7725 South Harlem Avenue, Bridgeview, IL 60645
http://www.northwesternbc.edu/

**CONTACT** Lawrence Schumacher, President
**Telephone:** 888-205-2283

**GENERAL INFORMATION** Private Institution. **Total program enrollment:** 331. **Application fee:** $25.

**PROGRAM(S) OFFERED**

• **Accounting Technology/Technician and Bookkeeping** • **Administrative Assistant and Secretarial Science, General** • **Business Administration and Management, General** *3 students enrolled* • **Computer and Information Sciences and Support Services, Other** *7 students enrolled* • **Electroneurodiagnostic/Electroencephalographic Technology/Technologist** *31 students enrolled* • **Health Information/Medical Records Technology/Technician** *8 students enrolled* • **Hospitality Administration/Management, General** • **Legal Assistant/Paralegal** *18 students enrolled* • **Massage Therapy/Therapeutic Massage** *16 students enrolled* • **Medical Insurance Coding Specialist/Coder** *7 students enrolled* • **Medical/Clinical Assistant** • **Pharmacy Technician/Assistant** *16 students enrolled* • **Phlebotomy/Phlebotomist** *20 students enrolled* • **Real Estate** • **Tourism and Travel Services Management**

**STUDENT SERVICES** Academic or career counseling, employment services for current students, placement services for program completers, remedial services.

## Northwestern College

4839 North Milwaukee Avenue, Chicago, IL 60630
http://www.northwesterncollege.edu/

**CONTACT** Lawrence Schumacher, President
**Telephone:** 773-777-4220

**GENERAL INFORMATION** Private Institution. Founded 1902. **Accreditation:** Regional (NCA); health information technology (AHIMA); medical assisting (AAMAE). **Total program enrollment:** 354. **Application fee:** $25.

**PROGRAM(S) OFFERED**

• **Accounting Technology/Technician and Bookkeeping** • **Business Administration and Management, General** *1 student enrolled* • **Computer Programming, Specific Applications** • **Computer and Information Sciences and Support Services, Other** *2 students enrolled* • **Electroneurodiagnostic/Electroencephalographic Technology/Technologist** *10 students enrolled* • **Health Information/Medical Records Technology/Technician** *3 students enrolled* • **Hospitality Administration/Management, General** • **Legal Assistant/Paralegal** *6 students enrolled* • **Management Information Systems, General** • **Massage Therapy/Therapeutic Massage** *5 students enrolled* • **Medical/Clinical Assistant** *3 students enrolled* • **Pharmacy Technician/Assistant** *4 students enrolled* • **Phlebotomy/Phlebotomist** *3 students enrolled* • **Real Estate**

**STUDENT SERVICES** Academic or career counseling, employment services for current students, placement services for program completers, remedial services.

## Northwestern University

Evanston, IL 60208
http://www.northwestern.edu/

**CONTACT** Henry S. Bienen, President
**Telephone:** 312-491-3741

**GENERAL INFORMATION** Private Institution. Founded 1851. **Accreditation:** Regional (NCA); audiology (ASHA); journalism and mass communications (ACEJMC); music (NASM); speech-language pathology (ASHA); theater (NAST). **Total program enrollment:** 16134. **Application fee:** $65.

**PROGRAM(S) OFFERED**

• **Accounting Technology/Technician and Bookkeeping** • **Business Administration, Management and Operations, Other** • **Business/Commerce, General** • **Communication and Media Studies, Other** • **Computer and Information Sciences and Support Services, Other** • **Finance, General** *9 students enrolled* • **Health/Medical Preparatory Programs, Other** *6 students enrolled*

**STUDENT SERVICES** Academic or career counseling, employment services for current students, placement services for program completers.

## Oakton Community College

1600 East Golf Road, Des Plaines, IL 60016-1268
http://www.oakton.edu/

**CONTACT** Margaret B. Lee, President
**Telephone:** 847-635-1600

**GENERAL INFORMATION** Public Institution. Founded 1969. **Accreditation:** Regional (NCA); health information technology (AHIMA); medical laboratory technology (NAACLS); physical therapy assisting (APTA). **Total program enrollment:** 3444. **Application fee:** $25.

**PROGRAM(S) OFFERED**

• **Accounting Technology/Technician and Bookkeeping** *2 students enrolled* • **Architectural Drafting and Architectural CAD/CADD** *3 students enrolled* • **Automobile/Automotive Mechanics Technology/Technician** *1 student enrolled* • **Banking and Financial Support Services** *2 students enrolled* • **Business Administration and Management, General** *2 students enrolled* • **CAD/CADD Drafting and/or Design Technology/Technician** *5 students enrolled* • **Child Care Provider/Assistant** *41 students enrolled* • **Commercial Photography** *4 students enrolled* • **Computer Programming, Vendor/Product Certification** *2 students enrolled* • **Computer Software Technology/Technician** *1 student enrolled* • **Computer Systems Networking and Telecommunications** *9 students enrolled* • **Computer Technology/Computer Systems Technology** *2 students enrolled* • **Construction Management** *4 students enrolled* • **Criminal Justice/Police Science** *5 students enrolled* • **Data Modeling/Warehousing and Database Administration** *1 student enrolled* • **Data Processing and Data Processing Technology/Technician** *1 student enrolled* • **Emergency Medical Technology/Technician (EMT Paramedic)** *6 students enrolled* • **Executive Assistant/Executive Secretary** *2 students enrolled* • **Fire Science/Firefighting** *1 student enrolled* • **Heating, Air Conditioning, Ventilation and Refrigeration Maintenance Technology/Technician (HAC, HACR, HVAC, HVACR)** *20 students enrolled* • **Human Resources Management/Personnel Administration, General** *7 students enrolled* • **Information Science/Studies** *13 students enrolled* • **International Marketing** *1 student enrolled* • **Investments and Securities** *1 student enrolled* • **Manufacturing Technology/Technician** *8 students enrolled* • **Mechanical Engineering/Mechanical Technology/Technician** *3 students enrolled* • **Medical Insurance Coding Specialist/Coder** *12 students enrolled* • **Medical Insurance Specialist/Medical Biller** *18 students enrolled* • **Medical Office Assistant/Specialist** *1 student enrolled* • **Medical Transcription/Transcriptionist** *2 students enrolled* • **Nurse/Nursing Assistant/Aide and Patient Care Assistant** *141 students enrolled* • **Nursing—Registered Nurse Training (RN, ASN, BSN, MSN)** *5 students enrolled* • **Operations Management and Supervision** *1 student enrolled* • **Perioperative/Operating Room and Surgical Nurse/Nursing** *10 students enrolled* • **Pharmacy Technician/Assistant** *98 students enrolled* • **Phlebotomy/Phlebotomist** *12 students enrolled* • **Public Administration** *1 student enrolled* • **Purchasing, Procurement/Acquisitions and Contracts Management** *1 student enrolled* • **Real Estate** *1 student enrolled* • **Sales, Distribution and Marketing Operations, General** *1 student enrolled* • **Substance Abuse/Addiction Counseling** *4 students enrolled* • **System Administration/Administrator** *3 students enrolled* • **Web Page, Digital/Multimedia and Information Resources Design** *2 students enrolled* • **Web/Multimedia Management and Webmaster** *2 students enrolled*

**STUDENT SERVICES** Academic or career counseling, daycare for children of students, employment services for current students, placement services for program completers, remedial services.

## Oehrlein School of Cosmetology

100 Meadow Avenue, East Peoria, IL 61611

**CONTACT** Sandra L. Gay, President
**Telephone:** 309-699-1561

**GENERAL INFORMATION** Private Institution. Founded 1972. **Total program enrollment:** 74. **Application fee:** $100.

**PROGRAM(S) OFFERED**
• **Cosmetology/Cosmetologist, General** *1500 hrs./$11,670*

**STUDENT SERVICES** Academic or career counseling, placement services for program completers.

## Olivet Nazarene University

One University Avenue, Bourbonnais, IL 60914-2271
http://www.olivet.edu/

**CONTACT** John C. Bowling, President
**Telephone:** 815-939-5011

**GENERAL INFORMATION** Private Institution (Affiliated with Church of the Nazarene). Founded 1907. **Accreditation:** Regional (NCA); home economics (AAFCS); music (NASM). **Total program enrollment:** 2667. **Application fee:** $25.

**STUDENT SERVICES** Academic or career counseling, employment services for current students, placement services for program completers, remedial services.

## Pacific College of Oriental Medicine-Chicago

3646 North Broadway, 2nd Floor, Chicago, IL 60613
http://www.pacificcollege.edu/

**CONTACT** Ruth A. Levy, Chief Operating Officer
**Telephone:** 773-477-4822

**GENERAL INFORMATION** Private Institution. Founded 2000. **Accreditation:** Acupuncture and Oriental Medicine (ACAOM). **Total program enrollment:** 152. **Application fee:** $50.

**PROGRAM(S) OFFERED**
• **Massage Therapy/Therapeutic Massage** *6 students enrolled*

**STUDENT SERVICES** Academic or career counseling, remedial services.

## Parkland College

2400 West Bradley Avenue, Champaign, IL 61821-1899
http://www.parkland.edu/

**CONTACT** Tom Ramage, President
**Telephone:** 217-351-2200

**GENERAL INFORMATION** Public Institution. Founded 1967. **Accreditation:** Regional (NCA); dental hygiene (ADA); practical nursing (NLN); radiologic technology: radiography (JRCERT); surgical technology (ARCST). **Total program enrollment:** 4410.

**PROGRAM(S) OFFERED**
• **Accounting** *5 students enrolled* • **Administrative Assistant and Secretarial Science, General** *1 student enrolled* • **Agricultural Power Machinery Operation** *1 student enrolled* • **Autobody/Collision and Repair Technology/Technician** *23 students enrolled* • **Automobile/Automotive Mechanics Technology/Technician** *14 students enrolled* • **Building/Property Maintenance and Management** *2 students enrolled* • **Business/Office Automation/Technology/Data Entry** *1 student enrolled* • **CAD/CADD Drafting and/or Design Technology/Technician** *1 student enrolled* • **Carpentry/Carpenter** *4 students enrolled* • **Child Care Provider/Assistant** *2 students enrolled* • **Computer Graphics** *3 students enrolled* • **Computer Programming, Specific Applications** *1 student enrolled* • **Computer Programming/Programmer, General** *3 students enrolled* • **Computer Systems Networking and Telecommunications** *7 students enrolled* • **Construction Trades, General** *6 students enrolled* • **Data Modeling/Warehousing and Database Administration** *1 student enrolled* • **Emergency Care Attendant (EMT Ambulance)** *9 students enrolled* • **Emergency Medical Technology/Technician (EMT Paramedic)** *8 students enrolled* • **Entrepreneurship/Entrepreneurial Studies** *2 students enrolled* • **Floriculture/Floristry Operations and Management** *1 student enrolled* • **Glazier** *1 student enrolled* • **Heating, Air Conditioning, Ventilation and Refrigeration Maintenance Technology/Technician (HAC, HACR, HVAC, HVACR)** *4 students enrolled* • **Horse Husbandry/Equine Science and Management** *2 students enrolled* • **Hotel/Motel Administration/Management** *1 student enrolled* • **Industrial Electronics Technology/Technician** *4 students enrolled* • **International Business/Trade/Commerce** *1 student enrolled* • **Licensed Practical/Vocational Nurse Training (LPN, LVN, Cert, Dipl, AAS)** *18 students enrolled* • **Massage Therapy/Therapeutic Massage** *26 students enrolled* • **Medical Transcription/Transcriptionist** *1 student enrolled* • **Medical/Clinical Assistant** *17 students enrolled* • **Nurse/Nursing Assistant/Aide and Patient Care Assistant** *41 students enrolled* • **System Administration/Administrator** *1 student enrolled* • **Teaching English as a Second or Foreign Language/ESL Language Instructor** *6 students enrolled* • **Truck and Bus Driver/Commercial Vehicle Operation** *5 students enrolled* • **Web Page, Digital/Multimedia and Information Resources Design** *3 students enrolled* • **Web/Multimedia Management and Webmaster** *1 student enrolled*

**STUDENT SERVICES** Academic or career counseling, daycare for children of students, employment services for current students, placement services for program completers, remedial services.

## Pivot Point Beauty School

1791 West Howard Street, Chicago, IL 60626
http://www.pivot-point.com/

**CONTACT** Janice Douglas, Director, Student Affairs
**Telephone:** 800-886-0500 Ext. 7351

**GENERAL INFORMATION** Private Institution. **Total program enrollment:** 188. **Application fee:** $150.

**PROGRAM(S) OFFERED**
• **Aesthetician/Esthetician and Skin Care Specialist** *750 hrs./$10,929* • **Cosmetology/Cosmetologist, General** *1500 hrs./$18,759* • **Teacher Education and Professional Development, Specific Subject Areas, Other** *500 hrs./$8349*

**STUDENT SERVICES** Academic or career counseling, placement services for program completers.

## Pivot Point Beauty School

3901 West Irving Park, Chicago, IL 60618
http://www.pivot-point.com/

**CONTACT** Janice Douglas, Student Services Director
**Telephone:** 773-463-3121

**GENERAL INFORMATION** Private Institution. **Total program enrollment:** 115. **Application fee:** $150.

**PROGRAM(S) OFFERED**
• **Aesthetician/Esthetician and Skin Care Specialist** *750 hrs./$10,062* • **Cosmetology/Cosmetologist, General** *1500 hrs./$18,759* • **Nail Technician/Specialist and Manicurist**

**STUDENT SERVICES** Academic or career counseling, placement services for program completers.

## Pivot Point International Cosmetology Research Center

525 Busse Road, Elk Grove Villiage, IL 60007-2116
http://www.pivot-point.com/

**CONTACT** Janice Douglas, Student Services Director
**Telephone:** 847-985-5900

**GENERAL INFORMATION** Private Institution. Founded 1988. **Total program enrollment:** 217. **Application fee:** $150.

*Pivot Point International Cosmetology Research Center (continued)*

**PROGRAM(S) OFFERED**

- **Aesthetician/Esthetician and Skin Care Specialist** *750 hrs./$10,929*
- **Cosmetology/Cosmetologist, General** *150 hrs./$18,759*

**STUDENT SERVICES** Academic or career counseling, placement services for program completers.

## Prairie State College

202 South Halsted Street, Chicago Heights, IL 60411-8226
http://www.prairiestate.edu/

**CONTACT** Eric Radtke, President
**Telephone:** 708-709-3500

**GENERAL INFORMATION** Public Institution. Founded 1958. **Accreditation:** Regional (NCA); dental hygiene (ADA). **Total program enrollment:** 1908.

**PROGRAM(S) OFFERED**

• **Accounting Technology/Technician and Bookkeeping** *2 students enrolled* • **Administrative Assistant and Secretarial Science, General** *5 students enrolled* • **Automobile/Automotive Mechanics Technology/Technician** *10 students enrolled* • **CAD/CADD Drafting and/or Design Technology/Technician** *2 students enrolled* • **Cabinetmaking and Millwork/Millwright** *4 students enrolled* • **Child Care Provider/Assistant** *21 students enrolled* • **Commercial Photography** *1 student enrolled* • **Computer Installation and Repair Technology/Technician** *2 students enrolled* • **Computer Systems Networking and Telecommunications** *7 students enrolled* • **Criminal Justice/Police Science** *1 student enrolled* • **Data Processing and Data Processing Technology/Technician** *2 students enrolled* • **E-Commerce/Electronic Commerce** *1 student enrolled* • **Electrician** *9 students enrolled* • **Emergency Care Attendant (EMT Ambulance)** *62 students enrolled* • **Emergency Medical Technology/Technician (EMT Paramedic)** *71 students enrolled* • **Fire Science/Firefighting** *38 students enrolled* • **Health and Physical Education, General** *8 students enrolled* • **Heating, Air Conditioning, Ventilation and Refrigeration Maintenance Technology/Technician (HAC, HACR, HVAC, HVACR)** *15 students enrolled* • **Industrial Mechanics and Maintenance Technology** *12 students enrolled* • **Kinesiology and Exercise Science** *7 students enrolled* • **Machine Tool Technology/Machinist** *4 students enrolled* • **Nurse/Nursing Assistant/Aide and Patient Care Assistant** *255 students enrolled* • **Operations Management and Supervision** *1 student enrolled* • **Prepress/Desktop Publishing and Digital Imaging Design** *3 students enrolled* • **Surgical Technology/Technologist** *15 students enrolled* • **Teacher Assistant/Aide** *2 students enrolled* • **Tool and Die Technology/Technician** *2 students enrolled* • **Web Page, Digital/Multimedia and Information Resources Design** *4 students enrolled* • **Web/Multimedia Management and Webmaster** *2 students enrolled* • **Welding Technology/Welder** *1 student enrolled*

**STUDENT SERVICES** Academic or career counseling, daycare for children of students, employment services for current students, placement services for program completers, remedial services.

## Professionals Choice Hair Design Academy

2719 West Jefferson Street, Joliet, IL 60435
http://www.pchairdesign.com/

**CONTACT** John Thompson, President
**Telephone:** 815-741-8224

**GENERAL INFORMATION** Private Institution. Founded 1983. **Total program enrollment:** 15. **Application fee:** $100.

**PROGRAM(S) OFFERED**

- **Cosmetology and Related Personal Grooming Arts, Other** *1500 hrs./$14,550*
- **Cosmetology, Barber/Styling, and Nail Instructor** *1000 hrs./$9070*
- **Cosmetology/Cosmetologist, General** *38 students enrolled*

**STUDENT SERVICES** Academic or career counseling, employment services for current students, placement services for program completers.

## Pyramid Career Institute

3057 N. Lincoln Avenue, Chicago, IL 60657-4207
http://www.pyramid-pci.com/

**CONTACT** Dr. Marianne King, Chief Administration Officer, Executive Director
**Telephone:** 773-975-9898

**GENERAL INFORMATION** Private Institution. **Total program enrollment:** 7. **Application fee:** $100.

**PROGRAM(S) OFFERED**

• **Business Operations Support and Secretarial Services, Other** *360 hrs./$3300* • **Business/Office Automation/Technology/Data Entry** *360 hrs./$3300* • **Tourism and Travel Services Marketing Operations**

**STUDENT SERVICES** Academic or career counseling, employment services for current students, placement services for program completers, remedial services.

## Quincy University

1800 College Avenue, Quincy, IL 62301-2699
http://www.quincy.edu/

**CONTACT** Robert Gervasi, PhD, President
**Telephone:** 217-228-5432

**GENERAL INFORMATION** Private Institution. Founded 1860. **Accreditation:** Regional (NCA); music (NASM). **Total program enrollment:** 1141. **Application fee:** $25.

**PROGRAM(S) OFFERED**

• **Business Administration and Management, General**

**STUDENT SERVICES** Academic or career counseling, employment services for current students, placement services for program completers, remedial services.

## Rasmussen College Aurora

2363 Sequoia Drive, Aurora, IL 60506
http://www.rasmussen.edu/

**CONTACT** Bob Ernst, Campus Director
**Telephone:** 630-888-3500

**GENERAL INFORMATION** Private Institution. **Total program enrollment:** 41. **Application fee:** $60.

**PROGRAM(S) OFFERED**

• **Massage Therapy/Therapeutic Massage** • **Medical Insurance Coding Specialist/Coder** • **Medical Transcription/Transcriptionist**

**STUDENT SERVICES** Academic or career counseling, employment services for current students, placement services for program completers, remedial services.

## Rasmussen College Rockford, Illinois

6000 East State Street, Fourth Floor, Rockford, IL 61108-2513
http://www.rasmussen.edu/

**CONTACT** Scott Vukoder, Campus Director
**Telephone:** 815-316-4800

**GENERAL INFORMATION** Private Institution. **Total program enrollment:** 540. **Application fee:** $60.

**PROGRAM(S) OFFERED**

• **Massage Therapy/Therapeutic Massage** • **Medical Insurance Coding Specialist/Coder** *1 student enrolled* • **Medical Transcription/Transcriptionist**

**STUDENT SERVICES** Academic or career counseling, employment services for current students, placement services for program completers, remedial services.

## Regency Beauty Institute

4374 East New York Street, Aurora, IL 60504
http://www.regencybeauty.com/

**CONTACT** J. Hayes Batson, President
**Telephone:** 630-723-5051

**GENERAL INFORMATION** Private Institution. **Total program enrollment:** 89. **Application fee:** $100.

**PROGRAM(S) OFFERED**
- **Cosmetology/Cosmetologist, General** *1500 hrs./$16,011*

**STUDENT SERVICES** Academic or career counseling, placement services for program completers.

## Regency Beauty Institute

517 Town Center Boulevard, Champaign, IL 61822
http://www.regencybeauty.com/

**CONTACT** J. Hayes Batson, President CEO
**Telephone:** 800-787-6456

**GENERAL INFORMATION** Private Institution. **Total program enrollment:** 93. **Application fee:** $100.

**PROGRAM(S) OFFERED**
- **Cosmetology/Cosmetologist, General** *1500 hrs./$16,011*

**STUDENT SERVICES** Academic or career counseling, placement services for program completers.

## Regency Beauty Institute

7411 South Cass Avenue, Darien, IL 60561
http://www.regencybeauty.com/

**CONTACT** J. Hayes Batson, President
**Telephone:** 630-824-4022

**GENERAL INFORMATION** Private Institution. **Total program enrollment:** 70. **Application fee:** $100.

**PROGRAM(S) OFFERED**
- **Cosmetology/Cosmetologist, General** *1500 hrs./$16,011*

**STUDENT SERVICES** Academic or career counseling, placement services for program completers.

## Regency Beauty Institute

10850 Lincoln Trail, Fairview Heights, IL 62208
http://www.regencybeauty.com/

**CONTACT** J. Hayes Batson, President CEO
**Telephone:** 800-787-6456

**GENERAL INFORMATION** Private Institution. **Total program enrollment:** 103. **Application fee:** $100.

**PROGRAM(S) OFFERED**
- **Cosmetology/Cosmetologist, General** *1500 hrs./$16,011*

**STUDENT SERVICES** Academic or career counseling, placement services for program completers.

## Regency Beauty Institute

2601 West Lake Avenue, Peoria, IL 61602
http://www.regencybeauty.com/

**CONTACT** J. Hayes Batson, President CEO
**Telephone:** 800-787-6456

**GENERAL INFORMATION** Private Institution. **Total program enrollment:** 73. **Application fee:** $100.

**PROGRAM(S) OFFERED**
- **Cosmetology/Cosmetologist, General** *1500 hrs./$16,011*

**STUDENT SERVICES** Academic or career counseling, placement services for program completers.

## Regency Beauty Institute

609 S. Randall Road, Elgin, IL 60123

**CONTACT** J. Hayes Batson
**Telephone:** 224-856-4045

**GENERAL INFORMATION** Private Institution. **Application fee:** $100.

**PROGRAM(S) OFFERED**
- **Cosmetology/Cosmetologist, General** *1500 hrs./$16,011*

**STUDENT SERVICES** Academic or career counseling, placement services for program completers.

## Regency Beauty Institute

2904 Colorado Avenue, Joliet, IL 60431

**GENERAL INFORMATION** Private Institution. **Total program enrollment:** 90. **Application fee:** $100.

**PROGRAM(S) OFFERED**
- **Cosmetology/Cosmetologist, General** *1500 hrs./$16,011*

**STUDENT SERVICES** Academic or career counseling, placement services for program completers.

## Regency Beauty Institute

657 Highgrove Place, Rockford, IL 61108

**GENERAL INFORMATION** Private Institution. **Total program enrollment:** 106. **Application fee:** $100.

**PROGRAM(S) OFFERED**
- **Cosmetology/Cosmetologist, General** *1500 hrs./$16,011*

**STUDENT SERVICES** Academic or career counseling, placement services for program completers.

## Rend Lake College

468 North Ken Gray Parkway, Ina, IL 62846-9801
http://www.rlc.edu/

**CONTACT** Mark S. Kern, President
**Telephone:** 618-437-5321

**GENERAL INFORMATION** Public Institution. Founded 1967. **Accreditation:** Regional (NCA); health information technology (AHIMA); medical laboratory technology (NAACLS). **Total program enrollment:** 1795.

**PROGRAM(S) OFFERED**
- **Agricultural Mechanization, General** *4 students enrolled* • **Applied Horticulture/Horticultural Operations, General** *6 students enrolled* • **Architectural Drafting and Architectural CAD/CADD** *8 students enrolled* • **Automobile/Automotive Mechanics Technology/Technician** *26 students enrolled* • **Business/Office Automation/Technology/Data Entry** *12 students*

*Rend Lake College (continued)*

*enrolled* • **CAD/CADD Drafting and/or Design Technology/Technician** *7 students enrolled* • **Child Care Provider/Assistant** *23 students enrolled* • **Computer Engineering Technology/Technician** *12 students enrolled* • **Computer Systems Networking and Telecommunications** *11 students enrolled* • **Construction Trades, General** *33 students enrolled* • **Cosmetology, Barber/Styling, and Nail Instructor** *3 students enrolled* • **Cosmetology/Cosmetologist, General** *24 students enrolled* • **Criminal Justice/Police Science** *2 students enrolled* • **Culinary Arts/Chef Training** *6 students enrolled* • **Diesel Mechanics Technology/Technician** *4 students enrolled* • **Electrical, Electronic and Communications Engineering Technology/Technician** *2 students enrolled* • **Food Service, Waiter/Waitress, and Dining Room Management/Manager** *23 students enrolled* • **Graphic Design** *4 students enrolled* • **Housing and Human Environments, Other** *17 students enrolled* • **Industrial Mechanics and Maintenance Technology** *2 students enrolled* • **Licensed Practical/Vocational Nurse Training (LPN, LVN, Cert, Dipl, AAS)** *6 students enrolled* • **Massage Therapy/Therapeutic Massage** *14 students enrolled* • **Medical Transcription/Transcriptionist** *6 students enrolled* • **Nursing—Registered Nurse Training (RN, ASN, BSN, MSN)** *47 students enrolled* • **Surgical Technology/Technologist** *2 students enrolled* • **Turf and Turfgrass Management** *1 student enrolled* • **Welding Technology/Welder** *28 students enrolled*

**STUDENT SERVICES** Academic or career counseling, daycare for children of students, employment services for current students, placement services for program completers, remedial services.

## Richland Community College

One College Park, Decatur, IL 62521-8513
http://www.richland.edu/

**CONTACT** Dr. Gayle Saunders, President
**Telephone:** 217-875-7200

**GENERAL INFORMATION** Public Institution. Founded 1971. **Accreditation:** Regional (NCA); surgical technology (ARCST). **Total program enrollment:** 1049.

**PROGRAM(S) OFFERED**

• **Accounting Technology/Technician and Bookkeeping** *2 students enrolled* • **Administrative Assistant and Secretarial Science, General** *8 students enrolled* • **Applied Horticulture/Horticultural Operations, General** *28 students enrolled* • **Automobile/Automotive Mechanics Technology/Technician** *4 students enrolled* • **Business Administration and Management, General** *37 students enrolled* • **Business/Office Automation/Technology/Data Entry** *12 students enrolled* • **Child Care Provider/Assistant** *9 students enrolled* • **Computer Programming, Vendor/Product Certification** *1 student enrolled* • **Computer Systems Networking and Telecommunications** *1 student enrolled* • **Construction Trades, General** *30 students enrolled* • **Corrections** *1 student enrolled* • **Criminal Justice/Police Science** *4 students enrolled* • **Electrical and Power Transmission Installation/Installer, General** *10 students enrolled* • **Emergency Medical Technology/Technician (EMT Paramedic)** *1 student enrolled* • **Family Systems** *4 students enrolled* • **Fire Science/Firefighting** *5 students enrolled* • **Fire Services Administration** *5 students enrolled* • **Food Service, Waiter/Waitress, and Dining Room Management/Manager** *26 students enrolled* • **Graphic Design** *2 students enrolled* • **Greenhouse Operations and Management** *1 student enrolled* • **Heating, Air Conditioning, Ventilation and Refrigeration Maintenance Technology/Technician (HAC, HACR, HVAC, HVACR)** *4 students enrolled* • **Housing and Human Environments, Other** *120 students enrolled* • **Industrial Electronics Technology/Technician** *2 students enrolled* • **Industrial Mechanics and Maintenance Technology** *2 students enrolled* • **Instrumentation Technology/Technician** *1 student enrolled* • **Legal Administrative Assistant/Secretary** *1 student enrolled* • **Licensed Practical/Vocational Nurse Training (LPN, LVN, Cert, Dipl, AAS)** *7 students enrolled* • **Lineworker** *1 student enrolled* • **Manufacturing Technology/Technician** *3 students enrolled* • **Marketing/Marketing Management, General** *1 student enrolled* • **Mechanical Drafting and Mechanical Drafting CAD/CADD** *8 students enrolled* • **Medical Insurance Coding Specialist/Coder** *3 students enrolled* • **Medical Office Assistant/Specialist** *2 students enrolled* • **Medical Transcription/Transcriptionist** *5 students enrolled* • **Pharmacy Technician/Assistant** *7 students enrolled* • **Prepress/Desktop Publishing and Digital Imaging Design** *1 student enrolled* • **Surgical Technology/Technologist** *6 students enrolled* • **System Administration/Administrator** *1 student enrolled* • **Turf and Turfgrass Management** *1 student enrolled* • **Web Page, Digital/Multimedia and Information Resources Design** *1 student enrolled*

**STUDENT SERVICES** Academic or career counseling, daycare for children of students, employment services for current students, placement services for program completers, remedial services.

## Robert Morris University

401 South State Street, Chicago, IL 60605
http://www.robertmorris.edu/

**CONTACT** Michael P. Viollt, President
**Telephone:** 312-935-6800

**GENERAL INFORMATION** Private Institution. Founded 1913. **Accreditation:** Regional (NCA); medical assisting (AAMAE). **Total program enrollment:** 4030. **Application fee:** $30.

**PROGRAM(S) OFFERED**

• **Accounting Technology/Technician and Bookkeeping** *43 students enrolled* • **Administrative Assistant and Secretarial Science, General** • **Business Administration and Management, General** *379 students enrolled* • **Commercial and Advertising Art** *95 students enrolled* • **Computer Systems Networking and Telecommunications** *105 students enrolled* • **Drafting and Design Technology/Technician, General** *22 students enrolled* • **Interior Design** • **Intermedia/Multimedia** • **Legal Administrative Assistant/Secretary** • **Legal Assistant/Paralegal** *88 students enrolled* • **Management Information Systems, General** • **Medical/Clinical Assistant** *222 students enrolled*

**STUDENT SERVICES** Academic or career counseling, employment services for current students, placement services for program completers.

## Rockford Business College

730 North Church Street, Rockford, IL 61103
http://www.rbcsuccess.com/

**CONTACT** Steve W. Gibson, President
**Telephone:** 815-965-8616

**GENERAL INFORMATION** Private Institution. Founded 1862. **Accreditation:** Medical assisting (AAMAE); state accredited or approved. **Total program enrollment:** 254. **Application fee:** $150.

**PROGRAM(S) OFFERED**

• **Administrative Assistant and Secretarial Science, General** • **Business Administration and Management, General** • **Computer Software and Media Applications, Other** • **Computer and Information Sciences and Support Services, Other** • **Legal Administrative Assistant/Secretary** • **Massage Therapy/Therapeutic Massage** *18 students enrolled* • **Medical Transcription/Transcriptionist** • **Medical/Clinical Assistant** • **Nurse/Nursing Assistant/Aide and Patient Care Assistant** *40 students enrolled* • **Pharmacy Technician/Assistant** • **Web Page, Digital/Multimedia and Information Resources Design** *1 student enrolled*

**STUDENT SERVICES** Academic or career counseling, employment services for current students, placement services for program completers.

## Rock Valley College

3301 North Mulford Road, Rockford, IL 61114-5699
http://www.rockvalleycollege.edu/

**CONTACT** Jack Becherer, President
**Telephone:** 815-921-7821

**GENERAL INFORMATION** Public Institution. Founded 1964. **Accreditation:** Regional (NCA); dental hygiene (ADA). **Total program enrollment:** 3569.

**PROGRAM(S) OFFERED**

• **Accounting Technology/Technician and Bookkeeping** *7 students enrolled* • **Administrative Assistant and Secretarial Science, General** *1 student enrolled* • **Airframe Mechanics and Aircraft Maintenance Technology/Technician** *9 students enrolled* • **Architectural Drafting and Architectural CAD/CADD** *1 student enrolled* • **Automobile/Automotive Mechanics Technology/Technician** *46 students enrolled* • **Business/Commerce, General** *1 student enrolled* • **Business/Office Automation/Technology/Data Entry** *4 students enrolled* • **Child Care Provider/Assistant** *1 student enrolled* • **Computer Programming, Specific Applications** *2 students enrolled* • **Computer Systems Networking and Telecommunications** *10 students enrolled* • **Construction Management** *4 students enrolled* • **Construction Trades, General** *16 students enrolled* • **Fire Protection and Safety Technology/Technician** *5 students enrolled* • **Fire Science/Firefighting** *5 students enrolled* • **Fire Services Administration** *2 students enrolled* • **Graphic and Printing Equipment Operator, General Production** *1* student enrolled • **Industrial Technology/Technician** *1 student enrolled* • **Licensed Practical/Vocational Nurse Training (LPN, LVN, Cert, Dipl, AAS)** *36 students enrolled* • **Medical Insurance Coding Specialist/Coder** *4 students enrolled* • **Medical Transcription/Transcriptionist** *4 students enrolled* • **Nurse/Nursing Assistant/Aide and Patient Care Assistant** *421 students enrolled* • **Radio and Television** *2 students enrolled* • **Selling Skills and Sales Operations** *1 student enrolled* • **Substance Abuse/Addiction Counseling** *8 students enrolled* • **Surgical Technology/Technologist** *4 students enrolled*

**STUDENT SERVICES** Academic or career counseling, employment services for current students, placement services for program completers, remedial services.

## Roosevelt University

430 South Michigan Avenue, Chicago, IL 60605-1394
http://www.roosevelt.edu/

**CONTACT** Charles R. Middleton, President
**Telephone:** 312-341-3500

**GENERAL INFORMATION** Private Institution. Founded 1945. **Accreditation:** Regional (NCA); counseling (ACA); music (NASM). **Total program enrollment:** 3891. **Application fee:** $25.

**PROGRAM(S) OFFERED**

• **Accounting and Related Services, Other** *3 students enrolled* • **Geography** *2 students enrolled* • **Health/Health Care Administration/Management** *1 student enrolled* • **Hospitality Administration/Management, General** *19 students enrolled* • **Human Resources Development** *82 students enrolled* • **Mental and Social Health Services and Allied Professions, Other** *9 students enrolled* • **Music Pedagogy** *1 student enrolled* • **Non-Profit/Public/Organizational Management** *4 students enrolled* • **Organizational Behavior Studies** *23 students enrolled* • **Real Estate** *1 student enrolled* • **Women's Studies** *2 students enrolled*

**STUDENT SERVICES** Academic or career counseling, employment services for current students, placement services for program completers, remedial services.

## Rosel School of Cosmetology

2444 West Devon Avenue, Chicago, IL 60659

**CONTACT** Rosel Baek, Owner Director
**Telephone:** 773-508-5600

**GENERAL INFORMATION** Private Institution. Founded 1989. **Total program enrollment:** 81. **Application fee:** $100.

**PROGRAM(S) OFFERED**

• **Aesthetician/Esthetician and Skin Care Specialist** *750 hrs./$7100*
• **Cosmetology and Related Personal Grooming Arts, Other** *250 hrs./$800*
• **Cosmetology, Barber/Styling, and Nail Instructor** *500 hrs./$2300*
• **Cosmetology/Cosmetologist, General** *1500 hrs./$8700* • **Nail Technician/Specialist and Manicurist** *350 hrs./$1300*

**STUDENT SERVICES** Academic or career counseling, employment services for current students, placement services for program completers.

## St. Augustine College

1333-1345 West Argyle, Chicago, IL 60640-3501
http://www.staugustinecollege.edu/

**CONTACT** Mr. Andrew C. Sund, President
**Telephone:** 773-878-8756

**GENERAL INFORMATION** Private Institution. Founded 1980. **Accreditation:** Regional (NCA); respiratory therapy technology (CoARC). **Total program enrollment:** 1018.

**PROGRAM(S) OFFERED**

• **Accounting Technology/Technician and Bookkeeping** *3 students enrolled*
• **Administrative Assistant and Secretarial Science, General** *1 student enrolled*
• **Computer and Information Sciences, General** *3 students enrolled* • **Cooking and Related Culinary Arts, General** *48 students enrolled* • **Early Childhood Education and Teaching** *51 students enrolled* • **Substance Abuse/Addiction Counseling** *3 students enrolled*

**STUDENT SERVICES** Academic or career counseling, daycare for children of students, placement services for program completers, remedial services.

## St. Johns Hospital School of Clinical Lab Science

800 E. Carpenter, Springfield, IL 62769
http://www.st-johns.org/

**CONTACT** Gilma Roncancio-Weemer, Coordinator
**Telephone:** 217-757-6788

**GENERAL INFORMATION** Private Institution. **Total program enrollment:** 5. **Application fee:** $15.

**PROGRAM(S) OFFERED**

• **Clinical Laboratory Science/Medical Technology/Technologist** *5 students enrolled*

**STUDENT SERVICES** Academic or career counseling.

## Saint Xavier University

3700 West 103rd Street, Chicago, IL 60655-3105
http://www.sxu.edu/

**CONTACT** Judith A. Dwyer, President
**Telephone:** 773-298-3000

**GENERAL INFORMATION** Private Institution. Founded 1847. **Accreditation:** Regional (NCA); music (NASM); speech-language pathology (ASHA). **Total program enrollment:** 2910. **Application fee:** $25.

**PROGRAM(S) OFFERED**

• **Accounting** • **Business/Commerce, General** • **Corrections and Criminal Justice, Other** • **Psychiatric/Mental Health Nurse/Nursing**

**STUDENT SERVICES** Academic or career counseling, employment services for current students, placement services for program completers, remedial services.

## Sanford-Brown College

1101 Eastport Plaza Drive, Collinsville, IL 62234
http://www.sanford-brown.edu/

**CONTACT** Athena Seidel, Campus President
**Telephone:** 618-344-5600

**GENERAL INFORMATION** Private Institution. **Total program enrollment:** 398. **Application fee:** $100.

**PROGRAM(S) OFFERED**

• **Accounting and Business/Management** *92 hrs./$22,381* • **Business Administration and Management, General** *73 hrs./$17,804* • **Massage Therapy/Therapeutic Massage** *71 hrs./$17,328* • **Medical Insurance Coding Specialist/Coder** *70 hrs./$16,321* • **Medical/Clinical Assistant** *68 hrs./$18,539*
• **Office Management and Supervision** *6 students enrolled*

**STUDENT SERVICES** Academic or career counseling, employment services for current students, placement services for program completers.

## Sauk Valley Community College

173 Illinois Route 2, Dixon, IL 61021
http://www.svcc.edu/

**CONTACT** Dr. George Mihel, President
**Telephone:** 815-288-5511

**GENERAL INFORMATION** Public Institution. Founded 1965. **Accreditation:** Regional (NCA); radiologic technology: radiography (JRCERT). **Total program enrollment:** 1092.

**PROGRAM(S) OFFERED**
• **Accounting** *11 students enrolled* • **Business Administration and Management, General** *9 students enrolled* • **Business/Office Automation/Technology/Data Entry** *8 students enrolled* • **CAD/CADD Drafting and/or Design Technology/Technician** *3 students enrolled* • **Child Care Provider/Assistant** *13 students enrolled* • **Communications Systems Installation and Repair Technology** *2 students enrolled* • **Computer Installation and Repair Technology/Technician** *1 student enrolled* • **Computer Programming/Programmer, General** *4 students enrolled* • **Computer Systems Networking and Telecommunications** *10 students enrolled* • **Design and Visual Communications, General** *10 students enrolled* • **Drafting and Design Technology/Technician, General** *2 students enrolled* • **Emergency Care Attendant (EMT Ambulance)** *71 students enrolled* • **Emergency Medical Technology/Technician (EMT Paramedic)** *3 students enrolled* • **General Office Occupations and Clerical Services** *10 students enrolled* • **Heating, Air Conditioning, Ventilation and Refrigeration Maintenance Technology/Technician (HAC, HACR, HVAC, HVACR)** *17 students enrolled* • **Industrial Electronics Technology/Technician** *5 students enrolled* • **Licensed Practical/Vocational Nurse Training (LPN, LVN, Cert, Dipl, AAS)** *15 students enrolled* • **Machine Tool Technology/Machinist** *1 student enrolled* • **Management Information Systems, General** *1 student enrolled* • **Medical Administrative/Executive Assistant and Medical Secretary** *4 students enrolled* • **Nurse/Nursing Assistant/Aide and Patient Care Assistant** *101 students enrolled* • **Office Management and Supervision** *8 students enrolled* • **Prepress/Desktop Publishing and Digital Imaging Design** *1 student enrolled* • **Selling Skills and Sales Operations** *4 students enrolled* • **Social Work** *1 student enrolled* • **System Administration/Administrator** *11 students enrolled* • **Truck and Bus Driver/Commercial Vehicle Operation** *18 students enrolled* • **Welding Technology/Welder** *91 students enrolled* • **Word Processing** *1 student enrolled*

**STUDENT SERVICES** Academic or career counseling, employment services for current students, placement services for program completers, remedial services.

## Shawnee Community College

8364 Shawnee College Road, Ullin, IL 62992-2206
http://www.shawneecc.edu/

**CONTACT** Larry E. Peterson, President
**Telephone:** 618-634-3200

**GENERAL INFORMATION** Public Institution. Founded 1967. **Accreditation:** Regional (NCA); health information technology (AHIMA); medical laboratory technology (NAACLS). **Total program enrollment:** 944.

**PROGRAM(S) OFFERED**
• **Automobile/Automotive Mechanics Technology/Technician** *1 student enrolled* • **Cosmetology/Cosmetologist, General** *8 students enrolled* • **Criminal Justice/Police Science** *2 students enrolled* • **Early Childhood Education and Teaching** *2 students enrolled* • **Information Science/Studies** *1 student enrolled* • **Licensed Practical/Vocational Nurse Training (LPN, LVN, Cert, Dipl, AAS)** *31 students enrolled* • **Massage Therapy/Therapeutic Massage** *4 students enrolled* • **Medical Administrative/Executive Assistant and Medical Secretary** *2 students enrolled* • **Medical Insurance Coding Specialist/Coder** *3 students enrolled* • **Medical Transcription/Transcriptionist** *1 student enrolled* • **Nurse/Nursing Assistant/Aide and Patient Care Assistant** *115 students enrolled* • **Psychiatric/Mental Health Services Technician** *1 student enrolled* • **Substance Abuse/Addiction Counseling** *2 students enrolled* • **Surgical Technology/Technologist** *3 students enrolled* • **Truck and Bus Driver/Commercial Vehicle Operation** *26 students enrolled* • **Welding Technology/Welder** *1 student enrolled*

**STUDENT SERVICES** Academic or career counseling, daycare for children of students, employment services for current students, placement services for program completers, remedial services.

## SOLEX Medical Academy

350 E. Dundee Road, Suite 207, Wheeling, IL 60090
massage.solex.edu/

**CONTACT** Leon E. Linton, Executive Director
**Telephone:** 847-229-9595 Ext. 103

**GENERAL INFORMATION** Private Institution. **Total program enrollment:** 11. **Application fee:** $150.

**PROGRAM(S) OFFERED**
• **Massage Therapy/Therapeutic Massage** *600 hrs./$7450*

**STUDENT SERVICES** Placement services for program completers.

## Soma Institute–The National School of Clinical Massage Therapy

14 E. Jackson Boulevard, Suite 1300, Chicago, IL 60604-2232
http://www.soma.edu/

**CONTACT** Joan Hannant, President
**Telephone:** 312-939-2723

**GENERAL INFORMATION** Private Institution.

**PROGRAM(S) OFFERED**
• **Massage Therapy/Therapeutic Massage** *300 hrs./$5150*

**STUDENT SERVICES** Academic or career counseling, placement services for program completers, remedial services.

## Southeastern Illinois College

3575 College Road, Harrisburg, IL 62946-4925
http://www.sic.edu/

**CONTACT** Dana Keating, Interim President
**Telephone:** 618-252-5400

**GENERAL INFORMATION** Public Institution. Founded 1960. **Accreditation:** Regional (NCA); health information technology (AHIMA); medical laboratory technology (NAACLS). **Total program enrollment:** 1105.

**PROGRAM(S) OFFERED**
• **Accounting Technology/Technician and Bookkeeping** *6 students enrolled* • **Applied Horticulture/Horticultural Operations, General** *5 students enrolled* • **Autobody/Collision and Repair Technology/Technician** *2 students enrolled* • **Automobile/Automotive Mechanics Technology/Technician** *35 students enrolled* • **Business Administration and Management, General** *4 students enrolled* • **Business/Office Automation/Technology/Data Entry** *9 students enrolled* • **CAD/CADD Drafting and/or Design Technology/Technician** *3 students enrolled* • **Carpentry/Carpenter** *3 students enrolled* • **Child Care Provider/Assistant** *1 student enrolled* • **Construction Trades, General** *16 students enrolled* • **Corrections** *1 student enrolled* • **Cosmetology/Cosmetologist, General** *25 students enrolled* • **Criminal Justice/Police Science** *1 student enrolled* • **Diesel Mechanics Technology/Technician** *3 students enrolled* • **Food Service, Waiter/Waitress, and Dining Room Management/Manager** *8 students enrolled* • **General Office Occupations and Clerical Services** *6 students enrolled* • **Health Professions and Related Clinical Sciences, Other** *1 student enrolled* • **Housing and Human Environments, Other** *35 students enrolled* • **Licensed Practical/Vocational Nurse Training (LPN, LVN, Cert, Dipl, AAS)** *44 students enrolled* • **Massage Therapy/Therapeutic Massage** *10 students enrolled* • **Medical Insurance Coding Specialist/Coder** *13 students enrolled* • **Medical Transcription/Transcriptionist** *13 students enrolled* • **Prepress/Desktop Publishing and Digital Imaging Design** *1 student enrolled* • **Psychiatric/Mental Health Services Technician** *3 students enrolled* • **Substance Abuse/Addiction Counseling** *3 students enrolled* • **Surgical Technology/Technologist** *3 students enrolled* • **Teacher Assistant/Aide** *1 student enrolled* • **Welding Technology/Welder** *3 students enrolled*

**STUDENT SERVICES** Academic or career counseling, daycare for children of students, placement services for program completers, remedial services.

## South Suburban College

15800 South State Street, South Holland, IL 60473-1270
http://www.southsuburbancollege.edu/

**CONTACT** George Dammer, President
**Telephone:** 708-596-2000

**GENERAL INFORMATION** Public Institution. Founded 1927. **Accreditation:** Regional (NCA); music (NASM); practical nursing (NLN); radiologic technology: radiography (JRCERT). **Total program enrollment:** 2175.

**PROGRAM(S) OFFERED**
• **Accounting Technology/Technician and Bookkeeping** *2 students enrolled* • **Accounting and Business/Management** *2 students enrolled* • **Administrative Assistant and Secretarial Science, General** *1 student enrolled* • **Biomedical Technology/Technician** *1 student enrolled* • **CAD/CADD Drafting and/or Design Technology/Technician** *1 student enrolled* • **Child Care Provider/Assistant** *52 students enrolled* • **Computer Programming/Programmer, General** *1 student enrolled* • **Computer Systems Networking and Telecommunications** *5 students enrolled* • **Construction Management** *1 student enrolled* • **Construction Trades, General** *18 students enrolled* • **Court Reporting/Court Reporter** *4 students enrolled* • **Criminal Justice/Police Science** *13 students enrolled* • **Diagnostic Medical Sonography/Sonographer and Ultrasound Technician** *10 students enrolled* • **Electrical, Electronic and Communications Engineering Technology/Technician** *2 students enrolled* • **Emergency Care Attendant (EMT Ambulance)** *71 students enrolled* • **Emergency Medical Technology/Technician (EMT Paramedic)** *82 students enrolled* • **Entrepreneurship/Entrepreneurial Studies** *4 students enrolled* • **Executive Assistant/Executive Secretary** *2 students enrolled* • **Kinesiology and Exercise Science** *8 students enrolled* • **Legal Assistant/Paralegal** *1 student enrolled* • **Licensed Practical/Vocational Nurse Training (LPN, LVN, Cert, Dipl, AAS)** *17 students enrolled* • **Massage Therapy/Therapeutic Massage** *16 students enrolled* • **Medical Insurance Coding Specialist/Coder** *1 student enrolled* • **Medical Radiologic Technology/Science—Radiation Therapist** *10 students enrolled* • **Medical/Clinical Assistant** *8 students enrolled* • **Nurse/Nursing Assistant/Aide and Patient Care Assistant** *239 students enrolled* • **Office Management and Supervision** *23 students enrolled* • **Pharmacy Technician/Assistant** *5 students enrolled* • **Phlebotomy/Phlebotomist** *15 students enrolled* • **Sign Language Interpretation and Translation** *1 student enrolled* • **Small Business Administration/Management** *4 students enrolled* • **Social Work** *1 student enrolled* • **Substance Abuse/Addiction Counseling** *1 student enrolled* • **Teacher Assistant/Aide** *7 students enrolled*

**STUDENT SERVICES** Academic or career counseling, daycare for children of students, employment services for current students, placement services for program completers, remedial services.

## Southwestern Illinois College

2500 Carlyle Road, Belleville, IL 62221-5899
http://www.southwestern.cc.il.us/

**CONTACT** Georgia Costello, President
**Telephone:** 618-235-2700

**GENERAL INFORMATION** Public Institution. Founded 1946. **Accreditation:** Regional (NCA); health information technology (AHIMA); medical assisting (AAMAE); medical laboratory technology (NAACLS); physical therapy assisting (APTA); radiologic technology: radiography (JRCERT); respiratory therapy technology (CoARC). **Total program enrollment:** 5358.

**PROGRAM(S) OFFERED**
• **Administrative Assistant and Secretarial Science, General** *11 students enrolled* • **Airline/Commercial/Professional Pilot and Flight Crew** *1 student enrolled* • **Applied Horticulture/Horticultural Operations, General** *12 students enrolled* • **Autobody/Collision and Repair Technology/Technician** *38 students enrolled* • **Business Administration and Management, General** *37 students enrolled* • **Business/Office Automation/Technology/Data Entry** *2 students enrolled* • **Carpentry/Carpenter** *58 students enrolled* • **Child Care Provider/Assistant** *32 students enrolled* • **Computer Installation and Repair Technology/Technician** *1 student enrolled* • **Computer Programming, Specific Applications** *49 students enrolled* • **Computer Systems Networking and Telecommunications** *77 students enrolled* • **Concrete Finishing/Concrete Finisher** *7 students enrolled* • **Construction Trades, General** *7 students enrolled* • **Criminal Justice/Law Enforcement Administration** *51 students enrolled* • **Criminal Justice/Police Science** *36 students enrolled* • **Culinary Arts/Chef Training** *21 students enrolled* • **Electrical, Electronic and Communications Engineering Technology/Technician** *13 students enrolled* • **Electrician** *36 students enrolled* • **Fire Science/Firefighting** *152 students enrolled* • **Fire Services Administration** *29 students enrolled* • **Floriculture/Floristry Operations and Management** *1 student enrolled* • **Food Preparation/Professional Cooking/Kitchen Assistant** *7 students enrolled* • **Health Unit Coordinator/Ward Clerk** *67 students enrolled* • **Heating, Air Conditioning, Ventilation and Refrigeration Maintenance Technology/Technician (HAC, HACR, HVAC, HVACR)** *55 students enrolled* • **Industrial Electronics Technology/Technician** *3 students enrolled* • **Machine Tool Technology/Machinist** *9 students enrolled* • **Mason/Masonry** *1 student enrolled* • **Massage Therapy/Therapeutic Massage** *25 students enrolled* • **Mechanical Drafting and Mechanical Drafting CAD/CADD** *7 students enrolled* • **Medical Insurance Coding Specialist/Coder** *15 students enrolled* • **Medical Transcription/Transcriptionist** *1 student enrolled* • **Medical/Clinical Assistant** *31 students enrolled* • **Music, General** *5 students enrolled* • **Nurse/Nursing Assistant/Aide and Patient Care Assistant** *270 students enrolled* • **Painting/Painter and Wall Coverer** *3 students enrolled* • **Parts, Warehousing, and Inventory Management Operations** *32 students enrolled* • **Phlebotomy/Phlebotomist** *19 students enrolled* • **Prepress/Desktop Publishing and Digital Imaging Design** *8 students enrolled* • **Restaurant/Food Services Management** *6 students enrolled* • **Sales, Distribution and Marketing Operations, General** *8 students enrolled* • **Security and Loss Prevention Services** *1 student enrolled* • **Sheet Metal Technology/Sheetworking** *7 students enrolled* • **Sign Language Interpretation and Translation** *22 students enrolled* • **Social Work** *1 student enrolled* • **Web Page, Digital/Multimedia and Information Resources Design** *25 students enrolled* • **Welding Technology/Welder** *228 students enrolled*

**STUDENT SERVICES** Academic or career counseling, daycare for children of students, employment services for current students, placement services for program completers, remedial services.

## Spanish Coalition for Jobs, Inc.

2011 West Pershing Road, Chicago, IL 60609
http://www.scj-usa.org/

**CONTACT** Mary Gonzalez Koenig, President
**Telephone:** 773-247-0707 Ext. 200

**GENERAL INFORMATION** Private Institution. Founded 1972. **Total program enrollment:** 121.

**PROGRAM(S) OFFERED**
• **Administrative Assistant and Secretarial Science, General** *36 hrs./$4600* • **Customer Service Management** *44 hrs./$4800* • **Medical/Clinical Assistant** *63 hrs./$9038*

**STUDENT SERVICES** Academic or career counseling, employment services for current students, placement services for program completers, remedial services.

## Sparks College

131 South Morgan Street, Shelbyville, IL 62565
http://www.sparkscollege.org/

**CONTACT** Judith A. Lehman, Director
**Telephone:** 217-774-5112

**GENERAL INFORMATION** Private Institution. Founded 1908. **Total program enrollment:** 20. **Application fee:** $50.

**PROGRAM(S) OFFERED**
• **Accounting and Related Services, Other** • **Accounting** *2 students enrolled* • **Administrative Assistant and Secretarial Science, General** • **Business/Office Automation/Technology/Data Entry** *1 student enrolled* • **Court Reporting/Court Reporter** *3 students enrolled* • **Legal Administrative Assistant/Secretary** *2 students enrolled* • **Medical Administrative/Executive Assistant and Medical Secretary** • **Medical Transcription/Transcriptionist** *3 students enrolled*

**STUDENT SERVICES** Academic or career counseling, placement services for program completers.

## Spoon River College

23235 North County 22, Canton, IL 61520-9801
http://www.spoonrivercollege.net/

**CONTACT** Dr. Robert Ritschel, President
**Telephone:** 309-647-4645

**GENERAL INFORMATION** Public Institution. Founded 1959. **Accreditation:** Regional (NCA). **Total program enrollment:** 890.

**PROGRAM(S) OFFERED**
• **Administrative Assistant and Secretarial Science, General** *3 students enrolled* • **Applied Horticulture/Horticultural Operations, General** *5 students enrolled*

*Spoon River College (continued)*

• **Automobile/Automotive Mechanics Technology/Technician** *7 students enrolled* • **Business Administration and Management, General** *2 students enrolled* • **Business/Office Automation/Technology/Data Entry** *2 students enrolled* • **Computer Installation and Repair Technology/Technician** *2 students enrolled* • **Computer Systems Networking and Telecommunications** *3 students enrolled* • **Computer and Information Systems Security** *1 student enrolled* • **Construction Trades, General** *4 students enrolled* • **Electrical, Electronic and Communications Engineering Technology/Technician** *8 students enrolled* • **Food Preparation/Professional Cooking/Kitchen Assistant** *14 students enrolled* • **Graphic Design** *3 students enrolled* • **Health Information/Medical Records Technology/Technician** *1 student enrolled* • **Industrial Electronics Technology/Technician** *5 students enrolled* • **Licensed Practical/Vocational Nurse Training (LPN, LVN, Cert, Dipl, AAS)** *18 students enrolled* • **Medical Insurance Coding Specialist/Coder** *8 students enrolled* • **Truck and Bus Driver/Commercial Vehicle Operation** *26 students enrolled* • **Web Page, Digital/Multimedia and Information Resources Design** *1 student enrolled* • **Welding Technology/Welder** *1 student enrolled*

**STUDENT SERVICES** Academic or career counseling, daycare for children of students, employment services for current students, placement services for program completers, remedial services.

## Taylor Business Institute

318 West Adams, Chicago, IL 60007
http://www.tbiil.edu/

**CONTACT** Janice C. Parker, President
**Telephone:** 312-658-5100

**GENERAL INFORMATION** Private Institution. Founded 1964. **Accreditation:** State accredited or approved. **Total program enrollment:** 318. **Application fee:** $25.

**PROGRAM(S) OFFERED**
• **Accounting** • **Criminal Justice/Law Enforcement Administration** • **Electrical, Electronic and Communications Engineering Technology/Technician** • **Medical Insurance Specialist/Medical Biller** • **Teaching English as a Second or Foreign Language/ESL Language Instructor**

**STUDENT SERVICES** Academic or career counseling, employment services for current students, placement services for program completers, remedial services.

## Trend Setter's College of Cosmetology

665 West Broadway, Bradley, IL 60915
http://www.trendsetterscollege.com/

**CONTACT** Lori Clark, CEO
**Telephone:** 815-932-5049

**GENERAL INFORMATION** Private Institution. Founded 1986. **Total program enrollment:** 44. **Application fee:** $100.

**PROGRAM(S) OFFERED**
• **Aesthetician/Esthetician and Skin Care Specialist** *750 hrs./$9850* • **Cosmetology, Barber/Styling, and Nail Instructor** *1000 hrs./$7500* • **Cosmetology/Cosmetologist, General** *1500 hrs./$17,900* • **Nail Technician/Specialist and Manicurist** *350 hrs./$3206*

**STUDENT SERVICES** Academic or career counseling, placement services for program completers.

## Tri-County Beauty Academy

219 North State Street, Litchfield, IL 62056

**CONTACT** Diane Riemann, Owner
**Telephone:** 217-324-9062

**GENERAL INFORMATION** Private Institution. Founded 1971. **Total program enrollment:** 25.

**PROGRAM(S) OFFERED**
• **Cosmetology, Barber/Styling, and Nail Instructor** *1000 hrs./$5650* • **Cosmetology/Cosmetologist, General** *1500 hrs./$9825*

## Trinity College of Nursing and Health Sciences

2122-25th Avenue, Rock Island, IL 61201
http://www.trinitycollegeqc.edu/

**CONTACT** Leanne Hullett, Dean
**Telephone:** 309-779-7700

**GENERAL INFORMATION** Private Institution. Founded 1994. **Accreditation:** Regional (NCA). **Total program enrollment:** 139. **Application fee:** $50.

**PROGRAM(S) OFFERED**
• **Emergency Medical Technology/Technician (EMT Paramedic)** *11 students enrolled* • **Surgical Technology/Technologist** *6 students enrolled*

**STUDENT SERVICES** Academic or career counseling, daycare for children of students, employment services for current students, placement services for program completers, remedial services.

## Triton College

2000 5th Avenue, River Grove, IL 60171-1995
http://www.triton.cc.il.us/

**CONTACT** Dr. Patricia Granados, President
**Telephone:** 708-456-0300

**GENERAL INFORMATION** Public Institution. Founded 1964. **Accreditation:** Regional (NCA); diagnostic medical sonography (JRCEDMS); nuclear medicine technology (JRCNMT); ophthalmic medical technology (JCAHPO); practical nursing (NLN); radiologic technology: radiography (JRCERT). **Total program enrollment:** 4379. **Application fee:** $10.

**PROGRAM(S) OFFERED**
• **Accounting Technology/Technician and Bookkeeping** *10 students enrolled* • **Administrative Assistant and Secretarial Science, General** *7 students enrolled* • **Applied Horticulture/Horticultural Operations, General** *2 students enrolled* • **Architectural Drafting and Architectural CAD/CADD** *2 students enrolled* • **Automobile/Automotive Mechanics Technology/Technician** *1 student enrolled* • **Baking and Pastry Arts/Baker/Pastry Chef** *4 students enrolled* • **Business Administration and Management, General** *2 students enrolled* • **CAD/CADD Drafting and/or Design Technology/Technician** *1 student enrolled* • **Child Care Provider/Assistant** *5 students enrolled* • **Computer Installation and Repair Technology/Technician** *1 student enrolled* • **Computer Technology/Computer Systems Technology** *7 students enrolled* • **Construction Management** *2 students enrolled* • **Criminal Justice/Law Enforcement Administration** *5 students enrolled* • **Culinary Arts/Chef Training** *1 student enrolled* • **Data Modeling/Warehousing and Database Administration** *1 student enrolled* • **Design and Visual Communications, General** *1 student enrolled* • **Diagnostic Medical Sonography/Sonographer and Ultrasound Technician** *7 students enrolled* • **Electrician** *1 student enrolled* • **Emergency Medical Technology/Technician (EMT Paramedic)** *12 students enrolled* • **Fashion Merchandising** *1 student enrolled* • **Fire Science/Firefighting** *1 student enrolled* • **Health Information/Medical Records Technology/Technician** *3 students enrolled* • **Heating, Air Conditioning, Ventilation and Refrigeration Maintenance Technology/Technician (HAC, HACR, HVAC, HVACR)** *22 students enrolled* • **Hotel/Motel Administration/Management** *1 student enrolled* • **Human Resources Management/Personnel Administration, General** *4 students enrolled* • **Interior Design** *2 students enrolled* • **Kinesiology and Exercise Science** *1 student enrolled* • **Landscaping and Groundskeeping** *3 students enrolled* • **Licensed Practical/Vocational Nurse Training (LPN, LVN, Cert, Dipl, AAS)** *21 students enrolled* • **Mechanic and Repair Technologies/Technicians, Other** *10 students enrolled* • **Nurse/Nursing Assistant/Aide and Patient Care Assistant** *172 students enrolled* • **Platemaker/Imager** *1 student enrolled* • **Security and Loss Prevention Services** *1 student enrolled* • **Substance Abuse/Addiction Counseling** *3 students enrolled* • **Surgical Technology/Technologist** *14 students enrolled* • **System Administration/Administrator** *4 students enrolled* • **Teacher Assistant/Aide** *2 students enrolled* • **Web Page, Digital/Multimedia and Information Resources Design** *2 students enrolled* • **Welding Technology/Welder** *1 student enrolled*

**STUDENT SERVICES** Academic or career counseling, daycare for children of students, employment services for current students, placement services for program completers, remedial services.

## Universal Technical Institute

601 Regency Drive, Glendale Heights, IL 60139-2208
http://www.uticorp.com/

**CONTACT** Pat Kellen, Campus President
**Telephone:** 630-529-2662

**GENERAL INFORMATION** Private Institution. Founded 1965. **Total program enrollment:** 1613.

**PROGRAM(S) OFFERED**
• **Automobile/Automotive Mechanics Technology/Technician** *97 hrs./$32,050* • **Diesel Mechanics Technology/Technician** *157 students enrolled*

## University of Phoenix–Chicago Campus

1500 McConner Parkway, Suite 700, Schaumburg, IL 60173-4399
http://www.phoenix.edu/

**CONTACT** William Pepicello, PhD, President
**Telephone:** 847-413-1922

**GENERAL INFORMATION** Private Institution. Founded 2002. **Accreditation:** Regional (NCA). **Total program enrollment:** 1223.

**STUDENT SERVICES** Academic or career counseling, remedial services.

## University of Spa & Cosmetology Arts

300 West Carpenter Street, Springfield, IL 62702
http://www.uscart.com/

**CONTACT** Lynne Lowder, Director of Admissions & Financial Aid
**Telephone:** 217-753-8990

**GENERAL INFORMATION** Private Institution. Founded 1978. **Total program enrollment:** 143. **Application fee:** $50.

**PROGRAM(S) OFFERED**
• **Aesthetician/Esthetician and Skin Care Specialist** *25 hrs./$6680* • **Cosmetology/Cosmetologist, General** *50 hrs./$11,200* • **Massage Therapy/Therapeutic Massage** *600 hrs./$8000* • **Nail Technician/Specialist and Manicurist** *350 hrs./$2625* • **Teacher Education and Professional Development, Specific Subject Areas, Other** *1000 hrs./$2245*

**STUDENT SERVICES** Academic or career counseling, employment services for current students, placement services for program completers.

## The Vanderschmidt School

4825 N. Scott Street, Suite 76, Schiller Park, IL 60176

**CONTACT** Alan Stutts, Executive Director
**Telephone:** 773-380-6800

**GENERAL INFORMATION** Private Institution. Founded 1950. **Total program enrollment:** 734. **Application fee:** $25.

**PROGRAM(S) OFFERED**
• **Medical Office Assistant/Specialist** *53 students enrolled* • **Medical Staff Services Technology/Technician**

**STUDENT SERVICES** Academic or career counseling, employment services for current students, placement services for program completers, remedial services.

## Vatterott College

501 North 3rd Street, Quincy, IL 62301
http://www.vatterott-college.edu/

**CONTACT** Leslie Fischer, Director
**Telephone:** 800-438-5621

**GENERAL INFORMATION** Private Institution. Founded 1969. **Total program enrollment:** 345.

**PROGRAM(S) OFFERED**
• **CAD/CADD Drafting and/or Design Technology/Technician** *16 students enrolled* • **Cosmetology/Cosmetologist, General** *7 students enrolled* • **Data Processing and Data Processing Technology/Technician** • **Electrician** *25 students enrolled* • **Heating, Air Conditioning, Ventilation and Refrigeration Maintenance Technology/Technician (HAC, HACR, HVAC, HVACR)** *18 students enrolled* • **Information Technology** *31 students enrolled* • **Medical Office Assistant/Specialist** *30 students enrolled*

**STUDENT SERVICES** Academic or career counseling, employment services for current students, placement services for program completers.

## Vee's School of Beauty Culture

2701 State Street, East St. Louis, IL 62205

**CONTACT** Versie Ruffin, President
**Telephone:** 618-274-1751

**GENERAL INFORMATION** Private Institution. **Total program enrollment:** 33. **Application fee:** $100.

**PROGRAM(S) OFFERED**
• **Salon/Beauty Salon Management/Manager** *21 students enrolled*

**STUDENT SERVICES** Academic or career counseling, placement services for program completers.

## Waubonsee Community College

Route 47 at Waubonsee Drive, Sugar Grove, IL 60554-9799
http://www.waubonsee.edu/

**CONTACT** Christine J. Sobek, President
**Telephone:** 630-466-7900 Ext. 2938

**GENERAL INFORMATION** Public Institution. Founded 1966. **Accreditation:** Regional (NCA). **Total program enrollment:** 3432.

**PROGRAM(S) OFFERED**
• **Accounting Technology/Technician and Bookkeeping** *4 students enrolled* • **Accounting** *1 student enrolled* • **Animation, Interactive Technology, Video Graphics and Special Effects** *2 students enrolled* • **Autobody/Collision and Repair Technology/Technician** *9 students enrolled* • **Building/Property Maintenance and Management** *1 student enrolled* • **Business Administration and Management, General** *2 students enrolled* • **Child Care Provider/Assistant** *1 student enrolled* • **Commercial Photography** *5 students enrolled* • **Computer Technology/Computer Systems Technology** *2 students enrolled* • **Criminal Justice/Police Science** *1 student enrolled* • **Data Entry/Microcomputer Applications, General** *1 student enrolled* • **Electrical, Electronic and Communications Engineering Technology/Technician** *4 students enrolled* • **Electrician** *16 students enrolled* • **Emergency Care Attendant (EMT Ambulance)** *91 students enrolled* • **Executive Assistant/Executive Secretary** *1 student enrolled* • **Fire Science/Firefighting** *1 student enrolled* • **Fire Services Administration** *1 student enrolled* • **General Office Occupations and Clerical Services** *1 student enrolled* • **Graphic Design** *2 students enrolled* • **Heating, Air Conditioning, Ventilation and Refrigeration Maintenance Technology/Technician (HAC, HACR, HVAC, HVACR)** *7 students enrolled* • **Hydraulics and Fluid Power Technology/Technician** *1 student enrolled* • **Industrial Mechanics and Maintenance Technology** *3 students enrolled* • **Kinesiology and Exercise Science** *1 student enrolled* • **Logistics and Materials Management** *1 student enrolled* • **Massage Therapy/Therapeutic Massage** *15 students enrolled* • **Medical Administrative/Executive Assistant and Medical Secretary** *4 students enrolled* • **Medical Transcription/Transcriptionist** *2 students enrolled* • **Medical/Clinical Assistant** *5 students enrolled* • **Nurse/Nursing Assistant/Aide and Patient Care Assistant** *234 students enrolled* • **Phlebotomy/Phlebotomist** *38 students enrolled* • **Radio and Television Broadcasting Technology/Technician** *8 students enrolled* • **Real Estate** *81 students enrolled* • **Security and Loss Prevention Services** *1 student enrolled* • **Sign Language Interpretation and Translation** *5 students enrolled* • **Substance Abuse/Addiction Counseling** *3 students enrolled* • **Surgical Technology/Technologist** *3 students enrolled* • **Survey Technology/Surveying** *1 student enrolled* • **System Administration/Administrator** *1 student enrolled* • **Tourism and Travel Services Management** *3 students enrolled* • **Web Page, Digital/Multimedia and Information Resources Design** *2 students enrolled* • **Welding Technology/Welder** *1 student enrolled* • **Word Processing** *1 student enrolled*

**STUDENT SERVICES** Academic or career counseling, daycare for children of students, employment services for current students, placement services for program completers, remedial services.

## Westwood College–Chicago River Oaks

80 River Oaks Drive, Suite D-49, Calumet City, IL 60409
http://www.westwood.edu/

**CONTACT** Bruce McKenzie, Executive Director
**Telephone:** 708-832-9760

**GENERAL INFORMATION** Private Institution. **Accreditation:** State accredited or approved. **Total program enrollment:** 538. **Application fee:** $25.

**PROGRAM(S) OFFERED**
• **Medical Insurance Coding Specialist/Coder** *11 students enrolled* • **Medical Staff Services Technology/Technician** *96 students enrolled*

**STUDENT SERVICES** Academic or career counseling, employment services for current students, placement services for program completers, remedial services.

## Worsham College of Mortuary Science

495 Northgate Parkway, Wheeling, IL 60090-2646
http://www.worshamcollege.com/

**CONTACT** Stephanie J. Kann, President
**Telephone:** 847-808-8444

**GENERAL INFORMATION** Private Institution. Founded 1911. **Accreditation:** Funeral service (ABFSE). **Total program enrollment:** 91. **Application fee:** $30.

**PROGRAM(S) OFFERED**
• **Funeral Service and Mortuary Science, General** *39 students enrolled*

**STUDENT SERVICES** Academic or career counseling, employment services for current students, placement services for program completers.

## Zarem/Golde ORT Technical Institute

3050 West Touhy Avenue, Chicago, IL 60645
http://www.zg-ort.org/

**CONTACT** Arthur A. Eldar, Director
**Telephone:** 847-324-5588 Ext. 18

**GENERAL INFORMATION** Private Institution. Founded 1991. **Total program enrollment:** 313. **Application fee:** $100.

**PROGRAM(S) OFFERED**
• **Accounting Technology/Technician and Bookkeeping** *32 hrs./$7200* • **Accounting** *32 students enrolled* • **CAD/CADD Drafting and/or Design Technology/Technician** *35 hrs./$7500* • **Computer Systems Networking and Telecommunications** *33 hrs./$7200* • **Drafting and Design Technology/Technician, General** *16 students enrolled* • **English Language and Literature, General** *720 hrs./$4500* • **Executive Assistant/Executive Secretary** • **Medical/Clinical Assistant** *33 hrs./$7400* • **Prepress/Desktop Publishing and Digital Imaging Design** *36 hrs./$7200*

**STUDENT SERVICES** Academic or career counseling, employment services for current students, placement services for program completers, remedial services.

# IOWA

## American College of Hairstyling

1531 First Avenue, SE, Cedar Rapids, IA 52402-5123
http://americancollegeofhair.com/

**CONTACT** T. L. Millis, President
**Telephone:** 319-362-1488

**GENERAL INFORMATION** Private Institution. Founded 1900. **Total program enrollment:** 17. **Application fee:** $150.

**PROGRAM(S) OFFERED**
• **Barbering/Barber** *400 hrs./$2400*

**STUDENT SERVICES** Academic or career counseling, employment services for current students, placement services for program completers, remedial services.

## American College of Hairstyling

603 East 6th Street, Des Moines, IA 50309
http://www.americancollegeofhair.com/

**CONTACT** T. L. Millis, President
**Telephone:** 515-244-0971

**GENERAL INFORMATION** Private Institution. **Total program enrollment:** 30. **Application fee:** $150.

**PROGRAM(S) OFFERED**
• **Barbering/Barber** *400 hrs./$2400*

**STUDENT SERVICES** Academic or career counseling, employment services for current students, placement services for program completers, remedial services.

## Bio-Chi Institute of Massage Therapy

1925 Geneva Street, Sioux City, IA 51103
http://www.bcimassage.com

**CONTACT** Lonnie Jensen, LMT, Director
**Telephone:** 712-252-1157

**GENERAL INFORMATION** Private Institution. **Total program enrollment:** 15. **Application fee:** $30.

**PROGRAM(S) OFFERED**
• **Massage Therapy/Therapeutic Massage**

**STUDENT SERVICES** Academic or career counseling, employment services for current students, placement services for program completers.

## Capri College

315 Second Avenue, SE, Cedar Rapids, IA 52401
http://www.capricollege.com/

**CONTACT** Charles Fiegen, Owner
**Telephone:** 319-364-1541

**GENERAL INFORMATION** Private Institution. Founded 1967. **Total program enrollment:** 191. **Application fee:** $50.

**PROGRAM(S) OFFERED**
• **Aesthetician/Esthetician and Skin Care Specialist** *24 hrs./$6560* • **Cosmetology and Related Personal Grooming Arts, Other** • **Cosmetology, Barber/Styling, and Nail Instructor** *34 hrs./$3457* • **Cosmetology/Cosmetologist, General** *70 hrs./$14,300* • **Health Professions and Related Clinical Sciences, Other** *21 students enrolled* • **Massage Therapy/Therapeutic Massage** *24 hrs./$6610* • **Nail Technician/Specialist and Manicurist** *360 hrs./$2354*

**STUDENT SERVICES** Academic or career counseling, placement services for program completers.

## Capri College

425 East 59th Street, Davenport, IA 52807
http://www.capricollege.com/

**CONTACT** Charles Fiegen, Owner
**Telephone:** 563-388-6642

**GENERAL INFORMATION** Private Institution. Founded 1987. **Total program enrollment:** 173. **Application fee:** $50.

**PROGRAM(S) OFFERED**
• **Aesthetician/Esthetician and Skin Care Specialist** *24 hrs./$6560* • **Cosmetology and Related Personal Grooming Arts, Other** • **Cosmetology, Barber/Styling, and Nail Instructor** *34 hrs./$3457* • **Cosmetology/Cosmetologist, General** *70 hrs./$14,300* • **Health Professions and Related Clinical Sciences,**

**Other** *10 students enrolled* • **Make-Up Artist/Specialist** *24 students enrolled* • **Massage Therapy/Therapeutic Massage** *24 hrs./$6610* • **Nail Technician/Specialist and Manicurist** *360 hrs./$2354*

**STUDENT SERVICES** Academic or career counseling, placement services for program completers.

## Capri College

395 Main Street, PO Box 873, Dubuque, IA 52004-0873
http://www.capricollege.com/

**CONTACT** Charles Fiegen, Owner
**Telephone:** 563-588-2379

**GENERAL INFORMATION** Private Institution. Founded 1966. **Total program enrollment:** 149. **Application fee:** $50.

**PROGRAM(S) OFFERED**
• **Aesthetician/Esthetician and Skin Care Specialist** *24 hrs./$6560* • **Cosmetology and Related Personal Grooming Arts, Other** *6 students enrolled* • **Cosmetology, Barber/Styling, and Nail Instructor** *34 hrs./$3457* • **Cosmetology/Cosmetologist, General** *70 hrs./$14,300* • **Health Professions and Related Clinical Sciences, Other** *25 students enrolled* • **Massage Therapy/Therapeutic Massage** *24 hrs./$6610* • **Nail Technician/Specialist and Manicurist** *360 hrs./$2354*

**STUDENT SERVICES** Academic or career counseling, placement services for program completers.

## Carlson College of Massage Therapy

11809 Country Road, X28, Anamosa, IA 52205
http://www.carlsoncollege.com

**CONTACT** Christina Rider, Chief Operating Officer, Owner
**Telephone:** 319-462-3402

**GENERAL INFORMATION** Private Institution. **Total program enrollment:** 43. **Application fee:** $50.

**PROGRAM(S) OFFERED**
• **Massage Therapy/Therapeutic Massage** *635 hrs./$8000*

## College of Hair Design

Squires Square, 722 Water Street, Suite 201, Waterloo, IA 50703
http://chd.net/

**CONTACT** Debra S. McFarland, President
**Telephone:** 319-232-9995 Ext. 100

**GENERAL INFORMATION** Private Institution. Founded 1957. **Total program enrollment:** 49. **Application fee:** $100.

**PROGRAM(S) OFFERED**
• **Barbering/Barber** *2100 hrs./$13,265* • **Massage Therapy/Therapeutic Massage** *720 hrs./$6770*

**STUDENT SERVICES** Placement services for program completers.

## Des Moines Area Community College

2006 South Ankeny Boulevard, Ankeny, IA 50021-8995
http://www.dmacc.edu/

**CONTACT** Robert J. Denson, President & CEO
**Telephone:** 515-964-6241

**GENERAL INFORMATION** Public Institution. Founded 1966. **Accreditation:** Regional (NCA); dental assisting (ADA); dental hygiene (ADA); medical laboratory technology (NAACLS); practical nursing (NLN). **Total program enrollment:** 7428.

**PROGRAM(S) OFFERED**
• **Accounting Technology/Technician and Bookkeeping** *16 students enrolled* • **Accounting** *1 student enrolled* • **Agricultural/Farm Supplies Retailing and Wholesaling** *30 students enrolled* • **Apparel and Accessories Marketing Operations** *10 students enrolled* • **Applied Horticulture/Horticultural Business Services, Other** *11 students enrolled* • **Architectural Drafting and Architectural CAD/CADD** *4 students enrolled* • **Autobody/Collision and Repair Technology/Technician** *14 students enrolled* • **Automobile/Automotive Mechanics Technology/Technician** *3 students enrolled* • **Cabinetmaking and Millwork/Millwright** *7 students enrolled* • **Carpentry/Carpenter** *4 students enrolled* • **Child Care Provider/Assistant** *5 students enrolled* • **Communications Systems Installation and Repair Technology** *2 students enrolled* • **Community Organization and Advocacy** *2 students enrolled* • **Computer Programming, Specific Applications** *3 students enrolled* • **Computer and Information Sciences and Support Services, Other** • **Computer/Information Technology Services Administration and Management, Other** *1 student enrolled* • **Culinary Arts/Chef Training** *1 student enrolled* • **Dental Assisting/Assistant** *30 students enrolled* • **Diesel Mechanics Technology/Technician** • **Dietitian Assistant** *5 students enrolled* • **Electrician** *14 students enrolled* • **Emergency Medical Technology/Technician (EMT Paramedic)** *3 students enrolled* • **Fire Protection and Safety Technology/Technician** *1 student enrolled* • **Funeral Service and Mortuary Science, General** *18 students enrolled* • **General Office Occupations and Clerical Services** *14 students enrolled* • **Health/Health Care Administration/Management** *6 students enrolled* • **Heating, Air Conditioning, Ventilation and Refrigeration Maintenance Technology/Technician (HAC, HACR, HVAC, HVACR)** *7 students enrolled* • **Hospitality Administration/Management, General** *2 students enrolled* • **Language Interpretation and Translation** *20 students enrolled* • **Legal Assistant/Paralegal** *5 students enrolled* • **Licensed Practical/Vocational Nurse Training (LPN, LVN, Cert, Dipl, AAS)** *138 students enrolled* • **Marketing/Marketing Management, General** *25 students enrolled* • **Mechanical Drafting and Mechanical Drafting CAD/CADD** • **Medical Administrative/Executive Assistant and Medical Secretary** *16 students enrolled* • **Medical/Clinical Assistant** *10 students enrolled* • **Nurse/Nursing Assistant/Aide and Patient Care Assistant** *1 student enrolled* • **Office Management and Supervision** *41 students enrolled* • **Phlebotomy/Phlebotomist** *32 students enrolled* • **Prepress/Desktop Publishing and Digital Imaging Design** • **Retailing and Retail Operations** *4 students enrolled* • **Selling Skills and Sales Operations** *9 students enrolled* • **Small Business Administration/Management** *7 students enrolled* • **Surgical Technology/Technologist** *4 students enrolled* • **Tool and Die Technology/Technician** *15 students enrolled* • **Welding Technology/Welder** *37 students enrolled*

**STUDENT SERVICES** Academic or career counseling, daycare for children of students, employment services for current students, placement services for program completers, remedial services.

## Ellsworth Community College

1100 College Avenue, Iowa Falls, IA 50126-1199
http://www.iavalley.cc.ia.us/ecc/

**CONTACT** Tim Wynes, Chancellor
**Telephone:** 800-322-9235

**GENERAL INFORMATION** Public Institution. Founded 1890. **Accreditation:** Regional (NCA). **Total program enrollment:** 689.

**PROGRAM(S) OFFERED**
• **Accounting Technology/Technician and Bookkeeping** • **Administrative Assistant and Secretarial Science, General** *4 students enrolled* • **Agriculture, General** *5 students enrolled* • **Business Administration and Management, General** *3 students enrolled* • **Computer Systems Networking and Telecommunications** • **Construction Trades, General** *1 student enrolled* • **Electrician** • **Horse Husbandry/Equine Science and Management** *7 students enrolled* • **Licensed Practical/Vocational Nurse Training (LPN, LVN, Cert, Dipl, AAS)** *21 students enrolled* • **Mason/Masonry** • **Nursing—Registered Nurse Training (RN, ASN, BSN, MSN)** *19 students enrolled* • **Psychiatric/Mental Health Services Technician** • **Sales, Distribution and Marketing Operations, General** *2 students enrolled*

**STUDENT SERVICES** Academic or career counseling, employment services for current students, placement services for program completers, remedial services.

## Emmaus Bible College

2570 Asbury Road, Dubuque, IA 52001-3097
http://www.emmaus.edu/

**CONTACT** Kenneth A. Daughters, President
**Telephone:** 563-588-8000

**GENERAL INFORMATION** Private Institution. Founded 1941. **Accreditation:** State accredited or approved. **Total program enrollment:** 225. **Application fee:** $25.

**PROGRAM(S) OFFERED**
• **Bible/Biblical Studies** *61 students enrolled*

**STUDENT SERVICES** Academic or career counseling, employment services for current students, remedial services.

## Faith Baptist Bible College and Theological Seminary

1900 Northwest 4th Street, Ankeny, IA 50021
http://www.faith.edu/

**CONTACT** James Maxwell, III, President
**Telephone:** 515-964-0601

**GENERAL INFORMATION** Private Institution (Affiliated with General Association of Regular Baptist Churches). Founded 1921. **Accreditation:** Regional (NCA); state accredited or approved. **Total program enrollment:** 322. **Application fee:** $25.

**PROGRAM(S) OFFERED**
• **Bible/Biblical Studies** *5 students enrolled*

**STUDENT SERVICES** Academic or career counseling, employment services for current students, placement services for program completers, remedial services.

## Grand View University

1200 Grandview Avenue, Des Moines, IA 50316-1599
http://www.grandview.edu/

**CONTACT** Kent L. Henning, President
**Telephone:** 515-263-2800

**GENERAL INFORMATION** Private Institution (Affiliated with Evangelical Lutheran Church in America). Founded 1896. **Accreditation:** Regional (NCA). **Total program enrollment:** 1539. **Application fee:** $35.

**PROGRAM(S) OFFERED**
• **Art Therapy/Therapist** *8 students enrolled* • **Business/Commerce, General** *2 students enrolled* • **Entrepreneurship/Entrepreneurial Studies** *6 students enrolled* • **Real Estate** *3 students enrolled* • **Spanish Language and Literature** *1 student enrolled* • **Sport and Fitness Administration/Management** *5 students enrolled*

**STUDENT SERVICES** Academic or career counseling, employment services for current students, placement services for program completers, remedial services.

## Hamilton Technical College

1011 East 53rd Street, Davenport, IA 52807-2653
http://www.hamiltontechcollege.com/

**CONTACT** Maryanne Hamilton, President
**Telephone:** 563-386-3570

**GENERAL INFORMATION** Private Institution. Founded 1969. **Accreditation:** State accredited or approved. **Total program enrollment:** 223. **Application fee:** $25.

**PROGRAM(S) OFFERED**
• **Manufacturing Technology/Technician** • **Medical Insurance Coding Specialist/Coder** *33 students enrolled* • **Medical/Clinical Assistant** *101 students enrolled*

**STUDENT SERVICES** Academic or career counseling, employment services for current students, placement services for program completers, remedial services.

## Hawkeye Community College

PO Box 8015, Waterloo, IA 50704-8015
http://www.hawkeyecollege.edu/

**CONTACT** Greg Schmitz, President
**Telephone:** 319-296-2320

**GENERAL INFORMATION** Public Institution. Founded 1966. **Accreditation:** Regional (NCA); dental assisting (ADA); dental hygiene (ADA); medical laboratory technology (NAACLS). **Total program enrollment:** 2858.

**PROGRAM(S) OFFERED**
• **Accounting** • **Administrative Assistant and Secretarial Science, General** *5 students enrolled* • **Agricultural/Farm Supplies Retailing and Wholesaling** *2 students enrolled* • **Animal/Livestock Husbandry and Production** *2 students enrolled* • **Applied Horticulture/Horticultural Operations, General** • **Autobody/Collision and Repair Technology/Technician** • **Child Care Provider/Assistant** • **Computer Systems Networking and Telecommunications** *3 students enrolled* • **Dental Assisting/Assistant** *16 students enrolled* • **Electrical, Electronic and Communications Engineering Technology/Technician** • **General Office Occupations and Clerical Services** *5 students enrolled* • **Heating, Air Conditioning, Ventilation and Refrigeration Maintenance Technology/Technician (HAC, HACR, HVAC, HVACR)** *8 students enrolled* • **Industrial Mechanics and Maintenance Technology** *12 students enrolled* • **Licensed Practical/Vocational Nurse Training (LPN, LVN, Cert, Dipl, AAS)** *295 students enrolled* • **Machine Tool Technology/Machinist** *1 student enrolled* • **Medical Administrative/Executive Assistant and Medical Secretary** *2 students enrolled* • **Natural Resources Management and Policy** *11 students enrolled* • **Nursing, Other** • **Optometric Technician/Assistant** *11 students enrolled* • **Sales, Distribution and Marketing Operations, General** *2 students enrolled* • **Truck and Bus Driver/Commercial Vehicle Operation** *22 students enrolled* • **Welding Technology/Welder**

**STUDENT SERVICES** Academic or career counseling, daycare for children of students, employment services for current students, placement services for program completers, remedial services.

## Indian Hills Community College

525 Grandview Avenue, Building #1, Ottumwa, IA 52501-1398
http://www.ihcc.cc.ia.us/

**CONTACT** Jim Lindenmayer, President
**Telephone:** 641-683-5111

**GENERAL INFORMATION** Public Institution. Founded 1966. **Accreditation:** Regional (NCA); health information technology (AHIMA); physical therapy assisting (APTA); radiologic technology: radiography (JRCERT). **Total program enrollment:** 2705.

**PROGRAM(S) OFFERED**
• **Accounting Technology/Technician and Bookkeeping** • **Administrative Assistant and Secretarial Science, General** *47 students enrolled* • **Applied Horticulture/Horticultural Operations, General** *7 students enrolled* • **Child Care Provider/Assistant** *13 students enrolled* • **Computer/Information Technology Services Administration and Management, Other** *6 students enrolled* • **Construction Trades, General** *6 students enrolled* • **Crop Production** • **Culinary Arts/Chef Training** *2 students enrolled* • **Electrical, Electronic and Communications Engineering Technology/Technician** *34 students enrolled* • **Emergency Medical Technology/Technician (EMT Paramedic)** *1 student enrolled* • **Health Unit Coordinator/Ward Clerk** *8 students enrolled* • **Industrial Electronics Technology/Technician** *28 students enrolled* • **Licensed Practical/Vocational Nurse Training (LPN, LVN, Cert, Dipl, AAS)** *64 students enrolled* • **Massage Therapy/Therapeutic Massage** *11 students enrolled* • **Mechanical Drafting and Mechanical Drafting CAD/CADD** • **Medical Insurance Coding Specialist/Coder** *5 students enrolled* • **Medical Transcription/Transcriptionist** *10 students enrolled*

**• Nursing—Registered Nurse Training (RN, ASN, BSN, MSN)** *79 students enrolled* **• Pharmacy Technician/Assistant** *4 students enrolled* **• Radiologic Technology/Science—Radiographer • Welding Technology/Welder** *19 students enrolled*

**STUDENT SERVICES** Academic or career counseling, daycare for children of students, employment services for current students, placement services for program completers, remedial services.

## Iowa Central Community College

330 Avenue M, Fort Dodge, IA 50501-5798
http://www.iccc.cc.ia.us/

**CONTACT** Chuck Peterson, President's Assistant
**Telephone:** 515-576-7201

**GENERAL INFORMATION** Public Institution. Founded 1966. **Accreditation:** Regional (NCA); medical laboratory technology (NAACLS); radiologic technology: radiography (JRCERT). **Total program enrollment:** 2714.

**PROGRAM(S) OFFERED**
**• Accounting** *14 students enrolled* **• Administrative Assistant and Secretarial Science, General** *2 students enrolled* **• Aeronautics/Aviation/Aerospace Science and Technology, General • Automobile/Automotive Mechanics Technology/Technician • Carpentry/Carpenter** *19 students enrolled* **• Computer Systems Networking and Telecommunications** *4 students enrolled* **• Criminal Justice/Police Science** *3 students enrolled* **• Emergency Medical Technology/Technician (EMT Paramedic) • Industrial Mechanics and Maintenance Technology** *5 students enrolled* **• Licensed Practical/Vocational Nurse Training (LPN, LVN, Cert, Dipl, AAS)** *54 students enrolled* **• Mechanical Drafting and Mechanical Drafting CAD/CADD** *13 students enrolled* **• Medical Transcription/Transcriptionist** *3 students enrolled* **• Medical/Clinical Assistant** *7 students enrolled* **• Prepress/Desktop Publishing and Digital Imaging Design** *1 student enrolled* **• Web Page, Digital/Multimedia and Information Resources Design • Welding Technology/Welder** *5 students enrolled*

**STUDENT SERVICES** Academic or career counseling, employment services for current students, placement services for program completers, remedial services.

## Iowa Lakes Community College

19 South 7th Street, Estherville, IA 51334-2295
http://www.iowalakes.edu/

**CONTACT** Harold Prior, President
**Telephone:** 712-362-2601

**GENERAL INFORMATION** Public Institution. Founded 1967. **Accreditation:** Regional (NCA); medical assisting (AAMAE). **Total program enrollment:** 1589.

**PROGRAM(S) OFFERED**
**• Accounting • Administrative Assistant and Secretarial Science, General** *4 students enrolled* **• Agricultural Production Operations, General** *1 student enrolled* **• Agricultural/Biological Engineering and Bioengineering • Autobody/Collision and Repair Technology/Technician** *12 students enrolled* **• Carpentry/Carpenter** *19 students enrolled* **• Child Care Provider/Assistant** *10 students enrolled* **• Commercial and Advertising Art** *1 student enrolled* **• Computer and Information Systems Security • Emergency Medical Technology/Technician (EMT Paramedic) • Energy Management and Systems Technology/Technician • General Office Occupations and Clerical Services** *5 students enrolled* **• Journalism** *2 students enrolled* **• Licensed Practical/Vocational Nurse Training (LPN, LVN, Cert, Dipl, AAS)** *95 students enrolled* **• Marine Maintenance/Fitter and Ship Repair Technology/Technician** *9 students enrolled* **• Massage Therapy/Therapeutic Massage** *8 students enrolled* **• Medical Administrative/Executive Assistant and Medical Secretary** *2 students enrolled* **• Medical/Clinical Assistant • Motorcycle Maintenance and Repair Technology/Technician** *7 students enrolled* **• Pharmacy Technician/Assistant** *3 students enrolled* **• Rehabilitation and Therapeutic Professions, Other • Sales, Distribution and Marketing Operations, General** *2 students enrolled* **• Surgical Technology/Technologist** *5 students enrolled* **• Vehicle and Vehicle Parts and Accessories Marketing Operations • Welding Technology/Welder** *8 students enrolled*

**STUDENT SERVICES** Academic or career counseling, employment services for current students, placement services for program completers, remedial services.

## Iowa School of Beauty

3305 70th Street, Des Moines, IA 50322
http://iowaschoolofbeauty.com/

**CONTACT** Mark Oswald, President
**Telephone:** 515-278-9939

**GENERAL INFORMATION** Private Institution. Founded 1923. **Total program enrollment:** 113. **Application fee:** $50.

**PROGRAM(S) OFFERED**
**• Aesthetician/Esthetician and Skin Care Specialist** *600 hrs./$6000* **• Cosmetology/Cosmetologist, General** *2100 hrs./$17,193* **• Nail Technician/Specialist and Manicurist** *325 hrs./$2975*

**STUDENT SERVICES** Academic or career counseling, placement services for program completers.

## Iowa School of Beauty

112 Nicholas Drive, Marshalltown, IA 50158
http://iowaschoolofbeauty.com/

**CONTACT** Mark Oswald, President
**Telephone:** 641-752-4223

**GENERAL INFORMATION** Private Institution. Founded 1923. **Total program enrollment:** 24. **Application fee:** $50.

**PROGRAM(S) OFFERED**
**• Cosmetology and Related Personal Grooming Arts, Other • Cosmetology/Cosmetologist, General** *2100 hrs./$17,193* **• Nail Technician/Specialist and Manicurist** *325 hrs./$2975*

**STUDENT SERVICES** Academic or career counseling, placement services for program completers.

## Iowa School of Beauty

609 West Second Street, Ottumwa, IA 52501
http://iowaschoolofbeauty.com/

**CONTACT** Mark Oswald, President
**Telephone:** 641-684-6504

**GENERAL INFORMATION** Private Institution. Founded 1923. **Total program enrollment:** 46. **Application fee:** $50.

**PROGRAM(S) OFFERED**
**• Cosmetology/Cosmetologist, General** *2100 hrs./$17,193* **• Nail Technician/Specialist and Manicurist** *325 hrs./$2975*

**STUDENT SERVICES** Academic or career counseling, placement services for program completers.

## Iowa School of Beauty

2524 Glenn Avenue, Sioux City, IA 51106
http://iowaschoolofbeauty.com/

**CONTACT** Mark Oswald, President
**Telephone:** 712-274-9733

**GENERAL INFORMATION** Private Institution. **Total program enrollment:** 35. **Application fee:** $50.

**PROGRAM(S) OFFERED**
**• Cosmetology/Cosmetologist, General** *2100 hrs./$17,193* **• Nail Technician/Specialist and Manicurist** *325 hrs./$2975*

**STUDENT SERVICES** Academic or career counseling, placement services for program completers.

## Iowa Western Community College

2700 College Road, Box 4-C, Council Bluffs, IA 51502
http://www.iwcc.edu/

**CONTACT** Dan Kinney, President
**Telephone:** 712-325-3200

**GENERAL INFORMATION** Public Institution. Founded 1966. **Accreditation:** Regional (NCA); dental assisting (ADA); dental hygiene (ADA); engineering technology (ABET/TAC). **Total program enrollment:** 3096.

**PROGRAM(S) OFFERED**
• **Accounting** *2 students enrolled* • **Administrative Assistant and Secretarial Science, General** *7 students enrolled* • **Automobile/Automotive Mechanics Technology/Technician** *2 students enrolled* • **Avionics Maintenance Technology/Technician** • **Child Care Provider/Assistant** *1 student enrolled* • **Computer/Information Technology Services Administration and Management, Other** • **Construction Trades, General** • **Dental Assisting/Assistant** *11 students enrolled* • **Diesel Mechanics Technology/Technician** • **Food Service, Waiter/Waitress, and Dining Room Management/Manager** *1 student enrolled* • **Licensed Practical/Vocational Nurse Training (LPN, LVN, Cert, Dipl, AAS)** *100 students enrolled* • **Medical Transcription/Transcriptionist** *2 students enrolled* • **Medical/Clinical Assistant** *8 students enrolled* • **Surgical Technology/Technologist** *11 students enrolled*

**STUDENT SERVICES** Academic or career counseling, daycare for children of students, employment services for current students, placement services for program completers, remedial services.

## Kaplan University, Cedar Falls

7009 Nordic Drive, Cedar Falls, IA 50613
http://www.cedarfalls.kaplanuniversity.edu

**CONTACT** Connie Reidy, Campus President
**Telephone:** 319-277-0220

**GENERAL INFORMATION** Private Institution. Founded 2000. **Total program enrollment:** 339.

**PROGRAM(S) OFFERED**
• **Accounting Technology/Technician and Bookkeeping** *2 students enrolled* • **Computer Systems Analysis/Analyst** *2 students enrolled* • **Computer and Information Sciences and Support Services, Other** *7 students enrolled* • **General Office Occupations and Clerical Services** *2 students enrolled* • **Licensed Practical/Vocational Nurse Training (LPN, LVN, Cert, Dipl, AAS)** *66 students enrolled*

**STUDENT SERVICES** Academic or career counseling, employment services for current students, placement services for program completers.

## Kaplan University, Cedar Rapids

3165 Edgewood Parkway, SW, Cedar Rapids, IA 52404
http://www.cedarrapids.kaplanuniversity.edu

**CONTACT** Susan Spivey, Campus President
**Telephone:** 319-363-0481

**GENERAL INFORMATION** Private Institution. Founded 1900. **Accreditation:** Regional (NCA); medical assisting (AAMAE). **Total program enrollment:** 335.

**PROGRAM(S) OFFERED**
• **Computer Systems Analysis/Analyst** *2 students enrolled* • **General Office Occupations and Clerical Services** *2 students enrolled* • **Licensed Practical/Vocational Nurse Training (LPN, LVN, Cert, Dipl, AAS)** *74 students enrolled*

**STUDENT SERVICES** Academic or career counseling, employment services for current students, placement services for program completers.

## Kaplan University, Council Bluffs

1751 Madison Avenue, Council Bluffs, IA 51503
http://www.councilbluffs.kaplanuniversity.edu

**CONTACT** Michael Zawisky, Executive Director
**Telephone:** 712-328-4212

**GENERAL INFORMATION** Private Institution. Founded 2004. **Total program enrollment:** 116. **Application fee:** $25.

**STUDENT SERVICES** Academic or career counseling, employment services for current students, placement services for program completers, remedial services.

## Kaplan University, Davenport Campus

1801 East Kimberly Road, Suite 1, Davenport, IA 52807-2095
http://www.ku-davenport.edu

**CONTACT** Ron Blumenthal, Senior Vice President, Administration
**Telephone:** 563-355-3500

**GENERAL INFORMATION** Private Institution. Founded 1937. **Accreditation:** Regional (NCA); medical assisting (AAMAE). **Total program enrollment:** 3954.

**PROGRAM(S) OFFERED**
• **Computer Programming/Programmer, General** *2 students enrolled* • **Computer and Information Sciences, General** *20 students enrolled* • **Corrections** *1 student enrolled* • **Criminal Justice/Safety Studies** *1 student enrolled* • **Legal Administrative Assistant/Secretary** *15 students enrolled* • **Legal Assistant/Paralegal** *3 students enrolled* • **Management Information Systems and Services, Other** *3 students enrolled* • **Medical/Clinical Assistant** *2 students enrolled* • **Tourism and Travel Services Management** *1 student enrolled* • **Web Page, Digital/Multimedia and Information Resources Design** *12 students enrolled*

**STUDENT SERVICES** Academic or career counseling, employment services for current students, placement services for program completers, remedial services.

## Kaplan University, Des Moines

4655 121st Street, Urbandale, IA 50323
http://www.desmoines.kaplanuniversity.edu

**CONTACT** Jeremy Wells, President
**Telephone:** 515-727-2100

**GENERAL INFORMATION** Private Institution. **Total program enrollment:** 540.

**PROGRAM(S) OFFERED**
• **Licensed Practical/Vocational Nurse Training (LPN, LVN, Cert, Dipl, AAS)** *90 students enrolled* • **Medical Transcription/Transcriptionist** *19 students enrolled*

**STUDENT SERVICES** Academic or career counseling, employment services for current students, placement services for program completers.

## Kaplan University, Mason City Campus

Plaza West, 2570 4th Street, SW, Mason City, IA 50401
http://www.ku-masoncity.edu

**CONTACT** Joe Albers, Executive Director
**Telephone:** 641-423-2530

**GENERAL INFORMATION** Private Institution. Founded 1900. **Total program enrollment:** 218. **Application fee:** $45.

**PROGRAM(S) OFFERED**
• **Computer and Information Sciences, General** *1 student enrolled* • **Licensed Practical/Vocational Nurse Training (LPN, LVN, Cert, Dipl, AAS)** *19 students enrolled*

**STUDENT SERVICES** Academic or career counseling, employment services for current students, placement services for program completers.

## Kirkwood Community College

PO Box 2068, Cedar Rapids, IA 52406-2068
http://www.kirkwood.cc.ia.us/

**CONTACT** Mick Starcevich, President
**Telephone:** 319-398-5411

**GENERAL INFORMATION** Public Institution. Founded 1966. **Accreditation:** Regional (NCA); dental assisting (ADA); dental hygiene (ADA); dental laboratory technology (ADA); electroneurodiagnostic technology (JR-CEND); health information technology (AHIMA); medical assisting (AAMAE); physical therapy assisting (APTA); surgical technology (ARCST). **Total program enrollment:** 8300.

**PROGRAM(S) OFFERED**
• **Administrative Assistant and Secretarial Science, General** *6 students enrolled* • **Agricultural Production Operations, General** *2 students enrolled* • **Agricultural/Farm Supplies Retailing and Wholesaling** *1 student enrolled* • **Animal Health** *17 students enrolled* • **Apparel and Accessories Marketing Operations** *1 student enrolled* • **Autobody/Collision and Repair Technology/Technician** *19 students enrolled* • **Business Administration and Management, General** *19 students enrolled* • **Business/Office Automation/Technology/Data Entry** *10 students enrolled* • **Carpentry/Carpenter** *12 students enrolled* • **Child Care Provider/Assistant** *5 students enrolled* • **Computer Programming, Specific Applications** *3 students enrolled* • **Construction Trades, General** *3 students enrolled* • **Culinary Arts/Chef Training** *2 students enrolled* • **Data Entry/Microcomputer Applications, General** *5 students enrolled* • **Dental Assisting/Assistant** *20 students enrolled* • **Fire Protection and Safety Technology/Technician** *1 student enrolled* • **Fire Science/Firefighting** *1 student enrolled* • **Floriculture/Floristry Operations and Management** *12 students enrolled* • **Health Information/Medical Records Technology/Technician** *4 students enrolled* • **Heating, Air Conditioning, Ventilation and Refrigeration Maintenance Technology/Technician (HAC, HACR, HVAC, HVACR)** *12 students enrolled* • **Licensed Practical/Vocational Nurse Training (LPN, LVN, Cert, Dipl, AAS)** *171 students enrolled* • **Marketing/Marketing Management, General** *2 students enrolled* • **Mason/Masonry** *8 students enrolled* • **Medical Transcription/Transcriptionist** *6 students enrolled* • **Medical/Clinical Assistant** *22 students enrolled* • **Plumbing Technology/Plumber** *13 students enrolled* • **Social Work, Other** *1 student enrolled* • **Surgical Technology/Technologist** *25 students enrolled* • **Surveying Engineering** *1 student enrolled* • **System Administration/Administrator** *15 students enrolled* • **Welding Technology/Welder** *5 students enrolled*

**STUDENT SERVICES** Academic or career counseling, daycare for children of students, employment services for current students, placement services for program completers, remedial services.

## La' James College of Hairstyling

6322 University Avenue, Cedar Falls, IA 50613
http://lajames.net/

**CONTACT** Cynthia Becher, President
**Telephone:** 319-277-2150

**GENERAL INFORMATION** Private Institution. Founded 1984. **Total program enrollment:** 91. **Application fee:** $50.

**PROGRAM(S) OFFERED**
• **Aesthetician/Esthetician and Skin Care Specialist** *600 hrs./$8860* • **Cosmetology, Barber/Styling, and Nail Instructor** *1000 hrs./$7565* • **Cosmetology/Cosmetologist, General** *2100 hrs./$18,215* • **Massage Therapy/Therapeutic Massage** *625 hrs./$8860* • **Nail Technician/Specialist and Manicurist** *350 hrs./$3925*

**STUDENT SERVICES** Academic or career counseling, employment services for current students, placement services for program completers.

## La' James College of Hairstyling

211 West 53rd Street, Davenport, IA 52807
http://lajames.net/

**CONTACT** Cynthia Becher, President
**Telephone:** 563-441-7900

**GENERAL INFORMATION** Private Institution. Founded 1986. **Total program enrollment:** 60. **Application fee:** $50.

**PROGRAM(S) OFFERED**
• **Aesthetician/Esthetician and Skin Care Specialist** *600 hrs./$8860* • **Cosmetology, Barber/Styling, and Nail Instructor** *1000 hrs./$7565* • **Cosmetology/Cosmetologist, General** *2100 hrs./$18,365* • **Massage Therapy/Therapeutic Massage** *625 hrs./$8860* • **Nail Technician/Specialist and Manicurist** *350 hrs./$3925*

**STUDENT SERVICES** Academic or career counseling, employment services for current students, placement services for program completers.

## La' James College of Hairstyling

6336 Hickman Road, Des Moines, IA 50322
http://lajames.net/

**CONTACT** Cynthia Becher, President
**Telephone:** 515-278-2208

**GENERAL INFORMATION** Private Institution. Founded 1925. **Total program enrollment:** 181. **Application fee:** $50.

**PROGRAM(S) OFFERED**
• **Aesthetician/Esthetician and Skin Care Specialist** *600 hrs./$8860* • **Cosmetology, Barber/Styling, and Nail Instructor** *1000 hrs./$7565* • **Cosmetology/Cosmetologist, General** *2100 hrs./$18,365* • **Massage Therapy/Therapeutic Massage** *625 hrs./$8860* • **Nail Technician/Specialist and Manicurist** *350 hrs./$3925*

**STUDENT SERVICES** Academic or career counseling, employment services for current students, placement services for program completers.

## La' James College of Hairstyling

2604 First Avenue, S, Fort Dodge, IA 50501
http://lajames.net/

**CONTACT** Cynthia Becher, President
**Telephone:** 515-576-3119

**GENERAL INFORMATION** Private Institution. Founded 1966. **Total program enrollment:** 83. **Application fee:** $50.

**PROGRAM(S) OFFERED**
• **Aesthetician/Esthetician and Skin Care Specialist** *600 hrs./$8860* • **Cosmetology, Barber/Styling, and Nail Instructor** *1000 hrs./$7565* • **Cosmetology/Cosmetologist, General** *2100 hrs./$18,365* • **Massage Therapy/Therapeutic Massage** *625 hrs./$8860* • **Nail Technician/Specialist and Manicurist** *350 hrs./$3925*

**STUDENT SERVICES** Academic or career counseling, employment services for current students, placement services for program completers.

## La' James College of Hairstyling

227 East Market Street, Iowa City, IA 52240
http://www.lajames.net/

**CONTACT** Cynthia Becher, President
**Telephone:** 319-338-3926

**GENERAL INFORMATION** Private Institution. Founded 1986. **Total program enrollment:** 94. **Application fee:** $50.

*La' James College of Hairstyling (continued)*

**PROGRAM(S) OFFERED**
• **Aesthetician/Esthetician and Skin Care Specialist** *600 hrs./$8860*
• **Cosmetology, Barber/Styling, and Nail Instructor** *1000 hrs./$7565*
• **Cosmetology/Cosmetologist, General** *2100 hrs./$18,365* • **Massage Therapy/Therapeutic Massage** *625 hrs./$8860* • **Nail Technician/Specialist and Manicurist** *350 hrs./$3925*

**STUDENT SERVICES** Academic or career counseling, employment services for current students, placement services for program completers.

## La' James College of Hairstyling and Cosmetology

24 Second Avenue, NE, Mason City, IA 50401
http://www.lajames.com/

**CONTACT** K. Rentz, College Administrator
**Telephone:** 641-424-2161

**GENERAL INFORMATION** Private Institution. Founded 1933. **Total program enrollment:** 111. **Application fee:** $50.

**PROGRAM(S) OFFERED**
• **Aesthetician/Esthetician and Skin Care Specialist** *600 hrs./$8300*
• **Cosmetology, Barber/Styling, and Nail Instructor** *1000 hrs./$4730*
• **Cosmetology/Cosmetologist, General** *2100 hrs./$17,650* • **Massage Therapy/Therapeutic Massage** *650 hrs./$11,350* • **Nail Technician/Specialist and Manicurist** *350 hrs./$3000*

**STUDENT SERVICES** Academic or career counseling, placement services for program completers.

## Maharishi University of Management

1000 North 4th Street, Fairfield, IA 52557
http://www.mum.edu/

**CONTACT** Bevan Morris, President
**Telephone:** 515-472-7000

**GENERAL INFORMATION** Private Institution. Founded 1971. **Accreditation:** Regional (NCA). **Total program enrollment:** 727. **Application fee:** $30.

**STUDENT SERVICES** Academic or career counseling, employment services for current students, placement services for program completers.

## Marshalltown Community College

3700 South Center Street, Marshalltown, IA 50158-4760
http://www.marshalltowncommunitycollege.com/

**CONTACT** Tim Wynes, Chancellor
**Telephone:** 641-752-7106

**GENERAL INFORMATION** Public Institution. Founded 1927. **Accreditation:** Regional (NCA); dental assisting (ADA). **Total program enrollment:** 930.

**PROGRAM(S) OFFERED**
• **Accounting Technology/Technician and Bookkeeping** • **Administrative Assistant and Secretarial Science, General** *3 students enrolled* • **Agricultural Production Operations, General** • **Business Administration and Management, General** • **Child Care Provider/Assistant** *1 student enrolled* • **Computer Programming, Specific Applications** • **Computer Systems Networking and Telecommunications** • **Construction Trades, General** *6 students enrolled* • **Dental Assisting/Assistant** *15 students enrolled* • **Industrial Mechanics and Maintenance Technology** • **Licensed Practical/Vocational Nurse Training (LPN, LVN, Cert, Dipl, AAS)** *38 students enrolled* • **Machine Shop Technology/Assistant** • **Nursing—Registered Nurse Training (RN, ASN, BSN, MSN)** • **Psychiatric/Mental Health Services Technician** • **Tool and Die Technology/Technician** *4 students enrolled*

**STUDENT SERVICES** Academic or career counseling, daycare for children of students, employment services for current students, placement services for program completers, remedial services.

## Mercy College of Health Sciences

928 Sixth Avenue, Des Moines, IA 50309-1239
http://www.mchs.edu/

**CONTACT** Barbara Q. Decker, President
**Telephone:** 515-643-3180

**GENERAL INFORMATION** Private Institution (Affiliated with Roman Catholic Church). Founded 1995. **Accreditation:** Regional (NCA); diagnostic medical sonography (JRCEDMS); surgical technology (ARCST). **Total program enrollment:** 381. **Application fee:** $25.

**PROGRAM(S) OFFERED**
• **Allied Health Diagnostic, Intervention, and Treatment Professions, Other** • **Medical/Clinical Assistant** *6 students enrolled* • **Nuclear Medical Technology/Technologist** *5 students enrolled* • **Surgical Technology/Technologist** *12 students enrolled*

**STUDENT SERVICES** Academic or career counseling, employment services for current students, remedial services.

## Muscatine Community College

152 Colorado Street, Muscatine, IA 52761-5396
http://www.eicc.edu/

**CONTACT** Patricia Keir, Chancellor
**Telephone:** 563-336-3309

**GENERAL INFORMATION** Public Institution. Founded 1929. **Accreditation:** Regional (NCA). **Total program enrollment:** 3238.

**PROGRAM(S) OFFERED**
• **Accounting** *7 students enrolled* • **Administrative Assistant and Secretarial Science, General** *24 students enrolled* • **Architectural Drafting and Architectural CAD/CADD** *3 students enrolled* • **Autobody/Collision and Repair Technology/Technician** *6 students enrolled* • **Automobile/Automotive Mechanics Technology/Technician** *13 students enrolled* • **Business Administration and Management, General** *49 students enrolled* • **Child Care Provider/Assistant** *8 students enrolled* • **Computer Programming, Specific Applications** *18 students enrolled* • **Construction Trades, General** • **Culinary Arts/Chef Training** *6 students enrolled* • **Dental Assisting/Assistant** *16 students enrolled* • **Diagnostic Medical Sonography/Sonographer and Ultrasound Technician** • **Emergency Medical Technology/Technician (EMT Paramedic)** *14 students enrolled* • **Environmental Engineering Technology/Environmental Technology** *8 students enrolled* • **Health Information/Medical Records Technology/Technician** *15 students enrolled* • **Heating, Air Conditioning, Ventilation and Refrigeration Maintenance Technology/Technician (HAC, HACR, HVAC, HVACR)** *6 students enrolled* • **Industrial Mechanics and Maintenance Technology** *1 student enrolled* • **Licensed Practical/Vocational Nurse Training (LPN, LVN, Cert, Dipl, AAS)** *28 students enrolled* • **Machine Tool Technology/Machinist** *7 students enrolled* • **Manufacturing Technology/Technician** • **Mechanical Drafting and Mechanical Drafting CAD/CADD** *4 students enrolled* • **Nuclear Medical Technology/Technologist** • **Truck and Bus Driver/Commercial Vehicle Operation** *57 students enrolled* • **Welding Technology/Welder** *10 students enrolled*

**STUDENT SERVICES** Academic or career counseling, daycare for children of students, employment services for current students, placement services for program completers, remedial services.

## Northeast Iowa Community College

Box 400, Calmar, IA 52132-0480
http://www.nicc.edu/

**CONTACT** Dr. Penelope H. Wills, President
**Telephone:** 563-562-3263

**GENERAL INFORMATION** Public Institution. Founded 1966. **Accreditation:** Regional (NCA); health information technology (AHIMA). **Total program enrollment:** 2103.

**PROGRAM(S) OFFERED**
• **Accounting Technology/Technician and Bookkeeping** *13 students enrolled*
• **Administrative Assistant and Secretarial Science, General** *16 students*

enrolled • **Agribusiness/Agricultural Business Operations** *1 student enrolled* • **Agricultural Production Operations, General** *1 student enrolled* • **Agricultural and Food Products Processing** • **Automobile/Automotive Mechanics Technology/Technician** *9 students enrolled* • **Business/Office Automation/ Technology/Data Entry** *4 students enrolled* • **Carpentry/Carpenter** *14 students enrolled* • **Child Care Provider/Assistant** *5 students enrolled* • **Cosmetology/ Cosmetologist, General** *8 students enrolled* • **Crop Production** • **Dairy Husbandry and Production** • **Dental Assisting/Assistant** *21 students enrolled* • **Diesel Mechanics Technology/Technician** *13 students enrolled* • **Drafting and Design Technology/Technician, General** *5 students enrolled* • **Electrician** *17 students enrolled* • **Emergency Medical Technology/Technician (EMT Paramedic)** • **Health Information/Medical Records Technology/Technician** *11 students enrolled* • **Heating, Air Conditioning, Ventilation and Refrigeration Maintenance Technology/Technician (HAC, HACR, HVAC, HVACR)** *8 students enrolled* • **Licensed Practical/Vocational Nurse Training (LPN, LVN, Cert, Dipl, AAS)** *116 students enrolled* • **Massage Therapy/Therapeutic Massage** *6 students enrolled* • **Medical Transcription/Transcriptionist** *17 students enrolled* • **Nail Technician/Specialist and Manicurist** *1 student enrolled* • **Retailing and Retail Operations** *4 students enrolled* • **Sales, Distribution and Marketing Operations, General** *1 student enrolled* • **Social Work** *1 student enrolled* • **Special Products Marketing Operations** • **Welding Technology/Welder** *18 students enrolled*

**STUDENT SERVICES** Academic or career counseling, daycare for children of students, employment services for current students, placement services for program completers, remedial services.

## North Iowa Area Community College

500 College Drive, Mason City, IA 50401-7299
http://www.niacc.edu/

**CONTACT** Debra Derr, President
**Telephone:** 641-423-1264

**GENERAL INFORMATION** Public Institution. Founded 1918. **Accreditation:** Regional (NCA); physical therapy assisting (APTA). **Total program enrollment:** 1852.

**PROGRAM(S) OFFERED**
• **Accounting Technology/Technician and Bookkeeping** *2 students enrolled* • **Accounting** *2 students enrolled* • **Administrative Assistant and Secretarial Science, General** *2 students enrolled* • **Agricultural Production Operations, General** *2 students enrolled* • **Business Administration and Management, General** *2 students enrolled* • **Carpentry/Carpenter** *7 students enrolled* • **Computer Systems Networking and Telecommunications** • **Early Childhood Education and Teaching** *3 students enrolled* • **Emergency Medical Technology/ Technician (EMT Paramedic)** *40 students enrolled* • **Entrepreneurship/ Entrepreneurial Studies** *3 students enrolled* • **Heating, Air Conditioning, Ventilation and Refrigeration Maintenance Technology/Technician (HAC, HACR, HVAC, HVACR)** *3 students enrolled* • **Legal Administrative Assistant/ Secretary** • **Licensed Practical/Vocational Nurse Training (LPN, LVN, Cert, Dipl, AAS)** *20 students enrolled* • **Medical Administrative/Executive Assistant and Medical Secretary** • **Medical/Clinical Assistant** *30 students enrolled* • **Nurse/Nursing Assistant/Aide and Patient Care Assistant** *190 students enrolled* • **Tool and Die Technology/Technician** *2 students enrolled* • **Welding Technology/Welder** *1 student enrolled*

**STUDENT SERVICES** Academic or career counseling, employment services for current students, placement services for program completers, remedial services.

## Northwest Iowa Community College

603 West Park Street, Sheldon, IA 51201-1046
http://www.nwicc.edu/

**CONTACT** Bill Giddings, President
**Telephone:** 712-324-5061

**GENERAL INFORMATION** Public Institution. Founded 1966. **Accreditation:** Regional (NCA); health information technology (AHIMA). **Total program enrollment:** 599. **Application fee:** $10.

**PROGRAM(S) OFFERED**
• **Accounting** • **Administrative Assistant and Secretarial Science, General** *9 students enrolled* • **Autobody/Collision and Repair Technology/Technician** • **Automobile/Automotive Mechanics Technology/Technician** *3 students enrolled* • **Carpentry/Carpenter** *4 students enrolled* • **Construction/Heavy Equipment/ Earthmoving Equipment Operation** *13 students enrolled* • **Licensed Practical/ Vocational Nurse Training (LPN, LVN, Cert, Dipl, AAS)** *42 students enrolled* • **Lineworker** *44 students enrolled* • **Machine Tool Technology/Machinist** *1 student enrolled* • **Mechanical Drafting and Mechanical Drafting CAD/CADD** *5 students enrolled* • **Retailing and Retail Operations** *2 students enrolled* • **Welding Technology/Welder** *5 students enrolled*

**STUDENT SERVICES** Academic or career counseling, employment services for current students, placement services for program completers, remedial services.

## Palmer College of Chiropractic

1000 Brady Street, Davenport, IA 52803-5287
http://www.palmer.edu/

**CONTACT** Donald Kern, President
**Telephone:** 563-884-5000

**GENERAL INFORMATION** Private Institution. Founded 1897. **Accreditation:** Regional (NCA). **Total program enrollment:** 2142. **Application fee:** $50.

**PROGRAM(S) OFFERED**
• **Allied Health and Medical Assisting Services, Other**

**STUDENT SERVICES** Academic or career counseling, employment services for current students.

## Professional Cosmetology Institute

627 Main Street, Ames, IA 50010
http://www.pciames.com/

**CONTACT** Angela Torgeson, President
**Telephone:** 515-232-7250 Ext. 2

**GENERAL INFORMATION** Private Institution. Founded 1978. **Total program enrollment:** 116.

**PROGRAM(S) OFFERED**
• **Aesthetician/Esthetician and Skin Care Specialist** *600 hrs./$7795* • **Cosmetology/Cosmetologist, General** *2100 hrs./$18,677* • **Massage Therapy/ Therapeutic Massage** *624 hrs./$10,113* • **Nail Technician/Specialist and Manicurist** *325 hrs./$4254*

**STUDENT SERVICES** Academic or career counseling, placement services for program completers, remedial services.

## St. Ambrose University

518 West Locust Street, Davenport, IA 52803-2898
http://www.sau.edu/

**CONTACT** Sr. Joan Lescinski CSJ, President
**Telephone:** 563-333-6000

**GENERAL INFORMATION** Private Institution. Founded 1882. **Accreditation:** Regional (NCA). **Total program enrollment:** 2721. **Application fee:** $25.

**PROGRAM(S) OFFERED**
• **Special Education and Teaching, General** *9 students enrolled*

**STUDENT SERVICES** Academic or career counseling, employment services for current students, placement services for program completers, remedial services.

## St. Luke's College

2720 Stone Park Boulevard, Sioux City, IA 51104
http://stlukescollege.edu/

**CONTACT** Michael D. Stiles, Chancellor
**Telephone:** 712-279-3149

**GENERAL INFORMATION** Private Institution. Founded 1967. **Accreditation:** Regional (NCA). **Total program enrollment:** 105. **Application fee:** $50.

**STUDENT SERVICES** Academic or career counseling, employment services for current students, placement services for program completers, remedial services.

## Southeastern Community College, North Campus

1500 West Agency Street, PO Box 180, West Burlington, IA 52655-0180
http://www.secc.cc.ia.us/

**CONTACT** Dr. Beverly Simone, President
**Telephone:** 319-752-2731

**GENERAL INFORMATION** Public Institution. Founded 1968. **Accreditation:** Regional (NCA); medical assisting (AAMAE). **Total program enrollment:** 1875.

**PROGRAM(S) OFFERED**
• **Accounting** • **Administrative Assistant and Secretarial Science, General** *2 students enrolled* • **Autobody/Collision and Repair Technology/Technician** *1 student enrolled* • **Automobile/Automotive Mechanics Technology/Technician** *4 students enrolled* • **Construction Trades, General** • **Electrical, Electronic and Communications Engineering Technology/Technician** *3 students enrolled* • **Information Technology** • **Licensed Practical/Vocational Nurse Training (LPN, LVN, Cert, Dipl, AAS)** *94 students enrolled* • **Machine Tool Technology/Machinist** *7 students enrolled* • **Mechanical Drafting and Mechanical Drafting CAD/CADD** *2 students enrolled* • **Medical/Clinical Assistant** *3 students enrolled* • **Radiologic Technology/Science—Radiographer** • **Welding Technology/Welder** *10 students enrolled*

**STUDENT SERVICES** Academic or career counseling, daycare for children of students, employment services for current students, placement services for program completers, remedial services.

## Southwestern Community College

1501 West Townline Street, Creston, IA 50801
http://www.iowa.edu/

**CONTACT** Dr. Barbara Crittenden, President
**Telephone:** 641-782-7081 Ext. 420

**GENERAL INFORMATION** Public Institution. Founded 1966. **Accreditation:** Regional (NCA). **Total program enrollment:** 696.

**PROGRAM(S) OFFERED**
• **Administrative Assistant and Secretarial Science, General** *1 student enrolled* • **Autobody/Collision and Repair Technology/Technician** *8 students enrolled* • **Automobile/Automotive Mechanics Technology/Technician** *10 students enrolled* • **Carpentry/Carpenter** *8 students enrolled* • **Civil Drafting and Civil Engineering CAD/CADD** *13 students enrolled* • **Computer Systems Networking and Telecommunications** *15 students enrolled* • **Computer and Information Sciences and Support Services, Other** *1 student enrolled* • **Computer and Information Sciences, Other** *1 student enrolled* • **Licensed Practical/Vocational Nurse Training (LPN, LVN, Cert, Dipl, AAS)** *64 students enrolled* • **Medical Transcription/Transcriptionist** *2 students enrolled*

**STUDENT SERVICES** Academic or career counseling, employment services for current students, placement services for program completers, remedial services.

## Total Look School of Cosmetology & Massage Therapy

806 W. Third Street, Cresco, IA 52136

**CONTACT** Pam Burnikel
**Telephone:** 563-547-3624

**GENERAL INFORMATION** Private Institution. **Total program enrollment:** 13. **Application fee:** $50.

**PROGRAM(S) OFFERED**
• **Cosmetology/Cosmetologist, General** *2100 hrs./$13,800* • **Massage Therapy/Therapeutic Massage** *600 hrs./$8300*

## Upper Iowa University

605 Washington Street, Box 1857, Fayette, IA 52142-1857
http://www.uiu.edu/

**CONTACT** Alan G. Walker, President
**Telephone:** 563-425-5200

**GENERAL INFORMATION** Private Institution. Founded 1857. **Accreditation:** Regional (NCA). **Total program enrollment:** 2552. **Application fee:** $15.

**PROGRAM(S) OFFERED**
• **Human Resources Management/Personnel Administration, General** *9 students enrolled* • **Management Information Systems, General** *1 student enrolled* • **Marketing, Other** *2 students enrolled* • **Organizational Behavior Studies** *2 students enrolled* • **Public Administration and Social Service Professions, Other**

**STUDENT SERVICES** Academic or career counseling, employment services for current students, remedial services.

## Vatterott College

6100 Thornton Avenue, Suite 290, Des Moines, IA 50321
http://www.vatterott-college.edu/

**CONTACT** Daniel Nieland, Director
**Telephone:** 515-309-9000

**GENERAL INFORMATION** Private Institution. **Accreditation:** State accredited or approved. **Total program enrollment:** 236.

**PROGRAM(S) OFFERED**
• **Dental Assisting/Assistant** *15 students enrolled* • **Medical Office Assistant/Specialist** *3 students enrolled* • **Medical/Clinical Assistant** *31 students enrolled*

**STUDENT SERVICES** Academic or career counseling, employment services for current students, placement services for program completers.

## Western Iowa Tech Community College

4647 Stone Avenue, PO Box 5199, Sioux City, IA 51102-5199
http://www.witcc.edu/

**CONTACT** Robert Dunker, President
**Telephone:** 712-274-6400

**GENERAL INFORMATION** Public Institution. Founded 1966. **Accreditation:** Regional (NCA); dental assisting (ADA); physical therapy assisting (APTA). **Total program enrollment:** 2096.

**PROGRAM(S) OFFERED**
• **Accounting Technology/Technician and Bookkeeping** *5 students enrolled* • **Administrative Assistant and Secretarial Science, General** *4 students enrolled* • **Agricultural/Farm Supplies Retailing and Wholesaling** • **Autobody/Collision and Repair Technology/Technician** • **Automobile/Automotive Mechanics Technology/Technician** • **Biomedical Technology/Technician** *1 student enrolled* • **Building/Property Maintenance and Management** *5 students enrolled* • **Business/Office Automation/Technology/Data Entry** *27 students enrolled* • **Carpentry/Carpenter** *11 students enrolled* • **Child Care Provider/Assistant** *7 students enrolled* • **Computer/Information Technology Services**

**Administration and Management, Other** • **Dental Assisting/Assistant** *24 students enrolled* • **Diesel Mechanics Technology/Technician** *5 students enrolled* • **Electrical, Electronic and Communications Engineering Technology/Technician** *2 students enrolled* • **Electrician** *14 students enrolled* • **Emergency Medical Technology/Technician (EMT Paramedic)** • **Heating, Air Conditioning, Ventilation and Refrigeration Maintenance Technology/Technician (HAC, HACR, HVAC, HVACR)** *51 students enrolled* • **Human Resources Management/Personnel Administration, General** *1 student enrolled* • **Industrial Mechanics and Maintenance Technology** • **Legal Administrative Assistant/Secretary** *2 students enrolled* • **Licensed Practical/Vocational Nurse Training (LPN, LVN, Cert, Dipl, AAS)** *100 students enrolled* • **Mechanical Drafting and Mechanical Drafting CAD/CADD** • **Medical Administrative/Executive Assistant and Medical Secretary** *40 students enrolled* • **Nurse/Nursing Assistant/Aide and Patient Care Assistant** *1 student enrolled* • **Pharmacy Technician/Assistant** • **Physical Therapist Assistant** *5 students enrolled* • **Retailing and Retail Operations** *3 students enrolled* • **Surgical Technology/Technologist** *5 students enrolled* • **Teacher Assistant/Aide** *2 students enrolled* • **Tool and Die Technology/Technician** • **Turf and Turfgrass Management** • **Veterinary/Animal Health Technology/Technician and Veterinary Assistant** *13 students enrolled* • **Web Page, Digital/Multimedia and Information Resources Design** • **Welding Technology/Welder** *12 students enrolled*

**STUDENT SERVICES** Academic or career counseling, employment services for current students, placement services for program completers, remedial services.

# KANSAS

## Academy of Hair Design

115 South Fifth Street, Salina, KS 67401
http://www.academyofhairsalina.com/

**CONTACT** Janet Reynolds, Chief Executive Officer
**Telephone:** 785-825-8155

**GENERAL INFORMATION** Private Institution. Founded 1967. **Total program enrollment:** 57. **Application fee:** $100.

**PROGRAM(S) OFFERED**
• **Aesthetician/Esthetician and Skin Care Specialist** *650 hrs./$5294* • **Cosmetology/Cosmetologist, General** *1500 hrs./$12,613* • **Nail Technician/Specialist and Manicurist** *350 hrs./$2896*

**STUDENT SERVICES** Academic or career counseling.

## Allen County Community College

1801 North Cottonwood Street, Iola, KS 66749-1607
http://www.allencc.net/

**CONTACT** John Masterson, President
**Telephone:** 620-365-5116 Ext. 100

**GENERAL INFORMATION** Public Institution. Founded 1923. **Accreditation:** Regional (NCA). **Total program enrollment:** 1272.

**PROGRAM(S) OFFERED**
• **Business Administration and Management, General** • **Computer Systems Networking and Telecommunications** • **Emergency Medical Technology/Technician (EMT Paramedic)** *24 students enrolled* • **Health Aide** *535 students enrolled* • **Hospital and Health Care Facilities Administration/Management** • **Management Information Systems and Services, Other** • **Medication Aide** *1 student enrolled* • **Sales, Distribution and Marketing Operations, General** • **Substance Abuse/Addiction Counseling**

**STUDENT SERVICES** Academic or career counseling, employment services for current students, remedial services.

## American Institute of Baking

1213 Bakers Way, Manhattan, KS 66502
http://www.aibonline.org/

**CONTACT** James Munyon, President
**Telephone:** 785-537-4750 Ext. 131

**GENERAL INFORMATION** Private Institution. Founded 1919. **Total program enrollment:** 182. **Application fee:** $45.

**PROGRAM(S) OFFERED**
• **Baking and Pastry Arts/Baker/Pastry Chef** *460 hrs./$9325* • **Electromechanical and Instrumentation and Maintenance Technologies/Technicians, Other** *300 hrs./$7175* • **Engineering, General** *20 students enrolled*

**STUDENT SERVICES** Employment services for current students, placement services for program completers.

## Barclay College

607 North Kingman, Haviland, KS 67059-0288
http://www.barclaycollege.edu/

**CONTACT** Dr. Herbert Frazier, President
**Telephone:** 620-862-5252

**GENERAL INFORMATION** Private Institution (Affiliated with Society of Friends). Founded 1917. **Accreditation:** Regional (NCA); state accredited or approved. **Total program enrollment:** 127. **Application fee:** $20.

**STUDENT SERVICES** Academic or career counseling, employment services for current students, remedial services.

## Barton County Community College

245 Northeast 30th Road, Great Bend, KS 67530-9283
http://www.bartonccc.edu/

**CONTACT** Carl Heilman, President
**Telephone:** 620-792-2701

**GENERAL INFORMATION** Public Institution. Founded 1969. **Accreditation:** Regional (NCA); medical laboratory technology (NAACLS). **Total program enrollment:** 1028.

**PROGRAM(S) OFFERED**
• **Agricultural Production Operations, General** • **Automobile/Automotive Mechanics Technology/Technician** *6 students enrolled* • **Business Administration and Management, General** • **Dietitian Assistant** *14 students enrolled* • **Emergency Medical Technology/Technician (EMT Paramedic)** • **Hazardous Materials Management and Waste Technology/Technician** *8 students enrolled* • **Home Health Aide/Home Attendant** • **Industrial Production Technologies/Technicians, Other** • **Licensed Practical/Vocational Nurse Training (LPN, LVN, Cert, Dipl, AAS)** *39 students enrolled* • **Medical Insurance Coding Specialist/Coder** • **Medical/Clinical Assistant** • **Medication Aide** • **Nurse/Nursing Assistant/Aide and Patient Care Assistant** • **Pre-Veterinary Studies** • **Security and Protective Services, Other**

**STUDENT SERVICES** Academic or career counseling, daycare for children of students, employment services for current students, placement services for program completers, remedial services.

## Bethel College

300 East 27th Street, North Newton, KS 67117
http://www.bethelks.edu/

**CONTACT** Barry C. Bartel, President
**Telephone:** 316-283-2500

**GENERAL INFORMATION** Private Institution (Affiliated with Mennonite Church USA). Founded 1887. **Accreditation:** Regional (NCA). **Total program enrollment:** 475. **Application fee:** $20.

*Bethel College (continued)*

**PROGRAM(S) OFFERED**
• **Physical Education Teaching and Coaching** • **Youth Ministry**

**STUDENT SERVICES** Academic or career counseling, employment services for current students, remedial services.

## BMSI Institute

8665 W. 96th Street, Suite 300, Overland Park, KS 66212
http://www.bmsi.edu/

**CONTACT** C. Michael Pizzuto, Owner
**Telephone:** 913-649-3322

**GENERAL INFORMATION** Private Institution. **Total program enrollment:** 10. **Application fee:** $60.

**PROGRAM(S) OFFERED**
• **Massage Therapy/Therapeutic Massage** *650 hrs./$9860*

**STUDENT SERVICES** Academic or career counseling.

## Brown Mackie College–Kansas City

9705 Lenexa Drive, Lenexa, KS 66215
http://www.brownmackie.edu/KansasCity/

**CONTACT** Susan Naples, President
**Telephone:** 913-768-1900

**GENERAL INFORMATION** Private Institution. Founded 1892. **Accreditation:** Regional (NCA). **Total program enrollment:** 457.

**PROGRAM(S) OFFERED**
• **Accounting** *1 student enrolled* • **Business Administration and Management, General** • **Computer Software Technology/Technician** • **Computer Systems Networking and Telecommunications** • **Criminal Justice/Law Enforcement Administration** • **Drafting and Design Technology/Technician, General** • **Legal Assistant/Paralegal** *1 student enrolled* • **Medical Office Assistant/Specialist** • **Medical/Clinical Assistant** *2 students enrolled* • **Nurse/Nursing Assistant/Aide and Patient Care Assistant** *57 students enrolled*

**STUDENT SERVICES** Academic or career counseling, employment services for current students, placement services for program completers, remedial services.

## Brown Mackie College–Salina

2106 South 9th Street, Salina, KS 67401-2810
http://www.brownmackie.edu/Salina/

**CONTACT** Danny Finuf, President
**Telephone:** 785-825-5422

**GENERAL INFORMATION** Private Institution. Founded 1892. **Accreditation:** Regional (NCA). **Total program enrollment:** 450.

**PROGRAM(S) OFFERED**
• **Accounting** *1 student enrolled* • **Advertising** • **Business Administration and Management, General** *10 students enrolled* • **CAD/CADD Drafting and/or Design Technology/Technician** *1 student enrolled* • **Computer Software Technology/Technician** *1 student enrolled* • **Computer Systems Networking and Telecommunications** • **Criminal Justice/Safety Studies** *2 students enrolled* • **Legal Assistant/Paralegal** *1 student enrolled* • **Medical Insurance Coding Specialist/Coder** *6 students enrolled* • **Medical/Clinical Assistant** *5 students enrolled* • **Nursing, Other** *85 students enrolled*

**STUDENT SERVICES** Academic or career counseling, employment services for current students, placement services for program completers, remedial services.

## Bryan Career College

1527 SW Fairlawn Road, Topeka, KS 66604
http://www.bryancollege.com/

**CONTACT** Brian Stewart, President
**Telephone:** 785-272-0889

**GENERAL INFORMATION** Private Institution. **Total program enrollment:** 187. **Application fee:** $30.

**PROGRAM(S) OFFERED**
• **Business Administration and Management, General** *21 students enrolled* • **Computer Programming/Programmer, General** *11 students enrolled* • **Computer Systems Networking and Telecommunications** *11 students enrolled* • **Medical Office Assistant/Specialist** *17 students enrolled* • **Medical/Clinical Assistant** *56 students enrolled*

**STUDENT SERVICES** Academic or career counseling, employment services for current students, placement services for program completers.

## B Street Design-School International Hair Styling–Overland Park

10324 Mastin Street, Overland Park, KS 66212

**CONTACT** Joe Hancock, President
**Telephone:** 913-782-4004

**GENERAL INFORMATION** Private Institution. Founded 1967. **Total program enrollment:** 94.

**PROGRAM(S) OFFERED**
• **Aesthetician/Esthetician and Skin Care Specialist** *650 hrs./$6650* • **Cosmetology/Cosmetologist, General** *1500 hrs./$12,750*

**STUDENT SERVICES** Placement services for program completers.

## B Street Design-School International Hair Styling–Topeka

3602 SW Topeka Boulevard, Topeka, KS 66611

**CONTACT** Nancy Sweatt, Director
**Telephone:** 785-267-7701

**GENERAL INFORMATION** Private Institution. **Total program enrollment:** 82.

**PROGRAM(S) OFFERED**
• **Cosmetology and Related Personal Grooming Arts, Other** *14 students enrolled* • **Cosmetology/Cosmetologist, General** *1500 hrs./$9250* • **Nail Technician/Specialist and Manicurist** *350 hrs./$1900*

**STUDENT SERVICES** Placement services for program completers.

## B Street Design-School International Hair Styling–Wichita

1675 South Rock Road, Wichita, KS 67207

**CONTACT** Mary Kay Mitchell, Director
**Telephone:** 316-681-2288

**GENERAL INFORMATION** Private Institution. **Total program enrollment:** 71.

**PROGRAM(S) OFFERED**
• **Aesthetician/Esthetician and Skin Care Specialist** *650 hrs./$6750* • **Cosmetology/Cosmetologist, General** *1500 hrs./$11,935* • **Nail Technician/Specialist and Manicurist** *350 hrs./$2100*

**STUDENT SERVICES** Placement services for program completers.

## Butler Community College

901 South Haverhill Road, El Dorado, KS 67042-3280
http://www.butlercc.edu/

**CONTACT** Dr. Jacqueline Vietti, President
**Telephone:** 316-321-2222

**GENERAL INFORMATION** Public Institution. Founded 1927. **Accreditation:** Regional (NCA). **Total program enrollment:** 3578.

**PROGRAM(S) OFFERED**
• **Administrative Assistant and Secretarial Science, General** *11 students enrolled* • **Animal/Livestock Husbandry and Production** *4 students enrolled* • **Animation, Interactive Technology, Video Graphics and Special Effects** • **Autobody/Collision and Repair Technology/Technician** *6 students enrolled* • **Automobile/Automotive Mechanics Technology/Technician** *10 students enrolled* • **CAD/CADD Drafting and/or Design Technology/Technician** *2 students enrolled* • **Child Care and Support Services Management** *4 students enrolled* • **Computer and Information Systems Security** • **Computer/Information Technology Services Administration and Management, Other** • **Drafting and Design Technology/Technician, General** • **Entrepreneurial and Small Business Operations, Other** • **Farm/Farm and Ranch Management** • **Fire Science/Firefighting** *1 student enrolled* • **Hospitality and Recreation Marketing Operations** • **Hotel/Motel Administration/Management** • **Legal Administrative Assistant/Secretary** • **Licensed Practical/Vocational Nurse Training (LPN, LVN, Cert, Dipl, AAS)** • **Machine Tool Technology/Machinist** • **Manufacturing Technology/Technician** • **Marketing/Marketing Management, General** • **Massage Therapy/Therapeutic Massage** *31 students enrolled* • **Medical Insurance Coding Specialist/Coder** *2 students enrolled* • **Medical Office Assistant/Specialist** *6 students enrolled* • **Medical Office Management/Administration** • **Medical Transcription/Transcriptionist** *2 students enrolled* • **Nursing—Registered Nurse Training (RN, ASN, BSN, MSN)** *86 students enrolled* • **Restaurant/Food Services Management** *2 students enrolled* • **Retailing and Retail Operations** • **Substance Abuse/Addiction Counseling** • **System, Networking, and LAN/WAN Management/Manager** • **Tourism and Travel Services Management** *1 student enrolled* • **Web/Multimedia Management and Webmaster** *1 student enrolled* • **Welding Technology/Welder** *11 students enrolled*

**STUDENT SERVICES** Academic or career counseling, daycare for children of students, employment services for current students, remedial services.

## Cloud County Community College

2221 Campus Drive, PO Box 1002, Concordia, KS 66901-1002
http://www.cloud.edu/

**CONTACT** Dr. Richard Underbakke, President
**Telephone:** 785-243-1435

**GENERAL INFORMATION** Public Institution. Founded 1965. **Accreditation:** Regional (NCA); practical nursing (NLN). **Total program enrollment:** 652.

**PROGRAM(S) OFFERED**
• **Administrative Assistant and Secretarial Science, General** *1 student enrolled* • **Agricultural Production Operations, General** *1 student enrolled* • **Business Administration and Management, General** • **Child Care and Support Services Management** *2 students enrolled* • **Criminal Justice/Police Science** *1 student enrolled* • **Emergency Care Attendant (EMT Ambulance)** *8 students enrolled* • **Graphic Design** • **Health Aide** • **Health Aides/Attendants/Orderlies, Other** *31 students enrolled* • **Health/Health Care Administration/Management** • **Home Health Aide/Home Attendant** • **Journalism** • **Legal Assistant/Paralegal** *1 student enrolled* • **Licensed Practical/Vocational Nurse Training (LPN, LVN, Cert, Dipl, AAS)** *15 students enrolled* • **Medication Aide** *22 students enrolled* • **Nurse/Nursing Assistant/Aide and Patient Care Assistant** *128 students enrolled* • **Radio and Television Broadcasting Technology/Technician** • **System, Networking, and LAN/WAN Management/Manager** • **Web Page, Digital/Multimedia and Information Resources Design**

**STUDENT SERVICES** Academic or career counseling, daycare for children of students, employment services for current students, placement services for program completers, remedial services.

## Coffeyville Community College

400 West 11th Street, Coffeyville, KS 67337-5063
http://www.coffeyville.edu/

**CONTACT** Don A. Woodburn, President
**Telephone:** 620-251-7700

**GENERAL INFORMATION** Public Institution. Founded 1923. **Accreditation:** Regional (NCA). **Total program enrollment:** 1121.

**PROGRAM(S) OFFERED**
• **Administrative Assistant and Secretarial Science, General** *3 students enrolled* • **Autobody/Collision and Repair Technology/Technician** *13 students enrolled* • **Automobile/Automotive Mechanics Technology/Technician** *10 students enrolled* • **Carpentry/Carpenter** *5 students enrolled* • **Computer Systems Networking and Telecommunications** • **Electrician** *9 students enrolled* • **Emergency Medical Technology/Technician (EMT Paramedic)** *9 students enrolled* • **Home Health Aide/Home Attendant** *13 students enrolled* • **Medication Aide** *46 students enrolled* • **Nurse/Nursing Assistant/Aide and Patient Care Assistant** *110 students enrolled* • **Welding Technology/Welder** *15 students enrolled*

**STUDENT SERVICES** Academic or career counseling, employment services for current students, remedial services.

## Colby Community College

1255 South Range, Colby, KS 67701-4099
http://www.colbycc.edu/

**CONTACT** Dr. Lynn Kreider, President
**Telephone:** 785-462-3984

**GENERAL INFORMATION** Public Institution. Founded 1964. **Accreditation:** Regional (NCA); physical therapy assisting (APTA). **Total program enrollment:** 746.

**PROGRAM(S) OFFERED**
• **Administrative Assistant and Secretarial Science, General** • **Emergency Medical Technology/Technician (EMT Paramedic)** *30 students enrolled* • **Health Aide** • **Health Aides/Attendants/Orderlies, Other** *13 students enrolled* • **Home Health Aide/Home Attendant** • **Licensed Practical/Vocational Nurse Training (LPN, LVN, Cert, Dipl, AAS)** *42 students enrolled* • **Medical Office Assistant/Specialist** *1 student enrolled* • **Medication Aide** *59 students enrolled* • **Nurse/Nursing Assistant/Aide and Patient Care Assistant** *65 students enrolled*

**STUDENT SERVICES** Academic or career counseling, remedial services.

## Cowley County Community College and Area Vocational–Technical School

125 South Second, PO Box 1147, Arkansas City, KS 67005-1147
http://www.cowley.cc.ks.us/

**CONTACT** Pat McAtee, President
**Telephone:** 620-442-0430

**GENERAL INFORMATION** Public Institution. Founded 1922. **Accreditation:** Regional (NCA). **Total program enrollment:** 1667.

**PROGRAM(S) OFFERED**
• **Administrative Assistant and Secretarial Science, General** • **Airframe Mechanics and Aircraft Maintenance Technology/Technician** *11 students enrolled* • **Automobile/Automotive Mechanics Technology/Technician** *9 students enrolled* • **Computer Systems Networking and Telecommunications** • **Cosmetology/Cosmetologist, General** *14 students enrolled* • **Criminal Justice/Police Science** • **Machine Shop Technology/Assistant** *7 students enrolled* • **Medical Office Assistant/Specialist** *1 student enrolled* • **System, Networking, and LAN/WAN Management/Manager** *1 student enrolled* • **Welding Technology/Welder** *18 students enrolled*

**STUDENT SERVICES** Academic or career counseling, employment services for current students, placement services for program completers, remedial services.

## Crums Beauty College

512 Poyntz Avenue, Box 663, Manhattan, KS 66502

**CONTACT** Bill Hancock, School Owner
**Telephone:** 785-776-4794

**GENERAL INFORMATION** Private Institution. **Total program enrollment:** 65. **Application fee:** $100.

**PROGRAM(S) OFFERED**
• **Aesthetician/Esthetician and Skin Care Specialist** *650 hrs./$3831* • **Cosmetology, Barber/Styling, and Nail Instructor** *300 hrs./$1300* • **Cosmetology/Cosmetologist, General** *1500 hrs./$11,500* • **Nail Technician/Specialist and Manicurist** *350 hrs./$1300*

**STUDENT SERVICES** Academic or career counseling, employment services for current students, placement services for program completers.

## Cutting Edge Hairstyling Academy

812 North Kansas Avenue, Topeka, KS 66608-1211
http://cuttingedge-kc.com/

**CONTACT** Douglas R. Rushing, President
**Telephone:** 913-321-0214

**GENERAL INFORMATION** Private Institution. Founded 1957. **Total program enrollment:** 180. **Application fee:** $100.

**PROGRAM(S) OFFERED**
• **Barbering/Barber** *1500 hrs./$13,683* • **Cosmetology/Cosmetologist, General** *74 students enrolled*

**STUDENT SERVICES** Academic or career counseling, placement services for program completers.

## Dodge City Community College

2501 North 14th Avenue, Dodge City, KS 67801-2399
http://www.dc3.edu/

**CONTACT** Richard K. Burke, PhD, President
**Telephone:** 620-225-1321

**GENERAL INFORMATION** Public Institution. Founded 1935. **Accreditation:** Regional (NCA); practical nursing (NLN). **Total program enrollment:** 695.

**PROGRAM(S) OFFERED**
• **Administrative Assistant and Secretarial Science, General** • **Agricultural/Farm Supplies Retailing and Wholesaling** *1 student enrolled* • **Agriculture, Agriculture Operations and Related Sciences, Other** • **Agriculture, General** • **Automobile/Automotive Mechanics Technology/Technician** *1 student enrolled* • **Child Care and Support Services Management** *1 student enrolled* • **Cosmetology/Cosmetologist, General** *12 students enrolled* • **Criminal Justice/Police Science** • **Data Processing and Data Processing Technology/Technician** *7 students enrolled* • **Diesel Mechanics Technology/Technician** *1 student enrolled* • **Equestrian/Equine Studies** *2 students enrolled* • **Farm/Farm and Ranch Management** • **Fire Science/Firefighting** *1 student enrolled* • **Floriculture/Floristry Operations and Management** • **Licensed Practical/Vocational Nurse Training (LPN, LVN, Cert, Dipl, AAS)** *23 students enrolled* • **Manufacturing Technology/Technician** • **Welding Technology/Welder** *1 student enrolled*

**STUDENT SERVICES** Academic or career counseling, daycare for children of students, employment services for current students, placement services for program completers, remedial services.

## Flint Hills Technical College

3301 West 18th Avenue, Emporia, KS 66801
http://www.fhtc.net/

**CONTACT** Dr. Dean Hollenbeck, President
**Telephone:** 620-343-4600 Ext. 1301

**GENERAL INFORMATION** Public Institution. Founded 1963. **Accreditation:** Dental assisting (ADA); state accredited or approved. **Total program enrollment:** 292.

**PROGRAM(S) OFFERED**
• **Administrative Assistant and Secretarial Science, General** *18 students enrolled* • **Automobile/Automotive Mechanics Technology/Technician** *17 students enrolled* • **Building/Property Maintenance and Management** *9 students enrolled* • **Commercial and Advertising Art** • **Computer Programming/Programmer, General** *10 students enrolled* • **Dental Assisting/Assistant** *23 students enrolled* • **Emergency Medical Technology/Technician (EMT Paramedic)** *23 students enrolled* • **Foodservice Systems Administration/Management** *7 students enrolled* • **Graphic and Printing Equipment Operator, General Production** *7 students enrolled* • **Health Professions and Related Clinical Sciences, Other** *12 students enrolled* • **Industrial Engineering** *12 students enrolled* • **Licensed Practical/Vocational Nurse Training (LPN, LVN, Cert, Dipl, AAS)** *30 students enrolled* • **Manufacturing Technology/Technician** *9 students enrolled* • **Nuclear Engineering Technology/Technician** *14 students enrolled*

**STUDENT SERVICES** Academic or career counseling, placement services for program completers, remedial services.

## Fort Scott Community College

2108 South Horton, Fort Scott, KS 66701
http://www.fortscott.edu/

**CONTACT** Dr. Clayton Tatro, President
**Telephone:** 620-223-2700

**GENERAL INFORMATION** Public Institution. Founded 1919. **Accreditation:** Regional (NCA). **Total program enrollment:** 891.

**PROGRAM(S) OFFERED**
• **Administrative Assistant and Secretarial Science, General** *3 students enrolled* • **Banking and Financial Support Services** • **Cosmetology/Cosmetologist, General** *6 students enrolled* • **Criminal Justice/Police Science** • **Data Processing and Data Processing Technology/Technician** • **Emergency Medical Technology/Technician (EMT Paramedic)** • **Farm/Farm and Ranch Management** • **Graphic and Printing Equipment Operator, General Production** • **Health Aide** • **Health Aides/Attendants/Orderlies, Other** • **Heating, Air Conditioning, Ventilation and Refrigeration Maintenance Technology/Technician (HAC, HACR, HVAC, HVACR)** *8 students enrolled* • **Home Health Aide/Home Attendant** • **Medical Administrative/Executive Assistant and Medical Secretary** • **Medication Aide** • **Phlebotomy/Phlebotomist** • **Retailing and Retail Operations** *1 student enrolled* • **Teacher Assistant/Aide** • **Truck and Bus Driver/Commercial Vehicle Operation** *286 students enrolled* • **Water Quality and Wastewater Treatment Management and Recycling Technology/Technician** *14 students enrolled*

**STUDENT SERVICES** Academic or career counseling, employment services for current students, placement services for program completers, remedial services.

## Garden City Community College

801 Campus Drive, Garden City, KS 67846-6399
http://www.gcccks.edu/

**CONTACT** Carol Ballantyne, President
**Telephone:** 620-276-7611

**GENERAL INFORMATION** Public Institution. Founded 1919. **Accreditation:** Regional (NCA). **Total program enrollment:** 908.

**PROGRAM(S) OFFERED**
• **Administrative Assistant and Secretarial Science, General** • **Automobile/Automotive Mechanics Technology/Technician** • **Cosmetology/Cosmetologist, General** *13 students enrolled* • **Emergency Care Attendant (EMT Ambulance)** • **Fire Science/Firefighting** • **Health Aide** • **Health Aides/Attendants/Orderlies, Other** • **Home Health Aide/Home Attendant** • **Licensed Practical/Vocational Nurse Training (LPN, LVN, Cert, Dipl, AAS)** *13 students enrolled* • **Manufacturing Technology/Technician** • **Medication Aide** • **Nail Technician/Specialist and Manicurist** • **Nurse/Nursing Assistant/Aide and Patient Care Assistant** • **Welding Technology/Welder**

**STUDENT SERVICES** Academic or career counseling, daycare for children of students, employment services for current students, remedial services.

## Hays Academy of Hair Design

119 West Tenth Street, Hays, KS 67601

**CONTACT** Summer Melvin, Owner
**Telephone:** 785-628-6624

**GENERAL INFORMATION** Private Institution. Founded 1977. **Total program enrollment:** 78. **Application fee:** $100.

**PROGRAM(S) OFFERED**
• **Cosmetology/Cosmetologist, General** *1500 hrs./$9900* • **Nail Technician/Specialist and Manicurist** *350 hrs./$3095*

**STUDENT SERVICES** Academic or career counseling, placement services for program completers.

## Highland Community College

606 West Main Street, Highland, KS 66035
http://www.highlandcc.edu/

**CONTACT** David E. Reist, President
**Telephone:** 785-442-6000

**GENERAL INFORMATION** Public Institution. Founded 1858. **Accreditation:** Regional (NCA). **Total program enrollment:** 1007.

**PROGRAM(S) OFFERED**
• **Administrative Assistant and Secretarial Science, General**

**STUDENT SERVICES** Academic or career counseling, employment services for current students, placement services for program completers, remedial services.

## Hutchinson Community College and Area Vocational School

1300 North Plum Street, Hutchinson, KS 67501-5894
http://www.hutchcc.edu/

**CONTACT** Edward E. Berger, President
**Telephone:** 620-665-3500

**GENERAL INFORMATION** Public Institution. Founded 1928. **Accreditation:** Regional (NCA); health information technology (AHIMA); radiologic technology: radiography (JRCERT). **Total program enrollment:** 2128.

**PROGRAM(S) OFFERED**
• **Administrative Assistant and Secretarial Science, General** *3 students enrolled* • **Agricultural Power Machinery Operation** • **Autobody/Collision and Repair Technology/Technician** *7 students enrolled* • **Automobile/Automotive Mechanics Technology/Technician** *7 students enrolled* • **Carpentry/Carpenter** *5 students enrolled* • **Child Care and Support Services Management** • **Computer and Information Sciences, General** *4 students enrolled* • **Criminal Justice/Police Science** *1 student enrolled* • **Health Information/Medical Records Technology/Technician** • **Licensed Practical/Vocational Nurse Training (LPN, LVN, Cert, Dipl, AAS)** *50 students enrolled* • **Machine Tool Technology/Machinist** • **Management Information Systems, General** • **Manufacturing Technology/Technician** *2 students enrolled* • **Medical Insurance Coding Specialist/Coder** *4 students enrolled* • **Medical Transcription/Transcriptionist** *5 students enrolled* • **Retailing and Retail Operations** • **Surgical Technology/Technologist** *9 students enrolled* • **Welding Technology/Welder** *4 students enrolled*

**STUDENT SERVICES** Academic or career counseling, daycare for children of students, employment services for current students, placement services for program completers, remedial services.

## Independence Community College

Brookside Drive and College Avenue, PO Box 708, Independence, KS 67301-0708
http://www.indycc.edu/

**CONTACT** Daniel Bain, President
**Telephone:** 620-331-4100

**GENERAL INFORMATION** Public Institution. Founded 1925. **Accreditation:** Regional (NCA). **Total program enrollment:** 515.

**PROGRAM(S) OFFERED**
• **Administrative Assistant and Secretarial Science, General** *3 students enrolled* • **Business Administration and Management, General** • **Cosmetology/Cosmetologist, General** *2 students enrolled* • **Drama and Dramatics/Theatre Arts, General** • **Emergency Care Attendant (EMT Ambulance)** *27 students enrolled* • **Foreign Languages and Literatures, General** *1 student enrolled* • **Health Aide** *74 students enrolled* • **Health Professions and Related Clinical Sciences, Other** *1 student enrolled* • **Health and Physical Education, General** *1 student enrolled* • **Home Health Aide/Home Attendant** *11 students enrolled* • **Retailing and Retail Operations** *1 student enrolled* • **Technical Theatre/Theatre Design and Technology** • **Word Processing** *1 student enrolled*

**STUDENT SERVICES** Academic or career counseling, daycare for children of students, remedial services.

## Johnson County Community College

12345 College Boulevard, Overland Park, KS 66210-1299
http://www.johnco.cc.ks.us/

**CONTACT** Terry Calaway, President
**Telephone:** 913-469-8500

**GENERAL INFORMATION** Public Institution. Founded 1967. **Accreditation:** Regional (NCA); dental hygiene (ADA); emergency medical services (JRCEMTP). **Total program enrollment:** 6737.

**PROGRAM(S) OFFERED**
• **Accounting Technology/Technician and Bookkeeping** *3 students enrolled* • **Administrative Assistant and Secretarial Science, General** *4 students enrolled* • **Aesthetician/Esthetician and Skin Care Specialist** • **Applied Horticulture/Horticultural Operations, General** *3 students enrolled* • **Automobile/Automotive Mechanics Technology/Technician** *7 students enrolled* • **Baking and Pastry Arts/Baker/Pastry Chef** • **Biology Technician/Biotechnology Laboratory Technician** *2 students enrolled* • **CAD/CADD Drafting and/or Design Technology/Technician** *10 students enrolled* • **Child Care and Support Services Management** *1 student enrolled* • **Civil Engineering Technology/Technician** • **Computer Programming, Specific Applications** *15 students enrolled* • **Computer Programming/Programmer, General** • **Computer Systems Networking and Telecommunications** *11 students enrolled* • **Construction Management** *13 students enrolled* • **Cosmetology/Cosmetologist, General** • **Criminal Justice/Law Enforcement Administration** *55 students enrolled* • **Data Modeling/Warehousing and Database Administration** • **Electrical and Power Transmission Installation/Installer, General** *3 students enrolled* • **Electrical/Electronics Equipment Installation and Repair, General** *8 students enrolled* • **Electrical/Electronics Maintenance and Repair Technology, Other** *2 students enrolled* • **Electrician** *12 students enrolled* • **Emergency Medical Technology/Technician (EMT Paramedic)** *41 students enrolled* • **Entrepreneurship/Entrepreneurial Studies** *2 students enrolled* • **Fashion Merchandising** *1 student enrolled* • **Fashion/Apparel Design** • **Ground Transportation, Other** *520 students enrolled* • **Heating, Air Conditioning, Ventilation and Refrigeration Maintenance Technology/Technician (HAC, HACR, HVAC, HVACR)** *13 students enrolled* • **Home Health Aide/Home Attendant** *27 students enrolled* • **Hotel/Motel Administration/Management** *1 student enrolled* • **Industrial Mechanics and Maintenance Technology** • **Interior Design** *1 student enrolled* • **Landscaping and Groundskeeping** *1 student enrolled* • **Language Interpretation and Translation** *6 students enrolled* • **Legal Assistant/Paralegal** *4 students enrolled* • **Licensed Practical/Vocational Nurse Training (LPN, LVN, Cert, Dipl, AAS)** *22 students enrolled* • **Marketing/Marketing Management, General** • **Mechanic and Repair Technologies/Technicians, Other** • **Medical Office Assistant/Specialist** • **Medical Transcription/Transcriptionist** *3 students enrolled* • **Medication Aide** *140 students enrolled* • **Nail Technician/Specialist and Manicurist** *5 students enrolled* • **Nurse/Nursing Assistant/Aide and Patient Care Assistant** *589 students enrolled* • **Restaurant, Culinary, and Catering Management/Manager** *3 students enrolled* • **Retailing and Retail Operations** *1 student enrolled* • **Selling Skills and Sales Operations** • **Sign Language Interpretation and Translation** *5 students enrolled* • **Web Page, Digital/Multimedia and Information Resources Design** • **Web/Multimedia Management and Webmaster** • **Welding Technology/Welder** *5 students enrolled*

**STUDENT SERVICES** Academic or career counseling, daycare for children of students, employment services for current students, placement services for program completers, remedial services.

## Kansas City Area Technical School

2220 North 59th Street, Kansas City, KS 66104
http://www.kckats.com/

**CONTACT** Barbara Schilling, Dean
**Telephone:** 913-627-4100

**GENERAL INFORMATION** Public Institution. Founded 1968. **Total program enrollment:** 244.

**PROGRAM(S) OFFERED**
• **Accounting Technology/Technician and Bookkeeping** *4 students enrolled* • **Administrative Assistant and Secretarial Science, General** *7 students enrolled* • **Animation, Interactive Technology, Video Graphics and Special Effects** *3 students enrolled* • **Autobody/Collision and Repair Technology/Technician** *57 hrs./$3300* • **Automobile/Automotive Mechanics Technology/Technician** *57 hrs./$3300* • **Building/Property Maintenance and Management** *1 student enrolled* • **CAD/CADD Drafting and/or Design Technology/Technician** *2 students enrolled* • **Carpentry/Carpenter** *10 students enrolled* • **Child Care Provider/Assistant** *6 students enrolled* • **Computer Installation and Repair Technology/Technician** *57 hrs./$3300* • **Computer Systems Networking and Telecommunications** • **Cosmetology/Cosmetologist, General** *59 hrs./$3984* • **Data Entry/Microcomputer Applications, General** *2 students enrolled* • **Food Preparation/Professional Cooking/Kitchen Assistant** *8 students enrolled* • **General Office Occupations and Clerical Services** *3 students enrolled* • **Heating, Air Conditioning, Ventilation and Refrigeration Maintenance Technology/Technician (HAC, HACR, HVAC, HVACR)** *57 hrs./$3300* • **Licensed Practical/Vocational Nurse Training (LPN, LVN, Cert, Dipl, AAS)** *46 hrs./$3880* • **Machine Tool Technology/Machinist** *6 students enrolled* • **Medical/Clinical Assistant** *5 students enrolled* • **Prepress/Desktop Publishing and Digital Imaging Design** *1 student enrolled* • **Welding Technology/Welder** *10 students enrolled*

**STUDENT SERVICES** Academic or career counseling, employment services for current students, placement services for program completers, remedial services.

## Kansas City Kansas Community College

7250 State Avenue, Kansas City, KS 66112-3003
http://www.kckcc.edu/

**CONTACT** Thomas R. Burke, President
**Telephone:** 913-334-1100

**GENERAL INFORMATION** Public Institution. Founded 1923. **Accreditation:** Regional (NCA); funeral service (ABFSE); physical therapy assisting (APTA); respiratory therapy technology (CoARC). **Total program enrollment:** 2053.

**PROGRAM(S) OFFERED**
• **Administrative Assistant and Secretarial Science, General** • **Computer Software Technology/Technician** • **Computer Systems Networking and Telecommunications** • **Corrections and Criminal Justice, Other** • **Corrections** • **Criminal Justice/Police Science** • **Emergency Care Attendant (EMT Ambulance)** • **Fire Protection and Safety Technology/Technician** • **Fire Services Administration** • **Substance Abuse/Addiction Counseling** • **Web Page, Digital/Multimedia and Information Resources Design**

**STUDENT SERVICES** Academic or career counseling, daycare for children of students, employment services for current students, remedial services.

## Kansas State University

Manhattan, KS 66506
http://www.ksu.edu/

**CONTACT** Jon Wefald, President
**Telephone:** 785-532-6250

**GENERAL INFORMATION** Public Institution. Founded 1863. **Accreditation:** Regional (NCA); art and design (NASAD); athletic training (JRCAT); computer science (ABET/CSAC); counseling (ACA); engineering technology (ABET/TAC); home economics (AAFCS); interior design: professional (CIDA); journalism and mass communications (ACEJMC); music (NASM); recreation and parks (NRPA); speech-language pathology (ASHA); theater (NAST). **Total program enrollment:** 18537. **Application fee:** $30.

**STUDENT SERVICES** Academic or career counseling, daycare for children of students, employment services for current students, placement services for program completers, remedial services.

## Kaw Area Technical School

5724 Huntoon, Topeka, KS 66604
http://www.kats.tec.ks.us/

**CONTACT** Roxanne Kelly, Dean
**Telephone:** 785-273-7140

**GENERAL INFORMATION** Private Institution. **Total program enrollment:** 172. **Application fee:** $25.

**PROGRAM(S) OFFERED**
• **Administrative Assistant and Secretarial Science, General** *8 students enrolled* • **Applied Horticulture/Horticultural Operations, General** *2 students enrolled* • **Autobody/Collision and Repair Technology/Technician** *48 hrs./$3264* • **Automobile/Automotive Mechanics Technology/Technician** *54 hrs./$4923* • **Building/Property Maintenance and Management** *12 students enrolled* • **CAD/CADD Drafting and/or Design Technology/Technician** *7 students enrolled* • **Cabinetmaking and Millwork/Millwright** *5 students enrolled* • **Child Care Provider/Assistant** *22 students enrolled* • **Civil Engineering Technology/Technician** • **Commercial Photography** *9 students enrolled* • **Computer Systems Networking and Telecommunications** *48 hrs./$3264* • **Diesel Mechanics Technology/Technician** *16 students enrolled* • **Electrical/Electronics Equipment Installation and Repair, General** *7 students enrolled* • **Food Preparation/Professional Cooking/Kitchen Assistant** *4 students enrolled* • **Graphic and Printing Equipment Operator, General Production** *22 students enrolled* • **Heating, Air Conditioning, Ventilation and Refrigeration Maintenance Technology/Technician (HAC, HACR, HVAC, HVACR)** *48 hrs./$3264* • **Home Furnishings and Equipment Installers** • **Industrial Mechanics and Maintenance Technology** *8 students enrolled* • **Legal Administrative Assistant/Secretary** *6 students enrolled* • **Licensed Practical/Vocational Nurse Training (LPN, LVN, Cert, Dipl, AAS)** *49 hrs./$3332* • **Machine Tool Technology/Machinist** *9 students enrolled* • **Medical Administrative/Executive Assistant and Medical Secretary** *8 students enrolled* • **Medication Aide** *177 students enrolled* • **Nurse/Nursing Assistant/Aide and Patient Care Assistant** *165 students enrolled* • **Parts, Warehousing, and Inventory Management Operations** *2 students enrolled* • **Surgical Technology/Technologist** *8 students enrolled* • **Welding Technology/Welder** *48 hrs./$3264*

**STUDENT SERVICES** Academic or career counseling, daycare for children of students, employment services for current students, placement services for program completers, remedial services.

## La Baron Hairdressing Academy

8119 Robinson, Overland Park, KS 66204
http://labarononline.com/

**CONTACT** Lois Wroble, President
**Telephone:** 913-642-0077

**GENERAL INFORMATION** Private Institution. Founded 1984. **Total program enrollment:** 24.

**PROGRAM(S) OFFERED**
• **Cosmetology/Cosmetologist, General** *1500 hrs./$10,457* • **Nail Technician/Specialist and Manicurist** *350 hrs./$1300*

**STUDENT SERVICES** Academic or career counseling, employment services for current students, placement services for program completers.

## Labette Community College

200 South 14th Street, Parsons, KS 67357-4299
http://www.labette.edu/

**CONTACT** Dr. George C. Knox, President
**Telephone:** 620-421-6700

**GENERAL INFORMATION** Public Institution. Founded 1923. **Accreditation:** Regional (NCA); radiologic technology: radiography (JRCERT). **Total program enrollment:** 670.

**PROGRAM(S) OFFERED**
• **Administrative Assistant and Secretarial Science, General** *1 student enrolled* • **Commercial and Advertising Art** *1 student enrolled* • **Computer Installation and Repair Technology/Technician** • **Computer Systems Networking and Telecommunications** • **Computer and Information Sciences, General** • **Corrections** • **Criminal Justice/Police Science** • **Legal Administrative Assistant/ Secretary** • **Licensed Practical/Vocational Nurse Training (LPN, LVN, Cert, Dipl, AAS)** *52 students enrolled* • **Management Information Systems, General**

**STUDENT SERVICES** Academic or career counseling, employment services for current students, remedial services.

## Manhattan Area Technical College

3136 Dickens Avenue, Manhattan, KS 66503-2499
http://www.matc.net/

**CONTACT** Dr. Robert J. Edleston, President
**Telephone:** 785-587-2800

**GENERAL INFORMATION** Public Institution. Founded 1965. **Accreditation:** Regional (NCA). **Total program enrollment:** 343. **Application fee:** $40.

**PROGRAM(S) OFFERED**
• **Administrative Assistant and Secretarial Science, General** *1 student enrolled* • **Autobody/Collision and Repair Technology/Technician** *12 students enrolled* • **Automobile/Automotive Mechanics Technology/Technician** *1 student enrolled* • **Carpentry/Carpenter** *6 students enrolled* • **Electrical and Power Transmission Installation/Installer, General** *16 students enrolled* • **Heating, Air Conditioning, Ventilation and Refrigeration Maintenance Technology/Technician (HAC, HACR, HVAC, HVACR)** *15 students enrolled* • **Licensed Practical/Vocational Nurse Training (LPN, LVN, Cert, Dipl, AAS)** *36 students enrolled* • **Welding Technology/Welder** *10 students enrolled*

**STUDENT SERVICES** Academic or career counseling, employment services for current students, placement services for program completers, remedial services.

## Manhattan Christian College

1415 Anderson Avenue, Manhattan, KS 66502-4081
http://www.mccks.edu/

**CONTACT** Kevin Ingram, President
**Telephone:** 785-539-3571

**GENERAL INFORMATION** Private Institution (Affiliated with Christian Churches and Churches of Christ). Founded 1927. **Accreditation:** Regional (NCA); state accredited or approved. **Total program enrollment:** 278. **Application fee:** $25.

**PROGRAM(S) OFFERED**
• **Bible/Biblical Studies**

**STUDENT SERVICES** Academic or career counseling, employment services for current students, placement services for program completers, remedial services.

## National American University

10310 Mastin, Overland Park, KS 66212
http://www.national.edu/

**CONTACT** Dr. Jerry Gallentine, University President/CEO
**Telephone:** 913-981-8700

**GENERAL INFORMATION** Private Institution. **Total program enrollment:** 69. **Application fee:** $25.

**STUDENT SERVICES** Academic or career counseling, employment services for current students, placement services for program completers, remedial services.

## Neosho County Community College

800 West 14th Street, Chanute, KS 66720-2699
http://www.neosho.edu/

**CONTACT** Dr. Vicky Smith, President
**Telephone:** 620-431-2820

**GENERAL INFORMATION** Public Institution. Founded 1936. **Accreditation:** Regional (NCA). **Total program enrollment:** 686.

**PROGRAM(S) OFFERED**
• **Accounting Technology/Technician and Bookkeeping** *13 students enrolled* • **Administrative Assistant and Secretarial Science, General** *2 students enrolled* • **Business Administration and Management, General** *9 students enrolled* • **Business/Commerce, General** • **Computer Programming/ Programmer, General** *1 student enrolled* • **Health and Physical Education/ Fitness, Other** • **Licensed Practical/Vocational Nurse Training (LPN, LVN, Cert, Dipl, AAS)** *123 students enrolled* • **Marketing/Marketing Management, General** *3 students enrolled* • **Medical Insurance Coding Specialist/Coder** *5 students enrolled* • **Medical/Health Management and Clinical Assistant/ Specialist** *12 students enrolled*

**STUDENT SERVICES** Academic or career counseling, remedial services.

## North Central Kansas Technical College

PO Box 507, 3033 US Highway 24, Beloit, KS 67420
http://www.ncktc.edu/

**CONTACT** Clark Coco, President
**Telephone:** 785-738-2276

**GENERAL INFORMATION** Public Institution. Founded 1963. **Accreditation:** Regional (NCA). **Total program enrollment:** 429. **Application fee:** $50.

**PROGRAM(S) OFFERED**
• **Administrative Assistant and Secretarial Science, General** *21 students enrolled* • **Autobody/Collision and Repair Technology/Technician** *35 hrs./$3207* • **Carpentry/Carpenter** *19 students enrolled* • **Diesel Mechanics Technology/ Technician** *69 hrs./$6400* • **Electrician** *14 students enrolled* • **Heating, Air Conditioning, Ventilation and Refrigeration Maintenance Technology/ Technician (HAC, HACR, HVAC, HVACR)** *17 students enrolled* • **Heavy Equipment Maintenance Technology/Technician** *35 hrs./$3886* • **Institutional Food Workers** *8 students enrolled* • **Licensed Practical/Vocational Nurse Training (LPN, LVN, Cert, Dipl, AAS)** *48 hrs./$2407* • **Management Information Systems, General** *2 students enrolled* • **Mason/Masonry** *10 students enrolled* • **Nurse/Nursing Assistant/Aide and Patient Care Assistant** *75 students enrolled* • **Nursing—Registered Nurse Training (RN, ASN, BSN, MSN)** *72 hrs./$4775* • **Pharmacy Technician/Assistant** *2 students enrolled* • **Retailing and Retail Operations** *13 students enrolled* • **Welding Technology/Welder** *37 hrs./$3207*

**STUDENT SERVICES** Academic or career counseling, employment services for current students, placement services for program completers, remedial services.

## Northeast Kansas Technical Center of Highland Community College

1501 West Riley Street, Atchison, KS 66002
http://www.nektc.net/

**CONTACT** Michael B. Rogg, Vice President of Trade and Technical Education
**Telephone:** 913-367-6204

**GENERAL INFORMATION** Public Institution. Founded 1965. **Accreditation:** State accredited or approved. **Total program enrollment:** 150.

**PROGRAM(S) OFFERED**
• **Administrative Assistant and Secretarial Science, General** *1116 hrs./$2877*
• **Autobody/Collision and Repair Technology/Technician** *2232 hrs./$2948*
• **Automobile/Automotive Mechanics Technology/Technician** *2232 hrs./$2948*
• **Carpentry/Carpenter** *4 students enrolled* • **Diesel Mechanics Technology/Technician** *2232 hrs./$2948* • **Electrician** *13 students enrolled* • **Heating, Air Conditioning, Ventilation and Refrigeration Maintenance Technology/Technician (HAC, HACR, HVAC, HVACR)** *5 students enrolled* • **Licensed Practical/Vocational Nurse Training (LPN, LVN, Cert, Dipl, AAS)** *1230 hrs./$6417* • **Medical/Clinical Assistant** *14 students enrolled* • **Welding Technology/Welder** *1116 hrs./$2920*

**STUDENT SERVICES** Academic or career counseling, employment services for current students, placement services for program completers, remedial services.

## Northwest Kansas Technical College

PO Box 668, 1209 Harrison Street, Goodland, KS 67735
http://www.nwktc.org/

**CONTACT** Kenneth A. Clouse, President
**Telephone:** 785-890-3641

**GENERAL INFORMATION** Public Institution. Founded 1964. **Accreditation:** State accredited or approved. **Total program enrollment:** 246. **Application fee:** $25.

**PROGRAM(S) OFFERED**
• **Administrative Assistant and Secretarial Science, General** *3 students enrolled*
• **Automobile/Automotive Mechanics Technology/Technician** *77 hrs./$9579*
• **Carpentry/Carpenter** *4 students enrolled* • **Civil Engineering Technology/Technician** *77 hrs./$5480* • **Computer Systems Networking and Telecommunications** *77 hrs./$5680* • **Cosmetology/Cosmetologist, General** *9 students enrolled* • **Diesel Mechanics Technology/Technician** *77 hrs./$5965* • **Electrician** *77 hrs./$5775* • **Heating, Air Conditioning, Ventilation and Refrigeration Maintenance Technology/Technician (HAC, HACR, HVAC, HVACR)** *4 students enrolled* • **Medical/Clinical Assistant** *5 students enrolled* • **Nail Technician/Specialist and Manicurist** • **Prepress/Desktop Publishing and Digital Imaging Design** *5 students enrolled* • **System, Networking, and LAN/WAN Management/Manager** • **Welding Technology/Welder** *46 hrs./$3600*

**STUDENT SERVICES** Academic or career counseling, daycare for children of students, employment services for current students, placement services for program completers, remedial services.

## Old Town Barber and Beauty College

1207 East Douglas Avenue, Wichita, KS 67211-1693
http://www.otbbcollege.com/

**CONTACT** Larry Nienhueser, Director Owner
**Telephone:** 316-264-4891 Ext. 11

**GENERAL INFORMATION** Private Institution. Founded 1955. **Total program enrollment:** 43. **Application fee:** $50.

**PROGRAM(S) OFFERED**
• **Barbering/Barber** *1500 hrs./$11,960* • **Cosmetology and Related Personal Grooming Arts, Other** *2000 hrs./$12,785* • **Cosmetology/Cosmetologist, General** *14 students enrolled*

**STUDENT SERVICES** Placement services for program completers.

## Ottawa University

1001 South Cedar, Ottawa, KS 66067-3399
http://www.ottawa.edu/

**CONTACT** Dr. Dennis Tyner, Vice President and Provost of the College
**Telephone:** 785-242-5200

**GENERAL INFORMATION** Private Institution. Founded 1865. **Accreditation:** Regional (NCA). **Total program enrollment:** 539. **Application fee:** $50.

**STUDENT SERVICES** Academic or career counseling, employment services for current students, placement services for program completers, remedial services.

## Ottawa University–Kansas City

4370 W. 109th Street, Suite 200, Overland Park, KS 66211
http://www.ottawa.edu/

**CONTACT** Terry Haines, Vice President and Provost Adult and Professional Studies
**Telephone:** 913-451-1431

**GENERAL INFORMATION** Private Institution (Affiliated with American Baptist Churches in the U.S.A.). **Total program enrollment:** 31. **Application fee:** $50.

**STUDENT SERVICES** Academic or career counseling.

## Pinnacle Career Institute

1601 West 23rd Street, Suite 200, Lawrence, KS 66046-2743
http://www.pcitraining.edu/

**CONTACT** Jeremy Cooper, Executive Director
**Telephone:** 785-841-9640

**GENERAL INFORMATION** Private Institution. **Total program enrollment:** 101. **Application fee:** $50.

**PROGRAM(S) OFFERED**
• **Business Operations Support and Secretarial Services, Other** *4 students enrolled* • **Health and Physical Education/Fitness, Other** *15 students enrolled*
• **Massage Therapy/Therapeutic Massage** *47 students enrolled* • **Medical Administrative/Executive Assistant and Medical Secretary** *6 students enrolled*
• **Medical/Clinical Assistant** *35 students enrolled*

**STUDENT SERVICES** Academic or career counseling, employment services for current students, placement services for program completers.

## Pittsburg State University

1701 South Broadway, Pittsburg, KS 66762
http://www.pittstate.edu/

**CONTACT** Tom W. Bryant, President
**Telephone:** 620-231-7000

**GENERAL INFORMATION** Public Institution. Founded 1903. **Accreditation:** Regional (NCA); counseling (ACA); engineering technology (ABET/TAC); home economics (AAFCS); music (NASM). **Total program enrollment:** 5873. **Application fee:** $30.

**PROGRAM(S) OFFERED**
• **Automobile/Automotive Mechanics Technology/Technician** • **Electrical/Electronics Equipment Installation and Repair, General** *12 students enrolled*

**STUDENT SERVICES** Academic or career counseling, employment services for current students, placement services for program completers, remedial services.

## Pratt Community College

348 NE State Road 61, Pratt, KS 67124-8317
http://www.prattcc.edu/

**CONTACT** Wm A. Wojciechowski, President
**Telephone:** 620-672-5641

**GENERAL INFORMATION** Public Institution. Founded 1938. **Accreditation:** Regional (NCA). **Total program enrollment:** 719.

**PROGRAM(S) OFFERED**
• **Automobile/Automotive Mechanics Technology/Technician** • **Electrical and Power Transmission Installation/Installer, General** • **Licensed Practical/ Vocational Nurse Training (LPN, LVN, Cert, Dipl, AAS)** *43 students enrolled*

**STUDENT SERVICES** Academic or career counseling, employment services for current students, placement services for program completers, remedial services.

## Regency Beauty Institute

12517 S. Rogers Road, Olathe, KS 66062
http://www.regencybeauty.com/

**CONTACT** J. Hayes Batson, President CEO
**Telephone:** 800-787-6456

**GENERAL INFORMATION** Private Institution. **Total program enrollment:** 62. **Application fee:** $100.

**PROGRAM(S) OFFERED**
• **Cosmetology/Cosmetologist, General** *1500 hrs./$16,011*

**STUDENT SERVICES** Academic or career counseling, placement services for program completers.

## Regency Beauty Institute

1930 SW Wanamaker Road, Suite A, Topeka, KS 66604

**GENERAL INFORMATION** Private Institution. **Total program enrollment:** 36. **Application fee:** $100.

**PROGRAM(S) OFFERED**
• **Cosmetology/Cosmetologist, General** *1500 hrs./$16,011*

**STUDENT SERVICES** Academic or career counseling, placement services for program completers.

## Salina Area Technical School

2562 Scanlan Avenue, Salina, KS 67401
http://www.salinatech.com/

**CONTACT** Duane Custer, Director
**Telephone:** 785-309-3100

**GENERAL INFORMATION** Public Institution. Founded 1965. **Total program enrollment:** 216.

**PROGRAM(S) OFFERED**
• **Administrative Assistant and Secretarial Science, General** *4 students enrolled* • **Autobody/Collision and Repair Technology/Technician** *42 hrs./$3466* • **Automobile/Automotive Mechanics Technology/Technician** *59 hrs./$10,359* • **CAD/CADD Drafting and/or Design Technology/Technician** *52 hrs./$3286* • **Carpentry/Carpenter** *6 students enrolled* • **Commercial and Advertising Art** *59 hrs./$6612* • **Dental Assisting/Assistant** *13 students enrolled* • **Diesel Mechanics Technology/Technician** *59 hrs./$6852* • **Heating, Air Conditioning, Ventilation and Refrigeration Maintenance Technology/Technician (HAC, HACR, HVAC, HVACR)** *17 students enrolled* • **Machine Tool Technology/Machinist** *5 students enrolled* • **Medical/Clinical Assistant** *5 students enrolled* • **Water Quality and Wastewater Treatment Management and Recycling Technology/ Technician** *29 students enrolled* • **Welding Technology/Welder** *49 hrs./$3416*

**STUDENT SERVICES** Academic or career counseling, employment services for current students, placement services for program completers, remedial services.

## Seward County Community College

PO Box 1137, Liberal, KS 67905-1137
http://www.sccc.edu/

**CONTACT** Dr. Duane Dunn, President
**Telephone:** 620-624-1951

**GENERAL INFORMATION** Public Institution. Founded 1969. **Accreditation:** Regional (NCA); medical laboratory technology (NAACLS); practical nursing (NLN); surgical technology (ARCST). **Total program enrollment:** 707.

**PROGRAM(S) OFFERED**
• **Administrative Assistant and Secretarial Science, General** *2 students enrolled* • **Agricultural Business and Management, General** • **Autobody/Collision and Repair Technology/Technician** *12 students enrolled* • **Automobile/Automotive Mechanics Technology/Technician** *14 students enrolled* • **Business, Management, Marketing, and Related Support Services, Other** • **Carpentry/ Carpenter** *6 students enrolled* • **Cosmetology/Cosmetologist, General** *12 students enrolled* • **Diesel Mechanics Technology/Technician** *10 students enrolled* • **Drafting and Design Technology/Technician, General** *3 students enrolled* • **Heating, Air Conditioning, Ventilation and Refrigeration Maintenance Technology/Technician (HAC, HACR, HVAC, HVACR)** *12 students enrolled* • **Licensed Practical/Vocational Nurse Training (LPN, LVN, Cert, Dipl, AAS)** *22 students enrolled* • **Machine Tool Technology/Machinist** *2 students enrolled* • **Medical/Clinical Assistant** *14 students enrolled* • **Parts, Warehousing, and Inventory Management Operations** *2 students enrolled* • **Surgical Technology/ Technologist** *3 students enrolled* • **Welding Technology/Welder** *12 students enrolled*

**STUDENT SERVICES** Academic or career counseling, employment services for current students, placement services for program completers, remedial services.

## Sidney's Hair Dressing College

916 E. Fourth Street, Hutchinson, KS 67501
http://www.sidneyshair.com/

**CONTACT** William Wyer, President
**Telephone:** 620-662-5481

**GENERAL INFORMATION** Private Institution. **Total program enrollment:** 67. **Application fee:** $100.

**PROGRAM(S) OFFERED**
• **Cosmetology/Cosmetologist, General** *1500 hrs./$12,400*

**STUDENT SERVICES** Academic or career counseling, employment services for current students, placement services for program completers.

## Southwestern College

100 College Street, Winfield, KS 67156-2499
http://www.sckans.edu/

**CONTACT** W. Richard Merriman, Jr., President
**Telephone:** 620-229-6000

**GENERAL INFORMATION** Private Institution. Founded 1885. **Accreditation:** Regional (NCA); music (NASM). **Total program enrollment:** 582. **Application fee:** $25.

**STUDENT SERVICES** Academic or career counseling, employment services for current students, placement services for program completers, remedial services.

## Tabor College

400 South Jefferson, Hillsboro, KS 67063
http://www.tabor.edu/

**CONTACT** Dr. Jules Glanzer, President
**Telephone:** 620-947-3121

**GENERAL INFORMATION** Private Institution. Founded 1908. **Accreditation:** Regional (NCA); music (NASM). **Total program enrollment:** 483. **Application fee:** $30.

**STUDENT SERVICES** Academic or career counseling, employment services for current students, placement services for program completers, remedial services.

## University of Saint Mary

4100 South Fourth Street Trafficway, Leavenworth, KS 66048-5082
http://www.stmary.edu/

**CONTACT** Diane Steele SCL, PhD, President
**Telephone:** 913-682-5151

**GENERAL INFORMATION** Private Institution. Founded 1923. **Accreditation:** Regional (NCA). **Total program enrollment:** 508. **Application fee:** $25.

**PROGRAM(S) OFFERED**
• **Health/Health Care Administration/Management** *2 students enrolled*

**STUDENT SERVICES** Academic or career counseling, daycare for children of students, employment services for current students, placement services for program completers, remedial services.

## Vatterott College

3639 North Comotara, Wichita, KS 67226
http://www.vatterott-college.edu/

**CONTACT** Diana Otis, Director
**Telephone:** 316-634-0066

**GENERAL INFORMATION** Private Institution. Founded 1969. **Total program enrollment:** 175.

**PROGRAM(S) OFFERED**
• **Computer Programming/Programmer, General** *15 students enrolled* • **Electrician** *14 students enrolled* • **Heating, Air Conditioning, Ventilation and Refrigeration Maintenance Technology/Technician (HAC, HACR, HVAC, HVACR)** *12 students enrolled* • **Information Technology** *9 students enrolled* • **Medical Office Assistant/Specialist** *15 students enrolled* • **Medical/Clinical Assistant** *28 students enrolled*

**STUDENT SERVICES** Academic or career counseling, employment services for current students, placement services for program completers.

## Vernon's Kansas School of Cosmetology–Central

501 East Pawnee, Suite 525, Wichita, KS 67211
http://www.vksc.edu/

**CONTACT** Fredrick J. Laurino, President
**Telephone:** 316-265-2629

**GENERAL INFORMATION** Private Institution. Founded 1938. **Total program enrollment:** 16. **Application fee:** $100.

**PROGRAM(S) OFFERED**
• **Cosmetology and Related Personal Grooming Arts, Other** *4 students enrolled* • **Cosmetology/Cosmetologist, General** *1500 hrs./$9980* • **Nail Technician/Specialist and Manicurist** *350 hrs./$2188*

**STUDENT SERVICES** Academic or career counseling, employment services for current students, placement services for program completers.

## Washburn University

1700 Southwest College Avenue, Topeka, KS 66621
http://www.washburn.edu/

**CONTACT** Jerry B. Farley, President
**Telephone:** 785-670-1010

**GENERAL INFORMATION** Public Institution. Founded 1865. **Accreditation:** Regional (NCA); art and design (NASAD); health information technology (AHIMA); music (NASM); physical therapy assisting (APTA); radiologic technology: radiography (JRCERT). **Total program enrollment:** 4412. **Application fee:** $20.

**PROGRAM(S) OFFERED**
• **Administrative Assistant and Secretarial Science, General** • **Diagnostic Medical Sonography/Sonographer and Ultrasound Technician** *23 students enrolled* • **Entrepreneurship/Entrepreneurial Studies** • **Health Information/Medical Records Technology/Technician** *4 students enrolled* • **Hospital and Health Care Facilities Administration/Management** • **Human Services, General** • **Legal Administrative Assistant/Secretary** • **Legal Assistant/Paralegal** *6 students enrolled* • **Legal Studies, General** • **Medical Insurance Coding Specialist/Coder** • **Medical Radiologic Technology/Science—Radiation Therapist** *71 students enrolled* • **Mental and Social Health Services and Allied Professions, Other** *4 students enrolled* • **Non-Profit/Public/Organizational Management** *2 students enrolled* • **Nursing, Other** *1 student enrolled* • **Office Management and Supervision** • **Political Science and Government, General** • **Purchasing, Procurement/Acquisitions and Contracts Management** • **Respiratory Care Therapy/Therapist** • **Social Work, Other** *1 student enrolled* • **Substance Abuse/Addiction Counseling** *10 students enrolled*

**STUDENT SERVICES** Academic or career counseling, employment services for current students, placement services for program completers, remedial services.

## Wichita Area Technical College

301 South Grove Street, Wichita, KS 67211
http://www.wichitatech.com/

**CONTACT** Pete Gustaf, President
**Telephone:** 316-677-9400

**GENERAL INFORMATION** Public Institution. Founded 1963. **Accreditation:** Dental assisting (ADA); medical laboratory technology (NAACLS); surgical technology (ARCST); state accredited or approved. **Total program enrollment:** 840.

**PROGRAM(S) OFFERED**
• **Autobody/Collision and Repair Technology/Technician** *15 students enrolled* • **Automobile/Automotive Mechanics Technology/Technician** *40 hrs./$5261* • **CAD/CADD Drafting and/or Design Technology/Technician** *5 students enrolled* • **Carpentry/Carpenter** *5 students enrolled* • **Dental Assisting/Assistant** *12 students enrolled* • **Diesel Mechanics Technology/Technician** *4 students enrolled* • **Dietitian Assistant** *4 students enrolled* • **Health Aide** *5 hrs./$425* • **Heating, Air Conditioning, Ventilation and Refrigeration Maintenance Technology/Technician (HAC, HACR, HVAC, HVACR)** *8 students enrolled* • **Licensed Practical/Vocational Nurse Training (LPN, LVN, Cert, Dipl, AAS)** *40 hrs./$3640* • **Machine Tool Technology/Machinist** *5 students enrolled* • **Mechanical Engineering/Mechanical Technology/Technician** *15 hrs./$2430* • **Medical/Clinical Assistant** *22 students enrolled* • **Sheet Metal Technology/Sheetworking** *15 hrs./$2822* • **Surgical Technology/Technologist** *23 students enrolled* • **Truck and Bus Driver/Commercial Vehicle Operation** *90 students enrolled* • **Welding Technology/Welder** *52 hrs./$4624* • **Woodworking, Other** *11 students enrolled*

**STUDENT SERVICES** Academic or career counseling, placement services for program completers, remedial services.

## Wichita State University

1845 North Fairmount, Wichita, KS 67260
http://www.wichita.edu/

**CONTACT** Donald L. Beggs, President
**Telephone:** 316-978-3456

**GENERAL INFORMATION** Public Institution. Founded 1895. **Accreditation:** Regional (NCA); audiology (ASHA); dance (NASD); dental hygiene (ADA); medical technology (NAACLS); music (NASM); speech-language pathology (ASHA). **Total program enrollment:** 9139. **Application fee:** $30.

**PROGRAM(S) OFFERED**
• **Art/Art Studies, General** • **Communication Disorders, General** *2 students enrolled* • **Criminal Justice/Safety Studies** *6 students enrolled* • **Emergency Medical Technology/Technician (EMT Paramedic)**

**STUDENT SERVICES** Academic or career counseling, daycare for children of students, employment services for current students, placement services for program completers, remedial services.

## Wichita Technical Institute

942 S West Street, Wichita, KS 67213-1626
http://www.wti.edu/

**CONTACT** J. Barry Mannion, President
**Telephone:** 316-943-2241

**GENERAL INFORMATION** Private Institution. **Total program enrollment:** 982.

**PROGRAM(S) OFFERED**
• **Computer Technology/Computer Systems Technology** *55 students enrolled* • **Electrical/Electronics Equipment Installation and Repair, General** *50 students enrolled* • **Heating, Air Conditioning and Refrigeration Technology/Technician (ACH/ACR/ACHR/HRAC/HVAC/AC Technology)** *66 students enrolled* • **Medical Insurance Coding Specialist/Coder** *46 students enrolled* • **Medical/Clinical Assistant** *209 students enrolled*

**STUDENT SERVICES** Academic or career counseling, employment services for current students, placement services for program completers.

## Wright Business School

8951 Metcalf Avenue, Overland Park, KS 66212

**CONTACT** John Mucci, President
**Telephone:** 913-385-7700

**GENERAL INFORMATION** Private Institution. **Total program enrollment:** 899. **Application fee:** $100.

**PROGRAM(S) OFFERED**
• **Accounting** *44 students enrolled* • **Administrative Assistant and Secretarial Science, General** *37 students enrolled* • **Computer Installation and Repair Technology/Technician** *10 students enrolled* • **Computer Technology/Computer Systems Technology** • **Computer and Information Systems Security** *39 students enrolled* • **Information Science/Studies** *32 students enrolled* • **Medical Insurance Coding Specialist/Coder** *53 students enrolled* • **Medical Transcription/Transcriptionist** *11 students enrolled* • **Medical/Clinical Assistant** *150 students enrolled* • **Surgical Technology/Technologist** *26 students enrolled*

**STUDENT SERVICES** Academic or career counseling, placement services for program completers.

## Xenon International School of Hair Design

3804 West Douglas, Wichita, KS 67203
http://www.xenonintl.com/

**CONTACT** Kim McIntosh, President
**Telephone:** 316-943-5516

**GENERAL INFORMATION** Private Institution. **Total program enrollment:** 156.

**PROGRAM(S) OFFERED**
• **Aesthetician/Esthetician and Skin Care Specialist** *650 hrs./$6100* • **Cosmetology, Barber/Styling, and Nail Instructor** *300 hrs./$2100* • **Cosmetology/Cosmetologist, General** *1500 hrs./$13,300* • **Nail Technician/Specialist and Manicurist** *350 hrs./$2200*

**STUDENT SERVICES** Academic or career counseling, employment services for current students, placement services for program completers.

## Z Hair Academy

2429 Iowa Street, Suite E, Lawrence, KS 66046
http://www.zcoz.com/about.htm

**CONTACT** Ron McKenzie, Co-Owner
**Telephone:** 785-749-1488

**GENERAL INFORMATION** Private Institution. **Total program enrollment:** 58. **Application fee:** $150.

**PROGRAM(S) OFFERED**
• **Cosmetology/Cosmetologist, General** *1500 hrs./$10,527*

# KENTUCKY

## Ashland Community and Technical College

1400 College Drive, Ashland, KY 41101-3683
http://www.ashland.kctcs.edu/

**CONTACT** Dr. Gregory D. Adkins, President/CEO
**Telephone:** 606-326-2000

**GENERAL INFORMATION** Public Institution. Founded 1937. **Accreditation:** Regional (SACS/CC); respiratory therapy technology (CoARC); surgical technology (ARCST); state accredited or approved. **Total program enrollment:** 1808.

**PROGRAM(S) OFFERED**
• **Automobile/Automotive Mechanics Technology/Technician** *8 students enrolled* • **Business Administration and Management, General** *14 students enrolled* • **Carpentry/Carpenter** *12 students enrolled* • **Child Care Provider/Assistant** *42 students enrolled* • **Computer and Information Sciences, General** *9 students enrolled* • **Cosmetology/Cosmetologist, General** *11 students enrolled* • **Culinary Arts/Chef Training** *15 students enrolled* • **Diesel Mechanics Technology/Technician** *36 students enrolled* • **Drafting and Design Technology/Technician, General** *9 students enrolled* • **Electrician** *127 students enrolled* • **Executive Assistant/Executive Secretary** *116 students enrolled* • **Heating, Air Conditioning, Ventilation and Refrigeration Maintenance Technology/Technician (HAC, HACR, HVAC, HVACR)** *16 students enrolled* • **Industrial Mechanics and Maintenance Technology** *29 students enrolled* • **Licensed Practical/Vocational Nurse Training (LPN, LVN, Cert, Dipl, AAS)** *6 students enrolled* • **Machine Shop Technology/Assistant** *17 students enrolled* • **Pharmacy Technician/Assistant** *1 student enrolled* • **Surgical Technology/Technologist** *2 students enrolled* • **Welding Technology/Welder** *142 students enrolled*

**STUDENT SERVICES** Academic or career counseling, daycare for children of students, employment services for current students, placement services for program completers, remedial services.

## ATA Career Education

10180 Linn Station Road, Suite A200, Louisville, KY 40223
http://www.atai.com/

**CONTACT** Donald A. Jones
**Telephone:** 502-371-8330 Ext. 363

**GENERAL INFORMATION** Private Institution. **Total program enrollment:** 320. **Application fee:** $25.

**PROGRAM(S) OFFERED**
• **Clinical/Medical Laboratory Science and Allied Professions, Other** • **Dental Assisting/Assistant** *52 students enrolled* • **Medical Insurance Coding Specialist/Coder** *128 students enrolled* • **Medical Reception/Receptionist** *49 students enrolled* • **Nursing, Other** • **System Administration/Administrator** *14 students enrolled*

**STUDENT SERVICES** Academic or career counseling, employment services for current students, placement services for program completers, remedial services.

## Barrett and Company School of Hair Design

973 Kimberly Square, Nicholasville, KY 40356

**CONTACT** Jamie B. Lovern, Director
**Telephone:** 859-885-9136

**GENERAL INFORMATION** Private Institution. Founded 1984. **Total program enrollment:** 87.

**PROGRAM(S) OFFERED**
• **Cosmetology and Related Personal Grooming Arts, Other** *1000 hrs./$6600* • **Cosmetology, Barber/Styling, and Nail Instructor** • **Cosmetology/Cosmetologist, General** *1800 hrs./$9535* • **Nail Technician/Specialist and Manicurist** *600 hrs./$3600*

**STUDENT SERVICES** Academic or career counseling.

## Beckfield College

16 Spiral Drive, Florence, KY 41042
http://www.beckfield.edu/

**CONTACT** Dr. Ronald A. Swanson, President
**Telephone:** 859-371-9393

**GENERAL INFORMATION** Private Institution. Founded 1984. **Accreditation:** State accredited or approved. **Total program enrollment:** 441. **Application fee:** $20.

**PROGRAM(S) OFFERED**
• **Legal Assistant/Paralegal** *3 students enrolled* • **Medical Office Assistant/Specialist** *13 students enrolled*

**STUDENT SERVICES** Academic or career counseling, employment services for current students, placement services for program completers, remedial services.

## Bellefonte Academy of Beauty

420 Belfont Street, Russell, KY 41169

**CONTACT** William C. Stull, Jr., School Director/Owner
**Telephone:** 606-833-5446

**GENERAL INFORMATION** Private Institution. **Total program enrollment:** 111.

**PROGRAM(S) OFFERED**
• **Cosmetology, Barber/Styling, and Nail Instructor** *1000 hrs./$6600* • **Cosmetology/Cosmetologist, General** *1800 hrs./$12,300* • **Nail Technician/Specialist and Manicurist** *600 hrs./$3900*

**STUDENT SERVICES** Academic or career counseling, placement services for program completers.

## Big Sandy Community and Technical College

One Bert T. Combs Drive, Prestonsburg, KY 41653-1815
http://www.bigsandy.kctcs.edu/

**CONTACT** Dr. George D. Edwards, President/CEO
**Telephone:** 606-886-3863 Ext. 0

**GENERAL INFORMATION** Public Institution. Founded 1964. **Accreditation:** Regional (SACS/CC); dental hygiene (ADA); state accredited or approved. **Total program enrollment:** 1929.

**PROGRAM(S) OFFERED**
• **Autobody/Collision and Repair Technology/Technician** *5 students enrolled* • **Automobile/Automotive Mechanics Technology/Technician** *49 students enrolled* • **Business Administration and Management, General** *63 students enrolled* • **Carpentry/Carpenter** *6 students enrolled* • **Communications Technology/Technician** *1 student enrolled* • **Computer and Information Sciences, General** *19 students enrolled* • **Cosmetology/Cosmetologist, General** *2 students enrolled* • **Diesel Mechanics Technology/Technician** *59 students enrolled* • **Drafting and Design Technology/Technician, General** *7 students enrolled* • **Electrician** *10 students enrolled* • **Engineering Technology, General** *35 students enrolled* • **Executive Assistant/Executive Secretary** *9 students enrolled* • **Heating, Air Conditioning, Ventilation and Refrigeration Maintenance Technology/Technician (HAC, HACR, HVAC, HVACR)** *4 students enrolled* • **Industrial Mechanics and Maintenance Technology** *18 students enrolled* • **Licensed Practical/Vocational Nurse Training (LPN, LVN, Cert, Dipl, AAS)** *32 students enrolled* • **Mason/Masonry** *2 students enrolled* • **Medical Administrative/Executive Assistant and Medical Secretary** *84 students enrolled* • **Respiratory Care Therapy/Therapist** *19 students enrolled* • **Survey Technology/Surveying** *9 students enrolled* • **Welding Technology/Welder** *2 students enrolled*

**STUDENT SERVICES** Academic or career counseling, remedial services.

## Bluegrass Community and Technical College

470 Cooper Drive, Lexington, KY 40506-0235
http://www.bluegrass.kctcs.edu/

**CONTACT** Dr. Augusta Julian, President/CEO
**Telephone:** 859-246-2400

**GENERAL INFORMATION** Public Institution. Founded 1965. **Accreditation:** Regional (SACS/CC); dental hygiene (ADA); dental laboratory technology (ADA). **Total program enrollment:** 5892.

**PROGRAM(S) OFFERED**
• **Aesthetician/Esthetician and Skin Care Specialist** *15 students enrolled* • **Applied Horticulture/Horticultural Operations, General** *14 students enrolled* • **Autobody/Collision and Repair Technology/Technician** *28 students enrolled* • **Automobile/Automotive Mechanics Technology/Technician** *66 students enrolled* • **Carpentry/Carpenter** *138 students enrolled* • **Cartography** *7 students enrolled* • **Child Care Provider/Assistant** *13 students enrolled* • **Cinematography and Film/Video Production** *24 students enrolled* • **Clinical/Medical Laboratory Technician** *14 students enrolled* • **Computer and Information Sciences, General** *48 students enrolled* • **Cosmetology/Cosmetologist, General** *6 students enrolled* • **Data Processing and Data Processing Technology/Technician** *5 students enrolled* • **Dental Hygiene/Hygienist** *18 students enrolled* • **Dental Laboratory Technology/Technician** *10 students enrolled* • **Drafting and Design Technology/Technician, General** *6 students enrolled* • **Electrician** *217 students enrolled* • **Engineering Technology, General** *209 students enrolled* • **Environmental Engineering Technology/Environmental Technology** *3 students enrolled* • **Equestrian/Equine Studies** *8 students enrolled* • **Executive Assistant/Executive Secretary** *55 students enrolled* • **Fire Science/Firefighting** *3 students enrolled* • **Heating, Air Conditioning, Ventilation and Refrigeration Maintenance Technology/Technician (HAC, HACR, HVAC, HVACR)** *5 students enrolled* • **Industrial Mechanics and Maintenance Technology** *33 students enrolled* • **Licensed Practical/Vocational Nurse Training (LPN, LVN, Cert, Dipl, AAS)** *175 students enrolled* • **Machine Shop Technology/Assistant** *62 students enrolled* • **Mason/Masonry** *38 students enrolled* • **Medical Administrative/Executive Assistant and Medical Secretary** *29 students enrolled* • **Medical/Clinical Assistant** *36 students enrolled* • **Respiratory Care Therapy/Therapist** *5 students enrolled* • **Securities Services Administration/Management** *7 students enrolled* • **Surgical Technology/Technologist** *20 students enrolled* • **Teacher Assistant/Aide** *2 students enrolled* • **Welding Technology/Welder** *3 students enrolled*

**STUDENT SERVICES** Academic or career counseling, employment services for current students, placement services for program completers, remedial services.

## Bowling Green Technical College

1845 Loop Drive, Bowling Green, KY 42101
http://www.bowlinggreen.kctcs.edu/

**CONTACT** Dr. Nathan L. Hodges, CEO/President
**Telephone:** 270-901-1000

**GENERAL INFORMATION** Public Institution. Founded 1938. **Accreditation:** Respiratory therapy technology (CoARC); state accredited or approved. **Total program enrollment:** 909.

**PROGRAM(S) OFFERED**
• **Autobody/Collision and Repair Technology/Technician** *27 students enrolled* • **Automobile/Automotive Mechanics Technology/Technician** *46 students enrolled* • **Communications Technology/Technician** *1 student enrolled* • **Computer Technology/Computer Systems Technology** *3 students enrolled* • **Computer and Information Sciences, General** *93 students enrolled* • **Culinary Arts/Chef Training** *17 students enrolled* • **Diagnostic Medical Sonography/Sonographer and Ultrasound Technician** *7 students enrolled* • **Drafting and Design Technology/Technician, General** *7 students enrolled* • **Electrician** *7 students enrolled* • **Electromechanical and Instrumentation and Maintenance Technologies/Technicians, Other** *9 students enrolled* • **Engineering Technology, General** *222 students enrolled* • **Executive Assistant/Executive Secretary** *146 students enrolled* • **Health Unit Coordinator/Ward Clerk** *9 students enrolled* • **Heating, Air Conditioning, Ventilation and Refrigeration Maintenance Technology/Technician (HAC, HACR, HVAC, HVACR)** *5 students enrolled* • **Industrial Mechanics and Maintenance Technology** *18 students enrolled* • **Licensed Practical/Vocational Nurse Training (LPN, LVN, Cert, Dipl, AAS)** *46 students enrolled* • **Machine Shop Technology/Assistant** *12 students enrolled* • **Medical Administrative/Executive Assistant and Medical Secretary** *83 students enrolled* • **Respiratory Care Therapy/Therapist** *2 students enrolled* • **Surgical Technology/Technologist** *13 students enrolled* • **Welding Technology/Welder** *41 students enrolled*

**STUDENT SERVICES** Academic or career counseling, placement services for program completers, remedial services.

## Brighton Center's Center for Employment Training

601 Washington Street, Suite 140, Newport, KY 41071

**CONTACT** Robert Brewster, Executive Director
**Telephone:** 859-491-8303 Ext. 2200

**GENERAL INFORMATION** Private Institution. **Total program enrollment:** 76.

**PROGRAM(S) OFFERED**
• **Business Operations Support and Secretarial Services, Other** *1020 hrs./$8107* • **Medical/Clinical Assistant** *1070 hrs./$8507*

**STUDENT SERVICES** Academic or career counseling, employment services for current students, placement services for program completers, remedial services.

## Brown Mackie College–Hopkinsville

4001 Ft. Cambell Boulevard, Hopkinsville, KY 42240
http://www.brownmackie.edu/Hopkinsville/

**CONTACT** Lesley Wilbert, Registrar
**Telephone:** 270-886-1302

**GENERAL INFORMATION** Private Institution. **Accreditation:** State accredited or approved. **Total program enrollment:** 268.

**PROGRAM(S) OFFERED**
• **Accounting** *1 student enrolled* • **Business Administration and Management, General** • **Computer Programming/Programmer, General** • **Computer Software and Media Applications, Other** • **Criminal Justice/Law Enforcement Administration** *2 students enrolled* • **Legal Assistant/Paralegal** *2 students enrolled* • **Medical Insurance Coding Specialist/Coder** *20 students enrolled* • **Medical/Clinical Assistant** *26 students enrolled*

**STUDENT SERVICES** Academic or career counseling, employment services for current students, placement services for program completers, remedial services.

## Brown Mackie College–Louisville

3605 Fern Valley Road, Louisville, KY 40219
http://www.brownmackie.edu/Louisville/

**CONTACT** Elyane Harney, President
**Telephone:** 502-968-7191

**GENERAL INFORMATION** Private Institution. Founded 1972. **Accreditation:** State accredited or approved. **Total program enrollment:** 906.

**PROGRAM(S) OFFERED**
• **Computer Systems Networking and Telecommunications** • **Electrical, Electronics and Communications Engineering** • **Medical/Clinical Assistant**

**STUDENT SERVICES** Academic or career counseling, employment services for current students, placement services for program completers, remedial services.

## Brown Mackie College–Northern Kentucky

309 Buttermilk Pike, Fort Mitchell, KY 41017-2191
http://www.brownmackie.edu/NorthernKentucky/

**CONTACT** Rick Lemmel, President
**Telephone:** 859-341-5627

**GENERAL INFORMATION** Private Institution. Founded 1927. **Accreditation:** State accredited or approved. **Total program enrollment:** 352.

**PROGRAM(S) OFFERED**
• **Health Services/Allied Health/Health Sciences, General** *1 student enrolled*
• **Nursing, Other** *58 students enrolled*

**STUDENT SERVICES** Academic or career counseling, employment services for current students, placement services for program completers, remedial services.

## Campbellsville University

1 University Drive, Campbellsville, KY 42718-2799
http://www.campbellsville.edu/

**CONTACT** Michael V. Carter, President
**Telephone:** 270-789-5000 Ext. 5000

**GENERAL INFORMATION** Private Institution (Affiliated with Kentucky Baptist Convention). Founded 1906. **Accreditation:** Regional (SACS/CC); music (NASM). **Total program enrollment:** 1581. **Application fee:** $20.

**STUDENT SERVICES** Academic or career counseling, employment services for current students, placement services for program completers, remedial services.

## Clear Creek Baptist Bible College

300 Clear Creek Road, Pineville, KY 40977-9754
http://www.ccbbc.edu/

**CONTACT** Donald S. Fox, President
**Telephone:** 606-337-3196

**GENERAL INFORMATION** Private Institution. Founded 1926. **Accreditation:** Regional (SACS/CC); state accredited or approved. **Total program enrollment:** 116. **Application fee:** $40.

**PROGRAM(S) OFFERED**
• **Theology/Theological Studies**

**STUDENT SERVICES** Academic or career counseling, daycare for children of students, employment services for current students, placement services for program completers, remedial services.

## Collins School of Cosmetology

111 West Chester Avenue, Middlesboro, KY 40965

**CONTACT** Reta Mc Daniel, Owner
**Telephone:** 606-248-3602

**GENERAL INFORMATION** Private Institution. **Total program enrollment:** 26. **Application fee:** $100.

**PROGRAM(S) OFFERED**
• **Aesthetician/Esthetician and Skin Care Specialist** • **Cosmetology, Barber/Styling, and Nail Instructor** • **Cosmetology/Cosmetologist, General** *1800 hrs./$8700* • **Nail Technician/Specialist and Manicurist** *600 hrs./$2800*

## Daymar College

4400 Breckenridge Lane, Suite 415, Louisville, KY 40218
http://www.daymarcollege.edu/

**CONTACT** Mark A. Gabis, President
**Telephone:** 502-495-1040

**GENERAL INFORMATION** Private Institution. Founded 2001. **Accreditation:** State accredited or approved. **Total program enrollment:** 422.

*Daymar College (continued)*

**PROGRAM(S) OFFERED**

• **Business/Office Automation/Technology/Data Entry** • **Computer and Information Sciences, General** • **Graphic Design** • **Health Information/Medical Records Technology/Technician** • **Medical Insurance Coding Specialist/Coder** *7 students enrolled* • **Medical Office Assistant/Specialist** *4 students enrolled* • **Medical Transcription/Transcriptionist** *3 students enrolled*

**STUDENT SERVICES** Academic or career counseling, employment services for current students, placement services for program completers, remedial services.

## Daymar College

76 Carothers Road, Newport, KY 41071
http://www.daymarcollege.edu/

**CONTACT** Mark A. Gabis, President
**Telephone:** 859-291-0800

**GENERAL INFORMATION** Private Institution. **Total program enrollment:** 76.

**PROGRAM(S) OFFERED**

• **Medical Insurance Coding Specialist/Coder** • **Medical Office Assistant/Specialist** *3 students enrolled*

**STUDENT SERVICES** Academic or career counseling, employment services for current students, placement services for program completers.

## Daymar College

3361 Buckland Square, Owensboro, KY 42301
http://www.daymarcollege.edu/

**CONTACT** Mark A. Gabis, President
**Telephone:** 270-926-4040

**GENERAL INFORMATION** Private Institution. Founded 1963. **Accreditation:** State accredited or approved. **Total program enrollment:** 247.

**PROGRAM(S) OFFERED**

• **Medical Insurance Specialist/Medical Biller** • **Medical Office Assistant/Specialist** *5 students enrolled* • **Office Management and Supervision**

**STUDENT SERVICES** Academic or career counseling, employment services for current students, placement services for program completers.

## Daymar College

509 South 30th Street, Paducah, KY 42001
http://www.daymarcollege.edu/

**CONTACT** Mark A. Gabis, President
**Telephone:** 270-444-9676 Ext. 203

**GENERAL INFORMATION** Private Institution. **Total program enrollment:** 104. **Application fee:** $75.

**PROGRAM(S) OFFERED**

• **Medical/Clinical Assistant**

**STUDENT SERVICES** Academic or career counseling, employment services for current students, placement services for program completers.

## Daymar College

509 South 30th Street, PO Box 8252, Paducah, KY 42001
http://www.daymarcollege.edu/college/paducah

**CONTACT** Mark Gabis, President
**Telephone:** 270-444-9676

**GENERAL INFORMATION** Private Institution. Founded 1964. **Accreditation:** State accredited or approved. **Total program enrollment:** 137.

**PROGRAM(S) OFFERED**

• **Business Administration and Management, General** • **Business/Office Automation/Technology/Data Entry** *88 hrs./$26,335* • **Computer Engineering Technology/Technician** • **Electrical and Electronic Engineering Technologies/Technicians, Other** • **Electrical, Electronic and Communications Engineering Technology/Technician** *96 hrs./$15,354* • **General Office Occupations and Clerical Services** • **Medical Insurance Specialist/Medical Biller** *88 hrs./$26,335* • **Pharmacy Technician/Assistant** *88 hrs./$26,335* • **Real Estate**

**STUDENT SERVICES** Academic or career counseling, employment services for current students, placement services for program completers.

## Donta School of Beauty Culture

515 West Oak Street, Louisville, KY 40203
http://www.beautyschooldirectory.com/

**CONTACT** Dale Jones, Owner
**Telephone:** 801-302-8801 Ext. 1021

**GENERAL INFORMATION** Private Institution. **Total program enrollment:** 84. **Application fee:** $100.

**PROGRAM(S) OFFERED**

• **Cosmetology/Cosmetologist, General** *1800 hrs./$14,800*

**STUDENT SERVICES** Academic or career counseling, employment services for current students, placement services for program completers.

## Draughons Junior College

2421 Fitzgerald Industrial Drive, Bowling Green, KY 42101
http://www.draughons.edu/

**CONTACT** Melva Hale, Director
**Telephone:** 270-843-6750

**GENERAL INFORMATION** Private Institution. Founded 1989. **Accreditation:** State accredited or approved. **Total program enrollment:** 300.

**PROGRAM(S) OFFERED**

• **Accounting** *1 student enrolled* • **Cardiovascular Technology/Technologist** *8 students enrolled* • **Computer Science** • **E-Commerce/Electronic Commerce** • **Health Information/Medical Records Technology/Technician** *3 students enrolled* • **Medical/Clinical Assistant** *10 students enrolled*

**STUDENT SERVICES** Academic or career counseling, employment services for current students, placement services for program completers, remedial services.

## Eastern Kentucky University

521 Lancaster Avenue, Richmond, KY 40475-3102
http://www.eku.edu/

**CONTACT** Doug Whitlock, President
**Telephone:** 859-622-1000

**GENERAL INFORMATION** Public Institution. Founded 1906. **Accreditation:** Regional (SACS/CC); athletic training (JRCAT); computer science (ABET/CSAC); counseling (ACA); cytotechnology (ASC); dietetics: postbaccalaureate internship (ADtA/CAADE); emergency medical services (JRCEMTP); health information administration (AHIMA); health information technology (AHIMA); home economics (AAFCS); medical assisting (AAMAE); medical laboratory technology (NAACLS); medical technology (NAACLS); music (NASM); recreation and parks (NRPA); speech-language pathology (ASHA). **Total program enrollment:** 11761. **Application fee:** $30.

**PROGRAM(S) OFFERED**

• **Real Estate**

**STUDENT SERVICES** Academic or career counseling, employment services for current students, placement services for program completers, remedial services.

## Elizabethtown Community and Technical College

620 College Street Road, Elizabethtown, KY 42701
http://www.elizabethtown.kctcs.edu/

**CONTACT** Dr. Thelma White, CEO/President
**Telephone:** 270-769-2371

**GENERAL INFORMATION** Public Institution. Founded 1966. **Accreditation:** State accredited or approved. **Total program enrollment:** 2675.

**PROGRAM(S) OFFERED**
• **Automobile/Automotive Mechanics Technology/Technician** *5 students enrolled* • **Business Administration and Management, General** *199 students enrolled* • **Carpentry/Carpenter** *25 students enrolled* • **Child Care Provider/Assistant** *104 students enrolled* • **Computer and Information Sciences, General** *82 students enrolled* • **Culinary Arts/Chef Training** *3 students enrolled* • **Diesel Mechanics Technology/Technician** *99 students enrolled* • **Drafting and Design Technology/Technician, General** *20 students enrolled* • **Electrician** *174 students enrolled* • **Emergency Medical Technology/Technician (EMT Paramedic)** *38 students enrolled* • **Engineering Technology, General** *69 students enrolled* • **Executive Assistant/Executive Secretary** *157 students enrolled* • **Fire Science/Firefighting** *11 students enrolled* • **Industrial Mechanics and Maintenance Technology** *18 students enrolled* • **Licensed Practical/Vocational Nurse Training (LPN, LVN, Cert, Dipl, AAS)** *263 students enrolled* • **Machine Shop Technology/Assistant** *21 students enrolled* • **Medical Administrative/Executive Assistant and Medical Secretary** *100 students enrolled* • **Plumbing Technology/Plumber** *33 students enrolled* • **Quality Control Technology/Technician** *11 students enrolled* • **Social Work** *12 students enrolled* • **Welding Technology/Welder** *82 students enrolled*

**STUDENT SERVICES** Academic or career counseling, remedial services.

## Employment Solutions

1165 Centre Parkway, Suite 120, Lexington, KY 40517
http://www.employmentsolutionsinc.org/

**CONTACT** Rick Christman, CEO
**Telephone:** 859-272-5225

**GENERAL INFORMATION** Private Institution. **Total program enrollment:** 214.

**PROGRAM(S) OFFERED**
• **Building/Property Maintenance and Management** *9 students enrolled* • **Cooking and Related Culinary Arts, General** *29 hrs./$6500* • **General Office Occupations and Clerical Services** *28 hrs./$6700* • **Mason/Masonry** *36 hrs./$6500*

**STUDENT SERVICES** Academic or career counseling, daycare for children of students, placement services for program completers, remedial services.

## Ezell's Beauty School

504 Maple Street, Murray, KY 42071

**CONTACT** Brenda J. Brown, Owner, Administrator
**Telephone:** 270-753-4723

**GENERAL INFORMATION** Private Institution. **Total program enrollment:** 37. **Application fee:** $100.

**PROGRAM(S) OFFERED**
• **Cosmetology, Barber/Styling, and Nail Instructor** *1000 hrs./$5500* • **Cosmetology/Cosmetologist, General** *1800 hrs./$10,050* • **Nail Technician/Specialist and Manicurist** *600 hrs./$6500*

**STUDENT SERVICES** Academic or career counseling.

## Galen Health Institutes

612 South 4th Street, Suite 400, Louisville, KY 40202
http://www.galened.com/

**CONTACT** Mark Vogt, President
**Telephone:** 502-410-6200

**GENERAL INFORMATION** Private Institution. Founded 1990. **Total program enrollment:** 883. **Application fee:** $100.

**PROGRAM(S) OFFERED**
• **Licensed Practical/Vocational Nurse Training (LPN, LVN, Cert, Dipl, AAS)** *1440 hrs./$16,420* • **Nursing—Registered Nurse Training (RN, ASN, BSN, MSN)** *80 hrs./$20,935*

**STUDENT SERVICES** Academic or career counseling, placement services for program completers.

## Gateway Community and Technical College

1025 Amsterdam Road, Covington, KY 41011
http://www.gateway.kctcs.edu/

**CONTACT** Dr. G. Edward Hughes, President
**Telephone:** 859-441-4500

**GENERAL INFORMATION** Public Institution. Founded 1961. **Accreditation:** State accredited or approved. **Total program enrollment:** 1158.

**PROGRAM(S) OFFERED**
• **Allied Health Diagnostic, Intervention, and Treatment Professions, Other** *3 students enrolled* • **Autobody/Collision and Repair Technology/Technician** *6 students enrolled* • **Automobile/Automotive Mechanics Technology/Technician** *17 students enrolled* • **Business Administration and Management, General** *56 students enrolled* • **Carpentry/Carpenter** *1 student enrolled* • **Child Care Provider/Assistant** *38 students enrolled* • **Communications Technology/Technician** *1 student enrolled* • **Computer and Information Sciences, General** *17 students enrolled* • **Cosmetology/Cosmetologist, General** *11 students enrolled* • **Electrician** *5 students enrolled* • **Executive Assistant/Executive Secretary** *3 students enrolled* • **Health Information/Medical Records Technology/Technician** *1 student enrolled* • **Health Unit Coordinator/Ward Clerk** *18 students enrolled* • **Heating, Air Conditioning, Ventilation and Refrigeration Maintenance Technology/Technician (HAC, HACR, HVAC, HVACR)** *3 students enrolled* • **Industrial Mechanics and Maintenance Technology** *9 students enrolled* • **Licensed Practical/Vocational Nurse Training (LPN, LVN, Cert, Dipl, AAS)** *221 students enrolled* • **Machine Shop Technology/Assistant** *6 students enrolled* • **Medical Administrative/Executive Assistant and Medical Secretary** *1 student enrolled* • **Medical/Clinical Assistant** *2 students enrolled*

**STUDENT SERVICES** Academic or career counseling, employment services for current students, placement services for program completers, remedial services.

## The Hair Design School

7285 Turfway Road, Florence, KY 41042
http://hairdesignschool.com/

**CONTACT** Michael Bouman, President/COO
**Telephone:** 502-491-0077

**GENERAL INFORMATION** Private Institution. Founded 1972. **Total program enrollment:** 98. **Application fee:** $100.

**PROGRAM(S) OFFERED**
• **Aesthetician/Esthetician and Skin Care Specialist** • **Cosmetology, Barber/Styling, and Nail Instructor** • **Cosmetology/Cosmetologist, General** *1800 hrs./$12,230* • **Nail Technician/Specialist and Manicurist** *9 students enrolled*

**STUDENT SERVICES** Academic or career counseling, placement services for program completers.

## The Hair Design School

1049 Bardstown Road, Louisville, KY 40204
http://hairdesignschool.com/

**CONTACT** Michael Bouman, President/COO
**Telephone:** 502-491-0077

**GENERAL INFORMATION** Private Institution. Founded 1987. **Total program enrollment:** 85. **Application fee:** $100.

**PROGRAM(S) OFFERED**
• **Cosmetology, Barber/Styling, and Nail Instructor** *1 student enrolled* • **Cosmetology/Cosmetologist, General** *1800 hrs./$12,230* • **Nail Technician/Specialist and Manicurist** *600 hrs./$2898*

**STUDENT SERVICES** Academic or career counseling, placement services for program completers.

## The Hair Design School

151 Chenoweth Lane, Louisville, KY 40207
http://hairdesignschool.com/

**CONTACT** Michael Bouman, President/COO
**Telephone:** 502-491-0077

**GENERAL INFORMATION** Private Institution. Founded 1965. **Total program enrollment:** 90. **Application fee:** $100.

**PROGRAM(S) OFFERED**
• **Aesthetician/Esthetician and Skin Care Specialist** • **Cosmetology, Barber/Styling, and Nail Instructor** • **Cosmetology/Cosmetologist, General** *1800 hrs./$12,230* • **Nail Technician/Specialist and Manicurist**

**STUDENT SERVICES** Academic or career counseling, placement services for program completers.

## The Hair Design School

3968 Park Drive, Louisville, KY 40216
http://hairdesignschool.com/

**CONTACT** Michael Bouman, President/COO
**Telephone:** 502-491-0077

**GENERAL INFORMATION** Private Institution. Founded 1972. **Total program enrollment:** 93. **Application fee:** $100.

**PROGRAM(S) OFFERED**
• **Cosmetology, Barber/Styling, and Nail Instructor** *2 students enrolled* • **Cosmetology/Cosmetologist, General** *1800 hrs./$12,230* • **Nail Technician/Specialist and Manicurist**

**STUDENT SERVICES** Academic or career counseling, placement services for program completers.

## The Hair Design School

4160 Bardstown Road, Louisville, KY 40218
http://hairdesignschool.com/

**CONTACT** Michael Bouman, President/COO
**Telephone:** 502-499-0070

**GENERAL INFORMATION** Private Institution. Founded 1972. **Total program enrollment:** 170. **Application fee:** $100.

**PROGRAM(S) OFFERED**
• **Aesthetician/Esthetician and Skin Care Specialist** *1000 hrs./$6600* • **Cosmetology, Barber/Styling, and Nail Instructor** *2 students enrolled* • **Cosmetology/Cosmetologist, General** *1800 hrs./$12,230* • **Nail Technician/Specialist and Manicurist** *600 hrs./$2898*

**STUDENT SERVICES** Academic or career counseling, placement services for program completers.

## The Hair Design School

640 Knox Boulevard, Radcliff, KY 40160
http://hairdesignschool.com/

**CONTACT** Michael Bouman, President/COO
**Telephone:** 270-765-3374

**GENERAL INFORMATION** Private Institution. **Total program enrollment:** 127. **Application fee:** $100.

**PROGRAM(S) OFFERED**
• **Aesthetician/Esthetician and Skin Care Specialist** *1000 hrs./$6600* • **Cosmetology, Barber/Styling, and Nail Instructor** • **Cosmetology/Cosmetologist, General** *1800 hrs./$12,230* • **Nail Technician/Specialist and Manicurist** *5 students enrolled*

**STUDENT SERVICES** Academic or career counseling, placement services for program completers.

## Hazard Community and Technical College

1 Community College Drive, Hazard, KY 41701-2403
http://www.hazard.kctcs.edu/

**CONTACT** Dr. Allen F. Goben, President/CEO
**Telephone:** 606-436-5721 Ext. 73503

**GENERAL INFORMATION** Public Institution. Founded 1968. **Accreditation:** Regional (SACS/CC); medical laboratory technology (NAACLS); physical therapy assisting (APTA); radiologic technology: radiography (JRCERT). **Total program enrollment:** 1466.

**PROGRAM(S) OFFERED**
• **Autobody/Collision and Repair Technology/Technician** *17 students enrolled* • **Automobile/Automotive Mechanics Technology/Technician** *40 students enrolled* • **Business Administration and Management, General** *70 students enrolled* • **Carpentry/Carpenter** *27 students enrolled* • **Child Care Provider/Assistant** *38 students enrolled* • **Computer and Information Sciences, General** *6 students enrolled* • **Construction/Heavy Equipment/Earthmoving Equipment Operation** *9 students enrolled* • **Cosmetology/Cosmetologist, General** *11 students enrolled* • **Crafts/Craft Design, Folk Art and Artisanry** *1 student enrolled* • **Diesel Mechanics Technology/Technician** *76 students enrolled* • **Drafting and Design Technology/Technician, General** *50 students enrolled* • **Electrician** *35 students enrolled* • **Executive Assistant/Executive Secretary** *1 student enrolled* • **Fire Science/Firefighting** *2 students enrolled* • **Heating, Air Conditioning, Ventilation and Refrigeration Maintenance Technology/Technician (HAC, HACR, HVAC, HVACR)** *5 students enrolled* • **Industrial Mechanics and Maintenance Technology** *2 students enrolled* • **Licensed Practical/Vocational Nurse Training (LPN, LVN, Cert, Dipl, AAS)** *119 students enrolled* • **Medical Administrative/Executive Assistant and Medical Secretary** *11 students enrolled* • **Survey Technology/Surveying** *25 students enrolled* • **Welding Technology/Welder** *15 students enrolled*

**STUDENT SERVICES** Academic or career counseling, employment services for current students, remedial services.

## Head's West Kentucky Beauty School

Briarwood Shopping Center, Madisonville, KY 42431

**CONTACT** Pat Wilson, Chief Administrator
**Telephone:** 270-825-3019

**GENERAL INFORMATION** Private Institution. Founded 1986. **Total program enrollment:** 22.

**PROGRAM(S) OFFERED**
• **Cosmetology, Barber/Styling, and Nail Instructor** *1000 hrs./$2800* • **Cosmetology/Cosmetologist, General** *1800 hrs./$9400* • **Nail Technician/Specialist and Manicurist** *600 hrs./$2550* • **Trade and Industrial Teacher Education**

## Henderson Community College

2660 South Green Street, Henderson, KY 42420-4623
http://www.henderson.kctcs.edu/

**CONTACT** Dr. Patrick Lake, President
**Telephone:** 270-827-1867

**GENERAL INFORMATION** Public Institution. Founded 1963. **Accreditation:** Regional (SACS/CC); dental hygiene (ADA); medical laboratory technology (NAACLS). **Total program enrollment:** 647.

**PROGRAM(S) OFFERED**

• **Agricultural Production Operations, General** *4 students enrolled* • **Child Care Provider/Assistant** *1 student enrolled* • **Clinical/Medical Laboratory Technician** *18 students enrolled* • **Computer and Information Sciences, General** *12 students enrolled* • **Engineering Technology, General** *36 students enrolled* • **Industrial Mechanics and Maintenance Technology** *6 students enrolled* • **Medical/Clinical Assistant** *24 students enrolled*

**STUDENT SERVICES** Academic or career counseling, daycare for children of students, employment services for current students, placement services for program completers, remedial services.

## Hopkinsville Community College

PO Box 2100, Hopkinsville, KY 42241-2100
http://www.hopcc.kctcs.edu/

**CONTACT** Dr. James E. Selbe, President
**Telephone:** 270-707-3700

**GENERAL INFORMATION** Public Institution. Founded 1965. **Accreditation:** Regional (SACS/CC). **Total program enrollment:** 1517.

**PROGRAM(S) OFFERED**

• **Agricultural Production Operations, General** *4 students enrolled* • **Business Administration and Management, General** *72 students enrolled* • **Child Care Provider/Assistant** *96 students enrolled* • **Computer and Information Sciences, General** *14 students enrolled* • **Drafting and Design Technology/Technician, General** *30 students enrolled* • **Electrician** *2 students enrolled* • **Engineering Technology, General** *34 students enrolled* • **Executive Assistant/Executive Secretary** *96 students enrolled* • **Industrial Mechanics and Maintenance Technology** *9 students enrolled* • **Licensed Practical/Vocational Nurse Training (LPN, LVN, Cert, Dipl, AAS)** *20 students enrolled* • **Machine Shop Technology/Assistant** *19 students enrolled*

**STUDENT SERVICES** Academic or career counseling, employment services for current students, placement services for program completers, remedial services.

## Interactive Learning Systems

11 Spiral Drive, Suite 8, Florence, KY 41042
http://www.ict-ils.edu/

**CONTACT** Elmer R. Smith, President
**Telephone:** 859-282-8989

**GENERAL INFORMATION** Private Institution. Founded 1980. **Total program enrollment:** 53. **Application fee:** $50.

**PROGRAM(S) OFFERED**

• **Accounting and Related Services, Other** *1 student enrolled* • **Administrative Assistant and Secretarial Science, General** • **Computer Programming/Programmer, General** • **Computer and Information Sciences, General** *10 students enrolled* • **Medical Insurance Coding Specialist/Coder** *6 students enrolled*

**STUDENT SERVICES** Academic or career counseling, employment services for current students, placement services for program completers, remedial services.

## J & M Academy of Cosmetology

110A Brighton Park Boulevard, Frankfort, KY 40601

**CONTACT** V. Michelle Whitaker, Director
**Telephone:** 502-695-9006

**GENERAL INFORMATION** Private Institution. Founded 1997. **Total program enrollment:** 14. **Application fee:** $100.

**PROGRAM(S) OFFERED**

• **Cosmetology, Barber/Styling, and Nail Instructor** *1000 hrs./$3300*
• **Cosmetology/Cosmetologist, General** *1800 hrs./$8920* • **Nail Technician/Specialist and Manicurist** *600 hrs./$3000*

## Jefferson Community and Technical College

109 East Broadway, Louisville, KY 40202-2005
http://www.jctc.kctcs.edu/

**CONTACT** Dr. Anthony Newberry, President and CEO
**Telephone:** 502-213-4000

**GENERAL INFORMATION** Public Institution. Founded 1968. **Accreditation:** Regional (SACS/CC); physical therapy assisting (APTA). **Total program enrollment:** 5128.

**PROGRAM(S) OFFERED**

• **Accounting Technology/Technician and Bookkeeping** *95 students enrolled* • **Aircraft Powerplant Technology/Technician** *30 students enrolled* • **Applied Horticulture/Horticultural Operations, General** *83 students enrolled* • **Autobody/Collision and Repair Technology/Technician** *13 students enrolled* • **Automobile/Automotive Mechanics Technology/Technician** *299 students enrolled* • **Business Administration and Management, General** *96 students enrolled* • **Cabinetmaking and Millwork/Millwright** *1 student enrolled* • **Carpentry/Carpenter** *170 students enrolled* • **Child Care Provider/Assistant** *213 students enrolled* • **Clinical/Medical Laboratory Technician** *2 students enrolled* • **Communications Technology/Technician** *12 students enrolled* • **Computer and Information Sciences, General** *55 students enrolled* • **Cosmetology/Cosmetologist, General** *9 students enrolled* • **Culinary Arts/Chef Training** *30 students enrolled* • **Electrician** *95 students enrolled* • **Electromechanical Technology/Electromechanical Engineering Technology** *5 students enrolled* • **Emergency Medical Technology/Technician (EMT Paramedic)** *4 students enrolled* • **Engineering Technology, General** *80 students enrolled* • **Executive Assistant/Executive Secretary** *109 students enrolled* • **Health Unit Coordinator/Ward Clerk** *22 students enrolled* • **Heating, Air Conditioning, Ventilation and Refrigeration Maintenance Technology/Technician (HAC, HACR, HVAC, HVACR)** *34 students enrolled* • **Industrial Mechanics and Maintenance Technology** *6 students enrolled* • **Licensed Practical/Vocational Nurse Training (LPN, LVN, Cert, Dipl, AAS)** *273 students enrolled* • **Machine Shop Technology/Assistant** *35 students enrolled* • **Mason/Masonry** *30 students enrolled* • **Medical/Clinical Assistant** *22 students enrolled* • **Plumbing Technology/Plumber** *35 students enrolled* • **Radiologic Technology/Science—Radiographer** *1 student enrolled* • **Real Estate** *25 students enrolled* • **Respiratory Care Therapy/Therapist** *1 student enrolled* • **Small Engine Mechanics and Repair Technology/Technician** *63 students enrolled* • **Surgical Technology/Technologist** *10 students enrolled* • **Teacher Assistant/Aide** *1 student enrolled* • **Upholstery/Upholsterer** *46 students enrolled* • **Welding Technology/Welder** *88 students enrolled*

**STUDENT SERVICES** Academic or career counseling, daycare for children of students, employment services for current students, placement services for program completers, remedial services.

## Jenny Lea Academy of Cosmetology

114 North Cumberland Avenue, Harlan, KY 40831

**CONTACT** Virginia Lewis, President
**Telephone:** 606-573-4276

**GENERAL INFORMATION** Private Institution. Founded 1980. **Total program enrollment:** 14. **Application fee:** $100.

**PROGRAM(S) OFFERED**

• **Cosmetology, Barber/Styling, and Nail Instructor** *1000 hrs./$4450*
• **Cosmetology/Cosmetologist, General** *1800 hrs./$9350* • **Nail Technician/Specialist and Manicurist** *600 hrs./$4050*

## Jenny Lea Academy of Cosmetology

74 Parkway Plaza Loop, Whitesburg, KY 41858

**CONTACT** Virginia Lewis, President
**Telephone:** 606-573-4276

**GENERAL INFORMATION** Private Institution. Founded 1984. **Total program enrollment:** 13. **Application fee:** $100.

**PROGRAM(S) OFFERED**
• **Cosmetology, Barber/Styling, and Nail Instructor** *1000 hrs./$4450*
• **Cosmetology/Cosmetologist, General** *1800 hrs./$9350*

## Kaufman's Beauty School

701 East High Street, Lexington, KY 40502
http://kaufmaneducation.com/

**CONTACT** Leslie Foster, Owner
**Telephone:** 859-266-5531

**GENERAL INFORMATION** Private Institution. Founded 1959. **Total program enrollment:** 109.

**PROGRAM(S) OFFERED**
• **Cosmetology, Barber/Styling, and Nail Instructor** *1000 hrs./$5990*
• **Cosmetology/Cosmetologist, General** *1800 hrs./$12,190* • **Nail Technician/ Specialist and Manicurist**

**STUDENT SERVICES** Placement services for program completers.

## Kentucky Community and Technical College System

300 North Main Street, Versailles, KY 40383
http://www.state.ky.us/agencies/kctcs/

**CONTACT** Dr. Michael B. McCall, President
**Telephone:** 859-256-3100

**GENERAL INFORMATION** Public Institution.

## Lexington Beauty College

90 Southport Drive, Lexington, KY 40503
http://lexingtonbeautycollege.com/

**CONTACT** Ann Halloran, President
**Telephone:** 859-252-7647

**GENERAL INFORMATION** Private Institution. Founded 1967. **Total program enrollment:** 24.

**PROGRAM(S) OFFERED**
• **Aesthetician/Esthetician and Skin Care Specialist** *1000 hrs./$7600*
• **Cosmetology, Barber/Styling, and Nail Instructor** *1000 hrs./$8000*
• **Cosmetology/Cosmetologist, General** *1800 hrs./$9913* • **Nail Technician/ Specialist and Manicurist** *600 hrs./$3695*

**STUDENT SERVICES** Academic or career counseling, employment services for current students, placement services for program completers.

## Lexington Healing Arts Academy

272 Southland Drive, Lexington, KY 40503
http://www.lexingtonhealingarts.com

**CONTACT** Bill Booker, Executive Director
**Telephone:** 859-252-5656

**GENERAL INFORMATION** Private Institution. **Application fee:** $50.

**PROGRAM(S) OFFERED**
• **Massage Therapy/Therapeutic Massage** *650 hrs.* • **Yoga Teacher Training/ Yoga Therapy** *200 hrs./$2500*

**STUDENT SERVICES** Academic or career counseling, placement services for program completers, remedial services.

## Madisonville Community College

2000 College Drive, Madisonville, KY 42431-9185
http://www.madcc.kctcs.edu/

**CONTACT** Dr. Judith Rhoads, President
**Telephone:** 270-821-2250

**GENERAL INFORMATION** Public Institution. Founded 1968. **Accreditation:** Regional (SACS/CC); physical therapy assisting (APTA). **Total program enrollment:** 1690.

**PROGRAM(S) OFFERED**
• **Business Administration and Management, General** *22 students enrolled* • **Carpentry/Carpenter** *41 students enrolled* • **Child Care Provider/Assistant** *32 students enrolled* • **Clinical/Medical Laboratory Technician** *20 students enrolled* • **Computer and Information Sciences, General** *2 students enrolled* • **Electrician** *1 student enrolled* • **Engineering Technology, General** *1 student enrolled* • **Heating, Air Conditioning, Ventilation and Refrigeration Maintenance Technology/ Technician (HAC, HACR, HVAC, HVACR)** *15 students enrolled* • **Industrial Mechanics and Maintenance Technology** *9 students enrolled* • **Licensed Practical/Vocational Nurse Training (LPN, LVN, Cert, Dipl, AAS)** *234 students enrolled* • **Machine Shop Technology/Assistant** *6 students enrolled* • **Mason/ Masonry** *28 students enrolled* • **Medical Administrative/Executive Assistant and Medical Secretary** *41 students enrolled* • **Medical Radiologic Technology/ Science—Radiation Therapist** *2 students enrolled* • **Mining Technology/ Technician** *10 students enrolled* • **Surgical Technology/Technologist** *23 students enrolled* • **Welding Technology/Welder** *14 students enrolled*

**STUDENT SERVICES** Academic or career counseling, employment services for current students, placement services for program completers, remedial services.

## Maysville Community and Technical College

1755 US 68, Maysville, KY 41056
http://www.maycc.kctcs.net/

**CONTACT** Dr. Edward Story, President
**Telephone:** 606-759-7141 Ext. 0

**GENERAL INFORMATION** Public Institution. Founded 1967. **Accreditation:** Regional (SACS/CC); respiratory therapy technology (CoARC). **Total program enrollment:** 1332.

**PROGRAM(S) OFFERED**
• **Applied Horticulture/Horticultural Operations, General** *5 students enrolled* • **Automobile/Automotive Mechanics Technology/Technician** *57 students enrolled* • **Business Administration and Management, General** *138 students enrolled* • **Carpentry/Carpenter** *46 students enrolled* • **Child Care Provider/ Assistant** *16 students enrolled* • **Computer and Information Sciences, General** *18 students enrolled* • **Diesel Mechanics Technology/Technician** *13 students enrolled* • **Electrician** *33 students enrolled* • **Electromechanical Technology/ Electromechanical Engineering Technology** *1 student enrolled* • **Energy Management and Systems Technology/Technician** *5 students enrolled* • **Engineering Technology, General** *58 students enrolled* • **Executive Assistant/Executive Secretary** *58 students enrolled* • **Heating, Air Conditioning, Ventilation and Refrigeration Maintenance Technology/Technician (HAC, HACR, HVAC, HVACR)** *15 students enrolled* • **Industrial Mechanics and Maintenance Technology** *3 students enrolled* • **Licensed Practical/Vocational Nurse Training (LPN, LVN, Cert, Dipl, AAS)** *157 students enrolled* • **Machine Shop Technology/ Assistant** *3 students enrolled* • **Mason/Masonry** *5 students enrolled* • **Medical Administrative/Executive Assistant and Medical Secretary** *10 students enrolled* • **Medical/Clinical Assistant** *38 students enrolled* • **Nurse/Nursing Assistant/ Aide and Patient Care Assistant** *6 students enrolled* • **Plumbing Technology/ Plumber** *73 students enrolled* • **Real Estate** *1 student enrolled* • **Small Engine Mechanics and Repair Technology/Technician** *38 students enrolled* • **Surgical Technology/Technologist** *6 students enrolled* • **Welding Technology/Welder** *72 students enrolled*

**STUDENT SERVICES** Academic or career counseling, employment services for current students, placement services for program completers, remedial services.

## Murray State University

113 Sparks Hall, Murray, KY 42071
http://www.murraystate.edu/

**CONTACT** Randy J. Dunn, President
**Telephone:** 270-809-3011

**GENERAL INFORMATION** Public Institution. Founded 1922. **Accreditation:** Regional (SACS/CC); art and design (NASAD); counseling (ACA); dietetics: postbaccalaureate internship (ADtA/CAADE); engineering technology (ABET/TAC); engineering-related programs (ABET/RAC); home economics (AAFCS); journalism and mass communications (ACEJMC); music (NASM); speech-language pathology (ASHA). **Total program enrollment:** 7493. **Application fee:** $30.

**STUDENT SERVICES** Academic or career counseling, employment services for current students, placement services for program completers, remedial services.

## National College

2376 Sir Barton Way, Lexington, KY 40509
http://www.national-college.edu/

**CONTACT** Frank Longaker, President
**Telephone:** 859-253-0621

**GENERAL INFORMATION** Private Institution. Founded 1947. **Accreditation:** Medical assisting (AAMAE); state accredited or approved. **Total program enrollment:** 1607. **Application fee:** $30.

**PROGRAM(S) OFFERED**
• **Accounting Technology/Technician and Bookkeeping** • **Business Administration and Management, General** *1 student enrolled* • **Business/Commerce, General** *12 students enrolled* • **Computer and Information Sciences and Support Services, Other** *9 students enrolled* • **Executive Assistant/Executive Secretary** *6 students enrolled* • **Health and Medical Administrative Services, Other** *90 students enrolled* • **Information Technology** • **Medical Office Assistant/Specialist** *1 student enrolled* • **Medical Transcription/Transcriptionist** *12 students enrolled* • **Pharmacy Technician/Assistant** *60 students enrolled* • **Phlebotomy/Phlebotomist** *6 students enrolled* • **Radio and Television Broadcasting Technology/Technician**

**STUDENT SERVICES** Academic or career counseling, employment services for current students, placement services for program completers, remedial services.

## Northern Kentucky University

Louie B Nunn Drive, Highland Heights, KY 41099
http://www.nku.edu/

**CONTACT** James C. Votruba, President
**Telephone:** 859-572-5100

**GENERAL INFORMATION** Public Institution. Founded 1968. **Accreditation:** Regional (SACS/CC); engineering technology (ABET/TAC); music (NASM); radiologic technology: radiography (JRCERT). **Total program enrollment:** 10047. **Application fee:** $40.

**STUDENT SERVICES** Academic or career counseling, daycare for children of students, employment services for current students, placement services for program completers, remedial services.

## Nu-Tek Academy of Beauty

Maysville Road, Mount Sterling, KY 40391

**CONTACT** Rebecca H. Taylor, CEO
**Telephone:** 859-498-4460

**GENERAL INFORMATION** Private Institution. Founded 1973. **Total program enrollment:** 30. **Application fee:** $200.

**PROGRAM(S) OFFERED**
• **Cosmetology, Barber/Styling, and Nail Instructor** *1000 hrs./$3200* • **Cosmetology/Cosmetologist, General** *1800 hrs./$9500* • **Nail Technician/Specialist and Manicurist** *600 hrs./$5700*

**STUDENT SERVICES** Academic or career counseling, placement services for program completers.

## Owensboro Community and Technical College

4800 New Hartford Road, Owensboro, KY 42303-1899
http://www.octc.kctcs.edu/

**CONTACT** Dr. Paula Gastenveld, President
**Telephone:** 270-686-4400

**GENERAL INFORMATION** Public Institution. Founded 1986. **Accreditation:** Regional (SACS/CC); radiologic technology: radiography (JRCERT); state accredited or approved. **Total program enrollment:** 1775.

**PROGRAM(S) OFFERED**
• **Agricultural Production Operations, General** *1 student enrolled* • **Autobody/Collision and Repair Technology/Technician** *12 students enrolled* • **Automobile/Automotive Mechanics Technology/Technician** *61 students enrolled* • **Business Administration and Management, General** *17 students enrolled* • **Carpentry/Carpenter** *20 students enrolled* • **Child Care Provider/Assistant** *62 students enrolled* • **Computer and Information Sciences, General** *20 students enrolled* • **Cosmetology/Cosmetologist, General** *6 students enrolled* • **Culinary Arts/Chef Training** *8 students enrolled* • **Diesel Mechanics Technology/Technician** *22 students enrolled* • **Drafting and Design Technology/Technician, General** *2 students enrolled* • **Electrician** *19 students enrolled* • **Emergency Medical Technology/Technician (EMT Paramedic)** *24 students enrolled* • **Engineering Technology, General** *34 students enrolled* • **Executive Assistant/Executive Secretary** *16 students enrolled* • **Heating, Air Conditioning, Ventilation and Refrigeration Maintenance Technology/Technician (HAC, HACR, HVAC, HVACR)** *19 students enrolled* • **Industrial Mechanics and Maintenance Technology** *58 students enrolled* • **Licensed Practical/Vocational Nurse Training (LPN, LVN, Cert, Dipl, AAS)** *32 students enrolled* • **Machine Shop Technology/Assistant** *21 students enrolled* • **Medical Administrative/Executive Assistant and Medical Secretary** *31 students enrolled* • **Surgical Technology/Technologist** *10 students enrolled* • **Welding Technology/Welder** *36 students enrolled*

**STUDENT SERVICES** Academic or career counseling, daycare for children of students, employment services for current students, placement services for program completers, remedial services.

## Pat Wilson's Beauty College

326 North Main, Henderson, KY 42420

**CONTACT** Pat Wilson, Director
**Telephone:** 270-826-5195

**GENERAL INFORMATION** Private Institution. Founded 1975. **Total program enrollment:** 42.

**PROGRAM(S) OFFERED**
• **Cosmetology and Related Personal Grooming Arts, Other** • **Cosmetology, Barber/Styling, and Nail Instructor** *1000 hrs./$2800* • **Cosmetology/Cosmetologist, General** *1800 hrs./$9400* • **Nail Technician/Specialist and Manicurist** *600 hrs./$2050* • **Technical Teacher Education**

**STUDENT SERVICES** Academic or career counseling, employment services for current students, placement services for program completers.

## PJ's College of Cosmetology

1901 Russelville Road, Suite 10, Bowling Green, KY 42101
http://gotopjs.com/

**CONTACT** Judith Stewart, President/Owner
**Telephone:** 317-846-8999 Ext. 320

**GENERAL INFORMATION** Private Institution. **Total program enrollment:** 263.

*PJ's College of Cosmetology (continued)*

**PROGRAM(S) OFFERED**

• **Cosmetology and Related Personal Grooming Arts, Other** *600 hrs./$8070* • **Cosmetology, Barber/Styling, and Nail Instructor** *1000 hrs./$10,088* • **Cosmetology/Cosmetologist, General** *1500 hrs./$14,870* • **Nail Technician/Specialist and Manicurist** *450 hrs./$6095*

**STUDENT SERVICES** Academic or career counseling, employment services for current students, placement services for program completers.

## PJ's College of Cosmetology

124 South Public Square, Glasgow, KY 42141
http://gotopjs.com/

**CONTACT** Judith Stewart, Owner/President
**Telephone:** 317-846-8999 Ext. 320

**GENERAL INFORMATION** Private Institution. **Total program enrollment:** 64.

**PROGRAM(S) OFFERED**

• **Cosmetology and Related Personal Grooming Arts, Other** *600 hrs./$8070* • **Cosmetology, Barber/Styling, and Nail Instructor** *1000 hrs./$10,088* • **Cosmetology/Cosmetologist, General** *1800 hrs./$15,400* • **Hair Styling/Stylist and Hair Design** • **Nail Technician/Specialist and Manicurist** *1 student enrolled*

**STUDENT SERVICES** Academic or career counseling, employment services for current students, placement services for program completers.

## Regency School of Hair Design

567 North Lake Drive, Prestonburg, KY 41653

**CONTACT** Edith Dotson, Co-Owner
**Telephone:** 606-886-6457

**GENERAL INFORMATION** Private Institution. **Total program enrollment:** 35. **Application fee:** $100.

**PROGRAM(S) OFFERED**

• **Cosmetology, Barber/Styling, and Nail Instructor** *1000 hrs./$3600* • **Cosmetology/Cosmetologist, General** *1800 hrs./$9362* • **Nail Technician/Specialist and Manicurist** *3 students enrolled*

## St. Catharine College

2735 Bardstown Road, St. Catharine, KY 40061-9499
http://www.sccky.edu/

**CONTACT** William D. Huston, President
**Telephone:** 859-336-5082

**GENERAL INFORMATION** Private Institution. Founded 1931. **Accreditation:** Regional (SACS/CC). **Total program enrollment:** 524. **Application fee:** $15.

**PROGRAM(S) OFFERED**

• **Child Care Provider/Assistant** • **Computer and Information Sciences, General** • **Pharmacy Technician/Assistant** *2 students enrolled*

**STUDENT SERVICES** Academic or career counseling, daycare for children of students, employment services for current students, placement services for program completers, remedial services.

## Somerset Community College

808 Monticello Street, Somerset, KY 42501-2973
http://www.somerset.kctcs.edu/

**CONTACT** Dr. Jo Marshall, President & CEO
**Telephone:** 877-629-9722

**GENERAL INFORMATION** Public Institution. Founded 1965. **Accreditation:** Regional (SACS/CC); medical laboratory technology (NAACLS); physical therapy assisting (APTA); state accredited or approved. **Total program enrollment:** 3162.

**PROGRAM(S) OFFERED**

• **Accounting Technology/Technician and Bookkeeping** *1 student enrolled* • **Aircraft Powerplant Technology/Technician** *37 students enrolled* • **Autobody/Collision and Repair Technology/Technician** *5 students enrolled* • **Automobile/Automotive Mechanics Technology/Technician** *64 students enrolled* • **Business Administration and Management, General** *1 student enrolled* • **Carpentry/Carpenter** *33 students enrolled* • **Child Care Provider/Assistant** *19 students enrolled* • **Clinical/Medical Laboratory Technician** *55 students enrolled* • **Communications Technology/Technician** *11 students enrolled* • **Cosmetology/Cosmetologist, General** *2 students enrolled* • **Diesel Mechanics Technology/Technician** *117 students enrolled* • **Drafting and Design Technology/Technician, General** *24 students enrolled* • **Electrician** *20 students enrolled* • **Engineering Technology, General** *26 students enrolled* • **Executive Assistant/Executive Secretary** *23 students enrolled* • **Heating, Air Conditioning, Ventilation and Refrigeration Maintenance Technology/Technician (HAC, HACR, HVAC, HVACR)** *8 students enrolled* • **Industrial Electronics Technology/Technician** *14 students enrolled* • **Industrial Mechanics and Maintenance Technology** *37 students enrolled* • **Licensed Practical/Vocational Nurse Training (LPN, LVN, Cert, Dipl, AAS)** *127 students enrolled* • **Machine Shop Technology/Assistant** *34 students enrolled* • **Medical Administrative/Executive Assistant and Medical Secretary** *120 students enrolled* • **Medical/Clinical Assistant** *11 students enrolled* • **Welding Technology/Welder** *38 students enrolled*

**STUDENT SERVICES** Academic or career counseling, employment services for current students, placement services for program completers, remedial services.

## Southeast Kentucky Community and Technical College

700 College Road, Cumberland, KY 40823-1099
http://www.soucc.kctcs.net/

**CONTACT** Dr. W. Bruce Ayers, President & CEO
**Telephone:** 606-589-2145

**GENERAL INFORMATION** Public Institution. Founded 1960. **Accreditation:** Regional (SACS/CC); medical laboratory technology (NAACLS); physical therapy assisting (APTA). **Total program enrollment:** 1676.

**PROGRAM(S) OFFERED**

• **Autobody/Collision and Repair Technology/Technician** *8 students enrolled* • **Automobile/Automotive Mechanics Technology/Technician** *19 students enrolled* • **Business Administration and Management, General** *21 students enrolled* • **Carpentry/Carpenter** *25 students enrolled* • **Clinical/Medical Laboratory Technician** *10 students enrolled* • **Computer and Information Sciences, General** *7 students enrolled* • **Construction/Heavy Equipment/Earthmoving Equipment Operation** *17 students enrolled* • **Diesel Mechanics Technology/Technician** *49 students enrolled* • **Drafting and Design Technology/Technician, General** *1 student enrolled* • **Electrician** *31 students enrolled* • **Engineering Technology, General** *8 students enrolled* • **Executive Assistant/Executive Secretary** *44 students enrolled* • **Heating, Air Conditioning, Ventilation and Refrigeration Maintenance Technology/Technician (HAC, HACR, HVAC, HVACR)** *22 students enrolled* • **Licensed Practical/Vocational Nurse Training (LPN, LVN, Cert, Dipl, AAS)** *34 students enrolled* • **Machine Shop Technology/Assistant** *2 students enrolled* • **Medical Radiologic Technology/Science—Radiation Therapist** *11 students enrolled* • **Medical/Clinical Assistant** *5 students enrolled* • **Mining Technology/Technician** *1 student enrolled* • **Surgical Technology/Technologist** *14 students enrolled* • **Welding Technology/Welder** *54 students enrolled*

**STUDENT SERVICES** Academic or career counseling, employment services for current students, placement services for program completers, remedial services.

## Southeast School of Cosmetology

19 Manchester Square, Manchester, KY 40962

**CONTACT** Betty S. Roberts, President
**Telephone:** 606-598-7901

**GENERAL INFORMATION** Private Institution. **Total program enrollment:** 51.

**PROGRAM(S) OFFERED**
• **Cosmetology, Barber/Styling, and Nail Instructor** *1000 hrs./$3390*
• **Cosmetology/Cosmetologist, General** *1800 hrs./$8500*

**STUDENT SERVICES** Academic or career counseling.

## Southwestern College of Business

8095 Connector Drive, Florence, KY 41042
http://www.swcollege.net/

**CONTACT** Tina M. Barnes, Executive Director
**Telephone:** 859-282-9999

**GENERAL INFORMATION** Private Institution. Founded 1978. **Accreditation:** State accredited or approved. **Total program enrollment:** 171. **Application fee:** $20.

**PROGRAM(S) OFFERED**
• **Blood Bank Technology Specialist** *24 students enrolled* • **Health and Medical Administrative Services, Other** *14 students enrolled* • **Information Science/Studies** • **Massage Therapy/Therapeutic Massage** *53 students enrolled* • **Medical/Clinical Assistant** *52 students enrolled*

**STUDENT SERVICES** Academic or career counseling, placement services for program completers.

## Spalding University

851 South Fourth Street, Louisville, KY 40203-2188
http://www.spalding.edu/

**CONTACT** Jo Ann Rooney, President
**Telephone:** 502-585-9911

**GENERAL INFORMATION** Private Institution (Affiliated with Roman Catholic Church). Founded 1814. **Accreditation:** Regional (SACS/CC). **Total program enrollment:** 1086. **Application fee:** $20.

**PROGRAM(S) OFFERED**
• **Nursing—Registered Nurse Training (RN, ASN, BSN, MSN)** • **Pastoral Studies/Counseling** • **Teaching English as a Second or Foreign Language/ESL Language Instructor**

**STUDENT SERVICES** Academic or career counseling, employment services for current students, remedial services.

## Spencerian College

4627 Dixie Highway, Louisville, KY 40216
http://www.spencerian.edu/

**CONTACT** Jan Gordon, Executive Director
**Telephone:** 502-447-1000

**GENERAL INFORMATION** Private Institution. Founded 1892. **Accreditation:** State accredited or approved. **Total program enrollment:** 834. **Application fee:** $100.

**PROGRAM(S) OFFERED**
• **Accounting Technology/Technician and Bookkeeping** *2 students enrolled* • **Blood Bank Technology Specialist** *29 students enrolled* • **Business, Management, Marketing, and Related Support Services, Other** *1 student enrolled* • **Business/Office Automation/Technology/Data Entry** *2 students enrolled* • **Clinical/Medical Laboratory Assistant** *36 students enrolled* • **Executive Assistant/Executive Secretary** *1 student enrolled* • **Health Information/Medical Records Technology/Technician** *14 students enrolled* • **Health Unit Coordinator/Ward Clerk** *4 students enrolled* • **Licensed Practical/Vocational Nurse Training (LPN, LVN, Cert, Dipl, AAS)** *146 students enrolled* • **Massage Therapy/Therapeutic Massage** *21 students enrolled* • **Medical Administrative/Executive Assistant and Medical Secretary** *4 students enrolled* • **Medical Radiologic Technology/Science—Radiation Therapist** *53 students enrolled* • **Medical Transcription/Transcriptionist** *8 students enrolled* • **Medical/Clinical Assistant** *14 students enrolled* • **Surgical Technology/Technologist** *27 students enrolled*

**STUDENT SERVICES** Academic or career counseling, employment services for current students, placement services for program completers, remedial services.

## Spencerian College–Lexington

2355 Harrodsburg Road, Lexington, KY 40504
http://www.spencerian.edu/

**CONTACT** Glen Sullivan, President
**Telephone:** 859-223-9608

**GENERAL INFORMATION** Private Institution. Founded 1997. **Accreditation:** State accredited or approved. **Total program enrollment:** 410. **Application fee:** $100.

**PROGRAM(S) OFFERED**
• **Allied Health and Medical Assisting Services, Other** • **Clinical/Medical Laboratory Technician** • **Computer Installation and Repair Technology/Technician** *1 student enrolled* • **Drafting and Design Technology/Technician, General** *10 students enrolled* • **Massage Therapy/Therapeutic Massage** *42 students enrolled* • **Medical Insurance Coding Specialist/Coder** *9 students enrolled* • **Medical Transcription/Transcriptionist** • **Medical/Clinical Assistant** *16 students enrolled* • **Phlebotomy/Phlebotomist** *26 students enrolled* • **Radiologic Technology/Science—Radiographer** *34 students enrolled*

**STUDENT SERVICES** Academic or career counseling, placement services for program completers.

## Sullivan College of Technology and Design

3901 Atkinson Square Drive, Louisville, KY 40218-4528
http://www.louisvilletech.com/

**CONTACT** David Winkler, Executive Director
**Telephone:** 502-456-6509

**GENERAL INFORMATION** Private Institution. Founded 1961. **Accreditation:** State accredited or approved. **Total program enrollment:** 404. **Application fee:** $100.

**PROGRAM(S) OFFERED**
• **Drafting and Design Technology/Technician, General** *26 students enrolled* • **Interior Design** *44 students enrolled*

**STUDENT SERVICES** Academic or career counseling, placement services for program completers, remedial services.

## Sullivan University

3101 Bardstown Road, Louisville, KY 40205
http://www.sullivan.edu/

**CONTACT** G. Stephen Coppock, Executive Vice President
**Telephone:** 502-456-6504

**GENERAL INFORMATION** Private Institution. Founded 1864. **Accreditation:** Regional (SACS/CC); medical assisting (AAMAE). **Total program enrollment:** 1715. **Application fee:** $100.

**PROGRAM(S) OFFERED**
• **Baking and Pastry Arts/Baker/Pastry Chef** *13 students enrolled* • **Business Administration and Management, General** *45 students enrolled* • **Child Care Provider/Assistant** *11 students enrolled* • **Computer and Information Sciences and Support Services, Other** *31 students enrolled* • **Culinary Arts/Chef Training** *4 students enrolled* • **Executive Assistant/Executive Secretary** *1 student enrolled* • **Legal Professions and Studies, Other** • **Medical Office Management/Administration** *2 students enrolled* • **Tourism and Travel Services Marketing Operations**

**STUDENT SERVICES** Academic or career counseling, employment services for current students, placement services for program completers.

## Thomas More College

333 Thomas More Parkway, Crestview Hills, KY 41017-3495
http://www.thomasmore.edu/

**CONTACT** Sr. Margaret A. Stallmeyer, CDP, President
**Telephone:** 859-341-5800

**GENERAL INFORMATION** Private Institution. Founded 1921. **Accreditation:** Regional (SACS/CC). **Total program enrollment:** 1418. **Application fee:** $25.

**PROGRAM(S) OFFERED**
• **Accounting** • **Religion/Religious Studies** *1 student enrolled*

**STUDENT SERVICES** Academic or career counseling, employment services for current students, placement services for program completers, remedial services.

## Trend Setter's Academy

7283 Dixie Highway, Louisville, KY 40258

**CONTACT** Franci Buckler, Financial Aid Director
**Telephone:** 502-937-6816

**GENERAL INFORMATION** Private Institution. Founded 1974. **Total program enrollment:** 63. **Application fee:** $100.

**PROGRAM(S) OFFERED**
• **Cosmetology, Barber/Styling, and Nail Instructor** *1000 hrs./$6100* • **Cosmetology/Cosmetologist, General** *1800 hrs./$10,800* • **Nail Technician/Specialist and Manicurist** *600 hrs./$3700*

**STUDENT SERVICES** Placement services for program completers.

## Trend Setter's Academy of Beauty Culture

622B Westport Road, Elizabethtown, KY 40601

**CONTACT** Deborah Livers, Financial Aid Director
**Telephone:** 270-765-5243

**GENERAL INFORMATION** Private Institution. Founded 1984. **Total program enrollment:** 37. **Application fee:** $100.

**PROGRAM(S) OFFERED**
• **Cosmetology, Barber/Styling, and Nail Instructor** *1000 hrs./$6100* • **Cosmetology/Cosmetologist, General** *1800 hrs./$10,800* • **Nail Technician/Specialist and Manicurist** *600 hrs./$3700*

**STUDENT SERVICES** Placement services for program completers.

## University of Louisville

2301 South Third Street, Louisville, KY 40292-0001
http://www.louisville.edu/

**CONTACT** James R. Ramsey, President
**Telephone:** 502-852-5555

**GENERAL INFORMATION** Public Institution. Founded 1798. **Accreditation:** Regional (SACS/CC); audiology (ASHA); computer science (ABET/CSAC); dental hygiene (ADA); interior design: professional (CIDA); music (NASM); radiologic technology: radiography (JRCERT); speech-language pathology (ASHA). **Total program enrollment:** 15250. **Application fee:** $40.

**PROGRAM(S) OFFERED**
• **Criminal Justice/Law Enforcement Administration** *31 students enrolled*

**STUDENT SERVICES** Academic or career counseling, employment services for current students, placement services for program completers, remedial services.

## Western Kentucky University

1906 College Heights Boulevard, Bowling Green, KY 42101
http://www.wku.edu/

**CONTACT** Gary A. Ransdell, President
**Telephone:** 270-745-0111

**GENERAL INFORMATION** Public Institution. Founded 1906. **Accreditation:** Regional (SACS/CC); art and design (NASAD); computer science (ABET/CSAC); dental hygiene (ADA); engineering technology (ABET/TAC); health information technology (AHIMA); home economics (AAFCS); journalism and mass communications (ACEJMC); music (NASM); recreation and parks (NRPA); speech-language pathology (ASHA). **Total program enrollment:** 14328. **Application fee:** $40.

**PROGRAM(S) OFFERED**
• **Accounting** *3 students enrolled* • **Canadian Studies** *1 student enrolled* • **Cartography** *20 students enrolled* • **Financial Planning and Services** *27 students enrolled* • **Public Relations/Image Management** *1 student enrolled*

**STUDENT SERVICES** Academic or career counseling, daycare for children of students, employment services for current students, placement services for program completers, remedial services.

## West Kentucky Community and Technical College

4810 Alben Barkley Drive, PO Box 7380, Paducah, KY 42002-7380
http://www.westkentucky.kctcs.edu/

**CONTACT** Dr. Barbara Veazey, President/CEO
**Telephone:** 270-554-9200 Ext. 0

**GENERAL INFORMATION** Public Institution. Founded 1932. **Accreditation:** Regional (SACS/CC); dental assisting (ADA); physical therapy assisting (APTA); state accredited or approved. **Total program enrollment:** 2126.

**PROGRAM(S) OFFERED**
• **Accounting Technology/Technician and Bookkeeping** *25 students enrolled* • **Aesthetician/Esthetician and Skin Care Specialist** *8 students enrolled* • **Applied Horticulture/Horticultural Operations, General** *59 students enrolled* • **Autobody/Collision and Repair Technology/Technician** *6 students enrolled* • **Barbering/Barber** *5 students enrolled* • **Business Administration and Management, General** *5 students enrolled* • **Carpentry/Carpenter** *103 students enrolled* • **Child Care Provider/Assistant** *17 students enrolled* • **Clinical/Medical Laboratory Technician** *25 students enrolled* • **Communications Technology/Technician** *37 students enrolled* • **Computer and Information Sciences, General** *18 students enrolled* • **Cosmetology/Cosmetologist, General** *8 students enrolled* • **Culinary Arts/Chef Training** *29 students enrolled* • **Dental Hygiene/Hygienist** *11 students enrolled* • **Diesel Mechanics Technology/Technician** *72 students enrolled* • **Drafting and Design Technology/Technician, General** *6 students enrolled* • **Electrician** *143 students enrolled* • **Emergency Medical Technology/Technician (EMT Paramedic)** *43 students enrolled* • **Engineering Technology, General** *5 students enrolled* • **Executive Assistant/Executive Secretary** *226 students enrolled* • **Fire Science/Firefighting** *2 students enrolled* • **Health/Medical Physics** *1 student enrolled* • **Heating, Air Conditioning, Ventilation and Refrigeration Maintenance Technology/Technician (HAC, HACR, HVAC, HVACR)** *32 students enrolled* • **Industrial Mechanics and Maintenance Technology** *10 students enrolled* • **Licensed Practical/Vocational Nurse Training (LPN, LVN, Cert, Dipl, AAS)** *373 students enrolled* • **Machine Shop Technology/Assistant** *17 students enrolled* • **Medical Radiologic Technology/Science—Radiation Therapist** *2 students enrolled* • **Medical/Clinical Assistant** *24 students enrolled* • **Nurse/Nursing Assistant/Aide and Patient Care Assistant** *23 students enrolled* • **Pharmacy Technician/Assistant** *5 students enrolled* • **Surgical Technology/Technologist** *6 students enrolled* • **Truck and Bus Driver/Commercial Vehicle Operation** *28 students enrolled* • **Welding Technology/Welder** *131 students enrolled*

**STUDENT SERVICES** Academic or career counseling, employment services for current students, placement services for program completers, remedial services.

# LOUISIANA

## Alden's School of Cosmetology

2080 Main Street, Baker, LA 70714

**CONTACT** Alden J. Hall
**Telephone:** 225-775-1800

**GENERAL INFORMATION** Private Institution. **Total program enrollment:** 37.

**PROGRAM(S) OFFERED**
• **Aesthetician/Esthetician and Skin Care Specialist** *750 hrs./$6150* • **Cosmetology and Related Personal Grooming Arts, Other** *40 hrs./$500* • **Cosmetology, Barber/Styling, and Nail Instructor** *500 hrs./$3800* • **Cosmetology/Cosmetologist, General** *1500 hrs./$9000* • **Hair Styling/Stylist and Hair Design** *1000 hrs./$6800* • **Nail Technician/Specialist and Manicurist** *500 hrs./$3500*

## American Commercial College

3014 Knight Street, Shreveport, LA 71105-2502
http://www.acc-careers.com/

**CONTACT** Brent Sheets, President
**Telephone:** 318-861-2112

**GENERAL INFORMATION** Private Institution. **Total program enrollment:** 84. **Application fee:** $150.

**PROGRAM(S) OFFERED**
• **Accounting Technology/Technician and Bookkeeping** *31 hrs./$12,750* • **Accounting** *10 students enrolled* • **Administrative Assistant and Secretarial Science, General** *29 hrs./$10,230* • **Business/Commerce, General** *9 students enrolled* • **Health Information/Medical Records Technology/Technician** *42 hrs./$12,750* • **Medical Insurance Specialist/Medical Biller** • **Medical Office Computer Specialist/Assistant** *31 hrs./$12,750* • **Medical Transcription/Transcriptionist** *38 hrs./$10,230* • **Medical/Clinical Assistant** *38 hrs./$10,230*

**STUDENT SERVICES** Employment services for current students, placement services for program completers.

## American School of Business

702 Professional Drive North, Shreveport, LA 71105

**CONTACT** Charles L. Harris, Jr., President
**Telephone:** 318-798-3333

**GENERAL INFORMATION** Private Institution. Founded 1985. **Total program enrollment:** 97. **Application fee:** $100.

**PROGRAM(S) OFFERED**
• **Accounting** *720 hrs./$8300* • **Administrative Assistant and Secretarial Science, General** *720 hrs./$8300* • **Computer Software and Media Applications, Other** *720 hrs./$8300* • **Health/Health Care Administration/Management** *720 hrs./$8300* • **Heating, Air Conditioning, Ventilation and Refrigeration Maintenance Technology/Technician (HAC, HACR, HVAC, HVACR)** *1080 hrs./$10,500* • **Medical Office Assistant/Specialist** *30 students enrolled* • **Medical Transcription/Transcriptionist** *900 hrs./$10,100*

**STUDENT SERVICES** Placement services for program completers.

## Ascension College

East Ascension Street, Gonzales, LA 70737
http://www.ascensioncollege.org/

**CONTACT** Dennis Kerr, President
**Telephone:** 225-647-6609

**GENERAL INFORMATION** Private Institution. Founded 1987. **Total program enrollment:** 142. **Application fee:** $100.

**PROGRAM(S) OFFERED**
• **Administrative Assistant and Secretarial Science, General** *58 hrs./$7995* • **Dental Assisting/Assistant** *72 hrs./$8895* • **Medical Office Assistant/Specialist** *16 students enrolled* • **Medical Office Computer Specialist/Assistant** *59 hrs./$7995* • **Medical/Clinical Assistant** *72 hrs./$9025* • **Nursing, Other** *118 hrs./$17,795*

**STUDENT SERVICES** Academic or career counseling, employment services for current students, placement services for program completers.

## Aveda Institute–Baton Rouge

2834 South Sherwood Forest Boulevard, Baton Rouge, LA 70816
http://www.avedainstitutes.com/

**CONTACT** Robert T. Blackwell, President
**Telephone:** 225-295-1435

**GENERAL INFORMATION** Private Institution. **Total program enrollment:** 103. **Application fee:** $200.

**PROGRAM(S) OFFERED**
• **Cosmetology/Cosmetologist, General** *1500 hrs./$16,000*

**STUDENT SERVICES** Academic or career counseling, employment services for current students, placement services for program completers.

## Aveda Institute–Covington

1355 Polders Lane, Covington, LA 70433
http://www.avedainstitutes.com/

**CONTACT** Robert Terry Blackwell, President/Chief Executive
**Telephone:** 985-892-9953 Ext. 1224

**GENERAL INFORMATION** Private Institution. **Total program enrollment:** 122. **Application fee:** $200.

**PROGRAM(S) OFFERED**
• **Aesthetician/Esthetician and Skin Care Specialist** *750 hrs./$7500* • **Cosmetology/Cosmetologist, General** *1500 hrs./$16,000* • **Nail Technician/Specialist and Manicurist**

**STUDENT SERVICES** Academic or career counseling, employment services for current students, placement services for program completers.

## Aveda Institute–Lafayette

2922 Johnston Street, Lafayette, LA 70503
http://www.beautybasicsinc.com/

**CONTACT** Terry Blackwell, President
**Telephone:** 337-233-0511

**GENERAL INFORMATION** Private Institution. Founded 1985. **Total program enrollment:** 100. **Application fee:** $200.

**PROGRAM(S) OFFERED**
• **Aesthetician/Esthetician and Skin Care Specialist** *750 hrs./$7500* • **Cosmetology/Cosmetologist, General** *1500 hrs./$16,000* • **Nail Technician/Specialist and Manicurist**

**STUDENT SERVICES** Academic or career counseling, employment services for current students, placement services for program completers.

## Ayers Institute

Shreveport, LA 71105
http://www.ayersinstitute.com/

**CONTACT** Bruce A. Busada, President
**Telephone:** 318-868-3000

**GENERAL INFORMATION** Private Institution. **Total program enrollment:** 363.

*Ayers Institute (continued)*

**PROGRAM(S) OFFERED**
• **Heating, Air Conditioning, Ventilation and Refrigeration Maintenance Technology/Technician (HAC, HACR, HVAC, HVACR)** *45 students enrolled* • **Medical/Clinical Assistant** *24 students enrolled* • **Pharmacy Technician/ Assistant** *64 students enrolled*

**STUDENT SERVICES** Academic or career counseling, placement services for program completers.

## Bastrop Beauty School

117 South Vine Street, Bastrop, LA 71220

**CONTACT** C. David Dumas, Owner-President
**Telephone:** 318-281-1157

**GENERAL INFORMATION** Private Institution. **Total program enrollment:** 41.

**PROGRAM(S) OFFERED**
• **Cosmetology, Barber/Styling, and Nail Instructor** *750 hrs./$3195* • **Cosmetology/Cosmetologist, General** *1500 hrs./$7694* • **Nail Technician/ Specialist and Manicurist** *600 hrs./$2215*

**STUDENT SERVICES** Academic or career counseling, placement services for program completers.

## Baton Rouge College

2834 South Sherwood Forest, Suite B12, Baton Rouge, LA 70816
http://brc.edu/

**CONTACT** Mohammad Ajmal, President
**Telephone:** 225-292-5464 Ext. 23

**GENERAL INFORMATION** Private Institution. **Total program enrollment:** 22.

**PROGRAM(S) OFFERED**
• **Legal Assistant/Paralegal** *12 students enrolled*

**STUDENT SERVICES** Placement services for program completers.

## Baton Rouge Community College

5310 Florida Boulevard, Baton Rouge, LA 70806
http://www.brcc.cc.la.us/

**CONTACT** Myrtle E.B. Dorsey, Chancellor
**Telephone:** 225-216-8000

**GENERAL INFORMATION** Public Institution. Founded 1995. **Accreditation:** Regional (SACS/CC). **Total program enrollment:** 4068. **Application fee:** $7.

**PROGRAM(S) OFFERED**
• **Business/Commerce, General** *11 students enrolled* • **Security and Protective Services, Other**

**STUDENT SERVICES** Academic or career counseling, employment services for current students, placement services for program completers, remedial services.

## Baton Rouge School of Computers

10425 Plaza Americana, Baton Rouge, LA 70816
http://www.brsc.edu/

**CONTACT** Betty D. Truxillo, Director
**Telephone:** 225-923-2524

**GENERAL INFORMATION** Private Institution. Founded 1979. **Accreditation:** State accredited or approved. **Total program enrollment:** 15.

**PROGRAM(S) OFFERED**
• **Computer Systems Networking and Telecommunications** *90 hrs./$25,000* • **Computer and Information Sciences and Support Services, Other** *16 students enrolled* • **Data Entry/Microcomputer Applications, General** *45 hrs./ $13,200* • **Data Entry/Microcomputer Applications, Other** *45 hrs./$12,500* • **System, Networking, and LAN/WAN Management/Manager** *90 hrs./$25,000* • **Web/Multimedia Management and Webmaster** *45 hrs./$12,000*

**STUDENT SERVICES** Employment services for current students, placement services for program completers.

## Blue Cliff College–Alexandria

1505 Metro Drive, Alexandria, LA 71301

**CONTACT** Michael Maise, Director
**Telephone:** 318-445-2778

**GENERAL INFORMATION** Private Institution. **Total program enrollment:** 165.

**PROGRAM(S) OFFERED**
• **Cosmetology and Related Personal Grooming Arts, Other** • **Massage Therapy/Therapeutic Massage** *20 students enrolled* • **Medical Office Assistant/ Specialist**

**STUDENT SERVICES** Academic or career counseling, employment services for current students, placement services for program completers, remedial services.

## Blue Cliff College–Baton Rouge

6160 Perkins Road, Suite 200, Baton Rouge, LA 70808
http://bluecliffcollege.com/

**CONTACT** Mr. Edward Moore, Owner/Campus Director
**Telephone:** 225-757-3770

**GENERAL INFORMATION** Private Institution. **Total program enrollment:** 25. **Application fee:** $25.

**PROGRAM(S) OFFERED**
• **Massage Therapy/Therapeutic Massage** *53 hrs./$11,530*

**STUDENT SERVICES** Academic or career counseling, placement services for program completers.

## Blue Cliff College–Houma

805 Barrow Street, Houma, LA 70360
http://www.bluecliffcollege.com/

**CONTACT** A. Michael Rowan, Director
**Telephone:** 985-601-4000

**GENERAL INFORMATION** Private Institution. **Total program enrollment:** 109.

**PROGRAM(S) OFFERED**
• **Allied Health and Medical Assisting Services, Other** *47 students enrolled* • **Cosmetology and Related Personal Grooming Arts, Other** • **Massage Therapy/Therapeutic Massage** *32 students enrolled*

**STUDENT SERVICES** Academic or career counseling.

## Blue Cliff College–Lafayette

100 Asma Boulevard, Suite 350, Lafayette, LA 70508-3862
http://www.bluecliffcollege.com/

**CONTACT** Hilda Jones, Director
**Telephone:** 337-269-0620

**GENERAL INFORMATION** Private Institution. **Total program enrollment:** 100.

**PROGRAM(S) OFFERED**
• **Massage Therapy/Therapeutic Massage** *85 students enrolled*

**STUDENT SERVICES** Academic or career counseling, placement services for program completers.

## Blue Cliff College–Metairie

3501 Severn Avenue, Suite 20, Metairie, LA 70002
http://www.bluecliffcollege.com/

**CONTACT** Vicki Gidney, Director
**Telephone:** 504-456-3141 Ext. 2225

**GENERAL INFORMATION** Private Institution. **Total program enrollment:** 134.

**PROGRAM(S) OFFERED**
• **Allied Health and Medical Assisting Services, Other** *42 students enrolled*
• **Massage Therapy/Therapeutic Massage** *64 students enrolled*

**STUDENT SERVICES** Academic or career counseling, placement services for program completers.

## Blue Cliff College–Shreveport

8731 Park Plaza Drive, Shreveport, LA 71105
http://www.bluecliffcollege.com/

**CONTACT** Michael Maise, Director
**Telephone:** 318-425-7941

**GENERAL INFORMATION** Private Institution. **Total program enrollment:** 91.

**PROGRAM(S) OFFERED**
• **Allied Health and Medical Assisting Services, Other** *24 students enrolled*
• **Cosmetology and Related Personal Grooming Arts, Other** • **Massage Therapy/Therapeutic Massage** *47 students enrolled*

**STUDENT SERVICES** Academic or career counseling, placement services for program completers.

## Bossier Parish Community College

2719 Airline Drive North, Bossier City, LA 71111-5801
http://www.bpcc.edu/

**CONTACT** Tom Carleton, Chancellor
**Telephone:** 318-678-6000

**GENERAL INFORMATION** Public Institution. Founded 1967. **Accreditation:** Regional (SACS/CC); medical assisting (AAMAE); physical therapy assisting (APTA); respiratory therapy technology (CoARC). **Total program enrollment:** 2681. **Application fee:** $15.

**PROGRAM(S) OFFERED**
• **Business/Commerce, General** *3 students enrolled* • **Computer and Information Sciences and Support Services, Other** • **Construction Engineering Technology/Technician** *2 students enrolled* • **Culinary Arts/Chef Training** *22 students enrolled* • **Drafting/Design Engineering Technologies/Technicians, Other** *3 students enrolled* • **Foods, Nutrition, and Wellness Studies, General** *2 students enrolled* • **Information Science/Studies** *2 students enrolled* • **Legal Administrative Assistant/Secretary** *3 students enrolled* • **Medical Office Assistant/Specialist** *15 students enrolled* • **Medical/Clinical Assistant** *15 students enrolled* • **Pharmacy Technician/Assistant** *6 students enrolled* • **Phlebotomy/Phlebotomist** *9 students enrolled* • **Recording Arts Technology/Technician** *26 students enrolled* • **Surgical Technology/Technologist** *15 students enrolled*

**STUDENT SERVICES** Academic or career counseling, employment services for current students, remedial services.

## Camelot College

2618 Wooddale Boulevard, Suite A, Baton Rouge, LA 70805
http://www.camelotcollege.com/

**CONTACT** Ronnie L. Williams, President/CEO
**Telephone:** 205-928-3005

**GENERAL INFORMATION** Private Institution. Founded 1986. **Accreditation:** State accredited or approved. **Total program enrollment:** 314.

**PROGRAM(S) OFFERED**
• **Cosmetology, Barber/Styling, and Nail Instructor** *720 hrs./$9554*
• **Cosmetology/Cosmetologist, General** *1500 hrs./$13,986* • **Data Processing and Data Processing Technology/Technician** *59 hrs./$11,488* • **Legal Assistant/Paralegal** *2008 hrs./$15,000* • **Medical/Clinical Assistant** *67 hrs./$11,288* • **Nail Technician/Specialist and Manicurist** *700 hrs./$5200*

**STUDENT SERVICES** Academic or career counseling, daycare for children of students, employment services for current students, placement services for program completers, remedial services.

## Cameron College

2740 Canal Street, New Orleans, LA 70119
http://www.cameroncollege.com/

**CONTACT** Eleanor Cameron, President
**Telephone:** 504-821-5881

**GENERAL INFORMATION** Private Institution. Founded 1981. **Accreditation:** State accredited or approved. **Total program enrollment:** 145. **Application fee:** $100.

**PROGRAM(S) OFFERED**
• **Health/Medical Preparatory Programs, Other** *901 hrs./$8945* • **Information Technology** *904 hrs./$8495* • **Medical Insurance Coding Specialist/Coder** *11 students enrolled* • **Medical Insurance Specialist/Medical Biller** *1020 hrs./$9975* • **Medical Office Assistant/Specialist** *924 hrs./$8495* • **Nurse/Nursing Assistant/Aide and Patient Care Assistant** • **Phlebotomy/Phlebotomist** *920 hrs./$7421*

**STUDENT SERVICES** Academic or career counseling, employment services for current students, placement services for program completers.

## Career Technical College

2319 Louisville Avenue, Monroe, LA 71201
http://www.careertc.edu/

**CONTACT** Cheryl Lokey, College Director
**Telephone:** 318-323-2889

**GENERAL INFORMATION** Private Institution. Founded 1985. **Accreditation:** Surgical technology (ARCST); state accredited or approved. **Total program enrollment:** 474. **Application fee:** $40.

**PROGRAM(S) OFFERED**
• **Massage Therapy/Therapeutic Massage** *8 students enrolled* • **Medical Office Management/Administration** *1 student enrolled* • **Medical/Clinical Assistant**

**STUDENT SERVICES** Academic or career counseling, employment services for current students, placement services for program completers, remedial services.

## Career Technical College

1227 Shreveport-Barksdale Highway, Shreveport, LA 71105

**CONTACT** Bill McGuire, Campus Director
**Telephone:** 318-629-2889

**GENERAL INFORMATION** Private Institution. **Total program enrollment:** 218. **Application fee:** $40.

*Career Technical College (continued)*

**PROGRAM(S) OFFERED**
• **Allied Health and Medical Assisting Services, Other** • **Massage Therapy/Therapeutic Massage**

**STUDENT SERVICES** Academic or career counseling, employment services for current students, placement services for program completers.

## Cloyd's Beauty School #1

603 Natchitoches Street, West Monroe, LA 71291-3131
http://cloydsbeautyschool.com/

**CONTACT** J. Rhett Mathieu, Chief Executive Officer
**Telephone:** 318-322-5314

**GENERAL INFORMATION** Public Institution. Founded 1955. **Total program enrollment:** 43. **Application fee:** $100.

**PROGRAM(S) OFFERED**
• **Cosmetology, Barber/Styling, and Nail Instructor** *750 hrs./$2900*
• **Cosmetology/Cosmetologist, General** *1500 hrs./$7450* • **Nail Technician/Specialist and Manicurist** *600 hrs./$2475*

**STUDENT SERVICES** Academic or career counseling, placement services for program completers.

## Cloyd's Beauty School #2

1311 Winnsboro Road, Monroe, LA 71202
http://cloydsbeautyschool.com/

**CONTACT** J. Rhett Mathieu, Chief Executive Officer
**Telephone:** 318-323-2138

**GENERAL INFORMATION** Public Institution. Founded 1977. **Total program enrollment:** 15. **Application fee:** $100.

**PROGRAM(S) OFFERED**
• **Cosmetology, Barber/Styling, and Nail Instructor** *750 hrs./$2900*
• **Cosmetology/Cosmetologist, General** *1500 hrs./$7450* • **Nail Technician/Specialist and Manicurist** *600 hrs./$2475*

**STUDENT SERVICES** Academic or career counseling, placement services for program completers.

## Cloyd's Beauty School #3

2514 Ferrand Street, Monroe, LA 71201-3539
http://cloydsbeautyschool.com/

**CONTACT** J. Rhett Mathieu, Chief Executive Officer
**Telephone:** 318-388-3710

**GENERAL INFORMATION** Private Institution. Founded 1955. **Total program enrollment:** 38. **Application fee:** $100.

**PROGRAM(S) OFFERED**
• **Aesthetician/Esthetician and Skin Care Specialist** *750 hrs./$3375*
• **Cosmetology, Barber/Styling, and Nail Instructor** *750 hrs./$2900*
• **Cosmetology/Cosmetologist, General** *1500 hrs./$7450* • **Nail Technician/Specialist and Manicurist** *600 hrs./$2475*

**STUDENT SERVICES** Academic or career counseling, placement services for program completers.

## Compass Career College

18175 Old Covington Highway, Hammond, LA 70403
http://www.com/passcareercollege.com/

**CONTACT** Phillip R. Moore, Director
**Telephone:** 985-419-2050

**GENERAL INFORMATION** Private Institution. **Total program enrollment:** 158. **Application fee:** $100.

**PROGRAM(S) OFFERED**
• **Health Aide** *6 students enrolled* • **Licensed Practical/Vocational Nurse Training (LPN, LVN, Cert, Dipl, AAS)** *1660 hrs./$19,415* • **Medical Insurance Coding Specialist/Coder** *700 hrs./$9850* • **Medical/Clinical Assistant** *825 hrs./$12,097* • **Nurse/Nursing Assistant/Aide and Patient Care Assistant** *125 hrs./$1000* • **Phlebotomy/Phlebotomist** *350 hrs./$3325*

**STUDENT SERVICES** Placement services for program completers.

## Cosmetology Training Center

2516 Johnston Street, Lafayette, LA 70503

**CONTACT** Lora Moreau, Owner Director
**Telephone:** 337-237-6868

**GENERAL INFORMATION** Private Institution. **Total program enrollment:** 100.

**PROGRAM(S) OFFERED**
• **Cosmetology, Barber/Styling, and Nail Instructor** *750 hrs./$2900*
• **Cosmetology/Cosmetologist, General** *1500 hrs./$10,500* • **Nail Technician/Specialist and Manicurist** *6 hrs./$2485*

## Crescent City Bartending School

209 North Broad Street, New Orleans, LA 70119
http://crescentschools.com/

**CONTACT** Ronnie Richard, Jr., President
**Telephone:** 504-822-3362

**GENERAL INFORMATION** Private Institution. Founded 1983. **Total program enrollment:** 496.

**PROGRAM(S) OFFERED**
• **Bartending/Bartender** *45 hrs./$795* • **Personal and Culinary Services, Other** *336 hrs./$3600*

**STUDENT SERVICES** Placement services for program completers.

## Delgado Community College

501 City Park Avenue, New Orleans, LA 70119-4399
http://www.dcc.edu/

**CONTACT** Dr. Ron D. Wright, Chancellor
**Telephone:** 504-361-6410

**GENERAL INFORMATION** Public Institution. Founded 1921. **Accreditation:** Regional (SACS/CC); emergency medical services (JRCEMTP); engineering technology (ABET/TAC); funeral service (ABFSE); health information technology (AHIMA); medical laboratory technology (NAACLS); physical therapy assisting (APTA); radiologic technology: radiography (JRCERT); respiratory therapy technology (CoARC). **Total program enrollment:** 6387. **Application fee:** $15.

**PROGRAM(S) OFFERED**
• **Applied Horticulture/Horticultural Operations, General** *5 students enrolled* • **Automobile/Automotive Mechanics Technology/Technician** *22 students enrolled* • **Baking and Pastry Arts/Baker/Pastry Chef** • **Culinary Arts/Chef Training** *8 students enrolled* • **Diagnostic Medical Sonography/Sonographer and Ultrasound Technician** *11 students enrolled* • **Diesel Mechanics Technology/Technician** • **Drafting and Design Technology/Technician, General** *11 students enrolled* • **Electrical/Electronics Maintenance and Repair Technology, Other** *2 students enrolled* • **Electrician** *15 students enrolled* • **Emergency Medical Technology/Technician (EMT Paramedic)** *16 students enrolled* • **Entrepreneurship/Entrepreneurial Studies** • **Fire Protection and Safety Technology/Technician** *9 students enrolled* • **Health Information/Medical Records Technology/Technician** *4 students enrolled* • **Hospitality Administration/Management, General** *2 students enrolled* • **Interior Design** • **Legal Administrative Assistant/Secretary** *5 students enrolled* • **Licensed Practical/Vocational Nurse Training (LPN, LVN, Cert, Dipl, AAS)** *40 students enrolled* • **Logistics and Materials Management** • **Massage Therapy/Therapeutic Massage** *12 students enrolled* • **Medical Radiologic Technology/Science—Radiation Therapist** • **Nuclear Medical Technology/Technologist** *6 students enrolled* • **Occupational Safety and Health Technology/Technician** *2 students enrolled* • **Ophthalmic Technician/Technologist** *10 students enrolled* • **Pharmacy Technician/Assistant** *9 students enrolled* • **Security and Protective**

**Services, Other** • **Sign Language Interpretation and Translation** *14 students enrolled* • **Surgical Technology/Technologist** *17 students enrolled* • **Web Page, Digital/Multimedia and Information Resources Design** *2 students enrolled*

**STUDENT SERVICES** Academic or career counseling, daycare for children of students, employment services for current students, placement services for program completers, remedial services.

## Delta College of Arts and Technology

7380 Exchange Place, Baton Rouge, LA 70806-3851
http://www.deltacollege.com/

**CONTACT** Billy L. Clark, President
**Telephone:** 225-928-7770

**GENERAL INFORMATION** Private Institution. **Accreditation:** State accredited or approved. **Total program enrollment:** 317. **Application fee:** $100.

**PROGRAM(S) OFFERED**
• **Administrative Assistant and Secretarial Science, General** *720 hrs./$8650* • **Commercial and Advertising Art** *1620 hrs./$18,900* • **Dental Assisting/Assistant** *756 hrs./$8650* • **Health Aide** • **Licensed Practical/Vocational Nurse Training (LPN, LVN, Cert, Dipl, AAS)** *1574 hrs./$22,096* • **Medical Insurance Coding Specialist/Coder** *720 hrs./$8650* • **Medical/Clinical Assistant** *786 hrs./$8650*

**STUDENT SERVICES** Academic or career counseling, employment services for current students, placement services for program completers.

## Delta College of Arts and Technology

2401 North Highway 190, Covington, LA 70433
http://www.deltacollege.com/

**CONTACT** Billy L. Clark, President
**Telephone:** 985-892-6651

**GENERAL INFORMATION** Private Institution. **Total program enrollment:** 97. **Application fee:** $100.

**PROGRAM(S) OFFERED**
• **Administrative Assistant and Secretarial Science, General** *720 hrs./$8650* • **Dental Assisting/Assistant** *756 hrs./$8650* • **Health and Medical Administrative Services, Other** *786 hrs./$8650* • **Licensed Practical/Vocational Nurse Training (LPN, LVN, Cert, Dipl, AAS)** *1594 hrs./$21,096* • **Massage Therapy/Therapeutic Massage** *674 hrs./$8650* • **Medical/Clinical Assistant** *786 hrs./$8650*

**STUDENT SERVICES** Academic or career counseling, placement services for program completers.

## Delta School of Business & Technology

517 Broad Street, Lake Charles, LA 70601
http://www.deltatech.edu/

**CONTACT** Gary Holt, President
**Telephone:** 337-439-5765 Ext. 1926

**GENERAL INFORMATION** Private Institution. **Accreditation:** State accredited or approved. **Total program enrollment:** 328.

**PROGRAM(S) OFFERED**
• **Accounting** • **Administrative Assistant and Secretarial Science, General** *4 students enrolled* • **Medical Office Assistant/Specialist** *10 students enrolled*

**STUDENT SERVICES** Academic or career counseling, daycare for children of students, employment services for current students, placement services for program completers.

## Demmon School of Beauty

1222 Ryan Street, Lake Charles, LA 70601

**CONTACT** Jim Haynes, President
**Telephone:** 337-439-9265

**GENERAL INFORMATION** Private Institution. **Total program enrollment:** 43. **Application fee:** $100.

**PROGRAM(S) OFFERED**
• **Cosmetology and Related Personal Grooming Arts, Other** *1500 hrs./$5900*

**STUDENT SERVICES** Placement services for program completers.

## Denham Springs Beauty School

923 Florida Boulevard, Denham Springs, LA 70726

**CONTACT** Frances Hand, Director
**Telephone:** 225-665-6188

**GENERAL INFORMATION** Private Institution. **Total program enrollment:** 88. **Application fee:** $100.

**PROGRAM(S) OFFERED**
• **Cosmetology/Cosmetologist, General** *1500 hrs./$9900* • **Nail Technician/Specialist and Manicurist** *600 hrs./$3250*

**STUDENT SERVICES** Academic or career counseling, placement services for program completers.

## Diesel Driving Academy

8136 Airline Highway, Baton Rouge, LA 70815
http://www.dieseldrivingacademy.com/

**CONTACT** Bruce A. Busada, President
**Telephone:** 318-636-6300

**GENERAL INFORMATION** Private Institution. **Total program enrollment:** 222.

**PROGRAM(S) OFFERED**
• **Truck and Bus Driver/Commercial Vehicle Operation** *495 hrs./$9900*

**STUDENT SERVICES** Placement services for program completers.

## Diesel Driving Academy

3523 Greenwood Drive, Shreveport, LA 71109
http://www.dieseldrivingacademy.com/

**CONTACT** Bruce A. Busada, President
**Telephone:** 318-636-6300

**GENERAL INFORMATION** Private Institution. **Total program enrollment:** 195.

**PROGRAM(S) OFFERED**
• **Truck and Bus Driver/Commercial Vehicle Operation** *495 hrs./$9900*

**STUDENT SERVICES** Placement services for program completers.

## D-Jay's School of Beauty Arts and Sciences

5131 Government Street, Baton Rouge, LA 70806

**CONTACT** Deborah Schilleci, President
**Telephone:** 225-272-6595

**GENERAL INFORMATION** Private Institution. **Total program enrollment:** 74.

*D-Jay's School of Beauty Arts and Sciences (continued)*

**PROGRAM(S) OFFERED**
- **Cosmetology, Barber/Styling, and Nail Instructor** *600 hrs./$3850*
- **Cosmetology/Cosmetologist, General** *1500 hrs./$12,500* • **Nail Technician/Specialist and Manicurist** *600 hrs./$3850*

**STUDENT SERVICES** Academic or career counseling, placement services for program completers.

## Eastern College of Health Vocations

3321 Hessmer Avenue, Suite 200, Metairie, LA 70002
http://www.echv.com/

**CONTACT** Joseph Dalto, III, Owner
**Telephone:** 504-736-0654

**GENERAL INFORMATION** Private Institution. Founded 1986. **Total program enrollment:** 107. **Application fee:** $100.

**PROGRAM(S) OFFERED**
- **Medical/Clinical Assistant** *736 hrs./$9160*

**STUDENT SERVICES** Academic or career counseling, placement services for program completers.

## Elaine P. Nunez Community College

3710 Paris Road, Chalmette, LA 70043-1249
http://www.nunez.edu/

**CONTACT** Thomas R. Warner, EdD, Chancellor
**Telephone:** 504-278-6245

**GENERAL INFORMATION** Public Institution. Founded 1992. **Accreditation:** Regional (SACS/CC). **Total program enrollment:** 641. **Application fee:** $10.

**PROGRAM(S) OFFERED**
- **Administrative Assistant and Secretarial Science, General** *4 students enrolled*
- **Carpentry/Carpenter** • **Child Care Provider/Assistant** *6 students enrolled*
- **Computer Technology/Computer Systems Technology** *1 student enrolled*
- **Culinary Arts/Chef Training** *3 students enrolled* • **Electrician** *1 student enrolled*
- **Emergency Medical Technology/Technician (EMT Paramedic)** *25 students enrolled* • **Heating, Air Conditioning, Ventilation and Refrigeration Maintenance Technology/Technician (HAC, HACR, HVAC, HVACR)** *1 student enrolled* • **Information Science/Studies** • **Legal Assistant/Paralegal** *7 students enrolled* • **Licensed Practical/Vocational Nurse Training (LPN, LVN, Cert, Dipl, AAS)** *26 students enrolled* • **Medical Insurance Coding Specialist/Coder** *8 students enrolled* • **Nurse/Nursing Assistant/Aide and Patient Care Assistant** *55 students enrolled*

**STUDENT SERVICES** Academic or career counseling, employment services for current students, placement services for program completers, remedial services.

## Grambling State University

PO Box 607, Grambling, LA 71245
http://www.gram.edu/

**CONTACT** Dr. Horace A. Judson, President
**Telephone:** 318-247-3811

**GENERAL INFORMATION** Public Institution. Founded 1901. **Accreditation:** Regional (SACS/CC); computer science (ABET/CSAC); engineering technology (ABET/TAC); journalism and mass communications (ACEJMC); music (NASM); recreation and parks (NRPA); theater (NAST). **Total program enrollment:** 4750. **Application fee:** $20.

**PROGRAM(S) OFFERED**
- **Legal Assistant/Paralegal** *1 student enrolled*

**STUDENT SERVICES** Academic or career counseling, employment services for current students, placement services for program completers, remedial services.

## Gretna Career College

1415 Whitney Avenue, Gretna, LA 70053-5835
http://www.gretnacareercollege.com/

**CONTACT** Nick Randazzo, President
**Telephone:** 504-366-5409

**GENERAL INFORMATION** Private Institution. Founded 1991. **Accreditation:** State accredited or approved. **Total program enrollment:** 103.

**PROGRAM(S) OFFERED**
- **Business Administration and Management, General** *114 hrs./$21,250*
- **Computer and Information Sciences and Support Services, Other** *17 students enrolled* • **Computer and Information Sciences, Other** *54 hrs./$10,575*
- **Medical Administrative/Executive Assistant and Medical Secretary** *112 hrs./$21,250* • **Medical Insurance Coding Specialist/Coder** *60 hrs./$10,575*
- **Medical Insurance Specialist/Medical Biller** *6 students enrolled* • **Medical Office Management/Administration** *108 hrs./$23,700* • **Medical/Clinical Assistant** *50 hrs./$10,575* • **Nurse/Nursing Assistant/Aide and Patient Care Assistant** *4 students enrolled*

**STUDENT SERVICES** Academic or career counseling, employment services for current students, placement services for program completers, remedial services.

## Guy's Shreveport Academy of Cosmetology

3954 Youree Drive, Shreveport, LA 71105
http://www.guysacademy.com/

**CONTACT** Claude Burch, Administrator
**Telephone:** 318-865-5591

**GENERAL INFORMATION** Private Institution. Founded 1954. **Total program enrollment:** 97.

**PROGRAM(S) OFFERED**
- **Aesthetician/Esthetician and Skin Care Specialist** *900 hrs./$9890*
- **Cosmetology, Barber/Styling, and Nail Instructor** *750 hrs./$1800*
- **Cosmetology/Cosmetologist, General** *1500 hrs./$14,124* • **Nail Technician/Specialist and Manicurist** *600 hrs./$4830*

**STUDENT SERVICES** Academic or career counseling, placement services for program completers.

## Herzing College

2400 Veterans Boulevard, Kenner, LA 70062
http://www.herzing.edu/

**CONTACT** Mark Aspiazu, President
**Telephone:** 504-733-0074

**GENERAL INFORMATION** Private Institution. Founded 1996. **Accreditation:** State accredited or approved. **Total program enrollment:** 125.

**PROGRAM(S) OFFERED**
- **Allied Health and Medical Assisting Services, Other** • **Medical Insurance Coding Specialist/Coder** *8 students enrolled*

**STUDENT SERVICES** Academic or career counseling, employment services for current students, placement services for program completers, remedial services.

## ITI Technical College

13944 Airline Highway, Baton Rouge, LA 70817
http://www.iticollege.edu/

**CONTACT** Mark Worthy, Vice President
**Telephone:** 225-752-4233

**GENERAL INFORMATION** Private Institution. Founded 1973. **Accreditation:** State accredited or approved. **Total program enrollment:** 426.

**PROGRAM(S) OFFERED**
• **CAD/CADD Drafting and/or Design Technology/Technician** *101 hrs./$27,350* • **Computer Technology/Computer Systems Technology** *100 hrs./$27,350* • **Drafting and Design Technology/Technician, General** • **Electrical, Electronic and Communications Engineering Technology/Technician** *7 students enrolled* • **Electrician** *9 students enrolled* • **Heating, Air Conditioning and Refrigeration Technology/Technician (ACH/ACR/ACHR/HRAC/HVAC/AC Technology)** *76 hrs./$19,350* • **Heating, Air Conditioning, Ventilation and Refrigeration Maintenance Technology/Technician (HAC, HACR, HVAC, HVACR)** *40 students enrolled* • **Instrumentation Technology/Technician** *105 hrs./$27,350* • **Manufacturing Technology/Technician** *105 hrs./$27,350* • **Office Management and Supervision** *103 hrs./$27,350*

**STUDENT SERVICES** Academic or career counseling, employment services for current students, placement services for program completers, remedial services.

## John Jay Beauty College

2844 Tennessee Avenue, Kenner, LA 70062
http://johnjaybeauty.com/

**CONTACT** John J. Grisaffi, President
**Telephone:** 504-467-2774 Ext. 12

**GENERAL INFORMATION** Private Institution. **Total program enrollment:** 124.

**PROGRAM(S) OFFERED**
• **Aesthetician/Esthetician and Skin Care Specialist** *750 hrs./$3700* • **Cosmetology, Barber/Styling, and Nail Instructor** *750 hrs./$2250* • **Cosmetology/Cosmetologist, General** *1500 hrs./$8400* • **Hair Styling/Stylist and Hair Design** • **Nail Technician/Specialist and Manicurist** *750 hrs./$2250*

**STUDENT SERVICES** Academic or career counseling, placement services for program completers.

## John Jay Charm and Beauty College

540 Robert East Lee Boulevard, New Orleans, LA 70124

**CONTACT** John J. Grisaffi, Jr., President
**Telephone:** 504-467-2774 Ext. 12

**GENERAL INFORMATION** Private Institution.

**PROGRAM(S) OFFERED**
• **Aesthetician/Esthetician and Skin Care Specialist** *750 hrs./$3700* • **Cosmetology and Related Personal Grooming Arts, Other** *750 hrs./$2250* • **Cosmetology, Barber/Styling, and Nail Instructor** *750 hrs./$2250* • **Cosmetology/Cosmetologist, General** *1500 hrs./$8400* • **Nail Technician/Specialist and Manicurist** *750 hrs./$2250*

**STUDENT SERVICES** Academic or career counseling, employment services for current students, placement services for program completers.

## Jonesville Beauty School

1112 First Street, Jonesville, LA 71343

**CONTACT** Tommy Callahan, CEO
**Telephone:** 318-336-2377

**GENERAL INFORMATION** Private Institution. **Total program enrollment:** 31.

**PROGRAM(S) OFFERED**
• **Cosmetology, Barber/Styling, and Nail Instructor** *750 hrs./$4500* • **Cosmetology/Cosmetologist, General** *1500 hrs./$12,500*

**STUDENT SERVICES** Academic or career counseling, placement services for program completers.

## Louisiana Academy of Beauty

550 East Laurel Street, Eunice, LA 70535

**CONTACT** Crystal Bihm, Financial Aid Administrator
**Telephone:** 337-457-9480

**GENERAL INFORMATION** Private Institution. Founded 1985. **Total program enrollment:** 48.

**PROGRAM(S) OFFERED**
• **Cosmetology, Barber/Styling, and Nail Instructor** *750 hrs./$4100* • **Cosmetology/Cosmetologist, General** *1500 hrs./$9000* • **Teacher Education and Professional Development, Specific Subject Areas, Other** *2 students enrolled*

**STUDENT SERVICES** Placement services for program completers.

## Louisiana Culinary Institute

5837 Essen Lane, Baton Rouge, LA 70810
http://www.louisianaculinary.com/

**GENERAL INFORMATION** Private Institution. **Total program enrollment:** 99. **Application fee:** $100.

**PROGRAM(S) OFFERED**
• **Culinary Arts/Chef Training** *56 hrs./$21,100*

**STUDENT SERVICES** Academic or career counseling, employment services for current students, placement services for program completers, remedial services.

## Louisiana Delta Community College

4014 LaSalle Street, Monroe, LA 71203
http://www.ladelta.cc.la.us

**CONTACT** Luke Robins, PhD, Chancellor
**Telephone:** 866-500-5322

**GENERAL INFORMATION** Public Institution. **Total program enrollment:** 809. **Application fee:** $15.

**PROGRAM(S) OFFERED**
• **Child Care Provider/Assistant** *2 students enrolled*

**STUDENT SERVICES** Academic or career counseling, employment services for current students, remedial services.

## Louisiana State University at Alexandria

8100 Highway 71 South, Alexandria, LA 71302-9121
http://www.lsua.edu/

**CONTACT** David P. Manuel, Chancellor
**Telephone:** 318-445-3672

**GENERAL INFORMATION** Public Institution. Founded 1960. **Accreditation:** Regional (SACS/CC); medical laboratory technology (NAACLS). **Total program enrollment:** 1284. **Application fee:** $20.

**PROGRAM(S) OFFERED**
• **Pharmacy Technician/Assistant** *8 students enrolled*

**STUDENT SERVICES** Academic or career counseling, daycare for children of students, employment services for current students, placement services for program completers, remedial services.

## Louisiana State University at Eunice

PO Box 1129, Eunice, LA 70535-1129
http://www.lsue.edu/

**CONTACT** William Nunez, Chancellor
**Telephone:** 337-457-7311

**GENERAL INFORMATION** Public Institution. Founded 1967. **Accreditation:** Regional (SACS/CC); radiologic technology: radiography (JRCERT);

*Louisiana State University at Eunice (continued)*

respiratory therapy technology (CoARC). **Total program enrollment:** 1609. **Application fee:** $25.

**PROGRAM(S) OFFERED**

• **Diagnostic Medical Sonography/Sonographer and Ultrasound Technician** • **Fire Protection, Other** *2 students enrolled* • **Fire Science/Firefighting** *2 students enrolled* • **Forensic Science and Technology** *9 students enrolled* • **General Office Occupations and Clerical Services** *3 students enrolled* • **Health Information/Medical Records Administration/Administrator** • **Health Information/Medical Records Technology/Technician** • **Quality Control and Safety Technologies/Technicians, Other**

**STUDENT SERVICES** Academic or career counseling, employment services for current students, placement services for program completers, remedial services.

## Louisiana Technical College–Acadian Campus

1933 West Hutchinson Avenue, Crowley, LA 70526
http://www.ltc.edu/

**CONTACT** Patricia Miers, Assistant Dean
**Telephone:** 337-788-7521

**GENERAL INFORMATION** Public Institution. Founded 1938. **Accreditation:** State accredited or approved. **Total program enrollment:** 122. **Application fee:** $5.

**PROGRAM(S) OFFERED**

• **Accounting Technology/Technician and Bookkeeping** *10 students enrolled* • **Administrative Assistant and Secretarial Science, General** *3 students enrolled* • **Automobile/Automotive Mechanics Technology/Technician** • **Diesel Mechanics Technology/Technician** *5 students enrolled* • **Drafting and Design Technology/Technician, General** *2 students enrolled* • **Health Aide** *6 students enrolled* • **Licensed Practical/Vocational Nurse Training (LPN, LVN, Cert, Dipl, AAS)** • **Machine Tool Technology/Machinist** *2 students enrolled* • **Mason/Masonry** • **Medical Administrative/Executive Assistant and Medical Secretary** *8 students enrolled* • **Nurse/Nursing Assistant/Aide and Patient Care Assistant** *40 students enrolled* • **Truck and Bus Driver/Commercial Vehicle Operation** *68 students enrolled* • **Welding Technology/Welder** *2 students enrolled*

**STUDENT SERVICES** Academic or career counseling, placement services for program completers, remedial services.

## Louisiana Technical College–Alexandria Campus

4311 South MacArthur, Alexandria, LA 71307-5698
http://www.ltc.edu/

**CONTACT** Mervin Birdwell, Regional Director/Campus Dean
**Telephone:** 318-487-5439 Ext. 116

**GENERAL INFORMATION** Public Institution. **Accreditation:** State accredited or approved. **Total program enrollment:** 252. **Application fee:** $5.

**PROGRAM(S) OFFERED**

• **Accounting Technology/Technician and Bookkeeping** *3 students enrolled* • **Administrative Assistant and Secretarial Science, General** *1 student enrolled* • **Appliance Installation and Repair Technology/Technician** *5 students enrolled* • **Autobody/Collision and Repair Technology/Technician** *3 students enrolled* • **Automobile/Automotive Mechanics Technology/Technician** *1 student enrolled* • **Diesel Mechanics Technology/Technician** • **Drafting and Design Technology/Technician, General** *6 students enrolled* • **Electrician** *6 students enrolled* • **Emergency Medical Technology/Technician (EMT Paramedic)** • **Health Aide** • **Heating, Air Conditioning, Ventilation and Refrigeration Maintenance Technology/Technician (HAC, HACR, HVAC, HVACR)** • **Industrial Electronics Technology/Technician** *3 students enrolled* • **Industrial Mechanics and Maintenance Technology** • **Licensed Practical/Vocational Nurse Training (LPN, LVN, Cert, Dipl, AAS)** *47 students enrolled* • **Machine Tool Technology/Machinist** • **Medical Administrative/Executive Assistant and Medical Secretary** • **Welding Technology/Welder** *3 students enrolled*

**STUDENT SERVICES** Academic or career counseling, placement services for program completers, remedial services.

## Louisiana Technical College–Ascension Campus

9697 Airline Highway, Sorrento, LA 70778-3007
http://www.ltc.edu/

**CONTACT** Donna Seale, Assistant Dean
**Telephone:** 225-675-5397

**GENERAL INFORMATION** Public Institution. **Accreditation:** State accredited or approved. **Total program enrollment:** 143. **Application fee:** $5.

**PROGRAM(S) OFFERED**

• **Accounting Technology/Technician and Bookkeeping** *2 students enrolled* • **Administrative Assistant and Secretarial Science, General** • **Automobile/Automotive Mechanics Technology/Technician** *6 students enrolled* • **Drafting and Design Technology/Technician, General** *6 students enrolled* • **Instrumentation Technology/Technician** *2 students enrolled* • **Welding Technology/Welder**

**STUDENT SERVICES** Academic or career counseling, placement services for program completers, remedial services.

## Louisiana Technical College–Avoyelles Campus

508 Choupique Street, Cottonport, LA 71327
http://www.ltc.edu/

**CONTACT** Jude Pitre, Campus Dean
**Telephone:** 318-876-2401

**GENERAL INFORMATION** Public Institution. **Accreditation:** Regional (SACS/CC); state accredited or approved. **Total program enrollment:** 163. **Application fee:** $5.

**PROGRAM(S) OFFERED**

• **Administrative Assistant and Secretarial Science, General** *3 students enrolled* • **Applied Horticulture/Horticultural Operations, General** *25 students enrolled* • **Autobody/Collision and Repair Technology/Technician** *2 students enrolled* • **Automobile/Automotive Mechanics Technology/Technician** *63 students enrolled* • **Barbering/Barber** • **Culinary Arts/Chef Training** *1 student enrolled* • **Diesel Mechanics Technology/Technician** *2 students enrolled* • **Industrial Electronics Technology/Technician** • **Licensed Practical/Vocational Nurse Training (LPN, LVN, Cert, Dipl, AAS)** *6 students enrolled* • **Mason/Masonry** *31 students enrolled* • **Nurse/Nursing Assistant/Aide and Patient Care Assistant** *14 students enrolled* • **Welding Technology/Welder** *5 students enrolled*

**STUDENT SERVICES** Academic or career counseling, placement services for program completers, remedial services.

## Louisiana Technical College–Bastrop Campus

729 Kammell Street, Bastrop, LA 71221-1120
http://www.ltc.edu/

**CONTACT** Norene R. Smith, Vice Chancellor/Provost
**Telephone:** 318-283-0836

**GENERAL INFORMATION** Public Institution. **Accreditation:** State accredited or approved. **Total program enrollment:** 101. **Application fee:** $5.

PROGRAM(S) OFFERED

• **Administrative Assistant and Secretarial Science, General** *10 students enrolled* • **Industrial Electronics Technology/Technician** *1 student enrolled* • **Licensed Practical/Vocational Nurse Training (LPN, LVN, Cert, Dipl, AAS)** *24 students enrolled* • **Nurse/Nursing Assistant/Aide and Patient Care Assistant** *52 students enrolled* • **Welding Technology/Welder** *35 students enrolled*

**STUDENT SERVICES** Academic or career counseling, placement services for program completers, remedial services.

## Louisiana Technical College–Baton Rouge Campus

3250 North Acadian Thruway East, Baton Rouge, LA 70805
http://www.ltc.edu/

**CONTACT** Dr. Kay McDaniel, Regional Director/Campus Dean
**Telephone:** 225-359-9201

**GENERAL INFORMATION** Public Institution. **Accreditation:** State accredited or approved. **Total program enrollment:** 591. **Application fee:** $5.

**PROGRAM(S) OFFERED**

• **Accounting Technology/Technician and Bookkeeping** *1 student enrolled* • **Administrative Assistant and Secretarial Science, General** *6 students enrolled* • **Automobile/Automotive Mechanics Technology/Technician** *11 students enrolled* • **Barbering/Barber** *10 students enrolled* • **Child Care Provider/Assistant** *5 students enrolled* • **Computer Systems Networking and Telecommunications** *8 students enrolled* • **Cosmetology/Cosmetologist, General** *4 students enrolled* • **Culinary Arts/Chef Training** *1 student enrolled* • **Drafting and Design Technology/Technician, General** *3 students enrolled* • **Heating, Air Conditioning, Ventilation and Refrigeration Maintenance Technology/Technician (HAC, HACR, HVAC, HVACR)** *7 students enrolled* • **Licensed Practical/Vocational Nurse Training (LPN, LVN, Cert, Dipl, AAS)** *46 students enrolled* • **Machine Tool Technology/Machinist** *6 students enrolled* • **Medical Administrative/Executive Assistant and Medical Secretary** *6 students enrolled* • **Printing Press Operator** *2 students enrolled* • **System Administration/Administrator** *8 students enrolled* • **Welding Technology/Welder** *5 students enrolled*

**STUDENT SERVICES** Academic or career counseling, daycare for children of students, employment services for current students, placement services for program completers, remedial services.

## Louisiana Technical College–Charles B. Coreil Campus

1124 Vocational Drive, PO Box 296, Ville Platte, LA 70586-0296
http://www.ltc.edu/

**CONTACT** Susan Fontenot, Assistant Dean
**Telephone:** 337-363-2197

**GENERAL INFORMATION** Public Institution. **Accreditation:** Regional (SACS/CC); state accredited or approved. **Total program enrollment:** 194. **Application fee:** $5.

**PROGRAM(S) OFFERED**

• **Accounting Technology/Technician and Bookkeeping** *1 student enrolled* • **Administrative Assistant and Secretarial Science, General** *2 students enrolled* • **Automobile/Automotive Mechanics Technology/Technician** *1 student enrolled* • **Health Aide** *6 students enrolled* • **Licensed Practical/Vocational Nurse Training (LPN, LVN, Cert, Dipl, AAS)** *21 students enrolled* • **Medical Administrative/Executive Assistant and Medical Secretary** *6 students enrolled* • **Medical/Clinical Assistant** • **Nurse/Nursing Assistant/Aide and Patient Care Assistant** *7 students enrolled* • **Welding Technology/Welder** *21 students enrolled*

**STUDENT SERVICES** Academic or career counseling, placement services for program completers, remedial services.

## Louisiana Technical College–Delta Ouachita Campus

609 Vocational Parkway, West, Ouachita Industrial Park, West Monroe, LA 71292-9064
http://www.ltc.edu/

**CONTACT** Norene Smith, Campus Dean-Regional Director
**Telephone:** 318-397-6100

**GENERAL INFORMATION** Public Institution. Founded 1941. **Accreditation:** State accredited or approved. **Total program enrollment:** 312. **Application fee:** $5.

**PROGRAM(S) OFFERED**

• **Administrative Assistant and Secretarial Science, General** *3 students enrolled* • **Automobile/Automotive Mechanics Technology/Technician** *7 students enrolled* • **Barbering/Barber** *10 students enrolled* • **Building/Property Maintenance and Management** • **Child Care Provider/Assistant** • **Data Processing and Data Processing Technology/Technician** • **Drafting and Design Technology/Technician, General** *2 students enrolled* • **Electrician** *19 students enrolled* • **Emergency Medical Technology/Technician (EMT Paramedic)** *26 students enrolled* • **Health Aide** • **Heating, Air Conditioning, Ventilation and Refrigeration Maintenance Technology/Technician (HAC, HACR, HVAC, HVACR)** *1 student enrolled* • **Industrial Electronics Technology/Technician** *5 students enrolled* • **Industrial Mechanics and Maintenance Technology** • **Instrumentation Technology/Technician** *2 students enrolled* • **Legal Assistant/Paralegal** • **Licensed Practical/Vocational Nurse Training (LPN, LVN, Cert, Dipl, AAS)** *57 students enrolled* • **Machine Tool Technology/Machinist** • **Medical Administrative/Executive Assistant and Medical Secretary** *6 students enrolled* • **Nurse/Nursing Assistant/Aide and Patient Care Assistant** *31 students enrolled* • **Precision Systems Maintenance and Repair Technologies, Other** *6 students enrolled* • **System Administration/Administrator** *2 students enrolled* • **Truck and Bus Driver/Commercial Vehicle Operation** *43 students enrolled* • **Welding Technology/Welder** *43 students enrolled*

**STUDENT SERVICES** Academic or career counseling, placement services for program completers, remedial services.

## Louisiana Technical College–Evangeline Campus

600 South Martin Luther King Drive, St. Martinville, LA 70582
http://www.ltc.edu/

**CONTACT** Millie Filer, Assistant Dean
**Telephone:** 337-394-6466

**GENERAL INFORMATION** Public Institution. **Accreditation:** State accredited or approved. **Total program enrollment:** 99. **Application fee:** $5.

**PROGRAM(S) OFFERED**

• **Accounting Technology/Technician and Bookkeeping** *1 student enrolled* • **Administrative Assistant and Secretarial Science, General** *2 students enrolled* • **Autobody/Collision and Repair Technology/Technician** *1 student enrolled* • **Child Care Provider/Assistant** *2 students enrolled* • **Health Aide** *4 students enrolled* • **Licensed Practical/Vocational Nurse Training (LPN, LVN, Cert, Dipl, AAS)** *11 students enrolled* • **Medical Administrative/Executive Assistant and Medical Secretary** *6 students enrolled* • **Nurse/Nursing Assistant/Aide and Patient Care Assistant** *54 students enrolled* • **Welding Technology/Welder** *23 students enrolled*

**STUDENT SERVICES** Academic or career counseling, placement services for program completers, remedial services.

## Louisiana Technical College–Florida Parishes Campus

PO Box 1300, Greensburg, LA 70441
http://www.ltc.edu/

**CONTACT** Sharon Hornsby, Campus Dean
**Telephone:** 225-222-4251

**GENERAL INFORMATION** Public Institution. **Accreditation:** State accredited or approved. **Total program enrollment:** 83. **Application fee:** $5.

*Louisiana Technical College–Florida Parishes Campus (continued)*

**PROGRAM(S) OFFERED**

• **Accounting Technology/Technician and Bookkeeping** *1 student enrolled* • **Administrative Assistant and Secretarial Science, General** *1 student enrolled* • **Automobile/Automotive Mechanics Technology/Technician** • **Building/ Property Maintenance and Management** *3 students enrolled* • **Criminal Justice/ Safety Studies** • **Electrician** *1 student enrolled* • **Health Aide** *5 students enrolled* • **Licensed Practical/Vocational Nurse Training (LPN, LVN, Cert, Dipl, AAS)** *18 students enrolled* • **Medical Administrative/Executive Assistant and Medical Secretary** *7 students enrolled* • **Nurse/Nursing Assistant/Aide and Patient Care Assistant** *16 students enrolled* • **Veterinary/Animal Health Technology/ Technician and Veterinary Assistant** • **Welding Technology/Welder** *2 students enrolled*

**STUDENT SERVICES** Academic or career counseling, placement services for program completers, remedial services.

## Louisiana Technical College–Folkes Campus

3337 Highway 10, Jackson, LA 70748
http://www.ltc.edu/

**CONTACT** Johnny Arceneaux, Campus Coordinator
**Telephone:** 225-634-2636

**GENERAL INFORMATION** Public Institution. **Accreditation:** State accredited or approved. **Total program enrollment:** 503. **Application fee:** $5.

**PROGRAM(S) OFFERED**

• **Accounting Technology/Technician and Bookkeeping** • **Administrative Assistant and Secretarial Science, General** *7 students enrolled* • **Applied Horticulture/Horticultural Operations, General** *3 students enrolled* • **Autobody/ Collision and Repair Technology/Technician** *4 students enrolled* • **Automobile/ Automotive Mechanics Technology/Technician** *28 students enrolled* • **Building/ Property Maintenance and Management** • **Carpentry/Carpenter** *63 students enrolled* • **Communications Systems Installation and Repair Technology** *9 students enrolled* • **Computer Installation and Repair Technology/Technician** *9 students enrolled* • **Culinary Arts/Chef Training** *5 students enrolled* • **Electrical/ Electronics Equipment Installation and Repair, General** • **Emergency Medical Technology/Technician (EMT Paramedic)** • **Heating, Air Conditioning, Ventilation and Refrigeration Maintenance Technology/Technician (HAC, HACR, HVAC, HVACR)** *3 students enrolled* • **Licensed Practical/Vocational Nurse Training (LPN, LVN, Cert, Dipl, AAS)** • **Mason/Masonry** *3 students enrolled* • **Printing Press Operator** *22 students enrolled* • **Small Engine Mechanics and Repair Technology/Technician** *7 students enrolled* • **System Administration/ Administrator** *40 students enrolled* • **Upholstery/Upholsterer** *1 student enrolled* • **Welding Technology/Welder** *48 students enrolled*

**STUDENT SERVICES** Academic or career counseling, employment services for current students, placement services for program completers, remedial services.

## Louisiana Technical College–Gulf Area Campus

1115 Clover Street, Abbeville, LA 70510
http://www.ltc.edu/

**CONTACT** Kenneth Posey, Assistant Dean
**Telephone:** 337-893-4984

**GENERAL INFORMATION** Public Institution. **Accreditation:** State accredited or approved. **Total program enrollment:** 225. **Application fee:** $5.

**PROGRAM(S) OFFERED**

• **Accounting Technology/Technician and Bookkeeping** *5 students enrolled* • **Administrative Assistant and Secretarial Science, General** *2 students enrolled* • **Autobody/Collision and Repair Technology/Technician** *1 student enrolled* • **Computer Installation and Repair Technology/Technician** *5 students enrolled* • **Cosmetology/Cosmetologist, General** *18 students enrolled* • **Diesel Mechanics Technology/Technician** *2 students enrolled* • **Drafting and Design Technology/Technician, General** *5 students enrolled* • **Electrician** *3 students enrolled* • **Health Aide** *3 students enrolled* • **Heating, Air Conditioning, Ventilation and Refrigeration Maintenance Technology/Technician (HAC, HACR, HVAC, HVACR)** *1 student enrolled* • **Licensed Practical/Vocational Nurse Training (LPN, LVN, Cert, Dipl, AAS)** *11 students enrolled* • **Medical Administrative/ Executive Assistant and Medical Secretary** *7 students enrolled* • **Medical/ Clinical Assistant** • **Nurse/Nursing Assistant/Aide and Patient Care Assistant** *49 students enrolled* • **Welding Technology/Welder** *16 students enrolled*

**STUDENT SERVICES** Academic or career counseling, employment services for current students, placement services for program completers, remedial services.

## Louisiana Technical College–Hammond Campus

111 Pride Avenue, Hammond, LA 70401
http://www.ltc.edu/

**CONTACT** Mack Jackson, Campus Dean
**Telephone:** 985-543-4120 Ext. 108

**GENERAL INFORMATION** Public Institution. Founded 1964. **Accreditation:** State accredited or approved. **Total program enrollment:** 171. **Application fee:** $5.

**PROGRAM(S) OFFERED**

• **Accounting Technology/Technician and Bookkeeping** *1 student enrolled* • **Administrative Assistant and Secretarial Science, General** *1 student enrolled* • **Autobody/Collision and Repair Technology/Technician** • **Automobile/ Automotive Mechanics Technology/Technician** *6 students enrolled* • **Barbering/ Barber** *6 students enrolled* • **Computer Systems Networking and Telecommunications** *1 student enrolled* • **Emergency Care Attendant (EMT Ambulance)** *6 students enrolled* • **Health Aide** *1 student enrolled* • **Licensed Practical/ Vocational Nurse Training (LPN, LVN, Cert, Dipl, AAS)** *5 students enrolled* • **Medical Administrative/Executive Assistant and Medical Secretary** *11 students enrolled* • **Welding Technology/Welder** *12 students enrolled*

**STUDENT SERVICES** Academic or career counseling, employment services for current students, placement services for program completers, remedial services.

## Louisiana Technical College–Huey P. Long Campus

303 South Jones Street, Winnfield, LA 71483
http://www.ltc.edu/

**CONTACT** Danny Keyes, Interim Campus Dean
**Telephone:** 318-628-4342

**GENERAL INFORMATION** Public Institution. Founded 1939. **Accreditation:** State accredited or approved. **Total program enrollment:** 107. **Application fee:** $5.

**PROGRAM(S) OFFERED**

• **Accounting Technology/Technician and Bookkeeping** • **Administrative Assistant and Secretarial Science, General** *8 students enrolled* • **Building/ Property Maintenance and Management** • **Carpentry/Carpenter** *1 student enrolled* • **Health Aide** *8 students enrolled* • **Licensed Practical/Vocational Nurse Training (LPN, LVN, Cert, Dipl, AAS)** *6 students enrolled* • **Medical Administrative/Executive Assistant and Medical Secretary** *8 students enrolled* • **Nurse/Nursing Assistant/Aide and Patient Care Assistant** *20 students enrolled* • **Welding Technology/Welder** *21 students enrolled*

**STUDENT SERVICES** Academic or career counseling, placement services for program completers, remedial services.

## Louisiana Technical College–Jefferson Campus

5200 Blaire Drive, Metairie, LA 70001
http://www.ltc.edu/

**CONTACT** Lesha Coulon, Interim Campus Assistant Dean
**Telephone:** 504-671-6700

**GENERAL INFORMATION** Public Institution. Founded 1949. **Accreditation:** State accredited or approved. **Total program enrollment:** 132. **Application fee:** $5.

**PROGRAM(S) OFFERED**

• **Accounting Technology/Technician and Bookkeeping** • **Administrative Assistant and Secretarial Science, General** • **Automobile/Automotive Mechanics**

**Technology/Technician** *1 student enrolled* • **Culinary Arts/Chef Training** • **Health Aide** • **Heating, Air Conditioning, Ventilation and Refrigeration Maintenance Technology/Technician (HAC, HACR, HVAC, HVACR)** • **Licensed Practical/ Vocational Nurse Training (LPN, LVN, Cert, Dipl, AAS)** *7 students enrolled* • **Medical/Clinical Assistant** • **Nurse/Nursing Assistant/Aide and Patient Care Assistant** *19 students enrolled* • **Phlebotomy/Phlebotomist** *8 students enrolled* • **Technical Theatre/Theatre Design and Technology** • **Welding Technology/ Welder**

**STUDENT SERVICES** Academic or career counseling, remedial services.

## Louisiana Technical College–Jumonville Campus

605 Hospital Road, PO Box 725, New Roads, LA 70760
http://www.ltc.edu/

**CONTACT** Amy Davis, Campus Dean
**Telephone:** 225-638-8613

**GENERAL INFORMATION** Public Institution. Founded 1952. **Accreditation:** Regional (SACS/CC); state accredited or approved. **Total program enrollment:** 73. **Application fee:** $5.

**PROGRAM(S) OFFERED**
• **Accounting Technology/Technician and Bookkeeping** *1 student enrolled* • **Administrative Assistant and Secretarial Science, General** *1 student enrolled* • **Aesthetician/Esthetician and Skin Care Specialist** • **Carpentry/Carpenter** *1 student enrolled* • **Cosmetology/Cosmetologist, General** *3 students enrolled* • **Health Aide** *9 students enrolled* • **Licensed Practical/Vocational Nurse Training (LPN, LVN, Cert, Dipl, AAS)** *10 students enrolled* • **Medical Administrative/ Executive Assistant and Medical Secretary** *6 students enrolled* • **Nail Technician/Specialist and Manicurist** • **Phlebotomy/Phlebotomist** *3 students enrolled* • **Welding Technology/Welder**

**STUDENT SERVICES** Academic or career counseling, placement services for program completers, remedial services.

## Louisiana Technical College–Lafayette Campus

1101 Bertrand Drive, Lafayette, LA 70502-4909
http://www.ltc.edu/

**CONTACT** Phyllis Dupuis, Campus Dean
**Telephone:** 337-262-5962

**GENERAL INFORMATION** Public Institution. Founded 1978. **Accreditation:** Medical laboratory technology (NAACLS); state accredited or approved. **Total program enrollment:** 583. **Application fee:** $5.

**PROGRAM(S) OFFERED**
• **Accounting Technology/Technician and Bookkeeping** *5 students enrolled* • **Administrative Assistant and Secretarial Science, General** *2 students enrolled* • **Aircraft Powerplant Technology/Technician** *4 students enrolled* • **Automobile/Automotive Mechanics Technology/Technician** *3 students enrolled* • **Barbering/Barber** *1 student enrolled* • **Child Care Provider/Assistant** *4 students enrolled* • **Computer Systems Networking and Telecommunications** *10 students enrolled* • **Culinary Arts/Chef Training** *1 student enrolled* • **Drafting and Design Technology/Technician, General** *2 students enrolled* • **Electrician** *6 students enrolled* • **Emergency Medical Technology/Technician (EMT Paramedic)** *5 students enrolled* • **Health Aide** *8 students enrolled* • **Heating, Air Conditioning, Ventilation and Refrigeration Maintenance Technology/Technician (HAC, HACR, HVAC, HVACR)** *7 students enrolled* • **Hotel/Motel Administration/ Management** *2 students enrolled* • **Industrial Electronics Technology/Technician** *7 students enrolled* • **Licensed Practical/Vocational Nurse Training (LPN, LVN, Cert, Dipl, AAS)** *29 students enrolled* • **Machine Tool Technology/Machinist** *8 students enrolled* • **Medical Administrative/Executive Assistant and Medical Secretary** *29 students enrolled* • **Nurse/Nursing Assistant/Aide and Patient Care Assistant** *56 students enrolled* • **Prepress/Desktop Publishing and Digital Imaging Design** *4 students enrolled* • **System Administration/Administrator** *1 student enrolled* • **Upholstery/Upholsterer** *1 student enrolled* • **Watchmaking and Jewelrymaking** *1 student enrolled* • **Welding Technology/Welder** *3 students enrolled*

**STUDENT SERVICES** Academic or career counseling, daycare for children of students, employment services for current students, placement services for program completers, remedial services.

## Louisiana Technical College–LaFourche Campus

1425 Tiger Drive, Thibodaux, LA 70302-1831
http://www.ltc.edu/

**CONTACT** Cynthia Poskey, Campus Administrator
**Telephone:** 985-447-0924

**GENERAL INFORMATION** Public Institution. **Accreditation:** State accredited or approved. **Total program enrollment:** 137. **Application fee:** $5.

**PROGRAM(S) OFFERED**
• **Accounting Technology/Technician and Bookkeeping** *2 students enrolled* • **Administrative Assistant and Secretarial Science, General** *4 students enrolled* • **Automobile/Automotive Mechanics Technology/Technician** *19 students enrolled* • **Carpentry/Carpenter** *17 students enrolled* • **Diesel Mechanics Technology/Technician** *1 student enrolled* • **Electrician** *31 students enrolled* • **Emergency Medical Technology/Technician (EMT Paramedic)** *1 student enrolled* • **Health Aide** *41 students enrolled* • **Licensed Practical/Vocational Nurse Training (LPN, LVN, Cert, Dipl, AAS)** *19 students enrolled* • **Medical Administrative/Executive Assistant and Medical Secretary** • **Truck and Bus Driver/Commercial Vehicle Operation** *120 students enrolled* • **Welding Technology/Welder** *91 students enrolled*

**STUDENT SERVICES** Academic or career counseling, employment services for current students, placement services for program completers, remedial services.

## Louisiana Technical College–Lamar Salter Campus

15014 Lake Charles Highway, Leesville, LA 71446
http://www.ltc.edu/

**CONTACT** Michael Kay, Campus Dean
**Telephone:** 337-537-3135 Ext. 201

**GENERAL INFORMATION** Public Institution. **Accreditation:** State accredited or approved. **Total program enrollment:** 185. **Application fee:** $5.

**PROGRAM(S) OFFERED**
• **Accounting Technology/Technician and Bookkeeping** • **Administrative Assistant and Secretarial Science, General** *1 student enrolled* • **Automobile/ Automotive Mechanics Technology/Technician** *2 students enrolled* • **Carpentry/ Carpenter** *2 students enrolled* • **Child Care Provider/Assistant** *1 student enrolled* • **Computer Installation and Repair Technology/Technician** *5 students enrolled* • **Data Processing and Data Processing Technology/Technician** • **Electrical/ Electronics Equipment Installation and Repair, General** • **Emergency Medical Technology/Technician (EMT Paramedic)** *18 students enrolled* • **Heating, Air Conditioning, Ventilation and Refrigeration Maintenance Technology/ Technician (HAC, HACR, HVAC, HVACR)** *1 student enrolled* • **Industrial Electronics Technology/Technician** • **Licensed Practical/Vocational Nurse Training (LPN, LVN, Cert, Dipl, AAS)** *22 students enrolled* • **Medical Administrative/Executive Assistant and Medical Secretary** *5 students enrolled* • **Small Engine Mechanics and Repair Technology/Technician** *5 students enrolled* • **Welding Technology/Welder** *4 students enrolled*

**STUDENT SERVICES** Daycare for children of students, employment services for current students, placement services for program completers, remedial services.

## Louisiana Technical College–Mansfield Campus

943 Oxford Road, Mansfield, LA 71052
http://www.ltc.edu/

**CONTACT** Jill H. Heard, Campus Dean
**Telephone:** 318-872-2243

**GENERAL INFORMATION** Public Institution. **Accreditation:** State accredited or approved. **Total program enrollment:** 108. **Application fee:** $5.

*Louisiana Technical College–Mansfield Campus (continued)*

**PROGRAM(S) OFFERED**

• **Accounting Technology/Technician and Bookkeeping** *1 student enrolled* • **Administrative Assistant and Secretarial Science, General** *7 students enrolled* • **Applied Horticulture/Horticultural Operations, General** *10 students enrolled* • **Health Aide** *11 students enrolled* • **Heating, Air Conditioning, Ventilation and Refrigeration Maintenance Technology/Technician (HAC, HACR, HVAC, HVACR)** • **Licensed Practical/Vocational Nurse Training (LPN, LVN, Cert, Dipl, AAS)** *22 students enrolled* • **Medical Administrative/Executive Assistant and Medical Secretary** *13 students enrolled* • **Welding Technology/Welder** *36 students enrolled*

**STUDENT SERVICES** Academic or career counseling, employment services for current students, placement services for program completers, remedial services.

## Louisiana Technical College–Morgan Smith Campus

1230 North Main Street, Jennings, LA 70546-1327
http://www.ltc.edu/

**CONTACT** Sanders J. Senegal, Interim Campus Dean
**Telephone:** 337-824-4811

**GENERAL INFORMATION** Public Institution. **Accreditation:** State accredited or approved. **Total program enrollment:** 73. **Application fee:** $5.

**PROGRAM(S) OFFERED**

• **Accounting Technology/Technician and Bookkeeping** *9 students enrolled* • **Administrative Assistant and Secretarial Science, General** *9 students enrolled* • **Automobile/Automotive Mechanics Technology/Technician** • **Electrician** • **Health Aide** • **Licensed Practical/Vocational Nurse Training (LPN, LVN, Cert, Dipl, AAS)** • **Medical Administrative/Executive Assistant and Medical Secretary** *10 students enrolled* • **Nurse/Nursing Assistant/Aide and Patient Care Assistant** *50 students enrolled* • **Welding Technology/Welder** *10 students enrolled*

**STUDENT SERVICES** Academic or career counseling, employment services for current students, placement services for program completers, remedial services.

## Louisiana Technical College–Natchitoches Campus

6587 Highway 1, Bypass, Natchitoches, LA 71457
http://www.ltc.edu/

**CONTACT** Carol Hebert, Campus Dean
**Telephone:** 318-357-3162

**GENERAL INFORMATION** Public Institution. Founded 1938. **Accreditation:** State accredited or approved. **Total program enrollment:** 154. **Application fee:** $5.

**PROGRAM(S) OFFERED**

• **Accounting Technology/Technician and Bookkeeping** • **Administrative Assistant and Secretarial Science, General** *2 students enrolled* • **Automobile/Automotive Mechanics Technology/Technician** • **Child Care Provider/Assistant** • **Cosmetology/Cosmetologist, General** *8 students enrolled* • **Data Processing and Data Processing Technology/Technician** *1 student enrolled* • **Heating, Air Conditioning, Ventilation and Refrigeration Maintenance Technology/Technician (HAC, HACR, HVAC, HVACR)** *1 student enrolled* • **Industrial Electronics Technology/Technician** *4 students enrolled* • **Industrial Mechanics and Maintenance Technology** *1 student enrolled* • **Licensed Practical/Vocational Nurse Training (LPN, LVN, Cert, Dipl, AAS)** *5 students enrolled* • **Medical Administrative/Executive Assistant and Medical Secretary** *5 students enrolled* • **Metal and Jewelry Arts** *4 students enrolled* • **Nurse/Nursing Assistant/Aide and Patient Care Assistant** *6 students enrolled*

**STUDENT SERVICES** Academic or career counseling, daycare for children of students, placement services for program completers, remedial services.

## Louisiana Technical College–North Central Campus

605 North Boundary West, Farmerville, LA 71241
http://www.ltc.edu/

**CONTACT** Norene Smith, Regional Director
**Telephone:** 318-368-3179

**GENERAL INFORMATION** Public Institution. Founded 1952. **Accreditation:** State accredited or approved. **Total program enrollment:** 80. **Application fee:** $5.

**PROGRAM(S) OFFERED**

• **Accounting Technology/Technician and Bookkeeping** • **Administrative Assistant and Secretarial Science, General** *2 students enrolled* • **Data Processing and Data Processing Technology/Technician** *2 students enrolled* • **Health Aide** *9 students enrolled* • **Licensed Practical/Vocational Nurse Training (LPN, LVN, Cert, Dipl, AAS)** *14 students enrolled* • **Medical Administrative/Executive Assistant and Medical Secretary** *7 students enrolled* • **Welding Technology/Welder**

**STUDENT SERVICES** Academic or career counseling, placement services for program completers, remedial services.

## Louisiana Technical College–Northeast Louisiana Campus

1710 Warren Street, Winnsboro, LA 71295
http://www.ltc.edu/

**CONTACT** Debbie M. Price, Campus Dean
**Telephone:** 318-435-2163 Ext. 11

**GENERAL INFORMATION** Public Institution. **Accreditation:** State accredited or approved. **Total program enrollment:** 99. **Application fee:** $5.

**PROGRAM(S) OFFERED**

• **Accounting Technology/Technician and Bookkeeping** *2 students enrolled* • **Administrative Assistant and Secretarial Science, General** • **Automobile/Automotive Mechanics Technology/Technician** • **Child Care Provider/Assistant** • **Data Processing and Data Processing Technology/Technician** • **Drafting and Design Technology/Technician, General** • **Emergency Medical Technology/Technician (EMT Paramedic)** • **Licensed Practical/Vocational Nurse Training (LPN, LVN, Cert, Dipl, AAS)** *1 student enrolled* • **Medical Administrative/Executive Assistant and Medical Secretary** • **Nurse/Nursing Assistant/Aide and Patient Care Assistant** *13 students enrolled* • **System Administration/Administrator** • **Welding Technology/Welder** *22 students enrolled*

**STUDENT SERVICES** Academic or career counseling, employment services for current students, placement services for program completers, remedial services.

## Louisiana Technical College–Northwest Louisiana Campus

814 Constable Street, Minden, LA 71058-0835
http://www.ltc.edu/

**CONTACT** Charles T. Strong, Campus Dean
**Telephone:** 318-371-3035 Ext. 07

**GENERAL INFORMATION** Public Institution. Founded 1952. **Accreditation:** State accredited or approved. **Total program enrollment:** 442. **Application fee:** $5.

**PROGRAM(S) OFFERED**

• **Accounting Technology/Technician and Bookkeeping** *2 students enrolled* • **Administrative Assistant and Secretarial Science, General** *4 students enrolled* • **Applied Horticulture/Horticultural Operations, General** *10 students enrolled* • **Automobile/Automotive Mechanics Technology/Technician** *2 students enrolled* • **Carpentry/Carpenter** *17 students enrolled* • **Construction/Heavy Equipment/Earthmoving Equipment Operation** *31 students enrolled* • **Data Processing and Data Processing Technology/Technician** *3 students enrolled* • **Drafting and Design Technology/Technician, General** *3 students enrolled* • **Heating, Air Conditioning, Ventilation and Refrigeration Maintenance**

**Technology/Technician (HAC, HACR, HVAC, HVACR)** *11 students enrolled* • **Hotel/Motel Administration/Management** • **Industrial Mechanics and Maintenance Technology** *17 students enrolled* • **Instrumentation Technology/Technician** *34 students enrolled* • **Licensed Practical/Vocational Nurse Training (LPN, LVN, Cert, Dipl, AAS)** *41 students enrolled* • **Machine Tool Technology/Machinist** *1 student enrolled* • **Medical Administrative/Executive Assistant and Medical Secretary** *7 students enrolled* • **Medical/Clinical Assistant** • **Nurse/Nursing Assistant/Aide and Patient Care Assistant** *15 students enrolled* • **Small Engine Mechanics and Repair Technology/Technician** *2 students enrolled* • **Welding Technology/Welder** *16 students enrolled*

**STUDENT SERVICES** Academic or career counseling, employment services for current students, placement services for program completers, remedial services.

## Louisiana Technical College–Oakdale Campus

Old Pelican Highway, Oakdale, LA 71463
http://www.ltc.edu/

**CONTACT** J. Darrell Rodriguez, Campus Dean
**Telephone:** 318-335-3944

**GENERAL INFORMATION** Public Institution. **Accreditation:** State accredited or approved. **Total program enrollment:** 234. **Application fee:** $5.

**PROGRAM(S) OFFERED**
• **Accounting Technology/Technician and Bookkeeping** *1 student enrolled* • **Administrative Assistant and Secretarial Science, General** *1 student enrolled* • **Apparel and Textile Manufacture** *8 students enrolled* • **Applied Horticulture/Horticultural Operations, General** • **Building/Property Maintenance and Management** • **Cabinetmaking and Millwork/Millwright** *3 students enrolled* • **Corrections** • **Criminal Justice/Safety Studies** *3 students enrolled* • **Forestry Technology/Technician** • **Licensed Practical/Vocational Nurse Training (LPN, LVN, Cert, Dipl, AAS)** *20 students enrolled* • **Medical Administrative/Executive Assistant and Medical Secretary** *2 students enrolled* • **Upholstery/Upholsterer** *3 students enrolled* • **Welding Technology/Welder** *3 students enrolled*

**STUDENT SERVICES** Academic or career counseling, placement services for program completers, remedial services.

## Louisiana Technical College–River Parishes Campus

PO Drawer AQ, Reserve, LA 70084
http://www.ltc.edu/

**CONTACT** Richard Cox, Campus Administrator
**Telephone:** 985-536-4418 Ext. 210

**GENERAL INFORMATION** Public Institution. **Accreditation:** State accredited or approved. **Total program enrollment:** 353. **Application fee:** $5.

**PROGRAM(S) OFFERED**
• **Accounting Technology/Technician and Bookkeeping** • **Administrative Assistant and Secretarial Science, General** *1 student enrolled* • **Drafting and Design Technology/Technician, General** • **Health Aide** *13 students enrolled* • **Heating, Air Conditioning, Ventilation and Refrigeration Maintenance Technology/Technician (HAC, HACR, HVAC, HVACR)** *9 students enrolled* • **Industrial Mechanics and Maintenance Technology** *1 student enrolled* • **Instrumentation Technology/Technician** *1 student enrolled* • **Licensed Practical/Vocational Nurse Training (LPN, LVN, Cert, Dipl, AAS)** *52 students enrolled* • **Medical/Clinical Assistant** *4 students enrolled* • **Welding Technology/Welder** *1 student enrolled*

**STUDENT SERVICES** Academic or career counseling, placement services for program completers, remedial services.

## Louisiana Technical College–Ruston Campus

PO Box 1070, 1010 James Street, Ruston, LA 71273-1070
http://www.ltc.edu/

**CONTACT** Doug Postel, Campus Dean
**Telephone:** 318-251-4145

**GENERAL INFORMATION** Public Institution. **Accreditation:** State accredited or approved. **Total program enrollment:** 87. **Application fee:** $5.

**PROGRAM(S) OFFERED**
• **Accounting Technology/Technician and Bookkeeping** *6 students enrolled* • **Administrative Assistant and Secretarial Science, General** *3 students enrolled* • **Carpentry/Carpenter** • **Data Processing and Data Processing Technology/Technician** • **Drafting and Design Technology/Technician, General** *5 students enrolled* • **Industrial Mechanics and Maintenance Technology** *5 students enrolled* • **Licensed Practical/Vocational Nurse Training (LPN, LVN, Cert, Dipl, AAS)** *18 students enrolled* • **Nurse/Nursing Assistant/Aide and Patient Care Assistant** *45 students enrolled* • **Welding Technology/Welder**

**STUDENT SERVICES** Academic or career counseling, employment services for current students, placement services for program completers, remedial services.

## Louisiana Technical College–Sabine Valley Campus

1255 Fisher Road, Many, LA 71449
http://www.ltc.edu/

**CONTACT** Laurie Morrow, Campus Dean
**Telephone:** 318-256-4101

**GENERAL INFORMATION** Public Institution. **Accreditation:** State accredited or approved. **Total program enrollment:** 79. **Application fee:** $5.

**PROGRAM(S) OFFERED**
• **Accounting Technology/Technician and Bookkeeping** *5 students enrolled* • **Administrative Assistant and Secretarial Science, General** *7 students enrolled* • **Automobile/Automotive Mechanics Technology/Technician** • **Data Processing and Data Processing Technology/Technician** *1 student enrolled* • **Medical Administrative/Executive Assistant and Medical Secretary** *9 students enrolled* • **Nurse/Nursing Assistant/Aide and Patient Care Assistant** *48 students enrolled* • **Welding Technology/Welder** *12 students enrolled*

**STUDENT SERVICES** Academic or career counseling, daycare for children of students, remedial services.

## Louisiana Technical College–Shelby M. Jackson Campus

PO Box 1465, Ferriday, LA 71334
http://www.ltc.edu/

**CONTACT** Mignonne Ater, Campus Dean
**Telephone:** 318-757-6501 Ext. 110

**GENERAL INFORMATION** Public Institution. **Accreditation:** State accredited or approved. **Total program enrollment:** 111. **Application fee:** $5.

**PROGRAM(S) OFFERED**
• **Accounting Technology/Technician and Bookkeeping** *1 student enrolled* • **Administrative Assistant and Secretarial Science, General** *4 students enrolled* • **Data Processing and Data Processing Technology/Technician** *2 students enrolled* • **Emergency Medical Technology/Technician (EMT Paramedic)** *7 students enrolled* • **Health Aide** *22 students enrolled* • **Heating, Air Conditioning, Ventilation and Refrigeration Maintenance Technology/Technician (HAC, HACR, HVAC, HVACR)** • **Licensed Practical/Vocational Nurse Training (LPN, LVN, Cert, Dipl, AAS)** *13 students enrolled* • **Medical Administrative/Executive Assistant and Medical Secretary** *4 students enrolled* • **Nurse/Nursing Assistant/Aide and Patient Care Assistant** *15 students enrolled* • **System Administration/Administrator** *1 student enrolled* • **Welding Technology/Welder** *2 students enrolled*

**STUDENT SERVICES** Academic or career counseling, employment services for current students, placement services for program completers, remedial services.

## Louisiana Technical College–Shreveport-Bossier Campus

2010 North Market Street, Shreveport, LA 71137-8527
http://www.ltc.edu/

**CONTACT** Angie Rymer, Dean
**Telephone:** 318-676-7811 Ext. 183

**GENERAL INFORMATION** Public Institution. **Accreditation:** Regional (SACS/CC); state accredited or approved. **Total program enrollment:** 541. **Application fee:** $5.

**PROGRAM(S) OFFERED**
• **Administrative Assistant and Secretarial Science, General** *4 students enrolled* • **Autobody/Collision and Repair Technology/Technician** *5 students enrolled* • **Automobile/Automotive Mechanics Technology/Technician** *7 students enrolled* • **Barbering/Barber** *17 students enrolled* • **Carpentry/Carpenter** *4 students enrolled* • **Computer Systems Networking and Telecommunications** *5 students enrolled* • **Culinary Arts/Chef Training** *3 students enrolled* • **Diesel Mechanics Technology/Technician** *6 students enrolled* • **Drafting and Design Technology/Technician, General** *1 student enrolled* • **Electrical/Electronics Equipment Installation and Repair, General** *2 students enrolled* • **Electrician** *6 students enrolled* • **Health Aide** *13 students enrolled* • **Heating, Air Conditioning, Ventilation and Refrigeration Maintenance Technology/Technician (HAC, HACR, HVAC, HVACR)** *11 students enrolled* • **Heavy/Industrial Equipment Maintenance Technologies, Other** *1 student enrolled* • **Licensed Practical/Vocational Nurse Training (LPN, LVN, Cert, Dipl, AAS)** *72 students enrolled* • **Machine Tool Technology/Machinist** *1 student enrolled* • **Nurse/Nursing Assistant/Aide and Patient Care Assistant** *1 student enrolled* • **Printing Press Operator** *1 student enrolled* • **Small Engine Mechanics and Repair Technology/Technician** *1 student enrolled* • **System Administration/Administrator** *1 student enrolled* • **Welding Technology/Welder** *8 students enrolled*

**STUDENT SERVICES** Academic or career counseling, employment services for current students, placement services for program completers, remedial services.

## Louisiana Technical College–Sullivan Campus

1710 Sullivan Drive, Bogalusa, LA 70427
http://www.ltc.edu/

**CONTACT** William S. Wainwright, Regional Director/Dean
**Telephone:** 985-732-6640 Ext. 100

**GENERAL INFORMATION** Public Institution. **Accreditation:** State accredited or approved. **Total program enrollment:** 382. **Application fee:** $5.

**PROGRAM(S) OFFERED**
• **Accounting Technology/Technician and Bookkeeping** *1 student enrolled* • **Administrative Assistant and Secretarial Science, General** *5 students enrolled* • **Automobile/Automotive Mechanics Technology/Technician** *2 students enrolled* • **Carpentry/Carpenter** *11 students enrolled* • **Child Care Provider/Assistant** • **Computer Programming/Programmer, General** • **Criminal Justice/Safety Studies** • **Diesel Mechanics Technology/Technician** *1 student enrolled* • **Drafting and Design Technology/Technician, General** *4 students enrolled* • **Electrician** • **Emergency Medical Technology/Technician (EMT Paramedic)** *13 students enrolled* • **Health Aide** • **Heating, Air Conditioning, Ventilation and Refrigeration Maintenance Technology/Technician (HAC, HACR, HVAC, HVACR)** *2 students enrolled* • **Licensed Practical/Vocational Nurse Training (LPN, LVN, Cert, Dipl, AAS)** *40 students enrolled* • **Machine Tool Technology/Machinist** • **Medical Administrative/Executive Assistant and Medical Secretary** *9 students enrolled* • **Nurse/Nursing Assistant/Aide and Patient Care Assistant** *179 students enrolled* • **Precision Systems Maintenance and Repair Technologies, Other** • **System Administration/Administrator** *3 students enrolled* • **Welding Technology/Welder** *11 students enrolled*

**STUDENT SERVICES** Academic or career counseling, placement services for program completers, remedial services.

## Louisiana Technical College–Tallulah Campus

Old Highway 65 South, Tallulah, LA 71284-1740
http://www.ltc.edu/

**CONTACT** Patrick Murphy, Campus Dean
**Telephone:** 318-574-4820

**GENERAL INFORMATION** Public Institution. **Accreditation:** Regional (SACS/CC); state accredited or approved. **Total program enrollment:** 168. **Application fee:** $5.

**PROGRAM(S) OFFERED**
• **Accounting Technology/Technician and Bookkeeping** • **Administrative Assistant and Secretarial Science, General** *2 students enrolled* • **Automobile/Automotive Mechanics Technology/Technician** *2 students enrolled* • **Carpentry/Carpenter** • **Computer Systems Analysis/Analyst** *1 student enrolled* • **Diesel Mechanics Technology/Technician** • **Industrial Mechanics and Maintenance Technology** • **Licensed Practical/Vocational Nurse Training (LPN, LVN, Cert, Dipl, AAS)** *16 students enrolled* • **Medical Administrative/Executive Assistant and Medical Secretary** *6 students enrolled* • **Nurse/Nursing Assistant/Aide and Patient Care Assistant** *81 students enrolled* • **System Administration/Administrator** *1 student enrolled* • **Welding Technology/Welder** *18 students enrolled*

**STUDENT SERVICES** Academic or career counseling, placement services for program completers, remedial services.

## Louisiana Technical College–Teche Area Campus

PO Box 11057, New Iberia, LA 70562-1057
http://www.ltc.edu/

**CONTACT** Annette L. Faulk, Campus Dean
**Telephone:** 337-373-0011

**GENERAL INFORMATION** Public Institution. **Accreditation:** State accredited or approved. **Total program enrollment:** 272. **Application fee:** $5.

**PROGRAM(S) OFFERED**
• **Accounting Technology/Technician and Bookkeeping** *2 students enrolled* • **Administrative Assistant and Secretarial Science, General** *1 student enrolled* • **Carpentry/Carpenter** *10 students enrolled* • **Child Care Provider/Assistant** *5 students enrolled* • **Computer Installation and Repair Technology/Technician** *7 students enrolled* • **Drafting and Design Technology/Technician, General** *9 students enrolled* • **Electrician** *4 students enrolled* • **Health Aide** *12 students enrolled* • **Heating, Air Conditioning, Ventilation and Refrigeration Maintenance Technology/Technician (HAC, HACR, HVAC, HVACR)** *5 students enrolled* • **Industrial Electronics Technology/Technician** *1 student enrolled* • **Industrial Mechanics and Maintenance Technology** *1 student enrolled* • **Licensed Practical/Vocational Nurse Training (LPN, LVN, Cert, Dipl, AAS)** *16 students enrolled* • **Machine Tool Technology/Machinist** *7 students enrolled* • **Medical Administrative/Executive Assistant and Medical Secretary** *17 students enrolled* • **System Administration/Administrator** *2 students enrolled* • **Welding Technology/Welder** *10 students enrolled*

**STUDENT SERVICES** Academic or career counseling, daycare for children of students, placement services for program completers, remedial services.

## Louisiana Technical College–T.H. Harris Campus

332 East South Street, Opelousas, LA 70570
http://www.ltc.edu/

**CONTACT** Allen Espree, Campus Dean
**Telephone:** 337-948-0239 Ext. 1

**GENERAL INFORMATION** Public Institution. **Accreditation:** State accredited or approved. **Total program enrollment:** 369. **Application fee:** $5.

### PROGRAM(S) OFFERED

• **Accounting Technology/Technician and Bookkeeping** *5 students enrolled* • **Administrative Assistant and Secretarial Science, General** *1 student enrolled* • **Automobile/Automotive Mechanics Technology/Technician** *1 student enrolled* • **Child Care Provider/Assistant** • **Computer Systems Networking and Telecommunications** *5 students enrolled* • **Cosmetology/Cosmetologist, General** *2 students enrolled* • **Diesel Mechanics Technology/Technician** *1 student enrolled* • **Drafting and Design Technology/Technician, General** *2 students enrolled* • **Electrician** *4 students enrolled* • **Health Aide** *6 students enrolled* • **Heating, Air Conditioning, Ventilation and Refrigeration Maintenance Technology/Technician (HAC, HACR, HVAC, HVACR)** *4 students enrolled* • **Industrial Electronics Technology/Technician** *1 student enrolled* • **Industrial Radiologic Technology/Technician** *42 students enrolled* • **Licensed Practical/Vocational Nurse Training (LPN, LVN, Cert, Dipl, AAS)** *38 students enrolled* • **Machine Tool Technology/Machinist** *3 students enrolled* • **Medical Administrative/Executive Assistant and Medical Secretary** *8 students enrolled* • **Nurse/Nursing Assistant/Aide and Patient Care Assistant** *1 student enrolled* • **Survey Technology/Surveying** • **System Administration/Administrator** *5 students enrolled* • **Welding Technology/Welder** *12 students enrolled*

**STUDENT SERVICES** Academic or career counseling, placement services for program completers, remedial services.

## Louisiana Technical College–West Jefferson Campus

475 Manhattan Boulevard, Harvey, LA 70058
http://www.ltc.edu/

**CONTACT** Pamela Thompson, Campus Assistant Dean
**Telephone:** 504-671-6800

**GENERAL INFORMATION** Public Institution. **Accreditation:** State accredited or approved. **Total program enrollment:** 65. **Application fee:** $5.

### PROGRAM(S) OFFERED

• **Autobody/Collision and Repair Technology/Technician** • **Barbering/Barber** • **Building/Property Maintenance and Management** *9 students enrolled* • **Carpentry/Carpenter** • **Cosmetology/Cosmetologist, General** • **Electrical and Power Transmission Installers, Other** • **Electrician** • **Health Aide** *5 students enrolled* • **Licensed Practical/Vocational Nurse Training (LPN, LVN, Cert, Dipl, AAS)** • **Machine Tool Technology/Machinist** • **Nurse/Nursing Assistant/Aide and Patient Care Assistant** *38 students enrolled* • **Pipefitting/Pipefitter and Sprinkler Fitter** • **Sheet Metal Technology/Sheetworking** • **Welding Technology/Welder**

**STUDENT SERVICES** Academic or career counseling, placement services for program completers, remedial services.

## Louisiana Technical College–Westside Campus

59125 Bayou Road, Plaquemine, LA 70765
http://www.ltc.edu/

**CONTACT** Mary Stewart, Campus Administrator
**Telephone:** 225-687-6392

**GENERAL INFORMATION** Public Institution. **Total program enrollment:** 69. **Application fee:** $5.

### PROGRAM(S) OFFERED

• **Computer Systems Networking and Telecommunications** • **Licensed Practical/Vocational Nurse Training (LPN, LVN, Cert, Dipl, AAS)** • **Medical Administrative/Executive Assistant and Medical Secretary** • **Medical/Clinical Assistant** *5 students enrolled* • **Nurse/Nursing Assistant/Aide and Patient Care Assistant** *6 students enrolled* • **System Administration/Administrator**

**STUDENT SERVICES** Academic or career counseling, placement services for program completers, remedial services.

## Louisiana Technical College–Young Memorial Campus

900 Youngs Road, Morgan City, LA 70381
http://www.ltc.edu/

**CONTACT** Karl Young, Campus Administrator
**Telephone:** 985-380-2436

**GENERAL INFORMATION** Public Institution. **Accreditation:** State accredited or approved. **Total program enrollment:** 139. **Application fee:** $5.

### PROGRAM(S) OFFERED

• **Accounting Technology/Technician and Bookkeeping** *1 student enrolled* • **Administrative Assistant and Secretarial Science, General** *1 student enrolled* • **Automobile/Automotive Mechanics Technology/Technician** *1 student enrolled* • **Carpentry/Carpenter** *3 students enrolled* • **Communications Systems Installation and Repair Technology** *1 student enrolled* • **Computer Systems Networking and Telecommunications** • **Diver, Professional and Instructor** *26 students enrolled* • **Drafting and Design Technology/Technician, General** • **Electrician** *9 students enrolled* • **Health Aide** • **Heating, Air Conditioning, Ventilation and Refrigeration Maintenance Technology/Technician (HAC, HACR, HVAC, HVACR)** *4 students enrolled* • **Licensed Practical/Vocational Nurse Training (LPN, LVN, Cert, Dipl, AAS)** *2 students enrolled* • **Marine Science/Merchant Marine Officer** *3953 students enrolled* • **Medical Administrative/Executive Assistant and Medical Secretary** • **Nurse/Nursing Assistant/Aide and Patient Care Assistant** *70 students enrolled* • **System Administration/Administrator** • **Truck and Bus Driver/Commercial Vehicle Operation** *1 student enrolled* • **Welding Technology/Welder** *49 students enrolled*

**STUDENT SERVICES** Academic or career counseling, placement services for program completers, remedial services.

## Medical Training College

4528 Bennington Avenue, Suite 10, Baton Rouge, LA 70808
http://www.mtcbr.com/

**CONTACT** Billy L. Clark, President
**Telephone:** 225-926-5820

**GENERAL INFORMATION** Private Institution. **Total program enrollment:** 74. **Application fee:** $100.

### PROGRAM(S) OFFERED

• **Dental Assisting/Assistant** *756 hrs./$9650* • **Health and Medical Administrative Services, Other** *816 hrs./$9650* • **Licensed Practical/Vocational Nurse Training (LPN, LVN, Cert, Dipl, AAS)** • **Massage Therapy/Therapeutic Massage** *756 hrs./$10,646* • **Medical/Clinical Assistant** *816 hrs./$9650*

**STUDENT SERVICES** Placement services for program completers.

## MedVance Institute

9255 Interline Avenue, Baton Rouge, LA 70809
http://www.medvance.org/

**CONTACT** John Hopkins, CEO
**Telephone:** 225-248-1015

**GENERAL INFORMATION** Private Institution. Founded 1970. **Accreditation:** Medical laboratory technology (NAACLS); state accredited or approved. **Total program enrollment:** 610. **Application fee:** $25.

### PROGRAM(S) OFFERED

• **Clinical/Medical Laboratory Technician** *100 hrs./$24,995* • **Health Information/Medical Records Technology/Technician** *67 hrs./$13,995* • **Medical Radiologic Technology/Science—Radiation Therapist** *130 hrs./$35,500* • **Medical/Clinical Assistant** *49 hrs./$11,995* • **Pharmacy Technician/Assistant** *49 hrs./$9995* • **Surgical Technology/Technologist** *98 hrs./$22,100*

**STUDENT SERVICES** Employment services for current students, placement services for program completers.

## Omega Institute of Cosmetology

229 S. Hollywood Road, Houma, LA 70360
http://omegainstitutes.com/

**CONTACT** Pricilla Marcel, Owner
**Telephone:** 985-876-9334

**GENERAL INFORMATION** Private Institution. **Total program enrollment:** 58. **Application fee:** $100.

**PROGRAM(S) OFFERED**
- **Aesthetician/Esthetician and Skin Care Specialist** *750 hrs./$6600*
- **Cosmetology, Barber/Styling, and Nail Instructor** *600 hrs./$4100*
- **Cosmetology/Cosmetologist, General** *1500 hrs./$10,850* • **Nail Technician/Specialist and Manicurist** *600 hrs./$3940*

**STUDENT SERVICES** Academic or career counseling, employment services for current students, placement services for program completers.

## Opelousas School of Cosmetology

529 East Vine Street, Opelousas, LA 70570

**CONTACT** Norma Prudhomme, Director Owner
**Telephone:** 337-942-6147

**GENERAL INFORMATION** Private Institution. **Total program enrollment:** 10.

**PROGRAM(S) OFFERED**
- **Cosmetology, Barber/Styling, and Nail Instructor** *1 student enrolled*
- **Cosmetology/Cosmetologist, General** *750 hrs./$2700*

**STUDENT SERVICES** Academic or career counseling, placement services for program completers.

## Our Lady of the Lake College

7434 Perkins Road, Baton Rouge, LA 70808
http://www.ololcollege.edu/

**CONTACT** Sandra Harper, President
**Telephone:** 225-768-1700

**GENERAL INFORMATION** Private Institution. Founded 1990. **Accreditation:** Regional (SACS/CC); medical laboratory technology (NAACLS); medical technology (NAACLS); physical therapy assisting (APTA); radiologic technology: radiography (JRCERT); surgical technology (ARCST). **Total program enrollment:** 656. **Application fee:** $35.

**PROGRAM(S) OFFERED**
- **Licensed Practical/Vocational Nurse Training (LPN, LVN, Cert, Dipl, AAS)** *1 student enrolled*

**STUDENT SERVICES** Academic or career counseling, remedial services.

## Pat Goins Beauty School

3138 Louisville Avenue, Monroe, LA 71201

**CONTACT** John Goins, President
**Telephone:** 318-322-2500

**GENERAL INFORMATION** Private Institution. **Total program enrollment:** 13.

**PROGRAM(S) OFFERED**
- **Cosmetology, Barber/Styling, and Nail Instructor** *750 hrs./$2925*
- **Cosmetology/Cosmetologist, General** *1500 hrs./$9250* • **Nail Technician/Specialist and Manicurist** *600 hrs./$3780*

**STUDENT SERVICES** Academic or career counseling, placement services for program completers.

## Pat Goins Benton Road Beauty School

1701 Old Minden Road, Suite 36, Bossier City, LA 71111

**CONTACT** John Goins, President
**Telephone:** 318-746-7674

**GENERAL INFORMATION** Private Institution. Founded 1969. **Total program enrollment:** 25.

**PROGRAM(S) OFFERED**
- **Cosmetology, Barber/Styling, and Nail Instructor** *750 hrs./$2925*
- **Cosmetology/Cosmetologist, General** *1500 hrs./$11,200* • **Nail Technician/Specialist and Manicurist** *600 hrs./$3780*

**STUDENT SERVICES** Academic or career counseling, placement services for program completers.

## Pat Goins Ruston Beauty School

213 West Alabama Avenue, Ruston, LA 71270

**CONTACT** John Goins, President
**Telephone:** 318-255-2717

**GENERAL INFORMATION** Private Institution. **Total program enrollment:** 27.

**PROGRAM(S) OFFERED**
- **Cosmetology, Barber/Styling, and Nail Instructor** *750 hrs./$2925*
- **Cosmetology/Cosmetologist, General** *1500 hrs./$11,200* • **Nail Technician/Specialist and Manicurist** *600 hrs./$3780*

**STUDENT SERVICES** Academic or career counseling, placement services for program completers.

## Pineville Beauty School

1008 Main Street, Pineville, LA 71360

**CONTACT** Michelle Hays, School Owner
**Telephone:** 318-445-1040

**GENERAL INFORMATION** Private Institution. **Total program enrollment:** 49.

**PROGRAM(S) OFFERED**
- **Cosmetology, Barber/Styling, and Nail Instructor** *750 hrs./$3750*
- **Cosmetology/Cosmetologist, General** *1500 hrs./$8545* • **Nail Technician/Specialist and Manicurist** *600 hrs./$3000*

## Remington College–Baton Rouge Campus

10551 Coursey Boulevard, Baton Rouge, LA 70816
http://www.remingtoncollege.edu/

**CONTACT** Mike Smith, President
**Telephone:** 225-236-3200

**GENERAL INFORMATION** Private Institution. **Accreditation:** State accredited or approved. **Total program enrollment:** 422. **Application fee:** $50.

**PROGRAM(S) OFFERED**
- **Electrical, Electronic and Communications Engineering Technology/Technician** • **Medical Insurance Coding Specialist/Coder** *39 students enrolled*
- **Medical/Clinical Assistant** *120 students enrolled* • **Pharmacy Technician/Assistant** *60 students enrolled*

**STUDENT SERVICES** Academic or career counseling, employment services for current students, placement services for program completers.

## Remington College–Lafayette Campus

303 Rue Louis XIV, Lafayette, LA 70508
http://www.remingtoncollege.edu/

**CONTACT** Jo Ann Boudreaux, Campus Vice President
**Telephone:** 337-981-4010

**GENERAL INFORMATION** Private Institution. Founded 1940. **Accreditation:** State accredited or approved. **Total program enrollment:** 458. **Application fee:** $50.

**PROGRAM(S) OFFERED**
• **Cosmetology/Cosmetologist, General** • **Electrical, Electronic and Communications Engineering Technology/Technician** • **Medical Insurance Coding Specialist/Coder** *30 students enrolled* • **Medical/Clinical Assistant** *130 students enrolled*

**STUDENT SERVICES** Academic or career counseling, employment services for current students, placement services for program completers.

## Remington College–Shreveport

2106 Bert Kouns Industrial Loop, Shreveport, LA 71118
http://www.remingtoncollege.edu/shreveport/

**CONTACT** Jerry Driskill, Campus President
**Telephone:** 318-671-4000

**GENERAL INFORMATION** Private Institution. **Total program enrollment:** 416. **Application fee:** $50.

**PROGRAM(S) OFFERED**
• **Electrical, Electronic and Communications Engineering Technology/Technician** • **Medical Insurance Coding Specialist/Coder** *9 students enrolled* • **Medical/Clinical Assistant** *31 students enrolled*

**STUDENT SERVICES** Academic or career counseling, employment services for current students, placement services for program completers.

## River Parishes Community College

PO Box 310, Sorrento, LA 70778
http://www.rpcc.edu/

**CONTACT** Dr. Joe Ben Welch, Chancellor
**Telephone:** 225-675-8270

**GENERAL INFORMATION** Public Institution. Founded 1997. **Accreditation:** Regional (SACS/CC). **Total program enrollment:** 518. **Application fee:** $10.

**STUDENT SERVICES** Academic or career counseling, remedial services.

## Ronnie and Dorman's School of Hair Design

2002 Johnston Street, Lafayette, LA 70503

**CONTACT** Freddie Gary, Director
**Telephone:** 337-232-1806

**GENERAL INFORMATION** Private Institution. Founded 1970. **Total program enrollment:** 22.

**PROGRAM(S) OFFERED**
• **Cosmetology/Cosmetologist, General** *1500 hrs./$8300*

**STUDENT SERVICES** Academic or career counseling, placement services for program completers.

## School of Urban Missions

511 Westbank Expy, Gretna, LA 70053
http://www.sum.edu/

**CONTACT** George Neau, Chancellor/President
**Telephone:** 510-567-6174

**GENERAL INFORMATION** Private Institution (Affiliated with Assembly of God Church). **Total program enrollment:** 88. **Application fee:** $20.

**PROGRAM(S) OFFERED**
• **Bible/Biblical Studies** *1 student enrolled*

**STUDENT SERVICES** Academic or career counseling, employment services for current students, remedial services.

## Southern University at Shreveport

3050 Martin Luther King, Jr. Drive, Shreveport, LA 71107
http://www.susla.edu/

**CONTACT** Dr. Ray L. Belton, Chancellor
**Telephone:** 318-670-6000

**GENERAL INFORMATION** Public Institution. Founded 1964. **Accreditation:** Regional (SACS/CC); dental hygiene (ADA); health information technology (AHIMA); medical laboratory technology (NAACLS); radiologic technology: radiography (JRCERT); surgical technology (ARCST). **Total program enrollment:** 1334. **Application fee:** $5.

**PROGRAM(S) OFFERED**
• **Aircraft Powerplant Technology/Technician** *7 students enrolled* • **Allied Health Diagnostic, Intervention, and Treatment Professions, Other** *7 students enrolled* • **Child Care and Support Services Management** *2 students enrolled* • **Child Development** *18 students enrolled* • **Computer Installation and Repair Technology/Technician** *7 students enrolled* • **Emergency Medical Technology/Technician (EMT Paramedic)** • **Hospitality Administration/Management, General** • **Information Science/Studies** • **Legal Assistant/Paralegal** *5 students enrolled* • **Phlebotomy/Phlebotomist** *16 students enrolled* • **Recording Arts Technology/Technician** *1 student enrolled* • **Renal/Dialysis Technologist/Technician** *6 students enrolled* • **Restaurant, Culinary, and Catering Management/Manager** *1 student enrolled* • **Web Page, Digital/Multimedia and Information Resources Design**

**STUDENT SERVICES** Academic or career counseling, employment services for current students, placement services for program completers, remedial services.

## Southern University System

Baton Rouge, LA 70813

**CONTACT** Ralph Slaughter, President
**Telephone:** 225-771-4680

**GENERAL INFORMATION** Public Institution.

## South Louisiana Beauty College

300 Howard Avenue, Houma, LA 70363
http://slbc-houma.com/

**CONTACT** Catherine Nagy, Owner
**Telephone:** 985-873-8978

**GENERAL INFORMATION** Private Institution. Founded 1974. **Total program enrollment:** 38.

**PROGRAM(S) OFFERED**
• **Cosmetology and Related Personal Grooming Arts, Other** *300 hrs./$1500*
• **Cosmetology, Barber/Styling, and Nail Instructor** *600 hrs./$3275*
• **Cosmetology/Cosmetologist, General** *1500 hrs./$9645* • **Hair Styling/Stylist and Hair Design** *300 hrs./$1500* • **Nail Technician/Specialist and Manicurist** *600 hrs./$3395* • **Permanent Cosmetics/Makeup and Tattooing**

**STUDENT SERVICES** Academic or career counseling, employment services for current students, placement services for program completers, remedial services.

## South Louisiana Community College

320 Devalcourt Street, Lafayette, LA 70506-2030
http://www.southlouisiana.edu

**CONTACT** Jan Brobst, Chancellor
**Telephone:** 337-521-8896

**GENERAL INFORMATION** Public Institution. **Total program enrollment:** 1497. **Application fee:** $5.

**STUDENT SERVICES** Academic or career counseling, remedial services.

## Stage One–the Hair School

209 West College Street, Lake Charles, LA 70605
http://www.stageoneinc.com/

**CONTACT** Peggy Guidry, President
**Telephone:** 337-474-0533

**GENERAL INFORMATION** Private Institution. **Total program enrollment:** 103. **Application fee:** $250.

**PROGRAM(S) OFFERED**
• **Cosmetology, Barber/Styling, and Nail Instructor** *750 hrs./$4200*
• **Cosmetology/Cosmetologist, General** *1500 hrs./$10,275*

**STUDENT SERVICES** Academic or career counseling, placement services for program completers.

## Stevenson's Academy of Hair Design

2039 Lapeyrouse Street, New Orleans, LA 70116
http://www.stevensonsacademy.com/

**CONTACT** Dorothy Stevenson, President
**Telephone:** 504-368-6377

**GENERAL INFORMATION** Private Institution. Founded 1973. **Total program enrollment:** 33. **Application fee:** $100.

**PROGRAM(S) OFFERED**
• **Aesthetician/Esthetician and Skin Care Specialist** *750 hrs./$6000* • **Barbering/Barber** *1500 hrs./$10,000* • **Cosmetology, Barber/Styling, and Nail Instructor** *750 hrs./$6000* • **Cosmetology/Cosmetologist, General** *1500 hrs./$11,000* • **Nail Technician/Specialist and Manicurist** *600 hrs./$5000*

**STUDENT SERVICES** Academic or career counseling, placement services for program completers.

## Unitech Training Academy

3605 Ambassador Caffery, Lafayette, LA 70503
http://www.unitechtrainingacademy.com/

**CONTACT** Deanna B. Head, President
**Telephone:** 337-988-6764

**GENERAL INFORMATION** Private Institution. **Total program enrollment:** 134. **Application fee:** $5.

**PROGRAM(S) OFFERED**
• **Blood Bank Technology Specialist** *620 hrs./$7810* • **Computer and Information Sciences, General** *1 student enrolled* • **Diagnostic Medical Sonography/Sonographer and Ultrasound Technician** *2792 hrs./$27,500* • **Health Unit Coordinator/Ward Clerk** • **Health and Medical Administrative Services, Other** *720 hrs./$9670* • **Medical Office Management/Administration** *20 students enrolled* • **Medical/Clinical Assistant** *1440 hrs./$19,565* • **Pharmacy Technician/Assistant** *21 students enrolled* • **Pharmacy, Pharmaceutical Sciences, and Administration, Other** *920 hrs./$13,735* • **Phlebotomy/Phlebotomist** *22 students enrolled* • **Physical Therapist Assistant** *17 students enrolled* • **Physical Therapy/Therapist** *480 hrs./$6595* • **Veterinary/Animal Health Technology/Technician and Veterinary Assistant**

**STUDENT SERVICES** Employment services for current students, placement services for program completers.

## Unitech Training Academy–Houma

1227 Grand Calliou, Houma, LA 70363
http://www.unitechtrainingacademy.com/

**CONTACT** Mrs. Deanna B. Head, President
**Telephone:** 985-223-1755

**GENERAL INFORMATION** Private Institution. **Total program enrollment:** 134. **Application fee:** $5.

**PROGRAM(S) OFFERED**
• **Blood Bank Technology Specialist** *620 hrs./$7810* • **Computer and Information Sciences, General** *4 students enrolled* • **Diagnostic Medical Sonography/Sonographer and Ultrasound Technician** *2792 hrs./$27,500* • **Health Unit Coordinator/Ward Clerk** *6 students enrolled* • **Health and Medical Administrative Services, Other** *720 hrs./$9670* • **Medical/Clinical Assistant** *1440 hrs./$19,565* • **Pharmacy, Pharmaceutical Sciences, and Administration, Other** *920 hrs./$13,735* • **Physical Therapy/Therapist** *480 hrs./$6595*

**STUDENT SERVICES** Employment services for current students, placement services for program completers.

## Unitech Training Academy–West Monroe Campus

111 Crosley Street, Suite 4, West Monroe, LA 71291
http://www.unitechtrainingacademy.com/

**CONTACT** Deanna B. Head, President
**Telephone:** 318-651-8001

**GENERAL INFORMATION** Private Institution. **Total program enrollment:** 108. **Application fee:** $5.

**PROGRAM(S) OFFERED**
• **Blood Bank Technology Specialist** *620 hrs./$7810* • **Computer and Information Sciences, General** *6 students enrolled* • **Diagnostic Medical Sonography/Sonographer and Ultrasound Technician** *2792 hrs./$27,500* • **Health Unit Coordinator/Ward Clerk** *3 students enrolled* • **Health and Medical Administrative Services, Other** *720 hrs./$9670* • **Medical Office Management/Administration** *25 students enrolled* • **Medical/Clinical Assistant** *1440 hrs./$19,565* • **Pharmacy Technician/Assistant** *35 students enrolled* • **Pharmacy, Pharmaceutical Sciences, and Administration, Other** *920 hrs./$13,735* • **Phlebotomy/Phlebotomist** *24 students enrolled* • **Physical Therapist Assistant** *30 students enrolled* • **Physical Therapy/Therapist** *480 hrs./$6595*

**STUDENT SERVICES** Employment services for current students, placement services for program completers.

## University of Louisiana at Monroe

700 University Avenue, Monroe, LA 71209-0001
http://www.ulm.edu/

**CONTACT** James E. Cofer, Sr., President
**Telephone:** 318-342-1000

**GENERAL INFORMATION** Public Institution. Founded 1931. **Accreditation:** Regional (SACS/CC); computer science (ABET/CSAC); counseling (ACA); dental hygiene (ADA); home economics (AAFCS); journalism and mass communications (ACEJMC); music (NASM); radiologic technology: radiography (JRCERT); speech-language pathology (ASHA). **Total program enrollment:** 6467. **Application fee:** $20.

**STUDENT SERVICES** Academic or career counseling, daycare for children of students, employment services for current students, placement services for program completers, remedial services.

## University of Phoenix–Louisiana Campus

1 Galleria Boulevard, Suite 725, Metairie, LA 70001-2082
http://www.phoenix.edu/

**CONTACT** William Pepicello, PhD, President
**Telephone:** 888-700-0867

**GENERAL INFORMATION** Private Institution. Founded 1976. **Accreditation:** Regional (NCA). **Total program enrollment:** 2006.

**PROGRAM(S) OFFERED**
• **Human Resources Management/Personnel Administration, General** *32 students enrolled*

**STUDENT SERVICES** Academic or career counseling, remedial services.

## Vanguard College of Cosmetology

3805 Pontchartrain Drive, Suite 16, Slidell, LA 70458
http://www.vanguardcollege.edu/

**CONTACT** Lisa B. Palermo, CEO
**Telephone:** 985-643-2614 Ext. 103

**GENERAL INFORMATION** Private Institution. Founded 1969. **Total program enrollment:** 124. **Application fee:** $50.

**PROGRAM(S) OFFERED**
• **Cosmetology, Barber/Styling, and Nail Instructor** *500 hrs./$4800*
• **Cosmetology/Cosmetologist, General** *1500 hrs./$16,900*

**STUDENT SERVICES** Academic or career counseling, placement services for program completers.

# MICRONESIA

## College of Micronesia–FSM

PO Box 159, Kolonia Pohnpei, FM 96941-0159
http://www.comfsm.fm/

**CONTACT** Spensin James, President
**Telephone:** 691-320-2480

**GENERAL INFORMATION** Public Institution. Founded 1963. **Accreditation:** Regional (WASC/ACCJC). **Total program enrollment:** 1867. **Application fee:** $10.

**PROGRAM(S) OFFERED**
• **Accounting Technology/Technician and Bookkeeping** *4 students enrolled* • **Agricultural and Food Products Processing** *2 students enrolled* • **Architectural Technology/Technician** *11 students enrolled* • **Carpentry/Carpenter** • **Community Health Services/Liaison/Counseling** *6 students enrolled* • **Electrical and Electronic Engineering Technologies/Technicians, Other** *1 student enrolled* • **Electrical and Power Transmission Installation/Installer, General** • **Kindergarten/Preschool Education and Teaching** • **Pre-Law Studies** *1 student enrolled*

**STUDENT SERVICES** Academic or career counseling, employment services for current students, remedial services.

# MINNESOTA

## Academy College

1101 East 78th Street, Suite 100, Minneapolis, MN 55420
http://www.academycollege.edu/

**CONTACT** Nancy Olson, Chief Executive Officer
**Telephone:** 952-851-0066

**GENERAL INFORMATION** Private Institution. Founded 1936. **Accreditation:** State accredited or approved. **Total program enrollment:** 125. **Application fee:** $30.

**PROGRAM(S) OFFERED**
• **Accounting** • **Air Transportation, Other** *9 students enrolled* • **Airline/Commercial/Professional Pilot and Flight Crew** *1 student enrolled* • **Commercial and Advertising Art** • **Data Processing and Data Processing Technology/Technician** • **Design and Visual Communications, General** • **Intermedia/Multimedia** • **Legal Administrative Assistant/Secretary** • **Medical Administrative/Executive Assistant and Medical Secretary** • **Medical Insurance Coding Specialist/Coder** *1 student enrolled* • **Medical/Clinical Assistant** *7 students enrolled* • **System, Networking, and LAN/WAN Management/Manager**

**STUDENT SERVICES** Academic or career counseling, employment services for current students, placement services for program completers.

## Alexandria Technical College

1601 Jefferson Street, Alexandria, MN 56308-3707
http://www.alextech.edu/

**CONTACT** Kevin Kopischke, President
**Telephone:** 320-762-0221

**GENERAL INFORMATION** Public Institution. Founded 1961. **Accreditation:** Regional (NCA); medical laboratory technology (NAACLS). **Total program enrollment:** 1503. **Application fee:** $20.

**PROGRAM(S) OFFERED**
• **Administrative Assistant and Secretarial Science, General** *7 students enrolled* • **Business Administration and Management, General** *1 student enrolled* • **Child Care and Support Services Management** *2 students enrolled* • **Computer Systems Networking and Telecommunications** *2 students enrolled* • **Criminal Justice/Police Science** *108 students enrolled* • **Health and Physical Education, General** *2 students enrolled* • **Human Resources Development** *1 student enrolled* • **Legal Administrative Assistant/Secretary** *2 students enrolled* • **Licensed Practical/Vocational Nurse Training (LPN, LVN, Cert, Dipl, AAS)** *41 students enrolled* • **Manufacturing Technology/Technician** *1 student enrolled* • **Mason/Masonry** *2 students enrolled* • **Medical Insurance Coding Specialist/Coder** *10 students enrolled* • **Phlebotomy/Phlebotomist** *6 students enrolled* • **Selling Skills and Sales Operations** *5 students enrolled* • **Truck and Bus Driver/Commercial Vehicle Operation** *24 students enrolled* • **Web Page, Digital/Multimedia and Information Resources Design** *3 students enrolled* • **Welding Technology/Welder** *19 students enrolled*

**STUDENT SERVICES** Academic or career counseling, employment services for current students, placement services for program completers, remedial services.

## American Indian OIC Incorporated

1845 E. Franklin Avenue, Minneapolis, MN 55404-2221
http://www.aioic.org/

**CONTACT** Lee Antell, President & CEO
**Telephone:** 612-341-3358 Ext. 100

**GENERAL INFORMATION** Private Institution. **Total program enrollment:** 48. **Application fee:** $35.

*American Indian OIC Incorporated (continued)*

**PROGRAM(S) OFFERED**

• **Administrative Assistant and Secretarial Science, General** *6 students enrolled* • **Community Organization and Advocacy** *4 students enrolled* • **Entrepreneurial and Small Business Operations, Other** *9 students enrolled* • **Finance, General** • **Medical Office Assistant/Specialist** *3 students enrolled* • **Nurse/Nursing Assistant/Aide and Patient Care Assistant** *22 students enrolled* • **Receptionist** *5 students enrolled*

**STUDENT SERVICES** Academic or career counseling, employment services for current students, placement services for program completers, remedial services.

## Anoka-Ramsey Community College

11200 Mississippi Boulevard, NW, Coon Rapids, MN 55433-3470
http://www.anokaramsey.edu/

**CONTACT** Patrick M. Johns, President
**Telephone:** 763-433-1240

**GENERAL INFORMATION** Public Institution. Founded 1965. **Accreditation:** Regional (NCA); physical therapy assisting (APTA). **Total program enrollment:** 3546. **Application fee:** $20.

**PROGRAM(S) OFFERED**

• **Accounting Technology/Technician and Bookkeeping** *2 students enrolled* • **Administrative Assistant and Secretarial Science, General** *1 student enrolled* • **Biology Technician/Biotechnology Laboratory Technician** *1 student enrolled* • **Business/Commerce, General** *26 students enrolled* • **Business/Office Automation/Technology/Data Entry** *2 students enrolled* • **Cartography** *2 students enrolled* • **Computer Systems Networking and Telecommunications** *11 students enrolled* • **Computer Technology/Computer Systems Technology** *3 students enrolled* • **Computer and Information Systems Security** *5 students enrolled* • **Health Services/Allied Health/Health Sciences, General** *7 students enrolled* • **Retailing and Retail Operations** *3 students enrolled*

**STUDENT SERVICES** Academic or career counseling, employment services for current students, placement services for program completers, remedial services.

## Anoka Technical College

1355 West Highway 10, Anoka, MN 55303
http://www.anokatech.edu/

**CONTACT** Anne Weyandt, President
**Telephone:** 763-576-4700

**GENERAL INFORMATION** Public Institution. Founded 1967. **Accreditation:** Regional (NCA). **Total program enrollment:** 979. **Application fee:** $20.

**PROGRAM(S) OFFERED**

• **Accounting Technology/Technician and Bookkeeping** *2 students enrolled* • **Architectural Drafting and Architectural CAD/CADD** *3 students enrolled* • **Automobile/Automotive Mechanics Technology/Technician** *1 student enrolled* • **Business Administration and Management, General** *2 students enrolled* • **Computer Hardware Technology/Technician** *5 students enrolled* • **Construction Management** *5 students enrolled* • **Court Reporting/Court Reporter** *5 students enrolled* • **Electrical, Electronic and Communications Engineering Technology/Technician** *1 student enrolled* • **Emergency Care Attendant (EMT Ambulance)** *3 students enrolled* • **Home Health Aide/Home Attendant** *1 student enrolled* • **Legal Administrative Assistant/Secretary** *11 students enrolled* • **Licensed Practical/Vocational Nurse Training (LPN, LVN, Cert, Dipl, AAS)** *48 students enrolled* • **Machine Tool Technology/Machinist** *10 students enrolled* • **Mechanical Drafting and Mechanical Drafting CAD/CADD** *4 students enrolled* • **Medical Insurance Coding Specialist/Coder** *14 students enrolled* • **Medical Reception/Receptionist** *2 students enrolled* • **Medical/Clinical Assistant** *12 students enrolled* • **Plumbing Technology/Plumber** *1 student enrolled* • **Receptionist** *1 student enrolled* • **Surgical Technology/Technologist** *18 students enrolled* • **Tool and Die Technology/Technician** *3 students enrolled* • **Welding Technology/Welder** *9 students enrolled*

**STUDENT SERVICES** Academic or career counseling, employment services for current students, placement services for program completers, remedial services.

## The Art Institutes International Minnesota

15 South 9th Street, Minneapolis, MN 55402-3137
http://www.artinstitutes.edu/minneapolis/

**CONTACT** William Johnson, President
**Telephone:** 612-332-3361

**GENERAL INFORMATION** Private Institution. Founded 1964. **Accreditation:** State accredited or approved. **Total program enrollment:** 1378. **Application fee:** $50.

**PROGRAM(S) OFFERED**

• **Culinary Arts/Chef Training** *45 students enrolled*

**STUDENT SERVICES** Academic or career counseling, employment services for current students, placement services for program completers, remedial services.

## Augsburg College

2211 Riverside Avenue, Minneapolis, MN 55454-1351
http://www.augsburg.edu/

**CONTACT** Paul Pribbenow, President
**Telephone:** 612-330-1000

**GENERAL INFORMATION** Private Institution. Founded 1869. **Accreditation:** Regional (NCA); music (NASM). **Total program enrollment:** 3070. **Application fee:** $25.

**STUDENT SERVICES** Academic or career counseling, employment services for current students, placement services for program completers, remedial services.

## Aveda Institute–Minneapolis

400 Central Avenue, Minneapolis, MN 55414
http://www.aveda.com/

**CONTACT** Teri Cipowski, Chancellor
**Telephone:** 612-378-7401

**GENERAL INFORMATION** Private Institution. Founded 1977. **Total program enrollment:** 499.

**PROGRAM(S) OFFERED**

• **Aesthetician/Esthetician and Skin Care Specialist** *600 hrs./$8450* • **Cosmetology/Cosmetologist, General** *1550 hrs./$17,650* • **Massage Therapy/Therapeutic Massage** *600 hrs./$8450*

**STUDENT SERVICES** Academic or career counseling, placement services for program completers, remedial services.

## Brown College

1440 Northland Drive, Mendota Heights, MN 55120
http://www.browncollege.edu/

**CONTACT** William Cowan, President
**Telephone:** 651-905-3400

**GENERAL INFORMATION** Private Institution. Founded 1946. **Accreditation:** State accredited or approved. **Total program enrollment:** 1257. **Application fee:** $50.

**STUDENT SERVICES** Academic or career counseling, employment services for current students, placement services for program completers, remedial services.

## Capella University

225 South 6th Street, 9th Floor, Minneapolis, MN 55402
http://www.capella.edu/

**CONTACT** Christopher Cassirer, University President
**Telephone:** 888-227-3552

**GENERAL INFORMATION** Private Institution. Founded 1993. **Accreditation:** Regional (NCA); counseling (ACA). **Total program enrollment:** 2240. **Application fee:** $75.

**PROGRAM(S) OFFERED**
• **Computer Systems Networking and Telecommunications** *1 student enrolled* • **Information Technology** *1 student enrolled*

**STUDENT SERVICES** Academic or career counseling, employment services for current students.

## Central Lakes College

501 West College Drive, Brainerd, MN 56401-3904
http://www.clcmn.edu/

**CONTACT** Dr. Larry Lundblad, President
**Telephone:** 218-855-8000

**GENERAL INFORMATION** Public Institution. Founded 1938. **Accreditation:** Regional (NCA); dental assisting (ADA). **Total program enrollment:** 2117. **Application fee:** $20.

**PROGRAM(S) OFFERED**
• **Accounting Technology/Technician and Bookkeeping** *4 students enrolled* • **American Sign Language (ASL)** *7 students enrolled* • **Automobile/Automotive Mechanics Technology/Technician** *9 students enrolled* • **Child Care Provider/Assistant** *1 student enrolled* • **Child Care and Support Services Management** *4 students enrolled* • **Commercial and Advertising Art** *7 students enrolled* • **Construction/Heavy Equipment/Earthmoving Equipment Operation** *57 students enrolled* • **Criminal Justice/Safety Studies** *9 students enrolled* • **Dental Assisting/Assistant** *28 students enrolled* • **Diesel Mechanics Technology/Technician** *14 students enrolled* • **Emergency Care Attendant (EMT Ambulance)** *1 student enrolled* • **Environmental Studies** *1 student enrolled* • **Farm/Farm and Ranch Management** *1 student enrolled* • **Floriculture/Floristry Operations and Management** *5 students enrolled* • **General Office Occupations and Clerical Services** *1 student enrolled* • **Greenhouse Operations and Management** *3 students enrolled* • **Landscaping and Groundskeeping** *10 students enrolled* • **Latin American Studies** *3 students enrolled* • **Licensed Practical/Vocational Nurse Training (LPN, LVN, Cert, Dipl, AAS)** *88 students enrolled* • **Machine Tool Technology/Machinist** *6 students enrolled* • **Marine Maintenance/Fitter and Ship Repair Technology/Technician** *10 students enrolled* • **Mechanical Drafting and Mechanical Drafting CAD/CADD** *1 student enrolled* • **Medical Administrative/Executive Assistant and Medical Secretary** *9 students enrolled* • **Photographic and Film/Video Technology/Technician and Assistant** *6 students enrolled* • **Welding Technology/Welder** *16 students enrolled*

**STUDENT SERVICES** Academic or career counseling, daycare for children of students, employment services for current students, placement services for program completers, remedial services.

## Century College

3300 Century Avenue North, White Bear Lake, MN 55110
http://www.century.edu/

**CONTACT** John O'Brien, Acting President
**Telephone:** 651-770-3200

**GENERAL INFORMATION** Public Institution. Founded 1970. **Accreditation:** Regional (NCA); dental assisting (ADA); dental hygiene (ADA); emergency medical services (JRCEMTP). **Total program enrollment:** 4355. **Application fee:** $20.

**PROGRAM(S) OFFERED**
• **Accounting Technology/Technician and Bookkeeping** *4 students enrolled* • **Accounting** *1 student enrolled* • **Administrative Assistant and Secretarial Science, General** *2 students enrolled* • **Applied Horticulture/Horticultural Operations, General** *4 students enrolled* • **Autobody/Collision and Repair Technology/Technician** *4 students enrolled* • **Automobile/Automotive Mechanics Technology/Technician** *7 students enrolled* • **Building/Property Maintenance and Management** *3 students enrolled* • **Computer Systems Networking and Telecommunications** *6 students enrolled* • **Computer Technology/Computer Systems Technology** *3 students enrolled* • **Cosmetology/Cosmetologist, General** *27 students enrolled* • **Dental Assisting/Assistant** *47 students enrolled* • **Dental Services and Allied Professions, Other** *1 student enrolled* • **Digital Communication and Media/Multimedia** *7 students enrolled* • **Emergency Medical Technology/Technician (EMT Paramedic)** *33 students enrolled* • **General Office Occupations and Clerical Services** *1 student enrolled* • **Greenhouse Operations and Management** *7 students enrolled* • **Heating, Air Conditioning, Ventilation and Refrigeration Maintenance Technology/Technician (HAC, HACR, HVAC, HVACR)** *8 students enrolled* • **Human Services, General** *6 students enrolled* • **Interior Design** *29 students enrolled* • **Landscaping and Groundskeeping** *3 students enrolled* • **Marketing/Marketing Management, General** *2 students enrolled* • **Medical Administrative/Executive Assistant and Medical Secretary** *2 students enrolled* • **Medical Office Assistant/Specialist** *8 students enrolled* • **Medical/Clinical Assistant** *33 students enrolled* • **Nail Technician/Specialist and Manicurist** *1 student enrolled* • **Orthotist/Prosthetist** *34 students enrolled* • **Pharmacy Technician/Assistant** *7 students enrolled* • **Quality Control Technology/Technician** *3 students enrolled* • **Special Products Marketing Operations** *1 student enrolled* • **Women's Studies** *3 students enrolled*

**STUDENT SERVICES** Academic or career counseling, daycare for children of students, employment services for current students, placement services for program completers, remedial services.

## The College of St. Scholastica

1200 Kenwood Avenue, Duluth, MN 55811-4199
http://www.css.edu/

**CONTACT** Larry Goodwin, President
**Telephone:** 218-723-6000

**GENERAL INFORMATION** Private Institution (Affiliated with Roman Catholic Church). Founded 1912. **Accreditation:** Regional (NCA); health information administration (AHIMA). **Total program enrollment:** 2986. **Application fee:** $25.

**PROGRAM(S) OFFERED**
• **Women's Studies** *1 student enrolled*

**STUDENT SERVICES** Academic or career counseling, employment services for current students, placement services for program completers.

## Concordia University, St. Paul

275 Syndicate Street North, St. Paul, MN 55104-5494
http://www.csp.edu/

**CONTACT** Robert A. Holst, President
**Telephone:** 651-641-8278

**GENERAL INFORMATION** Private Institution (Affiliated with Lutheran Church–Missouri Synod). Founded 1893. **Accreditation:** Regional (NCA). **Total program enrollment:** 2308. **Application fee:** $30.

**STUDENT SERVICES** Academic or career counseling, daycare for children of students, employment services for current students, placement services for program completers, remedial services.

## Cosmetology Careers Unlimited–Duluth

121 West Superior Street, Duluth, MN 55802
http://www.coscareers.com/

**CONTACT** Richard Shaffer, President
**Telephone:** 218-722-7484

**GENERAL INFORMATION** Private Institution. Founded 1927. **Total program enrollment:** 57. **Application fee:** $100.

**PROGRAM(S) OFFERED**
• **Aesthetician/Esthetician and Skin Care Specialist** *600 hrs./$6700* • **Cosmetology/Cosmetologist, General** *1550 hrs./$12,800*

**STUDENT SERVICES** Academic or career counseling, placement services for program completers.

## Cosmetology Careers Unlimited–Hibbing

110 East Howard Street, Hibbing, MN 55746
http://www.coscareers.com/

**CONTACT** Richard Shaffer, President
**Telephone:** 218-263-8354

**GENERAL INFORMATION** Private Institution. **Total program enrollment:** 37. **Application fee:** $100.

**PROGRAM(S) OFFERED**
• **Cosmetology/Cosmetologist, General** *1550 hrs./$12,800*

**STUDENT SERVICES** Academic or career counseling, placement services for program completers.

## Crown College

8700 College View Drive, St. Bonifacius, MN 55375-9001
http://www.crown.edu/

**CONTACT** Richard P. Mann, President
**Telephone:** 952-446-4100

**GENERAL INFORMATION** Private Institution (Affiliated with The Christian and Missionary Alliance). Founded 1916. **Accreditation:** Regional (NCA); state accredited or approved. **Total program enrollment:** 954. **Application fee:** $35.

**PROGRAM(S) OFFERED**
• **Bible/Biblical Studies** *1 student enrolled* • **General Office Occupations and Clerical Services** *8 students enrolled* • **System Administration/Administrator**

**STUDENT SERVICES** Academic or career counseling, employment services for current students, remedial services.

## Dakota County Technical College

1300 East 145th Street, Rosemount, MN 55068
http://www.dctc.edu/

**CONTACT** Ronald E. Thomas, President
**Telephone:** 651-423-8301

**GENERAL INFORMATION** Public Institution. Founded 1970. **Accreditation:** Regional (NCA); dental assisting (ADA); interior design: professional (CIDA); medical assisting (AAMAE). **Total program enrollment:** 1501. **Application fee:** $20.

**PROGRAM(S) OFFERED**
• **Accounting Technology/Technician and Bookkeeping** *3 students enrolled* • **Accounting** *1 student enrolled* • **Administrative Assistant and Secretarial Science, General** *3 students enrolled* • **Autobody/Collision and Repair Technology/Technician** *2 students enrolled* • **Automobile/Automotive Mechanics Technology/Technician** *2 students enrolled* • **Biomedical Technology/Technician** *1 student enrolled* • **Business Administration and Management, General** *8 students enrolled* • **Business/Office Automation/Technology/Data Entry** *1 student enrolled* • **Child Care Provider/Assistant** *9 students enrolled* • **Computer Systems Networking and Telecommunications** *2 students enrolled* • **Dental Assisting/Assistant** *23 students enrolled* • **Entrepreneurship/Entrepreneurial Studies** *6 students enrolled* • **Graphic Design** *2 students enrolled* • **Heavy Equipment Maintenance Technology/Technician** *2 students enrolled* • **Human Resources Development** *10 students enrolled* • **Kinesiology and Exercise Science** *2 students enrolled* • **Legal Administrative Assistant/Secretary** *1 student enrolled* • **Licensed Practical/Vocational Nurse Training (LPN, LVN, Cert, Dipl, AAS)** *62 students enrolled* • **Lineworker** *33 students enrolled* • **Marketing/Marketing Management, General** *2 students enrolled* • **Mason/Masonry** *10 students enrolled* • **Medical Administrative/Executive Assistant and Medical Secretary** *3 students enrolled* • **Medical Reception/Receptionist** *3 students enrolled* • **Medical Transcription/Transcriptionist** *3 students enrolled* • **Medical/Clinical Assistant** *22 students enrolled* • **Medium/Heavy Vehicle and Truck Technology/Technician** *3 students enrolled* • **Nurse/Nursing Assistant/Aide and Patient Care Assistant** *127 students enrolled* • **Photography** *1 student enrolled* • **Real Estate** *5 students enrolled* • **Receptionist** *2 students enrolled* • **Tourism and Travel Services Management** *23 students enrolled* • **Truck and Bus Driver/Commercial Vehicle Operation** *21 students enrolled* • **Welding Technology/Welder** *11 students enrolled* • **Woodworking, General** *16 students enrolled*

**STUDENT SERVICES** Academic or career counseling, employment services for current students, placement services for program completers, remedial services.

## Duluth Business University

4724 Mike Colalillo Drive, Duluth, MN 55807
http://www.dbumn.edu/

**CONTACT** James Gessner, President
**Telephone:** 218-722-4000

**GENERAL INFORMATION** Private Institution. Founded 1891. **Accreditation:** Dental assisting (ADA); medical assisting (AAMAE); state accredited or approved. **Total program enrollment:** 207. **Application fee:** $35.

**PROGRAM(S) OFFERED**
• **Health Information/Medical Records Technology/Technician** *12 students enrolled* • **Massage Therapy/Therapeutic Massage** *17 students enrolled* • **Medical/Clinical Assistant** *1 student enrolled* • **Phlebotomy/Phlebotomist** *4 students enrolled* • **Veterinary/Animal Health Technology/Technician and Veterinary Assistant**

**STUDENT SERVICES** Academic or career counseling, employment services for current students, placement services for program completers, remedial services.

## Dunwoody College of Technology

818 Dunwoody Boulevard, Minneapolis, MN 55403
http://www.dunwoody.edu/

**CONTACT** Dr. C. Ben Wright, President
**Telephone:** 612-374-5800

**GENERAL INFORMATION** Private Institution. Founded 1914. **Accreditation:** Regional (NCA). **Total program enrollment:** 1389. **Application fee:** $50.

**PROGRAM(S) OFFERED**
• **Appliance Installation and Repair Technology/Technician** *3 students enrolled* • **Building/Construction Site Management/Manager** *9 students enrolled* • **Building/Property Maintenance and Management** *8 students enrolled* • **CAD/CADD Drafting and/or Design Technology/Technician** • **Civil Drafting and Civil Engineering CAD/CADD** *2 students enrolled* • **Electrical, Electronic and Communications Engineering Technology/Technician** *11 students enrolled* • **Industrial Technology/Technician** • **Materials Engineering** • **Quality Control Technology/Technician** • **Sheet Metal Technology/Sheetworking** • **Survey Technology/Surveying** *5 students enrolled* • **Welding Technology/Welder** *21 students enrolled*

**STUDENT SERVICES** Academic or career counseling, employment services for current students, placement services for program completers, remedial services.

## East Metro Opportunities Industrialization Center

800 East Minnehaha Avenue, Suite 100, St. Paul, MN 55106
http://www.eastmetrooic.org/

**CONTACT** Barton Warren, Executive Director
**Telephone:** 651-291-5088

**GENERAL INFORMATION** Private Institution. Founded 1974. **Total program enrollment:** 120. **Application fee:** $50.

**PROGRAM(S) OFFERED**
• **Administrative Assistant and Secretarial Science, General** *1200 hrs./$9180* • **Business Operations Support and Secretarial Services, Other** *1 student enrolled* • **Business/Office Automation/Technology/Data Entry** *600 hrs./$4590* • **Computer Installation and Repair Technology/Technician** *600 hrs./$4590* • **Computer Systems Networking and Telecommunications** • **Computer and Information Sciences, General** • **Data Entry/Microcomputer Applications, General** *600 hrs./$4590* • **Electrical/Electronics Maintenance and Repair Technology, Other** *600 hrs./$4700* • **Receptionist** *900 hrs./$6885*

**STUDENT SERVICES** Academic or career counseling, employment services for current students, placement services for program completers, remedial services.

## Empire Beauty School–Eden Prairie

964 Prairie Center Drive, Eden Prairie, MN 55344
http://www.empire.edu

**CONTACT** Michael Bouman, President
**Telephone:** 952-906-2117

**GENERAL INFORMATION** Private Institution. **Total program enrollment:** 59. **Application fee:** $100.

**PROGRAM(S) OFFERED**
• **Cosmetology/Cosmetologist, General** *1550 hrs./$15,928*

## Everest Institute

1000 Blue Gentian Road, Suite 250, Eagan, MN 55121
http://www.everest.edu/

**CONTACT** Brian O'Hara, President
**Telephone:** 651-688-2145

**GENERAL INFORMATION** Private Institution. **Total program enrollment:** 859.

**PROGRAM(S) OFFERED**
• **Allied Health and Medical Assisting Services, Other** *720 hrs./$14,120* • **Health and Medical Administrative Services, Other** *720 hrs./$13,020* • **Massage Therapy/Therapeutic Massage** *720 hrs./$13,329* • **Medical Insurance Coding Specialist/Coder** *720 hrs./$13,020* • **Medical/Clinical Assistant** *148 students enrolled* • **Pharmacy Technician/Assistant** *720 hrs./$13,020*

**STUDENT SERVICES** Academic or career counseling, employment services for current students, placement services for program completers.

## Fond du Lac Tribal and Community College

2101 14th Street, Cloquet, MN 55720
http://www.fdltcc.edu/

**CONTACT** Larry Anderson, Interim President
**Telephone:** 218-879-0800

**GENERAL INFORMATION** Public Institution. Founded 1987. **Accreditation:** Regional (NCA). **Total program enrollment:** 771. **Application fee:** $20.

**PROGRAM(S) OFFERED**
• **Cartography** *1 student enrolled* • **Child Care Provider/Assistant** *6 students enrolled* • **Criminal Justice/Police Science** *80 students enrolled* • **Electrical and Power Transmission Installation/Installer, General** *2 students enrolled* • **Licensed Practical/Vocational Nurse Training (LPN, LVN, Cert, Dipl, AAS)** *1 student enrolled* • **Substance Abuse/Addiction Counseling** *28 students enrolled*

**STUDENT SERVICES** Academic or career counseling, daycare for children of students, remedial services.

## Globe University

8089 Globe Drive, Woodbury, MN 55125
http://www.globeuniversity.edu/

**CONTACT** Terry Myhre, President
**Telephone:** 651-332-8000

**GENERAL INFORMATION** Private Institution. Founded 1885. **Accreditation:** Medical assisting (AAMAE); state accredited or approved. **Total program enrollment:** 220. **Application fee:** $50.

**PROGRAM(S) OFFERED**
• **Accounting** *4 students enrolled* • **Allied Health and Medical Assisting Services, Other** *9 students enrolled* • **Business Administration and Management, General** *4 students enrolled* • **Computer Systems Networking and Telecommunications** • **Kinesiology and Exercise Science** *2 students enrolled* • **Legal Assistant/Paralegal** *3 students enrolled* • **Massage Therapy/Therapeutic Massage** *19 students enrolled* • **Medical Administrative/Executive Assistant and Medical Secretary**

**STUDENT SERVICES** Academic or career counseling, employment services for current students, placement services for program completers, remedial services.

## Hazelden Graduate School of Addiction Studies

PO Box 11, Center City, MN 55012
http://www.hazelden.org/

**CONTACT** Daniel McCormick
**Telephone:** 651-213-4000

**GENERAL INFORMATION** Private Institution. **Total program enrollment:** 64. **Application fee:** $30.

**PROGRAM(S) OFFERED**
• **Substance Abuse/Addiction Counseling** *8 students enrolled*

**STUDENT SERVICES** Academic or career counseling.

## Hennepin Technical College

9000 Brooklyn Boulevard, Brooklyn Park, MN 55445
http://www.hennepintech.edu/

**CONTACT** Cecilia Cervantes, President
**Telephone:** 952-995-1300

**GENERAL INFORMATION** Public Institution. Founded 1972. **Accreditation:** Regional (NCA); dental assisting (ADA). **Total program enrollment:** 2239. **Application fee:** $20.

**PROGRAM(S) OFFERED**
• **Accounting Technology/Technician and Bookkeeping** *13 students enrolled* • **Administrative Assistant and Secretarial Science, General** *4 students enrolled* • **Architectural Drafting and Architectural CAD/CADD** *4 students enrolled* • **Autobody/Collision and Repair Technology/Technician** *15 students enrolled* • **Automobile/Automotive Mechanics Technology/Technician** *22 students enrolled* • **Building/Property Maintenance and Management** *1 student enrolled* • **CAD/CADD Drafting and/or Design Technology/Technician** *3 students enrolled* • **Cabinetmaking and Millwork/Millwright** *9 students enrolled* • **Carpentry/Carpenter** *44 students enrolled* • **Child Care and Support Services Management** *8 students enrolled* • **Commercial Photography** *2 students enrolled* • **Computer Programming, Specific Applications** *5 students enrolled* • **Computer Systems Networking and Telecommunications** *1 student enrolled* • **Computer Technology/Computer Systems Technology** *1 student enrolled* • **Culinary Arts/Chef Training** *6 students enrolled* • **Data Modeling/Warehousing and Database Administration** *4 students enrolled* • **Dental Assisting/Assistant** *9 students enrolled* • **Digital Communication and Media/Multimedia** *2 students enrolled* • **Electrical, Electronic and Communications Engineering Technology/Technician** *8 students enrolled* • **Emergency Care Attendant (EMT Ambulance)** *8 students enrolled* • **Fire Protection and Safety Technology/Technician** *1 student enrolled* • **Fire Science/Firefighting** *7 students enrolled* • **Fire Services Administration** *1 student enrolled* • **Floriculture/Floristry Operations and Management** *4 students enrolled* • **General Office Occupations and Clerical Services** *53 students enrolled* • **Graphic and Printing Equipment Operator,**

*Hennepin Technical College (continued)*

**General Production** *1 student enrolled* • **Greenhouse Operations and Management** *2 students enrolled* • **Hazardous Materials Management and Waste Technology/Technician** *1 student enrolled* • **Health Unit Coordinator/Ward Clerk** *33 students enrolled* • **Heating, Air Conditioning, Ventilation and Refrigeration Maintenance Technology/Technician (HAC, HACR, HVAC, HVACR)** *40 students enrolled* • **Hydraulics and Fluid Power Technology/Technician** *4 students enrolled* • **Industrial Mechanics and Maintenance Technology** *8 students enrolled* • **Landscaping and Groundskeeping** *3 students enrolled* • **Licensed Practical/Vocational Nurse Training (LPN, LVN, Cert, Dipl, AAS)** *12 students enrolled* • **Machine Tool Technology/Machinist** *15 students enrolled* • **Marine Maintenance/Fitter and Ship Repair Technology/Technician** *1 student enrolled* • **Mechanical Drafting and Mechanical Drafting CAD/CADD** *4 students enrolled* • **Medical Administrative/Executive Assistant and Medical Secretary** *2 students enrolled* • **Medical Reception/Receptionist** *9 students enrolled* • **Medical Transcription/Transcriptionist** *3 students enrolled* • **Medium/Heavy Vehicle and Truck Technology/Technician** *11 students enrolled* • **Motorcycle Maintenance and Repair Technology/Technician** *2 students enrolled* • **Nurse/Nursing Assistant/Aide and Patient Care Assistant** *156 students enrolled* • **Plant Nursery Operations and Management** *1 student enrolled* • **Plastics Engineering Technology/Technician** *6 students enrolled* • **Prepress/Desktop Publishing and Digital Imaging Design** *2 students enrolled* • **Printing Press Operator** *5 students enrolled* • **Public Administration** *5 students enrolled* • **Real Estate** *2 students enrolled* • **Recording Arts Technology/Technician** *5 students enrolled* • **Small Engine Mechanics and Repair Technology/Technician** *3 students enrolled* • **Tool and Die Technology/Technician** *1 student enrolled* • **Welding Technology/Welder** *12 students enrolled*

**STUDENT SERVICES** Academic or career counseling, employment services for current students, placement services for program completers, remedial services.

## Herzing College

5700 West Broadway, Minneapolis, MN 55428
http://www.herzing.edu/

**CONTACT** John Slama, College President
**Telephone:** 763-535-3000

**GENERAL INFORMATION** Private Institution. Founded 1961. **Accreditation:** State accredited or approved. **Total program enrollment:** 182. **Application fee:** $25.

**PROGRAM(S) OFFERED**
• **Architectural Drafting and Architectural CAD/CADD** • **Dental Assisting/Assistant** *55 students enrolled* • **Health and Medical Administrative Services, Other** • **Mechanical Drafting and Mechanical Drafting CAD/CADD** • **Medical Insurance Coding Specialist/Coder** • **Medical Insurance Specialist/Medical Biller** *10 students enrolled* • **Medical/Clinical Assistant** *7 students enrolled*

**STUDENT SERVICES** Academic or career counseling, employment services for current students, placement services for program completers, remedial services.

## Hibbing Community College

1515 East 25th Street, Hibbing, MN 55746-3300
http://www.hcc.mnscu.edu/

**CONTACT** Kenneth Simberg, Provost
**Telephone:** 218-262-7200

**GENERAL INFORMATION** Public Institution. Founded 1916. **Accreditation:** Regional (NCA); dental assisting (ADA); medical laboratory technology (NAACLS). **Total program enrollment:** 1027. **Application fee:** $20.

**PROGRAM(S) OFFERED**
• **Administrative Assistant and Secretarial Science, General** *2 students enrolled* • **Appliance Installation and Repair Technology/Technician** *1 student enrolled* • **Automobile/Automotive Mechanics Technology/Technician** *6 students enrolled* • **Computer Installation and Repair Technology/Technician** *9 students enrolled* • **Computer Systems Networking and Telecommunications** *8 students enrolled* • **Culinary Arts/Chef Training** *1 student enrolled* • **Data Entry/Microcomputer Applications, General** *1 student enrolled* • **Dental Assisting/Assistant** *19 students enrolled* • **Health/Health Care Administration/Management** *1 student enrolled* • **Heating, Air Conditioning, Ventilation and Refrigeration Maintenance Technology/Technician (HAC, HACR, HVAC, HVACR)** *4 students enrolled* • **Medical Insurance Coding Specialist/Coder** *10 students enrolled* • **Nurse/Nursing Assistant/Aide and Patient Care Assistant** *63 students enrolled*

**STUDENT SERVICES** Academic or career counseling, employment services for current students, placement services for program completers, remedial services.

## High-Tech Institute

5100 Gamble Drive, St. Louis Park, MN 55416
http://www.high-techinstitute.com/

**CONTACT** Elizabeth Beseke, Campus President
**Telephone:** 952-417-2200

**GENERAL INFORMATION** Private Institution. Founded 1996. **Accreditation:** State accredited or approved. **Total program enrollment:** 400. **Application fee:** $50.

**PROGRAM(S) OFFERED**
• **Massage Therapy/Therapeutic Massage** *820 hrs./$11,961* • **Medical Insurance Specialist/Medical Biller** *720 hrs./$13,916* • **Medical Radiologic Technology/Science—Radiation Therapist** *810 hrs./$18,024* • **Medical/Clinical Assistant** *746 hrs./$12,150* • **Pharmacy Technician/Assistant** *720 hrs./$13,087* • **Surgical Technology/Technologist** *1340 hrs./$25,681*

**STUDENT SERVICES** Placement services for program completers.

## Ingenue Beauty School

17 South Fourth Street, Moorhead, MN 56560

**CONTACT** Rita L. Dickelman, President
**Telephone:** 218-236-7201

**GENERAL INFORMATION** Private Institution. **Total program enrollment:** 29. **Application fee:** $50.

**PROGRAM(S) OFFERED**
• **Cosmetology/Cosmetologist, General** *1550 hrs./$8100* • **Nail Technician/Specialist and Manicurist** *5 students enrolled*

**STUDENT SERVICES** Academic or career counseling, placement services for program completers.

## Inver Hills Community College

2500 East 80th Street, Inver Grove Heights, MN 55076-3224
http://www.inverhills.edu/

**CONTACT** Cheryl Frank, President
**Telephone:** 651-450-8500

**GENERAL INFORMATION** Public Institution. Founded 1969. **Accreditation:** Regional (NCA). **Total program enrollment:** 2206. **Application fee:** $20.

**PROGRAM(S) OFFERED**
• **Building/Construction Site Management/Manager** *2 students enrolled* • **Building/Home/Construction Inspection/Inspector** *4 students enrolled* • **Business Administration and Management, General** *2 students enrolled* • **Business/Office Automation/Technology/Data Entry** *1 student enrolled* • **Child Care Provider/Assistant** *1 student enrolled* • **Computer Technology/Computer Systems Technology** *1 student enrolled* • **Computer and Information Systems Security** *2 students enrolled* • **Criminal Justice/Safety Studies** *1 student enrolled* • **Emergency Medical Technology/Technician (EMT Paramedic)** *9 students enrolled* • **Human Resources Management/Personnel Administration, General** *8 students enrolled* • **Legal Assistant/Paralegal** *23 students enrolled* • **Nurse/Nursing Assistant/Aide and Patient Care Assistant** *143 students enrolled* • **Sales, Distribution and Marketing Operations, General** *4 students enrolled* • **Small Business Administration/Management** *3 students enrolled*

**STUDENT SERVICES** Academic or career counseling, daycare for children of students, employment services for current students, placement services for program completers, remedial services.

## Itasca Community College

1851 Highway 169 East, Grand Rapids, MN 55744
http://www.itascacc.edu/

**CONTACT** Dr. Sue Collins, President
**Telephone:** 218-327-4460

**GENERAL INFORMATION** Public Institution. Founded 1922. **Accreditation:** Regional (NCA). **Total program enrollment:** 811. **Application fee:** $20.

**PROGRAM(S) OFFERED**
• **Cartography** *4 students enrolled* • **Child Care Provider/Assistant** *12 students enrolled* • **Forest Management/Forest Resources Management** *4 students enrolled* • **Licensed Practical/Vocational Nurse Training (LPN, LVN, Cert, Dipl, AAS)** *34 students enrolled*

**STUDENT SERVICES** Academic or career counseling, daycare for children of students, employment services for current students, placement services for program completers, remedial services.

## Lake Superior College

2101 Trinity Road, Duluth, MN 55811
http://www.lsc.edu/

**CONTACT** Kathleen Nelson, President
**Telephone:** 800-432-2884

**GENERAL INFORMATION** Public Institution. Founded 1995. **Accreditation:** Regional (NCA); dental hygiene (ADA); medical laboratory technology (NAACLS); physical therapy assisting (APTA). **Total program enrollment:** 2299. **Application fee:** $20.

**PROGRAM(S) OFFERED**
• **Accounting Technology/Technician and Bookkeeping** *4 students enrolled* • **Administrative Assistant and Secretarial Science, General** *1 student enrolled* • **Athletic Training/Trainer** *1 student enrolled* • **Autobody/Collision and Repair Technology/Technician** *10 students enrolled* • **Automobile/Automotive Mechanics Technology/Technician** *6 students enrolled* • **Business Administration and Management, General** *2 students enrolled* • **Carpentry/Carpenter** *30 students enrolled* • **Civil Engineering Technology/Technician** *2 students enrolled* • **Communications Systems Installation and Repair Technology** *7 students enrolled* • **Computer Hardware Technology/Technician** *1 student enrolled* • **Computer Systems Networking and Telecommunications** *1 student enrolled* • **Electrical, Electronic and Communications Engineering Technology/Technician** *1 student enrolled* • **Electrician** *9 students enrolled* • **Human Resources Management/Personnel Administration, General** *1 student enrolled* • **Legal Administrative Assistant/Secretary** *4 students enrolled* • **Legal Assistant/Paralegal** *2 students enrolled* • **Licensed Practical/Vocational Nurse Training (LPN, LVN, Cert, Dipl, AAS)** *120 students enrolled* • **Machine Tool Technology/Machinist** *1 student enrolled* • **Massage Therapy/Therapeutic Massage** *24 students enrolled* • **Medical Administrative/Executive Assistant and Medical Secretary** *2 students enrolled* • **Medical Insurance Coding Specialist/Coder** *8 students enrolled* • **Medical Reception/Receptionist** *1 student enrolled* • **Medical Transcription/Transcriptionist** *4 students enrolled* • **Medical/Clinical Assistant** *13 students enrolled* • **Nurse/Nursing Assistant/Aide and Patient Care Assistant** *279 students enrolled* • **Phlebotomy/Phlebotomist** *21 students enrolled* • **Radio and Television Broadcasting Technology/Technician** *6 students enrolled* • **Radiologic Technology/Science—Radiographer** *5 students enrolled* • **Selling Skills and Sales Operations** *37 students enrolled* • **Surgical Technology/Technologist** *6 students enrolled* • **Web Page, Digital/Multimedia and Information Resources Design** *2 students enrolled*

**STUDENT SERVICES** Academic or career counseling, daycare for children of students, employment services for current students, placement services for program completers, remedial services.

## Le Cordon Bleu College of Culinary Arts

1315 Mendota Heights Road, Saint Paul, MN 55120
http://www.twincitiesculinary.com/

**CONTACT** Kevin Sanderson, President
**Telephone:** 651-675-4700

**GENERAL INFORMATION** Private Institution. **Total program enrollment:** 742. **Application fee:** $50.

**PROGRAM(S) OFFERED**
• **Baking and Pastry Arts/Baker/Pastry Chef** *104 hrs./$32,000* • **Culinary Arts/Chef Training** *33 hrs./$20,000*

**STUDENT SERVICES** Academic or career counseling, employment services for current students, placement services for program completers, remedial services.

## Leech Lake Tribal College

6945 Littlewolf Road NW, Cass Lake, MN 56633-0180
http://www.lltc.org/

**CONTACT** Dr. Leah Carpenter, President
**Telephone:** 218-335-4200

**GENERAL INFORMATION** Private Institution. Founded 1992. **Accreditation:** Regional (NCA). **Total program enrollment:** 188. **Application fee:** $15.

**PROGRAM(S) OFFERED**
• **Carpentry/Carpenter** *16 students enrolled*

**STUDENT SERVICES** Academic or career counseling, remedial services.

## Martin Luther College

1995 Luther Court, New Ulm, MN 56073
http://www.mlc-wels.edu/

**CONTACT** Mark G. Zarling, President
**Telephone:** 507-354-8221 Ext. 211

**GENERAL INFORMATION** Private Institution (Affiliated with Wisconsin Evangelical Lutheran Synod). Founded 1995. **Accreditation:** Regional (NCA). **Total program enrollment:** 712. **Application fee:** $25.

**PROGRAM(S) OFFERED**
• **Theology and Religious Vocations, Other** *36 students enrolled*

**STUDENT SERVICES** Academic or career counseling, employment services for current students, placement services for program completers, remedial services.

## Mayo School of Health Sciences

Siebens Building, 200 First Street, SW, Rochester, MN 55905
http://www.mayo.edu/mshs/

**CONTACT** Claire Bender, MD, Dean
**Telephone:** 507-284-3678

**GENERAL INFORMATION** Private Institution. Founded 1973. **Accreditation:** Regional (NCA); dietetics: postbaccalaureate internship (ADtA/CAADE); electroneurodiagnostic technology (JRCEND). **Total program enrollment:** 299. **Application fee:** $50.

**PROGRAM(S) OFFERED**
• **Cytogenetics/Genetics/Clinical Genetics Technology/Technologist** *17 students enrolled* • **Cytotechnology/Cytotechnologist** *1440 hrs./$3500* • **Diagnostic Medical Sonography/Sonographer and Ultrasound Technician** *22 students enrolled* • **Histologic Technology/Histotechnologist** *5 students enrolled* • **Medical Radiologic Technology/Science—Radiation Therapist** *1950 hrs./$1500* • **Nuclear Medical Technology/Technologist** *1853 hrs./$6500* • **Nurse Anesthetist** *2150 hrs./$9750* • **Physical Therapy/Therapist** *2700 hrs.*

**STUDENT SERVICES** Academic or career counseling, employment services for current students, placement services for program completers, remedial services.

## McNally Smith College of Music

19 Exchange Street East, Saint Paul, MN 55101
http://www.mcnallysmith.edu/

**CONTACT** Harry Chalmiers, President
**Telephone:** 651-291-0177

**GENERAL INFORMATION** Private Institution. Founded 1985. **Accreditation:** Music (NASM). **Total program enrollment:** 491. **Application fee:** $75.

**PROGRAM(S) OFFERED**
• **Engineering, Other** *7 students enrolled* • **Music Management and Merchandising** *1 student enrolled* • **Music Performance, General** *1 student enrolled*

**STUDENT SERVICES** Academic or career counseling, employment services for current students, remedial services.

## Mesabi Range Community and Technical College

1001 Chestnut Street West, Virginia, MN 55792-3448
http://www.mr.mnscu.edu/

**CONTACT** Dr. Tina Royer, Provost
**Telephone:** 218-741-3095

**GENERAL INFORMATION** Public Institution. Founded 1918. **Accreditation:** Regional (NCA). **Total program enrollment:** 912. **Application fee:** $20.

**PROGRAM(S) OFFERED**
• **Automobile/Automotive Mechanics Technology/Technician** *7 students enrolled* • **Business/Commerce, General** *1 student enrolled* • **Business/Office Automation/Technology/Data Entry** *5 students enrolled* • **Carpentry/Carpenter** *9 students enrolled* • **Child Care Provider/Assistant** *1 student enrolled* • **Graphic Communications, General** *4 students enrolled* • **Industrial Electronics Technology/Technician** *7 students enrolled* • **Industrial Mechanics and Maintenance Technology** *32 students enrolled* • **Licensed Practical/Vocational Nurse Training (LPN, LVN, Cert, Dipl, AAS)** *35 students enrolled* • **Mason/Masonry** *10 students enrolled* • **Substance Abuse/Addiction Counseling** *1 student enrolled* • **Welding Technology/Welder** *20 students enrolled*

**STUDENT SERVICES** Academic or career counseling, daycare for children of students, employment services for current students, placement services for program completers, remedial services.

## Metropolitan State University

700 East 7th Street, St. Paul, MN 55106-5000
http://www.metrostate.edu/

**CONTACT** Susan Hammersmith, President
**Telephone:** 651-793-1212

**GENERAL INFORMATION** Public Institution. Founded 1971. **Accreditation:** Regional (NCA). **Total program enrollment:** 2470. **Application fee:** $20.

**PROGRAM(S) OFFERED**
• **Criminal Justice/Law Enforcement Administration** *1 student enrolled* • **Criminal Justice/Police Science** *27 students enrolled*

**STUDENT SERVICES** Academic or career counseling.

## Minneapolis Business College

1711 West County Road B, Roseville, MN 55113
http://www.minneapolisbusinesscollege.edu/

**CONTACT** David B. Whitman, President
**Telephone:** 651-636-7406

**GENERAL INFORMATION** Private Institution. Founded 1874. **Accreditation:** State accredited or approved. **Total program enrollment:** 373. **Application fee:** $50.

**PROGRAM(S) OFFERED**
• **Accounting** *19 students enrolled* • **Administrative Assistant and Secretarial Science, General** *17 students enrolled* • **Commercial and Advertising Art** *26 students enrolled* • **Computer Programming/Programmer, General** *12 students enrolled* • **Legal Administrative Assistant/Secretary** *2 students enrolled* • **Medical/Clinical Assistant** *74 students enrolled* • **Tourism and Travel Services Management** *10 students enrolled*

**STUDENT SERVICES** Academic or career counseling, employment services for current students, placement services for program completers.

## Minneapolis Community and Technical College

1501 Hennepin Avenue, Minneapolis, MN 55403-1779
http://www.mctc.mnscu.edu/

**CONTACT** Phillip Davis, President
**Telephone:** 612-659-6000

**GENERAL INFORMATION** Public Institution. Founded 1965. **Accreditation:** Regional (NCA); dental assisting (ADA). **Total program enrollment:** 3922. **Application fee:** $20.

**PROGRAM(S) OFFERED**
• **Accounting Technology/Technician and Bookkeeping** *4 students enrolled* • **Aircraft Powerplant Technology/Technician** *7 students enrolled* • **Airframe Mechanics and Aircraft Maintenance Technology/Technician** *24 students enrolled* • **Allied Health and Medical Assisting Services, Other** *9 students enrolled* • **American Indian/Native American Studies** *1 student enrolled* • **Apparel and Textile Manufacture** *4 students enrolled* • **Architectural Drafting and Architectural CAD/CADD** *10 students enrolled* • **Banking and Financial Support Services** *2 students enrolled* • **Barbering/Barber** *1 student enrolled* • **Carpentry/Carpenter** *13 students enrolled* • **Child Care Provider/Assistant** *8 students enrolled* • **Child Care and Support Services Management** *4 students enrolled* • **Commercial Photography** *2 students enrolled* • **Community Health Services/Liaison/Counseling** *6 students enrolled* • **Computer Programming, Specific Applications** *2 students enrolled* • **Computer Systems Networking and Telecommunications** *4 students enrolled* • **Computer and Information Systems Security** *2 students enrolled* • **Cosmetology/Cosmetologist, General** *1 student enrolled* • **Criminal Justice/Police Science** *232 students enrolled* • **Culinary Arts/Chef Training** *2 students enrolled* • **Customer Service Support/Call Center/Teleservice Operation** *2 students enrolled* • **Data Modeling/Warehousing and Database Administration** *2 students enrolled* • **Dental Assisting/Assistant** *3 students enrolled* • **Dental Services and Allied Professions, Other** *20 students enrolled* • **Electrician** *16 students enrolled* • **Electroneurodiagnostic/Electroencephalographic Technology/Technologist** *6 students enrolled* • **Film/Cinema Studies** *1 student enrolled* • **Food Preparation/Professional Cooking/Kitchen Assistant** *1 student enrolled* • **Heating, Air Conditioning, Ventilation and Refrigeration Maintenance Technology/Technician (HAC, HACR, HVAC, HVACR)** *8 students enrolled* • **Human Services, General** *7 students enrolled* • **Legal Administrative Assistant/Secretary** *2 students enrolled* • **Library Assistant/Technician** *1 student enrolled* • **Licensed Practical/Vocational Nurse Training (LPN, LVN, Cert, Dipl, AAS)** *86 students enrolled* • **Machine Tool Technology/Machinist** *2 students enrolled* • **Medical Office Assistant/Specialist** *6 students enrolled* • **Nurse/Nursing Assistant/Aide and Patient Care Assistant** *309 students enrolled* • **Prepress/Desktop Publishing and Digital Imaging Design** *1 student enrolled* • **Public Administration** *5 students enrolled* • **Security and Protective Services, Other** *1 student enrolled* • **Substance Abuse/Addiction Counseling** *1 student enrolled* • **Watchmaking and Jewelrymaking** *13 students enrolled* • **Web Page, Digital/Multimedia and Information Resources Design** *1 student enrolled* • **Welding Technology/Welder** *2 students enrolled* • **Women's Studies** *11 students enrolled*

**STUDENT SERVICES** Academic or career counseling, employment services for current students, placement services for program completers, remedial services.

## Minnesota Cosmetology Education Center

704 Marie Avenue, South St. Paul, MN 55075
http://www.msccollege.edu/

**CONTACT** Terry Myhre, President
**Telephone:** 651-287-2180

**GENERAL INFORMATION** Private Institution. Founded 1978. **Total program enrollment:** 191. **Application fee:** $50.

**PROGRAM(S) OFFERED**

• **Cosmetology/Cosmetologist, General** *1550 hrs./$17,275* • **Nail Technician/Specialist and Manicurist** *25 students enrolled*

**STUDENT SERVICES** Academic or career counseling, employment services for current students, placement services for program completers.

## Minnesota School of Business–Brooklyn Center

5910 Shingle Creek Parkway, Brooklyn Center, MN 55430
http://www.msbcollege.edu/

**CONTACT** DeeAnn Kerr, Director
**Telephone:** 763-566-7777

**GENERAL INFORMATION** Private Institution. Founded 1989. **Accreditation:** State accredited or approved. **Total program enrollment:** 145. **Application fee:** $50.

**PROGRAM(S) OFFERED**

• **Accounting** • **Advertising** *1 student enrolled* • **Business Administration and Management, General** *4 students enrolled* • **Legal Administrative Assistant/Secretary** *1 student enrolled* • **Massage Therapy/Therapeutic Massage** *23 students enrolled* • **Medical Administrative/Executive Assistant and Medical Secretary** *2 students enrolled* • **Medical/Clinical Assistant** *14 students enrolled*

**STUDENT SERVICES** Academic or career counseling, employment services for current students, placement services for program completers, remedial services.

## Minnesota School of Business–Plymouth

1455 Country Road 101 North, Minneapolis, MN 55447
http://www.msbcollege.edu/

**CONTACT** Andy Hoeveler, Campus Director
**Telephone:** 763-476-2000

**GENERAL INFORMATION** Private Institution. Founded 2002. **Accreditation:** State accredited or approved. **Total program enrollment:** 140. **Application fee:** $50.

**PROGRAM(S) OFFERED**

• **Accounting** *1 student enrolled* • **Advertising** • **Allied Health and Medical Assisting Services, Other** *3 students enrolled* • **Business Administration and Management, General** *2 students enrolled* • **Health and Physical Education/Fitness, Other** *2 students enrolled* • **Legal Assistant/Paralegal** *2 students enrolled* • **Massage Therapy/Therapeutic Massage** *13 students enrolled* • **Medical Administrative/Executive Assistant and Medical Secretary**

**STUDENT SERVICES** Academic or career counseling, employment services for current students, placement services for program completers, remedial services.

## Minnesota School of Business–Richfield

1401 West 76th Street, Suite 500, Richfield, MN 55423
http://www.msbcollege.edu/

**CONTACT** Terry Myhre, President
**Telephone:** 612-861-2000

**GENERAL INFORMATION** Private Institution. Founded 1877. **Accreditation:** Medical assisting (AAMAE); state accredited or approved. **Total program enrollment:** 445. **Application fee:** $50.

**PROGRAM(S) OFFERED**

• **Accounting** *4 students enrolled* • **Administrative Assistant and Secretarial Science, General** • **Advertising** *2 students enrolled* • **Animation, Interactive Technology, Video Graphics and Special Effects** *7 students enrolled* • **Computer and Information Sciences, General** • **Design and Visual Communications, General** *2 students enrolled* • **Health and Physical Education/Fitness, Other** • **Legal Administrative Assistant/Secretary** *2 students enrolled* • **Massage Therapy/Therapeutic Massage** *1 student enrolled* • **Medical Administrative/Executive Assistant and Medical Secretary** • **Medical/Clinical Assistant** *8 students enrolled*

**STUDENT SERVICES** Academic or career counseling, employment services for current students, placement services for program completers, remedial services.

## Minnesota School of Business–Rochester

2521 Pennington Drive, NW, Rochester, MN 55901
http://www.msbcollege.edu/

**CONTACT** Shan Pollitt, Director
**Telephone:** 507-536-9500

**GENERAL INFORMATION** Private Institution. **Total program enrollment:** 291. **Application fee:** $50.

**PROGRAM(S) OFFERED**

• **Accounting** *3 students enrolled* • **Administrative Assistant and Secretarial Science, General** *16 students enrolled* • **Health and Physical Education/Fitness, Other** *1 student enrolled* • **Legal Assistant/Paralegal** • **Massage Therapy/Therapeutic Massage** *11 students enrolled* • **Medical Administrative/Executive Assistant and Medical Secretary** *4 students enrolled* • **Medical/Clinical Assistant** *9 students enrolled*

**STUDENT SERVICES** Academic or career counseling, employment services for current students, placement services for program completers, remedial services.

## Minnesota School of Business–St. Cloud

1201 2nd Street South, Waite Park, MN 56387
http://www.msbcollege.edu/

**CONTACT** James Beck, Campus Director
**Telephone:** 320-257-2000

**GENERAL INFORMATION** Private Institution. Founded 2004. **Total program enrollment:** 409. **Application fee:** $50.

**PROGRAM(S) OFFERED**

• **Accounting** *3 students enrolled* • **Advertising** *1 student enrolled* • **Business Administration and Management, General** *8 students enrolled* • **Health and Physical Education/Fitness, Other** *1 student enrolled* • **Legal Assistant/Paralegal** *2 students enrolled* • **Massage Therapy/Therapeutic Massage** *24 students enrolled* • **Medical Administrative/Executive Assistant and Medical Secretary** *2 students enrolled* • **Medical/Clinical Assistant** *17 students enrolled*

**STUDENT SERVICES** Academic or career counseling, employment services for current students, placement services for program completers, remedial services.

## Minnesota School of Business–Shakopee

1200 Shakopee Town Square, Shakopee, MN 55379
http://www.msbcollege.edu/

**CONTACT** Diana Igo, Campus Director
**Telephone:** 952-345-1200

**GENERAL INFORMATION** Private Institution. Founded 2004. **Total program enrollment:** 165. **Application fee:** $50.

**PROGRAM(S) OFFERED**

• **Accounting** • **Advertising** • **Business Administration and Management, General** *1 student enrolled* • **Kinesiology and Exercise Science** *1 student enrolled* • **Legal Assistant/Paralegal** *2 students enrolled* • **Massage Therapy/Therapeutic Massage** *22 students enrolled* • **Medical Administrative/Executive Assistant and Medical Secretary** *3 students enrolled* • **Medical/Clinical Assistant** *7 students enrolled*

**STUDENT SERVICES** Academic or career counseling, employment services for current students, placement services for program completers, remedial services.

## Minnesota State College–Southeast Technical

1250 Homer Road, PO Box 409, Winona, MN 55987
http://www.southeastmn.edu/

**CONTACT** James Johnson, President
**Telephone:** 507-453-2700

**GENERAL INFORMATION** Public Institution. Founded 1992. **Accreditation:** Regional (NCA). **Total program enrollment:** 1180. **Application fee:** $20.

**PROGRAM(S) OFFERED**
• **Accounting Technology/Technician and Bookkeeping** *1 student enrolled*
• **Administrative Assistant and Secretarial Science, General** *1 student enrolled*
• **Aesthetician/Esthetician and Skin Care Specialist** *2 students enrolled*
• **Autobody/Collision and Repair Technology/Technician** *2 students enrolled*
• **Automobile/Automotive Mechanics Technology/Technician** *9 students enrolled*
• **Business Administration and Management, General** *3 students enrolled*
• **Business/Office Automation/Technology/Data Entry** *1 student enrolled*
• **Carpentry/Carpenter** *9 students enrolled* • **Computer Programming, Specific Applications** *2 students enrolled* • **Computer Systems Networking and Telecommunications** *1 student enrolled* • **Cosmetology/Cosmetologist, General** *14 students enrolled* • **Drafting and Design Technology/Technician, General** *1 student enrolled* • **Electrical, Electronic and Communications Engineering Technology/Technician** *2 students enrolled* • **General Office Occupations and Clerical Services** *2 students enrolled* • **Health Unit Coordinator/Ward Clerk** *14 students enrolled* • **Heating, Air Conditioning, Ventilation and Refrigeration Maintenance Technology/Technician (HAC, HACR, HVAC, HVACR)** *16 students enrolled* • **Industrial Mechanics and Maintenance Technology** *5 students enrolled* • **Licensed Practical/Vocational Nurse Training (LPN, LVN, Cert, Dipl, AAS)** *121 students enrolled* • **Machine Shop Technology/Assistant** *1 student enrolled* • **Massage Therapy/Therapeutic Massage** *2 students enrolled* • **Medical Administrative/Executive Assistant and Medical Secretary** *10 students enrolled* • **Medical Transcription/Transcriptionist** *8 students enrolled* • **Musical Instrument Fabrication and Repair** *5 students enrolled* • **Nail Technician/Specialist and Manicurist** *1 student enrolled* • **Nurse/Nursing Assistant/Aide and Patient Care Assistant** *2 students enrolled* • **Retailing and Retail Operations** *1 student enrolled* • **Selling Skills and Sales Operations** *1 student enrolled* • **Small Engine Mechanics and Repair Technology/Technician** *4 students enrolled* • **Tool and Die Technology/Technician** *8 students enrolled* • **Truck and Bus Driver/Commercial Vehicle Operation** *35 students enrolled* • **Welding Technology/Welder** *4 students enrolled*

**STUDENT SERVICES** Academic or career counseling, employment services for current students, placement services for program completers, remedial services.

## Minnesota State Community and Technical College–Fergus Falls

1414 College Way, Fergus Falls, MN 56537-1009
http://www.minnesota.edu/

**CONTACT** Dr. Ann Valentine, President
**Telephone:** 218-736-1500

**GENERAL INFORMATION** Public Institution. Founded 1960. **Accreditation:** Regional (NCA); histologic technology (NAACLS); medical laboratory technology (NAACLS). **Total program enrollment:** 3241. **Application fee:** $20.

**PROGRAM(S) OFFERED**
• **Accounting Technology/Technician and Bookkeeping** *7 students enrolled* • **Accounting** *4 students enrolled* • **Administrative Assistant and Secretarial Science, General** *3 students enrolled* • **Autobody/Collision and Repair Technology/Technician** *7 students enrolled* • **Carpentry/Carpenter** *2 students enrolled* • **Child Care Provider/Assistant** *1 student enrolled* • **Communications Systems Installation and Repair Technology** *11 students enrolled* • **Computer Systems Networking and Telecommunications** *21 students enrolled* • **Cooking and Related Culinary Arts, General** *10 students enrolled* • **Corrections** *1 student enrolled* • **Cosmetology/Cosmetologist, General** *17 students enrolled* • **Dental Assisting/Assistant** *24 students enrolled* • **Electrical, Electronic and Communications Engineering Technology/Technician** *3 students enrolled* • **Entrepreneurship/Entrepreneurial Studies** *6 students enrolled* • **Fire Science/Firefighting** *15 students enrolled* • **Graphic Design** *12 students enrolled* • **Health Information/Medical Records Technology/Technician** *6 students enrolled* • **Heating, Air Conditioning, Ventilation and Refrigeration Maintenance Technology/Technician (HAC, HACR, HVAC, HVACR)** *9 students enrolled* • **Legal Administrative Assistant/Secretary** *1 student enrolled* • **Licensed Practical/Vocational Nurse Training (LPN, LVN, Cert, Dipl, AAS)** *32 students enrolled* • **Lineworker** *35 students enrolled* • **Manufacturing Technology/Technician** *1 student enrolled* • **Marine Maintenance/Fitter and Ship Repair Technology/Technician** *7 students enrolled* • **Massage Therapy/Therapeutic Massage** *18 students enrolled* • **Medical Administrative/Executive Assistant and Medical Secretary** *15 students enrolled* • **Medical Insurance Coding Specialist/Coder** *24 students enrolled* • **Medical Transcription/Transcriptionist** *21 students enrolled* • **Pharmacy Technician/Assistant** *2 students enrolled* • **Phlebotomy/Phlebotomist** *1 student enrolled* • **Plumbing Technology/Plumber** *29 students enrolled* • **Sales, Distribution and Marketing Operations, General** *1 student enrolled* • **Web Page, Digital/Multimedia and Information Resources Design** *6 students enrolled*

**STUDENT SERVICES** Academic or career counseling, daycare for children of students, employment services for current students, placement services for program completers, remedial services.

## Minnesota State University Mankato

228 Wiecking Center, Mankato, MN 56001
http://www.mnsu.edu/

**CONTACT** Richard Davenport, President
**Telephone:** 507-389-1866

**GENERAL INFORMATION** Public Institution. Founded 1868. **Accreditation:** Regional (NCA); art and design (NASAD); athletic training (JRCAT); counseling (ACA); dental hygiene (ADA); engineering technology (ABET/TAC); music (NASM); recreation and parks (NRPA); speech-language pathology (ASHA). **Total program enrollment:** 12071. **Application fee:** $20.

**PROGRAM(S) OFFERED**
• **Cartography** *2 students enrolled* • **Non-Profit/Public/Organizational Management** *9 students enrolled*

**STUDENT SERVICES** Academic or career counseling, daycare for children of students, employment services for current students, placement services for program completers, remedial services.

## Minnesota State University Moorhead

1104 7th Avenue South, Moorhead, MN 56563-0002
http://www.mnstate.edu/

**CONTACT** Edna Mora Szymanski, President
**Telephone:** 218-477-4000

**GENERAL INFORMATION** Public Institution. Founded 1885. **Accreditation:** Regional (NCA); art and design (NASAD); counseling (ACA); music (NASM); speech-language pathology (ASHA). **Total program enrollment:** 5968. **Application fee:** $20.

**PROGRAM(S) OFFERED**
• **Educational/Instructional Media Design** • **Publishing** *4 students enrolled*
• **Reading Teacher Education** *1 student enrolled* • **Special Education and Teaching, General** *6 students enrolled*

**STUDENT SERVICES** Academic or career counseling, daycare for children of students, employment services for current students, placement services for program completers, remedial services.

## Minnesota West Community and Technical College

1314 North Hiawatha Avenue, Pipestone, MN 56164
http://www.mnwest.edu/

**CONTACT** Dr. Richard Shrubb, President
**Telephone:** 320-564-4511

**GENERAL INFORMATION** Public Institution. Founded 1967. **Accreditation:** Regional (NCA); dental assisting (ADA); medical assisting (AAMAE);

medical laboratory technology (NAACLS). **Total program enrollment:** 1391. **Application fee:** $20.

**PROGRAM(S) OFFERED**

• **Accounting Technology/Technician and Bookkeeping** *3 students enrolled* • **Administrative Assistant and Secretarial Science, General** *3 students enrolled* • **Agricultural Production Operations, General** *4 students enrolled* • **Agricultural and Food Products Processing** *4 students enrolled* • **Autobody/Collision and Repair Technology/Technician** *17 students enrolled* • **Automobile/Automotive Mechanics Technology/Technician** *3 students enrolled* • **Business Administration, Management and Operations, Other** *1 student enrolled* • **Carpentry/Carpenter** *5 students enrolled* • **Child Care Provider/Assistant** *2 students enrolled* • **Child Care and Support Services Management** *6 students enrolled* • **Computer Installation and Repair Technology/Technician** *1 student enrolled* • **Computer and Information Systems Security** *3 students enrolled* • **Cosmetology/Cosmetologist, General** *18 students enrolled* • **Dental Assisting/Assistant** *7 students enrolled* • **Diesel Mechanics Technology/Technician** *6 students enrolled* • **Electrical and Power Transmission Installation/Installer, General** *3 students enrolled* • **Electrical and Power Transmission Installers, Other** *1 student enrolled* • **Farm/Farm and Ranch Management** *31 students enrolled* • **Heating, Air Conditioning, Ventilation and Refrigeration Maintenance Technology/Technician (HAC, HACR, HVAC, HVACR)** *8 students enrolled* • **Home Health Aide/Home Attendant** *356 students enrolled* • **Human Services, General** *1 student enrolled* • **Licensed Practical/Vocational Nurse Training (LPN, LVN, Cert, Dipl, AAS)** *68 students enrolled* • **Lineworker** *28 students enrolled* • **Machine Tool Technology/Machinist** *10 students enrolled* • **Massage Therapy/Therapeutic Massage** *15 students enrolled* • **Medical Administrative/Executive Assistant and Medical Secretary** *11 students enrolled* • **Medical Insurance Coding Specialist/Coder** *16 students enrolled* • **Medical Reception/Receptionist** *12 students enrolled* • **Medical/Clinical Assistant** *3 students enrolled* • **Nail Technician/Specialist and Manicurist** *4 students enrolled* • **Phlebotomy/Phlebotomist** *1 student enrolled* • **Plumbing Technology/Plumber** *7 students enrolled* • **Receptionist** *2 students enrolled* • **Small Engine Mechanics and Repair Technology/Technician** *17 students enrolled* • **Teacher Assistant/Aide** *2 students enrolled* • **Truck and Bus Driver/Commercial Vehicle Operation** *2 students enrolled*

**STUDENT SERVICES** Academic or career counseling, daycare for children of students, employment services for current students, placement services for program completers, remedial services.

## Model College of Hair Design

201 Eighth Avenue, S, St. Cloud, MN 56301
http://www.modelcollegeofhairdesign.com/

**CONTACT** Andy Smith, President
**Telephone:** 320-253-4222

**GENERAL INFORMATION** Private Institution. Founded 1952. **Total program enrollment:** 91. **Application fee:** $200.

**PROGRAM(S) OFFERED**

• **Aesthetician/Esthetician and Skin Care Specialist** *600 hrs./$5839* • **Cosmetology/Cosmetologist, General** *1500 hrs./$11,741* • **Nail Technician/Specialist and Manicurist** *350 hrs./$2339*

**STUDENT SERVICES** Academic or career counseling, placement services for program completers.

## National American University

112 West Market, Bloomington, MN 55425
http://www.national.edu/

**CONTACT** Jerry Gallentine, University President/CEO
**Telephone:** 952-356-3600

**GENERAL INFORMATION** Private Institution. **Total program enrollment:** 59. **Application fee:** $25.

**PROGRAM(S) OFFERED**

• **General Office Occupations and Clerical Services**

**STUDENT SERVICES** Academic or career counseling, employment services for current students, placement services for program completers, remedial services.

## National American University

6120 Earle Brown Drive, Suite 100, Brooklyn Center, MN 55430
http://www.national.edu/

**CONTACT** Dr. Jerry Gallentine, University President/CEO
**Telephone:** 763-852-7500

**GENERAL INFORMATION** Private Institution. **Total program enrollment:** 88. **Application fee:** $25.

**STUDENT SERVICES** Academic or career counseling, employment services for current students, placement services for program completers, remedial services.

## National American University

1500 West Highway 36, Roseville, MN 55113-4035
http://www.national.edu/

**CONTACT** Jerry Gallentine, University President/CEO
**Telephone:** 651-855-6300

**GENERAL INFORMATION** Private Institution. **Total program enrollment:** 87. **Application fee:** $25.

**PROGRAM(S) OFFERED**

• **Business Administration and Management, General** • **Massage Therapy/Therapeutic Massage** *4 students enrolled*

**STUDENT SERVICES** Academic or career counseling, employment services for current students, placement services for program completers, remedial services.

## Normandale Community College

9700 France Avenue South, Bloomington, MN 55431-4399
http://www.normandale.edu/

**CONTACT** Joe Opatz, President
**Telephone:** 952-487-8200

**GENERAL INFORMATION** Public Institution. Founded 1968. **Accreditation:** Regional (NCA); dental hygiene (ADA); music (NASM). **Total program enrollment:** 4525. **Application fee:** $20.

**PROGRAM(S) OFFERED**

• **Business Administration and Management, General** *2 students enrolled* • **Criminal Justice/Police Science** *2 students enrolled* • **Hotel/Motel Administration/Management** *3 students enrolled* • **Human Resources Management/Personnel Administration, General** *5 students enrolled* • **Manufacturing Technology/Technician** *1 student enrolled* • **Marketing/Marketing Management, General** *4 students enrolled* • **Nurse/Nursing Assistant/Aide and Patient Care Assistant** *201 students enrolled* • **Resort Management** *1 student enrolled* • **Restaurant/Food Services Management** *1 student enrolled* • **Small Business Administration/Management** *1 student enrolled*

**STUDENT SERVICES** Academic or career counseling, daycare for children of students, employment services for current students, placement services for program completers, remedial services.

## North Central University

910 Elliot Avenue, Minneapolis, MN 55404-1322
http://www.northcentral.edu/

**CONTACT** Gordon Anderson, President
**Telephone:** 612-343-4400

**GENERAL INFORMATION** Private Institution (Affiliated with Assemblies of God). Founded 1930. **Accreditation:** Regional (NCA). **Total program enrollment:** 986. **Application fee:** $25.

*North Central University (continued)*

**PROGRAM(S) OFFERED**

• **Bible/Biblical Studies** • **Pastoral Counseling and Specialized Ministries, Other** • **Religious/Sacred Music** • **Teaching English as a Second or Foreign Language/ESL Language Instructor** *9 students enrolled*

**STUDENT SERVICES** Academic or career counseling, employment services for current students, placement services for program completers, remedial services.

## North Hennepin Community College

7411 85th Avenue North, Brooklyn Park, MN 55445-2231
http://www.nhcc.edu/

**CONTACT** Ann Wynia, President
**Telephone:** 763-424-0702

**GENERAL INFORMATION** Public Institution. Founded 1966. **Accreditation:** Regional (NCA); medical laboratory technology (NAACLS). **Total program enrollment:** 2653. **Application fee:** $20.

**PROGRAM(S) OFFERED**

• **Accounting Technology/Technician and Bookkeeping** *10 students enrolled* • **Accounting** *26 students enrolled* • **Advertising** *1 student enrolled* • **Banking and Financial Support Services** *8 students enrolled* • **Building/Construction Site Management/Manager** *2 students enrolled* • **Building/Home/Construction Inspection/Inspector** *8 students enrolled* • **Business Administration and Management, General** *20 students enrolled* • **Business/Commerce, General** *136 students enrolled* • **Business/Corporate Communications** *21 students enrolled* • **Civil Engineering Technology/Technician** *5 students enrolled* • **Computer Programming, Specific Applications** *7 students enrolled* • **Data Entry/Microcomputer Applications, General** *3 students enrolled* • **E-Commerce/Electronic Commerce** *3 students enrolled* • **Legal Assistant/Paralegal** *19 students enrolled* • **Management Information Systems, General** *15 students enrolled* • **Selling Skills and Sales Operations** *7 students enrolled*

**STUDENT SERVICES** Academic or career counseling, employment services for current students, placement services for program completers, remedial services.

## Northland Community and Technical College–Thief River Falls

1101 Highway One East, Thief River Falls, MN 56701
http://www.northlandcollege.edu/

**CONTACT** Dr. Anne Temte, President
**Telephone:** 218-683-8800

**GENERAL INFORMATION** Public Institution. Founded 1965. **Accreditation:** Regional (NCA): **Total program enrollment:** 1879. **Application fee:** $20.

**PROGRAM(S) OFFERED**

• **Accounting Technology/Technician and Bookkeeping** *1 student enrolled* • **Administrative Assistant and Secretarial Science, General** *15 students enrolled* • **Agricultural Production Operations, General** *16 students enrolled* • **Animation, Interactive Technology, Video Graphics and Special Effects** *4 students enrolled* • **Architectural Drafting and Architectural CAD/CADD** *2 students enrolled* • **Automobile/Automotive Mechanics Technology/Technician** *6 students enrolled* • **Business Administration and Management, General** *1 student enrolled* • **Carpentry/Carpenter** *16 students enrolled* • **Cosmetology/Cosmetologist, General** *7 students enrolled* • **Electrical, Electronic and Communications Engineering Technology/Technician** *1 student enrolled* • **Farm/Farm and Ranch Management** *128 students enrolled* • **Fire Science/Firefighting** *6 students enrolled* • **Health and Physical Education, General** *1 student enrolled* • **Licensed Practical/Vocational Nurse Training (LPN, LVN, Cert, Dipl, AAS)** *50 students enrolled* • **Massage Therapy/Therapeutic Massage** *8 students enrolled* • **Medical Administrative/Executive Assistant and Medical Secretary** *11 students enrolled* • **Medical Insurance Coding Specialist/Coder** *26 students enrolled* • **Medical Transcription/Transcriptionist** *14 students enrolled* • **Medical/Clinical Assistant** *3 students enrolled* • **Operations Management and Supervision** *2 students enrolled* • **Pharmacy Technician/Assistant** *5 students enrolled* • **Phlebotomy/Phlebotomist** *6 students enrolled* • **Plumbing Technology/Plumber** *12 students enrolled* • **Special Products Marketing Operations** *25 students enrolled* • **Welding Technology/Welder** *4 students enrolled*

**STUDENT SERVICES** Academic or career counseling, daycare for children of students, employment services for current students, placement services for program completers, remedial services.

## Northwestern College

3003 Snelling Avenue North, St. Paul, MN 55113-1598
http://www.nwc.edu/

**CONTACT** Alan S. Cureton, President
**Telephone:** 651-631-5100

**GENERAL INFORMATION** Private Institution. Founded 1902. **Accreditation:** Regional (NCA); music (NASM). **Total program enrollment:** 2033. **Application fee:** $30.

**PROGRAM(S) OFFERED**

• **Bible/Biblical Studies** • **Pastoral Counseling and Specialized Ministries, Other** *2 students enrolled*

**STUDENT SERVICES** Academic or career counseling, employment services for current students, placement services for program completers, remedial services.

## Northwestern Health Sciences University

2501 West 84th Street, Bloomington, MN 55431-1599
http://www.nwhealth.edu/

**CONTACT** Dr. Mark Zeigler, President
**Telephone:** 952-888-4777

**GENERAL INFORMATION** Private Institution. Founded 1941. **Accreditation:** Regional (NCA); Acupuncture and Oriental Medicine (ACAOM). **Total program enrollment:** 777. **Application fee:** $50.

**PROGRAM(S) OFFERED**

• **Massage Therapy/Therapeutic Massage** *45 students enrolled*

**STUDENT SERVICES** Academic or career counseling, employment services for current students, placement services for program completers, remedial services.

## Northwest Technical College

905 Grant Avenue, SE, Bemidji, MN 56601-4907
http://bemidji.ntcmn.edu/

**CONTACT** Dr. Jon Quistgaard, President
**Telephone:** 218-333-6600

**GENERAL INFORMATION** Public Institution. Founded 1993. **Accreditation:** Regional (NCA); dental assisting (ADA); health information technology (AHIMA); medical assisting (AAMAE); medical laboratory technology (NAACLS); radiologic technology: radiography (JRCERT); surgical technology (ARCST). **Total program enrollment:** 501. **Application fee:** $20.

**PROGRAM(S) OFFERED**

• **Accounting Technology/Technician and Bookkeeping** *6 students enrolled* • **Administrative Assistant and Secretarial Science, General** *6 students enrolled* • **Business Administration and Management, General** *1 student enrolled* • **Business/Commerce, General** *13 students enrolled* • **Carpentry/Carpenter** *9 students enrolled* • **Construction Trades, General** *2 students enrolled* • **Dental Assisting/Assistant** *13 students enrolled* • **Engine Machinist** *8 students enrolled* • **Fire Services Administration** *2 students enrolled* • **Forestry Technology/Technician** *2 students enrolled* • **Health Information/Medical Records Technology/Technician** *1 student enrolled* • **Licensed Practical/Vocational Nurse Training (LPN, LVN, Cert, Dipl, AAS)** *40 students enrolled* • **Massage Therapy/Therapeutic Massage** *14 students enrolled* • **Medical Administrative/Executive Assistant and Medical Secretary** *5 students enrolled* • **Medical Insurance Coding Specialist/Coder** *7 students enrolled* • **Medical**

**Insurance Specialist/Medical Biller** *2 students enrolled* • **Medical Transcription/Transcriptionist** *5 students enrolled* • **Nurse/Nursing Assistant/Aide and Patient Care Assistant** *97 students enrolled* • **Sales, Distribution and Marketing Operations, General** *4 students enrolled*

**STUDENT SERVICES** Academic or career counseling, daycare for children of students, employment services for current students, placement services for program completers, remedial services.

## Oak Hills Christian College

1600 Oak Hills Road, SW, Bemidji, MN 56601-8832
http://www.oakhills.edu/

**CONTACT** Dr. Steven Hostetter, President
**Telephone:** 218-751-8670 Ext. 1295

**GENERAL INFORMATION** Private Institution. Founded 1946. **Accreditation:** State accredited or approved. **Total program enrollment:** 120. **Application fee:** $25.

**PROGRAM(S) OFFERED**
• **Bible/Biblical Studies** *4 students enrolled*

**STUDENT SERVICES** Academic or career counseling, employment services for current students, remedial services.

## Pine Technical College

900 4th Street SE, Pine City, MN 55063
http://www.pinetech.edu/

**CONTACT** Robert Musgrove, President
**Telephone:** 320-629-5100

**GENERAL INFORMATION** Public Institution. Founded 1965. **Accreditation:** Regional (NCA). **Total program enrollment:** 296. **Application fee:** $20.

**PROGRAM(S) OFFERED**
• **Accounting Technology/Technician and Bookkeeping** *2 students enrolled* • **Administrative Assistant and Secretarial Science, General** *2 students enrolled* • **American Sign Language (ASL)** *5 students enrolled* • **Automobile/Automotive Mechanics Technology/Technician** *1 student enrolled* • **Child Care Provider/Assistant** *1 student enrolled* • **Data Entry/Microcomputer Applications, General** *2 students enrolled* • **Gunsmithing/Gunsmith** *11 students enrolled* • **Home Health Aide/Home Attendant** *67 students enrolled* • **Human Services, General** *8 students enrolled* • **Licensed Practical/Vocational Nurse Training (LPN, LVN, Cert, Dipl, AAS)** *61 students enrolled* • **Machine Shop Technology/Assistant** *3 students enrolled* • **Machine Tool Technology/Machinist** *2 students enrolled* • **Medical Insurance Coding Specialist/Coder** *1 student enrolled*

**STUDENT SERVICES** Academic or career counseling, daycare for children of students, employment services for current students, remedial services.

## Rainy River Community College

1501 Highway 71, International Falls, MN 56649
http://www.rrcc.mnscu.edu/

**CONTACT** Wayne Merrell, Provost
**Telephone:** 218-285-7722

**GENERAL INFORMATION** Public Institution. Founded 1967. **Accreditation:** Regional (NCA). **Total program enrollment:** 234. **Application fee:** $20.

**PROGRAM(S) OFFERED**
• **Accounting Technology/Technician and Bookkeeping** *9 students enrolled* • **Administrative Assistant and Secretarial Science, General** *7 students enrolled* • **Health and Physical Education, General** *1 student enrolled* • **Licensed Practical/Vocational Nurse Training (LPN, LVN, Cert, Dipl, AAS)** *17 students enrolled* • **Nurse/Nursing Assistant/Aide and Patient Care Assistant** *17 students enrolled*

**STUDENT SERVICES** Academic or career counseling, employment services for current students, placement services for program completers, remedial services.

## Rasmussen College Brooklyn Park

8301 93rd Avenue North, Brooklyn Park, MN 55445-1512
http://www.rasmussen.edu/

**CONTACT** Cathy Plunkett, Campus Director
**Telephone:** 763-493-4500

**GENERAL INFORMATION** Private Institution. **Total program enrollment:** 642. **Application fee:** $60.

**PROGRAM(S) OFFERED**
• **Child Care and Support Services Management** *32 students enrolled* • **Computer Systems Networking and Telecommunications** *1 student enrolled* • **Massage Therapy/Therapeutic Massage** *3 students enrolled* • **Medical Insurance Coding Specialist/Coder** *19 students enrolled* • **Medical Transcription/Transcriptionist** *1 student enrolled*

**STUDENT SERVICES** Academic or career counseling, employment services for current students, placement services for program completers, remedial services.

## Rasmussen College Eagan

3500 Federal Drive, Eagan, MN 55122-1346
http://www.rasmussen.edu/

**CONTACT** RoxAnne Best, Campus Director
**Telephone:** 651-687-9000

**GENERAL INFORMATION** Private Institution. Founded 1904. **Accreditation:** Health information technology (AHIMA); state accredited or approved. **Total program enrollment:** 274. **Application fee:** $60.

**PROGRAM(S) OFFERED**
• **Child Care and Support Services Management** *15 students enrolled* • **Legal Administrative Assistant/Secretary** • **Medical Insurance Coding Specialist/Coder** *7 students enrolled* • **Medical Transcription/Transcriptionist** *1 student enrolled*

**STUDENT SERVICES** Academic or career counseling, employment services for current students, placement services for program completers, remedial services.

## Rasmussen College Eden Prairie

7905 Golden Triangle Drive, Suite 100, Eden Prairie, MN 55344
http://www.rasmussen.edu/

**CONTACT** Patty Sagert, Campus Director
**Telephone:** 952-545-2000

**GENERAL INFORMATION** Private Institution. Founded 1904. **Accreditation:** Regional (NCA); health information technology (AHIMA); state accredited or approved. **Total program enrollment:** 337. **Application fee:** $60.

**PROGRAM(S) OFFERED**
• **Child Care and Support Services Management** *14 students enrolled* • **Information Science/Studies** *1 student enrolled* • **Legal Administrative Assistant/Secretary** • **Massage Therapy/Therapeutic Massage** *2 students enrolled* • **Medical Administrative/Executive Assistant and Medical Secretary** *1 student enrolled* • **Medical Insurance Coding Specialist/Coder** *4 students enrolled*

**STUDENT SERVICES** Academic or career counseling, employment services for current students, placement services for program completers, remedial services.

## Rasmussen College Lake Elmo/Woodbury

8565 Eagle Point Circle, Lake Elmo, MN 55042
http://www.rasmussen.edu/

**CONTACT** Dwayne Bertotto, Campus Director
**Telephone:** 651-259-6600

**GENERAL INFORMATION** Private Institution. **Total program enrollment:** 212. **Application fee:** $60.

**PROGRAM(S) OFFERED**
• **Child Care and Support Services Management** *4 students enrolled* • **Massage Therapy/Therapeutic Massage** • **Medical Insurance Coding Specialist/Coder** • **Medical Transcription/Transcriptionist**

**STUDENT SERVICES** Academic or career counseling, employment services for current students, placement services for program completers, remedial services.

## Rasmussen College Mankato

501 Holly Lane, Mankato, MN 56001-6803
http://www.rasmussen.edu/

**CONTACT** Doug Gardner, Campus Director
**Telephone:** 507-625-6556

**GENERAL INFORMATION** Private Institution. Founded 1904. **Accreditation:** Health information technology (AHIMA); state accredited or approved. **Total program enrollment:** 307. **Application fee:** $60.

**PROGRAM(S) OFFERED**
• **Accounting** *2 students enrolled* • **Business/Commerce, General** • **Child Care and Support Services Management** • **Information Science/Studies** *1 student enrolled* • **Legal Administrative Assistant/Secretary** • **Licensed Practical/Vocational Nurse Training (LPN, LVN, Cert, Dipl, AAS)** *5 students enrolled* • **Massage Therapy/Therapeutic Massage** *7 students enrolled* • **Medical Administrative/Executive Assistant and Medical Secretary** • **Medical Insurance Coding Specialist/Coder** *3 students enrolled* • **Medical Transcription/Transcriptionist**

**STUDENT SERVICES** Academic or career counseling, employment services for current students, placement services for program completers, remedial services.

## Rasmussen College St. Cloud

226 Park Avenue South, St. Cloud, MN 56301-3713
http://www.rasmussen.edu/

**CONTACT** Liz Rian, Campus Director
**Telephone:** 320-251-5600

**GENERAL INFORMATION** Private Institution. Founded 1904. **Accreditation:** Regional (NCA); health information technology (AHIMA); state accredited or approved. **Total program enrollment:** 339. **Application fee:** $60.

**PROGRAM(S) OFFERED**
• **Accounting** • **Business Administration and Management, General** • **Child Care and Support Services Management** • **Information Science/Studies** *1 student enrolled* • **Massage Therapy/Therapeutic Massage** *5 students enrolled* • **Medical Administrative/Executive Assistant and Medical Secretary** *1 student enrolled* • **Medical Insurance Coding Specialist/Coder** • **Medical Transcription/Transcriptionist** *1 student enrolled*

**STUDENT SERVICES** Academic or career counseling, employment services for current students, placement services for program completers, remedial services.

## Regency Beauty Academy

40 Highway 10, Blaine, MN 55434
http://www.regencybeauty.com/

**CONTACT** J. Hayes Batson, President
**Telephone:** 763-533-3179

**GENERAL INFORMATION** Private Institution. Founded 1941. **Total program enrollment:** 125. **Application fee:** $100.

**PROGRAM(S) OFFERED**
• **Cosmetology/Cosmetologist, General** *1550 hrs./$16,011*

**STUDENT SERVICES** Academic or career counseling, placement services for program completers.

## Regency Beauty Institute

150 Cobblestone Lane, Burnsville, MN 55337
http://www.regencybeauty.com/

**CONTACT** J. Hayes Batson, Owner President
**Telephone:** 952-435-3882

**GENERAL INFORMATION** Private Institution. Founded 1986. **Total program enrollment:** 100. **Application fee:** $100.

**PROGRAM(S) OFFERED**
• **Cosmetology/Cosmetologist, General** *1550 hrs./$16,011*

**STUDENT SERVICES** Academic or career counseling, placement services for program completers.

## Regency Beauty Institute

5115 Burning Tree Road, Duluth, MN 55811
http://www.regencybeauty.com/

**CONTACT** J. Hayes Batson, President CEO
**Telephone:** 800-787-6456

**GENERAL INFORMATION** Private Institution. **Total program enrollment:** 57. **Application fee:** $100.

**PROGRAM(S) OFFERED**
• **Cosmetology/Cosmetologist, General** *1550 hrs./$16,011*

**STUDENT SERVICES** Academic or career counseling, placement services for program completers.

## Regency Beauty Institute

3000 White Bear Avenue, Suite 27, Maplewood, MN 55109
http://www.regencybeauty.com/

**CONTACT** J. Hayes Batson, President
**Telephone:** 651-773-3951

**GENERAL INFORMATION** Private Institution. **Total program enrollment:** 79. **Application fee:** $100.

**PROGRAM(S) OFFERED**
• **Cosmetology/Cosmetologist, General** *1550 hrs./$16,011*

**STUDENT SERVICES** Academic or career counseling, placement services for program completers.

## Regency Beauty Institute

12993 Ridgedale Drive, Suite 103, Minnetonka, MN 55305
http://www.regencybeauty.com/

**CONTACT** J. Hayes Batson, President
**Telephone:** 952-697-3000

**GENERAL INFORMATION** Private Institution. **Total program enrollment:** 51. **Application fee:** $100.

**PROGRAM(S) OFFERED**
• **Cosmetology/Cosmetologist, General** *1550 hrs./$16,011*

**STUDENT SERVICES** Academic or career counseling, placement services for program completers.

## Regency Beauty Institute

912 West Saint Germain Street, St. Cloud, MN 56301
http://www.regencybeauty.com/

**CONTACT** J. Hayes Batson, President
**Telephone:** 320-251-0500

**GENERAL INFORMATION** Private Institution. Founded 1991. **Total program enrollment:** 92. **Application fee:** $100.

**PROGRAM(S) OFFERED**
• **Cosmetology/Cosmetologist, General** *1550 hrs./$16,011*

**STUDENT SERVICES** Academic or career counseling, placement services for program completers.

## Ridgewater College

PO Box 1097, Willmar, MN 56201-1097
http://www.ridgewater.edu/

**CONTACT** Douglas Allen, President
**Telephone:** 800-722-1151

**GENERAL INFORMATION** Public Institution. Founded 1961. **Accreditation:** Regional (NCA); health information technology (AHIMA); practical nursing (NLN). **Total program enrollment:** 2527. **Application fee:** $20.

**PROGRAM(S) OFFERED**
• **Administrative Assistant and Secretarial Science, General** *9 students enrolled* • **Aesthetician/Esthetician and Skin Care Specialist** *3 students enrolled* • **Autobody/Collision and Repair Technology/Technician** *8 students enrolled* • **Commercial Photography** *13 students enrolled* • **Computer Systems Networking and Telecommunications** *1 student enrolled* • **Computer Technology/Computer Systems Technology** *1 student enrolled* • **Cosmetology/Cosmetologist, General** *30 students enrolled* • **Data Entry/Microcomputer Applications, General** *12 students enrolled* • **Digital Communication and Media/Multimedia** *1 student enrolled* • **Electromechanical Technology/Electromechanical Engineering Technology** *1 student enrolled* • **Emergency Medical Technology/Technician (EMT Paramedic)** *12 students enrolled* • **Farm/Farm and Ranch Management** *22 students enrolled* • **General Office Occupations and Clerical Services** *4 students enrolled* • **Health Aide** *5 students enrolled* • **Instrumentation Technology/Technician** *1 student enrolled* • **Insurance** *11 students enrolled* • **Licensed Practical/Vocational Nurse Training (LPN, LVN, Cert, Dipl, AAS)** *81 students enrolled* • **Machine Shop Technology/Assistant** *1 student enrolled* • **Machine Tool Technology/Machinist** *3 students enrolled* • **Massage Therapy/Therapeutic Massage** *28 students enrolled* • **Medical Administrative/Executive Assistant and Medical Secretary** *6 students enrolled* • **Medical Insurance Coding Specialist/Coder** *8 students enrolled* • **Medical Transcription/Transcriptionist** *3 students enrolled* • **Medical/Clinical Assistant** *26 students enrolled* • **Metallurgical Technology/Technician** *1 student enrolled* • **Nail Technician/Specialist and Manicurist** *1 student enrolled* • **Nurse/Nursing Assistant/Aide and Patient Care Assistant** *72 students enrolled* • **Prepress/Desktop Publishing and Digital Imaging Design** *5 students enrolled* • **Recording Arts Technology/Technician** *5 students enrolled* • **Selling Skills and Sales Operations** *3 students enrolled* • **Small Business Administration/Management** *6 students enrolled* • **Teacher Assistant/Aide** *1 student enrolled* • **Therapeutic Recreation/Recreational Therapy** *3 students enrolled* • **Tool and Die Technology/Technician** *1 student enrolled* • **Welding Technology/Welder** *28 students enrolled*

**STUDENT SERVICES** Academic or career counseling, employment services for current students, placement services for program completers, remedial services.

## Riverland Community College

1900 8th Avenue, NW, Austin, MN 55912
http://www.riverland.edu/

**CONTACT** Terry Leas, President
**Telephone:** 507-433-0600

**GENERAL INFORMATION** Public Institution. Founded 1940. **Accreditation:** Regional (NCA); radiologic technology: radiography (JRCERT). **Total program enrollment:** 1355. **Application fee:** $20.

**PROGRAM(S) OFFERED**
• **Animation, Interactive Technology, Video Graphics and Special Effects** *1 student enrolled* • **Business Administration and Management, General** *11 students enrolled* • **Carpentry/Carpenter** *17 students enrolled* • **Computer Systems Networking and Telecommunications** *3 students enrolled* • **Cosmetology/Cosmetologist, General** *30 students enrolled* • **Health Unit Coordinator/Ward Clerk** *2 students enrolled* • **Human Resources Development** *26 students enrolled* • **Legal Administrative Assistant/Secretary** *3 students enrolled* • **Licensed Practical/Vocational Nurse Training (LPN, LVN, Cert, Dipl, AAS)** *95 students enrolled* • **Machine Tool Technology/Machinist** *2 students enrolled* • **Massage Therapy/Therapeutic Massage** *10 students enrolled* • **Medical Administrative/Executive Assistant and Medical Secretary** *5 students enrolled* • **Medical Reception/Receptionist** *1 student enrolled* • **Pharmacy Technician/Assistant** *3 students enrolled* • **Prepress/Desktop Publishing and Digital Imaging Design** *1 student enrolled* • **Truck and Bus Driver/Commercial Vehicle Operation** *35 students enrolled* • **Web Page, Digital/Multimedia and Information Resources Design** *9 students enrolled* • **Web/Multimedia Management and Webmaster** *2 students enrolled* • **Welding Technology/Welder** *13 students enrolled*

**STUDENT SERVICES** Academic or career counseling, daycare for children of students, employment services for current students, placement services for program completers, remedial services.

## Rochester Community and Technical College

851 30th Avenue, SE, Rochester, MN 55904-4999
http://www.rctc.edu/

**CONTACT** Donald Supalla, President
**Telephone:** 507-285-7210

**GENERAL INFORMATION** Public Institution. Founded 1915. **Accreditation:** Regional (NCA); dental assisting (ADA); dental hygiene (ADA); health information technology (AHIMA); medical assisting (AAMAE); surgical technology (ARCST). **Total program enrollment:** 3257. **Application fee:** $20.

**PROGRAM(S) OFFERED**
• **Accounting Technology/Technician and Bookkeeping** *2 students enrolled* • **Administrative Assistant and Secretarial Science, General** *3 students enrolled* • **Architectural Drafting and Architectural CAD/CADD** *2 students enrolled* • **Business Administration and Management, General** *3 students enrolled* • **CAD/CADD Drafting and/or Design Technology/Technician** *28 students enrolled* • **Carpentry/Carpenter** *18 students enrolled* • **Child Care and Support Services Management** *3 students enrolled* • **Computer Graphics** *1 student enrolled* • **Computer Systems Networking and Telecommunications** *4 students enrolled* • **Criminal Justice/Police Science** *2 students enrolled* • **Customer Service Management** *1 student enrolled* • **Dental Assisting/Assistant** *11 students enrolled* • **Electrical, Electronic and Communications Engineering Technology/Technician** *2 students enrolled* • **Emergency Medical Technology/Technician (EMT Paramedic)** *1 student enrolled* • **General Office Occupations and Clerical Services** *1 student enrolled* • **Graphic Design** *2 students enrolled* • **Greenhouse Operations and Management** *3 students enrolled* • **Health Services/Allied Health/Health Sciences, General** *5 students enrolled* • **Health Unit Coordinator/Ward Clerk** *36 students enrolled* • **Heating, Air Conditioning, Ventilation and Refrigeration Maintenance Technology/Technician (HAC, HACR, HVAC, HVACR)** *10 students enrolled* • **Horse Husbandry/Equine Science and Management** *3 students enrolled* • **Human Resources Development** *1 student enrolled* • **Licensed Practical/Vocational Nurse Training (LPN, LVN, Cert, Dipl, AAS)** *27 students enrolled* • **Medical Informatics** *2 students enrolled* • **Medical Insurance Coding Specialist/Coder** *1 student enrolled* • **Medical Transcription/Transcriptionist** *12 students enrolled* • **Nurse/Nursing Assistant/Aide and Patient Care Assistant** *10 students enrolled* • **Photography** *1 student enrolled* • **Psychiatric/Mental Health Services Technician** *1 student enrolled* • **Retailing and Retail Operations** *7 students enrolled*

*Rochester Community and Technical College (continued)*

• **Teacher Assistant/Aide** *1 student enrolled* • **Turf and Turfgrass Management** *2 students enrolled* • **Veterinary/Animal Health Technology/Technician and Veterinary Assistant** *1 student enrolled*

**STUDENT SERVICES** Academic or career counseling, daycare for children of students, employment services for current students, placement services for program completers, remedial services.

## St. Catherine University

2004 Randolph Avenue, St. Paul, MN 55105-1789
http://www.stkate.edu/

**CONTACT** Andrea J. Lee, IHM, President
**Telephone:** 651-690-6000

**GENERAL INFORMATION** Private Institution. Founded 1905. **Accreditation:** Regional (NCA); diagnostic medical sonography (JRCEDMS); music (NASM). **Total program enrollment:** 3184.

**PROGRAM(S) OFFERED**

• **Hematology Technology/Technician** *16 students enrolled* • **Library Assistant/Technician** *7 students enrolled* • **Medical Insurance Coding Specialist/Coder** *1 student enrolled* • **Medical Insurance Specialist/Medical Biller** *5 students enrolled* • **Montessori Teacher Education** *11 students enrolled* • **Pastoral Studies/Counseling** *8 students enrolled*

**STUDENT SERVICES** Academic or career counseling, daycare for children of students, employment services for current students, remedial services.

## St. Cloud State University

720 4th Avenue South, St. Cloud, MN 56301-4498
http://www.stcloudstate.edu/

**CONTACT** Earl H. Potter, President
**Telephone:** 320-308-0121

**GENERAL INFORMATION** Public Institution. Founded 1869. **Accreditation:** Regional (NCA); art and design (NASAD); computer science (ABET/CSAC); counseling (ACA); journalism and mass communications (ACEJMC); music (NASM); speech-language pathology (ASHA); theater (NAST). **Total program enrollment:** 12702. **Application fee:** $20.

**PROGRAM(S) OFFERED**

• **School Librarian/School Library Media Specialist** *1 student enrolled* • **Survey Technology/Surveying** *3 students enrolled*

**STUDENT SERVICES** Academic or career counseling, daycare for children of students, employment services for current students, placement services for program completers, remedial services.

## St. Cloud Technical College

1540 Northway Drive, St. Cloud, MN 56303-1240
http://www.sctc.edu/

**CONTACT** Joyce M. Helens, President
**Telephone:** 320-308-5000

**GENERAL INFORMATION** Public Institution. Founded 1948. **Accreditation:** Regional (NCA); dental assisting (ADA); dental hygiene (ADA); surgical technology (ARCST). **Total program enrollment:** 2484. **Application fee:** $20.

**PROGRAM(S) OFFERED**

• **Accounting Technology/Technician and Bookkeeping** *5 students enrolled* • **Accounting** *5 students enrolled* • **Advertising** *1 student enrolled* • **Architectural Drafting and Architectural CAD/CADD** *12 students enrolled* • **Business Administration and Management, General** *3 students enrolled* • **Carpentry/Carpenter** *15 students enrolled* • **Child Care and Support Services Management** *1 student enrolled* • **Computer Programming, Specific Applications** *1 student enrolled* • **Computer Programming/Programmer, General** *1 student enrolled* • **Computer Systems Networking and Telecommunications** *3 students enrolled* • **Culinary Arts/Chef Training** *20 students enrolled* • **Dental Assisting/Assistant** *9 students enrolled* • **Electrical, Electronic and Communications Engineering Technology/Technician** *1 student enrolled* • **Farm/Farm and Ranch Management** *1 student enrolled* • **General Office Occupations and Clerical Services** *4 students enrolled* • **Graphic Communications, General** *7 students enrolled* • **Health Aide** *2 students enrolled* • **Heating, Air Conditioning, Ventilation and Refrigeration Maintenance Technology/Technician (HAC, HACR, HVAC, HVACR)** *15 students enrolled* • **Human Resources Development** *1 student enrolled* • **Legal Administrative Assistant/Secretary** *3 students enrolled* • **Licensed Practical/Vocational Nurse Training (LPN, LVN, Cert, Dipl, AAS)** *54 students enrolled* • **Mechanical Drafting and Mechanical Drafting CAD/CADD** *2 students enrolled* • **Medical Office Assistant/Specialist** *4 students enrolled* • **Plumbing Technology/Plumber** *20 students enrolled* • **Receptionist** *4 students enrolled* • **Sales, Distribution and Marketing Operations, General** *14 students enrolled* • **Surgical Technology/Technologist** *16 students enrolled* • **Water Quality and Wastewater Treatment Management and Recycling Technology/Technician** *17 students enrolled* • **Welding Technology/Welder** *18 students enrolled*

**STUDENT SERVICES** Academic or career counseling, daycare for children of students, employment services for current students, placement services for program completers, remedial services.

## Saint Mary's University of Minnesota

700 Terrace Heights, Winona, MN 55987-1399
http://www.smumn.edu/

**CONTACT** William Mann, Brother President
**Telephone:** 507-457-1600

**GENERAL INFORMATION** Private Institution. Founded 1912. **Accreditation:** Regional (NCA); nuclear medicine technology (JRCNMT). **Total program enrollment:** 2044. **Application fee:** $25.

**PROGRAM(S) OFFERED**

• **Accounting** • **Surgical Technology/Technologist** *20 students enrolled*

**STUDENT SERVICES** Academic or career counseling, employment services for current students, remedial services.

## Saint Paul College–A Community & Technical College

235 Marshall Avenue, St. Paul, MN 55102-1800
http://www.saintpaul.edu/

**CONTACT** Donovan Schwichtenberg, President
**Telephone:** 651-846-1600

**GENERAL INFORMATION** Public Institution. Founded 1919. **Accreditation:** Regional (NCA); medical laboratory technology (NAACLS); practical nursing (NLN). **Total program enrollment:** 2043. **Application fee:** $20.

**PROGRAM(S) OFFERED**

• **Administrative Assistant and Secretarial Science, General** *5 students enrolled* • **Aesthetician/Esthetician and Skin Care Specialist** *21 students enrolled* • **American Sign Language (ASL)** *28 students enrolled* • **Autobody/Collision and Repair Technology/Technician** *10 students enrolled* • **Automobile/Automotive Mechanics Technology/Technician** *8 students enrolled* • **Baking and Pastry Arts/Baker/Pastry Chef** *13 students enrolled* • **Cabinetmaking and Millwork/Millwright** *10 students enrolled* • **Carpentry/Carpenter** *16 students enrolled* • **Child Care Provider/Assistant** *9 students enrolled* • **Child Care and Support Services Management** *4 students enrolled* • **Computer Programming, Vendor/Product Certification** *1 student enrolled* • **Computer Systems Networking and Telecommunications** *2 students enrolled* • **Computer Technology/Computer Systems Technology** *1 student enrolled* • **Cosmetology/Cosmetologist, General** *18 students enrolled* • **Culinary Arts/Chef Training** *20 students enrolled* • **Electrical/Electronics Equipment Installation and Repair, General** *9 students enrolled* • **Food Preparation/Professional Cooking/Kitchen Assistant** *2 students enrolled* • **Health Unit Coordinator/Ward Clerk** *28 students enrolled* • **Human Resources Management/Personnel Administration, General** *2 students enrolled* • **International Marketing** *4 students enrolled* • **Ironworking/Ironworker** *20 students enrolled* • **Licensed Practical/Vocational Nurse Training (LPN, LVN, Cert, Dipl, AAS)** *42 students enrolled* • **Machine Shop Technology/Assistant** *2 students enrolled* • **Management Information Systems, General** *1 student enrolled* • **Massage Therapy/Therapeutic Massage** *19 students enrolled* • **Medical Insurance Coding Specialist/Coder** *17 students enrolled* • **Medical**

Reception/Receptionist *6 students enrolled* • **Medical Transcription/Transcriptionist** *3 students enrolled* • **Nurse/Nursing Assistant/Aide and Patient Care Assistant** *96 students enrolled* • **Painting/Painter and Wall Coverer** *11 students enrolled* • **Pipefitting/Pipefitter and Sprinkler Fitter** *58 students enrolled* • **Plumbing Technology/Plumber** *31 students enrolled* • **Sheet Metal Technology/Sheetworking** *35 students enrolled* • **Tool and Die Technology/Technician** *38 students enrolled* • **Watchmaking and Jewelrymaking** *15 students enrolled* • **Web Page, Digital/Multimedia and Information Resources Design** *4 students enrolled* • **Welding Technology/Welder** *19 students enrolled*

**STUDENT SERVICES** Academic or career counseling, daycare for children of students, employment services for current students, placement services for program completers, remedial services.

## Scot-Lewis School of Cosmetology

9801 James Circle, Bloomington, MN 55431
http://www.scotlewis.com/

**CONTACT** Michael Bouman, President/COO
**Telephone:** 952-881-9327

**GENERAL INFORMATION** Private Institution. Founded 1960. **Total program enrollment:** 96. **Application fee:** $100.

**PROGRAM(S) OFFERED**
• **Aesthetician/Esthetician and Skin Care Specialist** *600 hrs./$7900* • **Cosmetology/Cosmetologist, General** *1550 hrs./$15,928* • **Nail Technician/Specialist and Manicurist** *8 students enrolled*

**STUDENT SERVICES** Placement services for program completers.

## Scot Lewis School–St. Paul

1905 Suburban Avenue, Saint Paul, MN 55119-7003
http://www.scotlewis.com/

**CONTACT** Michael Bouman, President/COO
**Telephone:** 651-209-6930

**GENERAL INFORMATION** Private Institution. **Total program enrollment:** 70. **Application fee:** $100.

**PROGRAM(S) OFFERED**
• **Cosmetology/Cosmetologist, General** *1550 hrs./$15,928*

**STUDENT SERVICES** Placement services for program completers.

## South Central College

1920 Lee Boulevard, North Mankato, MN 56003
http://southcentral.edu/

**CONTACT** Keith Stover, President
**Telephone:** 507-389-7200

**GENERAL INFORMATION** Public Institution. Founded 1946. **Accreditation:** Regional (NCA); dental assisting (ADA); medical laboratory technology (NAACLS). **Total program enrollment:** 1858. **Application fee:** $20.

**PROGRAM(S) OFFERED**
• **Accounting Technology/Technician and Bookkeeping** *2 students enrolled* • **Administrative Assistant and Secretarial Science, General** *3 students enrolled* • **Autobody/Collision and Repair Technology/Technician** *8 students enrolled* • **Automobile/Automotive Mechanics Technology/Technician** *5 students enrolled* • **Child Care Provider/Assistant** *2 students enrolled* • **Child Care and Support Services Management** *1 student enrolled* • **Commercial and Advertising Art** *4 students enrolled* • **Computer Systems Networking and Telecommunications** *2 students enrolled* • **Computer Technology/Computer Systems Technology** *1 student enrolled* • **Cooking and Related Culinary Arts, General** *2 students enrolled* • **Dental Assisting/Assistant** *8 students enrolled* • **Emergency Medical Technology/Technician (EMT Paramedic)** *7 students enrolled* • **Farm/Farm and Ranch Management** *13 students enrolled* • **Graphic and Printing Equipment Operator, General Production** *2 students enrolled* • **Heating, Air Conditioning, Ventilation and Refrigeration Maintenance Technology/Technician (HAC, HACR, HVAC, HVACR)** *9 students enrolled* • **Industrial Safety Technology/Technician** *5 students enrolled* • **Licensed Practical/Vocational Nurse Training (LPN, LVN, Cert, Dipl, AAS)** *77 students enrolled* • **Machine Tool Technology/Machinist** *1 student enrolled* • **Marketing/Marketing Management, General** *2 students enrolled* • **Medical Insurance Coding Specialist/Coder** *18 students enrolled* • **Phlebotomy/Phlebotomist** *18 students enrolled* • **Receptionist** *4 students enrolled* • **Web Page, Digital/Multimedia and Information Resources Design** *3 students enrolled*

**STUDENT SERVICES** Academic or career counseling, daycare for children of students, employment services for current students, placement services for program completers, remedial services.

## Southwest Minnesota State University

1501 State Street, Marshall, MN 56258
http://www.smsu.edu/

**CONTACT** David C. Danahar, President
**Telephone:** 507-537-7021

**GENERAL INFORMATION** Public Institution. Founded 1963. **Accreditation:** Regional (NCA); music (NASM). **Total program enrollment:** 2530. **Application fee:** $20.

**STUDENT SERVICES** Academic or career counseling, daycare for children of students, employment services for current students, placement services for program completers, remedial services.

## Spa-A School

4411 Winnetka Avenue N, New Hope, MN 55428

**CONTACT** Angela Torgeson, President
**Telephone:** 763-536-0772

**GENERAL INFORMATION** Private Institution. **Total program enrollment:** 109.

**PROGRAM(S) OFFERED**
• **Aesthetician/Esthetician and Skin Care Specialist** *600 hrs./$7549* • **Cosmetology/Cosmetologist, General** *1550 hrs./$14,990* • **Nail Technician/Specialist and Manicurist** *350 hrs./$3229*

**STUDENT SERVICES** Academic or career counseling, placement services for program completers.

## Summit Academy Opportunities Industrialization Center

935 Olson Memorial Highway, Minneapolis, MN 55405
http://www.saoic.org/

**CONTACT** Louis King, President
**Telephone:** 612-377-0150

**GENERAL INFORMATION** Private Institution. **Total program enrollment:** 138.

**PROGRAM(S) OFFERED**
• **Administrative Assistant and Secretarial Science, General** *20 hrs./$4500* • **Carpentry/Carpenter** *20 hrs./$4500* • **Community Health Services/Liaison/Counseling** *20 hrs./$4500* • **Electrician** *20 hrs./$4500* • **Home Health Aide/Home Attendant** *33 students enrolled* • **Plumbing and Related Water Supply Services, Other** *20 hrs./$4500* • **Sheet Metal Technology/Sheetworking** *20 hrs./$4500*

**STUDENT SERVICES** Academic or career counseling, employment services for current students, placement services for program completers.

## University of Minnesota, Crookston

2900 University Avenue, Crookston, MN 56716-5001
http://www.umcrookston.edu/

**CONTACT** Charles Casey, Chancellor
**Telephone:** 800-862-6466

**GENERAL INFORMATION** Public Institution. Founded 1966. **Accreditation:** Regional (NCA). **Total program enrollment:** 1140. **Application fee:** $30.

**PROGRAM(S) OFFERED**
• **Industrial Technology/Technician** *1 student enrolled*

**STUDENT SERVICES** Academic or career counseling, daycare for children of students, employment services for current students, placement services for program completers, remedial services.

## University of Minnesota, Duluth

10 University Drive, Duluth, MN 55812-2496
http://www.d.umn.edu/

**CONTACT** Kathryn Martin, Chancellor
**Telephone:** 218-726-8000

**GENERAL INFORMATION** Public Institution. Founded 1947. **Accreditation:** Regional (NCA); computer science (ABET/CSAC); counseling (ACA); music (NASM); speech-language pathology (ASHA). **Total program enrollment:** 9655. **Application fee:** $35.

**PROGRAM(S) OFFERED**
• **Business Administration and Management, General** *1 student enrolled* • **Education/Teaching of Individuals with Autism** *1 student enrolled* • **Educational/Instructional Media Design** *17 students enrolled* • **Human Resources Management and Services, Other** *1 student enrolled*

**STUDENT SERVICES** Academic or career counseling, daycare for children of students, employment services for current students, placement services for program completers, remedial services.

## University of Minnesota, Twin Cities Campus

100 Church Street, SE, Minneapolis, MN 55455-0213
http://www.umn.edu/tc/

**CONTACT** Robert H. Bruininks, President
**Telephone:** 612-625-5000

**GENERAL INFORMATION** Public Institution. Founded 1851. **Accreditation:** Regional (NCA); audiology (ASHA); dance (NASD); dental hygiene (ADA); dietetics: undergraduate, postbaccalaureate internship (ADtA/CAADE); engineering-related programs (ABET/RAC); forestry (SAF); funeral service (ABFSE); interior design: professional (CIDA); journalism and mass communications (ACEJMC); medical technology (NAACLS); music (NASM); recreation and parks (NRPA); speech-language pathology (ASHA); theater (NAST). **Total program enrollment:** 36429. **Application fee:** $45.

**PROGRAM(S) OFFERED**
• **Accounting** *2 students enrolled* • **Adult and Continuing Education and Teaching** • **Building/Construction Finishing, Management, and Inspection, Other** *6 students enrolled* • **Business Administration and Management, General** *3 students enrolled* • **Communication Studies/Speech Communication and Rhetoric** • **Computer Science** *1 student enrolled* • **Computer Systems Networking and Telecommunications** • **Education/Teaching of Individuals with Autism** *2 students enrolled* • **Educational, Instructional, and Curriculum Supervision** • **Educational/Instructional Media Design** • **Engineering, Other** • **Human Resources Management/Personnel Administration, General** *44 students enrolled* • **Industrial Engineering** • **Language Interpretation and Translation** *18 students enrolled* • **Marketing, Other** *1 student enrolled* • **Mathematics and Statistics, Other** • **Medical Radiologic Technology/Science—Radiation Therapist** • **Physical Education Teaching and Coaching** *23 students enrolled* • **Sport and Fitness Administration/Management** • **Substance Abuse/Addiction Counseling** *12 students enrolled* • **Trade and Industrial Teacher Education** • **Wood Science and Wood Products/Pulp and Paper Technology**

**STUDENT SERVICES** Academic or career counseling, daycare for children of students, employment services for current students, placement services for program completers, remedial services.

## Vermilion Community College

1900 East Camp Street, Ely, MN 55731-1996
http://www.vcc.edu/

**CONTACT** Dr. Mary Koski, Provost
**Telephone:** 218-235-2100

**GENERAL INFORMATION** Public Institution. Founded 1922. **Accreditation:** Regional (NCA). **Total program enrollment:** 467. **Application fee:** $20.

**PROGRAM(S) OFFERED**
• **Criminal Justice/Police Science** *19 students enrolled* • **Entrepreneurship/Entrepreneurial Studies** *2 students enrolled* • **Forest Resources Production and Management** *1 student enrolled* • **Natural Resources/Conservation, General** *7 students enrolled* • **Parks, Recreation and Leisure Facilities Management** *5 students enrolled* • **Small Business Administration/Management** *1 student enrolled* • **Taxidermy/Taxidermist** *5 students enrolled*

**STUDENT SERVICES** Academic or career counseling, employment services for current students, placement services for program completers, remedial services.

## White Earth Tribal and Community College

202 -210 Main Street South, Mahnomen, MN 56557
http://www.wetcc.org/

**CONTACT** Dr. Robert Peacock, President
**Telephone:** 218-935-0417

**GENERAL INFORMATION** Private Institution. **Total program enrollment:** 62.

**STUDENT SERVICES** Academic or career counseling, employment services for current students, placement services for program completers, remedial services.

# MISSISSIPPI

## Academy of Hair Design

2003B South Commerce, Grenada, MS 38901
http://www.academyofhair.com/

**CONTACT** Andrea Calton, Administrative Asst.
**Telephone:** 662-226-2464

**GENERAL INFORMATION** Private Institution. **Total program enrollment:** 17.

**PROGRAM(S) OFFERED**
• **Cosmetology, Barber/Styling, and Nail Instructor** *2000 hrs./$13,833*
• **Cosmetology/Cosmetologist, General** *1500 hrs./$10,600*

**STUDENT SERVICES** Placement services for program completers.

## Academy of Hair Design

Cloverleaf Mall D-4, Hattiesburg, MS 39401
http://www.academyofhair.com/

**CONTACT** Andrea Calton, Administrative Assistant
**Telephone:** 601-583-1290

**GENERAL INFORMATION** Private Institution. **Total program enrollment:** 36.

**PROGRAM(S) OFFERED**
- **Cosmetology, Barber/Styling, and Nail Instructor** *750 hrs./$5250*
- **Cosmetology/Cosmetologist, General** *1500 hrs./$9200*

**STUDENT SERVICES** Placement services for program completers.

## Academy of Hair Design

1815 Terry Road, Jackson, MS 39204
http://www.academyofhair.com/

**CONTACT** Andrea Calton, Administrative Asst.
**Telephone:** 601-372-9800

**GENERAL INFORMATION** Private Institution. **Total program enrollment:** 41.

**PROGRAM(S) OFFERED**
- **Barbering/Barber** *1500 hrs./$9000* • **Cosmetology, Barber/Styling, and Nail Instructor** *2000 hrs./$13,833* • **Cosmetology/Cosmetologist, General** *1500 hrs./$9200*

**STUDENT SERVICES** Placement services for program completers.

## Academy of Hair Design

3167 Highway 80 East, Pearl, MS 39208
http://www.academyofhair.com/

**CONTACT** Andrea Calton, Administrative Asst.
**Telephone:** 601-939-4441

**GENERAL INFORMATION** Private Institution. **Total program enrollment:** 46.

**PROGRAM(S) OFFERED**
- **Cosmetology, Barber/Styling, and Nail Instructor** *2000 hrs./$13,833*
- **Cosmetology/Cosmetologist, General** *1500 hrs./$10,600*

## Antonelli College

1500 North 31st Avenue, Hattiesburg, MS 39401
http://antonellicollege.edu/

**CONTACT** Mary Ann Davis, President
**Telephone:** 601-583-4100

**GENERAL INFORMATION** Private Institution. **Accreditation:** State accredited or approved. **Total program enrollment:** 337.

**PROGRAM(S) OFFERED**
- **Business/Office Automation/Technology/Data Entry** *3 students enrolled*
- **Medical Administrative/Executive Assistant and Medical Secretary** *2 students enrolled*

**STUDENT SERVICES** Academic or career counseling, employment services for current students, placement services for program completers.

## Antonelli College

2323 Lakeland Drive, Jackson, MS 39232
http://www.antonellicollege.edu/

**CONTACT** Mary Ann Davis, President
**Telephone:** 601-362-9991

**GENERAL INFORMATION** Private Institution. **Accreditation:** State accredited or approved. **Total program enrollment:** 246. **Application fee:** $75.

**PROGRAM(S) OFFERED**
- **Business/Office Automation/Technology/Data Entry** • **Dental Assisting/Assistant** • **Medical/Clinical Assistant**

**STUDENT SERVICES** Academic or career counseling, employment services for current students, placement services for program completers.

## Belhaven College

1500 Peachtree Street, Jackson, MS 39202-1789
http://www.belhaven.edu/

**CONTACT** Roger Parrott, President
**Telephone:** 601-968-5940

**GENERAL INFORMATION** Private Institution. Founded 1883. **Accreditation:** Regional (SACS/CC); art and design (NASAD); music (NASM). **Total program enrollment:** 2435. **Application fee:** $25.

**PROGRAM(S) OFFERED**
- **Accounting** • **Bible/Biblical Studies** • **Business Administration and Management, General** • **Computer Science** • **Dance, General** *2 students enrolled*
- **Work and Family Studies**

**STUDENT SERVICES** Academic or career counseling, remedial services.

## Blue Cliff College–Gulfport

942 Beach Drive, Gulfport, MS 39507-1354
http://bluecliffcollege.com/

**CONTACT** Ted Little, Director
**Telephone:** 228-896-9727 Ext. 0000

**GENERAL INFORMATION** Private Institution. **Total program enrollment:** 138.

**PROGRAM(S) OFFERED**
- **Allied Health and Medical Assisting Services, Other** *27 students enrolled*
- **Cosmetology and Related Personal Grooming Arts, Other** • **Massage Therapy/Therapeutic Massage** *93 students enrolled*

**STUDENT SERVICES** Academic or career counseling, placement services for program completers.

## Chris Beauty College

1265 Pass Road, Gulfport, MS 39501
http://www.chrisbeautycollege.com/

**CONTACT** Donald O. Simmons, President Owner
**Telephone:** 228-864-2920

**GENERAL INFORMATION** Private Institution. Founded 1961. **Total program enrollment:** 91. **Application fee:** $35.

**PROGRAM(S) OFFERED**
- **Barbering/Barber** • **Cosmetology, Barber/Styling, and Nail Instructor** *750 hrs./$2250* • **Cosmetology/Cosmetologist, General** *1500 hrs./$8500* • **Nail Technician/Specialist and Manicurist** *350 hrs./$1750*

**STUDENT SERVICES** Academic or career counseling, placement services for program completers.

## Coahoma Community College

3240 Friars Point Road, Clarksdale, MS 38614-9799
http://www.ccc.cc.ms.us/

**CONTACT** Vivian M. Presley, President
**Telephone:** 662-627-2571

**GENERAL INFORMATION** Public Institution. Founded 1949. **Accreditation:** Regional (SACS/CC). **Total program enrollment:** 2057.

**PROGRAM(S) OFFERED**
• **Autobody/Collision and Repair Technology/Technician** *2 students enrolled* • **Barbering/Barber** *14 students enrolled* • **Carpentry/Carpenter** *2 students enrolled* • **Cosmetology/Cosmetologist, General** *5 students enrolled* • **Culinary Arts/Chef Training** *5 students enrolled* • **Heavy/Industrial Equipment Maintenance Technologies, Other** *1 student enrolled* • **Licensed Practical/Vocational Nurse Training (LPN, LVN, Cert, Dipl, AAS)** *22 students enrolled* • **Welding Technology/Welder** *12 students enrolled*

**STUDENT SERVICES** Academic or career counseling, employment services for current students, placement services for program completers, remedial services.

## Copiah-Lincoln Community College

PO Box 649, Wesson, MS 39191-0649
http://www.colin.edu/

**CONTACT** Dr. Ronnie Nettles, President
**Telephone:** 601-643-8306

**GENERAL INFORMATION** Public Institution. Founded 1928. **Accreditation:** Regional (SACS/CC); medical laboratory technology (NAACLS); radiologic technology: radiography (JRCERT). **Total program enrollment:** 2868.

**PROGRAM(S) OFFERED**
• **Administrative Assistant and Secretarial Science, General** *4 students enrolled* • **Automobile/Automotive Mechanics Technology/Technician** *7 students enrolled* • **Computer Systems Networking and Telecommunications** • **Construction/Heavy Equipment/Earthmoving Equipment Operation** • **Cosmetology/Cosmetologist, General** *23 students enrolled* • **Diesel Mechanics Technology/Technician** *7 students enrolled* • **Heating, Air Conditioning, Ventilation and Refrigeration Maintenance Technology/Technician (HAC, HACR, HVAC, HVACR)** *10 students enrolled* • **Heavy Equipment Maintenance Technology/Technician** • **Licensed Practical/Vocational Nurse Training (LPN, LVN, Cert, Dipl, AAS)** *46 students enrolled* • **Machine Shop Technology/Assistant** *1 student enrolled* • **Management Information Systems, General** • **Nurse/Nursing Assistant/Aide and Patient Care Assistant** *18 students enrolled* • **Truck and Bus Driver/Commercial Vehicle Operation** *9 students enrolled* • **Welding Technology/Welder** *20 students enrolled*

**STUDENT SERVICES** Academic or career counseling, daycare for children of students, employment services for current students, placement services for program completers, remedial services.

## Corinth Academy of Cosmetology

502 Cruise Street, Corinth, MS 38834

**CONTACT** Kathy Tollison, President
**Telephone:** 662-286-9200

**GENERAL INFORMATION** Private Institution. **Total program enrollment:** 22. **Application fee:** $100.

**PROGRAM(S) OFFERED**
• **Cosmetology, Barber/Styling, and Nail Instructor** *2000 hrs./$5080* • **Cosmetology/Cosmetologist, General** *1500 hrs./$4550* • **Nail Technician/Specialist and Manicurist** *350 hrs./$1250*

**STUDENT SERVICES** Academic or career counseling, placement services for program completers.

## Creations College of Cosmetology

2419 West Main Street, PO Box 2635, Tupelo, MS 38803
http://www.creationscosmetology.com/

**CONTACT** Carolyn Kennedy Bowen, Owner
**Telephone:** 662-844-9264

**GENERAL INFORMATION** Private Institution. Founded 1984. **Total program enrollment:** 51. **Application fee:** $100.

**PROGRAM(S) OFFERED**
• **Cosmetology/Cosmetologist, General** *1500 hrs./$7200*

**STUDENT SERVICES** Academic or career counseling.

## Day Spa Career College

3900 Bienville Boulevard, Ocean Spring, MS 39564

**CONTACT** Sandra Seymour, President, CEO
**Telephone:** 228-875-4809

**GENERAL INFORMATION** Private Institution. **Total program enrollment:** 37.

**PROGRAM(S) OFFERED**
• **Aesthetician/Esthetician and Skin Care Specialist** *6 students enrolled* • **Cosmetology and Related Personal Grooming Arts, Other** *1000 hrs./$5450* • **Cosmetology, Barber/Styling, and Nail Instructor** • **Cosmetology/Cosmetologist, General** *650 hrs./$7100* • **Nail Technician/Specialist and Manicurist** *1 student enrolled*

**STUDENT SERVICES** Academic or career counseling, placement services for program completers.

## Delta Beauty College

697 Delta Plaza, Greenville, MS 38701

**CONTACT** Kenny O'Neal, President
**Telephone:** 662-332-0587

**GENERAL INFORMATION** Private Institution. **Total program enrollment:** 43.

**PROGRAM(S) OFFERED**
• **Cosmetology, Barber/Styling, and Nail Instructor** *1 student enrolled* • **Cosmetology/Cosmetologist, General** *2000 hrs./$7587*

**STUDENT SERVICES** Academic or career counseling, placement services for program completers.

## Delta Technical College

1090 Main Street, Southaven, MS 38671
http://www.deltatechnicalcollege.com/

**CONTACT** Joan Hankins, Director of Education
**Telephone:** 662-280-1443

**GENERAL INFORMATION** Private Institution. **Total program enrollment:** 337.

**PROGRAM(S) OFFERED**
• **Aesthetician/Esthetician and Skin Care Specialist** *750 hrs./$6450* • **Heating, Air Conditioning, Ventilation and Refrigeration Maintenance Technology/Technician (HAC, HACR, HVAC, HVACR)** *720 hrs./$8975* • **Massage Therapy/Therapeutic Massage** *723 hrs./$8975* • **Medical/Clinical Assistant** *720 hrs./$9850*

**STUDENT SERVICES** Placement services for program completers.

## East Central Community College

PO Box 129, Decatur, MS 39327-0129
http://www.eccc.cc.ms.us/

**CONTACT** Phil Sutphin, President
**Telephone:** 601-635-2111

**GENERAL INFORMATION** Public Institution. Founded 1928. **Accreditation:** Regional (SACS/CC); surgical technology (ARCST). **Total program enrollment:** 1915.

**PROGRAM(S) OFFERED**
• **Administrative Assistant and Secretarial Science, General** *2 students enrolled* • **Autobody/Collision and Repair Technology/Technician** *5 students enrolled* • **Automobile/Automotive Mechanics Technology/Technician** *2 students enrolled* • **Carpentry/Carpenter** *10 students enrolled* • **Cooking and Related Culinary Arts, General** *2 students enrolled* • **Cosmetology/Cosmetologist, General** *17 students enrolled* • **Electrician** *2 students enrolled* • **Heating, Air Conditioning, Ventilation and Refrigeration Maintenance Technology/Technician (HAC, HACR, HVAC, HVACR)** *3 students enrolled* • **Licensed Practical/Vocational Nurse Training (LPN, LVN, Cert, Dipl, AAS)** *19 students enrolled* • **Machine Tool Technology/Machinist** *4 students enrolled* • **Nurse/Nursing Assistant/Aide and Patient Care Assistant** *24 students enrolled* • **Surgical Technology/Technologist** *5 students enrolled* • **Welding Technology/Welder** *15 students enrolled*

**STUDENT SERVICES** Academic or career counseling, daycare for children of students, employment services for current students, placement services for program completers, remedial services.

## East Mississippi Community College

PO Box 158, Scooba, MS 39358-0158
http://www.eastms.edu/

**CONTACT** Rick Young, President
**Telephone:** 662-476-5000

**GENERAL INFORMATION** Public Institution. Founded 1927. **Accreditation:** Regional (SACS/CC); funeral service (ABFSE). **Total program enrollment:** 2735.

**PROGRAM(S) OFFERED**
• **Administrative Assistant and Secretarial Science, General** *3 students enrolled* • **Automobile/Automotive Mechanics Technology/Technician** *5 students enrolled* • **Cosmetology/Cosmetologist, General** *18 students enrolled* • **Electrician** *15 students enrolled* • **Licensed Practical/Vocational Nurse Training (LPN, LVN, Cert, Dipl, AAS)** *29 students enrolled* • **Lineworker** *9 students enrolled* • **Machine Shop Technology/Assistant** *5 students enrolled* • **Management Information Systems, General** • **Nurse/Nursing Assistant/Aide and Patient Care Assistant** *21 students enrolled* • **Truck and Bus Driver/Commercial Vehicle Operation** *28 students enrolled* • **Welding Technology/Welder** *16 students enrolled*

**STUDENT SERVICES** Academic or career counseling, employment services for current students, placement services for program completers, remedial services.

## Final Touch Beauty School

832 Highway 19 N, Suite 510, Meridian, MS 39307

**CONTACT** Sue Mitchell, Owner
**Telephone:** 601-485-7733

**GENERAL INFORMATION** Private Institution. **Total program enrollment:** 68. **Application fee:** $100.

**PROGRAM(S) OFFERED**
• **Cosmetology, Barber/Styling, and Nail Instructor** *750 hrs./$3900* • **Cosmetology/Cosmetologist, General** *1500 hrs./$7500* • **Nail Technician/Specialist and Manicurist** *350 hrs./$2100*

**STUDENT SERVICES** Academic or career counseling, placement services for program completers.

## Foster's Cosmetology College

1813 Highway 15, N, Ripley, MS 38663

**CONTACT** Hazel L. Foster, Owner
**Telephone:** 662-837-9334

**GENERAL INFORMATION** Private Institution. Founded 1945. **Total program enrollment:** 15.

**PROGRAM(S) OFFERED**
• **Barbering/Barber** *1500 hrs./$7405* • **Cosmetology, Barber/Styling, and Nail Instructor** *600 hrs./$6400* • **Cosmetology/Cosmetologist, General** *1500 hrs./$7805*

**STUDENT SERVICES** Academic or career counseling, placement services for program completers.

## Gibson Barber and Beauty College

120 East Main Street, West Point, MS 39773

**CONTACT** Evelyn Gibson, Administrator
**Telephone:** 662-494-5444

**GENERAL INFORMATION** Private Institution. Founded 1985. **Total program enrollment:** 43. **Application fee:** $100.

**PROGRAM(S) OFFERED**
• **Barbering/Barber** *1500 hrs./$7800* • **Cosmetology and Related Personal Grooming Arts, Other** *750 hrs./$2200* • **Cosmetology, Barber/Styling, and Nail Instructor** *600 hrs./$2200* • **Cosmetology/Cosmetologist, General** *1500 hrs./$7300* • **Nail Technician/Specialist and Manicurist**

**STUDENT SERVICES** Placement services for program completers.

## Healing Touch School of Massage Therapy

4700 Hardy Street, Suite J-1, Hattiesburg, MS 39402
http://healingtouchms.com/

**CONTACT** Ibrahima Sidibe, Owner/Director/CFO
**Telephone:** 601-261-0111

**GENERAL INFORMATION** Private Institution. **Total program enrollment:** 12. **Application fee:** $25.

**PROGRAM(S) OFFERED**
• **Massage Therapy/Therapeutic Massage** *750 hrs./$10,500*

**STUDENT SERVICES** Academic or career counseling, placement services for program completers.

## Hinds Community College

PO Box 1100, Raymond, MS 39154-1100
http://www.hindscc.edu/

**CONTACT** Dr. V. Clyde Muse, President
**Telephone:** 601-857-5261

**GENERAL INFORMATION** Public Institution. Founded 1917. **Accreditation:** Regional (SACS/CC); dental assisting (ADA); health information technology (AHIMA); medical assisting (AAMAE); medical laboratory technology (NAACLS); physical therapy assisting (APTA); radiologic technology: radiography (JRCERT); respiratory therapy technology (CoARC). **Total program enrollment:** 6609.

**PROGRAM(S) OFFERED**
• **Administrative Assistant and Secretarial Science, General** *12 students enrolled* • **Agribusiness/Agricultural Business Operations** *3 students enrolled* • **Apparel and Textile Manufacture** • **Apparel and Textile Marketing Management** *8 students enrolled* • **Autobody/Collision and Repair Technology/Technician** *20 students enrolled* • **Automobile/Automotive Mechanics Technology/Technician** *12 students enrolled* • **Barbering/Barber** *15 students enrolled* • **Carpentry/Carpenter** *12 students enrolled* • **Cartography** *3 students enrolled* • **Communications Systems Installation and Repair Technology** *1 student enrolled* • **Computer Installation and Repair Technology/Technician** *1*

*Hinds Community College (continued)*

*student enrolled* • **Cooking and Related Culinary Arts, General** *1 student enrolled* • **Cosmetology/Cosmetologist, General** • **Dental Assisting/Assistant** *21 students enrolled* • **Diagnostic Medical Sonography/Sonographer and Ultrasound Technician** • **Diesel Mechanics Technology/Technician** *7 students enrolled* • **Drafting and Design Technology/Technician, General** • **Electrical, Electronic and Communications Engineering Technology/Technician** • **Electrician** *40 students enrolled* • **Emergency Medical Technology/Technician (EMT Paramedic)** *2 students enrolled* • **Engine Machinist** *1 student enrolled* • **Graphic and Printing Equipment Operator, General Production** *4 students enrolled* • **Heating, Air Conditioning, Ventilation and Refrigeration Maintenance Technology/Technician (HAC, HACR, HVAC, HVACR)** *10 students enrolled* • **Heavy Equipment Maintenance Technology/Technician** • **Hospitality Administration/Management, General** • **Institutional Food Workers** *7 students enrolled* • **Licensed Practical/Vocational Nurse Training (LPN, LVN, Cert, Dipl, AAS)** *98 students enrolled* • **Machine Shop Technology/Assistant** • **Machine Tool Technology/Machinist** *1 student enrolled* • **Mason/Masonry** *12 students enrolled* • **Meat Cutting/Meat Cutter** *1 student enrolled* • **Optometric Technician/Assistant** *1 student enrolled* • **Plumbing Technology/Plumber** *2 students enrolled* • **Surgical Technology/Technologist** *29 students enrolled* • **Tourism and Travel Services Management** • **Vehicle and Vehicle Parts and Accessories Marketing Operations** *4 students enrolled* • **Welding Technology/Welder** *29 students enrolled*

**STUDENT SERVICES** Academic or career counseling, daycare for children of students, employment services for current students, placement services for program completers, remedial services.

## Holmes Community College

PO Box 369, Goodman, MS 39079-0369
http://www.holmescc.edu/

**CONTACT** Dr. Glenn F. Boyce, President
**Telephone:** 662-472-2312

**GENERAL INFORMATION** Public Institution. Founded 1928. **Accreditation:** Regional (SACS/CC); emergency medical services (JRCEMTP); surgical technology (ARCST). **Total program enrollment:** 3838.

**PROGRAM(S) OFFERED**
• **Autobody/Collision and Repair Technology/Technician** *6 students enrolled* • **Automobile/Automotive Mechanics Technology/Technician** • **Business/Office Automation/Technology/Data Entry** • **Cosmetology/Cosmetologist, General** *9 students enrolled* • **Emergency Medical Technology/Technician (EMT Paramedic)** *7 students enrolled* • **Heating, Air Conditioning, Ventilation and Refrigeration Maintenance Technology/Technician (HAC, HACR, HVAC, HVACR)** *9 students enrolled* • **Licensed Practical/Vocational Nurse Training (LPN, LVN, Cert, Dipl, AAS)** *58 students enrolled* • **Surgical Technology/Technologist** *9 students enrolled* • **Welding Technology/Welder** *14 students enrolled*

**STUDENT SERVICES** Academic or career counseling, placement services for program completers, remedial services.

## ICS–The Wright Beauty College

2077 Highway 72, E, Corinth, MS 38834

**CONTACT** Linda Kay Richardson, Owner
**Telephone:** 662-287-0944

**GENERAL INFORMATION** Private Institution. Founded 1986. **Total program enrollment:** 34. **Application fee:** $100.

**PROGRAM(S) OFFERED**
• **Cosmetology, Barber/Styling, and Nail Instructor** *1 student enrolled* • **Cosmetology/Cosmetologist, General** *1500 hrs./$6400* • **Nail Technician/Specialist and Manicurist** *9 students enrolled* • **Trade and Industrial Teacher Education** *750 hrs./$3175*

**STUDENT SERVICES** Academic or career counseling.

## Itawamba Community College

602 West Hill Street, Fulton, MS 38843
http://www.icc.cc.ms.us/

**CONTACT** David C. Cole, PhD, President
**Telephone:** 601-862-8000

**GENERAL INFORMATION** Public Institution. Founded 1947. **Accreditation:** Regional (SACS/CC); health information technology (AHIMA); physical therapy assisting (APTA); radiologic technology: radiography (JRCERT); surgical technology (ARCST). **Total program enrollment:** 4805.

**PROGRAM(S) OFFERED**
• **Autobody/Collision and Repair Technology/Technician** *9 students enrolled* • **Automobile/Automotive Mechanics Technology/Technician** *3 students enrolled* • **Computer and Information Sciences, General** *1 student enrolled* • **Licensed Practical/Vocational Nurse Training (LPN, LVN, Cert, Dipl, AAS)** *40 students enrolled* • **Surgical Technology/Technologist** *5 students enrolled* • **Truck and Bus Driver/Commercial Vehicle Operation** *26 students enrolled* • **Welding Technology/Welder** *11 students enrolled*

**STUDENT SERVICES** Academic or career counseling, daycare for children of students, employment services for current students, placement services for program completers, remedial services.

## J & J Hair Design College

116 East Franklin Street, Carthage, MS 39051

**CONTACT** Ricky Jones, President Owner
**Telephone:** 601-267-3678

**GENERAL INFORMATION** Private Institution. **Total program enrollment:** 52. **Application fee:** $100.

**PROGRAM(S) OFFERED**
• **Barbering/Barber** *1500 hrs./$8450* • **Cosmetology and Related Personal Grooming Arts, Other** *80 hrs./$400* • **Cosmetology, Barber/Styling, and Nail Instructor** *1000 hrs./$5500* • **Hair Styling/Stylist and Hair Design** *2 students enrolled* • **Personal and Culinary Services, Other** *1 student enrolled* • **Salon/Beauty Salon Management/Manager** *80 hrs./$400*

**STUDENT SERVICES** Academic or career counseling, placement services for program completers.

## J & J Hair Design College

3905 Main Street, Moss Point, MS 39562

**CONTACT** Ricky Jones, President
**Telephone:** 228-864-4663

**GENERAL INFORMATION** Private Institution. **Total program enrollment:** 10. **Application fee:** $100.

**PROGRAM(S) OFFERED**
• **Barbering/Barber** *1500 hrs./$8300* • **Cosmetology, Barber/Styling, and Nail Instructor** *600 hrs./$3340*

**STUDENT SERVICES** Academic or career counseling, placement services for program completers.

## Jones County Junior College

900 South Court Street, Ellisville, MS 39437-3901
http://www.jcjc.edu/

**CONTACT** Jesse Smith, President
**Telephone:** 601-477-4000

**GENERAL INFORMATION** Public Institution. Founded 1928. **Accreditation:** Regional (SACS/CC); emergency medical services (JRCEMTP); radiologic technology: radiography (JRCERT). **Total program enrollment:** 3543.

**PROGRAM(S) OFFERED**
• **Administrative Assistant and Secretarial Science, General** *2 students enrolled* • **Agricultural and Food Products Processing** *11 students enrolled* • **Applied Horticulture/Horticultural Operations, General** *1 student enrolled* • **Automobile/Automotive Mechanics Technology/Technician** *10 students enrolled* • **Communications Systems Installation and Repair Technology** • **Cooking and Related Culinary Arts, General** *6 students enrolled* • **Cosmetology/Cosmetologist, General** *19 students enrolled* • **Diagnostic Medical Sonography/Sonographer and Ultrasound Technician** • **Electrician** *24 students enrolled* • **Engine Machinist** *1 student enrolled* • **Heating, Air Conditioning, Ventilation and Refrigeration Maintenance Technology/Technician (HAC, HACR, HVAC, HVACR)** *11 students enrolled* • **Licensed Practical/Vocational Nurse Training (LPN, LVN, Cert, Dipl, AAS)** *58 students enrolled* • **Machine Shop Technology/Assistant** *5 students enrolled* • **Nurse/Nursing Assistant/Aide and Patient Care Assistant** *30 students enrolled* • **Plastics Engineering Technology/Technician** • **Watchmaking and Jewelrymaking** *8 students enrolled* • **Welding Technology/Welder** *17 students enrolled*

**STUDENT SERVICES** Academic or career counseling, employment services for current students, placement services for program completers, remedial services.

## Magnolia College of Cosmetology

4725 I-55, Jackson, MS 39206
http://www.magnoliacollegeofcosmetology.com/

**CONTACT** Marie Wells Butler, Owner President
**Telephone:** 601-362-6940

**GENERAL INFORMATION** Private Institution. Founded 1985. **Total program enrollment:** 178. **Application fee:** $100.

**PROGRAM(S) OFFERED**
• **Aesthetician/Esthetician and Skin Care Specialist** *600 hrs./$6100* • **Cosmetology, Barber/Styling, and Nail Instructor** *750 hrs./$5100* • **Cosmetology/Cosmetologist, General** *1500 hrs./$13,500* • **Nail Technician/Specialist and Manicurist** *350 hrs./$2550*

**STUDENT SERVICES** Placement services for program completers.

## Meridian Community College

910 Highway 19 North, Meridian, MS 39307
http://www.meridiancc.edu/

**CONTACT** Scott D. Elliott, President
**Telephone:** 601-483-8241 Ext. 668

**GENERAL INFORMATION** Public Institution. Founded 1937. **Accreditation:** Regional (SACS/CC); dental hygiene (ADA); health information technology (AHIMA); medical laboratory technology (NAACLS); physical therapy assisting (APTA); practical nursing (NLN); radiologic technology: radiography (JRCERT). **Total program enrollment:** 2651.

**PROGRAM(S) OFFERED**
• **Administrative Assistant and Secretarial Science, General** *9 students enrolled* • **Carpentry/Carpenter** *18 students enrolled* • **Cosmetology/Cosmetologist, General** *26 students enrolled* • **Dental Assisting/Assistant** *6 students enrolled* • **Industrial Mechanics and Maintenance Technology** *8 students enrolled* • **Licensed Practical/Vocational Nurse Training (LPN, LVN, Cert, Dipl, AAS)** *32 students enrolled* • **Machine Tool Technology/Machinist** *3 students enrolled* • **Nurse/Nursing Assistant/Aide and Patient Care Assistant** *38 students enrolled* • **Surgical Technology/Technologist** *10 students enrolled* • **Truck and Bus Driver/Commercial Vehicle Operation** *29 students enrolled*

**STUDENT SERVICES** Academic or career counseling, employment services for current students, placement services for program completers, remedial services.

## Mississippi College of Beauty Culture

732 Sawmill Road, Laurel, MS 39440

**CONTACT** Robert Hatfield, President
**Telephone:** 601-428-7043

**GENERAL INFORMATION** Private Institution. **Total program enrollment:** 89.

**PROGRAM(S) OFFERED**
• **Cosmetology, Barber/Styling, and Nail Instructor** • **Cosmetology/Cosmetologist, General** *1500 hrs./$9100*

**STUDENT SERVICES** Placement services for program completers.

## Mississippi Delta Community College

PO Box 668, Highway 3 and Cherry Street, Moorhead, MS 38761-0668
http://www.msdelta.edu/

**CONTACT** Dr. Larry G. Bailey, President
**Telephone:** 662-246-6322

**GENERAL INFORMATION** Public Institution. Founded 1926. **Accreditation:** Regional (SACS/CC); dental hygiene (ADA); medical laboratory technology (NAACLS); radiologic technology: radiography (JRCERT). **Total program enrollment:** 2431.

**PROGRAM(S) OFFERED**
• **Agricultural Mechanization, General** *2 students enrolled* • **Agricultural Mechanization, Other** • **Automobile/Automotive Mechanics Technology/Technician** *3 students enrolled* • **Construction/Heavy Equipment/Earthmoving Equipment Operation** *11 students enrolled* • **Electrician** *12 students enrolled* • **Engine Machinist** *8 students enrolled* • **Heating, Air Conditioning, Ventilation and Refrigeration Maintenance Technology/Technician (HAC, HACR, HVAC, HVACR)** *11 students enrolled* • **Licensed Practical/Vocational Nurse Training (LPN, LVN, Cert, Dipl, AAS)** *21 students enrolled* • **Machine Shop Technology/Assistant** • **Mason/Masonry** *4 students enrolled* • **Nuclear Medical Technology/Technologist** *3 students enrolled* • **Sheet Metal Technology/Sheetworking** *5 students enrolled* • **Welding Technology/Welder** *11 students enrolled*

**STUDENT SERVICES** Academic or career counseling, employment services for current students, placement services for program completers, remedial services.

## Mississippi Gulf Coast Community College

PO Box 609, Perkinston, MS 39573-0609
http://www.mgccc.edu/

**CONTACT** Willis Lott, President
**Telephone:** 601-928-5211

**GENERAL INFORMATION** Public Institution. Founded 1911. **Accreditation:** Regional (SACS/CC); emergency medical services (JRCEMTP); funeral service (ABFSE); medical laboratory technology (NAACLS); radiologic technology: radiography (JRCERT). **Total program enrollment:** 5770.

**PROGRAM(S) OFFERED**
• **Administrative Assistant and Secretarial Science, General** *12 students enrolled* • **Aquaculture** • **Autobody/Collision and Repair Technology/Technician** *10 students enrolled* • **Automobile/Automotive Mechanics Technology/Technician** *6 students enrolled* • **Carpentry/Carpenter** • **Cosmetology/Cosmetologist, General** • **Drafting/Design Engineering Technologies/Technicians, Other** *1 student enrolled* • **Electrician** *20 students enrolled* • **Heating, Air Conditioning, Ventilation and Refrigeration Maintenance Technology/Technician (HAC, HACR, HVAC, HVACR)** *7 students enrolled* • **Industrial Mechanics and Maintenance Technology** *2 students enrolled* • **Landscaping and Groundskeeping** *11 students enrolled* • **Licensed Practical/Vocational Nurse Training (LPN, LVN, Cert, Dipl, AAS)** *89 students enrolled* • **Machine Shop Technology/Assistant** *13 students enrolled* • **Marine Maintenance/Fitter and Ship Repair Technology/Technician** *4 students enrolled* • **Marine Transportation, Other** • **Plumbing Technology/Plumber** *1 student enrolled* • **Restaurant/Food Services Management** *13 students enrolled* • **Surgical Technology/**

*Mississippi Gulf Coast Community College (continued)*

**Technologist** *10 students enrolled* • **Technical Teacher Education** • **Truck and Bus Driver/Commercial Vehicle Operation** *6 students enrolled* • **Welding Technology/Welder** *9 students enrolled*

**STUDENT SERVICES** Academic or career counseling, daycare for children of students, employment services for current students, placement services for program completers, remedial services.

## Mississippi State Board for Community and Junior Colleges

3825 Ridgewood Road, Jackson, MS 39211

**CONTACT** Eric Clark, Executive Director
**Telephone:** 601-432-6518

**GENERAL INFORMATION** Public Institution.

## Northeast Mississippi Community College

101 Cunningham Boulevard, Booneville, MS 38829
http://www.nemcc.edu/

**CONTACT** Johnny Allen, President
**Telephone:** 662-728-7751

**GENERAL INFORMATION** Public Institution. Founded 1948. **Accreditation:** Regional (SACS/CC); dental hygiene (ADA); medical assisting (AAMAE); medical laboratory technology (NAACLS); radiologic technology: radiography (JRCERT). **Total program enrollment:** 2685.

**PROGRAM(S) OFFERED**
• **Autobody/Collision and Repair Technology/Technician** *11 students enrolled* • **Automobile/Automotive Mechanics Technology/Technician** *15 students enrolled* • **Diesel Mechanics Technology/Technician** *2 students enrolled* • **Heating, Air Conditioning, Ventilation and Refrigeration Maintenance Technology/Technician (HAC, HACR, HVAC, HVACR)** *2 students enrolled* • **Licensed Practical/Vocational Nurse Training (LPN, LVN, Cert, Dipl, AAS)** *61 students enrolled* • **Machine Shop Technology/Assistant** • **Machine Tool Technology/Machinist** *4 students enrolled*

**STUDENT SERVICES** Academic or career counseling, daycare for children of students, employment services for current students, placement services for program completers, remedial services.

## Northwest Mississippi Community College

4975 Highway 51 North, Senatobia, MS 38668-1701
http://www.northwestms.edu/

**CONTACT** Gary Spears, President
**Telephone:** 662-562-3200

**GENERAL INFORMATION** Public Institution. Founded 1927. **Accreditation:** Regional (SACS/CC); funeral service (ABFSE). **Total program enrollment:** 5435.

**PROGRAM(S) OFFERED**
• **Administrative Assistant and Secretarial Science, General** *4 students enrolled* • **Autobody/Collision and Repair Technology/Technician** *9 students enrolled* • **Automobile/Automotive Mechanics Technology/Technician** • **Cosmetology/Cosmetologist, General** *39 students enrolled* • **Emergency Medical Technology/Technician (EMT Paramedic)** • **Licensed Practical/Vocational Nurse Training (LPN, LVN, Cert, Dipl, AAS)** *95 students enrolled* • **Nurse/Nursing Assistant/Aide and Patient Care Assistant** *9 students enrolled* • **Surgical Technology/Technologist** *10 students enrolled* • **Truck and Bus Driver/Commercial Vehicle Operation** • **Welding Technology/Welder** *12 students enrolled*

**STUDENT SERVICES** Academic or career counseling, employment services for current students, placement services for program completers, remedial services.

## Pearl River Community College

101 Highway 11 North, Poplarville, MS 39470
http://www.prcc.edu/

**CONTACT** William Lewis, President
**Telephone:** 601-403-1000

**GENERAL INFORMATION** Public Institution. Founded 1909. **Accreditation:** Regional (SACS/CC); dental assisting (ADA); dental hygiene (ADA); medical laboratory technology (NAACLS); physical therapy assisting (APTA); radiologic technology: radiography (JRCERT); surgical technology (ARCST). **Total program enrollment:** 3718.

**PROGRAM(S) OFFERED**
• **Administrative Assistant and Secretarial Science, General** *23 students enrolled* • **Barbering/Barber** *16 students enrolled* • **Computer Programming, Specific Applications** *11 students enrolled* • **Cosmetology/Cosmetologist, General** *17 students enrolled* • **Dental Assisting/Assistant** *12 students enrolled* • **Licensed Practical/Vocational Nurse Training (LPN, LVN, Cert, Dipl, AAS)** *60 students enrolled* • **Respiratory Care Therapy/Therapist** *20 students enrolled* • **Surgical Technology/Technologist** *20 students enrolled* • **Welding Technology/Welder** *54 students enrolled*

**STUDENT SERVICES** Academic or career counseling, employment services for current students, placement services for program completers, remedial services.

## Southwest Mississippi Community College

College Drive, Summit, MS 39666
http://www.smcc.cc.ms.us/

**CONTACT** Oliver Young, President
**Telephone:** 601-276-2000

**GENERAL INFORMATION** Public Institution. Founded 1918. **Accreditation:** Regional (SACS/CC). **Total program enrollment:** 1638.

**PROGRAM(S) OFFERED**
• **Administrative Assistant and Secretarial Science, General** *1 student enrolled* • **Automobile/Automotive Mechanics Technology/Technician** *3 students enrolled* • **Carpentry/Carpenter** *6 students enrolled* • **Computer Systems Networking and Telecommunications** *1 student enrolled* • **Cosmetology/Cosmetologist, General** *25 students enrolled* • **Heating, Air Conditioning, Ventilation and Refrigeration Maintenance Technology/Technician (HAC, HACR, HVAC, HVACR)** *3 students enrolled* • **Licensed Practical/Vocational Nurse Training (LPN, LVN, Cert, Dipl, AAS)** *48 students enrolled* • **Massage Therapy/Therapeutic Massage** *5 students enrolled* • **Nurse/Nursing Assistant/Aide and Patient Care Assistant** *18 students enrolled* • **Welding Technology/Welder** *11 students enrolled*

**STUDENT SERVICES** Academic or career counseling, employment services for current students, placement services for program completers, remedial services.

## Traxlers School of Hair

2845 Suncrest Drive, Jackson, MS 39212

**CONTACT** Thomas V. Traxlers, President
**Telephone:** 601-371-0226

**GENERAL INFORMATION** Private Institution. **Total program enrollment:** 54.

**PROGRAM(S) OFFERED**
• **Barbering/Barber** *1500 hrs./$8110* • **Cosmetology, Barber/Styling, and Nail Instructor** *10 hrs./$5250*

**STUDENT SERVICES** Placement services for program completers.

## University of Mississippi Medical Center

2500 North State Street, Jackson, MS 39216-4505
http://www.umc.edu/

**CONTACT** Daniel W. Jones, Vice Chancellor
**Telephone:** 601-984-1000

**GENERAL INFORMATION** Public Institution. Founded 1955. **Accreditation:** Regional (SACS/CC); cytotechnology (ASC); dental hygiene (ADA);

health information administration (AHIMA); medical technology (NAACLS). **Total program enrollment:** 1960. **Application fee:** $25.

**PROGRAM(S) OFFERED**

• **Nuclear Medical Technology/Technologist** *7 students enrolled*

**STUDENT SERVICES** Academic or career counseling.

## Virginia College at Jackson

5360 I-55 North, Jackson, MS 39211
http://www.vc.edu/

**CONTACT** David Podesta, Campus President
**Telephone:** 601-977-0960

**GENERAL INFORMATION** Private Institution. Founded 2000. **Accreditation:** State accredited or approved. **Total program enrollment:** 850.

**PROGRAM(S) OFFERED**

• **Administrative Assistant and Secretarial Science, General** *48 hrs./$14,496* • **Computer Systems Networking and Telecommunications** *14 students enrolled* • **Computer and Information Sciences and Support Services, Other** • **Cosmetology/Cosmetologist, General** *75 hrs./$15,525* • **Information Technology** *96 hrs./$30,816* • **Medical Insurance Coding Specialist/Coder** *60 hrs./$18,620* • **Medical Office Assistant/Specialist** *60 hrs./$18,620* • **Medical Office Management/Administration** *12 students enrolled* • **Medical/Clinical Assistant** *108 students enrolled* • **Pharmacy Technician/Assistant** *60 hrs./$18,620*

**STUDENT SERVICES** Academic or career counseling, employment services for current students, placement services for program completers.

## Virginia College Gulf Coast at Biloxi

920 Cedar Lake Road, Biloxi, MS 39532
http://www.vc.edu/site/campus.cfm?campus=gulfcoast

**CONTACT** Donald J. Newton, Campus President
**Telephone:** 228-392-2994 Ext. 3109

**GENERAL INFORMATION** Private Institution. **Total program enrollment:** 321. **Application fee:** $100.

**PROGRAM(S) OFFERED**

• **Administrative Assistant and Secretarial Science, General** *3 students enrolled* • **Medical Insurance Coding Specialist/Coder** *18 students enrolled* • **Medical/Clinical Assistant** *15 students enrolled* • **Pharmacy Technician/Assistant** *1 student enrolled*

**STUDENT SERVICES** Academic or career counseling, employment services for current students, placement services for program completers, remedial services.

# MISSOURI

## Academy of Hair Design

1834 S. Glenstone, Springfield, MO 65804

**GENERAL INFORMATION** Private Institution. **Total program enrollment:** 93. **Application fee:** $100.

**PROGRAM(S) OFFERED**

• **Aesthetician/Esthetician and Skin Care Specialist** *750 hrs./$7625* • **Barbering/Barber** *1000 hrs./$11,823* • **Cosmetology/Cosmetologist, General** *1500 hrs./$12,400* • **Nail Technician/Specialist and Manicurist** *400 hrs./$3763*

## Allied College

13723 Riverport Drive, Suite 103, Maryland Heights, MO 63043
http://www.hightechinstitute.edu/

**CONTACT** Heidi Wind, Campus President
**Telephone:** 314-595-3400

**GENERAL INFORMATION** Private Institution. **Accreditation:** State accredited or approved. **Total program enrollment:** 406. **Application fee:** $50.

**PROGRAM(S) OFFERED**

• **Dental Assisting/Assistant** *1210 hrs./$23,395* • **Massage Therapy/Therapeutic Massage** *1310 hrs./$24,241* • **Medical Insurance Specialist/Medical Biller** *1210 hrs./$23,274* • **Medical/Clinical Assistant** *1210 hrs./$23,950* • **Pharmacy Technician/Assistant** *1210 hrs./$2377* • **Surgical Technology/Technologist** *1620 hrs./$27,595*

**STUDENT SERVICES** Placement services for program completers.

## Allied College South

645 Gravois Bluffs Boulevard, Fenton, MO 63026
http://www.hightechinstitute.edu/

**CONTACT** Suzanne Marshall-Caby, Campus President
**Telephone:** 636-326-7300

**GENERAL INFORMATION** Private Institution. **Total program enrollment:** 448. **Application fee:** $50.

**PROGRAM(S) OFFERED**

• **Criminal Justice/Police Science** *1260 hrs./$26,789* • **Dental Assisting/Assistant** *1210 hrs./$23,398* • **Massage Therapy/Therapeutic Massage** *1310 hrs./$24,241* • **Medical Insurance Specialist/Medical Biller** *720 hrs./$11,316* • **Medical/Clinical Assistant** *1236 hrs./$23,950* • **Pharmacy Technician/Assistant** *3 students enrolled*

**STUDENT SERVICES** Placement services for program completers.

## American College of Hair Design

1400 South Limit, Sedalia, MO 65301

**CONTACT** Tahereh Benscoter, President
**Telephone:** 660-827-3295

**GENERAL INFORMATION** Private Institution. Founded 1961. **Total program enrollment:** 43. **Application fee:** $100.

**PROGRAM(S) OFFERED**

• **Aesthetician/Esthetician and Skin Care Specialist** *750 hrs./$5250* • **Cosmetology, Barber/Styling, and Nail Instructor** *600 hrs./$3702* • **Cosmetology/Cosmetologist, General** *1500 hrs./$9830*

**STUDENT SERVICES** Employment services for current students, placement services for program completers.

## Andrews Academy of Cosmetology

100 W. Main Street, Sullivan, MO 63080

**CONTACT** Annette S. Hill, Owner
**Telephone:** 573-468-3864

**GENERAL INFORMATION** Private Institution. **Total program enrollment:** 30. **Application fee:** $150.

**PROGRAM(S) OFFERED**

• **Cosmetology, Barber/Styling, and Nail Instructor** *600 hrs./$4675* • **Cosmetology/Cosmetologist, General** *1500 hrs./$10,475* • **Nail Technician/Specialist and Manicurist** *400 hrs./$3042*

**STUDENT SERVICES** Academic or career counseling.

## Aviation Institute of Maintenance–Kansas City

3130 Terrace Street, Kansas City, MO 64111
http://www.aviationmaintenance.edu/aviation-kansascity.asp

**CONTACT** David Meierotto
**Telephone:** 816-753-9920

**GENERAL INFORMATION** Private Institution. **Total program enrollment:** 117. **Application fee:** $25.

**STUDENT SERVICES** Academic or career counseling, employment services for current students, placement services for program completers.

## Baptist Bible College

628 East Kearney Street, Springfield, MO 65803-3498
http://www.gobbc.edu/

**CONTACT** Joseph Gleason, Registrar
**Telephone:** 417-268-6060

**GENERAL INFORMATION** Private Institution. Founded 1950. **Accreditation:** Regional (NCA); state accredited or approved. **Total program enrollment:** 454. **Application fee:** $40.

**PROGRAM(S) OFFERED**
• **Religion/Religious Studies** *3 students enrolled*

**STUDENT SERVICES** Academic or career counseling, daycare for children of students, employment services for current students, placement services for program completers, remedial services.

## Boonslick Area Vocational-Technical School

1694 Ashley Road, Boonville, MO 65233
http://www.btec.boonville.k12.mo.us/

**CONTACT** Dr. Paul E. Wootten, Director
**Telephone:** 660-882-5306

**GENERAL INFORMATION** Public Institution. Founded 1974. **Total program enrollment:** 26. **Application fee:** $30.

**PROGRAM(S) OFFERED**
• **Licensed Practical/Vocational Nurse Training (LPN, LVN, Cert, Dipl, AAS)** *1309 hrs./$11,080*

**STUDENT SERVICES** Academic or career counseling, employment services for current students, placement services for program completers, remedial services.

## Bryan College

237 South Florence Avenue, Springfield, MO 65806-2507

**CONTACT** Brian Stewart, President
**Telephone:** 417-862-5700

**GENERAL INFORMATION** Private Institution. **Total program enrollment:** 140. **Application fee:** $30.

**PROGRAM(S) OFFERED**
• **Animation, Interactive Technology, Video Graphics and Special Effects** • **Business Administration and Management, General** *1 student enrolled* • **Computer Programming/Programmer, General** • **Computer Systems Networking and Telecommunications** • **Health and Physical Education/Fitness, Other** *1 student enrolled* • **Medical Office Assistant/Specialist** *4 students enrolled* • **Tourism and Travel Services Management** *1 student enrolled*

**STUDENT SERVICES** Academic or career counseling, employment services for current students, placement services for program completers.

## Calvary Bible College and Theological Seminary

15800 Calvary Road, Kansas City, MO 64147-1341
http://www.calvary.edu/

**CONTACT** Elwood H. Chipchase, President
**Telephone:** 816-322-0110

**GENERAL INFORMATION** Private Institution. Founded 1932. **Accreditation:** Regional (NCA); state accredited or approved. **Total program enrollment:** 198. **Application fee:** $25.

**PROGRAM(S) OFFERED**
• **Bible/Biblical Studies** *3 students enrolled*

**STUDENT SERVICES** Academic or career counseling, employment services for current students, placement services for program completers, remedial services.

## Cape Girardeau Area Vocational Technical School

301 North Clark Avenue, Cape Girardeau, MO 63701
http://www.capectc.org/

**CONTACT** Rich Payne, Director
**Telephone:** 573-334-0826 Ext. 152

**GENERAL INFORMATION** Public Institution. Founded 1967. **Total program enrollment:** 61. **Application fee:** $20.

**PROGRAM(S) OFFERED**
• **Architectural Drafting and Architectural CAD/CADD** *6 students enrolled* • **Computer Systems Networking and Telecommunications** *900 hrs./$4150* • **Cooking and Related Culinary Arts, General** *3 students enrolled* • **Electrical/Electronics Equipment Installation and Repair, General** *900 hrs./$4150* • **Electrician** *900 hrs./$4150* • **Emergency Medical Technology/Technician (EMT Paramedic)** *1100 hrs./$4475* • **General Office Occupations and Clerical Services** *7 students enrolled* • **Licensed Practical/Vocational Nurse Training (LPN, LVN, Cert, Dipl, AAS)** *1320 hrs./$6462* • **Radio and Television Broadcasting Technology/Technician** *2 students enrolled* • **Respiratory Care Therapy/Therapist** *1320 hrs./$7286*

**STUDENT SERVICES** Academic or career counseling, employment services for current students, placement services for program completers, remedial services.

## Central Bible College

3000 North Grant Avenue, Springfield, MO 65803-1096
http://www.cbcag.edu/

**CONTACT** Gary A. Denbow, President
**Telephone:** 417-833-2551

**GENERAL INFORMATION** Private Institution. Founded 1922. **Accreditation:** State accredited or approved. **Total program enrollment:** 561. **Application fee:** $25.

**PROGRAM(S) OFFERED**
• **Bible/Biblical Studies**

**STUDENT SERVICES** Academic or career counseling, employment services for current students, placement services for program completers, remedial services.

## Central College of Cosmetology

Business Loop I44, St. Robert, MO 65583

**CONTACT** Joseph A. Nicholson, President
**Telephone:** 573-336-3888

**GENERAL INFORMATION** Private Institution. **Total program enrollment:** 81. **Application fee:** $100.

**PROGRAM(S) OFFERED**
• **Cosmetology and Related Personal Grooming Arts, Other** • **Cosmetology, Barber/Styling, and Nail Instructor** *600 hrs./$3100* • **Cosmetology/Cosmetologist, General** *1500 hrs./$7700* • **Nail Technician/Specialist and Manicurist** *400 hrs./$1900* • **Personal and Culinary Services, Other**

**STUDENT SERVICES** Academic or career counseling, employment services for current students, placement services for program completers.

## Chillicothe Beauty Academy

505 Elm Street, Chillicothe, MO 64601
http://www.chillicothecosmetology.com/

**CONTACT** Loolah W.D. Cox, Owner
**Telephone:** 660-646-4198

**GENERAL INFORMATION** Private Institution. Founded 1962. **Total program enrollment:** 17. **Application fee:** $100.

**PROGRAM(S) OFFERED**
• **Cosmetology, Barber/Styling, and Nail Instructor** • **Cosmetology/Cosmetologist, General** *1500 hrs./$12,500* • **Nail Technician/Specialist and Manicurist**

**STUDENT SERVICES** Academic or career counseling.

## Clinton Technical School

Fifth & Wilson, Clinton, MO 64735
http://clinton.k12.mo.us/

**CONTACT** Richard Wells, Director
**Telephone:** 660-885-6101

**GENERAL INFORMATION** Public Institution. **Total program enrollment:** 2.

**PROGRAM(S) OFFERED**
• **Computer Technology/Computer Systems Technology** • **General Office Occupations and Clerical Services** • **Heating, Air Conditioning, Ventilation and Refrigeration Maintenance Technology/Technician (HAC, HACR, HVAC, HVACR)** • **Machine Tool Technology/Machinist** • **Welding Technology/Welder**

**STUDENT SERVICES** Academic or career counseling, employment services for current students, placement services for program completers.

## Colorado Technical University North Kansas City

520 East 19th Avenue, North Kansas City, MO 64116
http://kc.coloradotech.edu/

**CONTACT** Paul Goddard, President
**Telephone:** 816-472-0275

**GENERAL INFORMATION** Private Institution. Founded 1992. **Accreditation:** Radiologic technology: radiography (JRCERT); state accredited or approved. **Total program enrollment:** 338. **Application fee:** $50.

**PROGRAM(S) OFFERED**
• **Health Information/Medical Records Technology/Technician** *15 students enrolled* • **Licensed Practical/Vocational Nurse Training (LPN, LVN, Cert, Dipl, AAS)** *33 students enrolled*

**STUDENT SERVICES** Academic or career counseling, employment services for current students, placement services for program completers, remedial services.

## Columbia Area Vocational Technical School

4203 South Providence Road, Columbia, MO 65203
http://www.career-center.org/

**CONTACT** Arden Boyer-Stephens, Director, Career, Technical & Adult Education
**Telephone:** 573-214-3809

**GENERAL INFORMATION** Private Institution. **Total program enrollment:** 38. **Application fee:** $50.

**PROGRAM(S) OFFERED**
• **Administrative Assistant and Secretarial Science, General** *600 hrs./$2400* • **Computer/Information Technology Services Administration and Management, Other** *600 hrs./$4400* • **Construction Trades, Other** *600 hrs./$2990* • **Electrician** *600 hrs./$2990* • **Licensed Practical/Vocational Nurse Training (LPN, LVN, Cert, Dipl, AAS)** *1485 hrs./$11,052* • **Surgical Technology/Technologist** *1416 hrs./$9140*

**STUDENT SERVICES** Academic or career counseling, employment services for current students, placement services for program completers, remedial services.

## Concorde Career Institute

3239 Broadway, Kansas City, MO 64111-2407
http://www.concordecareercolleges.com/

**CONTACT** Deborah Crow, Campus President
**Telephone:** 816-531-5223

**GENERAL INFORMATION** Private Institution. Founded 1983. **Accreditation:** Dental assisting (ADA); respiratory therapy technology (CoARC); state accredited or approved. **Total program enrollment:** 705.

**PROGRAM(S) OFFERED**
• **Dental Assisting/Assistant** *915 hrs./$12,175* • **Health and Medical Administrative Services, Other** *740 hrs./$11,564* • **Licensed Practical/Vocational Nurse Training (LPN, LVN, Cert, Dipl, AAS)** *1611 hrs./$21,517* • **Medical/Clinical Assistant** *740 hrs./$12,610* • **Respiratory Care Therapy/Therapist** *1695 hrs./$21,688* • **Respiratory Therapy Technician/Assistant** *1605 hrs./$23,084*

**STUDENT SERVICES** Academic or career counseling, employment services for current students, placement services for program completers, remedial services.

## Cosmetology Concepts Institute

217 North Ninth Street, Columbia, MO 65201
http://www.cosmetology-concepts.com/

**CONTACT** Terry Robb, Owner
**Telephone:** 573-449-7527

**GENERAL INFORMATION** Private Institution. Founded 1974. **Total program enrollment:** 47. **Application fee:** $100.

**PROGRAM(S) OFFERED**
• **Aesthetician/Esthetician and Skin Care Specialist** *1200 hrs./$7300* • **Cosmetology and Related Personal Grooming Arts, Other** • **Cosmetology/Cosmetologist, General** *1500 hrs./$9390* • **Nail Technician/Specialist and Manicurist** *400 hrs./$2035* • **Trade and Industrial Teacher Education** *400 hrs./$2035*

**STUDENT SERVICES** Academic or career counseling.

## Cox College of Nursing and Health Sciences

1423 North Jefferson, Springfield, MO 65802
http://www.coxcollege.edu/

**CONTACT** Dr. Anne Brett, President
**Telephone:** 417-269-3401

**GENERAL INFORMATION** Private Institution. Founded 1994. **Accreditation:** Regional (NCA). **Total program enrollment:** 206. **Application fee:** $45.

**PROGRAM(S) OFFERED**
• **Health Information/Medical Records Technology/Technician** *7 students enrolled* • **Medical Transcription/Transcriptionist** *15 students enrolled*

**STUDENT SERVICES** Academic or career counseling, daycare for children of students, remedial services.

## Crowder College

601 Laclede Avenue, Neosho, MO 64850-9160
http://www.crowder.edu/

**CONTACT** Alan Marble, President
**Telephone:** 417-451-3223

**GENERAL INFORMATION** Public Institution. Founded 1963. **Accreditation:** Regional (NCA). **Total program enrollment:** 1623. **Application fee:** $25.

**PROGRAM(S) OFFERED**
• **Agricultural Mechanization, Other** • **Agricultural Power Machinery Operation** • **Autobody/Collision and Repair Technology/Technician** • **Automobile/Automotive Mechanics Technology/Technician** • **Automotive Engineering Technology/Technician** *1 student enrolled* • **Computer Systems Analysis/Analyst** • **General Office Occupations and Clerical Services** • **Truck and Bus Driver/Commercial Vehicle Operation** *64 students enrolled*

**STUDENT SERVICES** Academic or career counseling, employment services for current students, placement services for program completers, remedial services.

## Divas Unlimited Academy

3306 Brown Road, St Louis, MO 63114

**CONTACT** Jane Hilton, President
**Telephone:** 314-428-3482

**GENERAL INFORMATION** Private Institution. **Total program enrollment:** 8. **Application fee:** $25.

**PROGRAM(S) OFFERED**
• **Aesthetician/Esthetician and Skin Care Specialist** *750 hrs./$5000* • **Cosmetology and Related Personal Grooming Arts, Other** *5 students enrolled* • **Cosmetology, Barber/Styling, and Nail Instructor** *600 hrs./$2800* • **Cosmetology/Cosmetologist, General** *1500 hrs./$11,850* • **Nail Technician/Specialist and Manicurist**

**STUDENT SERVICES** Placement services for program completers.

## East Central College

1964 Prairie Dell Road, Union, MO 63084
http://www.eastcentral.edu/

**CONTACT** Dr. Edward Jackson, President
**Telephone:** 636-583-5193

**GENERAL INFORMATION** Public Institution. Founded 1959. **Accreditation:** Regional (NCA). **Total program enrollment:** 1635.

**PROGRAM(S) OFFERED**
• **Accounting Technology/Technician and Bookkeeping** *1 student enrolled* • **Automobile/Automotive Mechanics Technology/Technician** *6 students enrolled* • **Business Operations Support and Secretarial Services, Other** *34 students enrolled* • **Business, Management, Marketing, and Related Support Services, Other** *23 students enrolled* • **Commercial and Advertising Art** *35 students enrolled* • **Computer Systems Networking and Telecommunications** *1 student enrolled* • **Construction Trades, General** • **Culinary Arts/Chef Training** *4 students enrolled* • **Drafting and Design Technology/Technician, General** *2 students enrolled* • **Emergency Medical Technology/Technician (EMT Paramedic)** *17 students enrolled* • **Fire Science/Firefighting** • **Heating, Air Conditioning, Ventilation and Refrigeration Maintenance Technology/Technician (HAC, HACR, HVAC, HVACR)** *7 students enrolled* • **Heavy/Industrial Equipment Maintenance Technologies, Other** *10 students enrolled* • **Legal Administrative Assistant/Secretary** *4 students enrolled* • **Machine Tool Technology/Machinist** *17 students enrolled* • **Medical Administrative/Executive Assistant and Medical Secretary** *13 students enrolled* • **Welding Technology/Welder**

**STUDENT SERVICES** Academic or career counseling, employment services for current students, placement services for program completers, remedial services.

## Elaine Steven Beauty College

2208 Chambers Road, St. Louis, MO 63136
http://www.elainestevenbeautycollege.com/

**CONTACT** Gina Kinion, President
**Telephone:** 314-868-8196

**GENERAL INFORMATION** Private Institution. Founded 1962. **Total program enrollment:** 150.

**PROGRAM(S) OFFERED**
• **Aesthetician/Esthetician and Skin Care Specialist** *750 hrs./$9550* • **Cosmetology, Barber/Styling, and Nail Instructor** *600 hrs./$1900* • **Cosmetology/Cosmetologist, General** *1500 hrs./$14,525* • **Nail Technician/Specialist and Manicurist** *400 hrs./$1600*

**STUDENT SERVICES** Academic or career counseling, placement services for program completers, remedial services.

## Eldon Career Center

Second and Pine, Eldon, MO 65026
http://www.eldoncareercenter.org/

**CONTACT** Willard Haley, Director
**Telephone:** 573-392-8060

**GENERAL INFORMATION** Public Institution. Founded 1968. **Total program enrollment:** 16. **Application fee:** $80.

**PROGRAM(S) OFFERED**
• **Autobody/Collision and Repair Technology/Technician** • **Automobile/Automotive Mechanics Technology/Technician** • **Building/Property Maintenance and Management** *1032 hrs./$2080* • **Business, Management, Marketing, and Related Support Services, Other** *1032 hrs./$2080* • **Business/Commerce, General** • **Construction Trades, Other** • **Drafting and Design Technology/Technician, General** • **Drafting/Design Engineering Technologies/Technicians, Other** *1032 hrs./$2080* • **Electrical/Electronics Maintenance and Repair Technology, Other** • **Graphic and Printing Equipment Operator, General Production** • **Licensed Practical/Vocational Nurse Training (LPN, LVN, Cert, Dipl, AAS)** *1480 hrs./$8400* • **Marine Maintenance/Fitter and Ship Repair Technology/Technician** • **Marine Transportation, Other** *1032 hrs./$2080*

**STUDENT SERVICES** Academic or career counseling, employment services for current students, placement services for program completers, remedial services.

## Everest College

3420 Rider Trail South, Earth City, MO 63045
http://www.everest.edu/

**CONTACT** Varghese Samuel, President
**Telephone:** 314-739-7333

**GENERAL INFORMATION** Private Institution. **Total program enrollment:** 370.

**PROGRAM(S) OFFERED**
• **Accounting Technology/Technician and Bookkeeping** *24 students enrolled* • **Accounting** *600 hrs./$10,775* • **Allied Health and Medical Assisting Services, Other** *125 students enrolled* • **Massage Therapy/Therapeutic Massage** *750 hrs./$14,790* • **Medical Administrative/Executive Assistant and Medical Secretary** *720 hrs./$13,526* • **Medical Insurance Specialist/Medical Biller** *720 hrs./$13,526* • **Medical Office Assistant/Specialist** *720 hrs./$14,541*

**STUDENT SERVICES** Employment services for current students, placement services for program completers.

## Everest College

1010 West Sunshine, Springfield, MO 65807-2488
http://www.everest.edu/campus/springfield

**CONTACT** Gary L. Myers, President
**Telephone:** 417-864-7220

**GENERAL INFORMATION** Private Institution. Founded 1976. **Accreditation:** Medical assisting (AAMAE); state accredited or approved. **Total program enrollment:** 343.

**PROGRAM(S) OFFERED**
• **Accounting** *4 students enrolled* • **Dental Assisting/Assistant** *23 students enrolled* • **Medical Insurance Coding Specialist/Coder** *1 student enrolled* • **Medical Office Assistant/Specialist** *28 students enrolled* • **Medical Transcription/Transcriptionist** *17 students enrolled*

**STUDENT SERVICES** Academic or career counseling, employment services for current students, placement services for program completers, remedial services.

## Fontbonne University

6800 Wydown Boulevard, St. Louis, MO 63105-3098
http://www.fontbonne.edu/

**CONTACT** Dennis C. Golden, President
**Telephone:** 314-862-3456

**GENERAL INFORMATION** Private Institution. Founded 1917. **Accreditation:** Regional (NCA); home economics (AAFCS); speech-language pathology (ASHA). **Total program enrollment:** 1990. **Application fee:** $25.

**PROGRAM(S) OFFERED**
• **General Merchandising, Sales, and Related Marketing Operations, Other** • **Selling Skills and Sales Operations** • **Spanish Language and Literature**

**STUDENT SERVICES** Academic or career counseling, employment services for current students, placement services for program completers, remedial services.

## Four Rivers Area Vocational-Technical School

550 East 11th Street, Washington, MO 63090
http://www.washington.k12.mo.us/schools/frcc/index.htm/

**CONTACT** Randy Kosark, Director
**Telephone:** 636-231-2131

**GENERAL INFORMATION** Public Institution. Founded 1966. **Total program enrollment:** 30.

**PROGRAM(S) OFFERED**
• **Autobody/Collision and Repair Technology/Technician** *2 students enrolled* • **Graphic Communications, General** • **Licensed Practical/Vocational Nurse Training (LPN, LVN, Cert, Dipl, AAS)** *30 students enrolled*

**STUDENT SERVICES** Academic or career counseling, employment services for current students, placement services for program completers.

## Franklin Technology Center

2020 Iowa Street, Joplin, MO 64804
http://ftcjoplin.com/

**CONTACT** Mark Lynch, Assistant Director
**Telephone:** 417-659-4400

**GENERAL INFORMATION** Private Institution. **Total program enrollment:** 217. **Application fee:** $50.

**PROGRAM(S) OFFERED**
• **Autobody/Collision and Repair Technology/Technician** *8 students enrolled* • **Automobile/Automotive Mechanics Technology/Technician** *4 students enrolled* • **Dental Assisting/Assistant** *13 students enrolled* • **General Office Occupations and Clerical Services** *900 hrs./$6150* • **Graphic and Printing Equipment Operator, General Production** *3 students enrolled* • **Health Information/Medical Records Technology/Technician** *20 students enrolled* • **Heating, Air Conditioning, Ventilation and Refrigeration Maintenance Technology/Technician (HAC, HACR, HVAC, HVACR)** *1050 hrs./$6170* • **Licensed Practical/Vocational Nurse Training (LPN, LVN, Cert, Dipl, AAS)** *1264 hrs./$9442* • **Machine Tool Technology/Machinist** *2 students enrolled* • **Medical/Clinical Assistant** *900 hrs./$7695* • **Pharmacy Technician/Assistant** *8 students enrolled* • **Respiratory Care Therapy/Therapist** *19 students enrolled* • **Surgical Technology/Technologist** *1090 hrs./$7377* • **Veterinary/Animal Health Technology/Technician and Veterinary Assistant** *900 hrs./$6430* • **Welding Technology/Welder** *9 students enrolled*

**STUDENT SERVICES** Academic or career counseling, placement services for program completers, remedial services.

## Grabber School of Hair Design

14560 Manchester, Suite 25, Ballwin, MO 63011

**CONTACT** Dennis Matteuzzi, Owner
**Telephone:** 314-428-0004

**GENERAL INFORMATION** Private Institution. **Total program enrollment:** 70.

**PROGRAM(S) OFFERED**
• **Cosmetology/Cosmetologist, General** *1500 hrs./$13,900* • **Nail Technician/Specialist and Manicurist** *400 hrs./$1550*

## Grand River Technical School

1200 Fair Street, Chillicothe, MO 64601
http://www.grts.org/

**CONTACT** Ron Wolf, Director
**Telephone:** 660-646-3414

**GENERAL INFORMATION** Private Institution. **Total program enrollment:** 78. **Application fee:** $100.

**PROGRAM(S) OFFERED**
• **Autobody/Collision and Repair Technology/Technician** *8 students enrolled* • **Automobile/Automotive Mechanics Technology/Technician** *3 students enrolled* • **Carpentry/Carpenter** *3 students enrolled* • **Child Care Provider/Assistant** *1 student enrolled* • **Diesel Mechanics Technology/Technician** *7 students enrolled* • **Electrical/Electronics Equipment Installation and Repair, General** *6 students enrolled* • **Emergency Medical Technology/Technician (EMT Paramedic)** *14 students enrolled* • **General Office Occupations and Clerical Services** *3 students enrolled* • **Health Aide** • **Industrial Mechanics and Maintenance Technology** *4 students enrolled* • **Welding Technology/Welder** *5 students enrolled*

**STUDENT SERVICES** Academic or career counseling, daycare for children of students, employment services for current students, placement services for program completers.

## Hair Academy 110

110 N. Franklin Street, Kirksville, MO 63501

**CONTACT** Tina M. Miller, Director
**Telephone:** 660-665-1028

**GENERAL INFORMATION** Private Institution. **Total program enrollment:** 28. **Application fee:** $50.

**PROGRAM(S) OFFERED**
• **Cosmetology, Barber/Styling, and Nail Instructor** *600 hrs./$3350* • **Cosmetology/Cosmetologist, General** *1500 hrs./$8980* • **Nail Technician/Specialist and Manicurist** *400 hrs./$2275*

**STUDENT SERVICES** Academic or career counseling, placement services for program completers.

## Hannibal Career and Technical Center

4500 McMasters Avenue, Hannibal, MO 63401
http://www.hannibal.tec.mo.us/

**CONTACT** Roger McGregor, Director
**Telephone:** 573-221-4430

**GENERAL INFORMATION** Public Institution. **Total program enrollment:** 27. **Application fee:** $15.

**PROGRAM(S) OFFERED**
• **Agriculture, General** • **Automobile/Automotive Mechanics Technology/Technician** *930 hrs./$4600* • **Business Administration, Management and Operations, Other** *930 hrs./$4600* • **Carpentry/Carpenter** • **Child Care Provider/Assistant** *930 hrs./$4600* • **Civil Engineering Technology/Technician** • **Computer Technology/Computer Systems Technology** • **Drafting and Design Technology/Technician, General** • **Health Aide** • **Industrial Mechanics and Maintenance Technology** *930 hrs./$4600* • **Licensed Practical/Vocational Nurse Training (LPN, LVN, Cert, Dipl, AAS)** *1500 hrs./$7980* • **Machine Tool Technology/Machinist** *930 hrs./$4600* • **Welding Technology/Welder**

**STUDENT SERVICES** Academic or career counseling, employment services for current students, placement services for program completers, remedial services.

## Hannibal-LaGrange College

2800 Palmyra Road, Hannibal, MO 63401-1999
http://www.hlg.edu/

**CONTACT** Woodrow Burt, President
**Telephone:** 573-221-3675

**GENERAL INFORMATION** Private Institution. Founded 1858. **Accreditation:** Regional (NCA). **Total program enrollment:** 841. **Application fee:** $25.

**STUDENT SERVICES** Academic or career counseling, employment services for current students, placement services for program completers.

## Heritage College

534 East 99th Street, Kansas City, MO 64131-4203
http://www.heritage-education.com/

**CONTACT** Larry Cartmill, Director
**Telephone:** 816-942-5474

**GENERAL INFORMATION** Private Institution. **Accreditation:** State accredited or approved. **Total program enrollment:** 702.

**PROGRAM(S) OFFERED**
• **Allied Health and Medical Assisting Services, Other** *94 hrs./$21,605* • **Health and Physical Education/Fitness, Other** *96 hrs./$19,431* • **Massage Therapy/Therapeutic Massage** *102 hrs./$21,450* • **Medical/Clinical Assistant** • **Pharmacy Technician/Assistant** *54 hrs./$12,039*

**STUDENT SERVICES** Academic or career counseling, employment services for current students, placement services for program completers.

## Hickey College

940 West Port Plaza, Suite 101, St. Louis, MO 63146
http://www.hickeycollege.edu/

**CONTACT** Christopher A. Gearin, President
**Telephone:** 314-434-2212 Ext. 125

**GENERAL INFORMATION** Private Institution. Founded 1933. **Accreditation:** State accredited or approved. **Total program enrollment:** 359. **Application fee:** $50.

**PROGRAM(S) OFFERED**
• **Accounting Technology/Technician and Bookkeeping** *21 students enrolled* • **Administrative Assistant and Secretarial Science, General** *44 students enrolled* • **Commercial and Advertising Art** *13 students enrolled* • **Computer and Information Sciences, General** *1 student enrolled* • **Legal Administrative Assistant/Secretary** *13 students enrolled*

**STUDENT SERVICES** Academic or career counseling, employment services for current students, placement services for program completers.

## High-Tech Institute

9001 State Line Road, Kansas City, MO 64114
http://www.high-techinstitute.com/

**CONTACT** Marilyn Knight, Campus President
**Telephone:** 816-444-4300

**GENERAL INFORMATION** Private Institution. Founded 2003. **Accreditation:** State accredited or approved. **Total program enrollment:** 192. **Application fee:** $50.

**PROGRAM(S) OFFERED**
• **Dental Assisting/Assistant** *720 hrs./$11,340* • **Massage Therapy/Therapeutic Massage** *820 hrs./$11,793* • **Medical Insurance Specialist/Medical Biller** *720 hrs./$11,316* • **Medical/Clinical Assistant** *746 hrs./$11,550* • **Surgical Technology/Technologist** *1160 hrs./$23,281*

**STUDENT SERVICES** Placement services for program completers.

## House of Heavilin Beauty College

12020 Blue Ridge Boulevard, Grandview, MO 64030
http://kc-hair.com/

**CONTACT** Jerry Heavilin, President
**Telephone:** 816-523-2471

**GENERAL INFORMATION** Private Institution. **Total program enrollment:** 42.

**PROGRAM(S) OFFERED**
• **Cosmetology, Barber/Styling, and Nail Instructor** *600 hrs./$1500* • **Cosmetology/Cosmetologist, General** *1500 hrs./$10,850* • **Nail Technician/Specialist and Manicurist**

**STUDENT SERVICES** Academic or career counseling, employment services for current students, placement services for program completers.

## House of Heavilin Beauty College

5720 Troost Avenue, Kansas City, MO 64110-2826
http://kc-hair.com/

**CONTACT** Jerry Heavilin, President
**Telephone:** 816-523-2471

**GENERAL INFORMATION** Private Institution. Founded 1953. **Total program enrollment:** 43.

**PROGRAM(S) OFFERED**
• **Cosmetology, Barber/Styling, and Nail Instructor** *600 hrs./$1695* • **Cosmetology/Cosmetologist, General** *1500 hrs./$11,700*

**STUDENT SERVICES** Academic or career counseling, employment services for current students, placement services for program completers.

## House of Heavilin Beauty School

1405 Smith, Blue Springs, MO 64015
http://kc-hair.com/

**CONTACT** Shara Burgess, Administrative Assistant
**Telephone:** 816-229-9000

**GENERAL INFORMATION** Private Institution. **Total program enrollment:** 118.

**PROGRAM(S) OFFERED**
• **Aesthetician/Esthetician and Skin Care Specialist** *750 hrs./$7150* • **Cosmetology, Barber/Styling, and Nail Instructor** *600 hrs./$1500*

• **Cosmetology/Cosmetologist, General** *1500 hrs./$11,700* • **Nail Technician/Specialist and Manicurist** *400 hrs./$1250*

**STUDENT SERVICES** Academic or career counseling, placement services for program completers.

## Independence College of Cosmetology

815 West 23rd Street, Independence, MO 64055
http://www.hair-skin-nails.com/

**CONTACT** Linda Clifford, Director
**Telephone:** 816-252-4247

**GENERAL INFORMATION** Private Institution. Founded 1960. **Total program enrollment:** 70. **Application fee:** $100.

**PROGRAM(S) OFFERED**
• **Aesthetician/Esthetician and Skin Care Specialist** *1500 hrs./$9368* • **Cosmetology and Related Personal Grooming Arts, Other** *22 students enrolled* • **Cosmetology, Barber/Styling, and Nail Instructor** *600 hrs./$3403* • **Cosmetology/Cosmetologist, General** *1500 hrs./$10,750* • **Teacher Education and Professional Development, Specific Subject Areas, Other** *2 students enrolled*

**STUDENT SERVICES** Academic or career counseling, placement services for program completers.

## Jefferson College

1000 Viking Drive, Hillsboro, MO 63050-2441
http://www.jeffco.edu/

**CONTACT** Wayne Watts, President
**Telephone:** 636-797-3000

**GENERAL INFORMATION** Public Institution. Founded 1963. **Accreditation:** Regional (NCA). **Total program enrollment:** 2694. **Application fee:** $20.

**PROGRAM(S) OFFERED**
• **Accounting Technology/Technician and Bookkeeping** *8 students enrolled* • **Administrative Assistant and Secretarial Science, General** *6 students enrolled* • **Automobile/Automotive Mechanics Technology/Technician** *2 students enrolled* • **Business/Commerce, General** • **CAD/CADD Drafting and/or Design Technology/Technician** • **Child Care and Support Services Management** *2 students enrolled* • **Civil Engineering Technology/Technician** • **Criminal Justice/Police Science** • **Emergency Medical Technology/Technician (EMT Paramedic)** *6 students enrolled* • **Fire Protection and Safety Technology/Technician** *47 students enrolled* • **Health Aide** • **Heating, Air Conditioning, Ventilation and Refrigeration Maintenance Technology/Technician (HAC, HACR, HVAC, HVACR)** *18 students enrolled* • **Industrial Mechanics and Maintenance Technology** • **Licensed Practical/Vocational Nurse Training (LPN, LVN, Cert, Dipl, AAS)** *69 students enrolled* • **Machine Tool Technology/Machinist** *2 students enrolled* • **Manufacturing Technology/Technician** • **Welding Technology/Welder** *3 students enrolled*

**STUDENT SERVICES** Academic or career counseling, daycare for children of students, employment services for current students, placement services for program completers, remedial services.

## Kansas City Art Institute

4415 Warwick Boulevard, Kansas City, MO 64111-1874
http://www.kcai.edu/

**CONTACT** Kathleen Collins, President
**Telephone:** 816-472-4852

**GENERAL INFORMATION** Private Institution. Founded 1885. **Accreditation:** Regional (NCA); art and design (NASAD). **Total program enrollment:** 651. **Application fee:** $35.

**PROGRAM(S) OFFERED**
• **Prepress/Desktop Publishing and Digital Imaging Design** *8 students enrolled* • **Web Page, Digital/Multimedia and Information Resources Design**

**STUDENT SERVICES** Academic or career counseling, employment services for current students, remedial services.

## Kennett Area Vocational Technical School

1400 W. Washington, Kennett, MO 63857
http://www.kennett.k12.mo.us/

**CONTACT** Terry Bruce, Director
**Telephone:** 573-717-1123

**GENERAL INFORMATION** Public Institution. **Total program enrollment:** 17. **Application fee:** $30.

**PROGRAM(S) OFFERED**
• **Licensed Practical/Vocational Nurse Training (LPN, LVN, Cert, Dipl, AAS)** *1350 hrs./$7418*

**STUDENT SERVICES** Academic or career counseling, employment services for current students, placement services for program completers.

## Kirksville Area Vocational Technical School

1103 South Cottage Grove, Kirksville, MO 63501

**CONTACT** Terri Jones, Vocational Director
**Telephone:** 660-665-2865

**GENERAL INFORMATION** Private Institution. **Total program enrollment:** 52. **Application fee:** $35.

**PROGRAM(S) OFFERED**
• **Administrative Assistant and Secretarial Science, General** *1020 hrs./$4435* • **Autobody/Collision and Repair Technology/Technician** *1 student enrolled* • **Automobile/Automotive Mechanics Technology/Technician** *5 students enrolled* • **Child Care Provider/Assistant** *1020 hrs./$4435* • **Computer Installation and Repair Technology/Technician** *1020 hrs./$4435* • **Construction Trades, Other** *1 student enrolled* • **Data Entry/Microcomputer Applications, General** *1020 hrs./$4435* • **Data Processing and Data Processing Technology/Technician** • **Graphic and Printing Equipment Operator, General Production** • **Legal Administrative Assistant/Secretary** *1 student enrolled* • **Licensed Practical/Vocational Nurse Training (LPN, LVN, Cert, Dipl, AAS)** *1337 hrs./$7490* • **Medical Administrative/Executive Assistant and Medical Secretary** *1020 hrs./$4435* • **Receptionist** *3 students enrolled*

**STUDENT SERVICES** Academic or career counseling, daycare for children of students, employment services for current students, placement services for program completers, remedial services.

## Lake Career and Technical Center

PO Box 1409, Township Road, Camdenton, MO 65020

**CONTACT** Gail White, Director
**Telephone:** 573-346-9260

**GENERAL INFORMATION** Public Institution. **Total program enrollment:** 8.

**PROGRAM(S) OFFERED**
• **Applied Horticulture/Horticultural Operations, General** • **Autobody/Collision and Repair Technology/Technician** • **Automobile/Automotive Mechanics Technology/Technician** *1 student enrolled* • **Business/Office Automation/Technology/Data Entry** • **Carpentry/Carpenter** • **Computer Technology/Computer Systems Technology** • **Culinary Arts/Chef Training** • **Graphic and Printing Equipment Operator, General Production** • **Health Aide** • **Marine Maintenance/Fitter and Ship Repair Technology/Technician** *9 students enrolled* • **Precision Metal Working, Other**

**STUDENT SERVICES** Academic or career counseling, employment services for current students, placement services for program completers, remedial services.

## Lebanon Technology and Career Center

Highway 64 Spur, Lebanon, MO 65536

**CONTACT** Keith Davis, Adult Director
**Telephone:** 417-532-5494

**GENERAL INFORMATION** Public Institution. Founded 1966. **Total program enrollment:** 38. **Application fee:** $30.

*Lebanon Technology and Career Center (continued)*

**PROGRAM(S) OFFERED**

• **Administrative Assistant and Secretarial Science, General** *1137 hrs./$3950* • **Autobody/Collision and Repair Technology/Technician** • **Automobile/Automotive Mechanics Technology/Technician** *925 hrs./$3950* • **Child Care Provider/Assistant** *925 hrs./$3950* • **Computer Technology/Computer Systems Technology** *600 hrs./$4150* • **Construction Engineering Technology/Technician** • **Licensed Practical/Vocational Nurse Training (LPN, LVN, Cert, Dipl, AAS)** *1425 hrs./$10,725* • **Machine Shop Technology/Assistant** • **Manufacturing Technology/Technician** *1 student enrolled* • **Restaurant, Culinary, and Catering Management/Manager** • **Welding Technology/Welder** *925 hrs./$4100*

**STUDENT SERVICES** Academic or career counseling, employment services for current students, placement services for program completers, remedial services.

## L'Ecole Culinaire

9811 South Forty Drive, St. Louis, MO 63124
http://www.lecoleculinaire.com/

**CONTACT** Jane McNamee, Director
**Telephone:** 314-587-2433

**GENERAL INFORMATION** Private Institution. **Total program enrollment:** 510.

**PROGRAM(S) OFFERED**

• **Cooking and Related Culinary Arts, General** *41 students enrolled*

**STUDENT SERVICES** Academic or career counseling, employment services for current students, placement services for program completers.

## Lex La-Ray Technical Center

2323 High School Drive, Lexington, MO 64067
http://www.lexington.k12.mo.us/

**CONTACT** James Judd, Superintendent
**Telephone:** 660-259-2264

**GENERAL INFORMATION** Public Institution. Founded 1975. **Total program enrollment:** 32. **Application fee:** $25.

**PROGRAM(S) OFFERED**

• **Autobody/Collision and Repair Technology/Technician** *1050 hrs./$6335* • **Automobile/Automotive Mechanics Technology/Technician** *1050 hrs./$6110* • **Carpentry/Carpenter** • **Computer Technology/Computer Systems Technology** • **Computer and Information Sciences and Support Services, Other** *1050 hrs./$6110* • **Construction Trades, Other** *1050 hrs./$6110* • **General Office Occupations and Clerical Services** *2 students enrolled* • **Licensed Practical/Vocational Nurse Training (LPN, LVN, Cert, Dipl, AAS)** *1435 hrs./$11,237* • **Machine Tool Technology/Machinist** *1 student enrolled* • **Nurse/Nursing Assistant/Aide and Patient Care Assistant** • **Welding Technology/Welder** *1050 hrs./$6270*

**STUDENT SERVICES** Academic or career counseling, employment services for current students, placement services for program completers, remedial services.

## Linn State Technical College

One Technology Drive, Linn, MO 65051-9606
http://www.linnstate.edu/

**CONTACT** Dr. Donald Claycomb, President
**Telephone:** 573-897-5000

**GENERAL INFORMATION** Public Institution. Founded 1961. **Accreditation:** Regional (NCA). **Total program enrollment:** 873.

**PROGRAM(S) OFFERED**

• **Aircraft Powerplant Technology/Technician** *3 students enrolled* • **Airframe Mechanics and Aircraft Maintenance Technology/Technician** *3 students enrolled* • **Autobody/Collision and Repair Technology/Technician** *7 students enrolled* • **Automobile/Automotive Mechanics Technology/Technician** *3 students enrolled* • **Civil Engineering Technology/Technician** • **Computer Systems Analysis/Analyst** • **Computer Systems Networking and Telecommunications** • **Construction/Heavy Equipment/Earthmoving Equipment Operation** *48 students enrolled* • **Electrician** *1 student enrolled* • **Manufacturing Technology/Technician**

**STUDENT SERVICES** Academic or career counseling, employment services for current students, placement services for program completers, remedial services.

## Massage Therapy Training Institute

9140 Ward Parkwway, Suite 100, Kansas City, MO 64114
http://www.massagetherapytraininginstitute.com/

**CONTACT** Don Farquharson, Executive Director
**Telephone:** 816-523-9140

**GENERAL INFORMATION** Private Institution. **Application fee:** $50.

**PROGRAM(S) OFFERED**

• **Health and Physical Education/Fitness, Other** *16 hrs./$6300* • **Massage Therapy/Therapeutic Massage** *37 hrs.*

**STUDENT SERVICES** Academic or career counseling, employment services for current students, placement services for program completers, remedial services.

## Merrell University of Beauty Arts and Science

1101R SW Boulevard, Jefferson City, MO 65109
http://merrelluniversity.edu/

**CONTACT** Christopher T. Elliott, School Administrator
**Telephone:** 573-635-4433 Ext. 226

**GENERAL INFORMATION** Private Institution. Founded 1985. **Total program enrollment:** 144.

**PROGRAM(S) OFFERED**

• **Aesthetician/Esthetician and Skin Care Specialist** *1200 hrs./$7530* • **Cosmetology, Barber/Styling, and Nail Instructor** *600 hrs./$1450* • **Cosmetology/Cosmetologist, General** *1500 hrs./$10,175* • **Nail Technician/Specialist and Manicurist** *400 hrs./$2950*

**STUDENT SERVICES** Academic or career counseling, employment services for current students, placement services for program completers.

## Messenger College

PO Box 4050, Joplin, MO 64803
http://www.messengercollege.edu/

**CONTACT** Ronald D. Cannon, DMin, MATS, BA, Executive Vice-President
**Telephone:** 417-624-7070 Ext. 156

**GENERAL INFORMATION** Private Institution. Founded 1987. **Accreditation:** State accredited or approved. **Total program enrollment:** 59. **Application fee:** $35.

**PROGRAM(S) OFFERED**

• **Theology and Religious Vocations, Other**

**STUDENT SERVICES** Academic or career counseling, employment services for current students, remedial services.

## Metro Business College

1732 North Kingshighway, Cape Girardeau, MO 63701
http://www.metrobusinesscollege.edu/

**CONTACT** George Holske, Chief Executive Officer
**Telephone:** 573-334-9181

**GENERAL INFORMATION** Private Institution. **Accreditation:** State accredited or approved. **Total program enrollment:** 434. **Application fee:** $25.

**PROGRAM(S) OFFERED**
• **Administrative Assistant and Secretarial Science, General** *11 students enrolled* • **Business/Office Automation/Technology/Data Entry** *30 students enrolled* • **Massage Therapy/Therapeutic Massage** *65 students enrolled* • **Medical Administrative/Executive Assistant and Medical Secretary** *75 students enrolled* • **Medical Office Assistant/Specialist** *15 students enrolled*

**STUDENT SERVICES** Academic or career counseling, employment services for current students, placement services for program completers.

## Metropolitan Community College–Blue River

20301 East 78 Highway, Independence, MO 64015
http://www.mcckc.edu/

**CONTACT** Joseph Seabrooks, President
**Telephone:** 816-655-6000

**GENERAL INFORMATION** Public Institution. Founded 1997. **Accreditation:** Regional (NCA). **Total program enrollment:** 1238.

**PROGRAM(S) OFFERED**
• **Accounting Technology/Technician and Bookkeeping** *1 student enrolled* • **Administrative Assistant and Secretarial Science, General** *1 student enrolled* • **Business Administration and Management, General** *1 student enrolled* • **Criminal Justice/Police Science** *50 students enrolled* • **Financial Planning and Services** *1 student enrolled* • **Fire Protection and Safety Technology/Technician** *51 students enrolled*

**STUDENT SERVICES** Academic or career counseling, employment services for current students, remedial services.

## Metropolitan Community College–Business & Technology Campus

1775 Universal Avenue, Kansas City, MO 64120
http://www.mcckc.edu/

**CONTACT** Deborah Goodall, President
**Telephone:** 816-482-5210

**GENERAL INFORMATION** Public Institution. Founded 1995. **Accreditation:** Regional (NCA). **Total program enrollment:** 222.

**PROGRAM(S) OFFERED**
• **Computer Programming, Specific Applications** *2 students enrolled* • **Environmental Engineering Technology/Environmental Technology** *1 student enrolled* • **Industrial Production Technologies/Technicians, Other** *90 students enrolled*

**STUDENT SERVICES** Academic or career counseling, remedial services.

## Metropolitan Community College–Longview

500 Southwest Longview Road, Lee's Summit, MO 64081-2105
http://www.mcckc.edu/

**CONTACT** Fred Grogan, President
**Telephone:** 816-672-2000

**GENERAL INFORMATION** Public Institution. Founded 1969. **Accreditation:** Regional (NCA). **Total program enrollment:** 2694.

**PROGRAM(S) OFFERED**
• **Accounting Technology/Technician and Bookkeeping** *1 student enrolled* • **Administrative Assistant and Secretarial Science, General** *2 students enrolled* • **Computer Programming, Specific Applications** *2 students enrolled* • **Geography, Other** *1 student enrolled* • **Psychiatric/Mental Health Services Technician** *1 student enrolled* • **Turf and Turfgrass Management** *2 students enrolled*

**STUDENT SERVICES** Academic or career counseling, daycare for children of students, employment services for current students, placement services for program completers, remedial services.

## Metropolitan Community College–Maple Woods

2601 Northeast Barry Road, Kansas City, MO 64156-1299
http://www.mcckc.edu/

**CONTACT** Merna Saliman, President
**Telephone:** 816-437-3000

**GENERAL INFORMATION** Public Institution. Founded 1969. **Accreditation:** Regional (NCA). **Total program enrollment:** 1880.

**PROGRAM(S) OFFERED**
• **Accounting Technology/Technician and Bookkeeping** *2 students enrolled* • **Administrative Assistant and Secretarial Science, General** *1 student enrolled* • **Computer and Information Sciences and Support Services, Other** *1 student enrolled* • **Sign Language Interpretation and Translation** *2 students enrolled*

**STUDENT SERVICES** Academic or career counseling, daycare for children of students, employment services for current students, placement services for program completers, remedial services.

## Metropolitan Community College–Penn Valley

3201 Southwest Trafficway, Kansas City, MO 64111
http://www.mcckc.edu/

**CONTACT** Bernard Franklin, President
**Telephone:** 816-759-4000

**GENERAL INFORMATION** Public Institution. Founded 1969. **Accreditation:** Regional (NCA); dental assisting (ADA); health information technology (AHIMA); physical therapy assisting (APTA); radiologic technology: radiography (JRCERT). **Total program enrollment:** 1434.

**PROGRAM(S) OFFERED**
• **Child Care Provider/Assistant** *13 students enrolled* • **Computer Programming, Specific Applications** *1 student enrolled* • **Dental Assisting/Assistant** *14 students enrolled* • **Emergency Medical Technology/Technician (EMT Paramedic)** *5 students enrolled* • **Health Information/Medical Records Technology/Technician** *16 students enrolled* • **Industrial Design** *7 students enrolled* • **Legal Assistant/Paralegal** *2 students enrolled* • **Licensed Practical/Vocational Nurse Training (LPN, LVN, Cert, Dipl, AAS)** *130 students enrolled* • **Medical Transcription/Transcriptionist** *5 students enrolled* • **Psychiatric/Mental Health Services Technician** *1 student enrolled* • **Surgical Technology/Technologist** *17 students enrolled*

**STUDENT SERVICES** Academic or career counseling, daycare for children of students, employment services for current students, placement services for program completers, remedial services.

## Metropolitan Community Colleges System

3200 Broadway, Kansas City, MO 64111-2429

**CONTACT** Jackie Snyder, Chancellor
**Telephone:** 816-759-1050

**GENERAL INFORMATION** Public Institution.

## Midwestern Baptist Theological Seminary

5001 North Oak Trafficway, Kansas City, MO 64118-4697
http://www.mbts.edu/

**CONTACT** R. Philip Roberts, PhD, President
**Telephone:** 816-414-3700

**GENERAL INFORMATION** Private Institution. Founded 1957. **Accreditation:** Regional (NCA). **Total program enrollment:** 416. **Application fee:** $25.

**PROGRAM(S) OFFERED**
• **Theology and Religious Vocations, Other** *2 students enrolled*

**STUDENT SERVICES** Academic or career counseling, employment services for current students, placement services for program completers.

## Midwest Institute

10910 Manchester Road, Kirkwood, MO 63122
http://www.midwestinstitute.com/

**CONTACT** Christine Shreffler, Director
**Telephone:** 314-965-8363

**GENERAL INFORMATION** Private Institution. Founded 1963. **Total program enrollment:** 91.

**PROGRAM(S) OFFERED**
• **Dental Assisting/Assistant** *29 hrs./$13,880* • **Heating, Air Conditioning, Ventilation and Refrigeration Maintenance Technology/Technician (HAC, HACR, HVAC, HVACR)** *37 hrs./$13,505* • **Massage Therapy/Therapeutic Massage** *10 students enrolled* • **Medical Office Assistant/Specialist** *33 hrs./$13,880* • **Medical Office Computer Specialist/Assistant** *17 students enrolled* • **Medical/Clinical Assistant** *33 hrs./$14,507* • **Pharmacy Technician/Assistant** *38 hrs./$13,880* • **Veterinary/Animal Health Technology/Technician and Veterinary Assistant** *32 hrs./$13,880*

**STUDENT SERVICES** Academic or career counseling, placement services for program completers.

## Mineral Area College

PO Box 1000, Park Hills, MO 63601-1000
http://www.mineralarea.edu/

**CONTACT** Dr. Steven Kurtz, President
**Telephone:** 573-431-4593

**GENERAL INFORMATION** Public Institution. Founded 1922. **Accreditation:** Regional (NCA). **Total program enrollment:** 1772. **Application fee:** $15.

**PROGRAM(S) OFFERED**
• **Administrative Assistant and Secretarial Science, General** *11 students enrolled* • **Applied Horticulture/Horticultural Operations, General** • **Autobody/Collision and Repair Technology/Technician** • **Automobile/Automotive Mechanics Technology/Technician** • **Business/Commerce, General** *1 student enrolled* • **Carpentry/Carpenter** • **Child Care Provider/Assistant** *2 students enrolled* • **Computer Programming/Programmer, General** • **Criminal Justice/Police Science** *34 students enrolled* • **Drafting and Design Technology/Technician, General** • **Emergency Medical Technology/Technician (EMT Paramedic)** *7 students enrolled* • **Floriculture/Floristry Operations and Management** *3 students enrolled* • **Graphic and Printing Equipment Operator, General Production** • **Heavy/Industrial Equipment Maintenance Technologies, Other** • **Licensed Practical/Vocational Nurse Training (LPN, LVN, Cert, Dipl, AAS)** *30 students enrolled* • **Nurse/Nursing Assistant/Aide and Patient Care Assistant** • **Operations Management and Supervision** *1 student enrolled* • **Radio and Television Broadcasting Technology/Technician** • **System, Networking, and LAN/WAN Management/Manager**

**STUDENT SERVICES** Academic or career counseling, employment services for current students, placement services for program completers, remedial services.

## Missouri Baptist University

One College Park Drive, St. Louis, MO 63141-8660
http://www.mobap.edu/

**CONTACT** R. Alton Lacey, President
**Telephone:** 877-434-1115

**GENERAL INFORMATION** Private Institution. Founded 1964. **Accreditation:** Regional (NCA); music (NASM). **Total program enrollment:** 1612. **Application fee:** $30.

**PROGRAM(S) OFFERED**
• **Business Administration and Management, General** • **Christian Studies** *4 students enrolled* • **Operations Management and Supervision** *1 student enrolled* • **Sport and Fitness Administration/Management** *2 students enrolled*

**STUDENT SERVICES** Academic or career counseling, employment services for current students, placement services for program completers.

## Missouri Beauty Academy

201 South Washington Street, Farmington, MO 63640

**CONTACT** Gary Schaefer, President
**Telephone:** 573-756-2730

**GENERAL INFORMATION** Private Institution. Founded 1935. **Total program enrollment:** 53. **Application fee:** $100.

**PROGRAM(S) OFFERED**
• **Adult and Continuing Education Administration** *600 hrs./$3500* • **Cosmetology/Cosmetologist, General** *50 hrs./$11,000* • **Trade and Industrial Teacher Education**

**STUDENT SERVICES** Academic or career counseling, placement services for program completers.

## Missouri College

10121 Manchester Road, St. Louis, MO 63122-1583
http://www.mocollege.com/

**CONTACT** Karl Petersen, President
**Telephone:** 314-768-7800

**GENERAL INFORMATION** Private Institution. Founded 1963. **Accreditation:** Dental assisting (ADA); state accredited or approved. **Total program enrollment:** 472. **Application fee:** $35.

**PROGRAM(S) OFFERED**
• **Administrative Assistant and Secretarial Science, General** *1 student enrolled* • **Dental Assisting/Assistant** *113 students enrolled* • **Massage Therapy/Therapeutic Massage** *77 students enrolled* • **Medical/Clinical Assistant** *167 students enrolled*

**STUDENT SERVICES** Academic or career counseling, employment services for current students, placement services for program completers.

## Missouri College of Cosmetology North

1035 W. Kearney, Springfield, MO 65803
http://www.missouricosmo.com/

**CONTACT** Jeffery Stanley, President
**Telephone:** 417-887-1501

**GENERAL INFORMATION** Private Institution. **Total program enrollment:** 150. **Application fee:** $100.

**PROGRAM(S) OFFERED**
• **Aesthetician/Esthetician and Skin Care Specialist** *750 hrs./$8400*
• **Cosmetology, Barber/Styling, and Nail Instructor** *600 hrs./$3700*
• **Cosmetology/Cosmetologist, General** *1500 hrs./$10,600* • **Nail Technician/Specialist and Manicurist** *400 hrs./$2545*

## Missouri Southern State University

3950 East Newman Road, Joplin, MO 64801-1595
http://www.mssu.edu/

**CONTACT** Dr. Bruce Speck, President
**Telephone:** 417-625-9300

**GENERAL INFORMATION** Public Institution. Founded 1937. **Accreditation:** Regional (NCA); dental hygiene (ADA); engineering technology (ABET/TAC); radiologic technology: radiography (JRCERT); respiratory therapy technology (CoARC). **Total program enrollment:** 3849. **Application fee:** $15.

**STUDENT SERVICES** Academic or career counseling, daycare for children of students, employment services for current students, placement services for program completers, remedial services.

## Missouri State University–West Plains

128 Garfield, West Plains, MO 65775
http://www.wp.missouristate.edu/

**CONTACT** Dr. Drew A. Bennett, Chancellor
**Telephone:** 417-255-7255

**GENERAL INFORMATION** Public Institution. Founded 1963. **Accreditation:** Regional (NCA). **Total program enrollment:** 1073. **Application fee:** $15.

**PROGRAM(S) OFFERED**
• **Business/Commerce, General**

**STUDENT SERVICES** Academic or career counseling, employment services for current students, placement services for program completers, remedial services.

## Missouri Tech

1167 Corporate Lake Drive, St. Louis, MO 63132-1716
http://www.motech.edu/

**CONTACT** Paul Dodge, President Owner
**Telephone:** 314-569-3600

**GENERAL INFORMATION** Private Institution. Founded 1932. **Accreditation:** State accredited or approved. **Total program enrollment:** 29.

**PROGRAM(S) OFFERED**
• **Computer Systems Networking and Telecommunications** • **Electrical/Electronics Maintenance and Repair Technology, Other**

**STUDENT SERVICES** Employment services for current students, placement services for program completers, remedial services.

## Missouri University of Science and Technology

1870 Miner Circle, Rolla, MO 65409
http://www.mst.edu/

**CONTACT** Dr. John F. Carney, III, Chancellor
**Telephone:** 573-341-4111

**GENERAL INFORMATION** Public Institution. Founded 1870. **Accreditation:** Regional (NCA); computer science (ABET/CSAC). **Total program enrollment:** 5306. **Application fee:** $35.

**PROGRAM(S) OFFERED**
• **Mining and Mineral Engineering** *3 students enrolled*

**STUDENT SERVICES** Academic or career counseling, employment services for current students, placement services for program completers.

## Missouri Western State University

4525 Downs Drive, St. Joseph, MO 64507-2294
http://www.missouriwestern.edu/

**CONTACT** Robert Vartabedian, President
**Telephone:** 816-271-4200

**GENERAL INFORMATION** Public Institution. Founded 1915. **Accreditation:** Regional (NCA); engineering technology (ABET/TAC); health information technology (AHIMA); music (NASM); physical therapy assisting (APTA). **Total program enrollment:** 3840. **Application fee:** $15.

**PROGRAM(S) OFFERED**
• **Health Information/Medical Records Technology/Technician** • **Legal Assistant/Paralegal** *10 students enrolled*

**STUDENT SERVICES** Academic or career counseling, daycare for children of students, employment services for current students, placement services for program completers, remedial services.

## Moberly Area Community College

101 College Avenue, Moberly, MO 65270-1304
http://www.macc.edu/

**CONTACT** Evelyn E. Jorgenson, President
**Telephone:** 660-263-4110

**GENERAL INFORMATION** Public Institution. Founded 1927. **Accreditation:** Regional (NCA). **Total program enrollment:** 2082.

**PROGRAM(S) OFFERED**
• **Child Care and Support Services Management** • **Computer and Information Sciences, General** • **Criminal Justice/Police Science** *29 students enrolled* • **Drafting and Design Technology/Technician, General** • **Electrical, Electronic and Communications Engineering Technology/Technician** • **General Office Occupations and Clerical Services** *2 students enrolled* • **Graphic Communications, General** • **Licensed Practical/Vocational Nurse Training (LPN, LVN, Cert, Dipl, AAS)** *31 students enrolled* • **Manufacturing Technology/Technician** • **Marketing/Marketing Management, General** *1 student enrolled* • **Welding Technology/Welder**

**STUDENT SERVICES** Academic or career counseling, employment services for current students, placement services for program completers, remedial services.

## National Academy of Beauty Arts

157 Concord Plaza, St. Louis, MO 63128

**CONTACT** Gary Schaefer, President
**Telephone:** 314-842-3616

**GENERAL INFORMATION** Private Institution. Founded 1967. **Total program enrollment:** 287. **Application fee:** $50.

**PROGRAM(S) OFFERED**
• **Aesthetician/Esthetician and Skin Care Specialist** *900 hrs./$8800* • **Cosmetology/Cosmetologist, General** *1500 hrs./$11,000* • **Trade and Industrial Teacher Education** *600 hrs./$3500*

**STUDENT SERVICES** Academic or career counseling, placement services for program completers.

## Neosho Beauty College

116 North Wood Street, Neosho, MO 64850
http://neoshobeautycollege.com/

**CONTACT** Erma Hill, President
**Telephone:** 417-451-7216

**GENERAL INFORMATION** Private Institution. Founded 1983. **Total program enrollment:** 43. **Application fee:** $50.

*Neosho Beauty College (continued)*

**PROGRAM(S) OFFERED**

• **Aesthetician/Esthetician and Skin Care Specialist** *9 students enrolled* • **Cosmetology, Barber/Styling, and Nail Instructor** *600 hrs./$1250* • **Cosmetology/Cosmetologist, General** *1500 hrs./$8850* • **Nail Technician/ Specialist and Manicurist** *400 hrs./$1450*

**STUDENT SERVICES** Academic or career counseling.

## New Dimension School of Hair Design

705 Illinois Street, Suite 12, Joplin, MO 64801

**CONTACT** Sharon A. Clements, Owner
**Telephone:** 417-782-2875

**GENERAL INFORMATION** Private Institution. Founded 1991. **Total program enrollment:** 24. **Application fee:** $100.

**PROGRAM(S) OFFERED**

• **Cosmetology and Related Personal Grooming Arts, Other** *43 students enrolled* • **Cosmetology, Barber/Styling, and Nail Instructor** *600 hrs./$786* • **Cosmetology/Cosmetologist, General** *1500 hrs./$9999* • **Nail Technician/ Specialist and Manicurist** *400 hrs./$2342*

**STUDENT SERVICES** Academic or career counseling, placement services for program completers.

## Nichols Career Center

609 Union, Jefferson City, MO 65101
http://www.jcps.k12.mo.us/education/school/school.php?sectionid=707/

**CONTACT** Mike Kriegshouser, Director
**Telephone:** 573-659-3100

**GENERAL INFORMATION** Private Institution. **Total program enrollment:** 74. **Application fee:** $15.

**PROGRAM(S) OFFERED**

• **Autobody/Collision and Repair Technology/Technician** • **Carpentry/Carpenter** • **Commercial and Advertising Art** *2 students enrolled* • **Computer Technology/ Computer Systems Technology** • **Construction Trades, General** *1050 hrs./ $3500* • **Dental Assisting/Assistant** *1167 hrs./$7600* • **Electrical/Electronics Equipment Installation and Repair, General** • **Graphic Communications, General** *1050 hrs./$3500* • **Graphic and Printing Equipment Operator, General Production** • **Heating, Air Conditioning, Ventilation and Refrigeration Maintenance Technology/Technician (HAC, HACR, HVAC, HVACR)** *1050 hrs./ $3500* • **Licensed Practical/Vocational Nurse Training (LPN, LVN, Cert, Dipl, AAS)** *1375 hrs./$10,549* • **Medical Radiologic Technology/Science—Radiation Therapist** *2834 hrs./$13,965* • **Welding Technology/Welder**

**STUDENT SERVICES** Academic or career counseling, employment services for current students, placement services for program completers, remedial services.

## North Central Missouri College

1301 Main Street, Trenton, MO 64683-1824
http://www.ncmissouri.edu/

**CONTACT** Dr. Neil Nuttall, President
**Telephone:** 660-359-3948

**GENERAL INFORMATION** Public Institution. Founded 1925. **Accreditation:** Regional (NCA). **Total program enrollment:** 821. **Application fee:** $15.

**PROGRAM(S) OFFERED**

• **Accounting Technology/Technician and Bookkeeping** *2 students enrolled* • **Agricultural Business and Management, General** • **Business Administration and Management, General** • **Business/Office Automation/Technology/Data Entry** • **Computer Programming/Programmer, General** *1 student enrolled* • **Health Information/Medical Records Technology/Technician** *4 students enrolled* • **Health Professions and Related Clinical Sciences, Other** • **Licensed Practical/Vocational Nurse Training (LPN, LVN, Cert, Dipl, AAS)** *68 students enrolled* • **Manufacturing Technology/Technician** *4 students enrolled* • **Marketing/Marketing Management, General** • **Medical Administrative/ Executive Assistant and Medical Secretary** • **Medical Transcription/ Transcriptionist** *1 student enrolled*

**STUDENT SERVICES** Academic or career counseling, employment services for current students, placement services for program completers, remedial services.

## Northwest Missouri State University

800 University Drive, Maryville, MO 64468-6001
http://www.nwmissouri.edu/

**CONTACT** Dean Hubbard, President
**Telephone:** 660-562-1212

**GENERAL INFORMATION** Public Institution. Founded 1905. **Accreditation:** Regional (NCA); home economics (AAFCS); music (NASM). **Total program enrollment:** 5541.

**PROGRAM(S) OFFERED**

• **Business Operations Support and Secretarial Services, Other** *2 students enrolled*

**STUDENT SERVICES** Academic or career counseling, employment services for current students, placement services for program completers, remedial services.

## Ozark Christian College

1111 North Main Street, Joplin, MO 64801-4804
http://www.occ.edu/

**CONTACT** Matthew Proctor, President
**Telephone:** 417-624-2518

**GENERAL INFORMATION** Private Institution. Founded 1942. **Accreditation:** State accredited or approved. **Total program enrollment:** 534. **Application fee:** $30.

**PROGRAM(S) OFFERED**

• **Bible/Biblical Studies** *7 students enrolled* • **Teaching English as a Second or Foreign Language/ESL Language Instructor** *5 students enrolled*

**STUDENT SERVICES** Academic or career counseling, remedial services.

## Ozarks Technical Community College

PO Box 5958, 1001 East Chestnut Expressway, Springfield, MO 65801
http://www.otc.edu/

**CONTACT** Hal Higdon, President
**Telephone:** 417-447-7500

**GENERAL INFORMATION** Public Institution. Founded 1990. **Accreditation:** Regional (NCA); dental assisting (ADA); dental hygiene (ADA); health information technology (AHIMA); physical therapy assisting (APTA). **Total program enrollment:** 5400.

**PROGRAM(S) OFFERED**

• **Autobody/Collision and Repair Technology/Technician** *1 student enrolled* • **Automobile/Automotive Mechanics Technology/Technician** *4 students enrolled* • **Business Administration and Management, General** *3 students enrolled* • **Child Care Provider/Assistant** *2 students enrolled* • **Culinary Arts/Chef Training** *3 students enrolled* • **Dental Assisting/Assistant** *4 students enrolled* • **Electrical, Electronic and Communications Engineering Technology/Technician** *2 students enrolled* • **Emergency Medical Technology/Technician (EMT Paramedic)** *4 students enrolled* • **Health Information/Medical Records Technology/Technician** *3 students enrolled* • **Heating, Air Conditioning and Refrigeration Technology/Technician (ACH/ACR/ACHR/HRAC/HVAC/AC Technology)** *2 students enrolled* • **Industrial Production Technologies/ Technicians, Other** *38 students enrolled* • **Instrumentation Technology/**

**Technician** *3 students enrolled* • **Licensed Practical/Vocational Nurse Training (LPN, LVN, Cert, Dipl, AAS)** *49 students enrolled* • **Management Information Systems, General** *1 student enrolled* • **Surgical Technology/Technologist** *10 students enrolled*

**STUDENT SERVICES** Academic or career counseling, daycare for children of students, employment services for current students, placement services for program completers, remedial services.

## Paris II Educational Center

6840 North Oak Trafficway, Gladstone, MO 64118
http://parisii.net/

**CONTACT** Garold Tingler, President
**Telephone:** 816-468-6666

**GENERAL INFORMATION** Private Institution. Founded 1983. **Total program enrollment:** 61.

**PROGRAM(S) OFFERED**
• **Aesthetician/Esthetician and Skin Care Specialist** *750 hrs./$6900*
• **Cosmetology, Barber/Styling, and Nail Instructor** *600 hrs./$3000*
• **Cosmetology/Cosmetologist, General** *1500 hrs./$10,575* • **Nail Technician/Specialist and Manicurist** *600 hrs./$4450* • **Teacher Education and Professional Development, Specific Subject Areas, Other** *4 students enrolled*

**STUDENT SERVICES** Academic or career counseling, employment services for current students, placement services for program completers.

## Patricia Stevens College

330 North Fourth Street, Suite 306, St. Louis, MO 63102
http://www.patriciastevenscollege.edu/

**CONTACT** Cynthia A. Musterman, President
**Telephone:** 314-421-0949 Ext. 10

**GENERAL INFORMATION** Private Institution. Founded 1947. **Accreditation:** State accredited or approved. **Total program enrollment:** 106. **Application fee:** $15.

**PROGRAM(S) OFFERED**
• **Administrative Assistant and Secretarial Science, General** *1 student enrolled*
• **Fashion Merchandising** • **Interior Design** *1 student enrolled* • **Tourism and Travel Services Management**

**STUDENT SERVICES** Academic or career counseling, employment services for current students, placement services for program completers, remedial services.

## Patsy and Robs Academy of Beauty

5065 Highway North, Cottleville, MO 63304
http://www.praob.edu

**CONTACT** Robert E. Bruner, President
**Telephone:** 636-447-0650

**GENERAL INFORMATION** Private Institution. **Total program enrollment:** 54. **Application fee:** $100.

**PROGRAM(S) OFFERED**
• **Cosmetology, Barber/Styling, and Nail Instructor** *600 hrs./$4000*
• **Cosmetology/Cosmetologist, General** *1500 hrs./$13,900* • **Nail Technician/Specialist and Manicurist** *400 hrs./$2700*

**STUDENT SERVICES** Placement services for program completers.

## Patsy and Rob's Academy of Beauty

18 NW Plaza, St. Ann, MO 63074
http://praob.edu/

**CONTACT** Robert E. Bruner, President/Director/Owner
**Telephone:** 314-298-8808

**GENERAL INFORMATION** Private Institution. Founded 1985. **Total program enrollment:** 83. **Application fee:** $100.

**PROGRAM(S) OFFERED**
• **Cosmetology, Barber/Styling, and Nail Instructor** *600 hrs./$4000*
• **Cosmetology/Cosmetologist, General** *1500 hrs./$13,900* • **Nail Technician/Specialist and Manicurist** *400 hrs./$2700*

**STUDENT SERVICES** Placement services for program completers.

## Pemiscot County Special School District

1317 W. State Highway 84, Hayti, MO 63851
http://www.pcssd.k12.mo.us

**CONTACT** Sandra Manley, Superintendent
**Telephone:** 573-359-2601

**GENERAL INFORMATION** Public Institution. **Total program enrollment:** 21. **Application fee:** $50.

**PROGRAM(S) OFFERED**
• **Licensed Practical/Vocational Nurse Training (LPN, LVN, Cert, Dipl, AAS)** *20 students enrolled*

## Pike/Lincoln Tech Center

PO Box 38, Eolia, MO 63344
http://pltc.k12.mo.us/

**CONTACT** Terry Robertson, Superintendent
**Telephone:** 573-485-2900

**GENERAL INFORMATION** Public Institution. Founded 1973. **Total program enrollment:** 49. **Application fee:** $100.

**PROGRAM(S) OFFERED**
• **Autobody/Collision and Repair Technology/Technician** *900 hrs./$5850*
• **Automobile/Automotive Mechanics Technology/Technician** *900 hrs./$5850*
• **Business/Office Automation/Technology/Data Entry** *900 hrs./$5850*
• **Carpentry/Carpenter** *1 student enrolled* • **Data Entry/Microcomputer Applications, General** • **Electrical/Electronics Equipment Installation and Repair, General** *1 student enrolled* • **General Office Occupations and Clerical Services** *2 students enrolled* • **Licensed Practical/Vocational Nurse Training (LPN, LVN, Cert, Dipl, AAS)** *1490 hrs./$8525* • **Prepress/Desktop Publishing and Digital Imaging Design** *900 hrs./$5850* • **Welding Technology/Welder** *900 hrs./$5850*

**STUDENT SERVICES** Academic or career counseling, employment services for current students, placement services for program completers, remedial services.

## Pinnacle Career Institute

1001 East 101st Terrace, Suite 325, Kansas City, MO 64134
http://www.pcitraining.edu/

**CONTACT** Barabette Hatcher, Executive Director
**Telephone:** 816-331-5700

**GENERAL INFORMATION** Private Institution. Founded 1953. **Accreditation:** State accredited or approved. **Total program enrollment:** 664. **Application fee:** $50.

**PROGRAM(S) OFFERED**
• **Athletic Training/Trainer** *85 students enrolled* • **Clinical/Medical Laboratory Assistant** • **Massage Therapy/Therapeutic Massage** *27 students enrolled*
• **Medical Insurance Coding Specialist/Coder** *103 students enrolled* • **Medical/Clinical Assistant** *39 students enrolled*

**STUDENT SERVICES** Academic or career counseling, employment services for current students, placement services for program completers, remedial services.

## Pinnacle Career Institute–North Kansas City

11500 N. Ambassador, Suite 221, Kansas City, MO 64153
http://www.pcitraining.edu

**CONTACT** Guy Genske, Executive Director
**Telephone:** 816-270-5300

**GENERAL INFORMATION** Private Institution. **Total program enrollment:** 72. **Application fee:** $50.

**PROGRAM(S) OFFERED**
• **Athletic Training/Trainer** • **Medical Insurance Coding Specialist/Coder** • **Medical/Clinical Assistant**

**STUDENT SERVICES** Academic or career counseling, employment services for current students, placement services for program completers, remedial services.

## Poplar Bluff School District–Practical Nurse Program

PO Box 47, Poplar Bluff, MO 63901
http://www.r1schools.org/

**CONTACT** Jean Winston, Director
**Telephone:** 573-785-2248

**GENERAL INFORMATION** Public Institution. Founded 1957. **Total program enrollment:** 25. **Application fee:** $40.

**PROGRAM(S) OFFERED**
• **Autobody/Collision and Repair Technology/Technician** *1044 hrs./$3700* • **Automobile/Automotive Mechanics Technology/Technician** *1044 hrs./$3700* • **Cosmetology/Cosmetologist, General** *1220 hrs./$4390* • **Heating, Air Conditioning, Ventilation and Refrigeration Maintenance Technology/ Technician (HAC, HACR, HVAC, HVACR)** *1044 hrs./$3700* • **Licensed Practical/Vocational Nurse Training (LPN, LVN, Cert, Dipl, AAS)** *1359 hrs./ $8700* • **Welding Technology/Welder** *1044 hrs./$3700*

**STUDENT SERVICES** Academic or career counseling, employment services for current students, placement services for program completers, remedial services.

## Professional Massage Training Center

229 E. Commercial, Springfield, MO 65803
http://www.pmtc.edu/

**CONTACT** Juliet Mee, President
**Telephone:** 417-863-7682

**GENERAL INFORMATION** Private Institution. **Total program enrollment:** 77. **Application fee:** $50.

**PROGRAM(S) OFFERED**
• **Massage Therapy/Therapeutic Massage** *900 hrs./$20,250*

**STUDENT SERVICES** Academic or career counseling, employment services for current students, placement services for program completers, remedial services.

## Ranken Technical College

4431 Finney Avenue, St. Louis, MO 63113
http://www.ranken.edu/

**CONTACT** Ben Ernst, President
**Telephone:** 314-371-0236

**GENERAL INFORMATION** Private Institution. Founded 1907. **Accreditation:** Regional (NCA). **Total program enrollment:** 1061. **Application fee:** $25.

**PROGRAM(S) OFFERED**
• **Autobody/Collision and Repair Technology/Technician** *18 students enrolled* • **Automobile/Automotive Mechanics Technology/Technician** *30 students enrolled* • **Business Administration and Management, General** *1 student enrolled* • **Carpentry/Carpenter** *28 students enrolled* • **Computer Engineering Technology/Technician** *1 student enrolled* • **Heating, Air Conditioning and Refrigeration Technology/Technician (ACH/ACR/ACHR/HRAC/HVAC/AC Technology)** *53 students enrolled* • **Heavy/Industrial Equipment Maintenance Technologies, Other** *12 students enrolled* • **Industrial Electronics Technology/ Technician** *36 students enrolled* • **Instrumentation Technology/Technician** *13 students enrolled* • **Machine Tool Technology/Machinist** *14 students enrolled* • **Mechanic and Repair Technologies/Technicians, Other** *14 students enrolled* • **Plumbing Technology/Plumber** *36 students enrolled* • **Welding Technology/ Welder** *25 students enrolled*

**STUDENT SERVICES** Academic or career counseling, employment services for current students, placement services for program completers, remedial services.

## Regency Beauty Institute

14133 E. US Highway 40, Kansas City, MO 64136
http://www.regencybeauty.com/

**CONTACT** J. Hayes Batson, President CEO
**Telephone:** 800-787-6456

**GENERAL INFORMATION** Private Institution. **Total program enrollment:** 100. **Application fee:** $100.

**PROGRAM(S) OFFERED**
• **Cosmetology/Cosmetologist, General** *1500 hrs./$16,011*

**STUDENT SERVICES** Academic or career counseling, placement services for program completers.

## Regency Beauty Institute

4468 Lemay Ferry Road, Mehlville, MO 64129
http://www.regencybeauty.com/

**CONTACT** J. Hayes Batson, President CEO
**Telephone:** 800-787-6456

**GENERAL INFORMATION** Private Institution. **Total program enrollment:** 47. **Application fee:** $100.

**PROGRAM(S) OFFERED**
• **Cosmetology/Cosmetologist, General** *1500 hrs./$16,011*

**STUDENT SERVICES** Academic or career counseling, placement services for program completers.

## Regency Beauty Institute

259 Salt Lick Road, St. Peters, MO 63376
http://www.regencybeauty.com/

**CONTACT** J. Hayes Batson, President CEO
**Telephone:** 800-787-6456

**GENERAL INFORMATION** Private Institution. **Total program enrollment:** 57. **Application fee:** $100.

**PROGRAM(S) OFFERED**
• **Cosmetology/Cosmetologist, General** *1500 hrs./$16,011*

**STUDENT SERVICES** Academic or career counseling, placement services for program completers.

## Rockhurst University

1100 Rockhurst Road, Kansas City, MO 64110-2561
http://www.rockhurst.edu/

**CONTACT** Rev. Thomas B. Curran, OSFS, President
**Telephone:** 816-501-4000

**GENERAL INFORMATION** Private Institution. Founded 1910. **Accreditation:** Regional (NCA); speech-language pathology (ASHA). **Total program enrollment:** 1841. **Application fee:** $25.

**PROGRAM(S) OFFERED**
• **Legal Assistant/Paralegal** *13 students enrolled*

**STUDENT SERVICES** Academic or career counseling, employment services for current students, placement services for program completers, remedial services.

## Rolla Technical Institute

1304 East Tenth Street, Rolla, MO 65401-3699
http://rolla.k12.mo.us/

**CONTACT** Jerry Giger, Superintendent
**Telephone:** 573-458-0160 Ext. 16008

**GENERAL INFORMATION** Public Institution. Founded 1967. **Total program enrollment:** 209. **Application fee:** $50.

**PROGRAM(S) OFFERED**
• **Computer Technology/Computer Systems Technology** *14 students enrolled* • **Emergency Medical Technology/Technician (EMT Paramedic)** *6 students enrolled* • **Fire Science/Firefighting** *2 students enrolled* • **Licensed Practical/Vocational Nurse Training (LPN, LVN, Cert, Dipl, AAS)** *39 students enrolled* • **Medical Administrative/Executive Assistant and Medical Secretary** *17 students enrolled* • **Respiratory Care Therapy/Therapist** *8 students enrolled*

**STUDENT SERVICES** Academic or career counseling, employment services for current students, placement services for program completers, remedial services.

## Saint Charles Community College

4601 Mid Rivers Mall Drive, St. Peters, MO 63376-0975
http://www.stchas.edu/

**CONTACT** John M. McGuire, President
**Telephone:** 636-922-8000

**GENERAL INFORMATION** Public Institution. Founded 1986. **Accreditation:** Regional (NCA); health information technology (AHIMA). **Total program enrollment:** 3736.

**PROGRAM(S) OFFERED**
• **Accounting Technology/Technician and Bookkeeping** *2 students enrolled* • **Child Care and Support Services Management** • **Computer Programming/Programmer, General** *2 students enrolled* • **Criminal Justice/Police Science** *1 student enrolled* • **Drafting and Design Technology/Technician, General** *3 students enrolled* • **Licensed Practical/Vocational Nurse Training (LPN, LVN, Cert, Dipl, AAS)** *26 students enrolled* • **Marketing/Marketing Management, General** *2 students enrolled* • **Office Management and Supervision** *10 students enrolled*

**STUDENT SERVICES** Academic or career counseling, daycare for children of students, employment services for current students, placement services for program completers, remedial services.

## St. Louis College of Health Careers

1297 North Highway Drive, Fenton, MO 63026
http://www.slchc.com/

**CONTACT** Dr. Rush L. Robinson, Academic Affairs
**Telephone:** 636-529-0000

**GENERAL INFORMATION** Private Institution. **Total program enrollment:** 130. **Application fee:** $35.

**PROGRAM(S) OFFERED**
• **Licensed Practical/Vocational Nurse Training (LPN, LVN, Cert, Dipl, AAS)** • **Massage Therapy/Therapeutic Massage** *3 students enrolled* • **Medical Insurance Specialist/Medical Biller** *5 students enrolled* • **Medical/Clinical Assistant** *33 students enrolled* • **Pharmacy Technician/Assistant**

**STUDENT SERVICES** Academic or career counseling, employment services for current students, placement services for program completers.

## St. Louis College of Health Careers

909 South Taylor Avenue, St. Louis, MO 63110-1511
http://www.slchc.com/

**CONTACT** Dr. Rush L. Robinson, PhD, Academic Affairs
**Telephone:** 314-652-0300

**GENERAL INFORMATION** Private Institution. Founded 1981. **Total program enrollment:** 315. **Application fee:** $35.

**PROGRAM(S) OFFERED**
• **Massage Therapy/Therapeutic Massage** *8 students enrolled* • **Medical Insurance Specialist/Medical Biller** *42 students enrolled* • **Medical/Clinical Assistant** *78 students enrolled* • **Nurse/Nursing Assistant/Aide and Patient Care Assistant** • **Pharmacy Technician/Assistant** *37 students enrolled*

**STUDENT SERVICES** Academic or career counseling, employment services for current students, placement services for program completers.

## St. Louis Community College

Cosand College Ctr, 300 S Broadway, St. Louis, MO 63102
http://www.stlcc.edu/

**CONTACT** Zelema Harris, Chancellor
**Telephone:** 314-539-5000

**GENERAL INFORMATION** Public Institution. **Accreditation:** Regional (NCA).

## St. Louis Community College at Florissant Valley

3400 Pershall Road, St. Louis, MO 63135-1499
http://www.stlcc.edu/

**CONTACT** Marcia Pfeiffer, President
**Telephone:** 314-513-4200

**GENERAL INFORMATION** Public Institution. Founded 1963. **Accreditation:** Regional (NCA); art and design (NASAD). **Total program enrollment:** 2561.

**PROGRAM(S) OFFERED**
• **Accounting Technology/Technician and Bookkeeping** *1 student enrolled* • **American Sign Language (ASL)** *18 students enrolled* • **Animation, Interactive Technology, Video Graphics and Special Effects** • **Biology Technician/Biotechnology Laboratory Technician** *5 students enrolled* • **Broadcast Journalism** • **Building/Property Maintenance and Management** • **Business Administration and Management, General** *1 student enrolled* • **Business/Commerce, General** *2 students enrolled* • **CAD/CADD Drafting and/or Design Technology/Technician** *2 students enrolled* • **Chemical Technology/Technician** • **Child Care Provider/Assistant** *35 students enrolled* • **Commercial Photography** • **Computer Programming/Programmer, General** • **Computer Systems Analysis/Analyst** • **Computer Systems Networking and Telecommunications** • **Computer and Information Sciences, General** *1 student enrolled* • **Construction Management** *3 students enrolled* • **Construction Trades, General** *14 students enrolled* • **Corrections** *1 student enrolled* • **Credit Management** • **Criminal Justice/Police Science** *1 student enrolled* • **Data Processing and Data Processing Technology/Technician** • **E-Commerce/Electronic Commerce** • **Electrical, Electronic and Communications Engineering Technology/Technician** • **Electrician** • **Emergency Medical Technology/Technician (EMT Paramedic)** • **Entrepreneurship/Entrepreneurial Studies** • **Fire Protection and Safety Technology/Technician** • **Graphic Design** • **Heavy Equipment Maintenance Technology/Technician** *2 students enrolled* • **Human Services, General** *3 students enrolled* • **Legal Assistant/Paralegal** *9 students enrolled* • **Plastics Engineering Technology/Technician** • **Plumbing Technology/Plumber** *1 student enrolled* • **Quality Control Technology/Technician** *19 students enrolled* • **Real Estate** • **Selling Skills and Sales Operations** • **Technical and Business**

*St. Louis Community College at Florissant Valley (continued)*

**Writing • Telecommunications Technology/Technician** *4 students enrolled* **• Tool and Die Technology/Technician** *1 student enrolled* **• Web Page, Digital/Multimedia and Information Resources Design • Welding Technology/Welder**

**STUDENT SERVICES** Academic or career counseling, daycare for children of students, employment services for current students, placement services for program completers, remedial services.

## St. Louis Community College at Forest Park

5600 Oakland Avenue, St. Louis, MO 63110-1316
http://www.stlcc.edu/

**CONTACT** Morris Johnson, President
**Telephone:** 314-644-9100

**GENERAL INFORMATION** Public Institution. Founded 1962. **Accreditation:** Regional (NCA); dental assisting (ADA); dental hygiene (ADA); funeral service (ABFSE); medical laboratory technology (NAACLS); radiologic technology: radiography (JRCERT). **Total program enrollment:** 2503.

**PROGRAM(S) OFFERED**
**• Accounting Technology/Technician and Bookkeeping** *1 student enrolled* **• Animation, Interactive Technology, Video Graphics and Special Effects • Automobile/Automotive Mechanics Technology/Technician** *13 students enrolled* **• Baking and Pastry Arts/Baker/Pastry Chef • Building/Home/Construction Inspection/Inspector** *3 students enrolled* **• Business Administration and Management, General • Business/Commerce, General** *3 students enrolled* **• Child Care Provider/Assistant** *10 students enrolled* **• Commercial Photography • Communications Technology/Technician** *2 students enrolled* **• Computer Programming/Programmer, General • Computer Systems Analysis/Analyst • Computer Systems Networking and Telecommunications • Computer and Information Sciences, General • Corrections** *1 student enrolled* **• Criminal Justice/Police Science** *2 students enrolled* **• Data Processing and Data Processing Technology/Technician • Dental Assisting/Assistant** *15 students enrolled* **• Diagnostic Medical Sonography/Sonographer and Ultrasound Technician • Diesel Mechanics Technology/Technician** *2 students enrolled* **• Emergency Medical Technology/Technician (EMT Paramedic) • Entrepreneurship/Entrepreneurial Studies • Fire Science/Firefighting • Funeral Direction/Service** *29 students enrolled* **• Graphic Design** *1 student enrolled* **• Health Information/Medical Records Technology/Technician** *11 students enrolled* **• Hotel/Motel Administration/Management** *1 student enrolled* **• Human Services, General** *1 student enrolled* **• International Business/Trade/Commerce • Medical Transcription/Transcriptionist** *1 student enrolled* **• Pharmacy Technician/Assistant** *14 students enrolled* **• Phlebotomy/Phlebotomist** *5 students enrolled* **• Prepress/Desktop Publishing and Digital Imaging Design • Respiratory Care Therapy/Therapist • Restaurant/Food Services Management** *2 students enrolled* **• Surgical Technology/Technologist** *1 student enrolled* **• Technical and Business Writing • Tourism and Travel Services Management** *20 students enrolled* **• Web Page, Digital/Multimedia and Information Resources Design**

**STUDENT SERVICES** Academic or career counseling, daycare for children of students, employment services for current students, placement services for program completers, remedial services.

## St. Louis Community College at Meramec

11333 Big Bend Boulevard, Kirkwood, MO 63122-5720
http://www.stlcc.edu/

**CONTACT** Paul Pai, President
**Telephone:** 314-984-7500

**GENERAL INFORMATION** Public Institution. Founded 1963. **Accreditation:** Regional (NCA); art and design (NASAD); physical therapy assisting (APTA). **Total program enrollment:** 4910.

**PROGRAM(S) OFFERED**
**• Accounting Technology/Technician and Bookkeeping** *7 students enrolled* **• Animation, Interactive Technology, Video Graphics and Special Effects • Applied Horticulture/Horticultural Operations, General** *2 students enrolled* **• Audiovisual Communications Technologies/Technicians, Other • Business Administration and Management, General • Business/Commerce, General** *1 student enrolled* **• Child Care Provider/Assistant** *5 students enrolled* **• Commercial Photography** *2 students enrolled* **• Computer Programming/Programmer, General** *1 student enrolled* **• Computer Systems Analysis/Analyst • Computer Systems Networking and Telecommunications • Computer and Information Sciences, General • Court Reporting/Court Reporter** *2 students enrolled* **• Criminal Justice/Police Science** *1 student enrolled* **• Data Processing and Data Processing Technology/Technician** *1 student enrolled* **• E-Commerce/Electronic Commerce • Entrepreneurship/Entrepreneurial Studies • Graphic Design** *5 students enrolled* **• Human Services, General** *3 students enrolled* **• Interior Design** *10 students enrolled* **• Legal Assistant/Paralegal** *32 students enrolled* **• Logistics and Materials Management** *1 student enrolled* **• Real Estate • Selling Skills and Sales Operations** *1 student enrolled* **• Technical and Business Writing • Web Page, Digital/Multimedia and Information Resources Design**

**STUDENT SERVICES** Academic or career counseling, daycare for children of students, employment services for current students, placement services for program completers, remedial services.

## St. Louis Community College at Wildwood

2645 Generations Drive, Wildwood, MO 63040
stlcc.edu

**CONTACT** Pam McIntyre, President
**Telephone:** 636-422-2000

**GENERAL INFORMATION** Public Institution. **Total program enrollment:** 592.

**STUDENT SERVICES** Academic or career counseling, employment services for current students, placement services for program completers, remedial services.

## St. Louis Hair Academy

3701 Kossuth Avenue, St. Louis, MO 63107

**CONTACT** Bessie Henderson, Director
**Telephone:** 314-533-3125

**GENERAL INFORMATION** Private Institution. Founded 1988. **Total program enrollment:** 9. **Application fee:** $100.

**PROGRAM(S) OFFERED**
**• Cosmetology, Barber/Styling, and Nail Instructor** *600 hrs./$2920* **• Cosmetology/Cosmetologist, General** *1500 hrs./$7950* **• Nail Technician/Specialist and Manicurist** *400 hrs./$1900*

**STUDENT SERVICES** Placement services for program completers.

## Saint Louis University

221 North Grand Boulevard, St. Louis, MO 63103-2097
http://www.slu.edu/

**CONTACT** Lawrence Biondi, SJ, President
**Telephone:** 314-977-2222

**GENERAL INFORMATION** Private Institution. Founded 1818. **Accreditation:** Regional (NCA); dietetics: postbaccalaureate internship (ADtA/CAADE); health information administration (AHIMA); medical technology (NAACLS); nuclear medicine technology (JRCNMT); speech-language pathology (ASHA). **Total program enrollment:** 9529. **Application fee:** $25.

**PROGRAM(S) OFFERED**
**• Computer and Information Sciences, General** *1 student enrolled* **• Elementary Education and Teaching** *1 student enrolled* **• Purchasing, Procurement/Acquisitions and Contracts Management** *1 student enrolled*

**STUDENT SERVICES** Academic or career counseling, employment services for current students, placement services for program completers, remedial services.

## Salem College of Hairstyling

1051 Kings Highway, Rolla, MO 65401

**CONTACT** Joseph A. Nicholson, Owner
**Telephone:** 573-368-3136

**GENERAL INFORMATION** Private Institution. **Total program enrollment:** 54. **Application fee:** $100.

**PROGRAM(S) OFFERED**
• **Cosmetology and Related Personal Grooming Arts, Other** • **Cosmetology, Barber/Styling, and Nail Instructor** *600 hrs./$3100* • **Cosmetology/Cosmetologist, General** *1500 hrs./$7700*

**STUDENT SERVICES** Academic or career counseling, employment services for current students, placement services for program completers.

## Saline County Career Center

900 W. Vest, Marshall, MO 65340-1698
http://www.marshallschools.com/sccc/

**CONTACT** Derek Lark, Director
**Telephone:** 660-886-6958

**GENERAL INFORMATION** Public Institution. **Total program enrollment:** 23.

**PROGRAM(S) OFFERED**
• **Automobile/Automotive Mechanics Technology/Technician** *1120 hrs./$3700* • **Business/Office Automation/Technology/Data Entry** *600 hrs./$1850* • **Carpentry/Carpenter** *1120 hrs./$3750* • **Culinary Arts/Chef Training** *600 hrs./$1850* • **General Office Occupations and Clerical Services** *5 students enrolled* • **Licensed Practical/Vocational Nurse Training (LPN, LVN, Cert, Dipl, AAS)** *1288 hrs./$6885*

**STUDENT SERVICES** Academic or career counseling, employment services for current students, placement services for program completers.

## Sanford-Brown College

1203 Smizer Mill Road, Fenton, MO 63026
http://www.sanford-brown.edu/

**CONTACT** Melissa Uding, President
**Telephone:** 636-651-1600

**GENERAL INFORMATION** Private Institution. Founded 1868. **Accreditation:** Radiologic technology: radiography (JRCERT); respiratory therapy technology (CoARC); state accredited or approved. **Total program enrollment:** 596. **Application fee:** $25.

**PROGRAM(S) OFFERED**
• **Emergency Medical Technology/Technician (EMT Paramedic)** *7 students enrolled* • **Massage Therapy/Therapeutic Massage** *1 student enrolled* • **Medical Insurance Specialist/Medical Biller** *34 students enrolled* • **Medical/Clinical Assistant** *61 students enrolled*

**STUDENT SERVICES** Employment services for current students, placement services for program completers.

## Sanford-Brown College

75 Village Square, Hazelwood, MO 63042
http://www.sanford-brown.edu/

**CONTACT** George Grayeb, Vice President Managing Director
**Telephone:** 314-687-2900

**GENERAL INFORMATION** Private Institution. Founded 1868. **Accreditation:** State accredited or approved. **Total program enrollment:** 566. **Application fee:** $25.

**PROGRAM(S) OFFERED**
• **Dental Assisting/Assistant** *3 students enrolled* • **Medical Insurance Specialist/Medical Biller** *22 students enrolled* • **Medical/Clinical Assistant** *86 students enrolled*

**STUDENT SERVICES** Employment services for current students, placement services for program completers.

## Sanford-Brown College

100 Richmond Center Boulevard, St. Peters, MO 63376
http://www.sanford-brown.edu/

**CONTACT** Julia Leeman, President
**Telephone:** 636-696-2300

**GENERAL INFORMATION** Private Institution. Founded 1868. **Accreditation:** State accredited or approved. **Total program enrollment:** 489. **Application fee:** $25.

**PROGRAM(S) OFFERED**
• **Licensed Practical/Vocational Nurse Training (LPN, LVN, Cert, Dipl, AAS)** *77 students enrolled* • **Massage Therapy/Therapeutic Massage** *26 students enrolled* • **Medical Insurance Coding Specialist/Coder** *44 students enrolled* • **Medical/Clinical Assistant** *74 students enrolled*

**STUDENT SERVICES** Employment services for current students, placement services for program completers.

## Semo Hairstyling Academy

904 Broadway, Cape Girardeau, MO 63701

**CONTACT** Eric Brown, President
**Telephone:** 573-651-0333

**GENERAL INFORMATION** Private Institution. **Total program enrollment:** 53. **Application fee:** $100.

**PROGRAM(S) OFFERED**
• **Barbering/Barber** *1000 hrs./$6550* • **Cosmetology/Cosmetologist, General** *1500 hrs./$8750*

**STUDENT SERVICES** Academic or career counseling, employment services for current students, placement services for program completers.

## Sikeston Career and Technology Center

1002 Virginia Street, Sikeston, MO 63801
http://www.sikeston.k12.mo.us/

**CONTACT** Stephen Borgsmiller, Superintendent
**Telephone:** 573-472-2581

**GENERAL INFORMATION** Public Institution. **Total program enrollment:** 53. **Application fee:** $75.

**PROGRAM(S) OFFERED**
• **Autobody/Collision and Repair Technology/Technician** *1080 hrs./$3700* • **Automobile/Automotive Mechanics Technology/Technician** • **Construction Trades, General** *1080 hrs./$3700* • **Drafting and Design Technology/Technician, General** • **General Office Occupations and Clerical Services** *600 hrs./$3500* • **Graphic and Printing Equipment Operator, General Production** *1080 hrs./$3700* • **Licensed Practical/Vocational Nurse Training (LPN, LVN, Cert, Dipl, AAS)** *1400 hrs./$8800* • **Welding Technology/Welder** *1080 hrs./$3700*

**STUDENT SERVICES** Academic or career counseling, employment services for current students, placement services for program completers, remedial services.

## South Central Area Vocational Technical School

610 East Olden, West Plains, MO 65775
http://mail.wphs.k12.mo.us/

**CONTACT** Karla Eslinger, Superintendent
**Telephone:** 417-256-2256

**GENERAL INFORMATION** Public Institution. Founded 1968. **Total program enrollment:** 79. **Application fee:** $25.

**PROGRAM(S) OFFERED**
• **Administrative Assistant and Secretarial Science, General** *900 hrs./$4000* • **Autobody/Collision and Repair Technology/Technician** *900 hrs./$4000* • **Automobile/Automotive Mechanics Technology/Technician** *3 students enrolled* • **Commercial and Advertising Art** *2 students enrolled* • **Computer Installation and Repair Technology/Technician** *1 student enrolled* • **Culinary Arts/Chef Training** *3 students enrolled* • **Drafting and Design Technology/Technician, General** *1 student enrolled* • **Emergency Medical Technology/Technician (EMT Paramedic)** *12 students enrolled* • **Heating, Air Conditioning, Ventilation and Refrigeration Maintenance Technology/Technician (HAC, HACR, HVAC, HVACR)** *600 hrs./$2850* • **Licensed Practical/Vocational Nurse Training (LPN, LVN, Cert, Dipl, AAS)** *1596 hrs./$9300* • **Machine Shop Technology/Assistant** *2 students enrolled* • **Surgical Technology/Technologist** *1300 hrs./$6170* • **Welding Technology/Welder** *900 hrs./$4000*

**STUDENT SERVICES** Academic or career counseling, remedial services.

## Southeast Missouri Hospital College of Nursing and Health Sciences

2001 William Street, Cape Girardeau, MO 63701
http://www.southeastmissourihospital.com/college/

**CONTACT** Tonya L. Buttry, President
**Telephone:** 573-334-6825 Ext. 21

**GENERAL INFORMATION** Private Institution. Founded 1928. **Accreditation:** Regional (NCA). **Total program enrollment:** 96. **Application fee:** $40.

**PROGRAM(S) OFFERED**
• **Surgical Technology/Technologist** *10 students enrolled*

## State Fair Community College

3201 West 16th Street, Sedalia, MO 65301-2199
http://www.sfccmo.edu/

**CONTACT** Marsha Drennon, President
**Telephone:** 660-530-5800 Ext. 7217

**GENERAL INFORMATION** Public Institution. Founded 1966. **Accreditation:** Regional (NCA); dental hygiene (ADA). **Total program enrollment:** 1866. **Application fee:** $25.

**PROGRAM(S) OFFERED**
• **Administrative Assistant and Secretarial Science, General** • **Automobile/Automotive Mechanics Technology/Technician** *2 students enrolled* • **Industrial Electronics Technology/Technician** *1 student enrolled* • **Industrial Mechanics and Maintenance Technology** • **Licensed Practical/Vocational Nurse Training (LPN, LVN, Cert, Dipl, AAS)** *35 students enrolled* • **Machine Tool Technology/Machinist** *2 students enrolled* • **Marine Maintenance/Fitter and Ship Repair Technology/Technician** • **Medical Administrative/Executive Assistant and Medical Secretary** *4 students enrolled* • **Welding Technology/Welder** *7 students enrolled*

**STUDENT SERVICES** Academic or career counseling, daycare for children of students, employment services for current students, placement services for program completers, remedial services.

## Texas County Technical Institute

6915 S. Hwy 63, Houston, MO 65483
http://www.texascountytech.edu/

**CONTACT** Charlotte Gray, Administrator/President
**Telephone:** 417-967-5466

**GENERAL INFORMATION** Private Institution. **Total program enrollment:** 189. **Application fee:** $45.

**PROGRAM(S) OFFERED**
• **Accounting** *52 hrs./$7975* • **Emergency Care Attendant (EMT Ambulance)** *9 students enrolled* • **Emergency Medical Technology/Technician (EMT Paramedic)** *1300 hrs./$9550* • **Licensed Practical/Vocational Nurse Training (LPN, LVN, Cert, Dipl, AAS)** *76 hrs./$16,985* • **Medical Administrative/Executive Assistant and Medical Secretary** *52 hrs./$7725* • **Nurse/Nursing Assistant/Aide and Patient Care Assistant** *41 students enrolled* • **Nursing—Registered Nurse Training (RN, ASN, BSN, MSN)** *69 hrs./$22,425* • **Occupational Health and Industrial Hygiene** *66 hrs./$10,120*

**STUDENT SERVICES** Academic or career counseling, placement services for program completers.

## Three Rivers Community College

2080 Three Rivers Boulevard, Poplar Bluff, MO 63901-2393
http://www.trcc.edu/

**CONTACT** Joseph T. Rozman, Interim President
**Telephone:** 573-840-9600

**GENERAL INFORMATION** Public Institution. Founded 1966. **Accreditation:** Regional (NCA); medical laboratory technology (NAACLS). **Total program enrollment:** 1860. **Application fee:** $20.

**PROGRAM(S) OFFERED**
• **Accounting Technology/Technician and Bookkeeping** • **Administrative Assistant and Secretarial Science, General** *8 students enrolled* • **Business/Office Automation/Technology/Data Entry** *1 student enrolled* • **Child Care and Support Services Management** • **Computer Technology/Computer Systems Technology** • **Criminal Justice/Police Science** *2 students enrolled* • **Electrical, Electronic and Communications Engineering Technology/Technician** • **Emergency Medical Technology/Technician (EMT Paramedic)** • **Environmental Engineering Technology/Environmental Technology** • **Hospitality Administration/Management, General** • **Industrial Electronics Technology/Technician** *2 students enrolled* • **Machine Shop Technology/Assistant** • **Marketing/Marketing Management, General** • **Occupational Safety and Health Technology/Technician** • **Office Management and Supervision** • **Quality Control Technology/Technician** • **Selling Skills and Sales Operations** • **Survey Technology/Surveying** *5 students enrolled* • **Web Page, Digital/Multimedia and Information Resources Design** *2 students enrolled*

**STUDENT SERVICES** Academic or career counseling, daycare for children of students, employment services for current students, placement services for program completers, remedial services.

## Trend Setters School of Cosmetology

835 S. Kings Highway, Cape Girardeau, MO 63703
http://www.trendsettersschool.com

**CONTACT** Wanda Verhines
**Telephone:** 573-335-9977

**GENERAL INFORMATION** Private Institution. **Total program enrollment:** 61. **Application fee:** $50.

**PROGRAM(S) OFFERED**
• **Cosmetology, Barber/Styling, and Nail Instructor** *600 hrs./$1600* • **Cosmetology/Cosmetologist, General** *1500 hrs./$7500* • **Nail Technician/Specialist and Manicurist** *400 hrs./$1100*

**STUDENT SERVICES** Academic or career counseling, employment services for current students, placement services for program completers.

## University of Missouri System

321 University Hall, Columbia, MO 65211
http://www.system.missiouri.edu/

**CONTACT** Gary Forsee, President
**Telephone:** 573-882-2011

**GENERAL INFORMATION** Public Institution.

## Vatterott College

5898 North Main Street, Joplin, MO 64801
http://www.vatterott-college.edu/

**CONTACT** Donna Goldthwaite, Campus Director
**Telephone:** 417-781-5633

**GENERAL INFORMATION** Private Institution. **Accreditation:** State accredited or approved. **Total program enrollment:** 247.

**PROGRAM(S) OFFERED**
• **Accounting Technology/Technician and Bookkeeping** *6 students enrolled* • **Administrative Assistant and Secretarial Science, General** *7 students enrolled* • **Aesthetician/Esthetician and Skin Care Specialist** *24 students enrolled* • **CAD/CADD Drafting and/or Design Technology/Technician** *8 students enrolled* • **Cosmetology/Cosmetologist, General** *20 students enrolled* • **Information Technology** *13 students enrolled* • **Medical Office Assistant/Specialist** *35 students enrolled* • **Nail Technician/Specialist and Manicurist** *3 students enrolled* • **Pharmacy Technician/Assistant** *14 students enrolled*

**STUDENT SERVICES** Academic or career counseling, employment services for current students, placement services for program completers.

## Vatterott College

8955 East 38th Terrace, Kansas City, MO 64129
http://www.vatterott-college.edu/

**CONTACT** Wayne Major, Director
**Telephone:** 816-861-1000

**GENERAL INFORMATION** Private Institution. **Accreditation:** State accredited or approved. **Total program enrollment:** 399.

**PROGRAM(S) OFFERED**
• **Administrative Assistant and Secretarial Science, General** *17 students enrolled* • **CAD/CADD Drafting and/or Design Technology/Technician** *24 students enrolled* • **Computer Programming/Programmer, General** *4 students enrolled* • **Electrician** *38 students enrolled* • **Heating, Air Conditioning, Ventilation and Refrigeration Maintenance Technology/Technician (HAC, HACR, HVAC, HVACR)** *68 students enrolled* • **Information Technology** *26 students enrolled* • **Medical Office Assistant/Specialist** *46 students enrolled* • **Pharmacy Technician/Assistant** *25 students enrolled* • **Plumbing Technology/Plumber** *6 students enrolled*

**STUDENT SERVICES** Academic or career counseling, employment services for current students, placement services for program completers.

## Vatterott College

927 East Terra Lane, O'Fallon, MO 63366
http://www.vatterott-college.edu/

**CONTACT** Robert Donnell, Campus Director
**Telephone:** 636-978-7488 Ext. 201

**GENERAL INFORMATION** Private Institution. **Total program enrollment:** 229.

**PROGRAM(S) OFFERED**
• **Cosmetology/Cosmetologist, General** *47 students enrolled* • **Electrician** *35 students enrolled* • **Heating, Air Conditioning, Ventilation and Refrigeration Maintenance Technology/Technician (HAC, HACR, HVAC, HVACR)** *41 students enrolled* • **Information Technology** *15 students enrolled* • **Medical Office Assistant/Specialist** *21 students enrolled*

**STUDENT SERVICES** Academic or career counseling, employment services for current students, placement services for program completers.

## Vatterott College

3925 Industrial Drive, St. Ann, MO 63074-1807
http://www.vatterott-college.edu/

**CONTACT** Raymond Ada, Regional Director of Compliance
**Telephone:** 314-264-1000 Ext. 1020

**GENERAL INFORMATION** Private Institution. Founded 1969. **Accreditation:** State accredited or approved. **Total program enrollment:** 755.

**PROGRAM(S) OFFERED**
• **CAD/CADD Drafting and/or Design Technology/Technician** *1 student enrolled* • **Computer Programming/Programmer, General** *15 students enrolled* • **Cosmetology/Cosmetologist, General** • **Dental Assisting/Assistant** *8 students enrolled* • **Electrician** *46 students enrolled* • **Heating, Air Conditioning, Ventilation and Refrigeration Maintenance Technology/Technician (HAC, HACR, HVAC, HVACR)** *88 students enrolled* • **Information Technology** *18 students enrolled* • **Medical Office Assistant/Specialist** *41 students enrolled* • **Plumbing Technology/Plumber** *17 students enrolled* • **Welding Technology/Welder** *32 students enrolled*

**STUDENT SERVICES** Academic or career counseling, employment services for current students, placement services for program completers.

## Vatterott College

3131 Frederick Avenue, St. Joseph, MO 64506
http://www.vatterott-college.edu/

**CONTACT** Andy Stufflebean, Director
**Telephone:** 816-364-5399

**GENERAL INFORMATION** Private Institution. **Accreditation:** State accredited or approved. **Total program enrollment:** 200.

**PROGRAM(S) OFFERED**
• **Administrative Assistant and Secretarial Science, General** *11 students enrolled* • **Cosmetology/Cosmetologist, General** *36 students enrolled* • **Information Technology** • **Massage Therapy/Therapeutic Massage** *20 students enrolled* • **Medical Office Assistant/Specialist** *26 students enrolled*

**STUDENT SERVICES** Academic or career counseling, employment services for current students, placement services for program completers.

## Vatterott College

12970 Maurer Industrial Drive, St. Louis, MO 63127
http://www.vatterott-college.edu/

**CONTACT** Lisa Dickerson, Director
**Telephone:** 314-843-4200

**GENERAL INFORMATION** Private Institution. **Accreditation:** State accredited or approved. **Total program enrollment:** 494.

**PROGRAM(S) OFFERED**
• **Building/Property Maintenance and Management** *19 students enrolled* • **CAD/CADD Drafting and/or Design Technology/Technician** *16 students enrolled* • **Computer Programming/Programmer, General** *11 students enrolled* • **Cosmetology/Cosmetologist, General** *24 students enrolled* • **Electrician** *72 students enrolled* • **Heating, Air Conditioning, Ventilation and Refrigeration Maintenance Technology/Technician (HAC, HACR, HVAC, HVACR)** *43 students enrolled* • **Information Technology** *31 students enrolled* • **Medical Office Assistant/Specialist** *12 students enrolled*

**STUDENT SERVICES** Academic or career counseling, employment services for current students, placement services for program completers.

## Vatterott College

1258 East Trafficway Street, Springfield, MO 65802
http://www.vatterott-college.edu/

**CONTACT** Rebecca Matney, Director
**Telephone:** 417-831-8116

**GENERAL INFORMATION** Private Institution. **Accreditation:** State accredited or approved. **Total program enrollment:** 329.

**PROGRAM(S) OFFERED**
• **Administrative Assistant and Secretarial Science, General** *2 students enrolled* • **Building/Property Maintenance and Management** • **CAD/CADD Drafting**

*Vatterott College (continued)*

**and/or Design Technology/Technician** *10 students enrolled* • **Dental Assisting/Assistant** *43 students enrolled* • **Heating, Air Conditioning, Ventilation and Refrigeration Maintenance Technology/Technician (HAC, HACR, HVAC, HVACR)** *25 students enrolled* • **Information Technology** *14 students enrolled* • **Legal Assistant/Paralegal** *19 students enrolled* • **Medical Office Assistant/Specialist** *17 students enrolled* • **Medical/Clinical Assistant** *54 students enrolled* • **Pharmacy Technician/Assistant** *9 students enrolled*

**STUDENT SERVICES** Academic or career counseling, employment services for current students, placement services for program completers.

## Washington University in St. Louis

One Brookings Drive, St. Louis, MO 63130-4899
http://www.wustl.edu/

**CONTACT** Mark Wrighton, Chancellor
**Telephone:** 314-935-5000

**GENERAL INFORMATION** Private Institution. Founded 1853. **Accreditation:** Regional (NCA); art and design (NASAD); audiology (ASHA). **Total program enrollment:** 11158. **Application fee:** $55.

**PROGRAM(S) OFFERED**
• **Communication, Journalism and Related Programs, Other** *1 student enrolled* • **Computer/Information Technology Services Administration and Management, Other** *2 students enrolled* • **Education, General** *1 student enrolled* • **Financial Planning and Services** *1 student enrolled*

**STUDENT SERVICES** Academic or career counseling, employment services for current students, placement services for program completers.

## Waynesville Technical Academy

810 Roosevelt, Waynesville, MO 65583
http://waynesville.k12.mo.us/

**CONTACT** Dr. Judene Blackburn, Superintendent
**Telephone:** 573-774-6106

**GENERAL INFORMATION** Private Institution. **Total program enrollment:** 49. **Application fee:** $100.

**PROGRAM(S) OFFERED**
• **Agriculture, General** • **Autobody/Collision and Repair Technology/Technician** *1080 hrs./$2960* • **Automobile/Automotive Mechanics Technology/Technician** *1 student enrolled* • **Carpentry/Carpenter** • **Communications Systems Installation and Repair Technology** *1 student enrolled* • **Computer Installation and Repair Technology/Technician** *1080 hrs./$2960* • **Computer Systems Analysis/Analyst** • **Culinary Arts/Chef Training** *2 students enrolled* • **Emergency Medical Technology/Technician (EMT Paramedic)** • **Graphic Communications, Other** *2 students enrolled* • **Graphic and Printing Equipment Operator, General Production** • **Health Aide** • **Heating, Air Conditioning, Ventilation and Refrigeration Maintenance Technology/Technician (HAC, HACR, HVAC, HVACR)** *1080 hrs./$2960* • **Hospitality and Recreation Marketing Operations** • **Licensed Practical/Vocational Nurse Training (LPN, LVN, Cert, Dipl, AAS)** *1587 hrs./$11,708* • **Mason/Masonry** *1080 hrs./$2960* • **Sales, Distribution and Marketing Operations, General** • **Welding Technology/Welder** *1080 hrs./$2960*

**STUDENT SERVICES** Academic or career counseling, employment services for current students, placement services for program completers.

## Webster University

470 East Lockwood Avenue, St. Louis, MO 63119-3194
http://www.webster.edu/

**CONTACT** Neil George, Interim President
**Telephone:** 314-961-2660

**GENERAL INFORMATION** Private Institution. Founded 1915. **Accreditation:** Regional (NCA); music (NASM). **Total program enrollment:** 6316. **Application fee:** $35.

**PROGRAM(S) OFFERED**
• **Ethics** *1 student enrolled* • **Web Page, Digital/Multimedia and Information Resources Design** *1 student enrolled*

**STUDENT SERVICES** Academic or career counseling, employment services for current students, placement services for program completers, remedial services.

# MONTANA

## Academy of Nail Skin and Hair

928 Broadwater Avenue, Suite B, Billings, MT 59101
http://academyofnailandskin.com/

**CONTACT** Brenda Zimmerer, Financial Aid Director
**Telephone:** 406-252-3232

**GENERAL INFORMATION** Private Institution. **Total program enrollment:** 130.

**PROGRAM(S) OFFERED**
• **Aesthetician/Esthetician and Skin Care Specialist** *650 hrs./$4350* • **Barbering/Barber** *1500 hrs./$6975* • **Cosmetology/Cosmetologist, General** *2000 hrs./$8375* • **Nail Technician/Specialist and Manicurist** *400 hrs./$1725*

**STUDENT SERVICES** Academic or career counseling.

## Blackfeet Community College

PO Box 819, Browning, MT 59417-0819
http://www.bfcc.org/

**CONTACT** John E. Salois, President
**Telephone:** 406-338-5441

**GENERAL INFORMATION** Private Institution. Founded 1974. **Accreditation:** Regional (NCCU/NCCU). **Total program enrollment:** 404. **Application fee:** $15.

**PROGRAM(S) OFFERED**
• **Construction Engineering Technology/Technician** *9 students enrolled* • **Construction/Heavy Equipment/Earthmoving Equipment Operation** *9 students enrolled* • **Consumer Services and Advocacy** *1 student enrolled* • **Corrections and Criminal Justice, Other** • **General Office Occupations and Clerical Services** • **Hazardous Materials Management and Waste Technology/Technician** *7 students enrolled* • **Hospitality Administration/Management, Other** *2 students enrolled* • **Physical Education Teaching and Coaching** *3 students enrolled*

**STUDENT SERVICES** Academic or career counseling, remedial services.

## Chief Dull Knife College

PO Box 98, 1 College Drive, Lame Deer, MT 59043-0098
http://www.cdkc.edu/

**CONTACT** Richard Littlebear, President
**Telephone:** 406-477-6215

**GENERAL INFORMATION** Private Institution. Founded 1975. **Accreditation:** Regional (NCCU/NCCU). **Total program enrollment:** 127.

**PROGRAM(S) OFFERED**
• **Administrative Assistant and Secretarial Science, General** • **Entrepreneurship/Entrepreneurial Studies**

**STUDENT SERVICES** Academic or career counseling, daycare for children of students, remedial services.

## Dahl's College of Beauty

716 Central Avenue, Great Falls, MT 59401

**CONTACT** Philip Belangie
**Telephone:** 406-454-3453

**GENERAL INFORMATION** Private Institution. **Total program enrollment:** 29. **Application fee:** $100.

**PROGRAM(S) OFFERED**
• **Cosmetology, Barber/Styling, and Nail Instructor** *650 hrs./$3500* • **Cosmetology/Cosmetologist, General** *1200 hrs./$8400* • **Nail Technician/Specialist and Manicurist** *350 hrs./$2100*

**STUDENT SERVICES** Academic or career counseling.

## Dawson Community College

Box 421, Glendive, MT 59330-0421
http://www.dawson.edu/

**CONTACT** Jim Cargill, President
**Telephone:** 406-377-3396

**GENERAL INFORMATION** Public Institution. Founded 1940. **Accreditation:** Regional (NCCU/NCCU). **Total program enrollment:** 292. **Application fee:** $30.

**PROGRAM(S) OFFERED**
• **Administrative Assistant and Secretarial Science, General** *1 student enrolled* • **Agricultural Power Machinery Operation** *2 students enrolled* • **Child Care Provider/Assistant** • **Criminal Justice/Police Science** • **Farm/Farm and Ranch Management** *10 students enrolled* • **Welding Technology/Welder** *3 students enrolled*

**STUDENT SERVICES** Academic or career counseling, remedial services.

## Flathead Valley Community College

777 Grandview Drive, Kalispell, MT 59901-2622
http://www.fvcc.edu/

**CONTACT** Jane Karas, President
**Telephone:** 406-756-3822

**GENERAL INFORMATION** Public Institution. Founded 1967. **Accreditation:** Regional (NCCU/NCCU); medical assisting (AAMAE). **Total program enrollment:** 958. **Application fee:** $15.

**PROGRAM(S) OFFERED**
• **Accounting** *1 student enrolled* • **Athletic Training/Trainer** *1 student enrolled* • **Business/Commerce, General** *2 students enrolled* • **Carpentry/Carpenter** • **Computer and Information Sciences, General** • **Entrepreneurship/Entrepreneurial Studies** *1 student enrolled* • **Executive Assistant/Executive Secretary** • **Graphic Communications, General** *1 student enrolled* • **Health Information/Medical Records Technology/Technician** *2 students enrolled* • **Heating, Air Conditioning, Ventilation and Refrigeration Maintenance Technology/Technician (HAC, HACR, HVAC, HVACR)** *1 student enrolled* • **Heavy Equipment Maintenance Technology/Technician** *4 students enrolled* • **Marketing/Marketing Management, General** *1 student enrolled* • **Medical Transcription/Transcriptionist** *3 students enrolled* • **Metal and Jewelry Arts** *3 students enrolled* • **Pharmacy Technician/Assistant** *5 students enrolled* • **Welding Technology/Welder**

**STUDENT SERVICES** Academic or career counseling, employment services for current students, placement services for program completers, remedial services.

## Fort Belknap College

PO Box 159, Harlem, MT 59526-0159
http://www.fbcc.edu/

**CONTACT** Carole Falcon-Chandler, President
**Telephone:** 406-353-2607 Ext. 222

**GENERAL INFORMATION** Public Institution. Founded 1984. **Accreditation:** Regional (NCCU/NCCU). **Total program enrollment:** 124. **Application fee:** $10.

**PROGRAM(S) OFFERED**
• **Carpentry/Carpenter** *4 students enrolled*

**STUDENT SERVICES** Academic or career counseling, employment services for current students, remedial services.

## Fort Peck Community College

PO Box 398, Poplar, MT 59255-0398
http://www.fpcc.edu/

**CONTACT** James E. Shanley, President
**Telephone:** 406-768-6300

**GENERAL INFORMATION** Public Institution. Founded 1978. **Accreditation:** Regional (NCCU/NCCU). **Total program enrollment:** 280. **Application fee:** $15.

**PROGRAM(S) OFFERED**
• **Accounting Technology/Technician and Bookkeeping** *2 students enrolled* • **Accounting** • **Automobile/Automotive Mechanics Technology/Technician** • **Building/Construction Finishing, Management, and Inspection, Other** *3 students enrolled* • **Business/Office Automation/Technology/Data Entry** • **Computer Programming/Programmer, General** • **Computer Systems Networking and Telecommunications** • **Computer Technology/Computer Systems Technology** *2 students enrolled* • **General Office Occupations and Clerical Services** *3 students enrolled* • **Ground Transportation, Other** *3 students enrolled* • **Hazardous Materials Management and Waste Technology/Technician** • **Health/Medical Preparatory Programs, Other** *2 students enrolled* • **Machine Tool Technology/Machinist** • **Medical Insurance Coding Specialist/Coder**

**STUDENT SERVICES** Academic or career counseling, daycare for children of students, employment services for current students, placement services for program completers, remedial services.

## Health Works Institute

111 S. Grand Avenue Annex 3, Bozeman, MT 59715
http://healthworksinstitute.com/

**CONTACT** Ruth Marion, Director
**Telephone:** 406-582-1555

**GENERAL INFORMATION** Private Institution. **Total program enrollment:** 24. **Application fee:** $25.

**PROGRAM(S) OFFERED**
• **Massage Therapy/Therapeutic Massage** *780 hrs./$11,296*

**STUDENT SERVICES** Academic or career counseling, employment services for current students.

## Miles Community College

2715 Dickinson, Miles City, MT 59301-4799
http://www.milescc.edu/

**CONTACT** Stefani Hicswa, President
**Telephone:** 800-541-9281

**GENERAL INFORMATION** Public Institution. Founded 1939. **Accreditation:** Regional (NCCU/NCCU). **Total program enrollment:** 328. **Application fee:** $30.

**PROGRAM(S) OFFERED**
• **Agricultural Business and Management, General** *3 students enrolled* • **Automotive Engineering Technology/Technician** • **Construction Engineering Technology/Technician** *3 students enrolled* • **Construction/Heavy Equipment/Earthmoving Equipment Operation** *14 students enrolled* • **Education, General** • **Medical Administrative/Executive Assistant and Medical Secretary** *3 students enrolled*

**STUDENT SERVICES** Academic or career counseling, employment services for current students, placement services for program completers, remedial services.

## Montana State University–Billings

1500 University Drive, Billings, MT 59101-0298
http://www.msubillings.edu/

**CONTACT** John Cech, Dean
**Telephone:** 406-247-3000

**GENERAL INFORMATION** Public Institution. Founded 1927. **Accreditation:** Regional (NCCU/NCCU); art and design (NASAD); music (NASM). **Total program enrollment:** 624. **Application fee:** $30.

**PROGRAM(S) OFFERED**
• **Accounting and Related Services, Other** • **Administrative Assistant and Secretarial Science, General** *3 students enrolled* • **Autobody/Collision and Repair Technology/Technician** *3 students enrolled* • **Automobile/Automotive Mechanics Technology/Technician** *3 students enrolled* • **Computer Systems Networking and Telecommunications** *2 students enrolled* • **Diesel Mechanics Technology/Technician** *1 student enrolled* • **Drafting and Design Technology/Technician, General** *1 student enrolled* • **Human Resources Management/Personnel Administration, General** *1 student enrolled* • **Medical Insurance Coding Specialist/Coder** *13 students enrolled* • **Sheet Metal Technology/Sheetworking** *4 students enrolled*

**STUDENT SERVICES** Academic or career counseling, daycare for children of students, employment services for current students, placement services for program completers, remedial services.

## Montana State University–Great Falls College of Technology

2100 16th Avenue, South, Great Falls, MT 59405
http://www.msugf.edu/

**CONTACT** Joseph M. Schaffer, Interim Dean/CEO
**Telephone:** 406-771-4300

**GENERAL INFORMATION** Public Institution. Founded 1969. **Accreditation:** Regional (NCCU/NCCU); dental assisting (ADA); dental hygiene (ADA); health information technology (AHIMA); medical assisting (AAMAE). **Total program enrollment:** 766. **Application fee:** $30.

**PROGRAM(S) OFFERED**
• **Accounting Technology/Technician and Bookkeeping** • **Administrative Assistant and Secretarial Science, General** *1 student enrolled* • **Business Administration and Management, General** • **Dental Assisting/Assistant** *11 students enrolled* • **Emergency Medical Technology/Technician (EMT Paramedic)** • **Entrepreneurship/Entrepreneurial Studies** *7 students enrolled* • **Health Information/Medical Records Technology/Technician** *15 students enrolled* • **Medical Insurance Specialist/Medical Biller** *7 students enrolled* • **Medical Transcription/Transcriptionist** *7 students enrolled* • **Surgical Technology/Technologist** *6 students enrolled* • **Welding Technology/Welder** *7 students enrolled*

**STUDENT SERVICES** Academic or career counseling, employment services for current students, placement services for program completers, remedial services.

## Montana State University–Northern

PO Box 7751, Havre, MT 59501-7751
http://www.msun.edu/

**CONTACT** Rolf Groseth, Interim Chancellor
**Telephone:** 406-265-3700

**GENERAL INFORMATION** Public Institution. Founded 1929. **Accreditation:** Regional (NCCU/NCCU); engineering technology (ABET/TAC). **Total program enrollment:** 905. **Application fee:** $30.

**PROGRAM(S) OFFERED**
• **Welding Technology/Welder** *6 students enrolled*

**STUDENT SERVICES** Academic or career counseling, employment services for current students, placement services for program completers, remedial services.

## Montana Tech–College of Technology

25 Basin Creek Road, Butte, MT 59701
http://www.mtech.edu/cot_tech/

**CONTACT** John Garic, Dean
**Telephone:** 406-496-3707

**GENERAL INFORMATION** Public Institution. Founded 1969. **Total program enrollment:** 351. **Application fee:** $30.

**PROGRAM(S) OFFERED**
• **Accounting Technology/Technician and Bookkeeping** • **Administrative Assistant and Secretarial Science, General** • **Automobile/Automotive Mechanics Technology/Technician** *4 students enrolled* • **Data Processing and Data Processing Technology/Technician** *1 student enrolled* • **Drafting and Design Technology/Technician, General** • **Medical Administrative/Executive Assistant and Medical Secretary**

**STUDENT SERVICES** Academic or career counseling, employment services for current students, placement services for program completers, remedial services.

## Montana University System

PO Box 203101, Helena, MT 59620-3101
http://www.oche.montana.edu

**CONTACT** Sheila Stearns, Commissioner
**Telephone:** 406-444-6570

**GENERAL INFORMATION** Public Institution.

## Salish Kootenai College

52000 Highway 93, PO Box 70, Pablo, MT 59855-0117
http://www.skc.edu/

**CONTACT** Joseph F. McDonald, President
**Telephone:** 406-275-4800

**GENERAL INFORMATION** Private Institution. Founded 1977. **Accreditation:** Regional (NCCU/NCCU); dental assisting (ADA). **Total program enrollment:** 592.

**PROGRAM(S) OFFERED**
• **Administrative Assistant and Secretarial Science, General** *10 students enrolled* • **American Indian/Native American Studies** *1 student enrolled* • **Carpentry/Carpenter** *3 students enrolled* • **Computer Science** *5 students enrolled* • **Construction/Heavy Equipment/Earthmoving Equipment Operation** *14 students enrolled* • **Dental Assisting/Assistant** *5 students enrolled* • **Medical Office Assistant/Specialist** *5 students enrolled*

**STUDENT SERVICES** Academic or career counseling, daycare for children of students, employment services for current students, placement services for program completers, remedial services.

## Stone Child College

RR1, Box 1082, Box Elder, MT 59521
http://www.montana.edu/wwwscc/

**CONTACT** Melody Henry, President
**Telephone:** 406-395-4313 Ext. 270

**GENERAL INFORMATION** Private Institution. Founded 1984. **Accreditation:** Regional (NCCU/NCCU). **Total program enrollment:** 158. **Application fee:** $10.

**PROGRAM(S) OFFERED**
• **Business/Commerce, General** *1 student enrolled* • **Carpentry/Carpenter** *2 students enrolled* • **Customer Service Management** • **Engineering Technology, General**

**STUDENT SERVICES** Academic or career counseling, daycare for children of students, employment services for current students, remedial services.

## The University of Montana

Missoula, MT 59812-0002
http://www.umt.edu/

**CONTACT** George M. Dennison, President
**Telephone:** 406-243-0211

**GENERAL INFORMATION** Public Institution. Founded 1893. **Accreditation:** Regional (NCCU/NCCU); art and design (NASAD); athletic training (JRCAT); computer science (ABET/CSAC); forestry (SAF); journalism and mass communications (ACEJMC); music (NASM); recreation and parks (NRPA); theater (NAST). **Total program enrollment:** 11322. **Application fee:** $30.

**PROGRAM(S) OFFERED**
• **Anthropology** *15 students enrolled* • **Building/Construction Finishing, Management, and Inspection, Other** *14 students enrolled* • **Computer Technology/Computer Systems Technology** *1 student enrolled* • **Construction/Heavy Equipment/Earthmoving Equipment Operation** *16 students enrolled* • **Culinary Arts/Chef Training** *5 students enrolled* • **Legal Professions and Studies, Other** *5 students enrolled* • **Licensed Practical/Vocational Nurse Training (LPN, LVN, Cert, Dipl, AAS)** *43 students enrolled* • **Marketing/Marketing Management, General** *2 students enrolled* • **Medical Reception/Receptionist** *3 students enrolled* • **Natural Resources and Conservation, Other** *3 students enrolled* • **Pharmacy Technician/Assistant** *11 students enrolled* • **Receptionist** *3 students enrolled* • **Science Technologies/Technicians, Other** *12 students enrolled* • **Small Engine Mechanics and Repair Technology/Technician** *6 students enrolled* • **Welding Technology/Welder** *1 student enrolled*

**STUDENT SERVICES** Academic or career counseling, daycare for children of students, employment services for current students, placement services for program completers, remedial services.

## The University of Montana–Helena College of Technology

1115 North Roberts Street, Helena, MT 59601
http://www.umhelena.edu/

**CONTACT** Daniel Bingham, PhD, CEO/Dean
**Telephone:** 406-444-6800

**GENERAL INFORMATION** Public Institution. Founded 1939. **Accreditation:** Regional (NCCU/NCCU). **Total program enrollment:** 571. **Application fee:** $30.

**PROGRAM(S) OFFERED**
• **Accounting Technology/Technician and Bookkeeping** *4 students enrolled* • **Administrative Assistant and Secretarial Science, General** *4 students enrolled* • **Computer Programming/Programmer, General** • **Construction Engineering Technology/Technician** • **Licensed Practical/Vocational Nurse Training (LPN, LVN, Cert, Dipl, AAS)** *21 students enrolled* • **Machine Tool Technology/Machinist** *2 students enrolled* • **Welding Technology/Welder** *6 students enrolled*

**STUDENT SERVICES** Academic or career counseling, employment services for current students, placement services for program completers, remedial services.

## The University of Montana Western

710 South Atlantic, Dillon, MT 59725-3598
http://www.umwestern.edu/

**CONTACT** Richard Storey, Chancellor
**Telephone:** 406-683-7011

**GENERAL INFORMATION** Public Institution. Founded 1893. **Accreditation:** Regional (NCCU/NCCU). **Total program enrollment:** 992. **Application fee:** $30.

**PROGRAM(S) OFFERED**
• **Child Care and Support Services Management** *3 students enrolled*

**STUDENT SERVICES** Academic or career counseling, daycare for children of students, employment services for current students, placement services for program completers, remedial services.

# NEBRASKA

## Capitol School of Hairstyling

2819 South 125th Avenue, Suite 268, Omaha, NE 68144
http://www.capitollook.com/

**CONTACT** Judy J. McCaig, President
**Telephone:** 402-333-3329 Ext. 514

**GENERAL INFORMATION** Private Institution. Founded 1923. **Total program enrollment:** 58. **Application fee:** $200.

**PROGRAM(S) OFFERED**
• **Aesthetician/Esthetician and Skin Care Specialist** *600 hrs./$8895* • **Cosmetology, Barber/Styling, and Nail Instructor** *300 hrs./$2545* • **Cosmetology/Cosmetologist, General** *2100 hrs./$15,295* • **Teacher Education and Professional Development, Specific Subject Areas, Other** *2 students enrolled*

**STUDENT SERVICES** Academic or career counseling, employment services for current students, placement services for program completers, remedial services.

## Central Community College–Grand Island Campus

PO Box 4903, Grand Island, NE 68802-4903
http://www.cccneb.edu/

**CONTACT** Dr. Greg Smith, College President
**Telephone:** 308-398-4222

**GENERAL INFORMATION** Public Institution. Founded 1976. **Accreditation:** Regional (NCA); dental assisting (ADA). **Total program enrollment:** 2262.

**PROGRAM(S) OFFERED**
• **Administrative Assistant and Secretarial Science, General** *53 students enrolled* • **Agricultural Business and Management, General** *7 students enrolled* • **Applied Horticulture/Horticultural Operations, General** *11 students enrolled* • **Autobody/Collision and Repair Technology/Technician** *86 students enrolled* • **Automobile/Automotive Mechanics Technology/Technician** *7 students enrolled* • **Building/Construction Finishing, Management, and Inspection, Other** *15 students enrolled* • **Business Administration and Management, General** *94 students enrolled* • **Child Care and Support Services Management** *56 students enrolled* • **Clinical/Medical Social Work** *13 students enrolled* • **Commercial and Advertising Art** *8 students enrolled* • **Computer and Information Sciences, General** *101 students enrolled* • **Dental Assisting/Assistant** *9 students enrolled* • **Diesel Mechanics Technology/Technician** • **Digital Communication and Media/Multimedia** *21 students enrolled* • **Drafting and Design Technology/Technician, General** *29 students enrolled* • **Electrical, Electronic and Communications Engineering Technology/Technician** *14 students enrolled* • **Electrician** *34 students enrolled* • **Health Information/Medical Records Technology/Technician** *5 students enrolled* • **Heating, Air Conditioning, Ventilation and Refrigeration Maintenance Technology/Technician (HAC, HACR, HVAC, HVACR)** *11 students enrolled* • **Industrial Mechanics and Maintenance Technology** *80 students enrolled* • **Legal Assistant/Paralegal** *5 students enrolled* • **Licensed Practical/Vocational Nurse Training (LPN, LVN, Cert, Dipl, AAS)** *65 students enrolled* • **Machine Tool Technology/Machinist** *14 students enrolled* • **Medical/Clinical Assistant** *1 student enrolled* • **Quality Control Technology/Technician** *1 student enrolled* • **Restaurant, Culinary, and Catering Management/Manager** • **Vehicle and Vehicle Parts and Accessories Marketing Operations** *1 student enrolled* • **Welding Technology/Welder** *20 students enrolled*

**STUDENT SERVICES** Academic or career counseling, daycare for children of students, employment services for current students, placement services for program completers, remedial services.

## Clarkson College

101 South 42nd Street, Omaha, NE 68131-2739
http://www.clarksoncollege.edu/

**CONTACT** Dr. Louis Burgher, President
**Telephone:** 402-552-3100

**GENERAL INFORMATION** Private Institution. Founded 1888. **Accreditation:** Regional (NCA); physical therapy assisting (APTA); radiologic technology: radiography (JRCERT). **Total program enrollment:** 460. **Application fee:** $35.

**PROGRAM(S) OFFERED**
- **Licensed Practical/Vocational Nurse Training (LPN, LVN, Cert, Dipl, AAS)** 6 *students enrolled*

**STUDENT SERVICES** Academic or career counseling, employment services for current students, placement services for program completers.

## College of Hair Design

304 South 11th Street, Lincoln, NE 68508
http://collegeofhairdesign.com/

**CONTACT** Alyce Howard, President
**Telephone:** 402-477-4040

**GENERAL INFORMATION** Private Institution. **Total program enrollment:** 230. **Application fee:** $25.

**PROGRAM(S) OFFERED**
- **Aesthetician/Esthetician and Skin Care Specialist** *700 hrs./$8000*
- **Barbering/Barber** *1100 hrs./$5000* • **Cosmetology, Barber/Styling, and Nail Instructor** *925 hrs./$5000* • **Cosmetology/Cosmetologist, General** *2100 hrs./ $16,513*

**STUDENT SERVICES** Academic or career counseling, employment services for current students, placement services for program completers.

## College of Saint Mary

7000 Mercy Road, Omaha, NE 68106
http://www.csm.edu/

**CONTACT** Dr. Maryanne Stevens, RSM, President
**Telephone:** 402-399-2400

**GENERAL INFORMATION** Private Institution. Founded 1923. **Accreditation:** Regional (NCA); health information administration (AHIMA); health information technology (AHIMA). **Total program enrollment:** 693. **Application fee:** $30.

**PROGRAM(S) OFFERED**
- **Business Administration and Management, General** *13 students enrolled*
- **Computer Systems Networking and Telecommunications** • **Health Information/Medical Records Technology/Technician** *9 students enrolled*
- **Nursing—Registered Nurse Training (RN, ASN, BSN, MSN)** *25 students enrolled*

**STUDENT SERVICES** Academic or career counseling, employment services for current students, remedial services.

## Concordia University, Nebraska

800 North Columbia Avenue, Seward, NE 68434-1599
http://www.cune.edu/

**CONTACT** Brian L. Friedrich, President and CEO
**Telephone:** 800-535-5494

**GENERAL INFORMATION** Private Institution (Affiliated with Lutheran Church–Missouri Synod). Founded 1894. **Accreditation:** Regional (NCA); music (NASM). **Total program enrollment:** 1210.

**STUDENT SERVICES** Academic or career counseling, employment services for current students, placement services for program completers.

## Creighton University

2500 California Plaza, Omaha, NE 68178-0001
http://www.creighton.edu/

**CONTACT** John P. Schlegel, President
**Telephone:** 402-280-2700

**GENERAL INFORMATION** Private Institution. Founded 1878. **Accreditation:** Regional (NCA); emergency medical services (JRCEMTP). **Total program enrollment:** 6274. **Application fee:** $40.

**PROGRAM(S) OFFERED**
- **Atmospheric Sciences and Meteorology, General** • **Computer Science**
- **Environmental Studies** • **Health/Health Care Administration/Management**
- **Health/Medical Preparatory Programs, Other** • **Human Resources Management/Personnel Administration, General** • **Journalism** *1 student enrolled* • **Organizational Communication, General** • **Theology/Theological Studies**

**STUDENT SERVICES** Academic or career counseling, daycare for children of students, employment services for current students, placement services for program completers.

## Grace University

1311 South Ninth Street, Omaha, NE 68108
http://www.graceuniversity.edu/

**CONTACT** James Eckman, PhD, President
**Telephone:** 402-449-2800

**GENERAL INFORMATION** Private Institution. Founded 1943. **Accreditation:** Regional (NCA); state accredited or approved. **Total program enrollment:** 314. **Application fee:** $35.

**PROGRAM(S) OFFERED**
- **Bible/Biblical Studies**

**STUDENT SERVICES** Academic or career counseling, employment services for current students, placement services for program completers, remedial services.

## Kaplan University, Lincoln

1821 K Street, Lincoln, NE 68508
http://www.lincoln.kaplanuniversity.edu

**CONTACT** Bruce Mallard, President
**Telephone:** 402-474-5315

**GENERAL INFORMATION** Private Institution. Founded 1884. **Accreditation:** Medical assisting (AAMAE); state accredited or approved. **Total program enrollment:** 277.

**PROGRAM(S) OFFERED**
- **General Office Occupations and Clerical Services** *20 students enrolled*
- **Licensed Practical/Vocational Nurse Training (LPN, LVN, Cert, Dipl, AAS)** *58 students enrolled* • **Tourism and Travel Services Management** *8 students enrolled*

**STUDENT SERVICES** Academic or career counseling, employment services for current students, placement services for program completers.

## Kaplan University, Omaha

5425 North 103rd Street, Omaha, NE 68134
http://www.omaha.kaplanuniversity.edu

**CONTACT** Sandra Muskopf, President
**Telephone:** 402-572-8500

**GENERAL INFORMATION** Private Institution. Founded 1891. **Accreditation:** Medical assisting (AAMAE); state accredited or approved. **Total program enrollment:** 490.

**PROGRAM(S) OFFERED**
• **Dental Assisting/Assistant** *10 students enrolled* • **Licensed Practical/Vocational Nurse Training (LPN, LVN, Cert, Dipl, AAS)** *144 students enrolled* • **Massage Therapy/Therapeutic Massage** *30 students enrolled*

**STUDENT SERVICES** Academic or career counseling, employment services for current students, placement services for program completers, remedial services.

## La'James International College

1660 North Grant, Fremont, NE 68025
http://www.lajamesinternational.com/

**CONTACT** Cynthia Becher, President
**Telephone:** 402-721-6500

**GENERAL INFORMATION** Private Institution. Founded 1958. **Total program enrollment:** 49. **Application fee:** $50.

**PROGRAM(S) OFFERED**
• **Aesthetician/Esthetician and Skin Care Specialist** *600 hrs./$8860* • **Barbering/Barber** *1 student enrolled* • **Cosmetology, Barber/Styling, and Nail Instructor** *925 hrs./$5350* • **Cosmetology/Cosmetologist, General** *2100 hrs./$17,600* • **Nail Technician/Specialist and Manicurist** *300 hrs./$3825*

**STUDENT SERVICES** Academic or career counseling, employment services for current students, placement services for program completers.

## Little Priest Tribal College

PO Box 270, Winnebago, NE 68071
http://www.lptc.bia.edu/

**CONTACT** Darla LaPointe, Interim President
**Telephone:** 402-878-2380 Ext. 100

**GENERAL INFORMATION** Private Institution. Founded 1996. **Accreditation:** Regional (NCA). **Total program enrollment:** 76. **Application fee:** $10.

**PROGRAM(S) OFFERED**
• **Computer and Information Sciences, General**

**STUDENT SERVICES** Academic or career counseling, remedial services.

## Metropolitan Community College

PO Box 3777, Omaha, NE 68103-0777
http://www.mccneb.edu/

**CONTACT** Randy Schmailzl, Interim President
**Telephone:** 402-457-2400

**GENERAL INFORMATION** Public Institution. Founded 1974. **Accreditation:** Regional (NCA); dental assisting (ADA). **Total program enrollment:** 5855.

**PROGRAM(S) OFFERED**
• **Accounting Technology/Technician and Bookkeeping** *6 students enrolled* • **Administrative Assistant and Secretarial Science, General** • **Applied Horticulture/Horticultural Operations, General** *5 students enrolled* • **Architectural Drafting and Architectural CAD/CADD** *8 students enrolled* • **Autobody/Collision and Repair Technology/Technician** • **Automobile/Automotive Mechanics Technology/Technician** • **Building/Construction Finishing, Management, and Inspection, Other** • **Business Administration and Management, General** *4 students enrolled* • **Business/Commerce, General** • **Child Care Provider/Assistant** *3 students enrolled* • **Child Care and Support Services Management** *1 student enrolled* • **Civil Engineering Technology/Technician** *2 students enrolled* • **Commercial Photography** • **Computer Systems Networking and Telecommunications** *12 students enrolled* • **Computer and Information Sciences, General** *1 student enrolled* • **Construction Trades, General** *1 student enrolled* • **Criminal Justice/Safety Studies** *2 students enrolled* • **Dental Assisting/Assistant** *24 students enrolled* • **Diesel Mechanics Technology/Technician** *1 student enrolled* • **Drafting and Design Technology/Technician, General** *7 students enrolled* • **Electrical, Electronic and Communications Engineering Technology/Technician** • **Electrician** *2 students enrolled* • **Film/Video and Photographic Arts, Other** *2 students enrolled* • **Financial Planning and Services** • **General Office Occupations and Clerical Services** *5 students enrolled* • **Heating, Air Conditioning, Ventilation and Refrigeration Maintenance Technology/Technician (HAC, HACR, HVAC, HVACR)** *19 students enrolled* • **Heavy/Industrial Equipment Maintenance Technologies, Other** *28 students enrolled* • **Human Services, General** • **Legal Assistant/Paralegal** *9 students enrolled* • **Licensed Practical/Vocational Nurse Training (LPN, LVN, Cert, Dipl, AAS)** *71 students enrolled* • **Lineworker** *1 student enrolled* • **Medical Administrative/Executive Assistant and Medical Secretary** • **Medical Office Assistant/Specialist** *7 students enrolled* • **Medical Transcription/Transcriptionist** • **Restaurant, Culinary, and Catering Management/Manager** *2 students enrolled* • **Sign Language Interpretation and Translation** *4 students enrolled* • **Substance Abuse/Addiction Counseling** *1 student enrolled* • **Technical Theatre/Theatre Design and Technology** *1 student enrolled* • **Welding Technology/Welder** *3 students enrolled*

**STUDENT SERVICES** Academic or career counseling, employment services for current students, placement services for program completers, remedial services.

## Mid-Plains Community College

601 West State Farm Road, North Platte, NE 69101
http://www.mpcc.edu/

**CONTACT** Dr. Michael R. Chipps, Area President
**Telephone:** 800-658-4308

**GENERAL INFORMATION** Public Institution. Founded 1973. **Accreditation:** Regional (NCA); dental assisting (ADA); medical laboratory technology (NAACLS). **Total program enrollment:** 959.

**PROGRAM(S) OFFERED**
• **Administrative Assistant and Secretarial Science, General** *1 student enrolled* • **Autobody/Collision and Repair Technology/Technician** *9 students enrolled* • **Automobile/Automotive Mechanics Technology/Technician** *27 students enrolled* • **Building/Construction Finishing, Management, and Inspection, Other** *1 student enrolled* • **Business Administration and Management, General** *1 student enrolled* • **Computer and Information Sciences, General** • **Dental Assisting/Assistant** *7 students enrolled* • **Diesel Mechanics Technology/Technician** *8 students enrolled* • **Electrical, Electronic and Communications Engineering Technology/Technician** • **Electrician** *8 students enrolled* • **Family and Consumer Sciences/Human Sciences, General** *1 student enrolled* • **Heating, Air Conditioning, Ventilation and Refrigeration Maintenance Technology/Technician (HAC, HACR, HVAC, HVACR)** *2 students enrolled* • **Licensed Practical/Vocational Nurse Training (LPN, LVN, Cert, Dipl, AAS)** *29 students enrolled* • **Welding Technology/Welder** *4 students enrolled*

**STUDENT SERVICES** Academic or career counseling, daycare for children of students, employment services for current students, remedial services.

## Myotherapy Institute

6020 South 58th Street, Lincoln, NE 68516
http://www.myotherapy.edu/

**CONTACT** Sue A. Kozisek, Director
**Telephone:** 402-421-7410

**GENERAL INFORMATION** Private Institution. **Accreditation:** State accredited or approved. **Total program enrollment:** 26. **Application fee:** $100.

**PROGRAM(S) OFFERED**
• **Massage Therapy/Therapeutic Massage** *3 students enrolled*

## Nebraska College of Technical Agriculture

RR3, Box 23A, Curtis, NE 69025-9205
http://www.ncta.unl.edu/

**CONTACT** Weldon Sleight, Dean
**Telephone:** 308-367-5200 Ext. 253

**GENERAL INFORMATION** Public Institution. Founded 1965. **Accreditation:** Regional (NCA). **Total program enrollment:** 285. **Application fee:** $25.

*Nebraska College of Technical Agriculture (continued)*

**PROGRAM(S) OFFERED**

• **Agricultural Business and Management, General** • **Agricultural Production Operations, General** *6 students enrolled* • **Applied Horticulture/Horticultural Operations, General** • **Veterinary/Animal Health Technology/Technician and Veterinary Assistant** *14 students enrolled*

**STUDENT SERVICES** Academic or career counseling, employment services for current students, placement services for program completers, remedial services.

## Nebraska Indian Community College

PO Box 428, Macy, NE 68039-0428
http://www.thenicc.edu/

**CONTACT** Michael Oltrogge, President
**Telephone:** 402-837-5078

**GENERAL INFORMATION** Public Institution. Founded 1979. **Accreditation:** Regional (NCA). **Total program enrollment:** 59. **Application fee:** $50.

**PROGRAM(S) OFFERED**

• **Data Entry/Microcomputer Applications, General** • **Early Childhood Education and Teaching**

**STUDENT SERVICES** Academic or career counseling, employment services for current students, remedial services.

## Nebraska Methodist College

720 North 87th Street, Omaha, NE 68114
http://www.methodistcollege.edu/

**CONTACT** Dr. Dennis Joslin, President
**Telephone:** 402-354-7000

**GENERAL INFORMATION** Private Institution (Affiliated with United Methodist Church). Founded 1891. **Accreditation:** Regional (NCA); diagnostic medical sonography (JRCEDMS). **Total program enrollment:** 454. **Application fee:** $25.

**PROGRAM(S) OFFERED**

• **Emergency Medical Technology/Technician (EMT Paramedic)** • **Health and Physical Education/Fitness, Other** • **Medical/Clinical Assistant** *14 students enrolled* • **Surgical Technology/Technologist** *15 students enrolled*

**STUDENT SERVICES** Academic or career counseling, employment services for current students, placement services for program completers, remedial services.

## Northeast Community College

801 East Benjamin Ave, PO Box 469, Norfolk, NE 68702-0469
http://www.northeast.edu/

**CONTACT** Dr. Bill Path, President
**Telephone:** 402-371-2020

**GENERAL INFORMATION** Public Institution. Founded 1973. **Accreditation:** Regional (NCA); physical therapy assisting (APTA). **Total program enrollment:** 2016.

**PROGRAM(S) OFFERED**

• **Accounting** • **Administrative Assistant and Secretarial Science, General** *7 students enrolled* • **Automobile/Automotive Mechanics Technology/Technician** • **Business Operations Support and Secretarial Services, Other** *1 student enrolled* • **Dairy Science** • **Early Childhood Education and Teaching** *1 student enrolled* • **General Office Occupations and Clerical Services** • **Health and Medical Administrative Services, Other** • **Legal Administrative Assistant/Secretary** • **Legal Assistant/Paralegal** • **Licensed Practical/Vocational Nurse Training (LPN, LVN, Cert, Dipl, AAS)** *44 students enrolled* • **Marketing/Marketing Management, General** *3 students enrolled* • **Medical Administrative/Executive Assistant and Medical Secretary** *2 students enrolled* • **Medical Insurance Coding Specialist/Coder** *8 students enrolled* • **Office Management and Supervision** *1 student enrolled* • **Recording Arts Technology/Technician** *17 students enrolled* • **Welding Technology/Welder** *14 students enrolled*

**STUDENT SERVICES** Academic or career counseling, daycare for children of students, employment services for current students, placement services for program completers, remedial services.

## Omaha School of Massage Therapy

9748 Park Drive, Omaha, NE 68127
http://www.osmt.com/

**CONTACT** Steve Carper, Campus President
**Telephone:** 402-331-3694

**GENERAL INFORMATION** Private Institution. Founded 1991. **Total program enrollment:** 119. **Application fee:** $25.

**PROGRAM(S) OFFERED**

• **Massage Therapy/Therapeutic Massage** *868 hrs./$10,925*

**STUDENT SERVICES** Academic or career counseling, employment services for current students, placement services for program completers, remedial services.

## Southeast Community College Area

1111 O Street, Suite 111, Lincoln, NE 68508-3614
http://www.southeast.edu/

**CONTACT** Jack Huck, President
**Telephone:** 402-471-3333

**GENERAL INFORMATION** Public Institution. **Total program enrollment:** 4935.

**PROGRAM(S) OFFERED**

• **Administrative Assistant and Secretarial Science, General** *2 students enrolled* • **Biology Technician/Biotechnology Laboratory Technician** • **Business Administration and Management, General** *2 students enrolled* • **Child Care and Support Services Management** *2 students enrolled* • **Commercial and Advertising Art** *1 student enrolled* • **Computer and Information Sciences, General** *5 students enrolled* • **Dental Assisting/Assistant** *32 students enrolled* • **Electrical, Electronic and Communications Engineering Technology/Technician** • **Licensed Practical/Vocational Nurse Training (LPN, LVN, Cert, Dipl, AAS)** *104 students enrolled* • **Machine Tool Technology/Machinist** • **Medical/Clinical Assistant** *28 students enrolled* • **Pharmacy Technician/Assistant** *11 students enrolled* • **Restaurant, Culinary, and Catering Management/Manager** • **Small Engine Mechanics and Repair Technology/Technician** *26 students enrolled* • **Truck and Bus Driver/Commercial Vehicle Operation** *82 students enrolled* • **Vehicle and Vehicle Parts and Accessories Marketing Operations** • **Welding Technology/Welder** *1 student enrolled*

**STUDENT SERVICES** Academic or career counseling, daycare for children of students, employment services for current students, placement services for program completers, remedial services.

## Universal College of Healing Arts

8702 North 30th Street, Omaha, NE 68112-1810
http://www.ucha.com/

**CONTACT** Paulette Genthon, Executive Director
**Telephone:** 402-556-4456

**GENERAL INFORMATION** Private Institution. **Total program enrollment:** 55. **Application fee:** $60.

**PROGRAM(S) OFFERED**

• **Massage Therapy/Therapeutic Massage** *27 students enrolled*

**STUDENT SERVICES** Academic or career counseling, placement services for program completers.

## University of Nebraska

3835 Holdrege Street, Lincoln, NE 68583-0743

**CONTACT** James B. Milliken, President
**Telephone:** 402-472-5242

**GENERAL INFORMATION** Public Institution.

## Vatterott College

5141 F Street, Omaha, NE 68117
http://www.vatterott-college.edu/

**CONTACT** Brian Carroll, Director
**Telephone:** 402-891-9411

**GENERAL INFORMATION** Private Institution. **Total program enrollment:** 276.

**PROGRAM(S) OFFERED**
• **Accounting Technology/Technician and Bookkeeping** *5 students enrolled* • **CAD/CADD Drafting and/or Design Technology/Technician** *3 students enrolled* • **Construction Engineering Technology/Technician** • **Dental Assisting/Assistant** *27 students enrolled* • **Graphic Design** *5 students enrolled* • **Heating, Air Conditioning, Ventilation and Refrigeration Maintenance Technology/Technician (HAC, HACR, HVAC, HVACR)** *30 students enrolled* • **Information Technology** *19 students enrolled* • **Medical Office Assistant/Specialist** *1 student enrolled* • **Medical/Clinical Assistant** *30 students enrolled* • **Pharmacy Technician/Assistant** *11 students enrolled* • **Psychiatric/Mental Health Services Technician** *3 students enrolled*

**STUDENT SERVICES** Academic or career counseling, employment services for current students, placement services for program completers.

## Western Nebraska Community College

371 College Drive, Sidney, NE 69162
http://www.wncc.net/

**CONTACT** Eileen E. Ely, President
**Telephone:** 308-635-3606

**GENERAL INFORMATION** Public Institution. Founded 1926. **Accreditation:** Regional (NCA); health information technology (AHIMA). **Total program enrollment:** 958.

**PROGRAM(S) OFFERED**
• **Accounting** • **Administrative Assistant and Secretarial Science, General** • **Airframe Mechanics and Aircraft Maintenance Technology/Technician** *5 students enrolled* • **Autobody/Collision and Repair Technology/Technician** • **Automobile/Automotive Mechanics Technology/Technician** • **Business Administration and Management, General** *3 students enrolled* • **Computer and Information Sciences, General** • **Cosmetology/Cosmetologist, General** *4 students enrolled* • **Electrical and Power Transmission Installation/Installer, General** *8 students enrolled* • **Health Information/Medical Records Technology/Technician** *1 student enrolled* • **Licensed Practical/Vocational Nurse Training (LPN, LVN, Cert, Dipl, AAS)** *26 students enrolled* • **Welding Technology/Welder** *1 student enrolled*

**STUDENT SERVICES** Academic or career counseling, daycare for children of students, employment services for current students, placement services for program completers, remedial services.

## Xenon International School of Hair Design II

333 South 78th Street, Omaha, NE 68114
http://xenonintl.com/

**CONTACT** Stacey Peters, Director
**Telephone:** 402-393-2933 Ext. 1007

**GENERAL INFORMATION** Private Institution. Founded 1987. **Total program enrollment:** 263.

**PROGRAM(S) OFFERED**
• **Aesthetician/Esthetician and Skin Care Specialist** *600 hrs./$9000* • **Cosmetology, Barber/Styling, and Nail Instructor** *925 hrs./$5000* • **Cosmetology/Cosmetologist, General** *2100 hrs./$16,000* • **Nail Technician/Specialist and Manicurist** *300 hrs./$1750*

**STUDENT SERVICES** Academic or career counseling, placement services for program completers.

# NEVADA

## Academy of Hair Design

4445 West Charleston Boulevard, Las Vegas, NV 89102

**CONTACT** Sandy Dunham, Director
**Telephone:** 702-878-1185 Ext. 21

**GENERAL INFORMATION** Private Institution. Founded 1972. **Total program enrollment:** 172. **Application fee:** $40.

**PROGRAM(S) OFFERED**
• **Aesthetician/Esthetician and Skin Care Specialist** *600 hrs./$7380* • **Barbering/Barber** *21 students enrolled* • **Cosmetology and Related Personal Grooming Arts, Other** *500 hrs./$4083* • **Cosmetology, Barber/Styling, and Nail Instructor** *1000 hrs./$5000* • **Cosmetology/Cosmetologist, General** *1800 hrs./$18,149* • **Hair Styling/Stylist and Hair Design** *1200 hrs./$12,735* • **Make-Up Artist/Specialist** *30 students enrolled*

**STUDENT SERVICES** Academic or career counseling, placement services for program completers.

## Academy of Medical and Business Careers

901 Rancho Lane, Suite 190, Las Vegas, NV 89106
http://www.academylasvegas.com/

**CONTACT** James W. Alexander, Chief Executive Officer
**Telephone:** 702-671-4242

**GENERAL INFORMATION** Private Institution. **Total program enrollment:** 545. **Application fee:** $20.

**PROGRAM(S) OFFERED**
• **Clinical/Medical Laboratory Assistant** *172 students enrolled* • **Massage Therapy/Therapeutic Massage** *720 hrs./$13,400* • **Medical Office Assistant/Specialist** *720 hrs./$12,775* • **Medical Office Management/Administration** *51 students enrolled* • **Medical/Clinical Assistant** *720 hrs./$13,000* • **Phlebotomy/Phlebotomist** *80 hrs./$1890*

**STUDENT SERVICES** Academic or career counseling, employment services for current students, placement services for program completers, remedial services.

## Career College of Northern Nevada

1195-A Corporate Boulevard, Reno, NV 89502
http://www.ccnn.edu/

**CONTACT** L. Nathan Clark, College President
**Telephone:** 775-856-2266

**GENERAL INFORMATION** Private Institution. Founded 1984. **Accreditation:** State accredited or approved. **Total program enrollment:** 358. **Application fee:** $25.

**PROGRAM(S) OFFERED**
• **Accounting Technology/Technician and Bookkeeping** • **Computer and Information Sciences and Support Services, Other** *1 student enrolled* • **Electrical and Electronic Engineering Technologies/Technicians, Other** *125 hrs./$26,250* • **Electrical/Electronics Maintenance and Repair Technology, Other**

*Career College of Northern Nevada (continued)*

76 *hrs./$15,855* • **Legal Administrative Assistant/Secretary** *1 student enrolled* • **Legal Assistant/Paralegal** *103 hrs./$21,525* • **Medical Insurance Coding Specialist/Coder** *45 students enrolled* • **Medical Insurance Specialist/Medical Biller** *56 hrs./$11,655* • **Medical/Clinical Assistant** *76 hrs./$15,960*

**STUDENT SERVICES** Academic or career counseling, employment services for current students, placement services for program completers, remedial services.

## Carson City Beauty Academy

2531 North Carson Street, Carson City, NV 89706

**CONTACT** Sandra Escover, President
**Telephone:** 702-885-9977

**GENERAL INFORMATION** Private Institution. Founded 1988. **Total program enrollment:** 115. **Application fee:** $100.

**PROGRAM(S) OFFERED**
• **Aesthetician/Esthetician and Skin Care Specialist** *600 hrs./$6700* • **Cosmetology/Cosmetologist, General** *1800 hrs./$14,950* • **Nail Technician/Specialist and Manicurist** *500 hrs./$3350*

**STUDENT SERVICES** Placement services for program completers.

## College of Southern Nevada

3200 East Cheyenne Avenue, North Las Vegas, NV 89030-4296
http://www.csn.edu/

**CONTACT** Dr. Michael Richards, President
**Telephone:** 702-651-5000

**GENERAL INFORMATION** Public Institution. Founded 1971. **Accreditation:** Regional (NCCU/NCCU); dental assisting (ADA); dental hygiene (ADA); diagnostic medical sonography (JRCEDMS); health information technology (AHIMA); medical laboratory technology (NAACLS); ophthalmic dispensing (COA); physical therapy assisting (APTA); practical nursing (NLN). **Total program enrollment:** 9356. **Application fee:** $5.

**PROGRAM(S) OFFERED**
• **Accounting Technology/Technician and Bookkeeping** *5 students enrolled* • **Automobile/Automotive Mechanics Technology/Technician** *2 students enrolled* • **Building/Construction Site Management/Manager** *1 student enrolled* • **Business Administration and Management, General** *5 students enrolled* • **Business/Commerce, General** *1 student enrolled* • **CAD/CADD Drafting and/or Design Technology/Technician** *4 students enrolled* • **Commercial Photography** *3 students enrolled* • **Computer Programming/Programmer, General** *6 students enrolled* • **Computer Systems Networking and Telecommunications** *3 students enrolled* • **Criminal Justice/Police Science** *1 student enrolled* • **Criminal Justice/Safety Studies** *1 student enrolled* • **Culinary Arts/Chef Training** *9 students enrolled* • **Customer Service Management** *5 students enrolled* • **Data Processing and Data Processing Technology/Technician** *3 students enrolled* • **Dental Assisting/Assistant** *9 students enrolled* • **Education/Teaching of Individuals with Hearing Impairments, Including Deafness** *1 student enrolled* • **Electrical, Electronic and Communications Engineering Technology/Technician** *1 student enrolled* • **Fire Science/Firefighting** *2 students enrolled* • **Graphic Design** *3 students enrolled* • **Health Information/Medical Records Technology/Technician** *3 students enrolled* • **Heating, Air Conditioning, Ventilation and Refrigeration Maintenance Technology/Technician (HAC, HACR, HVAC, HVACR)** *3 students enrolled* • **Hospitality Administration/Management, General** *2 students enrolled* • **Hotel/Motel Administration/Management** *3 students enrolled* • **Kindergarten/Preschool Education and Teaching** *1 student enrolled* • **Kinesiotherapy/Kinesiotherapist** *5 students enrolled* • **Legal Assistant/Paralegal** *5 students enrolled* • **Licensed Practical/Vocational Nurse Training (LPN, LVN, Cert, Dipl, AAS)** *25 students enrolled* • **Medical Office Assistant/Specialist** *8 students enrolled* • **Medical Radiologic Technology/Science—Radiation Therapist** *1 student enrolled* • **Music Management and Merchandising** *20 students enrolled* • **Ornamental Horticulture** *1 student enrolled* • **Pharmacy Technician/Assistant** *3 students enrolled* • **Pre-Veterinary Studies** *5 students enrolled* • **Prepress/Desktop Publishing and Digital Imaging Design** *1 student enrolled* • **Psychiatric/Mental Health Services Technician** *1 student enrolled* • **Restaurant/Food Services Management** *1 student enrolled* • **Surgical Technology/Technologist** *4 students enrolled* • **Tourism and Travel Services Management** *3 students enrolled* • **Water Quality and Wastewater Treatment Management and Recycling Technology/Technician** *2 students enrolled* • **Web Page, Digital/Multimedia and Information Resources Design** *1 student enrolled* • **Welding Technology/Welder** *1 student enrolled*

**STUDENT SERVICES** Academic or career counseling, daycare for children of students, employment services for current students, placement services for program completers, remedial services.

## Euphoria Institute of Beauty Arts & Sciences

11041 S. Eastern Avenue, Suite 112, Henderson, NV 89052
http://www.euphoriainstitute.com

**CONTACT** Kim Harney-Moore, Executive Director
**Telephone:** 702-932-8111

**GENERAL INFORMATION** Private Institution. **Total program enrollment:** 117. **Application fee:** $50.

**PROGRAM(S) OFFERED**
• **Aesthetician/Esthetician and Skin Care Specialist** *93 students enrolled* • **Cosmetology and Related Personal Grooming Arts, Other** *600 hrs./$8950* • **Cosmetology/Cosmetologist, General** *1800 hrs./$17,950*

**STUDENT SERVICES** Academic or career counseling, employment services for current students, placement services for program completers.

## Euphoria Institute of Beauty Arts & Sciences

9340 W. Sahara Avenue, Suite 205, Las Vegas, NV 89117
http://www.euphoriainstitute.com

**CONTACT** Cynthia Ford, Business Office Manager
**Telephone:** 702-341-8111

**GENERAL INFORMATION** Private Institution. **Total program enrollment:** 110. **Application fee:** $50.

**PROGRAM(S) OFFERED**
• **Aesthetician/Esthetician and Skin Care Specialist** *600 hrs./$9000* • **Cosmetology/Cosmetologist, General** *1800 hrs./$17,950*

**STUDENT SERVICES** Academic or career counseling, placement services for program completers.

## Expertise Cosmetology Institute

1911 Stella Lake Street, Las Vegas, NV 89106
http://www.expertisebeauty.com/

**CONTACT** Gwen Braimoh, Director/Owner
**Telephone:** 702-636-8686

**GENERAL INFORMATION** Private Institution. **Total program enrollment:** 76. **Application fee:** $100.

**PROGRAM(S) OFFERED**
• **Aesthetician/Esthetician and Skin Care Specialist** *600 hrs./$6910* • **Cosmetology, Barber/Styling, and Nail Instructor** *1000 hrs./$5400* • **Cosmetology/Cosmetologist, General** *1800 hrs./$14,970* • **Hair Styling/Stylist and Hair Design** *1200 hrs./$12,050* • **Nail Technician/Specialist and Manicurist** *600 hrs./$3375*

## Great Basin College

1500 College Parkway, Elko, NV 89801-3348
http://www.gbcnv.edu/

**CONTACT** Carl Diekhans, Interim President
**Telephone:** 775-738-8493

**GENERAL INFORMATION** Public Institution. Founded 1967. **Accreditation:** Regional (NCCU/NCCU). **Total program enrollment:** 964. **Application fee:** $10.

**PROGRAM(S) OFFERED**
• **Accounting Technology/Technician and Bookkeeping** *7 students enrolled* • **Business Administration and Management, General** *1 student enrolled* • **Business/Office Automation/Technology/Data Entry** • **Child Care and Support Services Management** • **Computer Graphics** *7 students enrolled* • **Computer/Information Technology Services Administration and Management, Other** • **Data Processing and Data Processing Technology/Technician** • **Diesel Mechanics Technology/Technician** *6 students enrolled* • **Early Childhood Education and Teaching** *1 student enrolled* • **Electrician** *8 students enrolled* • **Elementary Education and Teaching** *4 students enrolled* • **Industrial Mechanics and Maintenance Technology** • **Instrumentation Technology/Technician** *7 students enrolled* • **Language Interpretation and Translation** *1 student enrolled* • **Secondary Education and Teaching** *1 student enrolled* • **Web Page, Digital/Multimedia and Information Resources Design** • **Welding Technology/Welder** *8 students enrolled*

**STUDENT SERVICES** Academic or career counseling, daycare for children of students, employment services for current students, placement services for program completers, remedial services.

## High-Tech Institute

2320 South Rancho Drive, Las Vegas, NV 89102
http://www.high-techinstitute.com/

**CONTACT** Rose Frank, Campus President
**Telephone:** 702-385-6700

**GENERAL INFORMATION** Private Institution. Founded 2002. **Accreditation:** State accredited or approved. **Total program enrollment:** 639. **Application fee:** $50.

**PROGRAM(S) OFFERED**
• **Dental Assisting/Assistant** *720 hrs./$11,316* • **Massage Therapy/Therapeutic Massage** *820 hrs./$11,749* • **Medical Insurance Specialist/Medical Biller** *720 hrs./$11,092* • **Medical/Clinical Assistant** *746 hrs./$11,550* • **Pharmacy Technician/Assistant** *800 hrs./$11,513* • **Surgical Technology/Technologist** *1160 hrs./$23,257*

**STUDENT SERVICES** Placement services for program completers.

## Institute of Professional Careers

4472 S. Eastern Avenue, Las Vegas, NV 89119

**CONTACT** Sanjeeta Khurana, Chief Financial Officer
**Telephone:** 702-734-9900

**GENERAL INFORMATION** Private Institution. **Total program enrollment:** 6.

**PROGRAM(S) OFFERED**
• **Dental Assisting/Assistant** *776 hrs./$11,700*

**STUDENT SERVICES** Employment services for current students, placement services for program completers.

## Marinello School of Beauty

5001 East Bonanza, Suite 110, Las Vegas, NV 89110
http://www.marinello.com/

**CONTACT** Dr. Nagui Elyas, President
**Telephone:** 702-431-6200

**GENERAL INFORMATION** Private Institution. **Total program enrollment:** 285.

**PROGRAM(S) OFFERED**
• **Aesthetician/Esthetician and Skin Care Specialist** *600 hrs./$8475* • **Cosmetology/Cosmetologist, General** *1600 hrs./$16,635* • **Hair Styling/Stylist and Hair Design** • **Nail Technician/Specialist and Manicurist** *400 hrs./$3475*

**STUDENT SERVICES** Academic or career counseling, placement services for program completers.

## Nevada Career Academy

950 Industrial Way, Sparks, NV 89431-6092

**CONTACT** Gary Yasuda, President
**Telephone:** 775-348-7200

**GENERAL INFORMATION** Private Institution. **Total program enrollment:** 282. **Application fee:** $100.

**PROGRAM(S) OFFERED**
• **Dental Assisting/Assistant** *720 hrs./$12,564* • **Health/Health Care Administration/Management** *720 hrs./$10,810* • **Massage Therapy/Therapeutic Massage** *720 hrs./$11,128* • **Medical Administrative/Executive Assistant and Medical Secretary** *5 students enrolled* • **Medical/Clinical Assistant** *720 hrs./$10,845* • **Pharmacy Technician/Assistant** *900 hrs./$11,034*

**STUDENT SERVICES** Academic or career counseling, employment services for current students, placement services for program completers.

## Nevada Career Institute

3231 North Decatur Boulevard, Suite 219, Las Vegas, NV 89130

**CONTACT** Joanne Q. Leming, Director
**Telephone:** 702-893-3300

**GENERAL INFORMATION** Private Institution. **Total program enrollment:** 27. **Application fee:** $75.

**PROGRAM(S) OFFERED**
• **Massage Therapy/Therapeutic Massage** *720 hrs./$11,775* • **Medical Office Management/Administration** *720 hrs./$11,125* • **Medical/Clinical Assistant** *720 hrs./$11,125* • **Surgical Technology/Technologist** *1440 hrs./$23,100*

**STUDENT SERVICES** Employment services for current students, placement services for program completers, remedial services.

## Northwest Health Careers

7398 Smoke Ranch Road, Suite 100, Las Vegas, NV 89128
http://northwesthealthcareers.com/

**CONTACT** Dr. John Kenny, Chief Executive
**Telephone:** 702-254-7577

**GENERAL INFORMATION** Private Institution. **Total program enrollment:** 60. **Application fee:** $100.

**PROGRAM(S) OFFERED**
• **Allied Health and Medical Assisting Services, Other** *36 hrs./$11,087* • **Dental Assisting/Assistant** *31 hrs./$9913* • **Massage Therapy/Therapeutic Massage** *30 hrs./$9979* • **Medical Insurance Specialist/Medical Biller** *8 students enrolled* • **Medical Office Assistant/Specialist** • **Phlebotomy/Phlebotomist** *240 hrs./$2495*

**STUDENT SERVICES** Academic or career counseling, employment services for current students, placement services for program completers.

## Pima Medical Institute

3333 East Flamingo Road, Las Vegas, NV 89121
http://www.pmi.edu/

**CONTACT** Sam Gentile, Campus Director
**Telephone:** 702-458-9650

**GENERAL INFORMATION** Private Institution. Founded 2003. **Accreditation:** State accredited or approved. **Total program enrollment:** 963.

**PROGRAM(S) OFFERED**
• **Dental Assisting/Assistant** *720 hrs./$9530* • **Massage Therapy/Therapeutic Massage** • **Medical Administrative/Executive Assistant and Medical Secretary** *560 hrs./$6430* • **Medical/Clinical Assistant** *800 hrs./$9995* • **Pharmacy**

*Pima Medical Institute (continued)*

**Technician/Assistant** *800 hrs./$9380* • **Phlebotomy/Phlebotomist** *11 students enrolled* • **Respiratory Therapy Technician/Assistant** *91 hrs./$27,875* • **Veterinary/Animal Health Technology/Technician and Veterinary Assistant** *720 hrs./$9380*

**STUDENT SERVICES** Academic or career counseling, employment services for current students, placement services for program completers, remedial services.

## Prater Way College of Beauty

4750 Longley Lane, Suite 209, Reno, NV 89502
praterway.net

**CONTACT** Steve Mucciaro, Executive Director, Financial Aid
**Telephone:** 775-355-6677 Ext. 10

**GENERAL INFORMATION** Private Institution. **Total program enrollment:** 80.

**PROGRAM(S) OFFERED**
• **Aesthetician/Esthetician and Skin Care Specialist** *600 hrs./$6400* • **Cosmetology, Barber/Styling, and Nail Instructor** *1000 hrs./$7600* • **Cosmetology/Cosmetologist, General** *1800 hrs./$14,840* • **Hair Styling/Stylist and Hair Design** *1200 hrs./$8500* • **Nail Technician/Specialist and Manicurist** *500 hrs./$3400*

**STUDENT SERVICES** Academic or career counseling, placement services for program completers.

## Truckee Meadows Community College

7000 Dandini Boulevard, Reno, NV 89512-3901
http://www.tmcc.edu/

**CONTACT** Maria Sheehan, President
**Telephone:** 775-673-7000

**GENERAL INFORMATION** Public Institution. Founded 1971. **Accreditation:** Regional (NCCU/NCCU); dental assisting (ADA); dental hygiene (ADA); radiologic technology: radiography (JRCERT). **Total program enrollment:** 3296. **Application fee:** $10.

**PROGRAM(S) OFFERED**
• **Accounting Technology/Technician and Bookkeeping** • **Accounting and Related Services, Other** • **Administrative Assistant and Secretarial Science, General** *1 student enrolled* • **Architectural Drafting and Architectural CAD/CADD** • **Automobile/Automotive Mechanics Technology/Technician** *3 students enrolled* • **Baking and Pastry Arts/Baker/Pastry Chef** *1 student enrolled* • **Building/Construction Finishing, Management, and Inspection, Other** • **Business/Commerce, General** *3 students enrolled* • **Child Care and Support Services Management** • **Commercial and Advertising Art** *1 student enrolled* • **Computer Graphics** *3 students enrolled* • **Computer Systems Networking and Telecommunications** • **Cooking and Related Culinary Arts, General** *1 student enrolled* • **Criminal Justice/Law Enforcement Administration** *3 students enrolled* • **Culinary Arts/Chef Training** • **Dental Assisting/Assistant** *10 students enrolled* • **Diesel Mechanics Technology/Technician** • **Drafting and Design Technology/Technician, General** *1 student enrolled* • **Early Childhood Education and Teaching** • **Electrical, Electronic and Communications Engineering Technology/Technician** *2 students enrolled* • **Emergency Medical Technology/Technician (EMT Paramedic)** • **Environmental Control Technologies/Technicians, Other** • **Ethnic, Cultural Minority, and Gender Studies, Other** • **Fine Arts and Art Studies, Other** • **Fire Protection and Safety Technology/Technician** • **Graphic Communications, General** • **Heating, Air Conditioning, Ventilation and Refrigeration Maintenance Technology/Technician (HAC, HACR, HVAC, HVACR)** *1 student enrolled* • **Landscaping and Groundskeeping** • **Legal Administrative Assistant/Secretary** *4 students enrolled* • **Physical Sciences, Other** *1 student enrolled* • **Welding Technology/Welder** *1 student enrolled*

**STUDENT SERVICES** Academic or career counseling, daycare for children of students, employment services for current students, placement services for program completers, remedial services.

## University and Community College System of Nevada–System Office

2601 Enterprise Road, Reno, NV 89512
http://www.nevada.edu

**CONTACT** Dr. Jane Nichols, Vice Chancellor of Academic Affairs
**Telephone:** 775-784-4901

**GENERAL INFORMATION** Public Institution.

## University of Nevada, Las Vegas

4505 Maryland Parkway, Las Vegas, NV 89154-9900
http://www.unlv.edu/

**CONTACT** David B. Ashley, President
**Telephone:** 702-895-3011

**GENERAL INFORMATION** Public Institution. Founded 1957. **Accreditation:** Regional (NCCU/NCCU); art and design (NASAD); athletic training (JRCAT); computer science (ABET/CSAC); counseling (ACA); engineering-related programs (ABET/RAC); interior design: professional (CIDA); medical technology (NAACLS); music (NASM); nuclear medicine technology (JRCNMT); theater (NAST). **Total program enrollment:** 18490. **Application fee:** $60.

**PROGRAM(S) OFFERED**
• **Radiologic Technology/Science—Radiographer**

**STUDENT SERVICES** Academic or career counseling, daycare for children of students, employment services for current students, placement services for program completers, remedial services.

## University of Phoenix–Las Vegas Campus

7455 Washington Avenue, Suite 317, Las Vegas, NV 89128
http://www.phoenix.edu/

**CONTACT** William Pepicello, PhD, President
**Telephone:** 800-554-4665

**GENERAL INFORMATION** Private Institution. Founded 1994. **Accreditation:** Regional (NCA). **Total program enrollment:** 3288.

**STUDENT SERVICES** Academic or career counseling, remedial services.

## Western Nevada Community College

2201 West College Parkway, Carson City, NV 89703-7316
http://www.wncc.edu/

**CONTACT** Dr. Carol Lucey, President
**Telephone:** 775-445-3000

**GENERAL INFORMATION** Public Institution. Founded 1971. **Accreditation:** Regional (NCCU/NCCU). **Total program enrollment:** 1096. **Application fee:** $15.

**PROGRAM(S) OFFERED**
• **Accounting** *2 students enrolled* • **American Sign Language (ASL)** *3 students enrolled* • **Automobile/Automotive Mechanics Technology/Technician** *1 student enrolled* • **Business/Commerce, General** *13 students enrolled* • **Child Care Provider/Assistant** *1 student enrolled* • **Computer Systems Networking and Telecommunications** *4 students enrolled* • **Construction Trades, Other** *2 students enrolled* • **Corrections** • **Criminal Justice/Police Science** • **Drafting and Design Technology/Technician, General** *1 student enrolled* • **Health Information/Medical Records Technology/Technician** *1 student enrolled* • **Legal Assistant/Paralegal** • **Licensed Practical/Vocational Nurse Training (LPN, LVN, Cert, Dipl, AAS)** *1 student enrolled* • **Machine Tool Technology/Machinist** • **Science Technologies/Technicians, Other** • **Surgical Technology/Technologist** *13 students enrolled* • **Welding Technology/Welder** *1 student enrolled*

**STUDENT SERVICES** Academic or career counseling, daycare for children of students, employment services for current students, remedial services.

# NEW MEXICO

## The Art Center Design College

5000 Marble NE, Albuquerque, NM 87110
http://www.theartcenter.edu/

**CONTACT** Sharmon R. Woods, President
**Telephone:** 505-254-7575

**GENERAL INFORMATION** Private Institution. Founded 1989. **Accreditation:** State accredited or approved. **Total program enrollment:** 130. **Application fee:** $25.

**PROGRAM(S) OFFERED**
• **Interior Design**

**STUDENT SERVICES** Academic or career counseling, employment services for current students, placement services for program completers, remedial services.

## Brookline College

4201 Central Avenue NW, Suite J, Albuquerque, NM 87105-1649
http://brooklinecollege.edu/

**CONTACT** Cheryl Kindred, Director
**Telephone:** 505-880-2877

**GENERAL INFORMATION** Private Institution. **Accreditation:** State accredited or approved. **Total program enrollment:** 160. **Application fee:** $50.

**PROGRAM(S) OFFERED**
• **Business Administration and Management, General** *61 hrs./$23,375* • **Criminal Justice/Law Enforcement Administration** *64 hrs./$24,600* • **Legal Administrative Assistant/Secretary** • **Legal Assistant/Paralegal** *69 hrs./$26,425* • **Medical/Clinical Assistant** *28 hrs./$11,760* • **Security and Loss Prevention Services** *28 hrs./$12,260*

**STUDENT SERVICES** Academic or career counseling, daycare for children of students, employment services for current students, placement services for program completers, remedial services.

## Central New Mexico Community College

525 Buena Vista, SE, Albuquerque, NM 87106-4096
http://www.cnm.edu/

**CONTACT** Katharine Winograd, President
**Telephone:** 505-224-3000

**GENERAL INFORMATION** Public Institution. Founded 1965. **Accreditation:** Regional (NCA); dental assisting (ADA); engineering technology (ABET/TAC); medical laboratory technology (NAACLS); practical nursing (NLN). **Total program enrollment:** 7693.

**PROGRAM(S) OFFERED**
• **Accounting Technology/Technician and Bookkeeping** *33 students enrolled* • **Accounting** *4 students enrolled* • **Administrative Assistant and Secretarial Science, General** *8 students enrolled* • **Architectural Drafting and Architectural CAD/CADD** *21 students enrolled* • **Automobile/Automotive Mechanics Technology/Technician** *34 students enrolled* • **Baking and Pastry Arts/Baker/Pastry Chef** *32 students enrolled* • **Banking and Financial Support Services** *2 students enrolled* • **Blood Bank Technology Specialist** *65 students enrolled* • **Business Administration and Management, General** *23 students enrolled* • **Business Operations Support and Secretarial Services, Other** *20 students enrolled* • **Carpentry/Carpenter** *11 students enrolled* • **Cinematography and Film/Video Production** *24 students enrolled* • **Computer Systems Analysis/Analyst** *1 student enrolled* • **Culinary Arts/Chef Training** *34 students enrolled* • **Data Processing and Data Processing Technology/Technician** *1 student enrolled* • **Dental Assisting/Assistant** *16 students enrolled* • **Diesel Mechanics Technology/Technician** *24 students enrolled* • **Education, General** *13 students enrolled* • **Electrical, Electronic and Communications Engineering Technology/Technician** *19 students enrolled* • **Electrician** *131 students enrolled* • **Emergency Medical Technology/Technician (EMT Paramedic)** *7 students enrolled* • **Foodservice Systems Administration/Management** *29 students enrolled* • **Health Information/Medical Records Technology/Technician** *9 students enrolled* • **Health Unit Coordinator/Ward Clerk** *43 students enrolled* • **Health and Physical Education, General** *10 students enrolled* • **Heating, Air Conditioning, Ventilation and Refrigeration Maintenance Technology/Technician (HAC, HACR, HVAC, HVACR)** *40 students enrolled* • **Hematology Technology/Technician** *9 students enrolled* • **Landscaping and Groundskeeping** *3 students enrolled* • **Laser and Optical Technology/Technician** *10 students enrolled* • **Legal Assistant/Paralegal** *1 student enrolled* • **Legal Professions and Studies, Other** *5 students enrolled* • **Machine Shop Technology/Assistant** *7 students enrolled* • **Manufacturing Technology/Technician** *1 student enrolled* • **Nurse/Nursing Assistant/Aide and Patient Care Assistant** *52 students enrolled* • **Parks, Recreation and Leisure Studies** *2 students enrolled* • **Pharmacy Technician/Assistant** *6 students enrolled* • **Pipefitting/Pipefitter and Sprinkler Fitter** *43 students enrolled* • **Surgical Technology/Technologist** *11 students enrolled* • **Survey Technology/Surveying** *2 students enrolled* • **Truck and Bus Driver/Commercial Vehicle Operation** *65 students enrolled* • **Welding Technology/Welder** *28 students enrolled*

**STUDENT SERVICES** Academic or career counseling, daycare for children of students, employment services for current students, placement services for program completers, remedial services.

## Clovis Community College

417 Schepps Boulevard, Clovis, NM 88101-8381
http://www.clovis.edu/

**CONTACT** Dr. John Neibling, President
**Telephone:** 505-769-2811

**GENERAL INFORMATION** Public Institution. Founded 1990. **Accreditation:** Regional (NCA); radiologic technology: radiography (JRCERT). **Total program enrollment:** 773.

**PROGRAM(S) OFFERED**
• **Administrative Assistant and Secretarial Science, General** *3 students enrolled* • **Automobile/Automotive Mechanics Technology/Technician** *3 students enrolled* • **Business Administration and Management, General** *1 student enrolled* • **Carpentry/Carpenter** • **Cosmetology/Cosmetologist, General** *24 students enrolled* • **Electrical, Electronic and Communications Engineering Technology/Technician** *1 student enrolled* • **Heating, Air Conditioning, Ventilation and Refrigeration Maintenance Technology/Technician (HAC, HACR, HVAC, HVACR)** *3 students enrolled* • **Licensed Practical/Vocational Nurse Training (LPN, LVN, Cert, Dipl, AAS)** *73 students enrolled* • **Management Information Systems, General** *1 student enrolled* • **Sign Language Interpretation and Translation** • **Welding Technology/Welder** *2 students enrolled*

**STUDENT SERVICES** Academic or career counseling, daycare for children of students, employment services for current students, placement services for program completers, remedial services.

## Crownpoint Institute of Technology

PO Box 849, Crownpoint, NM 87313
http://www.citech.edu/academics.htm

**CONTACT** Elmer Guy, President
**Telephone:** 505-786-4100

**GENERAL INFORMATION** Private Institution. Founded 1979. **Accreditation:** Regional (NCA). **Total program enrollment:** 338.

**PROGRAM(S) OFFERED**
• **Accounting Technology/Technician and Bookkeeping** *12 students enrolled* • **Administrative Assistant and Secretarial Science, General** *7 students enrolled* • **Automotive Engineering Technology/Technician** *3 students enrolled* • **Building/Home/Construction Inspection/Inspector** *11 students enrolled* • **CAD/CADD Drafting and/or Design Technology/Technician** *3 students enrolled* • **Carpentry/Carpenter** *7 students enrolled* • **Computer Science** *9 students enrolled* • **Cooking and Related Culinary Arts, General** *14 students enrolled* • **Early Childhood Education and Teaching** *2 students enrolled* • **Electrician** *10 students enrolled* • **Environmental Science** • **Geography, Other** • **Horse Husbandry/Equine Science and Management** • **Nurse/Nursing Assistant/Aide**

*Crownpoint Institute of Technology (continued)*
**and Patient Care Assistant** *26 students enrolled* • **Small Business Administration/Management** • **Solar Energy Technology/Technician** • **Truck and Bus Driver/Commercial Vehicle Operation** *13 students enrolled*

**STUDENT SERVICES** Academic or career counseling, daycare for children of students, employment services for current students, placement services for program completers, remedial services.

## De Wolff College of Hair Styling and Cosmetology

6405 Lomas Avenue, NE, Albuquerque, NM 87110

**CONTACT** S. Washburn, President
**Telephone:** 505-296-4100

**GENERAL INFORMATION** Private Institution. Founded 1969. **Total program enrollment:** 112. **Application fee:** $100.

**PROGRAM(S) OFFERED**
• **Aesthetician/Esthetician and Skin Care Specialist** *600 hrs./$7999* • **Cosmetology and Related Personal Grooming Arts, Other** *600 hrs./$8300* • **Cosmetology, Barber/Styling, and Nail Instructor** *1000 hrs./$3556* • **Cosmetology/Cosmetologist, General** *1600 hrs./$12,459* • **Nail Technician/Specialist and Manicurist** *600 hrs./$4467* • **Trade and Industrial Teacher Education** *3 students enrolled*

**STUDENT SERVICES** Academic or career counseling, employment services for current students, placement services for program completers.

## Doña Ana Branch Community College

MSC-3DA, Box 30001, 3400 South Espina Street, Las Cruces, NM 88003-8001
http://dabcc-www.nmsu.edu/

**CONTACT** Margie Huerta, President
**Telephone:** 575-527-7500

**GENERAL INFORMATION** Public Institution. Founded 1973. **Accreditation:** Regional (NCA); dental assisting (ADA); emergency medical services (JRCEMTP); radiologic technology: radiography (JRCERT). **Total program enrollment:** 2791. **Application fee:** $20.

**PROGRAM(S) OFFERED**
• **Administrative Assistant and Secretarial Science, General** *15 students enrolled* • **Adult Development and Aging** • **Animation, Interactive Technology, Video Graphics and Special Effects** *3 students enrolled* • **Automobile/Automotive Mechanics Technology/Technician** • **Building/Property Maintenance and Management** *1 student enrolled* • **Carpentry/Carpenter** *2 students enrolled* • **Child Care Provider/Assistant** • **Commercial and Advertising Art** *8 students enrolled* • **Data Processing and Data Processing Technology/Technician** *3 students enrolled* • **Dental Assisting/Assistant** *14 students enrolled* • **Diagnostic Medical Sonography/Sonographer and Ultrasound Technician** *2 students enrolled* • **Digital Communication and Media/Multimedia** *4 students enrolled* • **Drafting and Design Technology/Technician, General** *2 students enrolled* • **Electrical, Electronic and Communications Engineering Technology/Technician** *10 students enrolled* • **Emergency Medical Technology/Technician (EMT Paramedic)** *3 students enrolled* • **General Office Occupations and Clerical Services** *3 students enrolled* • **Health Aide** *12 students enrolled* • **Heating, Air Conditioning, Ventilation and Refrigeration Maintenance Technology/Technician (HAC, HACR, HVAC, HVACR)** *13 students enrolled* • **Library Assistant/Technician** *8 students enrolled* • **Licensed Practical/Vocational Nurse Training (LPN, LVN, Cert, Dipl, AAS)** • **Lineworker** *2 students enrolled* • **Medical Insurance Specialist/Medical Biller** *11 students enrolled* • **Nurse/Nursing Assistant/Aide and Patient Care Assistant** *3 students enrolled* • **Photographic and Film/Video Technology/Technician and Assistant** *4 students enrolled* • **Pipefitting/Pipefitter and Sprinkler Fitter** • **Retailing and Retail Operations** • **Sales, Distribution and Marketing Operations, General** • **Water Quality and Wastewater Treatment Management and Recycling Technology/Technician** • **Web/Multimedia Management and Webmaster** *2 students enrolled* • **Welding Technology/Welder** *3 students enrolled*

**STUDENT SERVICES** Academic or career counseling, employment services for current students, placement services for program completers, remedial services.

## Eastern New Mexico University

1200 West University, Portales, NM 88130
http://www.enmu.edu/

**CONTACT** Steven Gamble, President
**Telephone:** 575-562-1011

**GENERAL INFORMATION** Public Institution. Founded 1934. **Accreditation:** Regional (NCA); home economics (AAFCS); music (NASM); speech-language pathology (ASHA). **Total program enrollment:** 2551.

**PROGRAM(S) OFFERED**
• **Agriculture, General**

**STUDENT SERVICES** Academic or career counseling, employment services for current students, placement services for program completers, remedial services.

## Eastern New Mexico University–Roswell

PO Box 6000, Roswell, NM 88202-6000
http://www.enmu.edu/

**CONTACT** Dr. John Madden, President
**Telephone:** 505-624-7000

**GENERAL INFORMATION** Public Institution. Founded 1958. **Accreditation:** Regional (NCA); emergency medical services (JRCEMTP); medical assisting (AAMAE). **Total program enrollment:** 1288.

**PROGRAM(S) OFFERED**
• **Accounting Technology/Technician and Bookkeeping** *1 student enrolled* • **Allied Health Diagnostic, Intervention, and Treatment Professions, Other** *2 students enrolled* • **Autobody/Collision and Repair Technology/Technician** *5 students enrolled* • **Automobile/Automotive Mechanics Technology/Technician** • **Blood Bank Technology Specialist** *1 student enrolled* • **Building/Property Maintenance and Management** *1 student enrolled* • **Child Care and Support Services Management** *11 students enrolled* • **Cinematography and Film/Video Production** • **Dental Assisting/Assistant** *3 students enrolled* • **Design and Visual Communications, General** • **Drafting and Design Technology/Technician, General** • **Electromechanical Technology/Electromechanical Engineering Technology** • **Emergency Medical Technology/Technician (EMT Paramedic)** *89 students enrolled* • **Food Preparation/Professional Cooking/Kitchen Assistant** *8 students enrolled* • **General Office Occupations and Clerical Services** *15 students enrolled* • **Graphic Design** • **Health Information/Medical Records Technology/Technician** *4 students enrolled* • **Heating, Air Conditioning, Ventilation and Refrigeration Maintenance Technology/Technician (HAC, HACR, HVAC, HVACR)** *1 student enrolled* • **Human Development, Family Studies, and Related Services, Other** • **Industrial Technology/Technician** • **Medical Office Management/Administration** • **Medical/Clinical Assistant** • **Nurse/Nursing Assistant/Aide and Patient Care Assistant** *43 students enrolled* • **Office Management and Supervision** • **Ornamental Horticulture** • **Parks, Recreation and Leisure Facilities Management** • **Pharmacy Technician/Assistant** • **Quality Control and Safety Technologies/Technicians, Other** *3 students enrolled* • **Sign Language Interpretation and Translation** • **Social Work** *1 student enrolled* • **Substance Abuse/Addiction Counseling** *2 students enrolled* • **Teacher Assistant/Aide** • **Veterinary/Animal Health Technology/Technician and Veterinary Assistant** *2 students enrolled* • **Welding Technology/Welder**

**STUDENT SERVICES** Academic or career counseling, daycare for children of students, employment services for current students, placement services for program completers, remedial services.

## Eastern New Mexico University–Ruidoso Instructional Center

709 Mechem Drive, Ruidoso, NM 88345
http://www.ruidoso.enmu.edu/

**CONTACT** Michael Elrod, Provost
**Telephone:** 505-257-2120

**GENERAL INFORMATION** Public Institution. **Total program enrollment:** 208.

**PROGRAM(S) OFFERED**
• **Accounting Technology/Technician and Bookkeeping** *2 students enrolled* • **Emergency Medical Technology/Technician (EMT Paramedic)** *4 students enrolled* • **Nurse/Nursing Assistant/Aide and Patient Care Assistant** *21 students enrolled* • **Social Work** *5 students enrolled*

**STUDENT SERVICES** Academic or career counseling, employment services for current students, remedial services.

## Luna Community College

PO Box 1510, Las Vegas, NM 87701
http://www.luna.edu/

**CONTACT** Dr. Pete Campos, President
**Telephone:** 505-454-2500

**GENERAL INFORMATION** Public Institution. **Accreditation:** Regional (NCA). **Total program enrollment:** 490.

**PROGRAM(S) OFFERED**
• **Accounting** • **Administrative Assistant and Secretarial Science, General** • **Autobody/Collision and Repair Technology/Technician** *5 students enrolled* • **Automobile/Automotive Mechanics Technology/Technician** *2 students enrolled* • **Business Administration and Management, General** *1 student enrolled* • **Carpentry/Carpenter** *1 student enrolled* • **Computer and Information Sciences, General** *4 students enrolled* • **Corrections** • **Cosmetology/Cosmetologist, General** *3 students enrolled* • **Criminal Justice/Police Science** • **Criminal Justice/Safety Studies** *1 student enrolled* • **Culinary Arts/Chef Training** *5 students enrolled* • **Dental Assisting/Assistant** *3 students enrolled* • **Drafting and Design Technology/Technician, General** • **Electrical, Electronic and Communications Engineering Technology/Technician** • **Electrician** • **Graphic Communications, Other** • **Kindergarten/Preschool Education and Teaching** • **Licensed Practical/Vocational Nurse Training (LPN, LVN, Cert, Dipl, AAS)** *26 students enrolled* • **Welding Technology/Welder** *3 students enrolled*

**STUDENT SERVICES** Academic or career counseling, daycare for children of students, placement services for program completers, remedial services.

## Massage Therapy Training Institute

2701 W. Picacho Avenue, Suite 4, Las Cruces, NM 88007
http://www.mtti.org/

**CONTACT** Timothy Gay, Administrator
**Telephone:** 505-523-6811

**GENERAL INFORMATION** Private Institution. **Total program enrollment:** 33.

**PROGRAM(S) OFFERED**
• **Massage Therapy/Therapeutic Massage** *720 hrs./$5999*

**STUDENT SERVICES** Academic or career counseling, placement services for program completers.

## Mesalands Community College

911 South Tenth Street, Tucumcari, NM 88401
http://www.mesalands.edu/

**CONTACT** Phillip Barry, President
**Telephone:** 575-461-4413

**GENERAL INFORMATION** Public Institution. Founded 1979. **Accreditation:** Regional (NCA). **Total program enrollment:** 335.

**PROGRAM(S) OFFERED**
• **Agribusiness/Agricultural Business Operations** *17 students enrolled* • **Agricultural Business and Management, General** • **Agricultural and Domestic Animals Services, Other** • **Automobile/Automotive Mechanics Technology/Technician** *1 student enrolled* • **Carpentry/Carpenter** • **Computer and Information Sciences, General** *52 students enrolled* • **Cosmetology/Cosmetologist, General** • **Diesel Mechanics Technology/Technician** *1 student enrolled* • **Pre-Nursing Studies** *2 students enrolled* • **Public Administration and Social Service Professions, Other** *39 students enrolled* • **Sculpture** *3 students enrolled* • **Truck and Bus Driver/Commercial Vehicle Operation** *20 students enrolled*

**STUDENT SERVICES** Academic or career counseling, remedial services.

## New Mexico Junior College

5317 Lovington Highway, Hobbs, NM 88240-9123
http://www.nmjc.edu/

**CONTACT** Steve McCleery, President
**Telephone:** 505-492-2787

**GENERAL INFORMATION** Public Institution. Founded 1965. **Accreditation:** Regional (NCA). **Total program enrollment:** 1005.

**PROGRAM(S) OFFERED**
• **Accounting** *1 student enrolled* • **Administrative Assistant and Secretarial Science, General** *4 students enrolled* • **Animation, Interactive Technology, Video Graphics and Special Effects** • **Automobile/Automotive Mechanics Technology/Technician** *1 student enrolled* • **CAD/CADD Drafting and/or Design Technology/Technician** *1 student enrolled* • **Computer and Information Sciences, General** • **Corrections** *35 students enrolled* • **Cosmetology/Cosmetologist, General** • **Criminal Justice/Police Science** • **Drafting and Design Technology/Technician, General** • **Early Childhood Education and Teaching** • **Environmental Control Technologies/Technicians, Other** • **Graphic Communications, Other** *1 student enrolled* • **Kindergarten/Preschool Education and Teaching** • **Licensed Practical/Vocational Nurse Training (LPN, LVN, Cert, Dipl, AAS)** *9 students enrolled* • **Nurse/Nursing Assistant/Aide and Patient Care Assistant** • **Truck and Bus Driver/Commercial Vehicle Operation** *104 students enrolled* • **Water Quality and Wastewater Treatment Management and Recycling Technology/Technician** • **Welding Technology/Welder**

**STUDENT SERVICES** Academic or career counseling, employment services for current students, placement services for program completers, remedial services.

## New Mexico State University–Alamogordo

2400 North Scenic Drive, Alamogordo, NM 88311-0477
http://alamo.nmsu.edu/

**CONTACT** Cheri Jimeno, President
**Telephone:** 575-439-3600

**GENERAL INFORMATION** Public Institution. Founded 1958. **Accreditation:** Regional (NCA); medical laboratory technology (NAACLS). **Total program enrollment:** 801. **Application fee:** $20.

**PROGRAM(S) OFFERED**
• **Administrative Assistant and Secretarial Science, General** • **Computer Systems Networking and Telecommunications** *3 students enrolled* • **Computer and Information Sciences and Support Services, Other** • **Data Processing and Data Processing Technology/Technician** *4 students enrolled* • **Education, General** • **Electrical, Electronic and Communications Engineering Technology/Technician** • **Emergency Medical Technology/Technician (EMT Paramedic)** • **Fire Services Administration** • **General Office Occupations and Clerical Services** *1 student enrolled* • **Graphic Design** *3 students enrolled* • **Legal Assistant/Paralegal** • **Medical Administrative/Executive Assistant and Medical Secretary** *2 students enrolled* • **Medical Office Assistant/Specialist** • **Optometric Technician/Assistant** • **Photographic and Film/Video Technology/Technician and Assistant** *1 student enrolled* • **Pre-Nursing Studies** *4 students enrolled*

**STUDENT SERVICES** Academic or career counseling, employment services for current students, placement services for program completers, remedial services.

## New Mexico State University–Carlsbad

1500 University Drive, Carlsbad, NM 88220-3509
http://www.cavern.nmsu.edu/

**CONTACT** Russell Hardy, President
**Telephone:** 575-234-9200

**GENERAL INFORMATION** Public Institution. Founded 1950. **Accreditation:** Regional (NCA). **Total program enrollment:** 525. **Application fee:** $20.

**PROGRAM(S) OFFERED**
• **Accounting Technology/Technician and Bookkeeping** • **Administrative Assistant and Secretarial Science, General** • **Animation, Interactive Technology,**

*New Mexico State University–Carlsbad (continued)*

**Video Graphics and Special Effects** *1 student enrolled* • **Computer Engineering Technology/Technician** • **Computer and Information Sciences and Support Services, Other** • **Data Processing and Data Processing Technology/Technician** • **Digital Communication and Media/Multimedia** *1 student enrolled* • **Emergency Medical Technology/Technician (EMT Paramedic)** • **Heating, Air Conditioning, Ventilation and Refrigeration Maintenance Technology/Technician (HAC, HACR, HVAC, HVACR)** • **Licensed Practical/Vocational Nurse Training (LPN, LVN, Cert, Dipl, AAS)** *22 students enrolled* • **Medical Transcription/Transcriptionist** • **Welding Technology/Welder** *1 student enrolled*

**STUDENT SERVICES** Academic or career counseling, employment services for current students, placement services for program completers, remedial services.

## New Mexico State University–Grants

1500 3rd Street, Grants, NM 87020-2025
http://grants.nmsu.edu/

**CONTACT** Felicia Casados, President
**Telephone:** 505-287-7981

**GENERAL INFORMATION** Public Institution. Founded 1968. **Accreditation:** Regional (NCA). **Total program enrollment:** 283. **Application fee:** $20.

**PROGRAM(S) OFFERED**
• **Administrative Assistant and Secretarial Science, General** • **Automobile/Automotive Mechanics Technology/Technician** • **Building/Property Maintenance and Management** • **Carpentry/Carpenter** • **Cartography** • **Computer Installation and Repair Technology/Technician** • **Computer Programming, Specific Applications** • **Computer and Information Sciences and Support Services, Other** *3 students enrolled* • **Corrections** *47 students enrolled* • **Data Processing and Data Processing Technology/Technician** *2 students enrolled* • **Drafting and Design Technology/Technician, General** • **Early Childhood Education and Teaching** *4 students enrolled* • **Education, General** • **Electrical, Electronic and Communications Engineering Technology/Technician** *3 students enrolled* • **Elementary Education and Teaching** • **Nurse/Nursing Assistant/Aide and Patient Care Assistant** *13 students enrolled* • **Welding Technology/Welder**

**STUDENT SERVICES** Academic or career counseling, daycare for children of students, employment services for current students, placement services for program completers, remedial services.

## Northern New Mexico College

921 Paseo de Oñate, Española, NM 87532
http://www.nnmc.edu/

**CONTACT** Jose Griego, PhD, President
**Telephone:** 505-747-2100

**GENERAL INFORMATION** Public Institution. Founded 1909. **Accreditation:** Regional (NCA); radiologic technology: radiography (JRCERT). **Total program enrollment:** 836.

**PROGRAM(S) OFFERED**
• **Accounting Technology/Technician and Bookkeeping** *10 students enrolled* • **Administrative Assistant and Secretarial Science, General** *9 students enrolled* • **Autobody/Collision and Repair Technology/Technician** • **Barbering/Barber** *3 students enrolled* • **Computer and Information Sciences, General** *8 students enrolled* • **Construction Trades, Other** • **Cosmetology/Cosmetologist, General** *4 students enrolled* • **Electrical, Electronic and Communications Engineering Technology/Technician** *4 students enrolled* • **Electrician** *5 students enrolled* • **Executive Assistant/Executive Secretary** • **Furniture Design and Manufacturing** • **General Office Occupations and Clerical Services** *6 students enrolled* • **Legal Administrative Assistant/Secretary** *3 students enrolled* • **Library Assistant/Technician** • **Machine Shop Technology/Assistant** • **Manufacturing Technology/Technician** • **Massage Therapy/Therapeutic Massage** *11 students enrolled* • **Medical Administrative/Executive Assistant and Medical Secretary** *5 students enrolled* • **Non-Profit/Public/Organizational Management** • **Nurse/Nursing Assistant/Aide and Patient Care Assistant** • **Technical Teacher Education** • **Welding Technology/Welder**

**STUDENT SERVICES** Academic or career counseling, daycare for children of students, employment services for current students, placement services for program completers, remedial services.

## Olympian University of Cosmetology

1810 East Tenth Street, Alamogordo, NM 88310
http://www.olympianuniversity.com/

**CONTACT** Michele Leon, Financial Aid Administrator
**Telephone:** 575-437-2221

**GENERAL INFORMATION** Private Institution. Founded 1985. **Total program enrollment:** 846. **Application fee:** $100.

**PROGRAM(S) OFFERED**
• **Aesthetician/Esthetician and Skin Care Specialist** *750 hrs./$12,500* • **Barbering/Barber** • **Cosmetology and Related Personal Grooming Arts, Other** *281 students enrolled* • **Cosmetology, Barber/Styling, and Nail Instructor** *13 students enrolled* • **Cosmetology/Cosmetologist, General** *1500 hrs./$16,095* • **Nail Technician/Specialist and Manicurist** • **Teacher Education and Professional Development, Specific Subject Areas, Other** *1000 hrs./$4000*

**STUDENT SERVICES** Academic or career counseling, employment services for current students, placement services for program completers.

## Pima Medical Institute

2201 San Pedro NE, Building 3, Suite 100, Albuquerque, NM 87110
http://www.pmi.edu/

**CONTACT** Holly Woelber, Director
**Telephone:** 505-881-1234

**GENERAL INFORMATION** Private Institution. Founded 1985. **Accreditation:** Radiologic technology: radiography (JRCERT); state accredited or approved. **Total program enrollment:** 781.

**PROGRAM(S) OFFERED**
• **Dental Assisting/Assistant** *720 hrs./$9280* • **Medical Administrative/Executive Assistant and Medical Secretary** *560 hrs./$6430* • **Medical Insurance Coding Specialist/Coder** *720 hrs./$7520* • **Medical/Clinical Assistant** *800 hrs./$9995* • **Pharmacy Technician/Assistant** *800 hrs./$9380* • **Physical Therapist Assistant** *15 students enrolled* • **Veterinary/Animal Health Technology/Technician and Veterinary Assistant** *720 hrs./$9180*

**STUDENT SERVICES** Academic or career counseling, employment services for current students, placement services for program completers, remedial services.

## Pima Medical Institute

3901 Georgia Street NE, Suite C-1, Albuquerque, NM 87110
http://www.pmi.edu/

**CONTACT** Holly Woelber, Director
**Telephone:** 505-881-1234

**GENERAL INFORMATION** Private Institution. **Total program enrollment:** 39.

**PROGRAM(S) OFFERED**
• **Massage Therapy/Therapeutic Massage** *720 hrs./$10,435*

**STUDENT SERVICES** Academic or career counseling, employment services for current students, placement services for program completers, remedial services.

## San Juan College

4601 College Boulevard, Farmington, NM 87402-4699
http://www.sanjuancollege.edu/

**CONTACT** Dr. Carol J. Spencer, President
**Telephone:** 505-326-3311

**GENERAL INFORMATION** Public Institution. Founded 1958. **Accreditation:** Regional (NCA); dental hygiene (ADA); engineering technology (ABET/TAC); health information technology (AHIMA); physical therapy assisting (APTA). **Total program enrollment:** 2545.

**PROGRAM(S) OFFERED**
• **Administrative Assistant and Secretarial Science, General** • **Airline/Commercial/Professional Pilot and Flight Crew** *14 students enrolled* • **Autobody/Collision and Repair Technology/Technician** *1 student enrolled* • **Automobile/Automotive Mechanics Technology/Technician** *31 students enrolled* • **Carpentry/Carpenter** • **Child Care Provider/Assistant** *25 students enrolled* • **Cosmetology/Cosmetologist, General** • **Criminal Justice/Police Science** *11 students enrolled* • **Data Processing and Data Processing Technology/Technician** • **Diesel Mechanics Technology/Technician** • **Education, General** • **Elementary Education and Teaching** *10 students enrolled* • **Emergency Medical Technology/Technician (EMT Paramedic)** • **Fire Science/Firefighting** • **Health Information/Medical Records Technology/Technician** *16 students enrolled* • **Industrial Mechanics and Maintenance Technology** *26 students enrolled* • **Machine Shop Technology/Assistant** • **Public Administration** • **Secondary Education and Teaching** *14 students enrolled* • **Social Work** • **Solar Energy Technology/Technician** *8 students enrolled* • **Survey Technology/Surveying** *1 student enrolled* • **Veterinary/Animal Health Technology/Technician and Veterinary Assistant** *3 students enrolled* • **Water Quality and Wastewater Treatment Management and Recycling Technology/Technician** • **Welding Technology/Welder** *1 student enrolled*

**STUDENT SERVICES** Academic or career counseling, daycare for children of students, employment services for current students, placement services for program completers, remedial services.

## Santa Fe Community College

6401 Richards Avenue, Santa Fe, NM 87508-4887
http://www.sfccnm.edu/

**CONTACT** Sheila Ortego, President
**Telephone:** 505-428-1000

**GENERAL INFORMATION** Public Institution. Founded 1983. **Accreditation:** Regional (NCA); dental assisting (ADA). **Total program enrollment:** 1016.

**PROGRAM(S) OFFERED**
• **Accounting Technology/Technician and Bookkeeping** *3 students enrolled* • **Computer and Information Sciences, General** *1 student enrolled* • **Construction Engineering Technology/Technician** *11 students enrolled* • **Culinary Arts/Chef Training** *5 students enrolled* • **Data Processing and Data Processing Technology/Technician** • **Dental Assisting/Assistant** *4 students enrolled* • **Design and Visual Communications, General** *3 students enrolled* • **Early Childhood Education and Teaching** • **Elementary Education and Teaching** *22 students enrolled* • **Fashion/Apparel Design** *1 student enrolled* • **Foods, Nutrition, and Wellness Studies, General** *4 students enrolled* • **Health and Physical Education, General** *7 students enrolled* • **Interior Design** *1 student enrolled* • **Legal Assistant/Paralegal** *4 students enrolled* • **Medical/Clinical Assistant** *4 students enrolled* • **Secondary Education and Teaching** *29 students enrolled* • **Sign Language Interpretation and Translation** • **Special Education and Teaching, General** *18 students enrolled* • **Substance Abuse/Addiction Counseling** *1 student enrolled* • **Water Quality and Wastewater Treatment Management and Recycling Technology/Technician** *2 students enrolled* • **Woodworking, General** *4 students enrolled*

**STUDENT SERVICES** Academic or career counseling, daycare for children of students, employment services for current students, placement services for program completers, remedial services.

## Southwestern Indian Polytechnic Institute

9169 Coors, NW, Box 10146, Albuquerque, NM 87184-0146
http://www.sipi.bia.edu/

**CONTACT** Dr. Jeffrey Hamley, President
**Telephone:** 505-346-2347

**GENERAL INFORMATION** Public Institution. Founded 1971. **Accreditation:** Regional (NCA); ophthalmic laboratory technology (COA). **Total program enrollment:** 363.

**PROGRAM(S) OFFERED**
• **Accounting Technology/Technician and Bookkeeping** *6 students enrolled* • **Business Administration and Management, General** *5 students enrolled* • **Business/Office Automation/Technology/Data Entry** • **Cartography** • **Computer Technology/Computer Systems Technology** • **Environmental Control Technologies/Technicians, Other** • **Food Preparation/Professional Cooking/Kitchen Assistant** *7 students enrolled* • **Graphic and Printing Equipment Operator, General Production** • **Optometric Technician/Assistant** *1 student enrolled* • **Survey Technology/Surveying** • **System, Networking, and LAN/WAN Management/Manager** *5 students enrolled* • **Teacher Education and Professional Development, Specific Levels and Methods, Other**

**STUDENT SERVICES** Academic or career counseling, employment services for current students, placement services for program completers, remedial services.

## Universal Therapeutic Massage Institute

3410 Aztec Road NE, Albuquerque, NM 87107-4403
http://www.utmi.com/

**CONTACT** Robert A. Paper, School Director
**Telephone:** 505-888-0020

**GENERAL INFORMATION** Private Institution. **Total program enrollment:** 98. **Application fee:** $100.

**PROGRAM(S) OFFERED**
• **Massage Therapy/Therapeutic Massage** *360 hrs./$4395*

**STUDENT SERVICES** Placement services for program completers.

## University of New Mexico

Albuquerque, NM 87131-2039
http://www.unm.edu/

**CONTACT** David J. Schmidly, President
**Telephone:** 505-277-0111

**GENERAL INFORMATION** Public Institution. Founded 1889. **Accreditation:** Regional (NCA); athletic training (JRCAT); computer science (ABET/CSAC); counseling (ACA); dance (NASD); dental hygiene (ADA); dietetics: postbaccalaureate internship (ADtA/CAADE); emergency medical services (JRCEMTP); home economics (AAFCS); medical technology (NAACLS); music (NASM); speech-language pathology (ASHA); theater (NAST). **Total program enrollment:** 18192. **Application fee:** $20.

**PROGRAM(S) OFFERED**
• **Nuclear Medical Technology/Technologist** *5 students enrolled*

**STUDENT SERVICES** Academic or career counseling, daycare for children of students, employment services for current students, placement services for program completers, remedial services.

## University of New Mexico–Gallup

200 College Road, Gallup, NM 87301-5603
http://www.gallup.unm.edu/

**CONTACT** Dr. Barry Cooney, Interim Executive Director
**Telephone:** 505-863-7500

**GENERAL INFORMATION** Public Institution. Founded 1968. **Accreditation:** Regional (NCA); dental assisting (ADA); health information technology (AHIMA); medical laboratory technology (NAACLS). **Total program enrollment:** 1207. **Application fee:** $15.

**PROGRAM(S) OFFERED**
• **Automobile/Automotive Mechanics Technology/Technician** *1 student enrolled* • **Building/Construction Finishing, Management, and Inspection, Other** *2 students enrolled* • **Carpentry/Carpenter** *1 student enrolled* • **Community Organization and Advocacy** *11 students enrolled* • **Cosmetology/Cosmetologist, General** *7 students enrolled* • **Data Processing and Data Processing Technology/Technician** *1 student enrolled* • **Dental Assisting/Assistant** *7 students enrolled* • **Drafting and Design Technology/Technician, General** *2 students enrolled* • **Early Childhood Education and Teaching** *1 student enrolled* • **Electrician** *1 student enrolled* • **Health Information/Medical Records Technology/Technician** *7 students enrolled* • **Medical Administrative/Executive**

*University of New Mexico–Gallup (continued)*

**Assistant and Medical Secretary** *2 students enrolled* • **Pre-Nursing Studies** *1 student enrolled* • **Public Health Education and Promotion** *1 student enrolled* • **Welding Technology/Welder** *4 students enrolled*

**STUDENT SERVICES** Academic or career counseling, daycare for children of students, placement services for program completers, remedial services.

## University of New Mexico–Los Alamos Branch

4000 University Drive, Los Alamos, NM 87544-2233
http://www.la.unm.edu/

**CONTACT** Cedric D. Page, Executive Director
**Telephone:** 505-662-5919

**GENERAL INFORMATION** Public Institution. Founded 1980. **Accreditation:** Regional (NCA). **Total program enrollment:** 150. **Application fee:** $10.

**PROGRAM(S) OFFERED**
• **Computer and Information Sciences, General** *2 students enrolled* • **Electromechanical Technology/Electromechanical Engineering Technology** *1 student enrolled*

**STUDENT SERVICES** Academic or career counseling, employment services for current students, placement services for program completers, remedial services.

## University of New Mexico–Taos

115 Civic Plaza Drive, Taos, NM 87571
http://taos.unm.edu/

**CONTACT** Dr. Catherine M. O'Neill, Executive Campus Director
**Telephone:** 505-737-6200

**GENERAL INFORMATION** Public Institution. Founded 1923. **Accreditation:** Regional (NCA). **Total program enrollment:** 376. **Application fee:** $15.

**PROGRAM(S) OFFERED**
• **Alternative and Complementary Medicine and Medical Systems, Other** *3 students enrolled* • **Computer and Information Sciences, General** *4 students enrolled* • **Culinary Arts/Chef Training** *4 students enrolled* • **Early Childhood Education and Teaching** *1 student enrolled* • **Social Work** *1 student enrolled*

**STUDENT SERVICES** Academic or career counseling, employment services for current students, placement services for program completers, remedial services.

## University of New Mexico–Valencia Campus

280 La Entrada, Los Lunas, NM 87031-7633
http://www.unm.edu/~unmvc/

**CONTACT** Alice V. Letteney, PhD, Executive Director
**Telephone:** 505-925-8500

**GENERAL INFORMATION** Public Institution. Founded 1981. **Accreditation:** Regional (NCA). **Total program enrollment:** 873. **Application fee:** $15.

**PROGRAM(S) OFFERED**
• **Art/Art Studies, General** *1 student enrolled* • **Business Administration and Management, General** *2 students enrolled* • **CAD/CADD Drafting and/or Design Technology/Technician** *3 students enrolled* • **Computer Technology/Computer Systems Technology** *1 student enrolled* • **Computer and Information Sciences, General** *1 student enrolled* • **Education, General** *2 students enrolled* • **General Office Occupations and Clerical Services** *2 students enrolled* • **Pharmacy Technician/Assistant** *2 students enrolled*

**STUDENT SERVICES** Academic or career counseling, daycare for children of students, employment services for current students, placement services for program completers, remedial services.

## University of Phoenix–New Mexico Campus

7471 Pan American Freeway NE, Albuquerque, NM 87109-4645
http://www.phoenix.edu/

**CONTACT** William Pepicello, PhD, President
**Telephone:** 800-333-8671

**GENERAL INFORMATION** Private Institution. **Accreditation:** Regional (NCA). **Total program enrollment:** 4357.

**PROGRAM(S) OFFERED**
• **Human Resources Management/Personnel Administration, General** *1 student enrolled*

**STUDENT SERVICES** Academic or career counseling, remedial services.

## Western New Mexico University

PO Box 680, Silver City, NM 88062-0680
http://www.wnmu.edu/

**CONTACT** Dr. John Counts, President
**Telephone:** 505-538-6336

**GENERAL INFORMATION** Public Institution. Founded 1893. **Accreditation:** Regional (NCA). **Total program enrollment:** 1405.

**PROGRAM(S) OFFERED**
• **Administrative Assistant and Secretarial Science, General** • **Automobile/Automotive Mechanics Technology/Technician** • **Banking and Financial Support Services** • **Computer Installation and Repair Technology/Technician** • **Construction Engineering Technology/Technician** • **Criminal Justice/Police Science** *7 students enrolled* • **Digital Communication and Media/Multimedia** • **Drafting and Design Technology/Technician, General** *1 student enrolled* • **Electrical, Electronic and Communications Engineering Technology/Technician** • **Kindergarten/Preschool Education and Teaching** *1 student enrolled* • **Welding Technology/Welder** *1 student enrolled*

**STUDENT SERVICES** Academic or career counseling, daycare for children of students, employment services for current students, placement services for program completers, remedial services.

# NORTH DAKOTA

## Bismarck State College

PO Box 5587, Bismarck, ND 58506-5587
http://www.bismarckstate.edu/

**CONTACT** Larry C. Skogen, President
**Telephone:** 701-224-5400

**GENERAL INFORMATION** Public Institution. Founded 1939. **Accreditation:** Regional (NCA); emergency medical services (JRCEMTP); medical laboratory technology (NAACLS); surgical technology (ARCST). **Total program enrollment:** 2485. **Application fee:** $35.

**PROGRAM(S) OFFERED**
• **Administrative Assistant and Secretarial Science, General** • **Autobody/Collision and Repair Technology/Technician** *13 students enrolled* • **Automobile/Automotive Mechanics Technology/Technician** *12 students enrolled* • **Business/Office Automation/Technology/Data Entry** *2 students enrolled* • **Carpentry/Carpenter** *19 students enrolled* • **Clinical/Medical Laboratory Science and Allied Professions, Other** *3 students enrolled* • **Commercial and Advertising Art** *2 students enrolled* • **Electrical, Electronic and Communications Engineering Technology/Technician** *4 students enrolled* • **Emergency Medical Technology/Technician (EMT Paramedic)** *16 students enrolled* • **Heating, Air Conditioning, Ventilation and Refrigeration Maintenance Technology/Technician (HAC, HACR, HVAC, HVACR)** *6 students enrolled* • **Hospitality Administration/Management, Other** • **Hotel/Motel Administration/Management** *1 student enrolled* • **Human Services, General** *2 students enrolled* • **Industrial Mechanics and Maintenance Technology** *1 student enrolled* • **Industrial Production**

**Technologies/Technicians, Other** *18 students enrolled* • **Industrial Technology/Technician** • **Licensed Practical/Vocational Nurse Training (LPN, LVN, Cert, Dipl, AAS)** *10 students enrolled* • **Lineworker** *33 students enrolled* • **Nuclear Engineering Technology/Technician** *1 student enrolled* • **Restaurant/Food Services Management** • **Survey Technology/Surveying** *2 students enrolled* • **Web Page, Digital/Multimedia and Information Resources Design** *1 student enrolled* • **Welding Technology/Welder** *6 students enrolled*

**STUDENT SERVICES** Academic or career counseling, employment services for current students, placement services for program completers, remedial services.

## Cankdeska Cikana Community College

PO Box 269, Fort Totten, ND 58335-0269
http://www.littlehoop.edu/

**CONTACT** Cynthia Lindquist, President
**Telephone:** 701-766-4415

**GENERAL INFORMATION** Public Institution. Founded 1974. **Accreditation:** Regional (NCA). **Total program enrollment:** 121.

**PROGRAM(S) OFFERED**
• **Carpentry/Carpenter** *2 students enrolled*

**STUDENT SERVICES** Academic or career counseling, daycare for children of students, remedial services.

## Dakota College at Bottineau

105 Simrall Boulevard, Bottineau, ND 58318-1198
http://www.misu-b.nodak.edu/

**CONTACT** Dr. Ken Grosz, Campus Dean
**Telephone:** 701-228-2277

**GENERAL INFORMATION** Public Institution. Founded 1906. **Accreditation:** Regional (NCA). **Total program enrollment:** 345. **Application fee:** $35.

**PROGRAM(S) OFFERED**
• **Accounting and Related Services, Other** • **Computer and Information Sciences and Support Services, Other** • **General Office Occupations and Clerical Services** *2 students enrolled* • **Greenhouse Operations and Management** • **Landscaping and Groundskeeping** *2 students enrolled* • **Licensed Practical/Vocational Nurse Training (LPN, LVN, Cert, Dipl, AAS)** *26 students enrolled* • **Marketing/Marketing Management, General** *1 student enrolled* • **Medical Insurance Coding Specialist/Coder** • **Medical Transcription/Transcriptionist** *1 student enrolled* • **Medical/Clinical Assistant** *2 students enrolled* • **Teacher Assistant/Aide** • **Turf and Turfgrass Management** *1 student enrolled* • **Urban Forestry** *1 student enrolled* • **Water Quality and Wastewater Treatment Management and Recycling Technology/Technician** *1 student enrolled* • **Web/Multimedia Management and Webmaster**

**STUDENT SERVICES** Academic or career counseling, employment services for current students, remedial services.

## Dickinson State University

291 Campus Drive, Dickinson, ND 58601-4896
http://www.dsu.nodak.edu/

**CONTACT** Richard McCallum, President
**Telephone:** 701-483-2507

**GENERAL INFORMATION** Public Institution. Founded 1918. **Accreditation:** Regional (NCA). **Total program enrollment:** 1891. **Application fee:** $35.

**PROGRAM(S) OFFERED**
• **Farm/Farm and Ranch Management** *1 student enrolled*

**STUDENT SERVICES** Academic or career counseling, employment services for current students, placement services for program completers, remedial services.

## Fort Berthold Community College

PO Box 490, 220 8th Avenue North, New Town, ND 58763-0490
http://www.fbcc.bia.edu/

**CONTACT** Russell Mason, Jr., President
**Telephone:** 701-627-4738 Ext. 286

**GENERAL INFORMATION** Private Institution. Founded 1973. **Accreditation:** Regional (NCA). **Total program enrollment:** 99. **Application fee:** $25.

**PROGRAM(S) OFFERED**
• **Administrative Assistant and Secretarial Science, General** *1 student enrolled* • **Film/Video and Photographic Arts, Other** *2 students enrolled* • **Plumbing and Related Water Supply Services, Other** *4 students enrolled*

**STUDENT SERVICES** Academic or career counseling, employment services for current students, placement services for program completers, remedial services.

## HairDesigners Academy

2011-13 South Washington Avenue, Grand Forks, ND 58201

**CONTACT** Mario Olivieri, Owner
**Telephone:** 701-772-2728

**GENERAL INFORMATION** Private Institution. Founded 1976. **Total program enrollment:** 51. **Application fee:** $100.

**PROGRAM(S) OFFERED**
• **Aesthetician/Esthetician and Skin Care Specialist** *600 hrs./$6450* • **Cosmetology/Cosmetologist, General** *1800 hrs./$8436* • **Massage Therapy/Therapeutic Massage** *750 hrs./$7100*

**STUDENT SERVICES** Academic or career counseling, placement services for program completers.

## Lake Region State College

1801 College Drive North, Devils Lake, ND 58301-1598
http://www.lrsc.nodak.edu/

**CONTACT** Mike Bower, President
**Telephone:** 701-662-1600

**GENERAL INFORMATION** Public Institution. Founded 1941. **Accreditation:** Regional (NCA). **Total program enrollment:** 419. **Application fee:** $35.

**PROGRAM(S) OFFERED**
• **Administrative Assistant and Secretarial Science, General** • **Automobile/Automotive Mechanics Technology/Technician** *5 students enrolled* • **Child Care Provider/Assistant** *1 student enrolled* • **Criminal Justice/Police Science** *60 students enrolled* • **Diesel Mechanics Technology/Technician** *5 students enrolled* • **General Merchandising, Sales, and Related Marketing Operations, Other** • **Language Interpretation and Translation** *3 students enrolled* • **Legal Assistant/Paralegal** • **Licensed Practical/Vocational Nurse Training (LPN, LVN, Cert, Dipl, AAS)** *20 students enrolled* • **Management Information Systems, General** • **Welding Technology/Welder** *2 students enrolled*

**STUDENT SERVICES** Academic or career counseling, daycare for children of students, employment services for current students, placement services for program completers, remedial services.

## Minot State University

500 University Avenue West, Minot, ND 58707-0002
http://www.minotstateu.edu/

**CONTACT** David Fuller, President
**Telephone:** 701-858-3000

**GENERAL INFORMATION** Public Institution. Founded 1913. **Accreditation:** Regional (NCA); audiology (ASHA); music (NASM); speech-language pathology (ASHA). **Total program enrollment:** 2350. **Application fee:** $35.

*Minot State University (continued)*

**PROGRAM(S) OFFERED**
• **Business/Office Automation/Technology/Data Entry** *3 students enrolled* • **Computer Programming/Programmer, General** *1 student enrolled* • **Computer and Information Sciences and Support Services, Other** • **Corrections and Criminal Justice, Other** • **Management Information Systems and Services, Other** • **Web Page, Digital/Multimedia and Information Resources Design** *9 students enrolled*

**STUDENT SERVICES** Academic or career counseling, employment services for current students, placement services for program completers, remedial services.

## Moler Barber College

16 S. Eighth Street, Fargo, ND 58103-1805

**CONTACT** Mary B. Cannon, President
**Telephone:** 701-232-6773

**GENERAL INFORMATION** Private Institution. **Total program enrollment:** 8. **Application fee:** $100.

**PROGRAM(S) OFFERED**
• **Barbering/Barber** *1550 hrs./$6074*

**STUDENT SERVICES** Academic or career counseling, placement services for program completers, remedial services.

## North Dakota State College of Science

800 North Sixth Street, Wahpeton, ND 58076
http://www.ndscs.nodak.edu/

**CONTACT** Dr. John Richman, President
**Telephone:** 701-671-2403

**GENERAL INFORMATION** Public Institution. Founded 1903. **Accreditation:** Regional (NCA); dental assisting (ADA); dental hygiene (ADA); health information technology (AHIMA). **Total program enrollment:** 1705. **Application fee:** $35.

**PROGRAM(S) OFFERED**
• **Administrative Assistant and Secretarial Science, General** *3 students enrolled* • **Autobody/Collision and Repair Technology/Technician** *7 students enrolled* • **Automobile/Automotive Mechanics Technology/Technician** • **Computer Programming, Specific Applications** • **Computer and Information Sciences, General** • **Culinary Arts/Chef Training** • **Dental Assisting/Assistant** *16 students enrolled* • **Diesel Mechanics Technology/Technician** *2 students enrolled* • **Health Information/Medical Records Technology/Technician** *8 students enrolled* • **Heating, Air Conditioning and Refrigeration Technology/Technician (ACH/ACR/ACHR/HRAC/HVAC/AC Technology)** *2 students enrolled* • **Heating, Air Conditioning, Ventilation and Refrigeration Maintenance Technology/Technician (HAC, HACR, HVAC, HVACR)** • **Machine Shop Technology/Assistant** • **Machine Tool Technology/Machinist** • **Pharmacy Technician/Assistant** • **Plumbing Technology/Plumber** *7 students enrolled* • **Small Engine Mechanics and Repair Technology/Technician** *7 students enrolled* • **Technical Teacher Education** • **Welding Technology/Welder**

**STUDENT SERVICES** Academic or career counseling, daycare for children of students, employment services for current students, placement services for program completers, remedial services.

## North Dakota State University

1301 North University Avenue, Fargo, ND 58105
http://www.ndsu.edu/

**CONTACT** Joseph A. Chapman, President
**Telephone:** 701-231-8011

**GENERAL INFORMATION** Public Institution. Founded 1890. **Accreditation:** Regional (NCA); art and design (NASAD); athletic training (JRCAT); computer science (ABET/CSAC); counseling (ACA); home economics (AAFCS); interior design: professional (CIDA); music (NASM); theater (NAST). **Total program enrollment:** 11004. **Application fee:** $35.

**PROGRAM(S) OFFERED**
• **Equestrian/Equine Studies** • **Finance, General** • **Human Resources Management/Personnel Administration, General** • **Marketing/Marketing Management, General**

**STUDENT SERVICES** Academic or career counseling, daycare for children of students, employment services for current students, remedial services.

## Rasmussen College Bismarck

1701 East Century Avenue, Bismarck, ND 58503
http://www.rasmussen.edu/

**CONTACT** Lorrie Laurin, Campus Director
**Telephone:** 701-530-9600

**GENERAL INFORMATION** Private Institution. **Total program enrollment:** 191. **Application fee:** $60.

**PROGRAM(S) OFFERED**
• **Accounting** • **Administrative Assistant and Secretarial Science, General** *1 student enrolled* • **Business Operations Support and Secretarial Services, Other** • **Executive Assistant/Executive Secretary** • **Medical Administrative/Executive Assistant and Medical Secretary** *1 student enrolled* • **Medical Insurance Coding Specialist/Coder** *10 students enrolled* • **Medical Transcription/Transcriptionist** *19 students enrolled*

**STUDENT SERVICES** Academic or career counseling, employment services for current students, placement services for program completers, remedial services.

## Rasmussen College Fargo

4012 19th Avenue, SW, Fargo, ND 58103
http://www.rasmussen.edu/

**CONTACT** Elizabeth Largent, Campus Director
**Telephone:** 701-277-3889

**GENERAL INFORMATION** Private Institution. Founded 1902. **Accreditation:** State accredited or approved. **Total program enrollment:** 423. **Application fee:** $60.

**PROGRAM(S) OFFERED**
• **Accounting** *2 students enrolled* • **Administrative Assistant and Secretarial Science, General** *3 students enrolled* • **Legal Administrative Assistant/Secretary** *2 students enrolled* • **Management Information Systems, General** *3 students enrolled* • **Medical Administrative/Executive Assistant and Medical Secretary** • **Medical Insurance Coding Specialist/Coder** *7 students enrolled* • **Medical Transcription/Transcriptionist** *6 students enrolled*

**STUDENT SERVICES** Academic or career counseling, employment services for current students, placement services for program completers, remedial services.

## RD Hairstyling College

124 North Fourth Street, Bismarck, ND 58501

**CONTACT** Jodi Zahn, Director
**Telephone:** 701-223-8804

**GENERAL INFORMATION** Private Institution. Founded 1973. **Total program enrollment:** 61. **Application fee:** $100.

**PROGRAM(S) OFFERED**
• **Cosmetology/Cosmetologist, General** *2100 hrs./$14,995* • **Nail Technician/Specialist and Manicurist** *350 hrs./$4000*

**STUDENT SERVICES** Academic or career counseling, placement services for program completers.

## Salon Professional Academy

1435 South University Drive, Fargo, ND 58103
http://www.thesalonprofessionalacademy.com/

**GENERAL INFORMATION** Private Institution. **Total program enrollment:** 101.

**PROGRAM(S) OFFERED**
• **Aesthetician/Esthetician and Skin Care Specialist** *600 hrs./$6390*
• **Cosmetology/Cosmetologist, General** *1800 hrs./$13,190* • **Nail Technician/Specialist and Manicurist** *350 hrs./$3690*

**STUDENT SERVICES** Placement services for program completers.

## Sitting Bull College

1341 92nd Street, Fort Yates, ND 58538-9701
http://www.sittingbull.edu/

**CONTACT** Laurel Vermillion, President
**Telephone:** 701-854-8000

**GENERAL INFORMATION** Private Institution. Founded 1973. **Accreditation:** Regional (NCA). **Total program enrollment:** 240. **Application fee:** $25.

**PROGRAM(S) OFFERED**
• **Business Administration and Management, General** • **Construction Trades, Other** *1 student enrolled* • **Criminal Justice/Law Enforcement Administration**
• **General Office Occupations and Clerical Services**

**STUDENT SERVICES** Academic or career counseling, daycare for children of students, employment services for current students, remedial services.

## Trinity Bible College

50 South 6th Avenue, Ellendale, ND 58436-7150
http://www.trinitybiblecollege.edu/

**CONTACT** Garnett Strom, President
**Telephone:** 888-822-2329

**GENERAL INFORMATION** Private Institution. Founded 1948. **Accreditation:** Regional (NCA); state accredited or approved. **Total program enrollment:** 250. **Application fee:** $25.

**STUDENT SERVICES** Academic or career counseling, employment services for current students, placement services for program completers, remedial services.

## Turtle Mountain Community College

Box 340, Belcourt, ND 58316-0340
http://www.turtle-mountain.cc.nd.us/

**CONTACT** Dr. James Davis, President
**Telephone:** 701-477-7862

**GENERAL INFORMATION** Private Institution. Founded 1972. **Accreditation:** Regional (NCA). **Total program enrollment:** 675.

**PROGRAM(S) OFFERED**
• **Administrative Assistant and Secretarial Science, General** *1 student enrolled*
• **Business, Management, Marketing, and Related Support Services, Other** *1 student enrolled* • **Computer and Information Sciences, General** *2 students enrolled* • **Construction Trades, General** *7 students enrolled* • **Early Childhood Education and Teaching** *6 students enrolled* • **Entrepreneurial and Small Business Operations, Other** *1 student enrolled* • **Industrial Production Technologies/Technicians, Other** *5 students enrolled* • **Information Technology** *3 students enrolled* • **Legal Assistant/Paralegal** *12 students enrolled*

**STUDENT SERVICES** Academic or career counseling, remedial services.

## United Tribes Technical College

3315 University Drive, Bismarck, ND 58504-7596
http://www.uttc.edu/

**CONTACT** David M. Gipp, President
**Telephone:** 701-255-3285 Ext. 1217

**GENERAL INFORMATION** Public Institution. Founded 1969. **Accreditation:** Regional (NCA); health information technology (AHIMA). **Total program enrollment:** 336.

**PROGRAM(S) OFFERED**
• **Arts Management** • **Business Administration and Management, General**
• **Criminal Justice/Safety Studies** • **General Office Occupations and Clerical Services** • **Medical Transcription/Transcriptionist** *6 students enrolled*

**STUDENT SERVICES** Academic or career counseling, daycare for children of students, employment services for current students, placement services for program completers, remedial services.

## University of North Dakota

264 Centennial Drive, Grand Forks, ND 58202
http://www.und.nodak.edu/

**CONTACT** Robert Kelley, President
**Telephone:** 800-225-5863

**GENERAL INFORMATION** Public Institution. Founded 1883. **Accreditation:** Regional (NCA); art and design (NASAD); athletic training (JRCAT); computer science (ABET/CSAC); cytotechnology (ASC); medical technology (NAACLS); music (NASM); speech-language pathology (ASHA); theater (NAST). **Total program enrollment:** 10194. **Application fee:** $35.

**PROGRAM(S) OFFERED**
• **Entrepreneurship/Entrepreneurial Studies** *12 students enrolled* • **Histologic Technology/Histotechnologist** *5 students enrolled* • **Non-Profit/Public/Organizational Management** *1 student enrolled*

**STUDENT SERVICES** Academic or career counseling, daycare for children of students, employment services for current students, placement services for program completers.

## Williston State College

Box 1326, Williston, ND 58802-1326
http://www.wsc.nodak.edu/

**CONTACT** Dr. Joseph McCann, President
**Telephone:** 701-774-4200

**GENERAL INFORMATION** Public Institution. Founded 1957. **Accreditation:** Regional (NCA); physical therapy assisting (APTA). **Total program enrollment:** 397. **Application fee:** $35.

**PROGRAM(S) OFFERED**
• **Administrative Assistant and Secretarial Science, General** *1 student enrolled*
• **Data Processing and Data Processing Technology/Technician**
• **Entrepreneurship/Entrepreneurial Studies** • **Health Information/Medical Records Technology/Technician** *7 students enrolled* • **Licensed Practical/Vocational Nurse Training (LPN, LVN, Cert, Dipl, AAS)** *31 students enrolled*
• **Marketing/Marketing Management, General** • **Massage Therapy/Therapeutic Massage** *2 students enrolled* • **Medical Transcription/Transcriptionist** • **Plant Sciences, Other** *3 students enrolled* • **Psychiatric/Mental Health Services Technician** *3 students enrolled* • **System, Networking, and LAN/WAN Management/Manager** *1 student enrolled* • **Teacher Assistant/Aide**

**STUDENT SERVICES** Academic or career counseling, daycare for children of students, remedial services.

# NORTHERN MARIANA ISLANDS

## Northern Marianas College

Box 501250, Saipan, MP 96950-1250
http://www.nmcnet.edu/

**CONTACT** Dr. Carmen Fernandez, President
**Telephone:** 670-234-5498 Ext. 1001

**GENERAL INFORMATION** Public Institution. Founded 1981. **Accreditation:** Regional (WASC/ACSCU). **Total program enrollment:** 568. **Application fee:** $25.

**PROGRAM(S) OFFERED**
• **Accounting Technology/Technician and Bookkeeping** *3 students enrolled* • **Administrative Assistant and Secretarial Science, General** • **Business Administration and Management, General** *1 student enrolled* • **Cinematography and Film/Video Production** • **Computer and Information Sciences, General** *2 students enrolled* • **Construction Trades, Other** • **Criminal Justice/Police Science** • **Early Childhood Education and Teaching** *1 student enrolled* • **Electrical/Electronics Equipment Installation and Repair, General** • **Fire Science/Firefighting** *25 students enrolled* • **Hospitality Administration/Management, General** • **Nurse/Nursing Assistant/Aide and Patient Care Assistant** *2 students enrolled* • **Renal/Dialysis Technologist/Technician** *1 student enrolled* • **Sales, Distribution and Marketing Operations, General** *3 students enrolled* • **Teacher Assistant/Aide** *22 students enrolled*

**STUDENT SERVICES** Academic or career counseling, employment services for current students, remedial services.

# OKLAHOMA

## American Beauty Institute

PO Box 1716, McAlester, OK 74502-1716
http://www.americanbeautyinstitutes.com/

**CONTACT** Donna Pope, Owner
**Telephone:** 918-420-4247

**GENERAL INFORMATION** Private Institution. **Total program enrollment:** 12.

**PROGRAM(S) OFFERED**
• **Cosmetology, Barber/Styling, and Nail Instructor** *1000 hrs./$3350* • **Cosmetology/Cosmetologist, General** *1500 hrs./$13,050* • **Nail Technician/Specialist and Manicurist** *600 hrs./$4900*

**STUDENT SERVICES** Academic or career counseling, placement services for program completers.

## American Broadcasting School

4511 SE 29th Street, Oklahoma City, OK 73115
http://www.radioschool.com/

**CONTACT** Delton L. Cockrell, Owner
**Telephone:** 405-672-6511

**GENERAL INFORMATION** Private Institution. **Total program enrollment:** 39.

**PROGRAM(S) OFFERED**
• **Radio and Television** *1032 hrs./$10,625*

**STUDENT SERVICES** Placement services for program completers.

## American Broadcasting School

7016 South Utica Avenue, Tulsa, OK 74136
http://www.radioschool.com/

**CONTACT** Delton Cockrell, Owner
**Telephone:** 918-293-9100

**GENERAL INFORMATION** Private Institution. Founded 1970. **Total program enrollment:** 26.

**PROGRAM(S) OFFERED**
• **Radio and Television** *1032 hrs./$10,625*

**STUDENT SERVICES** Placement services for program completers.

## American Institute of Medical Technology

7040 S. Yale Avenue, Suite 100, Tulsa, OK 74136
http://www.aimt-edu.com

**CONTACT** Manni Wallia, Campus Director
**Telephone:** 918-496-0800

**GENERAL INFORMATION** Private Institution. **Total program enrollment:** 69.

**PROGRAM(S) OFFERED**
• **Cardiovascular Technology/Technologist** *8 students enrolled* • **Diagnostic Medical Sonography/Sonographer and Ultrasound Technician** *111 hrs./$20,500* • **Electrocardiograph Technology/Technician** *30 hrs./$5150* • **Health Services/Allied Health/Health Sciences, General** *69 hrs./$9050* • **Nuclear Medical Technology/Technologist** *135 hrs./$20,750*

## Autry Technology Center

1201 West Willow Street, Enid, OK 73703
http://www.autrytech.com/

**CONTACT** James Strate, Superintendent
**Telephone:** 580-242-2750

**GENERAL INFORMATION** Private Institution. Founded 1967. **Total program enrollment:** 110.

**PROGRAM(S) OFFERED**
• **Accounting Technology/Technician and Bookkeeping** *1440 hrs./$1680* • **Autobody/Collision and Repair Technology/Technician** *15 students enrolled* • **Automobile/Automotive Mechanics Technology/Technician** *7 students enrolled* • **Business Administration, Management and Operations, Other** *6 students enrolled* • **Carpentry/Carpenter** *1 student enrolled* • **Cosmetology/Cosmetologist, General** *13 students enrolled* • **Dental Assisting/Assistant** *12 students enrolled* • **Drafting and Design Technology/Technician, General** *10 students enrolled* • **Emergency Medical Technology/Technician (EMT Paramedic)** • **Fire Science/Firefighting** *7 students enrolled* • **Foodservice Systems Administration/Management** *7 students enrolled* • **Graphic Communications, General** *1365 hrs./$1815* • **Graphic and Printing Equipment Operator, General Production** *8 students enrolled* • **Heating, Air Conditioning, Ventilation and Refrigeration Maintenance Technology/Technician (HAC, HACR, HVAC, HVACR)** *3 students enrolled* • **Heavy Equipment Maintenance Technology/Technician** *4 students enrolled* • **Industrial Electronics Technology/Technician** *4 students enrolled* • **Licensed Practical/Vocational Nurse Training (LPN, LVN, Cert, Dipl, AAS)** *1496 hrs./$2393* • **Management Information Systems and Services, Other** *13 students enrolled* • **Mechanical Drafting and Mechanical Drafting CAD/CADD** *1140 hrs./$1680* • **Medical Office Assistant/Specialist** *1308 hrs./$1680* • **Medical/Clinical Assistant** *14 students enrolled* • **Small Engine Mechanics and Repair Technology/Technician** *6 students enrolled* • **Surgical Technology/Technologist** *6 students enrolled* • **Welding Technology/Welder** *1425 hrs./$1680*

**STUDENT SERVICES** Academic or career counseling, employment services for current students, placement services for program completers, remedial services.

## Beauty Technical College

1600 Downing, Tahlequah, OK 74465

**CONTACT** Freda Poe, President
**Telephone:** 918-456-9431

**GENERAL INFORMATION** Private Institution. **Total program enrollment:** 29. **Application fee:** $100.

**PROGRAM(S) OFFERED**
• **Cosmetology, Barber/Styling, and Nail Instructor** *1000 hrs./$4950* • **Cosmetology/Cosmetologist, General** *1500 hrs./$7700* • **Nail Technician/Specialist and Manicurist** *600 hrs./$4700*

**STUDENT SERVICES** Academic or career counseling, employment services for current students, placement services for program completers, remedial services.

## Broken Arrow Beauty College

400 South Elm Place, Broken Arrow, OK 74012
http://babeautycollege.com/

**CONTACT** Frances Sells, President
**Telephone:** 918-251-9669

**GENERAL INFORMATION** Private Institution. Founded 1969. **Total program enrollment:** 51. **Application fee:** $75.

**PROGRAM(S) OFFERED**
• **Barbering/Barber** *1500 hrs./$10,388* • **Cosmetology, Barber/Styling, and Nail Instructor** *1000 hrs./$4000* • **Cosmetology/Cosmetologist, General** • **Facial Treatment Specialist/Facialist** *600 hrs./$3660* • **Nail Technician/Specialist and Manicurist** *600 hrs./$3660*

**STUDENT SERVICES** Academic or career counseling, placement services for program completers.

## Broken Arrow Beauty College–Tulsa

11122 E. 71st Street, Tulsa, OK 74133
http://babeautycollege.com/

**CONTACT** Frances Sells, President
**Telephone:** 918-294-8627

**GENERAL INFORMATION** Private Institution. **Total program enrollment:** 53. **Application fee:** $75.

**PROGRAM(S) OFFERED**
• **Aesthetician/Esthetician and Skin Care Specialist** *10 students enrolled* • **Cosmetology, Barber/Styling, and Nail Instructor** *1000 hrs./$4000* • **Cosmetology/Cosmetologist, General** *1500 hrs./$10,388* • **Facial Treatment Specialist/Facialist** *600 hrs./$3660* • **Nail Technician/Specialist and Manicurist** *600 hrs./$3660*

**STUDENT SERVICES** Placement services for program completers.

## Caddo-Kiowa Area Vocational Technical School

PO Box 190, Ft. Cobb, OK 73038
http://www.caddokiowa.com/

**CONTACT** Jerry L. Martin, Superintendent
**Telephone:** 405-643-5511

**GENERAL INFORMATION** Private Institution. **Total program enrollment:** 193.

**PROGRAM(S) OFFERED**
• **Allied Health and Medical Assisting Services, Other** *1050 hrs./$2410* • **Applied Horticulture/Horticultural Business Services, Other** *1 student enrolled* • **Autobody/Collision and Repair Technology/Technician** *2 students enrolled* • **Automobile/Automotive Mechanics Technology/Technician** *3 students enrolled* • **Business, Management, Marketing, and Related Support Services, Other** *2100 hrs./$2860* • **Carpentry/Carpenter** *2 students enrolled* • **Child Care Provider/Assistant** *5 students enrolled* • **Child Care and Support Services Management** *2100 hrs./$2410* • **Cosmetology/Cosmetologist, General** *1500 hrs./$2410* • **Criminal Justice/Law Enforcement Administration** *2 students enrolled* • **Culinary Arts/Chef Training** *3 students enrolled* • **Diesel Mechanics Technology/Technician** *2 students enrolled* • **Graphic and Printing Equipment Operator, General Production** *4 students enrolled* • **Heating, Air Conditioning, Ventilation and Refrigeration Maintenance Technology/Technician (HAC, HACR, HVAC, HVACR)** *4 students enrolled* • **Hotel/Motel Administration/Management** *2 students enrolled* • **Industrial Electronics Technology/Technician** *3 students enrolled* • **Licensed Practical/Vocational Nurse Training (LPN, LVN, Cert, Dipl, AAS)** *1452 hrs./$2410* • **Machine Shop Technology/Assistant** *2 students enrolled* • **Management Information Systems and Services, Other** *11 students enrolled* • **Occupational Therapist Assistant** *10 students enrolled* • **Physical Therapist Assistant** *10 students enrolled* • **Welding Technology/Welder** *2100 hrs./$2410*

**STUDENT SERVICES** Academic or career counseling, daycare for children of students, employment services for current students, placement services for program completers, remedial services.

## Canadian Valley Technology Center

6505 E. Highway 66, El Reno, OK 73036
http://www.cvtech.org/

**CONTACT** Dr. Greg Z. Winters, Superintendent
**Telephone:** 405-262-2629

**GENERAL INFORMATION** Public Institution. **Total program enrollment:** 265. **Application fee:** $25.

**PROGRAM(S) OFFERED**
• **Administrative Assistant and Secretarial Science, General** *50 students enrolled* • **Airframe Mechanics and Aircraft Maintenance Technology/Technician** • **Autobody/Collision and Repair Technology/Technician** *16 students enrolled* • **Automobile/Automotive Mechanics Technology/Technician** *12 students enrolled* • **Building/Property Maintenance and Management** • **Child Care Provider/Assistant** *1050 hrs./$1312* • **Computer Installation and Repair Technology/Technician** *17 students enrolled* • **Construction Trades, Other** *7 students enrolled* • **Cosmetology/Cosmetologist, General** *1050 hrs./$1312* • **Diesel Mechanics Technology/Technician** *8 students enrolled* • **Drafting and Design Technology/Technician, General** *17 students enrolled* • **Electrician** *13 students enrolled* • **Engineering Technology, General** *7 students enrolled* • **Graphic and Printing Equipment Operator, General Production** *1050 hrs./$1312* • **Health Aide** *1050 hrs./$1312* • **Heating, Air Conditioning, Ventilation and Refrigeration Maintenance Technology/Technician (HAC, HACR, HVAC, HVACR)** *11 students enrolled* • **Licensed Practical/Vocational Nurse Training (LPN, LVN, Cert, Dipl, AAS)** *1570 hrs./$4174* • **Machine Shop Technology/Assistant** *16 students enrolled* • **Medical Administrative/Executive Assistant and Medical Secretary** *7 students enrolled* • **Occupational Health and Industrial Hygiene** *8 students enrolled* • **Surgical Technology/Technologist** *18 students enrolled* • **Web Page, Digital/Multimedia and Information Resources Design** *12 students enrolled* • **Welding Technology/Welder** *1050 hrs./$1312*

**STUDENT SERVICES** Academic or career counseling, employment services for current students, placement services for program completers, remedial services.

## Career Point Institute

3138 South Garnett Road, Tulsa, OK 74146-1933

**CONTACT** Lawrence Earle, Board Chairman
**Telephone:** 918-627-8074

**GENERAL INFORMATION** Private Institution. **Total program enrollment:** 238.

**PROGRAM(S) OFFERED**
• **Accounting and Related Services, Other** *24 students enrolled* • **Accounting** *36 hrs./$14,350* • **Administrative Assistant and Secretarial Science, General** *36 hrs./$14,350* • **Computer Systems Analysis/Analyst** *2 students enrolled* • **General Office Occupations and Clerical Services** *2 students enrolled* • **Health Information/Medical Records Administration/Administrator** *54 students enrolled* • **Health Information/Medical Records Technology/Technician**

*Career Point Institute (continued)*

36 *hrs./$14,350* • **Legal Administrative Assistant/Secretary** 39 *hrs./$14,350* • **Medical Office Assistant/Specialist** 25 *hrs./$10,723* • **Medical/Clinical Assistant** 36 *hrs./$14,540*

**STUDENT SERVICES** Academic or career counseling, daycare for children of students, employment services for current students, placement services for program completers, remedial services.

## Carl Albert State College

1507 South McKenna, Poteau, OK 74953-5208
http://www.carlalbert.edu/

**CONTACT** Dr. Brandon Webb, President
**Telephone:** 918-647-1200

**GENERAL INFORMATION** Public Institution. Founded 1934. **Accreditation:** Regional (NCA); physical therapy assisting (APTA). **Total program enrollment:** 1428.

**PROGRAM(S) OFFERED**
• **Administrative Assistant and Secretarial Science, General** 2 *students enrolled* • **Child Care Provider/Assistant** 22 *students enrolled* • **Foodservice Systems Administration/Management** 4 *students enrolled* • **General Office Occupations and Clerical Services** 2 *students enrolled* • **Office Management and Supervision** 2 *students enrolled*

**STUDENT SERVICES** Academic or career counseling, daycare for children of students, employment services for current students, placement services for program completers, remedial services.

## CC's Cosmetology College

11630 East 21, Tulsa, OK 74129
http://www.ccscosmetology.edu/

**CONTACT** Chiquita Carter, Owner
**Telephone:** 918-234-9444

**GENERAL INFORMATION** Private Institution. **Total program enrollment:** 47. **Application fee:** $50.

**PROGRAM(S) OFFERED**
• **Aesthetician/Esthetician and Skin Care Specialist** 24 *hrs./$7194* • **Cosmetology, Barber/Styling, and Nail Instructor** 36 *hrs./$10,791* • **Cosmetology/Cosmetologist, General** 50 *hrs./$16,650* • **Nail Technician/Specialist and Manicurist** 24 *hrs./$7194*

**STUDENT SERVICES** Academic or career counseling, placement services for program completers.

## Central Oklahoma Area Vocational Technical School

3 Court Circle, Drumright, OK 74030
http://www.ctechok.org/

**CONTACT** Phil Waul, Superintendent
**Telephone:** 918-352-2551

**GENERAL INFORMATION** Private Institution. **Total program enrollment:** 102. **Application fee:** $100.

**PROGRAM(S) OFFERED**
• **Administrative Assistant and Secretarial Science, General** 7 *students enrolled* • **Allied Health and Medical Assisting Services, Other** 38 *students enrolled* • **Automobile/Automotive Mechanics Technology/Technician** 810 *hrs./$1013* • **Carpentry/Carpenter** 5 *students enrolled* • **Commercial and Advertising Art** 35 *students enrolled* • **Communications Systems Installation and Repair Technology** 3 *students enrolled* • **Computer and Information Sciences, General** 2 *students enrolled* • **Computer and Information Systems Security** 10 *students enrolled* • **Cosmetology, Barber/Styling, and Nail Instructor** 1500 *hrs./$1875* • **Cosmetology/Cosmetologist, General** 12 *students enrolled* • **Criminal Justice/Police Science** 4 *students enrolled* • **Diesel Mechanics Technology/Technician** 4 *students enrolled* • **Drafting and Design Technology/Technician, General** 2 *students enrolled* • **Electrician** 10 *students enrolled* • **Health Professions and Related Clinical Sciences, Other** 945 *hrs./$1181* • **Housing and Human Environments, Other** • **Licensed Practical/Vocational Nurse Training (LPN, LVN, Cert, Dipl, AAS)** 1500 *hrs./$4381* • **Machine Tool Technology/Machinist** 2 *students enrolled* • **Motorcycle Maintenance and Repair Technology/Technician** 4 *students enrolled* • **Printing Press Operator** 3 *students enrolled* • **Surgical Technology/Technologist** 1200 *hrs./$1500* • **Welding Technology/Welder** 1050 *hrs./$1313*

**STUDENT SERVICES** Academic or career counseling, remedial services.

## Central State Beauty Academy

8442 NW Expressway, Oklahoma City, OK 73162
http://www.centralstateacademy.com/

**CONTACT** Carol Fisher, President
**Telephone:** 405-722-4499

**GENERAL INFORMATION** Private Institution. Founded 1973. **Total program enrollment:** 94.

**PROGRAM(S) OFFERED**
• **Aesthetician/Esthetician and Skin Care Specialist** 600 *hrs./$4950* • **Cosmetology, Barber/Styling, and Nail Instructor** 1000 *hrs./$5100* • **Cosmetology/Cosmetologist, General** 50 *hrs./$10,785* • **Facial Treatment Specialist/Facialist** 18 *students enrolled* • **Nail Technician/Specialist and Manicurist** 600 *hrs./$3600*

**STUDENT SERVICES** Academic or career counseling, placement services for program completers.

## Central State Massage Academy

8494 Northwest Expressway, Oklahoma City, OK 73162

**CONTACT** Carol A. Fisher, President
**Telephone:** 405-722-4499

**GENERAL INFORMATION** Private Institution. **Total program enrollment:** 11.

**PROGRAM(S) OFFERED**
• **Massage Therapy/Therapeutic Massage** 42 *students enrolled*

**STUDENT SERVICES** Academic or career counseling, placement services for program completers.

## Chisholm Trail Area Vocational Technical Center

Route 1, Box 60, Omega, OK 73764
http://www.chisholmtrail.com/

**CONTACT** Max Thomas, Jr., Superintendent
**Telephone:** 405-729-8324 Ext. 221

**GENERAL INFORMATION** Private Institution. **Total program enrollment:** 44. **Application fee:** $20.

**PROGRAM(S) OFFERED**
• **Automobile/Automotive Mechanics Technology/Technician** 1050 *hrs./$2100* • **Business/Commerce, General** 5 *students enrolled* • **Computer Installation and Repair Technology/Technician** 6 *students enrolled* • **Computer Systems Networking and Telecommunications** 1020 *hrs./$2040* • **Graphic Communications, General** 840 *hrs./$1700* • **Health Professions and Related Clinical Sciences, Other** 3 *students enrolled* • **Licensed Practical/Vocational Nurse Training (LPN, LVN, Cert, Dipl, AAS)** 1500 *hrs./$5137* • **Medical/Clinical Assistant** 1050 *hrs./$1412* • **Phlebotomy/Phlebotomist** 600 *hrs./$1200*

**STUDENT SERVICES** Academic or career counseling, employment services for current students, placement services for program completers, remedial services.

## Claremore Beauty College

200 North Cherokee, Claremore, OK 74017
http://claremorebeautycollege.com/

**CONTACT** Denise Nelson, Owner
**Telephone:** 918-341-4370

**GENERAL INFORMATION** Private Institution. **Total program enrollment:** 13. **Application fee:** $100.

**PROGRAM(S) OFFERED**
• **Cosmetology, Barber/Styling, and Nail Instructor** *1000 hrs./$4400* • **Cosmetology/Cosmetologist, General** *1500 hrs./$7600* • **Nail Technician/Specialist and Manicurist** *600 hrs./$2800*

**STUDENT SERVICES** Academic or career counseling, employment services for current students, placement services for program completers.

## Clary Sage College

3131 South Sheridan, Tulsa, OK 74145
http://www.clarysagecollege.com/

**CONTACT** Teresa Knox, CEO
**Telephone:** 919-610-0027

**GENERAL INFORMATION** Private Institution. **Total program enrollment:** 105. **Application fee:** $100.

**PROGRAM(S) OFFERED**
• **Aesthetician/Esthetician and Skin Care Specialist** *600 hrs./$5940* • **Cosmetology, Barber/Styling, and Nail Instructor** *1000 hrs./$5280* • **Cosmetology/Cosmetologist, General** *1800 hrs./$15,423* • **Facial Treatment Specialist/Facialist** *61 students enrolled* • **Massage Therapy/Therapeutic Massage** *720 hrs./$7260* • **Nail Technician/Specialist and Manicurist** *600 hrs./$5940*

**STUDENT SERVICES** Academic or career counseling, employment services for current students, placement services for program completers.

## Community Care College

4242 South Sheridan, Tulsa, OK 74145
http://www.communitycarecollege.edu/

**CONTACT** Teresa Knox, CEO
**Telephone:** 919-610-0027

**GENERAL INFORMATION** Private Institution. Founded 1995. **Accreditation:** State accredited or approved. **Total program enrollment:** 175. **Application fee:** $100.

**PROGRAM(S) OFFERED**
• **Business Administration and Management, General** *940 hrs./$20,418* • **Dental Assisting/Assistant** *730 hrs./$9960* • **Early Childhood Education and Teaching** • **Massage Therapy/Therapeutic Massage** *810 hrs./$11,454* • **Medical/Clinical Assistant** *850 hrs./$12,614* • **Pharmacy Technician/Assistant** *19 students enrolled* • **Sport and Fitness Administration/Management** • **Surgical Technology/Technologist** *1270 hrs./$18,260* • **Veterinary/Animal Health Technology/Technician and Veterinary Assistant** *850 hrs./$12,118*

**STUDENT SERVICES** Academic or career counseling, daycare for children of students, employment services for current students, placement services for program completers.

## Connors State College

Route 1 Box 1000, Warner, OK 74469-9700
http://www.connorsstate.edu/

**CONTACT** Dr. Donnie L. Nero, President
**Telephone:** 918-463-2931

**GENERAL INFORMATION** Public Institution. Founded 1908. **Accreditation:** Regional (NCA). **Total program enrollment:** 1335.

**PROGRAM(S) OFFERED**
• **Child Development** *6 students enrolled* • **Equestrian/Equine Studies** *1 student enrolled*

**STUDENT SERVICES** Academic or career counseling, employment services for current students, remedial services.

## Eastern Oklahoma County Technology Center

4601 N. Choctaw Road, Choctaw, OK 73020-9017
http://www.eoctech.org/

**CONTACT** Dr. Terry Underwood, Superintendent
**Telephone:** 405-390-9591

**GENERAL INFORMATION** Public Institution. **Total program enrollment:** 90.

**PROGRAM(S) OFFERED**
• **Accounting Technology/Technician and Bookkeeping** *2 students enrolled* • **Administrative Assistant and Secretarial Science, General** *2 students enrolled* • **Allied Health and Medical Assisting Services, Other** *10 students enrolled* • **Automobile/Automotive Mechanics Technology/Technician** *915 hrs./$1056* • **Building/Property Maintenance and Management** *2 students enrolled* • **Carpentry/Carpenter** • **Child Care Provider/Assistant** *795 hrs./$1056* • **Child Care and Support Services Management** • **Computer Installation and Repair Technology/Technician** *1 student enrolled* • **Computer Systems Networking and Telecommunications** *720 hrs./$792* • **Digital Communication and Media/Multimedia** *6 students enrolled* • **Electrician** *4 students enrolled* • **Emergency Medical Technology/Technician (EMT Paramedic)** • **Fire Protection and Safety Technology/Technician** *23 students enrolled* • **Fire Protection, Other** *468 hrs./$528* • **Fire Science/Firefighting** *736 hrs./$3400* • **Graphic and Printing Equipment Operator, General Production** *4 students enrolled* • **Heating, Air Conditioning, Ventilation and Refrigeration Maintenance Technology/Technician (HAC, HACR, HVAC, HVACR)** *5 students enrolled* • **Mason/Masonry** *6 students enrolled* • **Nurse/Nursing Assistant/Aide and Patient Care Assistant** *496 hrs./$528* • **System, Networking, and LAN/WAN Management/Manager** *2 students enrolled* • **Welding Technology/Welder** *5 students enrolled*

**STUDENT SERVICES** Academic or career counseling, placement services for program completers, remedial services.

## Eastern Oklahoma State College

1301 West Main, Wilburton, OK 74578-4999
http://www.eosc.edu/

**CONTACT** Dr. Steve Smith, President
**Telephone:** 918-465-2361

**GENERAL INFORMATION** Public Institution. Founded 1908. **Accreditation:** Regional (NCA). **Total program enrollment:** 890. **Application fee:** $10.

**PROGRAM(S) OFFERED**
• **Orthoptics/Orthoptist** *2 students enrolled*

**STUDENT SERVICES** Academic or career counseling, employment services for current students, placement services for program completers, remedial services.

## Enid Beauty College

1601 East Broadway, Enid, OK 73701

**CONTACT** Lois Record, President
**Telephone:** 580-237-6677

**GENERAL INFORMATION** Private Institution. Founded 1963. **Total program enrollment:** 51. **Application fee:** $25.

**PROGRAM(S) OFFERED**
• **Cosmetology and Related Personal Grooming Arts, Other** *1000 hrs./$6600* • **Cosmetology/Cosmetologist, General** *1500 hrs./$10,800*

**STUDENT SERVICES** Academic or career counseling, placement services for program completers.

## Eve's College of Hairstyling

912 C Avenue, Lawton, OK 73501

**CONTACT** Tammy Graham, President
**Telephone:** 580-355-6620

**GENERAL INFORMATION** Private Institution. Founded 1962. **Total program enrollment:** 75. **Application fee:** $100.

**PROGRAM(S) OFFERED**
• **Cosmetology and Related Personal Grooming Arts, Other** *1 student enrolled* • **Cosmetology, Barber/Styling, and Nail Instructor** *1000 hrs./$4270* • **Cosmetology/Cosmetologist, General** *1500 hrs./$10,700* • **Nail Technician/Specialist and Manicurist** *600 hrs./$3450*

**STUDENT SERVICES** Placement services for program completers.

## 4-States Academy of Cosmetology

123 S. Wilson Street, Vinita, OK 74301

**CONTACT** Tanya Flock, CEO
**Telephone:** 918-542-8651

**GENERAL INFORMATION** Private Institution. **Total program enrollment:** 29. **Application fee:** $100.

**PROGRAM(S) OFFERED**
• **Aesthetician/Esthetician and Skin Care Specialist** *600 hrs./$4200* • **Cosmetology, Barber/Styling, and Nail Instructor** *1000 hrs./$6700* • **Cosmetology/Cosmetologist, General** *1500 hrs./$9400* • **Nail Technician/Specialist and Manicurist** *600 hrs./$4200*

**STUDENT SERVICES** Academic or career counseling, placement services for program completers.

## Francis Tuttle Area Vocational Technical Center

12777 North Rockwell Avenue, Oklahoma City, OK 73142-2789
http://www.francistuttle.com/

**CONTACT** Kay Martin, Superintendent
**Telephone:** 405-717-4900

**GENERAL INFORMATION** Public Institution. Founded 1982. **Total program enrollment:** 414.

**PROGRAM(S) OFFERED**
• **Accounting Technology/Technician and Bookkeeping** *12 students enrolled* • **Administrative Assistant and Secretarial Science, General** *13 students enrolled* • **Allied Health and Medical Assisting Services, Other** *35 students enrolled* • **Autobody/Collision and Repair Technology/Technician** *6 students enrolled* • **Automobile/Automotive Mechanics Technology/Technician** *1056 hrs./$1600* • **CAD/CADD Drafting and/or Design Technology/Technician** *4 students enrolled* • **Carpentry/Carpenter** *42 students enrolled* • **Child Care and Support Services Management** *5 students enrolled* • **Computer Installation and Repair Technology/Technician** *1716 hrs./$3600* • **Computer Programming/Programmer, General** *6 students enrolled* • **Computer Science** *22 students enrolled* • **Computer Systems Networking and Telecommunications** *1 student enrolled* • **Cosmetology and Related Personal Grooming Arts, Other** *50 students enrolled* • **Cosmetology/Cosmetologist, General** *1500 hrs./$2400* • **Customer Service Support/Call Center/Teleservice Operation** *5 students enrolled* • **Dental Assisting/Assistant** • **Food Preparation/Professional Cooking/Kitchen Assistant** *21 students enrolled* • **Graphic and Printing Equipment Operator, General Production** *10 students enrolled* • **Housing and Human Environments, Other** *9 students enrolled* • **Human Development, Family Studies, and Related Services, Other** *6 students enrolled* • **Human Resources Management and Services, Other** *3 students enrolled* • **Licensed Practical/Vocational Nurse Training (LPN, LVN, Cert, Dipl, AAS)** *1452 hrs./$2000* • **Machine Tool Technology/Machinist** *2 students enrolled* • **Management Information Systems and Services, Other** *2 students enrolled* • **Management Information Systems, General** *8 students enrolled* • **Manufacturing Technology/Technician** *6 students enrolled* • **Marketing, Other** *1 student enrolled* • **Mason/Masonry** • **Medical Office Management/Administration** *8 students enrolled* • **Medical/Clinical Assistant** *11 students enrolled* • **Orthotist/Prosthetist** *4 students enrolled* • **Printing Press Operator** • **Respiratory Care Therapy/Therapist** *28 students enrolled* • **Respiratory Therapy Technician/Assistant** *1880 hrs./$3280* • **Restaurant, Culinary, and Catering Management/Manager** *1056 hrs./$1600* • **Welding Technology/Welder** *4 students enrolled*

**STUDENT SERVICES** Academic or career counseling, daycare for children of students, placement services for program completers, remedial services.

## Gordon Cooper Technology Center

1. John C. Bruton Boulevard, Shawnee, OK 74801
http://www.gctech.org/

**CONTACT** Martin E. Lewis, Superintendent
**Telephone:** 405-273-7493

**GENERAL INFORMATION** Private Institution. **Total program enrollment:** 186.

**PROGRAM(S) OFFERED**
• **Accounting Technology/Technician and Bookkeeping** *1260 hrs./$1935* • **Administrative Assistant and Secretarial Science, General** *9 students enrolled* • **Applied Horticulture/Horticultural Operations, General** • **Autobody/Collision and Repair Technology/Technician** *9 students enrolled* • **Automobile/Automotive Mechanics Technology/Technician** *11 students enrolled* • **Building/Property Maintenance and Management** *21 students enrolled* • **Business/Office Automation/Technology/Data Entry** • **Carpentry/Carpenter** *4 students enrolled* • **Child Care Provider/Assistant** *1320 hrs./$1781* • **Computer Systems Networking and Telecommunications** *9 students enrolled* • **Diesel Mechanics Technology/Technician** *24 students enrolled* • **Drafting and Design Technology/Technician, General** *5 students enrolled* • **E-Commerce/Electronic Commerce** *8 students enrolled* • **Electrician** *11 students enrolled* • **Emergency Medical Technology/Technician (EMT Paramedic)** *12 students enrolled* • **Graphic Communications, Other** *11 students enrolled* • **Health Professions and Related Clinical Sciences, Other** *29 students enrolled* • **Heating, Air Conditioning, Ventilation and Refrigeration Maintenance Technology/Technician (HAC, HACR, HVAC, HVACR)** *10 students enrolled* • **Licensed Practical/Vocational Nurse Training (LPN, LVN, Cert, Dipl, AAS)** *1515 hrs./$3529* • **Machine Shop Technology/Assistant** *22 students enrolled* • **Mason/Masonry** *11 students enrolled* • **Web Page, Digital/Multimedia and Information Resources Design** *1320 hrs./$2002* • **Welding Technology/Welder** *1425 hrs./$1985*

**STUDENT SERVICES** Academic or career counseling, daycare for children of students, employment services for current students.

## Great Plains Technology Center

4500 West Lee Boulevard, Lawton, OK 73505
http://www.gptech.org/

**CONTACT** Jim Nisbett, Superintendent
**Telephone:** 580-355-6371

**GENERAL INFORMATION** Public Institution. Founded 1969. **Total program enrollment:** 221.

**PROGRAM(S) OFFERED**
• **Autobody/Collision and Repair Technology/Technician** • **Automobile/Automotive Mechanics Technology/Technician** *1170 hrs./$1462* • **Building/Property Maintenance and Management** • **Business, Management, Marketing, and Related Support Services, Other** *7 students enrolled* • **Computer Installation and Repair Technology/Technician** *1300 hrs./$1625* • **Computer Systems Networking and Telecommunications** *8 students enrolled* • **Criminal Justice/Law Enforcement Administration** *2 students enrolled* • **Culinary Arts/Chef Training** *4 students enrolled* • **Diesel Mechanics Technology/Technician** *5 students enrolled* • **Drafting and Design Technology/Technician, General** *5 students enrolled* • **Emergency Medical Technology/Technician (EMT Paramedic)** *9 students enrolled* • **Graphic and Printing Equipment Operator, General Production** *4 students enrolled* • **Health Information/Medical Records Technology/Technician** *4 students enrolled* • **Heating, Air Conditioning, Ventilation and Refrigeration Maintenance Technology/Technician (HAC, HACR, HVAC, HVACR)** *2370 hrs./$2962* • **Industrial Mechanics and Maintenance Technology** • **Licensed Practical/Vocational Nurse Training (LPN, LVN, Cert, Dipl, AAS)** *1497 hrs./$3340* • **Medical Radiologic Technology/Science—Radiation Therapist** *3000 hrs./$4757* • **Respiratory Care Therapy/Therapist** *21 students enrolled* • **Surgical Technology/Technologist** *1185 hrs./$1481* • **Welding Technology/Welder** *5 students enrolled*

**STUDENT SERVICES** Academic or career counseling, employment services for current students, placement services for program completers, remedial services.

## Green Country Technology Center

PO Box 1217, Okmulgee, OK 74447
http://gctcok.com/

**CONTACT** Danne Spurlock, Superintendent
**Telephone:** 918-758-0840

**GENERAL INFORMATION** Public Institution. **Total program enrollment:** 26.

**PROGRAM(S) OFFERED**
• **Building/Property Maintenance and Management** *14 students enrolled* • **CAD/CADD Drafting and/or Design Technology/Technician** *1050 hrs./$2625* • **Carpentry/Carpenter** *1050 hrs./$2625* • **Computer and Information Sciences, General** *12 students enrolled* • **Computer/Information Technology Services Administration and Management, Other** *17 students enrolled* • **Engineering, Other** *5 students enrolled* • **Health Aide** *11 students enrolled* • **Machine Tool Technology/Machinist** *1050 hrs./$2625* • **Management Information Systems and Services, Other** *1050 hrs./$2625* • **Nursing, Other** *27 students enrolled* • **Shoe, Boot and Leather Repair** *1250 hrs./$3125* • **Web Page, Digital/Multimedia and Information Resources Design** *1050 hrs./$2625*

**STUDENT SERVICES** Academic or career counseling, employment services for current students, placement services for program completers, remedial services.

## Heritage College of Hair Design

7100 I-35 Services Road, Suite 7118, Oklahoma City, OK 73149

**CONTACT** Cheryl Morris, Director
**Telephone:** 405-631-3399

**GENERAL INFORMATION** Private Institution. **Accreditation:** State accredited or approved. **Total program enrollment:** 767.

**PROGRAM(S) OFFERED**
• **Aesthetician/Esthetician and Skin Care Specialist** *95 hrs./$20,106* • **Allied Health and Medical Assisting Services, Other** *94 hrs./$22,850* • **Health and Physical Education/Fitness, Other** *96 hrs./$20,935* • **Massage Therapy/Therapeutic Massage** *95 hrs./$20,605* • **Pharmacy Technician/Assistant** *54 hrs./$12,053* • **Surgical Technology/Technologist** *96 hrs./$24,680*

**STUDENT SERVICES** Academic or career counseling, employment services for current students, placement services for program completers.

## High Plains Institute of Technology

3921 34th Street, Woodward, OK 73801
http://www.hptc.net/

**CONTACT** Don Bird, Superintendent
**Telephone:** 580-256-6618

**GENERAL INFORMATION** Private Institution. **Total program enrollment:** 50.

**PROGRAM(S) OFFERED**
• **Administrative Assistant and Secretarial Science, General** *2175 hrs./$4388* • **Automobile/Automotive Mechanics Technology/Technician** *1050 hrs./$1848* • **Building/Property Maintenance and Management** *1 student enrolled* • **Business/Office Automation/Technology/Data Entry** • **Carpentry/Carpenter** *1050 hrs./$1848* • **Computer Installation and Repair Technology/Technician** • **Diesel Mechanics Technology/Technician** *5 students enrolled* • **General Merchandising, Sales, and Related Marketing Operations, Other** *5 students enrolled* • **Health Aide** • **Information Technology** *9 students enrolled* • **Licensed Practical/Vocational Nurse Training (LPN, LVN, Cert, Dipl, AAS)** *19 students enrolled* • **Marketing/Marketing Management, General** *1050 hrs./$1852* • **Therapeutic Recreation/Recreational Therapy** *1050 hrs./$1853* • **Welding Technology/Welder** *1050 hrs./$1838*

**STUDENT SERVICES** Academic or career counseling, employment services for current students, placement services for program completers, remedial services.

## Hillsdale Free Will Baptist College

3701 South I-35 Service Road, PO Box 7208, Moore, OK 73160-1208
http://www.hc.edu/

**CONTACT** Timothy W. Eaton, President
**Telephone:** 405-912-9000

**GENERAL INFORMATION** Private Institution. Founded 1959. **Accreditation:** State accredited or approved. **Total program enrollment:** 196. **Application fee:** $20.

**STUDENT SERVICES** Academic or career counseling, employment services for current students, remedial services.

## Hollywood Cosmetology Center

1708 West Lindsey Street, Norman, OK 73072

**CONTACT** Crystal Burgess, Owner
**Telephone:** 405-364-3375

**GENERAL INFORMATION** Private Institution. Founded 1965. **Total program enrollment:** 11. **Application fee:** $100.

**PROGRAM(S) OFFERED**
• **Cosmetology and Related Personal Grooming Arts, Other** • **Cosmetology, Barber/Styling, and Nail Instructor** *1000 hrs./$2500* • **Cosmetology/Cosmetologist, General** *1500 hrs./$7025* • **Nail Technician/Specialist and Manicurist** *600 hrs./$2250*

**STUDENT SERVICES** Placement services for program completers.

## Indian Capital Technology Center–Muskogee

2403 N. 41st Street E, Muskogee, OK 74403
http://www.ictctech.com/

**CONTACT** Randy Cravens, Director
**Telephone:** 918-687-6383 Ext. 7900

**GENERAL INFORMATION** Public Institution. **Total program enrollment:** 114.

**PROGRAM(S) OFFERED**
• **Administrative Assistant and Secretarial Science, General** *1050 hrs./$1050* • **Autobody/Collision and Repair Technology/Technician** *21 students enrolled* • **Automobile/Automotive Mechanics Technology/Technician** *22 students enrolled* • **Business Administration and Management, General** *1050 hrs./$1050* • **Carpentry/Carpenter** *10 students enrolled* • **Cosmetology/Cosmetologist, General** *12 students enrolled* • **Culinary Arts/Chef Training** *8 students enrolled* • **Drafting/Design Engineering Technologies/Technicians, Other** *6 students enrolled* • **Electrical/Electronics Equipment Installation and Repair, General** *12 students enrolled* • **Electrician** *1050 hrs./$1050* • **Graphic Communications, General** *13 students enrolled* • **Heating, Air Conditioning, Ventilation and Refrigeration Maintenance Technology/Technician (HAC, HACR, HVAC, HVACR)** *1050 hrs./$1050* • **Hospitality Administration/Management, General** *9 students enrolled* • **Industrial Electronics Technology/Technician** *9 students enrolled* • **Information Resources Management/CIO Training** *11 students enrolled* • **Licensed Practical/Vocational Nurse Training (LPN, LVN, Cert, Dipl, AAS)** *1463 hrs./$3601* • **Machine Tool Technology/Machinist** *9 students enrolled* • **Radiation Biology/Radiobiology** *10 students enrolled* • **Radiologic Technology/Science—Radiographer** *2655 hrs./$2700* • **Welding Technology/Welder** *25 students enrolled*

**STUDENT SERVICES** Academic or career counseling, remedial services.

## Indian Capital Technology Center–Sallisaw

HC 61, Box 12, Sallisaw, OK 74955
http://www.icavts.tec.ok.us/

**CONTACT** Curtis Shumaker, Director
**Telephone:** 918-775-9119

**GENERAL INFORMATION** Public Institution. **Total program enrollment:** 43.

*Indian Capital Technology Center–Sallisaw (continued)*

**PROGRAM(S) OFFERED**

• **Administrative Assistant and Secretarial Science, General** *1050 hrs./$1050* • **Automobile/Automotive Mechanics Technology/Technician** *1050 hrs./$1050* • **Carpentry/Carpenter** *1050 hrs./$1050* • **Health Professions and Related Clinical Sciences, Other** *18 students enrolled* • **Heating, Air Conditioning, Ventilation and Refrigeration Maintenance Technology/Technician (HAC, HACR, HVAC, HVACR)** *1050 hrs./$1050* • **Information Resources Management/CIO Training** *18 students enrolled* • **Information Technology** *1050 hrs./$1050* • **Licensed Practical/Vocational Nurse Training (LPN, LVN, Cert, Dipl, AAS)** *1423 hrs./$3422* • **Upholstery/Upholsterer** *5 students enrolled*

**STUDENT SERVICES** Academic or career counseling, remedial services.

## Indian Capital Technology Center–Stilwell

Highway 59 N., Stilwell, OK 74960
http://icavts.tec.ok.us/

**CONTACT** Dan Collins, Director
**Telephone:** 918-696-3111

**GENERAL INFORMATION** Public Institution. **Total program enrollment:** 44.

**PROGRAM(S) OFFERED**

• **Administrative Assistant and Secretarial Science, General** *1050 hrs./$1235* • **Automobile/Automotive Mechanics Technology/Technician** *1050 hrs./$1050* • **Building/Construction Site Management/Manager** *2 students enrolled* • **Building/Property Maintenance and Management** *7 students enrolled* • **Construction Trades, General** *1050 hrs./$1050* • **Health Professions and Related Clinical Sciences, Other** *7 students enrolled* • **Health Services/Allied Health/Health Sciences, General** *1050 hrs./$1050* • **Licensed Practical/Vocational Nurse Training (LPN, LVN, Cert, Dipl, AAS)** *1423 hrs./$1423* • **Surgical Technology/Technologist** *1500 hrs./$1200*

**STUDENT SERVICES** Academic or career counseling, remedial services.

## Indian Capital Technology Center–Tahlequah

1400 South Hensley Drive, Tahlequah, OK 74464
http://www.ictctech.com/

**CONTACT** Denver Spears, Director
**Telephone:** 918-456-2594

**GENERAL INFORMATION** Public Institution. Founded 1972. **Total program enrollment:** 106.

**PROGRAM(S) OFFERED**

• **Administrative Assistant and Secretarial Science, General** *1050 hrs./$1435* • **Applied Horticulture/Horticultural Operations, General** *6 students enrolled* • **Autobody/Collision and Repair Technology/Technician** *6 students enrolled* • **Automobile/Automotive Mechanics Technology/Technician** *8 students enrolled* • **Building/Construction Site Management/Manager** *3 students enrolled* • **Computer Systems Networking and Telecommunications** *1050 hrs./$1050* • **Construction/Heavy Equipment/Earthmoving Equipment Operation** *1050 hrs./$2625* • **Heating, Air Conditioning, Ventilation and Refrigeration Maintenance Technology/Technician (HAC, HACR, HVAC, HVACR)** *1050 hrs./$1050* • **Heavy Equipment Maintenance Technology/Technician** *15 students enrolled* • **Information Resources Management/CIO Training** *6 students enrolled* • **Licensed Practical/Vocational Nurse Training (LPN, LVN, Cert, Dipl, AAS)** *1423 hrs./$1931* • **Nurse/Nursing Assistant/Aide and Patient Care Assistant** *11 students enrolled* • **Welding Technology/Welder** *1050 hrs./$1050*

**STUDENT SERVICES** Academic or career counseling, remedial services.

## Institute of Hair Design

1601½ N. Harrison, Shawnee, OK 74804

**CONTACT** Freda Poe, Owner
**Telephone:** 405-275-8000

**GENERAL INFORMATION** Private Institution. **Total program enrollment:** 30. **Application fee:** $100.

**PROGRAM(S) OFFERED**

• **Barbering/Barber** *1500 hrs./$7700* • **Cosmetology, Barber/Styling, and Nail Instructor** *600 hrs./$4950* • **Massage Therapy/Therapeutic Massage** *1000 hrs./$4700*

**STUDENT SERVICES** Academic or career counseling, employment services for current students, placement services for program completers, remedial services.

## Kiamichi Area Vocational-Technical School–Atoka

Highway 3 and 75 West, Atoka, OK 74525
http://www.kiamichi-atoka.tec.ok.us/

**CONTACT** Elaine Gee, Director
**Telephone:** 580-889-7321 Ext. 102

**GENERAL INFORMATION** Public Institution. **Total program enrollment:** 27.

**PROGRAM(S) OFFERED**

• **Administrative Assistant and Secretarial Science, General** *5 students enrolled* • **Automobile/Automotive Mechanics Technology/Technician** *2100 hrs./$1312* • **Business Administration and Management, General** *2100 hrs./$1312* • **Carpentry/Carpenter** *1 student enrolled* • **Child Care and Support Services Management** *2100 hrs./$1312* • **Computer Systems Networking and Telecommunications** *2100 hrs./$1312* • **Cosmetology/Cosmetologist, General** *1500 hrs./$1612* • **Licensed Practical/Vocational Nurse Training (LPN, LVN, Cert, Dipl, AAS)** *6 students enrolled* • **Welding Technology/Welder** *2100 hrs./$1312*

**STUDENT SERVICES** Academic or career counseling, daycare for children of students, employment services for current students, placement services for program completers, remedial services.

## Kiamichi Area Vocational-Technical School–Durant

810 Waldron Road, Durant, OK 74701
http://www.kiamichi-durant.tec.ok.us/

**CONTACT** Mike Goodwin, Director
**Telephone:** 580-924-7081

**GENERAL INFORMATION** Public Institution. Founded 1988. **Total program enrollment:** 107.

**PROGRAM(S) OFFERED**

• **Automobile/Automotive Mechanics Technology/Technician** *1050 hrs./$1313* • **Business Operations Support and Secretarial Services, Other** *1050 hrs./$1313* • **Computer Systems Networking and Telecommunications** *1050 hrs./$1313* • **Cooking and Related Culinary Arts, General** *1050 hrs./$1313* • **Data Processing and Data Processing Technology/Technician** • **Emergency Medical Technology/Technician (EMT Paramedic)** *7 students enrolled* • **General Office Occupations and Clerical Services** • **Licensed Practical/Vocational Nurse Training (LPN, LVN, Cert, Dipl, AAS)** *1508 hrs./$3375* • **Welding Technology/Welder** *1050 hrs./$1313*

**STUDENT SERVICES** Academic or career counseling, placement services for program completers, remedial services.

## Kiamichi Area Vocational-Technical School–McAlester

301 Kiamichi Drive, McAlester, OK 74501
http://www.kiamichi-mcalester.tec.ok.us/

**CONTACT** Eddie Coleman, Superintendent
**Telephone:** 918-426-0940

**GENERAL INFORMATION** Private Institution. **Total program enrollment:** 125.

**PROGRAM(S) OFFERED**
• **Business Administration and Management, General** *1050 hrs./$1313* • **Health Services/Allied Health/Health Sciences, General** *1050 hrs./$1313* • **Health/Health Care Administration/Management** *1050 hrs./$1313* • **Heating, Air Conditioning, Ventilation and Refrigeration Maintenance Technology/Technician (HAC, HACR, HVAC, HVACR)** *1050 hrs./$1313* • **Licensed Practical/Vocational Nurse Training (LPN, LVN, Cert, Dipl, AAS)** *1508 hrs./$3375* • **Welding Technology/Welder** *1050 hrs./$1313*

**STUDENT SERVICES** Academic or career counseling, daycare for children of students, employment services for current students, placement services for program completers, remedial services.

## Kiamichi Area Vocational-Technical School–Poteau

1509 South McKenna, Poteau, OK 74953
http://www.kiamichi-poteau.tec.ok.us/

**CONTACT** Eddie Coleman, Superintendent
**Telephone:** 918-465-2323

**GENERAL INFORMATION** Private Institution. **Total program enrollment:** 131.

**PROGRAM(S) OFFERED**
• **Allied Health and Medical Assisting Services, Other** *2100 hrs./$1712* • **Automobile/Automotive Mechanics Technology/Technician** *2100 hrs./$1312* • **Business/Office Automation/Technology/Data Entry** *2100 hrs./$1312* • **Electrician** *2100 hrs./$1312* • **Emergency Medical Technology/Technician (EMT Paramedic)** *13 students enrolled* • **Heating, Air Conditioning, Ventilation and Refrigeration Maintenance Technology/Technician (HAC, HACR, HVAC, HVACR)** *2100 hrs./$1312* • **Licensed Practical/Vocational Nurse Training (LPN, LVN, Cert, Dipl, AAS)** *18 students enrolled* • **Welding Technology/Welder** *2100 hrs./$1312*

**STUDENT SERVICES** Academic or career counseling, employment services for current students, placement services for program completers, remedial services.

## Kiamichi Area Vocational-Technical School–Stigler

1410 Military Road, Stigler, OK 74462-9601
http://www.kiamichi-stigler.tec.ok.us/

**CONTACT** Eddie Coleman, Superintendent
**Telephone:** 918-465-2323

**GENERAL INFORMATION** Private Institution. **Total program enrollment:** 25.

**PROGRAM(S) OFFERED**
• **Administrative Assistant and Secretarial Science, General** *2100 hrs./$1712* • **Automobile/Automotive Mechanics Technology/Technician** *2100 hrs./$1312* • **Carpentry/Carpenter** *2100 hrs./$1312* • **Licensed Practical/Vocational Nurse Training (LPN, LVN, Cert, Dipl, AAS)** *1508 hrs./$3790* • **Welding Technology/Welder** *2100 hrs./$1312*

**STUDENT SERVICES** Academic or career counseling, employment services for current students, placement services for program completers, remedial services.

## Kiamichi Area Vocational-Technical School–Talihina

Route 2, Highway 63A, Talihina, OK 74571
http://www.okktc.org/

**CONTACT** Eddie Coleman, Superintendent
**Telephone:** 918-465-2323

**GENERAL INFORMATION** Private Institution. **Total program enrollment:** 46.

**PROGRAM(S) OFFERED**
• **Administrative Assistant and Secretarial Science, General** *5 students enrolled* • **Automobile/Automotive Mechanics Technology/Technician** *1050 hrs./$1312* • **Business/Office Automation/Technology/Data Entry** *1050 hrs./$1712* • **Carpentry/Carpenter** *1050 hrs./$1312* • **Health Professions and Related Clinical Sciences, Other** *29 students enrolled* • **Health Services/Allied Health/Health Sciences, General** *1050 hrs./$1312* • **Licensed Practical/Vocational Nurse Training (LPN, LVN, Cert, Dipl, AAS)** *1508 hrs./$3790*

**STUDENT SERVICES** Academic or career counseling, employment services for current students, placement services for program completers, remedial services.

## Kiamichi Technology Center

107 South 15th, Hugo, OK 74743
http://www.okktc.org/

**CONTACT** Eddie Coleman, Superintendent
**Telephone:** 888-567-6807

**GENERAL INFORMATION** Private Institution. **Total program enrollment:** 65.

**PROGRAM(S) OFFERED**
• **Administrative Assistant and Secretarial Science, General** *13 students enrolled* • **Allied Health and Medical Assisting Services, Other** *1050 hrs./$1312* • **Autobody/Collision and Repair Technology/Technician** *1050 hrs./$1312* • **Building/Property Maintenance and Management** *1050 hrs./$1312* • **Business, Management, Marketing, and Related Support Services, Other** *1020 hrs./$1562* • **Child Care and Support Services Management** *1050 hrs./$1312* • **Computer Installation and Repair Technology/Technician** *1050 hrs./$1312* • **Diesel Mechanics Technology/Technician** *6 students enrolled* • **Family and Consumer Sciences/Human Sciences, Other** *13 students enrolled* • **Licensed Practical/Vocational Nurse Training (LPN, LVN, Cert, Dipl, AAS)** *23 students enrolled*

**STUDENT SERVICES** Academic or career counseling, employment services for current students, placement services for program completers, remedial services.

## Kiamichi Technology Center

Highway 70, N, Route 3, Box 177, Idabel, OK 74745
http://www.kiamichi-idabel.tec.ok.us/

**CONTACT** Eddie Coleman, Superintendent
**Telephone:** 580-286-7555

**GENERAL INFORMATION** Private Institution. **Total program enrollment:** 79.

**PROGRAM(S) OFFERED**
• **Allied Health and Medical Assisting Services, Other** *1050 hrs./$1313* • **Automobile/Automotive Mechanics Technology/Technician** *1050 hrs./$1313* • **Business, Management, Marketing, and Related Support Services, Other** *1050 hrs./$1313* • **Cosmetology/Cosmetologist, General** *1050 hrs./$1313* • **Licensed Practical/Vocational Nurse Training (LPN, LVN, Cert, Dipl, AAS)** *1508 hrs./$1803* • **Welding Technology/Welder** *1050 hrs./$1313*

**STUDENT SERVICES** Academic or career counseling, employment services for current students, placement services for program completers, remedial services.

## Meridian Technology Center

1312 South Sangre Road, Stillwater, OK 74074
http://www.meridian-technology.com/

**CONTACT** Doug Major, Superintendent
**Telephone:** 405-377-3333

**GENERAL INFORMATION** Public Institution. Founded 1973. **Total program enrollment:** 168.

*Meridian Technology Center (continued)*

**PROGRAM(S) OFFERED**

• **Accounting** *1 student enrolled* • **Administrative Assistant and Secretarial Science, General** *2 students enrolled* • **Autobody/Collision and Repair Technology/Technician** *7 students enrolled* • **Automobile/Automotive Mechanics Technology/Technician** *16 students enrolled* • **Banking and Financial Support Services** *1 student enrolled* • **Biology Technician/Biotechnology Laboratory Technician** *3 students enrolled* • **Carpentry/Carpenter** *8 students enrolled* • **Computer Installation and Repair Technology/Technician** *1 student enrolled* • **Computer Systems Networking and Telecommunications** *9 students enrolled* • **Cooking and Related Culinary Arts, General** *600 hrs./$1200* • **Cosmetology/Cosmetologist, General** *1000 hrs./$2000* • **Culinary Arts/Chef Training** *13 students enrolled* • **Drafting and Design Technology/Technician, General** *7 students enrolled* • **Electrical and Power Transmission Installation/Installer, General** *8 students enrolled* • **Electrician** *975 hrs./$1950* • **Emergency Medical Technology/Technician (EMT Paramedic)** • **Engineering, General** *1 student enrolled* • **Health Professions and Related Clinical Sciences, Other** *12 students enrolled* • **Heating, Air Conditioning, Ventilation and Refrigeration Maintenance Technology/Technician (HAC, HACR, HVAC, HVACR)** *8 students enrolled* • **Licensed Practical/Vocational Nurse Training (LPN, LVN, Cert, Dipl, AAS)** *1500 hrs./$3800* • **Machine Shop Technology/Assistant** *3 students enrolled* • **Manufacturing Technology/Technician** • **Mason/Masonry** *5 students enrolled* • **Massage Therapy/Therapeutic Massage** *20 students enrolled* • **Medical Informatics** *2 students enrolled* • **Pharmacy Technician/Assistant** *600 hrs./$1200* • **Radiologic Technology/Science—Radiographer** *3000 hrs./$4630* • **Web Page, Digital/Multimedia and Information Resources Design** *8 students enrolled* • **Welding Technology/Welder** *12 students enrolled*

**STUDENT SERVICES** Academic or career counseling, placement services for program completers, remedial services.

## Metro Area Vocational Technical School District 22

1900 Springlake Drive, Oklahoma City, OK 73111
http://www.metrotech.org/

**CONTACT** Dr. James Branscum, Superintendent
**Telephone:** 405-424-8324

**GENERAL INFORMATION** Public Institution. Founded 1969. **Total program enrollment:** 907. **Application fee:** $35.

**PROGRAM(S) OFFERED**

• **Accounting** *8 students enrolled* • **Administrative Assistant and Secretarial Science, General** *5 students enrolled* • **Autobody/Collision and Repair Technology/Technician** *1 student enrolled* • **Automobile/Automotive Mechanics Technology/Technician** *5 students enrolled* • **Avionics Maintenance Technology/Technician** *1980 hrs./$8784* • **Business Operations Support and Secretarial Services, Other** *990 hrs./$1980* • **Carpentry/Carpenter** *6 students enrolled* • **Child Care Provider/Assistant** *15 students enrolled* • **Computer Installation and Repair Technology/Technician** *10 students enrolled* • **Computer and Information Sciences and Support Services, Other** *750 hrs./$1500* • **Cosmetology/Cosmetologist, General** *1500 hrs./$3000* • **Culinary Arts/Chef Training** *9 students enrolled* • **Dental Assisting/Assistant** *8 students enrolled* • **Drafting and Design Technology/Technician, General** *1 student enrolled* • **Electrician** *4 students enrolled* • **Emergency Medical Technology/Technician (EMT Paramedic)** *12 students enrolled* • **Facial Treatment Specialist/Facialist** *5 students enrolled* • **Graphic Design** *4 students enrolled* • **Heating, Air Conditioning, Ventilation and Refrigeration Maintenance Technology/Technician (HAC, HACR, HVAC, HVACR)** *18 students enrolled* • **Legal Administrative Assistant/Secretary** *4 students enrolled* • **Licensed Practical/Vocational Nurse Training (LPN, LVN, Cert, Dipl, AAS)** *1509 hrs./$3018* • **Medical Administrative/Executive Assistant and Medical Secretary** • **Medical Radiologic Technology/Science—Radiation Therapist** *17 students enrolled* • **Medical/Clinical Assistant** *11 students enrolled* • **Nail Technician/Specialist and Manicurist** *10 students enrolled* • **Radiologic Technology/Science—Radiographer** *2775 hrs./$5550* • **Surgical Technology/Technologist** *1 student enrolled* • **Welding Technology/Welder** *2 students enrolled*

**STUDENT SERVICES** Academic or career counseling, daycare for children of students, employment services for current students, placement services for program completers, remedial services.

## Mid-America Technology Center

I35 & Highway 59, Wayne, OK 73095-0210
http://www.matech.org/

**CONTACT** Freddie C. Ricks, Superintendent
**Telephone:** 405-449-3391

**GENERAL INFORMATION** Public Institution. **Total program enrollment:** 55.

**PROGRAM(S) OFFERED**

• **Administrative Assistant and Secretarial Science, General** *1050 hrs./$1050* • **Allied Health and Medical Assisting Services, Other** *21 students enrolled* • **Applied Horticulture/Horticultural Operations, General** *1 student enrolled* • **Autobody/Collision and Repair Technology/Technician** *13 students enrolled* • **Automobile/Automotive Mechanics Technology/Technician** *13 students enrolled* • **Building/Property Maintenance and Management** *8 students enrolled* • **Carpentry/Carpenter** *5 students enrolled* • **Computer Installation and Repair Technology/Technician** *8 students enrolled* • **Cosmetology/Cosmetologist, General** *18 students enrolled* • **Criminal Justice/Police Science** *8 students enrolled* • **Diesel Mechanics Technology/Technician** *8 students enrolled* • **Drafting and Design Technology/Technician, General** *10 students enrolled* • **Electrician** *9 students enrolled* • **Engineering Technology, General** *1050 hrs./$1050* • **Engineering/Industrial Management** *1050 hrs./$1050* • **Equestrian/Equine Studies** *11 students enrolled* • **Health Services/Allied Health/Health Sciences, General** *1403 hrs./$1160* • **Heating, Air Conditioning, Ventilation and Refrigeration Maintenance Technology/Technician (HAC, HACR, HVAC, HVACR)** *7 students enrolled* • **Housing and Human Environments, Other** *6 students enrolled* • **Licensed Practical/Vocational Nurse Training (LPN, LVN, Cert, Dipl, AAS)** *27 students enrolled* • **Machine Tool Technology/Machinist** *8 students enrolled* • **Prepress/Desktop Publishing and Digital Imaging Design** *1050 hrs./$1050* • **Printing Press Operator** *8 students enrolled* • **Welding Technology/Welder** *1050 hrs./$1050*

**STUDENT SERVICES** Academic or career counseling, employment services for current students, placement services for program completers, remedial services.

## Mid-Del Technology Center

1621 Maple Drive, Midwest, OK 73110-4825
http://www.mid-del.tec.ok.us/

**CONTACT** John R. Matlock, Assistant Superintendent
**Telephone:** 405-739-1707 Ext. 365

**GENERAL INFORMATION** Public Institution. **Total program enrollment:** 69.

**PROGRAM(S) OFFERED**

• **Autobody/Collision and Repair Technology/Technician** *1 student enrolled* • **Automobile/Automotive Mechanics Technology/Technician** *2 students enrolled* • **Building/Property Maintenance and Management** • **Carpentry/Carpenter** • **Child Care Provider/Assistant** • **Computer Installation and Repair Technology/Technician** *4 students enrolled* • **Cosmetology/Cosmetologist, General** *1500 hrs./$2250* • **Drafting and Design Technology/Technician, General** *2 students enrolled* • **Electrician** *1 student enrolled* • **General Office Occupations and Clerical Services** *1050 hrs./$1575* • **Graphic and Printing Equipment Operator, General Production** *3 students enrolled* • **Health Professions and Related Clinical Sciences, Other** *1 student enrolled* • **Heating, Air Conditioning, Ventilation and Refrigeration Maintenance Technology/Technician (HAC, HACR, HVAC, HVACR)** *1050 hrs./$1575* • **Industrial Electronics Technology/Technician** • **Licensed Practical/Vocational Nurse Training (LPN, LVN, Cert, Dipl, AAS)** *1460 hrs./$3287* • **Mason/Masonry** *1 student enrolled* • **Plumbing Technology/Plumber** *1050 hrs./$1575* • **Welding Technology/Welder** *1050 hrs./$1575*

**STUDENT SERVICES** Academic or career counseling, employment services for current students, placement services for program completers, remedial services.

## Moore Norman Technology Center

4701 12th Avenue, NW, Norman, OK 73069
http://www.mntechnology.com/

**CONTACT** John Hunter, Superintendent
**Telephone:** 405-364-5763 Ext. 7260

**GENERAL INFORMATION** Private Institution. Founded 1972. **Total program enrollment:** 264. **Application fee:** $10.

**PROGRAM(S) OFFERED**
• **Accounting** *10 students enrolled* • **Adult Health Nurse/Nursing** *1438 hrs./$1725* • **Autobody/Collision and Repair Technology/Technician** *9 students enrolled* • **Automobile/Automotive Mechanics Technology/Technician** *1050 hrs./$1260* • **Business Administration and Management, General** *7 students enrolled* • **Carpentry/Carpenter** *8 students enrolled* • **Child Care Provider/Assistant** *9 students enrolled* • **Cinematography and Film/Video Production** *1050 hrs./$1260* • **Computer Programming, Specific Applications** *7 students enrolled* • **Computer Systems Networking and Telecommunications** *8 students enrolled* • **Construction Trades, Other** *8 students enrolled* • **Cosmetology/Cosmetologist, General** *1500 hrs./$1890* • **Data Processing and Data Processing Technology/Technician** • **Dental Assisting/Assistant** *9 students enrolled* • **Dental Laboratory Technology/Technician** *7 students enrolled* • **Diagnostic Medical Sonography/Sonographer and Ultrasound Technician** • **Drafting and Design Technology/Technician, General** *4 students enrolled* • **Electrician** *1050 hrs./$1260* • **Entrepreneurial and Small Business Operations, Other** *29 students enrolled* • **Graphic Design** *11 students enrolled* • **Hair Styling/Stylist and Hair Design** *32 students enrolled* • **Heating, Air Conditioning and Refrigeration Technology/Technician (ACH/ACR/ACHR/HRAC/HVAC/AC Technology)** *3 students enrolled* • **Licensed Practical/Vocational Nurse Training (LPN, LVN, Cert, Dipl, AAS)** *44 students enrolled* • **Machine Shop Technology/Assistant** *5 students enrolled* • **Massage Therapy/Therapeutic Massage** *4 students enrolled* • **Medical Office Management/Administration** *14 students enrolled* • **Pre-Medicine/Pre-Medical Studies** *21 students enrolled* • **Surgical Technology/Technologist** *16 students enrolled* • **System, Networking, and LAN/WAN Management/Manager** *1050 hrs./$2110* • **Web Page, Digital/Multimedia and Information Resources Design** *9 students enrolled* • **Welding Technology/Welder** *10 students enrolled*

**STUDENT SERVICES** Academic or career counseling, employment services for current students, placement services for program completers, remedial services.

## Murray State College

One Murray Campus, Tishomingo, OK 73460-3130
http://www.mscok.edu/

**CONTACT** Dr. Noble Jobe, President
**Telephone:** 580-371-2371

**GENERAL INFORMATION** Public Institution. Founded 1908. **Accreditation:** Regional (NCA); physical therapy assisting (APTA). **Total program enrollment:** 1206.

**PROGRAM(S) OFFERED**
• **Gunsmithing/Gunsmith** *6 students enrolled*

**STUDENT SERVICES** Academic or career counseling, daycare for children of students, employment services for current students, placement services for program completers, remedial services.

## Northeast Area Vocational Technical School

Highway 20, 6 Miles West of Pryor, Pryor, OK 74362
http://www.netechcenters.com/

**CONTACT** Dell Heavener, Superintendent
**Telephone:** 918-825-7040

**GENERAL INFORMATION** Private Institution. **Total program enrollment:** 79.

**PROGRAM(S) OFFERED**
• **Agribusiness/Agricultural Business Operations** *45 students enrolled*
• **Autobody/Collision and Repair Technology/Technician** *1 student enrolled*
• **Automobile/Automotive Mechanics Technology/Technician** *1 student enrolled*
• **Business Administration and Management, General** *6 students enrolled*
• **Business/Commerce, General** *1050 hrs./$800* • **Computer Science**
• **Construction Trades, General** *3 students enrolled* • **Cosmetology/Cosmetologist, General** *1050 hrs./$1200* • **Diesel Mechanics Technology/Technician** *1 student enrolled* • **Electrical and Electronic Engineering Technologies/Technicians, Other** *1050 hrs./$800* • **Food Preparation/Professional Cooking/Kitchen Assistant** *2 students enrolled* • **Health Professions and Related Clinical Sciences, Other** *4 students enrolled* • **Health Services/Allied Health/Health Sciences, General** *1050 hrs./$800* • **Licensed Practical/Vocational Nurse Training (LPN, LVN, Cert, Dipl, AAS)** *1401 hrs./$2963* • **Marketing, Other** • **Ornamental Horticulture** *1 student enrolled* • **Small Business Administration/Management** *36 students enrolled* • **Welding Technology/Welder** *1050 hrs./$800*

**STUDENT SERVICES** Academic or career counseling, employment services for current students, placement services for program completers, remedial services.

## Northeastern Oklahoma Agricultural and Mechanical College

200 I Street, NE, Miami, OK 74354-6434
http://www.neo.edu/

**CONTACT** Dr. Glenn E. Mayle, President
**Telephone:** 918-542-8441

**GENERAL INFORMATION** Public Institution. Founded 1919. **Accreditation:** Regional (NCA); medical laboratory technology (NAACLS); physical therapy assisting (APTA). **Total program enrollment:** 1348.

**PROGRAM(S) OFFERED**
• **Accounting Technology/Technician and Bookkeeping** *1 student enrolled*
• **Administrative Assistant and Secretarial Science, General** *1 student enrolled*
• **Child Care Provider/Assistant** *14 students enrolled* • **Computer Programming/Programmer, General** *1 student enrolled* • **Farm/Farm and Ranch Management** *2 students enrolled* • **General Office Occupations and Clerical Services** *1 student enrolled* • **Marketing/Marketing Management, General** *2 students enrolled* • **Medical Administrative/Executive Assistant and Medical Secretary** *1 student enrolled*

**STUDENT SERVICES** Academic or career counseling, placement services for program completers, remedial services.

## Northeast Technology Center–Afton

Highway 69, Afton, OK 74331
http://www.netechcenters.com/

**CONTACT** Dell Heavener, Superintendent
**Telephone:** 918-257-8324

**GENERAL INFORMATION** Public Institution. **Total program enrollment:** 105.

**PROGRAM(S) OFFERED**
• **Autobody/Collision and Repair Technology/Technician** *3 students enrolled*
• **Automobile/Automotive Mechanics Technology/Technician** *4 students enrolled*
• **Business Administration and Management, General** *1050 hrs./$800*
• **Carpentry/Carpenter** *1050 hrs./$800* • **Computer and Information Sciences, General** *1050 hrs./$800* • **Cosmetology/Cosmetologist, General** *2 students enrolled* • **Culinary Arts/Chef Training** *5 students enrolled* • **Diesel Mechanics Technology/Technician** *4 students enrolled* • **Electrician** *1050 hrs./$800* • **Health Services/Allied Health/Health Sciences, General** *13 students enrolled*
• **Licensed Practical/Vocational Nurse Training (LPN, LVN, Cert, Dipl, AAS)** *1401 hrs./$3091* • **Marine Maintenance/Fitter and Ship Repair Technology/Technician** *1050 hrs./$800* • **Mason/Masonry** *3 students enrolled* • **Small Business Administration/Management** *24 students enrolled* • **Welding Technology/Welder** *4 students enrolled*

**STUDENT SERVICES** Academic or career counseling, employment services for current students, placement services for program completers, remedial services.

## Northeast Technology Center–Kansas

Cherokee Turnpike & Highway 10, Kansas, OK 74347
http://www.netechcenters.com/

**CONTACT** Dell Heavener, Superintendent
**Telephone:** 918-868-3535

**GENERAL INFORMATION** Public Institution. **Total program enrollment:** 74.

**PROGRAM(S) OFFERED**
• **Automobile/Automotive Mechanics Technology/Technician** *1050 hrs./$800* • **Business/Office Automation/Technology/Data Entry** *1050 hrs./$800* • **Electrician** *1050 hrs./$800* • **Health Professions and Related Clinical Sciences, Other** *1050 hrs./$800* • **Licensed Practical/Vocational Nurse Training (LPN, LVN, Cert, Dipl, AAS)** *1401 hrs./$3091* • **Welding Technology/Welder** *1050 hrs./$800*

**STUDENT SERVICES** Academic or career counseling, employment services for current students, placement services for program completers, remedial services.

## Northern Oklahoma College

1220 East Grand Avenue, PO Box 310, Tonkawa, OK 74653-0310
http://www.north-ok.edu/

**CONTACT** Roger Stacy, President
**Telephone:** 580-628-6200

**GENERAL INFORMATION** Public Institution. Founded 1901. **Accreditation:** Regional (NCA). **Total program enrollment:** 2536. **Application fee:** $25.

**STUDENT SERVICES** Academic or career counseling, employment services for current students, placement services for program completers, remedial services.

## Northwest Technology Center

1801 South 11th Street, Alva, OK 73717
http://www.nwtechonline.com/

**CONTACT** Freelin Roberts, Superintendent
**Telephone:** 580-327-0344

**GENERAL INFORMATION** Public Institution. Founded 1972. **Total program enrollment:** 20.

**PROGRAM(S) OFFERED**
• **Administrative Assistant and Secretarial Science, General** *12 students enrolled* • **Autobody/Collision and Repair Technology/Technician** *1050 hrs./$1312* • **Automobile/Automotive Mechanics Technology/Technician** *1050 hrs./$1312* • **Business/Office Automation/Technology/Data Entry** *900 hrs./$1350* • **Computer Systems Networking and Telecommunications** *3 students enrolled* • **Culinary Arts and Related Services, Other** *900 hrs./$1125* • **Nurse/Nursing Assistant/Aide and Patient Care Assistant** *7 students enrolled* • **Personal and Culinary Services, Other** *4 students enrolled* • **Pre-Nursing Studies** *900 hrs./$1125* • **Web/Multimedia Management and Webmaster** *900 hrs./$1125*

**STUDENT SERVICES** Academic or career counseling, employment services for current students, placement services for program completers, remedial services.

## Northwest Technology Center

801 Vo-Tech Drive, Fairview, OK 73737
http://www.nwtechonline.com/

**CONTACT** Freelin Roberts, Superintendent
**Telephone:** 580-227-3708

**GENERAL INFORMATION** Public Institution. Founded 1969. **Total program enrollment:** 10.

**PROGRAM(S) OFFERED**
• **Administrative Assistant and Secretarial Science, General** *900 hrs./$1125* • **Automobile/Automotive Mechanics Technology/Technician** *1050 hrs./$1574* • **Culinary Arts and Related Services, Other** *900 hrs./$1125* • **Management Information Systems and Services, Other** *8 students enrolled* • **Nurse/Nursing Assistant/Aide and Patient Care Assistant** *3 students enrolled* • **Personal and Culinary Services, Other** *2 students enrolled* • **Pre-Nursing Studies** *900 hrs./$1125* • **Web/Multimedia Management and Webmaster** *1050 hrs./$1312* • **Welding Technology/Welder** *1050 hrs./$1312*

**STUDENT SERVICES** Academic or career counseling, employment services for current students, placement services for program completers, remedial services.

## Oklahoma City Community College

7777 South May Avenue, Oklahoma City, OK 73159-4419
http://www.occc.edu/

**CONTACT** Dr. Paul W. Sechrist, President
**Telephone:** 405-682-1611

**GENERAL INFORMATION** Public Institution. Founded 1969. **Accreditation:** Regional (NCA); emergency medical services (JRCEMTP); physical therapy assisting (APTA). **Total program enrollment:** 4631. **Application fee:** $25.

**PROGRAM(S) OFFERED**
• **Accounting Technology/Technician and Bookkeeping** *2 students enrolled* • **Architectural Drafting and Architectural CAD/CADD** *3 students enrolled* • **Banking and Financial Support Services** *3 students enrolled* • **Child Development** *26 students enrolled* • **Computer Installation and Repair Technology/Technician** *11 students enrolled* • **Computer Systems Networking and Telecommunications** *5 students enrolled* • **Computer and Information Systems Security** *4 students enrolled* • **Emergency Medical Technology/Technician (EMT Paramedic)** • **Foreign Languages and Literatures, General** *5 students enrolled* • **General Office Occupations and Clerical Services** *4 students enrolled* • **Health Information/Medical Records Administration/Administrator** *1 student enrolled* • **Legal Administrative Assistant/Secretary** *1 student enrolled* • **Web/Multimedia Management and Webmaster** *2 students enrolled*

**STUDENT SERVICES** Academic or career counseling, daycare for children of students, employment services for current students, placement services for program completers, remedial services.

## Oklahoma Health Academy

1939 N. Moore Avenue, Moore, OK 73160
http://www.oklahomahealthacademy.org/

**CONTACT** Michael Pugliese, President
**Telephone:** 405-912-2777

**GENERAL INFORMATION** Private Institution. **Total program enrollment:** 152. **Application fee:** $100.

**PROGRAM(S) OFFERED**
• **Dental Assisting/Assistant** *29 students enrolled* • **Massage Therapy/Therapeutic Massage** *11 students enrolled* • **Medical Office Assistant/Specialist** • **Medical/Clinical Assistant** *25 students enrolled* • **Surgical Technology/Technologist** *15 students enrolled*

**STUDENT SERVICES** Placement services for program completers, remedial services.

## Oklahoma Health Academy

2865 E. Skelly Drive, Suite 224, Tulsa, OK 74105
http://www.oklahomahealthacademy.org/

**CONTACT** Stephanie Thrasher, Director
**Telephone:** 918-748-9900

**GENERAL INFORMATION** Private Institution. **Total program enrollment:** 119. **Application fee:** $100.

**PROGRAM(S) OFFERED**
• **Dental Assisting/Assistant** *800 hrs./$9445* • **Massage Therapy/Therapeutic Massage** *900 hrs./$9445* • **Medical/Clinical Assistant** *800 hrs./$10,300*

**STUDENT SERVICES** Employment services for current students, placement services for program completers.

## Oklahoma School of Photography

2306 North Moore Avenue, Moore, OK 73160
http://www.photocareers.com/

**CONTACT** Jerry W. Cockrell, President
**Telephone:** 405-799-1411

**GENERAL INFORMATION** Private Institution. Founded 1972. **Total program enrollment:** 39.

**PROGRAM(S) OFFERED**
• **Design and Visual Communications, General** *1 student enrolled*
• **Photography** *32 students enrolled*

**STUDENT SERVICES** Academic or career counseling, placement services for program completers.

## Oklahoma State University

Stillwater, OK 74078
http://www.okstate.edu/

**CONTACT** President V. Burns Hargis, OSU System CEO and President
**Telephone:** 405-744-5000

**GENERAL INFORMATION** Public Institution. Founded 1890. **Accreditation:** Regional (NCA); athletic training (JRCAT); dietetics: postbaccalaureate internship (ADtA/CAADE); engineering technology (ABET/TAC); forestry (SAF); interior design: professional (CIDA); journalism and mass communications (ACEJMC); music (NASM); recreation and parks (NRPA); speech-language pathology (ASHA); theater (NAST). **Total program enrollment:** 17422. **Application fee:** $40.

**STUDENT SERVICES** Academic or career counseling, employment services for current students, placement services for program completers, remedial services.

## Oklahoma State University, Oklahoma City

900 North Portland, Oklahoma City, OK 73107-6120
http://www.osuokc.edu/

**CONTACT** Dr. Jerry D. Carroll, President
**Telephone:** 405-947-4421

**GENERAL INFORMATION** Public Institution. Founded 1961. **Accreditation:** Regional (NCA). **Total program enrollment:** 1911.

**PROGRAM(S) OFFERED**
• **Applied Horticulture/Horticultural Operations, General** *14 students enrolled*
• **Child Care and Support Services Management** *31 students enrolled* • **Fire Science/Firefighting** *7 students enrolled* • **Special Products Marketing Operations** *3 students enrolled*

**STUDENT SERVICES** Academic or career counseling, daycare for children of students, employment services for current students, placement services for program completers, remedial services.

## Oklahoma Technology Institute

9801 N. Broadway Extension, Oklahoma City, OK 73114

**CONTACT** Jeanne Fanning, Owner
**Telephone:** 405-842-9400 Ext. 27

**GENERAL INFORMATION** Private Institution. **Total program enrollment:** 38. **Application fee:** $100.

**PROGRAM(S) OFFERED**
• **Accounting Technology/Technician and Bookkeeping** *18 hrs./$4970*
• **Computer Hardware Engineering** *2 students enrolled* • **Computer Hardware Technology/Technician** • **Data Modeling/Warehousing and Database Administration** *29 hrs./$7785* • **Information Science/Studies** *43 hrs./$12,495* • **Massage Therapy/Therapeutic Massage** *25 hrs./$6765* • **Medical Insurance Coding Specialist/Coder** *25 hrs./$6715* • **Web/Multimedia Management and Webmaster** *32 hrs./$8550*

**STUDENT SERVICES** Academic or career counseling, employment services for current students, placement services for program completers, remedial services.

## Okmulgee School of Cosmetology

223 West 6th Street, Okmulgee, OK 74447

**CONTACT** Tanya Flock, CEO
**Telephone:** 918-756-5566

**GENERAL INFORMATION** Private Institution. **Total program enrollment:** 27. **Application fee:** $100.

**PROGRAM(S) OFFERED**
• **Aesthetician/Esthetician and Skin Care Specialist** *600 hrs./$4200*
• **Cosmetology, Barber/Styling, and Nail Instructor** *1000 hrs./$6700*
• **Cosmetology/Cosmetologist, General** *1500 hrs./$9400* • **Nail Technician/Specialist and Manicurist** *600 hrs./$4200*

**STUDENT SERVICES** Academic or career counseling, placement services for program completers.

## Pioneer Area Vocational Technical School

2101 North Ash, Ponca City, OK 74601
http://pioneertech.org/

**CONTACT** Dr. Steve Tiger, Superintendent/CEO
**Telephone:** 580-762-8336

**GENERAL INFORMATION** Private Institution. **Total program enrollment:** 71.

**PROGRAM(S) OFFERED**
• **Autobody/Collision and Repair Technology/Technician** *11 students enrolled*
• **Automobile/Automotive Mechanics Technology/Technician** *945 hrs./$1206*
• **Business Operations Support and Secretarial Services, Other** *1050 hrs./$2188* • **Carpentry/Carpenter** *7 students enrolled* • **Child Care Provider/Assistant** *1110 hrs./$1413* • **Computer Systems Networking and Telecommunications** *13 students enrolled* • **Cosmetology/Cosmetologist, General** *1500 hrs./$2625* • **Culinary Arts/Chef Training** *8 students enrolled* • **General Office Occupations and Clerical Services** *11 students enrolled* • **Health and Medical Administrative Services, Other** *1050 hrs./$1338* • **Industrial Mechanics and Maintenance Technology** *6 students enrolled* • **Licensed Practical/Vocational Nurse Training (LPN, LVN, Cert, Dipl, AAS)** *1500 hrs./$1900* • **Machine Shop Technology/Assistant** *9 students enrolled* • **Medical/Clinical Assistant** *12 students enrolled* • **Welding Technology/Welder** *17 students enrolled*

**STUDENT SERVICES** Academic or career counseling, daycare for children of students, remedial services.

## Platt College

112 Southwest 11th Street, Lawton, OK 73501
http://www.plattcollege.org/

**CONTACT** Michael Pugliese, President
**Telephone:** 580-355-4416

**GENERAL INFORMATION** Private Institution. **Total program enrollment:** 153. **Application fee:** $100.

**PROGRAM(S) OFFERED**
• **Dental Assisting/Assistant** *800 hrs./$10,300* • **Licensed Practical/Vocational Nurse Training (LPN, LVN, Cert, Dipl, AAS)** *1440 hrs./$19,945* • **Massage Therapy/Therapeutic Massage** *1000 hrs./$10,300* • **Medical/Clinical Assistant** *800 hrs./$10,300* • **Pharmacy Technician/Assistant** *800 hrs./$10,300*

**STUDENT SERVICES** Academic or career counseling, placement services for program completers, remedial services.

## Platt College

201 North Eastern Avenue, Moore, OK 73160
http://www.plattcollege.org/campuses/moore.htm

**CONTACT** Michael A. Pugliese, President
**Telephone:** 405-912-3260

**GENERAL INFORMATION** Private Institution. **Total program enrollment:** 156. **Application fee:** $100.

**PROGRAM(S) OFFERED**
• **Baking and Pastry Arts/Baker/Pastry Chef** *1050 hrs./$14,500* • **Licensed Practical/Vocational Nurse Training (LPN, LVN, Cert, Dipl, AAS)** *1570 hrs./ $23,600*

**STUDENT SERVICES** Academic or career counseling, employment services for current students, placement services for program completers.

## Platt College

2727 West Memorial Road, Oklahoma City, OK 73134-8034
http://www.plattcollege.org/

**CONTACT** Bob Kane, Director
**Telephone:** 405-749-2433

**GENERAL INFORMATION** Private Institution. Founded 2003. **Total program enrollment:** 380. **Application fee:** $100.

**PROGRAM(S) OFFERED**
• **Allied Health and Medical Assisting Services, Other** *800 hrs./$10,300* • **Culinary Arts/Chef Training** *900 hrs./$15,350* • **Medical/Clinical Assistant** *39 students enrolled* • **Nursing—Registered Nurse Training (RN, ASN, BSN, MSN)** *1140 hrs./$22,500* • **Restaurant/Food Services Management** *2370 hrs./ $33,000*

**STUDENT SERVICES** Academic or career counseling, employment services for current students, placement services for program completers, remedial services.

## Platt College

309 South Ann Arbor Avenue, Oklahoma City, OK 73128
http://www.plattcollege.org/

**CONTACT** Jane Nowlin, Director
**Telephone:** 405-946-7799

**GENERAL INFORMATION** Private Institution. Founded 1979. **Accreditation:** State accredited or approved. **Total program enrollment:** 257. **Application fee:** $100.

**PROGRAM(S) OFFERED**
• **Dental Assisting/Assistant** *800 hrs./$10,300* • **Licensed Practical/Vocational Nurse Training (LPN, LVN, Cert, Dipl, AAS)** *1570 hrs./$23,600* • **Medical Office Assistant/Specialist** *800 hrs./$10,300* • **Medical Transcription/ Transcriptionist** • **Medical/Clinical Assistant** *10 students enrolled* • **Pharmacy Technician/Assistant** *800 hrs./$10,300* • **Surgical Technology/Technologist** *1110 hrs./$19,400*

**STUDENT SERVICES** Academic or career counseling, employment services for current students, placement services for program completers, remedial services.

## Platt College

3801 South Sheridan Road, Tulsa, OK 74145-111
http://www.plattcollege.org/

**CONTACT** Mike Pugliese, President
**Telephone:** 918-663-9000

**GENERAL INFORMATION** Private Institution. Founded 1979. **Accreditation:** State accredited or approved. **Total program enrollment:** 369. **Application fee:** $100.

**PROGRAM(S) OFFERED**
• **Dental Assisting/Assistant** *800 hrs./$10,300* • **Licensed Practical/Vocational Nurse Training (LPN, LVN, Cert, Dipl, AAS)** *1570 hrs./$23,600* • **Medical/ Clinical Assistant** *800 hrs./$10,300* • **Nursing—Registered Nurse Training (RN, ASN, BSN, MSN)** *1540 hrs./$23,545* • **Pharmacy Technician/Assistant** *800 hrs./$10,300* • **Surgical Technology/Technologist** *1110 hrs./$19,400*

**STUDENT SERVICES** Academic or career counseling, employment services for current students, placement services for program completers, remedial services.

## Ponca City Beauty College

122 N. First Street, Ponca City, OK 74601

**CONTACT** Freda Poe, President
**Telephone:** 580-762-1470

**GENERAL INFORMATION** Private Institution. **Total program enrollment:** 44. **Application fee:** $100.

**PROGRAM(S) OFFERED**
• **Cosmetology, Barber/Styling, and Nail Instructor** *1000 hrs./$4950* • **Cosmetology/Cosmetologist, General** *1500 hrs./$7700* • **Nail Technician/ Specialist and Manicurist** *600 hrs./$4700*

**STUDENT SERVICES** Academic or career counseling, employment services for current students, placement services for program completers, remedial services.

## Pontotoc Technology Center

601 West 33rd, Ada, OK 74820
http://www.pontotoc.com/

**CONTACT** Greg Pierce, Superintendent
**Telephone:** 580-310-2200

**GENERAL INFORMATION** Public Institution. Founded 1987. **Total program enrollment:** 148. **Application fee:** $20.

**PROGRAM(S) OFFERED**
• **Automobile/Automotive Mechanics Technology/Technician** *25 students enrolled* • **Business/Commerce, General** *26 students enrolled* • **Computer and Information Systems Security** *33 students enrolled* • **Cosmetology/ Cosmetologist, General** *1500 hrs./$3750* • **Emergency Medical Technology/ Technician (EMT Paramedic)** *1412 hrs./$4130* • **Graphic Design** *1020 hrs./ $2550* • **Licensed Practical/Vocational Nurse Training (LPN, LVN, Cert, Dipl, AAS)** *1422 hrs./$6057* • **Nursing, Other** *19 students enrolled* • **Prepress/Desktop Publishing and Digital Imaging Design** *1050 hrs./$3350* • **Web Page, Digital/ Multimedia and Information Resources Design** *1020 hrs./$2550*

**STUDENT SERVICES** Academic or career counseling, employment services for current students, placement services for program completers, remedial services.

## Poteau Beauty College

2601 North Broadway, Poteau, OK 74953

**CONTACT** Shirley Smith, Owner
**Telephone:** 918-647-4119

**GENERAL INFORMATION** Private Institution. **Total program enrollment:** 46. **Application fee:** $100.

**PROGRAM(S) OFFERED**
• **Aesthetician/Esthetician and Skin Care Specialist** *600 hrs./$7866* • **Cosmetology and Related Personal Grooming Arts, Other** *2 students enrolled* • **Cosmetology, Barber/Styling, and Nail Instructor** *600 hrs./$6716* • **Cosmetology/Cosmetologist, General** *1500 hrs./$13,024* • **Nail Technician/ Specialist and Manicurist** *600 hrs./$6716*

**STUDENT SERVICES** Placement services for program completers.

## Pryor Beauty College

330 West Graham, Pryor, OK 74361

**CONTACT** Debbie Ailey, CEO
**Telephone:** 918-825-2795

**GENERAL INFORMATION** Private Institution. **Total program enrollment:** 72. **Application fee:** $100.

**PROGRAM(S) OFFERED**
• **Cosmetology, Barber/Styling, and Nail Instructor** *1000 hrs./$4950* • **Cosmetology/Cosmetologist, General** *1500 hrs./$7700* • **Nail Technician/Specialist and Manicurist** *600 hrs./$4700*

**STUDENT SERVICES** Academic or career counseling, employment services for current students, placement services for program completers, remedial services.

## Redlands Community College

1300 South Country Club Road, El Reno, OK 73036-5304
http://www.redlandscc.edu/

**CONTACT** Larry F. Devane, President
**Telephone:** 405-262-2552

**GENERAL INFORMATION** Public Institution. Founded 1938. **Accreditation:** Regional (NCA). **Total program enrollment:** 871. **Application fee:** $25.

**PROGRAM(S) OFFERED**
• **Child Development** *34 students enrolled*

**STUDENT SERVICES** Academic or career counseling, employment services for current students, placement services for program completers, remedial services.

## Red River Area Vocational-Technical School

3300 West Bois Darc, Duncan, OK 73533
http://www.redriver.tec.ok.us/

**CONTACT** Ken Layn, Superintendent
**Telephone:** 580-255-2903

**GENERAL INFORMATION** Public Institution. Founded 1977. **Total program enrollment:** 74.

**PROGRAM(S) OFFERED**
• **Autobody/Collision and Repair Technology/Technician** *975 hrs./$682* • **Automobile/Automotive Mechanics Technology/Technician** *915 hrs./$682* • **Carpentry/Carpenter** *3 students enrolled* • **Cosmetology/Cosmetologist, General** *16 students enrolled* • **Diesel Mechanics Technology/Technician** *5 students enrolled* • **Drafting and Design Technology/Technician, General** *8 students enrolled* • **Electrical/Electronics Equipment Installation and Repair, General** *3 students enrolled* • **Health Professions and Related Clinical Sciences, Other** *21 students enrolled* • **Heating, Air Conditioning, Ventilation and Refrigeration Maintenance Technology/Technician (HAC, HACR, HVAC, HVACR)** *1050 hrs./$682* • **Licensed Practical/Vocational Nurse Training (LPN, LVN, Cert, Dipl, AAS)** *1472 hrs./$2490* • **Machine Shop Technology/Assistant** *900 hrs./$682* • **Machine Tool Technology/Machinist** *6 students enrolled* • **Management Information Systems and Services, Other** *26 students enrolled* • **Welding Technology/Welder** *1050 hrs./$682*

**STUDENT SERVICES** Academic or career counseling, employment services for current students, placement services for program completers, remedial services.

## Rose State College

6420 Southeast 15th Street, Midwest City, OK 73110-2799
http://www.rose.edu/

**CONTACT** Terry D. Britton, President
**Telephone:** 405-733-7311

**GENERAL INFORMATION** Public Institution. Founded 1968. **Accreditation:** Regional (NCA); dental assisting (ADA); dental hygiene (ADA); health information technology (AHIMA); medical laboratory technology (NAACLS); radiologic technology: radiography (JRCERT). **Total program enrollment:** 2764.

**PROGRAM(S) OFFERED**
• **Broadcast Journalism** *1 student enrolled* • **Dental Assisting/Assistant** *1 student enrolled* • **Health Information/Medical Records Technology/Technician** *1 student enrolled* • **Operations Management and Supervision** *1 student enrolled*

**STUDENT SERVICES** Academic or career counseling, employment services for current students, placement services for program completers, remedial services.

## Seminole State College

PO Box 351, Seminole, OK 74818-0351
http://www.ssc.cc.ok.us/

**CONTACT** Dr. Jim Utterback, President
**Telephone:** 405-382-9950

**GENERAL INFORMATION** Public Institution. Founded 1931. **Accreditation:** Regional (NCA); medical laboratory technology (NAACLS). **Total program enrollment:** 1132. **Application fee:** $15.

**PROGRAM(S) OFFERED**
• **American Indian/Native American Studies** • **Child Development** *13 students enrolled*

**STUDENT SERVICES** Academic or career counseling, remedial services.

## Shawnee Beauty College

410 E. Main Street, Shawnee, OK 74801

**CONTACT** Freda Poe, Owner
**Telephone:** 405-275-3182

**GENERAL INFORMATION** Private Institution. **Total program enrollment:** 47. **Application fee:** $100.

**PROGRAM(S) OFFERED**
• **Cosmetology, Barber/Styling, and Nail Instructor** *1000 hrs./$4950* • **Cosmetology/Cosmetologist, General** *1500 hrs./$7700* • **Nail Technician/Specialist and Manicurist** *600 hrs./$4700*

**STUDENT SERVICES** Academic or career counseling, employment services for current students, placement services for program completers, remedial services.

## Southern Oklahoma Technology Center

2610 Sam Noble Parkway, Ardmore, OK 73401
http://www.sotc.org/

**CONTACT** Dr. David Powell, Superintendent
**Telephone:** 580-223-2070

**GENERAL INFORMATION** Private Institution. **Total program enrollment:** 85. **Application fee:** $20.

**PROGRAM(S) OFFERED**
• **Autobody/Collision and Repair Technology/Technician** *975 hrs./$2400* • **Automobile/Automotive Mechanics Technology/Technician** *915 hrs./$2400* • **Carpentry/Carpenter** *8 students enrolled* • **Computer Systems Networking and Telecommunications** *10 students enrolled* • **Computer and Information Sciences, General** *1080 hrs./$2400* • **Cosmetology/Cosmetologist, General** *1500 hrs./$2400* • **Diesel Mechanics Technology/Technician** *9 students enrolled* • **Drafting and Design Technology/Technician, General** *3 students enrolled* • **Health Services/Allied Health/Health Sciences, General** *525 hrs./$1200* • **Heating, Air Conditioning and Refrigeration Technology/Technician (ACH/ACR/ACHR/HRAC/HVAC/AC Technology)** *6 students enrolled* • **Home Health Aide/Home Attendant** *49 students enrolled* • **Licensed Practical/Vocational**

*Southern Oklahoma Technology Center (continued)*

**Nurse Training (LPN, LVN, Cert, Dipl, AAS)** *1496 hrs./$4457* • **Management Information Systems and Services, Other** *29 students enrolled* • **Medical/ Clinical Assistant** *31 students enrolled* • **Welding Technology/Welder** *12 students enrolled*

**STUDENT SERVICES** Academic or career counseling, placement services for program completers, remedial services.

## Southern School of Beauty

140 West Main Street, Durant, OK 74701

**CONTACT** Dale White, Owner
**Telephone:** 580-924-1049

**GENERAL INFORMATION** Private Institution. **Total program enrollment:** 19.

**PROGRAM(S) OFFERED**
• **Cosmetology, Barber/Styling, and Nail Instructor** *1000 hrs./$4300* • **Cosmetology/Cosmetologist, General** *1500 hrs./$8100* • **Nail Technician/ Specialist and Manicurist** *600 hrs./$4000*

**STUDENT SERVICES** Placement services for program completers.

## Southwest Area Vocational Technical Center

711 West Tamarack, Altus, OK 73521
http://www.swtc.org/

**CONTACT** Dr. C. June Knight, Superintendent
**Telephone:** 580-477-2250

**GENERAL INFORMATION** Private Institution. **Total program enrollment:** 63.

**PROGRAM(S) OFFERED**
• **Administrative Assistant and Secretarial Science, General** *1050 hrs./$2235* • **Airframe Mechanics and Aircraft Maintenance Technology/Technician** *10 students enrolled* • **Automobile/Automotive Mechanics Technology/Technician** *11 students enrolled* • **Avionics Maintenance Technology/Technician** *1200 hrs./ $2550* • **Building/Property Maintenance and Management** *5 students enrolled* • **Computer and Information Sciences and Support Services, Other** *8 students enrolled* • **Computer and Information Sciences, General** *5 students enrolled* • **Construction Trades, Other** *7 students enrolled* • **Electrical/Electronics Equipment Installation and Repair, General** *1050 hrs./$2235* • **Electrical/Electronics Maintenance and Repair Technology, Other** *1080 hrs./$3270* • **Health Professions and Related Clinical Sciences, Other** *4 students enrolled* • **Licensed Practical/Vocational Nurse Training (LPN, LVN, Cert, Dipl, AAS)** *1474 hrs./ $4242* • **Management Information Systems and Services, Other** *1050 hrs./ $2235*

**STUDENT SERVICES** Academic or career counseling, placement services for program completers, remedial services.

## Standard Beauty College of Oklahoma

28 East Second Street, Sand Springs, OK 74063
http://sandspringsbeautycollege.com/

**CONTACT** Myra L. Sellers, President
**Telephone:** 918-245-6627

**GENERAL INFORMATION** Private Institution. Founded 1977. **Total program enrollment:** 119. **Application fee:** $100.

**PROGRAM(S) OFFERED**
• **Aesthetician/Esthetician and Skin Care Specialist** *600 hrs./$3300* • **Cosmetology, Barber/Styling, and Nail Instructor** *1000 hrs./$4000* • **Cosmetology/Cosmetologist, General** *1500 hrs./$8850* • **Nail Technician/ Specialist and Manicurist** *600 hrs./$3300*

**STUDENT SERVICES** Academic or career counseling, placement services for program completers.

## State Barber and Hair Design College, Inc.

2514 South Agnew Avenue, Oklahoma City, OK 73108-6220
http://www.statebarber.com/

**CONTACT** Bobby Lewis, Owner
**Telephone:** 405-631-8621

**GENERAL INFORMATION** Private Institution. Founded 1975. **Total program enrollment:** 58. **Application fee:** $100.

**PROGRAM(S) OFFERED**
• **Barbering/Barber** *1500 hrs./$6250* • **Cosmetology, Barber/Styling, and Nail Instructor** *1000 hrs./$4000*

## Stillwater Beauty Academy

1684 Cimmaron Plaza, Stillwater, OK 74075

**CONTACT** Mary Whitby, Director
**Telephone:** 405-377-4100

**GENERAL INFORMATION** Private Institution. **Total program enrollment:** 29. **Application fee:** $100.

**PROGRAM(S) OFFERED**
• **Aesthetician/Esthetician and Skin Care Specialist** *600 hrs./$3685* • **Cosmetology, Barber/Styling, and Nail Instructor** *1000 hrs./$5200* • **Cosmetology/Cosmetologist, General** *12 hrs./$10,675* • **Nail Technician/ Specialist and Manicurist** *600 hrs./$3685* • **Technology Teacher Education/ Industrial Arts Teacher Education**

**STUDENT SERVICES** Academic or career counseling, placement services for program completers.

## Technical Institute of Cosmetology Arts and Sciences

2909A South Sheridan Road, Tulsa, OK 74129

**CONTACT** Brenda Cleveland, Administrator
**Telephone:** 918-660-8828 Ext. 10

**GENERAL INFORMATION** Private Institution. **Total program enrollment:** 22. **Application fee:** $100.

**PROGRAM(S) OFFERED**
• **Cosmetology, Barber/Styling, and Nail Instructor** *1000 hrs./$9873* • **Cosmetology/Cosmetologist, General** *1500 hrs./$14,810* • **Nail Technician/ Specialist and Manicurist** *600 hrs./$5700*

## Tri County Technology Center

6101 Nowata Road, Bartlesville, OK 74006-6029
http://www.tctc.org/

**CONTACT** Anita Risner, Superintendent
**Telephone:** 918-333-2422

**GENERAL INFORMATION** Public Institution. **Total program enrollment:** 132.

**PROGRAM(S) OFFERED**
• **Accounting Technology/Technician and Bookkeeping** *1050 hrs./$1575* • **Administrative Assistant and Secretarial Science, General** *12 students enrolled* • **Autobody/Collision and Repair Technology/Technician** *1050 hrs./ $1575* • **Automobile/Automotive Mechanics Technology/Technician** *15 students enrolled* • **Child Care Provider/Assistant** *8 students enrolled* • **Computer Systems Networking and Telecommunications** *11 students enrolled* • **Cosmetology/Cosmetologist, General** *1500 hrs./$2250* • **Culinary Arts/Chef Training** • **Dental Assisting/Assistant** *12 students enrolled* • **Drafting/Design Engineering Technologies/Technicians, Other** *8 students enrolled* • **General Merchandising, Sales, and Related Marketing Operations, Other** *15 students enrolled* • **Health Services/Allied Health/Health Sciences, General** *14 students enrolled* • **Licensed Practical/Vocational Nurse Training (LPN, LVN, Cert, Dipl,**

AAS) *1520 hrs./$3873* • **Machine Tool Technology/Machinist** *1050 hrs./$1575* • **Mechanical Drafting and Mechanical Drafting CAD/CADD** *1050 hrs./$1575* • **Printing Press Operator** *11 students enrolled* • **Welding Technology/Welder** *13 students enrolled*

**STUDENT SERVICES** Academic or career counseling, daycare for children of students, employment services for current students, placement services for program completers, remedial services.

## Tulsa Community College

6111 East Skelly Drive, Tulsa, OK 74135-6198
http://www.tulsacc.edu/

**CONTACT** Tom McKeon, President
**Telephone:** 918-595-7000

**GENERAL INFORMATION** Public Institution. Founded 1968. **Accreditation:** Regional (NCA); dental hygiene (ADA); health information technology (AHIMA); medical assisting (AAMAE); medical laboratory technology (NAACLS); physical therapy assisting (APTA); radiologic technology: radiography (JRCERT). **Total program enrollment:** 6897. **Application fee:** $20.

**PROGRAM(S) OFFERED**
• **Accounting Technology/Technician and Bookkeeping** *8 students enrolled* • **Applied Horticulture/Horticultural Operations, General** *1 student enrolled* • **Business Administration and Management, General** *1 student enrolled* • **Business Administration, Management and Operations, Other** *4 students enrolled* • **Business/Commerce, General** *1 student enrolled* • **CAD/CADD Drafting and/or Design Technology/Technician** *3 students enrolled* • **Child Development** *83 students enrolled* • **Clinical/Medical Laboratory Science and Allied Professions, Other** *7 students enrolled* • **Clinical/Medical Laboratory Technician** *24 students enrolled* • **Computer Programming, Specific Applications** *5 students enrolled* • **Electrical/Electronics Maintenance and Repair Technology, Other** *3 students enrolled* • **Fire Services Administration** *3 students enrolled* • **Health Aide** *77 students enrolled* • **Hospitality Administration/Management, Other** *1 student enrolled* • **Human Resources Management/Personnel Administration, General** *1 student enrolled* • **International Business/Trade/Commerce** *18 students enrolled* • **Management Information Systems and Services, Other** *20 students enrolled* • **Marketing/Marketing Management, General** *3 students enrolled* • **Medical/Clinical Assistant** *13 students enrolled* • **Office Management and Supervision** *1 student enrolled* • **Pharmacy Technician/Assistant** *10 students enrolled* • **Printmaking** *4 students enrolled* • **Quality Control Technology/Technician** *3 students enrolled* • **Social Work** *2 students enrolled*

**STUDENT SERVICES** Academic or career counseling, daycare for children of students, employment services for current students, placement services for program completers, remedial services.

## Tulsa Tech–Broken Arrow Campus

4600 South Olive Avenue, Broken Arrow, OK 74011-1706
http://www.tulsatech.com/

**CONTACT** Brad Wayman, Campus Director
**Telephone:** 918-828-3000

**GENERAL INFORMATION** Public Institution. Founded 1983. **Total program enrollment:** 31. **Application fee:** $15.

**PROGRAM(S) OFFERED**
• **Animation, Interactive Technology, Video Graphics and Special Effects** *600 hrs./$1500* • **Automobile/Automotive Mechanics Technology/Technician** *1050 hrs./$1050* • **Computer Programming, Specific Applications** *13 students enrolled* • **Industrial Mechanics and Maintenance Technology** *1050 hrs./$3500* • **Machine Shop Technology/Assistant** *1050 hrs./$2625* • **Small Engine Mechanics and Repair Technology/Technician** *7 students enrolled* • **Web Page, Digital/Multimedia and Information Resources Design** *600 hrs./$1900* • **Web/Multimedia Management and Webmaster** *600 hrs./$1500*

**STUDENT SERVICES** Academic or career counseling, placement services for program completers, remedial services.

## Tulsa Tech–Career Services Center

3420 South Memorial Drive, Tulsa, OK 74145
http://www.tulsatech.com/

**CONTACT** Sharon Schaub, Campus Director
**Telephone:** 918-828-1000

**GENERAL INFORMATION** Public Institution. Founded 1969. **Total program enrollment:** 142. **Application fee:** $15.

**PROGRAM(S) OFFERED**
• **Apparel and Textile Marketing Management** *26 students enrolled* • **Autobody/Collision and Repair Technology/Technician** *34 students enrolled* • **Automobile/Automotive Mechanics Technology/Technician** *1050 hrs./$2625* • **Carpentry/Carpenter** *1050 hrs./$2625* • **Commercial and Advertising Art** *11 students enrolled* • **Dental Assisting/Assistant** *50 students enrolled* • **Diesel Mechanics Technology/Technician** *12 students enrolled* • **Electrical/Electronics Equipment Installation and Repair, General** *1050 hrs./$2625* • **Entrepreneurship/Entrepreneurial Studies** *525 hrs./$1313* • **General Merchandising, Sales, and Related Marketing Operations, Other** *26 students enrolled* • **Graphic and Printing Equipment Operator, General Production** *11 students enrolled* • **Heating, Air Conditioning, Ventilation and Refrigeration Maintenance Technology/Technician (HAC, HACR, HVAC, HVACR)** *9 students enrolled* • **Interior Design** *22 students enrolled* • **Licensed Practical/Vocational Nurse Training (LPN, LVN, Cert, Dipl, AAS)** *1460 hrs./$5200* • **Mason/Masonry** *6 students enrolled* • **Medical/Clinical Assistant** *57 students enrolled* • **Ophthalmic Technician/Technologist** • **Photography** *15 students enrolled* • **Restaurant, Culinary, and Catering Management/Manager** *10 students enrolled* • **Surgical Technology/Technologist** *1200 hrs./$3000* • **Welding Technology/Welder** *15 students enrolled*

**STUDENT SERVICES** Academic or career counseling, placement services for program completers, remedial services.

## Tulsa Tech–Peoria Campus

3850 North Peoria, Tulsa, OK 74106
http://www.tulsatech.com/

**CONTACT** John Robinson, Campus Director
**Telephone:** 918-828-2000

**GENERAL INFORMATION** Private Institution. **Total program enrollment:** 135. **Application fee:** $15.

**PROGRAM(S) OFFERED**
• **Accounting Technology/Technician and Bookkeeping** *1050 hrs./$2625* • **Business/Office Automation/Technology/Data Entry** *12 students enrolled* • **Child Care Provider/Assistant** *15 students enrolled* • **Computer Systems Networking and Telecommunications** *600 hrs./$1500* • **Early Childhood Education and Teaching** *1050 hrs./$2625* • **Emergency Care Attendant (EMT Ambulance)** *86 students enrolled* • **Emergency Medical Technology/Technician (EMT Paramedic)** *1152 hrs./$4161* • **Health Information/Medical Records Technology/Technician** *600 hrs./$1500* • **Hospitality Administration/Management, General** *19 students enrolled* • **Legal Administrative Assistant/Secretary** *17 students enrolled* • **Medical Insurance Coding Specialist/Coder** *18 students enrolled* • **Medical Transcription/Transcriptionist** *13 students enrolled* • **Metal and Jewelry Arts** *3 students enrolled* • **System, Networking, and LAN/WAN Management/Manager** *5 students enrolled* • **Tourism and Travel Services Management** *14 students enrolled* • **Welding Technology/Welder** *1050 hrs./$2625*

**STUDENT SERVICES** Academic or career counseling, placement services for program completers, remedial services.

## Tulsa Welding School

2545 East 11th Street, Tulsa, OK 74104-3909
http://www.weldingschool.com/

**CONTACT** Debbie Burke, Vice President, School Director
**Telephone:** 918-587-6789

**GENERAL INFORMATION** Private Institution. Founded 1949. **Accreditation:** State accredited or approved. **Total program enrollment:** 796.

*Tulsa Welding School (continued)*

**PROGRAM(S) OFFERED**

• **Welding Technology/Welder** *405 hrs./$7815*

**STUDENT SERVICES** Academic or career counseling, employment services for current students, placement services for program completers.

## Vatterott College

4629 Northwest 23rd Street, Oklahoma City, OK 73127
http://www.vatterott-college.edu/

**CONTACT** sean kuhn, Director
**Telephone:** 405-945-0088

**GENERAL INFORMATION** Private Institution. **Accreditation:** State accredited or approved. **Total program enrollment:** 244.

**PROGRAM(S) OFFERED**

• **Accounting Technology/Technician and Bookkeeping** *7 students enrolled* • **Administrative Assistant and Secretarial Science, General** *17 students enrolled* • **Electrician** *6 students enrolled* • **Heating, Air Conditioning, Ventilation and Refrigeration Maintenance Technology/Technician (HAC, HACR, HVAC, HVACR)** *26 students enrolled* • **Information Technology** *11 students enrolled* • **Medical Office Assistant/Specialist** *71 students enrolled*

**STUDENT SERVICES** Academic or career counseling, employment services for current students, placement services for program completers.

## Vatterott College

555 South Memorial Drive, Tulsa, OK 74112
http://www.vatterott-college.edu/

**CONTACT** Traci Horton, Director
**Telephone:** 918-835-8288

**GENERAL INFORMATION** Private Institution. **Accreditation:** State accredited or approved. **Total program enrollment:** 116.

**PROGRAM(S) OFFERED**

• **Electrician** *12 students enrolled* • **Heating, Air Conditioning, Ventilation and Refrigeration Maintenance Technology/Technician (HAC, HACR, HVAC, HVACR)** *22 students enrolled* • **Information Technology** *11 students enrolled* • **Medical Office Assistant/Specialist** *15 students enrolled* • **Web Page, Digital/Multimedia and Information Resources Design** *12 students enrolled*

**STUDENT SERVICES** Academic or career counseling, employment services for current students, placement services for program completers.

## Virgil's Beauty College

111 South Ninth Street, Muskogee, OK 74401-6802
http://virgilsbeautycollege.com/

**CONTACT** Virgil Large, President Owner
**Telephone:** 918-682-9429

**GENERAL INFORMATION** Private Institution. Founded 1968. **Total program enrollment:** 38.

**PROGRAM(S) OFFERED**

• **Cosmetology, Barber/Styling, and Nail Instructor** *900 hrs./$6100* • **Cosmetology/Cosmetologist, General** *1500 hrs./$9600* • **Nail Technician/Specialist and Manicurist** *600 hrs./$3700*

**STUDENT SERVICES** Academic or career counseling, employment services for current students, placement services for program completers.

## Western Oklahoma State College

2801 North Main Street, Altus, OK 73521-1397
http://www.wosc.edu/

**CONTACT** Randy Cumby, President
**Telephone:** 580-477-2000

**GENERAL INFORMATION** Public Institution. Founded 1926. **Accreditation:** Regional (NCA); radiologic technology: radiography (JRCERT). **Total program enrollment:** 748. **Application fee:** $15.

**PROGRAM(S) OFFERED**

• **Child Development** *25 students enrolled*

**STUDENT SERVICES** Academic or career counseling, employment services for current students, remedial services.

## Western Technology Center

621 Sooner Drive, PO Box 1469, Burns Flat, OK 73624
http://www.wtc.tec.ok.us/

**CONTACT** Gene Orsack, Superintendent
**Telephone:** 580-562-3181

**GENERAL INFORMATION** Public Institution. Founded 1970. **Total program enrollment:** 126.

**PROGRAM(S) OFFERED**

• **Administrative Assistant and Secretarial Science, General** *15 students enrolled* • **Autobody/Collision and Repair Technology/Technician** *7 students enrolled* • **Automobile/Automotive Mechanics Technology/Technician** *9 students enrolled* • **Building/Property Maintenance and Management** *3 students enrolled* • **Computer Installation and Repair Technology/Technician** *12 students enrolled* • **Computer Programming, Specific Applications** • **Construction Trades, Other** *3 students enrolled* • **Cosmetology/Cosmetologist, General** *1500 hrs./$3000* • **Culinary Arts and Related Services, Other** *11 students enrolled* • **Dental Assisting/Assistant** *7 students enrolled* • **Diesel Mechanics Technology/Technician** *4 students enrolled* • **Health Professions and Related Clinical Sciences, Other** *37 students enrolled* • **Health/Health Care Administration/Management** *1210 hrs./$2420* • **Legal Administrative Assistant/Secretary** *1090 hrs./$2180* • **Licensed Practical/Vocational Nurse Training (LPN, LVN, Cert, Dipl, AAS)** *1500 hrs./$4027* • **Meat Cutting/Meat Cutter** *3 students enrolled* • **Printing Press Operator** *2 students enrolled* • **Vehicle Maintenance and Repair Technologies, Other** *1080 hrs./$2160* • **Welding Technology/Welder** *1425 hrs./$2850*

**STUDENT SERVICES** Academic or career counseling, employment services for current students, placement services for program completers, remedial services.

## Wes Watkins Area Vocational-Technical Center

Route 2, Box 159-1, Wetumka, OK 74883
http://www.wwtech.org/

**CONTACT** James R. Moore, Superintendent
**Telephone:** 405-452-5500

**GENERAL INFORMATION** Public Institution. Founded 1987. **Total program enrollment:** 114.

**PROGRAM(S) OFFERED**

• **Accounting Technology/Technician and Bookkeeping** *960 hrs./$2700* • **Allied Health Diagnostic, Intervention, and Treatment Professions, Other** *1231 hrs./$3078* • **Building/Property Maintenance and Management** • **Computer Installation and Repair Technology/Technician** *1050 hrs./$3051* • **Health Information/Medical Records Technology/Technician** *11 students enrolled* • **Health Professions and Related Clinical Sciences, Other** *24 students enrolled* • **Industrial Electronics Technology/Technician** *12 students enrolled* • **Licensed Practical/Vocational Nurse Training (LPN, LVN, Cert, Dipl, AAS)** *1497 hrs./$3000* • **Management Information Systems and Services, Other** *19 students* *enrolled* • **Mechanic and Repair Technologies/Technicians, Other** *5 students enrolled* • **Plumbing Technology/Plumber** *960 hrs./$2400* • **Surgical Technology/Technologist** *1185 hrs./$2963*

**STUDENT SERVICES** Academic or career counseling, employment services for current students, placement services for program completers, remedial services.

## Woodward Beauty College

502 Texas, Woodward, OK 73801

**CONTACT** Sherry Yauk, Owner Instructor
**Telephone:** 580-256-7520

**GENERAL INFORMATION** Private Institution. Founded 1952. **Total program enrollment:** 29. **Application fee:** $100.

**PROGRAM(S) OFFERED**
• **Cosmetology, Barber/Styling, and Nail Instructor** *1000 hrs./$6616* • **Cosmetology/Cosmetologist, General** *1500 hrs./$11,995* • **Facial Treatment Specialist/Facialist** *750 hrs./$7966* • **Nail Technician/Specialist and Manicurist** *600 hrs./$6016*

## Yukon Beauty College

1231 South 11th Street, Yukon, OK 73099

**CONTACT** Mary Whitby, CEO
**Telephone:** 405-354-3172

**GENERAL INFORMATION** Private Institution. **Total program enrollment:** 18. **Application fee:** $100.

**PROGRAM(S) OFFERED**
• **Aesthetician/Esthetician and Skin Care Specialist** *600 hrs./$3685* • **Cosmetology, Barber/Styling, and Nail Instructor** *1000 hrs./$5200* • **Cosmetology/Cosmetologist, General** *1500 hrs./$10,675* • **Nail Technician/Specialist and Manicurist** *600 hrs./$3685* • **Technology Teacher Education/Industrial Arts Teacher Education** *2 students enrolled*

**STUDENT SERVICES** Academic or career counseling, placement services for program completers.

# OREGON

## Abdill Career Schools

843 East Main, Suite 203, Medford, OR 97504
http://www.abdill.com/

**CONTACT** Owner
**Telephone:** 541-779-8384

**GENERAL INFORMATION** Private Institution. **Total program enrollment:** 85.

**PROGRAM(S) OFFERED**
• **Accounting Technology/Technician and Bookkeeping** *690 hrs./$7065* • **Accounting** *1 student enrolled* • **Dental Assisting/Assistant** *880 hrs./$9345* • **Insurance** • **Legal Assistant/Paralegal** *690 hrs./$7065* • **Medical Office Management/Administration** *830 hrs./$8745* • **Medical Radiologic Technology/Science—Radiation Therapist** *790 hrs./$8265* • **Medical Transcription/Transcriptionist** *2 students enrolled* • **Medical/Clinical Assistant** *880 hrs./$12,025* • **Phlebotomy/Phlebotomist** *5 students enrolled* • **Radiologic Technology/Science—Radiographer** *3 students enrolled* • **Real Estate** *1 student enrolled*

**STUDENT SERVICES** Academic or career counseling.

## Academy of Hair Design

305 Court Street NE, Salem, OR 97301

**CONTACT** Gene Snook, President
**Telephone:** 503-585-8122

**GENERAL INFORMATION** Private Institution. Founded 1967. **Total program enrollment:** 43. **Application fee:** $150.

**PROGRAM(S) OFFERED**
• **Barbering/Barber** *1350 hrs./$11,905* • **Cosmetology/Cosmetologist, General** *2300 hrs./$15,455* • **Hair Styling/Stylist and Hair Design** *1700 hrs./$13,860* • **Nail Technician/Specialist and Manicurist** *600 hrs./$5670*

**STUDENT SERVICES** Academic or career counseling, placement services for program completers.

## Apollo College–Portland

2600 SE 98th Avenue, Portland, OR 97266
http://www.apollocollege.edu/

**CONTACT** Bruce Capps, Executive Director
**Telephone:** 503-761-6100

**GENERAL INFORMATION** Private Institution. **Total program enrollment:** 1518. **Application fee:** $95.

**PROGRAM(S) OFFERED**
• **Dental Assisting/Assistant** *30 hrs./$11,940* • **Health Information/Medical Records Administration/Administrator** *30 hrs./$11,940* • **Licensed Practical/Vocational Nurse Training (LPN, LVN, Cert, Dipl, AAS)** *51 hrs./$22,704* • **Massage Therapy/Therapeutic Massage** *90 students enrolled* • **Medical Office Management/Administration** *2 students enrolled* • **Medical/Clinical Assistant** *30 hrs./$12,745* • **Pharmacy Technician/Assistant** *30 hrs./$11,940* • **Veterinary/Animal Health Technology/Technician and Veterinary Assistant** *30 hrs./$11,940*

**STUDENT SERVICES** Academic or career counseling, employment services for current students, placement services for program completers.

## Ashmead College

9600 SW Oak Street, Suite 400, Tigard, OR 97223
http://www.ashmeadcollege.com/

**CONTACT** Siri S. McElliott, School President
**Telephone:** 503-892-8100

**GENERAL INFORMATION** Private Institution. **Total program enrollment:** 154.

**PROGRAM(S) OFFERED**
• **Massage Therapy/Therapeutic Massage** *961 hrs./$16,634* • **Medical Insurance Specialist/Medical Biller** *4 students enrolled* • **Personal and Culinary Services, Other** *15 students enrolled*

**STUDENT SERVICES** Academic or career counseling, employment services for current students, placement services for program completers.

## BeauMonde College of Hair Design

1026 SW Salmon Street, Portland, OR 97205
http://www.beaumondecollege.com/

**CONTACT** Dianna Martin-Peterson, Administrator
**Telephone:** 503-226-7355

**GENERAL INFORMATION** Private Institution. Founded 1960. **Total program enrollment:** 169. **Application fee:** $100.

*BeauMonde College of Hair Design (continued)*

**PROGRAM(S) OFFERED**

• **Barbering/Barber** *1350 hrs./$14,835* • **Cosmetology and Related Personal Grooming Arts, Other** *1 student enrolled* • **Cosmetology, Barber/Styling, and Nail Instructor** *1000 hrs./$9235* • **Cosmetology/Cosmetologist, General** *1700 hrs./$19,010*

**STUDENT SERVICES** Academic or career counseling, placement services for program completers.

## Blue Mountain Community College

2411 Northwest Carden Avenue, PO Box 100, Pendleton, OR 97801-1000
http://www.bluecc.edu/

**CONTACT** John Turner, President
**Telephone:** 541-276-1260

**GENERAL INFORMATION** Public Institution. Founded 1962. **Accreditation:** Regional (NCCU/NCCU); dental assisting (ADA); engineering technology (ABET/TAC). **Total program enrollment:** 1019.

**PROGRAM(S) OFFERED**

• **Accounting Technology/Technician and Bookkeeping** *1 student enrolled* • **Administrative Assistant and Secretarial Science, General** *4 students enrolled* • **Adult Literacy Tutor/Instructor** • **Dental Assisting/Assistant** *11 students enrolled* • **Hospitality Administration/Management, General** • **Licensed Practical/Vocational Nurse Training (LPN, LVN, Cert, Dipl, AAS)** *28 students enrolled* • **Medical Administrative/Executive Assistant and Medical Secretary** *1 student enrolled* • **Retailing and Retail Operations** • **Small Business Administration/Management** • **Teacher Assistant/Aide** • **Welding Technology/Welder** *1 student enrolled*

**STUDENT SERVICES** Academic or career counseling, employment services for current students, remedial services.

## Cambridge College

4145 SW Watson Avenue, Suite 300, Beaverton, OR 97005-2162
http://www.hightechinstitute.edu/

**CONTACT** Leigh Christopherson, Campus President
**Telephone:** 503-646-6000

**GENERAL INFORMATION** Private Institution. **Total program enrollment:** 515. **Application fee:** $50.

**PROGRAM(S) OFFERED**

• **Dental Assisting/Assistant** *720 hrs./$11,740* • **Massage Therapy/Therapeutic Massage** *820 hrs./$11,683* • **Medical Insurance Specialist/Medical Biller** *720 hrs./$11,316* • **Medical/Clinical Assistant** *720 hrs./$11,550* • **Pharmacy Technician/Assistant** *720 hrs./$11,637* • **Surgical Technology/Technologist** *19 students enrolled*

**STUDENT SERVICES** Placement services for program completers.

## Central Oregon Community College

2600 Northwest College Way, Bend, OR 97701-5998
http://www.cocc.edu/

**CONTACT** Dr. James Middleton, President
**Telephone:** 541-383-7500

**GENERAL INFORMATION** Public Institution. Founded 1949. **Accreditation:** Regional (NCCU/NCCU); dental assisting (ADA); health information technology (AHIMA). **Total program enrollment:** 2131. **Application fee:** $25.

**PROGRAM(S) OFFERED**

• **Automobile/Automotive Mechanics Technology/Technician** *39 students enrolled* • **Business Administration and Management, General** • **Computer and Information Sciences, General** *2 students enrolled* • **Cooking and Related Culinary Arts, General** *3 students enrolled* • **Dental Assisting/Assistant** *18 students enrolled* • **Drafting and Design Technology/Technician, General** *1 student enrolled* • **Fire Science/Firefighting** *2 students enrolled* • **General Office Occupations and Clerical Services** *1 student enrolled* • **Health Information/Medical Records Technology/Technician** *5 students enrolled* • **Juvenile Corrections** • **Licensed Practical/Vocational Nurse Training (LPN, LVN, Cert, Dipl, AAS)** *31 students enrolled* • **Manufacturing Technology/Technician** • **Massage Therapy/Therapeutic Massage** *21 students enrolled* • **Medical Transcription/Transcriptionist** *1 student enrolled* • **Medical/Clinical Assistant** *15 students enrolled* • **Polymer/Plastics Engineering** • **Retailing and Retail Operations** *4 students enrolled* • **Substance Abuse/Addiction Counseling** *3 students enrolled*

**STUDENT SERVICES** Academic or career counseling, employment services for current students, placement services for program completers, remedial services.

## Chemeketa Community College

4000 Lancaster Drive NE, P.O. Box 14007, Salem, OR 97309
http://www.chemeketa.edu/

**CONTACT** Cheryl Roberts, President
**Telephone:** 503-399-5000

**GENERAL INFORMATION** Public Institution. Founded 1955. **Accreditation:** Regional (NCCU/NCCU); dental assisting (ADA); emergency medical services (JRCEMTP). **Total program enrollment:** 4711.

**PROGRAM(S) OFFERED**

• **Accounting Technology/Technician and Bookkeeping** • **Architectural Drafting and Architectural CAD/CADD** *1 student enrolled* • **Autobody/Collision and Repair Technology/Technician** *1 student enrolled* • **Automobile/Automotive Mechanics Technology/Technician** • **Building/Home/Construction Inspection/Inspector** • **Business/Office Automation/Technology/Data Entry** *4 students enrolled* • **Carpentry/Carpenter** • **Child Care and Support Services Management** *3 students enrolled* • **Criminal Justice/Safety Studies** *7 students enrolled* • **Crop Production** *3 students enrolled* • **Dental Assisting/Assistant** *18 students enrolled* • **Drafting and Design Technology/Technician, General** *4 students enrolled* • **Education/Teaching of Individuals with Speech or Language Impairments** *12 students enrolled* • **Electrical, Electronic and Communications Engineering Technology/Technician** *1 student enrolled* • **Fire Science/Firefighting** *1 student enrolled* • **Forestry, General** • **General Office Occupations and Clerical Services** *19 students enrolled* • **Health Information/Medical Records Technology/Technician** *6 students enrolled* • **Hospitality Administration/Management, General** *2 students enrolled* • **Hotel/Motel Administration/Management** *2 students enrolled* • **Licensed Practical/Vocational Nurse Training (LPN, LVN, Cert, Dipl, AAS)** *68 students enrolled* • **Machine Shop Technology/Assistant** *5 students enrolled* • **Medical/Clinical Assistant** *21 students enrolled* • **Pharmacy Technician/Assistant** *10 students enrolled* • **Retailing and Retail Operations** *2 students enrolled* • **Substance Abuse/Addiction Counseling** *1 student enrolled* • **Survey Technology/Surveying** • **Teacher Assistant/Aide** *4 students enrolled* • **Tourism and Travel Services Management** *2 students enrolled* • **Welding Technology/Welder** *1 student enrolled*

**STUDENT SERVICES** Academic or career counseling, daycare for children of students, employment services for current students, placement services for program completers, remedial services.

## Clackamas Community College

19600 South Molalla Avenue, Oregon City, OR 97045-7998
http://www.clackamas.edu/

**CONTACT** Dr. Joanne Truesdell, President
**Telephone:** 503-657-6958 Ext. 2313

**GENERAL INFORMATION** Public Institution. Founded 1966. **Accreditation:** Regional (NCCU/NCCU). **Total program enrollment:** 2572.

**PROGRAM(S) OFFERED**

• **Accounting Technology/Technician and Bookkeeping** *5 students enrolled* • **Administrative Assistant and Secretarial Science, General** *3 students enrolled* • **Applied Horticulture/Horticultural Operations, General** • **Autobody/Collision and Repair Technology/Technician** • **Automobile/Automotive Mechanics Technology/Technician** • **Business Administration and Management, General** *4 students enrolled* • **Clinical/Medical Laboratory Assistant** • **Computer Programming, Specific Applications** • **Computer Systems Networking and Telecommunications** *2 students enrolled* • **Construction Engineering Technology/Technician** • **Corrections** *2 students enrolled* • **Criminal Justice/Police Science** • **Dental Assisting/Assistant** *11 students enrolled* • **E-**

Commerce/Electronic Commerce • Electrical, Electronic and Communications Engineering Technology/Technician • Emergency Medical Technology/Technician (EMT Paramedic) *1 student enrolled* • Fire Science/Firefighting *1 student enrolled* • Hospitality Administration/Management, General • Human Development and Family Studies, General *7 students enrolled* • Human Resources Development *3 students enrolled* • Industrial Engineering *7 students enrolled* • Industrial Mechanics and Maintenance Technology • Industrial Technology/Technician • Juvenile Corrections *5 students enrolled* • Licensed Practical/Vocational Nurse Training (LPN, LVN, Cert, Dipl, AAS) • Logistics and Materials Management *80 students enrolled* • Machine Tool Technology/Machinist • Manufacturing Technology/Technician *2 students enrolled* • Marketing/Marketing Management, General • Medical Office Assistant/Specialist *4 students enrolled* • Medical/Clinical Assistant *14 students enrolled* • Office Management and Supervision *2 students enrolled* • Operations Management and Supervision *8 students enrolled* • Ornamental Horticulture • Publishing • Quality Control Technology/Technician • Recording Arts Technology/Technician *5 students enrolled* • Retailing and Retail Operations • Sales, Distribution and Marketing Operations, General • Security and Protective Services, Other • Social Work *5 students enrolled* • Survey Technology/Surveying *3 students enrolled* • Teacher Assistant/Aide *2 students enrolled* • Water Quality and Wastewater Treatment Management and Recycling Technology/Technician • Web Page, Digital/Multimedia and Information Resources Design *2 students enrolled* • Welding Technology/Welder *1 student enrolled*

**STUDENT SERVICES** Academic or career counseling, daycare for children of students, employment services for current students, remedial services.

## Clatsop Community College

1653 Jerome, Astoria, OR 97103-3698
http://www.clatsopcc.edu/

**CONTACT** Greg Hamann, President
**Telephone:** 503-325-0910

**GENERAL INFORMATION** Public Institution. Founded 1958. **Accreditation:** Regional (NCCU/NCCU). **Total program enrollment:** 385. **Application fee:** $15.

**PROGRAM(S) OFFERED**
• Automobile/Automotive Mechanics Technology/Technician *3 students enrolled* • Business/Office Automation/Technology/Data Entry • CAD/CADD Drafting and/or Design Technology/Technician *4 students enrolled* • Child Care Provider/Assistant *3 students enrolled* • Emergency Medical Technology/Technician (EMT Paramedic) *1 student enrolled* • General Office Occupations and Clerical Services *3 students enrolled* • Licensed Practical/Vocational Nurse Training (LPN, LVN, Cert, Dipl, AAS) *15 students enrolled* • Marine Science/Merchant Marine Officer *1 student enrolled* • Medical/Clinical Assistant *5 students enrolled* • Office Management and Supervision • Welding Technology/Welder *3 students enrolled*

**STUDENT SERVICES** Academic or career counseling, employment services for current students, remedial services.

## College of Cosmetology

357 East Main Street, Klamath Falls, OR 97601
http://collegeofcos.com/

**CONTACT** Roni Nelson, General Manager
**Telephone:** 541-882-6644

**GENERAL INFORMATION** Private Institution. **Total program enrollment:** 69.

**PROGRAM(S) OFFERED**
• Aesthetician/Esthetician and Skin Care Specialist *500 hrs./$3350* • Barbering/Barber *1350 hrs./$6850* • Cosmetology and Related Personal Grooming Arts, Other *850 hrs./$5200* • Cosmetology/Cosmetologist, General *2300 hrs./$14,748* • Hair Styling/Stylist and Hair Design *1700 hrs./$9960* • Nail Technician/Specialist and Manicurist *600 hrs./$3690*

**STUDENT SERVICES** Academic or career counseling.

## College of Hair Design Careers

3322 Lancaster Drive, NE, Salem, OR 97305-1354
http://www.collegeofhairdesigncareers.com/

**CONTACT** Cindy Long, Administrator
**Telephone:** 503-588-5888

**GENERAL INFORMATION** Private Institution. Founded 1983. **Total program enrollment:** 67. **Application fee:** $150.

**PROGRAM(S) OFFERED**
• Cosmetology and Related Personal Grooming Arts, Other *850 hrs./$5675* • Cosmetology/Cosmetologist, General *2300 hrs./$14,785* • Facial Treatment Specialist/Facialist *3 students enrolled* • Hair Styling/Stylist and Hair Design *1700 hrs./$9925* • Nail Technician/Specialist and Manicurist *600 hrs./$4050*

**STUDENT SERVICES** Academic or career counseling, placement services for program completers.

## College of Legal Arts

527 SW Hall Street, Suite 308, Portland, OR 97201
http://www.collegeoflegalarts.com/

**CONTACT** Joanna Russell, College President
**Telephone:** 503-223-5100

**GENERAL INFORMATION** Private Institution. Founded 1974. **Total program enrollment:** 49. **Application fee:** $50.

**PROGRAM(S) OFFERED**
• Corrections *42 hrs./$7950* • Court Reporting/Court Reporter *130 hrs./$9845* • Legal Assistant/Paralegal *45 hrs./$7950* • Medical Transcription/Transcriptionist *46 hrs./$7950*

**STUDENT SERVICES** Academic or career counseling, employment services for current students, placement services for program completers, remedial services.

## Columbia Gorge Community College

400 East Scenic Drive, The Dalles, OR 97058
http://www.cgcc.cc.or.us/

**CONTACT** Frank K. Toda, President
**Telephone:** 541-506-6000

**GENERAL INFORMATION** Public Institution. Founded 1977. **Accreditation:** Regional (NCCU/NCCU). **Total program enrollment:** 355.

**PROGRAM(S) OFFERED**
• Accounting *4 students enrolled* • Administrative Assistant and Secretarial Science, General • Business Administration and Management, General • Child Care and Support Services Management • Criminal Justice/Safety Studies *5 students enrolled* • Early Childhood Education and Teaching *1 student enrolled* • Electrical, Electronic and Communications Engineering Technology/Technician *15 students enrolled* • Emergency Medical Technology/Technician (EMT Paramedic) *1 student enrolled* • Marketing/Marketing Management, General *1 student enrolled* • Medical/Clinical Assistant *1 student enrolled* • Nursing—Registered Nurse Training (RN, ASN, BSN, MSN) *22 students enrolled* • Teacher Assistant/Aide

**STUDENT SERVICES** Academic or career counseling, employment services for current students, placement services for program completers, remedial services.

## Concorde Career Institute

1827 NE 44th Avenue, Portland, OR 97213
http://www.concorde.edu/

**CONTACT** Al Short, Campus President
**Telephone:** 503-281-4181

**GENERAL INFORMATION** Private Institution. **Total program enrollment:** 593.

*Concorde Career Institute (continued)*

**PROGRAM(S) OFFERED**

• **Dental Assisting/Assistant** *800 hrs./$13,360* • **Health Information/Medical Records Administration/Administrator** *720 hrs./$11,223* • **Health and Medical Administrative Services, Other** *69 students enrolled* • **Licensed Practical/Vocational Nurse Training (LPN, LVN, Cert, Dipl, AAS)** *1600 hrs./$23,448* • **Massage Therapy/Therapeutic Massage** *720 hrs./$11,196* • **Medical/Clinical Assistant** *900 hrs./$13,627* • **Surgical Technology/Technologist** *1220 hrs./$23,108*

**STUDENT SERVICES** Academic or career counseling, employment services for current students, placement services for program completers, remedial services.

## Corban College

5000 Deer Park Drive, SE, Salem, OR 97301-9392
http://www.corban.edu/

**CONTACT** Reno Hoff, President
**Telephone:** 503-581-8600

**GENERAL INFORMATION** Private Institution. Founded 1935. **Accreditation:** Regional (NCCU/NCCU). **Total program enrollment:** 776. **Application fee:** $40.

**STUDENT SERVICES** Academic or career counseling, employment services for current students, placement services for program completers.

## East West College of the Healing Arts

4531 SE Belmont Avenue, Portland, OR 97215-1635
http://www.eastwestcollege.com/

**CONTACT** David Slawson, Executive Director President
**Telephone:** 503-233-6500

**GENERAL INFORMATION** Private Institution. Founded 1972. **Application fee:** $25.

**PROGRAM(S) OFFERED**

• **Massage Therapy/Therapeutic Massage** *1002 hrs./$17,067*

**STUDENT SERVICES** Academic or career counseling, placement services for program completers.

## Eugene Bible College

2155 Bailey Hill Road, Eugene, OR 97405-1194
http://www.ebc.edu/

**CONTACT** Dr. David Cole, President
**Telephone:** 541-485-1780

**GENERAL INFORMATION** Private Institution (Affiliated with Open Bible Standard Churches). Founded 1925. **Accreditation:** State accredited or approved. **Total program enrollment:** 94. **Application fee:** $50.

**PROGRAM(S) OFFERED**

• **Bible/Biblical Studies** *7 students enrolled*

**STUDENT SERVICES** Academic or career counseling, employment services for current students, placement services for program completers, remedial services.

## Everest College

425 Southwest Washington Street, Portland, OR 97204
http://www.everest.edu/

**CONTACT** Mickey Sieracki, College President
**Telephone:** 503-222-3225

**GENERAL INFORMATION** Private Institution. Founded 1955. **Accreditation:** State accredited or approved. **Total program enrollment:** 371.

**PROGRAM(S) OFFERED**

• **Accounting Technology/Technician and Bookkeeping** *2 students enrolled* • **Accounting and Related Services, Other** *5 students enrolled* • **Allied Health and Medical Assisting Services, Other** *17 students enrolled* • **Business, Management, Marketing, and Related Support Services, Other** *10 students enrolled* • **Data Entry/Microcomputer Applications, General** *5 students enrolled* • **Legal Administrative Assistant/Secretary** *2 students enrolled* • **Medical Administrative/Executive Assistant and Medical Secretary** *13 students enrolled* • **Medical Insurance Coding Specialist/Coder** *63 students enrolled* • **Pharmacy Technician/Assistant** *6 students enrolled* • **Tourism and Travel Services Marketing Operations** *4 students enrolled*

**STUDENT SERVICES** Academic or career counseling, employment services for current students, placement services for program completers.

## Heald College–Portland

625 SW Broadway, 4th Floor, Portland, OR 97205
http://www.heald.edu/

**CONTACT** Jason Ferguson, Campus President
**Telephone:** 503-505-5400

**GENERAL INFORMATION** Private Institution. Founded 1863. **Accreditation:** Regional (WASC/ACCJC). **Total program enrollment:** 317.

**PROGRAM(S) OFFERED**

• **Business Administration, Management and Operations, Other** • **Computer and Information Sciences and Support Services, Other** *3 students enrolled* • **Medical/Clinical Assistant** *2 students enrolled*

**STUDENT SERVICES** Academic or career counseling, employment services for current students, placement services for program completers, remedial services.

## Klamath Community College

7390 South 6th Street, Klamath Falls, OR 97603
http://www.klamathcc.edu/

**CONTACT** Gerald Hamilton, President
**Telephone:** 541-882-3521

**GENERAL INFORMATION** Public Institution. Founded 1996. **Accreditation:** Regional (NCCU/NCCU). **Total program enrollment:** 427.

**PROGRAM(S) OFFERED**

• **Accounting Technology/Technician and Bookkeeping** *4 students enrolled* • **Administrative Assistant and Secretarial Science, General** • **Business Administration and Management, General** *3 students enrolled* • **Child Care Provider/Assistant** • **Computer and Information Sciences, General** *1 student enrolled* • **Corrections** • **Criminal Justice/Police Science** *1 student enrolled* • **Education, Other** • **Emergency Medical Technology/Technician (EMT Paramedic)** *1 student enrolled* • **Health Information/Medical Records Administration/Administrator** *2 students enrolled* • **Health Professions and Related Clinical Sciences, Other** • **Marketing/Marketing Management, General** *3 students enrolled* • **Nurse/Nursing Assistant/Aide and Patient Care Assistant** *51 students enrolled* • **Science Technologies/Technicians, Other** • **Welding Technology/Welder** *4 students enrolled*

**STUDENT SERVICES** Academic or career counseling, remedial services.

## Lane Community College

4000 East 30th Avenue, Eugene, OR 97405-0640
http://www.lanecc.edu/

**CONTACT** Mary Spilde, President
**Telephone:** 541-463-3000

**GENERAL INFORMATION** Public Institution. Founded 1964. **Accreditation:** Regional (NCCU/NCCU); dental assisting (ADA); dental hygiene (ADA). **Total program enrollment:** 5236.

**PROGRAM(S) OFFERED**

• **Accounting Technology/Technician and Bookkeeping** *1 student enrolled* • **Child Care Provider/Assistant** *1 student enrolled* • **Computer Programming/Programmer, General** *6 students enrolled* • **Construction Engineering Technology/Technician** *3 students enrolled* • **Corrections** *1 student enrolled* • **Data Entry/Microcomputer Applications, General** *3 students enrolled* • **Dental Assisting/Assistant** *22 students enrolled* • **Drafting and Design Technology/**

**Technician, General** *1 student enrolled* • **Emergency Medical Technology/Technician (EMT Paramedic)** *1 student enrolled* • **General Office Occupations and Clerical Services** *2 students enrolled* • **Health Information/Medical Records Technology/Technician** *18 students enrolled* • **Hotel/Motel Administration/Management** *3 students enrolled* • **Legal Administrative Assistant/Secretary** *3 students enrolled* • **Medical Administrative/Executive Assistant and Medical Secretary** *22 students enrolled* • **Sport and Fitness Administration/Management** *7 students enrolled* • **System, Networking, and LAN/WAN Management/Manager** *2 students enrolled*

**STUDENT SERVICES** Academic or career counseling, daycare for children of students, employment services for current students, placement services for program completers, remedial services.

## Linfield College–Adult Degree Program

Albany Center Linn-Benton Community College, Albany, OR 97321
http://www.linfield.edu/dce/

**CONTACT** Thomas L. Hellie, President
**Telephone:** 503-883-2447

**GENERAL INFORMATION** Private Institution. **Accreditation:** Regional (NCCU/NCCU). **Total program enrollment:** 43. **Application fee:** $100.

**PROGRAM(S) OFFERED**
• **Human Resources Management/Personnel Administration, General** *15 students enrolled* • **Management Information Systems, General** • **Marketing/Marketing Management, General** *3 students enrolled*

**STUDENT SERVICES** Academic or career counseling.

## Linn-Benton Community College

6500 Southwest Pacific Boulevard, Albany, OR 97321
http://www.linnbenton.edu/

**CONTACT** Dr. Rita Cavin, President
**Telephone:** 541-917-4999

**GENERAL INFORMATION** Public Institution. Founded 1966. **Accreditation:** Regional (NCCU/NCCU); dental assisting (ADA); medical assisting (AAMAE). **Total program enrollment:** 2996. **Application fee:** $25.

**PROGRAM(S) OFFERED**
• **Accounting Technology/Technician and Bookkeeping** *1 student enrolled* • **Agriculture, General** *2 students enrolled* • **Autobody/Collision and Repair Technology/Technician** *9 students enrolled* • **Automobile/Automotive Mechanics Technology/Technician** *1 student enrolled* • **Civil Engineering Technology/Technician** *3 students enrolled* • **Clinical/Medical Laboratory Science and Allied Professions, Other** *16 students enrolled* • **Computer Programming, Specific Applications** *1 student enrolled* • **Computer Technology/Computer Systems Technology** *3 students enrolled* • **Corrections** *3 students enrolled* • **Dental Assisting/Assistant** *15 students enrolled* • **Diesel Mechanics Technology/Technician** *4 students enrolled* • **Early Childhood Education and Teaching** *3 students enrolled* • **Emergency Medical Technology/Technician (EMT Paramedic)** *1 student enrolled* • **General Office Occupations and Clerical Services** *8 students enrolled* • **Heating, Air Conditioning, Ventilation and Refrigeration Maintenance Technology/Technician (HAC, HACR, HVAC, HVACR)** *12 students enrolled* • **Machine Tool Technology/Machinist** *9 students enrolled* • **Medical Administrative/Executive Assistant and Medical Secretary** *15 students enrolled* • **Medical Transcription/Transcriptionist** *8 students enrolled* • **Metallurgical Technology/Technician** *1 student enrolled* • **Nursing—Registered Nurse Training (RN, ASN, BSN, MSN)** *2 students enrolled* • **Office Management and Supervision** *2 students enrolled* • **Pharmacy Technician/Assistant** *21 students enrolled* • **Prepress/Desktop Publishing and Digital Imaging Design** *5 students enrolled* • **Radiologic Technology/Science—Radiographer** *25 students enrolled* • **Teacher Assistant/Aide** *3 students enrolled* • **Veterinary/Animal Health Technology/Technician and Veterinary Assistant** *15 students enrolled* • **Welding Technology/Welder** *2 students enrolled*

**STUDENT SERVICES** Academic or career counseling, daycare for children of students, employment services for current students, placement services for program completers, remedial services.

## Marylhurst University

17600 Pacific Highway, PO Box 261, Marylhurst, OR 97036-0261
http://www.marylhurst.edu/

**CONTACT** Judith A. Johansen, President
**Telephone:** 503-636-8141

**GENERAL INFORMATION** Private Institution. Founded 1893. **Accreditation:** Regional (NCCU/NCCU); music (NASM). **Total program enrollment:** 395. **Application fee:** $20.

**PROGRAM(S) OFFERED**
• **Business Administration and Management, General** *13 students enrolled* • **Communication Studies/Speech Communication and Rhetoric** *14 students enrolled* • **Interior Design** • **Music Pedagogy** • **Music Performance, General** • **Music Theory and Composition** • **Music, General** • **Organizational Communication, General** *3 students enrolled* • **Pastoral Studies/Counseling** *3 students enrolled* • **Real Estate** *2 students enrolled* • **Theology/Theological Studies**

**STUDENT SERVICES** Academic or career counseling, employment services for current students, placement services for program completers.

## Mount Angel Seminary

Saint Benedict, OR 97373
http://www.mtangel.edu/seminary/index.html

**CONTACT** Very Rev. Richard Paperini, President-Rector
**Telephone:** 503-845-3951

**GENERAL INFORMATION** Private Institution. Founded 1887. **Accreditation:** Regional (NCCU/NCCU). **Total program enrollment:** 131. **Application fee:** $27.

**PROGRAM(S) OFFERED**
• **Pre-Theology/Pre-Ministerial Studies** *6 students enrolled*

**STUDENT SERVICES** Academic or career counseling, remedial services.

## Mt. Hood Community College

26000 Southeast Stark Street, Gresham, OR 97030-3300
http://www.mhcc.cc.or.us/

**CONTACT** John J. Sygielski, President
**Telephone:** 503-491-6422

**GENERAL INFORMATION** Public Institution. Founded 1966. **Accreditation:** Regional (NCCU/NCCU); dental hygiene (ADA); funeral service (ABFSE); medical assisting (AAMAE); physical therapy assisting (APTA); surgical technology (ARCST). **Total program enrollment:** 3182. **Application fee:** $25.

**PROGRAM(S) OFFERED**
• **Accounting Technology/Technician and Bookkeeping** *4 students enrolled* • **Administrative Assistant and Secretarial Science, General** • **Airline/Commercial/Professional Pilot and Flight Crew** • **Applied Horticulture/Horticultural Operations, General** • **Architectural Drafting and Architectural CAD/CADD** • **Architectural Engineering Technology/Technician** *1 student enrolled* • **Automobile/Automotive Mechanics Technology/Technician** • **Business Administration and Management, General** • **Business/Office Automation/Technology/Data Entry** *9 students enrolled* • **Child Care Provider/Assistant** *2 students enrolled* • **Civil Engineering Technology/Technician** • **Computer and Information Sciences, General** • **Cosmetology/Cosmetologist, General** • **Dental Hygiene/Hygienist** • **Diesel Mechanics Technology/Technician** • **Electrical, Electronic and Communications Engineering Technology/Technician** • **Entrepreneurship/Entrepreneurial Studies** *3 students enrolled* • **Environmental Engineering Technology/Environmental Technology** • **Executive Assistant/Executive Secretary** • **Fishing and Fisheries Sciences and Management** • **Forestry Technology/Technician** • **Funeral Service and Mortuary Science, General** • **General Office Occupations and Clerical Services** *8 students enrolled* • **Graphic Design** • **Graphic and Printing Equipment Operator, General Production** • **Hospitality Administration/Management, General** • **Legal Administrative Assistant/Secretary** • **Licensed Practical/Vocational Nurse Training (LPN, LVN, Cert, Dipl, AAS)** *21 students enrolled* • **Machine Tool Technology/Machinist** • **Mechanical Drafting and Mechanical Drafting CAD/CADD** • **Mechanical Engineering/Mechanical Technology/Technician**

*Mt. Hood Community College (continued)*

• **Medical Administrative/Executive Assistant and Medical Secretary** • **Medical Transcription/Transcriptionist** • **Medical/Clinical Assistant** • **Mental Health Counseling/Counselor** • **Natural Resources/Conservation, General** • **Nursing—Registered Nurse Training (RN, ASN, BSN, MSN)** • **Photography** • **Physical Therapist Assistant** • **Precision Metal Working, Other** *26 students enrolled* • **Radio and Television Broadcasting Technology/Technician** • **Radio and Television** • **Respiratory Care Therapy/Therapist** • **Retailing and Retail Operations** *1 student enrolled* • **Sheet Metal Technology/Sheetworking** • **Surgical Technology/Technologist** • **Teacher Assistant/Aide** • **Tourism and Travel Services Management** • **Vehicle Maintenance and Repair Technologies, Other** • **Welding Technology/Welder** *3 students enrolled* • **Youth Services/Administration** *3 students enrolled*

**STUDENT SERVICES** Academic or career counseling, daycare for children of students, employment services for current students, placement services for program completers, remedial services.

## Northwest Christian University

828 East 11th Avenue, Eugene, OR 97401-3745
http://www.northwestchristian.edu/

**CONTACT** David Wilson, President
**Telephone:** 541-343-1641

**GENERAL INFORMATION** Private Institution. Founded 1895. **Accreditation:** Regional (NCCU/NCCU). **Total program enrollment:** 399.

**PROGRAM(S) OFFERED**
• **Teaching English as a Second or Foreign Language/ESL Language Instructor** *3 students enrolled*

**STUDENT SERVICES** Academic or career counseling, employment services for current students, placement services for program completers, remedial services.

## Northwest College of Hair Design

210 Se 4th Street, Hillsboro, OR 97123
http://www.nwcollege.edu/

**CONTACT** Shawn Meinung, Director of Education/Compliance
**Telephone:** 503-844-7320

**GENERAL INFORMATION** Private Institution. **Total program enrollment:** 79. **Application fee:** $100.

**PROGRAM(S) OFFERED**
• **Barbering/Barber** *1350 hrs./$10,968* • **Cosmetology, Barber/Styling, and Nail Instructor** • **Cosmetology/Cosmetologist, General** *2300 hrs./$16,810* • **Facial Treatment Specialist/Facialist** *500 hrs./$4543* • **Hair Styling/Stylist and Hair Design** *1700 hrs./$11,550* • **Nail Technician/Specialist and Manicurist** *600 hrs./$4620*

**STUDENT SERVICES** Academic or career counseling, employment services for current students.

## Northwest College of Hair Design

6128 SE King Road, Milwaukie, OR 97222

**CONTACT** Shawn Meinung, Director of Education/Compliance
**Telephone:** 503-659-2834

**GENERAL INFORMATION** Private Institution. **Total program enrollment:** 102. **Application fee:** $100.

**PROGRAM(S) OFFERED**
• **Barbering/Barber** *1350 hrs./$10,968* • **Cosmetology, Barber/Styling, and Nail Instructor** • **Cosmetology/Cosmetologist, General** *2300 hrs./$16,810* • **Facial Treatment Specialist/Facialist** *500 hrs./$4543* • **Hair Styling/Stylist and Hair Design** *1700 hrs./$11,550* • **Nail Technician/Specialist and Manicurist** *600 hrs./$4620*

**STUDENT SERVICES** Academic or career counseling, employment services for current students.

## Northwest Nannies Institute, Inc.

11830 SW Kerr Parkway, Suite 100, Lake Oswego, OR 97035
http://nwnanny.com/

**CONTACT** Linda Roffe, President
**Telephone:** 503-245-5288

**GENERAL INFORMATION** Private Institution. Founded 1984. **Total program enrollment:** 25. **Application fee:** $25.

**PROGRAM(S) OFFERED**
• **Child Care Provider/Assistant** *809 hrs./$6827*

**STUDENT SERVICES** Employment services for current students, placement services for program completers.

## Oregon Coast Community College

332 SW Coast Highway, Newport, OR 92365-4928
http://www.occc.cc.or.us

**CONTACT** Patrick O'Connor, President
**Telephone:** 541-265-2283

**GENERAL INFORMATION** Public Institution. Founded 1987. **Total program enrollment:** 117.

**PROGRAM(S) OFFERED**
• **Accounting Technology/Technician and Bookkeeping** • **Drafting and Design Technology/Technician, General** • **Education/Teaching of Individuals with Speech or Language Impairments** • **Hospitality Administration/Management, General** • **Licensed Practical/Vocational Nurse Training (LPN, LVN, Cert, Dipl, AAS)** *14 students enrolled*

**STUDENT SERVICES** Academic or career counseling, remedial services.

## Oregon Institute of Technology

3201 Campus Drive, Klamath Falls, OR 97601-8801
http://www.oit.edu/

**CONTACT** Christopher Maples, President
**Telephone:** 541-885-1000

**GENERAL INFORMATION** Public Institution. Founded 1947. **Accreditation:** Regional (NCCU/NCCU); dental hygiene (ADA); engineering technology (ABET/TAC); engineering-related programs (ABET/RAC); medical technology (NAACLS); radiologic technology: radiography (JRCERT). **Total program enrollment:** 1913. **Application fee:** $50.

**STUDENT SERVICES** Academic or career counseling, employment services for current students, placement services for program completers, remedial services.

## Oregon University System

PO Box 3175, Eugene, OR 97403-0175

**CONTACT** George Pernsteiner, Chancellor
**Telephone:** 541-346-5700

**GENERAL INFORMATION** Public Institution.

## Phagan's Beauty College

142 SW Second Street, Corvallis, OR 97333
http://www.phagans-schools.com/

**CONTACT** Karen Dieckman, Owner CEO
**Telephone:** 541-753-6466

**GENERAL INFORMATION** Private Institution. Founded 1953. **Total program enrollment:** 67. **Application fee:** $100.

**PROGRAM(S) OFFERED**

• **Aesthetician/Esthetician and Skin Care Specialist** *2 students enrolled* • **Barbering/Barber** *1350 hrs./$7830* • **Cosmetology and Related Personal Grooming Arts, Other** *4 students enrolled* • **Cosmetology, Barber/Styling, and Nail Instructor** *1000 hrs./$5940* • **Cosmetology/Cosmetologist, General** *1950 hrs./$11,115* • **Hair Styling/Stylist and Hair Design** *1700 hrs./$9720* • **Nail Technician/Specialist and Manicurist** *1 student enrolled*

**STUDENT SERVICES** Academic or career counseling.

## Phagan's Central Oregon Beauty College

355 NE Second, Bend, OR 97701
http://www.phagans-schools.com/

**CONTACT** Karen Dieckman, Owner CEO
**Telephone:** 541-382-6171

**GENERAL INFORMATION** Private Institution. **Total program enrollment:** 103. **Application fee:** $100.

**PROGRAM(S) OFFERED**

• **Aesthetician/Esthetician and Skin Care Specialist** *31 students enrolled* • **Barbering/Barber** *1350 hrs./$7830* • **Cosmetology and Related Personal Grooming Arts, Other** *7 students enrolled* • **Cosmetology, Barber/Styling, and Nail Instructor** *1000 hrs./$5940* • **Cosmetology/Cosmetologist, General** *1950 hrs./$11,115* • **Hair Styling/Stylist and Hair Design** *1700 hrs./$9720* • **Nail Technician/Specialist and Manicurist** *12 students enrolled*

**STUDENT SERVICES** Academic or career counseling.

## Phagan's Grants Pass College of Beauty

304 NE Agness Avenue, Suite F, Grants Pass, OR 97526
http://www.phagans-schools.com/

**CONTACT** Karen Dieckman, Owner CEO
**Telephone:** 541-479-6678

**GENERAL INFORMATION** Private Institution. **Total program enrollment:** 64. **Application fee:** $100.

**PROGRAM(S) OFFERED**

• **Aesthetician/Esthetician and Skin Care Specialist** • **Barbering/Barber** *1350 hrs./$7830* • **Cosmetology and Related Personal Grooming Arts, Other** *8 students enrolled* • **Cosmetology, Barber/Styling, and Nail Instructor** *1000 hrs./$5940* • **Cosmetology/Cosmetologist, General** *1950 hrs./$11,115* • **Hair Styling/Stylist and Hair Design** *1700 hrs./$9720* • **Nail Technician/Specialist and Manicurist** *9 students enrolled*

**STUDENT SERVICES** Academic or career counseling.

## Phagan's Medford Beauty School

2366 Poplar Drive, Medford, OR 97504
http://www.phagans-schools.com/

**CONTACT** Karen Dieckman, Owner CEO
**Telephone:** 541-772-6155

**GENERAL INFORMATION** Private Institution. Founded 1987. **Total program enrollment:** 67. **Application fee:** $100.

**PROGRAM(S) OFFERED**

• **Aesthetician/Esthetician and Skin Care Specialist** *4 students enrolled* • **Barbering/Barber** *1350 hrs./$7830* • **Cosmetology and Related Personal Grooming Arts, Other** *12 students enrolled* • **Cosmetology, Barber/Styling, and Nail Instructor** *1000 hrs./$5940* • **Cosmetology/Cosmetologist, General** *1950 hrs./$11,115* • **Hair Styling/Stylist and Hair Design** *1700 hrs./$9720* • **Nail Technician/Specialist and Manicurist** *8 students enrolled*

**STUDENT SERVICES** Academic or career counseling.

## Phagan's Newport Academy of Cosmetology

333 SW Seventh Street, Newport, OR 97365
http://www.phagans-schools.com/

**CONTACT** Karen Dieckman, Owner CEO
**Telephone:** 541-265-3083

**GENERAL INFORMATION** Private Institution. **Total program enrollment:** 22. **Application fee:** $100.

**PROGRAM(S) OFFERED**

• **Aesthetician/Esthetician and Skin Care Specialist** *2 students enrolled* • **Barbering/Barber** *1350 hrs./$7830* • **Cosmetology and Related Personal Grooming Arts, Other** • **Cosmetology, Barber/Styling, and Nail Instructor** *1000 hrs./$5940* • **Cosmetology/Cosmetologist, General** *1950 hrs./$11,115* • **Hair Styling/Stylist and Hair Design** *1700 hrs./$9720* • **Nail Technician/Specialist and Manicurist** *5 students enrolled*

**STUDENT SERVICES** Academic or career counseling.

## Phagan's School of Beauty

622 Lancaster, NE, Salem, OR 97301
http://www.phagans-schools.com/

**CONTACT** Karen Dieckman, Owner President
**Telephone:** 503-363-6800

**GENERAL INFORMATION** Private Institution. **Total program enrollment:** 56. **Application fee:** $100.

**PROGRAM(S) OFFERED**

• **Aesthetician/Esthetician and Skin Care Specialist** *1 student enrolled* • **Barbering/Barber** *1350 hrs./$7830* • **Cosmetology and Related Personal Grooming Arts, Other** *3 students enrolled* • **Cosmetology, Barber/Styling, and Nail Instructor** *1000 hrs./$5940* • **Cosmetology/Cosmetologist, General** *1950 hrs./$11,115* • **Hair Styling/Stylist and Hair Design** *1700 hrs./$9720* • **Nail Technician/Specialist and Manicurist** *2 students enrolled*

**STUDENT SERVICES** Academic or career counseling.

## Phagan's School of Hair Design

16550 SE McLoughlin Boulevard, Milwaukie, OR 97222
http://www.phagans.com/

**CONTACT** Barbara Climaldi, Director
**Telephone:** 503-652-2668

**GENERAL INFORMATION** Private Institution. Founded 1954. **Total program enrollment:** 86.

**PROGRAM(S) OFFERED**

• **Barbering/Barber** *1350 hrs./$10,850* • **Cosmetology and Related Personal Grooming Arts, Other** *1950 hrs./$14,850* • **Cosmetology, Barber/Styling, and Nail Instructor** *1000 hrs./$7800* • **Cosmetology/Cosmetologist, General** *2300 hrs./$17,700* • **Facial Treatment Specialist/Facialist** *2 students enrolled* • **Hair Styling/Stylist and Hair Design** *1700 hrs./$13,350* • **Nail Technician/Specialist and Manicurist** *1 student enrolled*

**STUDENT SERVICES** Academic or career counseling, placement services for program completers.

## Phagan's School of Hair Design

3301 NE Sandy Boulevard, Portland, OR 97232
http://www.phagans.com/

**CONTACT** Barbara Climaldi, President
**Telephone:** 503-239-0838

**GENERAL INFORMATION** Private Institution. Founded 1958. **Total program enrollment:** 167.

*Phagan's School of Hair Design (continued)*

**PROGRAM(S) OFFERED**

• **Barbering/Barber** *1350 hrs./$13,400* • **Cosmetology and Related Personal Grooming Arts, Other** *2300 hrs./$21,100* • **Cosmetology, Barber/Styling, and Nail Instructor** *1000 hrs./$9700* • **Cosmetology/Cosmetologist, General** *1950 hrs./$18,600* • **Facial Treatment Specialist/Facialist** *2 students enrolled* • **Hair Styling/Stylist and Hair Design** *1700 hrs./$16,100* • **Nail Technician/Specialist and Manicurist**

**STUDENT SERVICES** Academic or career counseling, placement services for program completers.

## Phagan's Tigard Beauty School

8820 SW Center Street, Tigard, OR 97223
http://www.phagansnw.com/

**CONTACT** John Olsen, CEO
**Telephone:** 503-639-6108

**GENERAL INFORMATION** Private Institution. Founded 1974. **Total program enrollment:** 44.

**PROGRAM(S) OFFERED**

• **Cosmetology and Related Personal Grooming Arts, Other** *2050 hrs./$12,072* • **Cosmetology/Cosmetologist, General** *2300 hrs./$15,055* • **Facial Treatment Specialist/Facialist** *850 hrs./$5710* • **Hair Styling/Stylist and Hair Design** *1950 hrs./$11,488* • **Nail Technician/Specialist and Manicurist** *600 hrs./$3950*

**STUDENT SERVICES** Academic or career counseling.

## Pioneer Pacific College

27501 Southwest Parkway Avenue, Wilsonville, OR 97070
http://www.pioneerpacific.edu/

**CONTACT** Don Moutos, President
**Telephone:** 503-682-3903

**GENERAL INFORMATION** Private Institution. Founded 1981. **Accreditation:** State accredited or approved. **Total program enrollment:** 792. **Application fee:** $50.

**PROGRAM(S) OFFERED**

• **Accounting** • **Baking and Pastry Arts/Baker/Pastry Chef** *22 students enrolled* • **Culinary Arts/Chef Training** *150 students enrolled* • **Licensed Practical/Vocational Nurse Training (LPN, LVN, Cert, Dipl, AAS)** *50 students enrolled* • **Massage Therapy/Therapeutic Massage** *21 students enrolled* • **Medical Insurance Specialist/Medical Biller** *66 students enrolled* • **Medical/Clinical Assistant** *178 students enrolled* • **Pharmacy Technician/Assistant** *42 students enrolled*

**STUDENT SERVICES** Academic or career counseling, employment services for current students, placement services for program completers.

## Portland Community College

PO Box 19000, Portland, OR 97280-0990
http://www.pcc.edu/

**CONTACT** Preston Pulliams, District President
**Telephone:** 503-244-6111

**GENERAL INFORMATION** Public Institution. Founded 1961. **Accreditation:** Regional (NCCU/NCCU); dental assisting (ADA); dental hygiene (ADA); dental laboratory technology (ADA); health information technology (AHIMA); medical laboratory technology (NAACLS); ophthalmic medical technology (JCAHPO); radiologic technology: radiography (JRCERT). **Total program enrollment:** 9892. **Application fee:** $25.

**PROGRAM(S) OFFERED**

• **Accounting Technology/Technician and Bookkeeping** • **Accounting** *14 students enrolled* • **Administrative Assistant and Secretarial Science, General** *10 students enrolled* • **Aircraft Powerplant Technology/Technician** *17 students enrolled* • **Airframe Mechanics and Aircraft Maintenance Technology/Technician** *23 students enrolled* • **American Sign Language (ASL)** *1 student enrolled* • **Autobody/Collision and Repair Technology/Technician** *15 students enrolled* • **Building/Home/Construction Inspection/Inspector** • **Business/Office Automation/Technology/Data Entry** • **Child Care and Support Services Management** *13 students enrolled* • **Civil Engineering Technology/Technician** • **Construction Engineering Technology/Technician** • **Dental Assisting/Assistant** *37 students enrolled* • **Design and Visual Communications, General** *6 students enrolled* • **Diesel Mechanics Technology/Technician** • **Drafting and Design Technology/Technician, General** *12 students enrolled* • **Education, Other** *8 students enrolled* • **Electrical, Electronic and Communications Engineering Technology/Technician** • **Emergency Medical Technology/Technician (EMT Paramedic)** • **Food Preparation/Professional Cooking/Kitchen Assistant** *8 students enrolled* • **General Office Occupations and Clerical Services** *1 student enrolled* • **Health and Physical Education, General** *9 students enrolled* • **Heating, Air Conditioning, Ventilation and Refrigeration Maintenance Technology/Technician (HAC, HACR, HVAC, HVACR)** *1 student enrolled* • **Interior Design** *6 students enrolled* • **Juvenile Corrections** *5 students enrolled* • **Landscaping and Groundskeeping** *1 student enrolled* • **Legal Assistant/Paralegal** *9 students enrolled* • **Machine Shop Technology/Assistant** • **Machine Tool Technology/Machinist** *4 students enrolled* • **Management Information Systems and Services, Other** *8 students enrolled* • **Management Information Systems, General** *2 students enrolled* • **Marketing/Marketing Management, General** *2 students enrolled* • **Mechanical Engineering/Mechanical Technology/Technician** • **Medical/Clinical Assistant** *24 students enrolled* • **Music Performance, General** *8 students enrolled* • **Office Management and Supervision** *5 students enrolled* • **Printing Press Operator** *1 student enrolled* • **Retailing and Retail Operations** *1 student enrolled* • **Security and Protective Services, Other** *2 students enrolled* • **Substance Abuse/Addiction Counseling** *1 student enrolled* • **Teacher Assistant/Aide** *6 students enrolled* • **Watchmaking and Jewelrymaking** *1 student enrolled* • **Web Page, Digital/Multimedia and Information Resources Design** *2 students enrolled* • **Welding Technology/Welder** *3 students enrolled*

**STUDENT SERVICES** Academic or career counseling, daycare for children of students, employment services for current students, placement services for program completers, remedial services.

## Rogue Community College

3345 Redwood Highway, Grants Pass, OR 97527-9298
http://www.roguecc.edu/

**CONTACT** Peter Angstadt, President
**Telephone:** 541-956-7500

**GENERAL INFORMATION** Public Institution. Founded 1970. **Accreditation:** Regional (NCCU/NCCU). **Total program enrollment:** 1669.

**PROGRAM(S) OFFERED**

• **Automobile/Automotive Mechanics Technology/Technician** • **Business/Commerce, General** *11 students enrolled* • **Child Care Provider/Assistant** • **Child Care and Support Services Management** *2 students enrolled* • **Computer Typography and Composition Equipment Operator** *5 students enrolled* • **Construction Engineering Technology/Technician** *7 students enrolled* • **Corrections** *1 student enrolled* • **Dental Assisting/Assistant** *9 students enrolled* • **Diesel Mechanics Technology/Technician** • **Electrical, Electronic and Communications Engineering Technology/Technician** *10 students enrolled* • **Emergency Medical Technology/Technician (EMT Paramedic)** *1 student enrolled* • **Fire Protection and Safety Technology/Technician** • **Fire Services Administration** • **Landscaping and Groundskeeping** • **Licensed Practical/Vocational Nurse Training (LPN, LVN, Cert, Dipl, AAS)** *15 students enrolled* • **Manufacturing Technology/Technician** *2 students enrolled* • **Massage Therapy/Therapeutic Massage** *10 students enrolled* • **Substance Abuse/Addiction Counseling** • **Welding Technology/Welder**

**STUDENT SERVICES** Academic or career counseling, daycare for children of students, employment services for current students, placement services for program completers, remedial services.

## Roseburg Beauty College

700 SE Stephens Street, Roseburg, OR 97470

**CONTACT** Kathy Pruitt, Director
**Telephone:** 541-673-5533

**GENERAL INFORMATION** Private Institution. **Total program enrollment:** 35.

**PROGRAM(S) OFFERED**
• **Barbering/Barber** *3 students enrolled* • **Cosmetology/Cosmetologist, General** *1950 hrs./$9555* • **Facial Treatment Specialist/Facialist** *500 hrs./$2850* • **Hair Styling/Stylist and Hair Design** *1700 hrs./$8525* • **Make-Up Artist/Specialist** *6 students enrolled* • **Nail Technician/Specialist and Manicurist** *600 hrs./$3400*

**STUDENT SERVICES** Academic or career counseling, placement services for program completers.

## Southwestern Oregon Community College

1988 Newmark Avenue, Coos Bay, OR 97420-2912
http://www.socc.edu/

**CONTACT** Patty M. Scott, EdD, Interim President
**Telephone:** 541-888-2525

**GENERAL INFORMATION** Public Institution. Founded 1961. **Accreditation:** Regional (NCCU/NCCU). **Total program enrollment:** 1135. **Application fee:** $30.

**PROGRAM(S) OFFERED**
• **Accounting Technology/Technician and Bookkeeping** *1 student enrolled* • **Child Care Provider/Assistant** • **Computer Programming, Vendor/Product Certification** *7 students enrolled* • **Computer Systems Analysis/Analyst** • **Computer Systems Networking and Telecommunications** *3 students enrolled* • **Emergency Medical Technology/Technician (EMT Paramedic)** • **General Office Occupations and Clerical Services** *2 students enrolled* • **Health and Physical Education, General** *1 student enrolled* • **Human Services, General** *1 student enrolled* • **Juvenile Corrections** *2 students enrolled* • **Medical Administrative/Executive Assistant and Medical Secretary** *7 students enrolled* • **Medical Reception/Receptionist** *4 students enrolled* • **Medical Transcription/Transcriptionist** *4 students enrolled* • **Medical/Clinical Assistant** • **Nursing, Other** • **Office Management and Supervision** *1 student enrolled* • **Pharmacy Technician/Assistant** *1 student enrolled* • **Retailing and Retail Operations** • **Sales, Distribution and Marketing Operations, General** • **Teacher Assistant/Aide** • **Turf and Turfgrass Management** *2 students enrolled* • **Web Page, Digital/Multimedia and Information Resources Design** • **Welding Technology/Welder**

**STUDENT SERVICES** Academic or career counseling, daycare for children of students, employment services for current students, placement services for program completers, remedial services.

## Springfield College of Beauty

727 Main Street, Springfield, OR 97477

**CONTACT** Dennis B. Zuniga, Owner
**Telephone:** 541-746-4473

**GENERAL INFORMATION** Private Institution. Founded 1958. **Total program enrollment:** 87. **Application fee:** $150.

**PROGRAM(S) OFFERED**
• **Cosmetology and Related Personal Grooming Arts, Other** *850 hrs./$4040* • **Cosmetology, Barber/Styling, and Nail Instructor** *1000 hrs./$3000* • **Cosmetology/Cosmetologist, General** *2300 hrs./$13,350* • **Hair Styling/Stylist and Hair Design** *1700 hrs./$8075*

**STUDENT SERVICES** Academic or career counseling, placement services for program completers.

## Tillamook Bay Community College

2510 First Street, Tillamook, OR 97141
http://www.tbcc.cc.or.us/

**CONTACT** Jon Carnahan, President
**Telephone:** 503-842-8222

**GENERAL INFORMATION** Public Institution. Founded 1984. **Accreditation:** Regional (NCCU/NCCU). **Total program enrollment:** 61.

**STUDENT SERVICES** Academic or career counseling, remedial services.

## Treasure Valley Community College

650 College Boulevard, Ontario, OR 97914-3423
http://www.tvcc.cc.or.us/

**CONTACT** James E. Sorensen, President
**Telephone:** 541-881-8822

**GENERAL INFORMATION** Public Institution. Founded 1962. **Accreditation:** Regional (NCCU/NCCU). **Total program enrollment:** 1206.

**PROGRAM(S) OFFERED**
• **Accounting Technology/Technician and Bookkeeping** *1 student enrolled* • **Business/Office Automation/Technology/Data Entry** • **Criminal Justice/Police Science** • **Fire Protection and Safety Technology/Technician** *7 students enrolled* • **Licensed Practical/Vocational Nurse Training (LPN, LVN, Cert, Dipl, AAS)** *29 students enrolled* • **Welding Technology/Welder** *3 students enrolled*

**STUDENT SERVICES** Academic or career counseling, daycare for children of students, employment services for current students, remedial services.

## Umpqua Community College

PO Box 967, Roseburg, OR 97470-0226
http://www.umpqua.edu/

**CONTACT** Dr. Blaine Nisson, President
**Telephone:** 541-440-4600

**GENERAL INFORMATION** Public Institution. Founded 1964. **Accreditation:** Regional (NCCU/NCCU). **Total program enrollment:** 1376. **Application fee:** $25.

**PROGRAM(S) OFFERED**
• **Automobile/Automotive Mechanics Technology/Technician** • **Business/Office Automation/Technology/Data Entry** • **Child Care and Support Services Management** • **Construction Trades, General** *2 students enrolled* • **Corrections** *1 student enrolled* • **Culinary Arts/Chef Training** *2 students enrolled* • **Dental Assisting/Assistant** *6 students enrolled* • **General Office Occupations and Clerical Services** *2 students enrolled* • **Heavy Equipment Maintenance Technology/Technician** • **Legal Assistant/Paralegal** *1 student enrolled* • **Licensed Practical/Vocational Nurse Training (LPN, LVN, Cert, Dipl, AAS)** • **Medical Insurance Coding Specialist/Coder** *9 students enrolled* • **Medical/Clinical Assistant** *23 students enrolled* • **Office Management and Supervision** • **Selling Skills and Sales Operations** • **Teacher Assistant/Aide** • **Welding Technology/Welder** *5 students enrolled*

**STUDENT SERVICES** Academic or career counseling, daycare for children of students, employment services for current students, placement services for program completers, remedial services.

## Valley Medical College

3886 Beverly Avenue NE, I-16, Salem, OR 97305
http://valleymedicalcollege.com/

**CONTACT** Van Brumbach, Director
**Telephone:** 503-363-9001

**GENERAL INFORMATION** Private Institution. **Total program enrollment:** 96. **Application fee:** $100.

**PROGRAM(S) OFFERED**
• **Licensed Practical/Vocational Nurse Training (LPN, LVN, Cert, Dipl, AAS)** *48 hrs./$15,148* • **Medical Administrative/Executive Assistant and Medical Secretary** *760 hrs./$7650* • **Medical Reception/Receptionist** *240 hrs./$2450* • **Medical/Clinical Assistant** *760 hrs./$7650* • **Phlebotomy/Phlebotomist** *237 hrs./$2020*

**STUDENT SERVICES** Academic or career counseling, employment services for current students, placement services for program completers.

## Warner Pacific College

2219 Southeast 68th Avenue, Portland, OR 97215-4099
http://www.warnerpacific.edu/

**CONTACT** Andrea Cook, PhD, Interim President
**Telephone:** 503-517-1000

**GENERAL INFORMATION** Private Institution (Affiliated with Church of God). Founded 1937. **Accreditation:** Regional (NCCU/NCCU). **Total program enrollment:** 942. **Application fee:** $50.

**PROGRAM(S) OFFERED**
• **American/United States Studies/Civilization**

**STUDENT SERVICES** Academic or career counseling, employment services for current students, placement services for program completers, remedial services.

## Western Culinary Institute

921 SW Morrison Street, Suite 400, Portland, OR 97205
http://www.wci.edu/

**CONTACT** Jon Alberts, President
**Telephone:** 503-223-2245

**GENERAL INFORMATION** Private Institution. Founded 1983. **Accreditation:** State accredited or approved. **Total program enrollment:** 822. **Application fee:** $50.

**PROGRAM(S) OFFERED**
• **Baking and Pastry Arts/Baker/Pastry Chef** *54 hrs./$22,000* • **Culinary Arts/Chef Training** *41 hrs./$16,000* • **Hospitality Administration/Management, Other** *92 hrs./$34,400*

**STUDENT SERVICES** Academic or career counseling, employment services for current students, placement services for program completers, remedial services.

## Western Oregon University

345 North Monmouth Avenue, Monmouth, OR 97361-1394
http://www.wou.edu/

**CONTACT** John P. Minahan, President
**Telephone:** 503-838-8000

**GENERAL INFORMATION** Public Institution. Founded 1856. **Accreditation:** Regional (NCCU/NCCU); music (NASM). **Total program enrollment:** 4214. **Application fee:** $50.

**STUDENT SERVICES** Academic or career counseling, daycare for children of students, employment services for current students, placement services for program completers, remedial services.

## Western States Chiropractic College

2900 Northeast 132nd Avenue, Portland, OR 97230-3099
http://www.wschiro.edu/

**CONTACT** Joseph Brimhall, DC, President
**Telephone:** 503-256-3180

**GENERAL INFORMATION** Private Institution. Founded 1904. **Accreditation:** Regional (NCCU/NCCU). **Total program enrollment:** 447. **Application fee:** $50.

**PROGRAM(S) OFFERED**
• **Massage Therapy/Therapeutic Massage** *9 students enrolled*

**STUDENT SERVICES** Academic or career counseling, employment services for current students, remedial services.

# SOUTH DAKOTA

## Dakota State University

820 North Washington, Madison, SD 57042-1799
http://www.dsu.edu/

**CONTACT** Douglas Knowlton, President
**Telephone:** 605-256-5111

**GENERAL INFORMATION** Public Institution. Founded 1881. **Accreditation:** Regional (NCA); health information administration (AHIMA); health information technology (AHIMA). **Total program enrollment:** 1165. **Application fee:** $20.

**PROGRAM(S) OFFERED**
• **Computer Programming/Programmer, General** • **Computer and Information Sciences, General** • **Design and Visual Communications, General** *1 student enrolled* • **Information Technology** • **Medical Insurance Coding Specialist/Coder** • **Non-Profit/Public/Organizational Management** • **Secondary Education and Teaching** *1 student enrolled* • **System Administration/Administrator** • **Teacher Education and Professional Development, Specific Levels and Methods, Other** *1 student enrolled* • **Web Page, Digital/Multimedia and Information Resources Design**

**STUDENT SERVICES** Academic or career counseling, employment services for current students, placement services for program completers, remedial services.

## Headlines Academy of Cosmetology

529 Main Street, Rapid City, SD 57701
http://headlinesacademy.com/

**CONTACT** Peggy Sproat, Owner
**Telephone:** 605-348-4247 Ext. 0

**GENERAL INFORMATION** Private Institution. **Total program enrollment:** 64.

**PROGRAM(S) OFFERED**
• **Aesthetician/Esthetician and Skin Care Specialist** *600 hrs./$6600* • **Cosmetology/Cosmetologist, General** *2100 hrs./$10,000* • **Massage Therapy/Therapeutic Massage** *600 hrs./$6400* • **Nail Technician/Specialist and Manicurist** *400 hrs./$3330*

**STUDENT SERVICES** Academic or career counseling, employment services for current students, placement services for program completers.

## Kilian Community College

300 East 6th Street, Sioux Falls, SD 57103
http://www.kilian.edu/

**CONTACT** Mark Millage, President
**Telephone:** 605-221-3100

**GENERAL INFORMATION** Private Institution. Founded 1977. **Accreditation:** Regional (NCA). **Total program enrollment:** 49. **Application fee:** $25.

**STUDENT SERVICES** Academic or career counseling, remedial services.

## Lake Area Technical Institute

230 11th Street, NE, Watertown, SD 57201
http://www.lakeareatech.edu/

**CONTACT** Debra Shephard, President
**Telephone:** 605-882-5284

**GENERAL INFORMATION** Public Institution. Founded 1964. **Accreditation:** Regional (NCA); dental assisting (ADA); medical assisting (AAMAE);

medical laboratory technology (NAACLS); physical therapy assisting (APTA). **Total program enrollment:** 1049. **Application fee:** $20.

**PROGRAM(S) OFFERED**

• **Aircraft Powerplant Technology/Technician** *5 students enrolled* • **Biology Technician/Biotechnology Laboratory Technician** *1 student enrolled* • **Cosmetology/Cosmetologist, General** *35 students enrolled* • **Dental Assisting/Assistant** *32 students enrolled* • **Human Services, General** *25 students enrolled* • **Licensed Practical/Vocational Nurse Training (LPN, LVN, Cert, Dipl, AAS)** *49 students enrolled* • **Medical/Clinical Assistant** *9 students enrolled* • **Welding Technology/Welder** *31 students enrolled*

**STUDENT SERVICES** Academic or career counseling, daycare for children of students, employment services for current students, placement services for program completers, remedial services.

## Mitchell Technical Institute

821 North Capital, Mitchell, SD 57301
http://www.mitchelltech.edu/

**CONTACT** Greg Von Wald, President
**Telephone:** 605-995-3023

**GENERAL INFORMATION** Public Institution. Founded 1968. **Accreditation:** Regional (NCA); medical assisting (AAMAE); medical laboratory technology (NAACLS). **Total program enrollment:** 615.

**PROGRAM(S) OFFERED**

• **Construction Trades, Other** *17 students enrolled* • **Culinary Arts/Chef Training** *11 students enrolled* • **Lineworker** *53 students enrolled* • **Plant Protection and Integrated Pest Management** *3 students enrolled*

**STUDENT SERVICES** Academic or career counseling, daycare for children of students, employment services for current students, placement services for program completers, remedial services.

## Mount Marty College

1105 West 8th Street, Yankton, SD 57078-3724
http://www.mtmc.edu/

**CONTACT** Dr. James Barry, President
**Telephone:** 800-658-4552

**GENERAL INFORMATION** Private Institution. Founded 1936. **Accreditation:** Regional (NCA). **Total program enrollment:** 738. **Application fee:** $35.

**PROGRAM(S) OFFERED**

• **Accounting** *2 students enrolled* • **Applied Horticulture/Horticultural Operations, General** *10 students enrolled* • **Business Administration and Management, General** *1 student enrolled*

**STUDENT SERVICES** Academic or career counseling, daycare for children of students, employment services for current students, placement services for program completers, remedial services.

## National American University

321 Kansas City Street, Rapid City, SD 57701
http://www.rapid.national.edu/

**CONTACT** Jerry Gallentine, University President/CEO
**Telephone:** 605-394-4800

**GENERAL INFORMATION** Private Institution. Founded 1941. **Accreditation:** Regional (NCA); medical assisting (AAMAE). **Total program enrollment:** 479. **Application fee:** $25.

**PROGRAM(S) OFFERED**

• **Computer and Information Sciences, General** *1 student enrolled* • **Veterinary/Animal Health Technology/Technician and Veterinary Assistant** *6 students enrolled*

**STUDENT SERVICES** Academic or career counseling, employment services for current students, placement services for program completers, remedial services.

## Northern State University

1200 South Jay Street, Aberdeen, SD 57401-7198
http://www.northern.edu/

**CONTACT** Laurie Nichols, Interim President
**Telephone:** 605-626-3011

**GENERAL INFORMATION** Public Institution. Founded 1901. **Accreditation:** Regional (NCA); music (NASM). **Total program enrollment:** 1760. **Application fee:** $20.

**PROGRAM(S) OFFERED**

• **Computer Programming, Other** • **Computer Software and Media Applications, Other** • **Computer and Information Sciences and Support Services, Other** • **Computer and Information Sciences, Other** *37 students enrolled* • **Computer/Information Technology Services Administration and Management, Other** *3 students enrolled* • **Data Modeling/Warehousing and Database Administration** *5 students enrolled* • **Educational Assessment, Evaluation, and Research, Other** • **Educational/Instructional Media Design** • **Web Page, Digital/Multimedia and Information Resources Design** *1 student enrolled* • **Web/Multimedia Management and Webmaster**

**STUDENT SERVICES** Academic or career counseling, daycare for children of students, employment services for current students, placement services for program completers, remedial services.

## Oglala Lakota College

490 Piya Wiconi Road, Kyle, SD 57752-0490
http://www.olc.edu/

**CONTACT** Thomas Shortbull, President
**Telephone:** 605-455-6000

**GENERAL INFORMATION** Public Institution. Founded 1970. **Accreditation:** Regional (NCA). **Total program enrollment:** 795. **Application fee:** $40.

**PROGRAM(S) OFFERED**

• **Accounting and Related Services, Other** • **American Indian/Native American Studies** *11 students enrolled* • **Business/Office Automation/Technology/Data Entry** *14 students enrolled* • **Carpentry/Carpenter** *1 student enrolled* • **Construction Trades, General** *6 students enrolled* • **Customer Service Management** • **Electrician** • **Entrepreneurship/Entrepreneurial Studies** *3 students enrolled* • **General Office Occupations and Clerical Services** • **Heating, Air Conditioning, Ventilation and Refrigeration Maintenance Technology/Technician (HAC, HACR, HVAC, HVACR)** • **Radio and Television** *1 student enrolled* • **Special Education and Teaching, General**

**STUDENT SERVICES** Remedial services.

## Presentation College

1500 North Main Street, Aberdeen, SD 57401-1299
http://www.presentation.edu/

**CONTACT** Lorraine Hale, President
**Telephone:** 605-225-1634

**GENERAL INFORMATION** Private Institution. Founded 1951. **Accreditation:** Regional (NCA); medical assisting (AAMAE); medical laboratory technology (NAACLS); radiologic technology: radiography (JRCERT); surgical technology (ARCST). **Total program enrollment:** 484. **Application fee:** $25.

**PROGRAM(S) OFFERED**

• **Medical Transcription/Transcriptionist** *9 students enrolled*

**STUDENT SERVICES** Academic or career counseling, employment services for current students, remedial services.

## Sinte Gleska University

101 Antelope Lake Circle, PO Box 105, Mission, SD 57555
http://www.sintegleska.edu/

**CONTACT** Lionel R. Bordeaux, President
**Telephone:** 605-856-8100

**GENERAL INFORMATION** Private Institution. Founded 1970. **Accreditation:** Regional (NCA). **Total program enrollment:** 431. **Application fee:** $20.

**PROGRAM(S) OFFERED**
**• Accounting Technology/Technician and Bookkeeping • Construction Trades, Other • Criminal Justice/Law Enforcement Administration • Criminal Justice/Police Science • Data Processing and Data Processing Technology/Technician** *1 student enrolled* **• Electrical, Electronic and Communications Engineering Technology/Technician** *9 students enrolled* **• General Office Occupations and Clerical Services** *5 students enrolled* **• Plumbing Technology/Plumber** *1 student enrolled*

**STUDENT SERVICES** Academic or career counseling, daycare for children of students, remedial services.

## Sisseton-Wahpeton Community College

Old Agency Box 689, Sisseton, SD 57262
http://www.swc.tc/

**CONTACT** Diana Canku, President
**Telephone:** 605-698-3966 Ext. 1100

**GENERAL INFORMATION** Public Institution. Founded 1979. **Accreditation:** Regional (NCA). **Total program enrollment:** 173.

**PROGRAM(S) OFFERED**
**• Computer Science • Construction Trades, General • Nursing, Other** *7 students enrolled*

**STUDENT SERVICES** Academic or career counseling, remedial services.

## South Dakota State University

PO Box 2201, Brookings, SD 57007
http://www.sdstate.edu/

**CONTACT** David L. Chicoine, President
**Telephone:** 605-688-4151

**GENERAL INFORMATION** Public Institution. Founded 1881. **Accreditation:** Regional (NCA); athletic training (JRCAT); counseling (ACA); home economics (AAFCS); journalism and mass communications (ACEJMC); music (NASM). **Total program enrollment:** 8775. **Application fee:** $20.

**PROGRAM(S) OFFERED**
**• Computer and Information Sciences, General** *2 students enrolled* **• Entrepreneurship/Entrepreneurial Studies** *1 student enrolled* **• Geography, Other** *1 student enrolled*

**STUDENT SERVICES** Academic or career counseling, employment services for current students, placement services for program completers, remedial services.

## Southeast Technical Institute

2320 N. Career Ave., Sioux Falls, SD 57107-1301
http://www.southeasttech.com/

**CONTACT** Jeff Holcomb, President
**Telephone:** 605-367-7624

**GENERAL INFORMATION** Public Institution. Founded 1968. **Accreditation:** Regional (NCA); cardiovascular technology (JRCECT); nuclear medicine technology (JRCNMT). **Total program enrollment:** 1660.

**PROGRAM(S) OFFERED**
**• Accounting Technology/Technician and Bookkeeping • Clinical/Medical Laboratory Science and Allied Professions, Other** *10 students enrolled* **• Computer and Information Sciences and Support Services, Other** *51 students enrolled* **• Executive Assistant/Executive Secretary** *9 students enrolled* **• Health Unit Coordinator/Ward Clerk • Heating, Air Conditioning and Refrigeration Technology/Technician (ACH/ACR/ACHR/HRAC/HVAC/AC Technology)** *10 students enrolled* **• Licensed Practical/Vocational Nurse Training (LPN, LVN, Cert, Dipl, AAS)** *47 students enrolled* **• Machine Shop Technology/Assistant** *9 students enrolled* **• Pharmacy Technician/Assistant** *10 students enrolled* **• Surgical Technology/Technologist** *29 students enrolled*

**STUDENT SERVICES** Academic or career counseling, daycare for children of students, employment services for current students, placement services for program completers, remedial services.

## Stewart School

604 N. West Avenue, Sioux Falls, SD 57104
http://www.stewartschool.com/

**CONTACT** Matthew Fiegen, Owner
**Telephone:** 605-336-2775 Ext. 3

**GENERAL INFORMATION** Private Institution. **Total program enrollment:** 146. **Application fee:** $50.

**PROGRAM(S) OFFERED**
**• Aesthetician/Esthetician and Skin Care Specialist** *600 hrs./$4439* **• Cosmetology/Cosmetologist, General** *2100 hrs./$9965* **• Nail Technician/Specialist and Manicurist** *400 hrs./$2408*

**STUDENT SERVICES** Academic or career counseling, placement services for program completers, remedial services.

## The University of South Dakota

414 East Clark Street, Vermillion, SD 57069-2390
http://www.usd.edu/

**CONTACT** Mr. James W. Abbott, President
**Telephone:** 605-677-5301

**GENERAL INFORMATION** Public Institution. Founded 1862. **Accreditation:** Regional (NCA); art and design (NASAD); audiology (ASHA); counseling (ACA); dental hygiene (ADA); dietetics: postbaccalaureate internship (ADtA/CAADE); journalism and mass communications (ACEJMC); music (NASM); speech-language pathology (ASHA); theater (NAST). **Total program enrollment:** 5544. **Application fee:** $20.

**PROGRAM(S) OFFERED**
**• Technical Theatre/Theatre Design and Technology**

**STUDENT SERVICES** Academic or career counseling, daycare for children of students, employment services for current students, placement services for program completers, remedial services.

## Western Dakota Technical Institute

800 Mickelson Drive, Rapid City, SD 57703
http://www.westerndakotatech.org/

**CONTACT** Dr. Craig Bailey, President
**Telephone:** 605-394-4034

**GENERAL INFORMATION** Public Institution. Founded 1968. **Accreditation:** Regional (NCA). **Total program enrollment:** 774. **Application fee:** $20.

**PROGRAM(S) OFFERED**
**• Clinical/Medical Laboratory Science and Allied Professions, Other** *12 students enrolled* **• General Office Occupations and Clerical Services • Health Unit Coordinator/Ward Clerk** *7 students enrolled* **• Licensed Practical/Vocational Nurse Training (LPN, LVN, Cert, Dipl, AAS)** *31 students enrolled* **• Medical Administrative/Executive Assistant and Medical Secretary** *4 students enrolled* **• Pharmacy Technician/Assistant** *39 students enrolled*

• **Rehabilitation and Therapeutic Professions, Other** *2 students enrolled* • **Security and Protective Services, Other** • **Surgical Technology/Technologist** *14 students enrolled* • **Welding Technology/Welder** *22 students enrolled*

**STUDENT SERVICES** Academic or career counseling, daycare for children of students, employment services for current students, placement services for program completers, remedial services.

# TENNESSEE

## American Baptist College of American Baptist Theological Seminary

1800 Baptist World Center Drive, Nashville, TN 37207
http://www.abcnash.edu/

**CONTACT** Forrest E. Harris, Sr., President
**Telephone:** 615-256-1463

**GENERAL INFORMATION** Private Institution. Founded 1924. **Accreditation:** State accredited or approved. **Total program enrollment:** 78. **Application fee:** $20.

## Aquinas College

4210 Harding Road, Nashville, TN 37205-2005
http://www.aquinascollege.edu/

**CONTACT** Sr. Mary Peter, OP, President
**Telephone:** 615-297-7545

**GENERAL INFORMATION** Private Institution. Founded 1961. **Accreditation:** Regional (SACS/CC). **Total program enrollment:** 330. **Application fee:** $25.

**STUDENT SERVICES** Academic or career counseling, remedial services.

## Arnold's Beauty School

1179 South Second Street, Milan, TN 38358

**CONTACT** Norma Arnold, Director
**Telephone:** 731-686-7351

**GENERAL INFORMATION** Private Institution. Founded 1941. **Total program enrollment:** 56.

**PROGRAM(S) OFFERED**
• **Cosmetology/Cosmetologist, General** *1500 hrs./$10,975*

**STUDENT SERVICES** Academic or career counseling, employment services for current students, placement services for program completers.

## The Art Institute of Tennessee–Nashville

100 CNA Drive, Nashville, TN 37214
http://www.artinstitutes.edu/nashville/

**CONTACT** Carol Menck, President
**Telephone:** 615-874-1067

**GENERAL INFORMATION** Private Institution. Founded 2006. **Total program enrollment:** 393. **Application fee:** $50.

**PROGRAM(S) OFFERED**
• **Culinary Arts/Chef Training** *8 students enrolled*

**STUDENT SERVICES** Academic or career counseling, employment services for current students, placement services for program completers, remedial services.

## Baptist College of Health Sciences

1003 Monroe Avenue, Memphis, TN 38104
http://www.bchs.edu/

**CONTACT** Bettysue McGarvey, DSN, President
**Telephone:** 901-572-2468

**GENERAL INFORMATION** Private Institution. Founded 1994. **Accreditation:** Regional (SACS/CC); diagnostic medical sonography (JRCEDMS); nuclear medicine technology (JRCNMT). **Total program enrollment:** 561. **Application fee:** $25.

**STUDENT SERVICES** Academic or career counseling, employment services for current students.

## Buchanan Beauty College

925 Sevier Street, Shelbyville, TN 37160

**CONTACT** Diana Buchanan, Director
**Telephone:** 931-684-4080

**GENERAL INFORMATION** Private Institution. **Total program enrollment:** 21. **Application fee:** $50.

**PROGRAM(S) OFFERED**
• **Aesthetician/Esthetician and Skin Care Specialist** *750 hrs./$4550*
• **Cosmetology and Related Personal Grooming Arts, Other** *300 hrs./$1650*
• **Cosmetology, Barber/Styling, and Nail Instructor** *300 hrs./$1800*
• **Cosmetology/Cosmetologist, General** *1500 hrs./$9725* • **Nail Technician/Specialist and Manicurist** *600 hrs./$3550*

**STUDENT SERVICES** Academic or career counseling.

## Career Beauty College

110 Waterloo Street, Lawrenceburg, TN 38464

**CONTACT** Karen Risner
**Telephone:** 931-766-9900

**GENERAL INFORMATION** Private Institution. **Total program enrollment:** 27. **Application fee:** $100.

**PROGRAM(S) OFFERED**
• **Cosmetology, Barber/Styling, and Nail Instructor** *100 hrs./$1750*
• **Cosmetology/Cosmetologist, General** *1500 hrs./$7000* • **Nail Technician/Specialist and Manicurist** *100 hrs./$2800*

## Chattanooga College–Medical, Dental and Technical Careers

3805 Brainerd Road, Chattanooga, TN 37411-3798
http://www.ecpconline.com/

**CONTACT** William G. Faour, Director
**Telephone:** 423-624-0077

**GENERAL INFORMATION** Private Institution. **Accreditation:** State accredited or approved. **Total program enrollment:** 189. **Application fee:** $75.

*Chattanooga College–Medical, Dental and Technical Careers (continued)*

**PROGRAM(S) OFFERED**

• **Data Processing and Data Processing Technology/Technician** *5 students enrolled* • **Health Information/Medical Records Technology/Technician** *51 students enrolled*

**STUDENT SERVICES** Academic or career counseling, employment services for current students, placement services for program completers.

## Chattanooga State Technical Community College

4501 Amnicola Highway, Chattanooga, TN 37406-1097
http://www.chattanoogastate.edu/

**CONTACT** James Catanzaro, President
**Telephone:** 423-697-4400

**GENERAL INFORMATION** Public Institution. Founded 1965. **Accreditation:** Regional (SACS/CC); dental assisting (ADA); dental hygiene (ADA); engineering technology (ABET/TAC); health information technology (AHIMA); physical therapy assisting (APTA). **Total program enrollment:** 3875. **Application fee:** $15.

**PROGRAM(S) OFFERED**

• **Administrative Assistant and Secretarial Science, General** • **Business/Office Automation/Technology/Data Entry** *13 students enrolled* • **Diagnostic Medical Sonography/Sonographer and Ultrasound Technician** *14 students enrolled* • **Drafting and Design Technology/Technician, General** *3 students enrolled* • **Engineering Technology, General** • **Management Information Systems, General** *2 students enrolled* • **Medical Radiologic Technology/Science—Radiation Therapist** *15 students enrolled* • **Nuclear Medical Technology/Technologist** *36 students enrolled* • **Pharmacy Technician/Assistant** *21 students enrolled*

**STUDENT SERVICES** Academic or career counseling, daycare for children of students, employment services for current students, placement services for program completers, remedial services.

## Cleveland State Community College

PO Box 3570, Cleveland, TN 37320-3570
http://www.clevelandstatecc.edu/

**CONTACT** Carl Hite, President
**Telephone:** 423-472-7141

**GENERAL INFORMATION** Public Institution. Founded 1967. **Accreditation:** Regional (SACS/CC); medical assisting (AAMAE). **Total program enrollment:** 1646. **Application fee:** $10.

**PROGRAM(S) OFFERED**

• **Administrative Assistant and Secretarial Science, General** *21 students enrolled* • **Criminal Justice/Police Science** *6 students enrolled* • **Emergency Medical Technology/Technician (EMT Paramedic)** *2 students enrolled*

**STUDENT SERVICES** Academic or career counseling, employment services for current students, placement services for program completers, remedial services.

## Columbia State Community College

PO Box 1315, Columbia, TN 38402-1315
http://www.columbiastate.edu/

**CONTACT** Janet F. Smith, President
**Telephone:** 931-540-2722

**GENERAL INFORMATION** Public Institution. Founded 1966. **Accreditation:** Regional (SACS/CC); emergency medical services (JRCEMTP); radiologic technology: radiography (JRCERT). **Total program enrollment:** 2342. **Application fee:** $10.

**PROGRAM(S) OFFERED**

• **Business Administration and Management, General** *17 students enrolled* • **Child Development** *10 students enrolled* • **Criminal Justice/Police Science** • **Emergency Medical Technology/Technician (EMT Paramedic)** *3 students enrolled* • **Music, Other** *1 student enrolled*

**STUDENT SERVICES** Academic or career counseling, employment services for current students, remedial services.

## Concorde Career College

5100 Poplar Avenue, Suite 132, Memphis, TN 38137
http://www.concordecareercolleges.com/

**CONTACT** Tommy Stewart, Campus President
**Telephone:** 901-761-9494

**GENERAL INFORMATION** Private Institution. Founded 1969. **Accreditation:** State accredited or approved. **Total program enrollment:** 1147.

**PROGRAM(S) OFFERED**

• **Dental Assisting/Assistant** *800 hrs./$12,201* • **Home Health Aide/Home Attendant** *124 students enrolled* • **Massage Therapy/Therapeutic Massage** *37 students enrolled* • **Medical Office Management/Administration** *108 students enrolled* • **Medical/Clinical Assistant** *720 hrs./$12,923* • **Nurse/Nursing Assistant/Aide and Patient Care Assistant** *488 hrs./$5235* • **Office Management and Supervision** *720 hrs./$11,471* • **Pharmacy Technician/Assistant** *47 students enrolled* • **Respiratory Care Therapy/Therapist** *1605 hrs./$23,013* • **Respiratory Therapy Technician/Assistant** *29 students enrolled* • **Surgical Technology/Technologist** *1220 hrs./$21,268*

**STUDENT SERVICES** Academic or career counseling, employment services for current students, placement services for program completers, remedial services.

## Crichton College

255 North Highland Street, Memphis, TN 38111
http://www.crichton.edu/

**CONTACT** Larry Lloyd, President
**Telephone:** 901-320-9700

**GENERAL INFORMATION** Private Institution. Founded 1941. **Accreditation:** Regional (SACS/CC). **Total program enrollment:** 762. **Application fee:** $25.

**PROGRAM(S) OFFERED**

• **Bible/Biblical Studies**

**STUDENT SERVICES** Academic or career counseling, employment services for current students, remedial services.

## Draughons Junior College

1860 Wilma Rudolph Boulevard, Clarksville, TN 37040
http://www.draughons.edu/

**CONTACT** Amye Melton, Campus Director
**Telephone:** 931-552-7600

**GENERAL INFORMATION** Private Institution. Founded 1987. **Accreditation:** State accredited or approved. **Total program enrollment:** 369.

**PROGRAM(S) OFFERED**

• **Accounting Technology/Technician and Bookkeeping** • **Accounting** • **Business Administration, Management and Operations, Other** • **Computer and Information Sciences, General** • **Criminal Justice/Law Enforcement Administration** • **Dental Assisting/Assistant** • **Health Information/Medical Records Administration/Administrator** • **Medical Insurance Coding Specialist/Coder** • **Medical/Clinical Assistant** *5 students enrolled* • **Pharmacy, Pharmaceutical Sciences, and Administration, Other**

**STUDENT SERVICES** Academic or career counseling, employment services for current students, placement services for program completers, remedial services.

## Draughons Junior College

1237 Commerce Park, Murfreesboro, TN 37130
http://www.draughons.edu/

**CONTACT** Mark A. Gabis, President
**Telephone:** 615-217-9347

**GENERAL INFORMATION** Private Institution. **Total program enrollment:** 370.

**PROGRAM(S) OFFERED**
• **Accounting** *1 student enrolled* • **Business Administration and Management, General** *1 student enrolled* • **Corrections and Criminal Justice, Other** • **Dental Assisting/Assistant** • **Health Information/Medical Records Administration/ Administrator** *1 student enrolled* • **Medical/Clinical Assistant** *4 students enrolled* • **Pharmacy Technician/Assistant**

**STUDENT SERVICES** Academic or career counseling, employment services for current students, placement services for program completers.

## Draughons Junior College

340 Plus Park Boulevard, Nashville, TN 37217
http://www.draughons.edu/

**CONTACT** Mark A. Gabis, President
**Telephone:** 615-361-7555

**GENERAL INFORMATION** Private Institution. Founded 1884. **Accreditation:** State accredited or approved. **Total program enrollment:** 266.

**PROGRAM(S) OFFERED**
• **Accounting** • **Business Administration, Management and Operations, Other** *1 student enrolled* • **Criminal Justice/Safety Studies** • **Dental Assisting/ Assistant** • **E-Commerce/Electronic Commerce** *1 student enrolled* • **Health Information/Medical Records Technology/Technician** • **Massage Therapy/ Therapeutic Massage** • **Medical Office Management/Administration** • **Medical/Clinical Assistant** • **Pharmacy Technician/Assistant**

**STUDENT SERVICES** Academic or career counseling, employment services for current students, placement services for program completers, remedial services.

## Dudley Nwani–The School

3532 W. Hamilton Road, Nashville, TN 37218
http://1wcu.org/

**CONTACT** Uchendi Nwani, CEO
**Telephone:** 615-496-3977

**GENERAL INFORMATION** Private Institution. **Total program enrollment:** 126. **Application fee:** $100.

**PROGRAM(S) OFFERED**
• **Barbering/Barber** *38 students enrolled* • **Cosmetology, Barber/Styling, and Nail Instructor** *1500 hrs./$12,900*

**STUDENT SERVICES** Placement services for program completers.

## Dyersburg State Community College

1510 Lake Road, Dyersburg, TN 38024
http://www.dscc.edu/

**CONTACT** Karen Bowyer, President
**Telephone:** 731-286-3200

**GENERAL INFORMATION** Public Institution. Founded 1969. **Accreditation:** Regional (SACS/CC). **Total program enrollment:** 1298. **Application fee:** $10.

**PROGRAM(S) OFFERED**
• **Child Development** *2 students enrolled* • **Health Information/Medical Records Technology/Technician** *4 students enrolled* • **Medical Transcription/ Transcriptionist** *3 students enrolled*

**STUDENT SERVICES** Academic or career counseling, employment services for current students, placement services for program completers, remedial services.

## Elite College of Cosmetology

459 N. Main Street, Lexington, TN 38351

**CONTACT** Melda Mills, Owner
**Telephone:** 731-968-5400

**GENERAL INFORMATION** Private Institution. **Total program enrollment:** 47.

**PROGRAM(S) OFFERED**
• **Cosmetology and Related Personal Grooming Arts, Other** *1500 hrs./$11,775* • **Nail Technician/Specialist and Manicurist** *600 hrs./$4450*

**STUDENT SERVICES** Placement services for program completers.

## Fayettville Beauty School

Southwest Public Square, PO Box 135, Fayetteville, TN 37334-0135
http://www.fayettevillebeautyschool.com/

**CONTACT** Rufus Hereford, Owner
**Telephone:** 931-433-1305

**GENERAL INFORMATION** Private Institution. Founded 1957. **Total program enrollment:** 9. **Application fee:** $100.

**PROGRAM(S) OFFERED**
• **Aesthetician/Esthetician and Skin Care Specialist** *750 hrs./$4665* • **Cosmetology, Barber/Styling, and Nail Instructor** *450 hrs./$2799* • **Cosmetology/Cosmetologist, General** *1500 hrs./$10,245* • **Nail Technician/ Specialist and Manicurist** *750 hrs./$4665*

**STUDENT SERVICES** Academic or career counseling, placement services for program completers.

## Franklin Academy

303 Keith Street Village Center, Cleveland, TN 37311
http://www.franklinacademy.edu/

**CONTACT** Patty Patterson, Executive Director
**Telephone:** 423-476-3742

**GENERAL INFORMATION** Private Institution. **Total program enrollment:** 30. **Application fee:** $25.

**PROGRAM(S) OFFERED**
• **Aesthetician/Esthetician and Skin Care Specialist** *$3850* • **Cosmetology/ Cosmetologist, General** *12 hrs./$8195* • **Nail Technician/Specialist and Manicurist** *$3100*

**STUDENT SERVICES** Academic or career counseling, placement services for program completers.

## High-Tech Institute

5865 Shelby Oaks Circle, Suite 100, Memphis, TN 38134
http://www.high-techinstitute.com/

**CONTACT** Catherine McClarin, Campus President
**Telephone:** 901-432-3800

**GENERAL INFORMATION** Private Institution. Founded 2003. **Accreditation:** State accredited or approved. **Total program enrollment:** 1014. **Application fee:** $50.

*High-Tech Institute (continued)*

**PROGRAM(S) OFFERED**

• **Massage Therapy/Therapeutic Massage** *820 hrs./$10,612* • **Medical Insurance Specialist/Medical Biller** *720 hrs./$10,831* • **Medical Radiologic Technology/Science—Radiation Therapist** *810 hrs./$12,834* • **Medical/Clinical Assistant** *1236 hrs./$21,350* • **Pharmacy Technician/Assistant** *720 hrs./$10,991* • **Surgical Technology/Technologist** *1 student enrolled*

**STUDENT SERVICES** Placement services for program completers.

## High-Tech Institute

560 Royal Parkway, Nashville, TN 37214
http://www.high-techinstitute.com/

**CONTACT** Michelle Bonocore, Operations Manager
**Telephone:** 615-232-3700

**GENERAL INFORMATION** Private Institution. Founded 1999. **Accreditation:** State accredited or approved. **Total program enrollment:** 605. **Application fee:** $50.

**PROGRAM(S) OFFERED**

• **Dental Assisting/Assistant** *720 hrs./$10,585* • **Massage Therapy/Therapeutic Massage** *820 hrs./$11,250* • **Medical Insurance Specialist/Medical Biller** *720 hrs./$10,831* • **Medical Radiologic Technology/Science—Radiation Therapist** *810 hrs./$12,834* • **Medical/Clinical Assistant** *1236 hrs./$21,350* • **Radiologic Technology/Science—Radiographer** *9 students enrolled* • **Surgical Technology/Technologist**

**STUDENT SERVICES** Placement services for program completers.

## Institute of Hair Design

205 Enterprise Drive, Adamsville, TN 38310
http://ihd4me.com/

**CONTACT** Cherry Johnson, Director
**Telephone:** 731-632-9533

**GENERAL INFORMATION** Private Institution. **Total program enrollment:** 53. **Application fee:** $100.

**PROGRAM(S) OFFERED**

• **Cosmetology/Cosmetologist, General** *1500 hrs./$11,950*

**STUDENT SERVICES** Placement services for program completers.

## Jackson State Community College

2046 North Parkway, Jackson, TN 38301-3797
http://www.jscc.edu/

**CONTACT** Dr. Bruce Blanding, President
**Telephone:** 731-424-3520

**GENERAL INFORMATION** Public Institution. Founded 1967. **Accreditation:** Regional (SACS/CC); emergency medical services (JRCEMTP); medical laboratory technology (NAACLS); physical therapy assisting (APTA); radiologic technology: radiography (JRCERT). **Total program enrollment:** 2151. **Application fee:** $10.

**PROGRAM(S) OFFERED**

• **Applied Horticulture/Horticultural Operations, General** • **Emergency Medical Technology/Technician (EMT Paramedic)** *12 students enrolled* • **Human Development, Family Studies, and Related Services, Other** *3 students enrolled* • **Manufacturing Technology/Technician**

**STUDENT SERVICES** Academic or career counseling, employment services for current students, placement services for program completers, remedial services.

## Jenny Lea Academy of Cosmetology and Aesthetics

222 E. Unaka Avenue, Johnson City, TN 37601

**CONTACT** Virginia Lewis, CEO
**Telephone:** 423-926-9095

**GENERAL INFORMATION** Private Institution. **Total program enrollment:** 87. **Application fee:** $100.

**PROGRAM(S) OFFERED**

• **Aesthetician/Esthetician and Skin Care Specialist** *750 hrs./$7095* • **Cosmetology, Barber/Styling, and Nail Instructor** *300 hrs./$2500* • **Cosmetology/Cosmetologist, General** *1500 hrs./$10,295* • **Nail Technician/Specialist and Manicurist** *650 hrs./$6095*

**STUDENT SERVICES** Academic or career counseling.

## John A. Gupton College

1616 Church Street, Nashville, TN 37203-2920
http://www.guptoncollege.edu/

**CONTACT** B. Steven Spann, President
**Telephone:** 615-327-3927

**GENERAL INFORMATION** Private Institution. Founded 1946. **Accreditation:** Regional (SACS/CC); funeral service (ABFSE). **Total program enrollment:** 64. **Application fee:** $20.

**PROGRAM(S) OFFERED**

• **Funeral Service and Mortuary Science, General** *11 students enrolled*

**STUDENT SERVICES** Academic or career counseling.

## Jon Nave University of Unisex Cosmetology

5128 Charlotte Avenue, Nashville, TN 37209
http://www.creativedesignsba.com/

**CONTACT** Dale Jones, Owner
**Telephone:** 801-302-8801 Ext. 1021

**GENERAL INFORMATION** Private Institution. **Total program enrollment:** 253. **Application fee:** $100.

**PROGRAM(S) OFFERED**

• **Aesthetician/Esthetician and Skin Care Specialist** *750 hrs./$7800* • **Cosmetology, Barber/Styling, and Nail Instructor** *300 hrs./$2200* • **Cosmetology/Cosmetologist, General** *1500 hrs./$15,900*

**STUDENT SERVICES** Academic or career counseling, employment services for current students, placement services for program completers.

## Kaplan Career Institute–Nashville Campus

750 Envious Lane, Nashville, TN 37217
http://www.kci-nashville.com

**CONTACT** Adam Butler, Executive Director
**Telephone:** 615-279-8300

**GENERAL INFORMATION** Private Institution. Founded 1981. **Accreditation:** State accredited or approved. **Total program enrollment:** 669.

**PROGRAM(S) OFFERED**

• **Criminal Justice/Law Enforcement Administration** *96 hrs./$29,500* • **Dental Assisting/Assistant** *55 hrs./$13,100* • **Legal Assistant/Paralegal** *44 hrs./$13,000* • **Massage Therapy/Therapeutic Massage** • **Medical Office Assistant/Specialist** *33 students enrolled* • **Medical Office Management/Administration** *50 hrs./$14,950* • **Medical/Clinical Assistant** *720 hrs./$14,330*

**STUDENT SERVICES** Academic or career counseling, employment services for current students, placement services for program completers.

## Last Minute Cuts School of Barbering and Cosmetology

2195 S. Third Street, Memphis, TN 38109
http://www.lastminutecuts.com/

**CONTACT** Quannah Harris, Director of Administrations
**Telephone:** 901-774-9699

**GENERAL INFORMATION** Private Institution.

**PROGRAM(S) OFFERED**
• **Barbering/Barber** *1500 hrs./$11,752* • **Cosmetology, Barber/Styling, and Nail Instructor** *1 student enrolled* • **Cosmetology/Cosmetologist, General** *1 student enrolled* • **Hair Styling/Stylist and Hair Design** • **Nail Technician/Specialist and Manicurist**

## McCollum and Ross–the Hair School

1433 Hollywood, Jackson, TN 38301
http://leadersinbeautyed.com/

**CONTACT** Ruby Klyce, Executive Director
**Telephone:** 901-323-6100

**GENERAL INFORMATION** Private Institution. **Total program enrollment:** 58.

**PROGRAM(S) OFFERED**
• **Cosmetology/Cosmetologist, General** *1500 hrs./$14,325*

**STUDENT SERVICES** Placement services for program completers.

## MedVance Institute

1025 Highway 111, Cookeville, TN 38501
http://www.medvance.edu/

**CONTACT** John Hopkins, CEO
**Telephone:** 931-526-3660

**GENERAL INFORMATION** Private Institution. Founded 1970. **Accreditation:** Medical laboratory technology (NAACLS); state accredited or approved. **Total program enrollment:** 377. **Application fee:** $25.

**PROGRAM(S) OFFERED**
• **Clinical/Medical Laboratory Technician** *99 hrs./$23,995* • **Health Information/Medical Records Technology/Technician** *67 hrs./$12,995* • **Medical Office Assistant/Specialist** *23 students enrolled* • **Medical Radiologic Technology/Science—Radiation Therapist** *130 hrs./$31,895* • **Medical/Clinical Assistant** *49 hrs./$9995* • **Pharmacy Technician/Assistant** *49 hrs./$10,000* • **Surgical Technology/Technologist** *98 hrs./$19,995*

**STUDENT SERVICES** Employment services for current students, placement services for program completers.

## MedVance Institute–Nashville

2400 Parman Place, Suite 3, Nashville, TN 37203
http://www.medvance.edu

**CONTACT** John Hopkins, CEO
**Telephone:** 615-320-5917

**GENERAL INFORMATION** Private Institution. **Total program enrollment:** 404. **Application fee:** $25.

**PROGRAM(S) OFFERED**
• **Biomedical Technology/Technician** *120 hrs./$25,500* • **Health Information/Medical Records Technology/Technician** *67 hrs./$13,500* • **Health Professions and Related Clinical Sciences, Other** *36 hrs./$9900* • **Medical Radiologic Technology/Science—Radiation Therapist** *130 hrs./$34,500* • **Medical/Clinical Assistant** *49 hrs./$12,500* • **Pharmacy Technician/Assistant** *16 students enrolled* • **Surgical Technology/Technologist** *98 hrs./$21,500*

**STUDENT SERVICES** Employment services for current students, placement services for program completers.

## Memphis Institute of Barbering

1309 Jackson Avenue, Memphis, TN 38107

**GENERAL INFORMATION** Private Institution. **Total program enrollment:** 61. **Application fee:** $100.

**PROGRAM(S) OFFERED**
• **Barbering/Barber** *1500 hrs./$9525*

## Middle Tennessee School of Cosmetology

868 East Tenth Street, Cookeville, TN 38501
http://www.midtncosmo.com/

**CONTACT** Richard Bundy, President
**Telephone:** 931-526-4515

**GENERAL INFORMATION** Private Institution. Founded 1950. **Total program enrollment:** 106. **Application fee:** $100.

**PROGRAM(S) OFFERED**
• **Aesthetician/Esthetician and Skin Care Specialist** *900 hrs./$8955*
• **Cosmetology, Barber/Styling, and Nail Instructor** *300 hrs./$1905*
• **Cosmetology/Cosmetologist, General** *1500 hrs./$11,795* • **Nail Technician/Specialist and Manicurist** *600 hrs./$5370*

**STUDENT SERVICES** Academic or career counseling, placement services for program completers.

## Miller-Motte Technical College

6020 Shallowford Road, Suite 100, Chattanooga, TN 37421
http://www.miller-motte.com/

**CONTACT** Alan Sussna, President
**Telephone:** 423-510-9675 Ext. 200

**GENERAL INFORMATION** Private Institution. **Total program enrollment:** 436. **Application fee:** $50.

**PROGRAM(S) OFFERED**
• **Cosmetology and Related Personal Grooming Arts, Other** *34 students enrolled* • **Cosmetology/Cosmetologist, General** *7 students enrolled* • **Data Entry/Microcomputer Applications, Other** *1 student enrolled* • **Dental Assisting/Assistant** • **Health Professions and Related Clinical Sciences, Other** *8 students enrolled* • **Massage Therapy/Therapeutic Massage** *31 students enrolled*

**STUDENT SERVICES** Academic or career counseling, employment services for current students, placement services for program completers, remedial services.

## Miller-Motte Technical College

1820 Business Park Drive, Clarksville, TN 37040
http://www.miller-motte.com/

**CONTACT** Gina Castleberry, Director
**Telephone:** 931-553-0071

**GENERAL INFORMATION** Private Institution. Founded 1916. **Accreditation:** Medical assisting (AAMAE); state accredited or approved. **Total program enrollment:** 405.

**PROGRAM(S) OFFERED**
• **Aesthetician/Esthetician and Skin Care Specialist** *20 students enrolled*
• **Computer and Information Sciences and Support Services, Other**
• **Cosmetology and Related Personal Grooming Arts, Other** *10 students enrolled* • **Massage Therapy/Therapeutic Massage** *11 students enrolled* • **Medical Office Assistant/Specialist** *4 students enrolled* • **Phlebotomy/Phlebotomist** *3 students enrolled*

**STUDENT SERVICES** Academic or career counseling, employment services for current students, placement services for program completers, remedial services.

## Miller-Motte Technical College

801 Space Park North, Goodlettsville, TN 37072
http://www.miller-motte.com/

**CONTACT** Kevin Suhr, Campus Administrator
**Telephone:** 615-859-8090

**GENERAL INFORMATION** Private Institution. **Total program enrollment:** 179. **Application fee:** $35.

**PROGRAM(S) OFFERED**
• **Electrician** *24 students enrolled* • **Heating, Air Conditioning and Refrigeration Technology/Technician (ACH/ACR/ACHR/HRAC/HVAC/AC Technology)** *39 students enrolled* • **Welding Technology/Welder** *10 students enrolled*

**STUDENT SERVICES** Academic or career counseling, employment services for current students, placement services for program completers.

## Motlow State Community College

PO Box 8500, Lynchburg, TN 37352-8500
http://www.mscc.cc.tn.us/

**CONTACT** MaryLou Apple, President
**Telephone:** 931-393-1500

**GENERAL INFORMATION** Public Institution. Founded 1969. **Accreditation:** Regional (SACS/CC). **Total program enrollment:** 2322. **Application fee:** $10.

**STUDENT SERVICES** Academic or career counseling, employment services for current students, placement services for program completers, remedial services.

## Mr. Wayne's School of Unisex Hair Design

170 South Willow Avenue, Cookeville, TN 38501
http://www.misterwaynes.com/

**CONTACT** Charles W. Fletcher, Owner
**Telephone:** 931-526-1478

**GENERAL INFORMATION** Private Institution. **Total program enrollment:** 18.

**PROGRAM(S) OFFERED**
• **Barbering/Barber** *1500 hrs./$10,000*

**STUDENT SERVICES** Academic or career counseling, placement services for program completers.

## Nashville Auto Diesel College

1524 Gallatin Road, Nashville, TN 37206-3298
http://www.nadcedu.com/

**CONTACT** Lisa Bacon, President
**Telephone:** 800-228-6232

**GENERAL INFORMATION** Private Institution. Founded 1919. **Accreditation:** State accredited or approved. **Total program enrollment:** 2380. **Application fee:** $100.

**PROGRAM(S) OFFERED**
• **Alternative Fuel Vehicle Technology/Technician** *156 students enrolled* • **Autobody/Collision and Repair Technology/Technician** *66 hrs./$23,500* • **Automobile/Automotive Mechanics Technology/Technician** *89 hrs./$28,300* • **Diesel Mechanics Technology/Technician** *79 hrs./$27,200* • **Engine Machinist** *17 students enrolled* • **Heavy Equipment Maintenance Technology/Technician** *7 students enrolled* • **Mechanic and Repair Technologies/Technicians, Other** *100 students enrolled* • **Medium/Heavy Vehicle and Truck Technology/Technician** *6 students enrolled* • **Vehicle Maintenance and Repair Technologies, Other** *80 hrs./$29,800*

**STUDENT SERVICES** Academic or career counseling, employment services for current students, placement services for program completers.

## Nashville College of Medical Careers

1556 Crestview Drive, Madison, TN 37115
http://www.nashvillecollege.com/

**CONTACT** A. Malek, President
**Telephone:** 615-868-2963

**GENERAL INFORMATION** Private Institution. **Total program enrollment:** 239. **Application fee:** $10.

**PROGRAM(S) OFFERED**
• **Medical Administrative/Executive Assistant and Medical Secretary** *44 students enrolled* • **Medical Insurance Coding Specialist/Coder** *36 hrs./$11,500* • **Medical Office Assistant/Specialist** *36 hrs./$11,500* • **Medical/Clinical Assistant** *36 hrs./$12,000*

**STUDENT SERVICES** Academic or career counseling, placement services for program completers.

## Nashville State Technical Community College

120 White Bridge Road, Nashville, TN 37209-4515
http://www.nscc.edu/

**CONTACT** George H. Van Allen, President
**Telephone:** 615-353-3333

**GENERAL INFORMATION** Public Institution. Founded 1970. **Accreditation:** Regional (SACS/CC); engineering technology (ABET/TAC). **Total program enrollment:** 2660. **Application fee:** $5.

**PROGRAM(S) OFFERED**
• **Child Development** *36 students enrolled* • **Culinary Arts/Chef Training** • **Drafting and Design Technology/Technician, General** *9 students enrolled* • **Electrician** *6 students enrolled* • **Entrepreneurship/Entrepreneurial Studies** *1 student enrolled* • **Landscaping and Groundskeeping** *7 students enrolled* • **Machine Tool Technology/Machinist** • **Music, Other** *22 students enrolled* • **Photography** *6 students enrolled* • **Robotics Technology/Technician** • **Surgical Technology/Technologist** *33 students enrolled* • **Technical and Business Writing** *1 student enrolled* • **Web Page, Digital/Multimedia and Information Resources Design** *2 students enrolled*

**STUDENT SERVICES** Academic or career counseling, employment services for current students, placement services for program completers, remedial services.

## National College

5042 Linbar Drive, Suite 200, Nashville, TN 37211
http://www.national-college.edu/

**CONTACT** Frank Longaker, President
**Telephone:** 615-333-3344

**GENERAL INFORMATION** Private Institution. Founded 1915. **Accreditation:** Medical assisting (AAMAE); state accredited or approved. **Total program enrollment:** 1021. **Application fee:** $30.

**PROGRAM(S) OFFERED**
• **Accounting Technology/Technician and Bookkeeping** *3 students enrolled* • **Business Administration and Management, General** • **Business/Commerce, General** *7 students enrolled* • **Computer and Information Sciences and Support Services, Other** *1 student enrolled* • **Data Entry/Microcomputer Applications, General** *2 students enrolled* • **Health and Medical Administrative Services, Other** *24 students enrolled* • **Hospitality Administration/Management, General** • **Information Technology** • **Medical Office Assistant/Specialist** • **Medical Transcription/Transcriptionist** • **Pharmacy Technician/Assistant** *14 students enrolled*

**STUDENT SERVICES** Academic or career counseling, employment services for current students, placement services for program completers, remedial services.

## Nave Cosmetology Academy

112 E. James Campbell Boulevard, Columbia, TN 38401

**CONTACT** Joyce Meadows, Owner
**Telephone:** 931-388-7717

**GENERAL INFORMATION** Private Institution. **Total program enrollment:** 143.

**PROGRAM(S) OFFERED**
• **Aesthetician/Esthetician and Skin Care Specialist** *750 hrs./$8000* • **Cosmetology/Cosmetologist, General** *1500 hrs./$12,800* • **Nail Technician/Specialist and Manicurist** *600 hrs./$4850*

**STUDENT SERVICES** Academic or career counseling, employment services for current students, placement services for program completers.

## New Concepts School of Cosmetology

1412 South Lee Highway, Cleveland, TN 37311

**CONTACT** Linda Luster, Owner
**Telephone:** 423-478-3231

**GENERAL INFORMATION** Private Institution. **Total program enrollment:** 16. **Application fee:** $50.

**PROGRAM(S) OFFERED**
• **Aesthetician/Esthetician and Skin Care Specialist** *5 students enrolled* • **Cosmetology, Barber/Styling, and Nail Instructor** • **Cosmetology/Cosmetologist, General** *1500 hrs./$8400* • **Nail Technician/Specialist and Manicurist** *1 student enrolled*

**STUDENT SERVICES** Placement services for program completers.

## New Directions Hair Academy

7106 Moores Lane, Brentwood, TN 37027
http://leadersinbeautyed.com/

**CONTACT** Ruby Klyce, Executive Director
**Telephone:** 901-323-6100

**GENERAL INFORMATION** Private Institution. **Total program enrollment:** 69.

**PROGRAM(S) OFFERED**
• **Aesthetician/Esthetician and Skin Care Specialist** *750 hrs./$8350* • **Cosmetology/Cosmetologist, General** *1500 hrs./$15,175* • **Nail Technician/Specialist and Manicurist** *600 hrs./$6770*

**STUDENT SERVICES** Placement services for program completers.

## New Directions Hair Academy

568 Colonial Road, Memphis, TN 38111
http://leadersinbeautyed.com/

**CONTACT** Ruby Klyce, Executive Director
**Telephone:** 901-323-6100

**GENERAL INFORMATION** Private Institution. **Total program enrollment:** 96.

**PROGRAM(S) OFFERED**
• **Aesthetician/Esthetician and Skin Care Specialist** *750 hrs./$8350* • **Cosmetology and Related Personal Grooming Arts, Other** *62 students enrolled* • **Cosmetology, Barber/Styling, and Nail Instructor** *1500 hrs./$15,175* • **Cosmetology/Cosmetologist, General** *68 students enrolled* • **Nail Technician/Specialist and Manicurist** *600 hrs./$6770*

**STUDENT SERVICES** Placement services for program completers.

## New Wave Hair Academy

3641 Brainerd Road, Chattanooga, TN 37411
http://leadersinbeautyed.com/

**CONTACT** Ruby Klyce, Executive Director
**Telephone:** 901-323-2100

**GENERAL INFORMATION** Private Institution. **Total program enrollment:** 116.

**PROGRAM(S) OFFERED**
• **Cosmetology/Cosmetologist, General** *1500 hrs./$14,325*

**STUDENT SERVICES** Placement services for program completers.

## New Wave Hair Academy

804 South Highland, Memphis, TN 38111
http://leadersinbeautyed.com/

**CONTACT** Ruby Klyce, Executive Director
**Telephone:** 901-323-2100

**GENERAL INFORMATION** Private Institution. **Total program enrollment:** 150.

**PROGRAM(S) OFFERED**
• **Cosmetology/Cosmetologist, General** *1500 hrs./$14,325*

**STUDENT SERVICES** Placement services for program completers.

## North Central Institute

168 Jack Miller Boulevard, Clarksville, TN 37042
http://www.nci.edu/

**CONTACT** John D. McCurdy, CEO
**Telephone:** 931-431-9700

**GENERAL INFORMATION** Private Institution. Founded 1988. **Accreditation:** State accredited or approved. **Total program enrollment:** 46. **Application fee:** $35.

**PROGRAM(S) OFFERED**
• **Aircraft Powerplant Technology/Technician** *88 hrs./$1577* • **Airframe Mechanics and Aircraft Maintenance Technology/Technician** *1960 hrs./$14,590* • **Avionics Maintenance Technology/Technician** *62 hrs./$5042*

**STUDENT SERVICES** Academic or career counseling, employment services for current students, placement services for program completers.

## Northeast State Technical Community College

PO Box 246, Blountville, TN 37617-0246
http://www.northeaststate.edu/

**CONTACT** William W. Locke, President
**Telephone:** 423-323-3191

**GENERAL INFORMATION** Public Institution. Founded 1966. **Accreditation:** Regional (SACS/CC); dental assisting (ADA); dental laboratory technology (ADA); medical assisting (AAMAE); medical laboratory technology (NAACLS). **Total program enrollment:** 2927. **Application fee:** $10.

**PROGRAM(S) OFFERED**
• **Accounting Technology/Technician and Bookkeeping** *17 students enrolled* • **Administrative Assistant and Secretarial Science, General** *2 students enrolled* • **Automobile/Automotive Mechanics Technology/Technician** *15 students enrolled* • **Chemical Technology/Technician** *8 students enrolled* • **Child Development** *8 students enrolled* • **Computer Programming, Vendor/Product Certification** • **Computer Systems Networking and Telecommunications** *2 students enrolled* • **Dental Assisting/Assistant** *11 students enrolled* • **Electrician** *20 students enrolled* • **Emergency Medical Technology/Technician (EMT**

*Northeast State Technical Community College (continued)*

**Paramedic)** *9 students enrolled* • **Heating, Air Conditioning, Ventilation and Refrigeration Maintenance Technology/Technician (HAC, HACR, HVAC, HVACR)** *18 students enrolled* • **Industrial Mechanics and Maintenance Technology** *9 students enrolled* • **Machine Shop Technology/Assistant** *8 students enrolled* • **Mechanical Drafting and Mechanical Drafting CAD/CADD** *8 students enrolled* • **Surgical Technology/Technologist** • **System, Networking, and LAN/WAN Management/Manager** • **Welding Technology/Welder** *8 students enrolled*

**STUDENT SERVICES** Academic or career counseling, employment services for current students, placement services for program completers, remedial services.

## Pellissippi State Technical Community College

PO Box 22990, Knoxville, TN 37933-0990
http://www.pstcc.edu/

**CONTACT** Dr. Allen G. Edwards, President
**Telephone:** 865-694-6400

**GENERAL INFORMATION** Public Institution. Founded 1974. **Accreditation:** Regional (SACS/CC); engineering technology (ABET/TAC). **Total program enrollment:** 4570. **Application fee:** $10.

**STUDENT SERVICES** Academic or career counseling, employment services for current students, placement services for program completers, remedial services.

## Plaza Beauty School

4682 Spottswood Avenue, Memphis, TN 38117
http://www.plazabeautyschool.com/

**CONTACT** Joan E. Sparks, Vice President
**Telephone:** 901-761-4445

**GENERAL INFORMATION** Private Institution. **Total program enrollment:** 89. **Application fee:** $100.

**PROGRAM(S) OFFERED**
• **Cosmetology/Cosmetologist, General** *1500 hrs./$12,550*

**STUDENT SERVICES** Academic or career counseling, placement services for program completers.

## Queen City College

1594 Fort Campbell Boulevard, Clarksville, TN 37042
http://www.queencitycollege.com/

**CONTACT** Laura E. Payne, Chief Administrator
**Telephone:** 931-645-2361

**GENERAL INFORMATION** Private Institution. Founded 1984. **Total program enrollment:** 141. **Application fee:** $100.

**PROGRAM(S) OFFERED**
• **Aesthetician/Esthetician and Skin Care Specialist** *750 hrs./$4013* • **Barbering/Barber** *1500 hrs./$6136* • **Cosmetology, Barber/Styling, and Nail Instructor** • **Cosmetology/Cosmetologist, General** *1500 hrs./$7201* • **Hair Styling/Stylist and Hair Design** • **Nail Technician/Specialist and Manicurist** *600 hrs./$2454*

**STUDENT SERVICES** Placement services for program completers.

## Regency Beauty Institute

5383 Mt View Road, Antioch, TN 37013

**CONTACT** J. Hayes Batson
**Telephone:** 615-916-2001

**GENERAL INFORMATION** Private Institution. **Total program enrollment:** 42. **Application fee:** $100.

**PROGRAM(S) OFFERED**
• **Cosmetology/Cosmetologist, General** *1500 hrs./$16,011*

**STUDENT SERVICES** Academic or career counseling, placement services for program completers.

## Remington College–Memphis Campus

2731 Nonconnah Boulevard, Memphis, TN 38132-2131
http://www.remingtoncollege.edu/

**CONTACT** Lori May, Campus President
**Telephone:** 901-345-1000

**GENERAL INFORMATION** Private Institution. **Accreditation:** State accredited or approved. **Total program enrollment:** 922. **Application fee:** $50.

**PROGRAM(S) OFFERED**
• **Medical Insurance Coding Specialist/Coder** *111 students enrolled* • **Medical/Clinical Assistant** *203 students enrolled* • **Pharmacy Technician/Assistant** *70 students enrolled*

**STUDENT SERVICES** Academic or career counseling, employment services for current students, placement services for program completers.

## Remington College–Nashville Campus

441 Donelson Pike, Suite 150, Nashville, TN 37214
http://www.remingtoncollege.edu/

**CONTACT** Larry Collins, Campus President
**Telephone:** 615-889-5520

**GENERAL INFORMATION** Private Institution. Founded 2003. **Total program enrollment:** 408. **Application fee:** $50.

**PROGRAM(S) OFFERED**
• **Cosmetology/Cosmetologist, General** • **Dental Assisting/Assistant** *87 students enrolled* • **Medical Insurance Coding Specialist/Coder** *13 students enrolled* • **Medical/Clinical Assistant** *158 students enrolled*

**STUDENT SERVICES** Academic or career counseling, employment services for current students, placement services for program completers.

## Reuben-Allen College

120 Center Park Drive, Knoxville, TN 37922
http://www.rosstheboss.com/

**CONTACT** Ross Badgett, Director
**Telephone:** 865-966-0400

**GENERAL INFORMATION** Private Institution. **Total program enrollment:** 49. **Application fee:** $100.

**PROGRAM(S) OFFERED**
• **Cosmetology/Cosmetologist, General** *1500 hrs./$10,650*

**STUDENT SERVICES** Academic or career counseling, placement services for program completers.

## Roane State Community College

276 Patton Lane, Harriman, TN 37748-5011
http://www.roanestate.edu/

**CONTACT** Gary Goff, President
**Telephone:** 865-354-3000

**GENERAL INFORMATION** Public Institution. Founded 1971. **Accreditation:** Regional (SACS/CC); dental hygiene (ADA); health information technology (AHIMA); ophthalmic dispensing (COA); physical therapy assisting (APTA); radiologic technology: radiography (JRCERT). **Total program enrollment:** 2977. **Application fee:** $10.

**PROGRAM(S) OFFERED**
• **Administrative Assistant and Secretarial Science, General** *1 student enrolled* • **Allied Health Diagnostic, Intervention, and Treatment Professions, Other** *10 students enrolled* • **Cartography** *7 students enrolled* • **Clinical/Medical Laboratory Science and Allied Professions, Other** *13 students enrolled* • **Computer and Information Sciences and Support Services, Other** • **Criminal Justice/Police Science** *1 student enrolled* • **Emergency Medical Technology/Technician (EMT Paramedic)** *19 students enrolled* • **Massage Therapy/Therapeutic Massage** *15 students enrolled* • **Medical Transcription/Transcriptionist** *9 students enrolled* • **Pharmacy Technician/Assistant** *8 students enrolled* • **Security and Protective Services, Other** *3 students enrolled*

**STUDENT SERVICES** Academic or career counseling, employment services for current students, placement services for program completers, remedial services.

## SAE Institute of Technology

7 Music Circle N, Nashville, TN 37203
http://www.sae-nashville.com/

**CONTACT** Prema Thiagarajah, Director
**Telephone:** 615-244-5848

**GENERAL INFORMATION** Private Institution. **Total program enrollment:** 168. **Application fee:** $100.

**PROGRAM(S) OFFERED**
• **Recording Arts Technology/Technician** *900 hrs./$18,900*

**STUDENT SERVICES** Academic or career counseling, placement services for program completers.

## Shear Academy

780 West Avenue, Crossville, TN 38555

**CONTACT** James Everitt, Owner
**Telephone:** 931-456-5391

**GENERAL INFORMATION** Private Institution. **Total program enrollment:** 21. **Application fee:** $25.

**PROGRAM(S) OFFERED**
• **Barbering/Barber** *1500 hrs./$8500* • **Cosmetology, Barber/Styling, and Nail Instructor** *450 hrs./$2000*

**STUDENT SERVICES** Placement services for program completers.

## South College

720 North Fifth Avenue, Knoxville, TN 37917
http://www.southcollegetn.edu/

**CONTACT** Stephen A. South, President
**Telephone:** 865-251-1800

**GENERAL INFORMATION** Private Institution. Founded 1882. **Accreditation:** Regional (SACS/CC); medical assisting (AAMAE); physical therapy assisting (APTA). **Total program enrollment:** 825. **Application fee:** $50.

**PROGRAM(S) OFFERED**
• **Administrative Assistant and Secretarial Science, General** *1 student enrolled* • **Medical Insurance Coding Specialist/Coder** *4 students enrolled* • **Nuclear Medical Technology/Technologist** *5 students enrolled*

**STUDENT SERVICES** Academic or career counseling, employment services for current students, placement services for program completers.

## Southern Adventist University

PO Box 370, Collegedale, TN 37315-0370
http://www.southern.edu/

**CONTACT** Gordon Bietz, President
**Telephone:** 423-236-2000

**GENERAL INFORMATION** Private Institution. Founded 1892. **Accreditation:** Regional (SACS/CC); music (NASM). **Total program enrollment:** 2211. **Application fee:** $25.

**STUDENT SERVICES** Academic or career counseling, employment services for current students, placement services for program completers, remedial services.

## Southern Institute of Cosmetology

3099 S. Perkin, Memphis, TN 38118-3239

**CONTACT** Nancy Ryall, President
**Telephone:** 901-363-3553

**GENERAL INFORMATION** Private Institution. **Total program enrollment:** 64. **Application fee:** $100.

**PROGRAM(S) OFFERED**
• **Cosmetology/Cosmetologist, General** *1500 hrs./$9400* • **Nail Technician/Specialist and Manicurist** *600 hrs./$2400*

**STUDENT SERVICES** Academic or career counseling, placement services for program completers.

## Southwest Tennessee Community College

PO Box 780, Memphis, TN 38101-0780
http://www.southwest.tn.edu/

**CONTACT** Nathan L. Essex, President
**Telephone:** 901-333-5000

**GENERAL INFORMATION** Public Institution. Founded 2000. **Accreditation:** Regional (SACS/CC); engineering technology (ABET/TAC); medical laboratory technology (NAACLS); physical therapy assisting (APTA); radiologic technology: radiography (JRCERT). **Total program enrollment:** 5298. **Application fee:** $10.

**PROGRAM(S) OFFERED**
• **Accounting Technology/Technician and Bookkeeping** *19 students enrolled* • **Architectural Engineering Technology/Technician** *9 students enrolled* • **Blood Bank Technology Specialist** *25 students enrolled* • **Business, Management, Marketing, and Related Support Services, Other** *28 students enrolled* • **Business/Commerce, General** *1 student enrolled* • **Child Care and Support Services Management** • **Child Development** *5 students enrolled* • **Computer Engineering Technology/Technician** *18 students enrolled* • **Computer Programming, Specific Applications** *28 students enrolled* • **Construction Trades, Other** • **Criminal Justice/Police Science** *1 student enrolled* • **Electrical, Electronic and Communications Engineering Technology/Technician** *22 students enrolled* • **Electrician** *4 students enrolled* • **Emergency Medical Technology/Technician (EMT Paramedic)** *142 students enrolled* • **Foodservice Systems Administration/Management** *7 students enrolled* • **Health and Medical Administrative Services, Other** • **Human Development, Family Studies, and Related Services, Other** *9 students enrolled* • **Industrial Technology/Technician** • **Landscaping and Groundskeeping** *4 students enrolled* • **Manufacturing Technology/Technician** • **Mechanic and Repair Technologies/Technicians, Other** *18 students enrolled* • **Pharmacy Technician/Assistant** *9 students enrolled*

*Southwest Tennessee Community College (continued)*

• **Quality Control Technology/Technician** *11 students enrolled* • **Security and Protective Services, Other** *3 students enrolled* • **Substance Abuse/Addiction Counseling** *18 students enrolled* • **Turf and Turfgrass Management**

**STUDENT SERVICES** Academic or career counseling, daycare for children of students, employment services for current students, placement services for program completers, remedial services.

## State University and Community College System of Tennessee

1415 Murfreesboro Road, Suite 350, Nashville, TN 37217-2829

**CONTACT** Dr. Charles W. Manning, Chancellor
**Telephone:** 615-366-4400

**GENERAL INFORMATION** Public Institution.

## Stylemasters Beauty Academy

223 North Cumberland, Lebanon, TN 37087
http://www.stylemasters.net/

**CONTACT** Richard J. Bundy, President
**Telephone:** 615-248-1927

**GENERAL INFORMATION** Private Institution. **Total program enrollment:** 315. **Application fee:** $100.

**PROGRAM(S) OFFERED**
• **Cosmetology, Barber/Styling, and Nail Instructor** *300 hrs./$1905*
• **Cosmetology/Cosmetologist, General** *1500 hrs./$11,795* • **Nail Technician/ Specialist and Manicurist** *600 hrs./$5370*

**STUDENT SERVICES** Academic or career counseling, employment services for current students, placement services for program completers.

## Styles and Profiles Beauty College

119 South Second Street, Selmer, TN 38375

**CONTACT** Phoebe M. Prather, Owner
**Telephone:** 731-645-9728

**GENERAL INFORMATION** Private Institution. **Total program enrollment:** 28. **Application fee:** $75.

**PROGRAM(S) OFFERED**
• **Cosmetology, Barber/Styling, and Nail Instructor** *300 hrs./$2297*
• **Cosmetology/Cosmetologist, General** *1500 hrs./$6949* • **Nail Technician/ Specialist and Manicurist** *600 hrs./$4499*

**STUDENT SERVICES** Academic or career counseling, employment services for current students.

## Tennessee Academy of Cosmetology

7020 East Shelby Drive, Suite 104, Memphis, TN 38125

**CONTACT** William Oxley, President
**Telephone:** 901-757-4166

**GENERAL INFORMATION** Private Institution. **Total program enrollment:** 48. **Application fee:** $100.

**PROGRAM(S) OFFERED**
• **Aesthetician/Esthetician and Skin Care Specialist** *750 hrs./$5828*
• **Cosmetology and Related Personal Grooming Arts, Other** *600 hrs./$4368*
• **Cosmetology/Cosmetologist, General** *1500 hrs./$11,920* • **Make-Up Artist/ Specialist** *142 students enrolled*

**STUDENT SERVICES** Academic or career counseling, placement services for program completers.

## Tennessee Academy of Cosmetology

7041 Stage Road, Suite 101, Memphis, TN 38133

**CONTACT** William Oxley, President
**Telephone:** 901-382-9085

**GENERAL INFORMATION** Private Institution. Founded 1984. **Total program enrollment:** 56. **Application fee:** $100.

**PROGRAM(S) OFFERED**
• **Aesthetician/Esthetician and Skin Care Specialist** *750 hrs./$5460*
• **Cosmetology and Related Personal Grooming Arts, Other** *600 hrs./$4368*
• **Cosmetology/Cosmetologist, General** *1500 hrs./$11,920*

**STUDENT SERVICES** Academic or career counseling, placement services for program completers.

## Tennessee School of Beauty

4704 Western Avenue, Knoxville, TN 37921
http://www.tennesseeschoolofbeauty.com/

**CONTACT** Adam J. Brown, President
**Telephone:** 865-588-7878

**GENERAL INFORMATION** Private Institution. Founded 1930. **Total program enrollment:** 290. **Application fee:** $100.

**PROGRAM(S) OFFERED**
• **Aesthetician/Esthetician and Skin Care Specialist** *750 hrs./$7495*
• **Cosmetology, Barber/Styling, and Nail Instructor** *300 hrs./$3995*
• **Cosmetology/Cosmetologist, General** *1500 hrs./$9995* • **Nail Technician/ Specialist and Manicurist** *600 hrs./$2645*

**STUDENT SERVICES** Academic or career counseling, placement services for program completers.

## Tennessee Technology Center at Athens

1635 Vo-Tech Drive, Athens, TN 37303
http://www.athens.tec.tn.us/

**CONTACT** Stewart Smith, Director
**Telephone:** 423-744-2814

**GENERAL INFORMATION** Public Institution. Founded 1965. **Total program enrollment:** 161.

**PROGRAM(S) OFFERED**
• **Autobody/Collision and Repair Technology/Technician** *2160 hrs./$3810*
• **Automobile/Automotive Mechanics Technology/Technician** *2160 hrs./$3810*
• **Business Operations Support and Secretarial Services, Other** *1296 hrs./ $2286* • **Electrical/Electronics Equipment Installation and Repair, General** *10 students enrolled* • **Electrician** *1728 hrs./$3048* • **Industrial Electronics Technology/Technician** *7 students enrolled* • **Industrial Mechanics and Maintenance Technology** *11 students enrolled* • **Licensed Practical/Vocational Nurse Training (LPN, LVN, Cert, Dipl, AAS)** *1296 hrs./$4586* • **Machine Tool Technology/Machinist** • **Pharmacy Technician/Assistant** • **Welding Technology/ Welder** *1296 hrs./$2286*

**STUDENT SERVICES** Academic or career counseling, employment services for current students, placement services for program completers, remedial services.

## Tennessee Technology Center at Covington

PO Box 249, Covington, TN 38019
http://www.covington.tec.tn.us/

**CONTACT** William N. Ray, Director
**Telephone:** 901-475-2526

**GENERAL INFORMATION** Public Institution. **Total program enrollment:** 134.

**PROGRAM(S) OFFERED**

• **Administrative Assistant and Secretarial Science, General** *1296 hrs./$2286* • **Computer and Information Sciences, General** *2160 hrs./$3810* • **Heating, Air Conditioning, Ventilation and Refrigeration Maintenance Technology/Technician (HAC, HACR, HVAC, HVACR)** *2160 hrs./$3810* • **Heavy/Industrial Equipment Maintenance Technologies, Other** *14 students enrolled* • **Industrial Mechanics and Maintenance Technology** *1728 hrs./$3048* • **Licensed Practical/Vocational Nurse Training (LPN, LVN, Cert, Dipl, AAS)** *1296 hrs./$5105* • **Machine Tool Technology/Machinist** *1944 hrs./$3674*

**STUDENT SERVICES** Academic or career counseling, employment services for current students, placement services for program completers, remedial services.

## Tennessee Technology Center at Crossville

910 Miller Avenue, Crossville, TN 38555
http://www.crossville.tec.tn.us/

**CONTACT** Donald Sadler, Director
**Telephone:** 931-484-7502

**GENERAL INFORMATION** Public Institution. Founded 1967. **Total program enrollment:** 259.

**PROGRAM(S) OFFERED**

• **Autobody/Collision and Repair Technology/Technician** *863 hrs./$3810* • **Automobile/Automotive Mechanics Technology/Technician** *2160 hrs./$5194* • **Automotive Engineering Technology/Technician** • **Business Operations Support and Secretarial Services, Other** *14 students enrolled* • **Business/Office Automation/Technology/Data Entry** *1296 hrs./$2286* • **Construction Trades, Other** *1 student enrolled* • **Drafting and Design Technology/Technician, General** *2 students enrolled* • **Heating, Air Conditioning, Ventilation and Refrigeration Maintenance Technology/Technician (HAC, HACR, HVAC, HVACR)** *1 student enrolled* • **Industrial Electronics Technology/Technician** *400 hrs./$3048* • **Industrial Mechanics and Maintenance Technology** *915 hrs./$3048* • **Licensed Practical/Vocational Nurse Training (LPN, LVN, Cert, Dipl, AAS)** *1164 hrs./$2586* • **Machine Shop Technology/Assistant** • **Mason/Masonry** *3 students enrolled* • **Surgical Technology/Technologist** *4 students enrolled* • **Welding Technology/Welder** *3 students enrolled*

**STUDENT SERVICES** Academic or career counseling, daycare for children of students, employment services for current students, placement services for program completers, remedial services.

## Tennessee Technology Center at Crump

Highway 64, West, Crump, TN 38327
http://www.crumpttc.edu/

**CONTACT** Dan Spears, Director
**Telephone:** 731-632-3393 Ext. 221

**GENERAL INFORMATION** Public Institution. Founded 1965. **Total program enrollment:** 225.

**PROGRAM(S) OFFERED**

• **Autobody/Collision and Repair Technology/Technician** *2160 hrs./$3406* • **Business Operations Support and Secretarial Services, Other** *16 students enrolled* • **Business/Office Automation/Technology/Data Entry** *2160 hrs./$2286* • **Commercial and Advertising Art** *6 students enrolled* • **Drafting and Design Technology/Technician, General** *2160 hrs./$2286* • **Electrical and Power Transmission Installation/Installer, General** *1728 hrs./$2286* • **Electrical/Electronics Equipment Installation and Repair, General** *16 students enrolled* • **Heating, Air Conditioning, Ventilation and Refrigeration Maintenance Technology/Technician (HAC, HACR, HVAC, HVACR)** *15 students enrolled* • **Industrial Electronics Technology/Technician** *1944 hrs./$2286* • **Industrial Mechanics and Maintenance Technology** *15 students enrolled* • **Licensed Practical/Vocational Nurse Training (LPN, LVN, Cert, Dipl, AAS)** *20 students enrolled* • **Machine Shop Technology/Assistant** *1944 hrs./$2286* • **Truck and Bus Driver/Commercial Vehicle Operation** *25 students enrolled*

**STUDENT SERVICES** Academic or career counseling, employment services for current students, placement services for program completers, remedial services.

## Tennessee Technology Center at Dickson

740 Highway 46, Dickson, TN 37055
http://www.dickson.tec.tn.us/

**CONTACT** Warner Taylor, Interim Director
**Telephone:** 615-441-6220

**GENERAL INFORMATION** Public Institution. Founded 1965. **Total program enrollment:** 374.

**PROGRAM(S) OFFERED**

• **Automobile/Automotive Mechanics Technology/Technician** *2160 hrs./$3810* • **Business Operations Support and Secretarial Services, Other** *1296 hrs./$2286* • **Computer Installation and Repair Technology/Technician** *2160 hrs./$3810* • **Cosmetology/Cosmetologist, General** *1500 hrs./$3048* • **Dental Assisting/Assistant** *15 students enrolled* • **Heating, Air Conditioning, Ventilation and Refrigeration Maintenance Technology/Technician (HAC, HACR, HVAC, HVACR)** *6 students enrolled* • **Heavy Equipment Maintenance Technology/Technician** *5 students enrolled* • **Industrial Mechanics and Maintenance Technology** *2592 hrs./$4572* • **Licensed Practical/Vocational Nurse Training (LPN, LVN, Cert, Dipl, AAS)** *1296 hrs./$4147* • **Machine Shop Technology/Assistant** *1 student enrolled* • **Mechanical Drafting and Mechanical Drafting CAD/CADD** • **Surgical Technology/Technologist** *11 students enrolled*

**STUDENT SERVICES** Academic or career counseling, employment services for current students, placement services for program completers, remedial services.

## Tennessee Technology Center at Elizabethton

425 Highway 91, PO Box 789, Elizabethton, TN 37644
http://www.elizabethton.tec.tn.us/

**CONTACT** Jerry Patton, Director
**Telephone:** 423-543-0070

**GENERAL INFORMATION** Public Institution. Founded 1965. **Total program enrollment:** 446.

**PROGRAM(S) OFFERED**

• **Automobile/Automotive Mechanics Technology/Technician** *2160 hrs./$3880* • **Business Operations Support and Secretarial Services, Other** *1296 hrs./$2286* • **Business/Office Automation/Technology/Data Entry** *2160 hrs./$3880* • **Dietetics/Dietitians** *34 students enrolled* • **Electrical/Electronics Equipment Installation and Repair, General** *1728 hrs./$3048* • **Health Aides/Attendants/Orderlies, Other** *116 students enrolled* • **Heating, Air Conditioning, Ventilation and Refrigeration Maintenance Technology/Technician (HAC, HACR, HVAC, HVACR)** • **Industrial Mechanics and Maintenance Technology** *20 students enrolled* • **Licensed Practical/Vocational Nurse Training (LPN, LVN, Cert, Dipl, AAS)** *1296 hrs./$5076* • **Welding Technology/Welder** *1296 hrs./$2286*

**STUDENT SERVICES** Academic or career counseling, employment services for current students, placement services for program completers, remedial services.

## Tennessee Technology Center at Harriman

1745 Harriman Highway, Harriman, TN 37748-1109
http://www.ttcharriman.edu/

**CONTACT** Mark Powers, Director
**Telephone:** 865-882-6703

**GENERAL INFORMATION** Public Institution. Founded 1970. **Total program enrollment:** 170.

**PROGRAM(S) OFFERED**

• **Automobile/Automotive Mechanics Technology/Technician** *2160 hrs./$2286* • **Business Operations Support and Secretarial Services, Other** *1296 hrs./$2286* • **Cosmetology/Cosmetologist, General** *1500 hrs./$2286* • **Diesel Mechanics Technology/Technician** *2160 hrs./$2286* • **Industrial Mechanics and Maintenance Technology** *1728 hrs./$2286* • **Information Technology** *4 students enrolled* • **Licensed Practical/Vocational Nurse Training (LPN, LVN, Cert, Dipl, AAS)** *1296 hrs./$4869* • **Machine Shop Technology/Assistant** *7 students enrolled*

**STUDENT SERVICES** Academic or career counseling, employment services for current students, placement services for program completers, remedial services.

## Tennessee Technology Center at Hartsville

716 McMurry Boulevard, Hartsville, TN 37074
http://hartsville.tec.tn.us/

**CONTACT** Mae W. Banks, Director
**Telephone:** 615-374-2147

**GENERAL INFORMATION** Public Institution. Founded 1965. **Total program enrollment:** 282.

**PROGRAM(S) OFFERED**
• **Automobile/Automotive Mechanics Technology/Technician** *2160 hrs./$3810* • **Business Operations Support and Secretarial Services, Other** *1296 hrs./$2286* • **Business/Office Automation/Technology/Data Entry** *2160 hrs./$3810* • **Drafting and Design Technology/Technician, General** *2160 hrs./$3810* • **Licensed Practical/Vocational Nurse Training (LPN, LVN, Cert, Dipl, AAS)** *1296 hrs./$3486* • **Machine Shop Technology/Assistant** *1944 hrs./$3810* • **Welding Technology/Welder** *9 students enrolled*

**STUDENT SERVICES** Academic or career counseling, employment services for current students, placement services for program completers, remedial services.

## Tennessee Technology Center at Hohenwald

813 West Main Street, Hohenwald, TN 38462-2201
http://www.hohenwald.tec.tn.us/

**CONTACT** Rick C. Brewer, Director
**Telephone:** 931-796-5351 Ext. 124

**GENERAL INFORMATION** Public Institution. Founded 1967. **Total program enrollment:** 330.

**PROGRAM(S) OFFERED**
• **Automobile/Automotive Mechanics Technology/Technician** *2160 hrs./$3810* • **Business Operations Support and Secretarial Services, Other** *1296 hrs./$2286* • **Business/Office Automation/Technology/Data Entry** *2160 hrs./$3810* • **Cosmetology/Cosmetologist, General** *1500 hrs./$2645* • **Drafting and Design Technology/Technician, General** *2 students enrolled* • **Early Childhood Education and Teaching** *3 students enrolled* • **Heavy/Industrial Equipment Maintenance Technologies, Other** • **Industrial Electronics Technology/Technician** • **Industrial Mechanics and Maintenance Technology** *1728 hrs./$3048* • **Licensed Practical/Vocational Nurse Training (LPN, LVN, Cert, Dipl, AAS)** *1296 hrs./$4946* • **Machine Shop Technology/Assistant** *2 students enrolled* • **Surgical Technology/Technologist** *12 students enrolled*

**STUDENT SERVICES** Academic or career counseling, daycare for children of students, employment services for current students, placement services for program completers, remedial services.

## Tennessee Technology Center at Jacksboro

Elkins Road, Jacksboro, TN 37757
http://www.jacksboro.tec.tn.us/

**CONTACT** David R. Browder, Director
**Telephone:** 423-566-9629 Ext. 100

**GENERAL INFORMATION** Public Institution. Founded 1967. **Total program enrollment:** 165.

**PROGRAM(S) OFFERED**
• **Administrative Assistant and Secretarial Science, General** *22 students enrolled* • **Automobile/Automotive Mechanics Technology/Technician** *2160 hrs./$3810* • **Business/Office Automation/Technology/Data Entry** *1296 hrs./$2247* • **Computer Installation and Repair Technology/Technician** *11 students enrolled* • **Computer Technology/Computer Systems Technology** *2160 hrs./$3810* • **Drafting and Design Technology/Technician, General** *5 students enrolled* • **Electrical/Electronics Equipment Installation and Repair, General** *9 students enrolled* • **Electrical/Electronics Maintenance and Repair Technology, Other** *1728 hrs./$3048* • **Licensed Practical/Vocational Nurse Training (LPN, LVN, Cert, Dipl, AAS)** *1296 hrs./$4786* • **Machine Tool Technology/Machinist** • **Welding Technology/Welder** *1296 hrs./$2247*

**STUDENT SERVICES** Academic or career counseling, employment services for current students, placement services for program completers, remedial services.

## Tennessee Technology Center at Jackson

2468 Westover Road, Jackson, TN 38301
http://www.jackson.tec.tn.us/

**CONTACT** Dr. Don Williams, Director
**Telephone:** 731-424-0691

**GENERAL INFORMATION** Public Institution. Founded 1965. **Total program enrollment:** 446.

**PROGRAM(S) OFFERED**
• **Autobody/Collision and Repair Technology/Technician** *13 students enrolled* • **Automobile/Automotive Mechanics Technology/Technician** *2150 hrs./$3180* • **Business Operations Support and Secretarial Services, Other** *1296 hrs./$2286* • **Computer Systems Analysis/Analyst** *1718 hrs./$3048* • **Drafting and Design Technology/Technician, General** *4 students enrolled* • **Electrical/Electronics Equipment Installation and Repair, General** *5 students enrolled* • **Electrician** *1 student enrolled* • **Heating, Air Conditioning, Ventilation and Refrigeration Maintenance Technology/Technician (HAC, HACR, HVAC, HVACR)** *1 student enrolled* • **Industrial Mechanics and Maintenance Technology** *11 students enrolled* • **Licensed Practical/Vocational Nurse Training (LPN, LVN, Cert, Dipl, AAS)** *1296 hrs./$4686* • **Machine Shop Technology/Assistant** *2 students enrolled* • **Machine Tool Technology/Machinist** *2150 hrs./$3810* • **Pharmacy Technician/Assistant** *11 students enrolled* • **Surgical Technology/Technologist** *14 students enrolled* • **Tool and Die Technology/Technician** *1 student enrolled* • **Welding Technology/Welder** *1296 hrs./$2286*

**STUDENT SERVICES** Academic or career counseling, employment services for current students, placement services for program completers, remedial services.

## Tennessee Technology Center at Knoxville

1100 Liberty Street, Knoxville, TN 37919
http://www.knoxville.tec.tn.us/

**CONTACT** Jeff Davis, Director
**Telephone:** 865-546-5567

**GENERAL INFORMATION** Public Institution. Founded 1968. **Total program enrollment:** 313.

**PROGRAM(S) OFFERED**
• **Autobody/Collision and Repair Technology/Technician** *10 students enrolled* • **Automobile/Automotive Mechanics Technology/Technician** *9 students enrolled* • **Business Operations Support and Secretarial Services, Other** *1296 hrs./$2286* • **Cosmetology/Cosmetologist, General** *1500 hrs./$2912* • **Dental Assisting/Assistant** *1296 hrs./$2286* • **Diesel Mechanics Technology/Technician** • **Drafting and Design Technology/Technician, General** *9 students enrolled* • **Electrician** *10 students enrolled* • **Heating, Air Conditioning, Ventilation and Refrigeration Maintenance Technology/Technician (HAC, HACR, HVAC, HVACR)** *1 student enrolled* • **Heavy/Industrial Equipment Maintenance Technologies, Other** *11 students enrolled* • **Industrial Electronics Technology/Technician** *1 student enrolled* • **Licensed Practical/Vocational Nurse Training (LPN, LVN, Cert, Dipl, AAS)** *1296 hrs./$3808* • **Machine Shop Technology/Assistant** • **Medical Administrative/Executive Assistant and Medical Secretary** *632 hrs./$1388* • **Medical/Clinical Assistant** *18 students enrolled* • **Surgical Technology/Technologist** *1498 hrs./$3048* • **Truck and Bus Driver/Commercial Vehicle Operation** *29 students enrolled* • **Welding Technology/Welder**

**STUDENT SERVICES** Academic or career counseling, employment services for current students, placement services for program completers, remedial services.

## Tennessee Technology Center at Livingston

740 Airport Road, PO Box 219, Livingston, TN 38570
http://www.livingston.tec.tn.us/

**CONTACT** Ralph Robbins, Director
**Telephone:** 931-823-5525 Ext. 0

**GENERAL INFORMATION** Public Institution. Founded 1966. **Total program enrollment:** 289.

**PROGRAM(S) OFFERED**
• **Autobody/Collision and Repair Technology/Technician** *5 students enrolled* • **Automobile/Automotive Mechanics Technology/Technician** *2592 hrs./$4572* • **Business Operations Support and Secretarial Services, Other** *1296 hrs./$2586* • **Business, Management, Marketing, and Related Support Services, Other** • **Business/Office Automation/Technology/Data Entry** *1728 hrs./$3048* • **Construction Trades, Other** *11 students enrolled* • **Cosmetology/Cosmetologist, General** *1500 hrs./$2912* • **Electrical/Electronics Equipment Installation and Repair, General** *1 student enrolled* • **Industrial Mechanics and Maintenance Technology** *2160 hrs./$3810* • **Licensed Practical/Vocational Nurse Training (LPN, LVN, Cert, Dipl, AAS)** *1296 hrs./$4760* • **Machine Shop Technology/Assistant** • **Pharmacy Technician/Assistant**

**STUDENT SERVICES** Academic or career counseling, employment services for current students, placement services for program completers, remedial services.

## Tennessee Technology Center at McKenzie

16940 Highland Drive, McKenzie, TN 38201
http://www.mckenzie.tec.tn.us/

**CONTACT** Elizabeth Check, Director
**Telephone:** 731-352-5364

**GENERAL INFORMATION** Public Institution. Founded 1964. **Total program enrollment:** 247.

**PROGRAM(S) OFFERED**
• **Automobile/Automotive Mechanics Technology/Technician** *2160 hrs./$3810* • **Business Operations Support and Secretarial Services, Other** *1296 hrs./$3894* • **Business/Office Automation/Technology/Data Entry** *2160 hrs./$3810* • **Drafting and Design Technology/Technician, General** • **Electrical/Electronics Equipment Installation and Repair, General** *4 students enrolled* • **Industrial Electronics Technology/Technician** *1728 hrs./$3048* • **Licensed Practical/Vocational Nurse Training (LPN, LVN, Cert, Dipl, AAS)** *1296 hrs./$2586* • **Welding Technology/Welder** *1296 hrs./$2286*

**STUDENT SERVICES** Academic or career counseling, employment services for current students, placement services for program completers, remedial services.

## Tennessee Technology Center at McMinnville

241 Vo Tech Drive, McMinnville, TN 37110
http://www.mcminnville.tec.tn.us/

**CONTACT** Marvin Lusk, Interim Director
**Telephone:** 931-473-5587

**GENERAL INFORMATION** Public Institution. **Total program enrollment:** 192.

**PROGRAM(S) OFFERED**
• **Administrative Assistant and Secretarial Science, General** *5 students enrolled* • **Automobile/Automotive Mechanics Technology/Technician** *2160 hrs./$3810* • **Business Operations Support and Secretarial Services, Other** *1296 hrs./$2286* • **Business/Office Automation/Technology/Data Entry** *2160 hrs./$3810* • **Industrial Electronics Technology/Technician** • **Industrial Mechanics and Maintenance Technology** *1728 hrs./$3048* • **Licensed Practical/Vocational Nurse Training (LPN, LVN, Cert, Dipl, AAS)** *1296 hrs./$5029* • **Machine Shop Technology/Assistant** *1944 hrs./$3810* • **Medical/Clinical Assistant** *14 students enrolled* • **Surgical Technology/Technologist** *13 students enrolled*

**STUDENT SERVICES** Academic or career counseling, employment services for current students, placement services for program completers, remedial services.

## Tennessee Technology Center at Memphis

550 Alabama Avenue, Memphis, TN 38105-3799
http://www.memphis.tec.tn.us/

**CONTACT** Lana Pierce, Director
**Telephone:** 901-543-6100

**GENERAL INFORMATION** Public Institution. Founded 1963. **Total program enrollment:** 696.

**PROGRAM(S) OFFERED**
• **Aircraft Powerplant Technology/Technician** *1918 hrs./$5296* • **Autobody/Collision and Repair Technology/Technician** *7 students enrolled* • **Automobile/Automotive Mechanics Technology/Technician** *4 students enrolled* • **Avionics Maintenance Technology/Technician** • **Barbering/Barber** *1500 hrs./$2974* • **Business Operations Support and Secretarial Services, Other** *1296 hrs./$2286* • **Business/Office Automation/Technology/Data Entry** *3 students enrolled* • **Commercial and Advertising Art** *19 students enrolled* • **Construction Trades, Other** *12 students enrolled* • **Cosmetology/Cosmetologist, General** *1500 hrs./$2974* • **Dental Assisting/Assistant** *24 students enrolled* • **Dental Laboratory Technology/Technician** *13 students enrolled* • **Diesel Mechanics Technology/Technician** *11 students enrolled* • **Drafting and Design Technology/Technician, General** *4 students enrolled* • **Graphic and Printing Equipment Operator, General Production** *1 student enrolled* • **Heating, Air Conditioning, Ventilation and Refrigeration Maintenance Technology/Technician (HAC, HACR, HVAC, HVACR)** *8 students enrolled* • **Industrial Electronics Technology/Technician** *20 students enrolled* • **Industrial Mechanics and Maintenance Technology** *3 students enrolled* • **Licensed Practical/Vocational Nurse Training (LPN, LVN, Cert, Dipl, AAS)** *1296 hrs./$2386* • **Machine Shop Technology/Assistant** *11 students enrolled* • **Mason/Masonry** *5 students enrolled* • **Nurse/Nursing Assistant/Aide and Patient Care Assistant** *22 students enrolled* • **Pharmacy Technician/Assistant** *14 students enrolled* • **Surgical Technology/Technologist** *1296 hrs./$2286* • **Truck and Bus Driver/Commercial Vehicle Operation** *77 students enrolled* • **Welding Technology/Welder** *15 students enrolled*

**STUDENT SERVICES** Academic or career counseling, employment services for current students, placement services for program completers, remedial services.

## Tennessee Technology Center at Morristown

821 West Louise Avenue, Morristown, TN 37813
http://www.morristown.tec.tn.us/

**CONTACT** B. Lynn Elkins, Director
**Telephone:** 423-586-5771

**GENERAL INFORMATION** Public Institution. Founded 1966. **Total program enrollment:** 443.

**PROGRAM(S) OFFERED**
• **Administrative Assistant and Secretarial Science, General** *1296 hrs./$2286* • **Aircraft Powerplant Technology/Technician** • **Autobody/Collision and Repair Technology/Technician** *2160 hrs./$3810* • **Automobile/Automotive Mechanics Technology/Technician** • **Business Operations Support and Secretarial Services, Other** *35 students enrolled* • **Business/Office Automation/Technology/Data Entry** *3 students enrolled* • **Computer Installation and Repair Technology/Technician** *2160 hrs./$3810* • **Drafting and Design Technology/Technician, General** *2 students enrolled* • **Electrician** *1728 hrs./$3048* • **Graphic and Printing Equipment Operator, General Production** *2 students enrolled* • **Heating, Air Conditioning, Ventilation and Refrigeration Maintenance Technology/Technician (HAC, HACR, HVAC, HVACR)** • **Industrial Mechanics and Maintenance Technology** *1728 hrs./$3048* • **Licensed Practical/Vocational Nurse Training (LPN, LVN, Cert, Dipl, AAS)** *1296 hrs./$4133* • **Machine Shop Technology/Assistant** *8 students enrolled* • **Mason/Masonry** • **Truck and Bus Driver/Commercial Vehicle Operation** *41 students enrolled* • **Welding Technology/Welder** *6 students enrolled*

**STUDENT SERVICES** Academic or career counseling, employment services for current students, placement services for program completers, remedial services.

## Tennessee Technology Center at Murfreesboro

1303 Old Fort Parkway, Murfreesboro, TN 37129-3312
http://www.ttcmurfreesboro.edu/

**CONTACT** Carol Puryear, Director
**Telephone:** 615-898-8010

**GENERAL INFORMATION** Public Institution. Founded 1969. **Total program enrollment:** 243.

**PROGRAM(S) OFFERED**
• **Automobile/Automotive Mechanics Technology/Technician** *2160 hrs./$3525* • **Business Operations Support and Secretarial Services, Other** *4 students enrolled* • **Business/Office Automation/Technology/Data Entry** *2160 hrs./$3810* • **Clinical/Medical Laboratory Science and Allied Professions, Other** *30 students enrolled* • **Dental Assisting/Assistant** *11 students enrolled* • **Drafting and Design Technology/Technician, General** *1728 hrs./$3048* • **Heating, Air**

*Tennessee Technology Center at Murfreesboro (continued)*

**Conditioning, Ventilation and Refrigeration Maintenance Technology/Technician (HAC, HACR, HVAC, HVACR)** *1728 hrs./$3048* • **Industrial Mechanics and Maintenance Technology** *1728 hrs./$3048* • **Licensed Practical/Vocational Nurse Training (LPN, LVN, Cert, Dipl, AAS)** *43 students enrolled* • **Machine Shop Technology/Assistant** *1944 hrs./$3810* • **Pharmacy Technician/Assistant** *9 students enrolled* • **Surgical Technology/Technologist** *12 students enrolled*

**STUDENT SERVICES** Academic or career counseling, employment services for current students, placement services for program completers, remedial services.

## Tennessee Technology Center at Nashville

100 White Bridge Road, Nashville, TN 37209
http://www.nashville.tec.tn.us/

**CONTACT** Johnny W. Williams, EdD, Director
**Telephone:** 615-425-5500 Ext. 5500

**GENERAL INFORMATION** Public Institution. Founded 1967. **Total program enrollment:** 536.

**PROGRAM(S) OFFERED**
• **Aesthetician/Esthetician and Skin Care Specialist** *864 hrs./$1524* • **Aircraft Powerplant Technology/Technician** *1918 hrs./$3674* • **Autobody/Collision and Repair Technology/Technician** *1 student enrolled* • **Automobile/Automotive Mechanics Technology/Technician** *2160 hrs./$3810* • **Business/Office Automation/Technology/Data Entry** *8 students enrolled* • **Child Care and Support Services Management** • **Clinical/Medical Laboratory Science and Allied Professions, Other** *33 students enrolled* • **Cosmetology/Cosmetologist, General** *1500 hrs./$2912* • **Dental Laboratory Technology/Technician** *4 students enrolled* • **Drafting and Design Technology/Technician, General** *7 students enrolled* • **Electrical and Power Transmission Installation/Installer, General** *3 students enrolled* • **Electrical/Electronics Equipment Installation and Repair, General** *5 students enrolled* • **Heating, Air Conditioning, Ventilation and Refrigeration Maintenance Technology/Technician (HAC, HACR, HVAC, HVACR)** *2160 hrs./$3810* • **Licensed Practical/Vocational Nurse Training (LPN, LVN, Cert, Dipl, AAS)** *1296 hrs./$4985* • **Machine Shop Technology/Assistant** *9 students enrolled* • **Management Information Systems, General** *4 students enrolled* • **Medical Insurance Specialist/Medical Biller** *5 students enrolled* • **Pharmacy Technician/Assistant** *14 students enrolled* • **Truck and Bus Driver/Commercial Vehicle Operation** *47 students enrolled* • **Welding Technology/Welder** *6 students enrolled*

**STUDENT SERVICES** Academic or career counseling, employment services for current students, placement services for program completers, remedial services.

## Tennessee Technology Center at Newbern

340 Washington Street, Newbern, TN 38059
http://www.newbern.tec.tn.us/

**CONTACT** Brian Collins, Director
**Telephone:** 731-627-2511

**GENERAL INFORMATION** Public Institution. **Total program enrollment:** 149.

**PROGRAM(S) OFFERED**
• **Automobile/Automotive Mechanics Technology/Technician** *2160 hrs./$3430* • **Business Operations Support and Secretarial Services, Other** *1296 hrs./$2058* • **Drafting and Design Technology/Technician, General** *2 students enrolled* • **Electrical/Electronics Equipment Installation and Repair, General** *1 student enrolled* • **Heating, Air Conditioning, Ventilation and Refrigeration Maintenance Technology/Technician (HAC, HACR, HVAC, HVACR)** *2160 hrs./$3430* • **Industrial Mechanics and Maintenance Technology** *2160 hrs./$5100* • **Licensed Practical/Vocational Nurse Training (LPN, LVN, Cert, Dipl, AAS)** *1296 hrs./$2358* • **Machine Shop Technology/Assistant** *1944 hrs./$2744*

**STUDENT SERVICES** Academic or career counseling, employment services for current students, placement services for program completers, remedial services.

## Tennessee Technology Center at Oneida/Huntsville

355 Scott High Drive, Huntsville, TN 37756
http://www.huntsville.tec.tn.us/

**CONTACT** Dwight E. Murphy, Director
**Telephone:** 423-663-4900

**GENERAL INFORMATION** Public Institution. Founded 1967. **Total program enrollment:** 79.

**PROGRAM(S) OFFERED**
• **Autobody/Collision and Repair Technology/Technician** *2160 hrs./$3810* • **Automobile/Automotive Mechanics Technology/Technician** *2160 hrs./$3810* • **Business Operations Support and Secretarial Services, Other** *1296 hrs./$2586* • **Business/Office Automation/Technology/Data Entry** *1 student enrolled* • **Cosmetology/Cosmetologist, General** *1500 hrs./$3048* • **Drafting and Design Technology/Technician, General** • **Industrial Electronics Technology/Technician** • **Licensed Practical/Vocational Nurse Training (LPN, LVN, Cert, Dipl, AAS)** *1296 hrs./$3717* • **Machine Shop Technology/Assistant** *1 student enrolled* • **Welding Technology/Welder** *1296 hrs./$2286*

**STUDENT SERVICES** Academic or career counseling, employment services for current students, placement services for program completers, remedial services.

## Tennessee Technology Center at Paris

312 South Wilson Street, Paris, TN 38242
http://www.paris.tec.tn.us/

**CONTACT** Brad White, Director
**Telephone:** 731-644-7365

**GENERAL INFORMATION** Public Institution. Founded 1971. **Total program enrollment:** 235.

**PROGRAM(S) OFFERED**
• **Autobody/Collision and Repair Technology/Technician** *2160 hrs./$3810* • **Business Operations Support and Secretarial Services, Other** *1296 hrs./$2286* • **Business/Office Automation/Technology/Data Entry** *2160 hrs./$4765* • **Child Care and Support Services Management** *10 students enrolled* • **Cosmetology/Cosmetologist, General** *2 students enrolled* • **Industrial Mechanics and Maintenance Technology** *1728 hrs./$3048* • **Licensed Practical/Vocational Nurse Training (LPN, LVN, Cert, Dipl, AAS)** *1296 hrs./$2586* • **Machine Shop Technology/Assistant** *12 students enrolled* • **Machine Tool Technology/Machinist** *1944 hrs./$3429* • **Motorcycle Maintenance and Repair Technology/Technician** *3 students enrolled* • **Robotics Technology/Technician** *5 students enrolled* • **Surgical Technology/Technologist** *9 students enrolled*

**STUDENT SERVICES** Academic or career counseling, employment services for current students, placement services for program completers, remedial services.

## Tennessee Technology Center at Pulaski

1233 East College Street, Pulaski, TN 38478
http://www.pulaski.tec.tn.us/

**CONTACT** James Dixon, Director
**Telephone:** 931-424-4014

**GENERAL INFORMATION** Public Institution. **Total program enrollment:** 81.

**PROGRAM(S) OFFERED**
• **Business, Management, Marketing, and Related Support Services, Other** *1296 hrs./$4506* • **Computer Technology/Computer Systems Technology** *3 students enrolled* • **Computer and Information Sciences and Support Services, Other** *2160 hrs./$3810* • **Electrical and Electronic Engineering Technologies/Technicians, Other** *1728 hrs./$3048* • **Heating, Air Conditioning and Refrigeration Technology/Technician (ACH/ACR/ACHR/HRAC/HVAC/AC Technology)** *2160 hrs./$3810* • **Heavy/Industrial Equipment Maintenance Technologies, Other** *1728 hrs./$3048* • **Licensed Practical/Vocational Nurse**

Training (LPN, LVN, Cert, Dipl, AAS) *1296 hrs./$2586* • Machine Tool Technology/Machinist *2 students enrolled* • Plastics Engineering Technology/ Technician *5 students enrolled* • Welding Technology/Welder *5 students enrolled*

**STUDENT SERVICES** Academic or career counseling, employment services for current students, placement services for program completers, remedial services.

## Tennessee Technology Center at Ripley

127 Industrial Drive, Ripley, TN 38063

**CONTACT** Brian Collins, Director
**Telephone:** 731-635-3368

**GENERAL INFORMATION** Public Institution. **Total program enrollment:** 142.

**PROGRAM(S) OFFERED**
• **Allied Health and Medical Assisting Services, Other** *864 hrs./$1524* • **Business Operations Support and Secretarial Services, Other** *1296 hrs./$2286* • **Computer Systems Analysis/Analyst** *2 students enrolled* • **Data Processing and Data Processing Technology/Technician** *2160 hrs./$3810* • **Drafting and Design Technology/Technician, General** • **Electrician** *1728 hrs./$3048* • **Licensed Practical/Vocational Nurse Training (LPN, LVN, Cert, Dipl, AAS)** *1296 hrs./$5425* • **Nursing, Other** *13 students enrolled* • **Truck and Bus Driver/ Commercial Vehicle Operation** *216 hrs./$926*

**STUDENT SERVICES** Academic or career counseling, employment services for current students, placement services for program completers, remedial services.

## Tennessee Technology Center at Shelbyville

1405 Madison Street, Shelbyville, TN 37160
http://www.shelbyville.tec.tn.us/

**CONTACT** Ivan Jones, Director
**Telephone:** 931-685-5013

**GENERAL INFORMATION** Public Institution. Founded 1964. **Total program enrollment:** 311.

**PROGRAM(S) OFFERED**
• **Autobody/Collision and Repair Technology/Technician** *2160 hrs./$3810* • **Automobile/Automotive Mechanics Technology/Technician** *8 students enrolled* • **Business Operations Support and Secretarial Services, Other** *1296 hrs./ $2286* • **Computer and Information Sciences, General** *2160 hrs./$3810* • **Drafting and Design Technology/Technician, General** *7 students enrolled* • **Electrical/Electronics Equipment Installation and Repair, General** *1728 hrs./ $3048* • **Heating, Air Conditioning, Ventilation and Refrigeration Maintenance Technology/Technician (HAC, HACR, HVAC, HVACR)** *6 students enrolled* • **Industrial Mechanics and Maintenance Technology** *2160 hrs./$3810* • **Licensed Practical/Vocational Nurse Training (LPN, LVN, Cert, Dipl, AAS)** *1296 hrs./$3596* • **Machine Shop Technology/Assistant** *6 students enrolled* • **Nurse/Nursing Assistant/Aide and Patient Care Assistant** *11 students enrolled* • **Truck and Bus Driver/Commercial Vehicle Operation** *25 students enrolled* • **Welding Technology/Welder** *10 students enrolled*

**STUDENT SERVICES** Academic or career counseling, employment services for current students, placement services for program completers, remedial services.

## Tennessee Technology Center at Whiteville

PO Box 489, Whiteville, TN 38075
http://www.whiteville.tec.tn.us/

**CONTACT** Jeff Sisk, Director
**Telephone:** 731-254-8521

**GENERAL INFORMATION** Public Institution. **Total program enrollment:** 156.

**PROGRAM(S) OFFERED**
• **Automobile/Automotive Mechanics Technology/Technician** *2160 hrs./$3810* • **Business Administration, Management and Operations, Other** *1296 hrs./ $2286* • **Business Operations Support and Secretarial Services, Other** *18 students enrolled* • **Business/Office Automation/Technology/Data Entry** *2160 hrs./$3810* • **Drafting and Design Technology/Technician, General** • **Electrician** • **Heating, Air Conditioning, Ventilation and Refrigeration Maintenance Technology/Technician (HAC, HACR, HVAC, HVACR)** *9 students enrolled* • **Industrial Electronics Technology/Technician** *11 students enrolled* • **Industrial Mechanics and Maintenance Technology** *1 student enrolled* • **Licensed Practical/Vocational Nurse Training (LPN, LVN, Cert, Dipl, AAS)** *1296 hrs./ $4158* • **Machine Tool Technology/Machinist** *1944 hrs./$3810* • **Nurse/Nursing Assistant/Aide and Patient Care Assistant** • **Welding Technology/Welder** *1296 hrs./$2286*

**STUDENT SERVICES** Academic or career counseling, employment services for current students, placement services for program completers, remedial services.

## Union University

1050 Union University Drive, Jackson, TN 38305-3697
http://www.uu.edu/

**CONTACT** David S. Dockery, President
**Telephone:** 731-668-1818

**GENERAL INFORMATION** Private Institution. Founded 1823. **Accreditation:** Regional (SACS/CC); art and design (NASAD); music (NASM). **Total program enrollment:** 2681. **Application fee:** $35.

**PROGRAM(S) OFFERED**
• **Christian Studies**

**STUDENT SERVICES** Academic or career counseling, employment services for current students, placement services for program completers.

## Vatterott College

2655 Dividend Drive, Memphis, TN 38132
http://www.vatterott-college.edu/

**CONTACT** Theresa Rice, Director
**Telephone:** 901-761-5730

**GENERAL INFORMATION** Private Institution. Founded 2004. **Accreditation:** State accredited or approved. **Total program enrollment:** 478.

**PROGRAM(S) OFFERED**
• **Cosmetology/Cosmetologist, General** *10 students enrolled* • **Electrician** *18 students enrolled* • **Heating, Air Conditioning, Ventilation and Refrigeration Maintenance Technology/Technician (HAC, HACR, HVAC, HVACR)** *75 students enrolled* • **Information Technology** *18 students enrolled* • **Medical Office Assistant/Specialist** *7 students enrolled*

**STUDENT SERVICES** Academic or career counseling, employment services for current students, placement services for program completers.

## Virginia College School of Business and Health at Chattanooga

721 Eastgate Loop Road, Chattanooga, TN 37411
http://www.vc.edu/site/campus.cfm?campus=chattanooga

**CONTACT** Don Newton, Campus Director
**Telephone:** 423-893-2000

**GENERAL INFORMATION** Private Institution. **Total program enrollment:** 413. **Application fee:** $100.

**PROGRAM(S) OFFERED**
• **Administrative Assistant and Secretarial Science, General** *4 students enrolled* • **Medical Insurance Coding Specialist/Coder** *6 students enrolled* • **Medical/ Clinical Assistant** *7 students enrolled* • **Pharmacy Technician/Assistant**

**STUDENT SERVICES** Academic or career counseling, placement services for program completers, remedial services.

## Visible School—Music and Worships Arts College

9817 Huff and Puff Road, Lakeland, TN 38002
http://www.visibleschool.com

**CONTACT** Ken Steorts, President
**Telephone:** 901-381-3939

**GENERAL INFORMATION** Private Institution. **Total program enrollment:** 90. **Application fee:** $40.

**PROGRAM(S) OFFERED**
• **Digital Communication and Media/Multimedia** • **Music Management and Merchandising** • **Music Performance, General** *3 students enrolled* • **Theology/Theological Studies**

**STUDENT SERVICES** Academic or career counseling, employment services for current students, placement services for program completers, remedial services.

## Volunteer Beauty Academy

1057-A Vendall Road, Dyersburg, TN 38024

**CONTACT** Dorothy H. Chitwood, President
**Telephone:** 731-285-1542

**GENERAL INFORMATION** Private Institution. **Total program enrollment:** 62. **Application fee:** $100.

**PROGRAM(S) OFFERED**
• **Cosmetology/Cosmetologist, General** *1500 hrs./$10,950*

**STUDENT SERVICES** Academic or career counseling, placement services for program completers.

## Volunteer Beauty Academy

1791B Gallatin Pike, N, Madison, TN 37115
http://www.volunteerbeauty.com/

**CONTACT** Dorothy H. Chitwood, President
**Telephone:** 615-865-4477

**GENERAL INFORMATION** Private Institution. **Total program enrollment:** 66. **Application fee:** $100.

**PROGRAM(S) OFFERED**
• **Aesthetician/Esthetician and Skin Care Specialist** *750 hrs./$6850* • **Cosmetology and Related Personal Grooming Arts, Other** *5 students enrolled* • **Cosmetology/Cosmetologist, General** *1500 hrs./$10,950* • **Nail Technician/Specialist and Manicurist** *600 hrs./$4000*

**STUDENT SERVICES** Academic or career counseling, placement services for program completers.

## Volunteer Beauty Academy

5666 Nolensville Road, Nashville, TN 37211
http://www.volunteerbeauty.com/

**CONTACT** Dorothy H. Chitwood, President
**Telephone:** 615-298-4600

**GENERAL INFORMATION** Private Institution. Founded 1985. **Total program enrollment:** 26. **Application fee:** $100.

**PROGRAM(S) OFFERED**
• **Cosmetology/Cosmetologist, General** *750 hrs./$2900*

**STUDENT SERVICES** Academic or career counseling, placement services for program completers.

## Volunteer Beauty Academy–System Office

5668 Nolensville Road, Nashville, TN 37211

**CONTACT** Dorothy Chitwood, President
**Telephone:** 615-860-4996

**GENERAL INFORMATION** Private Institution.

## Volunteer State Community College

1480 Nashville Pike, Gallatin, TN 37066-3188
http://www.volstate.edu/

**CONTACT** Dr. Warren Nichols, President
**Telephone:** 615-452-8600

**GENERAL INFORMATION** Public Institution. Founded 1970. **Accreditation:** Regional (SACS/CC); dental assisting (ADA); emergency medical services (JRCEMTP); health information technology (AHIMA); physical therapy assisting (APTA); radiologic technology: radiography (JRCERT); respiratory therapy technology (CoARC). **Total program enrollment:** 3530. **Application fee:** $10.

**PROGRAM(S) OFFERED**
• **Administrative Assistant and Secretarial Science, General** *6 students enrolled* • **Clinical/Medical Laboratory Science and Allied Professions, Other** *16 students enrolled* • **Dental Assisting/Assistant** *23 students enrolled* • **Diagnostic Medical Sonography/Sonographer and Ultrasound Technician** *11 students enrolled* • **Emergency Medical Technology/Technician (EMT Paramedic)** *157 students enrolled* • **Fire Science/Firefighting** *10 students enrolled* • **Logistics and Materials Management** *7 students enrolled*

**STUDENT SERVICES** Academic or career counseling, employment services for current students, placement services for program completers, remedial services.

## Walters State Community College

500 South Davy Crockett Parkway, Morristown, TN 37813-6899
http://www.ws.edu/

**CONTACT** Wade B. McCamey, President
**Telephone:** 423-585-2600

**GENERAL INFORMATION** Public Institution. Founded 1970. **Accreditation:** Regional (SACS/CC); physical therapy assisting (APTA); respiratory therapy technology (CoARC). **Total program enrollment:** 3241. **Application fee:** $10.

**PROGRAM(S) OFFERED**
• **Child Development** *4 students enrolled* • **Criminal Justice/Police Science** *148 students enrolled* • **Culinary Arts/Chef Training** *5 students enrolled* • **Emergency Medical Technology/Technician (EMT Paramedic)** *51 students enrolled* • **Health Information/Medical Records Technology/Technician** *19 students enrolled* • **Industrial Mechanics and Maintenance Technology** • **Management Information Systems and Services, Other** • **Medical Insurance Coding Specialist/Coder** *10 students enrolled* • **Medical Transcription/Transcriptionist** *9 students enrolled* • **Pharmacy Technician/Assistant** *14 students enrolled* • **Quality Control Technology/Technician** *1 student enrolled* • **Web Page, Digital/Multimedia and Information Resources Design**

**STUDENT SERVICES** Academic or career counseling, employment services for current students, placement services for program completers, remedial services.

## Watkins College of Art, Design, & Film

2298 MetroCenter Boulevard, Nashville, TN 37228
http://www.watkins.edu/

**CONTACT** Ellen L. Meyer, President
**Telephone:** 615-383-4848

**GENERAL INFORMATION** Private Institution. Founded 1885. **Accreditation:** Art and design (NASAD); interior design: professional (CIDA). **Total program enrollment:** 254. **Application fee:** $50.

**PROGRAM(S) OFFERED**
• **Cinematography and Film/Video Production** *1 student enrolled* • **Graphic Design**

**STUDENT SERVICES** Academic or career counseling, employment services for current students.

## West Tennessee Business College

1186 Highway 45 Bypass, Jackson, TN 38343
http://www.wtbc.com/

**CONTACT** Charlotte V. Burch, President
**Telephone:** 731-668-7240

**GENERAL INFORMATION** Private Institution. Founded 1888. **Total program enrollment:** 376. **Application fee:** $50.

**PROGRAM(S) OFFERED**
• **Administrative Assistant and Secretarial Science, General** *37 hrs./$11,470* • **Aesthetician/Esthetician and Skin Care Specialist** *750 hrs./$8275* • **Cosmetology/Cosmetologist, General** *1500 hrs./$11,275* • **General Office Occupations and Clerical Services** *1 student enrolled* • **Make-Up Artist/Specialist** *23 students enrolled* • **Medical Administrative/Executive Assistant and Medical Secretary** *43 students enrolled* • **Medical Insurance Coding Specialist/Coder** *34 hrs./$11,300* • **Medical Office Assistant/Specialist** *34 hrs./$10,540* • **Medical/Clinical Assistant** *37 hrs./$11,470* • **Nail Technician/Specialist and Manicurist** *12 students enrolled*

**STUDENT SERVICES** Employment services for current students, placement services for program completers.

## William R. Moore School of Technology

1200 Poplar Avenue, Memphis, TN 38104
http://www.williamrmoore.org/

**CONTACT** Don R. Smith, Director/Chief Administrative Officer
**Telephone:** 901-726-1977

**GENERAL INFORMATION** Private Institution. Founded 1939. **Total program enrollment:** 33.

**PROGRAM(S) OFFERED**
• **Computer Installation and Repair Technology/Technician** *3 students enrolled* • **Welding Technology/Welder** *9 students enrolled*

**STUDENT SERVICES** Academic or career counseling, placement services for program completers.

# TEXAS

## Abilene Christian University

ACU Box 29100, Abilene, TX 79699-9100
http://www.acu.edu/

**CONTACT** Royce Money, PhD, President
**Telephone:** 325-674-2000

**GENERAL INFORMATION** Private Institution (Affiliated with Church of Christ). Founded 1906. **Accreditation:** Regional (SACS/CC); home economics (AAFCS); journalism and mass communications (ACEJMC); music (NASM); speech-language pathology (ASHA). **Total program enrollment:** 3992. **Application fee:** $25.

**PROGRAM(S) OFFERED**
• **Social Sciences, Other**

**STUDENT SERVICES** Academic or career counseling, employment services for current students, placement services for program completers, remedial services.

## Academy at Austin

15635 Vision Drive, Suite 107, Pflugerville, TX 78660
http://www.theacademyaustin.com

**CONTACT** Oscar Perez, Dean
**Telephone:** 512-251-1644 Ext. 108

**GENERAL INFORMATION** Private Institution. **Total program enrollment:** 138. **Application fee:** $100.

**PROGRAM(S) OFFERED**
• **Aesthetician/Esthetician and Skin Care Specialist** *750 hrs./$7600* • **Cosmetology, Barber/Styling, and Nail Instructor** *250 hrs./$4600* • **Cosmetology/Cosmetologist, General** *1500 hrs./$16,975*

**STUDENT SERVICES** Academic or career counseling, placement services for program completers.

## Academy of Cosmetology

5416 Manchaca Road, Austin, TX 78745
http://academyofcosmetology.net/

**CONTACT** Rebecca Datcher, Administrator
**Telephone:** 512-444-2249

**GENERAL INFORMATION** Private Institution. **Total program enrollment:** 26. **Application fee:** $100.

**PROGRAM(S) OFFERED**
• **Aesthetician/Esthetician and Skin Care Specialist** *750 hrs./$4000* • **Cosmetology/Cosmetologist, General** *1500 hrs./$7723* • **Nail Technician/Specialist and Manicurist** *600 hrs./$2000*

**STUDENT SERVICES** Academic or career counseling, employment services for current students, placement services for program completers.

## Academy of Hair Design

348 Spring Hill Street, Jasper, TX 75951

**CONTACT** Minnie Richey
**Telephone:** 409-384-8200

**GENERAL INFORMATION** Private Institution. **Total program enrollment:** 56.

**PROGRAM(S) OFFERED**
• **Cosmetology, Barber/Styling, and Nail Instructor** *750 hrs./$4100* • **Cosmetology/Cosmetologist, General** *1500 hrs./$8325* • **Nail Technician/Specialist and Manicurist** *600 hrs./$3500*

**STUDENT SERVICES** Academic or career counseling, placement services for program completers.

## Academy of Hair Design

512 South Chestnut Building, Lufkin, TX 75901

**CONTACT** Carroll W. Lewing, President
**Telephone:** 936-634-8440

**GENERAL INFORMATION** Private Institution. **Total program enrollment:** 41.

**PROGRAM(S) OFFERED**
• **Cosmetology, Barber/Styling, and Nail Instructor** *7 students enrolled* • **Cosmetology/Cosmetologist, General** *750 hrs./$3800* • **Nail Technician/Specialist and Manicurist** *15 students enrolled*

**STUDENT SERVICES** Academic or career counseling, placement services for program completers.

## Academy of Hair Design

8140 Ninth Avenue, Port Arthur, TX 77642
http://academyofhairdesign@gmail.com/

**CONTACT** Minnie Richey, Owner
**Telephone:** 409-813-3100

**GENERAL INFORMATION** Private Institution. **Total program enrollment:** 61.

**PROGRAM(S) OFFERED**
• **Cosmetology, Barber/Styling, and Nail Instructor** *3 students enrolled* • **Cosmetology/Cosmetologist, General** *750 hrs./$3800* • **Nail Technician/ Specialist and Manicurist** *7 students enrolled*

**STUDENT SERVICES** Academic or career counseling, placement services for program completers.

## Academy of Health Care Professions

7517 Cameron Road, Suite 100, Austin, TX 78752
http://www.ahcp.edu/

**CONTACT** Lori Bjorgo, Director
**Telephone:** 512-892-2835

**GENERAL INFORMATION** Private Institution. **Total program enrollment:** 241. **Application fee:** $100.

**PROGRAM(S) OFFERED**
• **Allied Health and Medical Assisting Services, Other** *900 hrs./$10,500* • **Dental Assisting/Assistant** *750 hrs./$10,810* • **Medical Insurance Coding Specialist/Coder** *750 hrs./$10,500* • **Medical Radiologic Technology/ Science—Radiation Therapist** *1320 hrs./$18,400* • **Medical/Clinical Assistant** *35 students enrolled* • **Phlebotomy/Phlebotomist** *590 hrs./$7650*

**STUDENT SERVICES** Academic or career counseling, placement services for program completers.

## The Academy of Health Care Professions

1900 North Loop West, Suite 100, Houston, TX 77018
http://www.academyofhealth.com/

**CONTACT** A. John Emerald, Chief Executive Officer
**Telephone:** 713-425-3100

**GENERAL INFORMATION** Private Institution. Founded 1988. **Accreditation:** State accredited or approved. **Total program enrollment:** 370. **Application fee:** $100.

**PROGRAM(S) OFFERED**
• **Clinical/Medical Laboratory Technician** • **Dental Assisting/Assistant** *750 hrs./$10,810* • **Diagnostic Medical Sonography/Sonographer and Ultrasound Technician** *2144 hrs./$25,350* • **Health Information/Medical Records Administration/Administrator** *750 hrs./$10,500* • **Massage Therapy/ Therapeutic Massage** *500 hrs./$5500* • **Medical Radiologic Technology/ Science—Radiation Therapist** *1320 hrs./$18,400* • **Medical/Clinical Assistant** *900 hrs./$12,160* • **Surgical Technology/Technologist** *22 students enrolled*

**STUDENT SERVICES** Academic or career counseling, placement services for program completers.

## The Academy of Health Care Professions

8313 Southwest Freeway, Suite 300, Houston, TX 77074
http://www.ahcp.edu/

**CONTACT** John Emerald, CEO
**Telephone:** 713-470-2427

**GENERAL INFORMATION** Private Institution. **Total program enrollment:** 66. **Application fee:** $100.

**PROGRAM(S) OFFERED**
• **Dental Assisting/Assistant** *16 students enrolled* • **Medical Insurance Coding Specialist/Coder** *21 students enrolled* • **Radiologic Technology/Science—Radiographer** *51 students enrolled*

**STUDENT SERVICES** Academic or career counseling, placement services for program completers.

## The Academy of Health Care Professions

4738 N. W. Loop 410, San Antonio, TX 78229
http://ahcp.edu/

**CONTACT** A. John Emerald, CEO
**Telephone:** 210-298-3600

**GENERAL INFORMATION** Private Institution. **Total program enrollment:** 231. **Application fee:** $100.

**PROGRAM(S) OFFERED**
• **Dental Assisting/Assistant** *33 hrs./$10,810* • **Diagnostic Medical Sonography/Sonographer and Ultrasound Technician** *2144 hrs./$25,350* • **Health Information/Medical Records Administration/Administrator** *41 hrs./ $10,500* • **Medical Insurance Coding Specialist/Coder** *63 students enrolled* • **Medical/Clinical Assistant** *900 hrs./$12,160* • **Radiologic Technology/ Science—Radiographer** *1320 hrs./$16,733*

**STUDENT SERVICES** Academic or career counseling, placement services for program completers.

## Academy of Professional Careers

2201 South Western, Suite 102-103, Amarillo, TX 79109
http://www.academyofhealthcareers.com/

**CONTACT** Gary Yasuda, President
**Telephone:** 806-353-3500

**GENERAL INFORMATION** Private Institution. **Total program enrollment:** 199. **Application fee:** $100.

**PROGRAM(S) OFFERED**
• **Dental Assisting/Assistant** *720 hrs./$10,854* • **Health/Health Care Administration/Management** *720 hrs./$10,801* • **Medical Administrative/ Executive Assistant and Medical Secretary** *720 hrs./$10,585* • **Medical/ Clinical Assistant** *720 hrs./$11,033* • **Pharmacy Technician/Assistant** *720 hrs./ $10,819*

**STUDENT SERVICES** Academic or career counseling, employment services for current students, placement services for program completers.

## Advanced Barber College and Hair Design

2818 S. International, Weslaco, TX 78596

**CONTACT** Jaime Garza, Office Administrator
**Telephone:** 956-969-0341

**GENERAL INFORMATION** Private Institution. **Total program enrollment:** 57.

**PROGRAM(S) OFFERED**
• **Barbering/Barber** *1500 hrs./$7200* • **Cosmetology, Barber/Styling, and Nail Instructor** *1000 hrs./$5000* • **Education, Other** *5 students enrolled* • **Nail Technician/Specialist and Manicurist** *600 hrs./$3000* • **Personal and Culinary Services, Other** *9 students enrolled*

**STUDENT SERVICES** Placement services for program completers.

## Aeronautical Institute of Technologies

2502 West Ledbetter Drive, Dallas, TX 75233
http://www.fixthatplane.com

**CONTACT** James Cooper, School Director
**Telephone:** 214-333-9711

**GENERAL INFORMATION** Private Institution. **Total program enrollment:** 369. **Application fee:** $25.

**PROGRAM(S) OFFERED**
• **Airframe Mechanics and Aircraft Maintenance Technology/Technician** *96 hrs./$36,115* • **Avionics Maintenance Technology/Technician** *120 hrs./$43,600*

**STUDENT SERVICES** Academic or career counseling, placement services for program completers.

## Aims Academy

1711 S. Interstate 35E, Carrollton, TX 75006
http://www.aimsacademy.com/

**CONTACT** Crystal Elliott, President
**Telephone:** 972-323-6333

**GENERAL INFORMATION** Private Institution. **Total program enrollment:** 73. **Application fee:** $100.

**PROGRAM(S) OFFERED**
• **Bartending/Bartender** *56 hrs./$790* • **Culinary Arts/Chef Training** *1351 hrs./$28,985*

**STUDENT SERVICES** Academic or career counseling, placement services for program completers.

## Alamo Community College District System

811 West Houston, San Antonio, TX 78284

**CONTACT** Dr. Bruce H. Leslie, Chancellor
**Telephone:** 210-208-8000

**GENERAL INFORMATION** Public Institution.

## Allied Health Careers

5424 Highway 290 W, Suite 105, Austin, TX 78735
http://alliedhealthcareers.net/

**CONTACT** Dennis Childers, Director
**Telephone:** 512-892-5210

**GENERAL INFORMATION** Private Institution. **Total program enrollment:** 291. **Application fee:** $100.

**PROGRAM(S) OFFERED**
• **Allied Health and Medical Assisting Services, Other** *910 hrs./$19,446* • **Dental Assisting/Assistant** *910 hrs./$19,446* • **Health Services/Allied Health/Health Sciences, General** *1480 hrs./$35,286* • **Pharmacy Technician/Assistant** *910 hrs./$19,466*

**STUDENT SERVICES** Academic or career counseling, employment services for current students, placement services for program completers.

## Alvin Community College

3110 Mustang Road, Alvin, TX 77511-4898
http://www.alvincollege.edu/

**CONTACT** A. Rodney Allbright, President
**Telephone:** 281-756-3500

**GENERAL INFORMATION** Public Institution. Founded 1949. **Accreditation:** Regional (SACS/CC). **Total program enrollment:** 1319.

**PROGRAM(S) OFFERED**
• **Automobile/Automotive Mechanics Technology/Technician** *18 students enrolled* • **Business Administration and Management, General** *7 students enrolled* • **Business/Commerce, General** • **Cardiovascular Technology/Technologist** • **Chemical Technology/Technician** *45 students enrolled* • **Child Development** • **Clinical/Medical Laboratory Technician** • **Computer Programming/Programmer, General** *27 students enrolled* • **Computer Technology/Computer Systems Technology** *9 students enrolled* • **Corrections** • **Court Reporting/Court Reporter** *9 students enrolled* • **Criminal Justice/Police Science** • **Criminal Justice/Safety Studies** • **Criminalistics and Criminal Science** *2 students enrolled* • **Culinary Arts/Chef Training** *21 students enrolled* • **Diagnostic Medical Sonography/Sonographer and Ultrasound Technician** *1 student enrolled* • **Drafting and Design Technology/Technician, General** *15 students enrolled* • **Electrical, Electronic and Communications Engineering Technology/Technician** • **Electroneurodiagnostic/Electroencephalographic Technology/Technologist** • **Emergency Medical Technology/Technician (EMT Paramedic)** *2 students enrolled* • **General Office Occupations and Clerical Services** *1 student enrolled* • **Legal Assistant/Paralegal** *12 students enrolled* • **Licensed Practical/Vocational Nurse Training (LPN, LVN, Cert, Dipl, AAS)** *27 students enrolled* • **Medical Insurance Coding Specialist/Coder** *5 students enrolled* • **Ornamental Horticulture** *19 students enrolled* • **Prepress/Desktop Publishing and Digital Imaging Design** *22 students enrolled* • **Radio and Television** *5 students enrolled* • **Robotics Technology/Technician** • **Substance Abuse/Addiction Counseling** *2 students enrolled*

**STUDENT SERVICES** Academic or career counseling, daycare for children of students, employment services for current students, placement services for program completers, remedial services.

## Amarillo College

PO Box 447, Amarillo, TX 79178-0001
http://www.actx.edu/

**CONTACT** Dr. Steven W. Jones, President
**Telephone:** 806-371-5000

**GENERAL INFORMATION** Public Institution. Founded 1929. **Accreditation:** Regional (SACS/CC); dental hygiene (ADA); engineering technology (ABET/TAC); funeral service (ABFSE); medical laboratory technology (NAACLS); music (NASM); nuclear medicine technology (JRCNMT); physical therapy assisting (APTA); radiologic technology: radiation therapy technology (JRCERT); radiologic technology: radiography (JRCERT); surgical technology (ARCST). **Total program enrollment:** 3016.

**PROGRAM(S) OFFERED**
• **Administrative Assistant and Secretarial Science, General** *1 student enrolled* • **Aircraft Powerplant Technology/Technician** *13 students enrolled* • **Airframe Mechanics and Aircraft Maintenance Technology/Technician** *29 students enrolled* • **Autobody/Collision and Repair Technology/Technician** *10 students enrolled* • **Automobile/Automotive Mechanics Technology/Technician** *12 students enrolled* • **Business Administration and Management, General** *2 students enrolled* • **Business/Office Automation/Technology/Data Entry** *5 students enrolled* • **Child Care Provider/Assistant** *2 students enrolled* • **Child Care and Support Services Management** *7 students enrolled* • **Computer Programming/Programmer, General** *3 students enrolled* • **Criminal Justice/Police Science** • **Data Processing and Data Processing Technology/Technician** *54 students enrolled* • **Dental Assisting/Assistant** *8 students enrolled* • **Diesel Mechanics Technology/Technician** *31 students enrolled* • **Drafting and Design Technology/Technician, General** *14 students enrolled* • **Electrical, Electronic and Communications Engineering Technology/Technician** *3 students enrolled* • **Electromechanical Technology/Electromechanical Engineering Technology** *5 students enrolled* • **Emergency Medical Technology/Technician (EMT Paramedic)** *4 students enrolled* • **Fire Science/Firefighting** *13 students enrolled* • **Funeral Service and Mortuary Science, General** *36 students enrolled* • **Graphic Design** *1 student enrolled* • **Health Information/Medical Records Technology/Technician** *8 students enrolled* • **Instrumentation Technology/Technician** *8 students enrolled* • **Interior Design** • **Licensed Practical/Vocational Nurse Training (LPN, LVN, Cert, Dipl, AAS)** *68 students enrolled* • **Occupational Safety and Health Technology/Technician** • **Pharmacy Technician/Assistant** *10 students enrolled* • **Photographic and Film/Video Technology/Technician and Assistant** *1 student enrolled* • **Radio and Television Broadcasting Technology/Technician** *3 students enrolled* • **Real Estate** • **Substance Abuse/Addiction Counseling** *3 students enrolled* • **Surgical Technology/Technologist** *9 students enrolled* • **Welding Technology/Welder** *10 students enrolled*

**STUDENT SERVICES** Academic or career counseling, daycare for children of students, employment services for current students, placement services for program completers, remedial services.

## American Broadcasting School

712 N. Watson Road, Arlington, TX 76011
http://radioschool.com/

**CONTACT** Staci Cockrell, CEO
**Telephone:** 817-695-2474

**GENERAL INFORMATION** Private Institution. **Total program enrollment:** 63.

**PROGRAM(S) OFFERED**
• **Radio and Television** *1032 hrs./$11,125*

**STUDENT SERVICES** Placement services for program completers.

## American Commercial College

402 Butternut Street, Abilene, TX 79602
http://acc-careers.com/

**CONTACT** Tony Delgado, Director
**Telephone:** 325-672-8495

**GENERAL INFORMATION** Private Institution. **Total program enrollment:** 107. **Application fee:** $100.

**PROGRAM(S) OFFERED**
• **Accounting and Related Services, Other** *720 hrs./$10,080* • **Administrative Assistant and Secretarial Science, General** *720 hrs./$10,080* • **Health Information/Medical Records Technology/Technician** *900 hrs./$12,600* • **Medical Administrative/Executive Assistant and Medical Secretary** *720 hrs./$10,080* • **Medical Transcription/Transcriptionist** *900 hrs./$12,600* • **Medical/Clinical Assistant** *900 hrs./$12,600*

**STUDENT SERVICES** Academic or career counseling, placement services for program completers.

## American Commercial College

2007 34th Street, Lubbock, TX 79411
http://www.acc-careers.com/

**CONTACT** Michael J. Otto, Director
**Telephone:** 806-747-4339

**GENERAL INFORMATION** Private Institution. **Total program enrollment:** 28. **Application fee:** $100.

**PROGRAM(S) OFFERED**
• **Accounting Technology/Technician and Bookkeeping** *17 students enrolled* • **Administrative Assistant and Secretarial Science, General** *13 students enrolled* • **Computer Technology/Computer Systems Technology** *13 students enrolled* • **Data Processing and Data Processing Technology/Technician** *8 students enrolled* • **General Office Occupations and Clerical Services** *3 students enrolled* • **Medical Administrative/Executive Assistant and Medical Secretary** *30 students enrolled* • **Medical Transcription/Transcriptionist** *7 students enrolled* • **Medical/Clinical Assistant** *12 students enrolled*

**STUDENT SERVICES** Academic or career counseling, employment services for current students, placement services for program completers.

## American Commercial College

2115 East Eighth Street, Odessa, TX 79761
http://acc-careers.com/

**CONTACT** Shawn Clark, Director
**Telephone:** 432-362-6768

**GENERAL INFORMATION** Private Institution. **Total program enrollment:** 52. **Application fee:** $100.

**PROGRAM(S) OFFERED**
• **Accounting** *30 hrs./$10,080* • **Administrative Assistant and Secretarial Science, General** *2 students enrolled* • **Allied Health and Medical Assisting Services, Other** *42 students enrolled* • **Computer Science** *8 students enrolled* • **Executive Assistant/Executive Secretary** *30 hrs./$10,080* • **Medical Administrative/Executive Assistant and Medical Secretary** *12 students enrolled* • **Medical Insurance Specialist/Medical Biller** *39 hrs./$12,600* • **Medical Office Assistant/Specialist** *30 hrs./$10,080* • **Medical Transcription/Transcriptionist** *39 hrs./$12,600* • **Medical/Clinical Assistant** *39 hrs./$12,600*

**STUDENT SERVICES** Academic or career counseling, employment services for current students, placement services for program completers.

## American Commercial College

3177 Executive Drive, San Angelo, TX 76904
http://www.acc-careers.com/

**CONTACT** B. A. Reed, Director
**Telephone:** 325-942-6797

**GENERAL INFORMATION** Private Institution. **Total program enrollment:** 104. **Application fee:** $100.

**PROGRAM(S) OFFERED**
• **Accounting Technology/Technician and Bookkeeping** *720 hrs./$10,180* • **Accounting and Computer Science** *720 hrs./$10,180* • **Accounting** *4 students enrolled* • **Administrative Assistant and Secretarial Science, General** *720 hrs./$10,180* • **Business/Office Automation/Technology/Data Entry** *3 students enrolled* • **Data Entry/Microcomputer Applications, General** • **Executive Assistant/Executive Secretary** *5 students enrolled* • **Medical Office Computer Specialist/Assistant** *900 hrs./$12,700* • **Medical Office Management/Administration** *720 hrs./$10,180* • **Medical Transcription/Transcriptionist** *1 student enrolled* • **Medical/Clinical Assistant** *900 hrs./$12,700*

**STUDENT SERVICES** Academic or career counseling, placement services for program completers.

## American Commercial College

4317 Barnett Road, Wichita Falls, TX 76310
http://www.acc-careers.com/

**CONTACT** Kevin Laukhuf, Director
**Telephone:** 940-691-0454

**GENERAL INFORMATION** Private Institution. **Total program enrollment:** 112.

**PROGRAM(S) OFFERED**
• **Accounting Technology/Technician and Bookkeeping** *720 hrs./$10,080* • **Accounting and Business/Management** *720 hrs./$10,080* • **Allied Health and Medical Assisting Services, Other** *40 students enrolled* • **Business/Office Automation/Technology/Data Entry** • **Computer Installation and Repair Technology/Technician** *3 students enrolled* • **Computer Technology/Computer Systems Technology** *720 hrs./$10,080* • **Computer/Information Technology Services Administration and Management, Other** *6 students enrolled* • **Medical Office Assistant/Specialist** *720 hrs./$10,080* • **Medical Office Computer Specialist/Assistant** *13 students enrolled* • **Medical Transcription/Transcriptionist** *900 hrs./$12,600* • **Medical/Clinical Assistant** *900 hrs./$10,380*

**STUDENT SERVICES** Academic or career counseling, employment services for current students, placement services for program completers.

## Ames Academy

3863 SW Loop 820, Fort Worth, TX 76133
http://www.aimsacademy.com/

**CONTACT** Crystal Elliott, President
**Telephone:** 817-292-3559

**GENERAL INFORMATION** Private Institution. **Total program enrollment:** 65. **Application fee:** $100.

**PROGRAM(S) OFFERED**
• **Bartending/Bartender** *56 hrs./$790* • **Culinary Arts/Chef Training** *1351 hrs./$28,985*

**STUDENT SERVICES** Academic or career counseling, placement services for program completers.

## Anamarc Educational Institute

3210 Dyer, El Paso, TX 79930
http://www.anamarc.com/

**CONTACT** Marc Houde, Chief Administrator Officer
**Telephone:** 915-351-8100

**GENERAL INFORMATION** Private Institution. **Total program enrollment:** 627.

**PROGRAM(S) OFFERED**
• **Administrative Assistant and Secretarial Science, General** *27 hrs./$6473* • **Business Operations Support and Secretarial Services, Other** *8 students enrolled* • **Health Information/Medical Records Technology/Technician** *43 students enrolled* • **Human Development, Family Studies, and Related Services, Other** *14 students enrolled* • **Licensed Practical/Vocational Nurse Training (LPN, LVN, Cert, Dipl, AAS)** *63 hrs./$21,130* • **Medical Insurance Coding Specialist/Coder** *44 hrs./$11,621* • **Medical/Clinical Assistant** *47 hrs./$11,999* • **Nurse/Nursing Assistant/Aide and Patient Care Assistant** *120 hrs./$626* • **Nursing—Registered Nurse Training (RN, ASN, BSN, MSN)** *38 students enrolled* • **Phlebotomy/Phlebotomist** *26 hrs./$7320* • **Renal/Dialysis Technologist/Technician** *37 students enrolled*

**STUDENT SERVICES** Placement services for program completers.

## Angelina College

PO Box 1768, Lufkin, TX 75902-1768
http://www.angelina.cc.tx.us/

**CONTACT** Larry M. Phillips, President
**Telephone:** 936-639-1301

**GENERAL INFORMATION** Public Institution. Founded 1968. **Accreditation:** Regional (SACS/CC); radiologic technology: radiography (JRCERT). **Total program enrollment:** 2076.

**PROGRAM(S) OFFERED**
• **Administrative Assistant and Secretarial Science, General** *6 students enrolled* • **Automobile/Automotive Mechanics Technology/Technician** *5 students enrolled* • **Business Administration and Management, General** • **Business/Commerce, General** • **Business/Office Automation/Technology/Data Entry** *5 students enrolled* • **Child Care and Support Services Management** *4 students enrolled* • **Child Development** *5 students enrolled* • **Computer Systems Networking and Telecommunications** *1 student enrolled* • **Criminal Justice/Police Science** *59 students enrolled* • **Data Processing and Data Processing Technology/Technician** *4 students enrolled* • **Design and Visual Communications, General** *1 student enrolled* • **Diesel Mechanics Technology/Technician** *11 students enrolled* • **Drafting and Design Technology/Technician, General** *6 students enrolled* • **Electrical, Electronic and Communications Engineering Technology/Technician** *7 students enrolled* • **Electromechanical Technology/Electromechanical Engineering Technology** *14 students enrolled* • **Emergency Medical Technology/Technician (EMT Paramedic)** *1 student enrolled* • **Environmental Engineering Technology/Environmental Technology** • **Fire Science/Firefighting** *22 students enrolled* • **Human Services, General** *2 students enrolled* • **Licensed Practical/Vocational Nurse Training (LPN, LVN, Cert, Dipl, AAS)** *86 students enrolled* • **Machine Tool Technology/Machinist** *2 students enrolled* • **Nursing—Registered Nurse Training (RN, ASN, BSN, MSN)** • **Pharmacy Technician/Assistant** *16 students enrolled* • **Real Estate** *34 students enrolled* • **Substance Abuse/Addiction Counseling** • **Welding Technology/Welder** *14 students enrolled*

**STUDENT SERVICES** Academic or career counseling, employment services for current students, placement services for program completers, remedial services.

## Arlington Career Institute

901 Avenue K, Grand Prairie, TX 75050
http://www.arlingtonci.com/

**CONTACT** Jon Vecchio, Vice President
**Telephone:** 972-647-1607 Ext. 223

**GENERAL INFORMATION** Private Institution. **Total program enrollment:** 195. **Application fee:** $100.

**PROGRAM(S) OFFERED**
• **Allied Health and Medical Assisting Services, Other** *955 hrs./$10,413* • **Business/Commerce, General** *600 hrs./$7176* • **Court Reporting/Court Reporter** *3160 hrs./$28,959* • **Health and Medical Administrative Services, Other** *900 hrs./$10,464* • **Legal Assistant/Paralegal** *900 hrs./$11,853* • **Legal Professions and Studies, Other** *900 hrs./$10,865*

**STUDENT SERVICES** Academic or career counseling, employment services for current students, placement services for program completers.

## Arlington Medical Institute

2301 N. Collins, Suite 100, Arlington, TX 76011
http://arlingtonmedicalinst.com/

**CONTACT** Thad Smotherman, Director
**Telephone:** 817-460-6647

**GENERAL INFORMATION** Private Institution. **Total program enrollment:** 118. **Application fee:** $100.

**PROGRAM(S) OFFERED**
• **Medical/Clinical Assistant** *790 hrs./$10,200*

**STUDENT SERVICES** Academic or career counseling, employment services for current students, placement services for program completers, remedial services.

## The Art Institute of Dallas

8080 Park Lane, Suite 100, Dallas, TX 75231-5993
http://www.artinstitutes.edu/dallas

**CONTACT** Simon Lumley, President
**Telephone:** 214-692-8080

**GENERAL INFORMATION** Private Institution. Founded 1978. **Accreditation:** Regional (SACS/CC); interior design: professional (CIDA). **Total program enrollment:** 1082. **Application fee:** $50.

**PROGRAM(S) OFFERED**
• **Culinary Arts/Chef Training** *4 students enrolled*

**STUDENT SERVICES** Academic or career counseling, employment services for current students, placement services for program completers, remedial services.

## The Art Institute of Houston

1900 Yorktown, Houston, TX 77056-4115
http://www.artinstitutes.edu/houston

**CONTACT** Larry Horn, President
**Telephone:** 713-623-2040

**GENERAL INFORMATION** Private Institution. Founded 1978. **Accreditation:** Regional (SACS/CC). **Total program enrollment:** 1360. **Application fee:** $50.

**PROGRAM(S) OFFERED**
• **Culinary Arts and Related Services, Other** *11 students enrolled*

**STUDENT SERVICES** Academic or career counseling, employment services for current students, placement services for program completers, remedial services.

## ATI Career Training Center

3035 South Shiloh Road, Suite 150, Garland, TX 75041

**CONTACT** Carlo DeManero, Executive Director
**Telephone:** 972-535-5525

**GENERAL INFORMATION** Private Institution. **Total program enrollment:** 221. **Application fee:** $100.

*ATI Career Training Center (continued)*

**PROGRAM(S) OFFERED**

• **Automobile/Automotive Mechanics Technology/Technician** *1200 hrs./$22,850* • **Heating, Air Conditioning, Ventilation and Refrigeration Maintenance Technology/Technician (HAC, HACR, HVAC, HVACR)** *960 hrs./$18,100*

**STUDENT SERVICES** Employment services for current students, placement services for program completers.

## ATI Career Training Center

6531 Grapevine Highway, Suite 100, North Richland Hills, TX 76180
http://www.aticareertraining.edu/

**CONTACT** Darrell E. Testerman, Executive Director
**Telephone:** 817-284-1141

**GENERAL INFORMATION** Private Institution. **Total program enrollment:** 756. **Application fee:** $100.

**PROGRAM(S) OFFERED**

• **Athletic Training/Trainer** *7 students enrolled* • **Automobile/Automotive Mechanics Technology/Technician** *72 students enrolled* • **Dental Assisting/Assistant** *91 students enrolled* • **Heating, Air Conditioning, Ventilation and Refrigeration Maintenance Technology/Technician (HAC, HACR, HVAC, HVACR)** *17 students enrolled* • **Information Technology** *21 students enrolled* • **Massage Therapy/Therapeutic Massage** *161 students enrolled* • **Medical/Clinical Assistant** *97 students enrolled*

**STUDENT SERVICES** Academic or career counseling, employment services for current students, placement services for program completers.

## ATI Career Training Center

1100 E. Campbell Road, Suite 250, Richardson, TX 75081

**CONTACT** Gerald Brazell, Executive Director
**Telephone:** 214-646-8460

**GENERAL INFORMATION** Private Institution. **Total program enrollment:** 398. **Application fee:** $100.

**PROGRAM(S) OFFERED**

• **Business/Office Automation/Technology/Data Entry** *960 hrs./$16,700* • **Dental Assisting/Assistant** *968 hrs./$16,700* • **Medical/Clinical Assistant** *968 hrs./$16,700*

**STUDENT SERVICES** Employment services for current students, placement services for program completers.

## ATI Technical Training Center

6627 Maple Avenue, Dallas, TX 75235
http://www.aticareertraining.edu/

**CONTACT** Anthony DeVore, Executive Director
**Telephone:** 972-755-4508 Ext. 4550

**GENERAL INFORMATION** Private Institution. Founded 1965. **Total program enrollment:** 962. **Application fee:** $100.

**PROGRAM(S) OFFERED**

• **Automobile/Automotive Mechanics Technology/Technician** *1200 hrs./$23,630* • **Electrician** *720 hrs./$14,600* • **Heating, Air Conditioning, Ventilation and Refrigeration Maintenance Technology/Technician (HAC, HACR, HVAC, HVACR)** *960 hrs./$18,000* • **Industrial Electronics Technology/Technician** *52 students enrolled* • **Welding Technology/Welder** *960 hrs./$18,330*

**STUDENT SERVICES** Academic or career counseling, employment services for current students, placement services for program completers, remedial services.

## ATI Technical Training Center

6627 Maple Avenue, Dallas, TX 75235
http://www.aticareertraining.edu/

**CONTACT** Paulette Gallerson, Executive Director
**Telephone:** 214-902-8191

**GENERAL INFORMATION** Private Institution. **Accreditation:** State accredited or approved. **Total program enrollment:** 1234. **Application fee:** $100.

**PROGRAM(S) OFFERED**

• **Business/Office Automation/Technology/Data Entry** *70 hrs./$16,162* • **Computer and Information Sciences and Support Services, Other** *14 students enrolled* • **Dental Assisting/Assistant** *59 hrs./$16,590* • **Massage Therapy/Therapeutic Massage** *21 hrs./$8925* • **Medical/Clinical Assistant** *59 hrs./$16,590* • **Pharmacy Technician/Assistant** *49 hrs./$10,816* • **Respiratory Care Therapy/Therapist** *72 hrs./$39,895*

**STUDENT SERVICES** Academic or career counseling, employment services for current students, placement services for program completers.

## Austin Community College

5930 Middle Fiskville Road, Austin, TX 78752-4390
http://www.austincc.edu/

**CONTACT** Dr. Steve Kinslow, President/CEO
**Telephone:** 512-223-7000

**GENERAL INFORMATION** Public Institution. Founded 1972. **Accreditation:** Regional (SACS/CC); dental hygiene (ADA); diagnostic medical sonography (JRCEDMS); emergency medical services (JRCEMTP); medical laboratory technology (NAACLS); physical therapy assisting (APTA); radiologic technology: radiography (JRCERT); surgical technology (ARCST). **Total program enrollment:** 9328.

**PROGRAM(S) OFFERED**

• **Accounting Technology/Technician and Bookkeeping** *2 students enrolled* • **Administrative Assistant and Secretarial Science, General** • **Automobile/Automotive Mechanics Technology/Technician** *37 students enrolled* • **Banking and Financial Support Services** *2 students enrolled* • **Biology Technician/Biotechnology Laboratory Technician** *2 students enrolled* • **Business Administration and Management, General** *32 students enrolled* • **Carpentry/Carpenter** • **Child Care Provider/Assistant** *8 students enrolled* • **Commercial Photography** *7 students enrolled* • **Commercial and Advertising Art** • **Computer Programming/Programmer, General** *14 students enrolled* • **Computer Systems Networking and Telecommunications** *6 students enrolled* • **Criminal Justice/Police Science** *3 students enrolled* • **Culinary Arts/Chef Training** *6 students enrolled* • **Diagnostic Medical Sonography/Sonographer and Ultrasound Technician** *4 students enrolled* • **Drafting and Design Technology/Technician, General** *21 students enrolled* • **Electrical, Electronic and Communications Engineering Technology/Technician** *11 students enrolled* • **Emergency Medical Technology/Technician (EMT Paramedic)** *7 students enrolled* • **Environmental Engineering Technology/Environmental Technology** • **Fire Science/Firefighting** *55 students enrolled* • **Health and Physical Education, General** *3 students enrolled* • **Heating, Air Conditioning and Refrigeration Technology/Technician (ACH/ACR/ACHR/HRAC/HVAC/AC Technology)** *13 students enrolled* • **Heating, Air Conditioning, Ventilation and Refrigeration Maintenance Technology/Technician (HAC, HACR, HVAC, HVACR)** • **Hospitality Administration/Management, General** *4 students enrolled* • **Legal Assistant/Paralegal** • **Licensed Practical/Vocational Nurse Training (LPN, LVN, Cert, Dipl, AAS)** *54 students enrolled* • **Marketing/Marketing Management, General** *3 students enrolled* • **Medical Insurance Coding Specialist/Coder** *7 students enrolled* • **Motorcycle Maintenance and Repair Technology/Technician** *3 students enrolled* • **Pharmacy Technician/Assistant** *17 students enrolled* • **Photographic and Film/Video Technology/Technician and Assistant** *4 students enrolled* • **Prepress/Desktop Publishing and Digital Imaging Design** • **Radio and Television** • **Real Estate** *36 students enrolled* • **Sign Language Interpretation and Translation** *4 students enrolled* • **Small Engine Mechanics and Repair Technology/Technician** *1 student enrolled* • **Substance Abuse/Addiction Counseling** *5 students enrolled* • **Surgical Technology/Technologist** *3 students enrolled* • **Survey Technology/Surveying** *3 students enrolled* • **Technical and Business Writing** • **Therapeutic Recreation/Recreational Therapy** *1 student enrolled* • **Tourism and Travel Services Management** *6 students enrolled* • **Watchmaking and Jewelrymaking** *7 students enrolled* • **Welding Technology/Welder** *50 students enrolled*

**STUDENT SERVICES** Academic or career counseling, daycare for children of students, employment services for current students, remedial services.

## Baldwin Beauty School

3005 South Lamar, Austin, TX 78704

**CONTACT** Randy Baldwin, Vice President
**Telephone:** 512-441-6898

**GENERAL INFORMATION** Private Institution. **Total program enrollment:** 82.

**PROGRAM(S) OFFERED**
• **Cosmetology, Barber/Styling, and Nail Instructor** *750 hrs./$1800* • **Cosmetology/Cosmetologist, General** *1500 hrs./$8875* • **Facial Treatment Specialist/Facialist** *750 hrs./$6400* • **Nail Technician/Specialist and Manicurist** *600 hrs./$1900*

**STUDENT SERVICES** Academic or career counseling, placement services for program completers.

## Baldwin Beauty School

8440 Burnet Road, Suite 140, Austin, TX 78757

**CONTACT** Randy Baldwin, Vice President
**Telephone:** 512-458-4127

**GENERAL INFORMATION** Private Institution. **Total program enrollment:** 91.

**PROGRAM(S) OFFERED**
• **Cosmetology, Barber/Styling, and Nail Instructor** *750 hrs./$1800* • **Cosmetology/Cosmetologist, General** *1500 hrs./$9875* • **Facial Treatment Specialist/Facialist** *750 hrs./$6400* • **Nail Technician/Specialist and Manicurist** *600 hrs./$1900*

**STUDENT SERVICES** Academic or career counseling, placement services for program completers.

## Blinn College

902 College Avenue, Brenham, TX 77833-4049
http://www.blinn.edu/

**CONTACT** Dr. Daniel J. Holt, President
**Telephone:** 979-830-4000

**GENERAL INFORMATION** Public Institution. Founded 1883. **Accreditation:** Regional (SACS/CC); dental hygiene (ADA); physical therapy assisting (APTA); radiologic technology: radiography (JRCERT). **Total program enrollment:** 8391.

**PROGRAM(S) OFFERED**
• **Accounting Technology/Technician and Bookkeeping** *4 students enrolled* • **Administrative Assistant and Secretarial Science, General** *28 students enrolled* • **Business Administration and Management, General** • **Business/Office Automation/Technology/Data Entry** *3 students enrolled* • **Child Care Provider/Assistant** • **Computer Systems Networking and Telecommunications** *15 students enrolled* • **Criminal Justice/Police Science** *1 student enrolled* • **Criminal Justice/Safety Studies** • **Dental Hygiene/Hygienist** • **Emergency Medical Technology/Technician (EMT Paramedic)** • **Fire Science/Firefighting** *5 students enrolled* • **Health/Health Care Administration/Management** *21 students enrolled* • **Legal Administrative Assistant/Secretary** *4 students enrolled* • **Licensed Practical/Vocational Nurse Training (LPN, LVN, Cert, Dipl, AAS)** *45 students enrolled* • **Medical Administrative/Executive Assistant and Medical Secretary** *21 students enrolled* • **Medical Insurance Coding Specialist/Coder** • **Real Estate** *28 students enrolled* • **Welding Technology/Welder** *26 students enrolled*

**STUDENT SERVICES** Academic or career counseling, employment services for current students, remedial services.

## Bradford School of Business

4669 Southwest Freeway, Suite 100, Houston, TX 77027
http://www.bradfordschoolhouston.edu/

**CONTACT** Elbert Hamilton, Jr., Director of Education
**Telephone:** 713-629-1500

**GENERAL INFORMATION** Private Institution. Founded 1958. **Total program enrollment:** 150. **Application fee:** $50.

**PROGRAM(S) OFFERED**
• **Accounting** *4 students enrolled* • **Administrative Assistant and Secretarial Science, General** *1 student enrolled* • **Graphic Design** *12 students enrolled* • **Medical Administrative/Executive Assistant and Medical Secretary** *3 students enrolled* • **Medical/Clinical Assistant** *21 students enrolled*

**STUDENT SERVICES** Academic or career counseling, employment services for current students, placement services for program completers.

## Brazosport College

500 College Drive, Lake Jackson, TX 77566-3199
http://www.brazosport.edu/

**CONTACT** Millicent M. Valek, President
**Telephone:** 979-230-3000

**GENERAL INFORMATION** Public Institution. Founded 1968. **Accreditation:** Regional (SACS/CC). **Total program enrollment:** 1206.

**PROGRAM(S) OFFERED**
• **Administrative Assistant and Secretarial Science, General** • **Automobile/Automotive Mechanics Technology/Technician** *17 students enrolled* • **Chemical Technology/Technician** *1 student enrolled* • **Child Development** *4 students enrolled* • **Computer Hardware Technology/Technician** • **Computer Programming/Programmer, General** *5 students enrolled* • **Construction Engineering Technology/Technician** *2 students enrolled* • **Construction/Heavy Equipment/Earthmoving Equipment Operation** • **Criminal Justice/Police Science** *17 students enrolled* • **Drafting and Design Technology/Technician, General** *6 students enrolled* • **Electrician** *21 students enrolled* • **Emergency Medical Technology/Technician (EMT Paramedic)** *1 student enrolled* • **Heating, Air Conditioning, Ventilation and Refrigeration Maintenance Technology/Technician (HAC, HACR, HVAC, HVACR)** *8 students enrolled* • **Instrumentation Technology/Technician** *1 student enrolled* • **Licensed Practical/Vocational Nurse Training (LPN, LVN, Cert, Dipl, AAS)** *6 students enrolled* • **Machine Tool Technology/Machinist** *14 students enrolled* • **Occupational Safety and Health Technology/Technician** *6 students enrolled* • **Pipefitting/Pipefitter and Sprinkler Fitter** *9 students enrolled* • **Welding Technology/Welder**

**STUDENT SERVICES** Academic or career counseling, daycare for children of students, employment services for current students, placement services for program completers, remedial services.

## Brookhaven College

3939 Valley View Lane, Farmers Branch, TX 75244-4997
http://www.brookhavencollege.edu/

**GENERAL INFORMATION** Public Institution. Founded 1978. **Accreditation:** Regional (SACS/CC). **Total program enrollment:** 2407.

**PROGRAM(S) OFFERED**
• **Accounting Technology/Technician and Bookkeeping** • **Accounting** *36 students enrolled* • **Apparel and Accessories Marketing Operations** • **Automobile/Automotive Mechanics Technology/Technician** *63 students enrolled* • **Business Administration and Management, General** *12 students enrolled* • **Business/Office Automation/Technology/Data Entry** *9 students enrolled* • **Cartography** *1 student enrolled* • **Child Care Provider/Assistant** *2 students enrolled* • **Child Care and Support Services Management** *1 student enrolled* • **Computer Programming/Programmer, General** *1 student enrolled* • **Computer Systems Networking and Telecommunications** • **Data Processing and Data Processing Technology/Technician** *6 students enrolled* • **Design and Visual Communications, General** *9 students enrolled* • **E-Commerce/Electronic Commerce** • **Emergency Medical Technology/Technician (EMT Paramedic)** *9 students enrolled* • **Marketing/Marketing Management, General** *2 students enrolled* • **Receptionist** *10 students enrolled*

**STUDENT SERVICES** Academic or career counseling, employment services for current students, placement services for program completers, remedial services.

## Capital City Careers

4630 Westgate Boulevard, Austin, TX 78745
http://www.capcitycareers.com/

**CONTACT** Howard Roose, Director
**Telephone:** 512-892-2640

**GENERAL INFORMATION** Private Institution. Founded 1980. **Total program enrollment:** 48. **Application fee:** $100.

**PROGRAM(S) OFFERED**
• **Business Administration and Management, General** *960 hrs./$19,349* • **Legal Administrative Assistant/Secretary** *960 hrs./$20,696* • **Office Management and Supervision** *4 students enrolled*

**STUDENT SERVICES** Academic or career counseling, employment services for current students, placement services for program completers.

## Capital City Trade and Technical School

205 East Riverside Drive, Austin, TX 78704-1281

**CONTACT** Jim Davidson, Campus Director
**Telephone:** 512-444-3257

**GENERAL INFORMATION** Private Institution. Founded 1965. **Total program enrollment:** 318. **Application fee:** $100.

**PROGRAM(S) OFFERED**
• **Automobile/Automotive Mechanics Technology/Technician** *71 students enrolled* • **Drafting and Design Technology/Technician, General** *26 students enrolled* • **Heating, Air Conditioning and Refrigeration Technology/Technician (ACH/ACR/ACHR/HRAC/HVAC/AC Technology)** *59 students enrolled*

**STUDENT SERVICES** Academic or career counseling, employment services for current students, placement services for program completers.

## Career Centers of Texas–Brownsville

1900 North Expressway, Brownsville, TX 78521
http://careercenters.edu/

**CONTACT** Rolando Rodriguez, Executive Director
**Telephone:** 956-547-8200

**GENERAL INFORMATION** Private Institution. **Total program enrollment:** 781.

**PROGRAM(S) OFFERED**
• **Computer and Information Sciences and Support Services, Other** *54 hrs./$14,975* • **Heating, Air Conditioning and Refrigeration Technology/Technician (ACH/ACR/ACHR/HRAC/HVAC/AC Technology)** *66 hrs./$14,975* • **Medical Office Assistant/Specialist** *55 hrs./$14,975* • **Medical/Clinical Assistant** *720 hrs./$14,520*

**STUDENT SERVICES** Academic or career counseling, employment services for current students, placement services for program completers, remedial services.

## Career Centers of Texas–Corpus Christi

1620 S. Padre Island Drive, Corpus Christ, TX 78416
http://careercenters.edu/

**CONTACT** Jeriann Hix, President
**Telephone:** 361-852-2900

**GENERAL INFORMATION** Private Institution. **Total program enrollment:** 904.

**PROGRAM(S) OFFERED**
• **Computer and Information Sciences, General** *5 students enrolled* • **Dental Assisting/Assistant** *900 hrs./$14,900* • **Licensed Practical/Vocational Nurse Training (LPN, LVN, Cert, Dipl, AAS)** *1484 hrs./$23,232* • **Medical Insurance Specialist/Medical Biller** *740 hrs./$14,520* • **Medical Office Assistant/Specialist** *900 hrs./$14,520* • **Medical/Clinical Assistant** *740 hrs./$14,520* • **Nurse/Nursing Assistant/Aide and Patient Care Assistant** *66 students enrolled*

**STUDENT SERVICES** Academic or career counseling, employment services for current students, placement services for program completers.

## Career Centers of Texas–El Paso

8360 Burnham Road, Suite 100, El Paso, TX 79907
http://careercenters.edu/

**CONTACT** Richard Sambrano, Executive Director
**Telephone:** 915-595-1935

**GENERAL INFORMATION** Private Institution. **Total program enrollment:** 702.

**PROGRAM(S) OFFERED**
• **Computer and Information Sciences and Support Services, Other** *16 students enrolled* • **Dental Assisting/Assistant** *38 hrs./$14,820* • **Electrician** *37 students enrolled* • **Health Information/Medical Records Administration/Administrator** *38 hrs./$14,220* • **Health Information/Medical Records Technology/Technician** *37 hrs./$14,220* • **International Business/Trade/Commerce** *37 hrs./$14,220* • **Medical/Clinical Assistant** *43 hrs./$14,220* • **Pharmacy Technician/Assistant** *37 students enrolled* • **Surgical Technology/Technologist** *45 hrs./$22,905*

**STUDENT SERVICES** Academic or career counseling, employment services for current students, placement services for program completers.

## Career Centers of Texas–Ft. Worth

2001 Beach Street, Suite 201, Fort Worth, TX 76103-2310
http://careercenters.edu/

**CONTACT** Erik Stephan, Executive Director
**Telephone:** 817-413-2000

**GENERAL INFORMATION** Private Institution. **Total program enrollment:** 832.

**PROGRAM(S) OFFERED**
• **Computer and Information Sciences and Support Services, Other** • **Dental Assisting/Assistant** *55 hrs./$13,892* • **Medical Office Assistant/Specialist** *52 hrs./$13,030* • **Medical/Clinical Assistant** *720 hrs./$13,973* • **Pharmacy Technician/Assistant** *54 hrs./$13,705* • **Radiologic Technology/Science—Radiographer** *176 hrs./$32,862*

**STUDENT SERVICES** Academic or career counseling, employment services for current students, placement services for program completers, remedial services.

## Career Point Business School

485 Spencer Lane, San Antonio, TX 78201

**CONTACT** Lawrence D. Earle, Chairman of the Board
**Telephone:** 210-732-3000 Ext. 295

**GENERAL INFORMATION** Private Institution. **Total program enrollment:** 774.

**PROGRAM(S) OFFERED**
• **Accounting and Related Services, Other** *41 students enrolled* • **Administrative Assistant and Secretarial Science, General** *88 students enrolled* • **Computer Systems Analysis/Analyst** *45 students enrolled* • **General Office Occupations and Clerical Services** *34 students enrolled* • **Health Information/Medical Records Administration/Administrator** *132 students enrolled* • **Legal Studies, General** *72 students enrolled* • **Medical Office Assistant/Specialist** *195 students enrolled* • **Medical/Clinical Assistant** *270 students enrolled*

**STUDENT SERVICES** Academic or career counseling, daycare for children of students, employment services for current students, placement services for program completers, remedial services.

## Career Quest

5430 Fredericksburg Road, Suite 310, San Antonio, TX 78229
http://careerquestusa.com/

**CONTACT** Jeanne Martin, Director/CEO
**Telephone:** 210-366-2701

**GENERAL INFORMATION** Private Institution. **Total program enrollment:** 355. **Application fee:** $100.

**PROGRAM(S) OFFERED**
• **Area Studies, Other** *52 hrs./$23,400* • **Business Administration and Management, General** *22 students enrolled* • **Health Information/Medical Records Technology/Technician** *31 hrs./$14,229* • **Medical Administrative/Executive Assistant and Medical Secretary** *31 hrs./$14,229* • **Medical Insurance Specialist/Medical Biller** *36 students enrolled* • **Medical Office Assistant/Specialist** *31 hrs./$14,229* • **Medical Office Management/Administration** *3 students enrolled* • **Medical/Clinical Assistant** *36 students enrolled* • **Medical/Health Management and Clinical Assistant/Specialist** *42 hrs./$17,330* • **Tourism and Travel Services Management** *29 hrs./$14,229*

**STUDENT SERVICES** Academic or career counseling, placement services for program completers.

## CCI Training Center

770 E. Road To Six Flags, # 140, Arlington, TX 76011
http://www.cci-training.com

**CONTACT** Martin Zandi, Director
**Telephone:** 817-226-1900

**GENERAL INFORMATION** Private Institution. **Total program enrollment:** 17. **Application fee:** $100.

**PROGRAM(S) OFFERED**
• **Accounting Technology/Technician and Bookkeeping** *630 hrs./$11,550* • **Computer and Information Systems Security** *408 hrs./$7276* • **Health Information/Medical Records Technology/Technician** *606 hrs./$9668* • **Mechanical Engineering/Mechanical Technology/Technician** *392 hrs./$6550* • **System Administration/Administrator** *342 hrs./$6785*

**STUDENT SERVICES** Academic or career counseling, employment services for current students, placement services for program completers.

## Cedar Valley College

3030 North Dallas Avenue, Lancaster, TX 75134-3799
http://www.cedarvalleycollege.edu/cvc.htm

**CONTACT** Jennifer Wimbish, President
**Telephone:** 972-860-8258

**GENERAL INFORMATION** Public Institution. Founded 1977. **Accreditation:** Regional (SACS/CC). **Total program enrollment:** 1414.

**PROGRAM(S) OFFERED**
• **Accounting Technology/Technician and Bookkeeping** *1 student enrolled* • **Accounting** *22 students enrolled* • **Automobile/Automotive Mechanics Technology/Technician** *23 students enrolled* • **Business Administration and Management, General** *24 students enrolled* • **Business/Office Automation/Technology/Data Entry** *3 students enrolled* • **Computer Programming/Programmer, General** • **Computer Systems Networking and Telecommunications** • **Criminal Justice/Safety Studies** *21 students enrolled* • **Data Processing and Data Processing Technology/Technician** *5 students enrolled* • **Design and Visual Communications, General** *6 students enrolled* • **Diesel Mechanics Technology/Technician** *1 student enrolled* • **Graphic Design** *4 students enrolled* • **Heating, Air Conditioning, Ventilation and Refrigeration Maintenance Technology/Technician (HAC, HACR, HVAC, HVACR)** *22 students enrolled* • **Marketing/Marketing Management, General** *182 students enrolled* • **Motorcycle Maintenance and Repair Technology/Technician** *10 students enrolled* • **Music Management and Merchandising** • **Music Performance, General** *1 student enrolled* • **Nurse/Nursing Assistant/Aide and Patient Care Assistant** *5 students enrolled* • **Radio and Television Broadcasting Technology/Technician** *23 students enrolled* • **Real Estate** *44 students enrolled* • **Receptionist** *2 students enrolled* • **Small Engine Mechanics and Repair Technology/Technician** *1 student enrolled* • **Veterinary/Animal Health Technology/Technician and Veterinary Assistant** *46 students enrolled*

**STUDENT SERVICES** Academic or career counseling, employment services for current students, placement services for program completers, remedial services.

## Center for Employment Training–Socorro

10102 North Loop Drive, Socorro, TX 79927

**CONTACT** Rosie Guerrero, Director
**Telephone:** 408-287-7924

**GENERAL INFORMATION** Private Institution. **Total program enrollment:** 131.

**PROGRAM(S) OFFERED**
• **Business Operations Support and Secretarial Services, Other** *11 students enrolled* • **Business/Office Automation/Technology/Data Entry** *720 hrs./$7676* • **Medical Insurance Specialist/Medical Biller** *630 hrs./$7083* • **Transportation and Materials Moving, Other** • **Truck and Bus Driver/Commercial Vehicle Operation** *630 hrs./$8361*

**STUDENT SERVICES** Academic or career counseling, employment services for current students, placement services for program completers, remedial services.

## Central Texas Beauty College

1350 Palm Valley Road, Suite A, Round Rock, TX 68661
http://www.centraltexasbeautycollege.com/

**CONTACT** Robert Painter, Owner
**Telephone:** 512-244-2235

**GENERAL INFORMATION** Private Institution. **Total program enrollment:** 119. **Application fee:** $100.

**PROGRAM(S) OFFERED**
• **Cosmetology/Cosmetologist, General** *1500 hrs./$7895* • **Nail Technician/Specialist and Manicurist** *600 hrs./$3000*

## Central Texas Beauty College

2010 S. 57th Street, Temple, TX 76504-6948
http://www.centraltexasbeautycollege.com/

**CONTACT** Robert Painter, Owner
**Telephone:** 254-773-9911

**GENERAL INFORMATION** Private Institution. **Total program enrollment:** 99. **Application fee:** $100.

**PROGRAM(S) OFFERED**
• **Cosmetology/Cosmetologist, General** *1500 hrs./$7395* • **Nail Technician/Specialist and Manicurist** *600 hrs./$2800*

## Central Texas College

PO Box 1800, Killeen, TX 76540-1800
http://www.ctcd.edu/

**CONTACT** James R. Anderson, Chancellor
**Telephone:** 254-526-7161

**GENERAL INFORMATION** Public Institution. Founded 1967. **Accreditation:** Regional (SACS/CC); medical laboratory technology (NAACLS). **Total program enrollment:** 4163.

*Central Texas College (continued)*

**PROGRAM(S) OFFERED**

• **Administrative Assistant and Secretarial Science, General** • **Agricultural Business Technology** • **Airline/Commercial/Professional Pilot and Flight Crew** *5 students enrolled* • **Art/Art Studies, General** • **Autobody/Collision and Repair Technology/Technician** *1 student enrolled* • **Automobile/Automotive Mechanics Technology/Technician** *1 student enrolled* • **Building/Property Maintenance and Management** *2 students enrolled* • **Business Administration and Management, General** *16 students enrolled* • **Business/Office Automation/Technology/Data Entry** *11 students enrolled* • **Child Care Provider/Assistant** *11 students enrolled* • **Child Care and Support Services Management** • **Clinical/Medical Social Work** *4 students enrolled* • **Computer Programming/Programmer, General** • **Computer Technology/Computer Systems Technology** • **Cosmetology/Cosmetologist, General** *19 students enrolled* • **Criminal Justice/Police Science** • **Criminal Justice/Safety Studies** *16 students enrolled* • **Data Processing and Data Processing Technology/Technician** *6 students enrolled* • **Diesel Mechanics Technology/Technician** • **Drafting and Design Technology/Technician, General** *6 students enrolled* • **Electrical, Electronic and Communications Engineering Technology/Technician** • **Farm/Farm and Ranch Management** • **Fine/Studio Arts, General** • **Fire Protection and Safety Technology/Technician** • **Graphic and Printing Equipment Operator, General Production** *6 students enrolled* • **Health Information/Medical Records Technology/Technician** • **Heating, Air Conditioning, Ventilation and Refrigeration Maintenance Technology/Technician (HAC, HACR, HVAC, HVACR)** *10 students enrolled* • **Hospitality Administration/Management, General** *1 student enrolled* • **Licensed Practical/Vocational Nurse Training (LPN, LVN, Cert, Dipl, AAS)** • **Marketing/Marketing Management, General** • **Medical Administrative/Executive Assistant and Medical Secretary** *9 students enrolled* • **Military Technologies** • **Music, General** • **Nursing—Registered Nurse Training (RN, ASN, BSN, MSN)** *1 student enrolled* • **Office Management and Supervision** • **Radio and Television** *1 student enrolled* • **Real Estate** • **Restaurant/Food Services Management** *15 students enrolled* • **Substance Abuse/Addiction Counseling** • **System, Networking, and LAN/WAN Management/Manager** *69 students enrolled* • **Tourism and Travel Services Management** *1 student enrolled* • **Welding Technology/Welder**

**STUDENT SERVICES** Academic or career counseling, employment services for current students, placement services for program completers, remedial services.

## Central Texas Commercial College

9400 North Central Expressway, Suite 200, Dallas, TX 75231

**CONTACT** Dianne Day, Director
**Telephone:** 214-368-3680

**GENERAL INFORMATION** Private Institution. **Total program enrollment:** 26.

**PROGRAM(S) OFFERED**

• **Administrative Assistant and Secretarial Science, General** *22 students enrolled* • **Legal Administrative Assistant/Secretary** *10 students enrolled* • **Medical Office Assistant/Specialist** *7 students enrolled* • **Word Processing**

**STUDENT SERVICES** Academic or career counseling, employment services for current students, placement services for program completers.

## Champion Beauty College

4714 FM 1960 West, #104, Houston, TX 77069
championbeautycollege.com

**CONTACT** Jim Adams, Vice President
**Telephone:** 281-583-9117

**GENERAL INFORMATION** Private Institution. **Total program enrollment:** 26. **Application fee:** $100.

**PROGRAM(S) OFFERED**

• **Aesthetician/Esthetician and Skin Care Specialist** *750 hrs./$8350*
• **Cosmetology, Barber/Styling, and Nail Instructor** *750 hrs./$4788*
• **Cosmetology/Cosmetologist, General** *1500 hrs./$14,940* • **Massage Therapy/Therapeutic Massage** *300 hrs./$2850* • **Nail Technician/Specialist and Manicurist** *600 hrs./$3850*

**STUDENT SERVICES** Academic or career counseling, placement services for program completers.

## Charles and Sue's School of Hair Design

1711 Briarcrest Drive, Bryan, TX 77801
http://charlesandsues.com/

**CONTACT** Charles Fikes, President
**Telephone:** 979-776-4375

**GENERAL INFORMATION** Private Institution. Founded 1971. **Total program enrollment:** 18. **Application fee:** $50.

**PROGRAM(S) OFFERED**

• **Cosmetology, Barber/Styling, and Nail Instructor** *250 hrs./$1500*
• **Cosmetology/Cosmetologist, General** *1500 hrs./$12,960* • **Nail Technician/Specialist and Manicurist** *600 hrs./$3000*

**STUDENT SERVICES** Placement services for program completers.

## Cisco College

101 College Heights, Cisco, TX 76437-9321
http://www.cisco.edu/

**CONTACT** Colleen Smith, President
**Telephone:** 254-442-5000

**GENERAL INFORMATION** Public Institution. Founded 1940. **Accreditation:** Regional (SACS/CC); medical assisting (AAMAE); practical nursing (NLN). **Total program enrollment:** 1906.

**PROGRAM(S) OFFERED**

• **Administrative Assistant and Secretarial Science, General** • **Automobile/Automotive Mechanics Technology/Technician** *14 students enrolled* • **Building/Property Maintenance and Management** *5 students enrolled* • **Business Administration and Management, General** *9 students enrolled* • **Child Care Provider/Assistant** *12 students enrolled* • **Child Care and Support Services Management** • **Cosmetology, Barber/Styling, and Nail Instructor**
• **Cosmetology/Cosmetologist, General** *15 students enrolled* • **Criminal Justice/Safety Studies** *19 students enrolled* • **Fire Protection and Safety Technology/Technician** • **General Office Occupations and Clerical Services** *2 students enrolled* • **Heating, Air Conditioning, Ventilation and Refrigeration Maintenance Technology/Technician (HAC, HACR, HVAC, HVACR)** *7 students enrolled* • **Licensed Practical/Vocational Nurse Training (LPN, LVN, Cert, Dipl, AAS)** *52 students enrolled* • **Medical/Clinical Assistant** *10 students enrolled*
• **Pharmacy Technician/Assistant** *10 students enrolled* • **Real Estate** *11 students enrolled* • **Surgical Technology/Technologist** *11 students enrolled* • **Welding Technology/Welder** *13 students enrolled*

**STUDENT SERVICES** Academic or career counseling, employment services for current students, placement services for program completers, remedial services.

## Clarendon College

PO Box 968, Clarendon, TX 79226-0968
http://www.clarendoncollege.edu/

**CONTACT** William Auvenshine, President
**Telephone:** 806-874-3571 Ext. 163

**GENERAL INFORMATION** Public Institution. Founded 1898. **Accreditation:** Regional (SACS/CC). **Total program enrollment:** 587.

**PROGRAM(S) OFFERED**

• **Business/Office Automation/Technology/Data Entry** *6 students enrolled*
• **Computer Technology/Computer Systems Technology** *15 students enrolled*
• **Farm/Farm and Ranch Management** *18 students enrolled* • **Heating, Air Conditioning, Ventilation and Refrigeration Maintenance Technology/Technician (HAC, HACR, HVAC, HVACR)** *33 students enrolled* • **Licensed Practical/Vocational Nurse Training (LPN, LVN, Cert, Dipl, AAS)** *33 students enrolled* • **Web Page, Digital/Multimedia and Information Resources Design** *24 students enrolled*

**STUDENT SERVICES** Academic or career counseling, remedial services.

## Coastal Bend College

3800 Charco Road, Beeville, TX 78102-2197
http://www.cbc.cc.tx.us/

**CONTACT** Dr. Thomas Baynum, President
**Telephone:** 361-358-2838

**GENERAL INFORMATION** Public Institution. Founded 1965. **Accreditation:** Regional (SACS/CC); dental hygiene (ADA); health information technology (AHIMA). **Total program enrollment:** 1398.

**PROGRAM(S) OFFERED**
• **Accounting Technology/Technician and Bookkeeping** • **Applied Horticulture/Horticultural Operations, General** *10 students enrolled* • **Automobile/Automotive Mechanics Technology/Technician** • **Business, Management, Marketing, and Related Support Services, Other** • **Business/Office Automation/Technology/Data Entry** • **Carpentry/Carpenter** *20 students enrolled* • **Child Care Provider/Assistant** • **Computer and Information Sciences, General** • **Computer/Information Technology Services Administration and Management, Other** • **Construction Trades, Other** • **Corrections** • **Cosmetology, Barber/Styling, and Nail Instructor** • **Cosmetology/Cosmetologist, General** • **Criminal Justice/Police Science** *1 student enrolled* • **Data Processing and Data Processing Technology/Technician** *14 students enrolled* • **Drafting and Design Technology/Technician, General** *1 student enrolled* • **Electrical and Power Transmission Installation/Installer, General** • **Electrical/Electronics Equipment Installation and Repair, General** • **Electrician** • **Emergency Medical Technology/Technician (EMT Paramedic)** • **General Office Occupations and Clerical Services** • **Health Information/Medical Records Technology/Technician** • **Heating, Air Conditioning, Ventilation and Refrigeration Maintenance Technology/Technician (HAC, HACR, HVAC, HVACR)** *27 students enrolled* • **Hospital and Health Care Facilities Administration/Management** • **Housing and Human Environments, General** • **Licensed Practical/Vocational Nurse Training (LPN, LVN, Cert, Dipl, AAS)** • **Medical Administrative/Executive Assistant and Medical Secretary** • **Water Quality and Wastewater Treatment Management and Recycling Technology/Technician** *33 students enrolled* • **Welding Technology/Welder**

**STUDENT SERVICES** Academic or career counseling, employment services for current students, placement services for program completers, remedial services.

## College of Biblical Studies–Houston

6000 Dale Carnegie Drive, Houston, TX 77036
http://www.cbshouston.edu/

**CONTACT** Jay A. Quine, President
**Telephone:** 713-785-5995

**GENERAL INFORMATION** Private Institution. Founded 1979. **Accreditation:** State accredited or approved. **Total program enrollment:** 63. **Application fee:** $20.

**PROGRAM(S) OFFERED**
• **Bible/Biblical Studies** *16 students enrolled*

**STUDENT SERVICES** Academic or career counseling, remedial services.

## College of the Mainland

1200 Amburn Road, Texas City, TX 77591-2499
http://www.com.edu/

**CONTACT** Homer M. Hayes, PhD, President
**Telephone:** 409-938-1211

**GENERAL INFORMATION** Public Institution. Founded 1967. **Accreditation:** Regional (SACS/CC). **Total program enrollment:** 1093.

**PROGRAM(S) OFFERED**
• **Accounting Technology/Technician and Bookkeeping** • **Administrative Assistant and Secretarial Science, General** *1 student enrolled* • **Aesthetician/Esthetician and Skin Care Specialist** *5 students enrolled* • **Business Administration and Management, General** *5 students enrolled* • **Cartography** *4 students enrolled* • **Child Care and Support Services Management** *1 student enrolled* • **Child Development** *2 students enrolled* • **Computer Programming/Programmer, General** • **Computer Systems Networking and Telecommunications** • **Cosmetology/Cosmetologist, General** *7 students enrolled* • **Criminal Justice/Police Science** • **Drafting and Design Technology/Technician, General** • **Electrical, Electronic and Communications Engineering Technology/Technician** • **Emergency Medical Technology/Technician (EMT Paramedic)** *4 students enrolled* • **Fire Protection and Safety Technology/Technician** • **Licensed Practical/Vocational Nurse Training (LPN, LVN, Cert, Dipl, AAS)** *20 students enrolled* • **Medical Insurance Coding Specialist/Coder** *10 students enrolled* • **Medical Transcription/Transcriptionist** • **Nail Technician/Specialist and Manicurist** • **Pharmacy Technician/Assistant** *19 students enrolled* • **Real Estate** • **Web Page, Digital/Multimedia and Information Resources Design** *2 students enrolled* • **Web/Multimedia Management and Webmaster** • **Welding Technology/Welder**

**STUDENT SERVICES** Academic or career counseling, daycare for children of students, employment services for current students, placement services for program completers, remedial services.

## Collin County Community College District

4800 Preston Park Boulevard, Plano, TX 75093-8309
http://www.ccccd.edu/

**CONTACT** Cary Israel, President
**Telephone:** 972-881-5790

**GENERAL INFORMATION** Public Institution. Founded 1985. **Accreditation:** Regional (SACS/CC); dental hygiene (ADA). **Total program enrollment:** 8467.

**PROGRAM(S) OFFERED**
• **Administrative Assistant and Secretarial Science, General** *1 student enrolled* • **Animation, Interactive Technology, Video Graphics and Special Effects** *4 students enrolled* • **Biology Technician/Biotechnology Laboratory Technician** • **Business Administration and Management, General** *8 students enrolled* • **Business/Office Automation/Technology/Data Entry** *13 students enrolled* • **Child Care Provider/Assistant** *2 students enrolled* • **Child Care and Support Services Management** *2 students enrolled* • **Child Development** *1 student enrolled* • **Commercial and Advertising Art** • **Computer Programming/Programmer, General** • **Computer Systems Networking and Telecommunications** *5 students enrolled* • **Computer and Information Sciences, General** *2 students enrolled* • **Computer and Information Systems Security** *1 student enrolled* • **Criminal Justice/Police Science** *59 students enrolled* • **Drafting and Design Technology/Technician, General** *3 students enrolled* • **Electrical, Electronic and Communications Engineering Technology/Technician** • **Electrical/Electronics Drafting and Electrical/Electronics CAD/CADD** • **Electrical/Electronics Equipment Installation and Repair, General** • **Emergency Medical Technology/Technician (EMT Paramedic)** *13 students enrolled* • **Fire Protection and Safety Technology/Technician** *11 students enrolled* • **Fire Science/Firefighting** *50 students enrolled* • **Hospitality Administration/Management, General** *9 students enrolled* • **Interior Design** *3 students enrolled* • **Legal Assistant/Paralegal** *13 students enrolled* • **Medical Insurance Coding Specialist/Coder** *3 students enrolled* • **Medical Transcription/Transcriptionist** *4 students enrolled* • **Music Management and Merchandising** • **Music, General** *15 students enrolled* • **Real Estate** *14 students enrolled* • **Sales, Distribution and Marketing Operations, General** *2 students enrolled* • **Sign Language Interpretation and Translation** • **Telecommunications Technology/Technician** *2 students enrolled* • **Web Page, Digital/Multimedia and Information Resources Design**

**STUDENT SERVICES** Academic or career counseling, employment services for current students, placement services for program completers, remedial services.

## Commonwealth Institute of Funeral Service

415 Barren Springs Drive, Houston, TX 77090
http://www.commonwealthinst.org/

**CONTACT** Jason Altieri, President
**Telephone:** 281-873-0262

**GENERAL INFORMATION** Private Institution. Founded 1988. **Accreditation:** Funeral service (ABFSE). **Total program enrollment:** 112. **Application fee:** $50.

**PROGRAM(S) OFFERED**
• **Funeral Service and Mortuary Science, General** *18 students enrolled*

**STUDENT SERVICES** Academic or career counseling, employment services for current students, placement services for program completers.

## Computer Career Center

6101 Montana Avenue, El Paso, TX 79925
http://www.computercareercenter.com/

**CONTACT** Lee Chayes, President
**Telephone:** 915-779-8031

**GENERAL INFORMATION** Private Institution. Founded 1985. **Accreditation:** State accredited or approved. **Total program enrollment:** 206. **Application fee:** $100.

**PROGRAM(S) OFFERED**
• **Accounting Technology/Technician and Bookkeeping** • **Administrative Assistant and Secretarial Science, General** *900 hrs./$10,425* • **Commercial and Advertising Art** *900 hrs./$10,525* • **Computer Systems Networking and Telecommunications** *1110 hrs./$16,225* • **Legal Administrative Assistant/Secretary** • **Licensed Practical/Vocational Nurse Training (LPN, LVN, Cert, Dipl, AAS)** *1476 hrs./$24,255* • **Medical Administrative/Executive Assistant and Medical Secretary** *41 students enrolled* • **Medical/Clinical Assistant** *940 hrs./$11,455* • **Nurse/Nursing Assistant/Aide and Patient Care Assistant** *600 hrs./$7455*

**STUDENT SERVICES** Academic or career counseling, employment services for current students, placement services for program completers.

## Computer Labs

#3 Butterfield Trail, El Paso, TX 79906
http://www.cl.edu/

**CONTACT** Ruben Lopez, President
**Telephone:** 915-591-8899

**GENERAL INFORMATION** Private Institution. **Total program enrollment:** 10. **Application fee:** $100.

**PROGRAM(S) OFFERED**
• **Computer and Information Sciences and Support Services, Other** *980 hrs./$7930* • **Computer/Information Technology Services Administration and Management, Other** *1300 hrs./$13,000*

**STUDENT SERVICES** Academic or career counseling, placement services for program completers, remedial services.

## Concorde Career Institute

601 Ryan Plaza Drive, Suite 200, Arlington, TX 76011
http://www.concorde.edu/

**CONTACT** Rebecca Zielinski, Campus President
**Telephone:** 817-261-1594

**GENERAL INFORMATION** Private Institution. **Total program enrollment:** 767.

**PROGRAM(S) OFFERED**
• **Dental Assisting/Assistant** *720 hrs./$12,365* • **Health Information/Medical Records Administration/Administrator** *720 hrs./$10,751* • **Licensed Practical/Vocational Nurse Training (LPN, LVN, Cert, Dipl, AAS)** *1600 hrs./$22,434* • **Medical Insurance Coding Specialist/Coder** *63 students enrolled* • **Medical/Clinical Assistant** *720 hrs./$12,446* • **Surgical Technology/Technologist** *1220 hrs./$19,295*

**STUDENT SERVICES** Academic or career counseling, employment services for current students, placement services for program completers, remedial services.

## Conlee College of Cosmetology

402 Quinlan, Kerrville, TX 78028

**CONTACT** Angela Wollmann, CEO
**Telephone:** 830-896-2380

**GENERAL INFORMATION** Private Institution. Founded 1973. **Total program enrollment:** 23.

**PROGRAM(S) OFFERED**
• **Cosmetology, Barber/Styling, and Nail Instructor** *750 hrs./$3475* • **Cosmetology/Cosmetologist, General** *1500 hrs./$7200* • **Nail Technician/Specialist and Manicurist** *600 hrs./$2800*

**STUDENT SERVICES** Academic or career counseling, employment services for current students, placement services for program completers, remedial services.

## Coryell Cosmetology College

608 Leon Street, Gatesville, TX 76528

**CONTACT** Patsy Fountain, CEO
**Telephone:** 254-248-1716

**GENERAL INFORMATION** Private Institution. **Total program enrollment:** 35. **Application fee:** $100.

**PROGRAM(S) OFFERED**
• **Aesthetician/Esthetician and Skin Care Specialist** *5 students enrolled* • **Cosmetology/Cosmetologist, General** *1500 hrs./$7500*

**STUDENT SERVICES** Academic or career counseling, placement services for program completers.

## Cosmetology Career Center

8030 Spring Valley Road, Dallas, TX 75240
http://www.cccdallastexas.com/

**CONTACT** John W. Turnage, Owner
**Telephone:** 972-669-0494

**GENERAL INFORMATION** Private Institution. **Total program enrollment:** 338.

**PROGRAM(S) OFFERED**
• **Aesthetician/Esthetician and Skin Care Specialist** *750 hrs./$10,000* • **Cosmetology, Barber/Styling, and Nail Instructor** *750 hrs./$4500* • **Cosmetology/Cosmetologist, General** *1500 hrs./$18,000* • **Nail Technician/Specialist and Manicurist** *600 hrs./$4400*

**STUDENT SERVICES** Academic or career counseling, placement services for program completers.

## Culinary Academy of Austin

6020-B Dillard, Austin, TX 78752
http://www.culinaryacademyofaustin.com/

**CONTACT** Elizabeth Falto-Mannion, Owner
**Telephone:** 512-451-5743

**GENERAL INFORMATION** Private Institution. **Total program enrollment:** 47. **Application fee:** $75.

**PROGRAM(S) OFFERED**
• **Baking and Pastry Arts/Baker/Pastry Chef** *618 hrs./$11,500* • **Culinary Arts/Chef Training** *1401 hrs./$25,220*

**STUDENT SERVICES** Academic or career counseling, employment services for current students, placement services for program completers.

## Culinary Institute Alain & Marie LeNotre

7070 Allensby, Houston, TX 77022-4322
http://www.ciaml.com/

**CONTACT** Alain Lenotre, President
**Telephone:** 713-692-0077

**GENERAL INFORMATION** Private Institution. **Total program enrollment:** 103. **Application fee:** $50.

**PROGRAM(S) OFFERED**

• **Baking and Pastry Arts/Baker/Pastry Chef** *1122 hrs./$25,980* • **Cooking and Related Culinary Arts, General** *108 hrs./$37,222* • **Culinary Arts/Chef Training** *748 hrs./$17,325*

**STUDENT SERVICES** Academic or career counseling, employment services for current students, placement services for program completers, remedial services.

## Dallas Baptist University

3000 Mountain Creek Parkway, Dallas, TX 75211-9299
http://www.dbu.edu/

**CONTACT** Dr. Gary Cook, President
**Telephone:** 214-333-7100

**GENERAL INFORMATION** Private Institution (Affiliated with Baptist General Convention of Texas). Founded 1965. **Accreditation:** Regional (SACS/CC); music (NASM). **Total program enrollment:** 2766. **Application fee:** $25.

**STUDENT SERVICES** Academic or career counseling, employment services for current students, placement services for program completers, remedial services.

## Dallas Barber & Stylist College

8224 Park Lane, Suite 120, Dallas, TX 75231

**CONTACT** Sylvester Iwotor, Director
**Telephone:** 214-575-2168

**GENERAL INFORMATION** Private Institution. **Total program enrollment:** 87. **Application fee:** $100.

**PROGRAM(S) OFFERED**

• **Barbering/Barber** *1500 hrs./$8750* • **Cosmetology and Related Personal Grooming Arts, Other** • **Cosmetology, Barber/Styling, and Nail Instructor** *1000 hrs./$5440* • **Hair Styling/Stylist and Hair Design**

**STUDENT SERVICES** Placement services for program completers.

## Dallas County Community College District

701 Elm Street, Suite 400, Dallas, TX 75202-3250
http://www.dcccd.edu/

**CONTACT** Wright Lassiter, Chancellor
**Telephone:** 214-860-2135

**GENERAL INFORMATION** Public Institution. **Accreditation:** Regional (SACS/CC).

## Dallas Institute of Funeral Service

3909 South Buckner Boulevard, Dallas, TX 75227
http://www.dallasinstitute.edu/

**CONTACT** James M. Shoemake, President
**Telephone:** 214-388-5466

**GENERAL INFORMATION** Private Institution. Founded 1945. **Accreditation:** Funeral service (ABFSE). **Total program enrollment:** 132. **Application fee:** $50.

**PROGRAM(S) OFFERED**

• **Funeral Service and Mortuary Science, General**

**STUDENT SERVICES** Academic or career counseling, employment services for current students, remedial services.

## Dallas Nursing Institute

6200 Maple Avenue, Dallas, TX 75235
http://www.ntpci.com/

**CONTACT** Greg Davault, President
**Telephone:** 214-351-0223

**GENERAL INFORMATION** Private Institution. **Total program enrollment:** 149.

**PROGRAM(S) OFFERED**

• **Licensed Practical/Vocational Nurse Training (LPN, LVN, Cert, Dipl, AAS)** *46 hrs./$22,000*

**STUDENT SERVICES** Placement services for program completers.

## Del Mar College

101 Baldwin Boulevard, Corpus Christi, TX 78404-3897
http://www.delmar.edu/

**CONTACT** Joe Alaniz, Acting President
**Telephone:** 361-698-1255

**GENERAL INFORMATION** Public Institution. Founded 1935. **Accreditation:** Regional (SACS/CC); art and design (NASAD); dental assisting (ADA); dental hygiene (ADA); diagnostic medical sonography (JRCEDMS); engineering technology (ABET/TAC); health information technology (AHIMA); medical laboratory technology (NAACLS); music (NASM); physical therapy assisting (APTA); radiologic technology: radiography (JRCERT); surgical technology (ARCST); theater (NAST). **Total program enrollment:** 3314.

**PROGRAM(S) OFFERED**

• **Accounting Technology/Technician and Bookkeeping** *12 students enrolled* • **Administrative Assistant and Secretarial Science, General** *3 students enrolled* • **Aircraft Powerplant Technology/Technician** *9 students enrolled* • **Airframe Mechanics and Aircraft Maintenance Technology/Technician** *17 students enrolled* • **Architectural Drafting and Architectural CAD/CADD** *2 students enrolled* • **Automobile/Automotive Mechanics Technology/Technician** *18 students enrolled* • **Banking and Financial Support Services** *3 students enrolled* • **Building/Property Maintenance and Management** *9 students enrolled* • **Business Administration and Management, General** *4 students enrolled* • **Business/Commerce, General** *16 students enrolled* • **Chemical Technology/Technician** *22 students enrolled* • **Child Development** *3 students enrolled* • **Communications Systems Installation and Repair Technology** *9 students enrolled* • **Computer Programming/Programmer, General** *1 student enrolled* • **Cosmetology/Cosmetologist, General** *28 students enrolled* • **Criminal Justice/Police Science** *23 students enrolled* • **Criminalistics and Criminal Science** *9 students enrolled* • **Culinary Arts/Chef Training** *6 students enrolled* • **Dental Assisting/Assistant** *6 students enrolled* • **Diagnostic Medical Sonography/Sonographer and Ultrasound Technician** • **Diesel Mechanics Technology/Technician** *15 students enrolled* • **Drafting and Design Technology/Technician, General** *1 student enrolled* • **Emergency Medical Technology/Technician (EMT Paramedic)** *4 students enrolled* • **Family and Consumer Sciences/Human Sciences, General** *2 students enrolled* • **Finance, General** *3 students enrolled* • **Fire Protection and Safety Technology/Technician** *3 students enrolled* • **Food Service, Waiter/Waitress, and Dining Room Management/Manager** *1 student enrolled* • **General Office Occupations and Clerical Services** *2 students enrolled* • **Health Information/Medical Records Technology/Technician** *10 students enrolled* • **Heating, Air Conditioning, Ventilation and Refrigeration Maintenance Technology/Technician (HAC, HACR, HVAC, HVACR)** *24 students enrolled* • **Hotel/Motel Administration/Management** *1 student enrolled* • **Industrial Mechanics and Maintenance Technology** *1 student enrolled* • **Logistics and Materials Management** *8 students enrolled* • **Machine Tool Technology/Machinist** *4 students enrolled* • **Management Information Systems, General** *5 students enrolled* • **Medical Administrative/Executive Assistant and Medical Secretary** *1 student enrolled* • **Real Estate** *3 students enrolled* • **Sales, Distribution and Marketing Operations, General** *4 students enrolled* • **Sign Language Interpretation and Translation** *4 students enrolled* • **Surgical Technology/Technologist** *9 students enrolled* • **Welding Technology/Welder** *14 students enrolled*

**STUDENT SERVICES** Academic or career counseling, daycare for children of students, employment services for current students, placement services for program completers, remedial services.

## Eastfield College

3737 Motley Drive, Mesquite, TX 75150-2099
http://www.efc.dcccd.edu/

**CONTACT** Carol Brown, President
**Telephone:** 972-860-7002

**GENERAL INFORMATION** Public Institution. Founded 1970. **Accreditation:** Regional (SACS/CC). **Total program enrollment:** 2826.

**PROGRAM(S) OFFERED**
• **Accounting** • **Architectural Drafting and Architectural CAD/CADD** *4 students enrolled* • **Autobody/Collision and Repair Technology/Technician** *38 students enrolled* • **Automobile/Automotive Mechanics Technology/Technician** *77 students enrolled* • **Business Administration and Management, General** *10 students enrolled* • **Business/Office Automation/Technology/Data Entry** • **Child Care Provider/Assistant** *5 students enrolled* • **Child Care and Support Services Management** *5 students enrolled* • **Child Development** *1 student enrolled* • **Computer Programming/Programmer, General** *2 students enrolled* • **Computer Systems Networking and Telecommunications** • **Criminal Justice/Safety Studies** *8 students enrolled* • **Data Processing and Data Processing Technology/Technician** *5 students enrolled* • **Diesel Mechanics Technology/Technician** • **Drafting and Design Technology/Technician, General** *25 students enrolled* • **E-Commerce/Electronic Commerce** • **Electrical, Electronic and Communications Engineering Technology/Technician** *8 students enrolled* • **Electrical/Electronics Drafting and Electrical/Electronics CAD/CADD** • **Heating, Air Conditioning, Ventilation and Refrigeration Maintenance Technology/Technician (HAC, HACR, HVAC, HVACR)** *57 students enrolled* • **Mechanical Drafting and Mechanical Drafting CAD/CADD** *1 student enrolled* • **Prepress/Desktop Publishing and Digital Imaging Design** *6 students enrolled* • **Receptionist** *2 students enrolled* • **Sign Language Interpretation and Translation** • **Social Work** • **Substance Abuse/Addiction Counseling** *10 students enrolled* • **Telecommunications Technology/Technician**

**STUDENT SERVICES** Academic or career counseling, daycare for children of students, employment services for current students, placement services for program completers, remedial services.

## El Centro College

801 Main Street, Dallas, TX 75202-3604
http://www.ecc.dcccd.edu/

**CONTACT** Paul McCarthy, President
**Telephone:** 214-860-2037

**GENERAL INFORMATION** Public Institution. Founded 1966. **Accreditation:** Regional (SACS/CC); cardiovascular technology (JRCECT); diagnostic medical sonography (JRCEDMS); interior design: professional (CIDA); medical laboratory technology (NAACLS); radiologic technology: radiography (JRCERT). **Total program enrollment:** 1635.

**PROGRAM(S) OFFERED**
• **Accounting** *8 students enrolled* • **Apparel and Accessories Marketing Operations** *1 student enrolled* • **Baking and Pastry Arts/Baker/Pastry Chef** *8 students enrolled* • **Biology Technician/Biotechnology Laboratory Technician** • **Business Administration and Management, General** *10 students enrolled* • **Business/Office Automation/Technology/Data Entry** *1 student enrolled* • **Cardiovascular Technology/Technologist** *1 student enrolled* • **Computer Programming/Programmer, General** *2 students enrolled* • **Computer Systems Networking and Telecommunications** *13 students enrolled* • **Criminal Justice/Safety Studies** *1 student enrolled* • **Culinary Arts/Chef Training** *14 students enrolled* • **Data Processing and Data Processing Technology/Technician** *5 students enrolled* • **Diagnostic Medical Sonography/Sonographer and Ultrasound Technician** *2 students enrolled* • **Emergency Medical Technology/Technician (EMT Paramedic)** *86 students enrolled* • **Fashion/Apparel Design** *1 student enrolled* • **Interior Design** *3 students enrolled* • **Licensed Practical/Vocational Nurse Training (LPN, LVN, Cert, Dipl, AAS)** *17 students enrolled* • **Management Information Systems, General** • **Medical Transcription/Transcriptionist** *1 student enrolled* • **Medical/Clinical Assistant** *20 students enrolled* • **Receptionist** *1 student enrolled* • **Surgical Technology/Technologist** *13 students enrolled* • **Web Page, Digital/Multimedia and Information Resources Design** *4 students enrolled*

**STUDENT SERVICES** Academic or career counseling, employment services for current students, placement services for program completers, remedial services.

## El Paso Community College

PO Box 20500, El Paso, TX 79998-0500
http://www.epcc.edu/

**CONTACT** Dr. Richard Rhodes, President
**Telephone:** 915-831-2000

**GENERAL INFORMATION** Public Institution. Founded 1969. **Accreditation:** Regional (SACS/CC); dental assisting (ADA); dental hygiene (ADA); health information technology (AHIMA); medical assisting (AAMAE); medical laboratory technology (NAACLS); ophthalmic laboratory technology (COA); physical therapy assisting (APTA); surgical technology (ARCST). **Total program enrollment:** 9835. **Application fee:** $10.

**PROGRAM(S) OFFERED**
• **Accounting Technology/Technician and Bookkeeping** *12 students enrolled* • **Administrative Assistant and Secretarial Science, General** *17 students enrolled* • **Automobile/Automotive Mechanics Technology/Technician** *32 students enrolled* • **Business Administration and Management, General** *3 students enrolled* • **Business/Commerce, General** • **Business/Office Automation/Technology/Data Entry** *6 students enrolled* • **Child Development** *25 students enrolled* • **Cinematography and Film/Video Production** *2 students enrolled* • **Communications Systems Installation and Repair Technology** • **Community Health Services/Liaison/Counseling** *13 students enrolled* • **Computer Programming/Programmer, General** • **Computer and Information Sciences, General** *13 students enrolled* • **Computer/Information Technology Services Administration and Management, Other** • **Cosmetology/Cosmetologist, General** *27 students enrolled* • **Court Reporting/Court Reporter** *5 students enrolled* • **Criminal Justice/Safety Studies** *1 student enrolled* • **Culinary Arts/Chef Training** *1 student enrolled* • **Dental Assisting/Assistant** *4 students enrolled* • **Diagnostic Medical Sonography/Sonographer and Ultrasound Technician** *1 student enrolled* • **Drafting and Design Technology/Technician, General** *5 students enrolled* • **Electrical/Electronics Equipment Installation and Repair, General** • **Electrician** *44 students enrolled* • **Emergency Medical Technology/Technician (EMT Paramedic)** *6 students enrolled* • **Environmental Engineering Technology/Environmental Technology** • **Fashion Merchandising** • **Fashion/Apparel Design** • **Fine/Studio Arts, General** • **Fire Protection and Safety Technology/Technician** • **Fire Science/Firefighting** *47 students enrolled* • **Heating, Air Conditioning, Ventilation and Refrigeration Maintenance Technology/Technician (HAC, HACR, HVAC, HVACR)** *5 students enrolled* • **Hotel/Motel Administration/Management** • **Institutional Food Workers** *1 student enrolled* • **Interior Design** *5 students enrolled* • **International Business/Trade/Commerce** • **Legal Assistant/Paralegal** *1 student enrolled* • **Licensed Practical/Vocational Nurse Training (LPN, LVN, Cert, Dipl, AAS)** • **Machine Tool Technology/Machinist** *12 students enrolled* • **Manufacturing Technology/Technician** *10 students enrolled* • **Medical Insurance Coding Specialist/Coder** • **Medical Transcription/Transcriptionist** *2 students enrolled* • **Medical/Clinical Assistant** *1 student enrolled* • **Nurse/Nursing Assistant/Aide and Patient Care Assistant** *3 students enrolled* • **Nursing—Registered Nurse Training (RN, ASN, BSN, MSN)** • **Opticianry/Ophthalmic Dispensing Optician** *2 students enrolled* • **Optometric Technician/Assistant** • **Pharmacy Technician/Assistant** *14 students enrolled* • **Plastics Engineering Technology/Technician** • **Real Estate** • **Sign Language Interpretation and Translation** *14 students enrolled* • **Surgical Technology/Technologist** *5 students enrolled* • **System Administration/Administrator** *1 student enrolled* • **System, Networking, and LAN/WAN Management/Manager** *3 students enrolled* • **Tourism and Travel Services Marketing Operations** *4 students enrolled*

**STUDENT SERVICES** Academic or career counseling, daycare for children of students, employment services for current students, placement services for program completers, remedial services.

## Everest College

2801 East Division Street, Suite 250, Arlington, TX 76011
http://www.everest.edu/

**CONTACT** Kendra Williams, President
**Telephone:** 817-652-7790

**GENERAL INFORMATION** Private Institution. Founded 2003. **Accreditation:** State accredited or approved. **Total program enrollment:** 333.

**PROGRAM(S) OFFERED**
• **Medical Insurance Coding Specialist/Coder** *21 students enrolled* • **Pharmacy Technician/Assistant** *77 students enrolled*

**STUDENT SERVICES** Academic or career counseling, employment services for current students, placement services for program completers, remedial services.

## Everest College

6060 North Central Expressway, Suite 101, Dallas, TX 75206-5209
http://www.everest.edu/

**CONTACT** Stacy Pniewski, Acting College President
**Telephone:** 214-234-4850

**GENERAL INFORMATION** Private Institution. Founded 2003. **Accreditation:** State accredited or approved. **Total program enrollment:** 926.

**PROGRAM(S) OFFERED**
• **Medical Insurance Coding Specialist/Coder** *152 students enrolled*

**STUDENT SERVICES** Academic or career counseling, employment services for current students, placement services for program completers, remedial services.

## Everest College

5237 North Riverside Drive, Suite 100, Fort Worth, TX 76137
http://www.everest.edu/

**CONTACT** Marilyn Long, College President
**Telephone:** 817-838-3000

**GENERAL INFORMATION** Private Institution. Founded 2004. **Total program enrollment:** 236.

**PROGRAM(S) OFFERED**
• **Medical Insurance Specialist/Medical Biller** *123 students enrolled*
• **Pharmacy Technician/Assistant** *47 students enrolled*

**STUDENT SERVICES** Academic or career counseling, employment services for current students, placement services for program completers, remedial services.

## Everest Institute

9100 U.S. Highway 290 East, Suite 100, Austin, TX 78754
http://www.everest.edu/

**CONTACT** Joe Davila, School President
**Telephone:** 512-928-1933

**GENERAL INFORMATION** Private Institution. **Total program enrollment:** 1151.

**PROGRAM(S) OFFERED**
• **Dental Assisting/Assistant** *720 hrs./$15,000* • **Health and Medical Administrative Services, Other** *125 students enrolled* • **Heating, Air Conditioning and Refrigeration Technology/Technician (ACH/ACR/ACHR/HRAC/HVAC/AC Technology)** *720 hrs./$14,000* • **Heating, Air Conditioning, Ventilation and Refrigeration Maintenance Technology/Technician (HAC, HACR, HVAC, HVACR)** *122 students enrolled* • **Medical Administrative/Executive Assistant and Medical Secretary** *720 hrs./$13,110* • **Medical Insurance Coding Specialist/Coder** *720 hrs./$13,110* • **Medical/Clinical Assistant** *720 hrs./$14,081* • **Pharmacy Technician/Assistant** *720 hrs./$13,110*

**STUDENT SERVICES** Academic or career counseling, employment services for current students, placement services for program completers.

## Everest Institute

255 Northpoint Drive, Suite 100, Houston, TX 77060
http://www.everest.edu/campus/houston_greenspoint

**CONTACT** Anthonie Rich, School President
**Telephone:** 281-447-7037 Ext. 119

**GENERAL INFORMATION** Private Institution. **Total program enrollment:** 402.

**PROGRAM(S) OFFERED**
• **Dental Assisting/Assistant** *720 hrs./$14,298* • **Medical Administrative/Executive Assistant and Medical Secretary** *720 hrs./$13,100* • **Medical Insurance Specialist/Medical Biller** *336 students enrolled* • **Medical/Clinical Assistant** *720 hrs./$15,050* • **Pharmacy Technician/Assistant** *158 students enrolled*

**STUDENT SERVICES** Academic or career counseling, employment services for current students, placement services for program completers.

## Everest Institute

7151 Office City Drive, Suite 200, Houston, TX 77087
http://www.everest.edu/

**CONTACT** Wm. Greg Lotz, School President
**Telephone:** 713-645-7404

**GENERAL INFORMATION** Private Institution. **Total program enrollment:** 194.

**PROGRAM(S) OFFERED**
• **Medical Insurance Coding Specialist/Coder** *720 hrs./$13,494* • **Medical/Clinical Assistant** *720 hrs./$14,967* • **Pharmacy Technician/Assistant** *68 students enrolled*

**STUDENT SERVICES** Academic or career counseling, employment services for current students, placement services for program completers.

## Everest Institute

9700 Bissonnet Street, Westwood Technology Center, Houston, TX 77036-8001
http://www.everest.edu/

**CONTACT** Jeff Brown, President
**Telephone:** 713-772-4200

**GENERAL INFORMATION** Private Institution. **Total program enrollment:** 686.

**PROGRAM(S) OFFERED**
• **Computer Systems Networking and Telecommunications** *55 hrs./$15,656*
• **Electrical and Power Transmission Installers, Other** *59 hrs./$14,000*
• **Electrical, Electronic and Communications Engineering Technology/Technician** *23 students enrolled* • **Heating, Air Conditioning and Refrigeration Technology/Technician (ACH/ACR/ACHR/HRAC/HVAC/AC Technology)** *68 students enrolled* • **Heating, Air Conditioning, Ventilation and Refrigeration Maintenance Technology/Technician (HAC, HACR, HVAC, HVACR)** *56 hrs./$14,000* • **Medical Insurance Coding Specialist/Coder** *47 hrs./$13,547*
• **Medical Insurance Specialist/Medical Biller** *149 students enrolled* • **Medical Office Assistant/Specialist** *47 hrs./$14,927* • **Medical Office Management/Administration** *30 students enrolled* • **Medical/Clinical Assistant** *265 students enrolled* • **Pharmacy Technician/Assistant** *47 hrs./$14,260* • **Plumbing Technology/Plumber** *22 students enrolled*

**STUDENT SERVICES** Academic or career counseling, employment services for current students, placement services for program completers, remedial services.

## Everest Institute

3622 Fredricksburg Road, San Antonio, TX 78201-3841
http://www.everest.edu/

**CONTACT** Raymond Gutierrez, Campus President
**Telephone:** 210-732-7800

**GENERAL INFORMATION** Private Institution. Founded 1935. **Total program enrollment:** 1120.

**PROGRAM(S) OFFERED**
• **Heating, Air Conditioning, Ventilation and Refrigeration Maintenance Technology/Technician (HAC, HACR, HVAC, HVACR)** *600 hrs./$14,000* • **Medical Administrative/Executive Assistant and Medical Secretary** *720 hrs./$13,000* • **Medical/Clinical Assistant** *720 hrs./$14,120* • **Pharmacy Technician/Assistant** *720 hrs./$12,467*

**STUDENT SERVICES** Academic or career counseling, employment services for current students, placement services for program completers.

## Exposito School of Hair Design

3710 Mockingbird, Amarillo, TX 79109
http://expositoschoolofhair.com/

**CONTACT** Jan Exposito, Manager
**Telephone:** 806-355-9111

**GENERAL INFORMATION** Private Institution. **Total program enrollment:** 53.

**PROGRAM(S) OFFERED**
• **Cosmetology and Related Personal Grooming Arts, Other** *150 hrs./$700* • **Cosmetology/Cosmetologist, General** *1500 hrs./$9250* • **Nail Technician/Specialist and Manicurist** *600 hrs./$2228* • **Trade and Industrial Teacher Education** *750 hrs./$1800*

**STUDENT SERVICES** Academic or career counseling, placement services for program completers.

## Faris Computer School

1119 Kent Avenue, Nederland, TX 77627
http://www.fariscomputerschool.com/

**CONTACT** Lois Faris, Chief Administration Officer
**Telephone:** 409-722-4072

**GENERAL INFORMATION** Private Institution. **Total program enrollment:** 19.

**PROGRAM(S) OFFERED**
• **Administrative Assistant and Secretarial Science, General** *52 hrs./$9250* • **Business/Office Automation/Technology/Data Entry** *42 hrs./$8350* • **CAD/CADD Drafting and/or Design Technology/Technician** *54 hrs./$9200* • **Legal Administrative Assistant/Secretary** *52 hrs./$9225* • **Medical Administrative/Executive Assistant and Medical Secretary** *53 hrs./$9875*

**STUDENT SERVICES** Placement services for program completers.

## Fort Worth Beauty School

2820 Hemphill, Ft. Worth, TX 76110
http://fortworthbeautyschool.net/

**CONTACT** Sharon L. Gamblin, CEO
**Telephone:** 817-732-2232

**GENERAL INFORMATION** Private Institution. Founded 1957. **Total program enrollment:** 33. **Application fee:** $100.

**PROGRAM(S) OFFERED**
• **Cosmetology and Related Personal Grooming Arts, Other** *3 students enrolled* • **Cosmetology, Barber/Styling, and Nail Instructor** *750 hrs./$2815* • **Cosmetology/Cosmetologist, General** *1500 hrs./$10,000* • **Nail Technician/Specialist and Manicurist** *600 hrs./$2100*

**STUDENT SERVICES** Academic or career counseling, placement services for program completers.

## Franklin Beauty School

4965 Martin Luther King Jr. Boulevard, Houston, TX 77021
http://www.thefranklinbeautyschool.com/

**CONTACT** Ron B. Jemison, Sr., President
**Telephone:** 713-645-9060

**GENERAL INFORMATION** Private Institution. **Total program enrollment:** 115. **Application fee:** $75.

**PROGRAM(S) OFFERED**
• **Cosmetology and Related Personal Grooming Arts, Other** *600 hrs./$3000* • **Cosmetology, Barber/Styling, and Nail Instructor** *750 hrs./$3750* • **Cosmetology/Cosmetologist, General** *1500 hrs./$9752* • **Education, General** *24 students enrolled*

**STUDENT SERVICES** Placement services for program completers.

## Frank Phillips College

Box 5118, Borger, TX 79008-5118
http://www.fpctx.edu/

**CONTACT** Dr. Herbert J. Swender, President
**Telephone:** 806-457-4200

**GENERAL INFORMATION** Public Institution. Founded 1948. **Accreditation:** Regional (SACS/CC). **Total program enrollment:** 585.

**PROGRAM(S) OFFERED**
• **Accounting** • **Administrative Assistant and Secretarial Science, General** *1 student enrolled* • **Agricultural Business and Management, General** • **Animal/Livestock Husbandry and Production** *4 students enrolled* • **Business Administration and Management, General** *1 student enrolled* • **Computer and Information Systems Security** *3 students enrolled* • **Cosmetology/Cosmetologist, General** *6 students enrolled* • **Farm/Farm and Ranch Management** *3 students enrolled* • **Heating, Air Conditioning, Ventilation and Refrigeration Maintenance Technology/Technician (HAC, HACR, HVAC, HVACR)** *2 students enrolled* • **Industrial Technology/Technician** *7 students enrolled* • **Licensed Practical/Vocational Nurse Training (LPN, LVN, Cert, Dipl, AAS)** *16 students enrolled* • **Management Information Systems, General** *1 student enrolled* • **System, Networking, and LAN/WAN Management/Manager** *1 student enrolled* • **Welding Technology/Welder** *18 students enrolled*

**STUDENT SERVICES** Academic or career counseling, employment services for current students, placement services for program completers, remedial services.

## Galen Health Institute–San Antonio

6800 Park Ten Boulevard S, Suite 160, San Antonio, TX 78213
http://www.galened.com/

**CONTACT** Dr. Regina Aune, Dean
**Telephone:** 210-733-3056

**GENERAL INFORMATION** Private Institution. Founded 1991. **Total program enrollment:** 390. **Application fee:** $100.

**PROGRAM(S) OFFERED**
• **Licensed Practical/Vocational Nurse Training (LPN, LVN, Cert, Dipl, AAS)** *1440 hrs./$16,920*

**STUDENT SERVICES** Academic or career counseling, placement services for program completers.

## Galveston College

4015 Avenue Q, Galveston, TX 77550-7496
http://www.gc.edu/

**CONTACT** Dr. W. Myles Shelton, President
**Telephone:** 409-944-1220

**GENERAL INFORMATION** Public Institution. Founded 1967. **Accreditation:** Regional (SACS/CC); emergency medical services (JRCEMTP); nuclear medicine technology (JRCNMT); radiologic technology: radiation therapy technology (JRCERT); radiologic technology: radiography (JRCERT). **Total program enrollment:** 594.

**PROGRAM(S) OFFERED**
• **Accounting** • **Administrative Assistant and Secretarial Science, General** *4 students enrolled* • **Business Administration and Management, General** • **Computer Programming/Programmer, General** *1 student enrolled* • **Criminal Justice/Police Science** *21 students enrolled* • **Criminal Justice/Safety Studies** *1 student enrolled* • **Culinary Arts/Chef Training** *4 students enrolled* • **Emergency Medical Technology/Technician (EMT Paramedic)** *25 students enrolled* • **Licensed Practical/Vocational Nurse Training (LPN, LVN, Cert, Dipl, AAS)** *24 students enrolled* • **Medical Administrative/Executive Assistant and Medical Secretary** *3 students enrolled* • **Medical Radiologic Technology/Science—Radiation Therapist** *4 students enrolled* • **Phlebotomy/Phlebotomist** *6 students enrolled* • **Radiologic Technology/Science—Radiographer** *38 students enrolled* • **Surgical Technology/Technologist** *10 students enrolled*

**STUDENT SERVICES** Academic or career counseling, daycare for children of students, employment services for current students, placement services for program completers, remedial services.

## Grayson County College

6101 Grayson Drive, Denison, TX 75020-8299
http://www.grayson.edu/

**CONTACT** Dr. Alan Scheibmeir, President
**Telephone:** 903-465-6030

**GENERAL INFORMATION** Public Institution. Founded 1964. **Accreditation:** Regional (SACS/CC); dental assisting (ADA); medical laboratory technology (NAACLS). **Total program enrollment:** 1997.

**PROGRAM(S) OFFERED**
• **Accounting Technology/Technician and Bookkeeping** *3 students enrolled* • **Administrative Assistant and Secretarial Science, General** *6 students enrolled* • **Aesthetician/Esthetician and Skin Care Specialist** *6 students enrolled* • **Autobody/Collision and Repair Technology/Technician** *2 students enrolled* • **Business Administration and Management, General** *4 students enrolled* • **Computer Technology/Computer Systems Technology** *9 students enrolled* • **Cosmetology/Cosmetologist, General** *20 students enrolled* • **Data Processing and Data Processing Technology/Technician** • **Dental Assisting/Assistant** *17 students enrolled* • **Drafting and Design Technology/Technician, General** *10 students enrolled* • **Electrical, Electronic and Communications Engineering Technology/Technician** • **Emergency Medical Technology/Technician (EMT Paramedic)** *24 students enrolled* • **Food Science** *4 students enrolled* • **Heating, Air Conditioning and Refrigeration Technology/Technician (ACH/ACR/ACHR/HRAC/HVAC/AC Technology)** *19 students enrolled* • **Industrial Mechanics and Maintenance Technology** • **Licensed Practical/Vocational Nurse Training (LPN, LVN, Cert, Dipl, AAS)** *43 students enrolled* • **Machine Tool Technology/Machinist** • **Medical Administrative/Executive Assistant and Medical Secretary** *6 students enrolled* • **Nail Technician/Specialist and Manicurist** *4 students enrolled* • **Substance Abuse/Addiction Counseling** *10 students enrolled* • **Telecommunications Technology/Technician** *7 students enrolled* • **Welding Technology/Welder** *11 students enrolled*

**STUDENT SERVICES** Academic or career counseling, employment services for current students, placement services for program completers, remedial services.

## Hallmark Institute of Technology

10401 IH 10 West, San Antonio, TX 78230-1737
http://www.hallmarkinstitute.edu/

**CONTACT** Joe Fisher, President
**Telephone:** 210-690-9000 Ext. 244

**GENERAL INFORMATION** Private Institution. Founded 1969. **Accreditation:** State accredited or approved. **Total program enrollment:** 600. **Application fee:** $110.

**PROGRAM(S) OFFERED**
• **Avionics Maintenance Technology/Technician** *2070 hrs./$29,400* • **Business/Office Automation/Technology/Data Entry** *1488 hrs./$19,850* • **Computer Systems Networking and Telecommunications** *1472 hrs./$30,800* • **Electrical, Electronic and Communications Engineering Technology/Technician** *1472 hrs./$21,200* • **Medical/Clinical Assistant** *1488 hrs./$19,850*

**STUDENT SERVICES** Academic or career counseling, employment services for current students, placement services for program completers, remedial services.

## High-Tech Institute

4250 North Beltline Road, Irving, TX 75038
http://www.high-techinstitute.com/

**CONTACT** Cindy Bryant, Campus President
**Telephone:** 972-871-2824

**GENERAL INFORMATION** Private Institution. Founded 2000. **Accreditation:** State accredited or approved. **Total program enrollment:** 753. **Application fee:** $50.

**PROGRAM(S) OFFERED**
• **Criminal Justice/Police Science** *770 hrs./$13,469* • **Dental Assisting/Assistant** *746 hrs./$11,640* • **Massage Therapy/Therapeutic Massage** *51 students enrolled* • **Medical Insurance Specialist/Medical Biller** *720 hrs./$11,116* • **Medical/Clinical Assistant** *746 hrs./$11,550* • **Pharmacy Technician/Assistant** *720 hrs./$11,537* • **Surgical Technology/Technologist** *1160 hrs./$22,681*

**STUDENT SERVICES** Placement services for program completers.

## Hill College of the Hill Junior College District

PO Box 619, Hillsboro, TX 76645-0619
http://www.hillcollege.edu/

**CONTACT** Dr. Sheryl Smith Kappus, President
**Telephone:** 254-582-2555

**GENERAL INFORMATION** Public Institution. Founded 1923. **Accreditation:** Regional (SACS/CC). **Total program enrollment:** 1589.

**PROGRAM(S) OFFERED**
• **Administrative Assistant and Secretarial Science, General** *8 students enrolled* • **Autobody/Collision and Repair Technology/Technician** • **Automobile/Automotive Mechanics Technology/Technician** *24 students enrolled* • **Business Administration and Management, General** • **Business/Commerce, General** • **Child Care and Support Services Management** *10 students enrolled* • **Computer Programming/Programmer, General** *2 students enrolled* • **Construction Engineering Technology/Technician** *1 student enrolled* • **Corrections and Criminal Justice, Other** • **Corrections** *2 students enrolled* • **Cosmetology, Barber/Styling, and Nail Instructor** *2 students enrolled* • **Cosmetology/Cosmetologist, General** *21 students enrolled* • **Criminal Justice/Law Enforcement Administration** *1 student enrolled* • **Drafting and Design Technology/Technician, General** • **Emergency Medical Technology/Technician (EMT Paramedic)** *5 students enrolled* • **Facial Treatment Specialist/Facialist** *3 students enrolled* • **Fire Science/Firefighting** *28 students enrolled* • **Heating, Air Conditioning, Ventilation and Refrigeration Maintenance Technology/Technician (HAC, HACR, HVAC, HVACR)** *1 student enrolled* • **Industrial Electronics Technology/Technician** *2 students enrolled* • **Industrial Mechanics and Maintenance Technology** *1 student enrolled* • **Licensed Practical/Vocational Nurse Training (LPN, LVN, Cert, Dipl, AAS)** *38 students enrolled* • **Pharmacy Technician/Assistant** *4 students enrolled* • **Security and Loss Prevention Services** • **System, Networking, and LAN/WAN Management/Manager** *1 student enrolled* • **Teacher Assistant/Aide** • **Welding Technology/Welder** *37 students enrolled*

**STUDENT SERVICES** Academic or career counseling, employment services for current students, placement services for program completers, remedial services.

## Houston Community College System

3100 Main Street, PO Box 667517, Houston, TX 77266-7517
http://www.hccs.edu/

**CONTACT** Dr. Mary S. Spangler, Chancellor
**Telephone:** 713-718-2000

**GENERAL INFORMATION** Public Institution. Founded 1971. **Accreditation:** Regional (SACS/CC); dental assisting (ADA); emergency medical services (JRCEMTP); engineering technology (ABET/TAC); health information technology (AHIMA); histologic technology (NAACLS); medical laboratory technology (NAACLS); nuclear medicine technology (JRCNMT); physical therapy assisting (APTA); radiologic technology: radiography (JRCERT). **Total program enrollment:** 14056.

**PROGRAM(S) OFFERED**
• **Accounting** *7 students enrolled* • **Airframe Mechanics and Aircraft Maintenance Technology/Technician** • **Animation, Interactive Technology, Video Graphics and Special Effects** *10 students enrolled* • **Automobile/Automotive Mechanics Technology/Technician** *10 students enrolled* • **Baking and Pastry Arts/Baker/Pastry Chef** *4 students enrolled* • **Banking and Financial Support Services** *5 students enrolled* • **Biology Technician/Biotechnology Laboratory Technician** • **Business Administration and Management, General** *49 students enrolled* • **Business/Corporate Communications** • **Business/Office Automation/Technology/Data Entry** *56 students enrolled* • **Cardiovascular Technology/Technologist** • **Cartography** *4 students enrolled* • **Chemical Technology/Technician** *4 students enrolled* • **Child Care Provider/Assistant** *11 students enrolled* • **Child Care and Support Services Management** *4 students enrolled* • **Child Development** • **Cinematography and Film/Video Production** • **Commercial Photography** *1 student enrolled* • **Computer Engineering Technology/Technician** *4 students enrolled* • **Computer Programming/Programmer, General** • **Computer Systems Networking and Telecommunica-**

*Houston Community College System (continued)*

**tions** *12 students enrolled* • **Computer and Information Sciences, General** • **Construction Engineering Technology/Technician** *1 student enrolled* • **Cosmetology, Barber/Styling, and Nail Instructor** *1 student enrolled* • **Cosmetology/Cosmetologist, General** *2 students enrolled* • **Criminal Justice/Police Science** *28 students enrolled* • **Culinary Arts/Chef Training** *5 students enrolled* • **Dental Assisting/Assistant** *12 students enrolled* • **Diagnostic Medical Sonography/Sonographer and Ultrasound Technician** *11 students enrolled* • **Diesel Mechanics Technology/Technician** *9 students enrolled* • **Drafting and Design Technology/Technician, General** *10 students enrolled* • **Electrical and Power Transmission Installation/Installer, General** *11 students enrolled* • **Electrician** *7 students enrolled* • **Emergency Medical Technology/Technician (EMT Paramedic)** • **Facial Treatment Specialist/Facialist** *1 student enrolled* • **Fashion Merchandising** *8 students enrolled* • **Fashion/Apparel Design** *3 students enrolled* • **Fire Protection and Safety Technology/Technician** *3 students enrolled* • **Fire Science/Firefighting** *2 students enrolled* • **Health Information/Medical Records Technology/Technician** *7 students enrolled* • **Health and Physical Education, General** *6 students enrolled* • **Heating, Air Conditioning, Ventilation and Refrigeration Maintenance Technology/Technician (HAC, HACR, HVAC, HVACR)** *23 students enrolled* • **Hotel/Motel Administration/Management** • **International Business/Trade/Commerce** *3 students enrolled* • **Landscaping and Groundskeeping** • **Legal Assistant/Paralegal** • **Licensed Practical/Vocational Nurse Training (LPN, LVN, Cert, Dipl, AAS)** *79 students enrolled* • **Logistics and Materials Management** *1 student enrolled* • **Machine Shop Technology/Assistant** *11 students enrolled* • **Manufacturing Technology/Technician** *6 students enrolled* • **Marketing/Marketing Management, General** • **Medical Insurance Coding Specialist/Coder** *5 students enrolled* • **Medical/Clinical Assistant** *25 students enrolled* • **Music Management and Merchandising** *2 students enrolled* • **Music Performance, General** *4 students enrolled* • **Music Theory and Composition** • **Nuclear Medical Technology/Technologist** • **Occupational Therapist Assistant** *10 students enrolled* • **Ornamental Horticulture** • **Pharmacy Technician/Assistant** *37 students enrolled* • **Prepress/Desktop Publishing and Digital Imaging Design** *7 students enrolled* • **Psychiatric/Mental Health Services Technician** *5 students enrolled* • **Radio and Television Broadcasting Technology/Technician** *5 students enrolled* • **Radiologic Technology/Science—Radiographer** *18 students enrolled* • **Real Estate** *35 students enrolled* • **Restaurant/Food Services Management** *2 students enrolled* • **Sign Language Interpretation and Translation** *2 students enrolled* • **Surgical Technology/Technologist** *21 students enrolled* • **System Administration/Administrator** *3 students enrolled* • **System, Networking, and LAN/WAN Management/Manager** • **Tourism and Travel Services Management** *8 students enrolled* • **Veterinary/Animal Health Technology/Technician and Veterinary Assistant** *25 students enrolled* • **Welding Technology/Welder** *9 students enrolled*

**STUDENT SERVICES** Academic or career counseling, daycare for children of students, employment services for current students, placement services for program completers, remedial services.

## Houston's Training and Education Center

7457 Harwin, Suite 190, Houston, TX 77036
http://www.houston-tec.com/

**CONTACT** Stephanie Boutte-Phillips, School Director/CEO
**Telephone:** 713-783-2221

**GENERAL INFORMATION** Private Institution.

**PROGRAM(S) OFFERED**
• **Accounting Technology/Technician and Bookkeeping** *2 students enrolled* • **Clinical/Medical Laboratory Assistant** • **Data Entry/Microcomputer Applications, Other** *65 students enrolled* • **Executive Assistant/Executive Secretary** • **Medical Office Computer Specialist/Assistant** *93 students enrolled*

## Houston Training School

704 Shotwell Street, Houston, TX 77020

**CONTACT** Carolyn McAllister, President
**Telephone:** 281-535-0290

**GENERAL INFORMATION** Private Institution. Founded 1987. **Total program enrollment:** 32.

**PROGRAM(S) OFFERED**
• **Cosmetology and Related Personal Grooming Arts, Other** • **Cosmetology, Barber/Styling, and Nail Instructor** • **Cosmetology/Cosmetologist, General** *1500 hrs./$9700* • **Nail Technician/Specialist and Manicurist**

**STUDENT SERVICES** Academic or career counseling, placement services for program completers.

## Houston Training School–South

6969 Gulf Freeway, Suite 200, Houston, TX 77087

**CONTACT** C. McAllister, President
**Telephone:** 281-535-0290

**GENERAL INFORMATION** Private Institution. **Total program enrollment:** 349.

**PROGRAM(S) OFFERED**
• **Cosmetology and Related Personal Grooming Arts, Other** *150 hrs./$850* • **Cosmetology, Barber/Styling, and Nail Instructor** *750 hrs./$4800* • **Cosmetology/Cosmetologist, General** *1500 hrs./$9700* • **Multicultural Education** *720 hrs./$4510* • **Nail Technician/Specialist and Manicurist** *600 hrs./$3800*

**STUDENT SERVICES** Academic or career counseling, placement services for program completers.

## Howard College

1001 Birdwell Lane, Big Spring, TX 79720
http://www.howardcollege.edu/

**CONTACT** Cheryl T. Sparks, President
**Telephone:** 432-264-5000

**GENERAL INFORMATION** Public Institution. Founded 1945. **Accreditation:** Regional (SACS/CC); dental hygiene (ADA); health information technology (AHIMA). **Total program enrollment:** 1332.

**PROGRAM(S) OFFERED**
• **Accounting** • **Administrative Assistant and Secretarial Science, General** *14 students enrolled* • **Adult Development and Aging** • **Agriculture, General** *1 student enrolled* • **Business/Commerce, General** *24 students enrolled* • **Child Development** • **Computer and Information Sciences, General** *11 students enrolled* • **Corrections** • **Cosmetology, Barber/Styling, and Nail Instructor** • **Cosmetology/Cosmetologist, General** *30 students enrolled* • **Criminal Justice/Police Science** *13 students enrolled* • **Criminal Justice/Safety Studies** • **Drafting and Design Technology/Technician, General** *11 students enrolled* • **Emergency Medical Technology/Technician (EMT Paramedic)** • **Health Information/Medical Records Technology/Technician** • **Human Development and Family Studies, General** • **Industrial Technology/Technician** • **Licensed Practical/Vocational Nurse Training (LPN, LVN, Cert, Dipl, AAS)** *63 students enrolled* • **Marketing/Marketing Management, General** • **Medical Transcription/Transcriptionist** • **Medical/Clinical Assistant** *5 students enrolled* • **Nail Technician/Specialist and Manicurist** *3 students enrolled* • **Sign Language Interpretation and Translation** • **Surgical Technology/Technologist** *7 students enrolled*

**STUDENT SERVICES** Academic or career counseling, daycare for children of students, employment services for current students, placement services for program completers, remedial services.

## Howard Payne University

1000 Fisk Street, Brownwood, TX 76801-2715
http://www.hputx.edu/

**CONTACT** Dr. Lanny Hall, President
**Telephone:** 325-646-2502

**GENERAL INFORMATION** Private Institution (Affiliated with Baptist General Convention of Texas). Founded 1889. **Accreditation:** Regional (SACS/CC); music (NASM). **Total program enrollment:** 1046. **Application fee:** $25.

**PROGRAM(S) OFFERED**
• **Bible/Biblical Studies** *9 students enrolled* • **International Business/Trade/Commerce** *1 student enrolled*

**STUDENT SERVICES** Academic or career counseling, employment services for current students, remedial services.

## ICC Technical Institute

3333 Fannin, Suite 203, Houston, TX 77004

**CONTACT** Chi Do, Executive Director
**Telephone:** 713-522-7799

**GENERAL INFORMATION** Private Institution. **Total program enrollment:** 52. **Application fee:** $100.

**PROGRAM(S) OFFERED**
• **Cosmetology, Barber/Styling, and Nail Instructor** *1 student enrolled* • **Cosmetology/Cosmetologist, General** *1500 hrs./$6800* • **Facial Treatment Specialist/Facialist** *750 hrs./$3200* • **Nail Technician/Specialist and Manicurist** *600 hrs./$2150* • **Teacher Education and Professional Development, Specific Subject Areas, Other** *750 hrs./$3300*

**STUDENT SERVICES** Academic or career counseling, placement services for program completers, remedial services.

## Interactive Learning Systems

8585 North Stemmons Freeway, Twin Towers, #C15, Dallas, TX 75247
http://www.ict-ils.edu/

**CONTACT** Elmer R. Smith, President
**Telephone:** 214-637-3377

**GENERAL INFORMATION** Private Institution. **Total program enrollment:** 5. **Application fee:** $50.

**PROGRAM(S) OFFERED**
• **Accounting and Related Services, Other** *815 hrs./$8900* • **Administrative Assistant and Secretarial Science, General** *815 hrs./$8900* • **Computer Programming/Programmer, General** *1000 hrs./$12,630* • **Computer and Information Sciences, General** *815 hrs./$8900*

**STUDENT SERVICES** Academic or career counseling, employment services for current students, placement services for program completers, remedial services.

## Interactive Learning Systems

256 N. Sam Houston Parkway, Suite 130, Houston, TX 77060
http://www.ict-ils.edu/

**CONTACT** Elmer R. Smith, President
**Telephone:** 281-931-7717

**GENERAL INFORMATION** Private Institution. **Total program enrollment:** 18. **Application fee:** $50.

**PROGRAM(S) OFFERED**
• **Accounting and Related Services, Other** *815 hrs./$8900* • **Administrative Assistant and Secretarial Science, General** *815 hrs./$8900* • **Computer Programming/Programmer, General** *1000 hrs./$12,630* • **Computer and Information Sciences, General** *815 hrs./$8900*

**STUDENT SERVICES** Academic or career counseling, employment services for current students, placement services for program completers, remedial services.

## Interactive Learning Systems

6200 Hillcroft Avenue, Houston, TX 77042
http://www.ict-ils.edu/

**CONTACT** Elmer R. Smith, President
**Telephone:** 713-771-5336

**GENERAL INFORMATION** Private Institution. **Total program enrollment:** 25. **Application fee:** $50.

**PROGRAM(S) OFFERED**
• **Accounting and Related Services, Other** *815 hrs./$8900* • **Administrative Assistant and Secretarial Science, General** *815 hrs./$8900* • **Business Operations Support and Secretarial Services, Other** *4 students enrolled* • **Computer Programming/Programmer, General** *1000 hrs./$12,630* • **Computer and Information Sciences, General** *815 hrs./$8900*

**STUDENT SERVICES** Academic or career counseling, employment services for current students, placement services for program completers, remedial services.

## Interactive Learning Systems

1001 E. South Moore Street, Pasadena, TX 77502
http://www.ict-ils.edu/

**CONTACT** Elmer R. Smith, President
**Telephone:** 713-920-1120

**GENERAL INFORMATION** Private Institution. **Total program enrollment:** 26. **Application fee:** $50.

**PROGRAM(S) OFFERED**
• **Accounting and Related Services, Other** *815 hrs./$8900* • **Administrative Assistant and Secretarial Science, General** *815 hrs./$8900* • **Business Operations Support and Secretarial Services, Other** *6 students enrolled* • **Computer Programming/Programmer, General** *1000 hrs./$12,630* • **Computer and Information Sciences, General** *815 hrs./$8900*

**STUDENT SERVICES** Academic or career counseling, employment services for current students, placement services for program completers, remedial services.

## International Academy of Design & Technology

4511 Horizon Hill Boulevard, San Antonio, TX 78229-2263
http://www.iadtsanantonio.com/

**CONTACT** Lisa Kamenick, President
**Telephone:** 210-530-9449

**GENERAL INFORMATION** Private Institution. **Total program enrollment:** 352. **Application fee:** $50.

**PROGRAM(S) OFFERED**
• **Fashion/Apparel Design** • **Graphic Design**

**STUDENT SERVICES** Academic or career counseling, employment services for current students, placement services for program completers, remedial services.

## International Beauty College

2413 West Airport Freeway, Irving, TX 75062
http://www.jonesbeautycollege.com/

**CONTACT** Jennifer Jones, Director of Operations
**Telephone:** 972-770-1022

**GENERAL INFORMATION** Private Institution. **Total program enrollment:** 18. **Application fee:** $150.

**PROGRAM(S) OFFERED**
• **Aesthetician/Esthetician and Skin Care Specialist** *750 hrs./$6000*
• **Cosmetology, Barber/Styling, and Nail Instructor** *750 hrs./$6000*
• **Cosmetology/Cosmetologist, General** *1500 hrs./$8900* • **Nail Technician/Specialist and Manicurist** *7 students enrolled*

**STUDENT SERVICES** Placement services for program completers.

## International Beauty College 3

1225 Beltline Road, Suite 7, Garland, TX 75040

**CONTACT** Terry W. Jones, Administration Director
**Telephone:** 972-530-1103

**GENERAL INFORMATION** Private Institution. **Total program enrollment:** 43. **Application fee:** $50.

**PROGRAM(S) OFFERED**
• **Aesthetician/Esthetician and Skin Care Specialist** *750 hrs./$5600* • **Cosmetology/Cosmetologist, General** *1500 hrs./$7571* • **Nail Technician/Specialist and Manicurist** *600 hrs./$2900*

**STUDENT SERVICES** Academic or career counseling, placement services for program completers.

## International Business College

El Paso, TX
http://www.ibcelpaso.com

**CONTACT** Margie Aguilar, President
**Telephone:** 915-779-0900

**GENERAL INFORMATION** Private Institution.

## International Business College

4121 Montana Avenue, El Paso, TX 79903
http://www.ibcelpaso.edu/

**CONTACT** Jerry D. Foster, Chairman of the Board
**Telephone:** 915-842-0422

**GENERAL INFORMATION** Private Institution. Founded 1898. **Total program enrollment:** 218. **Application fee:** $100.

**PROGRAM(S) OFFERED**
• **Accounting** *42 hrs./$9600* • **Administrative Assistant and Secretarial Science, General** *13 students enrolled* • **Business Administration and Management, General** • **Computer Hardware Technology/Technician** *11 students enrolled* • **Computer Installation and Repair Technology/Technician** *46 hrs./$12,100* • **Customer Service Support/Call Center/Teleservice Operation** *2 students enrolled* • **General Office Occupations and Clerical Services** *44 hrs./$9200* • **Legal Administrative Assistant/Secretary** *4 students enrolled* • **Medical Insurance Coding Specialist/Coder** *41 hrs./$11,400* • **Medical Office Assistant/Specialist** *10 students enrolled* • **Medical/Clinical Assistant** *44 hrs./$11,400* • **Pharmacy Technician/Assistant** *48 hrs./$11,100*

**STUDENT SERVICES** Academic or career counseling, employment services for current students, placement services for program completers, remedial services.

## International Business College

1155 North Zaragosa Road, El Paso, TX 79907
http://www.ibcelpaso.edu/

**CONTACT** Jerry D. Foster, Chairman of the Board
**Telephone:** 915-859-0422

**GENERAL INFORMATION** Private Institution. **Total program enrollment:** 244. **Application fee:** $100.

**PROGRAM(S) OFFERED**
• **Accounting** *7 students enrolled* • **Administrative Assistant and Secretarial Science, General** *14 students enrolled* • **Business Administration and Management, General** *96 hrs./$19,800* • **Customer Service Support/Call Center/Teleservice Operation** *29 students enrolled* • **General Office Occupations and Clerical Services** *44 hrs./$9200* • **Health Information/Medical Records Technology/Technician** *18 students enrolled* • **Legal Administrative Assistant/Secretary** *48 hrs./$10,200* • **Medical Insurance Coding Specialist/Coder** *41 hrs./$11,400* • **Medical Office Assistant/Specialist** *10 students enrolled* • **Medical/Clinical Assistant** *44 hrs./$11,400* • **Pharmacy Technician/Assistant** *48 hrs./$11,100*

**STUDENT SERVICES** Academic or career counseling, employment services for current students, placement services for program completers, remedial services.

## Iverson Institute of Court Reporting

1200 Copeland Road, Suite 305, Arlington, TX 76011
http://www.iversonschool.edu/

**CONTACT** Akber Mithani, President/CEO
**Telephone:** 770-446-1333

**GENERAL INFORMATION** Private Institution. Founded 1986. **Total program enrollment:** 137. **Application fee:** $100.

**PROGRAM(S) OFFERED**
• **Administrative Assistant and Secretarial Science, General** *60 hrs./$8450* • **Computer Systems Networking and Telecommunications** *73 hrs./$11,200* • **Court Reporting/Court Reporter** *130 hrs./$31,150* • **General Office Occupations and Clerical Services** *42 hrs./$6900* • **Legal Assistant/Paralegal** *7 students enrolled* • **Medical Insurance Coding Specialist/Coder** *16 students enrolled* • **Medical Transcription/Transcriptionist** *81 hrs./$11,450* • **Medical/Clinical Assistant** *5 students enrolled* • **Pharmacy Technician/Assistant** • **Surgical Technology/Technologist** *67 hrs./$14,750*

**STUDENT SERVICES** Placement services for program completers.

## Jay's Technical Institute

10750 S. Gessner, Houston, TX 77071

**CONTACT** Ollie Hilliard, Chief Administrative Officer
**Telephone:** 713-772-2410 Ext. 110

**GENERAL INFORMATION** Private Institution. **Total program enrollment:** 127.

**PROGRAM(S) OFFERED**
• **Barbering/Barber** *1500 hrs./$9200* • **Cosmetology, Barber/Styling, and Nail Instructor** *250 hrs./$1625* • **Cosmetology/Cosmetologist, General** *1500 hrs./$8300* • **Facial Treatment Specialist/Facialist** *750 hrs./$4000* • **Hair Styling/Stylist and Hair Design** • **Nail Technician/Specialist and Manicurist**

**STUDENT SERVICES** Placement services for program completers.

## Jones Beauty College

129 Webb Chapel Road, Dallas, TX 75229
http://www.jonesbeautycollege.com/

**CONTACT** Jennifer Jones, Director of Operations
**Telephone:** 214-770-1020

**GENERAL INFORMATION** Private Institution. **Total program enrollment:** 19. **Application fee:** $150.

**PROGRAM(S) OFFERED**
• **Cosmetology, Barber/Styling, and Nail Instructor** *750 hrs./$6000* • **Cosmetology/Cosmetologist, General** *1500 hrs./$8900* • **Nail Technician/Specialist and Manicurist** *6 students enrolled*

**STUDENT SERVICES** Placement services for program completers.

## KD Studio

2600 Stemmons Freeway, #117, Dallas, TX 75207
http://www.kdstudio.com/

**CONTACT** Kathy Tyner, President
**Telephone:** 214-638-0484

**GENERAL INFORMATION** Private Institution. Founded 1979. **Accreditation:** Theater (NAST). **Total program enrollment:** 145. **Application fee:** $100.

**PROGRAM(S) OFFERED**
• **Drama and Dramatics/Theatre Arts, General**

**STUDENT SERVICES** Academic or career counseling.

## Kilgore College

1100 Broadway Boulevard, Kilgore, TX 75662-3299
http://www.kilgore.edu/

**CONTACT** William M. Holda, President
**Telephone:** 903-984-8531

**GENERAL INFORMATION** Public Institution. Founded 1935. **Accreditation:** Regional (SACS/CC); medical assisting (AAMAE); medical laboratory technology (NAACLS); physical therapy assisting (APTA); radiologic technology: radiography (JRCERT); surgical technology (ARCST). **Total program enrollment:** 2656.

**PROGRAM(S) OFFERED**
• **Accounting** *2 students enrolled* • **Autobody/Collision and Repair Technology/Technician** *5 students enrolled* • **Automobile/Automotive Mechanics Technology/Technician** *2 students enrolled* • **Business Administration and Management, General** *3 students enrolled* • **Business/Commerce, General** • **Child Care Provider/Assistant** *2 students enrolled* • **Child Care and Support Services Management** *1 student enrolled* • **Commercial Photography** *4 students enrolled* • **Commercial and Advertising Art** *3 students enrolled* • **Computer Installation and Repair Technology/Technician** *1 student enrolled* • **Computer Systems Networking and Telecommunications** *4 students enrolled* • **Computer and Information Sciences, General** • **Cosmetology/Cosmetologist, General** *3 students enrolled* • **Court Reporting/Court Reporter** *4 students enrolled* • **Criminal Justice/Police Science** *204 students enrolled* • **Diesel Mechanics Technology/Technician** *13 students enrolled* • **Drafting and Design Technology/Technician, General** *13 students enrolled* • **Electrical, Electronic and Communications Engineering Technology/Technician** • **Emergency Medical Technology/Technician (EMT Paramedic)** *3 students enrolled* • **Entrepreneurship/Entrepreneurial Studies** • **Executive Assistant/Executive Secretary** *34 students enrolled* • **Fashion and Fabric Consultant** • **Fire Science/Firefighting** *135 students enrolled* • **Heating, Air Conditioning, Ventilation and Refrigeration Maintenance Technology/Technician (HAC, HACR, HVAC, HVACR)** *41 students enrolled* • **Legal Assistant/Paralegal** *3 students enrolled* • **Licensed Practical/Vocational Nurse Training (LPN, LVN, Cert, Dipl, AAS)** *34 students enrolled* • **Management Information Systems, General** *5 students enrolled* • **Medical Administrative/Executive Assistant and Medical Secretary** *13 students enrolled* • **Medical/Clinical Assistant** *3 students enrolled* • **Metallurgical Technology/Technician** *4 students enrolled* • **Occupational Safety and Health Technology/Technician** *3 students enrolled* • **Surgical Technology/Technologist** • **Welding Technology/Welder** *19 students enrolled*

**STUDENT SERVICES** Academic or career counseling, daycare for children of students, employment services for current students, placement services for program completers, remedial services.

## Lamar Institute of Technology

855 East Lavaca, Beaumont, TX 77705
http://www.lit.edu/

**CONTACT** Dr. Paul Szuch, President
**Telephone:** 409-880-8321

**GENERAL INFORMATION** Public Institution. Founded 1995. **Accreditation:** Regional (SACS/CC); dental hygiene (ADA); health information technology (AHIMA). **Total program enrollment:** 1529.

**PROGRAM(S) OFFERED**
• **Administrative Assistant and Secretarial Science, General** *6 students enrolled* • **Child Care Provider/Assistant** • **Child Care and Support Services Management** • **Computer Technology/Computer Systems Technology** • **Computer and Information Sciences, General** *3 students enrolled* • **Criminal Justice/Police Science** *34 students enrolled* • **Diagnostic Medical Sonography/Sonographer and Ultrasound Technician** • **Diesel Mechanics Technology/Technician** *7 students enrolled* • **Emergency Medical Technology/Technician (EMT Paramedic)** • **Fire Science/Firefighting** *23 students enrolled* • **Heating, Air Conditioning and Refrigeration Technology/Technician (ACH/ACR/ACHR/HRAC/HVAC/AC Technology)** *11 students enrolled* • **Industrial Mechanics and Maintenance Technology** *4 students enrolled* • **Institutional Food Workers** *2 students enrolled* • **Instrumentation Technology/Technician** *1 student enrolled* • **Lineworker** *6 students enrolled* • **Machine Tool Technology/Machinist** *3 students enrolled* • **Public Administration** *7 students enrolled* • **Real Estate** • **Welding Technology/Welder** *11 students enrolled*

**STUDENT SERVICES** Academic or career counseling, employment services for current students, placement services for program completers, remedial services.

## Lamar State College–Orange

410 Front Street, Orange, TX 77630-5802
http://www.lsco.edu/

**CONTACT** Michael Shahan, President
**Telephone:** 409-883-7750

**GENERAL INFORMATION** Public Institution. Founded 1969. **Accreditation:** Regional (SACS/CC); dental assisting (ADA); medical laboratory technology (NAACLS). **Total program enrollment:** 1014.

**PROGRAM(S) OFFERED**
• **Accounting** *3 students enrolled* • **Administrative Assistant and Secretarial Science, General** *4 students enrolled* • **Business Administration and Management, General** *7 students enrolled* • **Chemical Technology/Technician** *18 students enrolled* • **Computer and Information Sciences, General** *14 students enrolled* • **Corrections** *7 students enrolled* • **Dental Assisting/Assistant** *19 students enrolled* • **Medical Administrative/Executive Assistant and Medical Secretary** *15 students enrolled* • **Pharmacy Technician/Assistant** *20 students enrolled*

**STUDENT SERVICES** Academic or career counseling, employment services for current students, placement services for program completers, remedial services.

## Lamar State College–Port Arthur

PO Box 310, Port Arthur, TX 77641-0310
http://www.lamarpa.edu/

**CONTACT** W. Sam Monroe, President
**Telephone:** 409-984-6342

**GENERAL INFORMATION** Public Institution. Founded 1909. **Accreditation:** Regional (SACS/CC); surgical technology (ARCST). **Total program enrollment:** 841.

**PROGRAM(S) OFFERED**
• **Accounting Technology/Technician and Bookkeeping** *3 students enrolled* • **Administrative Assistant and Secretarial Science, General** *4 students enrolled* • **Automobile/Automotive Mechanics Technology/Technician** *34 students enrolled* • **Business Administration and Management, General** • **Chemical Technology/Technician** *6 students enrolled* • **Child Care Provider/Assistant** *1 student enrolled* • **Computer Systems Networking and Telecommunications** *6 students enrolled* • **Cosmetology, Barber/Styling, and Nail Instructor** • **Cosmetology/Cosmetologist, General** *18 students enrolled* • **Data Processing and Data Processing Technology/Technician** *10 students enrolled* • **Electrical, Electronic and Communications Engineering Technology/Technician** • **Facial Treatment Specialist/Facialist** *7 students enrolled* • **Heating, Air Conditioning, Ventilation and Refrigeration Maintenance Technology/Technician (HAC, HACR, HVAC, HVACR)** *1 student enrolled* • **Legal Administrative Assistant/Secretary** • **Licensed Practical/Vocational Nurse Training (LPN, LVN, Cert, Dipl, AAS)** *99 students enrolled* • **Medical Administrative/Executive Assistant and Medical Secretary** *14 students enrolled* • **Nail Technician/**

*Lamar State College–Port Arthur (continued)*

**Specialist and Manicurist • Occupational Safety and Health Technology/Technician • Substance Abuse/Addiction Counseling • Surgical Technology/Technologist** *9 students enrolled*

**STUDENT SERVICES** Academic or career counseling, employment services for current students, placement services for program completers, remedial services.

## Laredo Beauty College

3002 North Malinche Avenue, Laredo, TX 78043

**CONTACT** Peggy Dietrick, Owner
**Telephone:** 956-723-2059

**GENERAL INFORMATION** Private Institution. Founded 1965. **Total program enrollment:** 133. **Application fee:** $100.

**PROGRAM(S) OFFERED**
**• Cosmetology and Related Personal Grooming Arts, Other • Cosmetology, Barber/Styling, and Nail Instructor** *750 hrs./$3675* **• Cosmetology/Cosmetologist, General** *1500 hrs./$8150* **• Nail Technician/Specialist and Manicurist** *600 hrs./$3050*

**STUDENT SERVICES** Placement services for program completers.

## Laredo Community College

West End Washington Street, Laredo, TX 78040-4395
http://www.laredo.edu/

**CONTACT** Juan L. Maldonado, President
**Telephone:** 956-721-5394

**GENERAL INFORMATION** Public Institution. Founded 1946. **Accreditation:** Regional (SACS/CC); medical laboratory technology (NAACLS); physical therapy assisting (APTA); radiologic technology: radiography (JRCERT). **Total program enrollment:** 2998.

**PROGRAM(S) OFFERED**
**• Accounting Technology/Technician and Bookkeeping** *3 students enrolled* **• Administrative Assistant and Secretarial Science, General** *2 students enrolled* **• Autobody/Collision and Repair Technology/Technician** *6 students enrolled* **• Automobile/Automotive Mechanics Technology/Technician** *11 students enrolled* **• Banking and Financial Support Services** *27 students enrolled* **• Child Care Provider/Assistant • Child Development** *7 students enrolled* **• Clinical/Medical Laboratory Technician** *14 students enrolled* **• Computer Installation and Repair Technology/Technician** *19 students enrolled* **• Computer/Information Technology Services Administration and Management, Other • Criminal Justice/Police Science** *44 students enrolled* **• Criminal Justice/Safety Studies • Diesel Mechanics Technology/Technician** *16 students enrolled* **• Electrical/Electronics Equipment Installation and Repair, General • Electrician** *16 students enrolled* **• Emergency Medical Technology/Technician (EMT Paramedic)** *2 students enrolled* **• Fire Protection and Safety Technology/Technician • Heating, Air Conditioning and Refrigeration Technology/Technician (ACH/ACR/ACHR/HRAC/HVAC/AC Technology)** *24 students enrolled* **• Heating, Air Conditioning, Ventilation and Refrigeration Maintenance Technology/Technician (HAC, HACR, HVAC, HVACR) • International Marketing** *4 students enrolled* **• Licensed Practical/Vocational Nurse Training (LPN, LVN, Cert, Dipl, AAS)** *23 students enrolled* **• Marketing/Marketing Management, General** *5 students enrolled* **• Medical/Clinical Assistant** *9 students enrolled* **• Nurse/Nursing Assistant/Aide and Patient Care Assistant** *37 students enrolled* **• Real Estate** *7 students enrolled* **• System Administration/Administrator** *35 students enrolled* **• Welding Technology/Welder** *2 students enrolled*

**STUDENT SERVICES** Academic or career counseling, daycare for children of students, employment services for current students, placement services for program completers, remedial services.

## Lee College

PO Box 818, Baytown, TX 77522-0818
http://www.lee.edu/

**CONTACT** Dennis Topper, Interim President
**Telephone:** 281-427-5611

**GENERAL INFORMATION** Public Institution. Founded 1934. **Accreditation:** Regional (SACS/CC); emergency medical services (JRCEMTP); health information technology (AHIMA). **Total program enrollment:** 1618.

**PROGRAM(S) OFFERED**
**• Accounting Technology/Technician and Bookkeeping** *1 student enrolled* **• Administrative Assistant and Secretarial Science, General** *69 students enrolled* **• Airline/Commercial/Professional Pilot and Flight Crew** *7 students enrolled* **• Applied Horticulture/Horticultural Operations, General** *57 students enrolled* **• Autobody/Collision and Repair Technology/Technician** *11 students enrolled* **• Automobile/Automotive Mechanics Technology/Technician** *32 students enrolled* **• Business Administration and Management, General** *14 students enrolled* **• Cabinetmaking and Millwork/Millwright** *32 students enrolled* **• Cartography** *4 students enrolled* **• Chemical Technology/Technician** *40 students enrolled* **• Computer Programming/Programmer, General • Computer Technology/Computer Systems Technology** *8 students enrolled* **• Computer and Information Sciences, General** *11 students enrolled* **• Construction Engineering Technology/Technician** *1 student enrolled* **• Cosmetology, Barber/Styling, and Nail Instructor** *1 student enrolled* **• Cosmetology/Cosmetologist, General** *11 students enrolled* **• Criminal Justice/Safety Studies • Culinary Arts/Chef Training** *37 students enrolled* **• Data Entry/Microcomputer Applications, General • Data Processing and Data Processing Technology/Technician** *17 students enrolled* **• Dental Laboratory Technology/Technician • Diesel Mechanics Technology/Technician • Drafting and Design Technology/Technician, General** *78 students enrolled* **• Electrician** *13 students enrolled* **• Heating, Air Conditioning, Ventilation and Refrigeration Maintenance Technology/Technician (HAC, HACR, HVAC, HVACR)** *31 students enrolled* **• Instrumentation Technology/Technician** *32 students enrolled* **• Licensed Practical/Vocational Nurse Training (LPN, LVN, Cert, Dipl, AAS)** *27 students enrolled* **• Machine Tool Technology/Machinist** *4 students enrolled* **• Medical Insurance Coding Specialist/Coder** *11 students enrolled* **• Medical Transcription/Transcriptionist** *1 student enrolled* **• Occupational Safety and Health Technology/Technician** *2 students enrolled* **• Pipefitting/Pipefitter and Sprinkler Fitter** *53 students enrolled* **• Prepress/Desktop Publishing and Digital Imaging Design** *1 student enrolled* **• Substance Abuse/Addiction Counseling** *1 student enrolled* **• System, Networking, and LAN/WAN Management/Manager** *27 students enrolled* **• Telecommunications Technology/Technician** *32 students enrolled* **• Truck and Bus Driver/Commercial Vehicle Operation** *54 students enrolled* **• Web Page, Digital/Multimedia and Information Resources Design** *18 students enrolled* **• Web/Multimedia Management and Webmaster • Welding Technology/Welder** *47 students enrolled*

**STUDENT SERVICES** Academic or career counseling, daycare for children of students, employment services for current students, placement services for program completers, remedial services.

## Lincoln Technical Institute

2501 Arkansas Lane, Grand Prairie, TX 75052
http://www.lincolnedu.com/

**CONTACT** Tim Bush, Executive Director
**Telephone:** 972-660-5701

**GENERAL INFORMATION** Private Institution. **Total program enrollment:** 481. **Application fee:** $100.

**PROGRAM(S) OFFERED**
**• Autobody/Collision and Repair Technology/Technician** *78 students enrolled* **• Automobile/Automotive Mechanics Technology/Technician** *245 students enrolled* **• Diesel Mechanics Technology/Technician** *115 students enrolled* **• Heating, Air Conditioning, Ventilation and Refrigeration Maintenance Technology/Technician (HAC, HACR, HVAC, HVACR)** *86 students enrolled* **• Mechanic and Repair Technologies/Technicians, Other**

**STUDENT SERVICES** Academic or career counseling, employment services for current students, placement services for program completers, remedial services.

## Lonestar College–North Harris

2700 W. W. Thorne Drive, Houston, TX 77073-3499
http://www.nhmccd.edu/

**CONTACT** Richard Carpenter, Chancellor
**Telephone:** 832-813-6500

**GENERAL INFORMATION** Public Institution. Founded 1972. **Accreditation:** Regional (SACS/CC); health information technology (AHIMA). **Total program enrollment:** 14107.

**PROGRAM(S) OFFERED**
• **Accounting** *37 students enrolled* • **Administrative Assistant and Secretarial Science, General** *2 students enrolled* • **Automobile/Automotive Mechanics Technology/Technician** *9 students enrolled* • **Biology Technician/Biotechnology Laboratory Technician** *2 students enrolled* • **Business Administration and Management, General** *44 students enrolled* • **Cartography** *9 students enrolled* • **Child Care and Support Services Management** *20 students enrolled* • **Computer and Information Sciences, General** *41 students enrolled* • **Cosmetology, Barber/Styling, and Nail Instructor** • **Cosmetology/Cosmetologist, General** • **Diagnostic Medical Sonography/Sonographer and Ultrasound Technician** *3 students enrolled* • **Educational/Instructional Media Design** • **Electrical and Power Transmission Installation/Installer, General** *2 students enrolled* • **Electrical, Electronic and Communications Engineering Technology/Technician** • **Emergency Medical Technology/Technician (EMT Paramedic)** *29 students enrolled* • **Facial Treatment Specialist/Facialist** *16 students enrolled* • **Fire Science/Firefighting** • **Graphic and Printing Equipment Operator, General Production** • **Health Information/Medical Records Technology/Technician** *6 students enrolled* • **Heating, Air Conditioning, Ventilation and Refrigeration Maintenance Technology/Technician (HAC, HACR, HVAC, HVACR)** • **Industrial Technology/Technician** *79 students enrolled* • **Interior Design** • **Legal Assistant/Paralegal** *13 students enrolled* • **Licensed Practical/Vocational Nurse Training (LPN, LVN, Cert, Dipl, AAS)** *106 students enrolled* • **Logistics and Materials Management** *9 students enrolled* • **Manufacturing Technology/Technician** • **Medical Administrative/Executive Assistant and Medical Secretary** *23 students enrolled* • **Medical Transcription/Transcriptionist** • **Medical/Clinical Assistant** *13 students enrolled* • **Nursing—Registered Nurse Training (RN, ASN, BSN, MSN)** *37 students enrolled* • **Pharmacy Technician/Assistant** *33 students enrolled* • **Psychiatric/Mental Health Services Technician** *14 students enrolled* • **Sign Language Interpretation and Translation** *9 students enrolled* • **Substance Abuse/Addiction Counseling** • **Surgical Technology/Technologist** *11 students enrolled* • **Survey Technology/Surveying** *7 students enrolled* • **Tourism and Travel Services Management** • **Veterinary/Animal Health Technology/Technician and Veterinary Assistant** *32 students enrolled* • **Welding Technology/Welder**

**STUDENT SERVICES** Academic or career counseling, daycare for children of students, employment services for current students, placement services for program completers, remedial services.

## Lubbock Hair Academy

2844 34th Street, Lubbock, TX 79410
http://www.lubbockhairacademy.com/

**CONTACT** Phillip Vivial, Chief Administrative Officer
**Telephone:** 806-795-0806

**GENERAL INFORMATION** Private Institution. **Total program enrollment:** 13.

**PROGRAM(S) OFFERED**
• **Barbering/Barber** *1500 hrs./$8673* • **Cosmetology and Related Personal Grooming Arts, Other** *300 hrs./$1473* • **Cosmetology, Barber/Styling, and Nail Instructor** *1000 hrs./$6233* • **Hair Styling/Stylist and Hair Design** *300 hrs./$1250* • **Nail Technician/Specialist and Manicurist** *600 hrs./$1873*

**STUDENT SERVICES** Academic or career counseling, placement services for program completers.

## Mai-trix Beauty College

5999 W. 34th Street, Suite 100, Houston, TX 77092
http://www.maitrixbeautycollege.com/

**CONTACT** Lynn Tran-Minh, Owner
**Telephone:** 713-957-0050

**GENERAL INFORMATION** Private Institution. **Total program enrollment:** 68.

**PROGRAM(S) OFFERED**
• **Cosmetology, Barber/Styling, and Nail Instructor** *750 hrs./$4535*
• **Cosmetology/Cosmetologist, General** *1500 hrs./$9274* • **Facial Treatment Specialist/Facialist** *750 hrs./$7224*

**STUDENT SERVICES** Academic or career counseling, placement services for program completers.

## Manuel and Theresa's School of Hair Design

220 N. Main Street, Bryan, TX 77803

**CONTACT** manuel rodriguez
**Telephone:** 979-821-2050

**GENERAL INFORMATION** Private Institution. **Total program enrollment:** 86. **Application fee:** $25.

**PROGRAM(S) OFFERED**
• **Cosmetology/Cosmetologist, General** *21 students enrolled*

**STUDENT SERVICES** Academic or career counseling, employment services for current students, placement services for program completers.

## McLennan Community College

1400 College Drive, Waco, TX 76708-1499
http://www.mclennan.edu/

**CONTACT** Dennis Michaelis, President
**Telephone:** 254-299-8000

**GENERAL INFORMATION** Public Institution. Founded 1965. **Accreditation:** Regional (SACS/CC); health information technology (AHIMA); medical laboratory technology (NAACLS); physical therapy assisting (APTA); radiologic technology: radiography (JRCERT). **Total program enrollment:** 3422.

**PROGRAM(S) OFFERED**
• **Accounting Technology/Technician and Bookkeeping** *2 students enrolled*
• **Business Administration and Management, General** *4 students enrolled*
• **Business/Office Automation/Technology/Data Entry** *5 students enrolled*
• **Carpentry/Carpenter** *1 student enrolled* • **Child Care and Support Services Management** *2 students enrolled* • **Child Development** *22 students enrolled*
• **Computer Programming/Programmer, General** • **Corrections** *6 students enrolled* • **Cosmetology/Cosmetologist, General** *36 students enrolled* • **Criminal Justice/Safety Studies** *17 students enrolled* • **Data Entry/Microcomputer Applications, General** *1 student enrolled* • **Electroneurodiagnostic/Electroencephalographic Technology/Technologist** *9 students enrolled*
• **Emergency Medical Technology/Technician (EMT Paramedic)** *28 students enrolled* • **Fire Science/Firefighting** *22 students enrolled* • **Health Information/Medical Records Technology/Technician** *3 students enrolled* • **Hospital and Health Care Facilities Administration/Management** *2 students enrolled*
• **Licensed Practical/Vocational Nurse Training (LPN, LVN, Cert, Dipl, AAS)** *46 students enrolled* • **Medical Administrative/Executive Assistant and Medical Secretary** *4 students enrolled* • **Medical Transcription/Transcriptionist** *5 students enrolled* • **Music Management and Merchandising** *2 students enrolled*
• **Psychiatric/Mental Health Services Technician** *8 students enrolled* • **Real Estate** *20 students enrolled* • **Sign Language Interpretation and Translation** *1 student enrolled* • **Substance Abuse/Addiction Counseling** *2 students enrolled*
• **System, Networking, and LAN/WAN Management/Manager** *1 student enrolled*
• **Web/Multimedia Management and Webmaster** *3 students enrolled*

**STUDENT SERVICES** Academic or career counseling, daycare for children of students, employment services for current students, remedial services.

## MedVance Institute

6220 Westpark Drive, Suite 180, Houston, TX 77057-7371
http://www.medvance.edu/

**CONTACT** John Hopkins, CEO
**Telephone:** 713-266-6594

**GENERAL INFORMATION** Private Institution. **Total program enrollment:** 455. **Application fee:** $25.

**PROGRAM(S) OFFERED**
• **Health Information/Medical Records Technology/Technician** *64 hrs./$14,200* • **Health Professions and Related Clinical Sciences, Other** *36 hrs./$9900* • **Medical Radiologic Technology/Science—Radiation Therapist** *130 hrs./ $36,400* • **Medical/Clinical Assistant** *48 hrs./$12,995* • **Pharmacy Technician/ Assistant** *44 hrs./$10,500* • **Surgical Technology/Technologist** *73 hrs./$22,900*

**STUDENT SERVICES** Employment services for current students, placement services for program completers.

## Metroplex Beauty School

519 North Galloway, Mesquite, TX 75149-3405

**CONTACT** Jimmy L. Culver, Owner Director
**Telephone:** 972-288-5485

**GENERAL INFORMATION** Private Institution. **Total program enrollment:** 56. **Application fee:** $100.

**PROGRAM(S) OFFERED**
• **Cosmetology, Barber/Styling, and Nail Instructor** *750 hrs./$2850* • **Cosmetology/Cosmetologist, General** *1500 hrs./$7600* • **Nail Technician/ Specialist and Manicurist** *600 hrs./$3000*

**STUDENT SERVICES** Placement services for program completers.

## Mid-Cities Barber College

2345 SW 3rd Street, #101, Grand Prairie, TX 75051-4892
http://www.midcitiesbarbercollege.com/

**CONTACT** Nachita G. Cano, Owner Manager
**Telephone:** 972-642-1892

**GENERAL INFORMATION** Private Institution. **Total program enrollment:** 29. **Application fee:** $15.

**PROGRAM(S) OFFERED**
• **Barbering/Barber** *1500 hrs./$8825* • **Cosmetology, Barber/Styling, and Nail Instructor** *1000 hrs./$5150*

**STUDENT SERVICES** Academic or career counseling, placement services for program completers.

## Midland College

3600 North Garfield, Midland, TX 79705-6399
http://www.midland.edu/

**CONTACT** Stephen Thomas, President
**Telephone:** 432-685-4500

**GENERAL INFORMATION** Public Institution. Founded 1969. **Accreditation:** Regional (SACS/CC); health information technology (AHIMA); radiologic technology: radiography (JRCERT). **Total program enrollment:** 1801.

**PROGRAM(S) OFFERED**
• **Cosmetology/Cosmetologist, General** *13 students enrolled*

**STUDENT SERVICES** Academic or career counseling, daycare for children of students, employment services for current students, placement services for program completers, remedial services.

## Milan Institute of Cosmetology

2400 SE 27th Avenue, East Campus, Amarillo, TX 79103
http://www.milaninstitute.edu/

**CONTACT** Gary Yasuda, President
**Telephone:** 806-371-7600

**GENERAL INFORMATION** Private Institution. **Total program enrollment:** 213. **Application fee:** $100.

**PROGRAM(S) OFFERED**
• **Aesthetician/Esthetician and Skin Care Specialist** *750 hrs./$8423* • **Cosmetology, Barber/Styling, and Nail Instructor** *250 hrs./$1587* • **Cosmetology/Cosmetologist, General** *1500 hrs./$15,338* • **Nail Technician/ Specialist and Manicurist** *10 students enrolled*

**STUDENT SERVICES** Academic or career counseling, employment services for current students, placement services for program completers.

## Milan Institute of Cosmetology

5403 Walzem Road, San Antonio, TX 78218
http://www.milaninstitute.edu/

**CONTACT** Gary Yasuda, President
**Telephone:** 210-656-1991

**GENERAL INFORMATION** Private Institution. **Total program enrollment:** 211. **Application fee:** $100.

**PROGRAM(S) OFFERED**
• **Aesthetician/Esthetician and Skin Care Specialist** *750 hrs./$8422* • **Cosmetology, Barber/Styling, and Nail Instructor** *250 hrs./$1587* • **Cosmetology/Cosmetologist, General** *1500 hrs./$15,822*

**STUDENT SERVICES** Academic or career counseling, employment services for current students, placement services for program completers.

## Milan Institute of Cosmetology

605 Southwest Military Drive, San Antonio, TX 78221
http://www.milaninstitute.edu

**CONTACT** Gary Yasuda, President
**Telephone:** 210-922-5900

**GENERAL INFORMATION** Private Institution. **Total program enrollment:** 244. **Application fee:** $100.

**PROGRAM(S) OFFERED**
• **Aesthetician/Esthetician and Skin Care Specialist** *750 hrs./$8422* • **Cosmetology, Barber/Styling, and Nail Instructor** *250 hrs./$1587* • **Cosmetology/Cosmetologist, General** *1500 hrs./$15,820*

**STUDENT SERVICES** Academic or career counseling, employment services for current students, placement services for program completers.

## Milan Institute of Cosmetology

6151 NW Loop 410, San Antonio, TX 78238
http://www.milaninstitute.edu/

**CONTACT** Gary Yasuda, President
**Telephone:** 210-647-5100

**GENERAL INFORMATION** Private Institution. **Total program enrollment:** 282. **Application fee:** $100.

**PROGRAM(S) OFFERED**
• **Aesthetician/Esthetician and Skin Care Specialist** *750 hrs./$8422* • **Cosmetology, Barber/Styling, and Nail Instructor** *250 hrs./$1587* • **Cosmetology/Cosmetologist, General** *1500 hrs./$15,820* • **Nail Technician/ Specialist and Manicurist** *5 students enrolled*

**STUDENT SERVICES** Academic or career counseling, employment services for current students, placement services for program completers.

## Mim's Classic Beauty College

5121 Blanco Road, San Antonio, TX 78216

**CONTACT** Neilana Mims Russell, Owner/Director
**Telephone:** 210-344-2041

**GENERAL INFORMATION** Private Institution. Founded 1928. **Total program enrollment:** 50.

**PROGRAM(S) OFFERED**
• **Cosmetology, Barber/Styling, and Nail Instructor** *750 hrs./$3100* • **Cosmetology/Cosmetologist, General** *1500 hrs./$10,525* • **Facial Treatment Specialist/Facialist** *750 hrs./$4300* • **Nail Technician/Specialist and Manicurist** *600 hrs./$3300*

**STUDENT SERVICES** Academic or career counseling, employment services for current students, placement services for program completers.

## MJ's Beauty Academy Inc.

3939 S. Polk Street, Suite 505, Dallas, TX 75224
http://www.mjsbeautyacademy.com/

**CONTACT** Margaret M. Jackson, Director
**Telephone:** 214-374-7500

**GENERAL INFORMATION** Private Institution. **Total program enrollment:** 44.

**PROGRAM(S) OFFERED**
• **Cosmetology and Related Personal Grooming Arts, Other** *300 hrs./$2585* • **Cosmetology, Barber/Styling, and Nail Instructor** *750 hrs./$4225* • **Cosmetology/Cosmetologist, General** *1500 hrs./$12,900* • **Nail Technician/Specialist and Manicurist** *600 hrs./$4075*

## Mountain View College

4849 West Illinois Avenue, Dallas, TX 75211-6599
http://www.mvc.dcccd.edu/

**CONTACT** Felix Zamora, President
**Telephone:** 214-860-8680

**GENERAL INFORMATION** Public Institution. Founded 1970. **Accreditation:** Regional (SACS/CC); health information technology (AHIMA). **Total program enrollment:** 1703.

**PROGRAM(S) OFFERED**
• **Accounting** *11 students enrolled* • **Air Traffic Controller** • **Architectural Drafting and Architectural CAD/CADD** *1 student enrolled* • **Business Administration and Management, General** *13 students enrolled* • **Business/Office Automation/Technology/Data Entry** • **Computer Programming/Programmer, General** • **Computer Systems Networking and Telecommunications** • **Criminal Justice/Safety Studies** *31 students enrolled* • **Data Processing and Data Processing Technology/Technician** *3 students enrolled* • **Drafting and Design Technology/Technician, General** *15 students enrolled* • **E-Commerce/Electronic Commerce** • **Electrical, Electronic and Communications Engineering Technology/Technician** *4 students enrolled* • **Medical Insurance Coding Specialist/Coder** • **Medical/Clinical Assistant** • **Receptionist** • **Welding Technology/Welder** *4 students enrolled*

**STUDENT SERVICES** Academic or career counseling, employment services for current students, placement services for program completers, remedial services.

## National Beauty College

149 W. Kingsley, Suite 230, Garland, TX 75401
http://nationalbeautycollege.com/

**CONTACT** Vonda M. Hutchings, Owner
**Telephone:** 972-278-2020

**GENERAL INFORMATION** Private Institution. **Total program enrollment:** 52. **Application fee:** $100.

**PROGRAM(S) OFFERED**
• **Cosmetology and Related Personal Grooming Arts, Other** *4 students enrolled* • **Cosmetology, Barber/Styling, and Nail Instructor** *25 hrs./$4275* • **Cosmetology/Cosmetologist, General** *50 hrs./$11,800* • **Education, Other** *1 student enrolled* • **Nail Technician/Specialist and Manicurist** *20 hrs./$4175*

**STUDENT SERVICES** Employment services for current students, placement services for program completers.

## Navarro College

3200 West 7th Avenue, Corsicana, TX 75110-4899
http://www.navarrocollege.edu/

**CONTACT** Dr. Richard M. Sanchez, President
**Telephone:** 903-874-6501

**GENERAL INFORMATION** Public Institution. Founded 1946. **Accreditation:** Regional (SACS/CC); medical laboratory technology (NAACLS). **Total program enrollment:** 3653.

**PROGRAM(S) OFFERED**
• **Accounting** *11 students enrolled* • **Administrative Assistant and Secretarial Science, General** *20 students enrolled* • **Agricultural Mechanization, General** *2 students enrolled* • **Business Administration and Management, General** *9 students enrolled* • **Business/Office Automation/Technology/Data Entry** • **Child Development** • **Computer Programming/Programmer, General** *7 students enrolled* • **Cosmetology/Cosmetologist, General** *23 students enrolled* • **Criminal Justice/Police Science** *34 students enrolled* • **Data Processing and Data Processing Technology/Technician** *8 students enrolled* • **Emergency Medical Technology/Technician (EMT Paramedic)** *39 students enrolled* • **Fire Science/Firefighting** *42 students enrolled* • **Heavy Equipment Maintenance Technology/Technician** *12 students enrolled* • **Intermedia/Multimedia** *3 students enrolled* • **Legal Assistant/Paralegal** *5 students enrolled* • **Licensed Practical/Vocational Nurse Training (LPN, LVN, Cert, Dipl, AAS)** *58 students enrolled* • **Medical Administrative/Executive Assistant and Medical Secretary** *21 students enrolled* • **Visual and Performing Arts, General**

**STUDENT SERVICES** Academic or career counseling, employment services for current students, remedial services.

## Neilson Beauty College

416 West Jefferson Boulevard, Dallas, TX 75208
http://www.neilsonbeautycollege.com/

**CONTACT** Yolanda Mendez, Owner
**Telephone:** 214-946-0458

**GENERAL INFORMATION** Private Institution. Founded 1929. **Total program enrollment:** 54.

**PROGRAM(S) OFFERED**
• **Cosmetology, Barber/Styling, and Nail Instructor** • **Cosmetology/Cosmetologist, General** *1500 hrs./$9324*

## North Central Texas College

1525 West California Street, Gainesville, TX 76240-4699
http://www.nctc.edu/

**CONTACT** Eddie Hadlock, President
**Telephone:** 940-668-7731

**GENERAL INFORMATION** Public Institution. Founded 1924. **Accreditation:** Regional (SACS/CC). **Total program enrollment:** 3306.

**PROGRAM(S) OFFERED**
• **Business Administration, Management and Operations, Other** *5 students enrolled* • **Computer Systems Networking and Telecommunications** • **Computer and Information Sciences, General** *3 students enrolled* • **Cosmetology/Cosmetologist, General** *7 students enrolled* • **Drafting and Design Technology/Technician, General** *2 students enrolled* • **Emergency Medical Technology/**

*North Central Texas College (continued)*

**Technician (EMT Paramedic)** • **Equestrian/Equine Studies** • **Farm/Farm and Ranch Management** *2 students enrolled* • **Nursing, Other** *23 students enrolled* • **Office Management and Supervision** *2 students enrolled* • **Surgical Technology/Technologist**

**STUDENT SERVICES** Academic or career counseling, employment services for current students, placement services for program completers, remedial services.

## Northeast Texas Community College

PO Box 1307, Mount Pleasant, TX 75456-1307
http://www.ntcc.edu/

**CONTACT** Bradley Johnson, President
**Telephone:** 903-434-8100

**GENERAL INFORMATION** Public Institution. Founded 1985. **Accreditation:** Regional (SACS/CC). **Total program enrollment:** 1192.

**PROGRAM(S) OFFERED**
• **Accounting** • **Administrative Assistant and Secretarial Science, General** *2 students enrolled* • **Autobody/Collision and Repair Technology/Technician** *6 students enrolled* • **Automobile/Automotive Mechanics Technology/Technician** • **Banking and Financial Support Services** • **Business Administration and Management, General** *2 students enrolled* • **Computer Programming/Programmer, General** • **Computer Science** • **Cosmetology/Cosmetologist, General** *19 students enrolled* • **Criminal Justice/Police Science** • **Criminal Justice/Safety Studies** *10 students enrolled* • **Culinary Arts and Related Services, Other** *3 students enrolled* • **Data Processing and Data Processing Technology/Technician** • **Diesel Mechanics Technology/Technician** • **Electrical and Power Transmission Installation/Installer, General** *1 student enrolled* • **Emergency Medical Technology/Technician (EMT Paramedic)** *11 students enrolled* • **Farm/Farm and Ranch Management** *2 students enrolled* • **Fire Science/Firefighting** *8 students enrolled* • **Heating, Air Conditioning, Ventilation and Refrigeration Maintenance Technology/Technician (HAC, HACR, HVAC, HVACR)** • **Legal Support Services, Other** *1 student enrolled* • **Licensed Practical/Vocational Nurse Training (LPN, LVN, Cert, Dipl, AAS)** *21 students enrolled* • **Medical Administrative/Executive Assistant and Medical Secretary** *8 students enrolled* • **Medical/Clinical Assistant** *3 students enrolled* • **Nail Technician/Specialist and Manicurist** • **Small Engine Mechanics and Repair Technology/Technician** • **Welding Technology/Welder** *2 students enrolled*

**STUDENT SERVICES** Academic or career counseling, employment services for current students, remedial services.

## North Lake College

5001 North MacArthur Boulevard, Irving, TX 75038-3899
http://www.northlakecollege.edu/

**CONTACT** Herlinda Glasscock, President
**Telephone:** 972-273-3000

**GENERAL INFORMATION** Public Institution. Founded 1977. **Accreditation:** Regional (SACS/CC). **Total program enrollment:** 3171.

**PROGRAM(S) OFFERED**
• **Accounting** *10 students enrolled* • **Banking and Financial Support Services** *2 students enrolled* • **Business Administration and Management, General** *4 students enrolled* • **Business/Commerce, General** *1 student enrolled* • **Business/Office Automation/Technology/Data Entry** *2 students enrolled* • **Computer Programming/Programmer, General** *3 students enrolled* • **Computer Systems Networking and Telecommunications** *15 students enrolled* • **Construction Engineering Technology/Technician** *1 student enrolled* • **Data Processing and Data Processing Technology/Technician** *13 students enrolled* • **Design and Visual Communications, General** *3 students enrolled* • **Electrical, Electronic and Communications Engineering Technology/Technician** *1 student enrolled* • **Electrician** *46 students enrolled* • **Graphic Design** *1 student enrolled* • **Heating, Air Conditioning, Ventilation and Refrigeration Maintenance Technology/Technician (HAC, HACR, HVAC, HVACR)** • **Hotel/Motel Administration/Management** *2 students enrolled* • **Logistics and Materials Management** *3 students enrolled* • **Management Information Systems, General** • **Radio and Television Broadcasting Technology/Technician** *5 students enrolled* • **Real Estate** *30 students enrolled* • **Receptionist** *3 students enrolled* • **Web Page, Digital/Multimedia and Information Resources Design**

**STUDENT SERVICES** Academic or career counseling, employment services for current students, placement services for program completers, remedial services.

## North West Beauty School

6770 Antoine Drive, Houston, TX 77091

**CONTACT** William E. Brooks, President
**Telephone:** 713-263-8333

**GENERAL INFORMATION** Private Institution. **Total program enrollment:** 91. **Application fee:** $100.

**PROGRAM(S) OFFERED**
• **Cosmetology, Barber/Styling, and Nail Instructor** *56 students enrolled* • **Cosmetology/Cosmetologist, General** *1500 hrs./$9405*

**STUDENT SERVICES** Academic or career counseling, employment services for current students, placement services for program completers.

## Northwest Educational Center

5812 Antoine Drive, Houston, TX 77091

**CONTACT** Edna Ryan, Executive
**Telephone:** 713-680-2929

**GENERAL INFORMATION** Private Institution. Founded 1985. **Total program enrollment:** 197. **Application fee:** $100.

**PROGRAM(S) OFFERED**
• **Business/Office Automation/Technology/Data Entry** *300 hrs./$1850* • **Executive Assistant/Executive Secretary** *900 hrs./$8500* • **Management Information Systems and Services, Other** *600 hrs./$6500* • **Massage Therapy/Therapeutic Massage** *500 hrs./$3025* • **Medical/Clinical Assistant** *900 hrs./$8500* • **Pharmacy Technician/Assistant** *900 hrs./$8500*

**STUDENT SERVICES** Academic or career counseling, employment services for current students, placement services for program completers.

## Northwest Vista College

3535 North Ellison Drive, San Antonio, TX 78251
http://www.accd.edu/nvc/

**CONTACT** Dr. Jacqueline E. Claunch, President
**Telephone:** 210-348-2001

**GENERAL INFORMATION** Public Institution. Founded 1995. **Accreditation:** Regional (SACS/CC). **Total program enrollment:** 3608.

**PROGRAM(S) OFFERED**
• **Community Health Services/Liaison/Counseling** *24 students enrolled* • **Computer Systems Networking and Telecommunications** *1 student enrolled* • **Computer and Information Sciences, General** *1 student enrolled* • **Pharmacy Technician/Assistant** *5 students enrolled* • **Teacher Assistant/Aide** *2 students enrolled* • **Water Quality and Wastewater Treatment Management and Recycling Technology/Technician** *9 students enrolled* • **Web Page, Digital/Multimedia and Information Resources Design** *10 students enrolled*

**STUDENT SERVICES** Academic or career counseling, employment services for current students, placement services for program completers, remedial services.

## Ocean Corporation

10840 Rockley Road, Houston, TX 77099
http://www.oceancorp.com/

**CONTACT** John S. Wood, President
**Telephone:** 281-776-3322

**GENERAL INFORMATION** Private Institution. Founded 1969. **Total program enrollment:** 334. **Application fee:** $100.

**PROGRAM(S) OFFERED**
• **Diver, Professional and Instructor** *1 hr./$1350* • **Quality Control Technology/Technician** *25 hrs./$14,800* • **Quality Control and Safety Technologies/Technicians, Other** *256 students enrolled*

**STUDENT SERVICES** Employment services for current students, placement services for program completers.

## Odessa College

201 West University Avenue, Odessa, TX 79764-7127
http://www.odessa.edu/

**CONTACT** Gregory D. Williams, President
**Telephone:** 432-335-6400

**GENERAL INFORMATION** Public Institution. Founded 1946. **Accreditation:** Regional (SACS/CC); medical laboratory technology (NAACLS); music (NASM); physical therapy assisting (APTA); radiologic technology: radiography (JRCERT); surgical technology (ARCST). **Total program enrollment:** 1229.

**PROGRAM(S) OFFERED**
• **Administrative Assistant and Secretarial Science, General** *5 students enrolled* • **Automobile/Automotive Mechanics Technology/Technician** *2 students enrolled* • **Building/Property Maintenance and Management** *2 students enrolled* • **Business Administration and Management, General** *6 students enrolled* • **Business/Office Automation/Technology/Data Entry** *6 students enrolled* • **Child Care Provider/Assistant** *1 student enrolled* • **Child Care and Support Services Management** • **Child Development** *1 student enrolled* • **Clinical/Medical Laboratory Technician** • **Commercial Photography** *9 students enrolled* • **Computer Programming/Programmer, General** • **Computer Systems Networking and Telecommunications** • **Cosmetology, Barber/Styling, and Nail Instructor** *1 student enrolled* • **Cosmetology/Cosmetologist, General** *17 students enrolled* • **Criminal Justice/Police Science** *8 students enrolled* • **Culinary Arts/Chef Training** *8 students enrolled* • **Diesel Mechanics Technology/Technician** *3 students enrolled* • **Electrical/Electronics Equipment Installation and Repair, General** *6 students enrolled* • **Emergency Medical Technology/Technician (EMT Paramedic)** *8 students enrolled* • **Fire Science/Firefighting** • **Home Health Aide/Home Attendant** • **Legal Administrative Assistant/Secretary** *1 student enrolled* • **Legal Assistant/Paralegal** *6 students enrolled* • **Licensed Practical/Vocational Nurse Training (LPN, LVN, Cert, Dipl, AAS)** • **Machine Tool Technology/Machinist** *9 students enrolled* • **Mechanical Drafting and Mechanical Drafting CAD/CADD** • **Medical Administrative/Executive Assistant and Medical Secretary** • **Occupational Safety and Health Technology/Technician** • **Petroleum Technology/Technician** • **Substance Abuse/Addiction Counseling** • **Surgical Technology/Technologist** • **Welding Technology/Welder** *12 students enrolled*

**STUDENT SERVICES** Academic or career counseling, daycare for children of students, employment services for current students, placement services for program completers, remedial services.

## Ogle's School of Hair Design

2200 West Park Row, Suite 106, Arlington, TX 76013-7401
http://www.ogleschool.com/

**CONTACT** Ashley Plumleigh, Assistant School Director
**Telephone:** 817-460-8181

**GENERAL INFORMATION** Private Institution. Founded 1973. **Total program enrollment:** 196. **Application fee:** $125.

**PROGRAM(S) OFFERED**
• **Aesthetician/Esthetician and Skin Care Specialist** *750 hrs./$7875*
• **Cosmetology and Related Personal Grooming Arts, Other** *150 hrs./$575*
• **Cosmetology, Barber/Styling, and Nail Instructor** *750 hrs./$7500*
• **Cosmetology/Cosmetologist, General** *1500 hrs./$16,300*

**STUDENT SERVICES** Academic or career counseling, placement services for program completers.

## Ogle's School of Hair Design

6333 East Mockingbird Lane, Suite 201, Dallas, TX 75214-2689
http://www.ogleschool.com/

**CONTACT** Marci Jackson, School Director
**Telephone:** 214-821-0819

**GENERAL INFORMATION** Private Institution. Founded 1980. **Total program enrollment:** 226. **Application fee:** $125.

**PROGRAM(S) OFFERED**
• **Aesthetician/Esthetician and Skin Care Specialist** *750 hrs./$7875*
• **Cosmetology and Related Personal Grooming Arts, Other** *150 hrs./$575*
• **Cosmetology, Barber/Styling, and Nail Instructor** *750 hrs./$7500*
• **Cosmetology/Cosmetologist, General** *1500 hrs./$16,300*

**STUDENT SERVICES** Academic or career counseling, placement services for program completers.

## Ogle's School of Hair Design

5063 Old Granbury Road, Fort Worth, TX 76133-2016
http://www.ogleschool.com/

**CONTACT** Debbie Kight, School Director
**Telephone:** 817-294-2950

**GENERAL INFORMATION** Private Institution. Founded 1980. **Total program enrollment:** 179. **Application fee:** $125.

**PROGRAM(S) OFFERED**
• **Aesthetician/Esthetician and Skin Care Specialist** *750 hrs./$7875*
• **Cosmetology and Related Personal Grooming Arts, Other** *150 hrs./$575*
• **Cosmetology, Barber/Styling, and Nail Instructor** *750 hrs./$7500*
• **Cosmetology/Cosmetologist, General** *1500 hrs./$16,300*

**STUDENT SERVICES** Academic or career counseling, placement services for program completers.

## Ogle's School of Hair Design

720b Arcadia, Hurst, TX 76053
http://www.ogleschool.com/

**CONTACT** Teresa Pahl, School Director
**Telephone:** 817-284-9231

**GENERAL INFORMATION** Private Institution. **Total program enrollment:** 141. **Application fee:** $125.

**PROGRAM(S) OFFERED**
• **Aesthetician/Esthetician and Skin Care Specialist** *750 hrs./$7875*
• **Cosmetology and Related Personal Grooming Arts, Other** *150 hrs./$575*
• **Cosmetology, Barber/Styling, and Nail Instructor** *750 hrs./$7500*
• **Cosmetology/Cosmetologist, General** *1500 hrs./$16,300*

**STUDENT SERVICES** Academic or career counseling, placement services for program completers.

## Palo Alto College

1400 West Villaret, San Antonio, TX 78224-2499
http://www.accd.edu/pac/htm/

**CONTACT** Ana M. Guzman, President
**Telephone:** 210-921-5000

**GENERAL INFORMATION** Public Institution. Founded 1987. **Accreditation:** Regional (SACS/CC). **Total program enrollment:** 2797.

**PROGRAM(S) OFFERED**
• **Administrative Assistant and Secretarial Science, General** *5 students enrolled*
• **Business Administration and Management, General** *7 students enrolled*
• **Computer and Information Sciences, General** *3 students enrolled* • **General Office Occupations and Clerical Services** *16 students enrolled* • **Landscaping**

*Palo Alto College (continued)*

**and Groundskeeping** *9 students enrolled* • **Logistics and Materials Management** *4 students enrolled* • **Teacher Assistant/Aide** *1 student enrolled* • **Turf and Turfgrass Management** *2 students enrolled*

**STUDENT SERVICES** Academic or career counseling, daycare for children of students, employment services for current students, placement services for program completers, remedial services.

## Panola College

1109 West Panola Street, Carthage, TX 75633-2397
http://www.panola.edu/

**CONTACT** Gregory Powell, President
**Telephone:** 903-693-2000

**GENERAL INFORMATION** Public Institution. Founded 1947. **Accreditation:** Regional (SACS/CC); health information technology (AHIMA). **Total program enrollment:** 958.

**PROGRAM(S) OFFERED**
• **Administrative Assistant and Secretarial Science, General** *3 students enrolled* • **Business/Commerce, General** *5 students enrolled* • **Business/Office Automation/Technology/Data Entry** • **Cosmetology, Barber/Styling, and Nail Instructor** *1 student enrolled* • **Cosmetology/Cosmetologist, General** *25 students enrolled* • **Environmental Engineering Technology/Environmental Technology** *1 student enrolled* • **Facial Treatment Specialist/Facialist** *5 students enrolled* • **General Office Occupations and Clerical Services** *5 students enrolled* • **Industrial Technology/Technician** • **Information Science/Studies** *2 students enrolled* • **Junior High/Intermediate/Middle School Education and Teaching** *6 students enrolled* • **Licensed Practical/Vocational Nurse Training (LPN, LVN, Cert, Dipl, AAS)** *68 students enrolled* • **Medical Insurance Coding Specialist/Coder** *5 students enrolled* • **Medical Office Management/Administration** • **Music, General** *2 students enrolled* • **Nail Technician/Specialist and Manicurist** *5 students enrolled* • **Nursing—Registered Nurse Training (RN, ASN, BSN, MSN)** *10 students enrolled* • **Welding Technology/Welder** *19 students enrolled*

**STUDENT SERVICES** Academic or career counseling, employment services for current students, placement services for program completers, remedial services.

## Paris Junior College

2400 Clarksville Street, Paris, TX 75460-6298
http://www.parisjc.edu/

**CONTACT** Pamela Anglin, EdD, President
**Telephone:** 903-785-7661

**GENERAL INFORMATION** Public Institution. Founded 1924. **Accreditation:** Regional (SACS/CC). **Total program enrollment:** 1903.

**PROGRAM(S) OFFERED**
• **Administrative Assistant and Secretarial Science, General** *2 students enrolled* • **Business/Office Automation/Technology/Data Entry** *4 students enrolled* • **Computer and Information Sciences, General** *1 student enrolled* • **Cosmetology/Cosmetologist, General** *8 students enrolled* • **Drafting and Design Technology/Technician, General** *5 students enrolled* • **Electrical, Electronic and Communications Engineering Technology/Technician** *8 students enrolled* • **Electromechanical Technology/Electromechanical Engineering Technology** *11 students enrolled* • **Heating, Air Conditioning, Ventilation and Refrigeration Maintenance Technology/Technician (HAC, HACR, HVAC, HVACR)** *22 students enrolled* • **Licensed Practical/Vocational Nurse Training (LPN, LVN, Cert, Dipl, AAS)** *56 students enrolled* • **Medical Insurance Coding Specialist/Coder** *18 students enrolled* • **Surgical Technology/Technologist** *11 students enrolled* • **System, Networking, and LAN/WAN Management/Manager** *1 student enrolled* • **Watchmaking and Jewelrymaking** *44 students enrolled* • **Welding Technology/Welder** *51 students enrolled*

**STUDENT SERVICES** Academic or career counseling, remedial services.

## Parker College of Chiropractic

2500 Walnut Hill Lane, Dallas, TX 75229-5668
http://www.parkercc.edu/

**CONTACT** Dr. Fabrizio Mancini, President
**Telephone:** 972-438-6932

**GENERAL INFORMATION** Private Institution. Founded 1982. **Accreditation:** Regional (SACS/CC). **Total program enrollment:** 946.

**PROGRAM(S) OFFERED**
• **Massage Therapy/Therapeutic Massage** *12 students enrolled*

**STUDENT SERVICES** Academic or career counseling, employment services for current students, placement services for program completers, remedial services.

## Paul Mitchell the School—Houston

744 Farm Road 1960 West G, Houston, TX 77090
http://www.paulmitchelltheschool.com/

**CONTACT** Sandy Matos, Owner
**Telephone:** 281-893-1960

**GENERAL INFORMATION** Private Institution. Founded 1982. **Total program enrollment:** 138. **Application fee:** $100.

**PROGRAM(S) OFFERED**
• **Cosmetology and Related Personal Grooming Arts, Other** *40 students enrolled* • **Cosmetology/Cosmetologist, General** *1500 hrs./$17,900*

**STUDENT SERVICES** Academic or career counseling, employment services for current students, placement services for program completers, remedial services.

## Paul Mitchell the School—San Antonio

5590 Summit Parkway, San Antonio, TX 78229
http://www.paulmitchelltheschool.com

**CONTACT** John Turnage, Owner
**Telephone:** 210-523-8333

**GENERAL INFORMATION** Private Institution. **Total program enrollment:** 181.

**PROGRAM(S) OFFERED**
• **Aesthetician/Esthetician and Skin Care Specialist** *750 hrs./$9000*
• **Cosmetology, Barber/Styling, and Nail Instructor** *750 hrs./$4500*
• **Cosmetology/Cosmetologist, General** *1500 hrs./$16,000*

**STUDENT SERVICES** Academic or career counseling, placement services for program completers.

## PCI Health Training Center

8101 John W. Carpenter Freeway, Dallas, TX 75247
http://www.pcihealth.net/

**CONTACT** Rhonda White, President
**Telephone:** 214-630-0568

**GENERAL INFORMATION** Private Institution. **Total program enrollment:** 854. **Application fee:** $100.

**PROGRAM(S) OFFERED**
• **Health Information/Medical Records Administration/Administrator** *239 students enrolled* • **Medical Office Assistant/Specialist** *600 hrs./$8195* • **Medical/Clinical Assistant** *900 hrs./$12,195* • **Mental and Social Health**

**Services and Allied Professions, Other** *29 students enrolled* • **Nurse/Nursing Assistant/Aide and Patient Care Assistant** *600 hrs./$8195* • **Psychiatric/Mental Health Services Technician** *900 hrs./$12,195*

**STUDENT SERVICES** Academic or career counseling, employment services for current students, placement services for program completers, remedial services.

## Pipo Academy of Hair Design

3000 Pershing Drive, El Paso, TX 79903

**CONTACT** Hector M. Barragan, Sr., Owner
**Telephone:** 915-565-3491

**GENERAL INFORMATION** Private Institution. **Total program enrollment:** 56.

**PROGRAM(S) OFFERED**
• **Cosmetology, Barber/Styling, and Nail Instructor** *750 hrs./$4500*
• **Cosmetology/Cosmetologist, General** *1500 hrs./$7950*

**STUDENT SERVICES** Academic or career counseling, placement services for program completers.

## Platt College

2974 LBJ Freeway, Suite 300, Dallas, TX 75234
http://www.plattcollege.org/

**CONTACT** Michael A. Pugliese, President
**Telephone:** 972-243-0900

**GENERAL INFORMATION** Private Institution. **Total program enrollment:** 262. **Application fee:** $100.

**PROGRAM(S) OFFERED**
• **Dental Assisting/Assistant** *800 hrs./$12,400* • **Licensed Practical/Vocational Nurse Training (LPN, LVN, Cert, Dipl, AAS)** *1580 hrs./$28,600* • **Medical Office Assistant/Specialist** *800 hrs./$12,400* • **Medical/Clinical Assistant** *800 hrs./$12,400* • **Pharmacy Technician/Assistant** *800 hrs./$12,400*

**STUDENT SERVICES** Placement services for program completers.

## Professional Careers Institute

6666 Harwin, Suite 160, Houston, TX 77036
pcitraining.org

**CONTACT** Sam Al-Rifai, Director
**Telephone:** 713-783-3999 Ext. 14

**GENERAL INFORMATION** Private Institution. **Total program enrollment:** 46. **Application fee:** $100.

**PROGRAM(S) OFFERED**
• **Administrative Assistant and Secretarial Science, General** *600 hrs./$5040* • **Allied Health and Medical Assisting Services, Other** *600 hrs./$7890* • **Medical Insurance Specialist/Medical Biller** *600 hrs./$7395* • **Pharmacy Technician/Assistant** *600 hrs./$7380*

**STUDENT SERVICES** Academic or career counseling, employment services for current students, placement services for program completers.

## Ranger College

1100 College Circle, Ranger, TX 76470
http://www.ranger.cc.tx.us/

**CONTACT** Mr. James McDonald, Interim President
**Telephone:** 254-647-3234

**GENERAL INFORMATION** Public Institution. Founded 1926. **Accreditation:** Regional (SACS/CC). **Total program enrollment:** 530.

**PROGRAM(S) OFFERED**
• **Administrative Assistant and Secretarial Science, General** *2 students enrolled* • **Cosmetology/Cosmetologist, General** *19 students enrolled* • **Data Processing and Data Processing Technology/Technician** *9 students enrolled* • **General Office Occupations and Clerical Services** *5 students enrolled* • **Licensed Practical/Vocational Nurse Training (LPN, LVN, Cert, Dipl, AAS)** *56 students enrolled* • **Welding Technology/Welder** *12 students enrolled*

**STUDENT SERVICES** Academic or career counseling, placement services for program completers, remedial services.

## Redstone Institute–Houston

8880 Telephone Road, Houston, TX 77061
http://www.redstone.edu/

**CONTACT** Roy Laney, School Director
**Telephone:** 713-644-7777

**GENERAL INFORMATION** Public Institution. Founded 1972. **Total program enrollment:** 100. **Application fee:** $25.

**PROGRAM(S) OFFERED**
• **Airframe Mechanics and Aircraft Maintenance Technology/Technician** *72 hrs./$33,352*

**STUDENT SERVICES** Academic or career counseling, employment services for current students, placement services for program completers.

## Regency Beauty Institute

500 E. Ben White Boulevard, Suite 100, Austin, TX 78704

**CONTACT** J. Hayes Batson
**Telephone:** 512-687-0938

**GENERAL INFORMATION** Private Institution. **Total program enrollment:** 27. **Application fee:** $100.

**PROGRAM(S) OFFERED**
• **Cosmetology/Cosmetologist, General** *1500 hrs./$16,011*

**STUDENT SERVICES** Academic or career counseling, placement services for program completers.

## Regency Beauty Institute

19770 North Freeway, Spring, TX 77373

**CONTACT** J. Hayes Batson
**Telephone:** 281-907-4294

**GENERAL INFORMATION** Private Institution. **Total program enrollment:** 32. **Application fee:** $100.

**PROGRAM(S) OFFERED**
• **Cosmetology/Cosmetologist, General** *1500 hrs./$17,011*

**STUDENT SERVICES** Academic or career counseling, placement services for program completers.

## Regency Beauty Institute

5968 Fairmont Parkway, Suite A, Pasadena, TX 77505

**CONTACT** J. Hayes Batson
**Telephone:** 281-810-5000

**GENERAL INFORMATION** Private Institution. **Total program enrollment:** 30. **Application fee:** $100.

**PROGRAM(S) OFFERED**
• **Cosmetology/Cosmetologist, General** *1500 hrs./$16,011*

**STUDENT SERVICES** Academic or career counseling, placement services for program completers.

## Remington College–Dallas Campus

1800 Eastgate Drive, Garland, TX 75041-5513
http://www.remingtoncollege.edu/

**CONTACT** Greenie Skip Walls, III, President
**Telephone:** 972-686-7878

**GENERAL INFORMATION** Private Institution. Founded 1987. **Accreditation:** State accredited or approved. **Total program enrollment:** 1417. **Application fee:** $50.

**PROGRAM(S) OFFERED**
• **Cosmetology/Cosmetologist, General** • **Medical Insurance Coding Specialist/Coder** *89 students enrolled* • **Medical/Clinical Assistant** *418 students enrolled* • **Pharmacy Technician/Assistant** *100 students enrolled*

**STUDENT SERVICES** Academic or career counseling, employment services for current students, placement services for program completers.

## Remington College–Fort Worth Campus

300 East Loop 820, Fort Worth, TX 76112
http://www.remingtoncollege.edu/

**CONTACT** Gregg Falcon, Campus President
**Telephone:** 817-451-0017

**GENERAL INFORMATION** Private Institution. **Accreditation:** State accredited or approved. **Total program enrollment:** 581. **Application fee:** $50.

**PROGRAM(S) OFFERED**
• **Cosmetology/Cosmetologist, General** • **Medical Insurance Coding Specialist/Coder** *14 students enrolled* • **Medical/Clinical Assistant** *159 students enrolled* • **Pharmacy Technician/Assistant** *52 students enrolled*

**STUDENT SERVICES** Academic or career counseling, employment services for current students, placement services for program completers.

## Remington College–Houston Campus

3110 Hayes Road, Suite 380, Houston, TX 77082
http://www.remingtoncollege.edu/houston/

**CONTACT** Hiram Nall, President
**Telephone:** 281-899-1240 Ext. 205

**GENERAL INFORMATION** Private Institution. **Accreditation:** State accredited or approved. **Total program enrollment:** 573. **Application fee:** $50.

**PROGRAM(S) OFFERED**
• **Electrical, Electronic and Communications Engineering Technology/Technician** • **Medical Insurance Coding Specialist/Coder** *72 students enrolled* • **Medical/Clinical Assistant** *173 students enrolled* • **Pharmacy Technician/Assistant** *53 students enrolled*

**STUDENT SERVICES** Academic or career counseling, employment services for current students, placement services for program completers.

## Remington College–Houston Southeast

20985 Interstate 45 South, Webster, TX 77598
http://www.remingtoncollege.edu/houstonsoutheast/

**CONTACT** Robert Doty, Campus President
**Telephone:** 281-554-1700

**GENERAL INFORMATION** Private Institution. **Total program enrollment:** 204. **Application fee:** $50.

**PROGRAM(S) OFFERED**
• **Cosmetology/Cosmetologist, General** • **Medical Insurance Coding Specialist/Coder** • **Medical/Clinical Assistant**

**STUDENT SERVICES** Academic or career counseling, employment services for current students, placement services for program completers.

## Remington College–North Houston Campus

11310 Greens Crossing Boulevard, Suite 300, Houston, TX 77067
http://www.remingtoncollege.edu/

**CONTACT** Andy Bossaler, Campus President
**Telephone:** 281-885-4450

**GENERAL INFORMATION** Private Institution. **Total program enrollment:** 698. **Application fee:** $50.

**PROGRAM(S) OFFERED**
• **Medical Insurance Coding Specialist/Coder** *53 students enrolled* • **Medical/Clinical Assistant** *211 students enrolled* • **Pharmacy Technician/Assistant** *51 students enrolled*

**STUDENT SERVICES** Academic or career counseling, employment services for current students, placement services for program completers.

## Richland College

12800 Abrams Road, Dallas, TX 75243-2199
http://www.rlc.dcccd.edu/

**CONTACT** Steve Mittelstet, President
**Telephone:** 972-238-6106

**GENERAL INFORMATION** Public Institution. Founded 1972. **Accreditation:** Regional (SACS/CC). **Total program enrollment:** 4403.

**PROGRAM(S) OFFERED**
• **Accounting** *50 students enrolled* • **Applied Horticulture/Horticultural Operations, General** *24 students enrolled* • **Business Administration and Management, General** *17 students enrolled* • **Business/Office Automation/Technology/Data Entry** *23 students enrolled* • **Computer Programming/Programmer, General** *5 students enrolled* • **Computer Systems Networking and Telecommunications** *10 students enrolled* • **Computer and Information Systems Security** *1 student enrolled* • **Data Processing and Data Processing Technology/Technician** *8 students enrolled* • **E-Commerce/Electronic Commerce** • **Electrical, Electronic and Communications Engineering Technology/Technician** *12 students enrolled* • **Floriculture/Floristry Operations and Management** *1 student enrolled* • **International Business/Trade/Commerce** *6 students enrolled* • **Landscaping and Groundskeeping** *2 students enrolled* • **Management Information Systems, General** • **Ornamental Horticulture** *1 student enrolled* • **Real Estate** *19 students enrolled* • **Receptionist** *8 students enrolled* • **Teacher Assistant/Aide** *3 students enrolled* • **Tourism and Travel Services Marketing Operations** *1 student enrolled* • **Web Page, Digital/Multimedia and Information Resources Design** *8 students enrolled*

**STUDENT SERVICES** Academic or career counseling, employment services for current students, placement services for program completers, remedial services.

## Ronny J's Barber Styling

443 Bruton Terrace Center, Dallas, TX 75227

**CONTACT** Abdu R. Ali, Chief Operations Officer
**Telephone:** 214-275-7151 Ext. 201

**GENERAL INFORMATION** Private Institution. **Total program enrollment:** 123.

**PROGRAM(S) OFFERED**
• **Barbering/Barber** *1500 hrs./$11,750* • **Cosmetology, Barber/Styling, and Nail Instructor** *1000 hrs./$9580*

## Royal Beauty Careers

5020 Farm Road 1960 West, A-12, Houston, TX 77069-4611
http://www.rb.edu/

**CONTACT** Nick Mithani, President
**Telephone:** 770-446-1333

**GENERAL INFORMATION** Private Institution. **Total program enrollment:** 166. **Application fee:** $100.

**PROGRAM(S) OFFERED**
• **Aesthetician/Esthetician and Skin Care Specialist** *750 hrs./$8552* • **Cosmetology, Barber/Styling, and Nail Instructor** *750 hrs./$7035* • **Cosmetology/Cosmetologist, General** *1500 hrs./$12,935* • **Nail Technician/Specialist and Manicurist** *600 hrs./$5626*

**STUDENT SERVICES** Academic or career counseling, employment services for current students, placement services for program completers.

## Royal Beauty Careers

1611 Spencer Highway, South Houston, TX 77587
http://www.rb.edu/

**CONTACT** Nick Mithani, President/CEO
**Telephone:** 770-446-1333

**GENERAL INFORMATION** Private Institution. Founded 1967. **Total program enrollment:** 129. **Application fee:** $100.

**PROGRAM(S) OFFERED**
• **Aesthetician/Esthetician and Skin Care Specialist** *750 hrs./$8552* • **Cosmetology, Barber/Styling, and Nail Instructor** *750 hrs./$7035* • **Cosmetology/Cosmetologist, General** *1500 hrs./$12,935* • **Nail Technician/Specialist and Manicurist** *600 hrs./$5626*

**STUDENT SERVICES** Placement services for program completers.

## St. Philip's College

1801 Martin Luther King Drive, San Antonio, TX 78203-2098
http://www.accd.edu/spc/

**CONTACT** Dr. Adena Williams Loston, President
**Telephone:** 210-531-3200

**GENERAL INFORMATION** Public Institution. Founded 1898. **Accreditation:** Regional (SACS/CC); health information technology (AHIMA); histologic technology (NAACLS); medical laboratory technology (NAACLS); physical therapy assisting (APTA); practical nursing (NLN); radiologic technology: radiography (JRCERT). **Total program enrollment:** 3106.

**PROGRAM(S) OFFERED**
• **Accounting Technology/Technician and Bookkeeping** *6 students enrolled* • **Administrative Assistant and Secretarial Science, General** *7 students enrolled* • **Aircraft Powerplant Technology/Technician** *15 students enrolled* • **Airframe Mechanics and Aircraft Maintenance Technology/Technician** *15 students enrolled* • **Architectural Drafting and Architectural CAD/CADD** *2 students enrolled* • **Autobody/Collision and Repair Technology/Technician** *9 students enrolled* • **Automobile/Automotive Mechanics Technology/Technician** *74 students enrolled* • **Business Administration and Management, General** *6 students enrolled* • **Child Development** *29 students enrolled* • **Computer Installation and Repair Technology/Technician** *10 students enrolled* • **Computer Programming/Programmer, General** *22 students enrolled* • **Computer Technology/Computer Systems Technology** *6 students enrolled* • **Construction Engineering Technology/Technician** *11 students enrolled* • **Culinary Arts/Chef Training** *9 students enrolled* • **Data Entry/Microcomputer Applications, General** *2 students enrolled* • **Diesel Mechanics Technology/Technician** *10 students enrolled* • **Electrician** *14 students enrolled* • **Health Information/Medical Records Technology/Technician** *6 students enrolled* • **Heating, Air Conditioning and Refrigeration Technology/Technician (ACH/ACR/ACHR/HRAC/HVAC/AC Technology)** *41 students enrolled* • **Histologic Technician** *5 students enrolled* • **Hotel/Motel Administration/Management** *2 students enrolled* • **Licensed Practical/Vocational Nurse Training (LPN, LVN, Cert, Dipl, AAS)** *157 students enrolled* • **Machine Tool Technology/Machinist** *7 students enrolled* • **Medical Administrative/Executive Assistant and Medical Secretary** *1 student enrolled* • **Medical Insurance Coding Specialist/Coder** *54 students enrolled* • **Pipefitting/Pipefitter and Sprinkler Fitter** *5 students enrolled* • **Surgical Technology/Technologist** *12 students enrolled* • **System, Networking, and LAN/WAN Management/Manager** *6 students enrolled* • **Welding Technology/Welder** *7 students enrolled*

**STUDENT SERVICES** Academic or career counseling, daycare for children of students, employment services for current students, placement services for program completers, remedial services.

## San Antonio Beauty College 3

4021 Naco Perrin Boulevard, San Antonio, TX 78217

**CONTACT** Ernestina Martinez, Executive Director
**Telephone:** 210-654-9734

**GENERAL INFORMATION** Private Institution. Founded 1965. **Total program enrollment:** 37. **Application fee:** $100.

**PROGRAM(S) OFFERED**
• **Aesthetician/Esthetician and Skin Care Specialist** *750 hrs./$9050* • **Cosmetology, Barber/Styling, and Nail Instructor** *750 hrs./$8250* • **Cosmetology/Cosmetologist, General** *1500 hrs./$14,829* • **Nail Technician/Specialist and Manicurist** *600 hrs./$6050*

**STUDENT SERVICES** Placement services for program completers.

## San Antonio Beauty College 4

2423 Jamar Street, Suite 2, San Antonio, TX 78226

**CONTACT** Mary Alice Escobedo, Executive Director
**Telephone:** 210-433-7222

**GENERAL INFORMATION** Private Institution. **Total program enrollment:** 27. **Application fee:** $100.

**PROGRAM(S) OFFERED**
• **Cosmetology and Related Personal Grooming Arts, Other** • **Cosmetology, Barber/Styling, and Nail Instructor** *750 hrs./$5847* • **Cosmetology/Cosmetologist, General** *1500 hrs./$14,929* • **Facial Treatment Specialist/Facialist** *750 hrs./$8445* • **Make-Up Artist/Specialist** • **Nail Technician/Specialist and Manicurist** *600 hrs./$7802*

**STUDENT SERVICES** Placement services for program completers.

## San Antonio College

1300 San Pedro Avenue, San Antonio, TX 78212-4299
http://www.accd.edu/

**CONTACT** Robert Zeigler, President
**Telephone:** 210-733-2000

**GENERAL INFORMATION** Public Institution. Founded 1925. **Accreditation:** Regional (SACS/CC); dental assisting (ADA); funeral service (ABFSE); medical assisting (AAMAE). **Total program enrollment:** 7404.

**PROGRAM(S) OFFERED**
• **Accounting Technology/Technician and Bookkeeping** *4 students enrolled* • **Administrative Assistant and Secretarial Science, General** *13 students enrolled* • **Banking and Financial Support Services** *15 students enrolled* • **Business Administration and Management, General** *16 students enrolled* • **Business/Office Automation/Technology/Data Entry** *61 students enrolled* • **Child Care and Support Services Management** *2 students enrolled* • **Child Development** *56 students enrolled* • **Computer Programming/Programmer, General** *3 students enrolled* • **Court Reporting/Court Reporter** *1 student enrolled* • **Criminal Justice/Police Science** *7 students enrolled* • **Dental Assisting/Assistant** *7 students enrolled* • **Emergency Medical Technology/Technician (EMT Paramedic)** *20 students enrolled* • **Fire Protection and Safety Technology/Technician** *75 students enrolled* • **Funeral Direction/Service** *8 students enrolled* • **Medical Transcription/Transcriptionist** *2 students enrolled* • **Medical/Clinical Assistant** *4 students enrolled* • **Occupational Safety and Health Technology/Technician** *1 student enrolled* • **Public Administration** *2 students enrolled* • **Real**

*San Antonio College (continued)*

**Estate** *33 students enrolled* • **Substance Abuse/Addiction Counseling** *9 students enrolled* • **System Administration/Administrator** *5 students enrolled* • **Teacher Assistant/Aide** *2 students enrolled*

**STUDENT SERVICES** Academic or career counseling, daycare for children of students, employment services for current students, placement services for program completers, remedial services.

## San Antonio College of Medical and Dental Assistants

4205 San Pedro Avenue, San Antonio, TX 78212
http://www.sacmda.com/

**CONTACT** Laura Bledsoe, President
**Telephone:** 210-366-5500

**GENERAL INFORMATION** Private Institution. **Total program enrollment:** 1094.

**PROGRAM(S) OFFERED**
• **Dental Assisting/Assistant** *38 hrs./$14,980* • **Electrical and Electronic Engineering Technologies/Technicians, Other** *71 hrs./$14,984* • **Medical Office Computer Specialist/Assistant** *38 hrs./$14,980* • **Medical/Clinical Assistant** *43 hrs./$14,860* • **Pharmacy Technician/Assistant** *39 hrs./$14,980* • **Phlebotomy/Phlebotomist** *22 hrs./$9564*

**STUDENT SERVICES** Academic or career counseling, employment services for current students, placement services for program completers.

## San Antonio College of Medical and Dental Assistants–South

3900 N. 23rd, Mcallen, TX 78231
http://www.sacmda.com/

**CONTACT** Leticia Ventura, President
**Telephone:** 956-630-1499

**GENERAL INFORMATION** Private Institution. **Total program enrollment:** 1199.

**PROGRAM(S) OFFERED**
• **Computer Systems Networking and Telecommunications** • **Computer and Information Sciences and Support Services, Other** *54 hrs./$13,900* • **Dental Assisting/Assistant** *38 hrs./$14,890* • **Electrician** *47 hrs./$14,890* • **Medical Administrative/Executive Assistant and Medical Secretary** *38 hrs./$14,890* • **Medical/Clinical Assistant** *43 hrs./$14,890* • **Pharmacy Technician/Assistant** *39 hrs./$13,900*

**STUDENT SERVICES** Academic or career counseling, employment services for current students, placement services for program completers.

## Sanford-Brown Institute

1250 Mockingbird Lane, Dallas, TX 75247
http://www.sbdallas.com/

**CONTACT** David Bowman, President
**Telephone:** 214-459-8490

**GENERAL INFORMATION** Private Institution. **Total program enrollment:** 992. **Application fee:** $25.

**PROGRAM(S) OFFERED**
• **Cardiovascular Technology/Technologist** *1860 hrs./$34,525* • **Diagnostic Medical Sonography/Sonographer and Ultrasound Technician** *1860 hrs./$34,525* • **Medical Insurance Coding Specialist/Coder** *900 hrs./$12,875* • **Medical/Clinical Assistant** *900 hrs./$14,875* • **Pharmacy Technician/Assistant** *900 hrs./$11,275* • **Surgical Technology/Technologist** *1200 hrs./$23,825*

**STUDENT SERVICES** Employment services for current students.

## Sanford-Brown Institute

10500 Forum Place Drive, Suite 200, Houston, TX 77036
http://www.careered.com/

**CONTACT** James C. Garrett, President
**Telephone:** 800-445-6108

**GENERAL INFORMATION** Private Institution. **Total program enrollment:** 819. **Application fee:** $25.

**PROGRAM(S) OFFERED**
• **Cardiovascular Technology/Technologist** *72 hrs./$36,465* • **Diagnostic Medical Sonography/Sonographer and Ultrasound Technician** *70 hrs./$36,423* • **Medical Insurance Coding Specialist/Coder** *44 hrs./$13,900* • **Medical/Clinical Assistant** *42 hrs./$13,747* • **Pharmacy Technician/Assistant** *38 hrs./$10,639* • **Surgical Technology/Technologist** *44 hrs./$19,835*

**STUDENT SERVICES** Academic or career counseling, employment services for current students, placement services for program completers, remedial services.

## Sanford-Brown Institute

2627 North Loop W, Suite 100, Houston, TX 77008
http://www.sbnorthloop.com/

**CONTACT** Marilyn D. Hall, Chief Administrator
**Telephone:** 832-325-4500

**GENERAL INFORMATION** Private Institution. **Total program enrollment:** 375. **Application fee:** $25.

**PROGRAM(S) OFFERED**
• **Medical Insurance Coding Specialist/Coder** *45 hrs./$13,744* • **Medical/Clinical Assistant** *41 hrs./$13,772* • **Pharmacy Technician/Assistant** *42 hrs./$10,649* • **Surgical Technology/Technologist** *44 hrs./$22,335*

**STUDENT SERVICES** Academic or career counseling, employment services for current students, placement services for program completers.

## San Jacinto College Central Campus

8060 Spencer Highway, Pasadena, TX 77505
http://www.sjcd.edu/

**CONTACT** Dr. William Lindemann, Chancellor
**Telephone:** 281-998-6150

**GENERAL INFORMATION** Public Institution. Founded 1961. **Accreditation:** Regional (SACS/CC); emergency medical services (JRCEMTP); medical laboratory technology (NAACLS); radiologic technology: radiography (JRCERT). **Total program enrollment:** 9786.

**PROGRAM(S) OFFERED**
• **Accounting** *6 students enrolled* • **Airline/Commercial/Professional Pilot and Flight Crew** *2 students enrolled* • **Autobody/Collision and Repair Technology/Technician** *2 students enrolled* • **Automobile/Automotive Mechanics Technology/Technician** *11 students enrolled* • **Aviation/Airway Management and Operations** *2 students enrolled* • **Business Administration and Management, General** *5 students enrolled* • **Business/Office Automation/Technology/Data Entry** *1 student enrolled* • **Cartography** *1 student enrolled* • **Chemical Technology/Technician** *27 students enrolled* • **Child Care and Support Services Management** *14 students enrolled* • **Child Development** *23 students enrolled* • **Commercial and Advertising Art** *5 students enrolled* • **Computer Programming/Programmer, General** *3 students enrolled* • **Computer and Information Sciences, General** *18 students enrolled* • **Cosmetology/Cosmetologist, General** *63 students enrolled* • **Criminal Justice/Police Science** *3 students enrolled* • **Culinary Arts/Chef Training** *3 students enrolled* • **Diesel Mechanics Technology/Technician** *12 students enrolled* • **Drafting and Design Technology/Technician, General** *15 students enrolled* • **Electrical and Power Transmission Installation/Installer, General** *14 students enrolled* • **Electrical, Electronic and Communications Engineering Technology/Technician** *3 students enrolled* • **Emergency Medical Technology/Technician (EMT Paramedic)** *17 students enrolled* • **Facial Treatment Specialist/Facialist** *22 students enrolled* • **Fire Science/Firefighting** *8 students enrolled* • **Food Preparation/Professional Cooking/Kitchen Assistant** *7 students enrolled* • **Health Information/Medical Records Technology/Technician** *11 students enrolled* • **Heating, Air Conditioning, Ventilation and Refrigeration Maintenance Technology/Technician (HAC,**

**HACR, HVAC, HVACR)** *16 students enrolled* • **Industrial Mechanics and Maintenance Technology** *1 student enrolled* • **Instrumentation Technology/Technician** *24 students enrolled* • **Interior Design** *9 students enrolled* • **International Business/Trade/Commerce** *5 students enrolled* • **Licensed Practical/Vocational Nurse Training (LPN, LVN, Cert, Dipl, AAS)** *129 students enrolled* • **Medical Administrative/Executive Assistant and Medical Secretary** *4 students enrolled* • **Medical Insurance Coding Specialist/Coder** *14 students enrolled* • **Medical/Clinical Assistant** *13 students enrolled* • **Occupational Safety and Health Technology/Technician** *5 students enrolled* • **Optometric Technician/Assistant** *6 students enrolled* • **Pharmacy Technician/Assistant** *34 students enrolled* • **Psychiatric/Mental Health Services Technician** *1 student enrolled* • **Radio and Television Broadcasting Technology/Technician** *6 students enrolled* • **Real Estate** *26 students enrolled* • **Substance Abuse/Addiction Counseling** *1 student enrolled* • **Surgical Technology/Technologist** *37 students enrolled* • **System, Networking, and LAN/WAN Management/Manager** *7 students enrolled* • **Web/Multimedia Management and Webmaster** *1 student enrolled* • **Welding Technology/Welder** *10 students enrolled*

**STUDENT SERVICES** Academic or career counseling, daycare for children of students, employment services for current students, placement services for program completers, remedial services.

## San Jacinto College District

4624 Fairmont Parkway, Pasadena, TX 77504-3323
http://www.sanjac.edu

**CONTACT** Dr. William Lindemann, Chancellor
**Telephone:** 281-998-6150

**GENERAL INFORMATION** Public Institution. Founded 1961. **Accreditation:** Regional (SACS/CC).

## School of Automotive Machinists

1911 Antoine Drive, Houston, TX 77055-1803
http://www.samracing.com/

**CONTACT** Linda Massingill, Executive Director
**Telephone:** 713-683-3817

**GENERAL INFORMATION** Private Institution. Founded 1985. **Total program enrollment:** 137. **Application fee:** $100.

**PROGRAM(S) OFFERED**
• **Automobile/Automotive Mechanics Technology/Technician** *541 hrs./$11,850* • **Engine Machinist** • **Machine Tool Technology/Machinist** • **Mechanic and Repair Technologies/Technicians, Other** *48 students enrolled*

**STUDENT SERVICES** Academic or career counseling, employment services for current students, placement services for program completers.

## Schreiner University

2100 Memorial Boulevard, Kerrville, TX 78028-5697
http://www.schreiner.edu/

**CONTACT** C. Timothy Summerlin, President
**Telephone:** 830-896-5411

**GENERAL INFORMATION** Private Institution. Founded 1923. **Accreditation:** Regional (SACS/CC). **Total program enrollment:** 930. **Application fee:** $25.

**PROGRAM(S) OFFERED**
• **Licensed Practical/Vocational Nurse Training (LPN, LVN, Cert, Dipl, AAS)** *52 students enrolled*

**STUDENT SERVICES** Academic or career counseling, employment services for current students, placement services for program completers, remedial services.

## Sebring Career Schools

6672 Highway 06 South, Houston, TX 77083

**CONTACT** M. Reese Moore, President
**Telephone:** 281-561-0592

**GENERAL INFORMATION** Private Institution. **Total program enrollment:** 101. **Application fee:** $100.

**PROGRAM(S) OFFERED**
• **Cosmetology and Related Personal Grooming Arts, Other** *49 students enrolled* • **Cosmetology, Barber/Styling, and Nail Instructor** *750 hrs./$3986* • **Cosmetology/Cosmetologist, General** *1500 hrs./$8084* • **Facial Treatment Specialist/Facialist** *750 hrs./$3986* • **Nail Technician/Specialist and Manicurist** *600 hrs./$3178*

**STUDENT SERVICES** Academic or career counseling, placement services for program completers.

## Sebring Career Schools

2212 Avenue I, Huntsville, TX 77340

**CONTACT** Reese Moore, President/Owner
**Telephone:** 936-291-6388

**GENERAL INFORMATION** Private Institution. **Total program enrollment:** 33. **Application fee:** $200.

**PROGRAM(S) OFFERED**
• **Cosmetology and Related Personal Grooming Arts, Other** *750 hrs./$6937* • **Cosmetology, Barber/Styling, and Nail Instructor** *600 hrs./$4818* • **Cosmetology/Cosmetologist, General** *1500 hrs./$10,877*

**STUDENT SERVICES** Academic or career counseling, employment services for current students, placement services for program completers.

## Seguin Beauty School

214 West San Antonio, New Braunfels, TX 78130
http://www.seguinbeautyschool.net/

**CONTACT** Joseph P. Evans, Administrator
**Telephone:** 830-372-0935

**GENERAL INFORMATION** Private Institution. **Total program enrollment:** 42.

**PROGRAM(S) OFFERED**
• **Cosmetology/Cosmetologist, General** *1500 hrs./$12,950*

**STUDENT SERVICES** Placement services for program completers.

## Seguin Beauty School

102 East Court Street, Seguin, TX 78155
http://www.seguinbeautyschool.net/

**CONTACT** Joseph P. Evans, Administrator
**Telephone:** 830-372-0935

**GENERAL INFORMATION** Private Institution. **Total program enrollment:** 50.

**PROGRAM(S) OFFERED**
• **Cosmetology/Cosmetologist, General** *1500 hrs./$12,950*

**STUDENT SERVICES** Placement services for program completers.

## Southeastern Career Institute

12005 Ford Road, Suite 100, Dallas, TX 75234
http://www.southeasterncareerinstitute.edu/

**CONTACT** Michelle Taylor, Executive Director
**Telephone:** 972-385-1446

**GENERAL INFORMATION** Private Institution. Founded 1987. **Accreditation:** State accredited or approved. **Total program enrollment:** 358.

**PROGRAM(S) OFFERED**
• **Allied Health and Medical Assisting Services, Other** *720 hrs./$13,732* • **Dental Assisting/Assistant** *900 hrs./$13,051* • **Legal Assistant/Paralegal** *460 hrs./$13,517* • **Medical Insurance Coding Specialist/Coder** *720 hrs./$12,789* • **Medical Office Assistant/Specialist** *37 students enrolled* • **Medical/Clinical Assistant** *86 students enrolled* • **Pharmacy Technician/Assistant** *720 hrs./$13,606*

**STUDENT SERVICES** Academic or career counseling, employment services for current students, placement services for program completers.

## Southeastern Career Institute–Midland

Westwood Village Shopping Center, 4320 W. Illinois Avenue, Midland, TX 79703
http://www.southeasterncareerinstitute.com/

**CONTACT** Marcy Raynes, Executive Director
**Telephone:** 432-681-3390

**GENERAL INFORMATION** Private Institution. **Total program enrollment:** 322. **Application fee:** $20.

**PROGRAM(S) OFFERED**
• **Computer Systems Networking and Telecommunications** *720 hrs./$12,930* • **Dental Assisting/Assistant** *900 hrs./$13,096* • **Electrical and Electronic Engineering Technologies/Technicians, Other** *900 hrs./$12,649* • **Management Information Systems, General** *24 students enrolled* • **Medical Office Assistant/Specialist** *720 hrs./$12,404* • **Medical/Clinical Assistant** *720 hrs./$13,631*

**STUDENT SERVICES** Academic or career counseling, employment services for current students, placement services for program completers.

## Southeast Texas Career Institute

975 Highway 327 East, Silsbee, TX 77656

**CONTACT** Lillie Cooper, Chief Administrative Officer
**Telephone:** 409-386-2020 Ext. 104

**GENERAL INFORMATION** Private Institution. **Total program enrollment:** 113. **Application fee:** $100.

**PROGRAM(S) OFFERED**
• **Cosmetology, Barber/Styling, and Nail Instructor** *750 hrs./$2000* • **Cosmetology/Cosmetologist, General** *600 hrs./$3000*

**STUDENT SERVICES** Academic or career counseling, placement services for program completers.

## Southern Careers Institute

2301 South Congress, Suite 27, Austin, TX 78704
http://www.scitexas.com/

**CONTACT** Joel P. Meck, President
**Telephone:** 512-448-4795

**GENERAL INFORMATION** Private Institution. **Total program enrollment:** 231. **Application fee:** $50.

**PROGRAM(S) OFFERED**
• **Accounting Technology/Technician and Bookkeeping** *806 hrs./$10,450* • **Administrative Assistant and Secretarial Science, General** *650 hrs./$8600* • **General Office Occupations and Clerical Services** *494 hrs./$5290* • **Medical Administrative/Executive Assistant and Medical Secretary** *780 hrs./$10,550* • **Medical/Clinical Assistant** *978 hrs./$10,950* • **Pharmacy Technician/Assistant** *848 hrs./$10,650*

**STUDENT SERVICES** Academic or career counseling, employment services for current students, placement services for program completers.

## Southern Careers Institute

5333 Everhart, Corpus Christi, TX 78411
http://www.scitexas.com/

**CONTACT** Joel P. Meck, President
**Telephone:** 512-448-4795

**GENERAL INFORMATION** Private Institution. **Total program enrollment:** 196. **Application fee:** $50.

**PROGRAM(S) OFFERED**
• **Accounting Technology/Technician and Bookkeeping** *806 hrs./$10,450* • **Administrative Assistant and Secretarial Science, General** *650 hrs./$8600* • **General Office Occupations and Clerical Services** *494 hrs./$5290* • **Medical Administrative/Executive Assistant and Medical Secretary** *780 hrs./$10,550* • **Medical/Clinical Assistant** *978 hrs./$10,950* • **Pharmacy Technician/Assistant** *848 hrs./$10,650*

**STUDENT SERVICES** Academic or career counseling, employment services for current students, placement services for program completers.

## Southern Careers Institute

1414 North Jackson Road, Pharr, TX 78577
http://www.scitexas.com/

**CONTACT** Joel P. Meck, President
**Telephone:** 512-448-4795

**GENERAL INFORMATION** Private Institution. **Total program enrollment:** 211. **Application fee:** $50.

**PROGRAM(S) OFFERED**
• **Accounting Technology/Technician and Bookkeeping** *806 hrs./$10,450* • **Administrative Assistant and Secretarial Science, General** *650 hrs./$8600* • **General Office Occupations and Clerical Services** *494 hrs./$5290* • **Medical Administrative/Executive Assistant and Medical Secretary** *780 hrs./$10,550* • **Medical/Clinical Assistant** *978 hrs./$10,950* • **Pharmacy Technician/Assistant** *848 hrs./$10,650*

**STUDENT SERVICES** Academic or career counseling, employment services for current students, placement services for program completers.

## Southern Careers Institute

1405 N. Main Avenue, Suite 100, San Antonio, TX 78212
http://www.scitexas.com/

**CONTACT** Joel P. Meck, President
**Telephone:** 512-448-4795

**GENERAL INFORMATION** Private Institution. **Total program enrollment:** 174. **Application fee:** $50.

**PROGRAM(S) OFFERED**
• **Accounting Technology/Technician and Bookkeeping** *806 hrs./$10,450* • **Administrative Assistant and Secretarial Science, General** *650 hrs./$8600* • **General Office Occupations and Clerical Services** *494 hrs./$5290* • **Medical Administrative/Executive Assistant and Medical Secretary** *780 hrs./$10,550* • **Medical/Clinical Assistant** *978 hrs./$10,950* • **Pharmacy Technician/Assistant** *848 hrs./$10,600*

**STUDENT SERVICES** Academic or career counseling, employment services for current students, placement services for program completers.

## South Plains College

1401 South College Avenue, Levelland, TX 79336-6595
http://www.southplainscollege.edu/

**CONTACT** Kelvin Sharp, President
**Telephone:** 806-894-9611 Ext. 2175

**GENERAL INFORMATION** Public Institution. Founded 1958. **Accreditation:** Regional (SACS/CC); health information technology (AHIMA); radiologic technology: radiography (JRCERT). **Total program enrollment:** 4364.

**PROGRAM(S) OFFERED**
• **Accounting Technology/Technician and Bookkeeping** *7 students enrolled* • **Administrative Assistant and Secretarial Science, General** *1 student enrolled* • **Autobody/Collision and Repair Technology/Technician** *21 students enrolled* • **Automobile/Automotive Mechanics Technology/Technician** *10 students enrolled* • **Business/Commerce, General** *9 students enrolled* • **Child Care and Support Services Management** *16 students enrolled* • **Computer and Information Sciences, General** *2 students enrolled* • **Cosmetology/Cosmetologist, General** *50 students enrolled* • **Criminal Justice/Law Enforcement Administration** *15 students enrolled* • **Diesel Mechanics Technology/Technician** *27 students enrolled* • **Drafting and Design Technology/Technician, General** • **Electrical/Electronics Equipment Installation and Repair, General** *11 students enrolled* • **Emergency Medical Technology/Technician (EMT Paramedic)** *58 students enrolled* • **Engineering Technology, General** *5 students enrolled* • **Executive Assistant/Executive Secretary** *8 students enrolled* • **Fire Science/Firefighting** *12 students enrolled* • **Health Information/Medical Records Technology/Technician** *4 students enrolled* • **Heating, Air Conditioning, Ventilation and Refrigeration Maintenance Technology/Technician (HAC, HACR, HVAC, HVACR)** *7 students enrolled* • **Licensed Practical/Vocational Nurse Training (LPN, LVN, Cert, Dipl, AAS)** *84 students enrolled* • **Machine Tool Technology/Machinist** *2 students enrolled* • **Music Performance, General** *27 students enrolled* • **Real Estate** *4 students enrolled* • **Surgical Technology/Technologist** *20 students enrolled* • **Welding Technology/Welder** *38 students enrolled*

**STUDENT SERVICES** Academic or career counseling, employment services for current students, placement services for program completers, remedial services.

## South Texas Barber College

3917 Ayers, Corpus Christi, TX 78415

**CONTACT** Juan A. Garcia, Owner
**Telephone:** 361-855-0262

**GENERAL INFORMATION** Private Institution. **Total program enrollment:** 34.

**PROGRAM(S) OFFERED**
• **Barbering/Barber** *1500 hrs./$7910* • **Cosmetology and Related Personal Grooming Arts, Other** *301 hrs./$1665* • **Cosmetology, Barber/Styling, and Nail Instructor** *1500 hrs./$4865* • **Nail Technician/Specialist and Manicurist** *600 hrs./$2865*

**STUDENT SERVICES** Academic or career counseling, placement services for program completers.

## South Texas College

3201 West Pecan, McAllen, TX 78501
http://www.southtexascollege.edu/

**CONTACT** Dr. Shirley A. Reed, President
**Telephone:** 956-872-8311

**GENERAL INFORMATION** Public Institution. Founded 1993. **Accreditation:** Regional (SACS/CC); health information technology (AHIMA). **Total program enrollment:** 6540.

**PROGRAM(S) OFFERED**
• **Administrative Assistant and Secretarial Science, General** *15 students enrolled* • **Automobile/Automotive Mechanics Technology/Technician** *32 students enrolled* • **Business/Commerce, General** *49 students enrolled* • **Child Care Provider/Assistant** *2 students enrolled* • **Child Development** *60 students enrolled* • **Computer Engineering Technology/Technician** *11 students enrolled* • **Computer Technology/Computer Systems Technology** *13 students enrolled* • **Computer and Information Sciences, General** *29 students enrolled* • **Culinary Arts/Chef Training** *7 students enrolled* • **Diesel Mechanics Technology/Technician** *30 students enrolled* • **Drafting and Design Technology/Technician, General** *24 students enrolled* • **Electrician** *9 students enrolled* • **Emergency Medical Technology/Technician (EMT Paramedic)** *129 students enrolled* • **Health Information/Medical Records Technology/Technician** *6 students enrolled* • **Heating, Air Conditioning, Ventilation and Refrigeration Maintenance Technology/Technician (HAC, HACR, HVAC, HVACR)** *31 students enrolled* • **Legal Administrative Assistant/Secretary** *6 students enrolled* • **Licensed Practical/Vocational Nurse Training (LPN, LVN, Cert, Dipl, AAS)** *149 students enrolled* • **Medical Insurance Coding Specialist/Coder** *5 students enrolled* • **Medical Transcription/Transcriptionist** *6 students enrolled* • **Medical/Clinical Assistant** *10 students enrolled* • **Nurse/Nursing Assistant/Aide and Patient Care Assistant** *47 students enrolled* • **Pharmacy Technician/Assistant** *8 students enrolled* • **Tool and Die Technology/Technician** *16 students enrolled*

**STUDENT SERVICES** Academic or career counseling, daycare for children of students, employment services for current students, placement services for program completers, remedial services.

## South Texas Vocational Technical Institute

2400 W. Daffodil Avenue, McAllen, TX 78501
http://www.stvt.edu/

**CONTACT** Javier Dimas, Executive Director
**Telephone:** 956-631-1107

**GENERAL INFORMATION** Private Institution. **Total program enrollment:** 151.

**PROGRAM(S) OFFERED**
• **Accounting Technology/Technician and Bookkeeping** *912 hrs./$12,680* • **Administrative Assistant and Secretarial Science, General** • **Business/Office Automation/Technology/Data Entry** *4 students enrolled* • **Child Development** *2 students enrolled* • **Clinical/Medical Laboratory Technician** • **Dental Assisting/Assistant** *12 hrs./$15,900* • **Home Health Aide/Home Attendant** • **Legal Administrative Assistant/Secretary** *2 students enrolled* • **Legal Assistant/Paralegal** *912 hrs./$13,620* • **Medical Administrative/Executive Assistant and Medical Secretary** *864 hrs./$12,658* • **Nurse/Nursing Assistant/Aide and Patient Care Assistant** *840 hrs./$12,614* • **Pharmacy Technician/Assistant** *1152 hrs./$12,660* • **Phlebotomy/Phlebotomist**

**STUDENT SERVICES** Academic or career counseling, placement services for program completers.

## South Texas Vo-Tech Institute

2419 East Haggar Avenue, Weslaco, TX 78596
http://www.stvt.edu/

**CONTACT** Jesse Hernandez, Executive Director
**Telephone:** 956-969-1564

**GENERAL INFORMATION** Private Institution. **Total program enrollment:** 251.

**PROGRAM(S) OFFERED**
• **Accounting** *912 hrs./$12,680* • **Administrative Assistant and Secretarial Science, General** • **Child Development** • **Clinical/Medical Laboratory Technician** *1224 hrs./$14,602* • **Dental Assisting/Assistant** *968 hrs./$15,900* • **General Office Occupations and Clerical Services** *768 hrs./$12,625* • **Home Health Aide/Home Attendant** • **Legal Administrative Assistant/Secretary** • **Legal Assistant/Paralegal** • **Medical Administrative/Executive Assistant and Medical Secretary** *864 hrs./$12,658* • **Nurse/Nursing Assistant/Aide and Patient Care Assistant** *840 hrs./$12,614* • **Pharmacy Technician/Assistant** *3 students enrolled* • **Phlebotomy/Phlebotomist**

**STUDENT SERVICES** Academic or career counseling, placement services for program completers.

## Southwest Career Institute

1414 Geronimo Drive, El Paso, TX 79925
swci-ep.com

**CONTACT** Yolanda Arriola, President
**Telephone:** 915-778-4001

**GENERAL INFORMATION** Private Institution. **Total program enrollment:** 200.

**PROGRAM(S) OFFERED**
• **Administrative Assistant and Secretarial Science, General** *15 students enrolled* • **Diesel Mechanics Technology/Technician** *13 students enrolled* • **Health Information/Medical Records Technology/Technician** *38 students enrolled* • **Medical/Clinical Assistant** *30 students enrolled*

**STUDENT SERVICES** Academic or career counseling, employment services for current students, placement services for program completers, remedial services.

## SouthWest Collegiate Institute for the Deaf

3200 Avenue C, Big Spring, TX 79720-7298
http://www.hc.cc.tx.us/

**CONTACT** Cheryl T. Sparks, President
**Telephone:** 432-264-3700

**GENERAL INFORMATION** Public Institution. Founded 1980. **Total program enrollment:** 94.

**PROGRAM(S) OFFERED**
• **Automobile/Automotive Mechanics Technology/Technician** • **Building/Property Maintenance and Management** *3 students enrolled* • **Business/Office Automation/Technology/Data Entry** *5 students enrolled* • **Computer and Information Sciences, General** • **Dental Laboratory Technology/Technician** • **Graphic and Printing Equipment Operator, General Production** *1 student enrolled* • **Sign Language Interpretation and Translation** *1 student enrolled* • **Welding Technology/Welder** *3 students enrolled*

**STUDENT SERVICES** Academic or career counseling, employment services for current students, placement services for program completers, remedial services.

## Southwest School of Business and Technical Careers

272 Commerical Street, Eagle Pass, TX 78852

**CONTACT** Al Salazar, Administrator
**Telephone:** 830-773-1373

**GENERAL INFORMATION** Private Institution. **Total program enrollment:** 50.

**PROGRAM(S) OFFERED**
• **Cosmetology, Barber/Styling, and Nail Instructor** *750 hrs./$3850* • **Cosmetology/Cosmetologist, General** *1500 hrs./$10,870* • **General Office Occupations and Clerical Services** *900 hrs./$5400* • **Nail Technician/Specialist and Manicurist** *600 hrs./$3100*

**STUDENT SERVICES** Employment services for current students, placement services for program completers, remedial services.

## Southwest School of Business and Technical Careers

602 West South Cross, San Antonio, TX 78221

**CONTACT** Ahmad Dib, President
**Telephone:** 830-626-7007

**GENERAL INFORMATION** Private Institution. Founded 1979. **Total program enrollment:** 379.

**PROGRAM(S) OFFERED**
• **Accounting Technology/Technician and Bookkeeping** *775 hrs./$10,520* • **Administrative Assistant and Secretarial Science, General** *900 hrs./$5400* • **General Office Occupations and Clerical Services** *575 hrs./$7240* • **Medical Office Assistant/Specialist** *800 hrs./$10,560* • **Medical/Clinical Assistant** *800 hrs./$10,900* • **Pharmacy Technician/Assistant** *775 hrs./$10,610*

**STUDENT SERVICES** Academic or career counseling, employment services for current students, placement services for program completers, remedial services.

## Southwest School of Business and Technical Careers–Cosmetology

505 East Travis, San Antonio, TX 78205

**CONTACT** Al Salazar, Administrator
**Telephone:** 210-731-8449

**GENERAL INFORMATION** Private Institution. **Total program enrollment:** 30.

**PROGRAM(S) OFFERED**
• **Cosmetology, Barber/Styling, and Nail Instructor** *750 hrs./$3850* • **Cosmetology/Cosmetologist, General** *1500 hrs./$10,970* • **Nail Technician/Specialist and Manicurist** *600 hrs./$3100*

**STUDENT SERVICES** Academic or career counseling, placement services for program completers, remedial services.

## Southwest Texas Junior College

2401 Garner Field Road, Uvalde, TX 78801-6297
http://www.swtjc.net/

**CONTACT** Ismael Sosa, Jr., President
**Telephone:** 830-278-4401

**GENERAL INFORMATION** Public Institution. Founded 1946. **Accreditation:** Regional (SACS/CC). **Total program enrollment:** 1859.

**PROGRAM(S) OFFERED**
• **Autobody/Collision and Repair Technology/Technician** *7 students enrolled* • **Automobile/Automotive Mechanics Technology/Technician** *12 students enrolled* • **Business/Office Automation/Technology/Data Entry** *3 students enrolled* • **Child Development** • **Construction Engineering Technology/Technician** *20 students enrolled* • **Cosmetology/Cosmetologist, General** *20 students enrolled* • **Criminal Justice/Police Science** • **Diesel Mechanics Technology/Technician** *3 students enrolled* • **Heating, Air Conditioning, Ventilation and Refrigeration Maintenance Technology/Technician (HAC, HACR, HVAC, HVACR)** *13 students enrolled* • **International Business/Trade/Commerce** • **Licensed Practical/Vocational Nurse Training (LPN, LVN, Cert, Dipl, AAS)** *78 students enrolled* • **Public Administration** *1 student enrolled* • **Welding Technology/Welder** *7 students enrolled* • **Wildlife and Wildlands Science and Management** *8 students enrolled*

**STUDENT SERVICES** Academic or career counseling, daycare for children of students, employment services for current students, placement services for program completers, remedial services.

## Star College of Cosmetology 2

520 E. Front Street, Tyler, TX 75702-8214

**CONTACT** Alan Krumdieck, CEO
**Telephone:** 903-596-7860

**GENERAL INFORMATION** Private Institution. **Total program enrollment:** 109.

**PROGRAM(S) OFFERED**
• **Aesthetician/Esthetician and Skin Care Specialist** *750 hrs./$5200* • **Cosmetology, Barber/Styling, and Nail Instructor** *750 hrs./$4000* • **Cosmetology/Cosmetologist, General** *1500 hrs./$8725* • **Nail Technician/Specialist and Manicurist** *600 hrs./$4000*

**STUDENT SERVICES** Academic or career counseling, placement services for program completers.

## State Beauty Academy

663 Oriole Boulevard, Duncanville, TX 75116
http://www.statebeautyacademy.net/

**CONTACT** Michael Rolfe, Director
**Telephone:** 972-298-0100

**GENERAL INFORMATION** Private Institution. **Total program enrollment:** 48.

**PROGRAM(S) OFFERED**
- **Cosmetology, Barber/Styling, and Nail Instructor** *750 hrs./$4825*
- **Cosmetology/Cosmetologist, General** *1500 hrs./$10,550*

**STUDENT SERVICES** Academic or career counseling, employment services for current students, placement services for program completers.

## Stephenville Beauty College

951 South Lillian Street, Stephenville, TX 76401

**CONTACT** Emilia Cuellar, President
**Telephone:** 254-968-2111

**GENERAL INFORMATION** Private Institution. **Total program enrollment:** 24.

**PROGRAM(S) OFFERED**
- **Cosmetology, Barber/Styling, and Nail Instructor** • **Cosmetology/Cosmetologist, General** *1500 hrs./$6777* • **Nail Technician/Specialist and Manicurist** *2 students enrolled*

**STUDENT SERVICES** Placement services for program completers.

## Sul Ross State University

East Highway 90, Alpine, TX 79832
http://www.sulross.edu/

**CONTACT** R. Vic Morgan, President
**Telephone:** 432-837-8011

**GENERAL INFORMATION** Public Institution. Founded 1920. **Accreditation:** Regional (SACS/CC). **Total program enrollment:** 1473. **Application fee:** $25.

**PROGRAM(S) OFFERED**
- **Equestrian/Equine Studies** • **Licensed Practical/Vocational Nurse Training (LPN, LVN, Cert, Dipl, AAS)** *5 students enrolled* • **Office Management and Supervision** *2 students enrolled*

**STUDENT SERVICES** Academic or career counseling, daycare for children of students, employment services for current students, placement services for program completers, remedial services.

## Tarrant County College District

1500 Houston Street, Fort Worth, TX 76102-6599
http://web.tccd.net/

**CONTACT** Leonardo de la Garza, Chancellor
**Telephone:** 817-515-5100

**GENERAL INFORMATION** Public Institution. Founded 1967. **Accreditation:** Regional (SACS/CC); dental hygiene (ADA); health information technology (AHIMA); physical therapy assisting (APTA); radiologic technology: radiography (JRCERT). **Total program enrollment:** 13623.

**PROGRAM(S) OFFERED**
- **Accounting Technology/Technician and Bookkeeping** *78 students enrolled*
- **Administrative Assistant and Secretarial Science, General** *16 students enrolled* • **Aircraft Powerplant Technology/Technician** *79 students enrolled* • **Applied Horticulture/Horticultural Operations, General** *7 students enrolled*
- **Architectural Engineering Technology/Technician** *2 students enrolled*
- **Autobody/Collision and Repair Technology/Technician** *19 students enrolled*
- **Automobile/Automotive Mechanics Technology/Technician** *18 students enrolled* • **Business Administration and Management, General** *1 student enrolled* • **Business/Commerce, General** *21 students enrolled* • **Business/Office Automation/Technology/Data Entry** *9 students enrolled* • **Cartography** *2 students enrolled* • **Child Care Provider/Assistant** *3 students enrolled* • **Child Care and Support Services Management** *2 students enrolled* • **Child Development**
- **Computer Programming/Programmer, General** *4 students enrolled* • **Computer Systems Networking and Telecommunications** *64 students enrolled* • **Computer Technology/Computer Systems Technology** *2 students enrolled* • **Computer and Information Sciences, General** *6 students enrolled* • **Criminal Justice/Police Science** *82 students enrolled* • **Criminal Justice/Safety Studies** • **Culinary Arts/Chef Training** *3 students enrolled* • **Dental Assisting/Assistant** *7 students enrolled*
- **Dietitian Assistant** *12 students enrolled* • **Drafting and Design Technology/Technician, General** *8 students enrolled* • **Electrical, Electronic and Communications Engineering Technology/Technician** *4 students enrolled*
- **Emergency Medical Technology/Technician (EMT Paramedic)** *9 students enrolled* • **Fashion Merchandising** *3 students enrolled* • **Fire Protection and Safety Technology/Technician** *66 students enrolled* • **Foodservice Systems Administration/Management** • **Graphic and Printing Equipment Operator, General Production** • **Heating, Air Conditioning and Refrigeration Technology/Technician (ACH/ACR/ACHR/HRAC/HVAC/AC Technology)** *51 students enrolled*
- **Hospital and Health Care Facilities Administration/Management** • **Hospitality Administration/Management, General** • **Legal Assistant/Paralegal** *4 students enrolled* • **Logistics and Materials Management** *55 students enrolled*
- **Manufacturing Technology/Technician** *1 student enrolled* • **Medical Insurance Coding Specialist/Coder** *9 students enrolled* • **Occupational Safety and Health Technology/Technician** *8 students enrolled* • **Operations Management and Supervision** *6 students enrolled* • **Pharmacy Technician/Assistant** *13 students enrolled* • **Prepress/Desktop Publishing and Digital Imaging Design** *3 students enrolled* • **Psychiatric/Mental Health Services Technician** *44 students enrolled*
- **Public Administration** *3 students enrolled* • **Quality Control Technology/Technician** • **Radio and Television Broadcasting Technology/Technician** *4 students enrolled* • **Real Estate** *40 students enrolled* • **Robotics Technology/Technician** *1 student enrolled* • **Sales, Distribution and Marketing Operations, General** *3 students enrolled* • **Sign Language Interpretation and Translation** *18 students enrolled* • **Small Business Administration/Management** *2 students enrolled* • **Small Engine Mechanics and Repair Technology/Technician** *4 students enrolled* • **Surgical Technology/Technologist** *20 students enrolled* • **Tourism and Travel Services Management** *3 students enrolled* • **Web Page, Digital/Multimedia and Information Resources Design** *3 students enrolled* • **Welding Technology/Welder** *12 students enrolled*

**STUDENT SERVICES** Academic or career counseling, employment services for current students, placement services for program completers, remedial services.

## Temple College

2600 South First Street, Temple, TX 76504-7435
http://www.templejc.edu/

**CONTACT** Glenda Barron, President
**Telephone:** 254-298-8282

**GENERAL INFORMATION** Public Institution. Founded 1926. **Accreditation:** Regional (SACS/CC); dental hygiene (ADA); medical laboratory technology (NAACLS). **Total program enrollment:** 1982.

**PROGRAM(S) OFFERED**
- **Administrative Assistant and Secretarial Science, General** *7 students enrolled*
- **Business Administration and Management, General** *28 students enrolled*
- **Cartography** • **Child Care and Support Services Management** *1 student enrolled* • **Child Development** *3 students enrolled* • **Computer Programming/Programmer, General** • **Computer and Information Sciences, General** *4 students enrolled* • **Criminal Justice/Safety Studies** *4 students enrolled* • **Data Entry/Microcomputer Applications, General** *4 students enrolled* • **Drafting and Design Technology/Technician, General** *1 student enrolled* • **Emergency Medical Technology/Technician (EMT Paramedic)** *11 students enrolled* • **Fire Science/Firefighting** • **Licensed Practical/Vocational Nurse Training (LPN, LVN, Cert, Dipl, AAS)** *60 students enrolled* • **Office Management and Supervision** • **Surgical Technology/Technologist** *17 students enrolled* • **System, Networking, and LAN/WAN Management/Manager** • **Web/Multimedia Management and Webmaster**

**STUDENT SERVICES** Academic or career counseling, employment services for current students, placement services for program completers, remedial services.

## Texarkana College

2500 North Robison Road, Texarkana, TX 75599-0001
http://www.texarkanacollege.edu/

**CONTACT** Frank Coleman, President
**Telephone:** 903-838-4541

**GENERAL INFORMATION** Public Institution. Founded 1927. **Accreditation:** Regional (SACS/CC). **Total program enrollment:** 2010.

**PROGRAM(S) OFFERED**
• **Administrative Assistant and Secretarial Science, General** *6 students enrolled* • **Autobody/Collision and Repair Technology/Technician** *19 students enrolled* • **Automobile/Automotive Mechanics Technology/Technician** *20 students enrolled* • **Business Administration and Management, General** *2 students enrolled* • **Business/Office Automation/Technology/Data Entry** • **Carpentry/Carpenter** • **Child Care and Support Services Management** • **Computer Programming/Programmer, General** *26 students enrolled* • **Cosmetology/Cosmetologist, General** *14 students enrolled* • **Criminal Justice/Law Enforcement Administration** *3 students enrolled* • **Culinary Arts/Chef Training** *11 students enrolled* • **Diesel Mechanics Technology/Technician** *13 students enrolled* • **Drafting and Design Technology/Technician, General** *15 students enrolled* • **Electrical, Electronic and Communications Engineering Technology/Technician** *7 students enrolled* • **Electrician** *41 students enrolled* • **Emergency Medical Technology/Technician (EMT Paramedic)** *27 students enrolled* • **General Office Occupations and Clerical Services** *8 students enrolled* • **Heating, Air Conditioning, Ventilation and Refrigeration Maintenance Technology/Technician (HAC, HACR, HVAC, HVACR)** *43 students enrolled* • **Licensed Practical/Vocational Nurse Training (LPN, LVN, Cert, Dipl, AAS)** *74 students enrolled* • **Marketing/Marketing Management, General** *3 students enrolled* • **Ornamental Horticulture** *4 students enrolled* • **Real Estate** *8 students enrolled* • **Small Engine Mechanics and Repair Technology/Technician** *8 students enrolled* • **Substance Abuse/Addiction Counseling** *2 students enrolled* • **Upholstery/Upholsterer** *2 students enrolled* • **Welding Technology/Welder** *31 students enrolled*

**STUDENT SERVICES** Academic or career counseling, employment services for current students, remedial services.

## Texas Barber College and Hairstyling School

9275 Richmond Avenue #180, Houston, TX 77063
http://www.texasbarbercolleges.com/

**CONTACT** Bradley David Bundy, President
**Telephone:** 713-953-0262

**GENERAL INFORMATION** Private Institution. **Total program enrollment:** 854.

**PROGRAM(S) OFFERED**
• **Aesthetician/Esthetician and Skin Care Specialist** *1 student enrolled* • **Barbering/Barber** *1500 hrs./$11,800* • **Cosmetology and Related Personal Grooming Arts, Other** *750 hrs./$5275* • **Cosmetology, Barber/Styling, and Nail Instructor** *1000 hrs./$7033* • **Cosmetology/Cosmetologist, General** *1500 hrs./$10,550* • **Nail Technician/Specialist and Manicurist** *600 hrs./$1500*

**STUDENT SERVICES** Academic or career counseling, placement services for program completers.

## Texas Careers–Beaumont

194 Gateway, Beaumont, TX 77701
http://www.texascareers.edu/

**CONTACT** Gregory Garrett, Executive Director
**Telephone:** 409-833-2722

**GENERAL INFORMATION** Private Institution. **Total program enrollment:** 442.

**PROGRAM(S) OFFERED**
• **Allied Health and Medical Assisting Services, Other** *135 students enrolled* • **Data Entry/Microcomputer Applications, General** *37 students enrolled* • **Dental Assisting/Assistant** *780 hrs./$14,245* • **Medical Office Assistant/Specialist** *720 hrs./$14,245* • **Medical/Clinical Assistant** *720 hrs./$14,245*

**STUDENT SERVICES** Academic or career counseling, employment services for current students, placement services for program completers.

## Texas Careers–Laredo

6410 McPherson, Laredo, TX 78041
http://www.texascareers.edu/

**CONTACT** Angie Keyes, Executive Director
**Telephone:** 956-717-5909

**GENERAL INFORMATION** Private Institution. **Total program enrollment:** 362. **Application fee:** $20.

**PROGRAM(S) OFFERED**
• **Business/Office Automation/Technology/Data Entry** *720 hrs./$14,695* • **International Business/Trade/Commerce** *772 hrs./$14,695* • **Medical Administrative/Executive Assistant and Medical Secretary** *720 hrs./$14,695* • **Medical/Clinical Assistant** *720 hrs./$14,575*

**STUDENT SERVICES** Academic or career counseling, employment services for current students, placement services for program completers.

## Texas Careers–Lubbock

1421 9th Street, Lubbock, TX 79401
http://www.texascareers.edu/

**CONTACT** James Hackney, President
**Telephone:** 806-765-7051

**GENERAL INFORMATION** Private Institution. **Total program enrollment:** 593.

**PROGRAM(S) OFFERED**
• **Dental Assisting/Assistant** *55 hrs./$14,483* • **Electrician** *73 hrs./$15,473* • **Medical Office Assistant/Specialist** *47 hrs./$14,483* • **Medical/Clinical Assistant** *720 hrs./$14,483* • **Nurse/Nursing Assistant/Aide and Patient Care Assistant** *48 hrs./$14,483*

**STUDENT SERVICES** Placement services for program completers.

## Texas Careers–San Antonio

1015 Jackson Keller, San Antonio, TX 78213
http://www.texascareers.edu/

**CONTACT** Lisa Ramirez, Executive Director
**Telephone:** 210-308-8584

**GENERAL INFORMATION** Private Institution. **Total program enrollment:** 958. **Application fee:** $20.

**PROGRAM(S) OFFERED**
• **Computer and Information Sciences and Support Services, Other** *720 hrs./$13,140* • **Legal Assistant/Paralegal** *900 hrs./$13,995* • **Licensed Practical/Vocational Nurse Training (LPN, LVN, Cert, Dipl, AAS)** *1544 hrs./$23,507* • **Medical Office Management/Administration** *720 hrs./$13,995* • **Medical/Clinical Assistant** *720 hrs./$13,995* • **Nurse/Nursing Assistant/Aide and Patient Care Assistant** *94 students enrolled*

**STUDENT SERVICES** Academic or career counseling, employment services for current students, placement services for program completers.

## Texas Christian University

2800 South University Drive, Fort Worth, TX 76129-0002
http://www.tcu.edu/

**CONTACT** Victor J. Boschini, Jr., Chancellor
**Telephone:** 817-257-7000

**GENERAL INFORMATION** Private Institution (Affiliated with Christian Church (Disciples of Christ)). Founded 1873. **Accreditation:** Regional (SACS/CC); athletic training (JRCAT); computer science (ABET/CSAC); interior design: professional (CIDA); journalism and mass communications (ACEJMC); music (NASM); speech-language pathology (ASHA). **Total program enrollment:** 7645. **Application fee:** $40.

**PROGRAM(S) OFFERED**
• **Farm/Farm and Ranch Management** *27 students enrolled*

**STUDENT SERVICES** Academic or career counseling, employment services for current students, placement services for program completers, remedial services.

## Texas College of Cosmetology

117 Sayles Boulevard, Abilene, TX 79605
http://texascollege.org/

**CONTACT** Steven Weilert, Owner
**Telephone:** 325-677-0532

**GENERAL INFORMATION** Private Institution. Founded 1988. **Total program enrollment:** 68. **Application fee:** $100.

**PROGRAM(S) OFFERED**
• **Aesthetician/Esthetician and Skin Care Specialist** *750 hrs./$5070* • **Cosmetology, Barber/Styling, and Nail Instructor** *750 hrs./$3338* • **Cosmetology/Cosmetologist, General** *1500 hrs./$8750* • **Nail Technician/Specialist and Manicurist** *600 hrs./$3220*

**STUDENT SERVICES** Academic or career counseling, placement services for program completers, remedial services.

## Texas College of Cosmetology

918 North Chadbourne, San Angelo, TX 76903
http://texascollege.org/

**CONTACT** Steve Weilert, President
**Telephone:** 325-659-2622

**GENERAL INFORMATION** Private Institution. **Total program enrollment:** 41. **Application fee:** $100.

**PROGRAM(S) OFFERED**
• **Aesthetician/Esthetician and Skin Care Specialist** *750 hrs./$3722* • **Cosmetology, Barber/Styling, and Nail Instructor** *750 hrs./$3577* • **Cosmetology/Cosmetologist, General** *1500 hrs./$7885* • **Nail Technician/Specialist and Manicurist** *600 hrs./$2839*

**STUDENT SERVICES** Academic or career counseling, placement services for program completers.

## Texas Culinary Academy

11400 Burnet Road, Suite 2100, Austin, TX 78758
http://www.txca.com/

**CONTACT** Julia Brooks, President
**Telephone:** 512-837-2665

**GENERAL INFORMATION** Private Institution. **Accreditation:** State accredited or approved. **Total program enrollment:** 948. **Application fee:** $100.

**PROGRAM(S) OFFERED**
• **Baking and Pastry Arts/Baker/Pastry Chef** *42 hrs./$28,725* • **Culinary Arts/Chef Training** *30 hrs./$13,046*

**STUDENT SERVICES** Academic or career counseling, employment services for current students, placement services for program completers, remedial services.

## Texas Health School

11211 Katy Freeway, Suite 170, Houston, TX 77079
http://texashealthschool.org/

**CONTACT** Jody M. Hawk, President
**Telephone:** 713-932-9333

**GENERAL INFORMATION** Private Institution. **Total program enrollment:** 149.

**PROGRAM(S) OFFERED**
• **Massage Therapy/Therapeutic Massage** *39 hrs./$6145* • **Medical/Clinical Assistant** *50 hrs./$10,935* • **Medication Aide** *140 hrs./$1700* • **Nurse/Nursing Assistant/Aide and Patient Care Assistant** *75 hrs./$887* • **Physical Therapist Assistant** *32 hrs./$6675*

**STUDENT SERVICES** Academic or career counseling, placement services for program completers.

## Texas School of Business–East Campus

12030 I-10 East Freeway, Houston, TX 77029
http://www.tsb.edu/

**CONTACT** Raymond Ada, Executive Director
**Telephone:** 713-455-8555

**GENERAL INFORMATION** Private Institution. **Total program enrollment:** 614.

**PROGRAM(S) OFFERED**
• **Allied Health and Medical Assisting Services, Other** *720 hrs./$14,933* • **Business Operations Support and Secretarial Services, Other** • **Medical Office Assistant/Specialist** *50 hrs./$14,933*

**STUDENT SERVICES** Academic or career counseling, placement services for program completers.

## Texas School of Business–Friendswood

17164 Blackhawk Boulevard, Friendswood, TX 77546
http://www.tsb.edu/

**CONTACT** Theo Anderson, Executive Director
**Telephone:** 281-648-0880

**GENERAL INFORMATION** Private Institution. **Total program enrollment:** 386.

**PROGRAM(S) OFFERED**
• **Allied Health and Medical Assisting Services, Other** *131 students enrolled* • **Business Operations Support and Secretarial Services, Other** *1 student enrolled* • **Dental Assisting/Assistant** *720 hrs./$14,933* • **Medical Office Assistant/Specialist** *720 hrs./$14,813* • **Medical/Clinical Assistant** *720 hrs./$14,813*

**STUDENT SERVICES** Academic or career counseling, placement services for program completers.

## Texas School of Business–North

711 Airtex Drive, Houston, TX 77073
http://www.tsb.edu/

**CONTACT** Kevin Prehn, President
**Telephone:** 281-443-8900

**GENERAL INFORMATION** Private Institution. **Total program enrollment:** 728.

**PROGRAM(S) OFFERED**
• **Accounting Technology/Technician and Bookkeeping** • **Allied Health and Medical Assisting Services, Other** *720 hrs./$14,933* • **Business/Office Automation/Technology/Data Entry** *29 students enrolled* • **Dental Assisting/**

*Texas School of Business–North (continued)*

**Assistant** *53 hrs./$14,933* • **Electrical/Electronics Maintenance and Repair Technology, Other** *7 students enrolled* • **Medical Office Assistant/Specialist** *50 hrs./$14,933* • **Pharmacy Technician/Assistant** *52 hrs./$14,933*

**STUDENT SERVICES** Academic or career counseling, employment services for current students, placement services for program completers.

## Texas School of Business–Southwest

6363 Richmond, Houston, TX 77057
http://www.tsb.edu/

**CONTACT** David Champllin, Executive Director
**Telephone:** 713-975-7527

**GENERAL INFORMATION** Private Institution. Founded 1984. **Total program enrollment:** 588. **Application fee:** $20.

**PROGRAM(S) OFFERED**
• **Accounting Technology/Technician and Bookkeeping** *1 student enrolled* • **Allied Health and Medical Assisting Services, Other** *720 hrs./$14,813* • **Business Operations Support and Secretarial Services, Other** *27 students enrolled* • **Dental Assisting/Assistant** *53 hrs./$14,813* • **Medical Office Assistant/Specialist** *50 hrs./$14,813* • **Pharmacy Technician/Assistant** *52 hrs./$14,933*

**STUDENT SERVICES** Academic or career counseling, placement services for program completers.

## Texas Southmost College

80 Fort Brown, Brownsville, TX 78520-4991
http://www.utb.edu/

**CONTACT** Juliet Garcia, President
**Telephone:** 956-882-8200

**GENERAL INFORMATION** Public Institution. Founded 1926. **Accreditation:** Regional (SACS/CC); medical laboratory technology (NAACLS); radiologic technology: radiography (JRCERT); respiratory therapy technology (CoARC).

**PROGRAM(S) OFFERED**
• **Accounting Technology/Technician and Bookkeeping** *10 students enrolled* • **Autobody/Collision and Repair Technology/Technician** *15 students enrolled* • **Automobile/Automotive Mechanics Technology/Technician** *33 students enrolled* • **Building/Construction Site Management/Manager** *40 students enrolled* • **Child Care Provider/Assistant** *23 students enrolled* • **Computer and Information Sciences, General** *6 students enrolled* • **Drafting and Design Technology/Technician, General** *13 students enrolled* • **Emergency Medical Technology/Technician (EMT Paramedic)** • **General Office Occupations and Clerical Services** *19 students enrolled* • **Heating, Air Conditioning, Ventilation and Refrigeration Maintenance Technology/Technician (HAC, HACR, HVAC, HVACR)** *26 students enrolled* • **International Marketing** *4 students enrolled* • **Legal Administrative Assistant/Secretary** *2 students enrolled* • **Licensed Practical/Vocational Nurse Training (LPN, LVN, Cert, Dipl, AAS)** *70 students enrolled* • **Machine Shop Technology/Assistant** • **Medical Administrative/Executive Assistant and Medical Secretary** *14 students enrolled*

**STUDENT SERVICES** Academic or career counseling, daycare for children of students, employment services for current students, placement services for program completers, remedial services.

## Texas State Technical College Harlingen

1902 North Loop 499, Harlingen, TX 78550-3697
http://www.harlingen.tstc.edu/

**CONTACT** Dr. Cesar Maldonado, President
**Telephone:** 956-364-4000

**GENERAL INFORMATION** Public Institution. Founded 1967. **Accreditation:** Regional (SACS/CC); dental assisting (ADA); dental hygiene (ADA); health information technology (AHIMA). **Total program enrollment:** 1880.

**PROGRAM(S) OFFERED**
• **Accounting Technology/Technician and Bookkeeping** *4 students enrolled* • **Administrative Assistant and Secretarial Science, General** *4 students enrolled* • **Agricultural Business and Management, General** • **Airframe Mechanics and Aircraft Maintenance Technology/Technician** *4 students enrolled* • **Autobody/Collision and Repair Technology/Technician** *7 students enrolled* • **Automobile/Automotive Mechanics Technology/Technician** *18 students enrolled* • **Business/Office Automation/Technology/Data Entry** *1 student enrolled* • **Commercial and Advertising Art** *2 students enrolled* • **Computer Technology/Computer Systems Technology** *4 students enrolled* • **Construction Engineering Technology/Technician** *3 students enrolled* • **Dental Assisting/Assistant** *21 students enrolled* • **Dental Laboratory Technology/Technician** *2 students enrolled* • **Electrical, Electronic and Communications Engineering Technology/Technician** • **Electromechanical Technology/Electromechanical Engineering Technology** • **Emergency Medical Technology/Technician (EMT Paramedic)** • **Heating, Air Conditioning, Ventilation and Refrigeration Maintenance Technology/Technician (HAC, HACR, HVAC, HVACR)** *9 students enrolled* • **Information Technology** • **Institutional Food Workers** *2 students enrolled* • **Machine Tool Technology/Machinist** *12 students enrolled* • **Medical Transcription/Transcriptionist** *14 students enrolled* • **Medical/Clinical Assistant** *10 students enrolled* • **Nurse/Nursing Assistant/Aide and Patient Care Assistant** • **Surgical Technology/Technologist** • **Teacher Assistant/Aide** *1 student enrolled* • **Telecommunications Technology/Technician** *5 students enrolled* • **Welding Technology/Welder** *32 students enrolled*

**STUDENT SERVICES** Academic or career counseling, daycare for children of students, employment services for current students, placement services for program completers, remedial services.

## Texas State Technical College Marshall

2650 East End Blvd. South, Marshall, TX 75671
http://www.marshall.tstc.edu/

**CONTACT** Mr. Randall Wooten, President
**Telephone:** 903-935-1010

**GENERAL INFORMATION** Public Institution. Founded 1991. **Total program enrollment:** 387.

**PROGRAM(S) OFFERED**
• **Diesel Mechanics Technology/Technician** *1 student enrolled* • **Industrial Technology/Technician** *6 students enrolled* • **Information Science/Studies** • **Mechanical Engineering/Mechanical Technology/Technician** *6 students enrolled* • **Occupational Safety and Health Technology/Technician** *1 student enrolled* • **Office Management and Supervision** *3 students enrolled* • **System, Networking, and LAN/WAN Management/Manager** • **Welding Technology/Welder** *17 students enrolled*

**STUDENT SERVICES** Academic or career counseling, employment services for current students, placement services for program completers, remedial services.

## Texas State Technical College System

3801 Campus Drive, System Admin, Waco, TX 76705-1607

**CONTACT** William Segura, Chancellor
**Telephone:** 254-799-3611

**GENERAL INFORMATION** Public Institution.

## Texas State Technical College Waco

3801 Campus Drive, Waco, TX 76705-1695
http://waco.tstc.edu/

**CONTACT** Elton E. Stuckly, Jr., President
**Telephone:** 800-792-8784

**GENERAL INFORMATION** Public Institution. Founded 1965. **Accreditation:** Regional (SACS/CC); dental assisting (ADA). **Total program enrollment:** 3200.

**PROGRAM(S) OFFERED**

• **Aircraft Powerplant Technology/Technician** *6 students enrolled* • **Airframe Mechanics and Aircraft Maintenance Technology/Technician** *9 students enrolled* • **Airline/Commercial/Professional Pilot and Flight Crew** *1 student enrolled* • **Autobody/Collision and Repair Technology/Technician** *38 students enrolled* • **Automobile/Automotive Mechanics Technology/Technician** *12 students enrolled* • **Cartography** *1 student enrolled* • **Chemical Technology/Technician** *22 students enrolled* • **Commercial and Advertising Art** *4 students enrolled* • **Computer Programming/Programmer, General** • **Computer Technology/Computer Systems Technology** *9 students enrolled* • **Computer and Information Systems Security** • **Construction Trades, General** • **Dental Assisting/Assistant** *64 students enrolled* • **Design and Visual Communications, General** • **Diesel Mechanics Technology/Technician** *26 students enrolled* • **Drafting and Design Technology/Technician, General** *1 student enrolled* • **Electrical, Electronic and Communications Engineering Technology/Technician** • **Heating, Air Conditioning and Refrigeration Technology/Technician (ACH/ACR/ACHR/HRAC/HVAC/AC Technology)** *14 students enrolled* • **Industrial Mechanics and Maintenance Technology** *9 students enrolled* • **Institutional Food Workers** *2 students enrolled* • **Instrumentation Technology/Technician** *1 student enrolled* • **Mechanical Engineering/Mechanical Technology/Technician** *7 students enrolled* • **Quality Control Technology/Technician** • **Radiation Protection/Health Physics Technician** *6 students enrolled* • **Robotics Technology/Technician** *6 students enrolled* • **System, Networking, and LAN/WAN Management/Manager** *2 students enrolled* • **Telecommunications Technology/Technician** *15 students enrolled* • **Turf and Turfgrass Management** *3 students enrolled* • **Web Page, Digital/Multimedia and Information Resources Design** • **Welding Technology/Welder** *6 students enrolled*

**STUDENT SERVICES** Academic or career counseling, employment services for current students, placement services for program completers, remedial services.

## Texas State Technical College West Texas

300 College Drive, Sweetwater, TX 79556-4108
http://www.westtexas.tstc.edu/

**CONTACT** Michael Reeser, President
**Telephone:** 325-235-7300

**GENERAL INFORMATION** Public Institution. Founded 1970. **Accreditation:** Regional (SACS/CC). **Total program enrollment:** 279.

**PROGRAM(S) OFFERED**

• **Aircraft Powerplant Technology/Technician** *5 students enrolled* • **Airframe Mechanics and Aircraft Maintenance Technology/Technician** *5 students enrolled* • **Autobody/Collision and Repair Technology/Technician** • **Automobile/Automotive Mechanics Technology/Technician** *4 students enrolled* • **Computer Engineering Technology/Technician** • **Computer Systems Networking and Telecommunications** *5 students enrolled* • **Construction Engineering Technology/Technician** • **Design and Visual Communications, General** • **Diesel Mechanics Technology/Technician** *6 students enrolled* • **Drafting and Design Technology/Technician, General** • **Electromechanical Technology/Electromechanical Engineering Technology** • **Emergency Medical Technology/Technician (EMT Paramedic)** • **Health Information/Medical Records Technology/Technician** • **Heating, Air Conditioning, Ventilation and Refrigeration Maintenance Technology/Technician (HAC, HACR, HVAC, HVACR)** *10 students enrolled* • **Licensed Practical/Vocational Nurse Training (LPN, LVN, Cert, Dipl, AAS)** *172 students enrolled* • **Machine Tool Technology/Machinist** • **Management Information Systems, General** • **Medical Insurance Coding Specialist/Coder** *7 students enrolled* • **Medical Transcription/Transcriptionist** *5 students enrolled* • **Restaurant, Culinary, and Catering Management/Manager** *2 students enrolled* • **Web Page, Digital/Multimedia and Information Resources Design** *1 student enrolled* • **Welding Technology/Welder** *10 students enrolled*

**STUDENT SERVICES** Academic or career counseling, employment services for current students, placement services for program completers, remedial services.

## Texas Vocational Schools

1921 East Red River, Victoria, TX 77901-5625
http://www.texasvocationalschools.com/

**CONTACT** Linda Simmons, Director
**Telephone:** 361-575-4768

**GENERAL INFORMATION** Private Institution. Founded 1967. **Total program enrollment:** 115. **Application fee:** $100.

**PROGRAM(S) OFFERED**

• **Administrative Assistant and Secretarial Science, General** *1080 hrs./$10,800* • **Business/Office Automation/Technology/Data Entry** *720 hrs./$7200* • **Legal Administrative Assistant/Secretary** *720 hrs./$7200* • **Medical Administrative/Executive Assistant and Medical Secretary** *720 hrs./$8582* • **Welding Technology/Welder** *720 hrs./$9360*

**STUDENT SERVICES** Employment services for current students, placement services for program completers.

## Toni & Guy Hairdressing Academy

2810 E. Trinity Mills Road, Suite 145, Carrollton, TX 75006
http://www.toniguy.com/

**CONTACT** Kent Movchan, Director
**Telephone:** 972-416-8396 Ext. 15

**GENERAL INFORMATION** Private Institution. **Total program enrollment:** 137. **Application fee:** $100.

**PROGRAM(S) OFFERED**

• **Cosmetology/Cosmetologist, General** *1500 hrs./$17,000*

**STUDENT SERVICES** Placement services for program completers.

## Touch of Class School of Cosmetology

111a Frontier Drive, Quinlan, TX 75474
http://www.tocsoc.com/

**CONTACT** Sharon Berry, Owner
**Telephone:** 903-455-1144

**GENERAL INFORMATION** Private Institution. **Total program enrollment:** 56. **Application fee:** $100.

**PROGRAM(S) OFFERED**

• **Cosmetology/Cosmetologist, General** *30 students enrolled*

## Trend Barber College

7725 W. Bellfort, Houston, TX 77071
http://trendbarbercollege.com/

**CONTACT** Obinna Mbachu, President
**Telephone:** 713-721-0000

**GENERAL INFORMATION** Private Institution. **Total program enrollment:** 83. **Application fee:** $35.

**PROGRAM(S) OFFERED**

• **Barbering/Barber** *1500 hrs./$10,485* • **Cosmetology, Barber/Styling, and Nail Instructor** *600 hrs./$3850* • **Nail Technician/Specialist and Manicurist**

**STUDENT SERVICES** Academic or career counseling, placement services for program completers, remedial services.

## Trinity Valley Community College

100 Cardinal Drive, Athens, TX 75751-2765
http://www.tvcc.edu/

**CONTACT** Dr. Glendon Forgey, President
**Telephone:** 903-675-6200

**GENERAL INFORMATION** Public Institution. Founded 1946. **Accreditation:** Regional (SACS/CC); surgical technology (ARCST). **Total program enrollment:** 2375.

**PROGRAM(S) OFFERED**

• **Accounting** *3 students enrolled* • **Administrative Assistant and Secretarial Science, General** *1 student enrolled* • **Applied Horticulture/Horticultural Operations, General** • **Autobody/Collision and Repair Technology/Technician** *30 students enrolled* • **Automobile/Automotive Mechanics Technology/Technician** *6 students enrolled* • **Business Administration and Management, General** *5*

*Trinity Valley Community College (continued)*

*students enrolled* • **Child Care and Support Services Management** *5 students enrolled* • **Computer Programming/Programmer, General** • **Computer Technology/Computer Systems Technology** *37 students enrolled* • **Computer and Information Sciences, General** *2 students enrolled* • **Corrections** • **Cosmetology/Cosmetologist, General** *22 students enrolled* • **Criminal Justice/Police Science** *2 students enrolled* • **Drafting and Design Technology/Technician, General** *54 students enrolled* • **Electrical, Electronic and Communications Engineering Technology/Technician** *43 students enrolled* • **Emergency Medical Technology/Technician (EMT Paramedic)** *6 students enrolled* • **Farm/Farm and Ranch Management** *3 students enrolled* • **Fire Science/Firefighting** *3 students enrolled* • **Heating, Air Conditioning, Ventilation and Refrigeration Maintenance Technology/Technician (HAC, HACR, HVAC, HVACR)** *31 students enrolled* • **Legal Administrative Assistant/Secretary** *1 student enrolled* • **Licensed Practical/Vocational Nurse Training (LPN, LVN, Cert, Dipl, AAS)** *48 students enrolled* • **Mason/Masonry** *24 students enrolled* • **Medical Administrative/Executive Assistant and Medical Secretary** • **Medical Transcription/Transcriptionist** *8 students enrolled* • **Nurse/Nursing Assistant/Aide and Patient Care Assistant** *24 students enrolled* • **Surgical Technology/Technologist** *4 students enrolled* • **Welding Technology/Welder** *11 students enrolled*

**STUDENT SERVICES** Academic or career counseling, employment services for current students, placement services for program completers, remedial services.

## Tri-State Cosmetology Institute 1

6800 Gateway E., Building 4A, El Paso, TX 79902
http://www.tristatecosmetology.com/

**CONTACT** Amy Parker, Owner
**Telephone:** 915-533-8274

**GENERAL INFORMATION** Private Institution. **Total program enrollment:** 246.

**PROGRAM(S) OFFERED**
• **Cosmetology, Barber/Styling, and Nail Instructor** *750 hrs./$4500* • **Cosmetology/Cosmetologist, General** *1500 hrs./$9287* • **Facial Treatment Specialist/Facialist** *750 hrs./$6500* • **Nail Technician/Specialist and Manicurist** *600 hrs./$4500*

**STUDENT SERVICES** Academic or career counseling, placement services for program completers.

## Tyler Junior College

PO Box 9020, Tyler, TX 75711-9020
http://www.tjc.edu/

**CONTACT** Mike Metke, President
**Telephone:** 903-510-2200

**GENERAL INFORMATION** Public Institution. Founded 1926. **Accreditation:** Regional (SACS/CC); dental hygiene (ADA); diagnostic medical sonography (JRCEDMS); health information technology (AHIMA); medical laboratory technology (NAACLS); ophthalmic laboratory technology (COA); radiologic technology: radiography (JRCERT); surgical technology (ARCST). **Total program enrollment:** 6099.

**PROGRAM(S) OFFERED**
• **Administrative Assistant and Secretarial Science, General** • **Automobile/Automotive Mechanics Technology/Technician** *12 students enrolled* • **Business Administration and Management, General** *17 students enrolled* • **Business/Office Automation/Technology/Data Entry** • **Cartography** • **Child Care Provider/Assistant** • **Child Care and Support Services Management** *6 students enrolled* • **Child Development** *8 students enrolled* • **Commercial Photography** *5 students enrolled* • **Commercial and Advertising Art** • **Computer Engineering Technology/Technician** • **Computer Programming/Programmer, General** • **Computer Systems Networking and Telecommunications** *1 student enrolled* • **Computer Technology/Computer Systems Technology** *6 students enrolled* • **Computer and Information Sciences, General** • **Criminal Justice/Police Science** • **Data Processing and Data Processing Technology/Technician** • **Diagnostic Medical Sonography/Sonographer and Ultrasound Technician** *11 students enrolled* • **Drafting and Design Technology/Technician, General** *7 students enrolled* • **Electrical, Electronic and Communications Engineering Technology/Technician** • **Emergency Medical Technology/Technician (EMT Paramedic)** *49 students enrolled* • **Farm/Farm and Ranch Management** • **Fire Protection and Safety Technology/Technician** • **Graphic Design** *5 students enrolled* • **Health Information/Medical Records Technology/Technician** • **Heating, Air Conditioning, Ventilation and Refrigeration Maintenance Technology/Technician (HAC, HACR, HVAC, HVACR)** • **Licensed Practical/Vocational Nurse Training (LPN, LVN, Cert, Dipl, AAS)** *134 students enrolled* • **Medical Administrative/Executive Assistant and Medical Secretary** *18 students enrolled* • **Medical Office Management/Administration** • **Medical Transcription/Transcriptionist** *8 students enrolled* • **Opticianry/Ophthalmic Dispensing Optician** • **Optometric Technician/Assistant** *15 students enrolled* • **Physical Education Teaching and Coaching** *4 students enrolled* • **Respiratory Care Therapy/Therapist** • **Sign Language Interpretation and Translation** *2 students enrolled* • **Substance Abuse/Addiction Counseling** • **Surgical Technology/Technologist** *10 students enrolled* • **Survey Technology/Surveying** *18 students enrolled* • **Telecommunications Technology/Technician** • **Welding Technology/Welder** *26 students enrolled*

**STUDENT SERVICES** Academic or career counseling, employment services for current students, placement services for program completers, remedial services.

## Universal Technical Institute

721 Lockhaven Drive, Houston, TX 77073-5598
http://www.uticorp.com/

**CONTACT** Ken Golaszewski, Campus President
**Telephone:** 281-443-6262

**GENERAL INFORMATION** Private Institution. Founded 1983. **Accreditation:** State accredited or approved. **Total program enrollment:** 1897.

**PROGRAM(S) OFFERED**
• **Autobody/Collision and Repair Technology/Technician** *162 students enrolled* • **Automobile/Automotive Mechanics Technology/Technician** *107 hrs./$34,350* • **Diesel Mechanics Technology/Technician** *146 students enrolled*

## University of Cosmetology Arts and Sciences

913 North 13th Street, Harlingen, TX 78550

**CONTACT** Sylvia R. Wall, Executive Director
**Telephone:** 956-412-1212

**GENERAL INFORMATION** Private Institution. **Total program enrollment:** 34. **Application fee:** $100.

**PROGRAM(S) OFFERED**
• **Aesthetician/Esthetician and Skin Care Specialist** *750 hrs./$9050* • **Cosmetology, Barber/Styling, and Nail Instructor** *750 hrs./$8250* • **Cosmetology/Cosmetologist, General** *1500 hrs./$14,829* • **Nail Technician/Specialist and Manicurist** *600 hrs./$6050*

**STUDENT SERVICES** Placement services for program completers.

## University of Cosmetology Arts and Sciences

PO Box 720391, McAllen, TX 78504

**CONTACT** Cindy Sandoval, President
**Telephone:** 956-687-9444

**GENERAL INFORMATION** Private Institution. Founded 1976. **Total program enrollment:** 157. **Application fee:** $100.

**PROGRAM(S) OFFERED**
• **Cosmetology, Barber/Styling, and Nail Instructor** *750 hrs./$7802* • **Cosmetology/Cosmetologist, General** *1500 hrs./$14,829* • **Facial Treatment Specialist/Facialist** *750 hrs./$8545* • **Hair Styling/Stylist and Hair Design** *150 hrs./$1777* • **Nail Technician/Specialist and Manicurist** *600 hrs./$5947*

**STUDENT SERVICES** Placement services for program completers.

## University of Phoenix–Dallas Campus

Churchill Tower, 12400 Coit Road, Suite 200, Dallas, TX 75251-2009
http://www.phoenix.edu/

**CONTACT** William Pepicello, PhD, President
**Telephone:** 972-385-1055

**GENERAL INFORMATION** Private Institution. Founded 2001. **Accreditation:** Regional (NCA). **Total program enrollment:** 1482.

**STUDENT SERVICES** Academic or career counseling, remedial services.

## University of Phoenix–Houston Campus

11451 Katy Freeway, Suite 100, Houston, TX 77079-2004
http://www.phoenix.edu/

**CONTACT** William Pepicello, PhD, President
**Telephone:** 713-465-9966

**GENERAL INFORMATION** Private Institution. Founded 2001. **Accreditation:** Regional (NCA). **Total program enrollment:** 2949.

**PROGRAM(S) OFFERED**
• **Business Administration and Management, General** *3 students enrolled* • **Human Resources Management/Personnel Administration, General** *17 students enrolled*

**STUDENT SERVICES** Academic or career counseling, remedial services.

## The University of Texas Anderson Cancer Center

1515 Holcombe Boulevard, Houston, TX 77030
http://www.mdanderson.org/

**CONTACT** John Mendelsohn, MD, President
**Telephone:** 800-392-1611

**GENERAL INFORMATION** Private Institution. **Total program enrollment:** 203.

**PROGRAM(S) OFFERED**
• **Clinical Laboratory Science/Medical Technology/Technologist** *9 students enrolled* • **Cytogenetics/Genetics/Clinical Genetics Technology/Technologist** *1 student enrolled* • **Cytotechnology/Cytotechnologist** • **Health/Medical Physics** *4 students enrolled* • **Medical Radiologic Technology/Science—Radiation Therapist**

**STUDENT SERVICES** Academic or career counseling.

## The University of Texas Health Science Center at San Antonio

7703 Floyd Curl Drive, San Antonio, TX 78229-3900
http://www.uthscsa.edu/

**CONTACT** Francisco G. Cigarroa, MD, President
**Telephone:** 210-567-2621

**GENERAL INFORMATION** Public Institution. Founded 1976. **Accreditation:** Regional (SACS/CC); dental hygiene (ADA); dental laboratory technology (ADA); emergency medical services (JRCEMTP); histologic technology (NAACLS); medical technology (NAACLS). **Total program enrollment:** 2589. **Application fee:** $45.

**PROGRAM(S) OFFERED**
• **Emergency Medical Technology/Technician (EMT Paramedic)** *131 students enrolled*

**STUDENT SERVICES** Academic or career counseling.

## Valley Grande Academy

1000 South Bridge Avenue, Weslaco, TX 78596
http://valleygrandeacademy.org/

**CONTACT** Anabell C. Cardona, President, CEO
**Telephone:** 956-973-1945

**GENERAL INFORMATION** Private Institution. Founded 1947. **Total program enrollment:** 439. **Application fee:** $100.

**PROGRAM(S) OFFERED**
• **Allied Health and Medical Assisting Services, Other** *44 students enrolled* • **Clinical/Medical Laboratory Assistant** *75 students enrolled* • **Electrocardiograph Technology/Technician** *44 students enrolled* • **Health Professions and Related Clinical Sciences, Other** *60 students enrolled* • **Licensed Practical/Vocational Nurse Training (LPN, LVN, Cert, Dipl, AAS)** *1530 hrs./$17,730* • **Medical Insurance Specialist/Medical Biller** *665 hrs./$7315* • **Medical Radiologic Technology/Science—Radiation Therapist** *970 hrs./$9700* • **Nurse/Nursing Assistant/Aide and Patient Care Assistant** *620 hrs./$6820* • **Pharmacy Technician/Assistant** *740 hrs./$8140* • **Physical Therapy/Therapist** *715 hrs./$7445*

**STUDENT SERVICES** Academic or career counseling, employment services for current students, placement services for program completers.

## Vatterott Education Center

9713 Harry Hines Boulevard, Suite 100, Dallas, TX 75220

**CONTACT** Rick Evans, Campus Director
**Telephone:** 214-352-8288

**GENERAL INFORMATION** Private Institution. **Total program enrollment:** 161.

**PROGRAM(S) OFFERED**
• **Allied Health and Medical Assisting Services, Other** *7 students enrolled* • **Cosmetology/Cosmetologist, General** *4 students enrolled* • **Heating, Air Conditioning, Ventilation and Refrigeration Maintenance Technology/Technician (HAC, HACR, HVAC, HVACR)** *5 students enrolled*

**STUDENT SERVICES** Academic or career counseling, employment services for current students, placement services for program completers.

## Velma B's Beauty Academy

1511 S. Ewing Avenue., Dallas, TX 75216
http://www.velmabs.com/

**CONTACT** Terry L. Brooks, Director
**Telephone:** 214-942-1541

**GENERAL INFORMATION** Private Institution. **Total program enrollment:** 54. **Application fee:** $100.

**PROGRAM(S) OFFERED**
• **Cosmetology, Barber/Styling, and Nail Instructor** *750 hrs./$4149* • **Cosmetology/Cosmetologist, General** *1500 hrs./$10,350*

**STUDENT SERVICES** Academic or career counseling, placement services for program completers.

## Vernon College

4400 College Drive, Vernon, TX 76384-4092
http://www.vernoncollege.edu/

**CONTACT** John B. Hardin, III, Interim President
**Telephone:** 940-552-6291

**GENERAL INFORMATION** Public Institution. Founded 1970. **Accreditation:** Regional (SACS/CC); health information technology (AHIMA). **Total program enrollment:** 800. **Application fee:** $10.

*Vernon College (continued)*

**PROGRAM(S) OFFERED**

• **Automobile/Automotive Mechanics Technology/Technician** • **Business/Commerce, General** *2 students enrolled* • **Business/Office Automation/Technology/Data Entry** • **Child Care Provider/Assistant** • **Child Care and Support Services Management** • **Child Development** • **Computer and Information Sciences, General** *2 students enrolled* • **Cosmetology/Cosmetologist, General** *28 students enrolled* • **Criminal Justice/Safety Studies** *1 student enrolled* • **Drafting and Design Technology/Technician, General** • **Electrical, Electronic and Communications Engineering Technology/Technician** *4 students enrolled* • **Emergency Medical Technology/Technician (EMT Paramedic)** *16 students enrolled* • **Farm/Farm and Ranch Management** • **Fire Science/Firefighting** *3 students enrolled* • **General Office Occupations and Clerical Services** *2 students enrolled* • **Health Information/Medical Records Technology/Technician** *5 students enrolled* • **Heating, Air Conditioning and Refrigeration Technology/Technician (ACH/ACR/ACHR/HRAC/HVAC/AC Technology)** *7 students enrolled* • **Language Interpretation and Translation** *2 students enrolled* • **Licensed Practical/Vocational Nurse Training (LPN, LVN, Cert, Dipl, AAS)** *82 students enrolled* • **Machine Tool Technology/Machinist** *3 students enrolled* • **Medical Administrative/Executive Assistant and Medical Secretary** *3 students enrolled* • **Medical Transcription/Transcriptionist** • **Pharmacy Technician/Assistant** *3 students enrolled* • **Surgical Technology/Technologist** *17 students enrolled* • **Welding Technology/Welder** *20 students enrolled*

**STUDENT SERVICES** Academic or career counseling, employment services for current students, placement services for program completers, remedial services.

## Victoria Beauty College, Inc.

1508 North Laurent Street, Victoria, TX 77901

**CONTACT** Rhonda Floyd, President Owner
**Telephone:** 361-575-4526

**GENERAL INFORMATION** Private Institution. **Total program enrollment:** 33.

**PROGRAM(S) OFFERED**

• **Cosmetology, Barber/Styling, and Nail Instructor** *750 hrs./$5050* • **Cosmetology/Cosmetologist, General** *1500 hrs./$10,000* • **Nail Technician/Specialist and Manicurist** *600 hrs./$5050*

**STUDENT SERVICES** Academic or career counseling, placement services for program completers.

## Victoria College

2200 East Red River, Victoria, TX 77901-4494
http://www.victoriacollege.edu/

**CONTACT** Dr. Thomas Butler, President
**Telephone:** 361-573-3291

**GENERAL INFORMATION** Public Institution. Founded 1925. **Accreditation:** Regional (SACS/CC); medical laboratory technology (NAACLS). **Total program enrollment:** 1326.

**PROGRAM(S) OFFERED**

• **Accounting Technology/Technician and Bookkeeping** • **Administrative Assistant and Secretarial Science, General** • **Business Administration and Management, General** *8 students enrolled* • **Business/Office Automation/Technology/Data Entry** *9 students enrolled* • **Chemical Technology/Technician** • **Child Care and Support Services Management** *2 students enrolled* • **Child Development** • **Computer Systems Analysis/Analyst** • **Computer Systems Networking and Telecommunications** *8 students enrolled* • **Criminal Justice/Police Science** *25 students enrolled* • **Drafting and Design Technology/Technician, General** • **Electrical, Electronic and Communications Engineering Technology/Technician** *3 students enrolled* • **Emergency Medical Technology/Technician (EMT Paramedic)** *21 students enrolled* • **Executive Assistant/Executive Secretary** • **Fire Science/Firefighting** *3 students enrolled* • **General Office Occupations and Clerical Services** • **Legal Assistant/Paralegal** • **Licensed Practical/Vocational Nurse Training (LPN, LVN, Cert, Dipl, AAS)** *129 students enrolled* • **Medical Administrative/Executive Assistant and Medical Secretary** • **Respiratory Care Therapy/Therapist** • **Web Page, Digital/Multimedia and Information Resources Design** *9 students enrolled* • **Welding Technology/Welder** *16 students enrolled*

**STUDENT SERVICES** Academic or career counseling, employment services for current students, remedial services.

## Virginia College at Austin

6301 East Highway 290, Austin, TX 78723
http://www.vc.edu/

**CONTACT** Harvey Giblin, President
**Telephone:** 512-371-3500

**GENERAL INFORMATION** Private Institution. Founded 2002. **Accreditation:** State accredited or approved. **Total program enrollment:** 282. **Application fee:** $100.

**PROGRAM(S) OFFERED**

• **Administrative Assistant and Secretarial Science, General** *7 students enrolled* • **Computer Engineering Technology/Technician** *8 students enrolled* • **Medical Insurance Coding Specialist/Coder** *23 students enrolled* • **Medical/Clinical Assistant** *41 students enrolled* • **Pharmacy Technician/Assistant** *17 students enrolled* • **Veterinary/Animal Health Technology/Technician and Veterinary Assistant** *12 students enrolled*

**STUDENT SERVICES** Academic or career counseling, employment services for current students, placement services for program completers, remedial services.

## Weatherford College

225 College Park Avenue, Weatherford, TX 76086-5699
http://www.wc.edu/

**CONTACT** Joseph C. Birmingham, President
**Telephone:** 817-594-5471

**GENERAL INFORMATION** Public Institution. Founded 1869. **Accreditation:** Regional (SACS/CC). **Total program enrollment:** 2284.

**PROGRAM(S) OFFERED**

• **Accounting Technology/Technician and Bookkeeping** *4 students enrolled* • **Child Development** *1 student enrolled* • **Computer Programming/Programmer, General** *9 students enrolled* • **Computer Systems Networking and Telecommunications** *1 student enrolled* • **Cosmetology/Cosmetologist, General** *11 students enrolled* • **Criminal Justice/Police Science** *9 students enrolled* • **Electrical, Electronic and Communications Engineering Technology/Technician** *1 student enrolled* • **Executive Assistant/Executive Secretary** *3 students enrolled* • **Fire Science/Firefighting** *3 students enrolled* • **General Office Occupations and Clerical Services** *2 students enrolled* • **Licensed Practical/Vocational Nurse Training (LPN, LVN, Cert, Dipl, AAS)** *46 students enrolled* • **Pharmacy Technician/Assistant** *12 students enrolled* • **Veterinary/Animal Health Technology/Technician and Veterinary Assistant** *6 students enrolled*

**STUDENT SERVICES** Academic or career counseling, employment services for current students, placement services for program completers, remedial services.

## Western Technical College

9451 Diana, El Paso, TX 79930-2610
http://www.wtc-ep.edu/

**CONTACT** Mary Cano, School Director
**Telephone:** 915-566-9621

**GENERAL INFORMATION** Private Institution. **Accreditation:** State accredited or approved. **Total program enrollment:** 438. **Application fee:** $100.

**PROGRAM(S) OFFERED**

• **Computer and Information Sciences and Support Services, Other** *1800 hrs./$28,404* • **Electrical, Electronic and Communications Engineering Technology/Technician** *1800 hrs./$25,704* • **Health and Medical Administrative Services, Other** *1000 hrs./$12,640* • **Massage Therapy/Therapeutic Massage** *600 hrs./$6552* • **Medical/Clinical Assistant** *1000 hrs./$11,640* • **Physical Therapist Assistant** *1732 hrs./$27,020*

**STUDENT SERVICES** Academic or career counseling, employment services for current students, placement services for program completers, remedial services.

## Western Technical College

9624 Plaza Circle, El Paso, TX 79927
http://www.wtc-ep.edu/

**CONTACT** Allan Sharpe, President
**Telephone:** 915-532-3737

**GENERAL INFORMATION** Private Institution. **Accreditation:** State accredited or approved. **Total program enrollment:** 609. **Application fee:** $100.

**PROGRAM(S) OFFERED**
• **Automobile/Automotive Mechanics Technology/Technician** *1500 hrs./$22,065* • **Clinical/Medical Laboratory Assistant** *1000 hrs./$11,640* • **Diesel Mechanics Technology/Technician** *1400 hrs./$20,594* • **Health Information/Medical Records Technology/Technician** *12 students enrolled* • **Heating, Air Conditioning and Refrigeration Technology/Technician (ACH/ACR/ACHR/HRAC/HVAC/AC Technology)** *1500 hrs./$22,065* • **Medical/Clinical Assistant** *127 students enrolled* • **Welding Technology/Welder** *1500 hrs./$24,810*

**STUDENT SERVICES** Employment services for current students, placement services for program completers, remedial services.

## Western Texas College

6200 College Avenue, Snyder, TX 79549-6105
http://www.wtc.edu/

**CONTACT** Mike Dreith, President
**Telephone:** 325-573-8511

**GENERAL INFORMATION** Public Institution. Founded 1969. **Accreditation:** Regional (SACS/CC). **Total program enrollment:** 406.

**PROGRAM(S) OFFERED**
• **Administrative Assistant and Secretarial Science, General** • **Business/Office Automation/Technology/Data Entry** *8 students enrolled* • **Child Care and Support Services Management** • **Computer Systems Networking and Telecommunications** *12 students enrolled* • **Criminal Justice/Police Science** • **Emergency Medical Technology/Technician (EMT Paramedic)** • **Heating, Air Conditioning, Ventilation and Refrigeration Maintenance Technology/Technician (HAC, HACR, HVAC, HVACR)** *11 students enrolled* • **Licensed Practical/Vocational Nurse Training (LPN, LVN, Cert, Dipl, AAS)** *15 students enrolled* • **Plant Nursery Operations and Management** *33 students enrolled* • **Turf and Turfgrass Management** *1 student enrolled* • **Welding Technology/Welder** *26 students enrolled*

**STUDENT SERVICES** Academic or career counseling, employment services for current students, placement services for program completers, remedial services.

## Westwood College–Dallas

Executive Plaza I, Suite 100, Dallas, TX 75243
http://www.westwood.edu/

**CONTACT** Paul Kepic, Executive Director
**Telephone:** 214-570-0100

**GENERAL INFORMATION** Private Institution. Founded 2002. **Accreditation:** State accredited or approved. **Total program enrollment:** 567. **Application fee:** $25.

**PROGRAM(S) OFFERED**
• **Medical Insurance Coding Specialist/Coder** *60 students enrolled* • **Medical/Clinical Assistant** *68 students enrolled*

**STUDENT SERVICES** Academic or career counseling, employment services for current students, placement services for program completers, remedial services.

## Westwood College–Ft. Worth

4232 North Freeway, Fort Worth, TX 76137
http://www.westwood.edu/

**CONTACT** David F. Bostick, Executive Director
**Telephone:** 817-547-9600

**GENERAL INFORMATION** Private Institution. **Total program enrollment:** 393. **Application fee:** $25.

**PROGRAM(S) OFFERED**
• **Medical Office Assistant/Specialist** *34 students enrolled* • **Medical/Clinical Assistant** *51 students enrolled*

**STUDENT SERVICES** Academic or career counseling, employment services for current students, placement services for program completers, remedial services.

## Westwood College–Houston South Campus

One Arena Place, 7322 Southwest Freeway, Suite 1900, Houston, TX 77074
http://www.westwood.edu/

**CONTACT** Rick Skinner, Executive Director
**Telephone:** 713-777-4433

**GENERAL INFORMATION** Private Institution. Founded 2003. **Accreditation:** State accredited or approved. **Total program enrollment:** 406. **Application fee:** $25.

**PROGRAM(S) OFFERED**
• **Medical Insurance Coding Specialist/Coder** *56 students enrolled* • **Medical/Clinical Assistant** *49 students enrolled*

**STUDENT SERVICES** Academic or career counseling, employment services for current students, placement services for program completers, remedial services.

## Wharton County Junior College

911 Boling Highway, Wharton, TX 77488-3298
http://www.wcjc.edu/

**CONTACT** Betty McCrohan, President
**Telephone:** 979-532-4560

**GENERAL INFORMATION** Public Institution. Founded 1946. **Accreditation:** Regional (SACS/CC); dental hygiene (ADA); health information technology (AHIMA); physical therapy assisting (APTA); radiologic technology: radiography (JRCERT). **Total program enrollment:** 2640.

**PROGRAM(S) OFFERED**
• **Administrative Assistant and Secretarial Science, General** *15 students enrolled* • **Architectural Drafting and Architectural CAD/CADD** *14 students enrolled* • **Automobile/Automotive Mechanics Technology/Technician** *10 students enrolled* • **Child Care and Support Services Management** • **Child Development** *2 students enrolled* • **Computer Systems Networking and Telecommunications** *4 students enrolled* • **Computer and Information Sciences, General** *4 students enrolled* • **Cosmetology/Cosmetologist, General** *19 students enrolled* • **Criminal Justice/Police Science** *48 students enrolled* • **Drafting and Design Technology/Technician, General** *9 students enrolled* • **Emergency Medical Technology/Technician (EMT Paramedic)** *5 students enrolled* • **Fire Science/Firefighting** *19 students enrolled* • **Heating, Air Conditioning, Ventilation and Refrigeration Maintenance Technology/Technician (HAC, HACR, HVAC, HVACR)** *4 students enrolled* • **Legal Assistant/Paralegal** *7 students enrolled* • **Licensed Practical/Vocational Nurse Training (LPN, LVN, Cert, Dipl, AAS)** *50 students enrolled* • **Surgical Technology/Technologist** *6 students enrolled*

**STUDENT SERVICES** Academic or career counseling, remedial services.

# UTAH

## American Institute of Medical-Dental Technology

1675 North Freedom Boulevard, Building 5A, Provo, UT 84604
http://www.ameritech.edu/

**CONTACT** Kenneth Bentley, CEO
**Telephone:** 801-377-2900

**GENERAL INFORMATION** Private Institution. Founded 1979. **Total program enrollment:** 100. **Application fee:** $50.

**PROGRAM(S) OFFERED**
• **Dental Assisting/Assistant** *34 hrs./$11,781* • **Massage Therapy/Therapeutic Massage** *5 students enrolled* • **Medical Office Management/Administration** *36 hrs./$12,301* • **Medical/Clinical Assistant** *37 hrs./$12,648* • **Pharmacy Technician/Assistant** *17 students enrolled* • **Surgical Technology/Technologist** *46 hrs./$17,332*

**STUDENT SERVICES** Academic or career counseling, placement services for program completers.

## AmeriTech College

12257 South Business Park Drive, Suite 108, Draper, UT 84020-6545
http://www.ameritech.edu/

**CONTACT** Ken Bentley, CEO
**Telephone:** 801-816-1444

**GENERAL INFORMATION** Private Institution. **Total program enrollment:** 363. **Application fee:** $50.

**PROGRAM(S) OFFERED**
• **Dental Laboratory Technology/Technician** *52 hrs./$16,265* • **Licensed Practical/Vocational Nurse Training (LPN, LVN, Cert, Dipl, AAS)** *43 hrs./$23,997* • **Nursing—Registered Nurse Training (RN, ASN, BSN, MSN)** *72 hrs./$42,499*

**STUDENT SERVICES** Academic or career counseling, placement services for program completers.

## The Art Institute of Salt Lake City

121 West Election Road, Draper, UT 84020-9492
http://www.artinstitutes.edu/SaltLakeCity/

**CONTACT** Ronald Moss, Campus President
**Telephone:** 800-978-0096

**GENERAL INFORMATION** Private Institution. **Total program enrollment:** 142. **Application fee:** $50.

**PROGRAM(S) OFFERED**
• **Baking and Pastry Arts/Baker/Pastry Chef** • **Culinary Arts/Chef Training** *1 student enrolled*

**STUDENT SERVICES** Academic or career counseling, employment services for current students.

## Bon Losee Academy of Hair Artistry

2230 North University Parkway, Building 5, Provo, UT 84604
http://bonlosee.com/

**CONTACT** Norma Child, Finance Officer
**Telephone:** 801-375-8000

**GENERAL INFORMATION** Private Institution. Founded 1987. **Total program enrollment:** 169. **Application fee:** $50.

**PROGRAM(S) OFFERED**
• **Aesthetician/Esthetician and Skin Care Specialist** *600 hrs./$6000*
• **Cosmetology/Cosmetologist, General** *2000 hrs./$12,500*

**STUDENT SERVICES** Academic or career counseling, placement services for program completers.

## Bridgerland Applied Technology Center

1301 North 600 West, Logan, UT 84321
http://www.batc.edu

**CONTACT** Richard L. Maughan, Campus President
**Telephone:** 435-753-6780

**GENERAL INFORMATION** Public Institution. Founded 1971. **Total program enrollment:** 227.

**PROGRAM(S) OFFERED**
• **Administrative Assistant and Secretarial Science, General** *21 students enrolled* • **Aesthetician/Esthetician and Skin Care Specialist** *4 students enrolled* • **Autobody/Collision and Repair Technology/Technician** • **Automobile/Automotive Mechanics Technology/Technician** *1590 hrs./$2033* • **CAD/CADD Drafting and/or Design Technology/Technician** *1500 hrs./$2033* • **Cabinetmaking and Millwork/Millwright** • **Carpentry/Carpenter** *4 students enrolled* • **Computer and Information Sciences, General** *1 student enrolled* • **Cosmetology/Cosmetologist, General** *2000 hrs./$3043* • **Criminal Justice/Police Science** *24 students enrolled* • **Dental Assisting/Assistant** *1530 hrs./$2033* • **Diesel Mechanics Technology/Technician** *10 students enrolled* • **E-Commerce/Electronic Commerce** • **Fashion Merchandising** *4 students enrolled* • **Fire Science/Firefighting** *1 student enrolled* • **Food Preparation/Professional Cooking/Kitchen Assistant** *1650 hrs./$2033* • **Industrial Electronics Technology/Technician** *24 students enrolled* • **Industrial Mechanics and Maintenance Technology** *10 students enrolled* • **Interior Design** • **Licensed Practical/Vocational Nurse Training (LPN, LVN, Cert, Dipl, AAS)** *48 students enrolled* • **Machine Tool Technology/Machinist** *1575 hrs./$2033* • **Meat Cutting/Meat Cutter** *2 students enrolled* • **Medical Administrative/Executive Assistant and Medical Secretary** *7 students enrolled* • **Medical Insurance Coding Specialist/Coder** *6 students enrolled* • **Medical Transcription/Transcriptionist** *13 students enrolled* • **Medical/Clinical Assistant** *17 students enrolled* • **Nail Technician/Specialist and Manicurist** *15 students enrolled* • **Pharmacy Technician/Assistant** *27 students enrolled* • **Truck and Bus Driver/Commercial Vehicle Operation** *24 students enrolled* • **Veterinary/Animal Health Technology/Technician and Veterinary Assistant** *13 students enrolled* • **Web Page, Digital/Multimedia and Information Resources Design** *4 students enrolled* • **Welding Technology/Welder** *15 students enrolled*

**STUDENT SERVICES** Academic or career counseling, employment services for current students, placement services for program completers, remedial services.

## Cameo College of Beauty Skin and Electrolysis

1600 South State Street, Salt Lake City, UT 84115
http://www.cameocollege.com/

**CONTACT** Brenda G. Scharman, Owner
**Telephone:** 801-747-5700

**GENERAL INFORMATION** Private Institution. Founded 1970. **Total program enrollment:** 108. **Application fee:** $50.

**PROGRAM(S) OFFERED**
• **Aesthetician/Esthetician and Skin Care Specialist** *600 hrs./$6450* • **Barbering/Barber** • **Cosmetology/Cosmetologist, General** *2000 hrs./$15,450* • **Electrolysis/Electrology and Electrolysis Technician** *600 hrs./$5250* • **Nail Technician/Specialist and Manicurist** *300 hrs./$1750*

**STUDENT SERVICES** Placement services for program completers.

## Careers Unlimited

1176 South 1480 West, Orem, UT 84058
http://www.ucdh.edu/

**CONTACT** Dave Owens, Financial Aid Director
**Telephone:** 801-426-8234

**GENERAL INFORMATION** Private Institution. **Total program enrollment:** 121. **Application fee:** $50.

**PROGRAM(S) OFFERED**
• **Dental Assisting/Assistant** *350 hrs./$3945* • **Dental Hygiene/Hygienist** *87 hrs./$49,950*

**STUDENT SERVICES** Academic or career counseling, employment services for current students, placement services for program completers.

## Certified Careers Institute

775 South 2000 East, Clearfield, UT 84015
http://www.cciutah.edu/

**CONTACT** Robert Enger, Director
**Telephone:** 801-774-9900

**GENERAL INFORMATION** Private Institution. Founded 1983. **Total program enrollment:** 86. **Application fee:** $100.

**PROGRAM(S) OFFERED**
• **Business Administration and Management, General** *900 hrs./$12,200* • **Dental Assisting/Assistant** *760 hrs./$13,650* • **Massage Therapy/Therapeutic Massage** *760 hrs./$12,900* • **Medical Office Assistant/Specialist** *880 hrs./ $12,900* • **Medical/Clinical Assistant** *910 hrs./$13,630* • **Web Page, Digital/ Multimedia and Information Resources Design** *900 hrs./$13,050*

**STUDENT SERVICES** Academic or career counseling, placement services for program completers.

## Certified Careers Institute

1455 West 2200 South, Suite 200, Salt Lake City, UT 84119
http://www.cciutah.edu/

**CONTACT** Robert Enger, Director
**Telephone:** 801-973-7008

**GENERAL INFORMATION** Private Institution. Founded 1983. **Total program enrollment:** 11. **Application fee:** $100.

**PROGRAM(S) OFFERED**
• **Business Administration and Management, General** *900 hrs./$12,200* • **Dental Assisting/Assistant** *760 hrs./$13,650* • **Massage Therapy/Therapeutic Massage** *760 hrs./$12,900* • **Medical Office Assistant/Specialist** *880 hrs./ $12,900* • **Medical/Clinical Assistant** *910 hrs./$13,630* • **Web Page, Digital/ Multimedia and Information Resources Design** *900 hrs./$13,050*

**STUDENT SERVICES** Academic or career counseling, placement services for program completers.

## College of Eastern Utah

451 East 400 North, Price, UT 84501-2699
http://www.ceu.edu/

**CONTACT** Mike King, Interim President
**Telephone:** 435-637-2120 Ext. 0

**GENERAL INFORMATION** Public Institution. Founded 1937. **Accreditation:** Regional (NCCU/NCCU). **Total program enrollment:** 1093. **Application fee:** $25.

**PROGRAM(S) OFFERED**
• **Accounting** *1 student enrolled* • **Administrative Assistant and Secretarial Science, General** *3 students enrolled* • **Automobile/Automotive Mechanics Technology/Technician** • **Building/Construction Finishing, Management, and Inspection, Other** • **Business Administration and Management, General** • **Business/Commerce, General** • **CAD/CADD Drafting and/or Design Technology/Technician** *4 students enrolled* • **Commercial and Advertising Art** • **Computer Systems Analysis/Analyst** • **Construction/Heavy Equipment/ Earthmoving Equipment Operation** • **Cosmetology/Cosmetologist, General** • **Data Processing and Data Processing Technology/Technician** • **Diesel Mechanics Technology/Technician** • **Early Childhood Education and Teaching** • **Electrical, Electronic and Communications Engineering Technology/ Technician** *6 students enrolled* • **Information Science/Studies** • **Licensed Practical/Vocational Nurse Training (LPN, LVN, Cert, Dipl, AAS)** *43 students enrolled* • **Mining Technology/Technician** • **Nursing—Registered Nurse Training (RN, ASN, BSN, MSN)** • **System Administration/Administrator** • **System, Networking, and LAN/WAN Management/Manager** • **Web Page, Digital/ Multimedia and Information Resources Design** • **Welding Technology/Welder**

**STUDENT SERVICES** Academic or career counseling, employment services for current students, placement services for program completers, remedial services.

## Dallas Roberts Academy of Hair Design & Aesthetics

1700 N. State Street, Suite 18, Provo, UT 84604
dallasroberts.com

**CONTACT** Craig Fletcher
**Telephone:** 801-375-1521

**GENERAL INFORMATION** Private Institution. **Total program enrollment:** 112. **Application fee:** $50.

**PROGRAM(S) OFFERED**
• **Aesthetician/Esthetician and Skin Care Specialist** *600 hrs./$4000* • **Cosmetology and Related Personal Grooming Arts, Other** *2000 hrs./$10,800*

## Davis Applied Technology Center

550 East 300 South, Kaysville, UT 84037
http://www.datc.net/

**CONTACT** Michael Bouwhuis, Campus President
**Telephone:** 801-593-2500

**GENERAL INFORMATION** Public Institution. Founded 1978. **Accreditation:** Regional (NCCU/NCCU). **Total program enrollment:** 497. **Application fee:** $40.

**PROGRAM(S) OFFERED**
• **Accounting** *3 students enrolled* • **Administrative Assistant and Secretarial Science, General** *5 students enrolled* • **Automobile/Automotive Mechanics Technology/Technician** • **CAD/CADD Drafting and/or Design Technology/ Technician** *1890 hrs./$3090* • **Computer Programming/Programmer, General** *1890 hrs./$3090* • **Cosmetology/Cosmetologist, General** *2000 hrs./$2562* • **Dental Assisting/Assistant** *17 students enrolled* • **Dental Services and Allied Professions, Other** • **Diesel Mechanics Technology/Technician** *6 students enrolled* • **Fire Science/Firefighting** *26 students enrolled* • **Food Preparation/ Professional Cooking/Kitchen Assistant** *7 students enrolled* • **Heating, Air Conditioning, Ventilation and Refrigeration Maintenance Technology/ Technician (HAC, HACR, HVAC, HVACR)** • **Industrial Electronics Technology/ Technician** *3 students enrolled* • **Industrial Mechanics and Maintenance Technology** • **Legal Assistant/Paralegal** *5 students enrolled* • **Licensed Practical/Vocational Nurse Training (LPN, LVN, Cert, Dipl, AAS)** *66 students enrolled* • **Machine Shop Technology/Assistant** *10 students enrolled* • **Machine Tool Technology/Machinist** *1575 hrs./$1995* • **Materials Engineering** *7 students enrolled* • **Medical Insurance Coding Specialist/Coder** • **Medical Office Management/Administration** • **Medical Transcription/Transcriptionist** *1 student enrolled* • **Medical/Clinical Assistant** *1890 hrs./$3090* • **Nail Technician/ Specialist and Manicurist** *7 students enrolled* • **Nurse/Nursing Assistant/Aide and Patient Care Assistant** *591 students enrolled* • **Phlebotomy/Phlebotomist** *57 students enrolled* • **Surgical Technology/Technologist** *1650 hrs./$2565* • **Teacher Assistant/Aide** *5 students enrolled* • **Web Page, Digital/Multimedia and Information Resources Design** *3 students enrolled* • **Welding Technology/ Welder**

**STUDENT SERVICES** Academic or career counseling, employment services for current students, placement services for program completers, remedial services.

## Dixie Applied Technology College

46 S. 1000 East, Saint George, UT 84770-3025
dixieatc.org/index.html

**CONTACT** Richard VanAusdal, Campus President
**Telephone:** 801-863-7605 Ext. 7605

**GENERAL INFORMATION** Public Institution. **Total program enrollment:** 12. **Application fee:** $40.

**PROGRAM(S) OFFERED**
• **Administrative Assistant and Secretarial Science, General** *1020 hrs./$1467* • **Autobody/Collision and Repair Technology/Technician** *1140 hrs./$1539* • **CAD/CADD Drafting and/or Design Technology/Technician** *1200 hrs./$2248* • **Diesel Mechanics Technology/Technician** *1200 hrs./$1710* • **Medical Administrative/Executive Assistant and Medical Secretary** *1049 hrs./$1696* • **Pharmacy Technician/Assistant** *600 hrs./$1010*

**STUDENT SERVICES** Academic or career counseling, employment services for current students, placement services for program completers, remedial services.

## Dixie State College of Utah

225 South 700 East, St. George, UT 84770-3876
http://www.dixie.edu/

**CONTACT** Stephen D. Nadauld, President
**Telephone:** 435-652-7500

**GENERAL INFORMATION** Public Institution. Founded 1911. **Accreditation:** Regional (NCCU/NCCU); dental hygiene (ADA); emergency medical services (JRCEMTP). **Total program enrollment:** 3484. **Application fee:** $35.

**PROGRAM(S) OFFERED**
• **Automobile/Automotive Mechanics Technology/Technician** *1 student enrolled* • **Business/Commerce, General** *1 student enrolled* • **Emergency Medical Technology/Technician (EMT Paramedic)** *83 students enrolled* • **Graphic and Printing Equipment Operator, General Production** • **Licensed Practical/Vocational Nurse Training (LPN, LVN, Cert, Dipl, AAS)** *77 students enrolled* • **Nurse/Nursing Assistant/Aide and Patient Care Assistant** *338 students enrolled* • **Phlebotomy/Phlebotomist** *58 students enrolled* • **Surgical Technology/Technologist** *8 students enrolled* • **Web Page, Digital/Multimedia and Information Resources Design** *2 students enrolled*

**STUDENT SERVICES** Academic or career counseling, employment services for current students, placement services for program completers, remedial services.

## Eagle Gate College

915 North 400 West, Layton, UT 84041
http://eaglegatecollege.edu/

**CONTACT** Karen Smith, Campus President
**Telephone:** 801-546-7500

**GENERAL INFORMATION** Private Institution. **Total program enrollment:** 67. **Application fee:** $40.

**PROGRAM(S) OFFERED**
• **Allied Health and Medical Assisting Services, Other** *7 students enrolled* • **Graphic Design** • **Medical Insurance Coding Specialist/Coder** *2 students enrolled* • **Pharmacy Technician/Assistant** *5 students enrolled*

**STUDENT SERVICES** Academic or career counseling, placement services for program completers.

## Eagle Gate College

5588 South Green Street, Murray, UT 84123
http://eaglegatecollege.edu/

**CONTACT** Janet Head, Campus President
**Telephone:** 801-333-8100 Ext. 8112

**GENERAL INFORMATION** Private Institution. **Total program enrollment:** 199. **Application fee:** $40.

**PROGRAM(S) OFFERED**
• **Dental Assisting/Assistant** *22 students enrolled* • **Medical Insurance Coding Specialist/Coder** *1 student enrolled* • **Medical/Clinical Assistant** *20 students enrolled* • **Pharmacy Technician/Assistant** *9 students enrolled*

**STUDENT SERVICES** Academic or career counseling, employment services for current students, placement services for program completers.

## Eagle Gate College

405 South Main Street, 7th Floor, Salt Lake City, UT 84111
http://eaglegatecollege.edu/

**CONTACT** Janet Head, Campus President
**Telephone:** 801-333-7120

**GENERAL INFORMATION** Private Institution. **Total program enrollment:** 102. **Application fee:** $40.

**PROGRAM(S) OFFERED**
• **Athletic Training/Trainer** *1 student enrolled* • **Commercial and Advertising Art** *1 student enrolled* • **Massage Therapy/Therapeutic Massage** *4 students enrolled* • **Medical/Clinical Assistant** *5 students enrolled* • **Pharmacy Technician/Assistant** *1 student enrolled* • **Resort Management** *2 students enrolled* • **Teaching English as a Second or Foreign Language/ESL Language Instructor** *20 students enrolled*

**STUDENT SERVICES** Academic or career counseling, employment services for current students, placement services for program completers.

## Everest College

3280 West 3500 South, West Valley City, UT 84119
http://www.everest.edu/

**CONTACT** Stephanie Byrd, President
**Telephone:** 801-840-4800

**GENERAL INFORMATION** Private Institution. Founded 1982. **Accreditation:** Medical assisting (AAMAE); state accredited or approved. **Total program enrollment:** 125.

**PROGRAM(S) OFFERED**
• **Administrative Assistant and Secretarial Science, General** • **Massage Therapy/Therapeutic Massage** *3 students enrolled* • **Medical Insurance Specialist/Medical Biller** *28 students enrolled* • **Medical/Clinical Assistant** *40 students enrolled* • **Pharmacy Technician/Assistant** *15 students enrolled* • **Tourism and Travel Services Management** *3 students enrolled*

**STUDENT SERVICES** Academic or career counseling, employment services for current students, placement services for program completers, remedial services.

## Fran Brown College of Beauty and Career Center

521 West 600 North, Layton, UT 84041
http://www.franschool.com/

**CONTACT** Fran Brown, Owner
**Telephone:** 801-546-1377

**GENERAL INFORMATION** Private Institution. **Total program enrollment:** 60. **Application fee:** $100.

**PROGRAM(S) OFFERED**

- **Aesthetician/Esthetician and Skin Care Specialist** *1200 hrs./$7400*
- **Cosmetology and Related Personal Grooming Arts, Other** *300 hrs./$1200*
- **Cosmetology, Barber/Styling, and Nail Instructor** *1000 hrs./$6500*
- **Cosmetology/Cosmetologist, General** *2000 hrs./$12,418*

**STUDENT SERVICES** Academic or career counseling, placement services for program completers.

## Francois D Hair Academy

111 W. 9000 S, Sandy, UT 84070
http://franciosd.com/

**CONTACT** Jeff Downward, President
**Telephone:** 801-561-2244

**GENERAL INFORMATION** Private Institution. **Total program enrollment:** 23. **Application fee:** $100.

**PROGRAM(S) OFFERED**

- **Aesthetician/Esthetician and Skin Care Specialist** *1200 hrs./$9600*
- **Cosmetology/Cosmetologist, General** *2000 hrs./$12,400*

**STUDENT SERVICES** Placement services for program completers.

## Hairitage College of Beauty

5414 South 900 East, Salt Lake City, UT 84117

**CONTACT** Shawn Trujillo, Owner
**Telephone:** 801-302-8801 Ext. 1021

**GENERAL INFORMATION** Private Institution. Founded 1979. **Total program enrollment:** 194. **Application fee:** $75.

**PROGRAM(S) OFFERED**

- **Aesthetician/Esthetician and Skin Care Specialist** *1200 hrs./$10,100*
- **Cosmetology/Cosmetologist, General** *2000 hrs./$14,925*

**STUDENT SERVICES** Academic or career counseling, placement services for program completers.

## Healing Mountain Massage School

455 S. 300 E, #103, Salt Lake City, UT 84111
http://www.healingmountain.org/

**CONTACT** Randall J. Nikola, School Director
**Telephone:** 801-355-6300 Ext. 7

**GENERAL INFORMATION** Private Institution. **Total program enrollment:** 15. **Application fee:** $100.

**PROGRAM(S) OFFERED**

- **Massage Therapy/Therapeutic Massage** *39 hrs./$9450*

**STUDENT SERVICES** Academic or career counseling, placement services for program completers.

## LDS Business College

411 East South Temple Street, Salt Lake City, UT 84111-1392
http://www.ldsbc.edu/

**CONTACT** J. Lawrence Richards, President
**Telephone:** 801-524-8100

**GENERAL INFORMATION** Private Institution (Affiliated with The Church of Jesus Christ of Latter-day Saints). Founded 1886. **Accreditation:** Regional (NCCU/NCCU); medical assisting (AAMAE). **Total program enrollment:** 1023. **Application fee:** $30.

**PROGRAM(S) OFFERED**

• **Accounting Technology/Technician and Bookkeeping** *120 students enrolled* • **Administrative Assistant and Secretarial Science, General** *13 students enrolled* • **Computer and Information Sciences and Support Services, Other** *1 student enrolled* • **Interior Design** *15 students enrolled* • **Medical Administrative/Executive Assistant and Medical Secretary** *3 students enrolled* • **Medical Insurance Coding Specialist/Coder** *2 students enrolled* • **Medical Transcription/Transcriptionist** *7 students enrolled* • **Medical/Clinical Assistant** *5 students enrolled* • **Sales, Distribution and Marketing Operations, General** *17 students enrolled* • **Web Page, Digital/Multimedia and Information Resources Design** *1 student enrolled*

**STUDENT SERVICES** Academic or career counseling, employment services for current students, placement services for program completers.

## Mountainland Applied Technology College

987 S. Geneva Road, Orem, UT 84058-5857
http://www.mlatc.edu/

**CONTACT** Clay E. Christensen, Campus President
**Telephone:** 801-863-6282

**GENERAL INFORMATION** Public Institution. **Total program enrollment:** 112. **Application fee:** $40.

**PROGRAM(S) OFFERED**

• **Administrative Assistant and Secretarial Science, General** *87 students enrolled* • **Athletic Training/Trainer** • **Automobile/Automotive Mechanics Technology/Technician** *163 students enrolled* • **Carpentry/Carpenter** *7 students enrolled* • **Clinical/Medical Laboratory Science and Allied Professions, Other** • **Computer Installation and Repair Technology/Technician** • **Computer and Information Sciences, General** • **Cosmetology/Cosmetologist, General** *42 students enrolled* • **Culinary Arts/Chef Training** *10 students enrolled* • **Dental Assisting/Assistant** *33 students enrolled* • **Diesel Mechanics Technology/Technician** *3 students enrolled* • **Electrician** • **Emergency Care Attendant (EMT Ambulance)** • **Emergency Medical Technology/Technician (EMT Paramedic)** *48 students enrolled* • **Fire Science/Firefighting** *4 students enrolled* • **Heating, Air Conditioning, Ventilation and Refrigeration Maintenance Technology/Technician (HAC, HACR, HVAC, HVACR)** • **Licensed Practical/Vocational Nurse Training (LPN, LVN, Cert, Dipl, AAS)** • **Medical Administrative/Executive Assistant and Medical Secretary** *5 students enrolled* • **Medical Insurance Coding Specialist/Coder** *1 student enrolled* • **Medical Transcription/Transcriptionist** • **Medical/Clinical Assistant** *38 students enrolled* • **Nurse/Nursing Assistant/Aide and Patient Care Assistant** *110 students enrolled* • **Pharmacy Technician/Assistant** *4 students enrolled* • **Plumbing Technology/Plumber** • **Truck and Bus Driver/Commercial Vehicle Operation** *25 students enrolled* • **Veterinary/Animal Health Technology/Technician and Veterinary Assistant** *5 students enrolled* • **Web Page, Digital/Multimedia and Information Resources Design** *9 students enrolled* • **Welding Technology/Welder**

**STUDENT SERVICES** Academic or career counseling, employment services for current students, placement services for program completers, remedial services.

## Myotherapy College of Utah

1174 East 2700 South, Suite 19, Salt Lake City, UT 84109
http://www.myotherapycollege.com/

**CONTACT** Susan C. Taylor, College Director
**Telephone:** 801-484-7624

**GENERAL INFORMATION** Private Institution. Founded 1987. **Total program enrollment:** 32. **Application fee:** $25.

**PROGRAM(S) OFFERED**

- **Massage Therapy/Therapeutic Massage** *39 hrs./$9530*

**STUDENT SERVICES** Placement services for program completers.

## Ogden Institute of Massage Therapy

3500 Harrison Boulevard #102, Ogden, UT 84403
http://oimt.net/

**CONTACT** Craig Anderson, Director
**Telephone:** 801-627-8227

**GENERAL INFORMATION** Private Institution. **Application fee:** $100.

**PROGRAM(S) OFFERED**
• **Massage Therapy/Therapeutic Massage** *44 hrs.*

**STUDENT SERVICES** Placement services for program completers.

## Ogden-Weber Applied Technology Center

559 East AVC Lane, Ogden, UT 84404-6704
http://www.owatc.com/

**CONTACT** Collette Mercier, Regional President
**Telephone:** 801-627-8300

**GENERAL INFORMATION** Public Institution. Founded 1971. **Accreditation:** Regional (NCCU/NCCU). **Total program enrollment:** 886. **Application fee:** $40.

**PROGRAM(S) OFFERED**
• **Accounting Technology/Technician and Bookkeeping** *11 students enrolled* • **Administrative Assistant and Secretarial Science, General** *12 students enrolled* • **Biomedical Technology/Technician** *1 student enrolled* • **CAD/CADD Drafting and/or Design Technology/Technician** *1500 hrs./$2385* • **Cabinetmaking and Millwork/Millwright** • **Carpentry/Carpenter** *5 students enrolled* • **Computer Installation and Repair Technology/Technician** *3 students enrolled* • **Computer and Information Sciences, General** *2 students enrolled* • **Cosmetology/Cosmetologist, General** *2000 hrs./$3159* • **Dental Assisting/Assistant** *15 students enrolled* • **Electrician** *1536 hrs./$4019* • **Food Preparation/Professional Cooking/Kitchen Assistant** *4 students enrolled* • **Heating, Air Conditioning, Ventilation and Refrigeration Maintenance Technology/Technician (HAC, HACR, HVAC, HVACR)** • **Industrial Electronics Technology/Technician** *1 student enrolled* • **Industrial Mechanics and Maintenance Technology** *1260 hrs./$2014* • **Licensed Practical/Vocational Nurse Training (LPN, LVN, Cert, Dipl, AAS)** *30 students enrolled* • **Machine Tool Technology/Machinist** *1200 hrs./$1921* • **Mason/Masonry** • **Materials Engineering** • **Medical Administrative/Executive Assistant and Medical Secretary** *5 students enrolled* • **Medical Insurance Coding Specialist/Coder** *7 students enrolled* • **Medical Transcription/Transcriptionist** *8 students enrolled* • **Medical/Clinical Assistant** *8 students enrolled* • **Nurse/Nursing Assistant/Aide and Patient Care Assistant** *110 hrs./$327* • **Pharmacy Technician/Assistant** *34 students enrolled* • **Phlebotomy/Phlebotomist** *45 students enrolled* • **Plumbing Technology/Plumber** *13 students enrolled* • **Real Estate** *144 students enrolled* • **Sheet Metal Technology/Sheetworking** *8 students enrolled* • **Transportation and Materials Moving, Other** • **Web Page, Digital/Multimedia and Information Resources Design** *11 students enrolled* • **Welding Technology/Welder** *3 students enrolled*

**STUDENT SERVICES** Academic or career counseling, daycare for children of students, employment services for current students, placement services for program completers, remedial services.

## Paul Mitchell the School—Provo

480 N. 900 East, Provo, UT 84606
http://www.paulmitchelltheschool.com

**CONTACT** Dennis Claybaugh, Director
**Telephone:** 801-302-8801 Ext. 1021

**GENERAL INFORMATION** Private Institution. **Total program enrollment:** 192. **Application fee:** $75.

**PROGRAM(S) OFFERED**
• **Cosmetology/Cosmetologist, General** *2000 hrs./$13,925*

**STUDENT SERVICES** Academic or career counseling, placement services for program completers, remedial services.

## Provo College

1450 West 820 North, Provo, UT 84601
http://www.provocollege.edu/

**CONTACT** Gordon C. Peters, Campus President
**Telephone:** 801-818-8900

**GENERAL INFORMATION** Private Institution. Founded 1984. **Accreditation:** Dental assisting (ADA); physical therapy assisting (APTA); state accredited or approved. **Total program enrollment:** 192. **Application fee:** $40.

**PROGRAM(S) OFFERED**
• **Dental Assisting/Assistant** *22 students enrolled* • **Pharmacy Technician/Assistant** *18 students enrolled*

**STUDENT SERVICES** Academic or career counseling, employment services for current students, placement services for program completers.

## Renaissance School of Therapeutic Massage

566 West 1350 South, Bountiful, UT 84010
http://www.renaissancemassageschool.com/

**CONTACT** Diana Young, Education Director
**Telephone:** 801-292-8515

**GENERAL INFORMATION** Private Institution. **Total program enrollment:** 6.

**PROGRAM(S) OFFERED**
• **Massage Therapy/Therapeutic Massage** *785 hrs./$10,705*

**STUDENT SERVICES** Academic or career counseling, employment services for current students, placement services for program completers.

## Salt Lake Community College

PO Box 30808, Salt Lake City, UT 84130-0808
http://www.slcc.edu/

**CONTACT** Cynthia Bioteau, President
**Telephone:** 801-957-4111

**GENERAL INFORMATION** Public Institution. Founded 1948. **Accreditation:** Regional (NCCU/NCCU); dental hygiene (ADA); medical laboratory technology (NAACLS); physical therapy assisting (APTA); practical nursing (NLN); radiologic technology: radiography (JRCERT). **Total program enrollment:** 8772. **Application fee:** $35.

**PROGRAM(S) OFFERED**
• **Accounting Technology/Technician and Bookkeeping** *18 students enrolled* • **Business Administration and Management, General** *3 students enrolled* • **Business/Office Automation/Technology/Data Entry** *14 students enrolled* • **Computer and Information Sciences and Support Services, Other** *23 students enrolled* • **Cosmetology/Cosmetologist, General** *79 students enrolled* • **Diesel Mechanics Technology/Technician** *1 student enrolled* • **Drafting and Design Technology/Technician, General** *26 students enrolled* • **Electrical and Power Transmission Installers, Other** *1 student enrolled* • **Electrical, Electronic and Communications Engineering Technology/Technician** *4 students enrolled* • **Finance, General** *1 student enrolled* • **General Office Occupations and Clerical Services** *8 students enrolled* • **Health Information/Medical Records Technology/Technician** *7 students enrolled* • **Health Unit Coordinator/Ward Clerk** *17 students enrolled* • **Health and Medical Administrative Services, Other** *12 students enrolled* • **Heating, Air Conditioning, Ventilation and Refrigeration Maintenance Technology/Technician (HAC, HACR, HVAC, HVACR)** *14 students enrolled* • **Industrial Electronics Technology/Technician** *5 students enrolled* • **Machine Shop Technology/Assistant** *19 students enrolled* • **Marketing/Marketing Management, General** *2 students enrolled* • **Mason/Masonry** *1 student enrolled* • **Medical Administrative/Executive Assistant and Medical Secretary** *10 students enrolled* • **Medical Insurance Specialist/Medical Biller** *37 students enrolled* • **Medical/Clinical Assistant** *28 students enrolled* • **Nurse/Nursing Assistant/Aide and Patient Care Assistant** *144 students enrolled* • **Prepress/Desktop Publishing and Digital Imaging Design** *2 students enrolled* • **Receptionist** *13 students enrolled* • **Surgical Technology/Technologist** 46

*students enrolled* • **System Administration/Administrator** *1 student enrolled* • **Truck and Bus Driver/Commercial Vehicle Operation** *194 students enrolled* • **Welding Technology/Welder** *5 students enrolled*

**STUDENT SERVICES** Academic or career counseling, daycare for children of students, employment services for current students, placement services for program completers, remedial services.

## Skinworks School of Advanced Skincare

2121 South, 230 East, Salt Lake City, UT 84115
http://www.skin-works.com/

**CONTACT** Dave Owens, FAC
**Telephone:** 801-530-0001

**GENERAL INFORMATION** Private Institution. **Total program enrollment:** 41. **Application fee:** $100.

**PROGRAM(S) OFFERED**
• **Aesthetician/Esthetician and Skin Care Specialist** *600 hrs./$5550* • **Cosmetology and Related Personal Grooming Arts, Other** *16 students enrolled* • **Cosmetology/Cosmetologist, General** *6 students enrolled*

**STUDENT SERVICES** Placement services for program completers.

## Snow College

150 East College Avenue, Ephraim, UT 84627-1203
http://www.snow.edu/

**CONTACT** Scott L. Wyatt, President
**Telephone:** 435-283-7000

**GENERAL INFORMATION** Public Institution. Founded 1888. **Accreditation:** Regional (NCCU/NCCU); music (NASM). **Total program enrollment:** 2291. **Application fee:** $30.

**PROGRAM(S) OFFERED**
• **Automobile/Automotive Mechanics Technology/Technician** • **Business/Commerce, General** *14 students enrolled* • **Construction Trades, Other** • **Cosmetology/Cosmetologist, General** • **Culinary Arts/Chef Training** • **Diesel Mechanics Technology/Technician** • **Drafting and Design Technology/Technician, General** • **Family Systems** *1 student enrolled* • **Licensed Practical/Vocational Nurse Training (LPN, LVN, Cert, Dipl, AAS)** *28 students enrolled* • **Nurse/Nursing Assistant/Aide and Patient Care Assistant** • **Teaching English as a Second or Foreign Language/ESL Language Instructor**

**STUDENT SERVICES** Academic or career counseling, daycare for children of students, employment services for current students, remedial services.

## Southern Utah University

351 West University Boulevard, Cedar City, UT 84720-2498
http://www.suu.edu/

**CONTACT** Michael Benson, President
**Telephone:** 435-586-7700

**GENERAL INFORMATION** Public Institution. Founded 1897. **Accreditation:** Regional (NCCU/NCCU); home economics (AAFCS); music (NASM). **Total program enrollment:** 5286. **Application fee:** $40.

**PROGRAM(S) OFFERED**
• **Animal/Livestock Husbandry and Production** *1 student enrolled* • **CAD/CADD Drafting and/or Design Technology/Technician** • **Civil Drafting and Civil Engineering CAD/CADD** *1 student enrolled* • **Geography, Other** *1 student enrolled* • **International Relations and Affairs** *2 students enrolled*

**STUDENT SERVICES** Academic or career counseling, daycare for children of students, employment services for current students, placement services for program completers, remedial services.

## Southwest Applied Technology Center

510 W. 800 South, Cedar City, UT 84720
http://www.swatc.org/studentservices/index.php?class=9999

**CONTACT** Dana L. Miller, Campus President
**Telephone:** 801-863-7605 Ext. 7605

**GENERAL INFORMATION** Public Institution. **Total program enrollment:** 39. **Application fee:** $40.

**PROGRAM(S) OFFERED**
• **Accounting Technology/Technician and Bookkeeping** • **Administrative Assistant and Secretarial Science, General** *1020 hrs./$1632* • **Automobile/Automotive Mechanics Technology/Technician** *1560 hrs./$2526* • **Computer Systems Networking and Telecommunications** *1170 hrs./$2865* • **Mason/Masonry** *600 hrs./$1100* • **Medical Administrative/Executive Assistant and Medical Secretary** *900 hrs./$1430* • **Nurse/Nursing Assistant/Aide and Patient Care Assistant** *140 students enrolled* • **Truck and Bus Driver/Commercial Vehicle Operation** *50 students enrolled* • **Welding Technology/Welder** *990 hrs./$1837*

**STUDENT SERVICES** Academic or career counseling, employment services for current students, placement services for program completers.

## Stacey's Hands of Champions

372150 250 West, Ogden, UT 84405
http://www.staceyscollege.com/

**CONTACT** Fay T. Stacey, President
**Telephone:** 801-394-5718

**GENERAL INFORMATION** Private Institution. **Total program enrollment:** 109. **Application fee:** $100.

**PROGRAM(S) OFFERED**
• **Cosmetology and Related Personal Grooming Arts, Other** *300 hrs./$2100* • **Cosmetology/Cosmetologist, General** *2000 hrs./$12,600*

**STUDENT SERVICES** Academic or career counseling, placement services for program completers.

## Uintah Basin Applied Technology Center

1100 East Lagoon (124-5), Roosevelt, UT 84066
http://www.ubatc.net/

**CONTACT** Paul Hacking, President
**Telephone:** 435-722-6900

**GENERAL INFORMATION** Public Institution. Founded 1968. **Total program enrollment:** 168.

**PROGRAM(S) OFFERED**
• **Accounting Technology/Technician and Bookkeeping** *1260 hrs./$1255* • **Automobile/Automotive Mechanics Technology/Technician** *1 student enrolled* • **Business Administration and Management, General** *900 hrs./$2479* • **CAD/CADD Drafting and/or Design Technology/Technician** *6 students enrolled* • **Carpentry/Carpenter** *20 students enrolled* • **Computer Installation and Repair Technology/Technician** *4 students enrolled* • **Computer and Information Sciences, General** • **Electrician** *3 students enrolled* • **Licensed Practical/Vocational Nurse Training (LPN, LVN, Cert, Dipl, AAS)** *900 hrs./$1692* • **Medical Administrative/Executive Assistant and Medical Secretary** *1500 hrs./$1255* • **Medical Transcription/Transcriptionist** *1380 hrs./$1255* • **Medical/Clinical Assistant** *1500 hrs./$1255* • **Nurse/Nursing Assistant/Aide and Patient Care Assistant** *61 students enrolled* • **Pharmacy Technician/Assistant** *10 students enrolled* • **Truck and Bus Driver/Commercial Vehicle Operation** *29 students enrolled* • **Welding Technology/Welder** *35 students enrolled*

**STUDENT SERVICES** Academic or career counseling, employment services for current students, placement services for program completers, remedial services.

## University of Phoenix–Utah Campus

5373 South Green Street, Salt Lake City, UT 84123-4617
http://www.phoenix.edu/

**CONTACT** William Pepicello, PhD, President
**Telephone:** 800-224-2844

**GENERAL INFORMATION** Private Institution. Founded 1984. **Accreditation:** Regional (NCA); counseling (ACA). **Total program enrollment:** 3396.

**STUDENT SERVICES** Academic or career counseling, remedial services.

## Utah Career College–Layton Campus

869 West Hill Field Road, Layton, UT 84041
http://www.utahcollege.edu/

**CONTACT** James Cox, Regional Director
**Telephone:** 801-660-6000

**GENERAL INFORMATION** Private Institution. **Total program enrollment:** 71. **Application fee:** $50.

**PROGRAM(S) OFFERED**
- **Legal Assistant/Paralegal** • **Massage Therapy/Therapeutic Massage** • **Medical Insurance Coding Specialist/Coder** • **Medical/Clinical Assistant**

**STUDENT SERVICES** Academic or career counseling, employment services for current students, placement services for program completers.

## Utah Career College–Orem Campus

898 N. 1200 West, Orem, UT 84057
http://www.utahcollege.edu/

**CONTACT** Terry Myhre
**Telephone:** 801-822-5800

**GENERAL INFORMATION** Private Institution. **Total program enrollment:** 11. **Application fee:** $50.

**PROGRAM(S) OFFERED**
- **Allied Health and Medical Assisting Services, Other** • **Health Information/Medical Records Administration/Administrator** • **Health and Physical Education, General** • **Legal Administrative Assistant/Secretary** • **Massage Therapy/Therapeutic Massage**

**STUDENT SERVICES** Academic or career counseling.

## Utah Career College–West Jordan Campus

1902 West 7800 South, West Jordan, UT 84088
http://www.utahcollege.edu/

**CONTACT** Terry Myhre, President
**Telephone:** 801-304-4224 Ext. 134

**GENERAL INFORMATION** Private Institution. **Accreditation:** Medical assisting (AAMAE); state accredited or approved. **Total program enrollment:** 108. **Application fee:** $50.

**PROGRAM(S) OFFERED**
- **Commercial and Advertising Art** *7 students enrolled* • **Legal Assistant/Paralegal** *1 student enrolled* • **Massage Therapy/Therapeutic Massage** *6 students enrolled* • **Medical Insurance Coding Specialist/Coder** *1 student enrolled* • **Medical/Clinical Assistant** *13 students enrolled* • **Pharmacy Technician/Assistant** *11 students enrolled*

**STUDENT SERVICES** Academic or career counseling, employment services for current students, placement services for program completers.

## Utah College of Massage Therapy

25 South 300 East, Salt Lake City, UT 84111
http://www.ucmt.com/

**CONTACT** Stephen Lazarus, Chief Operations Officer
**Telephone:** 801-521-3330

**GENERAL INFORMATION** Private Institution. Founded 1987. **Total program enrollment:** 85. **Application fee:** $100.

**PROGRAM(S) OFFERED**
- **Massage Therapy/Therapeutic Massage** *220 hrs./$4399*

**STUDENT SERVICES** Academic or career counseling, employment services for current students, placement services for program completers.

## Utah College of Massage Therapy, Inc.–Utah Valley

135 South State Street, Suite 12, Lindon, UT 84042
http://www.ucmt.com/

**CONTACT** Stephen Lazarus, Chief Operations Officer
**Telephone:** 801-796-0300

**GENERAL INFORMATION** Private Institution. **Total program enrollment:** 86. **Application fee:** $100.

**PROGRAM(S) OFFERED**
- **Massage Therapy/Therapeutic Massage** *51 hrs./$12,409*

**STUDENT SERVICES** Academic or career counseling, employment services for current students, placement services for program completers.

## Utah State University

Old Main Hill, Logan, UT 84322
http://www.usu.edu/

**CONTACT** Stan L. Albrecht, President
**Telephone:** 435-797-1000

**GENERAL INFORMATION** Public Institution. Founded 1888. **Accreditation:** Regional (NCCU/NCCU); audiology (ASHA); computer science (ABET/CSAC); dietetics: undergraduate, postbaccalaureate internship (ADtA/CAADE); engineering-related programs (ABET/RAC); forestry (SAF); interior design: professional (CIDA); music (NASM); recreation and parks (NRPA); speech-language pathology (ASHA). **Total program enrollment:** 12126. **Application fee:** $40.

**PROGRAM(S) OFFERED**
- **Agricultural Mechanization, General** *2 students enrolled* • **Dairy Science** • **Natural Resources Management and Policy** • **Ornamental Horticulture** *3 students enrolled*

**STUDENT SERVICES** Academic or career counseling, daycare for children of students, employment services for current students, placement services for program completers, remedial services.

## Utah State University–Continuing Education

Old Main Hill, Logan, UT 84322
http://www.usu.edu/

**CONTACT** Rhonda Menlove
**Telephone:** 435-797-1000

**GENERAL INFORMATION** Public Institution. **Total program enrollment:** 2574. **Application fee:** $40.

**STUDENT SERVICES** Academic or career counseling, employment services for current students, placement services for program completers, remedial services.

## Utah Valley University

800 West University Parkway, Orem, UT 84058-5999
http://www.uvu.edu/

**CONTACT** Elizabeth Hitch, Interim College President
**Telephone:** 801-863-8161

**GENERAL INFORMATION** Public Institution (Affiliated with Advent Christian Church). Founded 1941. **Accreditation:** Regional (NCCU/NCCU); computer science (ABET/CSAC); dental hygiene (ADA); engineering technology (ABET/TAC). **Total program enrollment:** 13215. **Application fee:** $35.

**PROGRAM(S) OFFERED**
• **Accounting** • **Administrative Assistant and Secretarial Science, General** *1 student enrolled* • **Autobody/Collision and Repair Technology/Technician** • **Automobile/Automotive Mechanics Technology/Technician** *2 students enrolled* • **Building/Home/Construction Inspection/Inspector** *2 students enrolled* • **Business Administration and Management, General** • **Cabinetmaking and Millwork/Millwright** • **Computer Programming/Programmer, General** *1 student enrolled* • **Computer Systems Networking and Telecommunications** *3 students enrolled* • **Construction Trades, General** • **Design and Visual Communications, General** *2 students enrolled* • **Diesel Mechanics Technology/Technician** *2 students enrolled* • **Electrical, Electronic and Communications Engineering Technology/Technician** • **Emergency Medical Technology/Technician (EMT Paramedic)** • **Fire Science/Firefighting** • **Kindergarten/Preschool Education and Teaching** *14 students enrolled* • **Lineworker** • **Welding Technology/Welder**

**STUDENT SERVICES** Academic or career counseling, daycare for children of students, employment services for current students, placement services for program completers, remedial services.

## Weber State University

1001 University Circle, Ogden, UT 84408-1001
http://www.weber.edu/

**CONTACT** Dr. F. Ann Millner, President
**Telephone:** 801-626-6000

**GENERAL INFORMATION** Public Institution. Founded 1889. **Accreditation:** Regional (NCCU/NCCU); dental hygiene (ADA); emergency medical services (JRCEMTP); engineering technology (ABET/TAC); health information administration (AHIMA); health information technology (AHIMA); medical laboratory technology (NAACLS); medical technology (NAACLS); music (NASM); respiratory therapy technology (CoARC). **Total program enrollment:** 9683. **Application fee:** $45.

**PROGRAM(S) OFFERED**
• **Business/Managerial Economics** *16 students enrolled* • **Computer Programming/Programmer, General** • **Computer Systems Networking and Telecommunications** • **Emergency Medical Technology/Technician (EMT Paramedic)** *15 students enrolled* • **Geography** *1 student enrolled* • **Health/Health Care Administration/Management** *1 student enrolled* • **Information Science/Studies** • **International Economics** • **Licensed Practical/Vocational Nurse Training (LPN, LVN, Cert, Dipl, AAS)** • **Management Information Systems, General** *7 students enrolled* • **Medical Insurance Coding Specialist/Coder** *4 students enrolled* • **Nursing—Registered Nurse Training (RN, ASN, BSN, MSN)**

**STUDENT SERVICES** Academic or career counseling, daycare for children of students, employment services for current students, placement services for program completers, remedial services.

# WASHINGTON

## Academy of Hair Design

208 South Wenatchee Avenue, Wenatchee, WA 98801
http://www.theacademyofhairdesign.com/

**CONTACT** Donald E. Crowell, President
**Telephone:** 509-662-9082

**GENERAL INFORMATION** Private Institution. Founded 1982. **Total program enrollment:** 40.

**PROGRAM(S) OFFERED**
• **Aesthetician/Esthetician and Skin Care Specialist** *700 hrs./$5130* • **Barbering/Barber** *1100 hrs./$7730* • **Cosmetology and Related Personal Grooming Arts, Other** *1300 hrs./$9200* • **Cosmetology, Barber/Styling, and Nail Instructor** *600 hrs./$4050* • **Cosmetology/Cosmetologist, General** *1800 hrs./$13,225* • **Nail Technician/Specialist and Manicurist** *700 hrs./$5130*

**STUDENT SERVICES** Academic or career counseling, placement services for program completers.

## Alpine College

10020 E. Knox Avenue, Suite 500, Spokane Valley, WA 99206
alpinecollege.edu

**CONTACT** Genevieve Taylor, Executive Director
**Telephone:** 509-892-0155

**GENERAL INFORMATION** Private Institution. **Total program enrollment:** 43. **Application fee:** $100.

**PROGRAM(S) OFFERED**
• **Medical Administrative/Executive Assistant and Medical Secretary** *26 hrs./$9219*

**STUDENT SERVICES** Academic or career counseling, employment services for current students, placement services for program completers, remedial services.

## The Art Institute of Seattle

2323 Elliott Avenue, Seattle, WA 98121-1642
http://www.artinstitutes.edu/seattle/

**CONTACT** Shelly Dubois, President
**Telephone:** 206-448-0900

**GENERAL INFORMATION** Private Institution. Founded 1982. **Accreditation:** Regional (NCCU/NCCU). **Total program enrollment:** 1478. **Application fee:** $50.

**PROGRAM(S) OFFERED**
• **Baking and Pastry Arts/Baker/Pastry Chef** *25 students enrolled* • **Food Preparation/Professional Cooking/Kitchen Assistant** *14 students enrolled* • **Interior Design** *18 students enrolled* • **Prepress/Desktop Publishing and Digital Imaging Design** *6 students enrolled*

**STUDENT SERVICES** Academic or career counseling, employment services for current students, placement services for program completers, remedial services.

## Ashmead College

5005 Pacific Highway East, Suite 20, Fife, WA 98424
http://ashmeadcollege.com/

**CONTACT** Lorine Hill, President
**Telephone:** 253-926-1435

**GENERAL INFORMATION** Private Institution. Founded 1974. **Total program enrollment:** 257.

**PROGRAM(S) OFFERED**
• **Massage Therapy/Therapeutic Massage** *961 hrs./$16,634*

**STUDENT SERVICES** Academic or career counseling, placement services for program completers.

## Ashmead College

2111 North Northgate Way, Suite 218, Seattle, WA 98133
http://ashmeadcollege.com/

**CONTACT** Meredyth Given, School President
**Telephone:** 206-440-3090

**GENERAL INFORMATION** Private Institution. **Total program enrollment:** 196.

*Ashmead College (continued)*

**PROGRAM(S) OFFERED**

• **Massage Therapy/Therapeutic Massage** *961 hrs./$16,634*

**STUDENT SERVICES** Academic or career counseling, employment services for current students, placement services for program completers.

## Ashmead College School of Massage

120 NE 136th Avenue, Stone Mill Center, Suite 220, Vancouver, WA 98684-6951
http://ashmeadcollege.com/

**CONTACT** Brad Kuchenruether, Campus President
**Telephone:** 360-885-3152

**GENERAL INFORMATION** Private Institution. **Total program enrollment:** 121.

**PROGRAM(S) OFFERED**

• **Massage Therapy/Therapeutic Massage** *1000 hrs./$17,988* • **Sport and Fitness Administration/Management** *20 students enrolled*

**STUDENT SERVICES** Academic or career counseling, placement services for program completers.

## Bates Technical College

1101 South Yakima Avenue, Tacoma, WA 98405-4895
http://www.bates.ctc.edu/

**CONTACT** David Borofsky, President
**Telephone:** 253-680-7000

**GENERAL INFORMATION** Public Institution. **Accreditation:** Regional (NCCU/NCCU); dental assisting (ADA). **Total program enrollment:** 2192. **Application fee:** $60.

**PROGRAM(S) OFFERED**

• **Accounting Technology/Technician and Bookkeeping** *2 students enrolled* • **Administrative Assistant and Secretarial Science, General** *2 students enrolled* • **Autobody/Collision and Repair Technology/Technician** *1 student enrolled* • **Banking and Financial Support Services** *1 student enrolled* • **Barbering/Barber** *7 students enrolled* • **Biology Technician/Biotechnology Laboratory Technician** *1 student enrolled* • **Cabinetmaking and Millwork/Millwright** *1 student enrolled* • **Carpentry/Carpenter** *1 student enrolled* • **Child Care Provider/Assistant** *3 students enrolled* • **Civil Engineering Technology/Technician** *1 student enrolled* • **Computer Systems Networking and Telecommunications** *1 student enrolled* • **Computer Technology/Computer Systems Technology** *6 students enrolled* • **Construction Trades, Other** *58 students enrolled* • **Construction/Heavy Equipment/Earthmoving Equipment Operation** *79 students enrolled* • **Dental Assisting/Assistant** *25 students enrolled* • **Dental Laboratory Technology/Technician** *1 student enrolled* • **Diesel Mechanics Technology/Technician** *5 students enrolled* • **Electrical/Electronics Equipment Installation and Repair, General** *1 student enrolled* • **Electrician** *1 student enrolled* • **Emergency Medical Technology/Technician (EMT Paramedic)** *59 students enrolled* • **Fashion/Apparel Design** *1 student enrolled* • **Fire Science/Firefighting** *3 students enrolled* • **Licensed Practical/Vocational Nurse Training (LPN, LVN, Cert, Dipl, AAS)** *23 students enrolled* • **Machine Tool Technology/Machinist** *4 students enrolled* • **Mechanic and Repair Technologies/Technicians, Other** *56 students enrolled* • **Mechanical Drafting and Mechanical Drafting CAD/CADD** *1 student enrolled* • **Mechanical Engineering/Mechanical Technology/Technician** *2 students enrolled* • **Medical Administrative/Executive Assistant and Medical Secretary** *8 students enrolled* • **Parts, Warehousing, and Inventory Management Operations** *4 students enrolled* • **Phlebotomy/Phlebotomist** *77 students enrolled* • **Radio and Television Broadcasting Technology/Technician** *2 students enrolled* • **Recording Arts Technology/Technician** *8 students enrolled* • **Small Engine Mechanics and Repair Technology/Technician** *1 student enrolled* • **Teacher Assistant/Aide** *3 students enrolled* • **Truck and Bus Driver/Commercial Vehicle Operation** *89 students enrolled* • **Vehicle and Vehicle Parts and Accessories Marketing Operations** *2 students enrolled* • **Web Page, Digital/Multimedia and Information Resources Design** *3 students enrolled* • **Welding Technology/Welder** *4 students enrolled*

**STUDENT SERVICES** Academic or career counseling, daycare for children of students, employment services for current students, placement services for program completers, remedial services.

## Bellevue College

3000 Landerholm Circle, SE, Bellevue, WA 98007-6484
http://www.bcc.ctc.edu/

**CONTACT** B. Jean Floten, President
**Telephone:** 425-564-1000

**GENERAL INFORMATION** Public Institution. Founded 1966. **Accreditation:** Regional (NCCU/NCCU); diagnostic medical sonography (JRCEDMS); radiologic technology: radiation therapy technology (JRCERT). **Total program enrollment:** 6096. **Application fee:** $28.

**PROGRAM(S) OFFERED**

• **Accounting Technology/Technician and Bookkeeping** *60 students enrolled* • **Business Administration and Management, General** *13 students enrolled* • **Computer Graphics** *2 students enrolled* • **Computer Programming/Programmer, General** *1 student enrolled* • **Computer Systems Networking and Telecommunications** *1 student enrolled* • **Computer and Information Sciences and Support Services, Other** • **Data Entry/Microcomputer Applications, General** *3 students enrolled* • **Data Modeling/Warehousing and Database Administration** *7 students enrolled* • **Early Childhood Education and Teaching** *1 student enrolled* • **Foreign Languages, Literatures, and Linguistics, Other** *1 student enrolled* • **General Office Occupations and Clerical Services** *38 students enrolled* • **Health Information/Medical Records Technology/Technician** *1 student enrolled* • **Human Resources Management/Personnel Administration, General** *2 students enrolled* • **Marketing/Marketing Management, General** *2 students enrolled* • **Medical Reception/Receptionist** *9 students enrolled* • **Medical/Health Management and Clinical Assistant/Specialist** *16 students enrolled* • **Nuclear Medical Technology/Technologist** *6 students enrolled* • **Nurse/Nursing Assistant/Aide and Patient Care Assistant** *12 students enrolled* • **Office Management and Supervision** *6 students enrolled* • **Parks, Recreation and Leisure Facilities Management** *1 student enrolled* • **Phlebotomy/Phlebotomist** *5 students enrolled* • **Prepress/Desktop Publishing and Digital Imaging Design** *4 students enrolled* • **Radiologic Technology/Science—Radiographer** • **Real Estate** *9 students enrolled* • **Sport and Fitness Administration/Management** *3 students enrolled* • **Substance Abuse/Addiction Counseling** *10 students enrolled* • **Web Page, Digital/Multimedia and Information Resources Design** *3 students enrolled*

**STUDENT SERVICES** Academic or career counseling, daycare for children of students, employment services for current students, placement services for program completers, remedial services.

## Bellingham Beauty School

211 West Holly Street, Bellingham, WA 98225
http://bellinghambeautyschool.edu/

**CONTACT** Betty Stock Kennard, President/Owner
**Telephone:** 360-734-1090

**GENERAL INFORMATION** Private Institution. Founded 1968. **Total program enrollment:** 37.

**PROGRAM(S) OFFERED**

• **Aesthetician/Esthetician and Skin Care Specialist** *650 hrs./$4550* • **Cosmetology, Barber/Styling, and Nail Instructor** *600 hrs./$3900* • **Cosmetology/Cosmetologist, General** *1800 hrs./$11,800* • **Nail Technician/Specialist and Manicurist** *650 hrs./$4550*

**STUDENT SERVICES** Academic or career counseling, placement services for program completers.

## Bellingham Technical College

3028 Lindbergh Avenue, Bellingham, WA 98225
http://www.btc.ctc.edu/

**CONTACT** Thomas Eckert, President
**Telephone:** 360-752-7000

**GENERAL INFORMATION** Public Institution. Founded 1957. **Accreditation:** Regional (NCCU/NCCU); dental assisting (ADA). **Total program enrollment:** 1177. **Application fee:** $37.

PROGRAM(S) OFFERED

• **Accounting Technology/Technician and Bookkeeping** *4 students enrolled* • **Appliance Installation and Repair Technology/Technician** *1 student enrolled* • **Automobile/Automotive Mechanics Technology/Technician** *9 students enrolled* • **Baking and Pastry Arts/Baker/Pastry Chef** *19 students enrolled* • **Building/Home/Construction Inspection/Inspector** *5 students enrolled* • **Business Administration and Management, General** *3 students enrolled* • **Computer Systems Networking and Telecommunications** *11 students enrolled* • **Culinary Arts/Chef Training** *3 students enrolled* • **Data Entry/Microcomputer Applications, General** *1 student enrolled* • **Dental Assisting/Assistant** *41 students enrolled* • **Diesel Mechanics Technology/Technician** *1 student enrolled* • **Early Childhood Education and Teaching** *5 students enrolled* • **General Office Occupations and Clerical Services** *2 students enrolled* • **Heavy/Industrial Equipment Maintenance Technologies, Other** *3 students enrolled* • **Hospitality Administration/Management, Other** *12 students enrolled* • **Human Resources Management/Personnel Administration, General** *3 students enrolled* • **Licensed Practical/Vocational Nurse Training (LPN, LVN, Cert, Dipl, AAS)** *61 students enrolled* • **Machine Shop Technology/Assistant** *4 students enrolled* • **Machine Tool Technology/Machinist** *2 students enrolled* • **Mechanical Drafting and Mechanical Drafting CAD/CADD** *1 student enrolled* • **Medical Administrative/Executive Assistant and Medical Secretary** *6 students enrolled* • **Medical Insurance Coding Specialist/Coder** *15 students enrolled* • **Medical Transcription/Transcriptionist** *1 student enrolled* • **Nurse/Nursing Assistant/Aide and Patient Care Assistant** *157 students enrolled* • **Operations Management and Supervision** *2 students enrolled* • **Receptionist** *1 student enrolled* • **Somatic Bodywork and Related Therapeutic Services, Other** *1 student enrolled* • **Sport and Fitness Administration/Management** *1 student enrolled* • **Surgical Technology/Technologist** *9 students enrolled* • **Teacher Assistant/Aide** *4 students enrolled* • **Truck and Bus Driver/Commercial Vehicle Operation** *39 students enrolled* • **Veterinary/Animal Health Technology/Technician and Veterinary Assistant** *17 students enrolled* • **Welding Technology/Welder** *15 students enrolled*

**STUDENT SERVICES** Academic or career counseling, employment services for current students, placement services for program completers, remedial services.

## Big Bend Community College

7662 Chanute Street, NE, Moses Lake, WA 98837-3299
http://www.bigbend.edu/

**CONTACT** William Bonaudi, President
**Telephone:** 509-793-2222

**GENERAL INFORMATION** Public Institution. Founded 1962. **Accreditation:** Regional (NCCU/NCCU). **Total program enrollment:** 1236. **Application fee:** $30.

PROGRAM(S) OFFERED

• **Accounting Technology/Technician and Bookkeeping** *3 students enrolled* • **Computer Programming, Vendor/Product Certification** *5 students enrolled* • **Early Childhood Education and Teaching** *1 student enrolled* • **Electrician** *1 student enrolled* • **General Office Occupations and Clerical Services** *16 students enrolled* • **Heavy/Industrial Equipment Maintenance Technologies, Other** *1 student enrolled* • **Licensed Practical/Vocational Nurse Training (LPN, LVN, Cert, Dipl, AAS)** *23 students enrolled* • **Medical Office Management/Administration** *4 students enrolled* • **Medical/Clinical Assistant** *3 students enrolled* • **Nurse/Nursing Assistant/Aide and Patient Care Assistant** *59 students enrolled* • **Office Management and Supervision** *2 students enrolled* • **Truck and Bus Driver/Commercial Vehicle Operation** *44 students enrolled* • **Vehicle Maintenance and Repair Technologies, Other** *40 students enrolled* • **Welding Technology/Welder** *1 student enrolled*

**STUDENT SERVICES** Academic or career counseling, daycare for children of students, employment services for current students, placement services for program completers, remedial services.

## BJ's Beauty and Barber College

5239 South Tacoma Way, Tacoma, WA 98409
http://www.bjsbeautyandbarbercollege.com/

**CONTACT** B. J. Boyer, Chief Executive Officer
**Telephone:** 253-473-4320

**GENERAL INFORMATION** Private Institution. Founded 1980. **Total program enrollment:** 67. **Application fee:** $100.

PROGRAM(S) OFFERED

• **Aesthetician/Esthetician and Skin Care Specialist** *600 hrs./$3264* • **Barbering/Barber** *1100 hrs./$7672* • **Cosmetology, Barber/Styling, and Nail Instructor** *300 hrs./$6264* • **Cosmetology/Cosmetologist, General** *1800 hrs./$10,718*

**STUDENT SERVICES** Employment services for current students, placement services for program completers.

## Cascadia Community College

19017 120th Avenue NE, Suite 102, Bothell, WA 98011
http://www.cascadia.ctc.edu/

**CONTACT** Dr. William Christopher, President
**Telephone:** 425-352-8000

**GENERAL INFORMATION** Public Institution. Founded 1999. **Accreditation:** Regional (NCCU/NCCU). **Total program enrollment:** 1212.

PROGRAM(S) OFFERED

• **Computer Programming/Programmer, General** *1 student enrolled* • **Computer Systems Networking and Telecommunications** *1 student enrolled* • **Computer and Information Sciences and Support Services, Other** *1 student enrolled* • **General Office Occupations and Clerical Services** *3 students enrolled* • **Phlebotomy/Phlebotomist** *2 students enrolled* • **Web/Multimedia Management and Webmaster** *2 students enrolled*

**STUDENT SERVICES** Academic or career counseling, employment services for current students, remedial services.

## Centralia College

600 Centralia College Boulevard, Centralia, WA 98531-4099
http://www.centralia.edu/

**CONTACT** James M. Walton, President
**Telephone:** 360-736-9391 Ext. 428

**GENERAL INFORMATION** Public Institution. Founded 1925. **Accreditation:** Regional (NCCU/NCCU). **Total program enrollment:** 1356.

PROGRAM(S) OFFERED

• **Administrative Assistant and Secretarial Science, General** *2 students enrolled* • **Building/Construction Finishing, Management, and Inspection, Other** *1 student enrolled* • **Clinical/Medical Laboratory Assistant** *1 student enrolled* • **Computer and Information Sciences and Support Services, Other** *1 student enrolled* • **Corrections** *1 student enrolled* • **Data Entry/Microcomputer Applications, General** *10 students enrolled* • **Forensic Science and Technology** *1 student enrolled* • **Health Unit Coordinator/Ward Clerk** *2 students enrolled* • **Legal Administrative Assistant/Secretary** *2 students enrolled* • **Licensed Practical/Vocational Nurse Training (LPN, LVN, Cert, Dipl, AAS)** *29 students enrolled* • **Marketing, Other** *2 students enrolled* • **Medical Administrative/Executive Assistant and Medical Secretary** *8 students enrolled* • **Medical/Clinical Assistant** *2 students enrolled* • **Mental and Social Health Services and Allied Professions, Other** *2 students enrolled* • **Pharmacy Technician/Assistant** *1 student enrolled* • **Phlebotomy/Phlebotomist** *2 students enrolled*

**STUDENT SERVICES** Academic or career counseling, daycare for children of students, employment services for current students, placement services for program completers, remedial services.

## Chetta's Academy of Hair and Nails

1222 E. Front ST, Port Angeles, WA 98362

**CONTACT** Chetta Wallace, Owner
**Telephone:** 360-417-0388

**GENERAL INFORMATION** Private Institution. **Total program enrollment:** 13.

PROGRAM(S) OFFERED

• **Cosmetology, Barber/Styling, and Nail Instructor** *600 hrs./$3500*
• **Cosmetology/Cosmetologist, General** *1800 hrs./$11,700*

## City University of Seattle

11900 Northeast First Street, Bellevue, WA 98005
http://www.cityu.edu/

**CONTACT** Edward Lee Gorsuch, II, President
**Telephone:** 425-637-1010 Ext. 3563

**GENERAL INFORMATION** Private Institution. Founded 1973. **Accreditation:** Regional (NCCU/NCCU). **Total program enrollment:** 1925. **Application fee:** $50.

**PROGRAM(S) OFFERED**
• **Accounting Technology/Technician and Bookkeeping** *7 students enrolled* • **Accounting** *2 students enrolled* • **Business, Management, Marketing, and Related Support Services, Other** *5 students enrolled* • **Marketing/Marketing Management, General** *2 students enrolled* • **Secondary Education and Teaching** *1 student enrolled*

## Clares Beauty College

104 North 4th Avenue, Pasco, WA 99301

**CONTACT** Richard D. Larson, Owner
**Telephone:** 509-547-8871

**GENERAL INFORMATION** Private Institution. **Total program enrollment:** 51.

**PROGRAM(S) OFFERED**
• **Cosmetology/Cosmetologist, General** *1800 hrs./$9323*

**STUDENT SERVICES** Academic or career counseling, employment services for current students, placement services for program completers, remedial services.

## Clark College

1933 Fort Vancouver Way, Vancouver, WA 98663-3598
http://www.clark.edu/

**CONTACT** Robert K. Knight, President
**Telephone:** 360-992-2000

**GENERAL INFORMATION** Public Institution. Founded 1933. **Accreditation:** Regional (NCCU/NCCU); dental hygiene (ADA); medical assisting (AAMAE). **Total program enrollment:** 4718.

**PROGRAM(S) OFFERED**
• **Accounting Technology/Technician and Bookkeeping** *3 students enrolled* • **Baking and Pastry Arts/Baker/Pastry Chef** *10 students enrolled* • **Business Administration and Management, General** *1 student enrolled* • **Business/Office Automation/Technology/Data Entry** *2 students enrolled* • **CAD/CADD Drafting and/or Design Technology/Technician** *4 students enrolled* • **Computer Systems Networking and Telecommunications** *1 student enrolled* • **Construction Engineering Technology/Technician** *1 student enrolled* • **Culinary Arts/Chef Training** *8 students enrolled* • **Data Entry/Microcomputer Applications, General** *29 students enrolled* • **Early Childhood Education and Teaching** *4 students enrolled* • **Electrical and Power Transmission Installation/Installer, General** *5 students enrolled* • **Electrical, Electronic and Communications Engineering Technology/Technician** *11 students enrolled* • **Emergency Care Attendant (EMT Ambulance)** *1 student enrolled* • **Executive Assistant/Executive Secretary** *5 students enrolled* • **General Office Occupations and Clerical Services** *8 students enrolled* • **Health Information/Medical Records Technology/Technician** *11 students enrolled* • **Human Resources Management/Personnel Administration, General** *6 students enrolled* • **Landscaping and Groundskeeping** *2 students enrolled* • **Legal Assistant/Paralegal** *2 students enrolled* • **Medical Insurance Coding Specialist/Coder** *19 students enrolled* • **Medical Reception/Receptionist** *9 students enrolled* • **Medical Transcription/Transcriptionist** *6 students enrolled* • **Medical/Clinical Assistant** *4 students enrolled* • **Nurse/Nursing Assistant/Aide and Patient Care Assistant** *14 students enrolled* • **Pharmacy Technician/Assistant** *48 students enrolled* • **Phlebotomy/Phlebotomist** *40 students enrolled* • **Plant Nursery Operations and Management** *2 students enrolled* • **Prepress/Desktop Publishing and Digital Imaging Design** *6 students enrolled* • **Receptionist** *1 student enrolled* • **Selling Skills and Sales Operations** *1 student enrolled* • **Small Business Administration/Management** *1 student enrolled* • **Substance Abuse/Addiction Counseling** *2 students enrolled* • **Telecommunications Technology/Technician** *7 students enrolled* • **Web Page, Digital/Multimedia and Information Resources Design** *3 students enrolled* • **Web/Multimedia Management and Webmaster** *1 student enrolled* • **Welding Technology/Welder** *95 students enrolled*

**STUDENT SERVICES** Academic or career counseling, daycare for children of students, employment services for current students, placement services for program completers, remedial services.

## Clover Park Technical College

4500 Steilacoom Boulevard, SW, Lakewood, WA 98499
http://www.cptc.edu/

**CONTACT** John Walstrum, President
**Telephone:** 253-589-5800

**GENERAL INFORMATION** Public Institution. Founded 1942. **Accreditation:** Regional (NCCU/NCCU); dental assisting (ADA); medical laboratory technology (NAACLS). **Total program enrollment:** 2302. **Application fee:** $43.

**PROGRAM(S) OFFERED**
• **Accounting Technology/Technician and Bookkeeping** *1 student enrolled* • **Aesthetician/Esthetician and Skin Care Specialist** *63 students enrolled* • **Airline/Commercial/Professional Pilot and Flight Crew** *2 students enrolled* • **Allied Health Diagnostic, Intervention, and Treatment Professions, Other** *11 students enrolled* • **Autobody/Collision and Repair Technology/Technician** *23 students enrolled* • **Automobile/Automotive Mechanics Technology/Technician** *15 students enrolled* • **Computer Systems Networking and Telecommunications** *6 students enrolled* • **Computer and Information Sciences and Support Services, Other** *35 students enrolled* • **Computer and Information Systems Security** *3 students enrolled* • **Construction Trades, Other** *20 students enrolled* • **Cosmetology/Cosmetologist, General** *7 students enrolled* • **Customer Service Support/Call Center/Teleservice Operation** *11 students enrolled* • **Data Processing and Data Processing Technology/Technician** *2 students enrolled* • **Dental Assisting/Assistant** *16 students enrolled* • **Dietitian Assistant** *2 students enrolled* • **Early Childhood Education and Teaching** *6 students enrolled* • **Fire Protection, Other** *4 students enrolled* • **Floriculture/Floristry Operations and Management** *14 students enrolled* • **General Office Occupations and Clerical Services** *1 student enrolled* • **Health Unit Coordinator/Ward Clerk** *72 students enrolled* • **Health and Medical Administrative Services, Other** *9 students enrolled* • **Human Resources Management/Personnel Administration, General** *3 students enrolled* • **Licensed Practical/Vocational Nurse Training (LPN, LVN, Cert, Dipl, AAS)** *74 students enrolled* • **Machine Tool Technology/Machinist** *1 student enrolled* • **Marketing/Marketing Management, General** *3 students enrolled* • **Massage Therapy/Therapeutic Massage** *46 students enrolled* • **Medical Insurance Coding Specialist/Coder** *23 students enrolled* • **Medical Office Assistant/Specialist** *17 students enrolled* • **Medical/Clinical Assistant** *27 students enrolled* • **Nail Technician/Specialist and Manicurist** *14 students enrolled* • **Nurse/Nursing Assistant/Aide and Patient Care Assistant** *126 students enrolled* • **Pharmacy Technician/Assistant** *7 students enrolled* • **Phlebotomy/Phlebotomist** *102 students enrolled* • **Prepress/Desktop Publishing and Digital Imaging Design** *2 students enrolled* • **Quality Control and Safety Technologies/Technicians, Other** *3 students enrolled* • **Restaurant, Culinary, and Catering Management/Manager** *1 student enrolled* • **Security and Protective Services, Other** *3 students enrolled* • **Substance Abuse/Addiction Counseling** *3 students enrolled* • **Telecommunications Technology/Technician** *2 students enrolled* • **Tourism and Travel Services Marketing Operations** *30 students enrolled* • **Upholstery/Upholsterer** *2 students enrolled* • **Web Page, Digital/Multimedia and Information Resources Design** *5 students enrolled* • **Welding Technology/Welder** *2 students enrolled*

**STUDENT SERVICES** Academic or career counseling, daycare for children of students, employment services for current students, remedial services.

## Columbia Basin College

2600 North 20th Avenue, Pasco, WA 99301-3397
http://www.columbiabasin.edu/

**CONTACT** Richard Cummins, President
**Telephone:** 509-547-0511

**GENERAL INFORMATION** Public Institution. Founded 1955. **Accreditation:** Regional (NCCU/NCCU); dental hygiene (ADA); emergency medical services (JRCEMTP). **Total program enrollment:** 3265. **Application fee:** $26.

**PROGRAM(S) OFFERED**

• **Accounting Technology/Technician and Bookkeeping** *11 students enrolled* • **Computer Programming/Programmer, General** *4 students enrolled* • **Drafting and Design Technology/Technician, General** *2 students enrolled* • **Health Unit Coordinator/Ward Clerk** *2 students enrolled* • **Licensed Practical/Vocational Nurse Training (LPN, LVN, Cert, Dipl, AAS)** *36 students enrolled* • **Marketing/ Marketing Management, General** *3 students enrolled* • **Medical Administrative/ Executive Assistant and Medical Secretary** *2 students enrolled* • **Medical Insurance Coding Specialist/Coder** *1 student enrolled* • **Medical Office Assistant/ Specialist** *5 students enrolled* • **Medical/Clinical Assistant** *12 students enrolled* • **Receptionist** *4 students enrolled* • **Teacher Assistant/Aide** *1 student enrolled*

**STUDENT SERVICES** Academic or career counseling, employment services for current students, placement services for program completers, remedial services.

## Cortiva Institute—Brenneke School of Massage

425 Pontius Ave N, #100, Seattle, WA 98109
http://www.brennekeschool.com/

**CONTACT** Dina Boon, President
**Telephone:** 206-282-1233

**GENERAL INFORMATION** Private Institution. Founded 1972. **Total program enrollment:** 103. **Application fee:** $100.

**PROGRAM(S) OFFERED**

• **Massage Therapy/Therapeutic Massage** *56 hrs./$10,900*

**STUDENT SERVICES** Academic or career counseling, placement services for program completers.

## Divers Institute of Technology

4315 11th Avenue, NW, PO Box 70667, Seattle, WA 98107-0667
http://www.diversinstitute.com/

**CONTACT** Stefanie Kilcup, Registrar
**Telephone:** 206-783-5542

**GENERAL INFORMATION** Private Institution. Founded 1968. **Total program enrollment:** 116. **Application fee:** $100.

**PROGRAM(S) OFFERED**

• **Diver, Professional and Instructor** *900 hrs./$20,300*

**STUDENT SERVICES** Academic or career counseling, employment services for current students, placement services for program completers.

## Edmonds Community College

20000 68th Avenue West, Lynnwood, WA 98036-5999
http://www.edcc.edu/

**CONTACT** Jack Oharah, President
**Telephone:** 425-640-1459

**GENERAL INFORMATION** Public Institution. Founded 1967. **Accreditation:** Regional (NCCU/NCCU). **Total program enrollment:** 3938. **Application fee:** $19.

**PROGRAM(S) OFFERED**

• **Accounting Technology/Technician and Bookkeeping** *20 students enrolled* • **Administrative Assistant and Secretarial Science, General** *4 students enrolled* • **Applied Horticulture/Horticultural Operations, General** *19 students enrolled* • **Audiovisual Communications Technologies/Technicians, Other** *5 students enrolled* • **Building/Home/Construction Inspection/Inspector** *7 students enrolled* • **Business Administration and Management, General** *66 students enrolled* • **Clinical/Medical Laboratory Assistant** *18 students enrolled* • **Computer Graphics** *1 student enrolled* • **Computer Programming, Vendor/ Product Certification** *3 students enrolled* • **Computer Programming/ Programmer, General** *5 students enrolled* • **Computer Systems Networking and Telecommunications** *6 students enrolled* • **Computer Technology/Computer Systems Technology** *7 students enrolled* • **Computer and Information Sciences and Support Services, Other** *4 students enrolled* • **Computer and Information Systems Security** *15 students enrolled* • **Construction Management** *10 students enrolled* • **Construction Trades, Other** *36 students enrolled* • **Culinary Arts/Chef Training** *3 students enrolled* • **Data Entry/Microcomputer Applications, General** *37 students enrolled* • **Data Modeling/Warehousing and Database Administration** *2 students enrolled* • **Data Processing and Data Processing Technology/ Technician** *1 student enrolled* • **E-Commerce/Electronic Commerce** *4 students enrolled* • **Early Childhood Education and Teaching** *7 students enrolled* • **Electrical, Electronic and Communications Engineering Technology/Technician** *3 students enrolled* • **Electrocardiograph Technology/Technician** *9 students enrolled* • **Engineering Technology, General** *47 students enrolled* • **Entrepreneurship/ Entrepreneurial Studies** *8 students enrolled* • **General Office Occupations and Clerical Services** *14 students enrolled* • **Graphic and Printing Equipment Operator, General Production** *6 students enrolled* • **Health Aides/Attendants/ Orderlies, Other** *2 students enrolled* • **Health Information/Medical Records Technology/Technician** *5 students enrolled* • **Health Professions and Related Clinical Sciences, Other** *7 students enrolled* • **Hospitality Administration/ Management, General** *7 students enrolled* • **Human Resources Management/ Personnel Administration, General** *12 students enrolled* • **Legal Assistant/ Paralegal** *44 students enrolled* • **Marketing/Marketing Management, General** *10 students enrolled* • **Medical Administrative/Executive Assistant and Medical Secretary** *3 students enrolled* • **Medical Reception/Receptionist** *22 students enrolled* • **Mental and Social Health Services and Allied Professions, Other** *4 students enrolled* • **Nurse/Nursing Assistant/Aide and Patient Care Assistant** *17 students enrolled* • **Office Management and Supervision** *6 students enrolled* • **Pharmacy Technician/Assistant** *14 students enrolled* • **Phlebotomy/ Phlebotomist** *14 students enrolled* • **Robotics Technology/Technician** *4 students enrolled* • **Substance Abuse/Addiction Counseling** *4 students enrolled* • **Tourism and Travel Services Management** *5 students enrolled* • **Tourism and Travel Services Marketing Operations** *6 students enrolled* • **Web Page, Digital/ Multimedia and Information Resources Design** *40 students enrolled* • **Web/ Multimedia Management and Webmaster** *7 students enrolled* • **Welding Technology/Welder** *1 student enrolled*

**STUDENT SERVICES** Academic or career counseling, daycare for children of students, employment services for current students, placement services for program completers, remedial services.

## Everest College

155 Washington Avenue, Suite 200, Bremerton, WA 98337
http://www.everest.edu/

**CONTACT** Janet O'Connell, School President
**Telephone:** 360-473-1120

**GENERAL INFORMATION** Private Institution. **Total program enrollment:** 150.

**PROGRAM(S) OFFERED**

• **Dental Assisting/Assistant** *720 hrs./$13,046* • **Massage Therapy/Therapeutic Massage** *720 hrs./$12,647* • **Medical Insurance Specialist/Medical Biller** *34 students enrolled* • **Medical Transcription/Transcriptionist** *720 hrs./$11,220* • **Medical/Clinical Assistant** *720 hrs./$14,369* • **Pharmacy Technician/ Assistant** *720 hrs./$13,310*

**STUDENT SERVICES** Academic or career counseling, employment services for current students, placement services for program completers.

## Everest College

906 Everett Mall Way, Everett, WA 98201
http://www.everest.edu/

**CONTACT** Kim Lothyan, School President
**Telephone:** 425-789-7960

**GENERAL INFORMATION** Private Institution. Founded 1922. **Total program enrollment:** 155.

**PROGRAM(S) OFFERED**

• **Dental Assisting/Assistant** *880 hrs./$13,046* • **Medical Insurance Specialist/ Medical Biller** *780 hrs./$11,220* • **Medical/Clinical Assistant** *720 hrs./$14,339* • **Pharmacy Technician/Assistant** *880 hrs./$13,310*

**STUDENT SERVICES** Academic or career counseling, employment services for current students, placement services for program completers.

## Everest College

981 Powell Avenue SW, Suite 200, Renton, WA 98055
http://www.everest.edu/

**CONTACT** Michele O'Neill, School President
**Telephone:** 425-255-3281

**GENERAL INFORMATION** Private Institution. **Total program enrollment:** 613.

**PROGRAM(S) OFFERED**
• **Dental Assisting/Assistant** *720 hrs./$13,589* • **Medical Administrative/Executive Assistant and Medical Secretary** *720 hrs./$13,542* • **Medical Insurance Coding Specialist/Coder** *720 hrs./$12,563* • **Medical Insurance Specialist/Medical Biller** *56 students enrolled* • **Medical Office Management/Administration** *57 students enrolled* • **Medical/Clinical Assistant** *720 hrs./$14,641* • **Pharmacy Technician/Assistant** *800 hrs./$13,698*

**STUDENT SERVICES** Academic or career counseling, employment services for current students, placement services for program completers, remedial services.

## Everest College

2156 Pacific Avenue, Tacoma, WA 98402
http://www.everest.edu/

**CONTACT** Timothy E. Allen, President
**Telephone:** 253-207-4000

**GENERAL INFORMATION** Private Institution. Founded 2003. **Total program enrollment:** 307.

**PROGRAM(S) OFFERED**
• **Dental Assisting/Assistant** *880 hrs./$13,046* • **Medical Insurance Specialist/Medical Biller** *780 hrs./$11,220* • **Medical/Clinical Assistant** *720 hrs./$14,371* • **Pharmacy Technician/Assistant** *880 hrs./$13,310*

**STUDENT SERVICES** Academic or career counseling, placement services for program completers.

## Everest College

120 Northeast 136th Avenue, Suite 130, Vancouver, WA 98684
http://www.everest.edu/

**CONTACT** Brad Kuchenreuther, President
**Telephone:** 360-254-3282

**GENERAL INFORMATION** Private Institution. Founded 1979. **Accreditation:** State accredited or approved. **Total program enrollment:** 234.

**PROGRAM(S) OFFERED**
• **Accounting and Related Services, Other** *2 students enrolled* • **Accounting** *6 students enrolled* • **Administrative Assistant and Secretarial Science, General** *4 students enrolled* • **Business/Office Automation/Technology/Data Entry** *2 students enrolled* • **Legal Administrative Assistant/Secretary** • **Medical Administrative/Executive Assistant and Medical Secretary** *23 students enrolled* • **Medical Insurance Coding Specialist/Coder** *40 students enrolled* • **Medical/Clinical Assistant** *20 students enrolled*

**STUDENT SERVICES** Academic or career counseling, employment services for current students, placement services for program completers.

## Everett Community College

2000 Tower Street, Everett, WA 98201-1327
http://www.evcc.ctc.edu/

**CONTACT** David N. Beyer, President
**Telephone:** 425-388-9100

**GENERAL INFORMATION** Public Institution. Founded 1941. **Accreditation:** Regional (NCCU/NCCU). **Total program enrollment:** 3326.

**PROGRAM(S) OFFERED**
• **Accounting Technology/Technician and Bookkeeping** *15 students enrolled* • **Administrative Assistant and Secretarial Science, General** *1 student enrolled* • **Business Administration and Management, General** *7 students enrolled* • **Business/Office Automation/Technology/Data Entry** *4 students enrolled* • **Computer Graphics** *3 students enrolled* • **Computer Systems Networking and Telecommunications** *4 students enrolled* • **Computer and Information Sciences and Support Services, Other** *10 students enrolled* • **Data Modeling/Warehousing and Database Administration** *4 students enrolled* • **Drafting and Design Technology/Technician, General** *5 students enrolled* • **Early Childhood Education and Teaching** *1 student enrolled* • **Entrepreneurship/Entrepreneurial Studies** *14 students enrolled* • **Fire Science/Firefighting** *13 students enrolled* • **General Office Occupations and Clerical Services** *8 students enrolled* • **Geography, Other** *3 students enrolled* • **Legal Administrative Assistant/Secretary** *8 students enrolled* • **Licensed Practical/Vocational Nurse Training (LPN, LVN, Cert, Dipl, AAS)** *11 students enrolled* • **Machine Tool Technology/Machinist** *7 students enrolled* • **Medical Insurance Coding Specialist/Coder** *23 students enrolled* • **Medical Office Management/Administration** *7 students enrolled* • **Medical Reception/Receptionist** *12 students enrolled* • **Medical Transcription/Transcriptionist** *90 students enrolled* • **Medical/Clinical Assistant** *24 students enrolled* • **Phlebotomy/Phlebotomist** *1 student enrolled* • **Web Page, Digital/Multimedia and Information Resources Design** *1 student enrolled* • **Web/Multimedia Management and Webmaster** *1 student enrolled* • **Welding Technology/Welder** *1 student enrolled* • **Word Processing** *1 student enrolled*

**STUDENT SERVICES** Academic or career counseling, daycare for children of students, employment services for current students, placement services for program completers, remedial services.

## Evergreen Beauty and Barber College

802 SE Everett Mall Way, Suite A, Everett, WA 98208
http://www.evergreenbeautybarber.com/

**CONTACT** Frank Trieu, President
**Telephone:** 425-423-9186

**GENERAL INFORMATION** Private Institution. **Total program enrollment:** 81. **Application fee:** $100.

**PROGRAM(S) OFFERED**
• **Aesthetician/Esthetician and Skin Care Specialist** *600 hrs./$7650* • **Barbering/Barber** *1100 hrs./$9350* • **Cosmetology, Barber/Styling, and Nail Instructor** *600 hrs./$5200* • **Cosmetology/Cosmetologist, General** *1800 hrs./$13,600* • **Nail Technician/Specialist and Manicurist** *600 hrs./$4400*

## Gene Juarez Academy of Beauty

10715 8th Avenue, NE, Seattle, WA 98125
http://www.genejuarezacademy.com/

**CONTACT** Moira Douglass, Executive Director of Administration
**Telephone:** 206-368-0210

**GENERAL INFORMATION** Private Institution. Founded 1987. **Total program enrollment:** 360.

**PROGRAM(S) OFFERED**
• **Cosmetology, Barber/Styling, and Nail Instructor** *500 hrs./$5100* • **Cosmetology/Cosmetologist, General** *1600 hrs./$15,295* • **Nail Technician/Specialist and Manicurist** *600 hrs./$5600*

**STUDENT SERVICES** Academic or career counseling, employment services for current students, placement services for program completers.

## Gene Juarez Academy of Beauty–Branch Campus

2222 South 314 Street, Federal Way, WA 98003
http://www.genejuarezacademy.com/

**CONTACT** Moira Douglass, Executive Director of Administration
**Telephone:** 253-839-4338

**GENERAL INFORMATION** Private Institution. **Total program enrollment:** 393.

**PROGRAM(S) OFFERED**

• **Cosmetology/Cosmetologist, General** *1600 hrs./$15,295*

**STUDENT SERVICES** Academic or career counseling, employment services for current students, placement services for program completers.

## Glen Dow Academy of Hair Design

309 West Riverside Avenue, Spokane, WA 99201
http://www.glendow.com/

**CONTACT** Martin A. Dow, CEO
**Telephone:** 509-624-3244 Ext. 1

**GENERAL INFORMATION** Private Institution. Founded 1969. **Total program enrollment:** 161. **Application fee:** $100.

**PROGRAM(S) OFFERED**

• **Aesthetician/Esthetician and Skin Care Specialist** *660 hrs./$3577* • **Cosmetology, Barber/Styling, and Nail Instructor** *600 hrs./$2688* • **Cosmetology/Cosmetologist, General** *1970 hrs./$12,157* • **Nail Technician/Specialist and Manicurist** *660 hrs./$3577*

**STUDENT SERVICES** Academic or career counseling.

## Grays Harbor College

1620 Edward P Smith Drive, Aberdeen, WA 98520-7599
http://www.ghc.ctc.edu/

**CONTACT** Dr. Ed Brewster, President
**Telephone:** 360-532-9020

**GENERAL INFORMATION** Public Institution. Founded 1930. **Accreditation:** Regional (NCCU/NCCU). **Total program enrollment:** 1183.

**PROGRAM(S) OFFERED**

• **Accounting Technology/Technician and Bookkeeping** *1 student enrolled* • **Automobile/Automotive Mechanics Technology/Technician** *7 students enrolled* • **Building/Property Maintenance and Management** *72 students enrolled* • **CAD/CADD Drafting and/or Design Technology/Technician** *5 students enrolled* • **Carpentry/Carpenter** *1 student enrolled* • **Computer Systems Networking and Telecommunications** *2 students enrolled* • **Computer and Information Sciences and Support Services, Other** *1 student enrolled* • **Criminal Justice/Police Science** *1 student enrolled* • **Data Entry/Microcomputer Applications, General** *56 students enrolled* • **Early Childhood Education and Teaching** *3 students enrolled* • **General Office Occupations and Clerical Services** *6 students enrolled* • **Health Information/Medical Records Technology/Technician** *7 students enrolled* • **Licensed Practical/Vocational Nurse Training (LPN, LVN, Cert, Dipl, AAS)** *21 students enrolled* • **Medical Insurance Coding Specialist/Coder** *6 students enrolled* • **Medical Transcription/Transcriptionist** *2 students enrolled* • **Office Management and Supervision** *4 students enrolled* • **Pharmacy Technician/Assistant** *6 students enrolled* • **Truck and Bus Driver/Commercial Vehicle Operation** *35 students enrolled* • **Water, Wetlands, and Marine Resources Management** *1 student enrolled* • **Welding Technology/Welder** *7 students enrolled*

**STUDENT SERVICES** Academic or career counseling, daycare for children of students, employment services for current students, placement services for program completers, remedial services.

## Green River Community College

12401 Southeast 320th Street, Auburn, WA 98092-3699
http://www.greenriver.edu/

**CONTACT** Richard A. Rutkowski, President
**Telephone:** 253-833-9111

**GENERAL INFORMATION** Public Institution. Founded 1965. **Accreditation:** Regional (NCCU/NCCU). **Total program enrollment:** 4420.

**PROGRAM(S) OFFERED**

• **Accounting Technology/Technician and Bookkeeping** *43 students enrolled* • **Air Traffic Controller** *38 students enrolled* • **Air Transportation, Other** *1 student enrolled* • **Airline/Commercial/Professional Pilot and Flight Crew** *63 students enrolled* • **Architectural Drafting and Architectural CAD/CADD** *4 students enrolled* • **Autobody/Collision and Repair Technology/Technician** *1 student enrolled* • **Automobile/Automotive Mechanics Technology/Technician** *46 students enrolled* • **Aviation/Airway Management and Operations** *9 students enrolled* • **Business Operations Support and Secretarial Services, Other** *33 students enrolled* • **Carpentry/Carpenter** *36 students enrolled* • **Computer and Information Sciences and Support Services, Other** *21 students enrolled* • **Computer and Information Systems Security** *3 students enrolled* • **Criminal Justice/Police Science** *5 students enrolled* • **Data Entry/Microcomputer Applications, General** *2 students enrolled* • **Drafting and Design Technology/Technician, General** *27 students enrolled* • **Early Childhood Education and Teaching** *35 students enrolled* • **Forensic Science and Technology** *4 students enrolled* • **General Office Occupations and Clerical Services** *86 students enrolled* • **Geography, Other** *5 students enrolled* • **Legal Administrative Assistant/Secretary** *1 student enrolled* • **Marketing/Marketing Management, General** *4 students enrolled* • **Mechanical Drafting and Mechanical Drafting CAD/CADD** *1 student enrolled* • **Medical Insurance Coding Specialist/Coder** *1 student enrolled* • **Medical Transcription/Transcriptionist** *1 student enrolled* • **Nurse/Nursing Assistant/Aide and Patient Care Assistant** *26 students enrolled* • **Office Management and Supervision** *4 students enrolled* • **System, Networking, and LAN/WAN Management/Manager** *3 students enrolled* • **Teacher Education and Professional Development, Specific Levels and Methods, Other** *4 students enrolled* • **Water Quality and Wastewater Treatment Management and Recycling Technology/Technician** *7 students enrolled* • **Welding Technology/Welder** *22 students enrolled*

**STUDENT SERVICES** Academic or career counseling, daycare for children of students, employment services for current students, placement services for program completers, remedial services.

## Greenwood Academy of Hair

8501 Greenwood Avenue, N, Seattle, WA 98103
http://greenwoodacademyofhair.edu/

**CONTACT** Patty Davis, Owners
**Telephone:** 206-782-0220 Ext. 5

**GENERAL INFORMATION** Private Institution. **Total program enrollment:** 26.

**PROGRAM(S) OFFERED**

• **Aesthetician/Esthetician and Skin Care Specialist** *32 students enrolled* • **Cosmetology/Cosmetologist, General** *1800 hrs./$13,040* • **Technical Teacher Education** *2 students enrolled*

## Heritage University

3240 Fort Road, Toppenish, WA 98948-9599
http://www.heritage.edu/

**CONTACT** Kathleen Ross, President
**Telephone:** 509-865-8500

**GENERAL INFORMATION** Private Institution. Founded 1982. **Accreditation:** Regional (NCCU/NCCU). **Total program enrollment:** 566.

**PROGRAM(S) OFFERED**

• **Accounting** • **Business Administration and Management, General** • **Computer Science** • **Licensed Practical/Vocational Nurse Training (LPN, LVN, Cert, Dipl, AAS)** *22 students enrolled* • **Natural Resources/Conservation, General** • **Science, Technology and Society**

**STUDENT SERVICES** Academic or career counseling, daycare for children of students, employment services for current students, placement services for program completers, remedial services.

## Highline Community College

2400 S. 240th Street, PO Box 98000, Des Moines, WA 98198-9800
http://www.highline.edu/

**CONTACT** Jack Bermingham, President
**Telephone:** 206-878-3710

**GENERAL INFORMATION** Public Institution. Founded 1961. **Accreditation:** Regional (NCCU/NCCU); medical assisting (AAMAE). **Total program enrollment:** 3356. **Application fee:** $24.

*Highline Community College (continued)*

**PROGRAM(S) OFFERED**

• **Accounting Technology/Technician and Bookkeeping** *7 students enrolled* • **Administrative Assistant and Secretarial Science, General** *37 students enrolled* • **Allied Health Diagnostic, Intervention, and Treatment Professions, Other** *9 students enrolled* • **Audiovisual Communications Technologies/Technicians, Other** *2 students enrolled* • **Computer Systems Networking and Telecommunications** *1 student enrolled* • **Customer Service Management** *8 students enrolled* • **Data Modeling/Warehousing and Database Administration** *1 student enrolled* • **Early Childhood Education and Teaching** *42 students enrolled* • **General Office Occupations and Clerical Services** *1 student enrolled* • **International Business/Trade/Commerce** *4 students enrolled* • **Legal Assistant/Paralegal** *14 students enrolled* • **Library Assistant/Technician** *5 students enrolled* • **Medical Insurance Coding Specialist/Coder** *4 students enrolled* • **Mental and Social Health Services and Allied Professions, Other** *6 students enrolled* • **Nurse/Nursing Assistant/Aide and Patient Care Assistant** *52 students enrolled* • **Office Management and Supervision** *3 students enrolled* • **Opticianry/Ophthalmic Dispensing Optician** *1 student enrolled* • **Phlebotomy/Phlebotomist** *15 students enrolled* • **Small Business Administration/Management** *1 student enrolled* • **System Administration/Administrator** *5 students enrolled* • **Tourism and Travel Services Management** *9 students enrolled*

**STUDENT SERVICES** Academic or career counseling, daycare for children of students, employment services for current students, placement services for program completers, remedial services.

## Inland Massage Institute

111 E. Magnesium Road, Suite F, Spokane, WA 99208-5923
http://www.inlandmassage.com/School.htm

**CONTACT** Patty McNulty, Director
**Telephone:** 509-465-3033

**GENERAL INFORMATION** Private Institution. **Total program enrollment:** 39. **Application fee:** $100.

**PROGRAM(S) OFFERED**

• **Massage Therapy/Therapeutic Massage** *37 students enrolled*

**STUDENT SERVICES** Academic or career counseling, placement services for program completers, remedial services.

## Interface Computer School

9921 North Nevada Street, Spokane, WA 99218
http://www.interfacecomputerschool.edu/

**CONTACT** David Wilson, President
**Telephone:** 509-467-1727

**GENERAL INFORMATION** Private Institution. Founded 1982. **Total program enrollment:** 67.

**PROGRAM(S) OFFERED**

• **Administrative Assistant and Secretarial Science, General** *35 hrs./$11,250* • **Business/Office Automation/Technology/Data Entry** *66 hrs./$21,465* • **Computer and Information Sciences and Support Services, Other** *35 hrs./$11,505* • **Computer and Information Systems Security** *1 student enrolled* • **Medical Insurance Coding Specialist/Coder** *35 hrs./$11,305* • **Medical Office Assistant/Specialist** *35 hrs./$13,459* • **System Administration/Administrator** *9 students enrolled* • **Web/Multimedia Management and Webmaster** *35 hrs./$11,405*

**STUDENT SERVICES** Academic or career counseling, employment services for current students, placement services for program completers, remedial services.

## International Air Academy

2901 East Mill Plain Boulevard, Vancouver, WA 98661-4899
http://www.aha.edu/

**CONTACT** Lynn Rullman, Co-President
**Telephone:** 360-695-2500

**GENERAL INFORMATION** Private Institution. Founded 1980. **Total program enrollment:** 297. **Application fee:** $75.

**PROGRAM(S) OFFERED**

• **Air Transportation, Other** *21 hrs./$4400* • **Culinary Arts/Chef Training** *52 hrs./$16,000* • **Hospitality Administration/Management, General** *52 hrs./$9000* • **Hotel/Motel Administration/Management** *22 students enrolled*

**STUDENT SERVICES** Academic or career counseling, placement services for program completers.

## Kaplan College–Renton Campus

500 Southwest 39th Street, Suite 155, Renton, WA 98057
http://www.kc-renton.com

**CONTACT** Mr. Andrew Rosen, CEO
**Telephone:** 425-291-3620

**GENERAL INFORMATION** Private Institution. **Total program enrollment:** 176.

**PROGRAM(S) OFFERED**

• **Criminal Justice/Law Enforcement Administration** *97 hrs./$23,526* • **Dental Assisting/Assistant** *52 hrs./$13,958* • **Medical Office Assistant/Specialist** *46 hrs./$12,933* • **Medical/Clinical Assistant** *720 hrs./$12,923*

**STUDENT SERVICES** Academic or career counseling, employment services for current students, placement services for program completers, remedial services.

## Kitchen Academy

360 Corporate Drive North, Seattle, WA 98188
http://www.KitchenAcademy.com

**CONTACT** Bruce Edwards, Campus Director
**Telephone:** 206-268-3888

**GENERAL INFORMATION** Private Institution. **Total program enrollment:** 68.

**PROGRAM(S) OFFERED**

• **Culinary Arts/Chef Training** *750 hrs./$19,812*

**STUDENT SERVICES** Employment services for current students, placement services for program completers.

## Lake Washington Technical College

11605 132nd Avenue NE, Kirkland, WA 98034-8506
http://www.lwtc.edu/

**CONTACT** Dr. Sharon McGavick, President
**Telephone:** 425-739-8100

**GENERAL INFORMATION** Public Institution. Founded 1949. **Accreditation:** Regional (NCCU/NCCU); dental assisting (ADA); dental hygiene (ADA); medical assisting (AAMAE). **Total program enrollment:** 1637.

**PROGRAM(S) OFFERED**

• **Accounting Technology/Technician and Bookkeeping** *1 student enrolled* • **Administrative Assistant and Secretarial Science, General** *7 students enrolled* • **Applied Horticulture/Horticultural Operations, General** *6 students enrolled* • **Architectural Drafting and Architectural CAD/CADD** *2 students enrolled* • **Autobody/Collision and Repair Technology/Technician** *3 students enrolled* • **Automobile/Automotive Mechanics Technology/Technician** *3 students enrolled* • **Business Operations Support and Secretarial Services, Other** *1 student enrolled* • **CAD/CADD Drafting and/or Design Technology/Technician** *1* student enrolled • **Computer Graphics** *6 students enrolled* • **Computer Programming/Programmer, General** *1 student enrolled* • **Computer Systems Networking and Telecommunications** *26 students enrolled* • **Computer and Information Systems Security** *1 student enrolled* • **Cosmetology/Cosmetologist, General** *15 students enrolled* • **Culinary Arts/Chef Training** *2 students enrolled* • **Data Entry/Microcomputer Applications, General** *21 students enrolled* • **Dental Assisting/Assistant** *12 students enrolled* • **Diesel Mechanics Technology/Technician** *2 students enrolled* • **Electrical, Electronic and Communications Engineering Technology/Technician** *3 students enrolled* • **Emergency Care Attendant (EMT Ambulance)** *5 students enrolled* • **Entrepreneurial and Small Business Operations, Other** *1 student enrolled* • **Floriculture/Floristry Operations and Management** *8 students enrolled* • **General Office Occupations and Clerical Services** *1 student enrolled* • **Human Resources Management/Personnel Administration, General** *13 students enrolled* • **Industrial Mechanics and Maintenance Technology** *3 students enrolled* • **Legal Administrative Assistant/Secretary** *2 students enrolled* • **Licensed Practical/Vocational Nurse Training (LPN, LVN, Cert, Dipl, AAS)** *14 students enrolled* • **Mechanical Drafting and Mechanical Drafting CAD/CADD** *14 students enrolled* • **Medical Transcription/Transcriptionist** *6 students enrolled* • **Medical/Clinical Assistant** *11 students enrolled* • **Mental and Social Health Services and Allied Professions, Other** *5 students enrolled* • **Motorcycle Maintenance and Repair Technology/Technician** *3 students enrolled* • **Nurse/Nursing Assistant/Aide and Patient Care Assistant** *56 students enrolled* • **Phlebotomy/Phlebotomist** *1 student enrolled* • **Sport and Fitness Administration/Management** *1 student enrolled* • **Web Page, Digital/Multimedia and Information Resources Design** *5 students enrolled* • **Welding Technology/Welder** *12 students enrolled*

**STUDENT SERVICES** Academic or career counseling, daycare for children of students, employment services for current students, placement services for program completers, remedial services.

## Lower Columbia College

PO Box 3010, Longview, WA 98632-0310
http://www.lcc.ctc.edu/

**CONTACT** James L. McLaughlin, President
**Telephone:** 360-442-2311

**GENERAL INFORMATION** Public Institution. Founded 1934. **Accreditation:** Regional (NCCU/NCCU); medical assisting (AAMAE). **Total program enrollment:** 2012. **Application fee:** $14.

**PROGRAM(S) OFFERED**

• **Accounting Technology/Technician and Bookkeeping** *2 students enrolled* • **Accounting and Related Services, Other** *5 students enrolled* • **Administrative Assistant and Secretarial Science, General** *1 student enrolled* • **Automobile/Automotive Mechanics Technology/Technician** *7 students enrolled* • **Business Administration and Management, General** *1 student enrolled* • **Business, Management, Marketing, and Related Support Services, Other** *1 student enrolled* • **Customer Service Support/Call Center/Teleservice Operation** *6 students enrolled* • **Diesel Mechanics Technology/Technician** *2 students enrolled* • **Early Childhood Education and Teaching** *3 students enrolled* • **Electrician** *1 student enrolled* • **Entrepreneurship/Entrepreneurial Studies** *2 students enrolled* • **Fire Science/Firefighting** *1 student enrolled* • **Fire Services Administration** *13 students enrolled* • **General Merchandising, Sales, and Related Marketing Operations, Other** *7 students enrolled* • **General Office Occupations and Clerical Services** *9 students enrolled* • **Licensed Practical/Vocational Nurse Training (LPN, LVN, Cert, Dipl, AAS)** *53 students enrolled* • **Machine Shop Technology/Assistant** *2 students enrolled* • **Marketing, Other** *1 student enrolled* • **Medical Administrative/Executive Assistant and Medical Secretary** *7 students enrolled* • **Medical Insurance Coding Specialist/Coder** *1 student enrolled* • **Medical Radiologic Technology/Science—Radiation Therapist** *2 students enrolled* • **Medical Reception/Receptionist** *3 students enrolled* • **Medical Transcription/Transcriptionist** *3 students enrolled* • **Medical/Clinical Assistant** *9 students enrolled* • **Mental and Social Health Services and Allied Professions, Other** *1 student enrolled* • **Nurse/Nursing Assistant/Aide and Patient Care Assistant** *67 students enrolled* • **Office Management and Supervision** *15 students enrolled* • **Pharmacy Technician/Assistant** *1 student enrolled* • **Teacher Assistant/Aide** *1 student enrolled* • **Veterinary/Animal Health Technology/Technician and Veterinary Assistant** *2 students enrolled* • **Water Quality and Wastewater Treatment Management and Recycling Technology/Technician** *1 student enrolled* • **Welding Technology/Welder** *1 student enrolled* • **Wood Science and Wood Products/Pulp and Paper Technology** *1 student enrolled*

**STUDENT SERVICES** Academic or career counseling, daycare for children of students, employment services for current students, remedial services.

## Milan Institute of Cosmetology

607 SE Everett Mall Way, #5, Everett, WA 98208
http://www.milaninstitute.edu/

**CONTACT** Patrick Davis, President
**Telephone:** 425-353-8193

**GENERAL INFORMATION** Private Institution. Founded 1965. **Total program enrollment:** 87. **Application fee:** $100.

**PROGRAM(S) OFFERED**

• **Aesthetician/Esthetician and Skin Care Specialist** *700 hrs./$9367*
• **Cosmetology, Barber/Styling, and Nail Instructor** *600 hrs./$6092*
• **Cosmetology/Cosmetologist, General** *1600 hrs./$13,723*

**STUDENT SERVICES** Academic or career counseling, employment services for current students, placement services for program completers.

## New Beginnings Beauty College

435 East Main Street, Auburn, WA 98002

**GENERAL INFORMATION** Private Institution. Founded 1992. **Total program enrollment:** 22.

**PROGRAM(S) OFFERED**

• **Cosmetology/Cosmetologist, General** *1800 hrs./$9000*

**STUDENT SERVICES** Academic or career counseling, placement services for program completers.

## North Seattle Community College

9600 College Way North, Seattle, WA 98103-3599
http://www.northseattle.edu/

**CONTACT** Ronald Lafayette, EdD, President
**Telephone:** 206-527-3600

**GENERAL INFORMATION** Public Institution. Founded 1970. **Accreditation:** Regional (NCCU/NCCU); medical assisting (AAMAE). **Total program enrollment:** 1984.

**PROGRAM(S) OFFERED**

• **Accounting Technology/Technician and Bookkeeping** *5 students enrolled* • **Civil Drafting and Civil Engineering CAD/CADD** *3 students enrolled* • **Communications Technology/Technician** *1 student enrolled* • **Customer Service Management** *3 students enrolled* • **Early Childhood Education and Teaching** *36 students enrolled* • **Electrical, Electronic and Communications Engineering Technology/Technician** *3 students enrolled* • **Emergency Medical Technology/Technician (EMT Paramedic)** *104 students enrolled* • **Entrepreneurial and Small Business Operations, Other** *12 students enrolled* • **Health Information/Medical Records Technology/Technician** *3 students enrolled* • **Industrial Electronics Technology/Technician** *2 students enrolled* • **Legal Administrative Assistant/Secretary** *3 students enrolled* • **Licensed Practical/Vocational Nurse Training (LPN, LVN, Cert, Dipl, AAS)** *42 students enrolled* • **Medical Transcription/Transcriptionist** *1 student enrolled* • **Medical/Clinical Assistant** *7 students enrolled* • **Nurse/Nursing Assistant/Aide and Patient Care Assistant** *41 students enrolled* • **Office Management and Supervision** *1 student enrolled* • **Pharmacy Technician/Assistant** *16 students enrolled* • **Phlebotomy/Phlebotomist** *93 students enrolled* • **Real Estate** *27 students enrolled*

**STUDENT SERVICES** Academic or career counseling, daycare for children of students, employment services for current students, placement services for program completers, remedial services.

## Northwest Hair Academy

615 S. First Street, Mt. Vernon, WA 98273
http://www.northwesthairacademy.com/

**CONTACT** D. Camp, Owner
**Telephone:** 360-336-6553 Ext. 106

**GENERAL INFORMATION** Private Institution. **Total program enrollment:** 192. **Application fee:** $150.

*Northwest Hair Academy (continued)*

**PROGRAM(S) OFFERED**
• **Cosmetology, Barber/Styling, and Nail Instructor** *600 hrs./$5595*
• **Cosmetology/Cosmetologist, General** *1800 hrs./$14,800* • **Technical Teacher Education** *6 students enrolled*

**STUDENT SERVICES** Academic or career counseling, employment services for current students, placement services for program completers.

## Northwest HVAC/R Association and Training Center

811 East Sprague, Suite 6, Spokane, WA 99202-2125
http://inwhvac.org/

**CONTACT** Tena Risley, Executive Director
**Telephone:** 509-747-8810

**GENERAL INFORMATION** Private Institution. **Total program enrollment:** 22. **Application fee:** $25.

**PROGRAM(S) OFFERED**
• **Heating, Air Conditioning, Ventilation and Refrigeration Maintenance Technology/Technician (HAC, HACR, HVAC, HVACR)** *900 hrs./$5870*

**STUDENT SERVICES** Academic or career counseling, employment services for current students, placement services for program completers.

## Northwest Indian College

2522 Kwina Road, Bellingham, WA 98226
http://www.nwic.edu/

**CONTACT** Cheryl Crazy Bull, President
**Telephone:** 360-676-2772

**GENERAL INFORMATION** Public Institution. Founded 1978. **Accreditation:** Regional (NCCU/NCCU). **Total program enrollment:** 303.

**PROGRAM(S) OFFERED**
• **American Indian/Native American Studies** *1 student enrolled* • **Computer Installation and Repair Technology/Technician** • **Early Childhood Education and Teaching** • **Substance Abuse/Addiction Counseling**

**STUDENT SERVICES** Academic or career counseling, employment services for current students, remedial services.

## Northwest University

5520 108th Avenue NE, Kirkland, WA 98033
http://www.northwestu.edu/

**CONTACT** Joseph Castleberry, President
**Telephone:** 425-822-8266

**GENERAL INFORMATION** Private Institution (Affiliated with Assemblies of God). Founded 1934. **Accreditation:** Regional (NCCU/NCCU). **Total program enrollment:** 1079. **Application fee:** $30.

**PROGRAM(S) OFFERED**
• **Christian Studies** *1 student enrolled* • **Teaching English as a Second or Foreign Language/ESL Language Instructor** *1 student enrolled*

**STUDENT SERVICES** Academic or career counseling, employment services for current students, placement services for program completers, remedial services.

## Olympic College

1600 Chester Avenue, Bremerton, WA 98337-1699
http://www.olympic.edu/

**CONTACT** Dr. David C. Mitchell, President
**Telephone:** 360-792-6050

**GENERAL INFORMATION** Public Institution. Founded 1946. **Accreditation:** Regional (NCCU/NCCU). **Total program enrollment:** 3405.

**PROGRAM(S) OFFERED**
• **Accounting Technology/Technician and Bookkeeping** *12 students enrolled* • **Administrative Assistant and Secretarial Science, General** *5 students enrolled* • **Aesthetician/Esthetician and Skin Care Specialist** *1 student enrolled* • **Animation, Interactive Technology, Video Graphics and Special Effects** *2 students enrolled* • **Automobile/Automotive Mechanics Technology/Technician** *15 students enrolled* • **Barbering/Barber** *1 student enrolled* • **Business Administration and Management, General** *25 students enrolled* • **CAD/CADD Drafting and/or Design Technology/Technician** *52 students enrolled* • **Computer Programming/Programmer, General** *11 students enrolled* • **Computer Systems Networking and Telecommunications** *3 students enrolled* • **Computer and Information Sciences and Support Services, Other** *9 students enrolled* • **Culinary Arts/Chef Training** *39 students enrolled* • **Customer Service Support/Call Center/Teleservice Operation** *6 students enrolled* • **Drafting and Design Technology/Technician, General** *11 students enrolled* • **Early Childhood Education and Teaching** *4 students enrolled* • **Electrical, Electronic and Communications Engineering Technology/Technician** *1 student enrolled* • **Fire Science/Firefighting** *23 students enrolled* • **Fire Services Administration** *23 students enrolled* • **Industrial Technology/Technician** *63 students enrolled* • **Legal Administrative Assistant/Secretary** *3 students enrolled* • **Licensed Practical/Vocational Nurse Training (LPN, LVN, Cert, Dipl, AAS)** *23 students enrolled* • **Marketing, Other** *5 students enrolled* • **Medical Reception/Receptionist** *13 students enrolled* • **Medical/Clinical Assistant** *14 students enrolled* • **Nurse/Nursing Assistant/Aide and Patient Care Assistant** *57 students enrolled* • **Phlebotomy/Phlebotomist** *24 students enrolled* • **Precision Metal Working, Other** *9 students enrolled* • **Substance Abuse/Addiction Counseling** *2 students enrolled* • **Welding Technology/Welder** *73 students enrolled* • **Youth Services/Administration** *3 students enrolled*

**STUDENT SERVICES** Academic or career counseling, daycare for children of students, employment services for current students, remedial services.

## Peninsula College

1502 East Lauridsen Boulevard, Port Angeles, WA 98362-2779
http://www.pc.ctc.edu/

**CONTACT** Thomas Keegan, President
**Telephone:** 360-452-9277

**GENERAL INFORMATION** Public Institution. Founded 1961. **Accreditation:** Regional (NCCU/NCCU). **Total program enrollment:** 1835.

**PROGRAM(S) OFFERED**
• **Accounting Technology/Technician and Bookkeeping** *15 students enrolled* • **Administrative Assistant and Secretarial Science, General** *3 students enrolled* • **Automobile/Automotive Mechanics Technology/Technician** *81 students enrolled* • **Building/Property Maintenance and Management** *2 students enrolled* • **Business Administration and Management, General** *2 students enrolled* • **Business/Office Automation/Technology/Data Entry** *1 student enrolled* • **Carpentry/Carpenter** *7 students enrolled* • **Child Care Provider/Assistant** *3 students enrolled* • **Computer Programming, Vendor/Product Certification** *1 student enrolled* • **Corrections** *7 students enrolled* • **Data Entry/Microcomputer Applications, General** *24 students enrolled* • **Early Childhood Education and Teaching** *3 students enrolled* • **Family and Consumer Sciences/Human Sciences, Other** *12 students enrolled* • **General Office Occupations and Clerical Services** *7 students enrolled* • **Legal Administrative Assistant/Secretary** *3 students enrolled* • **Massage Therapy/Therapeutic Massage** *10 students enrolled* • **Medical Administrative/Executive Assistant and Medical Secretary** *1 student enrolled* • **Medical Office Management/Administration** *25 students enrolled* • **Medical Reception/Receptionist** *1 student enrolled* • **Medical Transcription/Transcriptionist** *1 student enrolled* • **Medical/Clinical Assistant** *19 students enrolled* • **Plastics Engineering Technology/Technician** *1 student enrolled* • **Radiologic Technology/Science—Radiographer** *2 students enrolled* • **Receptionist** *5 students enrolled* • **Substance Abuse/Addiction Counseling** *7 students enrolled* • **Web Page, Digital/Multimedia and Information Resources Design** *2 students enrolled* • **Welding Technology/Welder** *33 students enrolled*

**STUDENT SERVICES** Academic or career counseling, daycare for children of students, employment services for current students, placement services for program completers, remedial services.

## Perry Technical Institute

2011 West Washington Avenue, Yakima, WA 98903-1296
http://www.perrytech.edu/

**CONTACT** Christine Cote, President
**Telephone:** 509-453-0374 Ext. 218

**GENERAL INFORMATION** Private Institution. Founded 1940. **Total program enrollment:** 449. **Application fee:** $35.

**PROGRAM(S) OFFERED**
• **Automobile/Automotive Mechanics Technology/Technician** *27 students enrolled* • **Business Administration and Management, General** • **Commercial and Advertising Art** *2016 hrs./$20,265* • **Communications Technologies/Technicians and Support Services, Other** *2688 hrs./$20,265* • **Electrician** *3130 hrs./$24,242* • **Heating, Air Conditioning, Ventilation and Refrigeration Maintenance Technology/Technician (HAC, HACR, HVAC, HVACR)** *2688 hrs./$20,742* • **Instrumentation Technology/Technician** *2688 hrs./$20,742* • **Machine Tool Technology/Machinist** *2688 hrs./$20,265* • **Medical Office Management/Administration**

**STUDENT SERVICES** Academic or career counseling, employment services for current students, placement services for program completers, remedial services.

## Pierce College

1601 39th Avenue Southeast, Puyallup, WA 98374-2222
http://www.pierce.ctc.edu/

**CONTACT** Tana Hasart, President
**Telephone:** 253-840-8400

**GENERAL INFORMATION** Public Institution. Founded 1967. **Accreditation:** Regional (NCCU/NCCU); dental hygiene (ADA). **Total program enrollment:** 1345.

**PROGRAM(S) OFFERED**
• **Accounting Technology/Technician and Bookkeeping** *4 students enrolled* • **Business Administration and Management, General** *4 students enrolled* • **Criminal Justice/Law Enforcement Administration** *1 student enrolled* • **General Office Occupations and Clerical Services** *3 students enrolled* • **Human Resources Management/Personnel Administration, General** *4 students enrolled* • **Marketing/Marketing Management, General** *17 students enrolled* • **Medical Administrative/Executive Assistant and Medical Secretary** *14 students enrolled* • **Medical Reception/Receptionist** *3 students enrolled* • **Retailing and Retail Operations** *1 student enrolled* • **Selling Skills and Sales Operations** *3 students enrolled* • **Small Business Administration/Management** *3 students enrolled*

**STUDENT SERVICES** Academic or career counseling, daycare for children of students, employment services for current students, placement services for program completers, remedial services.

## Pierce College at Fort Steilacoom

9401 Farwest Drive SW, Lakewood, WA 98498
http://www.pierce.ctc.edu/

**CONTACT** Denise Yochum, President
**Telephone:** 253-964-6500

**GENERAL INFORMATION** Public Institution. **Total program enrollment:** 2868.

**PROGRAM(S) OFFERED**
• **Baking and Pastry Arts/Baker/Pastry Chef** *4 students enrolled* • **Building/Property Maintenance and Management** *178 students enrolled* • **Business Administration and Management, General** *7 students enrolled* • **Computer Technology/Computer Systems Technology** *1 student enrolled* • **Computer and Information Sciences and Support Services, Other** *2 students enrolled* • **Criminal Justice/Law Enforcement Administration** *23 students enrolled* • **Data Entry/Microcomputer Applications, General** *31 students enrolled* • **Drafting and Design Technology/Technician, General** *14 students enrolled* • **Early Childhood Education and Teaching** *23 students enrolled* • **Forensic Science and Technology** *2 students enrolled* • **General Office Occupations and Clerical Services** *3 students enrolled* • **Marketing/Marketing Management, General** *10 students enrolled* • **Medical Administrative/Executive Assistant and Medical Secretary** *13 students enrolled* • **Medical Reception/Receptionist** *3 students enrolled* • **Psychiatric/Mental Health Services Technician** *12 students enrolled* • **Small Business Administration/Management** *3 students enrolled* • **Substance Abuse/Addiction Counseling** *4 students enrolled* • **Welding Technology/Welder** *47 students enrolled*

**STUDENT SERVICES** Academic or career counseling, daycare for children of students, employment services for current students, placement services for program completers, remedial services.

## Pima Medical Institute

555 South Renton Village Place, Suite 110, Renton, WA 98055
http://www.pmi.edu/

**CONTACT** Bob Panerio, Campus Director
**Telephone:** 425-228-9600

**GENERAL INFORMATION** Private Institution. **Total program enrollment:** 443.

**PROGRAM(S) OFFERED**
• **Dental Assisting/Assistant** *720 hrs./$10,110* • **Medical Administrative/Executive Assistant and Medical Secretary** *560 hrs./$6900* • **Medical/Clinical Assistant** *800 hrs./$10,400* • **Pharmacy Technician/Assistant** *800 hrs./$9780* • **Phlebotomy/Phlebotomist** *300 hrs./$2950* • **Veterinary/Animal Health Technology/Technician and Veterinary Assistant** *720 hrs./$9480*

**STUDENT SERVICES** Academic or career counseling, employment services for current students, placement services for program completers, remedial services.

## Pima Medical Institute

9709 Third Avenue NE, Suite 400, Seattle, WA 98115
http://www.pmi.edu/

**CONTACT** Carey Hochman, Director
**Telephone:** 206-322-6100

**GENERAL INFORMATION** Private Institution. Founded 1989. **Accreditation:** Radiologic technology: radiography (JRCERT); state accredited or approved. **Total program enrollment:** 457.

**PROGRAM(S) OFFERED**
• **Dental Assisting/Assistant** *720 hrs./$10,110* • **Medical Administrative/Executive Assistant and Medical Secretary** *560 hrs./$6900* • **Medical/Clinical Assistant** *800 hrs./$9780* • **Pharmacy Technician/Assistant** *800 hrs./$9780* • **Phlebotomy/Phlebotomist** *300 hrs./$2950* • **Veterinary/Animal Health Technology/Technician and Veterinary Assistant** *720 hrs./$10,152*

**STUDENT SERVICES** Academic or career counseling, employment services for current students, placement services for program completers, remedial services.

## Professional Beauty School

214 South Sixth Street, Sunnyside, WA 98944
http://professionalbeautyschool.com/

**CONTACT** Vicki Schroeder, Director
**Telephone:** 509-576-0966

**GENERAL INFORMATION** Private Institution. **Total program enrollment:** 16. **Application fee:** $100.

**PROGRAM(S) OFFERED**
• **Cosmetology, Barber/Styling, and Nail Instructor** *600 hrs./$4200*
• **Cosmetology/Cosmetologist, General** *1800 hrs./$10,000*

**STUDENT SERVICES** Academic or career counseling, placement services for program completers.

## Professional Beauty School

2105 West Lincoln Avenue, Yakima, WA 98902
http://professionalbeautyschool.com/

**CONTACT** Vicki Schroeder, Director
**Telephone:** 509-576-0966

**GENERAL INFORMATION** Private Institution. **Total program enrollment:** 33. **Application fee:** $100.

**PROGRAM(S) OFFERED**
• **Cosmetology, Barber/Styling, and Nail Instructor** *600 hrs./$4200* • **Cosmetology/Cosmetologist, General** *1800 hrs./$10,000*

**STUDENT SERVICES** Academic or career counseling, placement services for program completers.

## Renton Technical College

3000 NE Fourth Street, Renton, WA 98056-4195
http://www.rtc.edu/

**CONTACT** Dr. Donald Bressler, President
**Telephone:** 425-235-2352

**GENERAL INFORMATION** Public Institution. Founded 1942. **Accreditation:** Regional (NCCU/NCCU); dental assisting (ADA); surgical technology (ARCST). **Total program enrollment:** 1137.

**PROGRAM(S) OFFERED**
• **Accounting Technology/Technician and Bookkeeping** *1 student enrolled* • **Baking and Pastry Arts/Baker/Pastry Chef** *10 students enrolled* • **Banking and Financial Support Services** *9 students enrolled* • **Building/Property Maintenance and Management** *3 students enrolled* • **Business/Office Automation/Technology/Data Entry** *3 students enrolled* • **Clinical/Medical Laboratory Assistant** *17 students enrolled* • **Computer Systems Networking and Telecommunications** *30 students enrolled* • **Construction Trades, Other** *13 students enrolled* • **Data Processing and Data Processing Technology/Technician** *39 students enrolled* • **Dental Assisting/Assistant** *29 students enrolled* • **Drafting and Design Technology/Technician, General** *1 student enrolled* • **Early Childhood Education and Teaching** *14 students enrolled* • **Electrical/Electronics Equipment Installation and Repair, General** *3 students enrolled* • **Environmental Engineering Technology/Environmental Technology** *10 students enrolled* • **Health and Medical Administrative Services, Other** *32 students enrolled* • **Heating, Air Conditioning, Ventilation and Refrigeration Maintenance Technology/Technician (HAC, HACR, HVAC, HVACR)** *3 students enrolled* • **Heavy Equipment Maintenance Technology/Technician** *3 students enrolled* • **Legal Administrative Assistant/Secretary** *5 students enrolled* • **Licensed Practical/Vocational Nurse Training (LPN, LVN, Cert, Dipl, AAS)** *26 students enrolled* • **Massage Therapy/Therapeutic Massage** *20 students enrolled* • **Medical Administrative/Executive Assistant and Medical Secretary** *1 student enrolled* • **Medical Reception/Receptionist** *13 students enrolled* • **Medical/Clinical Assistant** *32 students enrolled* • **Musical Instrument Fabrication and Repair** *17 students enrolled* • **Nurse/Nursing Assistant/Aide and Patient Care Assistant** *95 students enrolled* • **Office Management and Supervision** *8 students enrolled* • **Optometric Technician/Assistant** *6 students enrolled* • **Personal and Culinary Services, Other** *50 students enrolled* • **Pharmacy Technician/Assistant** *18 students enrolled* • **Phlebotomy/Phlebotomist** *40 students enrolled* • **Precision Systems Maintenance and Repair Technologies, Other** *21 students enrolled* • **Receptionist** *18 students enrolled* • **Security and Protective Services, Other** *12 students enrolled* • **Surgical Technology/Technologist** *26 students enrolled* • **Survey Technology/Surveying** *19 students enrolled* • **Teacher Assistant/Aide** *4 students enrolled* • **Veterinary/Animal Health Technology/Technician and Veterinary Assistant** *11 students enrolled* • **Welding Technology/Welder** *12 students enrolled*

**STUDENT SERVICES** Academic or career counseling, daycare for children of students, employment services for current students, placement services for program completers, remedial services.

## Seattle Central Community College

1701 Broadway, Seattle, WA 98122-2400
http://www.seattlecentral.edu/

**CONTACT** Mildred Ollee, President
**Telephone:** 206-587-3800

**GENERAL INFORMATION** Public Institution. Founded 1966. **Accreditation:** Regional (NCCU/NCCU); ophthalmic laboratory technology (COA). **Total program enrollment:** 3866.

**PROGRAM(S) OFFERED**
• **Baking and Pastry Arts/Baker/Pastry Chef** *4 students enrolled* • **Data Modeling/Warehousing and Database Administration** *4 students enrolled* • **Early Childhood Education and Teaching** *1 student enrolled* • **Marine Science/Merchant Marine Officer** *9 students enrolled* • **Office Management and Supervision** *3 students enrolled* • **Substance Abuse/Addiction Counseling** *11 students enrolled* • **Surgical Technology/Technologist** *17 students enrolled* • **Web Page, Digital/Multimedia and Information Resources Design** *4 students enrolled* • **Web/Multimedia Management and Webmaster** *5 students enrolled*

**STUDENT SERVICES** Academic or career counseling, daycare for children of students, employment services for current students, placement services for program completers, remedial services.

## Seattle Vocational Institute

315 22nd Avenue, South, Seattle, WA 98144
http://sviweb.sccd.ctc.edu/

**CONTACT** Norward Brooks, Executive Dean
**Telephone:** 206-587-4950

**GENERAL INFORMATION** Private Institution. Founded 1988. **Total program enrollment:** 238.

**PROGRAM(S) OFFERED**
• **Accounting Technology/Technician and Bookkeeping** *18 students enrolled* • **Computer Installation and Repair Technology/Technician** *11 students enrolled* • **Construction Trades, Other** *27 students enrolled* • **Cosmetology/Cosmetologist, General** *27 students enrolled* • **Dental Assisting/Assistant** *24 students enrolled* • **General Office Occupations and Clerical Services** *32 students enrolled* • **Health Unit Coordinator/Ward Clerk** *1 student enrolled* • **Medical/Clinical Assistant** *1 student enrolled* • **Nurse/Nursing Assistant/Aide and Patient Care Assistant** *18 students enrolled* • **Phlebotomy/Phlebotomist** *38 students enrolled*

**STUDENT SERVICES** Academic or career counseling, daycare for children of students, employment services for current students, placement services for program completers, remedial services.

## Shoreline Community College

16101 Greenwood Avenue North, Shoreline, WA 98133-5696
http://www.shore.ctc.edu/

**CONTACT** Dr. Lee D. Lambert, President
**Telephone:** 206-546-4101

**GENERAL INFORMATION** Public Institution. Founded 1964. **Accreditation:** Regional (NCCU/NCCU); dental hygiene (ADA); health information technology (AHIMA); medical laboratory technology (NAACLS). **Total program enrollment:** 3104.

**PROGRAM(S) OFFERED**
• **Accounting Technology/Technician and Bookkeeping** *19 students enrolled* • **Automobile/Automotive Mechanics Technology/Technician** *16 students enrolled* • **Biology Technician/Biotechnology Laboratory Technician** *6 students enrolled* • **Business Administration and Management, General** *2 students enrolled* • **Business Operations Support and Secretarial Services, Other** *3 students enrolled* • **Business, Management, Marketing, and Related Support Services, Other** *1 student enrolled* • **CAD/CADD Drafting and/or Design Technology/Technician** *1 student enrolled* • **Clinical/Medical Laboratory Assistant** *14 students enrolled* • **Computer Graphics** *57 students enrolled* • **Computer and Information Sciences and Support Services, Other** *2 students enrolled* • **Cosmetology/Cosmetologist, General** *7 students enrolled* • **Data Entry/Microcomputer Applications, General** *3 students enrolled* • **Fashion Merchandising** *2 students enrolled* • **Health Aides/Attendants/Orderlies, Other**

14 students enrolled • **International Business/Trade/Commerce** *1 student enrolled* • **Logistics and Materials Management** *2 students enrolled* • **Machine Tool Technology/Machinist** *11 students enrolled* • **Manufacturing Technology/Technician** *20 students enrolled* • **Marketing, Other** *11 students enrolled* • **Marketing/Marketing Management, General** *1 student enrolled* • **Medical Insurance Specialist/Medical Biller** *13 students enrolled* • **Music, Other** *13 students enrolled* • **Phlebotomy/Phlebotomist** *7 students enrolled* • **Photographic and Film/Video Technology/Technician and Assistant** *9 students enrolled* • **Small Business Administration/Management** *3 students enrolled* • **Teacher Assistant/Aide** *1 student enrolled* • **Web Page, Digital/Multimedia and Information Resources Design** *1 student enrolled*

**STUDENT SERVICES** Academic or career counseling, daycare for children of students, employment services for current students, placement services for program completers, remedial services.

## Skagit Valley College

2405 College Way, Mount Vernon, WA 98273-5899
http://www.skagit.edu/

**CONTACT** Dr. Gary Tollefson, President
**Telephone:** 360-416-7600

**GENERAL INFORMATION** Public Institution. Founded 1926. **Accreditation:** Regional (NCCU/NCCU). **Total program enrollment:** 2503.

**PROGRAM(S) OFFERED**
• **Accounting Technology/Technician and Bookkeeping** *6 students enrolled* • **Automobile/Automotive Mechanics Technology/Technician** *2 students enrolled* • **Business/Office Automation/Technology/Data Entry** *4 students enrolled* • **Computer Programming/Programmer, General** *4 students enrolled* • **Computer Systems Networking and Telecommunications** *5 students enrolled* • **Criminal Justice/Law Enforcement Administration** *45 students enrolled* • **Culinary Arts/Chef Training** *1 student enrolled* • **Data Entry/Microcomputer Applications, General** *1 student enrolled* • **Data Processing and Data Processing Technology/Technician** *5 students enrolled* • **Early Childhood Education and Teaching** *12 students enrolled* • **Entrepreneurship/Entrepreneurial Studies** *1 student enrolled* • **General Office Occupations and Clerical Services** *3 students enrolled* • **Geography, Other** *2 students enrolled* • **Health Information/Medical Records Technology/Technician** *3 students enrolled* • **Legal Assistant/Paralegal** *2 students enrolled* • **Licensed Practical/Vocational Nurse Training (LPN, LVN, Cert, Dipl, AAS)** *84 students enrolled* • **Marine Maintenance/Fitter and Ship Repair Technology/Technician** *7 students enrolled* • **Marketing/Marketing Management, General** *6 students enrolled* • **Medical Reception/Receptionist** *6 students enrolled* • **Medical/Clinical Assistant** *12 students enrolled* • **Pharmacy Technician/Assistant** *15 students enrolled* • **Phlebotomy/Phlebotomist** *9 students enrolled* • **Sport and Fitness Administration/Management** *4 students enrolled* • **Teacher Assistant/Aide** *3 students enrolled* • **Vehicle Maintenance and Repair Technologies, Other** *5 students enrolled* • **Vehicle and Vehicle Parts and Accessories Marketing Operations** *1 student enrolled* • **Web Page, Digital/Multimedia and Information Resources Design** *2 students enrolled* • **Welding Technology/Welder** *19 students enrolled*

**STUDENT SERVICES** Academic or career counseling, daycare for children of students, employment services for current students, placement services for program completers, remedial services.

## South Puget Sound Community College

2011 Mottman Road, SW, Olympia, WA 98512-6292
http://www.spscc.ctc.edu/

**CONTACT** Gerald Pumphrey, President
**Telephone:** 360-596-5241

**GENERAL INFORMATION** Public Institution. Founded 1970. **Accreditation:** Regional (NCCU/NCCU); dental assisting (ADA); medical assisting (AAMAE). **Total program enrollment:** 2624.

**PROGRAM(S) OFFERED**
• **Accounting Technology/Technician and Bookkeeping** *8 students enrolled* • **Applied Horticulture/Horticultural Operations, General** *1 student enrolled* • **Architectural Drafting and Architectural CAD/CADD** *16 students enrolled* • **Banking and Financial Support Services** *1 student enrolled* • **Civil Drafting and Civil Engineering CAD/CADD** *14 students enrolled* • **Culinary Arts/Chef Training** *1 student enrolled* • **Licensed Practical/Vocational Nurse Training (LPN, LVN, Cert, Dipl, AAS)** *40 students enrolled* • **Mechanical Drafting and Mechanical Drafting CAD/CADD** *15 students enrolled* • **Medical Transcription/Transcriptionist** *3 students enrolled* • **Receptionist** *3 students enrolled*

**STUDENT SERVICES** Academic or career counseling, daycare for children of students, employment services for current students, placement services for program completers, remedial services.

## South Seattle Community College

6000 16th Avenue, SW, Seattle, WA 98106-1499
http://southseattle.edu/

**CONTACT** Jill Wakefield, President
**Telephone:** 206-764-5300

**GENERAL INFORMATION** Public Institution. Founded 1970. **Accreditation:** Regional (NCCU/NCCU). **Total program enrollment:** 2141.

**PROGRAM(S) OFFERED**
• **Applied Horticulture/Horticultural Operations, General** *2 students enrolled* • **Automobile/Automotive Mechanics Technology/Technician** *1 student enrolled* • **Baking and Pastry Arts/Baker/Pastry Chef** *3 students enrolled* • **Cosmetology/Cosmetologist, General** *1 student enrolled* • **Culinary Arts/Chef Training** *10 students enrolled* • **Landscaping and Groundskeeping** *2 students enrolled* • **Licensed Practical/Vocational Nurse Training (LPN, LVN, Cert, Dipl, AAS)** *72 students enrolled* • **Medical Office Assistant/Specialist** *2 students enrolled* • **Office Management and Supervision** *4 students enrolled* • **Web Page, Digital/Multimedia and Information Resources Design** *2 students enrolled* • **Welding Technology/Welder** *1 student enrolled*

**STUDENT SERVICES** Academic or career counseling, daycare for children of students, employment services for current students, placement services for program completers, remedial services.

## Spokane Community College

1810 North Greene Street, Spokane, WA 99217-5399
http://www.scc.spokane.edu/

**CONTACT** Joe Dunlap, President
**Telephone:** 509-533-8020

**GENERAL INFORMATION** Public Institution. Founded 1963. **Accreditation:** Regional (NCCU/NCCU); cardiovascular technology (JRCECT); dental assisting (ADA); health information technology (AHIMA); medical assisting (AAMAE); optometric technology (AOA); surgical technology (ARCST). **Total program enrollment:** 4411. **Application fee:** $15.

**PROGRAM(S) OFFERED**
• **Accounting Technology/Technician and Bookkeeping** *14 students enrolled* • **Aesthetician/Esthetician and Skin Care Specialist** *22 students enrolled* • **Automobile/Automotive Mechanics Technology/Technician** *11 students enrolled* • **Baking and Pastry Arts/Baker/Pastry Chef** *6 students enrolled* • **Banking and Financial Support Services** *1 student enrolled* • **Business Administration and Management, General** *3 students enrolled* • **CAD/CADD Drafting and/or Design Technology/Technician** *5 students enrolled* • **Carpentry/Carpenter** *1 student enrolled* • **Cosmetology, Barber/Styling, and Nail Instructor** *1 student enrolled* • **Data Processing and Data Processing Technology/Technician** *7 students enrolled* • **Dental Assisting/Assistant** *21 students enrolled* • **Electrical and Power Transmission Installation/Installer, General** *73 students enrolled* • **Electrician** *1 student enrolled* • **Entrepreneurship/Entrepreneurial Studies** *11 students enrolled* • **General Office Occupations and Clerical Services** *14 students enrolled* • **Health Unit Coordinator/Ward Clerk** *4 students enrolled* • **Legal Administrative Assistant/Secretary** *5 students enrolled* • **Legal Assistant/Paralegal** *3 students enrolled* • **Licensed Practical/Vocational Nurse Training (LPN, LVN, Cert, Dipl, AAS)** *107 students enrolled* • **Machine Tool Technology/Machinist** *3 students enrolled* • **Massage Therapy/Therapeutic Massage** *16 students enrolled* • **Medical Insurance Coding Specialist/Coder** *15 students enrolled* • **Medical Reception/Receptionist** *13 students enrolled* • **Medical Transcription/Transcriptionist** *8 students enrolled* • **Medical/Clinical Assistant** *18 students enrolled* • **Nail Technician/Specialist and Manicurist** *17 students enrolled* • **Optometric Technician/Assistant** *8 students enrolled* • **Pharmacy Technician/Assistant** *18 students enrolled* • **Receptionist** *8 students enrolled* • **Turf and Turfgrass Management** *1 student enrolled* • **Vehicle**

*Spokane Community College (continued)*

**Maintenance and Repair Technologies, Other** *5 students enrolled* • **Web Page, Digital/Multimedia and Information Resources Design** *34 students enrolled* • **Welding Technology/Welder** *16 students enrolled*

**STUDENT SERVICES** Academic or career counseling, daycare for children of students, employment services for current students, placement services for program completers, remedial services.

## Spokane Falls Community College

3410 West Fort George Wright Drive, Spokane, WA 99224-5288
http://www.spokanefalls.edu/

**CONTACT** Mark A. Palek, President
**Telephone:** 509-533-3500

**GENERAL INFORMATION** Public Institution. Founded 1967. **Accreditation:** Regional (NCCU/NCCU); physical therapy assisting (APTA). **Total program enrollment:** 4803. **Application fee:** $15.

**PROGRAM(S) OFFERED**

• **Business Administration and Management, General** *3 students enrolled* • **Computer Systems Networking and Telecommunications** *2 students enrolled* • **Computer Technology/Computer Systems Technology** *4 students enrolled* • **Computer and Information Systems Security** *4 students enrolled* • **Data Entry/Microcomputer Applications, General** *39 students enrolled* • **Early Childhood Education and Teaching** *1 student enrolled* • **General Office Occupations and Clerical Services** *7 students enrolled* • **Health Aides/Attendants/Orderlies, Other** *6 students enrolled* • **Home Health Aide/Home Attendant** *11 students enrolled* • **Interior Design** *14 students enrolled* • **Marketing, Other** *1 student enrolled* • **Office Management and Supervision** *4 students enrolled* • **Orthotist/Prosthetist** *1 student enrolled* • **Substance Abuse/Addiction Counseling** *2 students enrolled* • **Teacher Assistant/Aide** *5 students enrolled* • **Upholstery/Upholsterer** *20 students enrolled* • **Web Page, Digital/Multimedia and Information Resources Design** *1 student enrolled*

**STUDENT SERVICES** Academic or career counseling, daycare for children of students, employment services for current students, placement services for program completers, remedial services.

## Stylemasters College of Hair Design

1224 Commerce, Longview, WA 98632
http://stylemasters.edu/

**CONTACT** John Chilson, Owner
**Telephone:** 360-636-2720

**GENERAL INFORMATION** Private Institution. Founded 1975. **Total program enrollment:** 54.

**PROGRAM(S) OFFERED**

• **Cosmetology and Related Personal Grooming Arts, Other** *600 hrs./$4000* • **Cosmetology, Barber/Styling, and Nail Instructor** *600 hrs./$2100* • **Cosmetology/Cosmetologist, General** *1650 hrs./$11,430*

**STUDENT SERVICES** Academic or career counseling, employment services for current students, placement services for program completers, remedial services.

## Sunnyside Beauty Academy

440 Barnard Boulevard, Suite 2, Sunnyside, WA 98944

**GENERAL INFORMATION** Private Institution. **Total program enrollment:** 11. **Application fee:** $100.

**PROGRAM(S) OFFERED**

• **Aesthetician/Esthetician and Skin Care Specialist** *700 hrs./$4600* • **Cosmetology, Barber/Styling, and Nail Instructor** *600 hrs./$4500*

**STUDENT SERVICES** Academic or career counseling, placement services for program completers.

## Tacoma Community College

6501 South 19th Street, Tacoma, WA 98466
http://www.tacomacc.edu/

**CONTACT** Pamela Transue, President
**Telephone:** 253-566-5000

**GENERAL INFORMATION** Public Institution. Founded 1965. **Accreditation:** Regional (NCCU/NCCU); emergency medical services (JRCEMTP); health information technology (AHIMA); radiologic technology: radiography (JRCERT). **Total program enrollment:** 3538.

**PROGRAM(S) OFFERED**

• **Accounting Technology/Technician and Bookkeeping** *35 students enrolled* • **Applied Horticulture/Horticultural Operations, General** *31 students enrolled* • **Business Administration and Management, General** *2 students enrolled* • **Computer and Information Sciences and Support Services, Other** *7 students enrolled* • **Criminal Justice/Law Enforcement Administration** *1 student enrolled* • **Data Entry/Microcomputer Applications, General** *3 students enrolled* • **Drafting and Design Technology/Technician, General** *12 students enrolled* • **Emergency Care Attendant (EMT Ambulance)** *45 students enrolled* • **Emergency Medical Technology/Technician (EMT Paramedic)** *23 students enrolled* • **General Office Occupations and Clerical Services** *1 student enrolled* • **Health Information/Medical Records Technology/Technician** *1 student enrolled* • **Human Resources Management/Personnel Administration, General** *4 students enrolled* • **Legal Assistant/Paralegal** *4 students enrolled* • **Logistics and Materials Management** *11 students enrolled* • **Medical Administrative/Executive Assistant and Medical Secretary** *1 student enrolled* • **Medical Insurance Coding Specialist/Coder** *2 students enrolled* • **Medical Insurance Specialist/Medical Biller** *1 student enrolled* • **Medical Reception/Receptionist** *14 students enrolled* • **Medical Transcription/Transcriptionist** *7 students enrolled* • **Mental and Social Health Services and Allied Professions, Other** *27 students enrolled* • **Receptionist** *5 students enrolled* • **Retailing and Retail Operations** *5 students enrolled* • **Teacher Assistant/Aide** *30 students enrolled*

**STUDENT SERVICES** Academic or career counseling, daycare for children of students, employment services for current students, placement services for program completers, remedial services.

## Total Cosmetology Training Center

5303 North Market Street, Spokane, WA 99207-6231
http://totalcosmetology@comcast.net/

**CONTACT** Patty Stanley, Admissions Director
**Telephone:** 509-487-5500

**GENERAL INFORMATION** Private Institution. **Total program enrollment:** 41. **Application fee:** $100.

**PROGRAM(S) OFFERED**

• **Aesthetician/Esthetician and Skin Care Specialist** *650 hrs./$3675* • **Barbering/Barber** *1050 hrs./$5875* • **Cosmetology, Barber/Styling, and Nail Instructor** *600 hrs./$3400* • **Cosmetology/Cosmetologist, General** *1650 hrs./$10,158* • **Education, General** *2 students enrolled* • **Nail Technician/Specialist and Manicurist** *650 hrs./$3675*

**STUDENT SERVICES** Academic or career counseling, employment services for current students, placement services for program completers.

## Victoria's Academy of Cosmetology

314 W. Kennewick Avenue, Kennewick, WA 99336
victoriasacademy.com

**CONTACT** Victoria Kile
**Telephone:** 509-586-9979

**GENERAL INFORMATION** Private Institution. **Total program enrollment:** 47. **Application fee:** $100.

**PROGRAM(S) OFFERED**

• **Aesthetician/Esthetician and Skin Care Specialist** *14 students enrolled* • **Barbering/Barber** *1100 hrs./$5049* • **Cosmetology and Related Personal Grooming Arts, Other** *30 students enrolled* • **Cosmetology, Barber/Styling, and**

**Nail Instructor** *600 hrs./$2754* • **Cosmetology/Cosmetologist, General** *1700 hrs./$8981* • **Facial Treatment Specialist/Facialist** *650 hrs./$4218* • **Nail Technician/Specialist and Manicurist** *650 hrs./$4218*

**STUDENT SERVICES** Academic or career counseling, employment services for current students, placement services for program completers, remedial services.

## Walla Walla Community College

500 Tausick Way, Walla Walla, WA 99362-9267
http://www.wwcc.edu/home/

**CONTACT** Steven L. Vanausdle, President
**Telephone:** 509-522-2500

**GENERAL INFORMATION** Public Institution. Founded 1967. **Accreditation:** Regional (NCCU/NCCU); engineering technology (ABET/TAC). **Total program enrollment:** 2371.

**PROGRAM(S) OFFERED**
• **Accounting Technology/Technician and Bookkeeping** *10 students enrolled* • **Agricultural Production Operations, Other** *10 students enrolled* • **Agricultural and Domestic Animals Services, Other** *5 students enrolled* • **Autobody/Collision and Repair Technology/Technician** *2 students enrolled* • **Automobile/Automotive Mechanics Technology/Technician** *9 students enrolled* • **Banking and Financial Support Services** *1 student enrolled* • **Barbering/Barber** *1 student enrolled* • **Building/Property Maintenance and Management** *85 students enrolled* • **Carpentry/Carpenter** *10 students enrolled* • **Civil Engineering Technology/Technician** *6 students enrolled* • **Culinary Arts/Chef Training** *1 student enrolled* • **Data Entry/Microcomputer Applications, General** *8 students enrolled* • **Diesel Mechanics Technology/Technician** *2 students enrolled* • **Early Childhood Education and Teaching** *1 student enrolled* • **Electrician** *1 student enrolled* • **Emergency Medical Technology/Technician (EMT Paramedic)** *11 students enrolled* • **Engineering Technology, General** *7 students enrolled* • **Fire Science/Firefighting** *1 student enrolled* • **General Office Occupations and Clerical Services** *13 students enrolled* • **Heating, Air Conditioning, Ventilation and Refrigeration Maintenance Technology/Technician (HAC, HACR, HVAC, HVACR)** *19 students enrolled* • **Legal Administrative Assistant/Secretary** *1 student enrolled* • **Licensed Practical/Vocational Nurse Training (LPN, LVN, Cert, Dipl, AAS)** *55 students enrolled* • **Medical Administrative/Executive Assistant and Medical Secretary** *8 students enrolled* • **Nurse/Nursing Assistant/Aide and Patient Care Assistant** *256 students enrolled* • **Parks, Recreation, Leisure and Fitness Studies, Other** *3 students enrolled* • **Phlebotomy/Phlebotomist** *18 students enrolled* • **Teacher Assistant/Aide** *2 students enrolled* • **Truck and Bus Driver/Commercial Vehicle Operation** *32 students enrolled* • **Welding Technology/Welder** *37 students enrolled*

**STUDENT SERVICES** Academic or career counseling, daycare for children of students, employment services for current students, placement services for program completers, remedial services.

## Washington State University

Pullman, WA 99164
http://www.wsu.edu/

**CONTACT** Elson S. Floyd, President
**Telephone:** 509-335-3564

**GENERAL INFORMATION** Public Institution. Founded 1890. **Accreditation:** Regional (NCCU/NCCU); athletic training (JRCAT); audiology (ASHA); computer science (ABET/CSAC); forestry (SAF); interior design: professional (CIDA); music (NASM); speech-language pathology (ASHA). **Total program enrollment:** 20958. **Application fee:** $50.

**PROGRAM(S) OFFERED**
• **Child Development** *3 students enrolled* • **Family and Community Services** *5 students enrolled* • **Human Development, Family Studies, and Related Services, Other** *5 students enrolled* • **Technical and Business Writing** *1 student enrolled*

**STUDENT SERVICES** Academic or career counseling, daycare for children of students, employment services for current students, placement services for program completers.

## Wenatchee Valley College

1300 Fifth Street, Wenatchee, WA 98801-1799
http://www.wvc.edu/

**CONTACT** Mr. Jim Richardson, President
**Telephone:** 509-682-6800

**GENERAL INFORMATION** Public Institution. Founded 1939. **Accreditation:** Regional (NCCU/NCCU); medical laboratory technology (NAACLS); radiologic technology: radiography (JRCERT). **Total program enrollment:** 2095.

**PROGRAM(S) OFFERED**
• **Accounting Technology/Technician and Bookkeeping** *4 students enrolled* • **Administrative Assistant and Secretarial Science, General** *6 students enrolled* • **Agricultural Production Operations, Other** *47 students enrolled* • **Business Administration and Management, General** *1 student enrolled* • **Business/Office Automation/Technology/Data Entry** *2 students enrolled* • **Carpentry/Carpenter** *55 students enrolled* • **Computer Systems Networking and Telecommunications** *6 students enrolled* • **Data Entry/Microcomputer Applications, General** *5 students enrolled* • **Drafting and Design Technology/Technician, General** *10 students enrolled* • **Emergency Care Attendant (EMT Ambulance)** *19 students enrolled* • **General Office Occupations and Clerical Services** *2 students enrolled* • **Heating, Air Conditioning, Ventilation and Refrigeration Maintenance Technology/Technician (HAC, HACR, HVAC, HVACR)** *2 students enrolled* • **Industrial Electronics Technology/Technician** *8 students enrolled* • **Legal Administrative Assistant/Secretary** *1 student enrolled* • **Licensed Practical/Vocational Nurse Training (LPN, LVN, Cert, Dipl, AAS)** *53 students enrolled* • **Mechanic and Repair Technologies/Technicians, Other** *8 students enrolled* • **Medical Administrative/Executive Assistant and Medical Secretary** *1 student enrolled* • **Medical Office Assistant/Specialist** *9 students enrolled* • **Medical/Clinical Assistant** *20 students enrolled* • **Natural Resources/Conservation, General** *2 students enrolled* • **Nurse/Nursing Assistant/Aide and Patient Care Assistant** *109 students enrolled* • **Sign Language Interpretation and Translation** *1 student enrolled*

**STUDENT SERVICES** Academic or career counseling, daycare for children of students, employment services for current students, placement services for program completers, remedial services.

## Whatcom Community College

237 West Kellogg Road, Bellingham, WA 98226-8003
http://www.whatcom.ctc.edu/

**CONTACT** Kathi Hiyane-Brown, President
**Telephone:** 360-383-3000

**GENERAL INFORMATION** Public Institution. Founded 1970. **Accreditation:** Regional (NCCU/NCCU); medical assisting (AAMAE); physical therapy assisting (APTA). **Total program enrollment:** 2243.

**PROGRAM(S) OFFERED**
• **Accounting Technology/Technician and Bookkeeping** *3 students enrolled* • **Administrative Assistant and Secretarial Science, General** *1 student enrolled* • **Computer Systems Networking and Telecommunications** *1 student enrolled* • **Computer and Information Sciences and Support Services, Other** *1 student enrolled* • **Hospitality Administration/Management, General** *1 student enrolled* • **Legal Assistant/Paralegal** *2 students enrolled* • **Marketing, Other** *2 students enrolled* • **Medical Insurance Coding Specialist/Coder** *8 students enrolled* • **Medical/Clinical Assistant** *4 students enrolled* • **Teacher Assistant/Aide** *2 students enrolled*

**STUDENT SERVICES** Academic or career counseling, daycare for children of students, employment services for current students, remedial services.

## Yakima Beauty School Beautyworks

401 N. First Street, Yakima, WA 98901
http://yakimabeautyschool.edu/

**CONTACT** Mike Kennard, President
**Telephone:** 509-248-2288

**GENERAL INFORMATION** Private Institution. **Total program enrollment:** 37.

*Yakima Beauty School Beautyworks (continued)*

**PROGRAM(S) OFFERED**
• **Aesthetician/Esthetician and Skin Care Specialist** *650 hrs./$3900* • **Barbering/Barber** *2 students enrolled* • **Cosmetology, Barber/Styling, and Nail Instructor** *600 hrs./$3000* • **Cosmetology/Cosmetologist, General** *1800 hrs./$9000* • **Nail Technician/Specialist and Manicurist** *650 hrs./$3900*

**STUDENT SERVICES** Academic or career counseling, placement services for program completers.

## Yakima Valley Community College

PO Box 22520, Yakima, WA 98907-2520
http://www.yvcc.edu/

**CONTACT** Linda J. Kaminski, President
**Telephone:** 509-574-4600

**GENERAL INFORMATION** Public Institution. Founded 1928. **Accreditation:** Regional (NCCU/NCCU); dental hygiene (ADA); radiologic technology: radiography (JRCERT). **Total program enrollment:** 2608. **Application fee:** $20.

**PROGRAM(S) OFFERED**
• **Accounting Technology/Technician and Bookkeeping** *2 students enrolled* • **Administrative Assistant and Secretarial Science, General** *2 students enrolled* • **Agricultural Production Operations, Other** *1 student enrolled* • **Business Administration and Management, General** *3 students enrolled* • **Criminal Justice/Law Enforcement Administration** *1 student enrolled* • **Criminal Justice/Police Science** *2 students enrolled* • **Customer Service Support/Call Center/Teleservice Operation** *13 students enrolled* • **Data Entry/Microcomputer Applications, General** *7 students enrolled* • **Data Processing and Data Processing Technology/Technician** *1 student enrolled* • **Dental Assisting/Assistant** *7 students enrolled* • **Drafting and Design Technology/Technician, General** *5 students enrolled* • **General Office Occupations and Clerical Services** *1 student enrolled* • **Licensed Practical/Vocational Nurse Training (LPN, LVN, Cert, Dipl, AAS)** *59 students enrolled* • **Medical Insurance Coding Specialist/Coder** *2 students enrolled* • **Medical/Clinical Assistant** *13 students enrolled* • **Nurse/Nursing Assistant/Aide and Patient Care Assistant** *32 students enrolled* • **Pharmacy Technician/Assistant** *6 students enrolled* • **Radiologic Technology/Science—Radiographer** *2 students enrolled* • **Substance Abuse/Addiction Counseling** *9 students enrolled* • **Teacher Assistant/Aide** *15 students enrolled* • **Teacher Education and Professional Development, Specific Levels and Methods, Other** *5 students enrolled* • **Word Processing** *2 students enrolled*

**STUDENT SERVICES** Academic or career counseling, daycare for children of students, employment services for current students, placement services for program completers, remedial services.

# WISCONSIN

## Academy of Cosmetology

2310 W. Court Street, Janesville, WI 53548

**GENERAL INFORMATION** Private Institution. **Total program enrollment:** 51. **Application fee:** $10.

**PROGRAM(S) OFFERED**
• **Aesthetician/Esthetician and Skin Care Specialist** *450 hrs./$4661* • **Cosmetology, Barber/Styling, and Nail Instructor** *150 hrs./$1220* • **Cosmetology/Cosmetologist, General** *1800 hrs./$16,121* • **Nail Technician/Specialist and Manicurist** *300 hrs./$2508*

**STUDENT SERVICES** Academic or career counseling, employment services for current students, placement services for program completers.

## Advanced Institute of Hair Design

5655 South 27 Street, Milwaukee, WI 53221

**CONTACT** Penny Rushing, Chief Executive Officer
**Telephone:** 414-525-1700

**GENERAL INFORMATION** Private Institution. **Total program enrollment:** 150. **Application fee:** $35.

**PROGRAM(S) OFFERED**
• **Aesthetician/Esthetician and Skin Care Specialist** *600 hrs./$4274* • **Cosmetology/Cosmetologist, General** *1800 hrs./$16,357*

**STUDENT SERVICES** Academic or career counseling, placement services for program completers.

## Blackhawk Technical College

PO Box 5009, Janesville, WI 53547-5009
http://www.blackhawk.edu/

**CONTACT** Eric Larson, President
**Telephone:** 608-758-6900

**GENERAL INFORMATION** Public Institution. Founded 1968. **Accreditation:** Regional (NCA); dental assisting (ADA); dental hygiene (ADA); physical therapy assisting (APTA); radiologic technology: radiography (JRCERT). **Total program enrollment:** 1319. **Application fee:** $30.

**PROGRAM(S) OFFERED**
• **Carpentry/Carpenter** • **Computer Installation and Repair Technology/Technician** *7 students enrolled* • **Computer and Information Systems Security** *7 students enrolled* • **Criminal Justice/Police Science** *40 students enrolled* • **Dental Assisting/Assistant** *10 students enrolled* • **Electrician** *12 students enrolled* • **Emergency Medical Technology/Technician (EMT Paramedic)** *90 students enrolled* • **Farm/Farm and Ranch Management** *7 students enrolled* • **Industrial Mechanics and Maintenance Technology** *5 students enrolled* • **Landscaping and Groundskeeping** *4 students enrolled* • **Licensed Practical/Vocational Nurse Training (LPN, LVN, Cert, Dipl, AAS)** • **Lineworker** *17 students enrolled* • **Medical Insurance Coding Specialist/Coder** *5 students enrolled* • **Medical/Clinical Assistant** *19 students enrolled* • **Nurse/Nursing Assistant/Aide and Patient Care Assistant** *221 students enrolled* • **Plumbing Technology/Plumber** *6 students enrolled* • **Welding Technology/Welder** *12 students enrolled*

**STUDENT SERVICES** Academic or career counseling, daycare for children of students, employment services for current students, placement services for program completers, remedial services.

## Blue Sky School of Professional Massage and Therapeutic Bodywork

220 Oak Street, Grafton, WI 53024
http://www.BlueSkyMassage.com/

**CONTACT** Karen N. Lewis, Dean
**Telephone:** 262-692-9500

**GENERAL INFORMATION** Private Institution. **Total program enrollment:** 99. **Application fee:** $50.

**PROGRAM(S) OFFERED**
• **Massage Therapy/Therapeutic Massage** *27 hrs./$10,075*

## Carthage College

2001 Alford Park Drive, Kenosha, WI 53140
http://www.carthage.edu/

**CONTACT** F. Gregory Campbell, President
**Telephone:** 262-551-8500

**GENERAL INFORMATION** Private Institution (Affiliated with Evangelical Lutheran Church in America). Founded 1847. **Accreditation:** Regional (NCA); music (NASM). **Total program enrollment:** 2374. **Application fee:** $35.

**PROGRAM(S) OFFERED**
• **Legal Assistant/Paralegal** *45 students enrolled*

**STUDENT SERVICES** Academic or career counseling, employment services for current students, placement services for program completers.

## Chippewa Valley Technical College

620 West Clairemont Avenue, Eau Claire, WI 54701-6162
http://www.cvtc.edu/

**CONTACT** Bruce Barker, President
**Telephone:** 715-833-6200

**GENERAL INFORMATION** Public Institution. Founded 1912. **Accreditation:** Regional (NCA); diagnostic medical sonography (JRCEDMS); health information technology (AHIMA); medical laboratory technology (NAACLS); radiologic technology: radiography (JRCERT). **Total program enrollment:** 2868. **Application fee:** $30.

**PROGRAM(S) OFFERED**
• **Allied Health Diagnostic, Intervention, and Treatment Professions, Other** • **Allied Health and Medical Assisting Services, Other** *6 students enrolled* • **Autobody/Collision and Repair Technology/Technician** *19 students enrolled* • **Automobile/Automotive Mechanics Technology/Technician** *18 students enrolled* • **Building/Construction Finishing, Management, and Inspection, Other** *27 students enrolled* • **Child Care Provider/Assistant** *14 students enrolled* • **Criminal Justice/Police Science** *91 students enrolled* • **Dental Assisting/Assistant** *26 students enrolled* • **Electrical, Electronic and Communications Engineering Technology/Technician** • **Electrician** *13 students enrolled* • **Emergency Medical Technology/Technician (EMT Paramedic)** • **Farm/Farm and Ranch Management** • **General Office Occupations and Clerical Services** *13 students enrolled* • **Hair Styling/Stylist and Hair Design** *13 students enrolled* • **Heating, Air Conditioning, Ventilation and Refrigeration Maintenance Technology/Technician (HAC, HACR, HVAC, HVACR)** *13 students enrolled* • **Housing and Human Environments, Other** *48 students enrolled* • **Industrial Electronics Technology/Technician** • **Industrial Mechanics and Maintenance Technology** *11 students enrolled* • **Licensed Practical/Vocational Nurse Training (LPN, LVN, Cert, Dipl, AAS)** *90 students enrolled* • **Lineworker** *33 students enrolled* • **Massage Therapy/Therapeutic Massage** *19 students enrolled* • **Medical/Clinical Assistant** *45 students enrolled* • **Nurse/Nursing Assistant/Aide and Patient Care Assistant** • **Pharmacy Technician/Assistant** *13 students enrolled* • **Pipefitting/Pipefitter and Sprinkler Fitter** *1 student enrolled* • **Plumbing Technology/Plumber** *5 students enrolled* • **Renal/Dialysis Technologist/Technician** *12 students enrolled* • **Sheet Metal Technology/Sheetworking** *3 students enrolled* • **Small Engine Mechanics and Repair Technology/Technician** *19 students enrolled* • **Surgical Technology/Technologist** *12 students enrolled* • **Truck and Bus Driver/Commercial Vehicle Operation** *89 students enrolled* • **Welding Technology/Welder** *25 students enrolled*

**STUDENT SERVICES** Academic or career counseling, employment services for current students, placement services for program completers, remedial services.

## College of Menominee Nation

PO Box 1179, Keshena, WI 54135
http://www.menominee.edu/

**CONTACT** Verna Fowler, President
**Telephone:** 715-799-5600

**GENERAL INFORMATION** Private Institution. Founded 1993. **Accreditation:** Regional (NCA). **Total program enrollment:** 268.

**PROGRAM(S) OFFERED**
• **Carpentry/Carpenter** • **Criminal Justice/Police Science** *1 student enrolled*

**STUDENT SERVICES** Academic or career counseling, remedial services.

## Concordia University Wisconsin

12800 North Lake Shore Drive, Mequon, WI 53097-2402
http://www.cuw.edu/

**CONTACT** Patrick Ferry, President
**Telephone:** 262-243-5700

**GENERAL INFORMATION** Private Institution (Affiliated with Lutheran Church–Missouri Synod). Founded 1881. **Accreditation:** Regional (NCA). **Total program enrollment:** 3899. **Application fee:** $35.

**PROGRAM(S) OFFERED**
• **Allied Health and Medical Assisting Services, Other** *12 students enrolled* • **Theology and Religious Vocations, Other** *7 students enrolled*

**STUDENT SERVICES** Academic or career counseling, employment services for current students, placement services for program completers.

## Empire Beauty School–Milwaukee

5655 South 27th Street, Milwaukee, WI 53221
http://www.empire.edu

**CONTACT** Michael Bouman, President/COO
**Telephone:** 920-684-3028

**GENERAL INFORMATION** Private Institution. **Total program enrollment:** 107. **Application fee:** $100.

**PROGRAM(S) OFFERED**
• **Cosmetology/Cosmetologist, General** *1800 hrs./$14,930*

**STUDENT SERVICES** Academic or career counseling.

## Four Seasons Salon & Day Spa

128 W. 8th Street, Monroe, WI 53566

**CONTACT** Kristin Allison, President
**Telephone:** 608-329-7004

**GENERAL INFORMATION** Private Institution. **Total program enrollment:** 19.

**PROGRAM(S) OFFERED**
• **Cosmetology, Barber/Styling, and Nail Instructor** *150 hrs./$1500* • **Cosmetology/Cosmetologist, General** *1800 hrs./$9800* • **Nail Technician/Specialist and Manicurist** *300 hrs./$2650* • **Salon/Beauty Salon Management/Manager** *150 hrs./$1500*

**STUDENT SERVICES** Academic or career counseling, employment services for current students, placement services for program completers.

## Fox Valley Technical College

1825 North Bluemound, PO Box 2277, Appleton, WI 54912-2277
http://www.fvtc.edu/

**CONTACT** Dr. Susan May, President
**Telephone:** 920-735-5600

**GENERAL INFORMATION** Public Institution. Founded 1967. **Accreditation:** Regional (NCA); dental assisting (ADA). **Total program enrollment:** 2571. **Application fee:** $30.

**PROGRAM(S) OFFERED**
• **Accounting Technology/Technician and Bookkeeping** *13 students enrolled* • **Agricultural Production Operations, General** *7 students enrolled* • **Applied Horticulture/Horticultural Business Services, Other** *15 students enrolled* • **Autobody/Collision and Repair Technology/Technician** *1 student enrolled* • **Automobile/Automotive Mechanics Technology/Technician** *4 students enrolled* • **Cabinetmaking and Millwork/Millwright** *11 students enrolled* • **Carpentry/Carpenter** *24 students enrolled* • **Criminal Justice/Police Science** *81 students enrolled* • **Dental Assisting/Assistant** *39 students enrolled* • **Electrician** *14 students enrolled* • **Emergency Medical Technology/Technician (EMT Paramedic)** *50 students enrolled* • **Food Preparation/Professional Cooking/Kitchen Assistant** *1 student enrolled* • **General Office Occupations and Clerical**

*Fox Valley Technical College (continued)*

**Services** *44 students enrolled* • **Heavy Equipment Maintenance Technology/Technician** *7 students enrolled* • **Hydraulics and Fluid Power Technology/Technician** *1 student enrolled* • **Licensed Practical/Vocational Nurse Training (LPN, LVN, Cert, Dipl, AAS)** *50 students enrolled* • **Machine Shop Technology/Assistant** *8 students enrolled* • **Medical Insurance Coding Specialist/Coder** *39 students enrolled* • **Medical Transcription/Transcriptionist** *16 students enrolled* • **Medical/Clinical Assistant** *14 students enrolled* • **Nurse/Nursing Assistant/Aide and Patient Care Assistant** *461 students enrolled* • **Printing Press Operator** *16 students enrolled* • **Small Engine Mechanics and Repair Technology/Technician** *7 students enrolled* • **Truck and Bus Driver/Commercial Vehicle Operation** *145 students enrolled* • **Vehicle Maintenance and Repair Technologies, Other** *9 students enrolled* • **Welding Technology/Welder** *3 students enrolled*

**STUDENT SERVICES** Academic or career counseling, daycare for children of students, employment services for current students, placement services for program completers, remedial services.

## Gateway Technical College

3520 30th Avenue, Kenosha, WI 53144-1690
http://www.gtc.edu/

**CONTACT** Bryan Albrecht, President
**Telephone:** 262-564-2200

**GENERAL INFORMATION** Public Institution. Founded 1911. **Accreditation:** Regional (NCA); dental assisting (ADA); health information technology (AHIMA); physical therapy assisting (APTA); surgical technology (ARCST). **Total program enrollment:** 1824. **Application fee:** $30.

**PROGRAM(S) OFFERED**
• **Automobile/Automotive Mechanics Technology/Technician** *3 students enrolled* • **Building/Property Maintenance and Management** *5 students enrolled* • **Carpentry/Carpenter** • **Dental Assisting/Assistant** *9 students enrolled* • **Electrician** *8 students enrolled* • **Emergency Medical Technology/Technician (EMT Paramedic)** *169 students enrolled* • **General Office Occupations and Clerical Services** *8 students enrolled* • **Hair Styling/Stylist and Hair Design** *48 students enrolled* • **Health Unit Coordinator/Ward Clerk** *23 students enrolled* • **Industrial Electronics Technology/Technician** • **Industrial Mechanics and Maintenance Technology** • **Licensed Practical/Vocational Nurse Training (LPN, LVN, Cert, Dipl, AAS)** *127 students enrolled* • **Machine Tool Technology/Machinist** • **Mason/Masonry** *1 student enrolled* • **Mechanical Drafting and Mechanical Drafting CAD/CADD** *1 student enrolled* • **Medical Transcription/Transcriptionist** *2 students enrolled* • **Medical/Clinical Assistant** *45 students enrolled* • **Metal Building Assembly/Assembler** *6 students enrolled* • **Nurse/Nursing Assistant/Aide and Patient Care Assistant** *689 students enrolled* • **Nursing, Other** *11 students enrolled* • **Painting/Painter and Wall Coverer** *1 student enrolled* • **Pipefitting/Pipefitter and Sprinkler Fitter** • **Plumbing Technology/Plumber** *12 students enrolled* • **Welding Technology/Welder** *9 students enrolled*

**STUDENT SERVICES** Academic or career counseling, daycare for children of students, employment services for current students, placement services for program completers, remedial services.

## Gill-Tech Academy of Hair Design

423 West College Avenue, Appleton, WI 54911
http://www.gill-tech.com/

**CONTACT** Sheryl Bruemmer-Fisk, President
**Telephone:** 920-739-8684

**GENERAL INFORMATION** Private Institution. Founded 1984. **Total program enrollment:** 94. **Application fee:** $100.

**PROGRAM(S) OFFERED**
• **Aesthetician/Esthetician and Skin Care Specialist** *8 students enrolled* • **Cosmetology/Cosmetologist, General** *1800 hrs./$13,150* • **Facial Treatment Specialist/Facialist** *450 hrs./$4800* • **Nail Technician/Specialist and Manicurist** *300 hrs./$2350*

**STUDENT SERVICES** Academic or career counseling, placement services for program completers.

## Herzing College

5218 East Terrace Drive, Madison, WI 53718
http://www.herzing.edu/madison

**CONTACT** Donald G. Madelung, President
**Telephone:** 800-582-1227

**GENERAL INFORMATION** Private Institution. Founded 1948. **Accreditation:** Regional (NCA); state accredited or approved. **Total program enrollment:** 754. **Application fee:** $25.

**PROGRAM(S) OFFERED**
• **Medical Insurance Coding Specialist/Coder** *160 students enrolled* • **Medical Office Management/Administration** *38 students enrolled* • **Nursing—Registered Nurse Training (RN, ASN, BSN, MSN)** *36 students enrolled* • **Web Page, Digital/Multimedia and Information Resources Design**

**STUDENT SERVICES** Academic or career counseling, employment services for current students, placement services for program completers, remedial services.

## High-Tech Institute–Milwaukee

440 S. Executive Drive, Suite 200, Brookfield, WI 53005
http://www.hightechinstitute.edu/

**CONTACT** Jeff Engh, Operations Manager
**Telephone:** 262-373-7000

**GENERAL INFORMATION** Private Institution. Founded 2006. **Total program enrollment:** 519. **Application fee:** $50.

**PROGRAM(S) OFFERED**
• **Massage Therapy/Therapeutic Massage** *820 hrs./$11,383* • **Medical Insurance Specialist/Medical Biller** *1210 hrs./$23,336* • **Medical/Clinical Assistant** *746 hrs./$11,361* • **Surgical Technology/Technologist** *1620 hrs./$27,850*

**STUDENT SERVICES** Placement services for program completers.

## The Institute of Beauty and Wellness

342 North Water Street, Milwaukee, WI 53202

**CONTACT** Susan Haise, Owner
**Telephone:** 414-227-2889

**GENERAL INFORMATION** Private Institution. **Total program enrollment:** 94. **Application fee:** $50.

**PROGRAM(S) OFFERED**
• **Aesthetician/Esthetician and Skin Care Specialist** *450 hrs./$3723* • **Cosmetology/Cosmetologist, General** *1800 hrs./$18,450* • **Facial Treatment Specialist/Facialist** *59 students enrolled* • **Massage Therapy/Therapeutic Massage** *600 hrs./$6681* • **Nail Technician/Specialist and Manicurist** *300 hrs./$1663*

**STUDENT SERVICES** Academic or career counseling, employment services for current students, placement services for program completers, remedial services.

## Kaplan College–Milwaukee

111 W. Pleasant Street, Suite 101, Milwaukee, WI 53212

**CONTACT** Michael O'Herron, Executive Director
**Telephone:** 414-225-4600

**GENERAL INFORMATION** Private Institution. **Total program enrollment:** 678.

**PROGRAM(S) OFFERED**
• **Computer Systems Analysis/Analyst** *720 hrs./$12,420* • **Dental Assisting/Assistant** *900 hrs./$14,060* • **Medical Office Assistant/Specialist** *720 hrs./$13,060* • **Medical/Clinical Assistant** *720 hrs./$14,480* • **Pharmacy Technician/Assistant** *720 hrs./$13,750*

**STUDENT SERVICES** Academic or career counseling, employment services for current students, placement services for program completers, remedial services.

## Lac Courte Oreilles Ojibwa Community College

13466 West Trepania Road, Hayward, WI 54843-2181
http://www.lco.edu/

**CONTACT** Danielle Hornett, President
**Telephone:** 715-634-4790 Ext. 100

**GENERAL INFORMATION** Public Institution. Founded 1982. **Accreditation:** Regional (NCA); medical assisting (AAMAE). **Total program enrollment:** 317. **Application fee:** $10.

**PROGRAM(S) OFFERED**
• **Carpentry/Carpenter** *1 student enrolled* • **Child Care Provider/Assistant** • **Computer and Information Sciences, General** *2 students enrolled* • **Data Processing and Data Processing Technology/Technician** • **Hospitality and Recreation Marketing Operations** *1 student enrolled* • **Medical Transcription/Transcriptionist** • **Solar Energy Technology/Technician** *2 students enrolled*

**STUDENT SERVICES** Academic or career counseling, remedial services.

## Lakeshore Technical College

1290 North Avenue, Cleveland, WI 53015-1414
http://www.gotoltc.com/

**CONTACT** Michael Lanser, President
**Telephone:** 920-693-1000

**GENERAL INFORMATION** Public Institution. Founded 1967. **Accreditation:** Regional (NCA); dental hygiene (ADA); radiologic technology: radiography (JRCERT). **Total program enrollment:** 858. **Application fee:** $30.

**PROGRAM(S) OFFERED**
• **Autobody/Collision and Repair Technology/Technician** *9 students enrolled* • **Automobile/Automotive Mechanics Technology/Technician** *11 students enrolled* • **Carpentry/Carpenter** *6 students enrolled* • **Child Care Provider/Assistant** *6 students enrolled* • **Dairy Husbandry and Production** *11 students enrolled* • **Dental Assisting/Assistant** *16 students enrolled* • **Emergency Medical Technology/Technician (EMT Paramedic)** *49 students enrolled* • **Farm/Farm and Ranch Management** *10 students enrolled* • **General Office Occupations and Clerical Services** *5 students enrolled* • **Health Unit Coordinator/Ward Clerk** *22 students enrolled* • **Industrial Electronics Technology/Technician** *8 students enrolled* • **Industrial Mechanics and Maintenance Technology** *9 students enrolled* • **Licensed Practical/Vocational Nurse Training (LPN, LVN, Cert, Dipl, AAS)** *63 students enrolled* • **Machine Shop Technology/Assistant** *12 students enrolled* • **Machine Tool Technology/Machinist** *11 students enrolled* • **Mason/Masonry** *2 students enrolled* • **Medical Transcription/Transcriptionist** *2 students enrolled* • **Medical/Clinical Assistant** *18 students enrolled* • **Metal Building Assembly/Assembler** *4 students enrolled* • **Nurse/Nursing Assistant/Aide and Patient Care Assistant** *299 students enrolled* • **Nursing, Other** *4 students enrolled* • **Pharmacy Technician/Assistant** *26 students enrolled* • **Plumbing Technology/Plumber** *2 students enrolled* • **Sheet Metal Technology/Sheetworking** *1 student enrolled* • **Surgical Technology/Technologist** *4 students enrolled* • **Tool and Die Technology/Technician** *3 students enrolled* • **Welding Technology/Welder** *13 students enrolled*

**STUDENT SERVICES** Academic or career counseling, daycare for children of students, employment services for current students, placement services for program completers, remedial services.

## Lakeside School of Massage Therapy

6101 Odana Road, Madison, WI 53719
http://www.lakeside.edu/

**CONTACT** Carole Ostendorf, CEO
**Telephone:** 414-372-4345

**GENERAL INFORMATION** Private Institution. Founded 1983. **Total program enrollment:** 45. **Application fee:** $25.

**PROGRAM(S) OFFERED**
• **Massage Therapy/Therapeutic Massage** *41 hrs./$9794*

**STUDENT SERVICES** Academic or career counseling, placement services for program completers.

## Madison Area Technical College

3550 Anderson Street, Madison, WI 53704-2599
http://www.matcmadison.edu/matc/

**CONTACT** Bettsey Barhorst, President
**Telephone:** 608-246-6100

**GENERAL INFORMATION** Public Institution. Founded 1911. **Accreditation:** Regional (NCA); dental hygiene (ADA); medical laboratory technology (NAACLS); optometric technology (AOA); radiologic technology: radiography (JRCERT). **Total program enrollment:** 5274. **Application fee:** $35.

**PROGRAM(S) OFFERED**
• **Accounting Technology/Technician and Bookkeeping** *18 students enrolled* • **Allied Health Diagnostic, Intervention, and Treatment Professions, Other** *7 students enrolled* • **Applied Horticulture/Horticultural Operations, General** *25 students enrolled* • **Autobody/Collision and Repair Technology/Technician** *6 students enrolled* • **Baking and Pastry Arts/Baker/Pastry Chef** *10 students enrolled* • **Building/Property Maintenance and Management** *9 students enrolled* • **Carpentry/Carpenter** *26 students enrolled* • **Computer and Information Sciences and Support Services, Other** *9 students enrolled* • **Cosmetology and Related Personal Grooming Arts, Other** *32 students enrolled* • **Criminal Justice/Police Science** *86 students enrolled* • **Data Processing and Data Processing Technology/Technician** *7 students enrolled* • **Dental Assisting/Assistant** *24 students enrolled* • **Emergency Medical Technology/Technician (EMT Paramedic)** *264 students enrolled* • **Fire Science/Firefighting** *31 students enrolled* • **Graphic and Printing Equipment Operator, General Production** *3 students enrolled* • **Housing and Human Environments, Other** *23 students enrolled* • **Licensed Practical/Vocational Nurse Training (LPN, LVN, Cert, Dipl, AAS)** *1096 students enrolled* • **Massage Therapy/Therapeutic Massage** *19 students enrolled* • **Medical Insurance Coding Specialist/Coder** *13 students enrolled* • **Medical Transcription/Transcriptionist** *25 students enrolled* • **Medical/Clinical Assistant** *32 students enrolled* • **Nurse/Nursing Assistant/Aide and Patient Care Assistant** *2 students enrolled* • **Optometric Technician/Assistant** *9 students enrolled* • **Small Business Administration/Management** *19 students enrolled* • **Small Engine Mechanics and Repair Technology/Technician** *20 students enrolled* • **Surgical Technology/Technologist** *15 students enrolled* • **Web Page, Digital/Multimedia and Information Resources Design** *4 students enrolled* • **Welding Technology/Welder** *16 students enrolled*

**STUDENT SERVICES** Academic or career counseling, daycare for children of students, employment services for current students, placement services for program completers, remedial services.

## Martin's School of Hair Design

2310 West College Avenue, Appleton, WI 54914
http://www.mcofc.com/

**CONTACT** Michael Bouman, President/COO
**Telephone:** 920-684-3028

**GENERAL INFORMATION** Private Institution. Founded 1992. **Total program enrollment:** 54. **Application fee:** $100.

**PROGRAM(S) OFFERED**
• **Aesthetician/Esthetician and Skin Care Specialist** *600 hrs./$5700*
• **Cosmetology, Barber/Styling, and Nail Instructor** *5 students enrolled*
• **Cosmetology/Cosmetologist, General** *1800 hrs./$14,930* • **Nail Technician/Specialist and Manicurist** *2 students enrolled*

**STUDENT SERVICES** Academic or career counseling.

## Martin's School of Hair Design

2575 West Mason Street, Green Bay, WI 54304
http://www.mcofc.com/

**CONTACT** Michael Bouman, President/COO
**Telephone:** 920-684-3028

**GENERAL INFORMATION** Private Institution. Founded 1988. **Total program enrollment:** 102. **Application fee:** $100.

*Martin's School of Hair Design (continued)*

**PROGRAM(S) OFFERED**

• **Aesthetician/Esthetician and Skin Care Specialist** *600 hrs./$5700* • **Cosmetology, Barber/Styling, and Nail Instructor** *2 students enrolled* • **Cosmetology/Cosmetologist, General** *1800 hrs./$14,930* • **Massage Therapy/Therapeutic Massage** *40 students enrolled* • **Nail Technician/Specialist and Manicurist** *8 students enrolled*

**STUDENT SERVICES** Academic or career counseling.

## Martin's School of Hair Design

1034 South 18th Street, Manitowoc, WI 54220
http://www.mcofc.com/

**CONTACT** Michael Bouman, President/COO
**Telephone:** 920-684-3028

**GENERAL INFORMATION** Private Institution. Founded 1983. **Total program enrollment:** 99. **Application fee:** $100.

**PROGRAM(S) OFFERED**

• **Aesthetician/Esthetician and Skin Care Specialist** *41 students enrolled* • **Cosmetology, Barber/Styling, and Nail Instructor** *11 students enrolled* • **Cosmetology/Cosmetologist, General** *1800 hrs./$14,930* • **Nail Technician/Specialist and Manicurist** *3 students enrolled*

**STUDENT SERVICES** Academic or career counseling.

## Martin's School of Hair Design

620 West Murdock Avenue, Oshkosh, WI 54901
http://www.mcofc.com/

**CONTACT** Michael Bouman, President/COO
**Telephone:** 920-684-3028

**GENERAL INFORMATION** Private Institution. Founded 1981. **Total program enrollment:** 57. **Application fee:** $100.

**PROGRAM(S) OFFERED**

• **Cosmetology, Barber/Styling, and Nail Instructor** *1 student enrolled* • **Cosmetology/Cosmetologist, General** *1800 hrs./$14,930* • **Nail Technician/Specialist and Manicurist**

**STUDENT SERVICES** Academic or career counseling.

## Mid-State Technical College

500 32nd Street North, Wisconsin Rapids, WI 54494-5599
http://www.mstc.edu/

**CONTACT** John Clark, President
**Telephone:** 715-422-5500

**GENERAL INFORMATION** Public Institution. Founded 1917. **Accreditation:** Regional (NCA). **Total program enrollment:** 1245. **Application fee:** $30.

**PROGRAM(S) OFFERED**

• **Agricultural Production Operations, General** *5 students enrolled* • **Allied Health and Medical Assisting Services, Other** *8 students enrolled* • **Banking and Financial Support Services** *2 students enrolled* • **Business/Office Automation/Technology/Data Entry** *8 students enrolled* • **Carpentry/Carpenter** *3 students enrolled* • **Construction/Heavy Equipment/Earthmoving Equipment Operation** *7 students enrolled* • **Criminal Justice/Police Science** *25 students enrolled* • **Electrician** *5 students enrolled* • **Emergency Medical Technology/Technician (EMT Paramedic)** *30 students enrolled* • **Hair Styling/Stylist and Hair Design** *21 students enrolled* • **Health Unit Coordinator/Ward Clerk** *12 students enrolled* • **Industrial Mechanics and Maintenance Technology** *1 student enrolled* • **Ironworking/Ironworker** *2 students enrolled* • **Licensed Practical/Vocational Nurse Training (LPN, LVN, Cert, Dipl, AAS)** *8 students enrolled* • **Mason/Masonry** *1 student enrolled* • **Medical Transcription/Transcriptionist** *8 students enrolled* • **Medical/Clinical Assistant** *35 students enrolled* • **Metal Building Assembly/Assembler** *2 students enrolled* • **Nurse/Nursing Assistant/Aide and Patient Care Assistant** *293 students enrolled* • **Phlebotomy/Phlebotomist** *20 students enrolled* • **Pipefitting/Pipefitter and Sprinkler Fitter** *4 students enrolled* • **Plumbing Technology/Plumber** *4 students enrolled* • **Precision Systems Maintenance and Repair Technologies, Other** *5 students enrolled* • **Surgical Technology/Technologist** *8 students enrolled* • **Welding Technology/Welder** *10 students enrolled*

**STUDENT SERVICES** Academic or career counseling, employment services for current students, placement services for program completers, remedial services.

## Milwaukee Area Technical College

700 West State Street, Milwaukee, WI 53233-1443
http://www.matc.edu/

**CONTACT** Darnell E. Cole, President
**Telephone:** 414-297-6370

**GENERAL INFORMATION** Public Institution. Founded 1912. **Accreditation:** Regional (NCA); cardiovascular technology (JRCECT); dental hygiene (ADA); funeral service (ABFSE); medical laboratory technology (NAACLS); ophthalmic dispensing (COA); physical therapy assisting (APTA); practical nursing (NLN); radiologic technology: radiography (JRCERT); surgical technology (ARCST). **Total program enrollment:** 6042. **Application fee:** $30.

**PROGRAM(S) OFFERED**

• **Accounting Technology/Technician and Bookkeeping** *8 students enrolled* • **Aircraft Powerplant Technology/Technician** *2 students enrolled* • **Airframe Mechanics and Aircraft Maintenance Technology/Technician** *3 students enrolled* • **Allied Health Diagnostic, Intervention, and Treatment Professions, Other** • **Appliance Installation and Repair Technology/Technician** *7 students enrolled* • **Autobody/Collision and Repair Technology/Technician** *19 students enrolled* • **Automobile/Automotive Mechanics Technology/Technician** *28 students enrolled* • **Baking and Pastry Arts/Baker/Pastry Chef** • **Building/Construction Finishing, Management, and Inspection, Other** • **Cabinetmaking and Millwork/Millwright** • **Carpentry/Carpenter** *28 students enrolled* • **Child Care and Support Services Management** • **Communications Systems Installation and Repair Technology** • **Concrete Finishing/Concrete Finisher** • **Cosmetology and Related Personal Grooming Arts, Other** • **Culinary Arts/Chef Training** *8 students enrolled* • **Dental Assisting/Assistant** *33 students enrolled* • **Dental Laboratory Technology/Technician** *14 students enrolled* • **Diesel Mechanics Technology/Technician** *10 students enrolled* • **Drywall Installation/Drywaller** • **Electrical and Power Transmission Installation/Installer, General** *1 student enrolled* • **Electrician** • **Emergency Medical Technology/Technician (EMT Paramedic)** *95 students enrolled* • **Engineering Technologies/Technicians, Other** • **Foods, Nutrition, and Related Services, Other** • **Foodservice Systems Administration/Management** • **General Office Occupations and Clerical Services** *6 students enrolled* • **Glazier** • **Graphic Communications, Other** • **Graphic and Printing Equipment Operator, General Production** *2 students enrolled* • **Hair Styling/Stylist and Hair Design** *38 students enrolled* • **Health Unit Coordinator/Ward Clerk** *21 students enrolled* • **Heating, Air Conditioning, Ventilation and Refrigeration Maintenance Technology/Technician (HAC, HACR, HVAC, HVACR)** *29 students enrolled* • **Heavy Equipment Maintenance Technology/Technician** • **Human Development, Family Studies, and Related Services, Other** • **Industrial Electronics Technology/Technician** *7 students enrolled* • **Industrial Mechanics and Maintenance Technology** • **Language Interpretation and Translation** *1 student enrolled* • **Licensed Practical/Vocational Nurse Training (LPN, LVN, Cert, Dipl, AAS)** *139 students enrolled* • **Lineworker** *13 students enrolled* • **Machine Shop Technology/Assistant** *14 students enrolled* • **Machine Tool Technology/Machinist** • **Mason/Masonry** *1 student enrolled* • **Mechanic and Repair Technologies/Technicians, Other** *10 students enrolled* • **Mechanical Drafting and Mechanical Drafting CAD/CADD** *1 student enrolled* • **Medical Insurance Coding Specialist/Coder** *17 students enrolled* • **Medical/Clinical Assistant** *15 students enrolled* • **Metal Building Assembly/Assembler** • **Nurse/Nursing Assistant/Aide and Patient Care Assistant** *264 students enrolled* • **Opticianry/Ophthalmic Dispensing Optician** *2 students enrolled* • **Optometric Technician/Assistant** • **Painting/Painter and Wall Coverer** *14 students enrolled* • **Personal and Culinary Services, Other** *1 student enrolled* • **Pharmacy Technician/Assistant** • **Phlebotomy/Phlebotomist** *32 students enrolled* • **Pipefitting/Pipefitter and Sprinkler Fitter** *10 students enrolled* • **Plumbing and Related Water Supply Services, Other** *7 students enrolled* • **Renal/Dialysis Technologist/Technician** *11 students enrolled* • **Roofer** • **Small Business Administration/Management** *9 students enrolled* • **Tool and Die Technology/Technician** *1 student enrolled* • **Tourism and Travel Services Management** *2 students enrolled* • **Welding Technology/Welder** *25 students enrolled*

**STUDENT SERVICES** Academic or career counseling, daycare for children of students, employment services for current students, placement services for program completers, remedial services.

## Milwaukee Career College

3077 N. Mayfair Road, Suite 300, Milwaukee, WI 53222
http://www.mkecc.edu

**CONTACT** Jack Takahashi, President
**Telephone:** 414-257-2939

**GENERAL INFORMATION** Private Institution. **Total program enrollment:** 136. **Application fee:** $20.

**PROGRAM(S) OFFERED**
• **Computer Installation and Repair Technology/Technician** *650 hrs./$4800* • **Computer Systems Networking and Telecommunications** *140 hrs./$1730* • **Customer Service Support/Call Center/Teleservice Operation** *320 hrs./$2550* • **Medical Insurance Coding Specialist/Coder** *720 hrs./$10,800* • **Medical/Clinical Assistant** *720 hrs./$11,747* • **Pharmacy Technician/Assistant** *720 hrs./$10,800*

**STUDENT SERVICES** Academic or career counseling, employment services for current students, placement services for program completers.

## Moraine Park Technical College

235 North National Avenue, PO Box 1940, Fond du Lac, WI 54936-1940
http://www.morainepark.edu/

**CONTACT** Dr. Gayle Hytrek, President
**Telephone:** 920-922-8611

**GENERAL INFORMATION** Public Institution. Founded 1967. **Accreditation:** Regional (NCA); health information technology (AHIMA); practical nursing (NLN). **Total program enrollment:** 1287. **Application fee:** $30.

**PROGRAM(S) OFFERED**
• **Accounting Technology/Technician and Bookkeeping** *5 students enrolled* • **Applied Horticulture/Horticultural Business Services, Other** • **Autobody/Collision and Repair Technology/Technician** • **Automobile/Automotive Mechanics Technology/Technician** • **Blood Bank Technology Specialist** • **Building/Property Maintenance and Management** *75 students enrolled* • **Business Operations Support and Secretarial Services, Other** • **Business and Personal/Financial Services Marketing Operations** • **Cabinetmaking and Millwork/Millwright** *14 students enrolled* • **Child Care and Support Services Management** *1 student enrolled* • **Chiropractic Assistant/Technician** • **Computer Engineering, Other** • **Computer Systems Networking and Telecommunications** • **Computer and Information Sciences and Support Services, Other** • **Construction Trades, Other** • **Cosmetology/Cosmetologist, General** *9 students enrolled* • **Data Entry/Microcomputer Applications, Other** • **Dental Laboratory Technology/Technician** *6 students enrolled* • **Electrical and Power Transmission Installation/Installer, General** *31 students enrolled* • **Emergency Medical Technology/Technician (EMT Paramedic)** • **Environmental Control Technologies/Technicians, Other** • **Food Preparation/Professional Cooking/Kitchen Assistant** *1 student enrolled* • **General Merchandising, Sales, and Related Marketing Operations, Other** • **General Office Occupations and Clerical Services** *7 students enrolled* • **Health Information/Medical Records Technology/Technician** • **Health and Medical Administrative Services, Other** • **Heating, Air Conditioning and Refrigeration Technology/Technician (ACH/ACR/ACHR/HRAC/HVAC/AC Technology)** *14 students enrolled* • **Heating, Air Conditioning, Ventilation and Refrigeration Maintenance Technology/Technician (HAC, HACR, HVAC, HVACR)** • **Human Development, Family Studies, and Related Services, Other** • **Human Resources Management/Personnel Administration, General** • **Institutional Food Workers** • **Landscaping and Groundskeeping** • **Legal Administrative Assistant/Secretary** • **Licensed Practical/Vocational Nurse Training (LPN, LVN, Cert, Dipl, AAS)** *69 students enrolled* • **Lineworker** *14 students enrolled* • **Machine Shop Technology/Assistant** • **Machine Tool Technology/Machinist** *12 students enrolled* • **Management Information Systems and Services, Other** • **Management Sciences and Quantitative Methods, Other** • **Marine Maintenance/Fitter and Ship Repair Technology/Technician** *5 students enrolled* • **Marketing, Other** • **Mason/Masonry** *31 students enrolled* • **Mechanical Drafting and Mechanical Drafting CAD/CADD** *7 students enrolled* • **Medical Office Assistant/Specialist** *16 students enrolled* • **Medical Office Computer Specialist/Assistant** *30 students enrolled* • **Medical Transcription/Transcriptionist** *11 students enrolled* • **Medication Aide** *10 students enrolled* • **Nail Technician/Specialist and Manicurist** • **Nurse/Nursing Assistant/Aide and Patient Care Assistant** *242 students enrolled* • **Quality Control and Safety Technologies/Technicians, Other** • **Salon/Beauty Salon Management/Manager** • **Technical and Business Writing** • **Vehicle Maintenance and Repair Technologies, Other** • **Water Quality and Wastewater Treatment Management and Recycling Technology/Technician** • **Web Page, Digital/Multimedia and Information Resources Design** *5 students enrolled* • **Web/Multimedia Management and Webmaster** • **Welding Technology/Welder** *36 students enrolled*

**STUDENT SERVICES** Academic or career counseling, employment services for current students, placement services for program completers, remedial services.

## Nicolet Area Technical College

Box 518, Rhinelander, WI 54501-0518
http://www.nicoletcollege.edu/

**CONTACT** Adrian Lorbetske, President
**Telephone:** 715-365-4410

**GENERAL INFORMATION** Public Institution. Founded 1968. **Accreditation:** Regional (NCA). **Total program enrollment:** 555. **Application fee:** $30.

**PROGRAM(S) OFFERED**
• **Accounting and Related Services, Other** *8 students enrolled* • **Automobile/Automotive Mechanics Technology/Technician** *6 students enrolled* • **Business Administration and Management, General** *7 students enrolled* • **Business Administration, Management and Operations, Other** • **Child Care and Support Services Management** *28 students enrolled* • **Emergency Medical Technology/Technician (EMT Paramedic)** *72 students enrolled* • **Food Preparation/Professional Cooking/Kitchen Assistant** *11 students enrolled* • **General Office Occupations and Clerical Services** *8 students enrolled* • **Hair Styling/Stylist and Hair Design** *6 students enrolled* • **Information Technology** *1 student enrolled* • **Licensed Practical/Vocational Nurse Training (LPN, LVN, Cert, Dipl, AAS)** *25 students enrolled* • **Marketing/Marketing Management, General** *2 students enrolled* • **Medical/Clinical Assistant** *15 students enrolled* • **Nurse/Nursing Assistant/Aide and Patient Care Assistant** *117 students enrolled* • **Nursing, Other** *5 students enrolled* • **Receptionist** *9 students enrolled* • **Small Engine Mechanics and Repair Technology/Technician** *1 student enrolled* • **Welding Technology/Welder** *9 students enrolled*

**STUDENT SERVICES** Academic or career counseling, daycare for children of students, employment services for current students, placement services for program completers, remedial services.

## Northcentral Technical College

1000 West Campus Drive, Wausau, WI 54401-1899
http://www.ntc.edu/

**CONTACT** Dr. Lori Weyers, President
**Telephone:** 715-675-3331

**GENERAL INFORMATION** Public Institution. Founded 1912. **Accreditation:** Regional (NCA); dental hygiene (ADA); radiologic technology: radiography (JRCERT). **Total program enrollment:** 1401. **Application fee:** $30.

**PROGRAM(S) OFFERED**
• **Accounting Technology/Technician and Bookkeeping** • **Accounting** *14 students enrolled* • **Agricultural Mechanics and Equipment/Machine Technology** *1 student enrolled* • **Autobody/Collision and Repair Technology/Technician** *6 students enrolled* • **Automobile/Automotive Mechanics Technology/Technician** *7 students enrolled* • **Building/Construction Finishing, Management, and Inspection, Other** *20 students enrolled* • **Criminal Justice/Police Science** *18 students enrolled* • **Data Entry/Microcomputer Applications, General** *1 student enrolled* • **Emergency Medical Technology/Technician (EMT Paramedic)** *113 students enrolled* • **General Office Occupations and Clerical Services** *9 students enrolled* • **Heating, Air Conditioning, Ventilation and Refrigeration Maintenance Technology/Technician (HAC, HACR, HVAC, HVACR)** *2 students enrolled* • **Licensed Practical/Vocational Nurse Training (LPN, LVN, Cert, Dipl, AAS)** *105 students enrolled* • **Machine Shop Technology/Assistant** *17 students enrolled* • **Medical Insurance Coding Specialist/Coder** *23 students enrolled* • **Medical Transcription/Transcriptionist** *9 students enrolled* • **Medical/Clinical Assistant** *19 students enrolled* • **Nurse/Nursing Assistant/Aide and Patient Care Assistant** *391 students enrolled* • **Surgical Technology/Technologist** *13 students enrolled* • **Welding Technology/Welder** *31 students enrolled*

**STUDENT SERVICES** Academic or career counseling, daycare for children of students, employment services for current students, placement services for program completers, remedial services.

## Northeast Wisconsin Technical College

2740 W Mason Street, PO Box 19042, Green Bay, WI 54307-9042
http://www.nwtc.edu/

**CONTACT** H. Jeffery Rafn, President
**Telephone:** 920-498-5400

**GENERAL INFORMATION** Public Institution. Founded 1913. **Accreditation:** Regional (NCA); dental assisting (ADA); dental hygiene (ADA); engineering technology (ABET/TAC); health information administration (AHIMA); health information technology (AHIMA); medical laboratory technology (NAACLS); physical therapy assisting (APTA). **Total program enrollment:** 2664. **Application fee:** $30.

**PROGRAM(S) OFFERED**
• **Building/Construction Finishing, Management, and Inspection, Other** *8 students enrolled* • **Computer and Information Sciences and Support Services, Other** *2 students enrolled* • **Criminal Justice/Police Science** *26 students enrolled* • **Dental Assisting/Assistant** *17 students enrolled* • **Electrician** *15 students enrolled* • **Emergency Medical Technology/Technician (EMT Paramedic)** *112 students enrolled* • **Farm/Farm and Ranch Management** *14 students enrolled* • **General Office Occupations and Clerical Services** *23 students enrolled* • **Graphic and Printing Equipment Operator, General Production** *7 students enrolled* • **Industrial Mechanics and Maintenance Technology** *6 students enrolled* • **Licensed Practical/Vocational Nurse Training (LPN, LVN, Cert, Dipl, AAS)** *171 students enrolled* • **Lineworker** *33 students enrolled* • **Machine Shop Technology/Assistant** *36 students enrolled* • **Mechanic and Repair Technologies/Technicians, Other** • **Medical/Clinical Assistant** *33 students enrolled* • **Nurse/Nursing Assistant/Aide and Patient Care Assistant** *691 students enrolled* • **Nursing, Other** *12 students enrolled* • **Surgical Technology/Technologist** *43 students enrolled* • **Watchmaking and Jewelrymaking** *9 students enrolled* • **Welding Technology/Welder** *54 students enrolled*

**STUDENT SERVICES** Academic or career counseling, employment services for current students, placement services for program completers, remedial services.

## Ottawa University–Milwaukee

245 South Executive Drive, Suite 110, Brookfield, WI 53005
http://www.ottawa.edu/

**CONTACT** Robin Ware, Campus Executive Officer
**Telephone:** 262-879-0200

**GENERAL INFORMATION** Private Institution (Affiliated with American Baptist Churches in the U.S.A.). **Total program enrollment:** 14. **Application fee:** $50.

**STUDENT SERVICES** Academic or career counseling.

## Philadelphia Biblical University–Wisconsin Wilderness Campus

HC 60, Box 60, Cable, WI 54821
http://www.pbu.edu/programs/wwc/

**CONTACT** Mark Jalovick, Director
**Telephone:** 715-798-3525

**GENERAL INFORMATION** Private Institution. **Total program enrollment:** 32. **Application fee:** $25.

**PROGRAM(S) OFFERED**
• **Bible/Biblical Studies** *34 students enrolled*

**STUDENT SERVICES** Academic or career counseling, employment services for current students.

## Professional Hair Design Academy

3408 Mall Drive, Eau Claire, WI 54701-7633
http://www.phdacademy.com/

**CONTACT** William Rauckman, Chief Executive Officer
**Telephone:** 715-835-2345

**GENERAL INFORMATION** Private Institution. **Total program enrollment:** 69.

**PROGRAM(S) OFFERED**
• **Cosmetology and Related Personal Grooming Arts, Other** *288 hrs./$1900*
• **Cosmetology, Barber/Styling, and Nail Instructor** *150 hrs./$800*
• **Cosmetology/Cosmetologist, General** *1800 hrs./$11,091* • **Massage Therapy/Therapeutic Massage** *630 hrs./$6300* • **Nail Technician/Specialist and Manicurist** *300 hrs./$1700*

**STUDENT SERVICES** Academic or career counseling, employment services for current students, placement services for program completers.

## Rasmussen College Green Bay

940 South Taylor Street, Suite 100, Green Bay, WI 54303
http://www.rasmussen.edu/

**CONTACT** Scott Borley, Campus Director
**Telephone:** 920-593-8400

**GENERAL INFORMATION** Private Institution. **Total program enrollment:** 254. **Application fee:** $60.

**PROGRAM(S) OFFERED**
• **Child Care and Support Services Management** • **Massage Therapy/Therapeutic Massage** • **Medical Insurance Coding Specialist/Coder** • **Medical Transcription/Transcriptionist**

**STUDENT SERVICES** Academic or career counseling, employment services for current students, placement services for program completers, remedial services.

## Regency Beauty Institute

7995 West Layton Avenue, Greenfield, WI 53220

**GENERAL INFORMATION** Private Institution. **Total program enrollment:** 54. **Application fee:** $100.

**PROGRAM(S) OFFERED**
• **Cosmetology/Cosmetologist, General** *1799 hrs./$16,011*

**STUDENT SERVICES** Academic or career counseling, placement services for program completers.

## Regency Beauty Institute

2358 East Springs Drive, Madison, WI 53704
http://www.regencybeauty.com

**CONTACT** J. Hayes Batson, President
**Telephone:** 608-819-0469

**GENERAL INFORMATION** Private Institution. **Total program enrollment:** 90. **Application fee:** $100.

**PROGRAM(S) OFFERED**
• **Cosmetology/Cosmetologist, General** *1799 hrs./$16,011*

**STUDENT SERVICES** Academic or career counseling, placement services for program completers.

## St. Luke's Medical Center–School of Diagnostic Medical Sonography

2900 West Oklahoma Avenue, Milwaukee, WI 53215
http://www.aurorahealthcare.org/

**CONTACT** Laura Sorenson, Program Director
**Telephone:** 414-747-4360

**GENERAL INFORMATION** Private Institution. **Total program enrollment:** 9. **Application fee:** $25.

**PROGRAM(S) OFFERED**
• **Diagnostic Medical Sonography/Sonographer and Ultrasound Technician** *7 students enrolled*

## The Salon Professional Academy

3355 W. College Avenue, Appleton, WI 54915

**CONTACT** Josif Wittnik, President
**Telephone:** 920-968-0433

**GENERAL INFORMATION** Private Institution. **Total program enrollment:** 86.

**PROGRAM(S) OFFERED**
• **Aesthetician/Esthetician and Skin Care Specialist** *450 hrs./$4990*
• **Cosmetology and Related Personal Grooming Arts, Other** *1800 hrs./$13,000*
• **Cosmetology/Cosmetologist, General** *43 students enrolled* • **Nail Technician/Specialist and Manicurist** *300 hrs./$2890*

## Sanford-Brown College

6737 West Washington Street, Suite 2355, West Allis, WI 53214
http://www.sanford-brown.edu/

**CONTACT** Steve Guell, Chief Administrator
**Telephone:** 414-771-2200

**GENERAL INFORMATION** Private Institution. **Total program enrollment:** 748. **Application fee:** $35.

**PROGRAM(S) OFFERED**
• **Medical Insurance Coding Specialist/Coder** *105 students enrolled* • **Medical/Clinical Assistant** *198 students enrolled*

**STUDENT SERVICES** Academic or career counseling, employment services for current students, placement services for program completers.

## Southwest Wisconsin Technical College

1800 Bronson Boulevard, Fennimore, WI 53809-9778
http://www.swtc.edu/

**CONTACT** Karen R. Knox, President
**Telephone:** 608-822-3262

**GENERAL INFORMATION** Public Institution. Founded 1967. **Accreditation:** Regional (NCA). **Total program enrollment:** 811. **Application fee:** $30.

**PROGRAM(S) OFFERED**
• **Accounting Technology/Technician and Bookkeeping** *9 students enrolled*
• **Aesthetician/Esthetician and Skin Care Specialist** *8 students enrolled*
• **Autobody/Collision and Repair Technology/Technician** *17 students enrolled*
• **Business/Office Automation/Technology/Data Entry** *7 students enrolled*
• **Carpentry/Carpenter** *8 students enrolled* • **Child Care Provider/Assistant** *6 students enrolled* • **Criminal Justice/Police Science** *20 students enrolled* • **Dairy Husbandry and Production** *8 students enrolled* • **Dental Assisting/Assistant** *16 students enrolled* • **Electrician** *3 students enrolled* • **Engine Machinist** *11 students enrolled* • **Farm/Farm and Ranch Management** *23 students enrolled* • **General Office Occupations and Clerical Services** *16 students enrolled* • **Hair Styling/Stylist and Hair Design** *22 students enrolled* • **Industrial Electronics Technology/Technician** *7 students enrolled* • **Industrial Mechanics and Maintenance Technology** *1 student enrolled* • **Licensed Practical/Vocational Nurse Training (LPN, LVN, Cert, Dipl, AAS)** *51 students enrolled* • **Machine Shop Technology/Assistant** *9 students enrolled* • **Mason/Masonry** *12 students enrolled* • **Medical Insurance Coding Specialist/Coder** *41 students enrolled* • **Medical Transcription/Transcriptionist** *12 students enrolled* • **Medical/Clinical Assistant** *30 students enrolled* • **Nurse/Nursing Assistant/Aide and Patient Care Assistant** *235 students enrolled* • **Plumbing Technology/Plumber** *5 students enrolled* • **Welding Technology/Welder** *23 students enrolled*

**STUDENT SERVICES** Academic or career counseling, daycare for children of students, employment services for current students, placement services for program completers, remedial services.

## State College of Beauty Culture

527½ Washington Street, Wausau, WI 54403
http://www.statecollegeofbeauty.com/

**CONTACT** Andrea L. Burns, President
**Telephone:** 715-845-2888

**GENERAL INFORMATION** Private Institution. Founded 1967. **Total program enrollment:** 58. **Application fee:** $100.

**PROGRAM(S) OFFERED**
• **Aesthetician/Esthetician and Skin Care Specialist** *600 hrs./$6200*
• **Cosmetology/Cosmetologist, General** *1800 hrs./$11,500* • **Nail Technician/Specialist and Manicurist** *300 hrs./$3000*

**STUDENT SERVICES** Academic or career counseling, employment services for current students, placement services for program completers.

## University of Phoenix–Wisconsin Campus

20075 Watertower Boulevard, Brookfield, WI 53045-6608
http://www.phoenix.edu/

**CONTACT** William Pepicello, PhD, President
**Telephone:** 262-785-0608

**GENERAL INFORMATION** Private Institution. Founded 2001. **Accreditation:** Regional (NCA). **Total program enrollment:** 476.

**STUDENT SERVICES** Academic or career counseling, remedial services.

## University of Wisconsin–La Crosse

1725 State Street, La Crosse, WI 54601-3742
http://www.uwlax.edu/

**CONTACT** Joe Gow, Chancellor
**Telephone:** 608-785-8000

**GENERAL INFORMATION** Public Institution. Founded 1909. **Accreditation:** Regional (NCA); athletic training (JRCAT); medical technology (NAACLS); music (NASM); public health: community health education (CEPH); radiologic technology: radiation therapy technology (JRCERT); recreation and parks (NRPA). **Total program enrollment:** 8676. **Application fee:** $44.

**STUDENT SERVICES** Academic or career counseling, daycare for children of students, employment services for current students, placement services for program completers, remedial services.

## University of Wisconsin–Parkside

900 Wood Road, Box 2000, Kenosha, WI 53141-2000
http://www.uwp.edu/

**CONTACT** Lane Earns, Interim Chancellor
**Telephone:** 262-595-2573

**GENERAL INFORMATION** Public Institution. Founded 1968. **Accreditation:** Regional (NCA). **Total program enrollment:** 3696. **Application fee:** $44.

**STUDENT SERVICES** Academic or career counseling, daycare for children of students, employment services for current students, placement services for program completers, remedial services.

## University of Wisconsin–Stout

Menomonie, WI 54751
http://www.uwstout.edu/

**CONTACT** Charles Sorensen, Chancellor
**Telephone:** 715-232-1431

**GENERAL INFORMATION** Public Institution. Founded 1891. **Accreditation:** Regional (NCA); art and design (NASAD); dietetics: postbaccalaureate internship (ADtA/CAADE); interior design: professional (CIDA). **Total program enrollment:** 7141. **Application fee:** $44.

**STUDENT SERVICES** Academic or career counseling, daycare for children of students, employment services for current students, placement services for program completers, remedial services.

## University of Wisconsin–Superior

Belknap and Catlin, PO Box 2000, Superior, WI 54880-4500
http://www.uwsuper.edu/

**CONTACT** Julius E. Erlenbach, Chancellor
**Telephone:** 715-394-8101

**GENERAL INFORMATION** Public Institution. Founded 1893. **Accreditation:** Regional (NCA); counseling (ACA); music (NASM). **Total program enrollment:** 2035. **Application fee:** $44.

**STUDENT SERVICES** Academic or career counseling, daycare for children of students, employment services for current students, placement services for program completers, remedial services.

## University of Wisconsin System

1220 Linden Dr, 1720 Van Hise Hall, Madison, WI 53706-1559
http://www.uwsa.edu/

**CONTACT** Kevin Reilly, President
**Telephone:** 608-262-1234

**GENERAL INFORMATION** Public Institution. **Accreditation:** Regional (NCA).

## Waukesha County Technical College

800 Main Street, Pewaukee, WI 53072-4601
http://www.wctc.edu/

**CONTACT** Barbara Prindiville, PhD, President
**Telephone:** 262-691-5566

**GENERAL INFORMATION** Public Institution. Founded 1923. **Accreditation:** Regional (NCA); dental hygiene (ADA); surgical technology (ARCST). **Total program enrollment:** 2128. **Application fee:** $30.

**PROGRAM(S) OFFERED**

• **Allied Health and Medical Assisting Services, Other** *6 students enrolled* • **Autobody/Collision and Repair Technology/Technician** • **Automobile/Automotive Mechanics Technology/Technician** *10 students enrolled* • **Building/Property Maintenance and Management** *12 students enrolled* • **CAD/CADD Drafting and/or Design Technology/Technician** *5 students enrolled* • **Carpentry/Carpenter** *20 students enrolled* • **Computer Programming/Programmer, General** • **Computer Software and Media Applications, Other** *2 students enrolled* • **Computer Technology/Computer Systems Technology** • **Concrete Finishing/Concrete Finisher** *1 student enrolled* • **Criminal Justice/Police Science** *46 students enrolled* • **Data Processing and Data Processing Technology/Technician** *1 student enrolled* • **Dental Assisting/Assistant** *17 students enrolled* • **Electrician** • **Emergency Medical Technology/Technician (EMT Paramedic)** *156 students enrolled* • **Fire Science/Firefighting** *1 student enrolled* • **Food Preparation/Professional Cooking/Kitchen Assistant** *2 students enrolled* • **General Office Occupations and Clerical Services** *5 students enrolled* • **Graphic and Printing Equipment Operator, General Production** *1 student enrolled* • **Hair Styling/Stylist and Hair Design** *27 students enrolled* • **Health Unit Coordinator/Ward Clerk** *13 students enrolled* • **Heating, Air Conditioning, Ventilation and Refrigeration Maintenance Technology/Technician (HAC, HACR, HVAC, HVACR)** • **Industrial Electronics Technology/Technician** *1 student enrolled* • **Industrial Mechanics and Maintenance Technology** *13 students enrolled* • **Information Technology** *10 students enrolled* • **Language Interpretation and Translation** *11 students enrolled* • **Licensed Practical/Vocational Nurse Training (LPN, LVN, Cert, Dipl, AAS)** *72 students enrolled* • **Machine Shop Technology/Assistant** *1 student enrolled* • **Machine Tool Technology/Machinist** *4 students enrolled* • **Manufacturing Technology/Technician** *4 students enrolled* • **Mason/Masonry** *1 student enrolled* • **Medical Insurance Coding Specialist/Coder** *30 students enrolled* • **Medical Transcription/Transcriptionist** *7 students enrolled* • **Medical/Clinical Assistant** *30 students enrolled* • **Nurse/Nursing Assistant/Aide and Patient Care Assistant** *331 students enrolled* • **Operations Management and Supervision** *9 students enrolled* • **Phlebotomy/Phlebotomist** *16 students enrolled* • **Plumbing Technology/Plumber** • **Precision Production, Other** *9 students enrolled* • **Tool and Die Technology/Technician** *13 students enrolled* • **Truck and Bus Driver/Commercial Vehicle Operation** *26 students enrolled* • **Welding Technology/Welder** *19 students enrolled*

**STUDENT SERVICES** Academic or career counseling, daycare for children of students, employment services for current students, placement services for program completers, remedial services.

## Western Technical College

304 6th Street North, PO Box C-908, La Crosse, WI 54602-0908
http://www.westerntc.edu/

**CONTACT** J. Lee Rasch, EdD, President, District Director
**Telephone:** 608-785-9200

**GENERAL INFORMATION** Public Institution. Founded 1911. **Accreditation:** Regional (NCA); dental assisting (ADA); electroneurodiagnostic technology (JRCEND); health information technology (AHIMA); medical laboratory technology (NAACLS); physical therapy assisting (APTA); radiologic technology: radiography (JRCERT). **Total program enrollment:** 1837. **Application fee:** $30.

**PROGRAM(S) OFFERED**

• **Accounting Technology/Technician and Bookkeeping** *2 students enrolled* • **Building/Construction Finishing, Management, and Inspection, Other** *15 students enrolled* • **Computer and Information Sciences and Support Services, Other** *3 students enrolled* • **Criminal Justice/Law Enforcement Administration** *13 students enrolled* • **Dental Assisting/Assistant** *15 students enrolled* • **Emergency Medical Technology/Technician (EMT Paramedic)** *49 students enrolled* • **Farm/Farm and Ranch Management** • **Food Preparation/Professional Cooking/Kitchen Assistant** *5 students enrolled* • **General Office Occupations and Clerical Services** *11 students enrolled* • **Health Information/Medical Records Technology/Technician** *12 students enrolled* • **Heating, Air Conditioning, Ventilation and Refrigeration Maintenance Technology/Technician (HAC, HACR, HVAC, HVACR)** *11 students enrolled* • **Industrial Mechanics and Maintenance Technology** *12 students enrolled* • **Licensed Practical/Vocational Nurse Training (LPN, LVN, Cert, Dipl, AAS)** *59 students enrolled* • **Machine Shop Technology/Assistant** *4 students enrolled* • **Massage Therapy/Therapeutic Massage** *16 students enrolled* • **Medical Staff Services Technology/Technician** *11 students enrolled* • **Medical/Clinical Assistant** *37 students enrolled* • **Nurse/Nursing Assistant/Aide and Patient Care Assistant** *446 students enrolled* • **Surgical Technology/Technologist** *16 students enrolled* • **Teacher Assistant/Aide** • **Welding Technology/Welder** *24 students enrolled*

**STUDENT SERVICES** Academic or career counseling, daycare for children of students, employment services for current students, placement services for program completers, remedial services.

## Wisconsin Indianhead Technical College

505 Pine Ridge Drive, Shell Lake, WI 54871
http://www.witc.edu/

**CONTACT** Bob Meyer, President
**Telephone:** 715-468-2815

**GENERAL INFORMATION** Public Institution. Founded 1912. **Accreditation:** Regional (NCA). **Total program enrollment:** 1556. **Application fee:** $30.

**PROGRAM(S) OFFERED**

• **Accounting Technology/Technician and Bookkeeping** *23 students enrolled* • **Aesthetician/Esthetician and Skin Care Specialist** *15 students enrolled* • **Autobody/Collision and Repair Technology/Technician** *10 students enrolled*

• **Automobile/Automotive Mechanics Technology/Technician** *21 students enrolled* • **Building/Construction Finishing, Management, and Inspection, Other** *2 students enrolled* • **Business/Office Automation/Technology/Data Entry** *27 students enrolled* • **Communications Systems Installation and Repair Technology** *6 students enrolled* • **Computer Installation and Repair Technology/Technician** *2 students enrolled* • **Dairy Husbandry and Production** *9 students enrolled* • **Emergency Medical Technology/Technician (EMT Paramedic)** *155 students enrolled* • **Farm/Farm and Ranch Management** *10 students enrolled* • **Hair Styling/Stylist and Hair Design** *4 students enrolled* • **Industrial Mechanics and Maintenance Technology** *2 students enrolled* • **Licensed Practical/Vocational Nurse Training (LPN, LVN, Cert, Dipl, AAS)** *64 students enrolled* • **Machine Shop Technology/Assistant** *4 students enrolled* • **Mason/Masonry** *2 students enrolled* • **Massage Therapy/Therapeutic Massage** *44 students enrolled* • **Medical/Clinical Assistant** *49 students enrolled* • **Nurse/Nursing Assistant/Aide and Patient Care Assistant** *829 students enrolled* • **Plumbing Technology/Plumber** *9 students enrolled* • **Small Engine Mechanics and Repair Technology/Technician** *14 students enrolled* • **Welding Technology/Welder** *45 students enrolled*

**STUDENT SERVICES** Academic or career counseling, employment services for current students, placement services for program completers, remedial services.

# WYOMING

## Casper College

125 College Drive, Casper, WY 82601-4699
http://www.caspercollege.edu/

**CONTACT** Dr. Walter H. Nolte, President
**Telephone:** 307-268-2110

**GENERAL INFORMATION** Public Institution. Founded 1945. **Accreditation:** Regional (NCA); art and design (NASAD); music (NASM); radiologic technology: radiography (JRCERT); theater (NAST). **Total program enrollment:** 1943.

**PROGRAM(S) OFFERED**
• **Accounting Technology/Technician and Bookkeeping** *1 student enrolled* • **Autobody/Collision and Repair Technology/Technician** *2 students enrolled* • **Automobile/Automotive Mechanics Technology/Technician** *2 students enrolled* • **Business/Office Automation/Technology/Data Entry** • **Computer Programming, Vendor/Product Certification** • **Construction Trades, General** *3 students enrolled* • **Diesel Mechanics Technology/Technician** *12 students enrolled* • **Electrical, Electronic and Communications Engineering Technology/Technician** *10 students enrolled* • **Fire Science/Firefighting** *33 students enrolled* • **Geography, Other** *10 students enrolled* • **Health Unit Coordinator/Ward Clerk** • **Legal Assistant/Paralegal** *1 student enrolled* • **Machine Tool Technology/Machinist** *1 student enrolled* • **Medical Transcription/Transcriptionist** *2 students enrolled* • **Pharmacy Technician/Assistant** *5 students enrolled* • **Phlebotomy/Phlebotomist** *9 students enrolled* • **Rehabilitation and Therapeutic Professions, Other** *2 students enrolled* • **Retailing and Retail Operations** • **Statistics, Other** • **Substance Abuse/Addiction Counseling** *1 student enrolled* • **Teacher Assistant/Aide** *1 student enrolled* • **Water Quality and Wastewater Treatment Management and Recycling Technology/Technician** • **Welding Technology/Welder** *7 students enrolled*

**STUDENT SERVICES** Academic or career counseling, daycare for children of students, employment services for current students, placement services for program completers, remedial services.

## Central Wyoming College

2660 Peck Avenue, Riverton, WY 82501-2273
http://www.cwc.edu/

**CONTACT** Dr. Jo Anne McFarland, College President
**Telephone:** 800-735-8418

**GENERAL INFORMATION** Public Institution. Founded 1966. **Accreditation:** Regional (NCA); surgical technology (ARCST). **Total program enrollment:** 807.

**PROGRAM(S) OFFERED**
• **Accounting Technology/Technician and Bookkeeping** *1 student enrolled* • **Agricultural and Domestic Animals Services, Other** *5 students enrolled* • **American Indian/Native American Studies** • **Area Studies, Other** • **Art/Art Studies, General** • **Automobile/Automotive Mechanics Technology/Technician** • **Business Operations Support and Secretarial Services, Other** *1 student enrolled* • **Business/Office Automation/Technology/Data Entry** *1 student enrolled* • **Carpentry/Carpenter** *38 students enrolled* • **Computer Technology/Computer Systems Technology** • **Culinary Arts/Chef Training** *3 students enrolled* • **Dental Assisting/Assistant** • **Emergency Medical Technology/Technician (EMT Paramedic)** *39 students enrolled* • **Equestrian/Equine Studies** *11 students enrolled* • **Fire Science/Firefighting** • **Graphic Design** *1 student enrolled* • **Manufacturing Engineering** • **Medical Transcription/Transcriptionist** *1 student enrolled* • **Selling Skills and Sales Operations** *10 students enrolled* • **Web/Multimedia Management and Webmaster** • **Welding Technology/Welder**

**STUDENT SERVICES** Academic or career counseling, employment services for current students, placement services for program completers, remedial services.

## Cheeks International Academy of Beauty Culture

207 West 18 Street, Cheyenne, WY 82001
http://www.cheeksusa.com/

**CONTACT** Robert M. Stevenson, Financial Aid Administrator
**Telephone:** 307-637-8700

**GENERAL INFORMATION** Private Institution. **Total program enrollment:** 16. **Application fee:** $100.

**PROGRAM(S) OFFERED**
• **Aesthetician/Esthetician and Skin Care Specialist** *600 hrs./$5290*
• **Cosmetology, Barber/Styling, and Nail Instructor** *1000 hrs./$4600*
• **Cosmetology/Cosmetologist, General** *2000 hrs./$13,525* • **Hair Styling/Stylist and Hair Design** *1250 hrs./$8770* • **Nail Technician/Specialist and Manicurist** *400 hrs./$3125*

**STUDENT SERVICES** Academic or career counseling, placement services for program completers.

## Eastern Wyoming College

3200 West C Street, Torrington, WY 82240-1699
http://www.ewc.wy.edu/

**CONTACT** Dr. Thomas Armstrong, President
**Telephone:** 307-532-8200

**GENERAL INFORMATION** Public Institution. Founded 1948. **Accreditation:** Regional (NCA). **Total program enrollment:** 554.

**PROGRAM(S) OFFERED**
• **Aesthetician/Esthetician and Skin Care Specialist** *3 students enrolled* • **Child Care Provider/Assistant** • **Computer Systems Networking and Telecommunications** *2 students enrolled* • **Computer and Information Sciences and Support Services, Other** *2 students enrolled* • **Construction Trades, General** *7 students enrolled* • **Farm/Farm and Ranch Management** *4 students enrolled* • **General Office Occupations and Clerical Services** *2 students enrolled* • **Hair Styling/Stylist and Hair Design** *2 students enrolled* • **Machine Shop Technology/Assistant** *2 students enrolled* • **Nail Technician/Specialist and Manicurist** *2 students enrolled* • **Web Page, Digital/Multimedia and Information Resources Design** *1 student enrolled* • **Welding Technology/Welder**

**STUDENT SERVICES** Academic or career counseling, employment services for current students, placement services for program completers, remedial services.

## Laramie County Community College

1400 East College Drive, Cheyenne, WY 82007-3299
http://www.lccc.wy.edu/

**CONTACT** Darrel L. Hammon, President
**Telephone:** 307-778-5222 Ext. 1357

**GENERAL INFORMATION** Public Institution. Founded 1968. **Accreditation:** Regional (NCA); dental hygiene (ADA); practical nursing (NLN);

*Laramie County Community College (continued)*

radiologic technology: radiography (JRCERT). **Total program enrollment:** 1937. **Application fee:** $20.

**PROGRAM(S) OFFERED**

• **Autobody/Collision and Repair Technology/Technician** *1 student enrolled* • **Automobile/Automotive Mechanics Technology/Technician** *2 students enrolled* • **Business Operations Support and Secretarial Services, Other** *1 student enrolled* • **Civil Engineering Technology/Technician** • **Computer Hardware Technology/Technician** • **Computer Programming, Vendor/Product Certification** *4 students enrolled* • **Computer Programming/Programmer, General** *14 students enrolled* • **Computer Systems Analysis/Analyst** *4 students enrolled* • **Computer and Information Sciences and Support Services, Other** *2 students enrolled* • **Construction Trades, General** *1 student enrolled* • **Customer Service Support/Call Center/Teleservice Operation** *1 student enrolled* • **Data Modeling/Warehousing and Database Administration** • **Diagnostic Medical Sonography/Sonographer and Ultrasound Technician** • **Diesel Mechanics Technology/Technician** *6 students enrolled* • **Drafting and Design Technology/Technician, General** *7 students enrolled* • **Emergency Medical Technology/Technician (EMT Paramedic)** • **Nursing—Registered Nurse Training (RN, ASN, BSN, MSN)** *75 students enrolled* • **Public Administration** • **Web Page, Digital/Multimedia and Information Resources Design** *3 students enrolled*

**STUDENT SERVICES** Academic or career counseling, daycare for children of students, employment services for current students, placement services for program completers, remedial services.

## Northwest College

231 West 6th Street, Powell, WY 82435-1898
http://www.northwestcollege.edu/

**CONTACT** Paul B. Prestwich, President
**Telephone:** 307-754-6000

**GENERAL INFORMATION** Public Institution. Founded 1946. **Accreditation:** Regional (NCA); music (NASM); practical nursing (NLN). **Total program enrollment:** 1156.

**PROGRAM(S) OFFERED**

• **Administrative Assistant and Secretarial Science, General** • **Agricultural Production Operations, General** • **Anthropology** • **Archeology** • **CAD/CADD Drafting and/or Design Technology/Technician** *4 students enrolled* • **Chemistry, General** • **Commercial Photography** *29 students enrolled* • **Commercial and Advertising Art** • **Equestrian/Equine Studies** *14 students enrolled* • **General Office Occupations and Clerical Services** • **Graphic and Printing Equipment Operator, General Production** • **Health and Physical Education, General** *5 students enrolled* • **Information Science/Studies** • **Journalism** *5 students enrolled* • **Nursing—Registered Nurse Training (RN, ASN, BSN, MSN)** *27 students enrolled* • **Parks, Recreation and Leisure Studies** • **Prepress/Desktop Publishing and Digital Imaging Design** • **Welding Technology/Welder** *11 students enrolled*

**STUDENT SERVICES** Academic or career counseling, daycare for children of students, employment services for current students, remedial services.

## Sheridan College

PO Box 1500, Sheridan, WY 82801-1500
http://www.sheridan.edu/

**CONTACT** Kevin Drumm, President
**Telephone:** 307-674-6446 Ext. 0

**GENERAL INFORMATION** Public Institution. Founded 1948. **Accreditation:** Regional (NCA); dental hygiene (ADA); practical nursing (NLN). **Total program enrollment:** 1094.

**PROGRAM(S) OFFERED**

• **Administrative Assistant and Secretarial Science, General** *2 students enrolled* • **Building/Construction Finishing, Management, and Inspection, Other** • **Business/Commerce, General** • **CAD/CADD Drafting and/or Design Technology/Technician** *1 student enrolled* • **Construction Trades, General** *2 students enrolled* • **Criminal Justice/Safety Studies** *5 students enrolled* • **Culinary Arts/Chef Training** *1 student enrolled* • **Diesel Mechanics Technology/Technician** *16 students enrolled* • **Early Childhood Education and Teaching** *3 students enrolled* • **Engineering Technologies/Technicians, Other** • **Hospitality Administration/Management, General** *1 student enrolled* • **Licensed Practical/Vocational Nurse Training (LPN, LVN, Cert, Dipl, AAS)** *37 students enrolled* • **Machine Tool Technology/Machinist** *1 student enrolled* • **Massage Therapy/Therapeutic Massage** *6 students enrolled* • **Medical Transcription/Transcriptionist** *1 student enrolled* • **Welding Technology/Welder** *17 students enrolled*

**STUDENT SERVICES** Academic or career counseling, employment services for current students, placement services for program completers, remedial services.

## University of Wyoming

1000 East University Avenue, Laramie, WY 82070
http://www.uwyo.edu/

**CONTACT** Thomas Buchanan, President
**Telephone:** 307-766-1121

**GENERAL INFORMATION** Public Institution. Founded 1886. **Accreditation:** Regional (NCA); audiology (ASHA); computer science (ABET/CSAC); counseling (ACA); home economics (AAFCS); music (NASM); speech-language pathology (ASHA). **Total program enrollment:** 9251. **Application fee:** $40.

**PROGRAM(S) OFFERED**

• **Administration of Special Education** • **Child Development** *2 students enrolled* • **Real Estate** *32 students enrolled* • **Special Education and Teaching, General** • **Survey Technology/Surveying** *7 students enrolled*

**STUDENT SERVICES** Academic or career counseling, daycare for children of students, employment services for current students, placement services for program completers.

## Western Wyoming Community College

PO Box 428, Rock Springs, WY 82902-0428
http://www.wwcc.wy.edu/

**CONTACT** Karla Leach, President
**Telephone:** 307-382-1600

**GENERAL INFORMATION** Public Institution. Founded 1959. **Accreditation:** Regional (NCA); respiratory therapy technology (CoARC). **Total program enrollment:** 1029.

**PROGRAM(S) OFFERED**

• **Accounting** • **Automobile/Automotive Mechanics Technology/Technician** • **Diesel Mechanics Technology/Technician** *2 students enrolled* • **Electrical/Electronics Equipment Installation and Repair, General** *8 students enrolled* • **Foreign Languages and Literatures, General** *11 students enrolled* • **General Office Occupations and Clerical Services** *1 student enrolled* • **Heavy/Industrial Equipment Maintenance Technologies, Other** • **Industrial Mechanics and Maintenance Technology** *18 students enrolled* • **Kinesiology and Exercise Science** • **Licensed Practical/Vocational Nurse Training (LPN, LVN, Cert, Dipl, AAS)** *39 students enrolled* • **Management Information Systems, General** *9 students enrolled* • **Mechanic and Repair Technologies/Technicians, Other** *2 students enrolled* • **Medical Administrative/Executive Assistant and Medical Secretary** *1 student enrolled* • **Mining Technology/Technician** *13 students enrolled* • **Welding Technology/Welder** *3 students enrolled*

**STUDENT SERVICES** Academic or career counseling, daycare for children of students, employment services for current students, placement services for program completers, remedial services.

## WyoTech

4373 North Third Street, Laramie, WY 82072-9519
http://www.wyotech.com/

**CONTACT** W. Guy Warpness, President
**Telephone:** 307-742-3776

**GENERAL INFORMATION** Private Institution. Founded 1966. **Accreditation:** State accredited or approved. **Total program enrollment:** 1352. **Application fee:** $100.

**PROGRAM(S) OFFERED**
• **Autobody/Collision and Repair Technology/Technician** *1500 hrs./$25,700* • **Automobile/Automotive Mechanics Technology/Technician** *1500 hrs./$25,700* • **Diesel Mechanics Technology/Technician** *1501 hrs./$25,700* • **Precision Systems Maintenance and Repair Technologies, Other** *1500 hrs./$25,700*

**STUDENT SERVICES** Academic or career counseling, employment services for current students, placement services for program completers.

# Appendixes

# State Offices of Apprenticeship Contacts

### Alabama
Gregory Collins
State Director
USDOL/ETA/OA
Medical Forum Building
Room 648
950 22nd Street North
Birmingham, AL 35203
205-731-1308
E-mail: collins.gregory@dol.gov

### Alaska
John Hakala
State Director
USDOL/ETA/OA
605 West 4th Avenue, Room G-30
Anchorage, AK 99501
907-271-5035
E-mail: hakala.john@dol.gov

### Arizona
Colleen Henry
Acting State Director
USDOL/ETA/OA
230 North 1st Avenue, Suite 510
Phoenix, AZ 85025
602-514-7007
E-mail: henry.colleen@dol.gov

### Arkansas
Donald E. Reese
State Director
USDOL/ETA/OA
Federal Building, Room 3507
700 West Capitol Street
Little Rock, AR 72201-3204
501-324-5415
E-mail: reese.donald@dol.gov

### California
Rick Davis
State Director
USDOL/ETA/OA
2800 Cottage Way
Room W-1836
Sacramento, CA 95825-1846
916-978-4618
E-mail: davis.richard@dol.gov

### Colorado
Charles J. Noon (John)
State Director
USDOL/ETA/OA
U.S. Custom House
721 19th Street, Room 465
Denver, CO 80202-2517
303-844-6362
E-mail: noon.charles@dol.gov

### Florida
Nora Carlton
Acting State Director
USDOL/ETA/OA
400 West Bay Street, Suite 934
Jacksonville, FL 32202-4446
904-359-9252
Fax: 904-359-9251
E-mail: carlton.nora@dol.gov

### Georgia
Anita Reyes
State Director
USDOL/ETA/OA
61 Forsyth Street, SW
Room 6T80
Atlanta, GA 30303
404-302-5897

### Hawaii
Alfred Valles
State Director
USDOL/ETA/OA
300 Ala Moana Boulevard
Room 5-117
Honolulu, HI 96850
808-541-2519
E-mail: valles.alfred@dol.gov

### Idaho
William Kolber
State Director
USDOL/ETA/OA
1150 North Curtis Road, Suite 204
Boise, ID 83706-1234
208-321-2972
E-mail: kolber.william@dol.gov

### Illinois
David Wyatt
State Director
USDOL/ETA/OA
230 South Dearborn Street
Room 656
Chicago, IL 60604
312-596-5508
E-mail: wyatt.david@dol.gov

### Indiana
John Delgado
State Director
USDOL/ETA/OA
Federal Building and
U.S. Courthouse
46 East Ohio Street, Room 528
Indianapolis, IN 46204
317-226-7001
E-mail: delgado.john@dol.gov

## Iowa

Greer Sisson
State Director
USDOL/ETA/OA
210 Walnut Street, Room 715
Des Moines, IA 50309
515-284-4690
E-mail: sisson.greer@dol.gov

## Kansas

Neil Perry
Acting State Director
USDOL/ETA/OA
444 Southeast Quincy Street
Room 247
Topeka, KS 66683-3571
785-295-2624
E-mail: perry.neil@dol.gov

## Kentucky

John Delgado
Acting State Director
USDOL/ETA/OA
Federal Building, Room 168
600 Martin Luther King Place
Louisville, KY 40202
502-582-5223
E-mail: delgado.john@dol.gov

## Maryland

Robert Laudeman
State Director
USDOL/ETA/OA
Federal Building, Room 430-B
31 Hopkins Plaza
Baltimore, MD 21201
410-962-2676
E-mail: laudeman.robert@dol.gov

## Massachusetts

Jill Houser
Acting State Director
USDOL/ETA/OA
JFK Federal Building
Room E-370
Boston, MA 02203
617-788-0177
E-mail: houser.jill@dol.gov

## Michigan

Glenn Bivins
State Director
USDOL/ETA/OAELS-BAT
315 West Allegan, Room 209
Lansing, MI 48933
517-377-1746
E-mail: bivins.glenn@dol.gov

## Minnesota

David Wyatt
Acting State Director
USDOL/ETA/OA
316 North Robert Street
Room 144
St. Paul, MN 55101
312-596-5508
E-mail: wyatt.david@dol.gov

## Mississippi

Fred Westcott
State Director
USDOL/ETA/OA
Federal Building, Suite 515
100 West Capitol Street
Jackson, MS 39269
601-965-4346
E-mail: westcott.fred@dol.gov

## Missouri

Neil Perry
State Director
USDOL/ETA/OA
1222 Spruce Street, Room 9.102E
Robert A. Young Federal Building
St. Louis, MO 63103
314-539-2522
E-mail: perry.neil@dol.gov

## Nebraska

Tim Carson
State Director
USDOL/ETA/OA
Suite C-49
111 South 18th Plaza
Omaha, NE 68102-1322
402-221-3281
E-mail: carson.timothy@dol.gov

## Nevada

Colleen Henry
State Director
USDOL/ETA/OA
600 South Las Vegas Boulevard,
Suite 520
Las Vegas, NV 89101
702-388-6771
E-mail: henry.colleen@dol.gov

## New Hampshire

Charles Vaughan
State Director
USDOL/ETA/OA
55 Pleasant Street
Concord, NH 03301
603-225-1444
E-mail: vaughan.charles@dol.gov

## New Jersey

Joann A. Tomenchok
State Director
USDOL/ETA/OA
Metro Star Plaza, Suite 201A
190 Middlesex Essex Turnpike
Iselin, NJ 08830
732-750-9191
E-mail: tomenchok.joann@dol.gov

## New Mexico

Dennis Goodson
Acting State Director
USDOL/ETA/OA
500 4th Street NW, Suite 401
Albuquerque, NM 87102
505-248-6530
E-mail: goodson.dennis@dol.gov

## New York

Charles Vaughan
Acting State Director
USDOL/ETA/OA
55 Pleasant Street
Concord, NH 03301
603-225-1444
E-mail: vaughan.charles@dol.gov

## North Dakota

Barry Dutton
State Director
USDOL/ETA/OA
304 Broadway
Room 332
Bismarck, ND 58501-5900
701-250-4700
E-mail: dutton.barry@dol.gov

## Ohio

John Delgado
Acting State Director
USDOL/ETA/OA
200 North High Street, Room 605
Columbus, OH 43215
614-469-7375
E-mail: delgado.john@dol.gov

## Oklahoma

Cynthia McLain
State Director
USDOL/ETA/OA
215 Dean A. McGee Avenue
Suite 346
Oklahoma City, OK 73102
405-231-4338
E-mail: mclain.cynthia@dol.gov

## Pennsylvania

Thomas Bydlon
State Director
USDOL/ETA/OA
Federal Building
228 Walnut Street, Room 356
Harrisburg, PA 17108
717-221-3496
E-mail: bydlon.thomas@dol.gov

## Rhode Island

Howard Carney
State Director
USDOL/ETA/OA
Federal Building
100 Hartford Avenue
Providence, RI 02909
401-528-5198
E-mail: carney.howard@dol.gov

## South Carolina

Ronald Johnson
State Director
USDOL/ETA/OATELS-BAT
Strom Thurmond Federal Building
1835 Assembly Street, Room 838
Columbia, SC 29201
803-765-5547
E-mail: johnson.ronald@dol.gov

## South Dakota

Barry Dutton
Acting State Director
USDOL/ETA/OA
4804 South Minnesota, Room 103
Sioux Falls, SD 57108
701-250-4700
E-mail: dutton.barry@dol.gov

## Tennessee

Nathaniel Brown
State Director
USDOL/ETA/OA
Airport Executive Plaza
1321 Murfreesboro Road
Suite 541
Nashville, TN 37210
615-781-5318
E-mail: brown.nat@dol.gov

## Texas

Dennis Goodson
State Director
USDOL/ETA/OA
300 East 8th Street
Suite 914
Austin, TX 78701
512-916-5435
E-mail: goodson.dennis@dol.gov

## Utah

Juan Pelaez-Gary
State Director
USDOL/ETA/OA
125 South State Street, Room 2412
Salt Lake City, UT 84138
801-524-5450
E-mail: pelaez-gary.juan@dol.gov

## Virginia

James Walker
State Director
USDOL/ETA/OA
400 North 8th Street
Federal Building, Suite 404
Richmond, VA 23219-23240
804-771-2488
E-mail: walker.james@dol.gov

## Washington

Anne Wetmore
State Director
USDOL/ETA/OA
1111 Third Avenue, Suite 850
Seattle, WA 98101-3212
206-553-0076
E-mail: wetmore.anne@dol.gov

## West Virginia

Kenneth Milnes
State Director
USDOL/ETA/OA
405 Capitol Street, Suite 409
Charleston, WV 25301
304-347-5794
E-mail: milnes.kenneth@dol.gov

## Wisconsin

David Wyatt
Acting State Director
USDOL/ETA/OA
Suite 104
740 Regent Street
Madison, WI 53715-1233
608-441-5377
E-mail: wyatt.david@dol.gov

## Wyoming

Michael Ann Broad
State Director
USDOL/ETA/OA
American National Bank Building
1912 Capitol Avenue, Room 508
Cheyenne, WY 82001-3661
307-772-2448
E-mail: broad.michael@dol.gov

# Accrediting Organizations

The following accrediting bodies are recognized by the U.S. Department of Education or the Council for Higher Education Accreditation (CHEA).

## General Accreditation—Regional

General accreditation applies to an institution as a whole and is not limited to institutions or programs in a particular field of specialization.

Regional accreditation denotes accreditation of an institution as a whole by one of the six regional associations of schools and colleges, each of which covers a specified portion of the United States and its territories as indicated in the following listings.

### Middle States

Delaware, the District of Columbia, Maryland, New Jersey, New York, Pennsylvania, Puerto Rico, and the Virgin Islands

**Middle States Association of Colleges and Schools, Middle States Commission on Higher Education**

Elizabeth H. Sibolski, Acting President
3624 Market Street, 2nd Floor Annex
Philadelphia, PA 19104
Phone: 267-284-5000
Fax: 215-662-5950
E-mail: info@msche.org
Web site: www.msche.org

**New York State Board of Regents, New York State Education Department**

89 Washington Avenue
Room 110EB
Albany, NY 12234
Robert M. Bennett, Chancellor
Phone: 518-474-5889
Web site: www.regents.nysed.gov

### New England

Connecticut, Maine, Massachusetts, New Hampshire, Rhode Island, and Vermont

**New England Association of Schools and Colleges, Commission on Institutions of Higher Education (NEASC-CIHE)**

Barbara E. Brittingham, President/Director of the Commission
209 Burlington Road
Bedford, MA 01730
Phone: 781-271-0022
Fax: 781-271-0950
E-mail: CIHE@neasc.org
Web site: www.neasc.org

Colleges and institutions that offer programs leading to the associate degree but do not offer programs leading to a degree in liberal arts or general studies are covered by:

**New England Association of Schools and Colleges, Commission on Technical and Career Institutions**

Paul Bento, Director of the Commission
209 Burlington Road, Suite 201
Bedford, MA 01730-1433
Phone: 781-541-5416
E-mail: pbento@neasc.org
Web site: www.ctci.neasc.org

### North Central

Arizona, Arkansas, Colorado, Illinois, Indiana, Iowa, Kansas, Michigan, Minnesota, Missouri, Nebraska, New Mexico, North Dakota, Ohio, Oklahoma, South Dakota, West Virginia, Wisconsin, and Wyoming

**North Central Association of Colleges and Schools, The Higher Learning Commission (NCA-HLC)**

Sylvia Manning, President
30 North LaSalle Street, Suite 2400
Chicago, IL 60602
Phone: 312-263-0456
Fax: 312-263-7462
E-mail: info@hlcommission.org
Web site: www.ncahigherlearningcommission.org

### Northwest

Alaska, Idaho, Montana, Nevada, Oregon, Utah, and Washington

**Northwest Commission on Colleges and Universities (NWCCU)**

Sandra E. Elman, President
8060 165th Avenue, NE, Suite 100
Redmond, WA 98052
Dr. Sandra E. Elman, President
Phone: 425-558-4224
Fax: 425-376-0596
E-mail: selman@nwccu.org
Web site: www.nwccu.org

### Southern

Alabama, Florida, Georgia, Kentucky, Louisiana, Mississippi, North Carolina, South Carolina, Tennessee, Texas, and Virginia

**Southern Association of Colleges and Schools (SACS), Commission on Colleges**

Belle S. Wheelan, President
1866 Southern Lane
Decatur, GA 30033
Phone: 404-679-4500
Fax: 404-679-4558
E-mail: bwheelan@sacscoc.org
Web site: www.sacscoc.org

### Western

California, Hawaii, the Territories of Guam and American Samoa, the Commonwealth of the Northern Mariana Islands, the Republic of Palau, the Federated States of Micronesia, and the Republic of the Marshall Islands.

Institutions that offer one or more educational programs of at least one academic year in length at the postsecondary level are covered by:

**Western Associaton of Schools and Colleges, Accrediting Commission for Community and Junior Colleges (WASC-ACCJC)**

Barbara A. Beno, President
10 Commercial Boulevard, Suite 204
Novato, CA 94949
Phone: 415-506-0234
Fax: 415-506-0238
E-mail: accjc@accjc.org
Web site: www.accjc.org

Institutions that offer one or more educational programs of at least one academic year in length beyond the first two years of college are covered by:

**Western Association of Schools and Colleges, Accrediting Commission for Senior Colleges and Universities (WASC-ACSCU)**

Ralph A. Wolff, President and Executive Director
985 Atlantic Avenue, Suite 100
Alameda, CA 94501
Phone: 510-748-9001
Fax: 510-748-9797
E-mail: wascsr@wascsenior.org
Web site: www.wascweb.org

## Specialized Accreditation

Specialized accreditation applies to an institution or program limited to a particular field of academic or professional specialization or to a particular type of instruction. The following listings for the categories of specialized accreditation are organized alphabetically by field of specialization.

### Acupuncture and Oriental Medicine

**Accreditation Commission for Acupuncture and Oriental Medicine**

Dort S. Bigg, Executive Director
Maryland Trade Center #3
7501 Greenway Center Drive, Suite 760
Greenbelt, MD 20770
Phone: 301-313-0855
Fax: 301-313-0912
E-mail: coordinator@acaom.org
Web site: www.acaom.org

### Allied Health

**Accrediting Bureau of Health Education Schools**

Carol Moneymaker, Executive Director
7777 Leesburg Pike, Suite 314N
Falls Church, VA 22043
Phone: 703-917-9503
Fax: 703-917-4109
E-mail: info@abhes.org
Web site: www.abhes.org

**Commission on Accreditation of Allied Health Education Programs (CAAHEP)**

Kathleen Megivern, Executive Director
1361 Park Street
Clearwater, FL 33756
Phone: 727-210-2350
Fax: 727-210-2354
E-mail: mail@caahep.org
Web site: www.caahep.org

### Art and Design

Art and design institutions and units within institutions offering degree and nondegree programs in art, design, and art/design-related disciplines.

**National Association of Schools of Art and Design (NASAD), Commission on Accreditation**

Samuel Hope, Executive Director
Karen P. Moynahan, Associate Director
11250 Roger Bacon Drive, Suite 21
Reston, VA 20190-5243
Phone: 703-437-0700
Fax: 703-437-6312
E-mail: info@arts-accredit.org
Web site: www.arts-accredit.org

## Athletic Training

Athletic Training Programs for the athletic trainer.

**Commission on Accreditation of Allied Health Education Programs (CAAHEP)—see Allied Health**

In conjunction with:

**Joint Review Committee on Educational Programs in Athletic Training**

5142 South Andes Street
Centennial, CO 80015
Phone: 303-627-6229
Fax: 303-632-5915

## Audiology—see Speech-Language Pathology and Audiology

## Bible College Education

**Association for Biblical Higher Education (ABHE), Commission on Accreditation**

Ralph Enlow, Executive Director
5575 South Semoran Boulevard, Suite 26
Orlando, FL 32822
Phone: 407-207-0808
Fax: 407-207-0840
E-mail: info@abhe.org
Web site: www.abhe.org

## Business

Business private postsecondary institutions that are predominantly organized to train students for business careers, including business schools (one- or two-year noncollegiate postsecondary programs), junior colleges (associate degrees), and senior colleges (baccalaureate and master's degrees).

**Accrediting Council for Independent Colleges and Schools (ACICS)**

Albert Grey, Executive Director and CEO
750 First Street, NE, Suite 980
Washington, DC 20002
Phone: 202-336-6780
Fax: 202-842-2593
E-mail: info@acics.org
Web site: www.acics.org

## Christian Education

**Transnational Association of Christian Colleges and Schools (TRACS), Accreditation Commission**

Russell Guy Fitzgerald, Executive Director
15935 Forest Road
P.O. Box 328
Forest, VA 24551
Phone: 434-525-9539
Fax: 434-525-9538
E-mail: info@tracs.org
Web site: www.tracs.org

## Computer Science

**Accrediting Board for Engineering and Technology, Inc. (ABET)**

Michael Milligan, Executive Director
111 Market Place, Suite 1050
Baltimore, MD 21202
Phone: 410-347-7700
Fax: 410-625-2238
E-mail: info@abet.org
Web site: www.abet.org

## Construction

**American Council for Construction Education (ACCE)**

Michael Holland, Executive Vice President
1717 North Loop
1604 East, Suite 320
San Antonio, TX 78232
Phone: 210-495-6161
Fax: 210-495-6168
E-mail: acce@acce-hq.org
Web site: www.acce-hq.org

## Counseling

**Council for Accreditation of Counseling and Related Educational Programs (CACREP)**

Carol L. Bobby, Executive Director
1000 North Fairfax Street, Suite 510
Alexandria, VA 22314
Phone: 703-535-5990
Fax: 703-739-6209
E-mail: cacrep@cacrep.org
Web site: www.cacrep.org

## Cytopathology

**Commission on Accreditation of Allied Health Education Programs—see Allied Health**

In conjunction with:

**American Society of Cytopathology**

Elizabeth Jenkins, Executive Director
100 West 10th Street, Suite 605
Wilmington, DE 19801
Phone: 302-543-6583
Fax: 302-543-6597
E-mail: asc@cytopathology.org
Web site: www.cytopathology.org

## Dance

**National Association of Schools of Dance (NASD), Commission on Accreditation**

Samuel Hope, Executive Director
Karen P. Moynahan, Associate Director
11250 Roger Bacon Drive, Suite 21
Reston, VA 20190
Phone: 703-437-0700
Fax: 703-437-6312
E-mail: shope@arts-accredit.org
Web site: www.arts-accredit.org

## Dentistry

Programs leading to the first professional (D.D.S. or D.M.D.) degree and advanced programs in general dentistry and dental specialties. Dental Auxiliary Technologies: dental assisting, dental hygiene, and dental laboratory technology education programs.

**American Dental Association**

211 East Chicago Avenue
Chicago, IL 60611
Phone: 312-440-2500
Web site: www.ada.org

## Diagnostic Medical Sonography

**Commission on Accreditation of Allied Health Education Programs—see Allied Health**

In conjunction with:

**Joint Review Committee on Education in Diagnostic Medical Sonography**

2025 Woodlane Drive
St. Paul, MN 55125-2998
Phone: 651-731-1582
Fax: 651-731-0410
E-mail: jrc-dms@jcahpo.org
Web site: www.jrcdms.org

## Dietics

**American Dietetic Association, Commission on Accreditation for Dietetics Education (CADE-ADA)**

Ulric K. Chung, Senior Director
120 South Riverside Plaza, Suite 2000
Chicago, IL 60606
Phone: 800-877-1600 Ext. 5400 (toll-free)
Fax: 312-899-4817
E-mail: uchung@eatright.org
Web site: www.eatright.org/cade

## Distance Learning

**Distance Education and Training Council (DETC), Accrediting Commission**

Michael P. Cambert, Executive Director
1601 18th Street, NW, Suite 2
Washington, DC 20009
Phone: 202-234-5100
Fax: 202-332-1386
E-mail: detc@detc.org
Web site: www.detc.org

## Emergency Medical Services

**Commission on Accreditation of Allied Health Education Programs—see Allied Health**

In conjunction with:

**Joint Review Committee on Educational Programs for the EMT-Paramedic**

7108-C South Alton Way, Suite 150
Englewood, CO 80112-2106
Phone: 303-694-6191
Fax: 303-741-3655
Web site: www.caahep.org

## Engineering and Engineering Technology

**ABET, Inc.**

111 Market Place, Suite 1050
Baltimore, MD 21202
Phone: 410-347-7700
Fax: 410-625-2238
Web site: www.abet.org

## Environmental Health Science

**National Environmental Health Association**

720 South Colorado Boulevard, Suite 1000-N
Denver, CO 80246
Phone: 303-756-9090
Fax: 303-691-9490
E-mail: staff@neha.org
Web site: www.neha.org

**Society of American Foresters**

Terence Clark, Associate Director of Science & Education
5400 Grosvenor Lane
Bethesda, MD 20814
Phone: 301-897-8720 Ext. 123
Fax: 301-897-3690
E-mail: clarkt@safnet.org
Web site: www.safnet.org

## Funeral Service and Mortuary Science

**American Board of Funeral Service Education (ABFSE), Committee on Accreditation**
3414 Ashland Avenue, Suite G
St. Joseph, MO 64506
Phone: 816-233-3747
Fax: 816-233-3793
E-mail: exdir@abfse.org
Web site: www.abfse.org

## Health Information Administration and Technology

**American Health Information Management Association (AHIMA)**
Linda Kloss, Chief Executive Officer
233 North Michigan Avenue, 21st Floor
Chicago, IL 60601-5809
Phone: 312-233-1100
Fax: 312-233-1090
E-mail: info@ahima.org
Web site: www.ahima.org

## Histologic Technology

**American Association of Family & Consumer Sciences, Council for Accreditation**
Karen Tucker Thomas, Director of Credentialing and Professional Development
400 North Columbus Street, Suite 202
Alexandria, VA 22314
Phone: 703-706-4600 or 800-424-8080 (toll-free)
Fax: 703-706-4663
E-mail: accreditation@aafcs.org
Web site: www.aafcs.org

**National Accrediting Agency for Clinical Laboratory Sciences (NAACLS)**
Dianne M. Cearlock, Chief Executive Officer
5600 North River Road, Suite 720
Rosemont, IL 60018
Phone: 773-714-8880
Fax: 773-714-8886
E-mail: dcearlock@naacls.org
Web site: www.naacls.org

## Interior Design

**Council for Interior Design Accreditation (CIDA)**
Holly Mattson, Executive Director
206 Grandville Avenue, Suite 350
Grand Rapids, MI 49503
Phone: 616-458-0400
Fax: 616-458-0460
E-mail: info@accredit-id.org
Web site: www.accredit-id.org

## Liberal Studies

**American Academy for Liberal Education**
1050 17th Street, NW, Suite 400
Washington, DC 20036
Phone: 202-452-8611
Fax: 202-452-8620
E-mail: aaleinfo@aale.org
Web site: www.aale.org

## Library Science

**American Library Association (ALA), Committee on Accreditation (CoA)**
Karen O'Brien, Director, Office for Accreditation
50 East Huron Street
Chicago, IL 60611
Phone: 800-545-2433 Ext. 2432 (toll-free)
Fax: 312-280-2433
E-mail: kobrien@ala.org
Web site: www.ala.org/accreditation/

## Medical Assisting

**Accrediting Bureau of Health Education Schools (ABHES)**
Carol Moneymaker, Executive Director
7777 Leesburg Pike, Suite 314 N.
Falls Church, VA 22043
Phone: 703-917-9503
Fax: 703-907-4109
E-mail: info@abhes.org
Web site: www.abhes.org

**Commission on Accreditation of Allied Health Education Programs**
In conjunction with:
**American Association of Medical Assistants**
20 North Wacker Drive, Suite 1575
Chicago, IL 60606
Phone: 312-899-1500
Fax: 312-899-1259
Web site: www.aama-ntl.org

## Medical/Clinical Laboratory Technology

**National Accrediting Agency for Clinical Laboratory Sciences (NAACLS)**
Dianne M. Cearlock, Chief Executive Officer
5600 North River Road, Suite 720
Rosemont, IL 60018
Phone: 773-714-8880
Fax: 773-714-8886
E-mail: dcearlock@naacls.org
Web site: www.naacls.org

## Music

**National Association of Schools of Music (NASM), Commission on Accreditation**
Samuel Hope, Executive Director
11250 Roger Bacon Drive, Suite 21
Reston, VA 20190
Phone: 703-437-0700
Fax: 703-437-6312
E-mail: info@arts-accredit.org
Web site: www.arts-accredit.org

## Nuclear Medicine Technology

**Joint Review Committee on Educational Programs in Nuclear Medicine Technology (JRCNMT)**
Jan M. Winn, Executive Director
2000 West Danforth Road, Suite 130, #203
Edmond, OK 73003
Phone: 405-285-0546
Fax: 405-285-0546
E-mail: jrcnmt@coxinent.net
Web site: www.jrcnmt.org

## Nursing

**American College of Nurse-Midwives**
8403 Colesville Road, Suite 1550
Silver Spring, MD 20910
Phone: 240-485-1800
Fax: 240-485-1818
Web site: www.midwife.org

## Occupational Education

**Council on Occupational Education**
41 Perimeter Center East, NE, Suite 640
Atlanta, GA 30346
Phone: 404-396-3898
Fax: 404-396-3790
Web site: www.council.org

## Occupational Therapy

**Commission on Accreditation of Allied Health Education Programs—see Allied Health**
In conjunction with:
**American Occupational Therapy Association, Inc.**
4720 Montgomery Lane, P.O. Box 31220
Bethesda, MD 20824-1220
Phone: 301-652-2682
Fax: 301-652-7711
Web site: www.aota.org

## Ophthalmic Dispensing and Laboratory Technology

**Commission on Opticianry Accreditation**
Ellen Stoner, Director of Accreditation
P.O. Box 142
Florence, IN 47020
Phone: 703-468-0566
Fax: 888-306-9036
E-mail: ellen@coaccreditation.com
Web site: www.coaccreditation.com

## Ophthalmic Medical Technology

**Commission on Accreditation of Allied Health Education Programs—see Allied Health**
In conjunction with:
**Joint Commission on Allied Health Personnel in Ophthalmology® (JCAHPO)**
2025 Woodland Drive
St. Paul, MN 55125-2998
Phone: 651-731-2944 or 800-284-3937 (toll-free)
Fax: 651-731-0410
E-mail: jcahpo@jcahpo.org
Web site: www.jcahpo.org

## Optometry and Optometric Technology

**American Optometric Association (ADA), Accreditation Council on Optometric Education (ACOE)**
Joyce L. Urbek, Administrative Director
243 North Lindbergh Boulevard
St. Louis, MO 63141
Phone: 314-991-4100 Ext. 246
Fax: 314-991-4101
E-mail: acoe@aoa.org
Web site: www.theacoe.org

## Physical Therapy

**American Physical Therapy Association**
1111 North Fairfax Street
Alexandria, VA 22314-1488
Phone: 703-684-2782
Fax: 703-684-7343
Web site: www.apta.org

## Physician and Surgeon's Assistant Practice

**Commission on Accreditation of Allied Health Education Programs—see Allied Health**

In conjunction with:

**Accreditation Review Commission on Education for the Physician Assistant, Inc. (ARC-PA)**

John E. McCarty, Executive Director
12000 Findley Road, Suite 240
Duluth, GA 30097
Phone: 770-476-1224
Fax: 770-476-1738
E-mail: arc-pa@arc-pa.org
Web site: http://www.arc-pa.org

**Council on Education for Public Health**

800 Eye Street, NW, Suite 202
Washington, DC 20001-3710
Phone: 202-789-1050
Fax: 202-789-1895
Web site: www.ceph.org

## Radiologic Technology

**Joint Review Committee on Education Programs in Radiologic Technology**

Leslie Winter, Chief Executive Officer
20 North Wacker Drive, Suite 2850
Chicago, IL 60606
Phone: 312-704-5300
Fax: 312-704-5304
E-mail: mail@jrcert.org
Web site: www.jrcert.org

## Recreation

**Council on Rehabilitation Education (CORE), Commission on Standards and Accreditation**

Marvin D. Kuehn, Executive Director
300 North Martingdale Road, Suite 460
Schaumburg, IL 60173
Phone: 847-944-1345
Fax: 847-944-1324
E-mail: mkuehn@emporia.edu
Web site: www.core-rehab.org

**National Recreation & Park Association, Council on Accreditation (NRPA/COA)**

James O'Connor, Accreditation Manager
22377 Belmont Ridge Road
Ashburn, VA 20148
Phone: 703-858-2150
Fax: 703-858-0794
E-mail: jthorner@nrpa.org
Web site: www.councilonaccreditation.org

## Respiratory Therapy

**Commission on Accreditation of Allied Health Education Programs—see Allied Health**

In conjunction with:

**Committee on Accreditation for Respiratory Care**

1248 Harwood Road
Bedford, TX 76021-4244
Phone: 817-283-2835
Fax: 817-354-8519
Web site: www.coarc.com

## Speech-Language Pathology and Audiology

**American Speech-Language-Hearing Association (ASHA),
Council on Academic Accreditation in Audiology and Speech-Language Pathology**

Patrima Tice, Director of Accreditation
2700 Research Boulevard
Rockville, MD 20852
Phone: 301-296-5796
Fax: 301-296-8750
E-mail: ptice@asha.org
Web site:
www.asha.org/about/credentialing/accreditation

## Surgical Technology

**Commission on Accreditation of Allied Health Education Programs—see Allied Health**

In conjunction with:

**Accreditation Review Committee on Education in Surgical Technology and Surgical Assisting (ARC/STSA)**

Keith Orloff, Executive Director
6 West Dry Creek Circle, Suite 110
Littleton, CO 80120
Phone: 303-694-9262
Fax: 303-741-3655
Web site: www.arcst.org

## Technology Fields

**Accrediting Commission of Career Schools and Colleges (ACCSC)**
Michale S. McComis, Executive Director
2101 Wilson Boulevard, Suite 302
Arlington, VA 22201
Phone: 703-247-4212
Fax: 703-247-4533
E-mail: mccomis@accsc.org
Web site: www.accsc.org

## Theater and Theater-Related Disciplines

**National Association of Schools of Theatre (NAST)**
Samuel Hope, Executive Director
11250 Roger Bacon Drive, Suite 21
Reston, VA 20190-5248
Phone: 703-437-0700
Fax: 703-437-6312
E-mail: info@arts-accredit.org
Web site: http://nast.arts-accredit.org

# Indexes

# Career Training Programs

## ACCOUNTING

### Alaska

Charter College (Anchorage), 41
University of Alaska Southeast (Juneau), 42

### American Samoa

American Samoa Community College (Pago Pago), 43

### Arizona

Brown Mackie College–Tucson (Tucson), 46
Coconino Community College (Flagstaff), 48
Mohave Community College (Kingman), 52
Northern Arizona University (Flagstaff), 52
Pima Community College (Tucson), 54
Yavapai College (Prescott), 58

### Arkansas

Arkansas Northeastern College (Blytheville), 59
Crowley's Ridge Technical Institute (Forrest City), 62
North Arkansas College (Harrison), 64
Northwest Technical Institute (Springdale), 64
Ouachita Technical College (Malvern), 64
Pulaski Technical College (North Little Rock), 65
University of Arkansas Community College at Batesville (Batesville), 67

### California

Advanced College (South Gate), 69
Allan Hancock College (Santa Maria), 70
American Pacific College (Van Nuys), 72
American River College (Sacramento), 72
Antelope Valley College (Lancaster), 72
Bakersfield College (Bakersfield), 74
Barstow College (Barstow), 74
Cabrillo College (Aptos), 75
Cañada College (Redwood City), 77
Cambridge Career College (Yuba City), 77
Center for Employment Training–El Centro (El Centro), 78
Center for Employment Training–Gilroy (Gilroy), 79
Center for Employment Training–Sobrato (San Jose), 79
Center for Employment Training–Temecula (Temecula), 80
Cerritos College (Norwalk), 80
CET–Sacramento (Sacramento), 81
Chabot College (Hayward), 81
Chaffey College (Rancho Cucamonga), 81
Citrus College (Glendora), 82
City College of San Francisco (San Francisco), 82
Coastline Community College (Fountain Valley), 83
College of Alameda (Alameda), 84
College of Marin (Kentfield), 84
College of San Mateo (San Mateo), 84
College of the Desert (Palm Desert), 84
College of the Redwoods (Eureka), 85
College of the Sequoias (Visalia), 85
College of the Siskiyous (Weed), 85
Contra Costa College (San Pablo), 86
Cosumnes River College (Sacramento), 87
Crafton Hills College (Yucaipa), 87
Cuyamaca College (El Cajon), 88
Cypress College (Cypress), 88
De Anza College (Cupertino), 88
Diablo Valley College (Pleasant Hill), 89
East Los Angeles College (Monterey Park), 89
El Camino College (Torrance), 90
Empire College (Santa Rosa), 90
Evergreen Valley College (San Jose), 93
Feather River College (Quincy), 93
Folsom Lake College (Folsom), 93
Foothill College (Los Altos Hills), 93
Fresno City College (Fresno), 94
Fullerton College (Fullerton), 95
Gavilan College (Gilroy), 95
Glendale Community College (Glendale), 95
Golden Gate University (San Francisco), 96
Golden West College (Huntington Beach), 96
Hacienda La Puente Unified School District–Adult Education (City of Industry), 97
Hartnell College (Salinas), 97
Heald College–Concord (Concord), 97
Humphreys College (Stockton), 99
Intercoast Colleges (Burbank), 100
Intercoast Colleges (Riverside), 101
Intercoast Colleges (Santa Ana), 101
Intercoast Colleges (West Covina), 101
Irvine Valley College (Irvine), 101
Lake Tahoe Community College (South Lake Tahoe), 105
Laney College (Oakland), 105
Las Positas College (Livermore), 105
Liberty Training Institute (Los Angeles), 106
Long Beach City College (Long Beach), 106
Los Angeles Pierce College (Woodland Hills), 108
Los Angeles Southwest College (Los Angeles), 109
Los Angeles Trade-Technical College (Los Angeles), 109
Los Angeles Valley College (Van Nuys), 109
Los Medanos College (Pittsburg), 109
Mendocino College (Ukiah), 113
Merced College (Merced), 113
MiraCosta College (Oceanside), 114
Mission College (Santa Clara), 115
Moorpark College (Moorpark), 116
MTI College of Business & Technology (Sacramento), 117
Mt. San Antonio College (Walnut), 116
Mt. San Jacinto College (San Jacinto), 117
Napa Valley College (Napa), 118
Ohlone College (Fremont), 120
Orange Coast College (Costa Mesa), 121
Oxnard College (Oxnard), 121
Palomar College (San Marcos), 122
Porterville College (Porterville), 124
Premiere Career College (Irwindale), 125
Reedley College (Reedley), 125
Rio Hondo College (Whittier), 125
Riverside Community College District (Riverside), 126
Sacramento City College (Sacramento), 126
Saddleback College (Mission Viejo), 127
San Bernardino Valley College (San Bernardino), 128
San Diego City College (San Diego), 128
San Diego Mesa College (San Diego), 128
San Joaquin Delta College (Stockton), 129
San Jose City College (San Jose), 130
Santa Ana College (Santa Ana), 131
Santa Barbara City College (Santa Barbara), 131
Santa Monica College (Santa Monica), 132
Santa Rosa Junior College (Santa Rosa), 132
Shasta College (Redding), 133
Sierra College (Rocklin), 133
Skyline College (San Bruno), 133
Solano Community College (Suisun City), 134
Southern California Institute of Technology (Anaheim), 134
Southwestern College (Chula Vista), 134
Stanbridge College (Irvine), 135
Taft College (Taft), 135
Ventura Adult and Continuing Education (Ventura), 138
Ventura College (Ventura), 138
Victor Valley College (Victorville), 138
West Hills Community College–Lemoore (Lemoore), 141
West Los Angeles College (Culver City), 141
West Valley College (Saratoga), 141
Yuba College (Marysville), 142

### Colorado

Colorado Christian University (Lakewood), 145
Colorado Northwestern Community College (Rangely), 145
San Juan Basin Area Vocational School (Cortez), 152

### Hawaii

Hawaii Community College (Hilo), 154
Kapiolani Community College (Honolulu), 155
Kauai Community College (Lihue), 155
Leeward Community College (Pearl City), 155
Maui Community College (Kahului), 155

### Idaho

Eastern Idaho Technical College (Idaho Falls), 157

### Illinois

Brown Mackie College–Moline (Moline), 161
Carl Sandburg College (Galesburg), 162
City Colleges of Chicago, Harold Washington College (Chicago), 163
City Colleges of Chicago, Harry S. Truman College (Chicago), 163
City Colleges of Chicago, Olive-Harvey College (Chicago), 163
City Colleges of Chicago, Richard J. Daley College (Chicago), 164
City Colleges of Chicago, Wilbur Wright College (Chicago), 164
College of Lake County (Grayslake), 165
East-West University (Chicago), 167
Harper College (Palatine), 170
Heartland Community College (Normal), 171
Highland Community College (Freeport), 171
John Wood Community College (Quincy), 174

## ACCOUNTING TECHNOLOGY/TECHNICIAN AND BOOKKEEPING

## ACTING



## ADMINISTRATION OF SPECIAL EDUCATION



## ADMINISTRATIVE ASSISTANT AND SECRETARIAL SCIENCE, GENERAL

## ADULT AND CONTINUING EDUCATION ADMINISTRATION



## ADULT AND CONTINUING EDUCATION AND TEACHING



## ADULT DEVELOPMENT AND AGING

**Texas**
Academy of Health Care Professions (Austin), 348
Allied Health Careers (Austin), 349
American Commercial College (Odessa), 350
American Commercial College (Wichita Falls), 350
Arlington Career Institute (Grand Prairie), 351
Professional Careers Institute (Houston), 375
Southeastern Career Institute (Dallas), 380
Texas Careers–Beaumont (Beaumont), 384
Texas School of Business–East Campus (Houston), 385
Texas School of Business–Friendswood (Friendswood), 385
Texas School of Business–North (Houston), 385
Texas School of Business–Southwest (Houston), 386
Valley Grande Academy (Weslaco), 389
Vatterott Education Center (Dallas), 389

**Utah**
Eagle Gate College (Layton), 394
Utah Career College–Orem Campus (Orem), 398

**Wisconsin**
Chippewa Valley Technical College (Eau Claire), 415
Concordia University Wisconsin (Mequon), 415
Mid-State Technical College (Wisconsin Rapids), 418
Waukesha County Technical College (Pewaukee), 422

## ALLIED HEALTH DIAGNOSTIC, INTERVENTION, AND TREATMENT PROFESSIONS, OTHER

**Arizona**
GateWay Community College (Phoenix), 50
Phoenix College (Phoenix), 53

**California**
Loma Linda University (Loma Linda), 106

**Colorado**
Aims Community College (Greeley), 143

**Iowa**
Mercy College of Health Sciences (Des Moines), 196

**Kentucky**
Gateway Community and Technical College (Covington), 213

**Louisiana**
Southern University at Shreveport (Shreveport), 237

**New Mexico**
Eastern New Mexico University–Roswell (Roswell), 294

**Oklahoma**
Wes Watkins Area Vocational-Technical Center (Wetumka), 318

**Tennessee**
Roane State Community College (Harriman), 339

**Washington**
Clover Park Technical College (Lakewood), 402
Highline Community College (Des Moines), 405

**Wisconsin**
Chippewa Valley Technical College (Eau Claire), 415
Madison Area Technical College (Madison), 417
Milwaukee Area Technical College (Milwaukee), 418

## ALTERNATIVE AND COMPLEMENTARY MEDICINE AND MEDICAL SYSTEMS, OTHER

**Arizona**
Southwest Institute of Healing Arts (Tempe), 56

**New Mexico**
University of New Mexico–Taos (Taos), 298

## ALTERNATIVE FUEL VEHICLE TECHNOLOGY/TECHNICIAN

**California**
Long Beach City College (Long Beach), 106

**Tennessee**
Nashville Auto Diesel College (Nashville), 336

## AMERICAN INDIAN/NATIVE AMERICAN LANGUAGES, LITERATURES, AND LINGUISTICS

**Alaska**
Ilisagvik College (Barrow), 41
University of Alaska Fairbanks (Fairbanks), 42

## AMERICAN INDIAN/NATIVE AMERICAN STUDIES

**Arizona**
Phoenix College (Phoenix), 53

**Hawaii**
Hawai'i Pacific University (Honolulu), 154

**Minnesota**
Minneapolis Community and Technical College (Minneapolis), 246

**Montana**
Salish Kootenai College (Pablo), 284

**Oklahoma**
Seminole State College (Seminole), 315

**South Dakota**
Oglala Lakota College (Kyle), 329

**Washington**
Northwest Indian College (Bellingham), 408

**Wyoming**
Central Wyoming College (Riverton), 423

## AMERICAN SIGN LANGUAGE (ASL)

**Arizona**
Arizona Western College (Yuma), 44
Phoenix College (Phoenix), 53

**California**
American River College (Sacramento), 72
Antelope Valley College (Lancaster), 72
Berkeley City College (Berkeley), 74
College of Alameda (Alameda), 84
San Joaquin Delta College (Stockton), 129
Santa Ana College (Santa Ana), 131
Santiago Canyon College (Orange), 132

**Minnesota**
Central Lakes College (Brainerd), 241
Pine Technical College (Pine City), 251
Saint Paul College–A Community & Technical College (St. Paul), 254

**Missouri**
St. Louis Community College at Florissant Valley (St. Louis), 277

**Nevada**
Western Nevada Community College (Carson City), 292

**Oregon**
Portland Community College (Portland), 326

## AMERICAN/UNITED STATES STUDIES/CIVILIZATION

**Arizona**
Northern Arizona University (Flagstaff), 52

**Oregon**
Warner Pacific College (Portland), 328

## ANATOMY

**California**
Sacramento City Unified School District–Skills and Business Education Center (Sacramento), 126

## ANIMAL HEALTH

**Iowa**
Kirkwood Community College (Cedar Rapids), 195

## ANIMAL/LIVESTOCK HUSBANDRY AND PRODUCTION

**Arizona**
Mesa Community College (Mesa), 52
Scottsdale Community College (Scottsdale), 56

**California**
Bakersfield College (Bakersfield), 74
College of the Sequoias (Visalia), 85
Lassen Community College District (Susanville), 106
Modesto Junior College (Modesto), 115
Reedley College (Reedley), 125

**Illinois**
Black Hawk College (Moline), 160
John Wood Community College (Quincy), 174

**Iowa**
Hawkeye Community College (Waterloo), 192

**Kansas**
Butler Community College (El Dorado), 201

**Texas**
Frank Phillips College (Borger), 362

**Utah**
Southern Utah University (Cedar City), 397

## ANIMAL SCIENCES, GENERAL

**Arizona**
Northland Pioneer College (Holbrook), 53

## ANIMAL TRAINING

**Illinois**
Lake Land College (Mattoon), 176

## ANIMATION, INTERACTIVE TECHNOLOGY, VIDEO GRAPHICS AND SPECIAL EFFECTS

**Arizona**
Cochise College (Douglas), 47
East Valley Institute of Technology (Mesa), 49

**California**
American River College (Sacramento), 72
Antelope Valley College (Lancaster), 72
Butte College (Oroville), 75
Cabrillo College (Aptos), 75
Cerro Coso Community College (Ridgecrest), 80
City College of San Francisco (San Francisco), 82
De Anza College (Cupertino), 88
Diablo Valley College (Pleasant Hill), 89
Fullerton College (Fullerton), 95
Mt. San Antonio College (Walnut), 116
Ohlone College (Fremont), 120
Palomar College (San Marcos), 122
Palo Verde College (Blythe), 123
Platt College San Diego (San Diego), 124

## AQUACULTURE



## ARABIC LANGUAGE AND LITERATURE



## ARCHEOLOGY



## ARCHITECTURAL DRAFTING AND ARCHITECTURAL CAD/CADD

Muscatine Community College (Muscatine), 196

**Minnesota**

Anoka Technical College (Anoka), 240
Hennepin Technical College (Brooklyn Park), 243
Herzing College (Minneapolis), 244
Minneapolis Community and Technical College (Minneapolis), 246
Northland Community and Technical College–Thief River Falls (Thief River Falls), 250
Rochester Community and Technical College (Rochester), 253
St. Cloud Technical College (St. Cloud), 254

**Missouri**

Cape Girardeau Area Vocational Technical School (Cape Girardeau), 264

**Nebraska**

Metropolitan Community College (Omaha), 287

**Nevada**

Truckee Meadows Community College (Reno), 292

**New Mexico**

Central New Mexico Community College (Albuquerque), 293

**Oklahoma**

Oklahoma City Community College (Oklahoma City), 312

**Oregon**

Chemeketa Community College (Salem), 320
Mt. Hood Community College (Gresham), 323

**Texas**

Del Mar College (Corpus Christi), 359
Eastfield College (Mesquite), 360
Mountain View College (Dallas), 371
St. Philip's College (San Antonio), 377
Wharton County Junior College (Wharton), 391

**Washington**

Green River Community College (Auburn), 405
Lake Washington Technical College (Kirkland), 406
South Puget Sound Community College (Olympia), 411

## ARCHITECTURAL ENGINEERING TECHNOLOGY/TECHNICIAN

**Alaska**

University of Alaska Anchorage (Anchorage), 41

**Colorado**

Arapahoe Community College (Littleton), 143
Front Range Community College (Westminster), 147
Pikes Peak Community College (Colorado Springs), 150

**Oregon**

Mt. Hood Community College (Gresham), 323

**Tennessee**

Southwest Tennessee Community College (Memphis), 339

**Texas**

Tarrant County College District (Fort Worth), 383

## ARCHITECTURAL TECHNOLOGY/TECHNICIAN

**California**

Bakersfield College (Bakersfield), 74
Cerritos College (Norwalk), 80
Cosumnes River College (Sacramento), 87
East Los Angeles College (Monterey Park), 89
Fullerton College (Fullerton), 95
Glendale Community College (Glendale), 95
Golden West College (Huntington Beach), 96
Long Beach City College (Long Beach), 106
Los Angeles Harbor College (Wilmington), 107
Los Angeles Pierce College (Woodland Hills), 108
Los Angeles Trade-Technical College (Los Angeles), 109
Los Angeles Valley College (Van Nuys), 109
MiraCosta College (Oceanside), 114
Modesto Junior College (Modesto), 115
Mt. San Antonio College (Walnut), 116
Orange Coast College (Costa Mesa), 121
Rio Hondo College (Whittier), 125
Riverside Community College District (Riverside), 126
Saddleback College (Mission Viejo), 127
San Diego Mesa College (San Diego), 128
San Joaquin Delta College (Stockton), 129
Santa Rosa Junior College (Santa Rosa), 132
Southwestern College (Chula Vista), 134
Ventura College (Ventura), 138
West Valley College (Saratoga), 141

**Micronesia**

College of Micronesia–FSM (Kolonia Pohnpei), 239

## ARCHITECTURE AND RELATED SERVICES, OTHER

**Arizona**

Yavapai College (Prescott), 58

**California**

East Los Angeles College (Monterey Park), 89

## AREA, ETHNIC, CULTURAL, AND GENDER STUDIES, OTHER

**American Samoa**

American Samoa Community College (Pago Pago), 43

## AREA STUDIES, OTHER

**Texas**

Career Quest (San Antonio), 355

**Wyoming**

Central Wyoming College (Riverton), 423

## ART/ART STUDIES, GENERAL

**Alaska**

University of Alaska Southeast (Juneau), 42

**Arizona**

Chandler-Gilbert Community College (Chandler), 47
Estrella Mountain Community College (Avondale), 49
GateWay Community College (Phoenix), 50
Glendale Community College (Glendale), 50
Mesa Community College (Mesa), 52
Mohave Community College (Kingman), 52
Paradise Valley Community College (Phoenix), 53
Phoenix College (Phoenix), 53
Rio Salado College (Tempe), 55
Scottsdale Community College (Scottsdale), 56
South Mountain Community College (Phoenix), 56

**California**

Foothill College (Los Altos Hills), 93
Glendale Community College (Glendale), 95
Los Angeles Trade-Technical College (Los Angeles), 109
San Diego Mesa College (San Diego), 128
Santa Rosa Junior College (Santa Rosa), 132
Ventura College (Ventura), 138
Yuba College (Marysville), 142

**Kansas**

Wichita State University (Wichita), 208

**New Mexico**

University of New Mexico–Valencia Campus (Los Lunas), 298

**Texas**

Central Texas College (Killeen), 355

**Wyoming**

Central Wyoming College (Riverton), 423

## ARTS MANAGEMENT

**Illinois**

Columbia College Chicago (Chicago), 165

**North Dakota**

United Tribes Technical College (Bismarck), 301

## ART THERAPY/THERAPIST

**Iowa**

Grand View University (Des Moines), 192

## ASIAN BODYWORK THERAPY

**Arizona**

Southwest Institute of Healing Arts (Tempe), 56

## ASTRONOMY

**California**

Ohlone College (Fremont), 120

## ATHLETIC TRAINING/TRAINER

**Arizona**

Apollo College–Phoenix (Phoenix), 43

**California**

Career Networks Institute (Costa Mesa), 78
Santa Barbara Business College (Bakersfield), 131
Santa Barbara Business College (Santa Maria), 131

**Minnesota**

Lake Superior College (Duluth), 245

**Missouri**

Pinnacle Career Institute (Kansas City), 275
Pinnacle Career Institute–North Kansas City (Kansas City), 276

**Montana**

Flathead Valley Community College (Kalispell), 283

**Texas**

ATI Career Training Center (North Richland Hills), 352

**Utah**

Eagle Gate College (Salt Lake City), 394
Mountainland Applied Technology College (Orem), 395

## ATMOSPHERIC SCIENCES AND METEOROLOGY, GENERAL

**Nebraska**

Creighton University (Omaha), 286

## AUDIOLOGY/AUDIOLOGIST AND SPEECH-LANGUAGE PATHOLOGY/PATHOLOGIST

**California**

Cerritos College (Norwalk), 80
Los Angeles Southwest College (Los Angeles), 109
Orange Coast College (Costa Mesa), 121
Pasadena City College (Pasadena), 123
Santa Ana College (Santa Ana), 131

Poplar Bluff School District–Practical Nurse Program (Poplar Bluff), 276
Ranken Technical College (St. Louis), 276
Sikeston Career and Technology Center (Sikeston), 279
South Central Area Vocational Technical School (West Plains), 280
Waynesville Technical Academy (Waynesville), 282

**Montana**
Montana State University–Billings (Billings), 284

**Nebraska**
Central Community College–Grand Island Campus (Grand Island), 285
Metropolitan Community College (Omaha), 287
Mid-Plains Community College (North Platte), 287
Western Nebraska Community College (Sidney), 289

**New Mexico**
Eastern New Mexico University–Roswell (Roswell), 294
Luna Community College (Las Vegas), 295
Northern New Mexico College (Española), 296
San Juan College (Farmington), 296

**North Dakota**
Bismarck State College (Bismarck), 298
North Dakota State College of Science (Wahpeton), 300

**Oklahoma**
Autry Technology Center (Enid), 302
Caddo-Kiowa Area Vocational Technical School (Ft. Cobb), 303
Canadian Valley Technology Center (El Reno), 303
Francis Tuttle Area Vocational Technical Center (Oklahoma City), 306
Gordon Cooper Technology Center (Shawnee), 306
Great Plains Technology Center (Lawton), 306
Indian Capital Technology Center–Muskogee (Muskogee), 307
Indian Capital Technology Center–Tahlequah (Tahlequah), 308
Kiamichi Technology Center (Hugo), 309
Meridian Technology Center (Stillwater), 309
Metro Area Vocational Technical School District 22 (Oklahoma City), 310
Mid-America Technology Center (Wayne), 310
Mid-Del Technology Center (Midwest), 310
Moore Norman Technology Center (Norman), 311
Northeast Area Vocational Technical School (Pryor), 311
Northeast Technology Center–Afton (Afton), 311
Northwest Technology Center (Alva), 312
Pioneer Area Vocational Technical School (Ponca City), 313
Red River Area Vocational-Technical School (Duncan), 315
Southern Oklahoma Technology Center (Ardmore), 315
Tri County Technology Center (Bartlesville), 316
Tulsa Tech–Career Services Center (Tulsa), 317
Western Technology Center (Burns Flat), 318

**Oregon**
Chemeketa Community College (Salem), 320
Clackamas Community College (Oregon City), 320
Linn-Benton Community College (Albany), 323
Portland Community College (Portland), 326

**Tennessee**
Nashville Auto Diesel College (Nashville), 336
Tennessee Technology Center at Athens (Athens), 340
Tennessee Technology Center at Crossville (Crossville), 341
Tennessee Technology Center at Crump (Crump), 341
Tennessee Technology Center at Jackson (Jackson), 342
Tennessee Technology Center at Knoxville (Knoxville), 342
Tennessee Technology Center at Livingston (Livingston), 342
Tennessee Technology Center at Memphis (Memphis), 343
Tennessee Technology Center at Morristown (Morristown), 343
Tennessee Technology Center at Nashville (Nashville), 344
Tennessee Technology Center at Oneida/ Huntsville (Huntsville), 344
Tennessee Technology Center at Paris (Paris), 344
Tennessee Technology Center at Shelbyville (Shelbyville), 345

**Texas**
Amarillo College (Amarillo), 349
Central Texas College (Killeen), 355
Eastfield College (Mesquite), 360
Grayson County College (Denison), 363
Hill College of the Hill Junior College District (Hillsboro), 363
Kilgore College (Kilgore), 367
Laredo Community College (Laredo), 368
Lee College (Baytown), 368
Lincoln Technical Institute (Grand Prairie), 368
Northeast Texas Community College (Mount Pleasant), 372
St. Philip's College (San Antonio), 377
San Jacinto College Central Campus (Pasadena), 378
South Plains College (Levelland), 381
Southwest Texas Junior College (Uvalde), 382
Tarrant County College District (Fort Worth), 383
Texarkana College (Texarkana), 384
Texas Southmost College (Brownsville), 386
Texas State Technical College Harlingen (Harlingen), 386
Texas State Technical College Waco (Waco), 386
Texas State Technical College West Texas (Sweetwater), 387
Trinity Valley Community College (Athens), 387
Universal Technical Institute (Houston), 388

**Utah**
Bridgerland Applied Technology Center (Logan), 392
Dixie Applied Technology College (Saint George), 394
Utah Valley University (Orem), 399

**Washington**
Bates Technical College (Tacoma), 400
Clover Park Technical College (Lakewood), 402
Green River Community College (Auburn), 405
Lake Washington Technical College (Kirkland), 406
Walla Walla Community College (Walla Walla), 413

**Wisconsin**
Chippewa Valley Technical College (Eau Claire), 415
Fox Valley Technical College (Appleton), 415
Lakeshore Technical College (Cleveland), 417
Madison Area Technical College (Madison), 417
Milwaukee Area Technical College (Milwaukee), 418
Moraine Park Technical College (Fond du Lac), 419
Northcentral Technical College (Wausau), 419
Southwest Wisconsin Technical College (Fennimore), 421
Waukesha County Technical College (Pewaukee), 422
Wisconsin Indianhead Technical College (Shell Lake), 422

**Wyoming**
Casper College (Casper), 423
Laramie County Community College (Cheyenne), 423
WyoTech (Laramie), 424

## AUTOMOBILE/AUTOMOTIVE MECHANICS TECHNOLOGY/TECHNICIAN

**Alaska**
Alaska Vocational Technical Center (Seward), 41
University of Alaska Anchorage (Anchorage), 41
University of Alaska Fairbanks (Fairbanks), 42
University of Alaska Southeast (Juneau), 42

**American Samoa**
American Samoa Community College (Pago Pago), 43

**Arizona**
Arizona Automotive Institute (Glendale), 43
Arizona Western College (Yuma), 44
Central Arizona College (Coolidge), 47
Cochise College (Douglas), 47
Eastern Arizona College (Thatcher), 48
East Valley Institute of Technology (Mesa), 49
GateWay Community College (Phoenix), 50
Glendale Community College (Glendale), 50
Mesa Community College (Mesa), 52
Pima Community College (Tucson), 54
Yavapai College (Prescott), 58

**Arkansas**
Arkansas Northeastern College (Blytheville), 59
Arkansas State University (State University), 59
Arkansas State University–Beebe (Beebe), 59
Arkansas Tech University (Russellville), 60
Black River Technical College (Pocahontas), 61
Cossatot Community College of the University of Arkansas (De Queen), 61
Crowley's Ridge Technical Institute (Forrest City), 62
National Park Community College (Hot Springs), 63
North Arkansas College (Harrison), 64
Northwest Technical Institute (Springdale), 64
Ouachita Technical College (Malvern), 64
Ozarka College (Melbourne), 65
Pulaski Technical College (North Little Rock), 65
South Arkansas Community College (El Dorado), 66
Southern Arkansas University Tech (Camden), 66
University of Arkansas at Fort Smith (Fort Smith), 67

The Master's College and Seminary (Santa Clarita), 113
Patten University (Oakland), 123
Shasta Bible College (Redding), 132
William Jessup University (Rocklin), 142

**Colorado**
Colorado Christian University (Lakewood), 145

**Idaho**
Boise Bible College (Boise), 157

**Illinois**
Lincoln Christian College (Lincoln), 176

**Iowa**
Emmaus Bible College (Dubuque), 192
Faith Baptist Bible College and Theological Seminary (Ankeny), 192

**Kansas**
Manhattan Christian College (Manhattan), 205

**Louisiana**
School of Urban Missions (Gretna), 237

**Minnesota**
Crown College (St. Bonifacius), 242
North Central University (Minneapolis), 249
Northwestern College (St. Paul), 250
Oak Hills Christian College (Bemidji), 251

**Mississippi**
Belhaven College (Jackson), 257

**Missouri**
Calvary Bible College and Theological Seminary (Kansas City), 264
Central Bible College (Springfield), 264
Ozark Christian College (Joplin), 274

**Nebraska**
Grace University (Omaha), 286

**Oregon**
Eugene Bible College (Eugene), 322

**Tennessee**
Crichton College (Memphis), 332

**Texas**
College of Biblical Studies–Houston (Houston), 357
Howard Payne University (Brownwood), 364

**Wisconsin**
Philadelphia Biblical University–Wisconsin Wilderness Campus (Cable), 420

## BILINGUAL AND MULTILINGUAL EDUCATION

**Arizona**
Pima Community College (Tucson), 54

## BIOLOGY/BIOLOGICAL SCIENCES, GENERAL

**California**
Contra Costa College (San Pablo), 86
Los Angeles Pierce College (Woodland Hills), 108
Ohlone College (Fremont), 120
Palomar College (San Marcos), 122

## BIOLOGY TECHNICIAN/BIOTECHNOLOGY LABORATORY TECHNICIAN

**Arizona**
Pima Community College (Tucson), 54

**California**
American River College (Sacramento), 72
City College of San Francisco (San Francisco), 82
Contra Costa College (San Pablo), 86
East Los Angeles College (Monterey Park), 89
Foothill College (Los Altos Hills), 93
Laney College (Oakland), 105
Los Angeles Pierce College (Woodland Hills), 108
Merced College (Merced), 113
MiraCosta College (Oceanside), 114
Ohlone College (Fremont), 120
Pasadena City College (Pasadena), 123
San Diego City College (San Diego), 128
San Diego Mesa College (San Diego), 128
Skyline College (San Bruno), 133
Solano Community College (Suisun City), 134
Southwestern College (Chula Vista), 134
Ventura College (Ventura), 138
Victor Valley College (Victorville), 138
Western Career College (Emeryville), 140

**Colorado**
Community College of Aurora (Aurora), 146

**Kansas**
Johnson County Community College (Overland Park), 203

**Minnesota**
Anoka-Ramsey Community College (Coon Rapids), 240

**Missouri**
St. Louis Community College at Florissant Valley (St. Louis), 277

**Nebraska**
Southeast Community College Area (Lincoln), 288

**Oklahoma**
Meridian Technology Center (Stillwater), 309

**South Dakota**
Lake Area Technical Institute (Watertown), 328

**Texas**
Austin Community College (Austin), 352
Collin County Community College District (Plano), 357
El Centro College (Dallas), 360
Houston Community College System (Houston), 363
Lonestar College–North Harris (Houston), 369

**Washington**
Bates Technical College (Tacoma), 400
Shoreline Community College (Shoreline), 410

## BIOMEDICAL TECHNOLOGY/TECHNICIAN

**Illinois**
South Suburban College (South Holland), 187

**Iowa**
Western Iowa Tech Community College (Sioux City), 198

**Minnesota**
Dakota County Technical College (Rosemount), 242

**Tennessee**
MedVance Institute–Nashville (Nashville), 335

**Utah**
Ogden-Weber Applied Technology Center (Ogden), 396

## BLOOD BANK TECHNOLOGY SPECIALIST

**Arizona**
Mohave Community College (Kingman), 52

**Kentucky**
Southwestern College of Business (Florence), 219
Spencerian College (Louisville), 219

**Louisiana**
Unitech Training Academy (Lafayette), 238
Unitech Training Academy–Houma (Houma), 238
Unitech Training Academy–West Monroe Campus (West Monroe), 238

**New Mexico**
Central New Mexico Community College (Albuquerque), 293
Eastern New Mexico University–Roswell (Roswell), 294

**Tennessee**
Southwest Tennessee Community College (Memphis), 339

**Wisconsin**
Moraine Park Technical College (Fond du Lac), 419

## BROADCAST JOURNALISM

**Alaska**
University of Alaska, Prince William Sound Community College (Valdez), 42

**Arizona**
Scottsdale Community College (Scottsdale), 56

**California**
Long Beach City College (Long Beach), 106
San Diego City College (San Diego), 128
Santa Ana College (Santa Ana), 131
Santa Barbara City College (Santa Barbara), 131

**Missouri**
St. Louis Community College at Florissant Valley (St. Louis), 277

**Oklahoma**
Rose State College (Midwest City), 315

## BUILDING/CONSTRUCTION FINISHING, MANAGEMENT, AND INSPECTION, OTHER

**Arizona**
Eastern Arizona College (Thatcher), 48
GateWay Community College (Phoenix), 50

**Arkansas**
Southern Arkansas University Tech (Camden), 66

**Colorado**
Pikes Peak Community College (Colorado Springs), 150

**Idaho**
College of Southern Idaho (Twin Falls), 157

**Minnesota**
University of Minnesota, Twin Cities Campus (Minneapolis), 256

**Montana**
Fort Peck Community College (Poplar), 283
The University of Montana (Missoula), 285

**Nebraska**
Central Community College–Grand Island Campus (Grand Island), 285
Metropolitan Community College (Omaha), 287
Mid-Plains Community College (North Platte), 287

**Nevada**
Truckee Meadows Community College (Reno), 292

**New Mexico**
University of New Mexico–Gallup (Gallup), 297

**Utah**
College of Eastern Utah (Price), 393

**Washington**
Centralia College (Centralia), 401

**Wisconsin**
Chippewa Valley Technical College (Eau Claire), 415
Milwaukee Area Technical College (Milwaukee), 418

Northcentral Technical College (Wausau), 419
Northeast Wisconsin Technical College (Green Bay), 420
Western Technical College (La Crosse), 422
Wisconsin Indianhead Technical College (Shell Lake), 422

**Wyoming**
Sheridan College (Sheridan), 424

## BUILDING/CONSTRUCTION SITE MANAGEMENT/MANAGER

**California**
Cabrillo College (Aptos), 75
College of the Desert (Palm Desert), 84
Cosumnes River College (Sacramento), 87
Diablo Valley College (Pleasant Hill), 89
Fullerton College (Fullerton), 95
Hartnell College (Salinas), 97
Laney College (Oakland), 105
San Diego Mesa College (San Diego), 128
Santa Rosa Junior College (Santa Rosa), 132
Southwestern College (Chula Vista), 134
Ventura College (Ventura), 138
Victor Valley College (Victorville), 138

**Colorado**
Aims Community College (Greeley), 143

**Minnesota**
Dunwoody College of Technology (Minneapolis), 242
Inver Hills Community College (Inver Grove Heights), 244
North Hennepin Community College (Brooklyn Park), 250

**Nevada**
College of Southern Nevada (North Las Vegas), 290

**Oklahoma**
Indian Capital Technology Center–Stilwell (Stilwell), 308
Indian Capital Technology Center–Tahlequah (Tahlequah), 308

**Texas**
Texas Southmost College (Brownsville), 386

## BUILDING/HOME/CONSTRUCTION INSPECTION/INSPECTOR

**Alaska**
University of Alaska Southeast (Juneau), 42

**Arizona**
Northland Pioneer College (Holbrook), 53
Phoenix College (Phoenix), 53
Scottsdale Community College (Scottsdale), 56

**California**
Butte College (Oroville), 75
Cabrillo College (Aptos), 75
Coastline Community College (Fountain Valley), 83
College of San Mateo (San Mateo), 84
College of the Desert (Palm Desert), 84
College of the Sequoias (Visalia), 85
Cosumnes River College (Sacramento), 87
Diablo Valley College (Pleasant Hill), 89
Fresno City College (Fresno), 94
Laney College (Oakland), 105
Modesto Junior College (Modesto), 115
Mt. San Antonio College (Walnut), 116
Palomar College (San Marcos), 122
Pasadena City College (Pasadena), 123
Riverside Community College District (Riverside), 126
Saddleback College (Mission Viejo), 127
San Bernardino Valley College (San Bernardino), 128
San Diego Mesa College (San Diego), 128
Southwestern College (Chula Vista), 134

**Illinois**
City Colleges of Chicago, Kennedy-King College (Chicago), 163
Harper College (Palatine), 170
McHenry County College (Crystal Lake), 178

**Minnesota**
Inver Hills Community College (Inver Grove Heights), 244
North Hennepin Community College (Brooklyn Park), 250

**Missouri**
St. Louis Community College at Forest Park (St. Louis), 278

**New Mexico**
Crownpoint Institute of Technology (Crownpoint), 293

**Oregon**
Chemeketa Community College (Salem), 320
Portland Community College (Portland), 326

**Utah**
Utah Valley University (Orem), 399

**Washington**
Bellingham Technical College (Bellingham), 400
Edmonds Community College (Lynnwood), 403

## BUILDING/PROPERTY MAINTENANCE AND MANAGEMENT

**Alaska**
Alaska Vocational Technical Center (Seward), 41

**Arizona**
Central Arizona College (Coolidge), 47
Cochise College (Douglas), 47
Eastern Arizona College (Thatcher), 48
East Valley Institute of Technology (Mesa), 49
Northland Pioneer College (Holbrook), 53
Pima Community College (Tucson), 54

**California**
Center for Employment Training–Coachella (Coachella), 78
Center for Employment Training–El Centro (El Centro), 78
Center for Employment Training–Gilroy (Gilroy), 79
Center for Employment Training–Oxnard (Oxnard), 79
Center for Employment Training–Riverside (Riverside), 79
Center for Employment Training–Salinas (Salinas), 79
Center for Employment Training–San Diego (San Diego), 79
Center for Employment Training–Santa Maria (Santa Maria), 79
Center for Employment Training–Sobrato (San Jose), 79
Center for Employment Training–Watsonville (Watsonville), 80
San Joaquin Valley College (Bakersfield), 129
Vallecitos CET (Hayward), 137

**Colorado**
Pickens Technical College (Aurora), 150

**Hawaii**
Maui Community College (Kahului), 155

**Illinois**
Center for Employment Training–Chicago (Chicago), 162
College of DuPage (Glen Ellyn), 164
Harper College (Palatine), 170
Lake Land College (Mattoon), 176
Lincoln Land Community College (Springfield), 177
Parkland College (Champaign), 181
Waubonsee Community College (Sugar Grove), 189

**Iowa**
Western Iowa Tech Community College (Sioux City), 198

**Kansas**
Flint Hills Technical College (Emporia), 202
Kansas City Area Technical School (Kansas City), 204
Kaw Area Technical School (Topeka), 204

**Kentucky**
Employment Solutions (Lexington), 213

**Louisiana**
Louisiana Technical College–Delta Ouachita Campus (West Monroe), 229
Louisiana Technical College–Florida Parishes Campus (Greensburg), 229
Louisiana Technical College–Folkes Campus (Jackson), 230
Louisiana Technical College–Huey P. Long Campus (Winnfield), 230
Louisiana Technical College–Oakdale Campus (Oakdale), 233
Louisiana Technical College–West Jefferson Campus (Harvey), 235

**Minnesota**
Century College (White Bear Lake), 241
Dunwoody College of Technology (Minneapolis), 242
Hennepin Technical College (Brooklyn Park), 243

**Missouri**
Eldon Career Center (Eldon), 266
St. Louis Community College at Florissant Valley (St. Louis), 277
Vatterott College (St. Louis), 281
Vatterott College (Springfield), 281

**New Mexico**
Doña Ana Branch Community College (Las Cruces), 294
Eastern New Mexico University–Roswell (Roswell), 294
New Mexico State University–Grants (Grants), 296

**Oklahoma**
Canadian Valley Technology Center (El Reno), 303
Eastern Oklahoma County Technology Center (Choctaw), 305
Gordon Cooper Technology Center (Shawnee), 306
Great Plains Technology Center (Lawton), 306
Green Country Technology Center (Okmulgee), 307
High Plains Institute of Technology (Woodward), 307
Indian Capital Technology Center–Stilwell (Stilwell), 308
Kiamichi Technology Center (Hugo), 309
Mid-America Technology Center (Wayne), 310
Mid-Del Technology Center (Midwest), 310
Southwest Area Vocational Technical Center (Altus), 316
Western Technology Center (Burns Flat), 318
Wes Watkins Area Vocational-Technical Center (Wetumka), 318

**Texas**
Central Texas College (Killeen), 355
Cisco College (Cisco), 356

## BUSINESS ADMINISTRATION AND MANAGEMENT, GENERAL

**Kansas**
Allen County Community College (Iola), 199
Barton County Community College (Great Bend), 199
Brown Mackie College–Kansas City (Lenexa), 200
Brown Mackie College–Salina (Salina), 200
Bryan Career College (Topeka), 200
Cloud County Community College (Concordia), 201
Independence Community College (Independence), 203
Neosho County Community College (Chanute), 205

**Kentucky**
Ashland Community and Technical College (Ashland), 209
Big Sandy Community and Technical College (Prestonsburg), 210
Brown Mackie College–Hopkinsville (Hopkinsville), 211
Daymar College (Paducah), 212
Elizabethtown Community and Technical College (Elizabethtown), 213
Gateway Community and Technical College (Covington), 213
Hazard Community and Technical College (Hazard), 214
Hopkinsville Community College (Hopkinsville), 215
Jefferson Community and Technical College (Louisville), 215
Madisonville Community College (Madisonville), 216
Maysville Community and Technical College (Maysville), 216
National College (Lexington), 217
Owensboro Community and Technical College (Owensboro), 217
Somerset Community College (Somerset), 218
Southeast Kentucky Community and Technical College (Cumberland), 218
Sullivan University (Louisville), 219
West Kentucky Community and Technical College (Paducah), 220

**Louisiana**
Gretna Career College (Gretna), 226

**Minnesota**
Alexandria Technical College (Alexandria), 239
Anoka Technical College (Anoka), 240
Dakota County Technical College (Rosemount), 242
Globe University (Woodbury), 243
Inver Hills Community College (Inver Grove Heights), 244
Lake Superior College (Duluth), 245
Minnesota School of Business–Brooklyn Center (Brooklyn Center), 247
Minnesota School of Business–Plymouth (Minneapolis), 247
Minnesota School of Business–St. Cloud (Waite Park), 247
Minnesota School of Business–Shakopee (Shakopee), 247
Minnesota State College–Southeast Technical (Winona), 248
National American University (Roseville), 249
Normandale Community College (Bloomington), 249
North Hennepin Community College (Brooklyn Park), 250
Northland Community and Technical College–Thief River Falls (Thief River Falls), 250
Northwest Technical College (Bemidji), 250
Rasmussen College St. Cloud (St. Cloud), 252
Riverland Community College (Austin), 253
Rochester Community and Technical College (Rochester), 253
St. Cloud Technical College (St. Cloud), 254
University of Minnesota, Duluth (Duluth), 256
University of Minnesota, Twin Cities Campus (Minneapolis), 256

**Mississippi**
Belhaven College (Jackson), 257

**Missouri**
Bryan College (Springfield), 264
Metropolitan Community College–Blue River (Independence), 271
Missouri Baptist University (St. Louis), 272
North Central Missouri College (Trenton), 274
Ozarks Technical Community College (Springfield), 274
Ranken Technical College (St. Louis), 276
St. Louis Community College at Florissant Valley (St. Louis), 277
St. Louis Community College at Forest Park (St. Louis), 278
St. Louis Community College at Meramec (Kirkwood), 278

**Montana**
Montana State University–Great Falls College of Technology (Great Falls), 284

**Nebraska**
Central Community College–Grand Island Campus (Grand Island), 285
College of Saint Mary (Omaha), 286
Metropolitan Community College (Omaha), 287
Mid-Plains Community College (North Platte), 287
Southeast Community College Area (Lincoln), 288
Western Nebraska Community College (Sidney), 289

**Nevada**
College of Southern Nevada (North Las Vegas), 290
Great Basin College (Elko), 290

**New Mexico**
Brookline College (Albuquerque), 293
Central New Mexico Community College (Albuquerque), 293
Clovis Community College (Clovis), 293
Luna Community College (Las Vegas), 295
Southwestern Indian Polytechnic Institute (Albuquerque), 297
University of New Mexico–Valencia Campus (Los Lunas), 298

**North Dakota**
Sitting Bull College (Fort Yates), 301
United Tribes Technical College (Bismarck), 301

**Northern Mariana Islands**
Northern Marianas College (Saipan), 302

**Oklahoma**
Community Care College (Tulsa), 305
Indian Capital Technology Center–Muskogee (Muskogee), 307
Kiamichi Area Vocational-Technical School–Atoka (Atoka), 308
Kiamichi Area Vocational-Technical School–McAlester (McAlester), 308
Moore Norman Technology Center (Norman), 311
Northeast Area Vocational Technical School (Pryor), 311
Northeast Technology Center–Afton (Afton), 311
Tulsa Community College (Tulsa), 317

**Oregon**
Central Oregon Community College (Bend), 320
Clackamas Community College (Oregon City), 320
Columbia Gorge Community College (The Dalles), 321
Klamath Community College (Klamath Falls), 322
Marylhurst University (Marylhurst), 323
Mt. Hood Community College (Gresham), 323

**South Dakota**
Mount Marty College (Yankton), 329

**Tennessee**
Columbia State Community College (Columbia), 332
Draughons Junior College (Murfreesboro), 333
National College (Nashville), 336

**Texas**
Alvin Community College (Alvin), 349
Amarillo College (Amarillo), 349
Angelina College (Lufkin), 351
Austin Community College (Austin), 352
Blinn College (Brenham), 353
Brookhaven College (Farmers Branch), 353
Capital City Careers (Austin), 354
Career Quest (San Antonio), 355
Cedar Valley College (Lancaster), 355
Central Texas College (Killeen), 355
Cisco College (Cisco), 356
College of the Mainland (Texas City), 357
Collin County Community College District (Plano), 357
Del Mar College (Corpus Christi), 359
Eastfield College (Mesquite), 360
El Centro College (Dallas), 360
El Paso Community College (El Paso), 360
Frank Phillips College (Borger), 362
Galveston College (Galveston), 362
Grayson County College (Denison), 363
Hill College of the Hill Junior College District (Hillsboro), 363
Houston Community College System (Houston), 363
International Business College (El Paso), 366
Kilgore College (Kilgore), 367
Lamar State College–Orange (Orange), 367
Lamar State College–Port Arthur (Port Arthur), 367
Lee College (Baytown), 368
Lonestar College–North Harris (Houston), 369
McLennan Community College (Waco), 369
Mountain View College (Dallas), 371
Navarro College (Corsicana), 371
Northeast Texas Community College (Mount Pleasant), 372
North Lake College (Irving), 372
Odessa College (Odessa), 373
Palo Alto College (San Antonio), 373
Richland College (Dallas), 376
St. Philip's College (San Antonio), 377
San Antonio College (San Antonio), 377
San Jacinto College Central Campus (Pasadena), 378
Tarrant County College District (Fort Worth), 383
Temple College (Temple), 383
Texarkana College (Texarkana), 384
Trinity Valley Community College (Athens), 387
Tyler Junior College (Tyler), 388

University of Phoenix–Houston Campus (Houston), 389
Victoria College (Victoria), 390

**Utah**
Certified Careers Institute (Clearfield), 393
Certified Careers Institute (Salt Lake City), 393
College of Eastern Utah (Price), 393
Salt Lake Community College (Salt Lake City), 396
Uintah Basin Applied Technology Center (Roosevelt), 397
Utah Valley University (Orem), 399

**Washington**
Bellevue College (Bellevue), 400
Bellingham Technical College (Bellingham), 400
Clark College (Vancouver), 402
Edmonds Community College (Lynnwood), 403
Everett Community College (Everett), 404
Heritage University (Toppenish), 405
Lower Columbia College (Longview), 407
Olympic College (Bremerton), 408
Peninsula College (Port Angeles), 408
Perry Technical Institute (Yakima), 409
Pierce College at Fort Steilacoom (Lakewood), 409
Pierce College (Puyallup), 409
Shoreline Community College (Shoreline), 410
Spokane Community College (Spokane), 411
Spokane Falls Community College (Spokane), 412
Tacoma Community College (Tacoma), 412
Wenatchee Valley College (Wenatchee), 413
Yakima Valley Community College (Yakima), 414

**Wisconsin**
Nicolet Area Technical College (Rhinelander), 419

## BUSINESS ADMINISTRATION, MANAGEMENT AND OPERATIONS, OTHER

**Arizona**
Estrella Mountain Community College (Avondale), 49
GateWay Community College (Phoenix), 50
Mesa Community College (Mesa), 52
Paradise Valley Community College (Phoenix), 53
Pima Community College (Tucson), 54
Rio Salado College (Tempe), 55

**California**
Gemological Institute of America (Carlsbad), 95
Heald College–Concord (Concord), 97
Heald College–Fresno (Fresno), 97
Heald College–Hayward (Hayward), 98
Heald College–Rancho Cordova (Rancho Cordova), 98
Heald College–Roseville (Roseville), 98
Heald College–Salinas (Salinas), 98
Heald College–Stockton (Stockton), 99
Lake College (Redding), 105
Ventura Adult and Continuing Education (Ventura), 138

**Colorado**
Arapahoe Community College (Littleton), 143

**Hawaii**
Heald College–Honolulu (Honolulu), 155

**Illinois**
Northwestern University (Evanston), 180

**Minnesota**
Minnesota West Community and Technical College (Pipestone), 248

**Missouri**
Hannibal Career and Technical Center (Hannibal), 268

**Oklahoma**
Autry Technology Center (Enid), 302
Tulsa Community College (Tulsa), 317

**Oregon**
Heald College–Portland (Portland), 322

**Tennessee**
Draughons Junior College (Clarksville), 332
Draughons Junior College (Nashville), 333
Tennessee Technology Center at Whiteville (Whiteville), 345

**Texas**
North Central Texas College (Gainesville), 371

**Wisconsin**
Nicolet Area Technical College (Rhinelander), 419

## BUSINESS AND PERSONAL/FINANCIAL SERVICES MARKETING OPERATIONS

**Wisconsin**
Moraine Park Technical College (Fond du Lac), 419

## BUSINESS/COMMERCE, GENERAL

**Arizona**
Central Arizona College (Coolidge), 47
Chandler-Gilbert Community College (Chandler), 47
Cochise College (Douglas), 47
Eastern Arizona College (Thatcher), 48
Estrella Mountain Community College (Avondale), 49
GateWay Community College (Phoenix), 50
Glendale Community College (Glendale), 50
Mesa Community College (Mesa), 52
Mohave Community College (Kingman), 52
Paradise Valley Community College (Phoenix), 53
Phoenix College (Phoenix), 53
Rio Salado College (Tempe), 55
Scottsdale Community College (Scottsdale), 56
South Mountain Community College (Phoenix), 56
Yavapai College (Prescott), 58

**Arkansas**
Arkansas Northeastern College (Blytheville), 59
University of Arkansas Community College at Batesville (Batesville), 67
University of Arkansas Community College at Morrilton (Morrilton), 68

**California**
Allan Hancock College (Santa Maria), 70
American River College (Sacramento), 72
Antelope Valley College (Lancaster), 72
Bakersfield College (Bakersfield), 74
Berkeley City College (Berkeley), 74
Cabrillo College (Aptos), 75
Clovis Adult Education (Clovis), 82
College of the Redwoods (Eureka), 85
Columbia College (Sonora), 85
Diablo Valley College (Pleasant Hill), 89
Everest College (Alhambra), 91
Feather River College (Quincy), 93
Gavilan College (Gilroy), 95
Glendale Community College (Glendale), 95
Grossmont College (El Cajon), 96
Kaplan College–Panorama City Campus (Panorama City), 103
Long Beach City College (Long Beach), 106
Los Angeles Pierce College (Woodland Hills), 108
Los Medanos College (Pittsburg), 109
Mission College (Santa Clara), 115
Riverside Community College District (Riverside), 126
Sacramento City College (Sacramento), 126
San Diego City College (San Diego), 128
Santa Barbara Business College (Bakersfield), 131
Santa Barbara Business College (Santa Maria), 131
Santa Barbara Business College (Ventura), 131
Sierra College (Rocklin), 133
Solano Community College (Suisun City), 134
West Los Angeles College (Culver City), 141
West Valley College (Saratoga), 141

**Hawaii**
Maui Community College (Kahului), 155

**Illinois**
John A. Logan College (Carterville), 174
Kendall College (Chicago), 175
Moraine Valley Community College (Palos Hills), 178
Northwestern University (Evanston), 180
Rock Valley College (Rockford), 184
Saint Xavier University (Chicago), 185

**Iowa**
Grand View University (Des Moines), 192

**Kansas**
Neosho County Community College (Chanute), 205

**Kentucky**
National College (Lexington), 217

**Louisiana**
American Commercial College (Shreveport), 221
Baton Rouge Community College (Baton Rouge), 222
Bossier Parish Community College (Bossier City), 223

**Minnesota**
Anoka-Ramsey Community College (Coon Rapids), 240
Mesabi Range Community and Technical College (Virginia), 246
North Hennepin Community College (Brooklyn Park), 250
Northwest Technical College (Bemidji), 250
Rasmussen College Mankato (Mankato), 252

**Missouri**
Eldon Career Center (Eldon), 266
Jefferson College (Hillsboro), 269
Mineral Area College (Park Hills), 272
Missouri State University–West Plains (West Plains), 273
St. Louis Community College at Florissant Valley (St. Louis), 277
St. Louis Community College at Forest Park (St. Louis), 278
St. Louis Community College at Meramec (Kirkwood), 278

**Montana**
Flathead Valley Community College (Kalispell), 283
Stone Child College (Box Elder), 284

**Nebraska**
Metropolitan Community College (Omaha), 287

**Nevada**
College of Southern Nevada (North Las Vegas), 290
Truckee Meadows Community College (Reno), 292

## BUSINESS/CORPORATE COMMUNICATIONS



## BUSINESS FAMILY AND CONSUMER SCIENCES/HUMAN SCIENCES



## BUSINESS MACHINE REPAIRER



## BUSINESS, MANAGEMENT, MARKETING, AND RELATED SUPPORT SERVICES, OTHER



## BUSINESS/MANAGERIAL ECONOMICS



## BUSINESS/OFFICE AUTOMATION/TECHNOLOGY/DATA ENTRY

Spoon River College (Canton), 187

**Iowa**

Kirkwood Community College (Cedar Rapids), 195
Northeast Iowa Community College (Calmar), 196
Western Iowa Tech Community College (Sioux City), 198

**Kentucky**

Daymar College (Louisville), 211
Daymar College (Paducah), 212
Spencerian College (Louisville), 219

**Minnesota**

Anoka-Ramsey Community College (Coon Rapids), 240
Dakota County Technical College (Rosemount), 242
East Metro Opportunities Industrialization Center (St. Paul), 242
Inver Hills Community College (Inver Grove Heights), 244
Mesabi Range Community and Technical College (Virginia), 246
Minnesota State College–Southeast Technical (Winona), 248

**Mississippi**

Antonelli College (Hattiesburg), 257
Antonelli College (Jackson), 257
Holmes Community College (Goodman), 260

**Missouri**

Lake Career and Technical Center (Camdenton), 269
Metro Business College (Cape Girardeau), 271
North Central Missouri College (Trenton), 274
Pike/Lincoln Tech Center (Eolia), 275
Saline County Career Center (Marshall), 279
Three Rivers Community College (Poplar Bluff), 280

**Montana**

Fort Peck Community College (Poplar), 283

**Nevada**

Great Basin College (Elko), 290

**New Mexico**

Southwestern Indian Polytechnic Institute (Albuquerque), 297

**North Dakota**

Bismarck State College (Bismarck), 298
Minot State University (Minot), 299

**Oklahoma**

Gordon Cooper Technology Center (Shawnee), 306
High Plains Institute of Technology (Woodward), 307
Kiamichi Area Vocational-Technical School–Poteau (Poteau), 309
Kiamichi Area Vocational-Technical School–Talihina (Talihina), 309
Northeast Technology Center–Kansas (Kansas), 312
Northwest Technology Center (Alva), 312
Tulsa Tech–Peoria Campus (Tulsa), 317

**Oregon**

Chemeketa Community College (Salem), 320
Clatsop Community College (Astoria), 321
Mt. Hood Community College (Gresham), 323
Portland Community College (Portland), 326
Treasure Valley Community College (Ontario), 327
Umpqua Community College (Roseburg), 327

**South Dakota**

Oglala Lakota College (Kyle), 329

**Tennessee**

Chattanooga State Technical Community College (Chattanooga), 332
Tennessee Technology Center at Crossville (Crossville), 341
Tennessee Technology Center at Crump (Crump), 341
Tennessee Technology Center at Elizabethton (Elizabethton), 341
Tennessee Technology Center at Hartsville (Hartsville), 342
Tennessee Technology Center at Hohenwald (Hohenwald), 342
Tennessee Technology Center at Jacksboro (Jacksboro), 342
Tennessee Technology Center at Livingston (Livingston), 342
Tennessee Technology Center at McKenzie (McKenzie), 343
Tennessee Technology Center at McMinnville (McMinnville), 343
Tennessee Technology Center at Memphis (Memphis), 343
Tennessee Technology Center at Morristown (Morristown), 343
Tennessee Technology Center at Murfreesboro (Murfreesboro), 343
Tennessee Technology Center at Nashville (Nashville), 344
Tennessee Technology Center at Oneida/Huntsville (Huntsville), 344
Tennessee Technology Center at Paris (Paris), 344
Tennessee Technology Center at Whiteville (Whiteville), 345

**Texas**

Amarillo College (Amarillo), 349
American Commercial College (San Angelo), 350
American Commercial College (Wichita Falls), 350
Angelina College (Lufkin), 351
ATI Career Training Center (Richardson), 352
ATI Technical Training Center (Dallas), 352
Blinn College (Brenham), 353
Brookhaven College (Farmers Branch), 353
Cedar Valley College (Lancaster), 355
Center for Employment Training–Socorro (Socorro), 355
Central Texas College (Killeen), 355
Clarendon College (Clarendon), 356
Coastal Bend College (Beeville), 357
Collin County Community College District (Plano), 357
Eastfield College (Mesquite), 360
El Centro College (Dallas), 360
El Paso Community College (El Paso), 360
Faris Computer School (Nederland), 362
Hallmark Institute of Technology (San Antonio), 363
Houston Community College System (Houston), 363
McLennan Community College (Waco), 369
Mountain View College (Dallas), 371
Navarro College (Corsicana), 371
North Lake College (Irving), 372
Northwest Educational Center (Houston), 372
Odessa College (Odessa), 373
Panola College (Carthage), 374
Paris Junior College (Paris), 374
Richland College (Dallas), 376
San Antonio College (San Antonio), 377
San Jacinto College Central Campus (Pasadena), 378
South Texas Vocational Technical Institute (McAllen), 381
SouthWest Collegiate Institute for the Deaf (Big Spring), 382
Southwest Texas Junior College (Uvalde), 382
Tarrant County College District (Fort Worth), 383
Texarkana College (Texarkana), 384
Texas Careers–Laredo (Laredo), 384
Texas School of Business–North (Houston), 385
Texas State Technical College Harlingen (Harlingen), 386
Texas Vocational Schools (Victoria), 387
Tyler Junior College (Tyler), 388
Vernon College (Vernon), 389
Victoria College (Victoria), 390
Western Texas College (Snyder), 391

**Utah**

Salt Lake Community College (Salt Lake City), 396

**Washington**

Clark College (Vancouver), 402
Everest College (Vancouver), 404
Everett Community College (Everett), 404
Interface Computer School (Spokane), 406
Peninsula College (Port Angeles), 408
Renton Technical College (Renton), 410
Skagit Valley College (Mount Vernon), 411
Wenatchee Valley College (Wenatchee), 413

**Wisconsin**

Mid-State Technical College (Wisconsin Rapids), 418
Southwest Wisconsin Technical College (Fennimore), 421
Wisconsin Indianhead Technical College (Shell Lake), 422

**Wyoming**

Casper College (Casper), 423
Central Wyoming College (Riverton), 423

## BUSINESS OPERATIONS SUPPORT AND SECRETARIAL SERVICES, OTHER

**Arizona**

Pima Community College (Tucson), 54

**California**

Heald College–Concord (Concord), 97
Heald College–Fresno (Fresno), 97
Heald College–Hayward (Hayward), 98
Heald College–Salinas (Salinas), 98
Heald College–San Jose (Milpitas), 98
Heald College–Stockton (Stockton), 99
Santa Barbara Business College (Bakersfield), 131
Santa Barbara Business College (Santa Maria), 131
Santa Barbara Business College (Ventura), 131
Valley Career College (El Cajon), 137
Ventura Adult and Continuing Education (Ventura), 138

**Hawaii**

Heald College–Honolulu (Honolulu), 155

**Illinois**

Pyramid Career Institute (Chicago), 182

**Kansas**

Pinnacle Career Institute (Lawrence), 206

**Kentucky**

Brighton Center's Center for Employment Training (Newport), 211

**Minnesota**

East Metro Opportunities Industrialization Center (St. Paul), 242

**Missouri**
East Central College (Union), 266
Northwest Missouri State University (Maryville), 274

**Nebraska**
Northeast Community College (Norfolk), 288

**New Mexico**
Central New Mexico Community College (Albuquerque), 293

**North Dakota**
Rasmussen College Bismarck (Bismarck), 300

**Oklahoma**
Kiamichi Area Vocational-Technical School–Durant (Durant), 308
Metro Area Vocational Technical School District 22 (Oklahoma City), 310
Pioneer Area Vocational Technical School (Ponca City), 313

**Tennessee**
Tennessee Technology Center at Athens (Athens), 340
Tennessee Technology Center at Crossville (Crossville), 341
Tennessee Technology Center at Crump (Crump), 341
Tennessee Technology Center at Dickson (Dickson), 341
Tennessee Technology Center at Elizabethton (Elizabethton), 341
Tennessee Technology Center at Harriman (Harriman), 341
Tennessee Technology Center at Hartsville (Hartsville), 342
Tennessee Technology Center at Hohenwald (Hohenwald), 342
Tennessee Technology Center at Jackson (Jackson), 342
Tennessee Technology Center at Knoxville (Knoxville), 342
Tennessee Technology Center at Livingston (Livingston), 342
Tennessee Technology Center at McKenzie (McKenzie), 343
Tennessee Technology Center at McMinnville (McMinnville), 343
Tennessee Technology Center at Memphis (Memphis), 343
Tennessee Technology Center at Morristown (Morristown), 343
Tennessee Technology Center at Murfreesboro (Murfreesboro), 343
Tennessee Technology Center at Newbern (Newbern), 344
Tennessee Technology Center at Oneida/Huntsville (Huntsville), 344
Tennessee Technology Center at Paris (Paris), 344
Tennessee Technology Center at Ripley (Ripley), 345
Tennessee Technology Center at Shelbyville (Shelbyville), 345
Tennessee Technology Center at Whiteville (Whiteville), 345

**Texas**
Anamarc Educational Institute (El Paso), 351
Center for Employment Training–Socorro (Socorro), 355
Interactive Learning Systems (Houston), 365
Interactive Learning Systems (Pasadena), 365
Texas School of Business–East Campus (Houston), 385
Texas School of Business–Friendswood (Friendswood), 385
Texas School of Business–Southwest (Houston), 386

**Washington**
Green River Community College (Auburn), 405
Lake Washington Technical College (Kirkland), 406
Shoreline Community College (Shoreline), 410

**Wisconsin**
Moraine Park Technical College (Fond du Lac), 419

**Wyoming**
Central Wyoming College (Riverton), 423
Laramie County Community College (Cheyenne), 423

## CABINETMAKING AND MILLWORK/MILLWRIGHT

**Arizona**
Northland Pioneer College (Holbrook), 53
Pima Community College (Tucson), 54

**California**
Bakersfield College (Bakersfield), 74
Cerritos College (Norwalk), 80
College of the Redwoods (Eureka), 85
Fullerton College (Fullerton), 95
Long Beach City College (Long Beach), 106
Los Angeles Trade-Technical College (Los Angeles), 109
Palomar College (San Marcos), 122
Sierra College (Rocklin), 133

**Colorado**
Emily Griffith Opportunity School (Denver), 146
Pickens Technical College (Aurora), 150

**Idaho**
College of Southern Idaho (Twin Falls), 157

**Illinois**
Prairie State College (Chicago Heights), 182

**Iowa**
Des Moines Area Community College (Ankeny), 191

**Kansas**
Kaw Area Technical School (Topeka), 204

**Kentucky**
Jefferson Community and Technical College (Louisville), 215

**Louisiana**
Louisiana Technical College–Oakdale Campus (Oakdale), 233

**Minnesota**
Hennepin Technical College (Brooklyn Park), 243
Saint Paul College–A Community & Technical College (St. Paul), 254

**Texas**
Lee College (Baytown), 368

**Utah**
Bridgerland Applied Technology Center (Logan), 392
Ogden-Weber Applied Technology Center (Ogden), 396
Utah Valley University (Orem), 399

**Washington**
Bates Technical College (Tacoma), 400

**Wisconsin**
Fox Valley Technical College (Appleton), 415
Milwaukee Area Technical College (Milwaukee), 418
Moraine Park Technical College (Fond du Lac), 419

## CAD/CADD DRAFTING AND/OR DESIGN TECHNOLOGY/TECHNICIAN

**Alaska**
Charter College (Anchorage), 41
University of Alaska Anchorage (Anchorage), 41

**Arizona**
Arizona Western College (Yuma), 44
Cochise College (Douglas), 47
Coconino Community College (Flagstaff), 48
Eastern Arizona College (Thatcher), 48
Maricopa Skill Center (Phoenix), 51
Northland Pioneer College (Holbrook), 53

**Arkansas**
East Arkansas Community College (Forrest City), 62
North Arkansas College (Harrison), 64
University of Arkansas at Fort Smith (Fort Smith), 67

**California**
Brownson Technical School (Anaheim), 75
Martinez Adult School (Martinez), 112
Westech College (Pomona), 139

**Colorado**
Front Range Community College (Westminster), 147
Pickens Technical College (Aurora), 150
Pikes Peak Community College (Colorado Springs), 150

**Idaho**
College of Southern Idaho (Twin Falls), 157
Lewis-Clark State College (Lewiston), 158

**Illinois**
Black Hawk College (Moline), 160
College of Lake County (Grayslake), 165
Elgin Community College (Elgin), 167
Heartland Community College (Normal), 171
Illinois Valley Community College (Oglesby), 173
John A. Logan College (Carterville), 174
Kankakee Community College (Kankakee), 174
Kaskaskia College (Centralia), 175
Kishwaukee College (Malta), 175
Lake Land College (Mattoon), 176
Lewis and Clark Community College (Godfrey), 176
Lincoln Land Community College (Springfield), 177
McHenry County College (Crystal Lake), 178
Moraine Valley Community College (Palos Hills), 178
Morton College (Cicero), 179
Oakton Community College (Des Plaines), 180
Parkland College (Champaign), 181
Prairie State College (Chicago Heights), 182
Rend Lake College (Ina), 183
Sauk Valley Community College (Dixon), 186
Southeastern Illinois College (Harrisburg), 186
South Suburban College (South Holland), 187
Triton College (River Grove), 188
Vatterott College (Quincy), 189
Zarem/Golde ORT Technical Institute (Chicago), 190

**Kansas**
Brown Mackie College–Salina (Salina), 200
Butler Community College (El Dorado), 201
Johnson County Community College (Overland Park), 203
Kansas City Area Technical School (Kansas City), 204
Kaw Area Technical School (Topeka), 204
Salina Area Technical School (Salina), 207
Wichita Area Technical College (Wichita), 208

**Louisiana**
ITI Technical College (Baton Rouge), 226

**Minnesota**
Dunwoody College of Technology (Minneapolis), 242
Hennepin Technical College (Brooklyn Park), 243
Rochester Community and Technical College (Rochester), 253

**Missouri**
Jefferson College (Hillsboro), 269
St. Louis Community College at Florissant Valley (St. Louis), 277
Vatterott College (Joplin), 281
Vatterott College (Kansas City), 281
Vatterott College (St. Ann), 281
Vatterott College (St. Louis), 281
Vatterott College (Springfield), 281

**Nebraska**
Vatterott College (Omaha), 289

**Nevada**
College of Southern Nevada (North Las Vegas), 290

**New Mexico**
Crownpoint Institute of Technology (Crownpoint), 293
New Mexico Junior College (Hobbs), 295
University of New Mexico–Valencia Campus (Los Lunas), 298

**Oklahoma**
Francis Tuttle Area Vocational Technical Center (Oklahoma City), 306
Green Country Technology Center (Okmulgee), 307
Tulsa Community College (Tulsa), 317

**Oregon**
Clatsop Community College (Astoria), 321

**Texas**
Faris Computer School (Nederland), 362

**Utah**
Bridgerland Applied Technology Center (Logan), 392
College of Eastern Utah (Price), 393
Davis Applied Technology Center (Kaysville), 393
Dixie Applied Technology College (Saint George), 394
Ogden-Weber Applied Technology Center (Ogden), 396
Southern Utah University (Cedar City), 397
Uintah Basin Applied Technology Center (Roosevelt), 397

**Washington**
Clark College (Vancouver), 402
Grays Harbor College (Aberdeen), 405
Lake Washington Technical College (Kirkland), 406
Olympic College (Bremerton), 408
Shoreline Community College (Shoreline), 410
Spokane Community College (Spokane), 411

**Wisconsin**
Waukesha County Technical College (Pewaukee), 422

**Wyoming**
Northwest College (Powell), 424
Sheridan College (Sheridan), 424

## CANADIAN STUDIES

**Kentucky**
Western Kentucky University (Bowling Green), 220

## CARDIOVASCULAR TECHNOLOGY/TECHNOLOGIST

**California**
Associated Technical College (Los Angeles), 73
ATI College (Norwalk), 73
City College of San Francisco (San Francisco), 82
Grossmont College (El Cajon), 96
MCed Career College (Fresno), 113
Modern Technology School (Anaheim), 115
Orange Coast College (Costa Mesa), 121
Pacific College (Costa Mesa), 121
West Coast Ultrasound Institute (Beverly Hills), 139

**Kentucky**
Draughons Junior College (Bowling Green), 212

**Oklahoma**
American Institute of Medical Technology (Tulsa), 302

**Texas**
Alvin Community College (Alvin), 349
El Centro College (Dallas), 360
Houston Community College System (Houston), 363
Sanford-Brown Institute (Dallas), 378
Sanford-Brown Institute (Houston), 378

## CARPENTRY/CARPENTER

**Alaska**
Ilisagvik College (Barrow), 41
University of Alaska Fairbanks (Fairbanks), 42
University of Alaska Southeast (Juneau), 42

**Arizona**
Arizona Western College (Yuma), 44
Central Arizona College (Coolidge), 47
Cochise College (Douglas), 47
Coconino Community College (Flagstaff), 48
Eastern Arizona College (Thatcher), 48
GateWay Community College (Phoenix), 50
Northland Pioneer College (Holbrook), 53
Rio Salado College (Tempe), 55
Tohono O'odham Community College (Sells), 57

**Arkansas**
Cossatot Community College of the University of Arkansas (De Queen), 61
Crowley's Ridge Technical Institute (Forrest City), 62
National Park Community College (Hot Springs), 63

**California**
American River College (Sacramento), 72
Bakersfield College (Bakersfield), 74
Hartnell College (Salinas), 97
Laney College (Oakland), 105
Long Beach City College (Long Beach), 106
Los Angeles Trade-Technical College (Los Angeles), 109
Palomar College (San Marcos), 122
San Joaquin Delta College (Stockton), 129
Sierra College (Rocklin), 133

**Colorado**
Arapahoe Community College (Littleton), 143
Emily Griffith Opportunity School (Denver), 146
Pickens Technical College (Aurora), 150
San Juan Basin Area Vocational School (Cortez), 152

**Guam**
Guam Community College (Barrigada), 154

**Hawaii**
Hawaii Community College (Hilo), 154
Honolulu Community College (Honolulu), 155
Kauai Community College (Lihue), 155
Maui Community College (Kahului), 155

**Idaho**
Idaho State University (Pocatello), 158
North Idaho College (Coeur d'Alene), 159

**Illinois**
City Colleges of Chicago, Kennedy-King College (Chicago), 163
Kaskaskia College (Centralia), 175
Kishwaukee College (Malta), 175
Parkland College (Champaign), 181
Southeastern Illinois College (Harrisburg), 186
Southwestern Illinois College (Belleville), 187

**Iowa**
Des Moines Area Community College (Ankeny), 191
Iowa Central Community College (Fort Dodge), 193
Iowa Lakes Community College (Estherville), 193
Kirkwood Community College (Cedar Rapids), 195
Northeast Iowa Community College (Calmar), 196
North Iowa Area Community College (Mason City), 197
Northwest Iowa Community College (Sheldon), 197
Southwestern Community College (Creston), 198
Western Iowa Tech Community College (Sioux City), 198

**Kansas**
Coffeyville Community College (Coffeyville), 201
Hutchinson Community College and Area Vocational School (Hutchinson), 203
Kansas City Area Technical School (Kansas City), 204
Manhattan Area Technical College (Manhattan), 205
North Central Kansas Technical College (Beloit), 205
Northeast Kansas Technical Center of Highland Community College (Atchison), 206
Northwest Kansas Technical College (Goodland), 206
Salina Area Technical School (Salina), 207
Seward County Community College (Liberal), 207
Wichita Area Technical College (Wichita), 208

**Kentucky**
Ashland Community and Technical College (Ashland), 209
Big Sandy Community and Technical College (Prestonsburg), 210
Bluegrass Community and Technical College (Lexington), 210
Elizabethtown Community and Technical College (Elizabethtown), 213
Gateway Community and Technical College (Covington), 213
Hazard Community and Technical College (Hazard), 214
Jefferson Community and Technical College (Louisville), 215
Madisonville Community College (Madisonville), 216
Maysville Community and Technical College (Maysville), 216

## CARTOGRAPHY

## Child-Care Provider/Assistant

**Nebraska**
Metropolitan Community College (Omaha), 287

**Nevada**
Western Nevada Community College (Carson City), 292

**New Mexico**
Doña Ana Branch Community College (Las Cruces), 294
San Juan College (Farmington), 296

**North Dakota**
Lake Region State College (Devils Lake), 299

**Oklahoma**
Caddo-Kiowa Area Vocational Technical School (Ft. Cobb), 303
Canadian Valley Technology Center (El Reno), 303
Carl Albert State College (Poteau), 304
Eastern Oklahoma County Technology Center (Choctaw), 305
Gordon Cooper Technology Center (Shawnee), 306
Metro Area Vocational Technical School District 22 (Oklahoma City), 310
Mid-Del Technology Center (Midwest), 310
Moore Norman Technology Center (Norman), 311
Northeastern Oklahoma Agricultural and Mechanical College (Miami), 311
Pioneer Area Vocational Technical School (Ponca City), 313
Tri County Technology Center (Bartlesville), 316
Tulsa Tech–Peoria Campus (Tulsa), 317

**Oregon**
Clatsop Community College (Astoria), 321
Klamath Community College (Klamath Falls), 322
Lane Community College (Eugene), 322
Mt. Hood Community College (Gresham), 323
Northwest Nannies Institute, Inc. (Lake Oswego), 324
Rogue Community College (Grants Pass), 326
Southwestern Oregon Community College (Coos Bay), 327

**Texas**
Amarillo College (Amarillo), 349
Austin Community College (Austin), 352
Blinn College (Brenham), 353
Brookhaven College (Farmers Branch), 353
Central Texas College (Killeen), 355
Cisco College (Cisco), 356
Coastal Bend College (Beeville), 357
Collin County Community College District (Plano), 357
Eastfield College (Mesquite), 360
Houston Community College System (Houston), 363
Kilgore College (Kilgore), 367
Lamar Institute of Technology (Beaumont), 367
Lamar State College–Port Arthur (Port Arthur), 367
Laredo Community College (Laredo), 368
Odessa College (Odessa), 373
South Texas College (McAllen), 381
Tarrant County College District (Fort Worth), 383
Texas Southmost College (Brownsville), 386
Tyler Junior College (Tyler), 388
Vernon College (Vernon), 389

**Washington**
Bates Technical College (Tacoma), 400
Peninsula College (Port Angeles), 408

**Wisconsin**
Chippewa Valley Technical College (Eau Claire), 415
Lac Courte Oreilles Ojibwa Community College (Hayward), 417
Lakeshore Technical College (Cleveland), 417
Southwest Wisconsin Technical College (Fennimore), 421

**Wyoming**
Eastern Wyoming College (Torrington), 423

## CHILD DEVELOPMENT

**Arizona**
Arizona Western College (Yuma), 44
Central Arizona College (Coolidge), 47
Eastern Arizona College (Thatcher), 48
Northland Pioneer College (Holbrook), 53
Phoenix College (Phoenix), 53
Pima Community College (Tucson), 54
Scottsdale Community College (Scottsdale), 56
South Mountain Community College (Phoenix), 56

**Arkansas**
Arkansas Northeastern College (Blytheville), 59
Cossatot Community College of the University of Arkansas (De Queen), 61
Mid-South Community College (West Memphis), 63
NorthWest Arkansas Community College (Bentonville), 64
Ozarka College (Melbourne), 65
Pulaski Technical College (North Little Rock), 65
Rich Mountain Community College (Mena), 66
University of Arkansas at Monticello (Monticello), 67
University of Arkansas Community College at Morrilton (Morrilton), 68

**California**
Allan Hancock College (Santa Maria), 70
American River College (Sacramento), 72
Antelope Valley College (Lancaster), 72
Bakersfield College (Bakersfield), 74
Barstow College (Barstow), 74
Cabrillo College (Aptos), 75
Cañada College (Redwood City), 77
Cerritos College (Norwalk), 80
Cerro Coso Community College (Ridgecrest), 80
Chabot College (Hayward), 81
Chaffey College (Rancho Cucamonga), 81
Citrus College (Glendora), 82
City College of San Francisco (San Francisco), 82
College of Marin (Kentfield), 84
College of the Desert (Palm Desert), 84
College of the Redwoods (Eureka), 85
College of the Sequoias (Visalia), 85
College of the Siskiyous (Weed), 85
Columbia College (Sonora), 85
Contra Costa College (San Pablo), 86
Cosumnes River College (Sacramento), 87
Crafton Hills College (Yucaipa), 87
Cuesta College (San Luis Obispo), 87
Cuyamaca College (El Cajon), 88
De Anza College (Cupertino), 88
Diablo Valley College (Pleasant Hill), 89
East Los Angeles College (Monterey Park), 89
El Camino College (Torrance), 90
El Camino College Compton Center (Compton), 90
Feather River College (Quincy), 93
Folsom Lake College (Folsom), 93
Foothill College (Los Altos Hills), 93
Fresno City College (Fresno), 94
Fullerton College (Fullerton), 95
Gavilan College (Gilroy), 95
Glendale Community College (Glendale), 95
Grossmont College (El Cajon), 96
Hartnell College (Salinas), 97
Imperial Valley College (Imperial), 100
Irvine Valley College (Irvine), 101
Lake Tahoe Community College (South Lake Tahoe), 105
Las Positas College (Livermore), 105
Lassen Community College District (Susanville), 106
Long Beach City College (Long Beach), 106
Los Angeles City College (Los Angeles), 107
Los Angeles Mission College (Sylmar), 107
Los Angeles Pierce College (Woodland Hills), 108
Los Angeles Southwest College (Los Angeles), 109
Los Angeles Trade-Technical College (Los Angeles), 109
Los Angeles Valley College (Van Nuys), 109
Los Medanos College (Pittsburg), 109
Maxine Waters Employment Preparation Center (Los Angeles), 113
Mendocino College (Ukiah), 113
Merritt College (Oakland), 114
MiraCosta College (Oceanside), 114
Mission College (Santa Clara), 115
Modesto Junior College (Modesto), 115
Monterey Peninsula College (Monterey), 116
Moorpark College (Moorpark), 116
Mt. San Antonio College (Walnut), 116
Mt. San Jacinto College (San Jacinto), 117
Ohlone College (Fremont), 120
Orange Coast College (Costa Mesa), 121
Oxnard College (Oxnard), 121
Palomar College (San Marcos), 122
Palo Verde College (Blythe), 123
Pasadena City College (Pasadena), 123
Patten University (Oakland), 123
Porterville College (Porterville), 124
Reedley College (Reedley), 125
Rio Hondo College (Whittier), 125
Riverside Community College District (Riverside), 126
Sacramento City College (Sacramento), 126
Saddleback College (Mission Viejo), 127
San Bernardino Valley College (San Bernardino), 128
San Diego City College (San Diego), 128
San Diego Mesa College (San Diego), 128
San Diego Miramar College (San Diego), 129
San Joaquin Delta College (Stockton), 129
San Jose City College (San Jose), 130
Santa Ana College (Santa Ana), 131
Santa Barbara City College (Santa Barbara), 131
Santa Monica College (Santa Monica), 132
Santa Rosa Junior College (Santa Rosa), 132
Santiago Canyon College (Orange), 132
Shasta College (Redding), 133
Sierra College (Rocklin), 133
Skyline College (San Bruno), 133
Solano Community College (Suisun City), 134
Southwestern College (Chula Vista), 134

## CHINESE LANGUAGE AND LITERATURE



## CHINESE STUDIES



## CHIROPRACTIC ASSISTANT/TECHNICIAN



## CHRISTIAN STUDIES



## CINEMATOGRAPHY AND FILM/VIDEO PRODUCTION



## CIVIL DRAFTING AND CIVIL ENGINEERING CAD/CADD



## CIVIL ENGINEERING, GENERAL



## CIVIL ENGINEERING TECHNOLOGY/TECHNICIAN

**Wyoming**
Laramie County Community College (Cheyenne), 423

## CLASSICS AND LANGUAGES, LITERATURES AND LINGUISTICS, GENERAL

**California**
Butte College (Oroville), 75

## CLINICAL LABORATORY SCIENCE/MEDICAL TECHNOLOGY/TECHNOLOGIST

**Colorado**
The Colorado Center for Medical Laboratory Science (Denver), 145

**Illinois**
St. Johns Hospital School of Clinical Lab Science (Springfield), 185

**Texas**
The University of Texas Anderson Cancer Center (Houston), 389

## CLINICAL/MEDICAL LABORATORY ASSISTANT

**Alaska**
University of Alaska Fairbanks (Fairbanks), 42

**Arizona**
Eastern Arizona College (Thatcher), 48
Phoenix College (Phoenix), 53

**Arkansas**
Black River Technical College (Pocahontas), 61

**California**
Career College of San Diego (San Diego), 78
CSI Career College (Vacaville), 87
Institute for Business and Technology (Santa Clara), 100
Los Angeles ORT Technical Institute (Los Angeles), 108
Los Angeles ORT Technical Institute–Sherman Oaks Branch (Sherman Oaks), 108
Newbridge College–Long Beach (Long Beach), 119
Newbridge College–Santa Ana (Santa Ana), 119
Premiere Career College (Irwindale), 125
Sacramento City Unified School District–Skills and Business Education Center (Sacramento), 126

**Kentucky**
Spencerian College (Louisville), 219

**Missouri**
Pinnacle Career Institute (Kansas City), 275

**Nevada**
Academy of Medical and Business Careers (Las Vegas), 289

**Oregon**
Clackamas Community College (Oregon City), 320

**Texas**
Houston's Training and Education Center (Houston), 364
Valley Grande Academy (Weslaco), 389
Western Technical College (El Paso), 391

**Washington**
Centralia College (Centralia), 401
Edmonds Community College (Lynnwood), 403
Renton Technical College (Renton), 410
Shoreline Community College (Shoreline), 410

## CLINICAL/MEDICAL LABORATORY SCIENCE AND ALLIED PROFESSIONS, OTHER

**Arizona**
Phoenix College (Phoenix), 53
Pima Community College (Tucson), 54

**Colorado**
Red Rocks Community College (Lakewood), 151

**Kentucky**
ATA Career Education (Louisville), 209

**North Dakota**
Bismarck State College (Bismarck), 298

**Oklahoma**
Tulsa Community College (Tulsa), 317

**Oregon**
Linn-Benton Community College (Albany), 323

**South Dakota**
Southeast Technical Institute (Sioux Falls), 330
Western Dakota Technical Institute (Rapid City), 330

**Tennessee**
Roane State Community College (Harriman), 339
Tennessee Technology Center at Murfreesboro (Murfreesboro), 343
Tennessee Technology Center at Nashville (Nashville), 344
Volunteer State Community College (Gallatin), 346

**Utah**
Mountainland Applied Technology College (Orem), 395

## CLINICAL/MEDICAL LABORATORY TECHNICIAN

**Arizona**
Phoenix College (Phoenix), 53

**Arkansas**
Baptist Schools of Nursing and Allied Health (Little Rock), 61

**California**
Cabrillo College (Aptos), 75
Career Care Institute (Lancaster), 78
Kaplan College–Vista Campus (Vista), 104
Newbridge College–Long Beach (Long Beach), 119

**Colorado**
IntelliTec Medical Institute (Colorado Springs), 148

**Illinois**
Elgin Community College (Elgin), 167

**Kentucky**
Bluegrass Community and Technical College (Lexington), 210
Henderson Community College (Henderson), 215
Jefferson Community and Technical College (Louisville), 215
Madisonville Community College (Madisonville), 216
Somerset Community College (Somerset), 218
Southeast Kentucky Community and Technical College (Cumberland), 218
Spencerian College–Lexington (Lexington), 219
West Kentucky Community and Technical College (Paducah), 220

**Louisiana**
MedVance Institute (Baton Rouge), 235

**Oklahoma**
Tulsa Community College (Tulsa), 317

**Tennessee**
MedVance Institute (Cookeville), 335

**Texas**
The Academy of Health Care Professions (Houston), 348
Alvin Community College (Alvin), 349
Laredo Community College (Laredo), 368
Odessa College (Odessa), 373
South Texas Vocational Technical Institute (McAllen), 381
South Texas Vo-Tech Institute (Weslaco), 381

## CLINICAL/MEDICAL SOCIAL WORK

**Arizona**
Pima Community College (Tucson), 54

**Guam**
Guam Community College (Barrigada), 154

**Nebraska**
Central Community College–Grand Island Campus (Grand Island), 285

**Texas**
Central Texas College (Killeen), 355

## COMMERCIAL AND ADVERTISING ART

**Arizona**
Chandler-Gilbert Community College (Chandler), 47
East Valley Institute of Technology (Mesa), 49
Glendale Community College (Glendale), 50
Mesa Community College (Mesa), 52
Northland Pioneer College (Holbrook), 53
Paradise Valley Community College (Phoenix), 53
Phoenix College (Phoenix), 53
Yavapai College (Prescott), 58

**Arkansas**
Southern Arkansas University Tech (Camden), 66

**California**
Chabot College (Hayward), 81
Glendale Community College (Glendale), 95
ICDC College (Los Angeles), 99
Los Angeles ORT Technical Institute (Los Angeles), 108
Los Angeles ORT Technical Institute–Sherman Oaks Branch (Sherman Oaks), 108
Los Angeles Trade-Technical College (Los Angeles), 109
Orange Coast College (Costa Mesa), 121
Santa Ana College (Santa Ana), 131
Ventura Adult and Continuing Education (Ventura), 138

**Colorado**
Pickens Technical College (Aurora), 150

**Illinois**
College of DuPage (Glen Ellyn), 164
Robert Morris University (Chicago), 184

**Iowa**
Iowa Lakes Community College (Estherville), 193

**Kansas**
Flint Hills Technical College (Emporia), 202
Labette Community College (Parsons), 205
Salina Area Technical School (Salina), 207

**Louisiana**
Delta College of Arts and Technology (Baton Rouge), 225

**Minnesota**
Academy College (Minneapolis), 239
Central Lakes College (Brainerd), 241

## COMPUTER AND INFORMATION SCIENCES, GENERAL

Fullerton College (Fullerton), 95
Glendale Community College (Glendale), 95
Gnomon School of Visual Effects (Hollywood), 96
Mission College (Santa Clara), 115
Mt. San Antonio College (Walnut), 116
Ohlone College (Fremont), 120
Orange Coast College (Costa Mesa), 121
Palladium Technical Academy (El Monte), 122
Palomar College (San Marcos), 122
Saddleback College (Mission Viejo), 127
Santa Ana College (Santa Ana), 131
Santa Rosa Junior College (Santa Rosa), 132
Western Career College (Emeryville), 140
Western Career College (San Jose), 140

**Illinois**
Parkland College (Champaign), 181

**Minnesota**
Rochester Community and Technical College (Rochester), 253

**Nevada**
Great Basin College (Elko), 290
Truckee Meadows Community College (Reno), 292

**Washington**
Bellevue College (Bellevue), 400
Edmonds Community College (Lynnwood), 403
Everett Community College (Everett), 404
Lake Washington Technical College (Kirkland), 406
Shoreline Community College (Shoreline), 410

## COMPUTER HARDWARE ENGINEERING

**Oklahoma**
Oklahoma Technology Institute (Oklahoma City), 313

## COMPUTER HARDWARE TECHNOLOGY/ TECHNICIAN

**Arizona**
Maricopa Skill Center (Phoenix), 51

**Minnesota**
Anoka Technical College (Anoka), 240
Lake Superior College (Duluth), 245

**Oklahoma**
Oklahoma Technology Institute (Oklahoma City), 313

**Texas**
Brazosport College (Lake Jackson), 353
International Business College (El Paso), 366

**Wyoming**
Laramie County Community College (Cheyenne), 423

## COMPUTER/INFORMATION TECHNOLOGY SERVICES ADMINISTRATION AND MANAGEMENT, OTHER

**Arizona**
Chandler-Gilbert Community College (Chandler), 47
Estrella Mountain Community College (Avondale), 49
GateWay Community College (Phoenix), 50
Glendale Community College (Glendale), 50
Paradise Valley Community College (Phoenix), 53
Phoenix College (Phoenix), 53
Scottsdale Community College (Scottsdale), 56

**California**
TechSkills–Sacramento (Sacramento), 135

**Colorado**
Colorado Mountain College (Glenwood Springs), 145
Institute of Business & Medical Careers (Fort Collins), 148
Pikes Peak Community College (Colorado Springs), 150
Pueblo Community College (Pueblo), 151

**Iowa**
Des Moines Area Community College (Ankeny), 191
Indian Hills Community College (Ottumwa), 192
Iowa Western Community College (Council Bluffs), 194
Western Iowa Tech Community College (Sioux City), 198

**Kansas**
Butler Community College (El Dorado), 201

**Missouri**
Columbia Area Vocational Technical School (Columbia), 265
Washington University in St. Louis (St. Louis), 282

**Nevada**
Great Basin College (Elko), 290

**Oklahoma**
Green Country Technology Center (Okmulgee), 307

**South Dakota**
Northern State University (Aberdeen), 329

**Texas**
American Commercial College (Wichita Falls), 350
Coastal Bend College (Beeville), 357
Computer Labs (El Paso), 358
El Paso Community College (El Paso), 360
Laredo Community College (Laredo), 368

## COMPUTER INSTALLATION AND REPAIR TECHNOLOGY/TECHNICIAN

**Alaska**
University of Alaska Fairbanks (Fairbanks), 42

**Arizona**
Chandler-Gilbert Community College (Chandler), 47
Cochise College (Douglas), 47
East Valley Institute of Technology (Mesa), 49
Estrella Mountain Community College (Avondale), 49
Mohave Community College (Kingman), 52
Northland Pioneer College (Holbrook), 53
Paradise Valley Community College (Phoenix), 53
Rio Salado College (Tempe), 55
Yavapai College (Prescott), 58

**Arkansas**
Arkansas State University–Mountain Home (Mountain Home), 59
Crowley's Ridge Technical Institute (Forrest City), 62
Mid-South Community College (West Memphis), 63
Southern Arkansas University Tech (Camden), 66
University of Arkansas at Fort Smith (Fort Smith), 67

**California**
Advanced College (South Gate), 69
American Pacific College (Van Nuys), 72
Chabot College (Hayward), 81
El Camino College (Torrance), 90
Empire College (Santa Rosa), 90
Fresno City College (Fresno), 94
Los Angeles Southwest College (Los Angeles), 109
Los Angeles Trade-Technical College (Los Angeles), 109
Maxine Waters Employment Preparation Center (Los Angeles), 113
Merced College (Merced), 113
Modesto Junior College (Modesto), 115
Mt. San Antonio College (Walnut), 116
Palomar College (San Marcos), 122
Saddleback College (Mission Viejo), 127
San Bernardino Valley College (San Bernardino), 128
San Diego City College (San Diego), 128
Solano Community College (Suisun City), 134
Southwestern College (Chula Vista), 134
TechSkills–Sacramento (Sacramento), 135
Ventura Adult and Continuing Education (Ventura), 138
Victor Valley College (Victorville), 138

**Colorado**
Pickens Technical College (Aurora), 150

**Illinois**
City Colleges of Chicago, Richard J. Daley College (Chicago), 164
City Colleges of Chicago, Wilbur Wright College (Chicago), 164
College of DuPage (Glen Ellyn), 164
College of Lake County (Grayslake), 165
Elgin Community College (Elgin), 167
Highland Community College (Freeport), 171
Illinois Eastern Community Colleges, Lincoln Trail College (Robinson), 172
Joliet Junior College (Joliet), 174
Kankakee Community College (Kankakee), 174
Kishwaukee College (Malta), 175
Lewis and Clark Community College (Godfrey), 176
Morton College (Cicero), 179
Prairie State College (Chicago Heights), 182
Sauk Valley Community College (Dixon), 186
Southwestern Illinois College (Belleville), 187
Spoon River College (Canton), 187
Triton College (River Grove), 188

**Kansas**
Kansas City Area Technical School (Kansas City), 204
Labette Community College (Parsons), 205
Wright Business School (Overland Park), 209

**Kentucky**
Spencerian College–Lexington (Lexington), 219

**Louisiana**
Louisiana Technical College–Folkes Campus (Jackson), 230
Louisiana Technical College–Gulf Area Campus (Abbeville), 230
Louisiana Technical College–Lamar Salter Campus (Leesville), 231
Louisiana Technical College–Teche Area Campus (New Iberia), 234
Southern University at Shreveport (Shreveport), 237

**Minnesota**
East Metro Opportunities Industrialization Center (St. Paul), 242
Hibbing Community College (Hibbing), 244
Minnesota West Community and Technical College (Pipestone), 248

**Mississippi**
Hinds Community College (Raymond), 259

## COMPUTER PROGRAMMING, OTHER



## COMPUTER PROGRAMMING/PROGRAMMER, GENERAL

## COMPUTER PROGRAMMING, SPECIFIC APPLICATIONS



## COMPUTER PROGRAMMING, VENDOR/PRODUCT CERTIFICATION



## COMPUTER SCIENCE

## COMPUTER SOFTWARE AND MEDIA APPLICATIONS, OTHER

### Arizona
Central Arizona College (Coolidge), 47
Coconino Community College (Flagstaff), 48
Eastern Arizona College (Thatcher), 48
Pima Community College (Tucson), 54

### California
American Pacific College (Van Nuys), 72
Platt College San Diego (San Diego), 124
Vallecitos CET (Hayward), 137

### Illinois
Midstate College (Peoria), 178
Rockford Business College (Rockford), 184

### Kentucky
Brown Mackie College–Hopkinsville (Hopkinsville), 211

### Louisiana
American School of Business (Shreveport), 221

### South Dakota
Northern State University (Aberdeen), 329

### Wisconsin
Waukesha County Technical College (Pewaukee), 422

## COMPUTER SOFTWARE TECHNOLOGY/ TECHNICIAN

### Arizona
Coconino Community College (Flagstaff), 48

### Illinois
Brown Mackie College–Moline (Moline), 161
Oakton Community College (Des Plaines), 180

### Kansas
Brown Mackie College–Kansas City (Lenexa), 200
Brown Mackie College–Salina (Salina), 200
Kansas City Kansas Community College (Kansas City), 204

## COMPUTER SYSTEMS ANALYSIS/ANALYST

### Arizona
Chandler-Gilbert Community College (Chandler), 47
Estrella Mountain Community College (Avondale), 49
GateWay Community College (Phoenix), 50
Glendale Community College (Glendale), 50
Mohave Community College (Kingman), 52
Paradise Valley Community College (Phoenix), 53
Phoenix College (Phoenix), 53
Pima Community College (Tucson), 54
Rio Salado College (Tempe), 55
South Mountain Community College (Phoenix), 56

### California
Cerritos College (Norwalk), 80
Irvine Valley College (Irvine), 101
MTI College of Business & Technology (Sacramento), 117

### Iowa
Kaplan University, Cedar Falls (Cedar Falls), 194
Kaplan University, Cedar Rapids (Cedar Rapids), 194

### Louisiana
Louisiana Technical College–Tallulah Campus (Tallulah), 234

### Missouri
Crowder College (Neosho), 266
Linn State Technical College (Linn), 270
St. Louis Community College at Florissant Valley (St. Louis), 277
St. Louis Community College at Forest Park (St. Louis), 278
St. Louis Community College at Meramec (Kirkwood), 278
Waynesville Technical Academy (Waynesville), 282

### New Mexico
Central New Mexico Community College (Albuquerque), 293

### Oklahoma
Career Point Institute (Tulsa), 303

### Oregon
Southwestern Oregon Community College (Coos Bay), 327

### Tennessee
Tennessee Technology Center at Jackson (Jackson), 342
Tennessee Technology Center at Ripley (Ripley), 345

### Texas
Career Point Business School (San Antonio), 354
Victoria College (Victoria), 390

### Utah
College of Eastern Utah (Price), 393

### Wisconsin
Kaplan College–Milwaukee (Milwaukee), 416

### Wyoming
Laramie County Community College (Cheyenne), 423

## COMPUTER SYSTEMS NETWORKING AND TELECOMMUNICATIONS

### Alaska
University of Alaska Anchorage (Anchorage), 41

### Arizona
Arizona Western College (Yuma), 44
Chandler-Gilbert Community College (Chandler), 47
Cochise College (Douglas), 47
Estrella Mountain Community College (Avondale), 49
GateWay Community College (Phoenix), 50
Glendale Community College (Glendale), 50
Mesa Community College (Mesa), 52
Northland Pioneer College (Holbrook), 53
Paradise Valley Community College (Phoenix), 53
Phoenix College (Phoenix), 53
Pima Community College (Tucson), 54
Rio Salado College (Tempe), 55
Scottsdale Community College (Scottsdale), 56
South Mountain Community College (Phoenix), 56
Yavapai College (Prescott), 58

### Arkansas
Arkansas State University–Mountain Home (Mountain Home), 59
Bryan College (Rogers), 61
Mid-South Community College (West Memphis), 63
North Arkansas College (Harrison), 64
Ouachita Technical College (Malvern), 64
Phillips Community College of the University of Arkansas (Helena), 65
Southeast Arkansas College (Pine Bluff), 66
Southern Arkansas University Tech (Camden), 66

### California
Advanced College (South Gate), 69
Advanced Training Associates (El Cajon), 70
Allan Hancock College (Santa Maria), 70
American River College (Sacramento), 72
Antelope Valley College (Lancaster), 72
ATI College (Norwalk), 73
Butte College (Oroville), 75
Cabrillo College (Aptos), 75
Cerritos College (Norwalk), 80
Chaffey College (Rancho Cucamonga), 81
City College of San Francisco (San Francisco), 82
Coastline Community College (Fountain Valley), 83
Coleman University (San Diego), 83
College of Alameda (Alameda), 84
College of San Mateo (San Mateo), 84
Computer Tutor Business and Technical Institute (Modesto), 86
Contra Costa College (San Pablo), 86
Cosumnes River College (Sacramento), 87
Cuyamaca College (El Cajon), 88
De Anza College (Cupertino), 88
Diablo Valley College (Pleasant Hill), 89
Foothill College (Los Altos Hills), 93
Fresno City College (Fresno), 94
Grossmont College (El Cajon), 96
ICDC College (Los Angeles), 99
Institute of Technology (Clovis), 100
Las Positas College (Livermore), 105
Long Beach City College (Long Beach), 106
Los Angeles City College (Los Angeles), 107
MCed Career College (Fresno), 113
Mendocino College (Ukiah), 113
MiraCosta College (Oceanside), 114
Moorpark College (Moorpark), 116
Mt. San Antonio College (Walnut), 116
Mt. San Jacinto College (San Jacinto), 117
Ohlone College (Fremont), 120
Oxnard College (Oxnard), 121
Palomar College (San Marcos), 122
PCI College (Cerritos), 124
Sacramento City College (Sacramento), 126
Saddleback College (Mission Viejo), 127
San Diego City College (San Diego), 128
San Diego Mesa College (San Diego), 128
San Joaquin Delta College (Stockton), 129
San Jose City College (San Jose), 130
Santa Barbara City College (Santa Barbara), 131
Shasta College (Redding), 133
Sierra College (Rocklin), 133
Skyline College (San Bruno), 133
TechSkills–Sacramento (Sacramento), 135

### Colorado
Emily Griffith Opportunity School (Denver), 146
Pikes Peak Community College (Colorado Springs), 150
San Juan Basin Area Vocational School (Cortez), 152

### Guam
Guam Community College (Barrigada), 154

### Idaho
Boise State University (Boise), 157
College of Southern Idaho (Twin Falls), 157
Eastern Idaho Technical College (Idaho Falls), 157

### Illinois
Black Hawk College (Moline), 160
CALC Institute of Technology (Alton), 161
City Colleges of Chicago, Harry S. Truman College (Chicago), 163

Southeastern Career Institute–Midland (Midland), 380
Tarrant County College District (Fort Worth), 383
Texas State Technical College West Texas (Sweetwater), 387
Tyler Junior College (Tyler), 388
Victoria College (Victoria), 390
Weatherford College (Weatherford), 390
Western Texas College (Snyder), 391
Wharton County Junior College (Wharton), 391

**Utah**
Southwest Applied Technology Center (Cedar City), 397
Utah Valley University (Orem), 399
Weber State University (Ogden), 399

**Washington**
Bates Technical College (Tacoma), 400
Bellevue College (Bellevue), 400
Bellingham Technical College (Bellingham), 400
Cascadia Community College (Bothell), 401
Clark College (Vancouver), 402
Clover Park Technical College (Lakewood), 402
Edmonds Community College (Lynnwood), 403
Everett Community College (Everett), 404
Grays Harbor College (Aberdeen), 405
Highline Community College (Des Moines), 405
Lake Washington Technical College (Kirkland), 406
Olympic College (Bremerton), 408
Renton Technical College (Renton), 410
Skagit Valley College (Mount Vernon), 411
Spokane Falls Community College (Spokane), 412
Wenatchee Valley College (Wenatchee), 413
Whatcom Community College (Bellingham), 413

**Wisconsin**
Milwaukee Career College (Milwaukee), 419
Moraine Park Technical College (Fond du Lac), 419

**Wyoming**
Eastern Wyoming College (Torrington), 423

## COMPUTER TEACHER EDUCATION

**Arizona**
GateWay Community College (Phoenix), 50

## COMPUTER TECHNOLOGY/COMPUTER SYSTEMS TECHNOLOGY

**Arizona**
Cochise College (Douglas), 47
Coconino Community College (Flagstaff), 48

**Arkansas**
Arkansas State University–Beebe (Beebe), 59
Ouachita Technical College (Malvern), 64
Southeast Arkansas College (Pine Bluff), 66
University of Arkansas at Monticello (Monticello), 67
University of Arkansas Community College at Morrilton (Morrilton), 68

**California**
ICDC College (Los Angeles), 99
InfoTech Career College (Bellflower), 100
PCI College (Cerritos), 124
United Education Institute (Los Angeles), 136
Valley Career College (El Cajon), 137

**Hawaii**
Maui Community College (Kahului), 155

**Idaho**
Boise State University (Boise), 157

**Illinois**
College of DuPage (Glen Ellyn), 164
Heartland Community College (Normal), 171
Illinois Valley Community College (Oglesby), 173
Lake Land College (Mattoon), 176
Lincoln Land Community College (Springfield), 177
McHenry County College (Crystal Lake), 178
Morton College (Cicero), 179
Oakton Community College (Des Plaines), 180
Triton College (River Grove), 188
Waubonsee Community College (Sugar Grove), 189

**Kansas**
Wichita Technical Institute (Wichita), 209
Wright Business School (Overland Park), 209

**Kentucky**
Bowling Green Technical College (Bowling Green), 210

**Louisiana**
Elaine P. Nunez Community College (Chalmette), 226
ITI Technical College (Baton Rouge), 226

**Minnesota**
Anoka-Ramsey Community College (Coon Rapids), 240
Century College (White Bear Lake), 241
Hennepin Technical College (Brooklyn Park), 243
Inver Hills Community College (Inver Grove Heights), 244
Ridgewater College (Willmar), 253
Saint Paul College–A Community & Technical College (St. Paul), 254
South Central College (North Mankato), 255

**Missouri**
Clinton Technical School (Clinton), 265
Hannibal Career and Technical Center (Hannibal), 268
Lake Career and Technical Center (Camdenton), 269
Lebanon Technology and Career Center (Lebanon), 269
Lex La-Ray Technical Center (Lexington), 270
Nichols Career Center (Jefferson City), 274
Rolla Technical Institute (Rolla), 277
Three Rivers Community College (Poplar Bluff), 280

**Montana**
Fort Peck Community College (Poplar), 283
The University of Montana (Missoula), 285

**New Mexico**
Southwestern Indian Polytechnic Institute (Albuquerque), 297
University of New Mexico–Valencia Campus (Los Lunas), 298

**Oregon**
Linn-Benton Community College (Albany), 323

**Tennessee**
Tennessee Technology Center at Jacksboro (Jacksboro), 342
Tennessee Technology Center at Pulaski (Pulaski), 344

**Texas**
Alvin Community College (Alvin), 349
American Commercial College (Lubbock), 350
American Commercial College (Wichita Falls), 350
Central Texas College (Killeen), 355
Clarendon College (Clarendon), 356
Grayson County College (Denison), 363
Lamar Institute of Technology (Beaumont), 367
Lee College (Baytown), 368
St. Philip's College (San Antonio), 377
South Texas College (McAllen), 381
Tarrant County College District (Fort Worth), 383
Texas State Technical College Harlingen (Harlingen), 386
Texas State Technical College Waco (Waco), 386
Trinity Valley Community College (Athens), 387
Tyler Junior College (Tyler), 388

**Washington**
Bates Technical College (Tacoma), 400
Edmonds Community College (Lynnwood), 403
Pierce College at Fort Steilacoom (Lakewood), 409
Spokane Falls Community College (Spokane), 412

**Wisconsin**
Waukesha County Technical College (Pewaukee), 422

**Wyoming**
Central Wyoming College (Riverton), 423

## COMPUTER TYPOGRAPHY AND COMPOSITION EQUIPMENT OPERATOR

**Oregon**
Rogue Community College (Grants Pass), 326

## CONCRETE FINISHING/CONCRETE FINISHER

**Colorado**
Emily Griffith Opportunity School (Denver), 146

**Illinois**
Southwestern Illinois College (Belleville), 187

**Wisconsin**
Milwaukee Area Technical College (Milwaukee), 418
Waukesha County Technical College (Pewaukee), 422

## CONSTRUCTION ENGINEERING TECHNOLOGY/TECHNICIAN

**Illinois**
College of Lake County (Grayslake), 165
Danville Area Community College (Danville), 166
Kankakee Community College (Kankakee), 174

**Louisiana**
Bossier Parish Community College (Bossier City), 223

**Missouri**
Lebanon Technology and Career Center (Lebanon), 269

**Montana**
Blackfeet Community College (Browning), 282
Miles Community College (Miles City), 283
The University of Montana–Helena College of Technology (Helena), 285

**Nebraska**
Vatterott College (Omaha), 289

**New Mexico**
Santa Fe Community College (Santa Fe), 297
Western New Mexico University (Silver City), 298

**Oregon**
Clackamas Community College (Oregon City), 320
Lane Community College (Eugene), 322
Portland Community College (Portland), 326
Rogue Community College (Grants Pass), 326

**Texas**
Brazosport College (Lake Jackson), 353
Hill College of the Hill Junior College District (Hillsboro), 363
Houston Community College System (Houston), 363
Lee College (Baytown), 368
North Lake College (Irving), 372
St. Philip's College (San Antonio), 377
Southwest Texas Junior College (Uvalde), 382
Texas State Technical College Harlingen (Harlingen), 386
Texas State Technical College West Texas (Sweetwater), 387

**Washington**
Clark College (Vancouver), 402

## CONSTRUCTION/HEAVY EQUIPMENT/ EARTHMOVING EQUIPMENT OPERATION

**Arizona**
Central Arizona College (Coolidge), 47

**Arkansas**
North Arkansas College (Harrison), 64
Northwest Technical Institute (Springdale), 64

**California**
Butte College (Oroville), 75

**Colorado**
Emily Griffith Opportunity School (Denver), 146
Trinidad State Junior College (Trinidad), 153

**Illinois**
Joliet Junior College (Joliet), 174

**Iowa**
Northwest Iowa Community College (Sheldon), 197

**Kentucky**
Hazard Community and Technical College (Hazard), 214
Southeast Kentucky Community and Technical College (Cumberland), 218

**Louisiana**
Louisiana Technical College–Northwest Louisiana Campus (Minden), 232

**Minnesota**
Central Lakes College (Brainerd), 241

**Mississippi**
Copiah-Lincoln Community College (Wesson), 258
Mississippi Delta Community College (Moorhead), 261

**Missouri**
Linn State Technical College (Linn), 270

**Montana**
Blackfeet Community College (Browning), 282
Miles Community College (Miles City), 283
Salish Kootenai College (Pablo), 284
The University of Montana (Missoula), 285

**Oklahoma**
Indian Capital Technology Center–Tahlequah (Tahlequah), 308

**Texas**
Brazosport College (Lake Jackson), 353

**Utah**
College of Eastern Utah (Price), 393

**Washington**
Bates Technical College (Tacoma), 400

**Wisconsin**
Mid-State Technical College (Wisconsin Rapids), 418

## CONSTRUCTION MANAGEMENT

**Arizona**
Phoenix College (Phoenix), 53

**Illinois**
Oakton Community College (Des Plaines), 180
Rock Valley College (Rockford), 184
South Suburban College (South Holland), 187
Triton College (River Grove), 188

**Kansas**
Johnson County Community College (Overland Park), 203

**Minnesota**
Anoka Technical College (Anoka), 240

**Missouri**
St. Louis Community College at Florissant Valley (St. Louis), 277

**Washington**
Edmonds Community College (Lynnwood), 403

## CONSTRUCTION TRADES, GENERAL

**Alaska**
Ilisagvik College (Barrow), 41

**American Samoa**
American Samoa Community College (Pago Pago), 43

**Arizona**
Northland Pioneer College (Holbrook), 53
Tohono O'odham Community College (Sells), 57

**Arkansas**
North Arkansas College (Harrison), 64

**California**
Bakersfield College (Bakersfield), 74
College of the Redwoods (Eureka), 85
Cuesta College (San Luis Obispo), 87
El Camino College (Torrance), 90
Fresno City College (Fresno), 94
Fullerton College (Fullerton), 95
Hartnell College (Salinas), 97
Los Angeles Trade-Technical College (Los Angeles), 109
Maxine Waters Employment Preparation Center (Los Angeles), 113
Modesto Junior College (Modesto), 115
Orange Coast College (Costa Mesa), 121
Sacramento City Unified School District–Skills and Business Education Center (Sacramento), 126
San Jose City College (San Jose), 130
Shasta College (Redding), 133
Sierra College (Rocklin), 133
Vallecitos CET (Hayward), 137
Victor Valley College (Victorville), 138

**Colorado**
Emily Griffith Opportunity School (Denver), 146
Red Rocks Community College (Lakewood), 151
Redstone College–Denver (Broomfield), 152
Trinidad State Junior College (Trinidad), 153

**Illinois**
Illinois Central College (East Peoria), 172
Joliet Junior College (Joliet), 174
Kaskaskia College (Centralia), 175
Lake Land College (Mattoon), 176
Parkland College (Champaign), 181
Rend Lake College (Ina), 183
Richland Community College (Decatur), 184
Rock Valley College (Rockford), 184
Southeastern Illinois College (Harrisburg), 186
South Suburban College (South Holland), 187
Southwestern Illinois College (Belleville), 187
Spoon River College (Canton), 187

**Iowa**
Ellsworth Community College (Iowa Falls), 191
Indian Hills Community College (Ottumwa), 192
Iowa Western Community College (Council Bluffs), 194
Kirkwood Community College (Cedar Rapids), 195
Marshalltown Community College (Marshalltown), 196
Muscatine Community College (Muscatine), 196
Southeastern Community College, North Campus (West Burlington), 198

**Minnesota**
Northwest Technical College (Bemidji), 250

**Missouri**
East Central College (Union), 266
Nichols Career Center (Jefferson City), 274
St. Louis Community College at Florissant Valley (St. Louis), 277
Sikeston Career and Technology Center (Sikeston), 279

**Nebraska**
Metropolitan Community College (Omaha), 287

**North Dakota**
Turtle Mountain Community College (Belcourt), 301

**Oklahoma**
Indian Capital Technology Center–Stilwell (Stilwell), 308
Northeast Area Vocational Technical School (Pryor), 311

**Oregon**
Umpqua Community College (Roseburg), 327

**South Dakota**
Oglala Lakota College (Kyle), 329
Sisseton-Wahpeton Community College (Sisseton), 330

**Texas**
Texas State Technical College Waco (Waco), 386

**Utah**
Utah Valley University (Orem), 399

**Wyoming**
Casper College (Casper), 423
Eastern Wyoming College (Torrington), 423
Laramie County Community College (Cheyenne), 423
Sheridan College (Sheridan), 424

## CONSTRUCTION TRADES, OTHER

**Alaska**
Ilisagvik College (Barrow), 41

**Arizona**
Arizona Western College (Yuma), 44
Central Arizona College (Coolidge), 47
Coconino Community College (Flagstaff), 48
East Valley Institute of Technology (Mesa), 49
GateWay Community College (Phoenix), 50
Maricopa Skill Center (Phoenix), 51
Yavapai College (Prescott), 58

## Construction Trades, Other

**California**
Center for Employment Training–Gilroy (Gilroy), 79
Center for Employment Training–Salinas (Salinas), 79
Center for Employment Training–Watsonville (Watsonville), 80
Citrus College (Glendora), 82
Los Angeles Trade-Technical College (Los Angeles), 109
Santiago Canyon College (Orange), 132

**Colorado**
Emily Griffith Opportunity School (Denver), 146
Morgan Community College (Fort Morgan), 149

**Illinois**
Lincoln Technical Institute (Norridge), 177

**Missouri**
Columbia Area Vocational Technical School (Columbia), 265
Eldon Career Center (Eldon), 266
Kirksville Area Vocational Technical School (Kirksville), 269
Lex La-Ray Technical Center (Lexington), 270

**Nevada**
Western Nevada Community College (Carson City), 292

**New Mexico**
Northern New Mexico College (Española), 296

**North Dakota**
Sitting Bull College (Fort Yates), 301

**Northern Mariana Islands**
Northern Marianas College (Saipan), 302

**Oklahoma**
Canadian Valley Technology Center (El Reno), 303
Moore Norman Technology Center (Norman), 311
Southwest Area Vocational Technical Center (Altus), 316
Western Technology Center (Burns Flat), 318

**South Dakota**
Mitchell Technical Institute (Mitchell), 329
Sinte Gleska University (Mission), 330

**Tennessee**
Southwest Tennessee Community College (Memphis), 339
Tennessee Technology Center at Crossville (Crossville), 341
Tennessee Technology Center at Livingston (Livingston), 342
Tennessee Technology Center at Memphis (Memphis), 343

**Texas**
Coastal Bend College (Beeville), 357

**Utah**
Snow College (Ephraim), 397

**Washington**
Bates Technical College (Tacoma), 400
Clover Park Technical College (Lakewood), 402
Edmonds Community College (Lynnwood), 403
Renton Technical College (Renton), 410
Seattle Vocational Institute (Seattle), 410

**Wisconsin**
Moraine Park Technical College (Fond du Lac), 419

## CONSUMER SERVICES AND ADVOCACY

**Montana**
Blackfeet Community College (Browning), 282

## COOKING AND RELATED CULINARY ARTS, GENERAL

**Arizona**
Rio Salado College (Tempe), 55

**California**
Allan Hancock College (Santa Maria), 70
The Art Institute of California–Los Angeles (Santa Monica), 73
The Art Institute of California–Orange County (Santa Ana), 73
Bakersfield College (Bakersfield), 74
Cabrillo College (Aptos), 75
California School of Culinary Arts (Pasadena), 77
Cerritos College (Norwalk), 80
Chaffey College (Rancho Cucamonga), 81
College of the Desert (Palm Desert), 84
Contra Costa College (San Pablo), 86
Cuesta College (San Luis Obispo), 87
Cypress College (Cypress), 88
Diablo Valley College (Pleasant Hill), 89
Fresno City College (Fresno), 94
Glendale Community College (Glendale), 95
Grossmont College (El Cajon), 96
Laney College (Oakland), 105
Long Beach City College (Long Beach), 106
Los Angeles Mission College (Sylmar), 107
Los Angeles Trade-Technical College (Los Angeles), 109
Merced College (Merced), 113
Modesto Junior College (Modesto), 115
Mt. San Antonio College (Walnut), 116
Orange Coast College (Costa Mesa), 121
Oxnard College (Oxnard), 121
Palomar College (San Marcos), 122
Pasadena City College (Pasadena), 123
Riverside Community College District (Riverside), 126
Sacramento City Unified School District–Skills and Business Education Center (Sacramento), 126
Saddleback College (Mission Viejo), 127
San Diego Mesa College (San Diego), 128
San Joaquin Delta College (Stockton), 129
Santa Barbara City College (Santa Barbara), 131
Santa Rosa Junior College (Santa Rosa), 132
Shasta College (Redding), 133
Yuba College (Marysville), 142

**Colorado**
Mesa State College (Grand Junction), 149
Pikes Peak Community College (Colorado Springs), 150

**Hawaii**
Hawaii Community College (Hilo), 154
Kapiolani Community College (Honolulu), 155
Kauai Community College (Lihue), 155
Leeward Community College (Pearl City), 155
Maui Community College (Kahului), 155

**Illinois**
St. Augustine College (Chicago), 185

**Kentucky**
Employment Solutions (Lexington), 213

**Minnesota**
Minnesota State Community and Technical College–Fergus Falls (Fergus Falls), 248
South Central College (North Mankato), 255

**Mississippi**
East Central Community College (Decatur), 259
Hinds Community College (Raymond), 259
Jones County Junior College (Ellisville), 260

**Missouri**
Cape Girardeau Area Vocational Technical School (Cape Girardeau), 264
L'Ecole Culinaire (St. Louis), 270

**Nevada**
Truckee Meadows Community College (Reno), 292

**New Mexico**
Crownpoint Institute of Technology (Crownpoint), 293

**Oklahoma**
Kiamichi Area Vocational-Technical School–Durant (Durant), 308
Meridian Technology Center (Stillwater), 309

**Oregon**
Central Oregon Community College (Bend), 320

**Texas**
Culinary Institute Alain & Marie LeNotre (Houston), 358

## CORRECTIONS

**Arizona**
Northland Pioneer College (Holbrook), 53
Rio Salado College (Tempe), 55

**Arkansas**
Arkansas State University–Beebe (Beebe), 59

**California**
Chaffey College (Rancho Cucamonga), 81
Contra Costa College (San Pablo), 86
Diablo Valley College (Pleasant Hill), 89
Fresno City College (Fresno), 94
Grossmont College (El Cajon), 96
Imperial Valley College (Imperial), 100
Lassen Community College District (Susanville), 106
Merritt College (Oakland), 114
Riverside Community College District (Riverside), 126
Sacramento City College (Sacramento), 126
San Diego Miramar College (San Diego), 129
San Joaquin Delta College (Stockton), 129
Santa Ana College (Santa Ana), 131
Santa Rosa Junior College (Santa Rosa), 132
Solano Community College (Suisun City), 134
Southwestern College (Chula Vista), 134
West Los Angeles College (Culver City), 141

**Illinois**
Heartland Community College (Normal), 171
Richland Community College (Decatur), 184
Southeastern Illinois College (Harrisburg), 186

**Iowa**
Kaplan University, Davenport Campus (Davenport), 194

**Kansas**
Kansas City Kansas Community College (Kansas City), 204
Labette Community College (Parsons), 205

**Louisiana**
Louisiana Technical College–Oakdale Campus (Oakdale), 233

**Minnesota**
Minnesota State Community and Technical College–Fergus Falls (Fergus Falls), 248

**Missouri**
St. Louis Community College at Florissant Valley (St. Louis), 277
St. Louis Community College at Forest Park (St. Louis), 278

## CORRECTIONS AND CRIMINAL JUSTICE, OTHER



## COSMETOLOGY AND RELATED PERSONAL GROOMING ARTS, OTHER

## COSMETOLOGY, BARBER/STYLING, AND NAIL INSTRUCTOR

## COSMETOLOGY/COSMETOLOGIST, GENERAL

## COUNSELOR EDUCATION/SCHOOL COUNSELING AND GUIDANCE SERVICES



## COURT REPORTING/COURT REPORTER



## CRAFTS/CRAFT DESIGN, FOLK ART AND ARTISANRY

## CREDIT MANAGEMENT

### Missouri

St. Louis Community College at Florissant Valley (St. Louis), 277

## CRIMINALISTICS AND CRIMINAL SCIENCE

### Arizona

Mohave Community College (Kingman), 52

### Illinois

City Colleges of Chicago, Wilbur Wright College (Chicago), 164

### Texas

Alvin Community College (Alvin), 349
Del Mar College (Corpus Christi), 359

## CRIMINAL JUSTICE/LAW ENFORCEMENT ADMINISTRATION

### Arizona

Brookline College (Mesa), 46
Brookline College (Phoenix), 46
Brookline College (Tucson), 46
Tucson College (Tucson), 57

### Arkansas

Arkansas State University–Beebe (Beebe), 59
Arkansas State University–Mountain Home (Mountain Home), 59
Arkansas Tech University (Russellville), 60
East Arkansas Community College (Forrest City), 62
North Arkansas College (Harrison), 64
Ouachita Technical College (Malvern), 64
Southern Arkansas University Tech (Camden), 66
University of Arkansas at Fort Smith (Fort Smith), 67
University of Arkansas Community College at Morrilton (Morrilton), 68

### California

Everest College (Los Angeles), 91
Heald College–Concord (Concord), 97
Kaplan College–Bakersfield (Bakersfield), 103
Kaplan College–Stockton Campus (Stockton), 104

### Colorado

Arapahoe Community College (Littleton), 143
Colorado Northwestern Community College (Rangely), 145
Community College of Aurora (Aurora), 146
Pikes Peak Community College (Colorado Springs), 150
Pueblo Community College (Pueblo), 151
Trinidad State Junior College (Trinidad), 153

### Idaho

North Idaho College (Coeur d'Alene), 159

### Illinois

Kaskaskia College (Centralia), 175
Southwestern Illinois College (Belleville), 187
Taylor Business Institute (Chicago), 188
Triton College (River Grove), 188

### Kansas

Brown Mackie College–Kansas City (Lenexa), 200
Johnson County Community College (Overland Park), 203

### Kentucky

Brown Mackie College–Hopkinsville (Hopkinsville), 211
University of Louisville (Louisville), 220

### Minnesota

Metropolitan State University (St. Paul), 246

### Nevada

Truckee Meadows Community College (Reno), 292

### New Mexico

Brookline College (Albuquerque), 293

### North Dakota

Sitting Bull College (Fort Yates), 301

### Oklahoma

Caddo-Kiowa Area Vocational Technical School (Ft. Cobb), 303
Great Plains Technology Center (Lawton), 306

### South Dakota

Sinte Gleska University (Mission), 330

### Tennessee

Draughons Junior College (Clarksville), 332
Kaplan Career Institute–Nashville Campus (Nashville), 334

### Texas

Hill College of the Hill Junior College District (Hillsboro), 363
South Plains College (Levelland), 381
Texarkana College (Texarkana), 384

### Washington

Kaplan College–Renton Campus (Renton), 406
Pierce College at Fort Steilacoom (Lakewood), 409
Pierce College (Puyallup), 409
Skagit Valley College (Mount Vernon), 411
Tacoma Community College (Tacoma), 412
Yakima Valley Community College (Yakima), 414

### Wisconsin

Western Technical College (La Crosse), 422

## CRIMINAL JUSTICE/POLICE SCIENCE

### Alaska

University of Alaska Southeast (Juneau), 42

### Arizona

Central Arizona College (Coolidge), 47
Chandler-Gilbert Community College (Chandler), 47
Eastern Arizona College (Thatcher), 48
East Valley Institute of Technology (Mesa), 49
Glendale Community College (Glendale), 50
High-Tech Institute (Phoenix), 51
Mesa Community College (Mesa), 52
Northland Pioneer College (Holbrook), 53
Phoenix College (Phoenix), 53
Pima Community College (Tucson), 54
Rio Salado College (Tempe), 55
Scottsdale Community College (Scottsdale), 56
Yavapai College (Prescott), 58

### Arkansas

Arkansas State University–Beebe (Beebe), 59
East Arkansas Community College (Forrest City), 62
NorthWest Arkansas Community College (Bentonville), 64
Southern Arkansas University Tech (Camden), 66

### California

Allan Hancock College (Santa Maria), 70
Bakersfield College (Bakersfield), 74
Barstow College (Barstow), 74
Butte College (Oroville), 75
Cerro Coso Community College (Ridgecrest), 80
Chaffey College (Rancho Cucamonga), 81
Citrus College (Glendora), 82
City College of San Francisco (San Francisco), 82
College of Marin (Kentfield), 84
College of San Mateo (San Mateo), 84
College of the Canyons (Santa Clarita), 84
College of the Desert (Palm Desert), 84
College of the Redwoods (Eureka), 85
College of the Sequoias (Visalia), 85
Contra Costa College (San Pablo), 86
Cypress College (Cypress), 88
Diablo Valley College (Pleasant Hill), 89
East Los Angeles College (Monterey Park), 89
East San Gabriel Valley Regional Occupational Program & Technical Center (West Covina), 90
El Camino College (Torrance), 90
El Camino College Compton Center (Compton), 90
Fresno City College (Fresno), 94
Fullerton College (Fullerton), 95
Gavilan College (Gilroy), 95
Glendale Community College (Glendale), 95
Golden West College (Huntington Beach), 96
Grossmont College (El Cajon), 96
Hartnell College (Salinas), 97
Imperial Valley College (Imperial), 100
Irvine Valley College (Irvine), 101
Lake Tahoe Community College (South Lake Tahoe), 105
Lassen Community College District (Susanville), 106
Long Beach City College (Long Beach), 106
Los Angeles City College (Los Angeles), 107
Los Angeles Mission College (Sylmar), 107
Los Angeles Southwest College (Los Angeles), 109
Los Angeles Valley College (Van Nuys), 109
Los Medanos College (Pittsburg), 109
Martinez Adult School (Martinez), 112
Mendocino College (Ukiah), 113
Merced College (Merced), 113
Merritt College (Oakland), 114
MiraCosta College (Oceanside), 114
Modesto Junior College (Modesto), 115
Monterey Peninsula College (Monterey), 116
Mt. San Antonio College (Walnut), 116
Mt. San Jacinto College (San Jacinto), 117
Napa Valley College (Napa), 118
Ohlone College (Fremont), 120
Palomar College (San Marcos), 122
Porterville College (Porterville), 124
Reedley College (Reedley), 125
Rio Hondo College (Whittier), 125
Riverside Community College District (Riverside), 126
San Bernardino Valley College (San Bernardino), 128
San Diego Miramar College (San Diego), 129
Santa Barbara City College (Santa Barbara), 131
Santa Rosa Junior College (Santa Rosa), 132
Skyline College (San Bruno), 133
Solano Community College (Suisun City), 134
Southwestern College (Chula Vista), 134
Taft College (Taft), 135
Ventura College (Ventura), 138
Victor Valley College (Victorville), 138

### Colorado

Aims Community College (Greeley), 143
Arapahoe Community College (Littleton), 143
Colorado Mountain College (Glenwood Springs), 145
Delta-Montrose Area Vocational Technical Center (Delta), 146
Mesa State College (Grand Junction), 149

## CRIMINAL JUSTICE/SAFETY STUDIES

Le Cordon Bleu College of Culinary Arts (Saint Paul), 245
Minneapolis Community and Technical College (Minneapolis), 246
St. Cloud Technical College (St. Cloud), 254
Saint Paul College–A Community & Technical College (St. Paul), 254

**Mississippi**
Coahoma Community College (Clarksdale), 258

**Missouri**
East Central College (Union), 266
Lake Career and Technical Center (Camdenton), 269
Ozarks Technical Community College (Springfield), 274
Saline County Career Center (Marshall), 279
South Central Area Vocational Technical School (West Plains), 280
Waynesville Technical Academy (Waynesville), 282

**Montana**
The University of Montana (Missoula), 285

**Nevada**
College of Southern Nevada (North Las Vegas), 290
Truckee Meadows Community College (Reno), 292

**New Mexico**
Central New Mexico Community College (Albuquerque), 293
Luna Community College (Las Vegas), 295
Santa Fe Community College (Santa Fe), 297
University of New Mexico–Taos (Taos), 298

**North Dakota**
North Dakota State College of Science (Wahpeton), 300

**Oklahoma**
Caddo-Kiowa Area Vocational Technical School (Ft. Cobb), 303
Great Plains Technology Center (Lawton), 306
Indian Capital Technology Center–Muskogee (Muskogee), 307
Meridian Technology Center (Stillwater), 309
Metro Area Vocational Technical School District 22 (Oklahoma City), 310
Northeast Technology Center–Afton (Afton), 311
Pioneer Area Vocational Technical School (Ponca City), 313
Platt College (Oklahoma City), 314
Tri County Technology Center (Bartlesville), 316

**Oregon**
Pioneer Pacific College (Wilsonville), 326
Umpqua Community College (Roseburg), 327
Western Culinary Institute (Portland), 328

**South Dakota**
Mitchell Technical Institute (Mitchell), 329

**Tennessee**
The Art Institute of Tennessee–Nashville (Nashville), 331
Nashville State Technical Community College (Nashville), 336
Walters State Community College (Morristown), 346

**Texas**
Aims Academy (Carrollton), 349
Alvin Community College (Alvin), 349
Ames Academy (Fort Worth), 350
The Art Institute of Dallas (Dallas), 351
Austin Community College (Austin), 352
Culinary Academy of Austin (Austin), 358
Culinary Institute Alain & Marie LeNotre (Houston), 358
Del Mar College (Corpus Christi), 359
El Centro College (Dallas), 360
El Paso Community College (El Paso), 360
Galveston College (Galveston), 362
Houston Community College System (Houston), 363
Lee College (Baytown), 368
Odessa College (Odessa), 373
St. Philip's College (San Antonio), 377
San Jacinto College Central Campus (Pasadena), 378
South Texas College (McAllen), 381
Tarrant County College District (Fort Worth), 383
Texarkana College (Texarkana), 384
Texas Culinary Academy (Austin), 385

**Utah**
The Art Institute of Salt Lake City (Draper), 392
Mountainland Applied Technology College (Orem), 395
Snow College (Ephraim), 397

**Washington**
Bellingham Technical College (Bellingham), 400
Clark College (Vancouver), 402
Edmonds Community College (Lynnwood), 403
International Air Academy (Vancouver), 406
Kitchen Academy (Seattle), 406
Lake Washington Technical College (Kirkland), 406
Olympic College (Bremerton), 408
Skagit Valley College (Mount Vernon), 411
South Puget Sound Community College (Olympia), 411
South Seattle Community College (Seattle), 411
Walla Walla Community College (Walla Walla), 413

**Wisconsin**
Milwaukee Area Technical College (Milwaukee), 418

**Wyoming**
Central Wyoming College (Riverton), 423
Sheridan College (Sheridan), 424

## CUSTOMER SERVICE MANAGEMENT

**Arizona**
Northern Arizona University (Flagstaff), 52
Pima Community College (Tucson), 54
Rio Salado College (Tempe), 55

**Illinois**
Spanish Coalition for Jobs, Inc. (Chicago), 187

**Minnesota**
Rochester Community and Technical College (Rochester), 253

**Montana**
Stone Child College (Box Elder), 284

**Nevada**
College of Southern Nevada (North Las Vegas), 290

**South Dakota**
Oglala Lakota College (Kyle), 329

**Washington**
Highline Community College (Des Moines), 405
North Seattle Community College (Seattle), 407

## CUSTOMER SERVICE SUPPORT/CALL CENTER/TELESERVICE OPERATION

**Arizona**
Axia College (Phoenix), 46
Cochise College (Douglas), 47
Rio Salado College (Tempe), 55

**California**
College of the Siskiyous (Weed), 85
Sacramento City Unified School District–Skills and Business Education Center (Sacramento), 126

**Minnesota**
Minneapolis Community and Technical College (Minneapolis), 246

**Oklahoma**
Francis Tuttle Area Vocational Technical Center (Oklahoma City), 306

**Texas**
International Business College (El Paso), 366

**Washington**
Clover Park Technical College (Lakewood), 402
Lower Columbia College (Longview), 407
Olympic College (Bremerton), 408
Yakima Valley Community College (Yakima), 414

**Wisconsin**
Milwaukee Career College (Milwaukee), 419

**Wyoming**
Laramie County Community College (Cheyenne), 423

## CYTOGENETICS/GENETICS/CLINICAL GENETICS TECHNOLOGY/TECHNOLOGIST

**Minnesota**
Mayo School of Health Sciences (Rochester), 245

**Texas**
The University of Texas Anderson Cancer Center (Houston), 389

## CYTOTECHNOLOGY/CYTOTECHNOLOGIST

**California**
Loma Linda University (Loma Linda), 106

**Minnesota**
Mayo School of Health Sciences (Rochester), 245

**Texas**
The University of Texas Anderson Cancer Center (Houston), 389

## DAIRY HUSBANDRY AND PRODUCTION

**Iowa**
Northeast Iowa Community College (Calmar), 196

**Wisconsin**
Lakeshore Technical College (Cleveland), 417
Southwest Wisconsin Technical College (Fennimore), 421
Wisconsin Indianhead Technical College (Shell Lake), 422

## DAIRY SCIENCE

**Nebraska**
Northeast Community College (Norfolk), 288

**Utah**
Utah State University (Logan), 398

## DANCE, GENERAL

**Arizona**
Scottsdale Community College (Scottsdale), 56

## DENTAL HYGIENE/HYGIENIST



## DENTAL LABORATORY TECHNOLOGY/ TECHNICIAN



## DENTAL SERVICES AND ALLIED PROFESSIONS, OTHER



## DESIGN AND APPLIED ARTS, OTHER



## DESIGN AND VISUAL COMMUNICATIONS, GENERAL

## DIETETICS AND CLINICAL NUTRITION SERVICES, OTHER



## DIETETICS/DIETITIANS



## DIETETIC TECHNICIAN (DTR)



## DIETITIAN ASSISTANT

Yakima Valley Community College (Yakima), 414

**Wyoming**

Laramie County Community College (Cheyenne), 423

## DRAFTING/DESIGN ENGINEERING TECHNOLOGIES/TECHNICIANS, OTHER

**Alaska**

University of Alaska Anchorage (Anchorage), 41

**Arizona**

Glendale Community College (Glendale), 50
Mesa Community College (Mesa), 52
Scottsdale Community College (Scottsdale), 56

**Arkansas**

Southern Arkansas University Tech (Camden), 66

**California**

Ventura Adult and Continuing Education (Ventura), 138

**Idaho**

Idaho State University (Pocatello), 158

**Louisiana**

Bossier Parish Community College (Bossier City), 223

**Mississippi**

Mississippi Gulf Coast Community College (Perkinston), 261

**Missouri**

Eldon Career Center (Eldon), 266

**Oklahoma**

Indian Capital Technology Center–Muskogee (Muskogee), 307
Tri County Technology Center (Bartlesville), 316

## DRAMA AND DRAMATICS/THEATRE ARTS, GENERAL

**Arizona**

Mohave Community College (Kingman), 52

**California**

College of the Siskiyous (Weed), 85
Dell'Arte School of Physical Theatre (Blue Lake), 89
Foothill College (Los Altos Hills), 93
Grossmont College (El Cajon), 96
Santa Rosa Junior College (Santa Rosa), 132
West Los Angeles College (Culver City), 141

**Kansas**

Independence Community College (Independence), 203

**Texas**

KD Studio (Dallas), 367

## DRAWING

**California**

American River College (Sacramento), 72
De Anza College (Cupertino), 88
Merced College (Merced), 113
Ohlone College (Fremont), 120
San Diego Mesa College (San Diego), 128
Santa Rosa Junior College (Santa Rosa), 132

## DRYWALL INSTALLATION/DRYWALLER

**California**

American River College (Sacramento), 72

**Wisconsin**

Milwaukee Area Technical College (Milwaukee), 418

## EARLY CHILDHOOD EDUCATION AND TEACHING

**Alaska**

University of Alaska Anchorage (Anchorage), 41
University of Alaska Fairbanks (Fairbanks), 42
University of Alaska Southeast (Juneau), 42

**Arizona**

Arizona Western College (Yuma), 44
Cochise College (Douglas), 47
Coconino Community College (Flagstaff), 48
Eastern Arizona College (Thatcher), 48
Glendale Community College (Glendale), 50
Northland Pioneer College (Holbrook), 53
Paradise Valley Community College (Phoenix), 53
Phoenix College (Phoenix), 53
Pima Community College (Tucson), 54
South Mountain Community College (Phoenix), 56
Yavapai College (Prescott), 58

**Arkansas**

Arkansas State University–Beebe (Beebe), 59
NorthWest Arkansas Community College (Bentonville), 64
Phillips Community College of the University of Arkansas (Helena), 65
South Arkansas Community College (El Dorado), 66
University of Arkansas Community College at Batesville (Batesville), 67

**California**

Bethesda Christian University (Anaheim), 75
Institute of Technology (Clovis), 100
Shasta Bible College (Redding), 132
World Mission University (Los Angeles), 142

**Colorado**

Colorado Christian University (Lakewood), 145
Montessori Centre International Denver (Greenwood Village), 149

**Guam**

Guam Community College (Barrigada), 154

**Hawaii**

Hawaii Community College (Hilo), 154
Honolulu Community College (Honolulu), 155
Kauai Community College (Lihue), 155

**Illinois**

College of Lake County (Grayslake), 165
St. Augustine College (Chicago), 185
Shawnee Community College (Ullin), 186

**Iowa**

North Iowa Area Community College (Mason City), 197

**Nebraska**

Nebraska Indian Community College (Macy), 288
Northeast Community College (Norfolk), 288

**Nevada**

Great Basin College (Elko), 290
Truckee Meadows Community College (Reno), 292

**New Mexico**

Crownpoint Institute of Technology (Crownpoint), 293
New Mexico Junior College (Hobbs), 295
New Mexico State University–Grants (Grants), 296
Santa Fe Community College (Santa Fe), 297
University of New Mexico–Gallup (Gallup), 297
University of New Mexico–Taos (Taos), 298

**North Dakota**

Turtle Mountain Community College (Belcourt), 301

**Northern Mariana Islands**

Northern Marianas College (Saipan), 302

**Oklahoma**

Community Care College (Tulsa), 305
Tulsa Tech–Peoria Campus (Tulsa), 317

**Oregon**

Columbia Gorge Community College (The Dalles), 321
Linn-Benton Community College (Albany), 323

**Tennessee**

Tennessee Technology Center at Hohenwald (Hohenwald), 342

**Utah**

College of Eastern Utah (Price), 393

**Washington**

Bellevue College (Bellevue), 400
Bellingham Technical College (Bellingham), 400
Big Bend Community College (Moses Lake), 401
Clark College (Vancouver), 402
Clover Park Technical College (Lakewood), 402
Edmonds Community College (Lynnwood), 403
Everett Community College (Everett), 404
Grays Harbor College (Aberdeen), 405
Green River Community College (Auburn), 405
Highline Community College (Des Moines), 405
Lower Columbia College (Longview), 407
North Seattle Community College (Seattle), 407
Northwest Indian College (Bellingham), 408
Olympic College (Bremerton), 408
Peninsula College (Port Angeles), 408
Pierce College at Fort Steilacoom (Lakewood), 409
Renton Technical College (Renton), 410
Seattle Central Community College (Seattle), 410
Skagit Valley College (Mount Vernon), 411
Spokane Falls Community College (Spokane), 412
Walla Walla Community College (Walla Walla), 413

**Wyoming**

Sheridan College (Sheridan), 424

## E-COMMERCE/ELECTRONIC COMMERCE

**Arizona**

Mohave Community College (Kingman), 52

**California**

Butte College (Oroville), 75
Cabrillo College (Aptos), 75
Foothill College (Los Altos Hills), 93
Fullerton College (Fullerton), 95
Los Angeles City College (Los Angeles), 107
MiraCosta College (Oceanside), 114
Saddleback College (Mission Viejo), 127
San Diego City College (San Diego), 128
Santa Rosa Junior College (Santa Rosa), 132

**Colorado**

Pueblo Community College (Pueblo), 151

**Illinois**

Danville Area Community College (Danville), 166
Illinois Central College (East Peoria), 172
Moraine Valley Community College (Palos Hills), 178

San Bernardino Valley College (San Bernardino), 128
San Diego City College (San Diego), 128

**Guam**
Guam Community College (Barrigada), 154

**Illinois**
Illinois Eastern Community Colleges, Frontier Community College (Fairfield), 172
Richland Community College (Decatur), 184

**Kansas**
Johnson County Community College (Overland Park), 203
Manhattan Area Technical College (Manhattan), 205
Pratt Community College (Pratt), 207

**Micronesia**
College of Micronesia–FSM (Kolonia Pohnpei), 239

**Minnesota**
Fond du Lac Tribal and Community College (Cloquet), 243
Minnesota West Community and Technical College (Pipestone), 248

**Nebraska**
Western Nebraska Community College (Sidney), 289

**Oklahoma**
Meridian Technology Center (Stillwater), 309

**Tennessee**
Tennessee Technology Center at Crump (Crump), 341
Tennessee Technology Center at Nashville (Nashville), 344

**Texas**
Coastal Bend College (Beeville), 357
Houston Community College System (Houston), 363
Lonestar College–North Harris (Houston), 369
Northeast Texas Community College (Mount Pleasant), 372
San Jacinto College Central Campus (Pasadena), 378

**Washington**
Clark College (Vancouver), 402
Spokane Community College (Spokane), 411

**Wisconsin**
Milwaukee Area Technical College (Milwaukee), 418
Moraine Park Technical College (Fond du Lac), 419

## ELECTRICAL AND POWER TRANSMISSION INSTALLERS, OTHER

**Arizona**
Cochise College (Douglas), 47

**California**
Center for Employment Training–Santa Maria (Santa Maria), 79
Center for Employment Training–Sobrato (San Jose), 79

**Colorado**
Emily Griffith Opportunity School (Denver), 146

**Louisiana**
Louisiana Technical College–West Jefferson Campus (Harvey), 235

**Minnesota**
Minnesota West Community and Technical College (Pipestone), 248

**Texas**
[illegible]stitute (Houston), 361

**Utah**
Salt Lake Community College (Salt Lake City), 396

## ELECTRICAL, ELECTRONIC AND COMMUNICATIONS ENGINEERING TECHNOLOGY/TECHNICIAN

**Arizona**
Cochise College (Douglas), 47
East Valley Institute of Technology (Mesa), 49
Mesa Community College (Mesa), 52
Northland Pioneer College (Holbrook), 53
Rio Salado College (Tempe), 55

**Arkansas**
Arkansas State University (State University), 59
Arkansas State University–Mountain Home (Mountain Home), 59
Arkansas Tech University (Russellville), 60
East Arkansas Community College (Forrest City), 62
North Arkansas College (Harrison), 64
Northwest Technical Institute (Springdale), 64
Remington College–Little Rock Campus (Little Rock), 65
Southern Arkansas University Tech (Camden), 66

**California**
Imperial Valley College (Imperial), 100

**Colorado**
Front Range Community College (Westminster), 147
Pueblo Community College (Pueblo), 151
San Juan Basin Area Vocational School (Cortez), 152

**Guam**
Guam Community College (Barrigada), 154

**Hawaii**
Kauai Community College (Lihue), 155

**Idaho**
Boise State University (Boise), 157
College of Southern Idaho (Twin Falls), 157
Eastern Idaho Technical College (Idaho Falls), 157
North Idaho College (Coeur d'Alene), 159

**Illinois**
College of Lake County (Grayslake), 165
East-West University (Chicago), 167
Heartland Community College (Normal), 171
Illinois Central College (East Peoria), 172
John A. Logan College (Carterville), 174
Kaskaskia College (Centralia), 175
Kishwaukee College (Malta), 175
Lincoln Land Community College (Springfield), 177
Moraine Valley Community College (Palos Hills), 178
Rend Lake College (Ina), 183
South Suburban College (South Holland), 187
Southwestern Illinois College (Belleville), 187
Spoon River College (Canton), 187
Taylor Business Institute (Chicago), 188
Waubonsee Community College (Sugar Grove), 189

**Iowa**
Hawkeye Community College (Waterloo), 192
Indian Hills Community College (Ottumwa), 192
Southeastern Community College, North Campus (West Burlington), 198
Western Iowa Tech Community College (Sioux City), 198

**Kentucky**
Daymar College (Paducah), 212

**Louisiana**
ITI Technical College (Baton Rouge), 226
Remington College–Baton Rouge Campus (Baton Rouge), 236
Remington College–Lafayette Campus (Lafayette), 237
Remington College–Shreveport (Shreveport), 237

**Minnesota**
Anoka Technical College (Anoka), 240
Dunwoody College of Technology (Minneapolis), 242
Hennepin Technical College (Brooklyn Park), 243
Lake Superior College (Duluth), 245
Minnesota State College–Southeast Technical (Winona), 248
Minnesota State Community and Technical College–Fergus Falls (Fergus Falls), 248
Northland Community and Technical College–Thief River Falls (Thief River Falls), 250
Rochester Community and Technical College (Rochester), 253
St. Cloud Technical College (St. Cloud), 254

**Mississippi**
Hinds Community College (Raymond), 259

**Missouri**
Moberly Area Community College (Moberly), 273
Ozarks Technical Community College (Springfield), 274
St. Louis Community College at Florissant Valley (St. Louis), 277
Three Rivers Community College (Poplar Bluff), 280

**Nebraska**
Central Community College–Grand Island Campus (Grand Island), 285
Metropolitan Community College (Omaha), 287
Mid-Plains Community College (North Platte), 287
Southeast Community College Area (Lincoln), 288

**Nevada**
College of Southern Nevada (North Las Vegas), 290
Truckee Meadows Community College (Reno), 292

**New Mexico**
Central New Mexico Community College (Albuquerque), 293
Clovis Community College (Clovis), 293
Doña Ana Branch Community College (Las Cruces), 294
Luna Community College (Las Vegas), 295
New Mexico State University–Alamogordo (Alamogordo), 295
New Mexico State University–Grants (Grants), 296
Northern New Mexico College (Española), 296
Western New Mexico University (Silver City), 298

**North Dakota**
Bismarck State College (Bismarck), 298

**Oregon**
Chemeketa Community College (Salem), 320
Clackamas Community College (Oregon City), 320
Columbia Gorge Community College (The Dalles), 321

## ELECTRICAL, ELECTRONICS AND COMMUNICATIONS ENGINEERING



## ELECTRICAL/ELECTRONICS DRAFTING AND ELECTRICAL/ELECTRONICS CAD/CADD



## ELECTRICAL/ELECTRONICS EQUIPMENT INSTALLATION AND REPAIR, GENERAL

Mississippi Gulf Coast Community College (Perkinston), 261

**Missouri**

Cape Girardeau Area Vocational Technical School (Cape Girardeau), 264
Columbia Area Vocational Technical School (Columbia), 265
Linn State Technical College (Linn), 270
St. Louis Community College at Florissant Valley (St. Louis), 277
Vatterott College (Kansas City), 281
Vatterott College (O'Fallon), 281
Vatterott College (St. Ann), 281
Vatterott College (St. Louis), 281

**Nebraska**

Central Community College–Grand Island Campus (Grand Island), 285
Metropolitan Community College (Omaha), 287
Mid-Plains Community College (North Platte), 287

**Nevada**

Great Basin College (Elko), 290

**New Mexico**

Central New Mexico Community College (Albuquerque), 293
Crownpoint Institute of Technology (Crownpoint), 293
Luna Community College (Las Vegas), 295
Northern New Mexico College (Española), 296
University of New Mexico–Gallup (Gallup), 297

**Oklahoma**

Canadian Valley Technology Center (El Reno), 303
Central Oklahoma Area Vocational Technical School (Drumright), 304
Eastern Oklahoma County Technology Center (Choctaw), 305
Gordon Cooper Technology Center (Shawnee), 306
Indian Capital Technology Center–Muskogee (Muskogee), 307
Kiamichi Area Vocational-Technical School–Poteau (Poteau), 309
Meridian Technology Center (Stillwater), 309
Metro Area Vocational Technical School District 22 (Oklahoma City), 310
Mid-America Technology Center (Wayne), 310
Mid-Del Technology Center (Midwest), 310
Moore Norman Technology Center (Norman), 311
Northeast Technology Center–Afton (Afton), 311
Northeast Technology Center–Kansas (Kansas), 312
Vatterott College (Oklahoma City), 318
Vatterott College (Tulsa), 318

**South Dakota**

Oglala Lakota College (Kyle), 329

**Tennessee**

Miller-Motte Technical College (Goodlettsville), 336
Nashville State Technical Community College (Nashville), 336
Northeast State Technical Community College (Blountville), 337
Southwest Tennessee Community College (Memphis), 339
Tennessee Technology Center at Athens (Athens), 340
Tennessee Technology Center at Jackson (Jackson), 342
Tennessee Technology Center at Knoxville (Knoxville), 342
Tennessee Technology Center at Morristown (Morristown), 343
Tennessee Technology Center at Ripley (Ripley), 345
Tennessee Technology Center at Whiteville (Whiteville), 345
Vatterott College (Memphis), 345

**Texas**

ATI Technical Training Center (Dallas), 352
Brazosport College (Lake Jackson), 353
Career Centers of Texas–El Paso (El Paso), 354
Coastal Bend College (Beeville), 357
El Paso Community College (El Paso), 360
Houston Community College System (Houston), 363
Laredo Community College (Laredo), 368
Lee College (Baytown), 368
North Lake College (Irving), 372
St. Philip's College (San Antonio), 377
San Antonio College of Medical and Dental Assistants–South (Mcallen), 378
South Texas College (McAllen), 381
Texarkana College (Texarkana), 384
Texas Careers–Lubbock (Lubbock), 384

**Utah**

Mountainland Applied Technology College (Orem), 395
Ogden-Weber Applied Technology Center (Ogden), 396
Uintah Basin Applied Technology Center (Roosevelt), 397

**Washington**

Bates Technical College (Tacoma), 400
Big Bend Community College (Moses Lake), 401
Lower Columbia College (Longview), 407
Perry Technical Institute (Yakima), 409
Spokane Community College (Spokane), 411
Walla Walla Community College (Walla Walla), 413

**Wisconsin**

Blackhawk Technical College (Janesville), 414
Chippewa Valley Technical College (Eau Claire), 415
Fox Valley Technical College (Appleton), 415
Gateway Technical College (Kenosha), 416
Mid-State Technical College (Wisconsin Rapids), 418
Milwaukee Area Technical College (Milwaukee), 418
Northeast Wisconsin Technical College (Green Bay), 420
Southwest Wisconsin Technical College (Fennimore), 421
Waukesha County Technical College (Pewaukee), 422

## ELECTROCARDIOGRAPH TECHNOLOGY/ TECHNICIAN

**California**

Cabrillo College (Aptos), 75
CSI Career College (Vacaville), 87
Cuesta College (San Luis Obispo), 87
Orange Coast College (Costa Mesa), 121

**Illinois**

College of DuPage (Glen Ellyn), 164
Joliet Junior College (Joliet), 174

**Oklahoma**

American Institute of Medical Technology (Tulsa), 302

**Texas**

Valley Grande Academy (Weslaco), 389

**Washington**

Edmonds Community College (Lynnwood), 403

## ELECTROLYSIS/ELECTROLOGY AND ELECTROLYSIS TECHNICIAN

**Arkansas**

Bee Jay's Academy (Little Rock), 61

**Utah**

Cameo College of Beauty Skin and Electrolysis (Salt Lake City), 392

## ELECTROMECHANICAL AND INSTRUMENTATION AND MAINTENANCE TECHNOLOGIES/TECHNICIANS, OTHER

**Arkansas**

University of Arkansas at Monticello (Monticello), 67

**Kansas**

American Institute of Baking (Manhattan), 199

**Kentucky**

Bowling Green Technical College (Bowling Green), 210

## ELECTROMECHANICAL TECHNOLOGY/ ELECTROMECHANICAL ENGINEERING TECHNOLOGY

**Arizona**

Mesa Community College (Mesa), 52
The Refrigeration School (Phoenix), 55

**Arkansas**

Northwest Technical Institute (Springdale), 64
University of Arkansas at Monticello (Monticello), 67

**California**

Chaffey College (Rancho Cucamonga), 81
Los Angeles Trade-Technical College (Los Angeles), 109
Skyline College (San Bruno), 133

**Illinois**

Black Hawk College (Moline), 160

**Kentucky**

Jefferson Community and Technical College (Louisville), 215
Maysville Community and Technical College (Maysville), 216

**Minnesota**

Ridgewater College (Willmar), 253

**New Mexico**

Eastern New Mexico University–Roswell (Roswell), 294
University of New Mexico–Los Alamos Branch (Los Alamos), 298

**Texas**

Amarillo College (Amarillo), 349
Angelina College (Lufkin), 351
Paris Junior College (Paris), 374
Texas State Technical College Harlingen (Harlingen), 386
Texas State Technical College West Texas (Sweetwater), 387

## ELECTRONEURODIAGNOSTIC/ ELECTROENCEPHALOGRAPHIC TECHNOLOGY/TECHNOLOGIST

**Arizona**

GateWay Community College (Phoenix), 50

**California**

Orange Coast College (Costa Mesa), 121

## Electroneurodiagnostic/Electroencephalographic Technology/Technologist



## ELEMENTARY EDUCATION AND TEACHING



## EMERGENCY CARE ATTENDANT (EMT AMBULANCE)



## EMERGENCY MEDICAL TECHNOLOGY/ TECHNICIAN (EMT PARAMEDIC)

**Wisconsin**
Southwest Wisconsin Technical College (Fennimore), 421

## ENGLISH LANGUAGE AND LITERATURE, GENERAL

**Illinois**
BIR Training Center (Chicago), 160
Zarem/Golde ORT Technical Institute (Chicago), 190

## ENTREPRENEURIAL AND SMALL BUSINESS OPERATIONS, OTHER

**Arizona**
Northland Pioneer College (Holbrook), 53
**Kansas**
Butler Community College (El Dorado), 201
**Minnesota**
American Indian OIC Incorporated (Minneapolis), 239
**North Dakota**
Turtle Mountain Community College (Belcourt), 301
**Oklahoma**
Moore Norman Technology Center (Norman), 311
**Washington**
Lake Washington Technical College (Kirkland), 406
North Seattle Community College (Seattle), 407

## ENTREPRENEURSHIP/ENTREPRENEURIAL STUDIES

**Alaska**
Alaska Pacific University (Anchorage), 41
University of Alaska Anchorage (Anchorage), 41
University of Alaska Southeast (Juneau), 42
**Arizona**
Eastern Arizona College (Thatcher), 48
Glendale Community College (Glendale), 50
Northern Arizona University (Flagstaff), 52
South Mountain Community College (Phoenix), 56
**Colorado**
Morgan Community College (Fort Morgan), 149
**Illinois**
College of DuPage (Glen Ellyn), 164
Elgin Community College (Elgin), 167
Joliet Junior College (Joliet), 174
Kaskaskia College (Centralia), 175
Lake Land College (Mattoon), 176
Parkland College (Champaign), 181
South Suburban College (South Holland), 187
**Iowa**
Grand View University (Des Moines), 192
North Iowa Area Community College (Mason City), 197
**Kansas**
Johnson County Community College (Overland Park), 203
Washburn University (Topeka), 208
**Louisiana**
Delgado Community College (New Orleans), 224
**Minnesota**
Dakota County Technical College (Rosemount), 242
Minnesota State Community and Technical College–Fergus Falls (Fergus Falls), 248
Vermilion Community College (Ely), 256
**Missouri**
St. Louis Community College at Florissant Valley (St. Louis), 277
St. Louis Community College at Forest Park (St. Louis), 278
St. Louis Community College at Meramec (Kirkwood), 278
**Montana**
Chief Dull Knife College (Lame Deer), 282
Flathead Valley Community College (Kalispell), 283
Montana State University–Great Falls College of Technology (Great Falls), 284
**North Dakota**
University of North Dakota (Grand Forks), 301
Williston State College (Williston), 301
**Oklahoma**
Tulsa Tech–Career Services Center (Tulsa), 317
**Oregon**
Mt. Hood Community College (Gresham), 323
**South Dakota**
Oglala Lakota College (Kyle), 329
South Dakota State University (Brookings), 330
**Tennessee**
Nashville State Technical Community College (Nashville), 336
**Texas**
Kilgore College (Kilgore), 367
**Washington**
Edmonds Community College (Lynnwood), 403
Everett Community College (Everett), 404
Lower Columbia College (Longview), 407
Skagit Valley College (Mount Vernon), 411
Spokane Community College (Spokane), 411

## ENVIRONMENTAL CONTROL TECHNOLOGIES/TECHNICIANS, OTHER

**Alaska**
University of Alaska Southeast (Juneau), 42
**Arizona**
Paradise Valley Community College (Phoenix), 53
**Nevada**
Truckee Meadows Community College (Reno), 292
**New Mexico**
New Mexico Junior College (Hobbs), 295
Southwestern Indian Polytechnic Institute (Albuquerque), 297
**Wisconsin**
Moraine Park Technical College (Fond du Lac), 419

## ENVIRONMENTAL ENGINEERING TECHNOLOGY/ENVIRONMENTAL TECHNOLOGY

**Arizona**
Pima Community College (Tucson), 54
**Arkansas**
NorthWest Arkansas Community College (Bentonville), 64
**Illinois**
City Colleges of Chicago, Wilbur Wright College (Chicago), 164
**Iowa**
Muscatine Community College (Muscatine), 196
**Kentucky**
Bluegrass Community and Technical College (Lexington), 210
**Missouri**
Metropolitan Community College–Business & Technology Campus (Kansas City), 271
Three Rivers Community College (Poplar Bluff), 280
**Oregon**
Mt. Hood Community College (Gresham), 323
**Texas**
Angelina College (Lufkin), 351
Austin Community College (Austin), 352
El Paso Community College (El Paso), 360
Panola College (Carthage), 374
**Washington**
Renton Technical College (Renton), 410

## ENVIRONMENTAL/ENVIRONMENTAL HEALTH ENGINEERING

**California**
East San Gabriel Valley Regional Occupational Program & Technical Center (West Covina), 90

## ENVIRONMENTAL SCIENCE

**California**
De Anza College (Cupertino), 88
**New Mexico**
Crownpoint Institute of Technology (Crownpoint), 293

## ENVIRONMENTAL STUDIES

**California**
Sacramento City College (Sacramento), 126
**Minnesota**
Central Lakes College (Brainerd), 241
**Nebraska**
Creighton University (Omaha), 286

## EQUESTRIAN/EQUINE STUDIES

**Arizona**
Cochise College (Douglas), 47
Scottsdale Community College (Scottsdale), 56
**California**
College of the Sequoias (Visalia), 85
Feather River College (Quincy), 93
Los Angeles Pierce College (Woodland Hills), 108
Mt. San Antonio College (Walnut), 116
Shasta College (Redding), 133
**Idaho**
College of Southern Idaho (Twin Falls), 157
**Kansas**
Dodge City Community College (Dodge City), 202
**Kentucky**
Bluegrass Community and Technical College (Lexington), 210
**North Dakota**
North Dakota State University (Fargo), 300
**Oklahoma**
Connors State College (Warner), 305
Mid-America Technology Center (Wayne), 310
**Texas**
North Central Texas College (Gainesville), 371
Sul Ross State University (Alpine), 383
**Wyoming**
Central Wyoming College (Riverton), 423
Northwest College (Powell), 424

## Fire Protection and Safety Technology/Technician

**California**
Casa Loma College–Van Nuys (Van Nuys), 78

**Colorado**
Red Rocks Community College (Lakewood), 151
San Juan Basin Area Vocational School (Cortez), 152

**Illinois**
College of DuPage (Glen Ellyn), 164
Lincoln Land Community College (Springfield), 177
Rock Valley College (Rockford), 184

**Iowa**
Des Moines Area Community College (Ankeny), 191
Kirkwood Community College (Cedar Rapids), 195

**Kansas**
Kansas City Kansas Community College (Kansas City), 204

**Louisiana**
Delgado Community College (New Orleans), 224

**Minnesota**
Hennepin Technical College (Brooklyn Park), 243

**Missouri**
Jefferson College (Hillsboro), 269
Metropolitan Community College–Blue River (Independence), 271
St. Louis Community College at Florissant Valley (St. Louis), 277

**Nevada**
Truckee Meadows Community College (Reno), 292

**Oklahoma**
Eastern Oklahoma County Technology Center (Choctaw), 305

**Oregon**
Rogue Community College (Grants Pass), 326
Treasure Valley Community College (Ontario), 327

**Texas**
Central Texas College (Killeen), 355
Cisco College (Cisco), 356
College of the Mainland (Texas City), 357
Collin County Community College District (Plano), 357
Del Mar College (Corpus Christi), 359
El Paso Community College (El Paso), 360
Houston Community College System (Houston), 363
Laredo Community College (Laredo), 368
San Antonio College (San Antonio), 377
Tarrant County College District (Fort Worth), 383
Tyler Junior College (Tyler), 388

## FIRE PROTECTION, OTHER

**Arizona**
East Valley Institute of Technology (Mesa), 49

**Louisiana**
Louisiana State University at Eunice (Eunice), 227

**Oklahoma**
Eastern Oklahoma County Technology Center (Choctaw), 305

**Washington**
Clover Park Technical College (Lakewood), 402

## FIRE SCIENCE/FIREFIGHTING

**Alaska**
University of Alaska Fairbanks (Fairbanks), 42

**Arizona**
Arizona Western College (Yuma), 44
Cochise College (Douglas), 47
Coconino Community College (Flagstaff), 48
Eastern Arizona College (Thatcher), 48
Glendale Community College (Glendale), 50
Mesa Community College (Mesa), 52
Mohave Community College (Kingman), 52
Northland Pioneer College (Holbrook), 53
Paradise Valley Community College (Phoenix), 53
Phoenix College (Phoenix), 53
Pima Community College (Tucson), 54
Rio Salado College (Tempe), 55
Scottsdale Community College (Scottsdale), 56
Yavapai College (Prescott), 58

**Arkansas**
Southern Arkansas University Tech (Camden), 66

**California**
Allan Hancock College (Santa Maria), 70
American River College (Sacramento), 72
Antelope Valley College (Lancaster), 72
Bakersfield College (Bakersfield), 74
Butte College (Oroville), 75
Cabrillo College (Aptos), 75
Chabot College (Hayward), 81
Chaffey College (Rancho Cucamonga), 81
City College of San Francisco (San Francisco), 82
College of San Mateo (San Mateo), 84
College of the Canyons (Santa Clarita), 84
College of the Desert (Palm Desert), 84
College of the Sequoias (Visalia), 85
College of the Siskiyous (Weed), 85
Columbia College (Sonora), 85
Cosumnes River College (Sacramento), 87
Crafton Hills College (Yucaipa), 87
East Los Angeles College (Monterey Park), 89
El Camino College (Torrance), 90
Fresno City College (Fresno), 94
Glendale Community College (Glendale), 95
Imperial Valley College (Imperial), 100
Lake Tahoe Community College (South Lake Tahoe), 105
Las Positas College (Livermore), 105
Long Beach City College (Long Beach), 106
Los Angeles Valley College (Van Nuys), 109
Los Medanos College (Pittsburg), 109
Merced College (Merced), 113
Modesto Junior College (Modesto), 115
Monterey Peninsula College (Monterey), 116
Mt. San Antonio College (Walnut), 116
Oxnard College (Oxnard), 121
Palomar College (San Marcos), 122
Palo Verde College (Blythe), 123
Pasadena City College (Pasadena), 123
Rio Hondo College (Whittier), 125
Riverside Community College District (Riverside), 126
San Diego Miramar College (San Diego), 129
San Joaquin Delta College (Stockton), 129
Santa Ana College (Santa Ana), 131
Santa Rosa Junior College (Santa Rosa), 132
Sierra College (Rocklin), 133
Solano Community College (Suisun City), 134
Southwestern College (Chula Vista), 134
Yuba College (Marysville), 142

**Colorado**
Aims Community College (Greeley), 143
Community College of Aurora (Aurora), 146
Pikes Peak Community College (Colorado Springs), 150
Pueblo Community College (Pueblo), 151

**Guam**
Guam Community College (Barrigada), 154

**Hawaii**
Honolulu Community College (Honolulu), 155

**Illinois**
Elgin Community College (Elgin), 167
Illinois Eastern Community Colleges, Frontier Community College (Fairfield), 172
Joliet Junior College (Joliet), 174
Lewis and Clark Community College (Godfrey), 176
Lincoln Land Community College (Springfield), 177
McHenry County College (Crystal Lake), 178
Oakton Community College (Des Plaines), 180
Prairie State College (Chicago Heights), 182
Richland Community College (Decatur), 184
Rock Valley College (Rockford), 184
Southwestern Illinois College (Belleville), 187
Triton College (River Grove), 188
Waubonsee Community College (Sugar Grove), 189

**Iowa**
Kirkwood Community College (Cedar Rapids), 195

**Kansas**
Butler Community College (El Dorado), 201
Dodge City Community College (Dodge City), 202
Garden City Community College (Garden City), 202

**Kentucky**
Bluegrass Community and Technical College (Lexington), 210
Elizabethtown Community and Technical College (Elizabethtown), 213
Hazard Community and Technical College (Hazard), 214
West Kentucky Community and Technical College (Paducah), 220

**Louisiana**
Louisiana State University at Eunice (Eunice), 227

**Minnesota**
Hennepin Technical College (Brooklyn Park), 243
Minnesota State Community and Technical College–Fergus Falls (Fergus Falls), 248
Northland Community and Technical College–Thief River Falls (Thief River Falls), 250

**Missouri**
East Central College (Union), 266
Rolla Technical Institute (Rolla), 277
St. Louis Community College at Forest Park (St. Louis), 278

**Nevada**
College of Southern Nevada (North Las Vegas), 290

**New Mexico**
San Juan College (Farmington), 296

**Northern Mariana Islands**
Northern Marianas College (Saipan), 302

**Oklahoma**
Autry Technology Center (Enid), 302
Eastern Oklahoma County Technology Center (Choctaw), 305
Oklahoma State University, Oklahoma City (Oklahoma City), 313

## FIRE SERVICES ADMINISTRATION



## FISHING AND FISHERIES SCIENCES AND MANAGEMENT



## FLORICULTURE/FLORISTRY OPERATIONS AND MANAGEMENT



## FOOD PREPARATION/PROFESSIONAL COOKING/KITCHEN ASSISTANT



## FOOD SCIENCE



## FOODSERVICE SYSTEMS ADMINISTRATION/MANAGEMENT

Merritt College (Oakland), 114
Mission College (Santa Clara), 115
Orange Coast College (Costa Mesa), 121
San Diego Mesa College (San Diego), 128
Santa Rosa Junior College (Santa Rosa), 132

**Illinois**
City Colleges of Chicago, Harold Washington College (Chicago), 163

**Kansas**
Flint Hills Technical College (Emporia), 202

**New Mexico**
Central New Mexico Community College (Albuquerque), 293

**Oklahoma**
Autry Technology Center (Enid), 302
Carl Albert State College (Poteau), 304

**Tennessee**
Southwest Tennessee Community College (Memphis), 339

**Texas**
Tarrant County College District (Fort Worth), 383

**Wisconsin**
Milwaukee Area Technical College (Milwaukee), 418

## FOOD SERVICE, WAITER/WAITRESS, AND DINING ROOM MANAGEMENT/MANAGER

**Illinois**
College of Lake County (Grayslake), 165
Harper College (Palatine), 170
Illinois Central College (East Peoria), 172
Illinois Eastern Community Colleges, Lincoln Trail College (Robinson), 172
Illinois Valley Community College (Oglesby), 173
Kaskaskia College (Centralia), 175
Lake Land College (Mattoon), 176
Rend Lake College (Ina), 183
Richland Community College (Decatur), 184
Southeastern Illinois College (Harrisburg), 186

**Iowa**
Iowa Western Community College (Council Bluffs), 194

**Texas**
Del Mar College (Corpus Christi), 359

## FOODS, NUTRITION, AND RELATED SERVICES, OTHER

**Wisconsin**
Milwaukee Area Technical College (Milwaukee), 418

## FOODS, NUTRITION, AND WELLNESS STUDIES, GENERAL

**Arizona**
Central Arizona College (Coolidge), 47
Glendale Community College (Glendale), 50
Mesa Community College (Mesa), 52

**California**
Chaffey College (Rancho Cucamonga), 81
Fresno City College (Fresno), 94
Mt. San Antonio College (Walnut), 116
Orange Coast College (Costa Mesa), 121
Saddleback College (Mission Viejo), 127
San Diego Mesa College (San Diego), 128

**Louisiana**
Bossier Parish Community College (Bossier City), 223

**New Mexico**
Santa Fe Community College (Santa Fe), 297

## FOREIGN LANGUAGES AND LITERATURES, GENERAL

**Kansas**
Independence Community College (Independence), 203

**Oklahoma**
Oklahoma City Community College (Oklahoma City), 312

**Wyoming**
Western Wyoming Community College (Rock Springs), 424

## FOREIGN LANGUAGES, LITERATURES, AND LINGUISTICS, OTHER

**Alaska**
University of Alaska Fairbanks (Fairbanks), 42

**Arizona**
Pima Community College (Tucson), 54

**California**
College of San Mateo (San Mateo), 84

**Washington**
Bellevue College (Bellevue), 400

## FORENSIC SCIENCE AND TECHNOLOGY

**Arizona**
Coconino Community College (Flagstaff), 48
Mesa Community College (Mesa), 52
Phoenix College (Phoenix), 53
Pima Community College (Tucson), 54
Scottsdale Community College (Scottsdale), 56

**Arkansas**
Arkansas State University–Mountain Home (Mountain Home), 59
NorthWest Arkansas Community College (Bentonville), 64
Southeast Arkansas College (Pine Bluff), 66
University of Arkansas Community College at Morrilton (Morrilton), 68

**California**
City College of San Francisco (San Francisco), 82
Diablo Valley College (Pleasant Hill), 89
Grossmont College (El Cajon), 96
Long Beach City College (Long Beach), 106
Los Angeles City College (Los Angeles), 107
Riverside Community College District (Riverside), 126
San Diego Miramar College (San Diego), 129

**Hawaii**
Hawai'i Pacific University (Honolulu), 154

**Illinois**
Illinois Central College (East Peoria), 172
Illinois Valley Community College (Oglesby), 173

**Louisiana**
Louisiana State University at Eunice (Eunice), 227

**Washington**
Centralia College (Centralia), 401
Green River Community College (Auburn), 405
Pierce College at Fort Steilacoom (Lakewood), 409

## FOREST MANAGEMENT/FOREST RESOURCES MANAGEMENT

**Minnesota**
Itasca Community College (Grand Rapids), 245

## FOREST RESOURCES PRODUCTION AND MANAGEMENT

**Minnesota**
Vermilion Community College (Ely), 256

## FORESTRY, GENERAL

**California**
Bakersfield College (Bakersfield), 74
Citrus College (Glendora), 82
Columbia College (Sonora), 85
Modesto Junior College (Modesto), 115
Reedley College (Reedley), 125

**Oregon**
Chemeketa Community College (Salem), 320

## FORESTRY, OTHER

**Hawaii**
Hawaii Community College (Hilo), 154

## FORESTRY TECHNOLOGY/TECHNICIAN

**Illinois**
College of Lake County (Grayslake), 165
Harper College (Palatine), 170

**Louisiana**
Louisiana Technical College–Oakdale Campus (Oakdale), 233

**Minnesota**
Northwest Technical College (Bemidji), 250

**Oregon**
Mt. Hood Community College (Gresham), 323

## FRENCH LANGUAGE AND LITERATURE

**California**
City College of San Francisco (San Francisco), 82
College of San Mateo (San Mateo), 84
Diablo Valley College (Pleasant Hill), 89
Foothill College (Los Altos Hills), 93
Grossmont College (El Cajon), 96
Palomar College (San Marcos), 122
West Valley College (Saratoga), 141

## FUNERAL DIRECTION/SERVICE

**Missouri**
St. Louis Community College at Forest Park (St. Louis), 278

**Texas**
San Antonio College (San Antonio), 377

## FUNERAL SERVICE AND MORTUARY SCIENCE, GENERAL

**Illinois**
Worsham College of Mortuary Science (Wheeling), 190

**Iowa**
Des Moines Area Community College (Ankeny), 191

**Oregon**
Mt. Hood Community College (Gresham), 323

**Tennessee**
John A. Gupton College (Nashville), 334

**Texas**
Amarillo College (Amarillo), 349
Commonwealth Institute of Funeral Service (Houston), 357
Dallas Institute of Funeral Service (Dallas), 359

## FURNITURE DESIGN AND MANUFACTURING

**New Mexico**
Northern New Mexico College (Española), 296

Southern Careers Institute (Corpus Christi), 380
Southern Careers Institute (Pharr), 380
Southern Careers Institute (San Antonio), 380
South Texas Vo-Tech Institute (Weslaco), 381
Southwest School of Business and Technical Careers (Eagle Pass), 382
Southwest School of Business and Technical Careers (San Antonio), 382
Texarkana College (Texarkana), 384
Texas Southmost College (Brownsville), 386
Vernon College (Vernon), 389
Victoria College (Victoria), 390
Weatherford College (Weatherford), 390

**Utah**
Salt Lake Community College (Salt Lake City), 396

**Washington**
Bellevue College (Bellevue), 400
Bellingham Technical College (Bellingham), 400
Big Bend Community College (Moses Lake), 401
Cascadia Community College (Bothell), 401
Clark College (Vancouver), 402
Clover Park Technical College (Lakewood), 402
Edmonds Community College (Lynnwood), 403
Everett Community College (Everett), 404
Grays Harbor College (Aberdeen), 405
Green River Community College (Auburn), 405
Highline Community College (Des Moines), 405
Lake Washington Technical College (Kirkland), 406
Lower Columbia College (Longview), 407
Peninsula College (Port Angeles), 408
Pierce College at Fort Steilacoom (Lakewood), 409
Pierce College (Puyallup), 409
Seattle Vocational Institute (Seattle), 410
Skagit Valley College (Mount Vernon), 411
Spokane Community College (Spokane), 411
Spokane Falls Community College (Spokane), 412
Tacoma Community College (Tacoma), 412
Walla Walla Community College (Walla Walla), 413
Wenatchee Valley College (Wenatchee), 413
Yakima Valley Community College (Yakima), 414

**Wisconsin**
Chippewa Valley Technical College (Eau Claire), 415
Fox Valley Technical College (Appleton), 415
Gateway Technical College (Kenosha), 416
Lakeshore Technical College (Cleveland), 417
Milwaukee Area Technical College (Milwaukee), 418
Moraine Park Technical College (Fond du Lac), 419
Nicolet Area Technical College (Rhinelander), 419
Northcentral Technical College (Wausau), 419
Northeast Wisconsin Technical College (Green Bay), 420
Southwest Wisconsin Technical College (Fennimore), 421
Waukesha County Technical College (Pewaukee), 422
Western Technical College (La Crosse), 422

**Wyoming**
Eastern Wyoming College (Torrington), 423
Northwest College (Powell), 424
Western Wyoming Community College (Rock Springs), 424

## GEOGRAPHY

**Arizona**
Mesa Community College (Mesa), 52

**California**
Foothill College (Los Altos Hills), 93
Los Angeles Trade-Technical College (Los Angeles), 109
Rio Hondo College (Whittier), 125

**Illinois**
Roosevelt University (Chicago), 185

**Utah**
Weber State University (Ogden), 399

## GEOGRAPHY, OTHER

**California**
American River College (Sacramento), 72
Antelope Valley College (Lancaster), 72
City College of San Francisco (San Francisco), 82
Columbia College (Sonora), 85
Cosumnes River College (Sacramento), 87
Diablo Valley College (Pleasant Hill), 89
Foothill College (Los Altos Hills), 93
Los Angeles Pierce College (Woodland Hills), 108
Los Angeles Trade-Technical College (Los Angeles), 109
Mt. San Jacinto College (San Jacinto), 117
Palomar College (San Marcos), 122
San Diego Mesa College (San Diego), 128
Southwestern College (Chula Vista), 134
West Valley College (Saratoga), 141

**Colorado**
Colorado Northwestern Community College (Rangely), 145

**Illinois**
Illinois Central College (East Peoria), 172

**Missouri**
Metropolitan Community College–Longview (Lee's Summit), 271

**New Mexico**
Crownpoint Institute of Technology (Crownpoint), 293

**South Dakota**
South Dakota State University (Brookings), 330

**Utah**
Southern Utah University (Cedar City), 397

**Washington**
Everett Community College (Everett), 404
Green River Community College (Auburn), 405
Skagit Valley College (Mount Vernon), 411

**Wyoming**
Casper College (Casper), 423

## GEOLOGY/EARTH SCIENCE, GENERAL

**California**
Ohlone College (Fremont), 120

## GEOTECHNICAL ENGINEERING

**Alaska**
University of Alaska Anchorage (Anchorage), 41

## GERMAN LANGUAGE AND LITERATURE

**California**
City College of San Francisco (San Francisco), 82
College of San Mateo (San Mateo), 84
Diablo Valley College (Pleasant Hill), 89
Grossmont College (El Cajon), 96

## GLAZIER

**Colorado**
Emily Griffith Opportunity School (Denver), 146

**Illinois**
Parkland College (Champaign), 181

**Wisconsin**
Milwaukee Area Technical College (Milwaukee), 418

## GRAPHIC AND PRINTING EQUIPMENT OPERATOR, GENERAL PRODUCTION

**Arkansas**
Phillips Community College of the University of Arkansas (Helena), 65

**Idaho**
Idaho State University (Pocatello), 158
Lewis-Clark State College (Lewiston), 158

**Illinois**
Harper College (Palatine), 170
Kaskaskia College (Centralia), 175
Lake Land College (Mattoon), 176
Rock Valley College (Rockford), 184

**Kansas**
Flint Hills Technical College (Emporia), 202
Fort Scott Community College (Fort Scott), 202
Kaw Area Technical School (Topeka), 204

**Minnesota**
Hennepin Technical College (Brooklyn Park), 243
South Central College (North Mankato), 255

**Mississippi**
Hinds Community College (Raymond), 259

**Missouri**
Eldon Career Center (Eldon), 266
Franklin Technology Center (Joplin), 267
Kirksville Area Vocational Technical School (Kirksville), 269
Lake Career and Technical Center (Camdenton), 269
Mineral Area College (Park Hills), 272
Nichols Career Center (Jefferson City), 274
Sikeston Career and Technology Center (Sikeston), 279
Waynesville Technical Academy (Waynesville), 282

**New Mexico**
Southwestern Indian Polytechnic Institute (Albuquerque), 297

**Oklahoma**
Autry Technology Center (Enid), 302
Caddo-Kiowa Area Vocational Technical School (Ft. Cobb), 303
Canadian Valley Technology Center (El Reno), 303
Eastern Oklahoma County Technology Center (Choctaw), 305
Francis Tuttle Area Vocational Technical Center (Oklahoma City), 306
Great Plains Technology Center (Lawton), 306
Mid-Del Technology Center (Midwest), 310
Tulsa Tech–Career Services Center (Tulsa), 317

**Oregon**
Mt. Hood Community College (Gresham), 323

**Tennessee**
Tennessee Technology Center at Memphis (Memphis), 343
Tennessee Technology Center at Morristown (Morristown), 343

Louisiana Technical College–Morgan Smith Campus (Jennings), 232
Louisiana Technical College–North Central Campus (Farmerville), 232
Louisiana Technical College–River Parishes Campus (Reserve), 233
Louisiana Technical College–Shelby M. Jackson Campus (Ferriday), 233
Louisiana Technical College–Shreveport-Bossier Campus (Shreveport), 234
Louisiana Technical College–Sullivan Campus (Bogalusa), 234
Louisiana Technical College–Teche Area Campus (New Iberia), 234
Louisiana Technical College–T.H. Harris Campus (Opelousas), 234
Louisiana Technical College–West Jefferson Campus (Harvey), 235
Louisiana Technical College–Young Memorial Campus (Morgan City), 235

**Minnesota**
Ridgewater College (Willmar), 253
St. Cloud Technical College (St. Cloud), 254

**Missouri**
Grand River Technical School (Chillicothe), 267
Hannibal Career and Technical Center (Hannibal), 268
Jefferson College (Hillsboro), 269
Lake Career and Technical Center (Camdenton), 269
Waynesville Technical Academy (Waynesville), 282

**New Mexico**
Doña Ana Branch Community College (Las Cruces), 294

**Oklahoma**
Canadian Valley Technology Center (El Reno), 303
Green Country Technology Center (Okmulgee), 307
High Plains Institute of Technology (Woodward), 307
Tulsa Community College (Tulsa), 317

## HEALTH AIDES/ATTENDANTS/ORDERLIES, OTHER

**Kansas**
Cloud County Community College (Concordia), 201
Colby Community College (Colby), 201
Fort Scott Community College (Fort Scott), 202
Garden City Community College (Garden City), 202

**Tennessee**
Tennessee Technology Center at Elizabethton (Elizabethton), 341

**Washington**
Edmonds Community College (Lynnwood), 403
Shoreline Community College (Shoreline), 410
Spokane Falls Community College (Spokane), 412

## HEALTH AND MEDICAL ADMINISTRATIVE SERVICES, OTHER

**Alaska**
University of Alaska Fairbanks (Fairbanks), 42

**Arizona**
GateWay Community College (Phoenix), 50
Phoenix College (Phoenix), 53
Pima Community College (Tucson), 54

**California**
Adelante Career Institute (Van Nuys), 69
American Career College (Anaheim), 71
American Career College (Los Angeles), 71
American Career College (Norco), 71
Antelope Valley Medical College (Lancaster), 72
Center for Employment Training–Salinas (Salinas), 79
Concorde Career College (Garden Grove), 86
Concorde Career Institute (North Hollywood), 86
Concorde Career Institute (San Diego), 86
Everest College (Alhambra), 91
Kaplan College–Modesto Campus (Salida), 103
Kaplan College–Stockton Campus (Stockton), 104
Sacramento City Unified School District–Skills and Business Education Center (Sacramento), 126
Skyline College (San Bruno), 133
Westech College (Pomona), 139
Western Career College (Sacramento), 140

**Colorado**
Concorde Career Institute (Denver), 146

**Kentucky**
National College (Lexington), 217
Southwestern College of Business (Florence), 219

**Louisiana**
Delta College of Arts and Technology (Covington), 225
Medical Training College (Baton Rouge), 235
Unitech Training Academy (Lafayette), 238
Unitech Training Academy–Houma (Houma), 238
Unitech Training Academy–West Monroe Campus (West Monroe), 238

**Minnesota**
Everest Institute (Eagan), 243
Herzing College (Minneapolis), 244

**Missouri**
Concorde Career Institute (Kansas City), 265

**Nebraska**
Northeast Community College (Norfolk), 288

**Oklahoma**
Pioneer Area Vocational Technical School (Ponca City), 313

**Oregon**
Concorde Career Institute (Portland), 321

**Tennessee**
National College (Nashville), 336
Southwest Tennessee Community College (Memphis), 339

**Texas**
Arlington Career Institute (Grand Prairie), 351
Everest Institute (Austin), 361
Western Technical College (El Paso), 390

**Utah**
Salt Lake Community College (Salt Lake City), 396

**Washington**
Clover Park Technical College (Lakewood), 402
Renton Technical College (Renton), 410

**Wisconsin**
Moraine Park Technical College (Fond du Lac), 419

## HEALTH AND PHYSICAL EDUCATION/ FITNESS, OTHER

**Arizona**
Cortiva Institute—School of Massage Therapy (Scottsdale), 48
Phoenix College (Phoenix), 53
Pima Community College (Tucson), 54

**Arkansas**
Bryan College (Rogers), 61

**California**
Santa Barbara Business College (Ventura), 131

**Colorado**
Emily Griffith Opportunity School (Denver), 146
Heritage College (Denver), 148

**Kansas**
Neosho County Community College (Chanute), 205
Pinnacle Career Institute (Lawrence), 206

**Minnesota**
Minnesota School of Business–Plymouth (Minneapolis), 247
Minnesota School of Business–Richfield (Richfield), 247
Minnesota School of Business–Rochester (Rochester), 247
Minnesota School of Business–St. Cloud (Waite Park), 247

**Missouri**
Bryan College (Springfield), 264
Heritage College (Kansas City), 268
Massage Therapy Training Institute (Kansas City), 270

**Nebraska**
Nebraska Methodist College (Omaha), 288

**Oklahoma**
Heritage College of Hair Design (Oklahoma City), 307

## HEALTH AND PHYSICAL EDUCATION, GENERAL

**California**
Contra Costa College (San Pablo), 86
De Anza College (Cupertino), 88
Foothill College (Los Altos Hills), 93
Grossmont College (El Cajon), 96
Los Angeles Southwest College (Los Angeles), 109
MiraCosta College (Oceanside), 114
Mt. San Antonio College (Walnut), 116
Santa Ana College (Santa Ana), 131
West Valley College (Saratoga), 141

**Colorado**
Arapahoe Community College (Littleton), 143
Heritage College (Denver), 148

**Illinois**
McHenry County College (Crystal Lake), 178
Prairie State College (Chicago Heights), 182

**Kansas**
Independence Community College (Independence), 203

**Minnesota**
Alexandria Technical College (Alexandria), 239
Northland Community and Technical College–Thief River Falls (Thief River Falls), 250
Rainy River Community College (International Falls), 251

**New Mexico**
Central New Mexico Community College (Albuquerque), 293
Santa Fe Community College (Santa Fe), 297

**Oregon**
Portland Community College (Portland), 326
Southwestern Oregon Community College (Coos Bay), 327

## HEALTH/HEALTH-CARE ADMINISTRATION/ MANAGEMENT



## HEALTH INFORMATION/MEDICAL RECORDS ADMINISTRATION/ADMINISTRATOR



## HEALTH INFORMATION/MEDICAL RECORDS TECHNOLOGY/TECHNICIAN

University of New Mexico–Gallup (Gallup), 297

**North Dakota**
North Dakota State College of Science (Wahpeton), 300
Williston State College (Williston), 301

**Oklahoma**
Career Point Institute (Tulsa), 303
Great Plains Technology Center (Lawton), 306
Rose State College (Midwest City), 315
Tulsa Tech–Peoria Campus (Tulsa), 317
Wes Watkins Area Vocational-Technical Center (Wetumka), 318

**Oregon**
Central Oregon Community College (Bend), 320
Chemeketa Community College (Salem), 320
Lane Community College (Eugene), 322

**Tennessee**
Chattanooga College–Medical, Dental and Technical Careers (Chattanooga), 331
Draughons Junior College (Nashville), 333
Dyersburg State Community College (Dyersburg), 333
MedVance Institute (Cookeville), 335
MedVance Institute–Nashville (Nashville), 335
Walters State Community College (Morristown), 346

**Texas**
Amarillo College (Amarillo), 349
American Commercial College (Abilene), 350
Anamarc Educational Institute (El Paso), 351
Career Centers of Texas–El Paso (El Paso), 354
Career Quest (San Antonio), 355
CCI Training Center (Arlington), 355
Central Texas College (Killeen), 355
Coastal Bend College (Beeville), 357
Del Mar College (Corpus Christi), 359
Houston Community College System (Houston), 363
Howard College (Big Spring), 364
International Business College (El Paso), 366
Lonestar College–North Harris (Houston), 369
McLennan Community College (Waco), 369
MedVance Institute (Houston), 370
St. Philip's College (San Antonio), 377
San Jacinto College Central Campus (Pasadena), 378
South Plains College (Levelland), 381
South Texas College (McAllen), 381
Southwest Career Institute (El Paso), 382
Texas State Technical College West Texas (Sweetwater), 387
Tyler Junior College (Tyler), 388
Vernon College (Vernon), 389
Western Technical College (El Paso), 391

**Utah**
Salt Lake Community College (Salt Lake City), 396

**Washington**
Bellevue College (Bellevue), 400
Clark College (Vancouver), 402
Edmonds Community College (Lynnwood), 403
Grays Harbor College (Aberdeen), 405
North Seattle Community College (Seattle), 407
Skagit Valley College (Mount Vernon), 411
Tacoma Community College (Tacoma), 412

**Wisconsin**
Moraine Park Technical College (Fond du Lac), 419
Western Technical College (La Crosse), 422

## HEALTH/MEDICAL CLAIMS EXAMINER

**California**
Four-D Success Academy (Colton), 94
Ladera Career Paths Training Centers (Los Angeles), 104

## HEALTH/MEDICAL PHYSICS

**Kentucky**
West Kentucky Community and Technical College (Paducah), 220

**Texas**
The University of Texas Anderson Cancer Center (Houston), 389

## HEALTH/MEDICAL PREPARATORY PROGRAMS, OTHER

**California**
Bakersfield College (Bakersfield), 74

**Illinois**
Northwestern University (Evanston), 180

**Louisiana**
Cameron College (New Orleans), 223

**Montana**
Fort Peck Community College (Poplar), 283

**Nebraska**
Creighton University (Omaha), 286

## HEALTH PROFESSIONS AND RELATED CLINICAL SCIENCES, OTHER

**Arizona**
Paradise Valley Community College (Phoenix), 53

**California**
Career Networks Institute (Costa Mesa), 78
Charles R. Drew University of Medicine and Science (Los Angeles), 81
Citrus College (Glendora), 82
City College of San Francisco (San Francisco), 82
Cuesta College (San Luis Obispo), 87
MTI College of Business & Technology (Sacramento), 117
National Holistic Institute (Emeryville), 118
San Jose City College (San Jose), 130
Western Career College (Sacramento), 140

**Colorado**
Red Rocks Community College (Lakewood), 151
San Juan Basin Area Vocational School (Cortez), 152

**Idaho**
College of Southern Idaho (Twin Falls), 157

**Illinois**
Southeastern Illinois College (Harrisburg), 186

**Iowa**
Capri College (Cedar Rapids), 190
Capri College (Davenport), 190
Capri College (Dubuque), 191

**Kansas**
Flint Hills Technical College (Emporia), 202
Independence Community College (Independence), 203

**Missouri**
North Central Missouri College (Trenton), 274

**Oklahoma**
Central Oklahoma Area Vocational Technical School (Drumright), 304
Chisholm Trail Area Vocational Technical Center (Omega), 304
Gordon Cooper Technology Center (Shawnee), 306
Indian Capital Technology Center–Sallisaw (Sallisaw), 307
Indian Capital Technology Center–Stilwell (Stilwell), 308
Kiamichi Area Vocational-Technical School–Talihina (Talihina), 309
Meridian Technology Center (Stillwater), 309
Mid-Del Technology Center (Midwest), 310
Northeast Area Vocational Technical School (Pryor), 311
Northeast Technology Center–Kansas (Kansas), 312
Red River Area Vocational-Technical School (Duncan), 315
Southwest Area Vocational Technical Center (Altus), 316
Western Technology Center (Burns Flat), 318
Wes Watkins Area Vocational-Technical Center (Wetumka), 318

**Oregon**
Klamath Community College (Klamath Falls), 322

**Tennessee**
MedVance Institute–Nashville (Nashville), 335
Miller-Motte Technical College (Chattanooga), 335

**Texas**
MedVance Institute (Houston), 370
Valley Grande Academy (Weslaco), 389

**Washington**
Edmonds Community College (Lynnwood), 403

## HEALTH SERVICES/ALLIED HEALTH/HEALTH SCIENCES, GENERAL

**Alaska**
Ilisagvik College (Barrow), 41

**Arkansas**
Arkansas State University–Mountain Home (Mountain Home), 59
East Arkansas Community College (Forrest City), 62
National Park Community College (Hot Springs), 63
North Arkansas College (Harrison), 64
Ozarka College (Melbourne), 65
Phillips Community College of the University of Arkansas (Helena), 65
Southern Arkansas University Tech (Camden), 66

**California**
Academy of Hair Design (Poway), 69
Citrus College (Glendora), 82
College of Marin (Kentfield), 84
Contra Costa College (San Pablo), 86
MiraCosta College (Oceanside), 114

**Illinois**
Lincoln Technical Institute (Norridge), 177

**Kentucky**
Brown Mackie College–Northern Kentucky (Fort Mitchell), 211

**Minnesota**
Anoka-Ramsey Community College (Coon Rapids), 240
Rochester Community and Technical College (Rochester), 253

**Oklahoma**
American Institute of Medical Technology (Tulsa), 302
Indian Capital Technology Center–Stilwell (Stilwell), 308
Kiamichi Area Vocational-Technical School–McAlester (McAlester), 308

## HEALTH TEACHER EDUCATION



## HEALTH UNIT COORDINATOR/WARD CLERK



## HEATING, AIR CONDITIONING AND REFRIGERATION TECHNOLOGY/TECHNICIAN (ACH/ACR/ACHR/HRAC/HVAC/AC TECHNOLOGY)



## HEATING, AIR CONDITIONING, VENTILATION AND REFRIGERATION MAINTENANCE TECHNOLOGY/TECHNICIAN (HAC, HACR, HVAC, HVACR)

## HEAVY EQUIPMENT MAINTENANCE TECHNOLOGY/TECHNICIAN

**Oklahoma**
Autry Technology Center (Enid), 302
Indian Capital Technology Center–Tahlequah (Tahlequah), 308
**Oregon**
Umpqua Community College (Roseburg), 327
**Tennessee**
Nashville Auto Diesel College (Nashville), 336
Tennessee Technology Center at Dickson (Dickson), 341
**Texas**
Navarro College (Corsicana), 371
**Washington**
Renton Technical College (Renton), 410
**Wisconsin**
Fox Valley Technical College (Appleton), 415
Milwaukee Area Technical College (Milwaukee), 418

## HEAVY/INDUSTRIAL EQUIPMENT MAINTENANCE TECHNOLOGIES, OTHER

**Arkansas**
University of Arkansas Community College at Hope (Hope), 67
**Louisiana**
Louisiana Technical College–Shreveport-Bossier Campus (Shreveport), 234
**Mississippi**
Coahoma Community College (Clarksdale), 258
**Missouri**
East Central College (Union), 266
Mineral Area College (Park Hills), 272
Ranken Technical College (St. Louis), 276
**Nebraska**
Metropolitan Community College (Omaha), 287
**Tennessee**
Tennessee Technology Center at Covington (Covington), 340
Tennessee Technology Center at Hohenwald (Hohenwald), 342
Tennessee Technology Center at Knoxville (Knoxville), 342
Tennessee Technology Center at Pulaski (Pulaski), 344
**Washington**
Bellingham Technical College (Bellingham), 400
Big Bend Community College (Moses Lake), 401
**Wyoming**
Western Wyoming Community College (Rock Springs), 424

## HEMATOLOGY TECHNOLOGY/TECHNICIAN

**Minnesota**
St. Catherine University (St. Paul), 254
**New Mexico**
Central New Mexico Community College (Albuquerque), 293

## HERBALISM/HERBALIST

**Arizona**
Southwest Institute of Healing Arts (Tempe), 56

## HISTOLOGIC TECHNICIAN

**Arizona**
Phoenix College (Phoenix), 53
Pima Community College (Tucson), 54
**Texas**
St. Philip's College (San Antonio), 377

## HISTOLOGIC TECHNOLOGY/HISTOTECHNOLOGIST

**Arizona**
Phoenix College (Phoenix), 53
**Arkansas**
Baptist Schools of Nursing and Allied Health (Little Rock), 61
**Minnesota**
Mayo School of Health Sciences (Rochester), 245
**North Dakota**
University of North Dakota (Grand Forks), 301

## HISTORIC PRESERVATION AND CONSERVATION

**Colorado**
Colorado Mountain College (Glenwood Springs), 145

## HOME FURNISHINGS AND EQUIPMENT INSTALLERS

**Kansas**
Kaw Area Technical School (Topeka), 204

## HOME HEALTH AIDE/HOME ATTENDANT

**Arizona**
Pima Community College (Tucson), 54
**California**
Allan Hancock College (Santa Maria), 70
Antelope Valley College (Lancaster), 72
Butte College (Oroville), 75
Citrus College (Glendora), 82
College of the Canyons (Santa Clarita), 84
College of the Desert (Palm Desert), 84
Imperial Valley College (Imperial), 100
Lake Tahoe Community College (South Lake Tahoe), 105
Long Beach City College (Long Beach), 106
MiraCosta College (Oceanside), 114
Palo Verde College (Blythe), 123
Santa Barbara City College (Santa Barbara), 131
**Colorado**
Emily Griffith Opportunity School (Denver), 146
**Illinois**
College of DuPage (Glen Ellyn), 164
**Kansas**
Barton County Community College (Great Bend), 199
Cloud County Community College (Concordia), 201
Coffeyville Community College (Coffeyville), 201
Colby Community College (Colby), 201
Fort Scott Community College (Fort Scott), 202
Garden City Community College (Garden City), 202
Independence Community College (Independence), 203
Johnson County Community College (Overland Park), 203
**Minnesota**
Anoka Technical College (Anoka), 240
Minnesota West Community and Technical College (Pipestone), 248
Pine Technical College (Pine City), 251
Summit Academy Opportunities Industrialization Center (Minneapolis), 255
**Oklahoma**
Southern Oklahoma Technology Center (Ardmore), 315
**Tennessee**
Concorde Career College (Memphis), 332
**Texas**
Odessa College (Odessa), 373
South Texas Vocational Technical Institute (McAllen), 381
South Texas Vo-Tech Institute (Weslaco), 381
**Washington**
Spokane Falls Community College (Spokane), 412

## HOMEOPATHIC MEDICINE/HOMEOPATHY

**Colorado**
Front Range Community College (Westminster), 147

## HORSE HUSBANDRY/EQUINE SCIENCE AND MANAGEMENT

**Illinois**
Parkland College (Champaign), 181
**Iowa**
Ellsworth Community College (Iowa Falls), 191
**Minnesota**
Rochester Community and Technical College (Rochester), 253
**New Mexico**
Crownpoint Institute of Technology (Crownpoint), 293

## HORTICULTURAL SCIENCE

**Arizona**
Eastern Arizona College (Thatcher), 48
Northland Pioneer College (Holbrook), 53

## HOSPITAL AND HEALTH-CARE FACILITIES ADMINISTRATION/MANAGEMENT

**California**
Cypress College (Cypress), 88
Premiere Career College (Irwindale), 125
**Illinois**
City Colleges of Chicago, Wilbur Wright College (Chicago), 164
College of DuPage (Glen Ellyn), 164
**Kansas**
Allen County Community College (Iola), 199
Washburn University (Topeka), 208
**Texas**
Coastal Bend College (Beeville), 357
McLennan Community College (Waco), 369
Tarrant County College District (Fort Worth), 383

## HOSPITALITY ADMINISTRATION/MANAGEMENT, GENERAL

**Arizona**
Cochise College (Douglas), 47
Northern Arizona University (Flagstaff), 52
Pima Community College (Tucson), 54
Scottsdale Community College (Scottsdale), 56
Scottsdale Culinary Institute (Scottsdale), 56
**Arkansas**
East Arkansas Community College (Forrest City), 62
National Park Community College (Hot Springs), 63
NorthWest Arkansas Community College (Bentonville), 64
University of Arkansas at Monticello (Monticello), 67
**California**
California Culinary Academy (San Francisco), 76

California School of Culinary Arts (Pasadena), 77
Cypress College (Cypress), 88
Empire College (Santa Rosa), 90
Glendale Community College (Glendale), 95
Grossmont College (El Cajon), 96
Heald College–Fresno (Fresno), 97
Laney College (Oakland), 105
Los Angeles Mission College (Sylmar), 107
MiraCosta College (Oceanside), 114
Monterey Peninsula College (Monterey), 116
Mt. San Antonio College (Walnut), 116
Pasadena City College (Pasadena), 123
Santa Barbara City College (Santa Barbara), 131
Santa Rosa Junior College (Santa Rosa), 132

**Colorado**
Front Range Community College (Westminster), 147

**Hawaii**
Hawaii Community College (Hilo), 154
Heald College–Honolulu (Honolulu), 155
Maui Community College (Kahului), 155

**Illinois**
Elgin Community College (Elgin), 167
Joliet Junior College (Joliet), 174
Moraine Valley Community College (Palos Hills), 178
Northwestern Business College–Southwestern Campus (Bridgeview), 180
Northwestern College (Chicago), 180
Roosevelt University (Chicago), 185

**Iowa**
Des Moines Area Community College (Ankeny), 191

**Louisiana**
Delgado Community College (New Orleans), 224
Southern University at Shreveport (Shreveport), 237

**Mississippi**
Hinds Community College (Raymond), 259

**Missouri**
Three Rivers Community College (Poplar Bluff), 280

**Nevada**
College of Southern Nevada (North Las Vegas), 290

**Northern Mariana Islands**
Northern Marianas College (Saipan), 302

**Oklahoma**
Indian Capital Technology Center–Muskogee (Muskogee), 307
Tulsa Tech–Peoria Campus (Tulsa), 317

**Oregon**
Blue Mountain Community College (Pendleton), 320
Chemeketa Community College (Salem), 320
Clackamas Community College (Oregon City), 320
Mt. Hood Community College (Gresham), 323
Oregon Coast Community College (Newport), 324

**Tennessee**
National College (Nashville), 336

**Texas**
Austin Community College (Austin), 352
Central Texas College (Killeen), 355
Collin County Community College District (Plano), 357
Tarrant County College District (Fort Worth), 383

**Washington**
Edmonds Community College (Lynnwood), 403
International Air Academy (Vancouver), 406
Whatcom Community College (Bellingham), 413

**Wyoming**
Sheridan College (Sheridan), 424

## HOSPITALITY ADMINISTRATION/MANAGEMENT, OTHER

**California**
Mt. Diablo Adult Education (Concord), 116

**Montana**
Blackfeet Community College (Browning), 282

**North Dakota**
Bismarck State College (Bismarck), 298

**Oklahoma**
Tulsa Community College (Tulsa), 317

**Oregon**
Western Culinary Institute (Portland), 328

**Washington**
Bellingham Technical College (Bellingham), 400

## HOSPITALITY AND RECREATION MARKETING OPERATIONS

**Arizona**
Northland Pioneer College (Holbrook), 53
Phoenix College (Phoenix), 53

**Colorado**
Pueblo Community College (Pueblo), 151

**Idaho**
Lewis-Clark State College (Lewiston), 158

**Kansas**
Butler Community College (El Dorado), 201

**Missouri**
Waynesville Technical Academy (Waynesville), 282

**Wisconsin**
Lac Courte Oreilles Ojibwa Community College (Hayward), 417

## HOTEL/MOTEL ADMINISTRATION/MANAGEMENT

**Arizona**
Central Arizona College (Coolidge), 47
Estrella Mountain Community College (Avondale), 49
Phoenix College (Phoenix), 53
Scottsdale Community College (Scottsdale), 56

**Arkansas**
East Arkansas Community College (Forrest City), 62

**California**
Chaffey College (Rancho Cucamonga), 81
Long Beach City College (Long Beach), 106
Los Angeles Mission College (Sylmar), 107
San Diego Mesa College (San Diego), 128

**Guam**
Guam Community College (Barrigada), 154

**Hawaii**
Hawaii Community College (Hilo), 154
Kauai Community College (Lihue), 155
Maui Community College (Kahului), 155
Travel Institute of the Pacific (Honolulu), 156

**Illinois**
College of DuPage (Glen Ellyn), 164
Elgin Community College (Elgin), 167
Harper College (Palatine), 170
Lincoln Land Community College (Springfield), 177
Parkland College (Champaign), 181
Triton College (River Grove), 188

**Kansas**
Butler Community College (El Dorado), 201
Johnson County Community College (Overland Park), 203

**Louisiana**
Louisiana Technical College–Lafayette Campus (Lafayette), 231
Louisiana Technical College–Northwest Louisiana Campus (Minden), 232

**Minnesota**
Normandale Community College (Bloomington), 249

**Missouri**
St. Louis Community College at Forest Park (St. Louis), 278

**Nevada**
College of Southern Nevada (North Las Vegas), 290

**North Dakota**
Bismarck State College (Bismarck), 298

**Oklahoma**
Caddo-Kiowa Area Vocational Technical School (Ft. Cobb), 303

**Oregon**
Chemeketa Community College (Salem), 320
Lane Community College (Eugene), 322

**Texas**
Del Mar College (Corpus Christi), 359
El Paso Community College (El Paso), 360
Houston Community College System (Houston), 363
North Lake College (Irving), 372
St. Philip's College (San Antonio), 377

**Washington**
International Air Academy (Vancouver), 406

## HOUSING AND HUMAN ENVIRONMENTS, GENERAL

**Texas**
Coastal Bend College (Beeville), 357

## HOUSING AND HUMAN ENVIRONMENTS, OTHER

**Arizona**
Cochise College (Douglas), 47
Northland Pioneer College (Holbrook), 53

**Colorado**
Emily Griffith Opportunity School (Denver), 146

**Illinois**
Illinois Central College (East Peoria), 172
Illinois Eastern Community Colleges, Lincoln Trail College (Robinson), 172
Illinois Valley Community College (Oglesby), 173
Kaskaskia College (Centralia), 175
Lake Land College (Mattoon), 176
Rend Lake College (Ina), 183
Richland Community College (Decatur), 184
Southeastern Illinois College (Harrisburg), 186

**Oklahoma**
Central Oklahoma Area Vocational Technical School (Drumright), 304
Francis Tuttle Area Vocational Technical Center (Oklahoma City), 306
Mid-America Technology Center (Wayne), 310

**Wisconsin**
Chippewa Valley Technical College (Eau Claire), 415

Madison Area Technical College (Madison), 417

## HUMAN DEVELOPMENT AND FAMILY STUDIES, GENERAL

**California**
Napa Valley College (Napa), 118

**Oregon**
Clackamas Community College (Oregon City), 320

**Texas**
Howard College (Big Spring), 364

## HUMAN DEVELOPMENT, FAMILY STUDIES, AND RELATED SERVICES, OTHER

**Arizona**
Central Arizona College (Coolidge), 47
Glendale Community College (Glendale), 50

**New Mexico**
Eastern New Mexico University–Roswell (Roswell), 294

**Oklahoma**
Francis Tuttle Area Vocational Technical Center (Oklahoma City), 306

**Tennessee**
Jackson State Community College (Jackson), 334
Southwest Tennessee Community College (Memphis), 339

**Texas**
Anamarc Educational Institute (El Paso), 351

**Washington**
Washington State University (Pullman), 413

**Wisconsin**
Milwaukee Area Technical College (Milwaukee), 418
Moraine Park Technical College (Fond du Lac), 419

## HUMAN NUTRITION

**California**
Sacramento City Unified School District–Skills and Business Education Center (Sacramento), 126

## HUMAN RESOURCES DEVELOPMENT

**Illinois**
Roosevelt University (Chicago), 185

**Minnesota**
Alexandria Technical College (Alexandria), 239
Dakota County Technical College (Rosemount), 242
Riverland Community College (Austin), 253
Rochester Community and Technical College (Rochester), 253
St. Cloud Technical College (St. Cloud), 254

**Oregon**
Clackamas Community College (Oregon City), 320

## HUMAN RESOURCES MANAGEMENT AND SERVICES, OTHER

**California**
Ventura Adult and Continuing Education (Ventura), 138

**Minnesota**
University of Minnesota, Duluth (Duluth), 256

**Oklahoma**
Francis Tuttle Area Vocational Technical Center (Oklahoma City), 306

## HUMAN RESOURCES MANAGEMENT/ PERSONNEL ADMINISTRATION, GENERAL

**Arizona**
Axia College (Phoenix), 46
Northern Arizona University (Flagstaff), 52
Pima Community College (Tucson), 54
University of Phoenix–Phoenix Campus (Phoenix), 57

**California**
Golden Gate University (San Francisco), 96
Institute of Technology (Clovis), 100
San Joaquin Valley College–Online (Visalia), 130
University of Phoenix–Bay Area Campus (Pleasanton), 137
University of Phoenix–Sacramento Valley Campus (Sacramento), 137
University of Phoenix–San Diego Campus (San Diego), 137
University of Phoenix–Southern California Campus (Costa Mesa), 137

**Colorado**
Arapahoe Community College (Littleton), 143
University of Phoenix–Denver Campus (Lone Tree), 153

**Illinois**
Harper College (Palatine), 170
Joliet Junior College (Joliet), 174
Lewis and Clark Community College (Godfrey), 176
Moraine Valley Community College (Palos Hills), 178
Oakton Community College (Des Plaines), 180
Triton College (River Grove), 188

**Iowa**
Upper Iowa University (Fayette), 198
Western Iowa Tech Community College (Sioux City), 198

**Louisiana**
University of Phoenix–Louisiana Campus (Metairie), 239

**Minnesota**
Inver Hills Community College (Inver Grove Heights), 244
Lake Superior College (Duluth), 245
Normandale Community College (Bloomington), 249
Saint Paul College–A Community & Technical College (St. Paul), 254
University of Minnesota, Twin Cities Campus (Minneapolis), 256

**Montana**
Montana State University–Billings (Billings), 284

**Nebraska**
Creighton University (Omaha), 286

**New Mexico**
University of Phoenix–New Mexico Campus (Albuquerque), 298

**North Dakota**
North Dakota State University (Fargo), 300

**Oklahoma**
Tulsa Community College (Tulsa), 317

**Oregon**
Linfield College–Adult Degree Program (Albany), 323

**Texas**
University of Phoenix–Houston Campus (Houston), 389

**Washington**
Bellevue College (Bellevue), 400
Bellingham Technical College (Bellingham), 400
Clark College (Vancouver), 402
Clover Park Technical College (Lakewood), 402
Edmonds Community College (Lynnwood), 403
Lake Washington Technical College (Kirkland), 406
Pierce College (Puyallup), 409
Tacoma Community College (Tacoma), 412

**Wisconsin**
Moraine Park Technical College (Fond du Lac), 419

## HUMAN SERVICES, GENERAL

**Arizona**
Phoenix College (Phoenix), 53

**California**
Allan Hancock College (Santa Maria), 70
American River College (Sacramento), 72
Bakersfield College (Bakersfield), 74
Berkeley City College (Berkeley), 74
Cabrillo College (Aptos), 75
Cañada College (Redwood City), 77
Cerritos College (Norwalk), 80
Chabot College (Hayward), 81
College of San Mateo (San Mateo), 84
College of the Desert (Palm Desert), 84
College of the Sequoias (Visalia), 85
Contra Costa College (San Pablo), 86
Cosumnes River College (Sacramento), 87
Cypress College (Cypress), 88
Diablo Valley College (Pleasant Hill), 89
East Los Angeles College (Monterey Park), 89
Fresno City College (Fresno), 94
Lassen Community College District (Susanville), 106
Long Beach City College (Long Beach), 106
Los Angeles City College (Los Angeles), 107
Los Angeles Southwest College (Los Angeles), 109
Mendocino College (Ukiah), 113
Merced College (Merced), 113
Merritt College (Oakland), 114
Modesto Junior College (Modesto), 115
Monterey Peninsula College (Monterey), 116
Mt. San Jacinto College (San Jacinto), 117
Napa Valley College (Napa), 118
Rio Hondo College (Whittier), 125
Riverside Community College District (Riverside), 126
Sacramento City College (Sacramento), 126
Saddleback College (Mission Viejo), 127
San Bernardino Valley College (San Bernardino), 128
San Diego City College (San Diego), 128
San Joaquin Delta College (Stockton), 129
Santa Rosa Junior College (Santa Rosa), 132
Solano Community College (Suisun City), 134

**Hawaii**
Honolulu Community College (Honolulu), 155
Maui Community College (Kahului), 155

**Kansas**
Washburn University (Topeka), 208

**Minnesota**
Century College (White Bear Lake), 241
Minneapolis Community and Technical College (Minneapolis), 246
Minnesota West Community and Technical College (Pipestone), 248
Pine Technical College (Pine City), 251

**Missouri**
St. Louis Community College at Florissant Valley (St. Louis), 277

## HYDRAULICS AND FLUID POWER TECHNOLOGY/TECHNICIAN



## HYPNOTHERAPY/HYPNOTHERAPIST



## ILLUSTRATION



## INDUSTRIAL DESIGN



## INDUSTRIAL ELECTRONICS TECHNOLOGY/ TECHNICIAN



## INDUSTRIAL ENGINEERING



## INDUSTRIAL MECHANICS AND MAINTENANCE TECHNOLOGY

## INDUSTRIAL PRODUCTION TECHNOLOGIES/ TECHNICIANS, OTHER

**California**
Antelope Valley College (Lancaster), 72
**Kansas**
Barton County Community College (Great Bend), 199
**Missouri**
Metropolitan Community College–Business & Technology Campus (Kansas City), 271
Ozarks Technical Community College (Springfield), 274
**North Dakota**
Bismarck State College (Bismarck), 298
Turtle Mountain Community College (Belcourt), 301

## INDUSTRIAL RADIOLOGIC TECHNOLOGY/ TECHNICIAN

**Louisiana**
Louisiana Technical College–T.H. Harris Campus (Opelousas), 234

## INDUSTRIAL SAFETY TECHNOLOGY/ TECHNICIAN

**Alaska**
University of Alaska Fairbanks (Fairbanks), 42
**California**
Cuyamaca College (El Cajon), 88
Las Positas College (Livermore), 105
Southwestern College (Chula Vista), 134
**Minnesota**
South Central College (North Mankato), 255

## INDUSTRIAL TECHNOLOGY/TECHNICIAN

**Arizona**
GateWay Community College (Phoenix), 50
Northland Pioneer College (Holbrook), 53
**Arkansas**
Phillips Community College of the University of Arkansas (Helena), 65
**California**
San Joaquin Valley College (Visalia), 130
**Idaho**
Boise State University (Boise), 157
**Illinois**
Highland Community College (Freeport), 171
Illinois Eastern Community Colleges, Wabash Valley College (Mount Carmel), 173
Rock Valley College (Rockford), 184
**Minnesota**
Dunwoody College of Technology (Minneapolis), 242
University of Minnesota, Crookston (Crookston), 256
**New Mexico**
Eastern New Mexico University–Roswell (Roswell), 294
**North Dakota**
Bismarck State College (Bismarck), 298
**Oregon**
Clackamas Community College (Oregon City), 320
**Tennessee**
Southwest Tennessee Community College (Memphis), 339
**Texas**
Frank Phillips College (Borger), 362
Howard College (Big Spring), 364
Lonestar College–North Harris (Houston), 369
Panola College (Carthage), 374
Texas State Technical College Marshall (Marshall), 386
**Washington**
Olympic College (Bremerton), 408

## INFORMATION RESOURCES MANAGEMENT/ CIO TRAINING

**Arkansas**
Ozarka College (Melbourne), 65
**Oklahoma**
Indian Capital Technology Center–Muskogee (Muskogee), 307
Indian Capital Technology Center–Sallisaw (Sallisaw), 307
Indian Capital Technology Center–Tahlequah (Tahlequah), 308

## INFORMATION SCIENCE/STUDIES

**Alaska**
Alaska Vocational Technical Center (Seward), 41
**Arizona**
Eastern Arizona College (Thatcher), 48
Northland Pioneer College (Holbrook), 53
**Arkansas**
Arkansas State University–Mountain Home (Mountain Home), 59
Southeast Arkansas College (Pine Bluff), 66
**Colorado**
Front Range Community College (Westminster), 147
**Illinois**
City Colleges of Chicago, Harold Washington College (Chicago), 163
City Colleges of Chicago, Harry S. Truman College (Chicago), 163
City Colleges of Chicago, Kennedy-King College (Chicago), 163
City Colleges of Chicago, Olive-Harvey College (Chicago), 163
City Colleges of Chicago, Richard J. Daley College (Chicago), 164
City Colleges of Chicago, Wilbur Wright College (Chicago), 164
Dominican University (River Forest), 167
Harper College (Palatine), 170
John A. Logan College (Carterville), 174
Lake Land College (Mattoon), 176
MacCormac College (Chicago), 177
Oakton Community College (Des Plaines), 180
Shawnee Community College (Ullin), 186
**Kansas**
Wright Business School (Overland Park), 209
**Kentucky**
Southwestern College of Business (Florence), 219
**Louisiana**
Bossier Parish Community College (Bossier City), 223
Elaine P. Nunez Community College (Chalmette), 226
Southern University at Shreveport (Shreveport), 237
**Minnesota**
Rasmussen College Eden Prairie (Eden Prairie), 251
Rasmussen College Mankato (Mankato), 252
Rasmussen College St. Cloud (St. Cloud), 252
**Oklahoma**
Oklahoma Technology Institute (Oklahoma City), 313
**Texas**
Panola College (Carthage), 374
Texas State Technical College Marshall (Marshall), 386
**Utah**
College of Eastern Utah (Price), 393
Weber State University (Ogden), 399
**Wyoming**
Northwest College (Powell), 424

## INFORMATION TECHNOLOGY

**Alaska**
Ilisagvik College (Barrow), 41
**Arizona**
Cochise College (Douglas), 47
South Mountain Community College (Phoenix), 56
**California**
Allan Hancock College (Santa Maria), 70
Antelope Valley College (Lancaster), 72
Butte College (Oroville), 75
Chaffey College (Rancho Cucamonga), 81
College of Alameda (Alameda), 84
College of the Desert (Palm Desert), 84
Cosumnes River College (Sacramento), 87
Crafton Hills College (Yucaipa), 87
El Camino College (Torrance), 90
Empire College (Santa Rosa), 90
Laney College (Oakland), 105
Los Angeles Trade-Technical College (Los Angeles), 109
Los Medanos College (Pittsburg), 109
Moorpark College (Moorpark), 116
Mt. San Jacinto College (San Jacinto), 117
Napa Valley College (Napa), 118
Palo Verde College (Blythe), 123
Pasadena City College (Pasadena), 123
Reedley College (Reedley), 125
Rio Hondo College (Whittier), 125
Sacramento City College (Sacramento), 126
San Diego Mesa College (San Diego), 128
San Diego Miramar College (San Diego), 129
San Joaquin Delta College (Stockton), 129
Santa Ana College (Santa Ana), 131
Stanbridge College (Irvine), 135
West Los Angeles College (Culver City), 141
**Hawaii**
Hawaii Community College (Hilo), 154
Kapiolani Community College (Honolulu), 155
**Illinois**
Vatterott College (Quincy), 189
**Iowa**
Southeastern Community College, North Campus (West Burlington), 198
**Kansas**
Vatterott College (Wichita), 208
**Kentucky**
National College (Lexington), 217
**Louisiana**
Cameron College (New Orleans), 223
**Minnesota**
Capella University (Minneapolis), 241
**Mississippi**
Virginia College at Jackson (Jackson), 263
**Missouri**
Vatterott College (Joplin), 281
Vatterott College (Kansas City), 281
Vatterott College (O'Fallon), 281
Vatterott College (St. Ann), 281
Vatterott College (St. Joseph), 281
Vatterott College (St. Louis), 281
Vatterott College (Springfield), 281

## KINESIOTHERAPY/KINESIOTHERAPIST

### Nevada
College of Southern Nevada (North Las Vegas), 290

## KOREAN LANGUAGE AND LITERATURE

### California
Foothill College (Los Altos Hills), 93

## LABOR AND INDUSTRIAL RELATIONS

### California
Laney College (Oakland), 105
Los Angeles Trade-Technical College (Los Angeles), 109
San Diego City College (San Diego), 128

## LANDSCAPING AND GROUNDSKEEPING

### Arizona
Glendale Community College (Glendale), 50
Mesa Community College (Mesa), 52
Phoenix College (Phoenix), 53

### California
American River College (Sacramento), 72
Butte College (Oroville), 75
Cabrillo College (Aptos), 75
City College of San Francisco (San Francisco), 82
College of Marin (Kentfield), 84
College of San Mateo (San Mateo), 84
College of the Sequoias (Visalia), 85
Cosumnes River College (Sacramento), 87
Cuyamaca College (El Cajon), 88
Diablo Valley College (Pleasant Hill), 89
Los Angeles Pierce College (Woodland Hills), 108
Maxine Waters Employment Preparation Center (Los Angeles), 113
Mendocino College (Ukiah), 113
Merritt College (Oakland), 114
MiraCosta College (Oceanside), 114
Mt. San Antonio College (Walnut), 116
Saddleback College (Mission Viejo), 127
San Diego Mesa College (San Diego), 128
San Joaquin Delta College (Stockton), 129
Santa Rosa Junior College (Santa Rosa), 132
Solano Community College (Suisun City), 134
Southwestern College (Chula Vista), 134

### Idaho
North Idaho College (Coeur d'Alene), 159

### Illinois
College of DuPage (Glen Ellyn), 164
College of Lake County (Grayslake), 165
Harper College (Palatine), 170
Lincoln Land Community College (Springfield), 177
McHenry County College (Crystal Lake), 178
Triton College (River Grove), 188

### Kansas
Johnson County Community College (Overland Park), 203

### Minnesota
Central Lakes College (Brainerd), 241
Century College (White Bear Lake), 241
Hennepin Technical College (Brooklyn Park), 243

### Mississippi
Mississippi Gulf Coast Community College (Perkinston), 261

### Nevada
Truckee Meadows Community College (Reno), 292

### New Mexico
Central New Mexico Community College (Albuquerque), 293

### North Dakota
Dakota College at Bottineau (Bottineau), 299

### Oregon
Portland Community College (Portland), 326
Rogue Community College (Grants Pass), 326

### Tennessee
Nashville State Technical Community College (Nashville), 336
Southwest Tennessee Community College (Memphis), 339

### Texas
Houston Community College System (Houston), 363
Palo Alto College (San Antonio), 373
Richland College (Dallas), 376

### Washington
Clark College (Vancouver), 402
South Seattle Community College (Seattle), 411

### Wisconsin
Blackhawk Technical College (Janesville), 414
Moraine Park Technical College (Fond du Lac), 419

## LANGUAGE INTERPRETATION AND TRANSLATION

### Arizona
Cochise College (Douglas), 47
Pima Community College (Tucson), 54

### California
Riverside Community College District (Riverside), 126
Southwestern College (Chula Vista), 134

### Iowa
Des Moines Area Community College (Ankeny), 191

### Kansas
Johnson County Community College (Overland Park), 203

### Minnesota
University of Minnesota, Twin Cities Campus (Minneapolis), 256

### Nevada
Great Basin College (Elko), 290

### North Dakota
Lake Region State College (Devils Lake), 299

### Texas
Vernon College (Vernon), 389

### Wisconsin
Milwaukee Area Technical College (Milwaukee), 418
Waukesha County Technical College (Pewaukee), 422

## LASER AND OPTICAL TECHNOLOGY/TECHNICIAN

### Arizona
Pima Community College (Tucson), 54

### California
Las Positas College (Livermore), 105
San Jose City College (San Jose), 130

### New Mexico
Central New Mexico Community College (Albuquerque), 293

## LATIN AMERICAN STUDIES

### Minnesota
Central Lakes College (Brainerd), 241

## LEGAL ADMINISTRATIVE ASSISTANT/SECRETARY

### Alaska
University of Alaska Anchorage (Anchorage), 41

### Arizona
Brookline College (Mesa), 46
Brookline College (Phoenix), 46
Brookline College (Tucson), 46
Maricopa Skill Center (Phoenix), 51
Mohave Community College (Kingman), 52
Northland Pioneer College (Holbrook), 53
Phoenix College (Phoenix), 53

### Arkansas
Pulaski Technical College (North Little Rock), 65

### California
Allan Hancock College (Santa Maria), 70
Butte College (Oroville), 75
Cerritos College (Norwalk), 80
College of the Sequoias (Visalia), 85
Cypress College (Cypress), 88
East Los Angeles College (Monterey Park), 89
Empire College (Santa Rosa), 90
Golden West College (Huntington Beach), 96
Humphreys College (Stockton), 99
Imperial Valley College (Imperial), 100
Kensington College (Santa Ana), 104
Long Beach City College (Long Beach), 106
Los Angeles Mission College (Sylmar), 107
Los Angeles Southwest College (Los Angeles), 109
MTI Business College (Stockton), 117
MTI College (Orange), 117
MTI College of Business & Technology (Sacramento), 117
Palomar College (San Marcos), 122
Sacramento City Unified School District–Skills and Business Education Center (Sacramento), 126
Sage College (Moreno Valley), 127
San Diego City College (San Diego), 128
San Diego Mesa College (San Diego), 128
Santa Ana College (Santa Ana), 131
Santa Barbara Business College (Bakersfield), 131
Santa Barbara Business College (Santa Maria), 131
Santa Barbara Business College (Ventura), 131
Santa Rosa Junior College (Santa Rosa), 132
Southwestern College (Chula Vista), 134
Ventura Adult and Continuing Education (Ventura), 138
Yuba College (Marysville), 142

### Idaho
Academy of Professional Careers (Boise), 156
Lewis-Clark State College (Lewiston), 158

### Illinois
Black Hawk College (Moline), 160
Harper College (Palatine), 170
John A. Logan College (Carterville), 174
Kaskaskia College (Centralia), 175
Lewis and Clark Community College (Godfrey), 176
Lincoln Land Community College (Springfield), 177
MacCormac College (Chicago), 177
Moraine Valley Community College (Palos Hills), 178
Richland Community College (Decatur), 184
Robert Morris University (Chicago), 184
Rockford Business College (Rockford), 184
Sparks College (Shelbyville), 187

## LEGAL ASSISTANT/PARALEGAL

## Machine Tool Technology/Machinist

**Oregon**
Clackamas Community College (Oregon City), 320
Linn-Benton Community College (Albany), 323
Mt. Hood Community College (Gresham), 323
Portland Community College (Portland), 326

**Tennessee**
Nashville State Technical Community College (Nashville), 336
Tennessee Technology Center at Athens (Athens), 340
Tennessee Technology Center at Covington (Covington), 340
Tennessee Technology Center at Jacksboro (Jacksboro), 342
Tennessee Technology Center at Jackson (Jackson), 342
Tennessee Technology Center at Paris (Paris), 344
Tennessee Technology Center at Pulaski (Pulaski), 344
Tennessee Technology Center at Whiteville (Whiteville), 345

**Texas**
Angelina College (Lufkin), 351
Brazosport College (Lake Jackson), 353
Del Mar College (Corpus Christi), 359
El Paso Community College (El Paso), 360
Grayson County College (Denison), 363
Lamar Institute of Technology (Beaumont), 367
Lee College (Baytown), 368
Odessa College (Odessa), 373
St. Philip's College (San Antonio), 377
School of Automotive Machinists (Houston), 379
South Plains College (Levelland), 381
Texas State Technical College Harlingen (Harlingen), 386
Texas State Technical College West Texas (Sweetwater), 387
Vernon College (Vernon), 389

**Utah**
Bridgerland Applied Technology Center (Logan), 392
Davis Applied Technology Center (Kaysville), 393
Ogden-Weber Applied Technology Center (Ogden), 396

**Washington**
Bates Technical College (Tacoma), 400
Bellingham Technical College (Bellingham), 400
Clover Park Technical College (Lakewood), 402
Everett Community College (Everett), 404
Perry Technical Institute (Yakima), 409
Shoreline Community College (Shoreline), 410
Spokane Community College (Spokane), 411

**Wisconsin**
Gateway Technical College (Kenosha), 416
Lakeshore Technical College (Cleveland), 417
Milwaukee Area Technical College (Milwaukee), 418
Moraine Park Technical College (Fond du Lac), 419
Waukesha County Technical College (Pewaukee), 422

**Wyoming**
Casper College (Casper), 423
Sheridan College (Sheridan), 424

## MAKE-UP ARTIST/SPECIALIST

**Arkansas**
Phillips Community College of the University of Arkansas (Helena), 65

**California**
Academy of Hair Design (Poway), 69
Bay Vista College of Beauty (National City), 74
Elegance Academy of Makeup (Los Angeles), 90
Je Boutique College of Beauty (El Cajon), 102
Lola Beauty College (Garden Grove), 106
Make-up Designory (Burbank), 110
Manchester Beauty College (Fresno), 110
Royale College of Beauty (Temecula), 126
Thanh Le College School of Cosmetology (Garden Grove), 135

**Illinois**
Mr. John's School of Cosmetology (Decatur), 179

**Iowa**
Capri College (Davenport), 190

**Nevada**
Academy of Hair Design (Las Vegas), 289

**Oregon**
Roseburg Beauty College (Roseburg), 326

**Tennessee**
Tennessee Academy of Cosmetology (Memphis), 340
West Tennessee Business College (Jackson), 347

**Texas**
San Antonio Beauty College 4 (San Antonio), 377

## MANAGEMENT INFORMATION SYSTEMS AND SERVICES, OTHER

**Arkansas**
Black River Technical College (Pocahontas), 61
Southeast Arkansas College (Pine Bluff), 66

**Iowa**
Kaplan University, Davenport Campus (Davenport), 194

**Kansas**
Allen County Community College (Iola), 199

**North Dakota**
Minot State University (Minot), 299

**Oklahoma**
Autry Technology Center (Enid), 302
Caddo-Kiowa Area Vocational Technical School (Ft. Cobb), 303
Francis Tuttle Area Vocational Technical Center (Oklahoma City), 306
Green Country Technology Center (Okmulgee), 307
Northwest Technology Center (Fairview), 312
Red River Area Vocational-Technical School (Duncan), 315
Southern Oklahoma Technology Center (Ardmore), 315
Southwest Area Vocational Technical Center (Altus), 316
Tulsa Community College (Tulsa), 317
Wes Watkins Area Vocational-Technical Center (Wetumka), 318

**Oregon**
Portland Community College (Portland), 326

**Tennessee**
Walters State Community College (Morristown), 346

**Texas**
Northwest Educational Center (Houston), 372

**Wisconsin**
Moraine Park Technical College (Fond du Lac), 419

## MANAGEMENT INFORMATION SYSTEMS, GENERAL

**Alaska**
University of Alaska Anchorage (Anchorage), 41
University of Alaska, Prince William Sound Community College (Valdez), 42
University of Alaska Southeast (Juneau), 42

**Arizona**
Chandler-Gilbert Community College (Chandler), 47
East Valley Institute of Technology (Mesa), 49
Estrella Mountain Community College (Avondale), 49
GateWay Community College (Phoenix), 50
Glendale Community College (Glendale), 50
Mesa Community College (Mesa), 52
Northern Arizona University (Flagstaff), 52
Phoenix College (Phoenix), 53
Rio Salado College (Tempe), 55
Scottsdale Community College (Scottsdale), 56
South Mountain Community College (Phoenix), 56

**Arkansas**
Arkansas State University–Mountain Home (Mountain Home), 59
Arkansas Tech University (Russellville), 60
East Arkansas Community College (Forrest City), 62
Northwest Technical Institute (Springdale), 64
Phillips Community College of the University of Arkansas (Helena), 65
Pulaski Technical College (North Little Rock), 65

**California**
Heald College–Concord (Concord), 97

**Colorado**
Aims Community College (Greeley), 143
Community College of Aurora (Aurora), 146
Front Range Community College (Westminster), 147
Red Rocks Community College (Lakewood), 151

**Illinois**
Northwestern College (Chicago), 180
Robert Morris University (Chicago), 184
Sauk Valley Community College (Dixon), 186

**Iowa**
Upper Iowa University (Fayette), 198

**Kansas**
Hutchinson Community College and Area Vocational School (Hutchinson), 203
Labette Community College (Parsons), 205
North Central Kansas Technical College (Beloit), 205

**Minnesota**
North Hennepin Community College (Brooklyn Park), 250
Saint Paul College–A Community & Technical College (St. Paul), 254

**Mississippi**
Copiah-Lincoln Community College (Wesson), 258
East Mississippi Community College (Scooba), 259

**Missouri**
Ozarks Technical Community College (Springfield), 274

## MANAGEMENT SCIENCES AND QUANTITATIVE METHODS, OTHER



## MANUFACTURING ENGINEERING



## MANUFACTURING TECHNOLOGY/ TECHNICIAN



## MARINE MAINTENANCE/FITTER AND SHIP REPAIR TECHNOLOGY/TECHNICIAN



## MARINE SCIENCE/MERCHANT MARINE OFFICER



## MARINE TRANSPORTATION, OTHER

## MARKETING/MARKETING MANAGEMENT, GENERAL



## MARKETING, OTHER



## MASON/MASONRY

Kaplan Career Institute–Nashville Campus (Nashville), 334
Miller-Motte Technical College (Chattanooga), 335
Miller-Motte Technical College (Clarksville), 335
Roane State Community College (Harriman), 339

**Texas**
The Academy of Health Care Professions (Houston), 348
ATI Career Training Center (North Richland Hills), 352
ATI Technical Training Center (Dallas), 352
Champion Beauty College (Houston), 356
High-Tech Institute (Irving), 363
Northwest Educational Center (Houston), 372
Parker College of Chiropractic (Dallas), 374
Texas Health School (Houston), 385
Western Technical College (El Paso), 390

**Utah**
American Institute of Medical-Dental Technology (Provo), 392
Certified Careers Institute (Clearfield), 393
Certified Careers Institute (Salt Lake City), 393
Eagle Gate College (Salt Lake City), 394
Everest College (West Valley City), 394
Healing Mountain Massage School (Salt Lake City), 395
Myotherapy College of Utah (Salt Lake City), 395
Ogden Institute of Massage Therapy (Ogden), 396
Renaissance School of Therapeutic Massage (Bountiful), 396
Utah Career College–Layton Campus (Layton), 398
Utah Career College–Orem Campus (Orem), 398
Utah Career College–West Jordan Campus (West Jordan), 398
Utah College of Massage Therapy, Inc.–Utah Valley (Lindon), 398
Utah College of Massage Therapy (Salt Lake City), 398

**Washington**
Ashmead College (Fife), 399
Ashmead College School of Massage (Vancouver), 400
Ashmead College (Seattle), 399
Clover Park Technical College (Lakewood), 402
Cortiva Institute—Brenneke School of Massage (Seattle), 403
Everest College (Bremerton), 403
Inland Massage Institute (Spokane), 406
Peninsula College (Port Angeles), 408
Renton Technical College (Renton), 410
Spokane Community College (Spokane), 411

**Wisconsin**
Blue Sky School of Professional Massage and Therapeutic Bodywork (Grafton), 414
Chippewa Valley Technical College (Eau Claire), 415
High-Tech Institute–Milwaukee (Brookfield), 416
The Institute of Beauty and Wellness (Milwaukee), 416
Lakeside School of Massage Therapy (Madison), 417
Madison Area Technical College (Madison), 417
Martin's School of Hair Design (Green Bay), 417
Professional Hair Design Academy (Eau Claire), 420
Rasmussen College Green Bay (Green Bay), 420
Western Technical College (La Crosse), 422
Wisconsin Indianhead Technical College (Shell Lake), 422

**Wyoming**
Sheridan College (Sheridan), 424

## MASS COMMUNICATION/MEDIA STUDIES

**California**
Bakersfield College (Bakersfield), 74
City College of San Francisco (San Francisco), 82
Glendale Community College (Glendale), 95
Los Angeles Pierce College (Woodland Hills), 108
Los Angeles Valley College (Van Nuys), 109

## MATERIALS ENGINEERING

**Minnesota**
Dunwoody College of Technology (Minneapolis), 242

**Utah**
Davis Applied Technology Center (Kaysville), 393
Ogden-Weber Applied Technology Center (Ogden), 396

## MATHEMATICS AND STATISTICS, OTHER

**Minnesota**
University of Minnesota, Twin Cities Campus (Minneapolis), 256

## MATHEMATICS, GENERAL

**California**
Cuyamaca College (El Cajon), 88
Los Angeles Pierce College (Woodland Hills), 108
Ohlone College (Fremont), 120

## MATHEMATICS TEACHER EDUCATION

**Alaska**
University of Alaska Southeast (Juneau), 42

## MEAT CUTTING/MEAT CUTTER

**Arizona**
Maricopa Skill Center (Phoenix), 51

**Mississippi**
Hinds Community College (Raymond), 259

**Oklahoma**
Western Technology Center (Burns Flat), 318

**Utah**
Bridgerland Applied Technology Center (Logan), 392

## MECHANICAL DRAFTING AND MECHANICAL DRAFTING CAD/CADD

**Arizona**
High-Tech Institute (Phoenix), 51
Mesa Community College (Mesa), 52

**California**
College of the Redwoods (Eureka), 85
De Anza College (Cupertino), 88
Diablo Valley College (Pleasant Hill), 89
Hartnell College (Salinas), 97
Long Beach City College (Long Beach), 106
Los Angeles Valley College (Van Nuys), 109
Merced College (Merced), 113
Mission College (Santa Clara), 115
Orange Coast College (Costa Mesa), 121
San Joaquin Delta College (Stockton), 129
Sierra College (Rocklin), 133

**Colorado**
IntelliTec College (Grand Junction), 148

**Illinois**
City Colleges of Chicago, Harry S. Truman College (Chicago), 163
City Colleges of Chicago, Wilbur Wright College (Chicago), 164
Kankakee Community College (Kankakee), 174
Kaskaskia College (Centralia), 175
Kishwaukee College (Malta), 175
Moraine Valley Community College (Palos Hills), 178
Morton College (Cicero), 179
Richland Community College (Decatur), 184
Southwestern Illinois College (Belleville), 187

**Iowa**
Des Moines Area Community College (Ankeny), 191
Indian Hills Community College (Ottumwa), 192
Iowa Central Community College (Fort Dodge), 193
Muscatine Community College (Muscatine), 196
Northwest Iowa Community College (Sheldon), 197
Southeastern Community College, North Campus (West Burlington), 198
Western Iowa Tech Community College (Sioux City), 198

**Minnesota**
Anoka Technical College (Anoka), 240
Central Lakes College (Brainerd), 241
Hennepin Technical College (Brooklyn Park), 243
Herzing College (Minneapolis), 244
St. Cloud Technical College (St. Cloud), 254

**Oklahoma**
Autry Technology Center (Enid), 302
Tri County Technology Center (Bartlesville), 316

**Oregon**
Mt. Hood Community College (Gresham), 323

**Tennessee**
Northeast State Technical Community College (Blountville), 337
Tennessee Technology Center at Dickson (Dickson), 341

**Texas**
Eastfield College (Mesquite), 360
Odessa College (Odessa), 373

**Washington**
Bates Technical College (Tacoma), 400
Bellingham Technical College (Bellingham), 400
Green River Community College (Auburn), 405
Lake Washington Technical College (Kirkland), 406
South Puget Sound Community College (Olympia), 411

**Wisconsin**
Gateway Technical College (Kenosha), 416
Milwaukee Area Technical College (Milwaukee), 418
Moraine Park Technical College (Fond du Lac), 419

## MECHANICAL ENGINEERING

**Alaska**
University of Alaska Anchorage (Anchorage), 41

## MEDICAL/HEALTH MANAGEMENT AND CLINICAL ASSISTANT/SPECIALIST



## MEDICAL INFORMATICS



## MEDICAL INSURANCE CODING SPECIALIST/CODER

## MEDICAL INSURANCE SPECIALIST/MEDICAL BILLER



## MEDICAL OFFICE ASSISTANT/SPECIALIST

## MEDICAL OFFICE COMPUTER SPECIALIST/ ASSISTANT

Houston's Training and Education Center (Houston), 364
San Antonio College of Medical and Dental Assistants (San Antonio), 378

**Wisconsin**
Moraine Park Technical College (Fond du Lac), 419

## MEDICAL OFFICE MANAGEMENT/ ADMINISTRATION

**Arizona**
Apollo College–Phoenix (Phoenix), 43
Tucson College (Tucson), 57

**Arkansas**
Arkansas State University–Mountain Home (Mountain Home), 59
Ouachita Technical College (Malvern), 64
University of Arkansas Community College at Hope (Hope), 67

**California**
Concorde Career Institute (San Bernardino), 86
Everest College (Alhambra), 91
Everest College (Gardena), 91
Everest College (Ontario), 92
Everest College (Reseda), 92
Everest College (San Bernardino), 92
Glendale Career College (Glendale), 95
LA College International (Los Angeles), 104
Martinez Adult School (Martinez), 112
Maxine Waters Employment Preparation Center (Los Angeles), 113
Meridian Institute (Los Angeles), 114
Modern Technology School (Anaheim), 115
MTI Business College (Stockton), 117
San Joaquin Valley College (Rancho Cordova), 129
San Joaquin Valley College (Rancho Cucamonga), 130
San Joaquin Valley College (Salida), 130
San Joaquin Valley College (Visalia), 130
San Joaquin Valley College–Online (Visalia), 130
Valley College of Medical Careers (West Hills), 138
Western Career College (Emeryville), 140
Western Career College (San Jose), 140
Western Career College (San Leandro), 140
Western Career College (Stockton), 140
Western Career College (Walnut Creek), 141

**Colorado**
Aims Community College (Greeley), 143
Arapahoe Community College (Littleton), 143
Pikes Peak Community College (Colorado Springs), 150
Red Rocks Community College (Lakewood), 151

**Idaho**
Apollo College–Boise (Boise), 156

**Illinois**
Brown Mackie College–Moline (Moline), 161
Computer Systems Institute (Skokie), 165
Everest College (Chicago), 169
John Wood Community College (Quincy), 174

**Kansas**
Butler Community College (El Dorado), 201

**Kentucky**
Sullivan University (Louisville), 219

**Louisiana**
Career Technical College (Monroe), 223
Gretna Career College (Gretna), 226
Unitech Training Academy (Lafayette), 238
Unitech Training Academy–West Monroe Campus (West Monroe), 238

**Mississippi**
Virginia College at Jackson (Jackson), 263

**Nevada**
Academy of Medical and Business Careers (Las Vegas), 289
Nevada Career Institute (Las Vegas), 291

**New Mexico**
Eastern New Mexico University–Roswell (Roswell), 294

**Oklahoma**
Francis Tuttle Area Vocational Technical Center (Oklahoma City), 306
Moore Norman Technology Center (Norman), 311

**Oregon**
Abdill Career Schools (Medford), 319
Apollo College–Portland (Portland), 319

**Tennessee**
Concorde Career College (Memphis), 332
Draughons Junior College (Nashville), 333
Kaplan Career Institute–Nashville Campus (Nashville), 334

**Texas**
American Commercial College (San Angelo), 350
Career Quest (San Antonio), 355
Everest Institute (Houston), 361
Panola College (Carthage), 374
Texas Careers–San Antonio (San Antonio), 384
Tyler Junior College (Tyler), 388

**Utah**
American Institute of Medical-Dental Technology (Provo), 392
Davis Applied Technology Center (Kaysville), 393

**Washington**
Big Bend Community College (Moses Lake), 401
Everest College (Renton), 404
Everett Community College (Everett), 404
Peninsula College (Port Angeles), 408
Perry Technical Institute (Yakima), 409

**Wisconsin**
Herzing College (Madison), 416

## MEDICAL RADIOLOGIC TECHNOLOGY/ SCIENCE—RADIATION THERAPIST

**Arizona**
The Bryman School of Arizona (Phoenix), 46
GateWay Community College (Phoenix), 50

**California**
Central California School (San Luis Obispo), 80
Loma Linda University (Loma Linda), 106
Modern Technology School (Anaheim), 115

**Colorado**
Anthem College Aurora (Aurora), 143

**Illinois**
College of DuPage (Glen Ellyn), 164
South Suburban College (South Holland), 187

**Kansas**
Washburn University (Topeka), 208

**Kentucky**
Madisonville Community College (Madisonville), 216
Southeast Kentucky Community and Technical College (Cumberland), 218
Spencerian College (Louisville), 219
West Kentucky Community and Technical College (Paducah), 220

**Louisiana**
Delgado Community College (New Orleans), 224
MedVance Institute (Baton Rouge), 235

**Minnesota**
High-Tech Institute (St. Louis Park), 244
Mayo School of Health Sciences (Rochester), 245
University of Minnesota, Twin Cities Campus (Minneapolis), 256

**Missouri**
Nichols Career Center (Jefferson City), 274

**Nevada**
College of Southern Nevada (North Las Vegas), 290

**Oklahoma**
Great Plains Technology Center (Lawton), 306
Metro Area Vocational Technical School District 22 (Oklahoma City), 310

**Oregon**
Abdill Career Schools (Medford), 319

**Tennessee**
Chattanooga State Technical Community College (Chattanooga), 332
High-Tech Institute (Memphis), 333
High-Tech Institute (Nashville), 334
MedVance Institute (Cookeville), 335
MedVance Institute–Nashville (Nashville), 335

**Texas**
Academy of Health Care Professions (Austin), 348
The Academy of Health Care Professions (Houston), 348
Galveston College (Galveston), 362
MedVance Institute (Houston), 370
The University of Texas Anderson Cancer Center (Houston), 389
Valley Grande Academy (Weslaco), 389

**Washington**
Lower Columbia College (Longview), 407

## MEDICAL RECEPTION/RECEPTIONIST

**Arizona**
Northland Pioneer College (Holbrook), 53

**California**
North-West College (Glendale), 119
North-West College (Pomona), 120
North-West College (West Covina), 120

**Kentucky**
ATA Career Education (Louisville), 209

**Minnesota**
Anoka Technical College (Anoka), 240
Dakota County Technical College (Rosemount), 242
Hennepin Technical College (Brooklyn Park), 243
Lake Superior College (Duluth), 245
Minnesota West Community and Technical College (Pipestone), 248
Riverland Community College (Austin), 253
Saint Paul College–A Community & Technical College (St. Paul), 254

**Montana**
The University of Montana (Missoula), 285

**Oregon**
Southwestern Oregon Community College (Coos Bay), 327
Valley Medical College (Salem), 327

**Washington**
Bellevue College (Bellevue), 400
Clark College (Vancouver), 402

## MEDICAL STAFF SERVICES TECHNOLOGY/ TECHNICIAN

### California



### Illinois



### Wisconsin



## MEDICAL TRANSCRIPTION/ TRANSCRIPTIONIST

### Arizona



### Arkansas



### California



### Colorado



### Idaho



### Illinois



### Iowa



### Kansas



### Kentucky



### Louisiana



### Minnesota



### Missouri



### Montana



### Nebraska



### New Mexico



### North Dakota



### Oklahoma



### Oregon



### South Dakota



### Tennessee



### Texas

## MONTESSORI TEACHER EDUCATION

**Colorado**
Montessori Education Center of the Rockies (Boulder), 149

**Minnesota**
St. Catherine University (St. Paul), 254

## MOTORCYCLE MAINTENANCE AND REPAIR TECHNOLOGY/TECHNICIAN

**Arizona**
Motorcycle Mechanics Institute–Division of Universal Technical Institute (Phoenix), 52

**California**
WyoTech (Fremont), 142

**Idaho**
North Idaho College (Coeur d'Alene), 159

**Iowa**
Iowa Lakes Community College (Estherville), 193

**Minnesota**
Hennepin Technical College (Brooklyn Park), 243

**Oklahoma**
Central Oklahoma Area Vocational Technical School (Drumright), 304

**Tennessee**
Tennessee Technology Center at Paris (Paris), 344

**Texas**
Austin Community College (Austin), 352
Cedar Valley College (Lancaster), 355

**Washington**
Lake Washington Technical College (Kirkland), 406

## MOVEMENT AND MIND-BODY THERAPIES AND EDUCATION, OTHER

**Arizona**
Southwest Institute of Healing Arts (Tempe), 56

## MULTICULTURAL EDUCATION

**Texas**
Houston Training School–South (Houston), 364

## MUSICAL INSTRUMENT FABRICATION AND REPAIR

**Arizona**
Roberto–Venn School of Luthiery (Phoenix), 56

**Minnesota**
Minnesota State College–Southeast Technical (Winona), 248

**Washington**
Renton Technical College (Renton), 410

## MUSIC, GENERAL

**Arizona**
Glendale Community College (Glendale), 50
Mesa Community College (Mesa), 52
Paradise Valley Community College (Phoenix), 53
Phoenix College (Phoenix), 53
Scottsdale Community College (Scottsdale), 56

**California**
College of the Desert (Palm Desert), 84
Cypress College (Cypress), 88
Glendale Community College (Glendale), 95
Grossmont College (El Cajon), 96
Las Positas College (Livermore), 105
MiraCosta College (Oceanside), 114
Mission College (Santa Clara), 115
Ohlone College (Fremont), 120
Palomar College (San Marcos), 122
Riverside Community College District (Riverside), 126
San Diego Mesa College (San Diego), 128
William Jessup University (Rocklin), 142

**Colorado**
Naropa University (Boulder), 149

**Illinois**
City Colleges of Chicago, Harold Washington College (Chicago), 163
Southwestern Illinois College (Belleville), 187

**Oregon**
Marylhurst University (Marylhurst), 323

**Texas**
Central Texas College (Killeen), 355
Collin County Community College District (Plano), 357
Panola College (Carthage), 374

## MUSIC MANAGEMENT AND MERCHANDISING

**Arizona**
Mesa Community College (Mesa), 52

**California**
Allan Hancock College (Santa Maria), 70
American River College (Sacramento), 72
Antelope Valley College (Lancaster), 72
Chaffey College (Rancho Cucamonga), 81
Citrus College (Glendora), 82
Cypress College (Cypress), 88
Diablo Valley College (Pleasant Hill), 89
Foothill College (Los Altos Hills), 93
Fullerton College (Fullerton), 95
Golden West College (Huntington Beach), 96
Long Beach City College (Long Beach), 106
Los Angeles City College (Los Angeles), 107
Los Angeles Pierce College (Woodland Hills), 108
Los Angeles Valley College (Van Nuys), 109
Los Medanos College (Pittsburg), 109
MiraCosta College (Oceanside), 114
Mt. San Jacinto College (San Jacinto), 117
Ohlone College (Fremont), 120
Orange Coast College (Costa Mesa), 121
Sacramento City College (Sacramento), 126
San Diego City College (San Diego), 128
San Diego Mesa College (San Diego), 128
Santa Ana College (Santa Ana), 131
Santa Barbara City College (Santa Barbara), 131
Southwestern College (Chula Vista), 134

**Minnesota**
McNally Smith College of Music (Saint Paul), 246

**Nevada**
College of Southern Nevada (North Las Vegas), 290

**Tennessee**
Visible School—Music and Worships Arts College (Lakeland), 346

**Texas**
Cedar Valley College (Lancaster), 355
Collin County Community College District (Plano), 357
Houston Community College System (Houston), 363
McLennan Community College (Waco), 369

## MUSIC, OTHER

**Arizona**
Conservatory of Recording Arts and Sciences (Tempe), 48
Mesa Community College (Mesa), 52
Phoenix College (Phoenix), 53

**California**
Musicians Institute (Hollywood), 118

**Tennessee**
Columbia State Community College (Columbia), 332
Nashville State Technical Community College (Nashville), 336

**Washington**
Shoreline Community College (Shoreline), 410

## MUSIC PEDAGOGY

**Illinois**
Roosevelt University (Chicago), 185

**Oregon**
Marylhurst University (Marylhurst), 323

## MUSIC PERFORMANCE, GENERAL

**Arizona**
Phoenix College (Phoenix), 53

**California**
La Sierra University (Riverside), 105
Los Angeles Music Academy (Pasadena), 108
Musicians Institute (Hollywood), 118

**Minnesota**
McNally Smith College of Music (Saint Paul), 246

**Oregon**
Marylhurst University (Marylhurst), 323
Portland Community College (Portland), 326

**Tennessee**
Visible School—Music and Worships Arts College (Lakeland), 346

**Texas**
Cedar Valley College (Lancaster), 355
Houston Community College System (Houston), 363
South Plains College (Levelland), 381

## MUSIC TEACHER EDUCATION

**Illinois**
DePaul University (Chicago), 167

## MUSIC THEORY AND COMPOSITION

**Oregon**
Marylhurst University (Marylhurst), 323

**Texas**
Houston Community College System (Houston), 363

## NAIL TECHNICIAN/SPECIALIST AND MANICURIST

**Arizona**
Arizona Academy of Beauty (Tucson), 43
Arizona Academy of Beauty–North (Tucson), 43
Artistic Beauty Colleges–Chandler (Chandler), 44
Artistic Beauty Colleges–Flagstaff (Flagstaff), 45
Artistic Beauty Colleges–Phoenix (Glendale), 45
Artistic Beauty Colleges–Phoenix North Central (Phoenix), 45
Artistic Beauty Colleges–Prescott (Prescott), 45
Artistic Beauty Colleges–Scottsdale (Scottsdale), 45
Artistic Beauty Colleges–Tucson (Tucson), 45
Artistic Beauty Colleges–Tucson North (Tucson), 45
Artistic Beauty School (Glendale), 45

## NURSING, OTHER



## NURSING—REGISTERED NURSE TRAINING (RN, ASN, BSN, MSN)



## NUTRITION SCIENCES



## OCCUPATIONAL AND ENVIRONMENTAL HEALTH NURSING



## OCCUPATIONAL HEALTH AND INDUSTRIAL HYGIENE



## OCCUPATIONAL SAFETY AND HEALTH TECHNOLOGY/TECHNICIAN



## OCCUPATIONAL THERAPIST ASSISTANT

## OFFICE MANAGEMENT AND SUPERVISION

**Alaska**
Ilisagvik College (Barrow), 41
University of Alaska Anchorage (Anchorage), 41

**Arizona**
Arizona Western College (Yuma), 44
Cochise College (Douglas), 47
GateWay Community College (Phoenix), 50
Glendale Community College (Glendale), 50

**Arkansas**
Arkansas State University–Mountain Home (Mountain Home), 59

**California**
Career College Consultants (Los Angeles), 78
Chabot College (Hayward), 81
Chaffey College (Rancho Cucamonga), 81
Citrus College (Glendora), 82
City College of San Francisco (San Francisco), 82
College of the Desert (Palm Desert), 84
Fresno City College (Fresno), 94
Golden West College (Huntington Beach), 96
Laney College (Oakland), 105
Los Angeles Southwest College (Los Angeles), 109
Los Angeles Trade-Technical College (Los Angeles), 109
Los Medanos College (Pittsburg), 109
MiraCosta College (Oceanside), 114
Mission College (Santa Clara), 115
Modesto Junior College (Modesto), 115
Ohlone College (Fremont), 120
Pasadena City College (Pasadena), 123
Rio Hondo College (Whittier), 125
Sacramento City College (Sacramento), 126
Saddleback College (Mission Viejo), 127
San Joaquin Delta College (Stockton), 129
Santa Ana College (Santa Ana), 131
Santa Monica College (Santa Monica), 132
Santa Rosa Junior College (Santa Rosa), 132
Solano Community College (Suisun City), 134
Southwestern College (Chula Vista), 134
Ventura College (Ventura), 138
Walter J. M.D. Institute, an Educational Center (Los Angeles), 139
Westech College (Pomona), 139
West Valley College (Saratoga), 141
Yuba College (Marysville), 142

**Colorado**
Arapahoe Community College (Littleton), 143
Community College of Aurora (Aurora), 146
Front Range Community College (Westminster), 147
Mesa State College (Grand Junction), 149
Pikes Peak Community College (Colorado Springs), 150

**Illinois**
College of Lake County (Grayslake), 165
Danville Area Community College (Danville), 166
Elgin Community College (Elgin), 167
Kaskaskia College (Centralia), 175
Lincoln College (Lincoln), 177
Sanford-Brown College (Collinsville), 185
Sauk Valley Community College (Dixon), 186
South Suburban College (South Holland), 187

**Iowa**
Des Moines Area Community College (Ankeny), 191

**Kansas**
Washburn University (Topeka), 208

**Kentucky**
Daymar College (Owensboro), 212

**Louisiana**
ITI Technical College (Baton Rouge), 226

**Missouri**
Saint Charles Community College (St. Peters), 277
Three Rivers Community College (Poplar Bluff), 280

**Nebraska**
Northeast Community College (Norfolk), 288

**New Mexico**
Eastern New Mexico University–Roswell (Roswell), 294

**Oklahoma**
Carl Albert State College (Poteau), 304
Tulsa Community College (Tulsa), 317

**Oregon**
Clackamas Community College (Oregon City), 320
Clatsop Community College (Astoria), 321
Linn-Benton Community College (Albany), 323
Portland Community College (Portland), 326
Southwestern Oregon Community College (Coos Bay), 327
Umpqua Community College (Roseburg), 327

**Tennessee**
Concorde Career College (Memphis), 332

**Texas**
Capital City Careers (Austin), 354
Central Texas College (Killeen), 355
North Central Texas College (Gainesville), 371
Sul Ross State University (Alpine), 383
Temple College (Temple), 383
Texas State Technical College Marshall (Marshall), 386

**Washington**
Bellevue College (Bellevue), 400
Big Bend Community College (Moses Lake), 401
Edmonds Community College (Lynnwood), 403
Grays Harbor College (Aberdeen), 405
Green River Community College (Auburn), 405
Highline Community College (Des Moines), 405
Lower Columbia College (Longview), 407
North Seattle Community College (Seattle), 407
Renton Technical College (Renton), 410
Seattle Central Community College (Seattle), 410
South Seattle Community College (Seattle), 411
Spokane Falls Community College (Spokane), 412

## OPERATIONS MANAGEMENT AND SUPERVISION

**Arizona**
Eastern Arizona College (Thatcher), 48
GateWay Community College (Phoenix), 50
Rio Salado College (Tempe), 55

**Illinois**
Joliet Junior College (Joliet), 174
McHenry County College (Crystal Lake), 178
Oakton Community College (Des Plaines), 180
Prairie State College (Chicago Heights), 182

**Minnesota**
Northland Community and Technical College–Thief River Falls (Thief River Falls), 250

**Missouri**
Mineral Area College (Park Hills), 272
Missouri Baptist University (St. Louis), 272

**Oklahoma**
Rose State College (Midwest City), 315

**Oregon**
Clackamas Community College (Oregon City), 320

**Texas**
Tarrant County College District (Fort Worth), 383

**Washington**
Bellingham Technical College (Bellingham), 400

**Wisconsin**
Waukesha County Technical College (Pewaukee), 422

## OPHTHALMIC LABORATORY TECHNOLOGY/TECHNICIAN

**California**
North-West College (West Covina), 120

## OPHTHALMIC TECHNICIAN/TECHNOLOGIST

**Louisiana**
Delgado Community College (New Orleans), 224

**Oklahoma**
Tulsa Tech–Career Services Center (Tulsa), 317

## OPTICIANRY/OPHTHALMIC DISPENSING OPTICIAN

**California**
American Career College (Anaheim), 71
American Career College (Los Angeles), 71
American Career College (Norco), 71
Coast Career Institute (Los Angeles), 83
InfoTech Career College (Bellflower), 100
Martinez Adult School (Martinez), 112

**Colorado**
Emily Griffith Opportunity School (Denver), 146

**Texas**
El Paso Community College (El Paso), 360
Tyler Junior College (Tyler), 388

**Washington**
Highline Community College (Des Moines), 405

**Wisconsin**
Milwaukee Area Technical College (Milwaukee), 418

## OPTOMETRIC TECHNICIAN/ASSISTANT

**California**
National Career Education (Citrus Heights), 118
Sacramento City Unified School District–Skills and Business Education Center (Sacramento), 126

**Iowa**
Hawkeye Community College (Waterloo), 192

**Mississippi**
Hinds Community College (Raymond), 259

**New Mexico**
New Mexico State University–Alamogordo (Alamogordo), 295
Southwestern Indian Polytechnic Institute (Albuquerque), 297

**Texas**
El Paso Community College (El Paso), 360

San Jacinto College Central Campus (Pasadena), 378
Tyler Junior College (Tyler), 388

**Washington**
Renton Technical College (Renton), 410
Spokane Community College (Spokane), 411

**Wisconsin**
Madison Area Technical College (Madison), 417
Milwaukee Area Technical College (Milwaukee), 418

## ORGANIZATIONAL BEHAVIOR STUDIES

**Arizona**
Estrella Mountain Community College (Avondale), 49
GateWay Community College (Phoenix), 50
Mesa Community College (Mesa), 52
Paradise Valley Community College (Phoenix), 53
Rio Salado College (Tempe), 55

**Colorado**
Colorado Christian University (Lakewood), 145

**Illinois**
Roosevelt University (Chicago), 185

**Iowa**
Upper Iowa University (Fayette), 198

## ORGANIZATIONAL COMMUNICATION, GENERAL

**Nebraska**
Creighton University (Omaha), 286

**Oregon**
Marylhurst University (Marylhurst), 323

## ORNAMENTAL HORTICULTURE

**California**
Southwestern College (Chula Vista), 134

**Illinois**
College of DuPage (Glen Ellyn), 164

**Nevada**
College of Southern Nevada (North Las Vegas), 290

**New Mexico**
Eastern New Mexico University–Roswell (Roswell), 294

**Oklahoma**
Northeast Area Vocational Technical School (Pryor), 311

**Oregon**
Clackamas Community College (Oregon City), 320

**Texas**
Alvin Community College (Alvin), 349
Houston Community College System (Houston), 363
Richland College (Dallas), 376
Texarkana College (Texarkana), 384

**Utah**
Utah State University (Logan), 398

## ORTHOPTICS/ORTHOPTIST

**Arizona**
Maricopa Skill Center (Phoenix), 51

**Oklahoma**
Eastern Oklahoma State College (Wilburton), 305

## ORTHOTIST/PROSTHETIST

**California**
Grossmont College (El Cajon), 96

**Minnesota**
Century College (White Bear Lake), 241

**Oklahoma**
Francis Tuttle Area Vocational Technical Center (Oklahoma City), 306

**Washington**
Spokane Falls Community College (Spokane), 412

## PAINTING

**Arizona**
Northern Arizona University (Flagstaff), 52

## PAINTING/PAINTER AND WALL COVERER

**Arizona**
GateWay Community College (Phoenix), 50

**Colorado**
Emily Griffith Opportunity School (Denver), 146

**Illinois**
City Colleges of Chicago, Kennedy-King College (Chicago), 163
Southwestern Illinois College (Belleville), 187

**Minnesota**
Saint Paul College–A Community & Technical College (St. Paul), 254

**Wisconsin**
Gateway Technical College (Kenosha), 416
Milwaukee Area Technical College (Milwaukee), 418

## PARKS, RECREATION AND LEISURE FACILITIES MANAGEMENT

**Arizona**
Northland Pioneer College (Holbrook), 53

**California**
Butte College (Oroville), 75
Modesto Junior College (Modesto), 115
Mt. San Antonio College (Walnut), 116
Palomar College (San Marcos), 122

**Minnesota**
Vermilion Community College (Ely), 256

**New Mexico**
Eastern New Mexico University–Roswell (Roswell), 294

**Washington**
Bellevue College (Bellevue), 400

## PARKS, RECREATION AND LEISURE STUDIES

**Arizona**
Northern Arizona University (Flagstaff), 52
Scottsdale Community College (Scottsdale), 56

**California**
Palomar College (San Marcos), 122
San Joaquin Delta College (Stockton), 129

**New Mexico**
Central New Mexico Community College (Albuquerque), 293

**Wyoming**
Northwest College (Powell), 424

## PARKS, RECREATION, LEISURE AND FITNESS STUDIES, OTHER

**Alaska**
University of Alaska Southeast (Juneau), 42

**Washington**
Walla Walla Community College (Walla Walla), 413

## PARTS, WAREHOUSING, AND INVENTORY MANAGEMENT OPERATIONS

**Arizona**
Southwest Skill Center (Avondale), 57

**California**
Proteus (Visalia), 125

**Illinois**
Harper College (Palatine), 170
Illinois Valley Community College (Oglesby), 173
Lake Land College (Mattoon), 176
Southwestern Illinois College (Belleville), 187

**Kansas**
Kaw Area Technical School (Topeka), 204
Seward County Community College (Liberal), 207

**Washington**
Bates Technical College (Tacoma), 400

## PASTORAL COUNSELING AND SPECIALIZED MINISTRIES, OTHER

**California**
William Jessup University (Rocklin), 142

**Colorado**
Nazarene Bible College (Colorado Springs), 150

**Minnesota**
North Central University (Minneapolis), 249
Northwestern College (St. Paul), 250

## PASTORAL STUDIES/COUNSELING

**California**
Trinity Life Bible College (Sacramento), 135

**Illinois**
Dominican University (River Forest), 167

**Kentucky**
Spalding University (Louisville), 219

**Minnesota**
St. Catherine University (St. Paul), 254

**Oregon**
Marylhurst University (Marylhurst), 323

## PERIOPERATIVE/OPERATING ROOM AND SURGICAL NURSE/NURSING

**Arizona**
GateWay Community College (Phoenix), 50

**Illinois**
Oakton Community College (Des Plaines), 180

## PERMANENT COSMETICS/MAKEUP AND TATTOOING

**Louisiana**
South Louisiana Beauty College (Houma), 237

## PERSONAL AND CULINARY SERVICES, OTHER

**Arizona**
Estrella Mountain Community College (Avondale), 49
GateWay Community College (Phoenix), 50
Mesa Community College (Mesa), 52
Paradise Valley Community College (Phoenix), 53
Rio Salado College (Tempe), 55

**California**
Coachella Valley Beauty College (La Quinta), 83
Fresno City College (Fresno), 94
Universal College of Beauty (Compton), 136

**Louisiana**
Crescent City Bartending School (New Orleans), 224

## PHOTOGRAPHIC AND FILM/VIDEO TECHNOLOGY/TECHNICIAN AND ASSISTANT

**California**
Platt College San Diego (San Diego), 124

**Illinois**
College of DuPage (Glen Ellyn), 164

**Minnesota**
Central Lakes College (Brainerd), 241

**New Mexico**
Doña Ana Branch Community College (Las Cruces), 294
New Mexico State University–Alamogordo (Alamogordo), 295

**Texas**
Amarillo College (Amarillo), 349
Austin Community College (Austin), 352

**Washington**
Shoreline Community College (Shoreline), 410

## PHOTOGRAPHY

**Arizona**
Mohave Community College (Kingman), 52
Northland Pioneer College (Holbrook), 53

**California**
Antelope Valley College (Lancaster), 72
Butte College (Oroville), 75
Citrus College (Glendora), 82
College of the Canyons (Santa Clarita), 84
Cosumnes River College (Sacramento), 87
Cypress College (Cypress), 88
Fresno City College (Fresno), 94
Glendale Community College (Glendale), 95
Mt. San Jacinto College (San Jacinto), 117
Santa Ana College (Santa Ana), 131
Santa Rosa Junior College (Santa Rosa), 132
West Valley College (Saratoga), 141

**Colorado**
Pickens Technical College (Aurora), 150

**Illinois**
Columbia College Chicago (Chicago), 165

**Minnesota**
Dakota County Technical College (Rosemount), 242
Rochester Community and Technical College (Rochester), 253

**Oklahoma**
Oklahoma School of Photography (Moore), 313
Tulsa Tech–Career Services Center (Tulsa), 317

**Oregon**
Mt. Hood Community College (Gresham), 323

**Tennessee**
Nashville State Technical Community College (Nashville), 336

## PHYSICAL EDUCATION TEACHING AND COACHING

**Arizona**
Pima Community College (Tucson), 54

**Kansas**
Bethel College (North Newton), 199

**Minnesota**
University of Minnesota, Twin Cities Campus (Minneapolis), 256

**Montana**
Blackfeet Community College (Browning), 282

**Texas**
Tyler Junior College (Tyler), 388

## PHYSICAL SCIENCES

**California**
San Diego Mesa College (San Diego), 128

## PHYSICAL SCIENCES, OTHER

**Nevada**
Truckee Meadows Community College (Reno), 292

## PHYSICAL THERAPIST ASSISTANT

**Arizona**
Apollo College–Phoenix (Phoenix), 43
Pima Medical Institute (Mesa), 54
Pima Medical Institute (Tucson), 55

**California**
Adelante Career Institute (Van Nuys), 69
ICDC College (Los Angeles), 99
Meridian Institute (Los Angeles), 114
MiraCosta College (Oceanside), 114
Pacific College (Costa Mesa), 121
Ventura Adult and Continuing Education (Ventura), 138

**Iowa**
Western Iowa Tech Community College (Sioux City), 198

**Louisiana**
Unitech Training Academy (Lafayette), 238
Unitech Training Academy–West Monroe Campus (West Monroe), 238

**New Mexico**
Pima Medical Institute (Albuquerque), 296

**Oklahoma**
Caddo-Kiowa Area Vocational Technical School (Ft. Cobb), 303

**Oregon**
Mt. Hood Community College (Gresham), 323

**Texas**
Texas Health School (Houston), 385
Western Technical College (El Paso), 390

## PHYSICAL THERAPY/THERAPIST

**California**
Advanced College (South Gate), 69

**Louisiana**
Unitech Training Academy (Lafayette), 238
Unitech Training Academy–Houma (Houma), 238
Unitech Training Academy–West Monroe Campus (West Monroe), 238

**Minnesota**
Mayo School of Health Sciences (Rochester), 245

**Texas**
Valley Grande Academy (Weslaco), 389

## PHYSICIAN ASSISTANT

**California**
Charles R. Drew University of Medicine and Science (Los Angeles), 81
Foothill College (Los Altos Hills), 93

**Colorado**
Red Rocks Community College (Lakewood), 151

## PHYSIOLOGY, PATHOLOGY, AND RELATED SCIENCES, OTHER

**California**
National Polytechnic College of Engineering and Oceaneering (Wilmington), 118

## PIPEFITTING/PIPEFITTER AND SPRINKLER FITTER

**Alaska**
Ilisagvik College (Barrow), 41

**Arizona**
Central Arizona College (Coolidge), 47
GateWay Community College (Phoenix), 50

**Colorado**
Emily Griffith Opportunity School (Denver), 146

**Louisiana**
Louisiana Technical College–West Jefferson Campus (Harvey), 235

**Minnesota**
Saint Paul College–A Community & Technical College (St. Paul), 254

**New Mexico**
Central New Mexico Community College (Albuquerque), 293
Doña Ana Branch Community College (Las Cruces), 294

**Texas**
Brazosport College (Lake Jackson), 353
Lee College (Baytown), 368
St. Philip's College (San Antonio), 377

**Wisconsin**
Chippewa Valley Technical College (Eau Claire), 415
Gateway Technical College (Kenosha), 416
Mid-State Technical College (Wisconsin Rapids), 418
Milwaukee Area Technical College (Milwaukee), 418

## PLANT NURSERY OPERATIONS AND MANAGEMENT

**Arizona**
Glendale Community College (Glendale), 50

**California**
American River College (Sacramento), 72
Cabrillo College (Aptos), 75
College of the Redwoods (Eureka), 85
Cosumnes River College (Sacramento), 87
Cuyamaca College (El Cajon), 88
Mendocino College (Ukiah), 113
Merritt College (Oakland), 114
MiraCosta College (Oceanside), 114
Mt. San Antonio College (Walnut), 116
Santa Rosa Junior College (Santa Rosa), 132

**Illinois**
College of DuPage (Glen Ellyn), 164
Harper College (Palatine), 170
Joliet Junior College (Joliet), 174

**Minnesota**
Hennepin Technical College (Brooklyn Park), 243

**Texas**
Western Texas College (Snyder), 391

**Washington**
Clark College (Vancouver), 402

## PLANT PROTECTION AND INTEGRATED PEST MANAGEMENT

**South Dakota**
Mitchell Technical Institute (Mitchell), 329

## PLANT SCIENCES, OTHER

**North Dakota**
Williston State College (Williston), 301

## PREPRESS/DESKTOP PUBLISHING AND DIGITAL IMAGING DESIGN

**Arizona**
Coconino Community College (Flagstaff), 48

**California**
American Pacific College (Van Nuys), 72
Antelope Valley College (Lancaster), 72
Chaffey College (Rancho Cucamonga), 81
College of Marin (Kentfield), 84
Cypress College (Cypress), 88
Long Beach City College (Long Beach), 106
Palomar College (San Marcos), 122
Platt College San Diego (San Diego), 124
Santa Ana College (Santa Ana), 131
Ventura Adult and Continuing Education (Ventura), 138
West Valley College (Saratoga), 141

**Illinois**
College of DuPage (Glen Ellyn), 164
Elgin Community College (Elgin), 167
Illinois Central College (East Peoria), 172
Joliet Junior College (Joliet), 174
Lake Land College (Mattoon), 176
Lewis and Clark Community College (Godfrey), 176
Prairie State College (Chicago Heights), 182
Richland Community College (Decatur), 184
Sauk Valley Community College (Dixon), 186
Southeastern Illinois College (Harrisburg), 186
Southwestern Illinois College (Belleville), 187
Zarem/Golde ORT Technical Institute (Chicago), 190

**Iowa**
Des Moines Area Community College (Ankeny), 191
Iowa Central Community College (Fort Dodge), 193

**Kansas**
Kansas City Area Technical School (Kansas City), 204
Northwest Kansas Technical College (Goodland), 206

**Louisiana**
Louisiana Technical College–Lafayette Campus (Lafayette), 231

**Minnesota**
Hennepin Technical College (Brooklyn Park), 243
Minneapolis Community and Technical College (Minneapolis), 246
Ridgewater College (Willmar), 253
Riverland Community College (Austin), 253

**Missouri**
Kansas City Art Institute (Kansas City), 269
Pike/Lincoln Tech Center (Eolia), 275
St. Louis Community College at Forest Park (St. Louis), 278

**Nevada**
College of Southern Nevada (North Las Vegas), 290

**Oklahoma**
Mid-America Technology Center (Wayne), 310
Pontotoc Technology Center (Ada), 314

**Oregon**
Linn-Benton Community College (Albany), 323

**Texas**
Alvin Community College (Alvin), 349
Austin Community College (Austin), 352
Eastfield College (Mesquite), 360
Houston Community College System (Houston), 363
Lee College (Baytown), 368
Tarrant County College District (Fort Worth), 383

**Utah**
Salt Lake Community College (Salt Lake City), 396

**Washington**
The Art Institute of Seattle (Seattle), 399
Bellevue College (Bellevue), 400
Clark College (Vancouver), 402
Clover Park Technical College (Lakewood), 402

**Wyoming**
Northwest College (Powell), 424

## PRE-THEOLOGY/PRE-MINISTERIAL STUDIES

**California**
Trinity Life Bible College (Sacramento), 135

**Oregon**
Mount Angel Seminary (Saint Benedict), 323

## PRE-VETERINARY STUDIES

**Kansas**
Barton County Community College (Great Bend), 199

**Nevada**
College of Southern Nevada (North Las Vegas), 290

## PRINTING PRESS OPERATOR

**Louisiana**
Louisiana Technical College–Baton Rouge Campus (Baton Rouge), 229
Louisiana Technical College–Folkes Campus (Jackson), 230
Louisiana Technical College–Shreveport-Bossier Campus (Shreveport), 234

**Minnesota**
Hennepin Technical College (Brooklyn Park), 243

**Oklahoma**
Central Oklahoma Area Vocational Technical School (Drumright), 304
Francis Tuttle Area Vocational Technical Center (Oklahoma City), 306
Mid-America Technology Center (Wayne), 310
Tri County Technology Center (Bartlesville), 316
Western Technology Center (Burns Flat), 318

**Oregon**
Portland Community College (Portland), 326

**Wisconsin**
Fox Valley Technical College (Appleton), 415

## PRINTMAKING

**Arizona**
Northern Arizona University (Flagstaff), 52

**Oklahoma**
Tulsa Community College (Tulsa), 317

## PSYCHIATRIC/MENTAL HEALTH NURSE/NURSING

**California**
Hacienda La Puente Unified School District–Adult Education (City of Industry), 97

**Illinois**
Saint Xavier University (Chicago), 185

## PSYCHIATRIC/MENTAL HEALTH SERVICES TECHNICIAN

**California**
Cypress College (Cypress), 88
Mission College (Santa Clara), 115
Mt. San Antonio College (Walnut), 116
Napa Valley College (Napa), 118
Porterville College (Porterville), 124
San Bernardino Valley College (San Bernardino), 128
San Joaquin Delta College (Stockton), 129
Santa Rosa Junior College (Santa Rosa), 132
West Hills Community College (Coalinga), 141

**Colorado**
Pueblo Community College (Pueblo), 151

**Idaho**
College of Southern Idaho (Twin Falls), 157
North Idaho College (Coeur d'Alene), 159

**Illinois**
City Colleges of Chicago, Wilbur Wright College (Chicago), 164
Elgin Community College (Elgin), 167
Illinois Central College (East Peoria), 172
Illinois Eastern Community Colleges, Frontier Community College (Fairfield), 172
Moraine Valley Community College (Palos Hills), 178
Shawnee Community College (Ullin), 186
Southeastern Illinois College (Harrisburg), 186

**Iowa**
Ellsworth Community College (Iowa Falls), 191
Marshalltown Community College (Marshalltown), 196

**Minnesota**
Rochester Community and Technical College (Rochester), 253

**Missouri**
Metropolitan Community College–Longview (Lee's Summit), 271
Metropolitan Community College–Penn Valley (Kansas City), 271

**Nebraska**
Vatterott College (Omaha), 289

**Nevada**
College of Southern Nevada (North Las Vegas), 290

**North Dakota**
Williston State College (Williston), 301

**Texas**
Houston Community College System (Houston), 363
Lonestar College–North Harris (Houston), 369
McLennan Community College (Waco), 369
PCI Health Training Center (Dallas), 374
San Jacinto College Central Campus (Pasadena), 378
Tarrant County College District (Fort Worth), 383

**Washington**
Pierce College at Fort Steilacoom (Lakewood), 409

## PUBLIC ADMINISTRATION

**Arizona**
Northland Pioneer College (Holbrook), 53
Rio Salado College (Tempe), 55

**California**
Los Angeles Trade-Technical College (Los Angeles), 109
Palomar College (San Marcos), 122

**Illinois**
Oakton Community College (Des Plaines), 180

**Minnesota**
Hennepin Technical College (Brooklyn Park), 243

## SURGICAL TECHNOLOGY/TECHNOLOGIST

Mercy College of Health Sciences (Des Moines), 196
Western Iowa Tech Community College (Sioux City), 198

**Kansas**
Hutchinson Community College and Area Vocational School (Hutchinson), 203
Kaw Area Technical School (Topeka), 204
Seward County Community College (Liberal), 207
Wichita Area Technical College (Wichita), 208
Wright Business School (Overland Park), 209

**Kentucky**
Ashland Community and Technical College (Ashland), 209
Bluegrass Community and Technical College (Lexington), 210
Bowling Green Technical College (Bowling Green), 210
Jefferson Community and Technical College (Louisville), 215
Madisonville Community College (Madisonville), 216
Maysville Community and Technical College (Maysville), 216
Owensboro Community and Technical College (Owensboro), 217
Southeast Kentucky Community and Technical College (Cumberland), 218
Spencerian College (Louisville), 219
West Kentucky Community and Technical College (Paducah), 220

**Louisiana**
Bossier Parish Community College (Bossier City), 223
Delgado Community College (New Orleans), 224
MedVance Institute (Baton Rouge), 235

**Minnesota**
Anoka Technical College (Anoka), 240
High-Tech Institute (St. Louis Park), 244
Lake Superior College (Duluth), 245
St. Cloud Technical College (St. Cloud), 254
Saint Mary's University of Minnesota (Winona), 254

**Mississippi**
East Central Community College (Decatur), 259
Hinds Community College (Raymond), 259
Holmes Community College (Goodman), 260
Itawamba Community College (Fulton), 260
Meridian Community College (Meridian), 261
Mississippi Gulf Coast Community College (Perkinston), 261
Northwest Mississippi Community College (Senatobia), 262
Pearl River Community College (Poplarville), 262

**Missouri**
Allied College (Maryland Heights), 263
Columbia Area Vocational Technical School (Columbia), 265
Franklin Technology Center (Joplin), 267
High-Tech Institute (Kansas City), 268
Metropolitan Community College–Penn Valley (Kansas City), 271
Ozarks Technical Community College (Springfield), 274
St. Louis Community College at Forest Park (St. Louis), 278
South Central Area Vocational Technical School (West Plains), 280
Southeast Missouri Hospital College of Nursing and Health Sciences (Cape Girardeau), 280

**Montana**
Montana State University–Great Falls College of Technology (Great Falls), 284

**Nebraska**
Nebraska Methodist College (Omaha), 288

**Nevada**
College of Southern Nevada (North Las Vegas), 290
High-Tech Institute (Las Vegas), 291
Nevada Career Institute (Las Vegas), 291
Western Nevada Community College (Carson City), 292

**New Mexico**
Central New Mexico Community College (Albuquerque), 293

**Oklahoma**
Autry Technology Center (Enid), 302
Canadian Valley Technology Center (El Reno), 303
Central Oklahoma Area Vocational Technical School (Drumright), 304
Community Care College (Tulsa), 305
Great Plains Technology Center (Lawton), 306
Heritage College of Hair Design (Oklahoma City), 307
Indian Capital Technology Center–Stilwell (Stilwell), 308
Metro Area Vocational Technical School District 22 (Oklahoma City), 310
Moore Norman Technology Center (Norman), 311
Oklahoma Health Academy (Moore), 312
Platt College (Oklahoma City), 314
Platt College (Tulsa), 314
Tulsa Tech–Career Services Center (Tulsa), 317
Wes Watkins Area Vocational-Technical Center (Wetumka), 318

**Oregon**
Cambridge College (Beaverton), 320
Concorde Career Institute (Portland), 321
Mt. Hood Community College (Gresham), 323

**South Dakota**
Southeast Technical Institute (Sioux Falls), 330
Western Dakota Technical Institute (Rapid City), 330

**Tennessee**
Concorde Career College (Memphis), 332
High-Tech Institute (Memphis), 333
High-Tech Institute (Nashville), 334
MedVance Institute (Cookeville), 335
MedVance Institute–Nashville (Nashville), 335
Nashville State Technical Community College (Nashville), 336
Northeast State Technical Community College (Blountville), 337
Tennessee Technology Center at Crossville (Crossville), 341
Tennessee Technology Center at Dickson (Dickson), 341
Tennessee Technology Center at Hohenwald (Hohenwald), 342
Tennessee Technology Center at Jackson (Jackson), 342
Tennessee Technology Center at Knoxville (Knoxville), 342
Tennessee Technology Center at McMinnville (McMinnville), 343
Tennessee Technology Center at Memphis (Memphis), 343
Tennessee Technology Center at Murfreesboro (Murfreesboro), 343
Tennessee Technology Center at Paris (Paris), 344

**Texas**
The Academy of Health Care Professions (Houston), 348
Amarillo College (Amarillo), 349
Austin Community College (Austin), 352
Career Centers of Texas–El Paso (El Paso), 354
Cisco College (Cisco), 356
Concorde Career Institute (Arlington), 358
Del Mar College (Corpus Christi), 359
El Centro College (Dallas), 360
El Paso Community College (El Paso), 360
Galveston College (Galveston), 362
High-Tech Institute (Irving), 363
Houston Community College System (Houston), 363
Howard College (Big Spring), 364
Iverson Institute of Court Reporting (Arlington), 366
Kilgore College (Kilgore), 367
Lamar State College–Port Arthur (Port Arthur), 367
Lonestar College–North Harris (Houston), 369
MedVance Institute (Houston), 370
North Central Texas College (Gainesville), 371
Odessa College (Odessa), 373
Paris Junior College (Paris), 374
St. Philip's College (San Antonio), 377
Sanford-Brown Institute (Dallas), 378
Sanford-Brown Institute (Houston), 378
San Jacinto College Central Campus (Pasadena), 378
South Plains College (Levelland), 381
Tarrant County College District (Fort Worth), 383
Temple College (Temple), 383
Texas State Technical College Harlingen (Harlingen), 386
Trinity Valley Community College (Athens), 387
Tyler Junior College (Tyler), 388
Vernon College (Vernon), 389
Wharton County Junior College (Wharton), 391

**Utah**
American Institute of Medical-Dental Technology (Provo), 392
Davis Applied Technology Center (Kaysville), 393
Dixie State College of Utah (St. George), 394
Salt Lake Community College (Salt Lake City), 396

**Washington**
Bellingham Technical College (Bellingham), 400
Renton Technical College (Renton), 410
Seattle Central Community College (Seattle), 410

**Wisconsin**
Chippewa Valley Technical College (Eau Claire), 415
High-Tech Institute–Milwaukee (Brookfield), 416
Lakeshore Technical College (Cleveland), 417
Madison Area Technical College (Madison), 417
Mid-State Technical College (Wisconsin Rapids), 418
Northcentral Technical College (Wausau), 419

**Louisiana**
Baton Rouge School of Computers (Baton Rouge), 222
**Minnesota**
Academy College (Minneapolis), 239
**Missouri**
Mineral Area College (Park Hills), 272
**New Mexico**
Southwestern Indian Polytechnic Institute (Albuquerque), 297
**North Dakota**
Williston State College (Williston), 301
**Oklahoma**
Eastern Oklahoma County Technology Center (Choctaw), 305
Moore Norman Technology Center (Norman), 311
Tulsa Tech–Peoria Campus (Tulsa), 317
**Oregon**
Lane Community College (Eugene), 322
**Tennessee**
Northeast State Technical Community College (Blountville), 337
**Texas**
Central Texas College (Killeen), 355
El Paso Community College (El Paso), 360
Frank Phillips College (Borger), 362
Hill College of the Hill Junior College District (Hillsboro), 363
Houston Community College System (Houston), 363
Lee College (Baytown), 368
McLennan Community College (Waco), 369
Paris Junior College (Paris), 374
St. Philip's College (San Antonio), 377
San Jacinto College Central Campus (Pasadena), 378
Temple College (Temple), 383
Texas State Technical College Marshall (Marshall), 386
Texas State Technical College Waco (Waco), 386
**Utah**
College of Eastern Utah (Price), 393
**Washington**
Green River Community College (Auburn), 405

## SYSTEMS ENGINEERING

**California**
ATI College (Norwalk), 73

## TAXATION

**California**
Butte College (Oroville), 75
Chaffey College (Rancho Cucamonga), 81
De Anza College (Cupertino), 88
Los Angeles Pierce College (Woodland Hills), 108
Los Angeles Southwest College (Los Angeles), 109
MiraCosta College (Oceanside), 114
Mt. San Jacinto College (San Jacinto), 117
Saddleback College (Mission Viejo), 127
San Diego City College (San Diego), 128
San Joaquin Delta College (Stockton), 129
Yuba College (Marysville), 142

## TAXIDERMY/TAXIDERMIST

**Minnesota**
Vermilion Community College (Ely), 256

## TEACHER ASSISTANT/AIDE

**Alaska**
University of Alaska Fairbanks (Fairbanks), 42
**Arizona**
Chandler-Gilbert Community College (Chandler), 47
Cochise College (Douglas), 47
Mesa Community College (Mesa), 52
Northland Pioneer College (Holbrook), 53
**California**
Antelope Valley College (Lancaster), 72
Chaffey College (Rancho Cucamonga), 81
Fresno City College (Fresno), 94
Los Angeles Mission College (Sylmar), 107
Los Angeles Southwest College (Los Angeles), 109
Mission College (Santa Clara), 115
Mt. San Antonio College (Walnut), 116
Porterville College (Porterville), 124
Riverside Community College District (Riverside), 126
Saddleback College (Mission Viejo), 127
West Hills Community College (Coalinga), 141
**Colorado**
Front Range Community College (Westminster), 147
**Idaho**
College of Southern Idaho (Twin Falls), 157
**Illinois**
College of Lake County (Grayslake), 165
Illinois Eastern Community Colleges, Frontier Community College (Fairfield), 172
Kankakee Community College (Kankakee), 174
Moraine Valley Community College (Palos Hills), 178
Prairie State College (Chicago Heights), 182
Southeastern Illinois College (Harrisburg), 186
South Suburban College (South Holland), 187
Triton College (River Grove), 188
**Iowa**
Western Iowa Tech Community College (Sioux City), 198
**Kansas**
Fort Scott Community College (Fort Scott), 202
**Kentucky**
Bluegrass Community and Technical College (Lexington), 210
Jefferson Community and Technical College (Louisville), 215
**Minnesota**
Minnesota West Community and Technical College (Pipestone), 248
Ridgewater College (Willmar), 253
Rochester Community and Technical College (Rochester), 253
**New Mexico**
Eastern New Mexico University–Roswell (Roswell), 294
**North Dakota**
Dakota College at Bottineau (Bottineau), 299
Williston State College (Williston), 301
**Northern Mariana Islands**
Northern Marianas College (Saipan), 302
**Oregon**
Blue Mountain Community College (Pendleton), 320
Chemeketa Community College (Salem), 320
Clackamas Community College (Oregon City), 320
Columbia Gorge Community College (The Dalles), 321
Linn-Benton Community College (Albany), 323
Mt. Hood Community College (Gresham), 323
Portland Community College (Portland), 326
Southwestern Oregon Community College (Coos Bay), 327
Umpqua Community College (Roseburg), 327
**Texas**
Hill College of the Hill Junior College District (Hillsboro), 363
Northwest Vista College (San Antonio), 372
Palo Alto College (San Antonio), 373
Richland College (Dallas), 376
San Antonio College (San Antonio), 377
Texas State Technical College Harlingen (Harlingen), 386
**Utah**
Davis Applied Technology Center (Kaysville), 393
**Washington**
Bates Technical College (Tacoma), 400
Bellingham Technical College (Bellingham), 400
Columbia Basin College (Pasco), 402
Lower Columbia College (Longview), 407
Renton Technical College (Renton), 410
Shoreline Community College (Shoreline), 410
Skagit Valley College (Mount Vernon), 411
Spokane Falls Community College (Spokane), 412
Tacoma Community College (Tacoma), 412
Walla Walla Community College (Walla Walla), 413
Whatcom Community College (Bellingham), 413
Yakima Valley Community College (Yakima), 414
**Wisconsin**
Western Technical College (La Crosse), 422
**Wyoming**
Casper College (Casper), 423

## TEACHER EDUCATION AND PROFESSIONAL DEVELOPMENT, SPECIFIC LEVELS AND METHODS, OTHER

**Arizona**
Pima Community College (Tucson), 54
**California**
Universal College of Beauty (Compton), 136
**New Mexico**
Southwestern Indian Polytechnic Institute (Albuquerque), 297
**South Dakota**
Dakota State University (Madison), 328
**Washington**
Green River Community College (Auburn), 405
Yakima Valley Community College (Yakima), 414

## TEACHER EDUCATION AND PROFESSIONAL DEVELOPMENT, SPECIFIC SUBJECT AREAS, OTHER

**Arizona**
International Academy of Hair Design (Tempe), 51
**Arkansas**
Velvatex College of Beauty Culture (Little Rock), 68
**California**
North Adrians Beauty College (Modesto), 119
Universal College of Beauty (Compton), 136

**Idaho**
College of Southern Idaho (Twin Falls), 157
**Illinois**
Cannella School of Hair Design (Blue Island), 161
Cannella School of Hair Design (Chicago), 161
Cannella School of Hair Design (Elgin), 162
Cannella School of Hair Design (Elmhurst), 162
Concept College of Cosmetology (Danville), 166
Concept College of Cosmetology (Urbana), 166
Hair Professionals Career College (Palos Hills), 170
Hair Professionals School of Cosmetology (Oswego), 170
Hebrew Theological College (Skokie), 171
Pivot Point Beauty School (Chicago), 181
University of Spa & Cosmetology Arts (Springfield), 189
**Louisiana**
Louisiana Academy of Beauty (Eunice), 227
**Missouri**
Independence College of Cosmetology (Independence), 269
Paris II Educational Center (Gladstone), 275
**Nebraska**
Capitol School of Hairstyling (Omaha), 285
**New Mexico**
Olympian University of Cosmetology (Alamogordo), 296
**Texas**
ICC Technical Institute (Houston), 365

## TEACHING ASSISTANTS/AIDES, OTHER

**Arizona**
Northland Pioneer College (Holbrook), 53

## TEACHING ENGLISH AS A SECOND OR FOREIGN LANGUAGE/ESL LANGUAGE INSTRUCTOR

**Arkansas**
Cossatot Community College of the University of Arkansas (De Queen), 61
**California**
Advanced Training Associates (El Cajon), 70
Silicon Valley University (San Jose), 133
**Colorado**
Front Range Community College (Westminster), 147
**Hawaii**
Hawai'i Pacific University (Honolulu), 154
**Illinois**
College of Lake County (Grayslake), 165
Parkland College (Champaign), 181
Taylor Business Institute (Chicago), 188
**Kentucky**
Spalding University (Louisville), 219
**Minnesota**
North Central University (Minneapolis), 249
**Missouri**
Ozark Christian College (Joplin), 274
**Oregon**
Northwest Christian University (Eugene), 324
**Utah**
Eagle Gate College (Salt Lake City), 394
Snow College (Ephraim), 397
**Washington**
Northwest University (Kirkland), 408

## TECHNICAL AND BUSINESS WRITING

**Arizona**
Pima Community College (Tucson), 54
**California**
American River College (Sacramento), 72
De Anza College (Cupertino), 88
Los Angeles Pierce College (Woodland Hills), 108
**Illinois**
College of DuPage (Glen Ellyn), 164
College of Lake County (Grayslake), 165
**Missouri**
St. Louis Community College at Florissant Valley (St. Louis), 277
St. Louis Community College at Forest Park (St. Louis), 278
St. Louis Community College at Meramec (Kirkwood), 278
**Tennessee**
Nashville State Technical Community College (Nashville), 336
**Texas**
Austin Community College (Austin), 352
**Washington**
Washington State University (Pullman), 413
**Wisconsin**
Moraine Park Technical College (Fond du Lac), 419

## TECHNICAL TEACHER EDUCATION

**Arkansas**
Hot Springs Beauty College (Hot Springs), 62
Margaret's Hair Academy (Morrilton), 63
**Idaho**
Headmasters School of Hair Design (Lewiston), 158
The School of Hairstyling (Pocatello), 159
**Kentucky**
Pat Wilson's Beauty College (Henderson), 217
**Mississippi**
Mississippi Gulf Coast Community College (Perkinston), 261
**New Mexico**
Northern New Mexico College (Española), 296
**North Dakota**
North Dakota State College of Science (Wahpeton), 300
**Washington**
Greenwood Academy of Hair (Seattle), 405
Northwest Hair Academy (Mt. Vernon), 407

## TECHNICAL THEATRE/THEATRE DESIGN AND TECHNOLOGY

**California**
El Camino College (Torrance), 90
MiraCosta College (Oceanside), 114
Modesto Junior College (Modesto), 115
Monterey Peninsula College (Monterey), 116
Mt. San Jacinto College (San Jacinto), 117
Palomar College (San Marcos), 122
Pasadena City College (Pasadena), 123
San Diego City College (San Diego), 128
Santa Ana College (Santa Ana), 131
**Colorado**
Community College of Denver (Denver), 146
Red Rocks Community College (Lakewood), 151
**Kansas**
Independence Community College (Independence), 203
**Louisiana**
Louisiana Technical College–Jefferson Campus (Metairie), 230
**Nebraska**
Metropolitan Community College (Omaha), 287
**South Dakota**
The University of South Dakota (Vermillion), 330

## TECHNOLOGY TEACHER EDUCATION/ INDUSTRIAL ARTS TEACHER EDUCATION

**Oklahoma**
Stillwater Beauty Academy (Stillwater), 316
Yukon Beauty College (Yukon), 319

## TELECOMMUNICATIONS TECHNOLOGY/ TECHNICIAN

**California**
Associated Technical College (Los Angeles), 73
**Missouri**
St. Louis Community College at Florissant Valley (St. Louis), 277
**Texas**
Collin County Community College District (Plano), 357
Eastfield College (Mesquite), 360
Grayson County College (Denison), 363
Lee College (Baytown), 368
Texas State Technical College Harlingen (Harlingen), 386
Texas State Technical College Waco (Waco), 386
Tyler Junior College (Tyler), 388
**Washington**
Clark College (Vancouver), 402
Clover Park Technical College (Lakewood), 402

## THEOLOGICAL AND MINISTERIAL STUDIES, OTHER

**California**
Hope International University (Fullerton), 99

## THEOLOGY AND RELIGIOUS VOCATIONS, OTHER

**California**
Trinity Life Bible College (Sacramento), 135
William Jessup University (Rocklin), 142
**Minnesota**
Martin Luther College (New Ulm), 245
**Missouri**
Messenger College (Joplin), 270
Midwestern Baptist Theological Seminary (Kansas City), 272
**Wisconsin**
Concordia University Wisconsin (Mequon), 415

## THEOLOGY/THEOLOGICAL STUDIES

**Kentucky**
Clear Creek Baptist Bible College (Pineville), 211
**Nebraska**
Creighton University (Omaha), 286
**Oregon**
Marylhurst University (Marylhurst), 323
**Tennessee**
Visible School—Music and Worships Arts College (Lakeland), 346

## THERAPEUTIC RECREATION/RECREATIONAL THERAPY

**California**
Fremont College (Cerritos), 94

**Minnesota**
Ridgewater College (Willmar), 253

**Oklahoma**
High Plains Institute of Technology (Woodward), 307

**Texas**
Austin Community College (Austin), 352

## TOOL AND DIE TECHNOLOGY/TECHNICIAN

**Arizona**
Mesa Community College (Mesa), 52

**Illinois**
Elgin Community College (Elgin), 167
John A. Logan College (Carterville), 174
Prairie State College (Chicago Heights), 182

**Iowa**
Des Moines Area Community College (Ankeny), 191
Marshalltown Community College (Marshalltown), 196
North Iowa Area Community College (Mason City), 197
Western Iowa Tech Community College (Sioux City), 198

**Minnesota**
Anoka Technical College (Anoka), 240
Hennepin Technical College (Brooklyn Park), 243
Minnesota State College–Southeast Technical (Winona), 248
Ridgewater College (Willmar), 253
Saint Paul College–A Community & Technical College (St. Paul), 254

**Missouri**
St. Louis Community College at Florissant Valley (St. Louis), 277

**Tennessee**
Tennessee Technology Center at Jackson (Jackson), 342

**Texas**
South Texas College (McAllen), 381

**Wisconsin**
Lakeshore Technical College (Cleveland), 417
Milwaukee Area Technical College (Milwaukee), 418
Waukesha County Technical College (Pewaukee), 422

## TOURISM AND TRAVEL SERVICES MANAGEMENT

**Alaska**
Career Academy (Anchorage), 41

**Arizona**
Northern Arizona University (Flagstaff), 52

**California**
Empire College (Santa Rosa), 90

**Colorado**
Colorado Mountain College (Glenwood Springs), 145

**Guam**
Guam Community College (Barrigada), 154

**Hawaii**
Hawai'i Pacific University (Honolulu), 154
Kapiolani Community College (Honolulu), 155
Travel Institute of the Pacific (Honolulu), 156

**Illinois**
Illinois Central College (East Peoria), 172
Moraine Valley Community College (Palos Hills), 178
Northwestern Business College–Southwestern Campus (Bridgeview), 180
Waubonsee Community College (Sugar Grove), 189

**Iowa**
Kaplan University, Davenport Campus (Davenport), 194

**Kansas**
Butler Community College (El Dorado), 201

**Minnesota**
Dakota County Technical College (Rosemount), 242
Minneapolis Business College (Roseville), 246

**Mississippi**
Hinds Community College (Raymond), 259

**Missouri**
Bryan College (Springfield), 264
Patricia Stevens College (St. Louis), 275
St. Louis Community College at Forest Park (St. Louis), 278

**Nebraska**
Kaplan University, Lincoln (Lincoln), 286

**Nevada**
College of Southern Nevada (North Las Vegas), 290

**Oklahoma**
Tulsa Tech–Peoria Campus (Tulsa), 317

**Oregon**
Chemeketa Community College (Salem), 320
Mt. Hood Community College (Gresham), 323

**Texas**
Austin Community College (Austin), 352
Career Quest (San Antonio), 355
Central Texas College (Killeen), 355
Houston Community College System (Houston), 363
Lonestar College–North Harris (Houston), 369
Tarrant County College District (Fort Worth), 383

**Utah**
Everest College (West Valley City), 394

**Washington**
Edmonds Community College (Lynnwood), 403
Highline Community College (Des Moines), 405

**Wisconsin**
Milwaukee Area Technical College (Milwaukee), 418

## TOURISM AND TRAVEL SERVICES MARKETING OPERATIONS

**Arizona**
Phoenix College (Phoenix), 53

**California**
Berkeley City College (Berkeley), 74
Butte College (Oroville), 75
Chabot College (Hayward), 81
City College of San Francisco (San Francisco), 82
Columbia College (Sonora), 85
Cypress College (Cypress), 88
Foothill College (Los Altos Hills), 93
Los Angeles Mission College (Sylmar), 107
Los Medanos College (Pittsburg), 109
MiraCosta College (Oceanside), 114
Saddleback College (Mission Viejo), 127
San Diego Mesa College (San Diego), 128
Santiago Canyon College (Orange), 132
Southwestern College (Chula Vista), 134
West Los Angeles College (Culver City), 141

**Colorado**
Arapahoe Community College (Littleton), 143

**Illinois**
College of DuPage (Glen Ellyn), 164
Lincoln College (Lincoln), 177
MacCormac College (Chicago), 177
Pyramid Career Institute (Chicago), 182

**Kentucky**
Sullivan University (Louisville), 219

**Oregon**
Everest College (Portland), 322

**Texas**
El Paso Community College (El Paso), 360
Richland College (Dallas), 376

**Washington**
Clover Park Technical College (Lakewood), 402
Edmonds Community College (Lynnwood), 403

## TOURISM PROMOTION OPERATIONS

**Alaska**
University of Alaska Southeast (Juneau), 42

## TRADE AND INDUSTRIAL TEACHER EDUCATION

**Arizona**
Toni & Guy Hairdressing Academy (Scottsdale), 57

**Arkansas**
Arkansas Beauty School (Conway), 58
Margaret's Hair Academy (Morrilton), 63

**California**
California Hair Design Academy (San Diego), 76
Lancaster Beauty School (Lancaster), 105

**Illinois**
Cameo Beauty Academy (Oak Lawn), 161

**Kentucky**
Head's West Kentucky Beauty School (Madisonville), 214

**Minnesota**
University of Minnesota, Twin Cities Campus (Minneapolis), 256

**Mississippi**
ICS–The Wright Beauty College (Corinth), 260

**Missouri**
Cosmetology Concepts Institute (Columbia), 265
Missouri Beauty Academy (Farmington), 272
National Academy of Beauty Arts (St. Louis), 273

**New Mexico**
De Wolff College of Hair Styling and Cosmetology (Albuquerque), 294

**Texas**
Exposito School of Hair Design (Amarillo), 362

## TRANSPORTATION AND MATERIALS MOVING, OTHER

**California**
Center for Employment Training–Salinas (Salinas), 79
Center for Employment Training–Sobrato (San Jose), 79
Center for Employment Training–Temecula (Temecula), 80
Southwestern College (Chula Vista), 134

**Texas**
Center for Employment Training–Socorro (Socorro), 355

**Utah**
Ogden-Weber Applied Technology Center (Ogden), 396

## TRUCK AND BUS DRIVER/COMMERCIAL VEHICLE OPERATION

**Alaska**
Ilisagvik College (Barrow), 41

**Arizona**
American Institute of Technology (Phoenix), 43
Glendale Community College (Glendale), 50
HDS Truck Driving Institute (Tucson), 50
Mohave Community College (Kingman), 52
Pima Community College (Tucson), 54

**Arkansas**
Arkansas Northeastern College (Blytheville), 59
Arkansas State University–Newport (Newport), 59
Crowley's Ridge Technical Institute (Forrest City), 62
North Arkansas College (Harrison), 64
Northwest Technical Institute (Springdale), 64
Ouachita Technical College (Malvern), 64
South Arkansas Community College (El Dorado), 66

**California**
California Career Schools (Anaheim), 76
Center for Employment Training–El Centro (El Centro), 78
Center for Employment Training–Gilroy (Gilroy), 79
Center for Employment Training–Oxnard (Oxnard), 79
Center for Employment Training–Santa Maria (Santa Maria), 79
CET–Sacramento (Sacramento), 81
Proteus (Visalia), 125
Sacramento City Unified School District–Skills and Business Education Center (Sacramento), 126

**Idaho**
Boise State University (Boise), 157
Eastern Idaho Technical College (Idaho Falls), 157

**Illinois**
City Colleges of Chicago, Harold Washington College (Chicago), 163
Danville Area Community College (Danville), 166
Elgin Community College (Elgin), 167
Illinois Eastern Community Colleges, Frontier Community College (Fairfield), 172
Illinois Eastern Community Colleges, Wabash Valley College (Mount Carmel), 173
Illinois Valley Community College (Oglesby), 173
John Wood Community College (Quincy), 174
Kaskaskia College (Centralia), 175
Lincoln Land Community College (Springfield), 177
Parkland College (Champaign), 181
Sauk Valley Community College (Dixon), 186
Shawnee Community College (Ullin), 186
Spoon River College (Canton), 187

**Iowa**
Hawkeye Community College (Waterloo), 192
Muscatine Community College (Muscatine), 196

**Kansas**
Fort Scott Community College (Fort Scott), 202
Wichita Area Technical College (Wichita), 208

**Kentucky**
West Kentucky Community and Technical College (Paducah), 220

**Louisiana**
Diesel Driving Academy (Baton Rouge), 225
Diesel Driving Academy (Shreveport), 225
Louisiana Technical College–Acadian Campus (Crowley), 228
Louisiana Technical College–Delta Ouachita Campus (West Monroe), 229
Louisiana Technical College–LaFourche Campus (Thibodaux), 231
Louisiana Technical College–Young Memorial Campus (Morgan City), 235

**Minnesota**
Alexandria Technical College (Alexandria), 239
Dakota County Technical College (Rosemount), 242
Minnesota State College–Southeast Technical (Winona), 248
Minnesota West Community and Technical College (Pipestone), 248
Riverland Community College (Austin), 253

**Mississippi**
Copiah-Lincoln Community College (Wesson), 258
East Mississippi Community College (Scooba), 259
Itawamba Community College (Fulton), 260
Meridian Community College (Meridian), 261
Mississippi Gulf Coast Community College (Perkinston), 261
Northwest Mississippi Community College (Senatobia), 262

**Missouri**
Crowder College (Neosho), 266

**Nebraska**
Southeast Community College Area (Lincoln), 288

**New Mexico**
Central New Mexico Community College (Albuquerque), 293
Crownpoint Institute of Technology (Crownpoint), 293
Mesalands Community College (Tucumcari), 295
New Mexico Junior College (Hobbs), 295

**Tennessee**
Tennessee Technology Center at Crump (Crump), 341
Tennessee Technology Center at Knoxville (Knoxville), 342
Tennessee Technology Center at Memphis (Memphis), 343
Tennessee Technology Center at Morristown (Morristown), 343
Tennessee Technology Center at Nashville (Nashville), 344
Tennessee Technology Center at Ripley (Ripley), 345
Tennessee Technology Center at Shelbyville (Shelbyville), 345

**Texas**
Center for Employment Training–Socorro (Socorro), 355
Lee College (Baytown), 368

**Utah**
Bridgerland Applied Technology Center (Logan), 392
Mountainland Applied Technology College (Orem), 395
Salt Lake Community College (Salt Lake City), 396
Southwest Applied Technology Center (Cedar City), 397
Uintah Basin Applied Technology Center (Roosevelt), 397

**Washington**
Bates Technical College (Tacoma), 400
Bellingham Technical College (Bellingham), 400
Big Bend Community College (Moses Lake), 401
Grays Harbor College (Aberdeen), 405
Walla Walla Community College (Walla Walla), 413

**Wisconsin**
Chippewa Valley Technical College (Eau Claire), 415
Fox Valley Technical College (Appleton), 415
Waukesha County Technical College (Pewaukee), 422

## TURF AND TURFGRASS MANAGEMENT

**Arizona**
Northland Pioneer College (Holbrook), 53

**California**
College of the Desert (Palm Desert), 84
Cuyamaca College (El Cajon), 88
Mt. San Antonio College (Walnut), 116
Mt. San Jacinto College (San Jacinto), 117

**Illinois**
Harper College (Palatine), 170
Illinois Eastern Community Colleges, Wabash Valley College (Mount Carmel), 173
Rend Lake College (Ina), 183
Richland Community College (Decatur), 184

**Iowa**
Western Iowa Tech Community College (Sioux City), 198

**Minnesota**
Rochester Community and Technical College (Rochester), 253

**Missouri**
Metropolitan Community College–Longview (Lee's Summit), 271

**North Dakota**
Dakota College at Bottineau (Bottineau), 299

**Oregon**
Southwestern Oregon Community College (Coos Bay), 327

**Tennessee**
Southwest Tennessee Community College (Memphis), 339

**Texas**
Palo Alto College (San Antonio), 373
Texas State Technical College Waco (Waco), 386
Western Texas College (Snyder), 391

**Washington**
Spokane Community College (Spokane), 411

## UPHOLSTERY/UPHOLSTERER

**Arizona**
Central Arizona College (Coolidge), 47
Northland Pioneer College (Holbrook), 53

**Arkansas**
Arkansas State University–Beebe (Beebe), 59

## WELDING TECHNOLOGY/WELDER

### Word Processing

**California**
Pomona Unified School District Adult and Career Education (Pomona), 124
Vallecitos CET (Hayward), 137

**Illinois**
Elgin Community College (Elgin), 167
Joliet Junior College (Joliet), 174
Lincoln Land Community College (Springfield), 177
Sauk Valley Community College (Dixon), 186
Waubonsee Community College (Sugar Grove), 189

**Kansas**
Independence Community College (Independence), 203

**Texas**
Central Texas Commercial College (Dallas), 356

**Washington**
Everett Community College (Everett), 404
Yakima Valley Community College (Yakima), 414

### WORK AND FAMILY STUDIES

**Mississippi**
Belhaven College (Jackson), 257

### YOGA TEACHER TRAINING/YOGA THERAPY

**Arizona**
Scottsdale Community College (Scottsdale), 56
Southwest Institute of Healing Arts (Tempe), 56

**Kentucky**
Lexington Healing Arts Academy (Lexington), 216

### YOUTH MINISTRY

**California**
William Jessup University (Rocklin), 142

**Kansas**
Bethel College (North Newton), 199

### YOUTH SERVICES/ADMINISTRATION

**Oregon**
Mt. Hood Community College (Gresham), 323

**Washington**
Olympic College (Bremerton), 408

# Alphabetical Listing of Vo-Tech Schools